ORGANISATIONAL

BEHAVIOUR and

MANAGEMENT

ORGANISATIONAL BEHAVIOUR and MANAGEMENT

JOHN IVANCEVICH
University of Houston

MARA OLEKALNS
University of Melbourne

MICHAEL MATTESON
University of Houston

The McGraw-Hill Companies, Inc.

Sydney New York San Francisco Auckland
Bangkok Bogotá Caracas Hong Kong
Kuala Lumpur Lisbon London Madrid
Mexico City Milan New Delhi San Juan
Seoul Singapore Taipei Toronto

Irwin/McGraw-Hill

A Division of The McGraw-Hill Companies

Reprinted 1999

Copyright © 1997 McGraw-Hill Book Company Australia Pty Limited/
Richard D. Irwin, Inc.

Additional owners of copyright are named in on-page credits.

National Library of Australia Cataloguing-in-Publication Data:

Ivancevich, John M.
  Organisational behaviour and management.

   1st Australasian ed.
   Includes index.
   ISBN 0 256 19921 3.

   1. Organisational behaviour — Australia. 2. Organisational behaviour —
New Zealand. I. Matteson, Michael T. II. Olekalns, Mara. III Title.

302.350994

Published in Australia by
McGraw-Hill Book Company Australia Pty Limited
4 Barcoo Street, Roseville NSW 2069, Australia

Publisher: Ann Nolan
Production coordinator: Katrina Hutchins
Designer: Megan Smith
Editor: Valerie Marlborough

Printer: Star Printery, Sydney

This book is dedicated to Philip.
Friendship, support and encouragement
overcome all obstacles.

We shall cease from exploration
And the end of all our exploring
Will be to arrive where we started
And know the place for the first time.
T. S. Eliot *Four Quartets*

CONTENTS

Preface

PART 1

THE FIELD OF ORGANISATIONAL BEHAVIOUR 1

1   **Introduction to organisational behaviour 2**
The origins of management 6
A brief lesson in history 6
Scientific management 6
Functions of management 7
The origins of organisational behaviour 8
The Hawthorne studies 8
The importance of studying organisational behaviour 9
Leaders and organisational behaviour 10
A model for managing organisations: Behaviour, structure and processes 12
The organisation's environment 12
The individual in the organisation 12
Interpersonal influence and group behaviour 15
Organisational processes 17
Organisational structure and design 19
Performance outcomes: Individual, group and organisational 20
Summary of key points 21
Review and discussion questions 21
Endnotes 21
Reading 1 Organisational behaviour revisited 22

2   **Managing behaviour in organisations 32**
Effective management 33
A brief history of effectiveness: Two perspectives on effectiveness 35
The goal approach 35

The systems theory approach 37
The time dimension model of organisational effectiveness 40
Criteria of effectiveness 41
Quality 41
Productivity 43
Efficiency 43
Satisfaction 43
Adaptiveness 43
Development 44
Management functions and effectiveness 44
Planning effective performance 46
Organising effective performance 47
Leading effective performance 48
Controlling effective performance 49
Studying organisational effectiveness 50
Summary of key points 51
Review and discussion questions 52
Endnotes 53
Reading 2 Rounding out the manager's job 54
Exercise 2 Initial view of organisational behaviour 68

PART 2

THE INDIVIDUAL IN THE ORGANISATION 71

3   **Understanding behaviour at work 72**
The basis for understanding work behaviour 74
Dispositional and situational explanations 76
Dispositions and situations together 81
Transactional approaches 82
Understanding behaviour 83
The basis for explaining behaviour 83
Perception 83

Social perception 85
Behaviour and organisational
    outcomes 87
Attitudes 87
Attitudes and job satisfaction 91
Satisfaction and job performance 93
Motivation and behaviour 94
Summary of key points 94
Review and discussion questions 95
Endnotes 96
Reading 3 Hiring for the organisation,
    not the job 97
Exercise 3 Testing your assumptions
    about people 111
Case 3   Bob Knowlton 114

4   **Motivation: An individual perspective** 120
The starting point: The individual 123
Motivation theories: A classification
    system 124
Need–value–motive theories 124
Need fulfilment 125
Intrinsic motivation 129
Cognitive-choice theories 130
Expectancy theory 130
Attribution theory 135
Self-regulation theories 135
Goal setting 135
Control theory 138
Resource allocation theories 140
*Factors influencing cost–benefit
    analysis* 141
*Motivation from a resource allocation
    perspective* 141
Motivation and the psychological
    contract 142
Reviewing motivation 144
Summary of key points 145
Review and discussion questions 146
Endnotes 147
Reading 4 Motivation: A diagnostic
    approach 149
Exercise 4 Goal setting: How to do it 160
Case 4   FAB Sweets Limited 161

5   **Motivation: An organisational
    perspective** 165
Improving performance 166
Job design 166
*Organisational behaviour
    management* 170
Evaluating performance 175
Purposes of evaluation 177
Focus of evaluation 177
Performance evaluation methods 178
Improving evaluations 180
Intrinsic and extrinsic rewards 182
Satisfaction with rewards 182
Rewards affect organisational
    concerns 185
Turnover 185
Abenteeism 186
Organisational commitment 186
A model of individual rewards 186
Summary of key points 188
Review and discussion questions 189
Endnotes 190
Reading 5 The folly of rewarding A,
    while hoping for B 191
Exercise 5 Job design 199
Case 5   Vaccino 203

6   **Occupational stress** 206
Understanding stress 207
The general adaptation syndrome 209
Stress and work: A model 210
Work and life stressors 211
Group and organisational stressors 212
Physical environment stressors 213
Individual stressors 213
Life stressors 216
Perceiving, appraising and coping with
    stress 218
Stress moderators 218
Type A behaviour pattern 219
Locus of control and hardiness 220
Pessimism, optimism and affectivity 220
Social support 221
Stress consequences 223

Individual consequences **223**

Organisational consequences **224**

Burnout: The professional stress syndrome **224**

Stress prevention and management **225**

Maximising person–environment fit **226**

Organisational stress prevention and management programs **227**

Individual stress prevention and management **228**

Ensuring program success **229**

Summary of key points **230**

Review and discussion questions **231**

Endnotes **231**

Reading 6   Who beats stress best — and how **234**

Exercise 6A   Behaviour Activity Profile — a Type A measure **239**

Exercise 6B   Health Risk Appraisal **242**

Case 6   The case of the missing time **245**

PART 3

INTERPERSONAL INFLUENCE AND GROUP BEHAVIOUR **249**

7   Group behaviour **250**

The nature of groups **251**

An integrated model of group formation and development **253**

Types of groups **253**

Formal groups **254**

Informal groups **255**

Joining groups **255**

Why people form groups **255**

Becoming a member **256**

Two models of group development **257**

Tuckman's five-stage model **257**

Gersick's Punctuated Equilibrium Model **259**

Group roles and norms **260**

Group socialisation **261**

Group roles **262**

Group norms **262**

Group performance **264**

Criteria of group effectiveness **264**

Process losses **266**

Group cohesion **267**

Teams at work **269**

Team characteristics **269**

Team effectiveness **271**

Summary of key points **273**

Review and discussion questions **274**

Endnotes **274**

Reading 7   The design of work teams **275**

Exercise 7   What to do with Johnny Rocco **292**

Case 7   International Superannuation Specialists **295**

8   Intergroup behaviour and conflict **298**

Interdependence: The key to understanding conflict **299**

Social interdependence **299**

Determinants of competition **300**

Determinants of cooperation **302**

Organisations as resource dilemmas **302**

Traditional versus contemporary perspectives on conflict **303**

A realistic view of intergroup conflict **304**

Functional conflict **304**

Dysfunctional conflict **305**

Conflict and organisational performance **305**

A model of conflict **305**

Stages of conflict **307**

Why intergroup conflict occurs **308**

Interdependence **308**

Differences in goals **310**

Differences in perceptions **311**

The increased demand for specialists **312**

Interpersonal factors **312**

The consequences of dysfunctional intergroup conflict **312**

Changes within groups **313**

Changes between groups **313**

The consequences of conflict **315**

Managing intergroup conflict **316**
  Altering structural variables **317**
  *Changing perceptions of
    interdependence* **317**
  Using symbolic management **317**
Conflict stimulation **317**
  *Bringing outside individuals into the
    group* **319**
  Altering the organisation's structure **319**
  Stimulating competition **319**
  Making use of programmed conflict **320**
Summary of key points **320**
Review and discussion questions **321**
Endnotes **322**
Reading 8 How to design a conflict
    management procedure
    that fits your dispute **323**
Exercise 8 Pemberton's dilemma **337**
Case 8   Rainbow Medical Centre **341**

9 Alternative dispute resolution 345
Negotiation **346**
  A definition of negotiation **346**
  Negotiating styles **347**
  Factors affecting strategy selection **349**
  Approaches to negotiation **350**
  More on integrative bargaining **354**
  Factors affecting negotiation outcomes **355**
  Moving towards effective negotiations **358**
Mediation **360**
  Stages and strategies in mediating **361**
  Improving mediator effectiveness **362**
Effective conflict management **364**
  Justice and conflict management **365**
  Conflict management goals **365**
  Managing conflicts **366**
Summary of key points **366**
Review and discussion questions **367**
Endnotes **367**
Reading 9 Negotiating rationally:
    The power and impact of the
    negotiator's frame **370**
Exercise 9 World Bank: An exercise in
    intergroup negotiation **377**
Case 9   Olympic television rights **379**

10 Organisational power and politics 386
The concept of power **387**
Sources of power **388**
  Interpersonal power **388**
  Positive power **391**
  Structural and situational power **391**
Positive power: Empowerment **395**
Interpersonal influence and politics **396**
  The mechanisms of social influence **396**
  Influence and conformity **397**
  Social influence strategies **398**
Organisational influence and politics **399**
  *Interpersonal influence in
    organisations* **399**
  Playing politics **402**
Ethics, power and politics **405**
Summary of key points **408**
Review and discussion questions **409**
Endnotes **409**
Reading 10 Leadership: The art of
    empowering others **411**
Exercise 10 How political are you? **421**
Case 10   Missouri campus bitterly
    divided over how to
    reallocate funds **422**

11 Leadership 427
Leadership defined **429**
  Is leadership important? **430**
Trait theories **431**
  Intelligence **432**
  Personality **433**
  Physical traits **433**
  Do traits predict effectiveness? **433**
Personal-behavioural theories **434**
  *The University of Michigan studies:
    Job-centred and employee-centred
    leadership* **434**
  *The Ohio State studies: Initiating structure
    and consideration* **435**
Situational theories **436**
  The contingency leadership model **436**
  House's path-goal model **439**
  *Hersey-Blanchard situational leadership
    theory* **441**

Comparing the situational
approaches **444**
Personal power and leadership **445**
Charismatic leadership **446**
Transformational leadership **448**
Leader attributions and their
consequences **451**
The attribution theory of leadership **451**
Leader–Member Exchange approach **454**
Do leaders matter? **455**
Are leaders necessary? **455**
The romance of leadership **456**
Substitutes for leadership **456**
Participative leadership **458**
The Vroom–Jago model of leadership **459**
Strategic leadership **463**
Organisational performance **464**
Organisational life cycles **464**
Changes over time **465**
Is leader behaviour a cause or an
effect? **465**
Summary of key points **466**
Review and discussion questions **466**
Endnotes **467**
Reading 11 Leading learning **470**
Exercise 11 Task and people
orientations **480**
Case 11 The Council of Adult
Education **481**

PART 4

ORGANISATIONAL PROCESSES **495**

12 Decision making **496**
Types of decisions **497**
Understanding decision making **499**
Types of outcomes **499**
Types of problems **499**
Types of approaches **500**
The decision-making process **501**
*Establishing specific goals and objectives,
and measuring results* **501**
Problem identification and definition **501**
Consideration of causes **503**

Development of alternative solutions **503**
Evaluation of solutions **504**
Solution selection **505**
Implementation **505**
Follow-up **506**
The decision-making context **506**
Ill-defined decision problems:
Unknown outcomes **507**
Structuring the problem **508**
Solving the problem **508**
Well-defined decision problems:
Known alternatives **509**
Individual decision rules **509**
Applying decision rules **511**
Limits to rational decision making **511**
Errors in estimating probabilities **511**
*Motivational factors in decision
making* **514**
Group decision making **518**
*Individual versus group decision
making* **518**
Creativity in group decision making **519**
Techniques for stimulating creativity **521**
Brainstorming **521**
The Delphi technique **521**
The nominal group technique **522**
Strategic decision making **523**
Stages in strategic decision making **523**
*Other issues in strategic decision
making* **525**
Summary of key points **526**
Review and discussion questions **527**
Endnotes **528**
Reading 12 Agreement and thinking
alike: Ingredients for poor
decisions **529**
Exercise 12 Group decision making **534**
Case 12 Kooyong appoints a new
vice-principal **537**

13 Communication **542**
The importance of communication **543**
The communication process **544**
The elements of communication **544**
Non-verbal messages **546**

Communication in organisations **547**

Interpersonal communication **547**

Blocks to effective sending **547**

Blocks to effective listening **549**

*Improving interpersonal
communication* **550**

*A managerial perspective on interpersonal
communication* **552**

Communicating within
organisations **553**

Downward communication **553**

Upward communication **555**

Horizontal communication **556**

Diagonal communication **558**

Communication networks **558**

Improving communication in
organisations **559**

Following up **560**

Regulating information flow **560**

Utilising feedback **560**

Empathy **560**

Repetition **561**

Encouraging mutual trust **561**

Effective timing **561**

Simplifying language **561**

Using the grapevine **562**

Promoting ethical communications **562**

Benchmarks for excellent
communication **562**

*The chief executive champions
communication* **563**

Actions and words match **563**

*Be committed to two-way
communication* **563**

*Face-to-face communication is
emphasised* **563**

*Communication is everyone's
responsibility* **563**

Do not avoid bad news **563**

Have a communication strategy **564**

Multicultural communication **565**

Summary of key points **566**

Review and discussion questions **567**

Endnotes **567**

Reading 13 Active listening **569**

Exercise 13 Your communication
style **577**

Case 13 A case of misunderstanding:
Mr Hart and Mr Bing **580**

**14 Organisational culture and
socialisation 582**

Organisational culture **583**

Organisational culture defined **583**

*Societal values and organisational
culture* **585**

Organisational culture and its effects **587**

Creating organisational culture **588**

Influencing culture change **589**

Socialisation and culture **591**

Socialisation stages **591**

Socialisation strategies **595**

Learning about the organisation **597**

Characteristics of effective
socialisation **599**

Effective anticipatory socialisation **599**

Effective accommodation socialisation **599**

Effective role management socialisation **601**

Mentors and socialisation **601**

Socialising a culturally diverse
workforce **603**

Socialisation as an integration
strategy **605**

Summary of key points **605**

Review and discussion questions **606**

Endnotes **606**

Reading 14 Levels of culture **608**

Exercise 14 Assessing and considering
organisational culture **618**

Case 14 The Consolidated Life case:
Caught between corporate
cultures **619**

**15 Organisational change and
development 623**

Forces for change **624**

External forces **624**

Internal forces **625**

Understanding the change process **626**

Lewin's Field Theory **627**

*Field Theory and the implementation
    of change* **628**
  Resistance revisited **632**
Change: Evolution or revolution? **634**
  Change by evolution **634**
  Change as punctuated equilibrium **635**
Organisational development:
    Planned change **636**
Change through organisation
    development **638**
  Organising arrangements **638**
  Social factors **642**
  Changing technology **644**
  Multifaceted approaches **645**
Implementing the method **646**
Evaluating the program **646**
The role of change agents **647**
Summary of key points **648**
Review and discussion questions **649**
Endnotes **649**
Reading 15 Why transformation efforts
              fail **651**
Exercise 15 Organisation development at
              J. P. Hunt **658**
Case 15   Community Services Victoria:
              New management and
              quality of service **659**

PART 5

ORGANISATIONAL STRUCTURE AND DESIGN **667**

16 Organisational structure and design 668
  Designing an organisational
    structure **669**
  Division of labour **671**
  Delegation of authority **671**
  Departmentalisation **672**
    Functional departmentalisation **673**
    Territorial departmentalisation **674**
    Product departmentalisation **674**

Customer departmentalisation **675**
*Mixed and changing
    departmentalisation* **675**
Span of control **676**
  Required contact **676**
  Degree of specialisation **677**
  Ability to communicate **677**
Dimensions of structure **677**
  Formalisation **677**
  Centralisation **679**
  Complexity **679**
Organisational design models **680**
  The mechanistic model **680**
  The organic model **681**
Matrix organisation design **682**
  Advantages of matrix organisation **683**
  Different forms of matrix organisation **684**
Multinational structure and design **685**
Organisational design and organisational
    behaviour **687**
  Job and work design **687**
  Occupational stress **687**
  Organisational communication **688**
  Justice and conflict at work **688**
  *Organisational change and
      innovation* **688**
A final word **688**
Summary of key points **689**
Review and discussion questions **690**
Endnotes **690**
Reading 16 The new enterprise
              architecture **692**
Exercise 16 Paper Plane Corporation **702**

Appendix A Selected functions of
              management **704**
Appendix B Quantitative and qualitative
              research techniques for studying
              organisational behaviour and
              management practice **717**
Glossary of terms **729**
Index **743**

PREFACE

Just as *Organisational Behaviour and Management* reaches its fourth US edition, we have finished the first Australasian adaptation. What makes this adaptation different from its US counterpart? Also, are Australia and New Zealand so different from other Westernised societies that the principles of organisational behaviour will be fundamentally altered? In answer, I would reply that there are more similarities than differences between our society and work values, and those of other Western countries. This means that the theories and models we see in US texts — because they represent an international research effort — will also be relevant to how we manage people within the Australasian workforce. Why, then, write an Australasian adaptation? First and foremost, my students demand local content. Especially for those students with limited work experience, examples bring theory to life; Australasian examples make the material more relevant to their study now, and their future place in an Australasian workforce. Beyond that, it is important for students to see that Australasian researchers contribute to research and theory in the field of organisational behaviour.

In writing this adaptation, I have incorporated the three principles that have guided my teaching of organisational behaviour over the past decade. The first of these is a strong commitment to demonstrating how fundamental theory can be applied in the workplace. The second is a recognition that organisational behaviour is a dynamic and changing field, as we see by the growth of research in this field. The third is the importance of connecting theory to practice, making the abstract 'real'. By teaching these skills to our students we can ensure that they will leave our classes equipped to improve the workplace.

This adaptation extends the theory found in the US edition in several ways. First, the biggest failing of many organisational behaviour texts is the cursory attention to the theory that underlies management practice. Can we hope that our students will become flexible and creative managers, if they have simply rote-learned a set of principles or 'rules'? I think not. To develop individuals who are skilled people managers, we must give our students a greater understanding of how and why these rules have developed. To increase students' understanding of organisational behaviour, I have introduced basic psychological theory in the text to lay the groundwork for understanding the behaviour of individuals and groups at work.

A second and vital part of teaching organisational behaviour is to introduce students to state-of-the-art research. This demonstrates clearly that our knowledge about how to manage people at work continues to grow. By challenging existing theories, current research encourages our students to think critically about the principles that we teach them — how they were developed, their limitations and the conditions under which they will be relevant. Also, it is here that local content can shine. The Inaugural Industrial/Organisational Psychology Conference in 1995 highlighted the large number of Australian and New Zealand researchers concerned about understanding the problems and challenges faced in the workplace. Introducing students to New Zealand and

Australian research highlights the role that we have played — and continue to play — in increasing the understanding of individual behaviour at work.

Finally, our students must be able to apply the theories that we teach to real-life problems. Only when they can connect the abstract to the everyday problems that they will encounter at work, will they become effective managers. Providing examples of how Australasian businesses deal with 'people issues' is one way to demonstrate this connection. More importantly, students learn about the practical side of work through participating in experiential exercises and analysing cases studies. These are integral to the US edition and are included in the Australasian adaptation.

As the US authors have said, with *Organisational Behaviour and Management (OBM)*, students become involved participants in learning about behaviour and management within work settings. We have designed the book with instructional flexibility in mind. *OBM* combines text, readings, self-learning exercises, group participation exercises and cases. These elements are aimed at students interested in understanding, interpreting and attempting to predict the behaviour of people working in organisations.

Organisational functioning is complex. No single theory or model of organisational behaviour has emerged as the best or most practical. Thus, managers must be able to probe and diagnose organisational situations when they attempt to understand, interpret and predict behaviour. *OBM* devotes considerable attention to encouraging the development of these probing and diagnostic skills. The first step in this development is for each reader to increase his or her own self-awareness. Before a person can diagnose why another person (a friend, subordinate or competitor) is behaving in a particular way, he or she must conduct a self-analysis. This introspective first step is built into each chapter's content and into learning elements found at the end of *OBM*'s chapters. The content and these elements encourage the students to relate their own knowledge and experience to the text, readings, exercises and cases in the book.

Learning objectives open each chapter to start the reader thinking about concepts, practices and concerns. At the end of each chapter is a summary of the main points covered in the chapter, and also review and discussion questions to test the students' understanding. A glossary of terms is provided at the end of the book.

FRAMEWORK OF THE BOOK

The book is organised into five parts containing a total of sixteen chapters and two appendices. The framework highlights behaviours, structure and processes that are part of organisational life. The five parts are:

Part I

The field of organisational behaviour. The first chapter of *OBM*, 'Introduction to organisational behaviour', introduces the field of organisational behaviour and explores the how, what, why and when of organisational behaviour as viewed and practised by managers. Chapter 2, 'Managing behaviour in organisations', places organisational behaviour within the broader context, establishing that one of the aims of better people management is a more effective and efficient organisation.

Part 2

The individual in the organisation. These four chapters focus on the individual, including such topics as 'Understanding behaviour at work' (Chapter 3), 'Motivation: An individual perspective' (Chapter 4), 'Motivation: An organisational perspective' (Chapter 5), and 'Occupational stress' (Chapter 6). I have departed from the US edition by including material on job design, which considers the relationship between organisational systems and individual motivation, in Chapter 5.

Part 3

Interpersonal influence and group behaviour. These two topics are explored in a five-chapter sequence: Chapter 7, 'Group behaviour'; Chapter 8, 'Intergroup behaviour and conflict'; Chapter 9, 'Alternative dispute resolution'; Chapter 10, 'Organisational power and politics'; and Chapter 11, 'Leadership'.

Part 4

Organisational processes. The following four chapters make up this part: Chapter 12, 'Decision making'; Chapter 13, 'Communication'; Chapter 14, 'Organisational culture and socialisation' and Chapter 15, 'Organisational change and development'.

Part 5

Organisational structure and design. Issues in organisational design are discussed in the final chapter, 'Organisational structure and design'.

FEATURES

I have incorporated several of the new and improved features found in the fourth US edition. There are several new readings, exercises and cases. Among these, you will find a number based on Australasian companies. Four of these were prepared by Masters students analysing the companies that they work for. In addition, there is a substantial amount of new material to be found in this adaptation. I have introduced and discussed new theories, models and recent advances in organisational behaviour — resource allocation theories of motivation, strategic leadership and strategic decision making are some examples. The chapter on organisational change, while retaining the material on organisational development, introduces material on individual responses to change; and the chapter on motivational systems extends earlier discussions of reinforcement theory by linking it to organisational behaviour management principles. Finally, in this adaptation, I have included a new chapter on alternative dispute resolution, an area that is becoming increasingly important to the field of organisational behaviour.

Encounters

There are numerous Encounters interspersed throughout the text. Unlike the US edition, many of these Encounters have a strong research orientation. It is easy for research, wherever conducted, to become lost among the many concepts we discuss in the body of the book. Browsing through other adaptations, I found it hard to distinguish between local and international content. Since one of my aims in this adaptation was to highlight the work done in Australasia, I chose to discuss the research in Encounters. In this adaptation, I have included three research-based types of encounters:

- Local Encounters, which showcase research from Australia and New Zealand;
- Global Encounters, which focus on research conducted in Europe, Asia and Japan;
- Management Encounters, which highlight a current issue in international research.

In addition, you will find Organisational Encounters in most chapters. These Encounters report on the experience of businesses in Australia and New Zealand: they present problems and issues facing organisations, and discuss how organisations have successfully overcome these problems.

Readings

This book contains carefully selected classic or contemporary readings from a variety of sources (e.g. *Academy of Management Executive, Harvard Business Review, Issues and Observations* and *Organizational Dynamics*). Each of the readings is tied to a chapter's content.

Exercises

OBM also includes end-of-chapter self-learning and group exercises. Some of the exercises allow the individual student to participate in a way that enhances self-knowledge. These self-learning exercises illustrate how to gather and use feedback properly and emphasise the uniqueness of perceptions, values, personality and communication abilities. In addition, a number of exercises apply theories and principles from the text in group activities. Working in groups is part of organisational life; so these exercises introduce a touch of reality. Group interaction can generate debates, lively discussions, the testing of personal ideas and the sharing of information.

Furthermore, the exercise are designed to involve the instructor in the learning process. Your participation allows you to try out techniques and patterns of behaviour, and to integrate exercise materials with the text. None of the exercises requires advance preparation for the instructor, although some require returning to a particular section or model in the chapter for information. The main objective is to get the reader involved. We want an involved, thinking, questioning reader.

For instructors who wish to go beyond the exercises provided in this book, several excellent resources are available. Johnston and Johnston's *Joining Together: Group Skills*, Pfeffer and Jones's *Handbooks of Structured Experiences* and the *Journal of Management Education* are all wonderful resources.

Cases

OBM contains full-length cases. These realistic, dynamic cases link theory, research and practice. They provide an inside view of various organisational settings and dynamics. The cases, like the real world, do not have one 'right' solution. Instead, each case challenges students to experience the complexity of the work environment as if they were managers. The cases are also an invaluable teaching tool. They encourage the individual student to probe, diagnose and creatively solve real problems. Group participation and learning are encouraged, meanwhile, through in-class discussion and debate. The questions at the end of each case can be used to guide classroom discussion.

Many of the cases focus on a specific issue. However, as we all know, organisational life is not that simple. It would be a rare occasion on which there was only one issue contributing to an organisational problem. For this reason, it is important that students also undertake some integrated cases — cases that cover several, interwoven areas. Four of the Australasian cases provide such an opportunity. Although these cases have been included as end-of-chapter material, the chapter topic highlights the major, rather than the only, problem. An additional challenge for students is to uncover the remaining problems and consider how these interact.

A case analysis should be conducted as follows:

1. Read the case quickly.
2. Reread the case using the following model:
   a. Define the major problem in organisational behaviour and management terms.
   b. If information is incomplete — which it is likely to be — make realistic assumptions.
   c. Outline the probable causes of the problem.
   d. Consider the costs and benefits of each possible solution.
   e. Choose a solution and describe how you would implement it.
   f. Go over the case again. Make sure that the questions at the end are answered and make sure that your solution is efficient, feasible, ethical and legally defensible, and one that can be defended in classroom debate.

Marginal notations

Marginal notations are used to highlight the main points and to encourage the reader to think of how the ideas and concepts fit together. These marginal notations connect the text with the end-of-chapter readings, exercises and cases. Every reading, exercise and case elaborates some point made in the chapter that precedes it; the marginal notation draws attention to these discussions by indicating the relevant reading, exercise or case. The following symbols were chosen for easy reference:

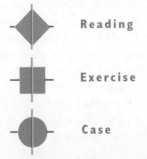

Reading

Exercise

Case

Thus the instructor can use the marginal notations to determine the best point in a lecture to incorporate each of the readings, exercises and cases. They also help students, when they are reading and reviewing the chapter, to understand how each reading, exercise and case fits into the overall framework of ideas in that chapter.

The marginal notations serve to tie together, to integrate and to stimulate organised thinking. Thus, these notations help to put the reader in the position of fitting the parts, pieces and ideas together to improve learning.

SUPPLEMENTARY MATERIALS

OBM includes a variety of supplementary materials, designed to provide additional classroom support. These materials are as follows :

Instructor's Manual and Test Bank

The instuctor's manual is organised to follow each chapter of the text. It includes chapter objectives, chapter synopses, chapter outlines with tips and ideas, and project and classroom speaker ideas. Encounter discussion questions and suggested answers are also provided to help you incorporate these dynamic features into your lecture presentations. Suggested transparencies, term exam topics and reading, exercise and case notes are also included. The test bank section has been completely updated to reflect changes to the Australasian edition. There are approximately 1200 true/false, multiple-choice and essay questions. Each question is classified according to level of difficulty and contains a page reference to the text. Additionally, the test bank includes questions that test students on concepts presented in the readings to enhance the integrative nature of the text.

Powerpoint

A Powerpoint slide presentation includes slides corresponding to the lecture notes found in the Instructor's Manual and Test Bank.

ACKNOWLEDGEMENTS

I would like to thank the academics who were prepared to give freely of their time to review and make suggestions about this adaptation. I have incorporated as many of the suggestions as were feasible in this edition, and will continue to think about how other suggestions may be used to improve this text in the future. I would here like to acknowledge the suggestions and comments made by Phillip Boyle of the University of Queensland, Lorraine Carey of the University of Tasmania, Julie Connell of the University of Newcastle, Ray Cooksey of the University of New England, Cherie England of James Cook University, Jane George-Falvy of the Australian Graduate School of Management, John Griffiths of La Trobe University, Pamela Hedges of Curtin University of Technology, Loretta Inglise of Monash University, Sandy Kiffin-Petersen of the University of Western Australia, Ann Lawrence of Deakin University, Wayne Mortensen of Victoria University of Technology, Peter Oswald of Victoria University of Technology and Cecil Pearson of Murdoch University.

PART I

THE FIELD OF
organisational
behaviour

1

Introduction to organisational behaviour

2

Managing behaviour in organisations

Culture is not life in its entirety, but just the moment of security, strength, and clarity.

— Jose Ortega y Gasset *Meditations on Quixote*

INTRODUCTION TO ORGANISATIONAL BEHAVIOUR

Learning objectives

- Define *the power of human resources.*
- Describe *the disciplines that have contributed to the field of organisational behaviour.*
- Discuss *the importance of understanding behaviour in organisations.*
- Explain *the 'Hawthorne Effect' in an organisational setting.*
- Identify *the characteristics of what is referred to as the 'new psychological contract'.*

Chapter

Imagine going to work in an office, plant or store and finding co-workers who are excited about their jobs, managers who listen carefully to worker comments about the job and a general atmosphere that is vibrant. What a pleasant setting it is where people want to work hard, have pride in the job they are doing, trust each other and share ideas on how to improve performance — a setting in which groups work together, solve problems, set high-quality standards and enjoy the diversity of each co-worker's family, ethnic and religious background.

Is this just an illusion or a dream of an ideal work setting? This is a sketch of a work setting that any manager would cherish, enjoy and strive to maintain. It is a picture of the kind of workplace that managers should use as a target to achieve. This is the kind of workplace that will have to be created if a company, entrepreneur or institution is to survive in the coming years.

There are a number of forces that are reshaping the nature of managing within organisations. A limited number of companies have recognised these forces and are working to channel their managerial talents to accomplish goals by using their knowledge about each of five major forces.[1]

The forces at work are the *power of human resources*. The way people (managers, technicians and staff specialists) work, think and behave dictates the direction and success of a company. Unfortunately, there is a shrinking workforce and a shortage of technically skilled workers. Managing the human resource as valuable assets to be maintained and improved is now more important than ever.

To compete effectively in the mid-1990s and into the 21st century, *globalism* must be understood and addressed. Global competition characterised by networks that bring together countries, institutions and people is beginning to dominate the global economy. Of the twenty-five largest industrial corporations in the world, eight are American, six are Japanese and three are German.[2] As a result of global integration, the growth rate of world trade has increased faster than that of world gross domestic product. That is, the trading of goods and services among nations has been increasing faster than the actual world production of goods. To survive the fast-paced changes, companies must make not only capital investments but also investments in people. How well a company recruits, selects, retains and motivates a skilled workforce will have a major impact on its ability to compete in the more globally interdependent world.

The *culturally diverse* workforce is a reality in Australia. As the complexion of Australia's workforce changes, managers and co-workers need to learn more about each other so that a receptive work culture is created.

The *rapidity of change* is another crucial force to recognise. The fax machine, genetic engineering, microchips, crumbling socialist empires and a reconfigured Commonwealth of Independent States (e.g. Russia, Ukraine, Georgia) are some of the changes sweeping the world. Understanding, accommodating and using change is now a part of a manager's job requirement.

The new worker–employer *psychological contract* is another force. From the employer's view, employees do not have lifetime jobs, guaranteed advancement or raises and assurance that their job roles will be fixed. Employees believe that employers must be honest, open and fair, and also be willing to give workers a larger say in their jobs. Employees also want organisations to pay more attention to their family situations and physical and mental health. Employees want employers to appreciate the humanness of workers.

The five forces — power of human resources, globalism, cultural diversity, the rapidity of change and a new worker–employer psychological contract — are inevitable. Resisting the reality of these forces will be likely to lead to unnecessary conflict, reduced managerial and non-managerial performance and lost opportunities. In managerial terms, failing to cope and deal with these forces will be likely to result in job dissatisfaction, poor morale, reduced commitment, lower work quality, burnout, poor judgement and a host of unhealthy consequences. A further consideration, beginning to emerge as the next force, is the relationship between how organisations do business and the environment. The greening of organisations will be a potent force in the next few decades, and we take a closer look at this issue in our Organisational Encounter.

ORGANISATIONAL Encounter

Organisational greening

Conservationist, Tasmanian MP and Senate candidate Bob Brown, for example, argues that unless capitalist countries can stop looking for endless growth, they must eventually collapse as they arrive at the limits of natural resources.

James, D. (1995). Business faces a new environment, *Business Review Weekly*, January 30, 54.

What issues will face companies in the future? Environmental protection is shaping up as a key issue in the management of organisations as we approach the year 2000. According to a recent survey of 176 top-level managers in Australia, some of the key factors shaping our business environment include:

- increased global pollution;
- increased international sanctions to influence national environmental policies;
- increased willingness by consumers to protect the environment by accepting higher costs;
- substantially increased environmental regulation.

These views are echoed by international business leaders, who predict that environmental spending will increase 50–100% over the next decade, while government regulations will also become tighter. Already many companies have board members responsible for environmental management: 50% of companies in England, 75% of companies in Germany and 100% of companies in the Netherlands have made such appointments. Australia's 27% does not compare well with these international figures.

Is this an accurate analysis? And what are the implications for business? David James, writing for the *Business Review Weekly*, looks more closely at the environmental debate. According to him, there are three themes in the argument:

1. There is a confusion between growth and consumption. The challenge for management is to move from physical resource-based to skill-based wealth creation. Growth without consumption can occur if we are innovative in the utilisation of technology.

2. There is a mistaken belief that capitalism is to blame for environmental problems. James points to several well-known environmental disasters — Chernobyl, the Aral Sea, The Yangtze River and Copsa Mica — all of which are the result of industrialisation. It seems that the way of the future is not necessarily to abandon capitalism, but to develop improved environmental controls.

3. Multinationals, operating in a global financial marketplace, ignore the environment. If this is the case, James argues that with a little thought the situation can be changed. Because multinationals require investment funds, it is possible to control their actions through how these funds are placed. Demanding environmental responsibility as a precondition for investment will help manage multinationals.

Source: James, D. (1995). Business faces a new environment challenge, *Business Review Weekly*, January 30; Lacsniak, G. R., Pecotich, A. & Spadaccini, A. (1995). Towards 2000: A tougher future for Australian business? *Asia Pacific Journal of Management*, 11, 67–90.

Exhibit 1.1
Organisations
and management
in society

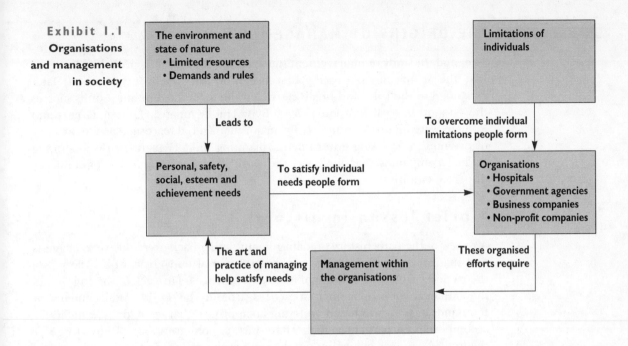

Source: Adapted and modified from Wren, D. A. (1979). *The Evolution of Management Thought*. New York: John Wiley & Sons, p. 10.

The purpose of this book is to help you learn how to manage individuals and groups as resources of organisations. These resources are operating in a world surrounded by change. Organisations are essential to the way our society operates in the world. In industry, education, health care and defence, organisations have created impressive gains for our standard of living and our worldwide image. The size of the organisations with which you deal daily should illustrate the tremendous political, economic and social powers they separately possess. For example, your university has much economic, political and social power in its community. If a large company announced that it was closing its plant in your community, the resulting impact might be devastating economically. On the other hand, if General Motors announced it was opening an automobile assembly plant in your community, the impact would probably be very positive. Exhibit 1.1 illustrates the role that organisations play in our changing world.

Organisations are, however, much more than means for providing goods and services.[3] They create the settings in which most of us spend our lives. In this respect, they have profound influence on our behaviour. However, because large-scale organisations have developed only in recent times, we are just now beginning to recognise the necessity for studying them. Researchers have just begun the process of developing ways to study the behaviour of people in organisations.

THE ORIGINS OF MANAGEMENT

The modern study of management started around 1990.[4] It is probable, however, that the management process first began in the family organisation, later expanded to the tribe and finally pervaded the formalised political units such as those found in early Babylonia (5000 BC). The Egyptians, Chinese, Greeks and Romans were all noted in history for major managerial feats such as the building of pyramids, organising governments, planning military manoeuvres, operating trading companies that traversed the world and controlling a geographically dispersed empire.

A brief lesson in history

A review of the early history of management dating back over 7000 years suggests that management as a process was based on trial and error, with little or no theory and virtually no sharing of ideas and practices. This lack of sharing slowed the influence of management practices around the world. Management for thousands of years was based on trying an approach that seemed to be suited for accomplishing a particular goal. There was no common body of knowledge or theoretical basis for managing the Roman Empire or building the great pyramid of Cheops. Exhibit 1.2 presents a select few of the early management contributions.

The period between 1700 and 1785 is referred to as the Industrial Revolution in England.[5] As a nation, England changed dramatically from a rural society to the workshop of the world. It was the first nation to successfully make the transition from a rural–agrarian society to an industrial–commercial society.[6] Management of the workshops of England was characterised by an emphasis on efficiency, strict controls and rigid rules and procedures.

Industrialisation

A new industrial era began in the United States around the time of the Civil War. There was a dramatic expansion of mechanical industries such as the railroad. In addition, large industrial manufacturing complexes grew in importance. Attempts to better plan, organise and control the work of these complexes led managers to discuss their situations and present papers at meetings. The first modern-era management articles were published in engineering journals.

In 1881, a new way to study management started with a US$100 000 gift by Joseph Wharton to the University of Pennsylvania to establish a management department in a college. The management curriculum at the time covered topics such as strikes, business law, the nature of stocks and bonds and principles of work cooperation.

Scientific management

In 1886, an engineer, Frederick W. Taylor, presented a paper entitled 'The engineer as an economist' at a national meeting of engineers. This paper and others presented by Taylor expressed his philosophy of **scientific management**.[7] Taylor's major thesis was that the maximum good for society can come only through the cooperation of management and labour in the application of scientific methods. He stated that the principles of management were:

Exhibit 1.2	Approximate Time	Contributing Group or Individual	Management Contribution
A select view of management in history	5000 BC	Sumerians	Kept records of work achievements
	4000 BC	Egyptians	Practised planning, organising and controlling
	2600 BC	Egyptians	Decentralised organisations
	1100 BC	Chinese	Recognised and practised organisation design
	350 BC	Greeks	Applied scientific methods
	325 BC	Alexander the Great	Used staff to advise and counsel
	AD 280	Diocletian	Delegation of authority
	AD 1776	Adam Smith	Applied principle of work specialisation
	AD 1881	Joseph Wharton	Established first college course of study in business management

- develop a science for each element of an employee's work, which replaces the old rule-of-thumb method;
- scientifically select and then train, teach and develop the worker, whereas in the past a worker chose the work to do and was self-trained;
- heartily cooperate with each other to ensure that all work done was in accordance with the principles of science;
- assure an almost equal division of the work and the responsibility between management and non-managers.

These four principles constituted Taylor's concept of scientific management. Some regard him as the father of all present-day management. Even if this is considered an exaggerated viewpoint, Taylor was a key figure in the promotion of the role of management in organisations. He has had a lasting impact on a unified, coherent way to improve how managers perform their jobs.

Functions of management

Henri Fayol, a French industrialist, presented what is considered the first comprehensive statement of a general theory of management. First published in France in 1916,[8] Fayol's *Administrative Industrielle et Générale* was largely ignored in the United States until it was translated into English in 1949.

Fayol attributed his success in managing a large mining company to his system of management, which he believed could be taught and learned. He emphasised the importance of carefully practising efficient planning, organising, commanding, coordinating and controlling.

Fayol's approach was a significant contribution in that it presented three important developments that have had a lasting impact on the field:

1. Management is a separate body of knowledge that can be applied in any type of organisation.
2. A theory of management can be learned and taught.
3. There is a need for teaching management at colleges.

7

Three of Fayol's functions — planning, organising and controlling — are introduced in Appendix A. These three of his five functions portray the building blocks of managing people in organisations.

THE ORIGINS OF ORGANISATIONAL BEHAVIOUR

The more contemporary study of what people do within organisations was developed in the mid to late 1940s. The behavioural sciences — psychology, sociology and cultural anthropology — have provided the principles, scientific rigour and models for what we refer to today as organisational behaviour. Therefore, it is important to note that organisational behaviour provides a multidisciplinary view of what people do in organisational settings.

Each of the disciplines that constitute organisational behaviour provides a slightly different focus, analytical framework and theme for helping managers answer questions about themselves, non-managers and environmental forces (e.g. competition, legal requirements and social–political changes).

The Hawthorne studies

A team of Harvard University researchers were asked to study the activities of work groups at Western Electric's Hawthorne plant outside Chicago (Cicero, Illinois).[9] Before the team arrived, an initial study at the plant examined the effects of illumination on worker output. It was proposed that 'illumination' would affect the work group's output. One group of female workers completed its job tasks in a test room where the illumination level remained constant. The other study group was placed in a test room where the amount of illumination was changed (increased and decreased).

In the test room where illumination was varied, worker output increased when illumination increased. This, of course, was an expected result. However, output also increased when illumination was decreased. In addition, productivity increased in the control group test room, even though illumination remained constant throughout the study.

The Harvard team was called in to solve the mystery. The team concluded that something more than an economic approach to improve worker output was occurring within the work groups. The researchers conducted additional studies on the impact of rest pauses, shorter working days, incentives and type of supervision on output. They also uncovered what is referred to as the 'Hawthorne Effect' operating within the study groups.[10] That is, the workers felt important because someone was observing and studying them at work. Thus, they produced more because of being observed and studied.

Elton Mayo, Fritz Roethlisberger and William Dickson were the leaders of the Harvard study team. They continued their work at the Hawthorne plant from 1924 to 1932. Eight years of study included over 20 000 Western Electric employees.

The Harvard researchers found that individual behaviours were modified within and by work groups. In a study referred to as the 'bank wiring room', the Harvard researchers were again faced with some perplexing results. The study group completed only two terminals per worker daily. This was considered to be a low level of output.

The bank wiring room workers appeared to be restricting output. The work group was being friendly, got along well on and off the job, and helped each other. There appeared to be a practice of protecting the slower workers. The fast producers did not want to outperform the slowest producers. The slow producers were part of the team and fast workers were instructed to 'slow it down'. The group formed an informal production norm of only two completed boards per day.

The Harvard researchers learned that economic rewards did not totally explain worker behaviour. Workers were observant, complied with norms and respected the informal social structure of their group. It was also learned that social pressures could restrict output.

The Hawthorne studies are perhaps the most cited research in the applied behavioural science area. They are not referred to as the most rigorous series of studies. For example, it was determined that workers were replaced in the experimental groups when they did not produce adequately. Nonetheless, the Hawthorne studies did point out that workers are more complex than economic theories of the time proposed. Workers respond to group norms, social pressures and observation. In 1924 to 1932, these were important revelations that changed the way management viewed workers.

THE IMPORTANCE OF STUDYING ORGANISATIONAL BEHAVIOUR

Reading I
Organisational
behaviour
revisited

Why do employees behave as they do in organisations? Why is one individual or group more productive than another? Why do managers continually seek ways to design jobs and delegate authority? These and similar questions are important to the relatively new field of study known as **organisational behaviour**. Understanding the behaviour of people in organisations has become increasingly important as management concerns — such as employee productivity, the quality of work life, job stress and career progression — continue to make front-page news.

Clearly understanding that organisational behaviour (OB) has evolved from multiple disciplines, we will use the following definition of OB throughout this book:

The study of human behaviour, attitudes and performance within an organisational setting; drawing on theory, methods and principles from such disciplines as psychology, sociology and cultural anthropology to learn about *individual* perceptions, values, learning capacities and actions while working in *groups* and within the total *organisation*; analysing the external environment's effect on the organisation and its human resources, missions, objectives and strategies.

This multidisciplinary anchored view of organisational behaviour illustrates a number of points:

1. OB is a *way of thinking*. Behaviour is viewed as operating at individual, group and organisational levels. This approach suggests that when studying OB, we must identify clearly the level of analysis being used — individual, group and/or organisational.

2. OB is *multidisciplinary*. This means that it utilises principles, models, theories and methods from other disciplines. The study of OB is not a discipline or a generally accepted science with an established theoretical foundation. It is a field that only now is beginning to grow and develop in stature and impact.
3. There is a distinctly *humanistic orientation* within organisational behaviour. People and their attitudes, perceptions, learning capacities, feelings and goals are of major importance to the organisation.
4. The field of OB is *performance-oriented*. Why is performance low or high? How can performance be improved? Can training enhance on-the-job performance? These are important issues facing practising managers.
5. The *external environment* is seen as having significant impact on organisational behaviour.
6. Since the field of OB relies heavily on recognised disciplines, the role of the *scientific method* is deemed important in studying variables and relationships. As the scientific method has been used in conducting research on organisational behaviour, a set of principles and guidelines on what constitutes good research has emerged.[11]
7. The field has a distinctive *applications orientation*; it is concerned with providing useful answers to questions which arise in the context of managing organisations.[12]

Leaders and organisational behaviour

Leaders of workers, managers and administrators in organisations are being challenged by many changes occurring within and outside of institutions. Terms such as 'transformation', 'cultural diversity', 'global competitiveness' and 're-engineering' are freely used by experts and non-experts. Each of these concepts points out that leaders are being asked to perform effectively in a changing world. The make-up of the workforce is changing as more and more minorities and women enter organisations and expect to be treated fairly. The differences in ethnicity, gender and background require leaders to deal with individuals whose values, concerns and needs are different from those that existed in the workforce in the 1960s. The importance of dealing with *diversity* and finding ways to capitalise on it is a challenge facing leaders.

In addition to the changing make-up of the workforce is the increased emphasis that consumers place on *value*.[13] The trend among consumers is to consider the total value of a product or service. Today, more than ever, customers expect organisations to be responsive to their needs, to provide prompt service and delivery, and to provide top-quality goods or services at the best price possible. Xerox shows an understanding of the value hierarchy for its customers. Exhibit 1.3 illustrates levels of customer service value for its customers. The outer band designates the supplementary services, the middle level focuses on specific value-added services and the core level has just two words: FIX IT.

Along with an increasingly diverse workforce and demanding customers, leaders must contend with changes in both domestic and global markets and competition. Today, there is the global market, which consists of richer, more educated and more demanding customers in every competitive country. The global market wants a world of easy access to products and services. Leaders

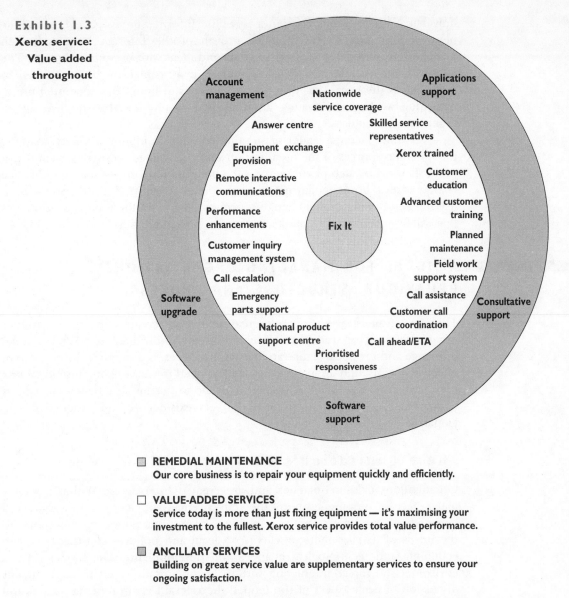

Exhibit 1.3
Xerox service:
Value added
throughout

☐ **REMEDIAL MAINTENANCE**
Our core business is to repair your equipment quickly and efficiently.

☐ **VALUE-ADDED SERVICES**
Service today is more than just fixing equipment — it's maximising your investment to the fullest. Xerox service provides total value performance.

☐ **ANCILLARY SERVICES**
Building on great service value are supplementary services to ensure your ongoing satisfaction.

Source: Bond, W. A (1994). *Touchstone.* New York: John Wiley & Sons, p. 13.

must assure customers that their high-quality goods or services will be available when the consumer wants them and at a competitive price. Establishing the work team, department or organisation that can respond and compete globally is what leaders are being asked to accomplish. The Global Encounter points out some of the dramatic changes and trends that are occurring that require managers to be prepared for globalisation more than ever before.

For over three decades, the development of the integrated circuit has permitted an increasing amount of information to be processed or stored in a single microchip. The leaders within organisations are asked to efficiently use and manage the available information technology so that the company can compete globally. The Internet is an example of an electronic information-sharing system. A national web of high-speed networks links business, state, university and regional computer systems. Information is passed from one network to another. The dramatic growth of the Internet has resulted in managers around the world sharing data and ideas with like-minded peers. The length of time it takes an idea to circulate or a problem to be considered by peers across the ocean has dropped from weeks to hours. The potential use in managing workers, motivating an individual or altering the structure of an organisation is endless.

Everything facing a leader in an organisation is in motion. Properly aligning the human resources of the organisation with the changes occurring requires an understanding of such phenomena as the organisation's environment, individual characteristics, group behaviour, organisational structure and design, decision making and organisational change processes. These are the topics and concepts that will be covered in this book and they are presented in Exhibit 1.4 (p. 14).

A MODEL FOR MANAGING ORGANISATIONS: BEHAVIOUR, STRUCTURE AND PROCESSES

This text frames a set of reference points to create a way to consider organisations. The study of the environment, individual and interpersonal influence and group structure and design processes, is done with the concept of effectiveness in mind. Managers and leaders need to view the organisational task they face in terms of effectiveness in order to accomplish that goal. Unless effectiveness is achieved over time, the very existence of the enterprise is in jeopardy.

The organisation's environment

Organisations exist in societies and are created by societies. Within a society many factors impinge upon the effectiveness of an organisation, and management must be responsive to them. Every organisation must respond to the needs of its customers or clients, to legal and political constraints and to economic and technological changes and developments. The model reflects environmental forces interacting within the organisation and throughout our discussion of each aspect of the model, the relevant environmental factors will be identified and examined.

The individual in the organisation

Individual performance is the foundation of organisational performance. Understanding individual behaviour therefore is critical for effective management, as illustrated in this account:

Ted Johnson has been a field representative for a major drug manufacturer since he graduated from university 7 years ago. He makes daily calls on physicians, hospitals, clinics and pharmacies as a representative of the many drugs his company manufactures. During his time in the field, prescription rates and sales for all of his company's major drugs have increased, and he has won three national sales awards given by the company. Yesterday Ted was promoted to sales

GLOBAL · Encounter

The realities of competing globally
The reality of the interdependence of global markets is changing the way business is transacted and how people work at home and abroad.

As globalisation takes hold, companies around the world will have to adapt and prepare for the way business is conducted and how organisations are going to be led. A few safe comments about what leaders can expect to be faced with to compete in domestic and foreign markets are the following:

Flatter hierachies. Fewer bureaucratic administrators so that faster reaction times and freer flow of ideas exist is beginning to be more widely practised. Asea Brown Bover (ABB), the Zurich-based manufacturing company, has one layer of managers between the executives and the operating employees.

More joint ventures and partnerships. These alliances conserve capital, and bring a company new technologies and local contacts to conduct business. AT&T is attempting to form an alliance with Unisource, a consortium of European telephone companies, to break into the still highly protected European telecom market.

Increased use of teams. Employees formed into quick-action teams to solve problems and to start new operations are used at Texas Instruments, Unilever and General Electric (GE) Appliances.

Nurturing innovation. The leader is expected to set the tone to help establish a culture that recognises and records innovation. Staying and thinking into the future stimulates others working with the leader. Andy Grove (CEO) has shifted Intel's mission and focus from memories to microprocessors to systems.

Information age. The information era that is emerging is based on the blending of computers, telephones and televisions into a telecommunications industry. It is this industry that is the driving force behind the global economy. Managers will have, in the palms of their hands, picocomputers that will allow them to have at their disposal information, data bases, files and contacts while they move around. At Pitney Bowes, technicians now carry wireless terminals connected to the wireless Ardis network. The set-up tells technicians where the next service call is, as well as information about the last date of service for the customer. If parts are needed, they can be ordered over the Ardis system and immediately shipped. The system has improved customer satisfaction and increased productivity by over 12% on average per technician.

Source: 'Tearing up today's organization chart', *Business Week*, Special Issue on 21st Century Capitalism, Fall 1994, 80–86; 'Enter the McFord', *Economist*, July 23, 1994, 69; and 'Borderless Management', *Business Week*, May 23, 1994, 24–26.

manager for a seven-district region. He no longer will be selling but instead will be managing fifteen other representatives. Ted accepted the promotion because he believes he knows how to motivate and lead salespeople. He commented: 'I know the personality of the salesperson. They are special people. I know what it takes to get them to perform. Remember, I am one. I know their values and attitudes and what it takes to motivate them. I know I can motivate a sales force.'

In his new job, Ted Johnson will be trying to maximise the individual performance of fifteen sales representatives. In doing so he will be dealing with several facets of individual behaviour. Our model includes four important influences on individual behaviour and motivation in organisations: individual characteristics, individual motivation, rewards and stress.

Individual characteristics

Because organisational performance depends on individual performance, managers such as Ted Johnson must have more than a passing knowledge of the

Exhibit 1.4
A framework for
the study of
organisational
behaviour and
management

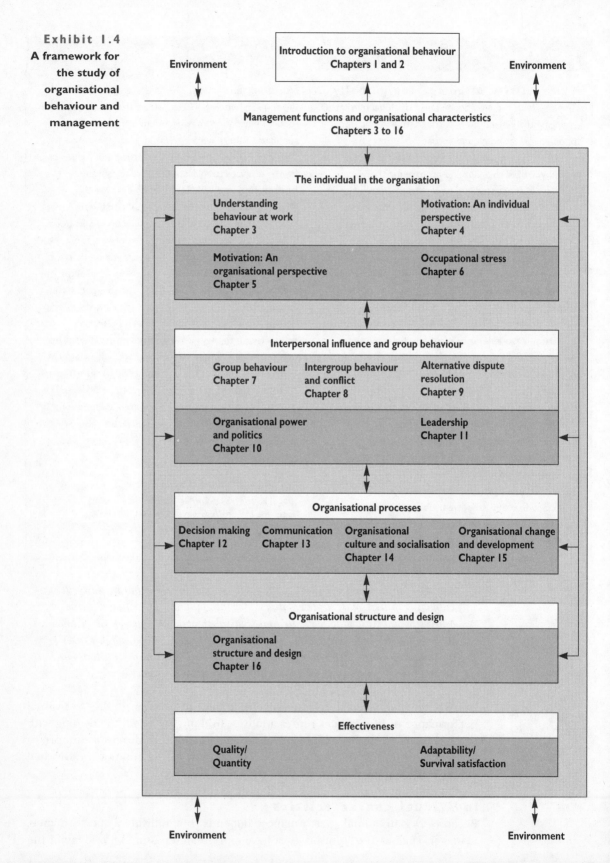

determinants of individual performance. Psychology and social psychology contribute a great deal of relevant knowledge about the relationships among attitudes, perceptions, personality, values and individual performance. Managers cannot ignore the necessity for acquiring and acting on knowledge of the individual characteristics of both their subordinates and themselves.

Individual motivation

Motivation and ability to work interact to determine performance. Motivation theory attempts to explain and predict how the behaviour of individuals is aroused, started, sustained and stopped. Unlike Ted Johnson, not all managers and behavioural scientists agree on what is the 'best' theory of motivation. In fact, motivation is so complex that it may be impossible to have an all-encompassing theory of how it occurs. However, managers must still try to understand it. They must be concerned with motivation because they must be concerned with performance.

Rewards

One of the most powerful influences on individual performance is an organisation's reward system. Management can use rewards (or punishment) to increase performance by present employees. Management also can use rewards to attract skilled employees to join the organisation. Pay cheques, raises and bonuses are important aspects of the reward system, but they are not the only aspects. Ted Johnson makes this point very clear in the account when he states, 'I know what it takes to get them to perform.' Performance of the work itself can provide employees with rewards, particularly if job performance leads to a sense of personal responsibility, autonomy and meaningfulness.

Stress

Stress is an important result of the interaction between the job and the individual. Stress in this context is a state of imbalance within an individual that often manifests itself in such symptoms as insomnia, excessive perspiration, nervousness and irritability. Whether stress is positive or negative depends on the individual's tolerance level. People react differently to situations that outwardly would seem to induce the same physical and psychological demands. Some individuals respond positively through increased motivation and commitment to finish the job. Other individuals respond less desirably by turning to such outlets as alcoholism and drug abuse. It is to be hoped that Ted Johnson will respond positively to the stresses of his new job.

Management's responsibility in managing stress has not been clearly defined, but there is growing evidence that organisations are devising programs to deal with work-induced stress.

Interpersonal influence and group behaviour

Interpersonal influence and group behaviour are also powerful forces affecting organisational performance. The effects of these forces are illustrated in the following account:

Kelly McCaul spent 2½ years as a teller in the busiest branch of First National Bank. During that time she developed close personal friendships with her co-workers. These friendships extended off the job as well. Kelly and her friends formed a wine-and-cheese club and were the top team in the bankwide bowling league. In addition, several of the friends took ski trips together each winter.

Two months ago Kelly was promoted to branch manager. She was excited about the new challenge but was a little surprised that she got the promotion since some other likely candidates in the branch had been with the bank longer. She began the job with a great deal of optimism and believed her friends would be genuinely happy for her and supportive of her efforts. However, since she became branch manager, things haven't seemed quite the same. Kelly can't spend nearly as much time with her friends because she is often away from the branch attending management meetings at the main office. A training course she must attend two evenings a week has caused her to miss the last two wine-and-cheese club meetings and she senses that some of her friends have been acting a little differently toward her lately.

Recently, Kelly said, 'I didn't know that being part of the management team could make that much difference. Frankly, I never really thought about it. I guess I was naive. I'm seeing a totally different perspective of the business and have to deal with problems I never knew about.'

Kelly McCaul's promotion has made her a member of more than one group. She is a member of her old group of friends at the branch and also a member of the management team. She is finding out that group behaviour and expectations have a strong impact on individual behaviour and interpersonal influence. Our model includes five important aspects of group and interpersonal influence on organisation behaviour: group behaviour, intergroup behaviour and conflict, alternative dispute resolution, organisational power and politics, and leadership.

Group behaviour

Groups form because of managerial action and also because of individual efforts. Managers create work groups to carry out assigned jobs and tasks. Such groups, created by managerial decisions, are termed **formal groups**. The group that Kelly McCaul manages at her branch is a formal group. Groups also form as a consequence of employees' actions. Such groups, termed **informal groups**, develop around common interests and friendships. The wine-and-cheese club at Kelly McCaul's branch is an informal group. Though not sanctioned by management, groups of this kind can affect organisational and individual performance. The effect can be positive or negative, depending on the intention of the group's members. If the group at Kelly's branch decided informally to slow the work pace, this norm would exert pressure on individuals who wanted to remain a part of the group. Effective managers recognise the consequences of individuals' need for affiliation.

Intergroup behaviour, conflict and conflict management

As groups function and interact with other groups, they develop their own unique set of characteristics, including structure, cohesiveness, roles, norms and processes. As a result, groups may cooperate or compete with other groups and intergroup competition can lead to conflict. If the management of Kelly's bank instituted an incentive program with cash bonuses to the branch bringing in the most new customers, this might lead to competition and conflict among the branches. While conflict among groups can have beneficial results for an organisation, too much or the wrong kinds of intergroup conflict can have very negative results. Thus, managing intergroup conflict is an important aspect of managing organisational behaviour. One of the challenges for managers is to ensure that conflicts are resolved functionally. They may choose to use strategies targeted directly at resolving the conflict, or they may decide that structural changes to the organisations are better able to address the sources of conflict.

Alternative dispute resolution

Negotiation and mediation are two important strategies for resolving conflicts. In negotiations, two individuals try to directly resolve conflicts. By adopting strategies that help them to understand the other person's needs and values, negotiators are able to resolve conflict effectively. Sometimes, negotiations break down. To help resolve stalemates, it is possible to involve a neutral third party — a mediator. The mediator's role is to help manage the process of resolving conflicts, rather than determining how the conflict will be resolved.

Power and politics

Power is the ability to get someone to do something you want done or to make things happen in the way you want them to happen. Many people in our society are very uncomfortable with the concept of power, and some are very offended by it. This is because the essence of power is control over others. To many Australians, control over others is an offensive thought. However, power is a reality in organisations. Managers derive power from both organisational and individual sources. Kelly McCaul has power by virtue of her position in the formal hierarchy of the bank. She controls performance evaluations and salary increases. However, she may also have power because her co-workers respect and admire the abilities and expertise she possesses. Managers therefore must become comfortable with the concept of power as a reality in organisations and managerial roles.

Leadership

Leaders exist within all organisations. Like the bank's Kelly McCaul, leaders may be found in formal groups, but they may also be found in informal groups. Leaders may be managers or non-managers. The importance of effective leadership for obtaining individual, group and organisational performance is so critical that it has stimulated a great deal of effort to determine the causes of such leadership. Some people believe that effective leadership depends on traits and certain behaviours — separately and in combination. Other people believe that one leadership style is effective in all situations. Still others believe that each situation requires a specific leadership style.

Organisational processes

Certain behavioural processes give life to an organisation. When these processes do not function well, unfortunate problems can arise, as illustrated in this account:

When she began to major in marketing as a first-year university student, Debra Washney knew that some day she would work in that field. Once she completed her MBA, she was more positive than ever that marketing would be her life's work. Because of her excellent academic record, she received several outstanding job offers. She decided to accept the job offer she received from one of the nation's largest consulting firms. She believed this job would allow her to gain experience in several areas of marketing and to engage in a variety of exciting work. On her last day on campus, she told her favourite professor: 'This has got to be one of the happiest days of my life, getting such a great career opportunity.'

Recently, while visiting the university placement office, the professor was surprised to hear that Debra had told the placement director that she was looking for another job. Since she had been with the consulting company less than a year, the professor was somewhat surprised. He decided to call Debra and find out why she wanted to change jobs. This is what she told him: 'I guess you can say my first experience with the real world was a "reality shock". Since being with this company, I have done nothing but gather data on phone surveys. All day long I sit and talk on the phone, asking questions and checking off the answers. In graduate school I was trained to be a manager, but here I am doing what any high school graduate can do. I talked to my boss and he said that all employees have to pay their dues. Well, why didn't they tell me this while they were recruiting me? To say there was a conflict between the recruiting information and the real world would be a gross understatement. I'm an adult — why didn't they provide me with realistic job information and then let me decide if I wanted it? A little bit of accurate communication would have gone a long way.'

Our model includes four behavioural processes that contribute to effective organisational performance: communication, decision making, culture and socialisation and organisational change and development.

Communication process

Organisational survival is related to the ability of management to receive, transmit and act on information. The communication process links the organisation to its environment as well as to its parts. Information flows to and from the organisation and within the organisation. Information integrates the activities of the organisation with the demands of the environment. But information also integrates the internal activities of the organisation. Debra Washney's problem arose because the information that flowed from the organisation was different from the information that flowed *within* the organisation.

Decision-making process

The quality of decision making in an organisation depends on selecting proper goals and identifying means for achieving them. With good integration of behavioural and structural factors, management can increase the probability that high-quality decisions will be made. Debra Washney's experience illustrates inconsistent decision making by different organisational units (personnel and marketing) in the hiring of new employees. Organisations rely on individual decisions as well as group decisions, and effective management requires knowledge of both types of decisions.

These days it is common to read about managerial decisions that are considered unethical. It is now accepted that most decisions made in an organisation are permeated by ethics.[14] Managers are powerful and, where power exists, there is potential for good and evil. Recent headlines emphasise the ethical nature of decision making: 'Large brokerage house pays large bonuses to top managers for months before declaring bankruptcy'; 'Lawyers and arbitrators trade inside information'; and 'How companies spy on employees'.[15]

The power of managers is clearly portrayed in making decisions about employees' wellbeing, distributing organisational resources and designing and implementing rules and policies. In Debra Washney's case, she claims that the consulting company did not provide a realistic job preview. She is making a statement that suggests unethical behaviour on the part of the individuals who interviewed her for the job. Was this the right thing for the company to do? Debra suggests that it was not the right thing or the ethical way to conduct an interview. Ethical dilemmas will be discussed throughout the book because managers and workers must make decisions every day that have an ethical component.

Culture and socialisation processes

Whenever we join organisations, we need to make some adaptations to the norms and rules that govern behaviour — the organisation's culture. The process of learning these rules is called 'socialisation', and effective socialisation is an important determinant of organisational commitment and job satisfaction. Early experiences are critical and organisations that provide misleading information are likely to have the same experience as those who employed Deborah Washney. It is likely that, when employers provide an overly optimistic picture of life with the company, their recruits will experience 'reality shock'.

Organisational change and development processes

Managers sometimes must consider the possibility that effective organisational functioning can be improved by making significant changes in the total organisation. Organisational change and development represent planned attempts to improve overall individual, group and organisational performance. Debra Washney might well have been spared the disappointment she experienced had an organisational development effort uncovered and corrected the inconsistent communication and decision making that brought about Debra's unhappiness. Concerted, planned and evaluative efforts to improve organisational functioning have great potential for success.

Organisational structure and design

To work effectively in organisations managers must have a clear understanding of the organisational structure. Viewing an organisation chart on a piece of paper or framed on a wall, one sees only a configuration of positions, job duties and lines of authority among the parts of an organisation. However, organisational structures can be far more complex than that, as illustrated in the following account:

> *Dr John Rice was recently appointed dean of the business school at a major university. Prior to arriving on campus, Rice spent several weeks studying the*

funding, programs, faculty, students and organisational structure of the business school. He was trying to develop a list of priorities for things he believed would require immediate attention during his first year as dean. The vice-chancellor of the university had requested that he have such a list of priorities available when he arrived on campus.

During his first official meeting with the vice-chancellor, Rice was asked the question he fully expected to be asked: 'What will be your number one priority?' Rice replied: 'Although money is always a problem, I believe the most urgent need is to reorganise the business school. At present, students can major in only one of two departments — accounting and business administration. The accounting department has twenty faculty members. The business administration department has forty-three faculty members, including fifteen in marketing, sixteen in management and twelve in finance. I foresee a college with four departments — accounting, management, marketing and finance — each with its own chairperson. First, I believe such a structure will enable us to better meet the needs of our students. Specifically, it will facilitate the development of programs of majors in each of the four areas. Students must be able to major in one of the four functional areas if they are going to be prepared adequately for the job market. Finally, I believe such an organisational structure will enable us to more easily recruit faculty since they will be joining a group with interests similar to their own.'

As this account indicates, an organisation's structure is the formal pattern of activities and interrelationships among the various subunits of the organisation. Our model includes two important aspects of organisational structure: the actual structure of the organisation itself and job design.

The structure of the organisation refers to the components of the organisation and how these components fit together. Dr Rice plans to alter the basic structure of the business school. The result of his efforts will be a new structure of tasks and authority relationships that he believes will channel the behaviour of individuals and groups towards higher levels of performance in the business school.

Performance outcomes: Individual, group and organisational

Individual performance contributes to group performance, which, in turn, contributes to organisational performance. In truly effective organisations, however, management helps create a positive synergy: that is, a whole that is greater than the sum of its parts.

No one measure or criterion adequately reflects effectiveness at any level. The next chapter introduces the idea that organisational effectiveness must be considered in terms of multiple measures within a time frame. But ineffective performance at any level is a signal to management to take corrective actions. All of management's corrective actions will focus on elements of organisational behaviour, structure or processes.

SUMMARY OF KEY POINTS

Define the power of human resources. The key to an organisation's success is the institution's human resources. Organisations need human resources that work hard, think creatively and perform excellently. Rewarding, encouraging and nurturing the human resources in a timely and meaningful manner is what is required. Thus, the power of human resources refers to their importance.

Describe the disciplines that have contributed to the field of organisational behaviour. A number of contributing disciplines stand out such as psychology, sociology and cultural anthropology. Psychology has contributed information and data about motivation, personality, perception, job satisfaction and work stress. Sociology has offered information about group dynamics, communication problems, organisational change and formal organisation structure. Cultural anthropology has contributed information about culture, comparative attitudes and cross-cultural studies.

Discuss the importance of understanding behaviour in organisations. The behaviour of employees is the key to achieving effectiveness. People behave in many predictable and unpredictable ways. Each person has a unique behavioural pattern. Managers must observe, respond to and cope with the array of behaviour patterns displayed by employees.

Explain the 'Hawthorne Effect' in an organisational setting. The Hawthorne Effect is the behaviour or reaction of a person who is being observed. Individuals who are being observed are likely to react in a non-routine way because they are being watched or are a part of an experiment.

Identify the characteristics of what is referred to as the 'new psychological contract'. Employers and employees enter into a psychological contract. The employer believes that no worker is guaranteed a lifelong job or pay raise. If the worker's performance is good and profit is earned, then employment continues and pay raises are provided. Employees today believe that employers should be honest, concerned about their families and interested in their overall health. These assumptions are the basis of what is called the new psychological agreement.

REVIEW AND DISCUSSION QUESTIONS

1. Why is management so necessary in any organisation — hospital, bank or school?

2. Why is it useful to distinguish three levels of behaviour — individual, group and organisational — when discussing behaviour in organisations?

3. 'As organisations increase in size and complexity, managing the behaviour of organisational members becomes more difficult.' Do you agree or disagree with this statement? Why?

4. What knowledge about human behaviour in the workplace was uncovered by the Hawthorne studies?

5. Organisations are characterised by their goal-directed behaviour. So are people. How is the study of organisations similar to the study of people? How is it different?

6. What is *new* about how employees view management responsibilities in the 1990s?

7. Frequently, organisations are described in terms used to refer to personality characteristics — dynamic, greedy, creative, conservative and so on. Is this a valid way to describe organisations? Does this mean that the people in the organisation possess the same characteristics?

8. Organisations are influenced by the environment in which they operate; in turn, organisations influence their environments. List examples of both types of influence that you can recall from personal experience.

9. What are the characteristics of what we refer to as a 'healthy' organisation?

10. What behavioural sciences have contributed to the field of study that is called organisational behaviour? Explain.

ENDNOTES

1 Peterson, J. L. (1994). *The Road to 2015*. Corte Madera, CA: Waite Group Press.
2 Hardy, E. S. (1995). The Forbes 500, *Forbes*, April 24, 208–275.

3 See Urwick, L. F. (1976). That word *organization*, *Academy of Management Review*, 89–91.

4 Ivancevich, J. M., Lorenzi, P., Skinner, S. J., & Crosby, P. B. (1994). *Management: Quality and Competitiveness*. Burr Ridge, IL: Irwin.

5 Peterson, J. L. (1994). *The Road to 2015*. Corte Madera, CA: Waite Group Press.

6 George, C. S., Jnr. (1968). *The History of Management Thought*. Englewood Cliffs, NJ: Prentice Hall.

7 Banta, M. (1993). *Taylored Lives: Narrative Productions in the Age of Taylor, Veblen and Ford*. Chicago: Chicago University Press.

8 Fayol, H. (1929). *General and Industrial Management*, trans. J. A. Conbrough. Geneva: International Management Institute.

9 Mayo, E. (1945). *The Social Problems of Industrial Civilization*. Boston: Harvard University Press.

10 Roethlisberger, F. J., & Dickson, W. J. (1939).

Management and the Worker. Cambridge, MA: Harvard University Press.

11 Lawler III, E. E. (1985). Challenging traditional research assumptions. In E. E. Lawler III, A. M. Mohrman, Jr., S. A. Mohrman, G. E. Ledford, Jr., & T. G. Cummings (Eds.) *Doing Business That Is Useful for Theory and Practice*. San Francisco: Jossey-Bass.

12 Martin, R. (1993). The new behaviorism: A critique of economics and organization, *Human Relations*, 1085–1101.

13 Landsburg, S. E. (1993). *The Armchair Economist*. New York: Free Press.

14 Edmonson, W. F. (1990). A Code of Ethics: Do Corporate Executives and Employees Need It?, Fulton, MS.: Itawamba Community College Press.

15 Bylinsky, G. (1991). How companies spy on employees, *Fortune*, November 4, 131–140.

READING I   ORGANIZATIONAL BEHAVIOR REVISITED

Malcolm Warner [1,2]

Source: *Human Relations* 47, no. 10(1994), pp. 1151–65.

Introduction

Many textbooks in the field do still deal with the various stages through which theorizing about organizations has passed, covering approximately 100 years of development from Max Weber's early work up to the present. Organisational Behavior may be said in this sense to have developed on 'the shoulders of giants'. There is a long line of intellectual ancestors, some nearer and some further away, often confounding neat categorization and periodization, a problem to be discussed early in this paper. As a distinct subdiscipline, it is nonetheless relatively recent although many of its component parts derive from the late nineteenth and early twentieth century. Another view might see the origins of the subject as going much further back if we look at the history of the subfields which make up Organizational Behavior (such as the theory of the firm within economics).

In order to critically reexamine the field, it would probably be most useful to initially discuss its overall *chronology*, followed by an examination of the problems of categorization and periodization. In looking at the time frame, we can see the evolution of the different schools and indeed, there is less controversy here as there is probably more of a consensus in many cases that *x* clearly preceded *y*; for example, most scholars would agree that Scientific Management came before, say, Human Relations, although there may be overlaps and ebbs and flows of each school's influence (see Kelly, 1983). It is, even so, relatively problematic to draw the boundaries between the periods often delineated in the textbooks. Moreover, the dates of publication of influential works may not be meaningful as those of original first printing, subsequent editions, or translations may mislead. Weber (lived 1864 to 1920), for example, although published in German before the First World War, was not translated into English as far as his organisational writing in *The Theory of Social and Economic Organizations* were concerned until after the Second World War (that is, in 1947). A similar problem arises with Fayol (lived 1841 to 1925), with a similar long lag in publications.

Chronology, categorization, and periodization

Let us first deal with the Classical approaches, then Human Relations, and in turn what became known as Organizational Behavior essentially in the post-1945 period, with its subsequent developments and critiques (see Exhibit 1.5). All such approaches in turn were criticized by those who rejected the mainstream paradigm. Early studies of organizations dating from the turn of the century, for example, are easier to classify than later developments. By this we mean the body of work covering Scientific Management and Management Theory, which was the first to claim universality in its coverage and potential application. Moving into the 1920s and 1930s, we find a distinctive set of studies characterizing the inter-war period, namely the beginnings of Human Relations. The influence of the workgroup then became an important variable in the mainstream paradigm (and may even pre-date the inter-war years). The discovery of the Hawthorne effect, whereby an experimental impact was achieved by the researchers' intervention in the situation (between 1927 and 1932) superimposed a unity onto the analysis (see Mayo, 1993; Roethlisberger and Dickson, 1939). We can say what appears to be novel in particular contribution, for example as with the Hawthorne Studies, although what the ultimate and wider impact might have been is harder to say (see Gillespie, 1991). Even if we determine x as being influential, later interpretations may point out a possible misunderstanding of which factors were operative in its context, and that its distinctive claim to fame may be unsubstantiated. Furthermore, it may only be an exemplification of an already understandable theory.

Putting the 'people factor' into the heart of the subject to create Human Relations became a concern of many writers on organizations active in the inter-war years (see Follett, 1941; Child, 1969). The First World War had earlier seen the authorities trying to boost worker motivation vis-à-vis the war-effort. Such developments (and similar practices occurred during World War II) continued over into the subsequent peacetime period after 1918 (and after 1945, respectively). Organizational Behavior as a specific focus of academic attention and as part of the curriculum was however to be a specifically post-World War II phenomenon (see March, 1965). As Human Relations began to appear outmoded, Organizational Behavior's star rose. It emerged as 'the study of the structure and functioning of organizations and the behavior of groups and individuals within them', and an 'interdisciplinary quasi-independent science,

Exhibit 1.5	**Chronology of the development of organizational behavior as a field**
post 1870	Pre-Scientific Management
post 1890	Scientific Management
	Management Theory
post 1920	Human Relations
post 1945	Organizational Behavior
	Systems Theory
	Neo-Human Relations
	Decision-Making Theory
post 1960	Human Resources
	Organizational Development
	Organization Design
post 1970	Organization Culture
	Cross-Cultural Studies
	Alternative Organizational Theory

drawing primarily on the disciplines of sociology and psychology, but also on economics, political science, social anthropology, and production engineering' (see Pugh, Mansfield, and Warner, 1975, p. 1), with a permeability to new knowledge inputs, both theoretical and empirical vis-à-vis the individual disciplines on which it drew, especially empirically-based sociological, psychological, and other related studies. By the 1950s, distinctive emphases in the field had emerged. One area of interest became the fief of Organizational Psychologists, or Managerial Psychologists, as many of the new scholars in the field came to be known. In Managerial Economics, a new and robust Behavioral Theory of the Firm emerged (see Cyert and March, 1963). The Human Resources model (see Miles, 1965) was introduced not long after. The Contingency Approach soon took roots, as it was argued that there was no 'one best way' to run an organization.

It is probably very difficult to underestimate the contribution of Systems thinking to modern Organizational Behavior when looking at this period. A great deal of post-1945 thinking about organizations hinges on its relevance and use. General Systems Theory linked the environment to the functioning of the organization (Bertalanffy, 1950). Systems as such, or their component subsystems, could be delineated and studied (Dunlop, 1950). Although originally a biological construct, it became a dominating concept across many fields of knowledge after the Second World War. Following from early mainstream contributions to the field emphasizing the Open Systems approach (see Katz and Kahn, 1966), work in Organizational Design for example has advanced further (see Nystrom and Starbuck, 1981; Daft, 1992). Interest in Organizational Learning built on March and Olsen's (1976) work, with later contributions by Nystrom and Starbuck (1984) and others on how organizations must 'un-learn' to survive, or face decline. Organizational Decision-Making and Organizational Development and Culture also became important sub-areas of study (see Butler, 1991). In the active decades of the post-war period after 1945, it looked as if Organizational Behavior was heading in a clear direction, at least as far as positivist social science was concerned. It was from these decades that the dominant paradigm, the 'commonality of perspective', emerged and was consolidated (see Burrell and Morgan, 1979, p. 25). The 'functionalist paradigm', to quote their observations directly, 'has provided the dominant framework for the conduct of academic sociology and the study of organizations. It represents a perspective which is firmly rooted in the *sociology of regulation* and approaches its subject matter from an objectivist point of view' (1979, p. 25). The mainstream and its component parts are set out in Exhibit 1.6.

By the 1970s, the mainstream writers on organizations still expected that the field would develop along a number of meaningful and interdependent paths. They believed that Organizational Behavior would increasingly

---

Exhibit 1.6 Mainstream organizational behavior theorists: A summary

Mainstream Theorists	Examples include:
Scientific Management	
General Management	
Structural	
Group	
Individual	
Technology	
Economic	

---

become international, which it appears partly to have accomplished, with greater emphasis on multinational firms, as well as on developments such as participative management, employee commitment, and the growing influence of lower participants in organizations, albeit in the conditions of full employment prevailing at that time, which are now less prevalent. While it is clear that the themes of worker participation and self-management were prominent in the late 1960s and 1970s (see Strauss and Rosenstein, 1970; I.D.E., 1981) and throughout the following decade, they were less evident as we moved into the late 1980s (see Kochan et al., 1986; Schuler, 1989). Even so, a moderate degree of interest in participative management continued (see Macy et al., 1989; I.D.E., 1993) and the search for the holy grail of business success, as the emphasis on the performance variable (in a word, greater profitability of enterprises) grew in the tighter economic climate of the last decade. Such research promoted interest in good people-management (in its new guise of Human Resource Management — HRM — which had replaced personnel administration in its old usage and industrial relations as well in many instances), as found in, what were at the time, successful firms (see for example Peters and Waterman, 1982; Soeters, 1986, and subsequent publications) as did work on profit-sharing (see Poole, 1989). Developing human capital, whether at managerial or workplace level, became de rigueur by the end of the decade (see, for example, Kanter, 1990; Heller, 1992).

If there had been critics of all or part of the dominant paradigm all along, those *within* the Organizational Behavior network felt very confident the mainstream would prevail. Indeed, the flow of books and journal articles seemed to reinforce this confidence. The hegemony of the mainstream in North America appeared to be firmly established, and as the study of organizations in this vein diffused especially to Britain and the rest of Europe, conditions were right for this kind of knowledge transfer, as new institutions like the new business schools were being set up. The paradigm was not necessarily only North American in origin. Its roots were partly elsewhere: indeed some contributions were British for example, stemming from work done in the First World War in Ergonomics. It is only to note that the specific forms the paradigm took, or were expressed in, were largely anchored in

North American publications, such as the early classic Organizational Behaviour texts, with publication dates in the 1950s and 1960s, depending on their mainly sociological or psychological provenance, respectively. This particular potential bias will be commented upon again later in the paper. Apart from monographs and journal articles reporting both empirical theory and field research, it was mainly textbooks which provided the synthesis of individual, group, and structural levels of analysis which gave the field its distinctive flavor. A summary of their different approaches has been usefully provided by Morgan's *Images of Organizations* (1986), although there is probably no one text which would fully satisfy even those within the mainstream paradigm, or the post-mainstream theorists outside it, for whom the above work is too enmeshed in a philosophical position they would decidedly abjure.

Within the mainstream paradigm, Social Science was to be the main instrument by which Social Engineering was to be achieved, within organizations and even beyond them (see Popper, 1945), although the former term sometimes seemed too 'radical' a concept for the ears of American policymakers who were to fund such research, and the term Behavioral Science was used instead. It was indeed as a consequence of such caution that the term Organizational Behavior was coined. As its semantic flavor was not necessarily acceptable to all researchers, some preferred to avoid the involvement with Behaviorism, and all its connotations, and used terms like Organization Studies, although sometimes Organization Theory was used interchangeably with it. The onward march of Organizational Behavior broadly defined (see Aronoff, 1975), however, seemed to be in tune with the optimism of the times, as the post-war economic growth underpinned the foundations of both private prosperity and public confidence in the West. Several events were to undermine this state of affairs. Among these were, respectively, the anti-Vietnam protests especially on US campuses in the 1960s, the events of 1968 first in Paris, then worldwide, and lastly, the oil price shock of the early 1970s. The dissatisfied theorists in the field believed a different view of the world was needed, and with it an alternative perspective, or set of perspectives. While the historical origins of these new approaches, such as ethnomethodology, have yet to be written up,

Exhibit 1.7 Successive waves of managerial ideologies		
Managerial Ideology	Dates	Tenor
Industrial Betterment	1870–1900	N
Scientific Management	1900–1923	R
Welfare Capitalism/ human relations	1923–1955	N
Systems Rationalism	1955–1980	R
Organizational Culture	1980 —	N

Key: N = Normative control ideologies; R = Rational control ideologies (from Barley & Kanda, (1992), p. 364).

the dates of their publication point to the above period (see Burrell & Morgan, 1979). Thus, a result of such influences, a number of critiques of mainstream Organizational Behavior came to the forefront. Some had philosophical and methodological objections to the then current theories at hand; others developed radical criticisms of, for example, their contradictions.

Barley and Kunda (1992) have recently shed light on the succession of what they call 'managerial ideologies' in which the main schools of management thought are encapsulated in yet another way — namely, as an alternation between ideologies of normative and rational control. These waves are set out in Exhibit 1.7. 'Cultural antinomies', they argue, 'generate inherently unstable interpretations of social life and economic cycles occasion social tensions that highlight the antinomies' contradictions' (1992, p. 393). Emphasizing the *cyclical* nature of Organizational Behavior, there is an implicit assumption here that the next wave will involve the reemergence of a rational control ideology. This theoretical model differs from the *unilinear* one stressing the evolution of OB into an integrated, interdisciplinary field, as well as from the 'rise and fall' interpretation stressing the consolidation of the mainstream paradigm and then its disintegration.

In the Discussion section which follows, we go on to critically examine the limitations of the mainstream work in OB vis-à-vis its generalizability, its cultural biases, and the gap between theorists and practicing managers. We go on to argue that no single model has yet been presented which takes into account all the factors feeding into the evolution of OB as an area of study, especially the growing division between macro- and micro-level work.

Discussion

Early management thought, for example, 'observed practices in leading organizations and attempted to rationalize and explain them, as is true of all schools of organizational theory. It set forth general principles that appeared to be consistent with observed practices and then promoted them with vigor' (Perrow, 1970, p. 14). While critics may find such writings in the area rather *simpliste*, possibly with the exception of Weber (see Bendix, 1963) or Taylor (see Nelson, 1980), these were the earliest steps in looking at management practices and trying to *generalize* from them. Such ideas were often put forward as 'scientific,' and taught in the newly emerging business schools.

In constructing the mainstream paradigm, writers on organizations with *practical* experience were some of the first to set out general principles of management. F. W. Taylor (lived 1856 to 1915), for example, virtually invented time-and-motion study and production control methods (see Merkle, 1988; Spender, 1989). Two other classic exponents of this approach remain noteworthy, such as Henri Fayol (lived 1841 to 1925) (1949) who laid down proverbial axioms, like 'one man, one boss' and so on, and Chester Barnard (lived 1886 to 1961) who set out the functions of the executive vis-à-vis the formal as well as the informal workings of the organization, emphasizing common goals (1938), who was another major contributor to this tradition. Strauss et al. (1974, pp. 4–5) have suggested that these early management writers greatly influenced both organizational practice and performance because they helped 'to simplify and expedite organizational communication and to improve the quality of information used in decision-making'. More recently, Williamson (1990, p. v) has suggested that classical work like Barnards's has a 'timeless character,' and 'continues to have far-reaching and lasting impact on the study of organization' (1990, p. vi).

As they were based on observation, there did appear to be a match between the trial-and-error pragmatism found in real-life organizations and the principles adduced by those who had studied them (1970, p. 15). Applications of the generalizations derived probably did in turn affect subsequent practice (see Argyris and Schon, 1978). Often, real-life experiments preceded theory (see Warner, 1984).

While OB findings were seen by many academics and practitioners as objective knowledge, this was not universally accepted (see Bacharach, 1989, on evaluation criteria). Critics of the mainstream paradigm in the 1970s and 1980s, like Silverman (1970) and followers, put forward what they called the Social Action approach. They argued that people's behavior was a result of their perceptions and beliefs. They also accused those who had produced much of the research that had constituted the main paradigm of the period, for example Woodward's work (1958, 1965) which emphasized technology, or that of the Aston Group, which concentrated on structure *reification*, and misplaced objectivity. Clegg and Dunkerley (1980, p. 260) claimed that the Aston research was a 'fetishistic exercise in objectification'. Pugh et al. (1968), Blau and Schonherr (1971), and Child (1972) had pointed to contextual variables such as size and technology, as well as ownership, to highlight how an organization's structure might be differentiated from another. While defenders of the Aston School, as Pugh and colleagues have been called (see Donaldson, 1985), have been unambiguous, others have been strictly critical. Even those within the original research group later became more ambiguous and stressed the role of strategic Choice emphasizing the role of the dominant coalition in organizations (see Child, 1972 and subsequent work). Many of the studies under attack were seen as cross-sectional, neglecting longitudinal factors and underplaying *processual* variables (see Weick, 1979).

Writers such as Burrell and Morgan (1979) even set out a competing paradigm which was based on alternative organizational approaches, such as Anti-Organizational, Neo-Marxian Radical Structuralist, and Radical Organizational Theories. Critical theoretical research emphasized macro-level variables such as class, status, and power, as well as race and gender (see Flax, 1990; Alvesson and Billing, 1992). The use of explanations of organizational life as based on '*metaphors*' was put forward by Morgan (1986, p. 12), for it 'may lead us to see and understand organizations in distinctive yet partial ways'. Such a reading, he suggests, takes us away from the onesided view and we must then get to understand how different perspectives 'may co-exist in a complementing or even paradoxical way' (1985, p. 13) when studying the ways organizations work. Clegg (1990) subsequently characterized Post-Modernism as everything Modernist theory was not, and pointed to a New Jerusalem (see 1990, p. 181). Debunking Fordist notions of mass production was in turn another Post-Organizational Behavior response invoking notions like 'flexible specialization' (see Piore and Sable, 1984; Loveridge and Pitt, 1990; Campbell and Warner, 1992). New technology, it was argued, could increasingly render small as beautiful. Critical Management Theorists have also recently invoked social theorists like Foucault and Habermas to emancipate the subject from mainstream influence (see Alvesson and Willmott, 1992).

A further problem in evaluating Organizational Behavior as a field is that, while on the one hand it aimed at generalizability, given the contingency chosen, it was mostly based on one-country studies. A preponderance of sources cited in most papers, monographs, and texts, for example, were from the US, as is the authorship of the published works themselves. In this sense, many contributions to the subject could be said to be culture-biased. In the light of the above observations, some felt that Organizational Behavior should take into account and pay more attention to the variety of national cultures (see Roberts, 1970; Tayeb, 1988). In turn, research has surfaced which has conceptualized this cross-cultural contingency, under the heading of the 'societal effect' — for example, some observers suggested (see Maurice, Sorge, and Warner, 1980; Sorge and Warner, 1986) that British, French, and West German organizational structures were different, even when controlling for technology, size, and other variables. A very large-scale cross-cultural research study covering most important nation-states was carried out by Hofstede (1980), whose book *Culture's Consequences* was to prove particularly influential if not controversial in its subfield, with a further synthesis later appearing in *Cultures and Organizations* (1991).

Schein (1965) had earlier developed links between the concepts of internal Organization Culture and leadership at the micro-level. Building on previous work (Jaques, 1951), writers such as Argyris and Schon (1978), Morgan (1986,

1989), and more recently Czarniawska-Joerges (1992) explored the concept of Organization culture emphasizing for example symbols, values, and subcultures, although the roots may be found back in Roethlisberger and Dixon's (1939) work on the Hawthorne experiments. Bridging the leadership and cross-cultural fields, the work of several researchers (for example Smith and Peterson, 1988) has shown how managers operate with different sets of cultural assumptions. They reveal how there may be discrepancies between the host-country culture and that of the multinational firm itself. Drawing on Western European research, a rival to the North American hegemony of the *Administrative Science Quarterly* (the ASQ, as it is known in the field) has appeared, namely *Organization Studies* (OS) sponsored by the European Group of Organizational Sociologists (EGOS), which has tried to offer a wider cultural perspective in the field. Pragmatic interest in how Japan as an industrial society has achieved its outstanding and envied economic success in recent years has also led to a high incidence of books and research papers based on that culture, or comparative between Western and Japanese enterprises (see for example Ouchi, 1981; Aoki, 1988; Whitehill, 1990). Hofstede and Bond (1988) compared cultural goals with economic growth rates in the 'little dragon' economies; whereas Whitley (1990) more recently matched up national economic values with forms of business organization in the East Asian context and other studies have looked at managerial behavior in the Pacific Basin (see for example Redding, 1990; Fruin, 1992; Warner, 1992).

Defending the mainstream, Donaldson (1985: pp. 155 ff) has argued that we can still have 'a value-neutral way of describing an organization. There is no implication that having a low score on say formalization is either ineffective or morally wrong. Indeed the modern contingency view has to a degree arisen as a rejection of classical management theories ...' (1985, pp. 156–57). This view strongly emphasizes that the structure most suitable for firms depends on the situational contingencies. Ring-fencing the field, the author goes on to argue that 'Organizations sociology is neither the study of the whole world nor of the entirety of sociology. It is a modest enquiry into organizations which is slowly enabling people to better understand how their aims may be helped or hindered through certain collective arrangements. As such, the results of these enquiries make a contribution to social discourse, widely valued by different members of society' (1985, p. 174). On the other hand, many scholars take another view and there have been fierce debates in recent years on a wide range of issues — quantitative vs. qualitative, positivist vs. antipositivist, and so on (see Clegg and Dunkerley, 1980, as well as Morgan (1986) for the content and flavor of some of these controversies). There is also the clash between those who see control as a value and those who favor autonomy as their preferred aim (see Brown, 1992). Critics of the field also include the practitioners who find much of the literature to be 'ivory-tower' and therefore of no great relevance to the professional manager in the firing line. This line of attack is often part of a general onslaught on the North American-style business schools' approach and their philosophy. Indeed, one such blast even has the title *What They Don't Teach You at the Harvard Business School* (McCormack, 1984), although it is not a formalized, systematic critique of Organizational Behavior as such or its component parts.

Some writers on organization do not, however, see the gap between theorists and managers as too wide, given for example the widespread diffusion of Organizational Development notions (see Beer and Walton, 1987). Theorists and practitioners in this vein have developed Neo-Human Relations micro-level techniques such as T-groups, team-building, assertiveness training, and so on (see Beer and Walton, 1987). In the related leadership field itself, later OB contributions sought a new synthesis (see Hunt, 1991), following in the empirical, multilevel research-tradition. However, more-broadly based studies have appeared, aimed at an informed practitioner audience, for example Tichy and Devanna's (1990) work on the 'transformational leader,' as well as Kotter's (1990) analysis of how leadership differs from management, and how the former can achieve change in business organizations by first conceiving a 'vision' and then communicating it to everyone else in the firm. One commentator (Morgan, 1986) even attributes an intuitive appreciation of concepts learned through experience to the practitioner — 'Effective managers and professionals in all walks of life, whether they be business executives, public administrators, organizational consultants, politicians, or trade unionists, have become skilled in the art of "reading" the situation that they are attempting to organize or manage' (1986, p. 11). It is also true to say that some of the most original studies (the Hawthorne experiment, the Tavistock Institute's work, and so on) have been market-led and initiated on management's behalf, with interesting theoretical spin-offs. Many insightful studies have therefore emerged and still result from such projects. On the other hand, a number of texts invoke Lewin's dictum — 'There is nothing as practical as a good theory' (cited in Pugh et al., 1975, p. 16) — in their attempt to show the proximity of theory and practice and to rescue theory from too abstract a role in the organizational context.

Finally, it is clear that categorization of the types of theorists used in this paper is not totally inclusive. Any division into macro-or micro-(or even meso-) levels will inevitably overlap with one or more of the periodizations we have set out above. Nonetheless, we would conclude that macro-level work would be more likely to coincide with the research of structural theorists, for example, whereas micro-level work might be found more readily with, say, the contribution of individual and group theorists. While some theorists had hoped for greater integration of all levels of analysis with Organizational Behavior as an emergent interdisciplinary endeavor, it is clear that this has not come to pass. A pragmatic compromise seems to be the most probable outcome in the circumstances of growing fragmentation of research-agenda. The pressure of market forces does seem to be aiding this process, for while a good number of academics still lean towards macro-level contributions, many more are likely to find both public and corporate research funds and sponsorship for work at the micro-level, especially where these have potential applications in the workplace.

Concluding remarks

We can therefore conclude from the reexamination of the chronology, categorization, and periodization of how the field developed that a unilinear view cannot be substantiated, and that by the 1990s, Organizational Behavior had become a good deal more theoretically and methodologically divergent than in past years. It is probably doubtful if the earlier dominance of the mainstream paradigm could be revived in what some writers on Post-Modernism have called 'the sociology of the consumer society' (see Bauman, 1992, pp. 110–11). The mainstream had in any case become excessively dependent on multivariate, empirical studies adopting the Contingency Approach. It had also failed to achieve an adequate level of conceptual integration, given the growing division between macro- and micro-level studies in the subject. Organizational Sociologists veered in one direction; Organizational Psychologists in the other. Nonetheless, qualitative studies in depth now stood head-high alongside quantitative multivariate analyses as a wider range of methodologies was given prominence (notwithstanding the contribution of the Alternative theorists), and many of the prestigious journals in the field had for example explicitly reflected the growing variety of papers submitted. There had also been a growing interest in many other parts of the world and different cultures, as we have seen, as well as the wider issues, such as global competition (see Ohmae, 1990; Porter, 1990; Sklair, 1991).

From the above evidence, it is premature to conclude that theorizing about organizations is in an intellectual cul-de-sac. There may yet be ways of rediscovering and renewing connections with its past, the 'recurring themes and problematics' with the possibility of a pragmatic mediation between 'competing perspectives and paradigms' (see Reed, 1993, p. 179). Even if the fierce debates and paradigm wars of the 1980s have somewhat abated, the dust has probably not yet settled.

Acknowledgment

I would like to thank the following colleagues for their helpful comments on earlier drafts of this paper: Professor John Child, Dr Matthew Jones, and Professor Roger Mansfield.

Endnotes

1   Malcolm Warner is a Fellow of Wolfson College and a faculty member of the Judge Institute of Management Studies, University of Cambridge.
2   Requests for reprints should be addressed to Malcolm Warner, Judge Institute of Management Studies, University of Cambridge, Mill Lane, Cambridge CB2 1RX, United Kingdom.

References

Alvesson, M., and Y. D. Billing, 1992. Gender and organization: Towards a differentiated understanding. *Organization Studies* 13: 73–103.

Arnoff, C. 1975. The rise of the behavioral perspective in selected general management textbooks: An empirical investigation through content analysis. *Academy of Management Journal* 18: 753–66.

Aoki, M. 1988. *Information, incentives and bargaining in the Japanese economy*. Cambridge: Cambridge University Press.

Argyris, C., and D. A. Schon, 1978. *Organizational learning: A theory of action perspective*. Reading: Addison-Wesley.

Bacharach, S. B. 1989. Organizational theories: Some criteria for evaluation. *The Academy of Management Review* 14: 496–515.

Barley, S. R., and G. Kunda, 1992. Design and devotion: Surges of rational and normative ideologies of control in managerial discourse. *Administrative Science Quarterly* 37: 363–99.

Barnard, C. I. 1938. *The functions of the executive*. Boston: Harvard University Press.

Bauman, Z. 1991. *Intimations of postmodernity*. London: Routledge.

Bedeian, A. G. 1987. Organization theory: Current controversies, issues and directions. In C. L. Cooper and I. T. Robertson, eds., *International Review of Industrial and Organizational Psychology*. Chichester: Wiley, 110–140.

Beer, M., and A. E. Walton, 1987. Organizational change and development. *Annual Review of Psychology* 38: 339–67.

Bendix, R. 1963. *Work and authority in industry*. New York: Harper and Row.

Bertalanffy, L. Von. 1950. The Theory of Open Systems in Physics and Biology. *Science* 111: 23–29.

Blau, P. M., and R. A. Schonenherr, 1971. *The structure of organizations*. New York: Basic Books.

Brown, R. 1992. *Understanding industrial organizations*. London: Routledge.

Burrell, G., and G. Morgan, 1979. *Sociological paradigms and organizational analysis*. London: Routledge.

Butler, R. 1991. *Designing organizations*. London: Routledge.

Campbell, A., and J. M. Warner, 1992. *New technology, skills and management*. London: Routledge.

Child, J. 1969. *British management thought*. London: George Allen and Unwin.

___. 1972. Organizational structure, environment and performance: The role of strategic choice. *Sociology* 6:1–22.

___. 1981. Culture, contingency and capitalism in the cross-cultural study of organizations. In L. L. Cummings and B. Straw, eds., *Research in Organizational Behavior*, vol. 3. Greenwich, CT: JIA Press, 303–56.

Clegg, S. R. 1990. *Modern organizations: Organization studies in the post-modern world.* London: Sage.

Clegg, S., and D. Dunkerley, 1980. *Organization, class and control.* London: Routledge and Kegan Paul.

Cyert, R. M., and J. G. March, 1963. *A behavioral theory of the firm.* New York: Wiley.

Czarniawska-Joerges, B. 1992. *Exploring complex organizations: A cultural perspective.* London: Sage.

Daft, R. L. 1992. *Organization theory and design.* St. Paul and New York: West Publishing.

Donaldson, L. 1985. *In defence of organization theory: A reply to the critics.* Cambridge: Cambridge University Press.

Dunlop, J. D. 1950. *Industrial relations systems.* New York: Holt, Rinehart and Winston.

Fayol, H. 1949. *General and industrial management* (translation). London: Pitman.

Flax, J. 1990. *Thinking fragments: Psychoanalysis, feminism and post-modernism in the contemporary west.* Berkeley: University of California Press.

Follett, M. P. 1941. In L. Urwich and H. C. Metcalf, eds., *Dynamic administration: Collected papers.* London: Pitman.

Fruin, M. 1992. *The Japanese enterprise system.* Oxford: Oxford University Press.

Gillespie, R. 1991. *Manufacturing knowledge: A history of the Hawthorne experiments.* Cambridge: Cambridge University Press.

Hofstede, G. 1980. *Culture's consequences.* London: Sage.

___. 1991. *Cultures and organizations: Software of the mind.* Maidenhead: McGraw Hill.

Hofstede, G., and M. H. Bond, 1988. The Confucius connection: From cultural roots to economic growth. *Organizational Dynamics* 16, 4–21.

Hollway, W. 1991. *Work psychology and organizational behaviour.* London: Sage.

Hunt, J. G. 1991. *Leadership: A new synthesis.* London: Sage.

I.D.E. Group. 1981. *Industrial democracy in Europe.* Oxford: Oxford University Press.

___. 1993. *Industrial democracy revisited.* Oxford: Oxford University Press.

Jaques, E. 1951. *The changing culture of a factory.* London: Tavistock.

Kanter, R. M. 1990. *When giants learn to dance: Mastering the challenges of strategy, management and careers in the 1990s.* London: Unwin.

Katz, D., and R. H. Kahn, 1966. *The social psychology of organizations.* New York: Wiley.

Kelly, J. 1983. *Scientific management, job design and work performance.* London: Academic Press.

Kochan, T. A., H. C. Katz, and R. B. McKersie, 1986. *The transformation of American Industrial Relations.* New York: Basic Books.

Kotter, J. P. 1990. *A force for change: How leadership differs from management.* London and New York: The Free Press.

Loveridge, R., and M. Pitt, eds. 1990. *The strategic management of technological innovation.* Chicester: Wiley.

Macy, B., M. Peterson, and L. Norton, 1989. A test of participation theory in a work-re-design field setting. *Human Relations* 42, 1095–1165.

March, J. G., ed. 1965. *Handbook of organizations.* Chicago: Rand McNally.

March, J. G., and H. A. Simon, 1958. *Organizations.* New York: Wiley.

March, J. G., and J. P. Olsen, 1976. *Ambiguity and choice in organizations.* Bergen: Unversitetsforlaget.

Maurice, M., A. Sorge, and M. Warner, 1980. Societal differences in organizing manufacturing units: A comparison of France, West Germany and Great Britain. *Organization Studies* 1, 59–86.

Mayo, E. 1933. *The human problems of industrial civilization.* New York: Macmillan.

McClelland, D. C. 1985. *Human motivation.* Glenview, IL: Scott Foresman.

McCormick, M. H. 1984. *What they don't teach you at the Harvard Business School.* London: Collins.

Merkle, J. A. 1980. *Management and ideology: The legacy of the scientific management movement.* Berkeley: University of California Press.

Miles, R. 1965. Human relations or human resources. *Harvard Business Review* 43, 148–63.

Morgan, G. 1986. *Images of organizations.* London: Sage.

___. 1989. *Creative organization theory: A resource book.* London: Sage.

Nelson, D. 1980. *Frederick Taylor and the rise of scientific management.* Madison: University of Wisconsin Press.

Nystrom, P. C., and W. H. Starbuck, eds. 1981. *Handbook of organizational design* (2 vols.). Oxford: Oxford University Press.

___. 1984. To avoid organizational crises: Unlearn. *Organizational Dynamics* 12, 53–65.

Ohmae, K. 1990. *The borderless world.* New York: Harper Business.

Ouchi, W. G. 1981. *Theory Z: How American business can meet the Japanese challenge.* Reading, MA: Addison Wesley.

Perrow, C. 1970. *Organizational analysis.* London: Tavistock.

Peters, T. J. , and R. H. Waterman, Jr. 1982. *In Search of Excellence: Lessons from America's best-run companies.* London and New York: Harper & Row.

Piore, M., and C. Sabel, 1984. *The second industrial divide.* New York: Basic Books.

Poole, M. 1989. *The impact of economic democracy.* London: Routledge.

Popper, K. R. 1945. *The open society and its enemies* (vol. 2). London: Routledge and Kegan Paul.

Porter, M. E. 1990. *The competitive advantage of nations.* New York: Free Press.

Pugh, D. S., D. J. Hickson, C. R. Hinings, and C. Turner, 1968. Dimensions of organization structure. *Administrative Science Quarterly* 13, 65–105.

Pugh, D.S., R. Mansfield, and M. Warner, 1975. *Research in organizational behaviour.* London: Heinemann.

Reed, M. I. 1993. Organization and modernity: Continuity and discontinuity in organization theory. In J. Hassard and M. Parker, eds., *Postmodernism and organizations.* London: Sage, 163–82.

Redding, S. G. 1990. *The spirit of Chinese capitalism.* Berlin: de Gruyter.

Roberts, K. H. 1970. On looking at an elephant. An evaluation of cross-cultural research related to organization. *Psychological Bulletin* 74, 327–50.

Roethlisberger, F. J., and W. J. Dickson, 1939. *Management and the worker.* Cambridge, Harvard University Press

Schein, E. H. 1965. *Organizational psychology.* Englewood Cliffs, NJ: Prentice Hall.

Schuler, R. S. 1989. Strategic HRM and industrial relations. *Human Relations* 42, 157–84.

Silverman, D., 1970. *The theory of organizations.* London: Heinemann.

Sklair, L. 1991. *Sociology of the global system.* Hemel Hempstead: Harvest Wheatsheaf.

Smith, P. B., and M. E. Peterson, 1988. *Leadership, organizations and culture.* London: Sage.

Snow, C. C., R. E. Miles, and H. J. Coleman, Jr., 1992. Managing 21st century organizations. *Organizational Dynamics*, Winter, 5–20.

Soeters, J. L. 1986. Excellent companies as social movements. *Journal of Management Studies* 23, 300–12.

Sorge, A., and M. Warner, 1986. *Comparative factory organization.* Aldershot: Gower Press.

Spender, J. C. 1989. *Industry recipes: The nature and sources of managerial power.* Oxford: Basil Blackwell.

Strauss, G., and E. Rosenstein, 1970. Workers' participation: A critical view. *Industrial Relations* 9, 197–214.

Strauss, G., R. Miles, C. C. Snow, and A. S. Tannenbaum, 1974. *Organizational behavior: Research and issues.* Madison, WI: Industrial Relations Research Association.

Tayeb, M. 1988. *Organizations and national culture: A comparative analysis.* London: Sage.

Taylor, F. W. 1911. *Principles of scientific management.* New York: Harper.

Tichy, N. M., and M. A. Devanna, 1990. *The tranformational leader.* New York and Chichester: Wiley.

Warner, M. 1984. *Organizations and experiments: Designing new ways of managing work.* Chichester: Wiley.

___. 1992. *How Chinese managers learn: Management and industrial training in China.* London: Macmillan.

Weber, M. 1947. *The theory of social and economic organization* (translation), Glencoe: Free Press.

Weick, K. E. 1979. *The social psychology of organizing.* Reading, MA: Addison Wesley.

Whitehill, A. M. 1990. *Japanese management: Tradition and transition.* London: Routledge.

Whitley, R. 1990. East Asian enterprise structures and the comparative analysis of business organizations. *Organization Studies* 11, 47–74.

Williamson, O. E., ed. 1990. *Organization theory: From Chester Barnard to the present and beyond.* Oxford: Oxford University Press.

Woodward, J. 1985. *Management and technology.* London: HMSO.

___. 1965. *Industrial organization: Theory and practice.* London: Oxford University Press.

MANAGING BEHAVIOUR IN ORGANISATIONS

Learning objectives

- Define *quality and explain its relationship to organisational effectiveness criteria.*

- Describe *the goal approach to defining and measuring effectiveness.*

- Explain *how managers attempt to measure what is called satisfaction.*

- Discuss *how an organisation's mission is used to determine whether it is effective.*

- Explain *the interrelationships between planning and organising as viewed by managers.*

- Compare *an intuitive approach to studying the behaviour of employees with a more systematic approach.*

Chapter 2

EFFECTIVE MANAGEMENT

Over the past two decades, the public has shown increased interest in learning about what constitutes effective management, total quality improvement and healthy organisations. *Theory Z*[1] *In Search of Excellence*,[2] *Made in America*,[3] *Quality or Else*[4] and *World Class Quality*[5] are some of the popular and practitioner-oriented how-to-be-effective books. The concern with such topics as effectiveness, quality and excellence, however, is not a new phenomenon.[6] For centuries economists, philosophers, engineers, military generals, government leaders and managers have attempted to define, measure, analyse and capture the essence of effectiveness. Adam Smith wrote in the *Wealth of Nations* over two centuries ago that efficiency of operations can be achieved most easily through high degrees of specialisation.

Whether — and how — managers can influence effectiveness are difficult to determine. There is still confusion about how to manage within organisations so that organisational effectiveness is the final result. Problems of definition, criteria identification and finding the best model to guide research and practice continue to hinder, block and discourage practitioners and researchers. Instead of simply ignoring effectiveness because of underlying confusion, we believe important insights can be found by attempting to clarify various perspectives.

From the standpoint of society, the effectiveness of business organisations is critical. Publications that report business and economic events occasionally survey opinions about business performance. One such survey is reported in the Organisational Encounter on Australia's most successful companies.

As noted in the previous chapter, the field of organisational behaviour identified three levels of analysis: individual, group and organisational. Theorists and researchers in organisational behaviour have accumulated a vast amount of information about each of these levels. These three levels of analysis also coincide with the three levels of managerial responsibility. That is, managers are responsible for the effectiveness of individuals, groups of individuals and organisations themselves.

Levi Strauss & Co. is considered by most observers to be an effective company. During California's frenzied Gold Rush in 1853, Levi Strauss, a Bavarian immigrant, arrived in San Francisco aboard a clipper ship.[7] He quickly discovered that the prospectors wanted sturdy pants that could survive the rigours of digging for gold. So he created the world's first jeans. Word of the quality of the pants spread like wildfire and the Levi's legend was born. Today the company enjoys annual sales of US$6 billion.

Levi's has emphasised quality, being socially responsible, and using the most talented people the company can recruit. The value of each individual, the effective leadership of work groups and the success of the enterprise have been emphasised at Levi Strauss since its founding. Long before a stream of companies paid attention to flatter hierarchies, cultural diversity, empowerment, quality and globalisation, Levi's was leading the way. Levi's embraced the view that every organisational decision should be grounded in what is ethically right.[8]

Levi's management has presented its values-based philosophy of what it aspires to be in terms of effectiveness. The firm believes that if specific values are practised, effectiveness within the firm and in competitive markets will result.[9]

ORGANISATIONAL · Encounter

Making it to the top

Who are the leading companies in Australia today? Based on net revenue, profit after tax, employees and total assets, the top five are BHP, Coles Myer, Telstra, News Corp and Woolworths. All five were in the top position in the previous year, too. There are, however, many ways to measure effectiveness and success. Let us look at a few to see how these and other companies fared.

Criterion	Top 1	2	3	4	5
Net profit	Reserve Bank	Telstra	NAB	BHP	News Corp
Most improved profits	Westpac	Shell	NAB	ANZ Bank	Brambles
Most improved revenue	Tattersalls	Qld Treasury Corp	Pacific Dunlop	BHP	Woolworths
Sector leaders/ public sector	BHP	Coles Myer	News Corp	Woolworths	NAB
Sector leaders/ private sector	Tattersalls	MLC Life	Ansett	Common-wealth Life Treasury	Mitre 10 State Super
Sector leaders/ government	Telstra	NZ Dairy	TAB NSW	Corp Vic	NSW
Top R&D spenders	CSIRO	CRA	BHP	Ericsson	Telstra
Top employers	Coles Myer	Woolworths	Telstra	BHP	Pacific Dunlop
New Zealand's top 5	Fletcher Challenge	NZ Dairy	Air NZ	Telecom NZ	Carter Holt Harvey

BHP: Broken Hill Propriety Company Limited
NAB: National Australia Bank
ANZ: Australia and New Zealand Banking Group Ltd
MLC: Mutual Life and Citizens Assurance Company Ltd
TAB: Totalizator Agency Board

CSIRO: Commonwealth Scientific and Industrial Research Organisation
Air NZ: Air New Zealand

Source: Quality shines through in tougher times, *Business Review Weekly*, October 23, 1995.

A few of Levi's value principles are:
- **Behaviours.** Management must exemplify 'directness, openness to influence, commitment to the success of others and willingness to acknowledge our own contributions to problems.'
- **Diversity.** Levi's 'values a diverse workforce (age, sex, ethnic group and so on) at all levels of the organisation ... Differing points of view will be sought; diversity will be valued and honestly rewarded, not suppressed.'
- **Recognition.** Levi's 'will provide greater recognition — both financial and public — for individuals and teams that contribute to our success'.
- **Ethical practices.** Management should epitomise 'the stated standards of ethical behaviour. We must provide clarity about our expectations and must enforce those standards throughout the corporation'.
- **Empowerment.** Management must 'increase the authority and responsibility of those closest to our products and customers. By actively pushing the responsibility, trust and recognition into the organisation, we can harness and release the capabilities of our people'.

Levi's is not offered as a perfect company. Like every company, there are problems. Being slow to adopt new fashion trends is a criticism that is well founded. Despite problems, Levi's appears to have enough leaders and managers pulling together and creating a unique philosophy for dealing with customers and employees. The Levi's corporate culture is recognised by many to be very effective for permitting individuals and groups to perform at their most effective levels.

Perhaps the modern-era starting point of understanding effectiveness was the scientific management views proposed by Frederick Taylor. Taylor's work used motion and time studies to find the one best way to do an effective (efficient) job. In Taylor's viewpoint, the principle of specialisation was causally linked to effectiveness.

The historical search for organisational effectiveness is briefly traced in Exhibit 2.1. In this presentation, the word 'attributes' is used to encompass both predictor variables (that predict) and indicator variables (that are of interest and indicate).[10]

As Exhibit 2.1 indicates, numerous perspectives, philosophies and issues surround organisational effectiveness. Each has contributed to the notion that a universal, overarching view of effectiveness is not likely to be found. Instead, viewpoints that are insightful, practical and relevant seem to offer the manager within organisations the most hope in managing organisational behaviour.

A BRIEF HISTORY OF EFFECTIVENESS: TWO PERSPECTIVES ON EFFECTIVENESS

Since no viewpoint of effectiveness is universally accepted, we have decided to use multiple perspectives. Two of the most popular perspectives are the goal approach and the systems theory approach. Both of these views have guided researchers and intrigued practitioners.

The goal approach

The **goal approach** to defining and measuring effectiveness is the oldest and most widely used evaluation technique.[11] In the view of this approach, an organisation exists to accomplish goals. An early but influential practitioner and writer on management and organisational behaviour stated: 'What we mean by effectiveness ... is the accomplishment of recognised objectives of cooperative effort. The degree of accomplishment indicates the degree of effectiveness'.[12] The idea that organisations, as well as individuals and groups, should be evaluated in terms of goal accomplishment has widespread appeal. The goal approach reflects purposefulness, rationality and achievement — the fundamental tenets of contemporary Western societies.

Many management practices are based on the goal approach. One widely used practice is management by objectives. Using this practice, managers specify in advance the goals they expect their subordinates to accomplish and periodically evaluate the degree to which the subordinates have accomplished these goals. The actual specifics of management by objectives vary from case to case. In some instances, the manager and subordinate discuss the objectives and

Exhibit 2.1 **Tracing the history of organisational research**

Management Concept	Pioneers	Philosophical Position	Attributes
Scientific management	Frederick Taylor (1911)	Motion and time studies; finding most efficient way	Minimise cost, task specialisation, maximise quantity (output)
Principles of management	Henri Fayol (1916–1925)	Management principles; training in use of principles	Order, equity, scalar chairs, division of work, discipline
Human relations	Elton Mayo (1933)	Psychological factors, job satisfaction, team work	Paying attention to worker's needs and satisfaction
Decision making	Herbert Simon (1947)	Bounded rationality, optimisation of goals	Hierarchy of goals, effective use of resources
Sociotechnical	E. L. Trist and K. W. Bamforth (1951)	Social systems view means that organisation is an open system	Fit between social/technological factors
Behavioural	Douglas McGregor (1961) Rensis Likert (1967)	Individual needs and the importance of participative management	Cohesiveness, loyalty, commitment and employee satisfaction,
Strategic management	Alfred Chandler (1962)	Establish strategy, then structure is established	Strategy/structure fit needed to adapt to environmental changes
Contingency theory	P. R. Lawrence and J. W. Lorsch (1967)	Structure firm to meet environmental demands	Integration fit and differentiation fit
*Quality	Deming (1951 in Japan) and Juran (1954 in Japan)	Train and educate people how to detect and eliminate defects. Quality principles must be applied to everything done in and by a company	Instil pride in quality in employees and focus on customer satisfaction
Empowerment	No specific person (highlighted in report in 1984)	Giving workers a say and power in what they do will increase their ownership in the job	Employees feel more responsible, show more initiative and are more satisfied
Proactive performance	Peters (1987)	Responsiveness to change, customers and the need for social support	Integrate people, leaders that are change-oriented, autonomous units, focus on new market creation, flat structure

*Quality started to be much more recognised in the United States across industries and companies around 1980. *Source:* Portions of Exhibit 2.1 are modified from M. Wilson (1990). *Deming Management at Work.* New York: Putnam, pp. 11–13; Lewin, A. Y., & Minton, J. W. (1986). Determining organizational effectiveness: Another look and an agenda for research, *Management Science*, May, 516–517; Ketchum, L. D. (1984). How redesigned plants really work, *National Productivity Review*, 246–254.

attempt to reach mutual agreement. In other instances, the manager simply assigns the goals. The idea of management by objectives is to specify in advance the goals to be sought. Yet the goal approach, for all of its appeal and apparent simplicity, has problems.[13] These are some of its more widely recognised difficulties:

- Goal achievement is not readily measurable for organisations that do not produce tangible outputs. For example, the stated goal of a college may be to provide a liberal education at a fair price. The question is: How would one know whether the college achieves that goal? What is a liberal education? What is a fair price? For that matter, what is education?
- Organisations attempt to achieve more than one goal, and achievement of one goal often precludes or diminishes their ability to achieve other goals. A business firm may state that its goal is to attain a maximum profit and to provide absolutely safe working conditions. These two goals are in conflict because each of these goals is achieved at the expense of the other.
- The very existence of a common set of official goals to which all members are committed is questionable. Various researchers have noted the difficulty of obtaining consensus among managers as to the specific goals of their organisation.[14]
- Sometimes, even if stated goals are achieved, the organisation is considered to be ineffective.

Despite the problems of the goal approach, it continues to exert a powerful influence on the development of management and organisational behaviour theory and practice. Saying that managers should achieve the goals of the organisation is easy. Knowing how to do this is more difficult. The alternative to the goal approach is the systems theory approach. Through systems theory, the concept of effectiveness can be defined in terms that enable managers to take a broader view of the organisation and to understand the causes of individual, group and organisational effectiveness.

The systems theory approach

Systems theory enables you to describe the behaviour of organisations both internally and externally. Internally, you can see how and why people within organisations perform their individual and group tasks. Externally, you can relate the transactions of organisations with other organisations and institutions. All organisations acquire resources from the outside environment of which they are a part and, in turn, provide goods and services demanded by the larger environment. Managers must deal simultaneously with the internal and external aspects of organisational behaviour. This complex process can be simplified, for analytical purposes, by employing the basic concepts of systems theory.

In systems theory, the organisation is seen as one element of a number of elements that act interdependently. The flow of inputs and outputs is the basic starting point in describing the organisation. In the simplest terms, the organisation takes resources (inputs) from the larger system (environment), processes these resources and returns them in changed form (output). Exhibit 2.2 displays the fundamental elements of the organisation as a system.

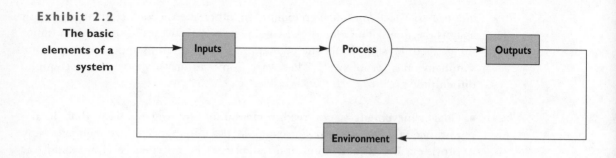

Exhibit 2.2
The basic
elements of a
system

An example of a systems explanation of organisational behaviour is found in companies doing business in Germany. In April 1991 Germany's federal government passed a new packaging law that is the toughest in the world.[15] Starting in December 1991 companies had to take back and recycle packaging used during transport or arrange for someone else to do so. By 1 July 1995, 80% of the packaging had to be collected. Germany's law applies to everyone. The environmental clean-up will influence how business is done in every company doing business in Germany. Hewlett-Packard, an American computer company, has redesigned its packaging worldwide to make it easier to recycle in Germany. Where possible, it has switched to cardboard, has hired designers to alter products and has conducted marketing research surveys to determine if German consumers would accept products in reused boxes (they would). The inputs, processes and outputs of Hewlett-Packard are influenced by the external environmental requirement.

Germany plans to extend recycling to manufacturers of cars and of electronic goods such as computers and televisions. Volkswagen has already practised to the point of stripping down a car in 20 minutes. Systems theory can also describe the behaviour of individuals and groups. The inputs of individual behaviour are causes that arise from the workplace. For example, the cause could be the directives of a manager to perform a certain task. The input (cause) is then acted on by the individual's mental and psychological processes to produce a particular outcome. The outcome that the manager prefers is, of course, compliance with the directive, but depending on the states of the individual's processes, the outcome could be non-compliance. Similarly, you can describe the behaviour of a group in systems theory terms. For example, the behaviour of a group of employees to unionise (outcome) could be explained in terms of perceived managerial unfairness in the assignment of work (input) and the state of the group's cohesiveness (process). We use the term 'systems theory' throughout this text to describe and explain the behaviour of individuals and groups in organisations.

Systems theory and feedback

The concept of the organisation as a system related to a larger system introduces the importance of feedback. As mentioned, the organisation is dependent on the environment not only for its inputs but also for the acceptance of its outputs. It is critical, therefore, that the organisation develop means for adjusting to environmental demands. The means for adjustment are information channels that enable the organisation to recognise these demands. In business organisations, for example, market research is an important feedback mechanism. Other forms of feedback are customer complaints, employee comments and financial reports. In simplest terms, feedback refers to information that reflects the outcomes of an act or a series of acts by an individual, a group or an organisation. Throughout this text, you will see the importance of responding to the content of the feedback information.

Examples of the input-output cycle

The business firm has two major categories of inputs: human and natural resources. Human inputs consist of the people who work in the firm. They contribute their time and energy to the organisation in exchange for wages and other rewards, tangible and intangible. Natural resources consist of the non-human inputs processed or used in combination with the human element to provide other resources. A steel mill must have people and blast furnaces (along with other tools and machinery) to process iron ore into steel and steel products. A car manufacturer takes steel, rubber, plastics and fabrics and — in combination with people, tools and equipment — uses them to make cars. A business firm survives as long as its output is purchased in the market in sufficient quantities and at prices that enable it to replenish its depleted stock of inputs.

Similarly, a university uses resources to teach students, to do research and to provide technical information to society. The survival of a university depends on its ability to attract students' tuition and taxpayers' dollars in sufficient amounts to pay the salaries of its faculty and staff as well as the costs of other resources. If a university's output is rejected by the larger environment, so that students enrol elsewhere and taxpayers support other public endeavours, or if a university is guilty of expending too great an amount of resources in relation to its output, it will cease to exist. Like a business firm, a university must provide the right output at the right price if it is to survive.[16]

Systems theory emphasises two important considerations:

1. The ultimate survival of the organisation depends on its ability to adapt to the demands of its environment.
2. In meeting these demands, the total cycle of input-process-output must be the focus of managerial attention.

Therefore, the criteria of effectiveness must reflect each of these two considerations and you must define effectiveness accordingly. The systems approach accounts for the fact that resources have to be devoted to activities that have little to do with achieving the organisation's primary goal.[17] In other words, adapting to the environment and maintaining the input-process-output flow require that resources be allocated to activities that are only indirectly related to that goal.

The 'learning organisation' has evolved out of the systems view of organisations. The systems view has encouraged the feeling that everyone on the organisation is involved in achieving the goals of the firm.[18] Thus, the effectiveness of an organisation is, to a large extent, dependent on how well everyone is able to work together to achieve the goals.

An organisation learns by acquiring knowledge, distributing information and interpreting information in a manner that results in learning, adaptation and change becoming a part of the firm's culture. According to Senge, organisational learning is both generative and facilitative. *Generative learning* is learning how to learn.[19] *Facilitative learning* is learning to learn through teaching. When a system fosters both types of learning, the overall level of organisational learning is likely to accelerate.

Senge suggests that people learn faster by using what he calls 'microworlds'. A microworld compresses time and space so that it becomes possible to experiment and to learn when the consequences of our decisions are in the future and are distant parts (e.g. in another plant or laboratory) of the organisation.[20] Aeronautical engineers who use wind tunnels to test products are engaged in microworld learning. Managers using whitewater rafting as a team-building training exercise are using the microworld. Using role-playing exercises in a university course to help develop interpersonal skills is a form of microworld laboratory.

THE TIME DIMENSION MODEL OF ORGANISATIONAL EFFECTIVENESS

The concept of organisational effectiveness presented in this book relies on the previous discussion of systems theory, but we must develop one additional point: the dimension of time. Recall that two main conclusions of systems theory are: (1) effectiveness criteria must reflect the entire input-process-output cycle, not simply output and (2) effectiveness criteria must reflect the interrelationships between the organisation and its outside environment. Thus:

1. Organisational effectiveness is an all-encompassing concept that includes a number of component concepts.
2. The managerial task is to maintain the optimal balance among these components.

Much additional research is needed to develop knowledge about the components of effectiveness. There is little consensus about these relevant components, about the interrelationships among them and about the effects of managerial action on them.[21]

According to systems theory, an organisation is an element of a larger system, the environment. With the passage of time, every organisation takes, processes and returns resources to the environment. The ultimate criterion of organisational effectiveness is whether the organisation survives in the environment. Survival requires adaptation and adaptation often involves predictable sequences. As the organisation ages, it will probably pass through different phases. It forms, develops, matures and declines in relation to environmental circumstances. Organisations and entire industries rise and fall. Today, the personal-computer industry is on the rise and the steel industry is declining. Marketing experts acknowledge the existence of product-market life cycles. Organisations also seem to have life cycles. Consequently, the appropriate criteria of effectiveness must reflect the stage of the organisation's life cycle.[22]

Managers and others with interests in the organisation must have indicators that assess the probability of the organisation's survival. In actual practice, managers use a number of short-run indicators of long-run survival. Among these indicators are measurements of productivity, efficiency, accidents, turnover, absenteeism, quality, rate of return, morale and employee satisfaction.[23] The overarching criterion that cuts across each time dimension is *quality*. Unless quality is perceived by customers, there will be no survival. Any of these criteria can be relevant for particular purposes. For simplicity, we will use four criteria of short-run effectiveness as representatives of all such criteria. They are quality, production, efficiency and satisfaction.

Three intermediate criteria in the time dimension model are quality, adaptiveness and development. The final two long-run criteria are quality and survival. The relationships between these criteria and the time dimension are shown in Exhibit 2.3.

Exhibit 2.3
Time dimension model of effectiveness

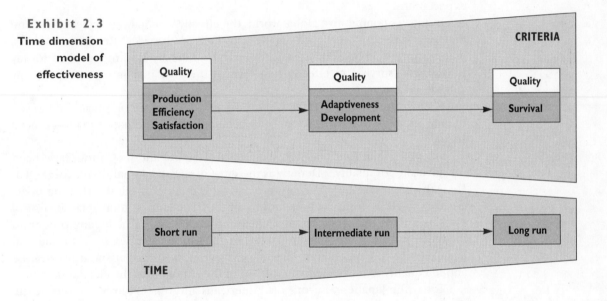

CRITERIA OF EFFECTIVENESS

In the time dimension model, criteria of effectiveness are typically stated in terms of the short run, the intermediate run and the long run. Short-run criteria are those referring to the results of actions concluded in a year or less. Intermediate-run criteria are applicable when you judge the effectiveness of an individual, group or organisation for a longer time period, perhaps 5 years. Long-run criteria are those for which the indefinite future is applicable. We will discuss six general categories of effectiveness criteria, beginning with those of a short-run nature.

Quality

J. M. Juran and W. Edwards Deming, in 1950, were prophets without honour in their own country, the United States. These two Americans emphasised the importance of quality. There is now a belief that, in order to survive, organisations must design products, make products and treat customers in a close-to-perfection way. Close-to-perfection means that quality is now an imperative.[24]

More than any other single event, the 1980 NBC White Paper, 'If Japan Can ... Why Can't We?' illustrates the importance of quality. The television show illustrated how, in 30 years, the Japanese had risen from the ashes of World War II to economic gianthood with products of superior quality. That is, Japanese organisational effectiveness centred on the notion of quality. The Japanese interpret quality as it relates to the customer's perception. Customers compare the actual performance of the product or evaluate the service being provided to their own set of expectations. The product or service either passes or fails. Thus, quality has nothing to do with how shiny or good looking something is or with how much it costs. *Quality* is defined as meeting customers' needs and expectations.

In today's competitive global world, the effective company is typically the one that provides customers with quality products or services. Retailers, bankers, manufacturers, lawyers, doctors, airlines and others are finding out that, to stay in business (survival in effectiveness terms), the customer must be kept happy and satisfied.

Each of the criteria of effectiveness discussed above are significant. However, the one element that executives now recognise as being perhaps the most crucial is quality.

For more than four decades, W. Edwards Deming and J. M. Juran have been the advocates of quality.[25] Deming is the guru of statistical quality control (SQC). He is the namesake of Japan's most prestigious quality award, the Deming prize, created in 1951. Juran is best known for his concept of total quality control (TQC). This is the application of quality principles to all company programs, including satisfying internal customers. In 1954 Juran first described his method in Japan. He has become an important inspiration to the Japanese because he applied quality to everyone from the top of the company to the clerical staff.

Today the Japanese, Europeans, Americans and others who want to compete on the international level have learned a lot about Deming's, Juran's and other quality improvement methods. Managers have learned that simply paying lip service to quality and what it means is not enough. If managers are to be effective over the short and long run, they must translate quality improvement into results: more satisfied customers, a more involved workforce, better designed products and more creative approaches to solving problems. Competition is sparking a long-overdue concern about quality. In many organisations, quality is now the top priority in the short, intermediate and long run.[26]

In December 1994, IBM stopped shipping personal computers (PCs) based on Intel's Pentium chip because of a quality problem. Quality is a top priority at IBM as it attempts to capture more of the PC market. Pentium PCs, at the time of IBM stoppages, were the hottest selling computers.[27] However, IBM laboratory tests indicated that Pentium chips could generate errors in high-intensity mathematical calculations.

A quality flaw in Pentium chips could ruin IBM's attempts to become a competitive force in PCs. IBM claims that it is watching out for its customers. The IBM laboratory tests found that, if a Pentium PC was turned on and it ran through random calculations, an error would occur once in 9 billion tries. The chip, about the size of a 35 millimetre slide, contains 3.3 million transistors. To fix the flaw, Pentium designers are inserting the missing transistors into a new chip.

The IBM stoppage of shipment created strained relations between the company and the supplier, Intel. Andrew Grove, chief executive officer at Intel, stated that IBM overreacted in stopping shipment considering a one-in-a-billion chance of a quality problem.[28] This debate and concern illustrates how important quality is in terms of competition, public relations and overall image.

Productivity

As used here, **production** reflects the ability of the organisation to produce the quantity of output that the environment demands. The concept excludes any consideration of efficiency, which is defined below. The measures of production include profit, sales, market share, students graduated, patients released, documents processed, clients served and the like. These measures relate directly to the output consumed by the organisation's customers and clients.

Efficiency

Efficiency is defined as the ratio of outputs to inputs. This short-run criterion focuses attention on the entire input-process-output cycle, yet it emphasises the input and process elements. Among the measures of efficiency are rate of return on capital or assets, unit cost, scrappage and waste, downtime and occupancy rates and cost per patient, per student or per client. Measures of efficiency inevitably must be in ratio terms; the ratios of benefit to cost or to time are the general forms of these measures.

Satisfaction

The idea of the organisation as a social system requires that some consideration be given to the benefits received by its participants as well as by its customers and clients. 'Satisfaction' and 'morale' are similar terms referring to the extent to which the organisation meets the needs of employees. We use the term **satisfaction** to refer to this criterion. Measures of satisfaction include employee attitudes, turnover, absenteeism, tardiness and grievances.

Adaptiveness

Adaptiveness is the extent to which the organisation can and does respond to internal and external changes. Adaptiveness in this context refers to management's ability to sense changes in the environment as well as changes within the organisation itself. Ineffectiveness in achieving production, efficiency and satisfaction can signal the need to adapt managerial practices and policies. Or the environment may demand different outputs or provide different inputs, thus necessitating change. To the extent that the organisation cannot or does not adapt, its survival is jeopardised. How can you really know whether the organisation is effectively adaptive? There are short-run measures of effectiveness, but there are no specific and concrete measures of adaptiveness.

Management can implement policies that encourage a sense of readiness for change and certain managerial practices, if implemented, facilitate adaptiveness. For example, managers can invest in employee-training programs and career counselling. They can encourage and reward innovation and risk-taking behaviour. Yet, when the time comes for an adaptive response, the organisation either adapts or does not adapt — and that is the ultimate measure.

Development

Development measures the ability of the organisation to increase its capacity to deal with environmental demands. An organisation must invest in itself to increase its chances of survival in the long run. The usual development efforts are training programs for managerial and non-managerial personnel. More recently the range of organisational development has expanded to include a number of psychological and sociological approaches. Time considerations enable you to evaluate effectiveness in the short, intermediate and long run. For example, you could evaluate a particular organisation as effective in terms of production, satisfaction and efficiency criteria but as ineffective in terms of adaptiveness and development. A manufacturer of buggy whips may be optimally effective because it can produce buggy whips better and faster than any other producer in the short run but still have little chance of survival because no one wants to buy its products. Thus, maintaining optimal balance means, in part, balancing the organisation's performance over time. The time dimensions model of effectiveness enables us to understand the work of managers in organisations. The basic job of managers is to identify and influence the causes of individual, group and organisational effectiveness in the short, intermediate and long run. Let us examine the nature of managerial work in that light.

MANAGEMENT FUNCTIONS AND EFFECTIVENESS

Whether the focus is one of Australia's top ten companies, such as Coles Myer, or a small family-run business, two factors are important — understanding people and managing effectively.[29] People in any organisation want to be treated as more than just faceless employees. Douglas McGregor, a pioneer in the field of management, informed the public about the importance of recognising people decades ago. People want attention and recognition. Federal Express has a rule that managers are not to sit idly at their desks. They must, as Peters and Waterman (well known for their book *In Search of Excellence*, which analyses the relationship between management style and company performance) encourage, walk around, talk to employees and above all else listen to what people are saying. The organisations in which people work and managers practise the art and science of management may be large, medium or small. Coles Myer is a large company, while Charmaine's Ice Cream in Melbourne is a small company. They are both private for-profit companies that must use and efficiently manage their employee talents to earn a profit. The size of these two companies as well as the markets in which they conduct business are significantly different. Myron Fottler has provided a framework as displayed in Exhibit 2.4 for considering how management is practised similarly and differently across organisations.[30] His framework identified four categories:

1. private for-profit: business firms dependent on the market environment (BHP, Woolworths);
2. private non-profit: organisations dependent on public contributions and/or government grants to operate (Arts Council);
3. private quasi-public: organisations created by legislatures to provide goods and services (NZ Dairy, Telstra);
4. public: government agency (Reserve Bank, Australia Post).

In each of these four types of organisations, managers are faced with environmental constraints; legal requirements; customer, client or public demands; and resource needs. Consequently, how to manage demands, resources, environmental changes and people effectively may differ. Even within each category managing people differs. Managing people effectively in any of the four types of organisations involves the application of the planning, organising, leading and controlling functions of management. These functions are portrayed in Exhibit 2.4. The managerial responses to macro and micro environmental factors will be unique for the particular organisation. However, exactly how planning or leading is done is largely determined by the type of organisation and environment in which the manager must operate to survive.

Exhibit 2.4
Organisation types, environmental dependencies and management response

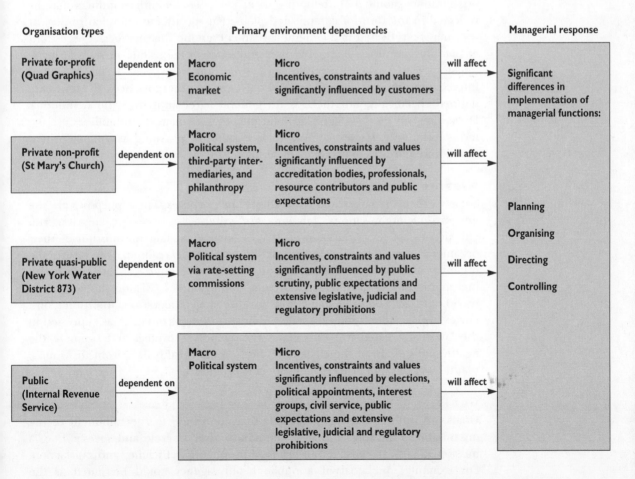

Source: Fottler, M. D. (1981). Is management really generic? *Academy of Management Review*, January, 4.

Management is defined as a process, a series of actions, activities or operations that lead to some end. The concept of management developed here is based on the assumption that the necessity for managing arises whenever work is specialised and is undertaken by two or more persons. Under such circumstances, the specialised work must be coordinated and this creates the necessity for performing managerial work. The nature of managerial work in any organisation, then, is to coordinate the work of others by performing four management functions: planning, organising, leading and controlling. In each case, the desired outcome of the function is to improve work performance.

Planning effective performance

The planning function includes defining the ends to be achieved and determining appropriate means to achieve the defined ends. Planning activities can be complex or simple, implicit or explicit, impersonal or personal. For example, the sales manager who is forecasting the demand for the company's major product may rely on complex econometric models or on casual conversations with salespersons in the field. The intended outcomes of planning activities are mutual understandings about what the members of the organisation should be attempting to achieve. These understandings may be reflected in the form of complicated plans that specify the intended results, or they may be reflected in a general agreement among the members. Discussions of planning are often hampered by the absence of definitions of such terms as 'mission', 'goal', and 'objective'. In some instances, the terms are used interchangeably, particularly goal and objective. In other instances, the terms are defined specifically, but there is no general agreement over the definitions. Depending on their backgrounds and purposes, managers and authors use the terms differently. However, the pivotal position of planning as a management function requires us to make the meanings of these key concepts very explicit.

Mission

Society expects organisations to serve specific purposes. These purposes are the missions of organisations. **Missions** are criteria for assessing the long-run effectiveness of an organisation. Effective managers state the mission of their organisation in terms of those conditions that, if realised, will assure the organisation's survival. Statements of mission are found in laws, articles of incorporation and in other extraorganisational sources. Mission statements are broad, abstract and value-laden and thus are subject to various interpretations. For example, the mission of a state public health department — as expressed in the law that created it — mandates the agency to protect and promote the health and welfare of the citizens of the Commonwealth. It is from this source that the organisation will create its specific programs.

Goals

Goals are future states or conditions that contribute to the fulfilment of the organisation's mission. A goal is somewhat more concrete and specific than a mission. Goals can be stated in terms of production, efficiency and satisfaction. For example, one goal of a public health agency could be stated as the eradication of measles as a health hazard by the end of 2000. In a business setting, a goal might be to have viable sales outlets established in every major population centre of the country by the end of 1999. It is entirely possible for an organisation to have multiple goals that contribute to its mission. For example, a hospital may pursue patient care, research and training. Universities typically state three significant goals: teaching, research and community service. The existence of multiple goals places great pressure on managers not only to coordinate the routine operations of the units that strive for these goals but also to plan and allocate scarce resources to the goals.

Objectives

Objectives refer to statements of accomplishment that are to be achieved in the short run, usually a year. The public health agency's objective can be stated as to reduce the incidence of measles from 6 per 10 000 to 4 per 10 000 by the end of the current year. The company seeking to have sales outlets in all major population centres could state its current year's objective as to have opened and begun operations in Melbourne, Sydney, Brisbane and Adelaide. Thus, goals are derived from the organisation's mission and objectives are derived from the goals. A coherent set of missions, goals and objectives defines the scope and direction of the organisation's activities. Planning involves specifying not only where the organisation is going, but also how it is to get there. Alternatives must be analysed and evaluated in terms of criteria that follow from the mission, goals and objectives. Thus, managers by their own decisions can affect how they and their organisations will be evaluated. Managers determine what ends are legitimate and, therefore, what criteria are relevant. And once the determination of appropriate means has been completed, the next managerial function — organising — must be undertaken.

Organising effective performance

The organising function includes all managerial activities that are taken to translate the required planned activities into a structure of tasks and authority. In a practical sense, the organising function involves specific activities.

Defining the nature and content of each job in the organisation

The tangible results of this activity are job specifications, position descriptions or task definitions. These indicate what is expected of job holders in terms of responsibilities, outcomes and objectives. In turn, the skills, abilities and training required to meet the defined expectations are also specified.

Determining the bases for grouping jobs together

The essence of defining jobs is specialisation, that is, dividing the work. But once the overall task has been subdivided into jobs, the jobs must be put into groups or departments. The managerial decision involves selecting the appropriate bases. For example, all the jobs that require similar machinery may be grouped together, or the manager may decide to group all the jobs according to the product or service they produce.

Deciding the size of the group

The purpose of grouping jobs is to enable a person to supervise the group's activities. Obviously, there is a limit to the number of jobs that one person can supervise, but the precise number will vary depending on the situation. For example, it is possible to supervise more jobs that are similar and simple than jobs that are dissimilar and complex. The supervisor of hourly workers can manage up to twenty-five or thirty employees, but the director of research scientists can manage far fewer, perhaps only eight to ten.

Delegating authority to the assigned manager

The preceding activities create groups of jobs with defined tasks. It then becomes necessary to determine the extent to which managers of the groups are allowed to make decisions and use the resources of the group without higher approval. This is authority.

Once the structure of task and authority is in place, it must be given life. People perform jobs and management must recruit and select the appropriate individual who will perform the jobs. The process of finding and placing people in jobs is termed 'staffing'. In some large organisations, specialised units such as personnel perform staffing activities. An important cause of individual effectiveness is a good fit between job requirements and individual abilities. Thus, even when staffing is performed by a specialised unit, the activity remains an important management responsibility. The interrelationships between planning and organising are apparent. The planning function results in the determination of organisational ends and means; that is, it defines the whats and hows. The organising function results in the determination of the whos; that is who will do what with whom to achieve the desired end results. The structure of tasks and authority should facilitate the fulfilment of planned results if the next management function, leading, is performed properly.

Leading effective performance

Reading 2
Rounding out the manager's job

Leading involves the manager in close, day-to-day contact with individuals and groups. Thus, leading is uniquely personal and interpersonal. Even though planning and organising provide guidelines and directives in the form of plans, job descriptions, organisation charts and policies, it is people who do the work. And people frequently are unpredictable. They have unique needs, aspirations, personalities and attitudes. Thus, they each perceive the workplace and their jobs differently. Managers must take into account these unique perceptions and behaviours and somehow direct them toward common purposes. Leading places the manager squarely in the arena of individual and group behaviour. To function in this arena, the manager must have knowledge of individual differences and motivation, group behaviour, power and politics. In short, being a leader requires knowledge of ways to influence individuals and groups to accept and pursue organisational objectives, often at the expense of personal objectives. Leading involves the day-to-day interactions between managers and their subordinates. In these interactions the full panorama of human behaviour is evident: individuals work, play, communicate, compete, accept and reject others, join groups, leave groups, receive rewards and cope with stress. Of all the management functions, leading is the one most humanly oriented.

Culture and managerial effectiveness

Do the criteria for assessing managerial effectiveness differ across cultures? In this research Chike Okechuku compares managers from the People's Republic of China (PRC), Hong Kong and Canada on six managerial attributes — supervisory ability, achievement motivation, intellectual ability, self-actualisation, self-assurance and decisiveness — and also investigates the relationship of these characteristics to perceived effectiveness.

Many researchers argue that cultural differences contribute significantly to differences in both managerial and employee attitudes and behaviours. On this basis, we would expect these traits to be valued differently in different countries and that, as a result, the relationship between these traits and perceived effectiveness would also differ. However, an alternative point of view is that, as a result of industrialisation, attitudes are common across organisations and cultures. Okechuku's analysis of cultural differences leads to the hypothesis that, whereas in Canada and the PRC all six traits should be important to assessments of effectiveness, in Hong Kong a different culture will result in minimal importance being placed on achievement motivation and self-actualisation.

When superiors rated organisational managers, the three countries differed along all dimensions. PRC managers were not only rated as more effective than Canadian managers, but were also rated as possessing higher levels of all six attributes. And Canadian managers were rated as more effective than Hong Kong managers, and were also rated as possessing higher levels of all the attributes except achievement motivation.

We can also ask what contributed to perceived effectiveness, and whether there were cultural differences. The table below summarises the traits that predicted effectiveness.

	All Countries	Canada	PRC	Hong Kong
Supervisory ability	yes	yes	yes	yes
Achievement motivation	not a predictor	not a predictor	yes	not a predictor
Intellectual ability	yes	yes	yes	not a predictor
Self-actualisation	yes	yes	yes	not a predictor
Self-assurance	yes	yes	not a predictor	yes
Decisiveness	yes	yes	yes	not a predictor

As you can see, Canada and the PRC are very similar in terms of the factors that predict managerial effectiveness. However, the pattern in Hong Kong is very different. What implications does this have for doing business in Hong Kong? What factors do you think might be important in Hong Kong? Under what conditions would you predict a shift in attitudes?

Source: Okechuku, C. (1994). The relationship between six managerial characteristics to the assessment of managerial effectiveness in Canada, Hong Kong and People's Republic of China, *Journal of Occupational and Organizational Psychology,* **67**, 79–86.

Controlling effective performance

The controlling function includes activities that managers undertake to assure that actual outcomes are consistent with planned outcomes. Three basic conditions must exist to undertake control: standards, information and corrective action.

Standards

Norms of acceptable outcomes, standards, must be spelled out. These standards reflect goals and objectives and are usually found in accounting, production, marketing, financial and budgeting documents. In more specific ways standards are reflected in procedures, performance criteria, rules of conduct, professional ethics and work rules. Standards therefore reflect desirable levels of achievement.

Information

Actual and planning outcomes must be compared using appropriate and reliable information. Many organisations have developed sophisticated information systems that provide managers with control data. Prime examples are standard cost accounting and quality control systems used extensively by modern manufacturing companies. In other instances the sources of information consist of nothing more than managers' observations of the behaviour of people assigned to their departments.

Corrective action

If actual outcomes are ineffective, managers must take corrective action. Without the ability to take corrective action, the controlling function has no point or purpose. Corrective action is made possible through the organising function — if managers have been assigned the authority to take action. Simply stated, managers undertake control to determine whether intended results are achieved and if not, why not. The conclusions managers reach because of their controlling activities are that the planning function is faulty or that the organising function is faulty, or both.

Controlling, then, is the completion of a logical sequence. The activities that controlling comprises include employee selection and placement, materials inspection, performance evaluation, financial statement analysis and other well-recognised managerial techniques. Describing management in terms of the four functions of planning, organising, leading and controlling is certainly not complete. Nothing in this description indicates the specific behaviours or activities associated with each function. Nor is there any recognition of the relative importance of these functions for overall organisational effectiveness. However, these four functions conveniently and adequately define management.

STUDYING ORGANISATIONAL EFFECTIVENESS

The literature has revealed that the majority of organisational effectiveness studies have used quantitative research designs. Case studies, field studies and occasionally field experiments have been used to analyse effectiveness.[31] On the other hand, qualitative research methods have been employed for the most part to study and learn about organisational culture. Using archival data, researching material artefacts, interpreting language and using on-site participants to research stories and myths are popular qualitative procedures.[32] Appendix B presents specific techniques that are used by researchers to study organisations. Even though years of research have been conducted, there are still many unanswered questions about behaviour within organisational settings.

Practising managers are still searching for answers about what to do or how to proceed so that effectiveness is the result. They also must learn about when and where to intervene in order to change and use culture to accomplish goals. The manager needs road maps that only reliable and valid research can help provide. The techniques provided in Appendix B offer some general research guidelines for scientifically studying organisational behaviour to understand effectiveness, culture and other important variables.

Each reader of this book has already formed opinions about the behaviour of people. It is common practice to watch the behaviours of others and to reach a conclusion about why a person behaved in a particular way. There is also a lot of guessing about what a person will do next. It is to be hoped that by studying, learning and coming into contact with theory and research about organisational behaviour, some of the guessing will be replaced by educated opinions, logic and learning of principles. Guessing, hoping for the best and casual approaches to explaining and predicting behaviour in organisations are not sufficient in a world that has become economically competitive. Managers cannot afford to rely on guesses. A statement made years ago captures the notion that behaviour is not always some random event:

> *Behaviour generally is predictable if we know how the person perceived the situation and what is important to him or her ... An observer often sees behaviour as non-rational because the observer does not have access to the same information or does not perceive the environment in the same way.*[33]

Exercise 2
Initial view of organisational behaviour

Before going on to other chapters in the text, you may wish to complete Exercise 2 at the end of this chapter. The exercise will assess your initial view of organisational behaviour, as well as your viewpoints about relevant topics. When you complete the course, complete the exercise again and see if your views have changed.

SUMMARY OF KEY POINTS

Define quality and explain its relationship to organisational effectiveness criteria. Definitions of quality are abundant. We opted for a straightforward definition: Quality is meeting customers' needs and expectations. The perception of customers (e.g. patients, clients or students) is the focal point of our definition. The technological aspects of a product or the elegance of providing a service are not included in our definition. Instead, needs and expectations being met is the key. The importance of quality is that it is the core concept that overarches any effectiveness criteria. Production in terms of quantity is important, but the quality of this output is more important. The crumbled Soviet Union found this out in that it produced large quantities of goods, but they were generally of low quality. The results of 70-plus years of this type of production thinking are still unfolding in what is now called the Commonwealth of Independent States (CIS).

Describe the goal approach to defining and measuring effectiveness. The goal approach is based on the idea that organisations are rational, purposive entities that pursue specific missions, goals and objectives. For example, how well Ansett Australia is performing — that is, how effective it is — would be reviewed and analysed in terms of how the mission, goals and objectives are being accomplished in the short, intermediate and long run.

Explain how managers attempt to measure what is called satisfaction. Managers do not generally walk around handing out behavioural science-type questionnaires or attitude surveys to determine satisfaction. They do, however, engage in observation, listening and talking with employees. Attempting to acquire insight about attitudes, feelings and emotions coupled with examining records of absenteeism, tardiness, accident rates, turnover and grievances provides managers with a general picture of the degree and type of satisfaction among workers.

Discuss how an organisation's mission is used to determine whether it is effective. The mission statement is considered a long-term signpost to measure effectiveness. The mission is usually worded, presented and implemented with the intention of enhancing the survival probability of the company. One problem with instilling this kind of orientation is that writing an inspiring and meaningful mission statement is difficult. The state public health department mission statement is clear, but is it inspiring?

Explain the interrelationships between planning and organising as viewed by managers. It is to be hoped that a plan provides a clear set of organisational goals and, more importantly, strategies for how the organisation will achieve those goals. The organising function provides a guide to who will do the jobs to accomplish the plans. Planning initiates a call, that is a signal that individuals must be assembled, instructed and provided with resources to achieve the mission, goals and objectives of the institution.

Compare an intuitive approach to studying the behaviour of employees with a more systematic approach. The text will attempt to convince you that intuition is practised by everyone, but, in terms of dealing with the behaviour of employees, it is better to learn more by using a systematic approach. One systematic approach starts with thinking about the effectiveness criteria of an organisation. What are they and how do we accomplish them? We are firm advocates of the fact that managing people is an art. However, knowing what the literature has to

say, what other managers have learned, and how people interact in organisations has a scientific basis. The educated man or woman who will manage others in the future needs a lot of intuition, but he or she also needs to use any scientifically derived hints, pointers or principles that are available.

REVIEW AND DISCUSSION QUESTIONS

1. Why is perception such an important factor when the quality of a product or of a service is being considered?

2. Why are mission statements so difficult to compose and put down in writing?

3. There have been many success stories reported in literature about how someone achieved business, career or personal goals by using intuition. Is there any place for the systematic study of achieving success as a manager in an organisation such as Quad Graphics (Exhibit 2.4)?

4. What are the main differences in taking a goal or a systems approach when interpreting organisational effectiveness?

5. What would be some of the potential negative consequences for a person who does not plan for his or her career?

6. Can a manager ever conclude that she has accurately measured and knows the job satisfaction of her fifteen employees? Explain.

7. How would you determine whether a large public hospital in your city (community or regional) is effective?

8. 'People are paid to be productive, not to be satisfied.' Do you agree with this statement? What are its implications in terms of achieving organisational effectiveness?

9. Why is quality considered such an important, overarching concept throughout the industrialised world?

10. Today in the fast-paced, globalising environment, it is important for an organisation of any size to be adaptive. What does this mean now to a company such as General Motors, who, in 1991, experienced a 12% reduction in new car sales in the United States?

ENDNOTES

1 Ouchi, W. G. (1981). *Theory Z*. Reading, MA.: Addison-Wesley Publishing.

2 Peters, T. J., & Waterman, R. H., Jnr. (1982). *In Search of Excellence*. New York: Harper & Row.

3 Dertouzos, M. K. (1989). *Made in America*. Cambridge, MA.: The MIT Press.

4 Dobyns, L., & Crawford-Mason, C. (1991). *Quality or Else*. Boston, MA.: Houghton-Mifflin.

5 Bhote, K. R. (1991). *World Class Quality*. New York: AMACOM.

6 Lewin, A. Y., & Minton, J. W. (1986). Determining organizational effectiveness: Another look and an agenda for research, *Management Science*. 514–535.

7 Roessing, W. (1994). Blue jean boss, *Sky*, August, 65–70.

8 Mitchell, R., & O'Neal, M. (1994). Managing by values, *Business Week*, August 1, 46–52.

9 Levi Strauss & Co., Annual Report, 1994.

10 This terminology is taken from Lewin, A. Y., & Minton, J. W. (1986). Determining organizational effectiveness: Another look and an agenda for research, *Management Science*, 514–535; and Cameron, K. S. (1981). Effectiveness as paradox: Consensus and conflict in concepts of organisational effectiveness, *Management Science*, 539–553.

11 Strasser, S., Eveland, J. D., Cummins, G., Deniston, O. L., & Romani, J. H. (1981). Conceptualizing the goal and systems models of organizational effectiveness, *Journal of Management Studies*, 323.

12 Barnard, C. I. (1938). *The Functions of the Executive*. Cambridge, MA.: Harvard University Press, p. 55.

13 Harrison, E. F. (1978). *Management and Organization*. Boston: Houghton Mifflin, pp. 404–414. This is an excellent survey of the limitations of the goal approach.

14 Gaertner, G. H., & Ramnarayan, S. (1983). Organizational effectiveness: An alternative perspective, *Academy of Management Review*, 97–107.

15 Recycling in Germany: A wall of waste, *Economist*, November 30, 1991, 73.

16 Cameron, K. (1978). Measuring organizational effectiveness in institutions of higher education, *Administrative Science Quarterly*, 604–629.

17 Etzioni, A. (1971). Two approaches to organizational analysis: A critique and a suggestion. In J. Ghorpade (Ed.) *Assessment of Organizational Effectiveness*. Santa Monica, CA: Goodyear Publishing.

18 Dumaine, B. (1994). Mr. Learning Organization, *Fortune*, October 7, 147–155.

19 Senge, P. M. (1990). *The Learning Organization*. New York: Doubleday.

20 Benson, T. E. (1993). The learning organization: Heading towards places unimaginable, *Industry Week*, January 4, 18.

21 Zammuto, R. F. (1984). A comparison of multiple constituency models of organizational effectiveness, *Academy of Management Review*, 606–616.

22 Cameron, K. S., & Whetton, D. A. (1981). Perceptions of organizational effectiveness over organizational life cycles, *Administrative Science Quarterly*, 525–544; Quinn, R. E., & Cameron, K. S. (1983). Organizational life cycles and shifting criteria of effectiveness: Some preliminary evidence, *Management Science*, 33–51.

23 Campbell, J. P. (1979). On the nature of organizational effectiveness. In P. S. Goodman & J. M. Pennings (Eds.) *New Perspectives on Organizational Effectiveness*. San Francisco, Jossey-Bass, pp. 36–39.

24 The quality imperative, *Business Week*, October 25, 1991, 7–11.

25 Denning, W. E., & Juran, J. M. (1991). Dueling pioneers, *Business Week*, October 25, 1991, 17.

26 Berry, T. H. (1991). *Managing the Total Quality Transformation*. New York: McGraw-Hill, p. 2.

27 Maney, K. (1994). Intel may get a chip on its shoulder, *USA Today*, December 13, 3B.

28 Horovitz, B. (1994). Intel needs damage control, *USA Today*, December 13, 35.

29 Storey, H. J. (1989). *Inside America's Fastest Growing Companies*. New York: John Wiley & Sons, pp. 135–136.

30 Fottler, M. D. (1981). Is management really generic? *Academy of Management Review*, 1–12.

31 Lawler, E. E., III, Mohrman, A. M., Mohrman, S. J., Ledford, G. E., Jnr., Cummings, T. G., & Associates. (1985). *Doing Research That Is Useful for Theory and Practice*. San Francisco: Jossey-Bass.

32 Van Maanen, J., Dabbs, J. M., & Faulkner, R. R. (Eds.) *Varieties of Qualitative Research*. Beverly Hills, CA: Sage Publications.

33 Lawler, E. E., III, & Rhode, J. G. (1976). *Information and Control in Organizations*. Pacific Palisades, CA: Goodyear, p. 22.

READING 2 ROUNDING OUT THE MANAGER'S JOB

Henry Mintzberg

Source: *Sloan Management Review*, Fall 1994, pp.11–26.

Tom Peters tells us that good managers are doers. (Wall Street says they 'do deals'.) Michael Porter suggests that they are thinkers. Not so, argue Abraham Zaleznik and Warren Bennis: good managers are really leaders. Yet, for the better part of this century, the classical writers — Henri Fayol and Lyndell Urwick, among others — kept telling us that good managers are essentially controllers.

It is a curiosity of the management literature that its best-known writers all seem to emphasize one particular part of the manager's job to the exclusion of the others. Together, perhaps, they cover all the parts, but even that does not describe the whole job of managing.

If you turn to the more formalized literature, you will find all kinds of lists — of tasks or roles or 'competencies'. But a list is not a model (even if presented in the form of a circle, meaning the ends have been joined), and so the integrated work of managing still gets lost in the process of describing it. And without such a model, we can neither understand the job properly nor deal with its many important needs — for design, selection, training, and support.

To play with a metaphor, if the toughest nut to crack in our knowledge of management has been the manager's job itself, then that may well be because we have done just that. We have been so intent on breaking the job into pieces that we never come to grips with the whole thing. It is time, therefore, to consider the integrated job of managing.

That is what I set out to do several years ago, after becoming discouraged with all those lists and circles (including one from my own initial study of managerial work, first published in 1973).[1] I did not feel the need to go find out what managers do. We knew that already, I believed, based on a considerable body of research and publication over the past decades. Our need was for a framework to put all this together, a model of managing, if you like. People had to be able to 'see' the job in one place, in order to deal with its component parts comprehensively and interactively. In fact, as my ideas developed, the metaphor of the nut came alive, for the model has taken the form of an interacting set of concentric circles.

Using this model, I began to spend time with managers at work, both to check out and to flesh out the model especially as it applies to different managerial jobs and styles. I have been spending a day with each of a number of managers — observation reinforced by interviewing — not to draw any definitive conclusions so much as to get a flavor for as wide a variety of managerial jobs and styles as possible. So far they number 23, ranging from the head of one of Europe's largest state health care systems to the 'front country' manager of a Canadian mountain park. (Examples used throughout this paper will give a sense of the variety of managers I have studied so far.)

This article presents the model, building the image of the manager's job from the inside out, beginning at the center with the person and his or her frame and working out from there, layer by layer. Once this description is complete, I shall discuss briefly the jobs and styles of some of the managers I have observed to give a sense of how readers might use the model to better appreciate their own jobs or those of the managers around them. I shall also comment on the effective practice of managerial work, concluding, as you may have already guessed, that this is one job that has to be 'well rounded'!

The person in the job

We begin at the center, with the person who comes to the job. People are not neutral when they take on a new managerial job, mere putty to be molded into the required shape. Indeed, greater appreciation of this fact would allow us to be more careful in how we select managers in the first place. Or else more flexible in how we let them mold their jobs to themselves in the second.

Exhibit 2.5 shows that an individual comes to a managerial job with a set of *values*, by this stage in life probably rather firmly set — for example, that the radio station he manages should provide intelligent fare. He or she also brings a body of *experience* that, on one hand has forged a set of skills or *competencies*, perhaps honed by training and, on the other, has provided a base of *knowledge* — that comes, for example, from spending 35 years on a major police force before becoming its commissioner. That knowledge is, of course, used directly, but it is also converted into a set of *mental models*, key means by which managers interpret the world around them — for example, how the head nurse on a hospital ward perceives the behavior of the surgeons with whom she must work. Together, all these characteristics greatly determine how any manager approaches a given job — his or her *style* of managing. Style will come to life as we begin to see *how* a manager carries out what his or her job requires.

Exhibit 2.5 **The person in the job**

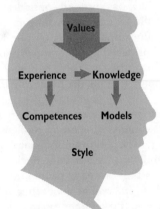

The frame of the job

Embed the person depicted in a given managerial job and you get managerial work. At the core of it is some kind of *frame* for the job, the mental set the incumbent assumes to carry it out. Frame is strategy, to be sure, possibly even vision, but it is more than that. We can show it as three increasingly specific components, emanating from the person concentrically in Exhibit 2.6.

First is *purpose*, namely what the manager is seeking to do fundamentally with the unit he or she is supposed to manage — for example, to increase the state funding for a hospital or to open more stores in a retail chain. As depicted around the circle, a manager may *create* a unit, *maintain* the effective functioning of a unit already created, *adapt* the unit to some new conditions, or *recreate* in some more ambitious way a unit previously created. To use a metaphor, a manager may build the track in the first place, keep the unit on track (or put it back on track), improve or shift the track, or else rebuild the track. The head nurse seeks to keep her unit running smoothly; the chief executive of the state

Exhibit 2.6 **The frame of the job**

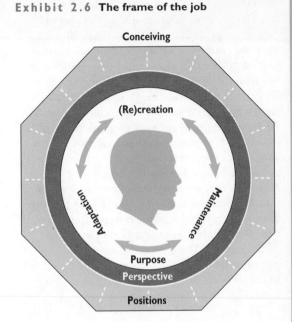

health care system accepts a government mandate for major restructuring.

The two circles beyond purpose describe two further dimensions of frame, encompassing both strategy and structure. First is *perspective*, equivalent to what Peter Drucker has called a 'theory of the business' (or of any unit being managed).[2] Perspective is the overall approach to the management of the unit, including such notions as 'vision' and 'culture'. Second are *positions*, which, in contrast, are more concrete, closer to Michael Porter's view of strategy and perhaps many consulting companies' view of structure. These positions consider specific locations for the unit in its environment, and specific ways of doing its work, such as the products produced, the markets served, the structures and systems designed, the facilities provided.[3]

Alain Noël, who studied the relationship between the frames and the work of the chief executives of three small companies, has said that managers have 'occupations' and they have 'preoccupations'.[4] Frame describes the preoccupations, while roles (discussed later) describe the occupations. But frame does give rise to a first role in this model as well, which I call *conceiving*, namely thinking through the purpose, perspective, and positions of a particular unit to be managed over a particular period of time.

Different managers conceive their frames in different ways. In other words, the style of performing this first role can vary significantly. First, the frame can be *imposed* by some outside person or force, or else it can be developed by the manager him- or herself. And second, that frame may range from being rather *sharp* to rather *vague*, for example from 'cutting costs by 10 percent before year end' to 'getting this place in order'. The frame of any managerial job, as suggested by its placement in the center of the rounding model, is a kind of magnet for the behaviors that surround it. So long as the frame is rather sharp, it holds those behaviors together tightly. But when the frame is vague the different issues considered and the different activities performed risk flying off in all directions. That is presumably why there has been so much demand in recent years for clearer 'vision' in strategic thinking.

Exhibit 2.7 Four styles of conceiving the frame

| | Clarity of Frame | |
	Vague	Sharp
Imposed	Passive style	Driven style
Invented	Opportunistic style	Determined style

(Selection of Frame)

As shown in Exhibit 2.7, these two sets of dimensions produce four broad styles of conceiving the frame. A frame that is self-selected but vague allows the manager wide latitude to maneuver but offers little real sense of direction. Managerial style is likely to become *opportunistic*, as in the case of a health care manager who uses any possible means to bring his unit under control. But having a vague frame imposed on the manager (such as 'empower your people') may provide little real help and risks evoking a *passive* style of management (unless, of course, the manager sharpens it). A sharp frame that the manager selects would tend to lead to a *determined*, sometimes 'visionary', style of management. For

example, the head of a fashion museum sees her role as the preservation of a national heritage. A sharp frame that is, in contrast, imposed, could well lead to a *driven* style of management, as in the example of that chief executive of the state medical system who tries to honor the government's intentions.

The agenda of the work

Given a person in a particular managerial job with a particular frame, the question arises of how this is manifested in the form of specific activities. That happens through the *agenda* to carry out the work, and the associated role of *scheduling*, which has received considerable attention in the literature of management, for example, in the empirical work of John Kotter.[5] Agenda is considered in two respects here, again shown as concentric circles (in Exhibit 2.8), the inner one more general, the outer one more specific.

First, the frame gets manifested as a set of current *issues*, in effect, whatever is of concern to the manager, broken down into manageable units — what Tom Peters likes to call 'chucks'. Ask any manager about his or her work, and the almost inevitable first reply will be about the 'issues' of central concern, those things 'on the plate' as the saying goes — promoting public exhibitions at the museum and developing a state-of-the-art storage facility for its clothing, for example. Or take a look at the agendas of meetings and you will likewise see a list of issues (rather than decisions). These, in effect, operationalize the

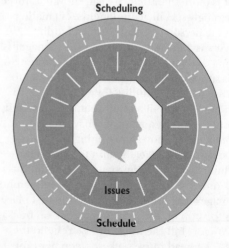

Exhibit 2.8 The agenda of the work

frame (as well as change it, of course by feeding in new concerns).

As already noted, the sharper the frame, the more integrated the issues. The more realizable they may be as well, since it is a vague frame that gives rise to that all-too-common phenomenon of the unattainable 'wish list' in an organization. Sometimes a frame can be so sharp, and the issues therefore so tightly integrated, that they all reduce to what Noël has called one 'magnificent' obsession.[6] In effect, all the concerns of the manager revolve around one central issue, for example, imposing those changes on the state health care system or expanding that retail chain.

Second, the frame and the issues get manifested in the more tangible *schedule*, the specific allocations of managerial time on a day-by-day basis. Also included here, however implicitly, is the setting of priorities among the issues. The scheduling of time and the prioritization of issues are obviously of great concern to all managers, and, in fact, are themselves significant consumers of managerial time. Accordingly, a great deal of attention has been devoted to these concerns, including numerous courses on 'time management'.

The core in context

If we label the person in the job with a frame manifested by an agenda (i.e. all the circles so far discussed), the central *core* of the manager's job, then we turn next to the context in which this core is embedded, the milieu in which the work is practiced.

The context of the job is depicted in Exhibit 2.9 by the lines that surround the core. I have so far been using the word 'unit' rather freely. Let me be more specific. A manager, by definition, has formal authority over an organizational unit, whether that be a whole organization in the case of a chief executive or a division, department, or branch, and so on, in the case of a manager within the hierarchy. Context can thus be split into three areas, labelled inside, within, and outside on Exhibit 2.9.

Inside refers to the unit being managed, shown below the manager to represent his or her formal authority over its people and activities — the hospital ward in the case of the head nurse, for example. *Within*, shown to the right, refers to the rest of the organization, other members and other units with which the manager must work but over which he or she has no formal authority

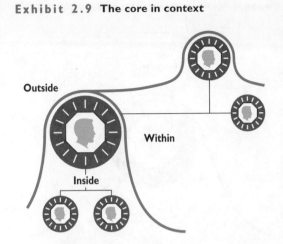

Exhibit 2.9 The core in context

Outside

Within

Inside

— the doctors, the kitchen, the physiotherapists in the rest of the hospital, to continue with the same example. (Of course, in the case of the chief executive, there is no inside separate from within: that person has authority over the entire organization.) And *outside* refers to the rest of the context not formally part of the organization, with which the manager must work — in this example, patients' relatives, long-term care institutions to which some of the unit's patients are discharged, nursing associations, and so on. The importance of this distinction (for convenience, we shall mostly refer to inside versus outside) is that much of managerial work is clearly directed either to the unit itself, for which the manager has official responsibility, or at its various boundary contexts, through which the manager must act without that responsibility.

Managing on three levels

We are now ready to address the actual behaviors that managers engage in to do their jobs. In other words, we turn now from the largely cerebral roles of conceiving and scheduling at the core to the more tangible roles of getting things done. The essence of the model, designed to enable us to 'see' managerial work comprehensively, is that these roles are carried out on three successive levels, each inside and outside the unit. Again this is depicted by concentric circles of increasing specificity shown in Exhibit 2.10.

From the outside (or most tangible level) in, managers can manage *action* directly, they can manage *people* to encourage them to take the necessary actions, and they can manage

Exhibit 2.10 Three levels of evoking action

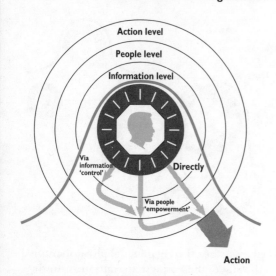

information to influence the people in turn to take their necessary actions. In other words, the ultimate objective of managerial work, and of the functioning of any organizational unit, the taking of action, can be managed directly, indirectly through people, or even more indirectly by information through people. The manager can thus choose to intervene at any of the three levels, but once done, he or she must work through the remaining ones. Later we shall see that the level a given manager favors becomes an important determinant of his or her managerial style, especially distinguishing so-called 'doers' who prefer direct action, 'leaders' who prefer working through people, and 'administrators' who prefer to work by information.

The discussion that follows describes managerial behavior in terms of roles, each pertaining to a given level and directed either inside or outside the unit (or both). We shall begin with the innermost circle, of information, containing the most conceptual roles, and work out to the more tangible or specific ones.

In presenting these roles, it should be emphasized that all managers perform all of them as the essence of their work. Styles of managers do vary, to be sure, but not in *whether* these roles are performed so much as in *which* of them is favored and how they are performed. This model of roles on levels directed inside and outside the unit thus provides the basis for understanding different styles of managing as well as different contexts in which that managing takes place.

Managing by information

To manage by information is to sit two steps removed from the purpose of managerial work. The manager processes information to drive other people who, in turn, are supposed to ensure that necessary actions are taken. In other words, here the managers' own activities focus neither on people nor on actions *per se*, but rather on information as an indirect way to make things happen. Ironically while this was the classic perception of managerial work for the first half of this century (as I discuss later), in recent years, it has also become a newly popular, in some quarters almost obsessional, view, epitomized by the so-called 'bottom line' approach to management.

The manager's various informational behaviors may be grouped into two broad roles, here labeled communicating and controlling, shown in Exhibit 2.11.

Exhibit 2.11 The information roles

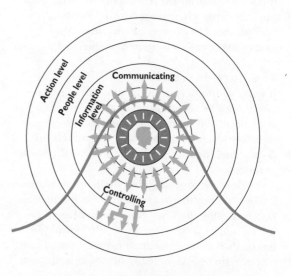

Communicating refers to the collection and dissemination of information. In Exhibit 2.11, communicating is shown by double arrows to indicate that managers devote a great deal of effort to the two-way flow of information with the people all around them — employees inside their own units, others in the rest of the organization, and especially, as the empirical evidence makes abundantly clear, a great number of outsiders with whom they maintain regular contact. Thus the head of one regional division of the national police force spent a good part of his day passing information back and forth between the central headquarters and the people on his staff.

Managers 'scan' their environments, they monitor their own units, and they share with and disseminate to others considerable amounts of the information they pick up. A point worth emphasizing, and one emphasized in almost every serious study of managerial work, is that the formal information — in other words, information capable of being processed in a computer — does not play a particularly dominant role here. Oral information — much of it too early or too 'soft' to formalize, such as gossip and hearsay — and even nonverbal information, namely what is seen and 'felt' but not heard, forms a critical part of every serious managerial job (or, at least, every managerial job performed seriously).

In my initial study, I described managers as 'nerve centers' of their units, who use their status of office to gain access to a wide variety of informational sources. Inside the unit, everyone else is a specialist who generally knows more about his or her specialty than the manager. But, because the manager is connected to all those specialists, he or she should have the broadest base of knowledge about the unit in general. This should apply to the head of an 800 000-person health care system, with regard to broad policy issues, no less than to the clinical director of one of its hospital units, with regard to the service rendered there. And externally, by virtue of their status, managers have access to other managers who are themselves nerve centers of their own units. And so they tend to be exposed to powerful sources of external information and thus emerge as external nerve centers as well. The health care chief executive can thus talk to people running health care systems in other countries and so gain access to an array of information perhaps inaccessible even to his more influential reports.

The result of all this is that a considerable amount of the manager's information turns out to be privileged, especially when we consider how much of it is oral and nonverbal. Accordingly, to function effectively with the people around them, managers have to spend considerable time sharing their information, both with outsiders (in a kind of spokesperson role) and with insiders (in a kind of disseminator role).

I found in my initial study of chief executives that perhaps 40 percent of their time was devoted almost exclusively to the communicating role —

just to gaining and sharing information — leaving aside the information processing aspects of all the other roles. In other words, the job of managing is fundamentally one of processing information, notably by talking and especially listening. Thus Exhibit 2.11 shows the inner core (the person in the job, conceiving and scheduling) connected to the outer rings (the more tangible roles of managing people and action) through what can be called the membrane of information processing all around the job.

What can be called the *controlling* role describes the managers' efforts, not just to gain and share information, but to use it in a directive way inside their units: to evoke or provoke general action by the people who report to them. They do this in three broad ways: they develop systems, they design structures, and they impose directives. Each of these seeks to control how other people work, especially with regard to the allocation of resources, and so what actions they are inclined to take.

First, developing systems is the most general of these three, and the closest to conceiving. It uses information to control people's behaviors. Managers often take charge of establishing and even running such systems in their units, including those of planning and performance control (such as budgeting). The head nurse, for example, dispensed with one of the hospital's key control systems and instead developed her own. Robert Simons has noted how chief executives tend to select one such system and make it key to their exercise of control, in a manner he calls 'interactive'.[7]

Second, managers exercise control through designing the structures of their units. By establishing responsibilities and defining hierarchical authority, they again exercise control rather passively, through the processing of information. People are informed of their duties, which in turn is expected to drive them to carry out the appropriate actions. Thus, a day spent with the head of an international environmental organization involved considerable attention to reorganization.

Third is imposing directives, which is the most direct of the three, closest to the people and actions, although still informational in nature. Managers pronounce: they make specific choices and give specific orders, usually in the process of 'delegating' particular responsibilities and 'authorizing' particular requests. In effect, managers manage by transmitting information to people so that they can act. Thus, a deputy minister in the Canadian government met with a number of his policy analysis people to provide rather specific comments about his wishes on drafts of reports they had submitted to him.

If a full decision-making process can be considered in the three stages of diagnosing, designing, and deciding — in other words, identifying issues, working out possible solutions, and selecting one[8] — then here we are dealing with a restricted view of decision making. Delegating means mostly diagnosing ('Would you please handle this problem in this context'), while authorizing means mostly deciding ('OK, you can proceed'). Either way, the richest part of the process, the stage of designing possible solutions, resides with the person being controlled rather than with the manager him- or herself, whose own behavior remains rather passive. Thus the manager as controller seems less an *actor* with sleeves rolled up, digging in, than a *reviewer* who sits back in the office and passes judgment. That is why this role is characterized as informational; I will describe a richer approach to decision making in the section on action roles.

The controlling role is shown in Exhibit 2.11 propelling down into the manager's own unit, since that is where formal authority is exercised. The single-headed arrows represent the imposed directives, while the pitchfork shape symbolizes both the design of structure and the development of systems. The proximity of the controlling role in Exhibit 2.11 to the manager's agenda reflects the fact that informational control is the most direct way to operationalize the agenda, for example, by using budgets to impose priorities or delegation to assign responsibilities.

The controlling role is, of course, what people have in mind when they refer to the 'administrative' aspect of managerial work. Interestingly, it encompasses almost the entire set of activities described by the classical writers. In the 1930s, for example, Gulick and Urwick popularized the acronym POSDCORB (planning, organizing, staffing, directing, coordinating, reporting and budgeting).[9] Planning, organizing, directing, and budgeting are all clearly focused here, while reporting, coordinating, and staffing have important, although not exclusive,

controlling aspects (staffing in the sense of deciding). Thus it must be concluded that the long-popular description of managerial work was not so much wrong as narrow, focusing almost exclusively on one restricted aspect of the job: informational control of the unit through the exercise of formal authority.

Managing through people

To manage through people, instead of by information, is to move one step closer to action, but still to remain removed from it. That is because here the focus of managerial attention becomes affect instead of effect. Other people become the means to get things done, not the manger him- or herself, or even the substance of the manager's thoughts.

After several decades of POSDCORB thinking and Taylorist technique, the Hawthorne experiments of the 1930s demonstrated with dramatic impact that management has to do with more than just the passive informational control of subordinates.[10] People entered the scene, or at least they entered the textbooks, as entities to be 'motivated' and later 'empowered'. Influencing began to replace informing and commitment began to vie with calculation for the attention of the manager. Indeed, in the 1960s and 1970s especially, the management of people, quite independent of content — of the strategies to be realized, the information to be processed, even the actions to be taken — became a virtual obsession of the literature, whether by the label of 'human relations', 'Theory Y', or 'participative management' (and later 'quality of work life', to be replaced by 'total quality management').

For a long time, however, these people remained 'subordinates' in more ways than one. 'Participation' kept them subordinate, for this was always considered to be granted at the behest of the managers still fully in control (compared with the more constitutional involvement of certain professionals, such as doctors in hospitals, or even of certain European workers who, under 'codetermination', gained legal representation on boards of directors). So does the currently popular term 'empowerment', which implies that power is being granted, thanks to the managers. (Hospital directors do not 'empower' physicians!) People also remained subordinates because the whole focus was on those inside the unit, not outside it. Not until serious research on managerial work began did it become evident

Exhibit 2.12 The people roles

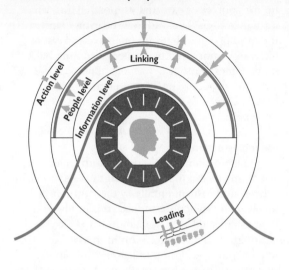

how important to managers were contacts with individuals outside their units (who, for example, go entirely without mention in POSDCORB!) Virtually every single study of how all kinds of managers spent their time has indicated that outsiders, of an enormously wide variety, generally take as much of managers' attention as so-called 'subordinates'. We shall thus describe two people roles here, shown in Exhibit 2.12, one internal, called leading, and one external called linking.

The *leading* role has probably received more attention in the literature of management than all the other roles combined. And so we need not dwell on it here. But neither can we ignore it: managers certainly do much more than lead the people in their own units, and leading certainly infuses much else of what managers do (as, in fact, do all the roles, as we have already noted about communicating). But their work just as certainly cannot be understood without this dimension.[11] We can describe the role of leading on three levels, as indicated in Exhibit 2.12.

First, managers lead on the *individual* level, 'one on one', as the expression goes. They encourage and drive the people of their units — — motivate them, inspire them, coach them, nurture them, push them, mentor them, and so on. All managers, from the chief executive of the major police force to the front-country manager in the mountain park, stop to chat with their people informally during the day to encourage them in their work. Second, managers lead on the *group* level, especially by building and

managing teams, an effort that has received considerable attention in recent years. Again, team meetings, including team building, figured in many of my observations, for example, the head of a London film company who brought film-making teams together for both effective and affective purposes. And third, they lead on the *unit* level, especially with regard to the creating and maintenance of culture, another subject of increasing attention in recent years (thanks especially to the Japanese). Managers, for example, engage in many acts of a symbolic nature ('figurehead' duties) to sustain culture, as when the head of the national police force visited its officer training institute (as he does frequently) to imbue the force's norms and attitudes in its graduating class.

All managers seem to spend time on all three levels of leadership, although, again, styles do vary according to context and personality. If the communicating role describes the manager as the nerve center of the unit, then the leading role must characterize him or her as its 'energy center', a concept perhaps best captured in Maeterlinck's wonderful description of the 'spirit of the hive'.[12] Given the right managerial 'chemistry' (in the case of Maeterlinck's queen bee, quite literally!), it may be the manager's mere presence that somehow draws things together. By exuding that mystical substance, the leader unites his or her people, galvanizing them into action to accomplish the unit's mission and adapt it to a changing world.

The excess attention to the role of leading has probably been matched by the inadequate attention to the role of *linking*. For, as already noted, in their sheer allocation of time, managers have been shown to be external linkers as much as they are internal leaders. In 1964, Leonard Sayles emphasized this in his path-breaking book, and I repeated it in 1973, as did John Kotter in 1982.[13] Yet, still the point seems hardly appreciated. Indeed, now more than ever, it must be understood, given the great growth of joint ventures and other collaborating and networking relationships between organizations, as well as the gradual reconception of the 'captive' employee as an autonomous 'agent' who supplies labor.

Exhibit 2.12 suggests a small model of the linking role. The arrows go in and out to indicate that the manager is both an advocate of its influence outside the unit and, in turn, a recipient of much of the influence exerted on it from the outside. In the middle are two parallel lines to represent the buffering aspect of this role — that managers must regulate the receipt of external influence to protect their units. To use a popular term, they are the 'gatekeepers' of influence. Or, to add a metaphor, the manager acts as a kind of valve between the unit and its environment. Nowhere was this clearer than in my observation of three levels of management in a national park system — a regional director, the head of one mountain park, and the front-country manager of the park. They sit in an immensely complex array of forces — developers who want to enhance their business opportunities, environmentalists who want to preserve the natural habitat, tourists who want to enjoy the beauty, truckers who want to drive through the park unimpeded, politicians who want to avoid negative publicity, etc. It is a delicate balancing, or buffering, act indeed!

All managers, as emphasized in other research and my studies cited earlier, appear to spend a great deal of time 'networking' — building vast arrays of contacts and intricate coalitions of supporters beyond their own units, whether within the rest of the organization or outside, in the world at large. To all these contacts, the manager represents the unit externally, promotes its needs, and lobbies for its causes. In response, these people are expected to provide a steady inflow of information to the unit as well as various means of support and specific favors for it. This networking was most evident in the case of the film company managing director, who even in one day exhibited an impressive network of contacts in order to negotiate her complex contracts with various media in different countries.

In turn, people intent on influencing the behavior of an organization or one of its subunits will often exercise pressure directly on its manager, expecting that person to transmit the influence inside, as was most pointedly clear in the work of the parks managers. Here, then, the managerial job becomes one of delicate balance, a tricky act of mediation. Those managers who let external influence pass inside too freely — who act like sieves — are apt to drive their people crazy. (Of course, those who act like sponges and absorb all the influence personally are apt to drive themselves crazy!) And those who block out all influence — who act like lead to x-rays — are apt to detach their units from reality (and so dry up the sources of external support). Thus, what influence to pass on and how, bearing in mind the quid pro quo that influence exerted out is likely to be mirrored by influence coming back in, becomes another key aspect of managerial style, worthy of greatly increased attention in both the study of the job and the training of its occupants.

Managing action

If managers manage passively by information and affectively through people, then they also manage actively and instrumentally by their own direct involvement in action. Indeed, this has been a long-established view of managerial work, although the excess attention in this century, first to controlling and then to leading, and more recently to conceiving (of planned strategy), has obscured its importance. Leonard Sayles, however, has long and steadily insisted on this, beginning with his 1964 book and culminating in *The Working Leader* (published in 1993), in which he makes his strongest statement yet, insisting that managers must be the focal points for action in and by their units.[14] Their direct involvement must, in his view, take precedence over the pulling force of leadership and the pushing force of controllership.

I shall refer to this involvement as the *doing* role. But, in using this label — a popular one in the managerial vernacular ('Mary Ann's a doer!') — it is necessary to point out that managers, in fact, hardly ever 'do' anything. Many barely even dial their own telephones! As already noted, watch a manager and you will see someone whose work consists almost exclusively of talking and listening, alongside, of course, watching and 'feeling'. (That, incidentally, is why I show the manager at the core of the model as a head and not a full body!)

What 'doing' presumably means, therefore, is getting closer to the action, ultimately being just one step removed from it. Managers as doers manage the carrying out of action directly, instead of indirectly through managing people or by processing information. In effect, a 'doer' is really someone who gets it done (or, as the French put it with their expression *faire faire*, to make something get made). And the managerial vernacular is, in fact, full of expressions that reflect just this: 'doing deals', 'championing change', 'fighting fires', 'juggling projects'. In the terms of decision making introduced earlier, here the manager diagnoses and designs as well as decides: he or she gets deeply and fully involved in the management of particular activities. Thus, in the day I spent with the head of the small retail chain, I saw a steady stream of all sorts of people coming and going, most involved with some aspect of store development or store operations, and there to get specific instructions on how to proceed next. He was not delegating or authorizing, but very clearly managing specific developmental projects step by step.

Just as they communicate all around the circle, so too do managers 'do' all around it, as shown in Exhibit 2.13. They manage projects and solve problems, or put out fires, inside their units, and they 'do deals' and negotiate agreements with outsiders. Let us consider each in turn.

Exhibit 2.13 The action roles

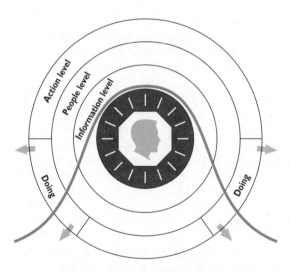

Doing inside involves projects and problems. This does not imply that projects are independent of problems, or that either is exclusively internal. Rather, it means that much 'doing' has to do with changing the unit itself, both proactively and reactively. Managers champion change to exploit opportunities for their units, and they handle its problems and resolve its crises, often with 'hands on' involvement. Indeed , the president of a large French systems company spent part of his day in a meeting on a very specific customer contract. Asked why he attended, he said it was a leading-edge project that could well change his company. He was being informed, to be sure, but also

'doing' (more than controlling): he was an active member of the team.

The difference between deciding in the controlling role and acting in the doing role is the difference, in effect, between sitting in a managerial office and passing judgment on the issues floating by — 'Roberta, please handle this', 'No, Joe, you can't do that' — and getting out of the office and actively engaging an issue from its initial identification to its final resolution. Here the manager becomes a true designer (or, in the example above, a partner in the design), not of abstract strategies or of generalized structures, but of tangible projects of change. And the evidence, in fact, is that managers at all levels typically juggle many such projects concurrently, perhaps several dozen in the case of chief executives. Hence the popularity of the term 'project management'.

Managers 'do' inside in two other respects as well. For one thing, they substitute, sometimes doing the routine work of their units in place of other people. (The front-country manager spent part of the day cruising a river for the body of a person who had a few days earlier gone over a waterfall in a boat!) Of course, when managers are replacing absent employees, this may be considered another aspect of handling problems. Second, some managers continue to do regular work after they have become managers. For example, the head nurse saw a patient (just as the Pope leads prayers, or a dean might teach a class). Done for its own sake, this might be considered separate from managerial work. But such things are often done for very managerial reasons as well. This may be an effective way of 'keeping in touch' with the unit's work and finding out about its problems, in which case it falls under the role of communicating. Or it may be done to demonstrate involvement and commitment with others in the unit. In which case it falls under the role of culture building in the role of leading.

Doing outside takes place in terms of deals and negotiations. Again, these are two sides of the same coin, in that managers negotiate in order to 'do deals', and also negotiate once the deal is done. And, again as well, there is no shortage of evidence on the importance of negotiating as well as dealing in managerial work. Most evident in my observations was the managing director of the film company, who was working on one intricate deal after another that day. This was a small company and making deals was a key part of her job. In larger organizations, senior managers may have all kinds of specialized negotiators supporting them (for example, lawyers for contracts and labor relations specialists for union bargaining). Yet that does not release them from having to spend considerable time on negotiations themselves, especially when critical moments arise. After all, they are the ones who have the authority to commit the resources of their unit, and it is they who are the nerve centers of its information as well as the energy centers of its activity, not to mention the conceptual centers of its strategy. All around the circles, therefore, action connects to people who connect to information, which connects to the frame.

The well-rounded job of managing

I opened this article by noting that the best-known writers of management all seem to emphasize one aspect of the job — in the terms we now have, 'doing' for Tom Peters, 'conceiving' for Michael Porter, 'leading' for Abraham Zaleznik and Warren Bennis, 'controlling' for the classical writers, and so on. Now it can be appreciated why all may well be wrong: heeding the advice of any one of them must lead to the lopsided practice of managerial work. Like an unbalanced wheel at resonant frequency, the job risks flying out of control. That is why it is important to show all of the components of managerial work on a single integrated diagram, as in Exhibit 2.14, to remind people, at a glance, that these components form one job and cannot be separated.

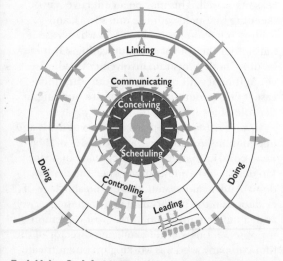

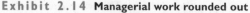

Exhibit 2.14 Managerial work rounded out

Acceptance of Tom Peters' urging — '"Don't think, do" is the phrase I favor'[15] — could lead to the centrifugal explosion of the job, as it flies off in all directions, free of a strong frame anchoring it at the core. But acceptance of the spirit of Michael Porter's opposite writings — that what matters most is conception of the frame, especially of strategic positions — could produce a result no better: centripetal implosion, as the job closes in on itself cerebrally, free of the tangible connection to its outer actions. Thinking is heavy and can wear down the incumbent, while acting is light and cannot keep him or her in place. Only together do they provide the balance that seems so characteristic of effective management.

Too much leading produces a job free of content — aimless, frameless, and actionless — while too much linking produces a job detached from its internal roots — public relations instead of public service. The manager who only communicates or only conceives never gets anything done, while the manager who only 'does' ends up doing it all alone. And, of course, we all know what happens to managers who believe their job is merely to control (or, these days, to their organizations, as the detached managers escape in their golden parachutes). If I combine the more cerebral roles, we end up with a 'think-link-lead-do' model. Or, as someone who read this description remarked, 'Well then, management is a form of thinking and leading by doing'.

A bad pun may thus make for good practice: the manager must practice a well-rounded job. Or, if you prefer, anyone who wants to hold this job must swallow the whole pill (which may not, in fact, be a bad metaphor, since the outer coating of doing provides the immediate effect, while each successive layer in this time-release capsule provides deeper, less accessible, but more long-term effects). The different roles are somewhat substitutable, to be sure, for example, pushing employees through controlling by systems instead of pulling them through leading by culture. But, more important, they are complementary.

In fact, while we may be able to separate the components of this job conceptually, I maintain that they cannot be separated behaviorally. In other words, it may be useful, even necessary, to delineate the parts for purposes of design, selection, training and support. But this job cannot be practiced as a set of independent parts. As noted, the core is a kind of magnet that holds the rest together, while the communication ring acts as a membrane that allows the flow of information between inner thinking and outer behaviors, which themselves tie people to action.

Indeed, the most interesting aspects of this job may well fall on the edges, between the component parts. For example, Andrew Grove, president of Intel, likes to describe what he does as 'nudging', a perfect blend of controlling, leading and doing.[16] This can mean pushing people, tangibly but not aggressively, as might happen with pure doing, and not coldly, as with pure controlling but with a sense of leading. There are similar edges between the inside and the outside, thinking and behaving, and communicating and controlling, as we shall see.

Managers who try to 'do' outside without 'doing' inside inevitably get themselves into trouble. Just consider all those chief executives who 'did the deal', acquired the company or whatever, and then dropped it into the laps of others for execution. Likewise, it makes no more sense to conceive and then fail to lead and do (as has been the tendency in so-called 'strategic planning', where controlling has often been considered sufficient for 'implementation') than it makes sense to do or to lead without thinking through the frame in which to embed these activities. A single managerial job may be carried out by a small team, but only if its members are so tightly knitted together — especially by that ring of communication — that they act as a single entity.

Earlier I mentioned how leading, while identifiable as some activities, tends to infuse almost all managerial work. But the same is true of communicating, as noted, and of conceiving (which cannot be saved for some ethereal mountain retreat), and of scheduling. Likewise, just as the core role of conceiving cannot be separated from the surface role of doing, so too can the inside roles of controlling, leading, and doing not be separated from the outside ones of linking and doing. In fact, at the limit, they blend into one another. Leading and controlling have been described here as inside roles, linking as an outside role. But a manager with considerable influence over an outsider — say, a captive supplier — can exercise leadership as well as direct control, while one whose own employees begin to act as free agents may have to relate to

them as a linker more than a leader (as the chief of any clinical service in a hospital can tell you).

Managing in style

To describe the various components that make up the job of managing as integrated, infused, and well rounded is not to imply that all managers do all of them with equal emphasis. Managerial work does vary, according to the needs of a particular job and the approach of its particular incumbent. Different managers end up emphasizing different things in different ways. Paradoxically, however, this may best be understood through a systematic framework of what they all do in common. Accordingly, I use the model in Exhibit 2.14 to consider briefly some questions of managerial *style* (including the effect of context). Style is considered to impact on managerial work in three ways: *which* roles a particular manager favors, *how* he or she performs these roles, and what kind of *relationship* exists among these roles.

First, and most obviously, managers in different contexts have to emphasize different roles. For example, as noted above, the managers of autonomous professionals, as in hospitals or universities, tend to favor linking over leading (let alone controlling), since professionals tend to come to their work naturally empowered. In other words, they need little encouragement or supervision although they do require considerable external support. However, when experts must work in teams, as in some research laboratories or in professional sports, leadership becomes rather critical, particularly at the group level. Entrepreneurs, in contrast, who run their own businesses, tend to emphasize doing (alongside conceiving), as they involve themselves deeply in specific issues. Interestingly, the same thing tends to be true of first-line managers, even in conventional big businesses, for example, foremen in factories who must resolve steady streams of operating problems. Senior executives of large diversified firms, on the other hand, give greater attention to controlling, particularly through their systems of performance control and their decisions to authorize major capital expenditures.

Of course, regardless of the context, individual managers are often personally predisposed to favor particular roles or aspects of the job. Considering this from the inside out, we can, for example, distinguish a *conceptual* style of management, which focuses on the development of the frame, an *administrative* style, which concerns itself primarily with controlling, an *interpersonal* style, which favors leading on the inside or linking on the outside, and an *action* style, which is concerned mainly with tangible doing. And as we move out in this order, the overall style of managing can be described as less *opaque*, more *visible*.

Even in how they respond to requests, managers can exhibit subtle yet significant variations in style. Asked for advice by an employee, for example, a manager may respond as a communicator ('Payroll has some data on this'), a controller ('Don't do it'), or a leader ('How do *you* feel about it?'). Of course, the doer may say, 'Just leave it with me'! All kinds of opportunities arise in managing to substitute, combine, and give nuance to the different roles.

Second, regardless of which roles or aspects of the job a particular manager emphasizes, his or her personal style is manifested particularly in *how* these are performed. We have already seen this, for example, in different approaches to linking at the extremes (the sieve, the lead, the sponge), and the different approaches to conceiving the frame (passive, driven, opportunistic, and determined styles). Similarly, we saw different predispositions to leading (favoring the individual, group, or unit level). Other obvious variations in style can be delineated according to how each of the remaining components of the model might be carried out.

A final aspect of managerial style has to do with the interrelationships among the various components of managerial work. For example, an important distinction can be made between *deductive* and *inductive* approaches to managerial work. The former proceeds from the core out, as the conceived frame is implemented through scheduling that uses information to drive people to get action done. We can call this a *cerebral* style of managing — highly deliberate — noting that it has been popular from the early POSDCORB writers to the current proponents of strategic planning and bottom-line thinking. But there is an alternate, emergent view of the management process as well, which proceeds inductively from the outer surface to the inner core. We might label it an *insightful* style. As Karl Weick puts it, managers act in order to think. They try things to gain experience, retain what works, and then, by

interpreting the results, gradually evolve their frames.[17]

Of course, the preferred approach may well vary with context as well as personal inclination. When a situation is well understood, the cerebral style seems logical, while, under conditions of ambiguity, the insightful style may make more sense. Part of our problem in recent years, in educating managers as well as in their own practice, has been a predisposition toward the cerebral style in situations of increasing ambiguity that require inductive insight. Even 'doing' is one step removed from the action: How then is a manager who relies on controlling — three steps removed — to come to serious grips with any real problem in an organization?

Clearly, there is an infinity of possible contexts within which management can be practiced. But just as clearly, perhaps, a model such as the one presented here can help to order them and so come to grips with the difficult requirements of designing managerial jobs, selecting the right people to fill them, and training people accordingly. It is in these areas that we are in greatest need of rich theory, and this kind of description may be one step toward the development of it. In particular, the model may help in the hitherto intractable problem of delineating a useful list of *competences* that underlie the effective performance of managerial work.

To give some idea of the flesh that might be put on the skeleton of this model, let me describe briefly a few of the managers I have observed. This gives a sense of how context and personal predisposition interact with the various components of the job to define reality.

■ Ann was director of nursing services for a hospital near London; Peter was the manager of a district in the National Health Service of England. The difference in their work was marked. Ann can be described as 'managing down', Peter as 'managing up'.

Ann was intimately connected to the delivery of health care on a daily basis, knowledgeable about every imaginable detail of her hospital's operations. It is people like her who keep the system running. She conceived and she managed outside, to be sure, and her relationships with the autonomous doctors are best described as linking. But mostly she seemed to maintain the internal operations by a certain amount of 'doing' combined with a good deal of leading as well as some controlling, all infused with the 'spirit of the hive'.

■ Peter, in contrast, managed largely up, being more concerned with the administrative intricacies of the hierarchy under which he sat than the district over which he ostensibly had authority. District management is necessarily detached from the daily delivery of health care, and so managing inside seemed to be restricted largely to formalized controlling, particularly with regard to systems of resource allocation. I found less 'doing' here and not a great deal of leading. Outside linking seemed to be the focus, to maintain good ties with the upper echelons of the hierarchy. As a result, buffering came naturally to this job. If Ann's style could be described as involved and insightful, then Peter's was cerebral and deductive.

■ Carol ran a film company in London, producing quality films mostly for television. She could afford to manage neither exclusively up nor exclusively down, although she had to use a different style for each. Trying to capture both the what and the how, I described her work as 'hard dealing and soft leading'. Carol seemed to be a doer above all, specifically on the outside, using a vast array of contacts to 'do the deals' of film contracts. But once the deal was done, a team had to be assembled and its work, by competent professionals, had to be not so much controlled as monitored, to ensure that it remained responsive to the client's needs. Thus Carol's outside work was focused and intense — 'doing' in detail and with a vengeance — while her inside work seemed to be gentler and somewhat more indirect — leading rather than doing. And her overall orientation had to be rather opportunistic, for this is a highly fashionable business. But there was a frame here too, not crystal clear perhaps, but sharp enough to help select the projects and maintain a sense of unity in the company. Carol's own style would appear to be more insightful than cerebral and more inductive than deductive.

■ Norman ran a large, Canadian national police force, where he had spent his career. Linking was important: this is a highly sensitive job in which informing and buffering are critical. And so, in his words, he arranged for 'no surprises',

especially for the politicians. But above all, he protected and strengthened the culture of the force, which is legendary. This served as his frame, in a way, on which he laid his own liberal stamp. Controlling is obviously not absent from the job of police commissioner, but this one tilted especially toward the collective level of leading.

■ Fabienne was the head nurse of a surgical ward in a Canadian hospital. The contrast between her job and Norman's is marked, except in its essence — the importance placed on the leading role. There was much less formality in her job and much less movement: she managed on her feet mostly in the nursing station around which all revolved. If Norman was 'on top' of things hierarchically and colloquially, then Fabienne was in the middle of them. This allowed her to solve problems quickly and informally. Linking was relatively less important here; indeed, Fabienne was 'not crazy about the whole PR thing' as she put it. Instead she could be described as 'doing' to lead (in contrast to Norman's and Carol's linking to lead), blending her different activities into a central frame that she described as a 'caring' style of management: she believed in serving her nurses much as she once served her patients. Management as 'blended care' would seem to be most effective, especially in contrast to the all-too-common style of management as interventionist cure![18]

These are but a few of the managers in context, but their brief profiles may give a sense of the richness with which the work and the style of managing can be described. We have a long way to go in understanding this most important of jobs. I can only hope that closing this initial circle may be one helpful way to proceed.

References

1 H. Mintzberg, *The Nature of Managerial Work* (New York: Harper and Row, 1973); and H. Mintzberg, 'The Manager's Job: Folklore and Fact', *Harvard Business Review*, July–August 1975, pp. 49–61.

2 P. F. Drucker, *Management: Tasks, Responsibilities, Practices* (New York: Harper and Row, 1973).

3 M. E. Porter, *Competitive Strategy* (New York: Free Press, 1980). For a comparison of strategy as perspective and position, see: H. Mintzberg, 'Five P's for Strategy', *California Management Review*, Fall 1987, pp. 11–24.

4   A. Noël, 'Strategic Cores and Magnificent
     Obsessions: Discovering Strategy Formation
     through Daily Activities of CEOs', *Strategic
     Management Journal* 10 (1989), pp. 33–49.

5   J. P. Kotter, *The General Manager* (New York: Free
     Press, 1982).

6   Noël (1989).

7   See R. Simons, 'Strategic Orientation and Top
     Management Attention to Control Systems',
     Strategic Management Journal 12 (1991), pp. 49–62;
     and R. Simons, 'The Role of Management
     Control Systems in Creating Competitive
     Advantage: New Perspectives', *Accounting,
     Organizations and Society* 15 (1990), pp. 127–43.

8   See H. Simon's discussion of intelligence,
     design, and choice, in *The New Science of
     Management Decision* (Englewood Cliffs, NJ:
     Prentice Hall, 1960).

9   H. Gulick and L. F. Urwick, *Paper on the Science of
     Administration* (New York, Columbia University,
     1937); see also H. Fayol, *Administration
     industrielle et générale* (Paris: Dunod, 1916);
     English translation, *General and Industrial
     Administration* (London: Pelman, 1949).

10   See F. W. Roethlisberger and W. J. Dickson,
     Management and the Worker (Cambridge, MA:
     Harvard University Press, 1939).

11   See Karl Weick's criticism of my inclusion of
     leading as a role in my 1973 book in: K. Weick,
     'Review Essay of *The Nature of Managerial Work*',
     Administrative Science Quarterly 19 (1974),
     pp. 111–18.

12   M. Maeterlinck, *The Life of the Bee* (New York:
     Dodd, Mead and Company, 1918).

13   L. R. Sayles, *Managerial Behavior: Administration
     in Complex Organizations* (New York: McGraw-
     Hill, 1964); Mintzberg (1973); and Kotter
     (1982).

14   L. R. Sayles, *The Working Leader* (New York: Free
     Press, 1993).

15   T. Peters, 'The Case for Experimentation: or,
     You Can't Plan Your Way to Unplanning a
     Formerly Planned Economy' (Palo Alto, CA:
     pamphlet issued by Tom Peters Group,
     1990).

16   A. Grove, *High Output Management* (New York:
     Random House, 1983).

17   K. E. Weick, *The Social Psychology of Organizing*
     (Reading, MA: Addison-Wesley, 1979). See also:
     H. Mintzberg, 'Crafting Strategy', *Harvard
     Business Review,* July–August 1987, pp. 66–75.

18   See H. Mintzberg, 'Managing as Blended Care',
     Journal of Nursing Administration (forthcoming,
     1994).

EXERCISE 2   INITIAL VIEW OF ORGANISATIONAL BEHAVIOUR

Source: Adapted from Weinberg, R., & Nord, W. (1982).
Coping with 'It's all common sense', *Exchange: The
Organizational Behavior Teaching Journal,* **7**, no. 2, 29–32.
Used with permission.

Now that you have read Chapters 1 and 2, which
set the tone for the book, complete the following
exercise. This should be used as your beginning
baseline assumptions, opinions and
understanding of organisational behaviour. Once
you have completed the course (book), we will
take another look at your assumptions, opinions
and understanding.

This exercise contains 20 pairs of statements
about organisational behaviour. For each pair,
circle the letter preceding the statement which
you think is most accurate. Circle only one letter
in each pair.

After you have circled the letter, indicate how
certain you are of your choice by writing 1, 2, 3 or
4 on the line following each item according to
the following procedure.

- Place a '1' if you are *very uncertain* that your
  choice is correct.
- Place a '2' if you are *somewhat uncertain* that
  your choice is correct.
- Place a '3' if you are *somewhat certain* that your
  choice is correct.
- Place a '4' if you are *very certain* that your
  choice is correct.
- Do not skip any pairs.

1. **a.**   A supervisor is well advised to treat, as much as possible, all members of
     his/her group exactly the same way.
   b.   A supervisor is well advised to adjust his/her behaviour according to the
     unique characteristics of the members of his/her group.   3

2. **a.** Generally speaking, individual motivation is greatest if the person has set goals for himself/herself that are *difficult* to achieve.
   b. Generally speaking, individual motivation is greatest if the person has set goals for himself/herself that are *easy* to achieve.

   3

3. **a.** A major reason why organisations are not as productive as they could be these days is that managers are too concerned with managing the work group rather than the individual.
   b. A major reason why organisations are not as productive as they could be these days is that managers are too concerned with managing the individual rather than the work group .

   4

4. **a.** Supervisors who, sometime prior to becoming a supervisor, have perfomed the job of the people they are currently supervising are apt to be more effective supervisors than those who have never performed that particular job.
   b. Supervisors who, sometime prior to becoming a supervisor, have perfomed the job of the people they are currently supervising are apt to be less effective supervisors than those who have never performed that particular job.

   1

5. **a.** On almost every matter relevant to the work, managers are well advised to be completely honest and open with their subordinates.
   b. There are very few matters in the workplace where managers are well advised to be completely honest and open with their subordinates.

   2

6. **a.** One's need for power is a better predictor of managerial advancement than one's motivation to do the work well.
   b. One's motivation to do the work well is a better predictor of managerial advancement than one's need for power.

   3

7. **a.** When people fail at something, they try harder the next time.
   b. When people fail at something, they quit trying.

   1

8. **a.** Performing well as a manager depends most on how much education you have.
   b. Performing well as a manager depends most on how much experience you have.

   3

9. **a.** The most effective leaders are those who give more emphasis to getting the work done than they do to relating to people.
   b. The most effective leaders are those who give more emphasis to relating to people than they do to getting the work done.

   3

10. **a.** It is very important for a leader to 'stick to his/her guns'.
    b. It is *not* very important for a leader to 'stick to his/her guns'.

    1   *don't know what it means*

11. **a.** Pay is the most important factor in determining how hard people work.
    b. The nature of the task people are doing is the most important factor in determining how hard people work.

    4

12. **a.** Pay is the most important factor in determining how satisfied people are at work.
    b. The nature of the task is the most important factor in determining how satisfied people are at work.

    3

13. a. Generally speaking, it is correct to say that a person's attitudes cause his/her behaviour.
    b. Generally speaking, it is correct to say that a person's attitudes are primarily rationalisations for his/her behaviour.

    _4_

14. a. Satisfied workers produce more than workers who are not satisfied.
    b. Satisfied workers produce no more than workers who are not satisfied.

    _4_

15. a. The notion that most semiskilled workers desire work that is interesting and meaningful is most likely incorrect.
    b. The notion that most semiskilled workers desire work that is interesting and meaningful is most likely correct.

    _2_

16. a. People welcome change for the better.
    b. Even if change if for the better, people will resist it.

    _2_

17. a. Leaders are born, not made.
    b. Leaders are made, not born.

    _2_

18. a. Groups make better decisions than individuals.
    b. Individuals make better decisions than groups.

    _2_

19. a. The statement 'A manager's authority needs to be commensurate with his/her responsibility' is, practically speaking, a very meaningful statement.
    b. The statement 'A manager's authority needs to be commensurate with his/her responsibility' is, practically speaking, a basically meaningless statement.

    _2_

20. a. A major reason for the relative decline in North American productivity is that the division of labour and job specialisation has gone too far.
    b. A major reason for the relative decline in North American productivity is that the division of labour and job specialisation has not been carried far enough.

    _1_

THE *individual* IN THE *organisation*

3

Understanding behaviour at work

4

Motivation: An individual perspective

5

Motivation: An organisational perspective

6

Occupational stress

To know when one's self is interested, is the first condition of interesting other people.

— Walter Pater *Marius the Epicurean, Ch. 6*

UNDERSTANDING BEHAVIOUR AT WORK

Learning objectives

- Identify *the major individual variables that influence work behaviour.*

- Describe *the influence of personality and situations on behaviour.*

- Describe *organisational implications of personality and situation-based explanations of behaviour.*

- Distinguish *between stereotyping and prejudice.*

- Describe *how attributions influence our behaviour.*

- Explain *what an attitude is and identify its three components.*

- Discuss *the relationship between job satisfaction and performance.*

- Identify *two important personality factors.*

Any attempt to learn why people behave as they do in organisations requires some understanding of individual differences. Managers spend considerable time making judgements about the fit between individuals, job tasks and effectiveness. Such judgements are influenced typically by both the manager's and the subordinate's characteristics. Making decisions about who will perform what tasks in a particular manner — without some understanding of behaviour — can lead to irreversible long-run problems.

Each employee is different in many respects. A manager needs to ask how such differences influence the behaviour and performance of subordinates. This chapter highlights some of the individual differences that can explain why one person is a significantly better performer than another person. Differences among people require forms of adjustment for both the individual and those for whom that person will work. Managers who ignore such differences often become involved in practices which hinder achieving organisational and personal goals.

One of the tasks facing managers and organisations is to understand or explain differences in performance, and to remedy poor performance. For example, Jenni and Daniel both joined a large accounting firm 5 years ago. Today, Daniel is a partner, but Jenni is not. How the organisation explains this difference will have a strong effect on how it responds. The senior management may reason that Jenni lacks the skills to become a partner: that men are simply better suited to this role than women, partly because they are distracted by family concerns:

> The fact that women continue to take primary responsibility for child care is a major cause of work distraction, absenteeism and turnover among women ... Those that do return [from maternity leave] are often reluctant to work long hours and weekends or to take on certain job assignments because they involve too much travel. I know one woman who recently turned down a promotion to partner because it would mean relocating her family.[1]

If this is the explanation, then the organisation is unlikely to consider its management practices and try to understand how, for example, organisational culture affects promotion prospects for women. It may, however, be that senior managers recognise that factors such as power differences and the composition of management teams make it difficult for women to make it to the top.

Managers can offer one of two possible explanations for employee performance: *individual* factors such as skills, abilities and personality, and *organisational* factors such as task design and reward systems. Exhibit 3.1 summarises these variables and suggests that effective managerial practice

Exhibit 3.1
Variables that influence work behaviour

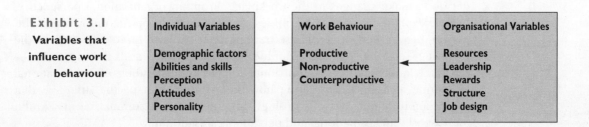

Individual Variables	Work Behaviour	Organisational Variables
Demographic factors	Productive	Resources
Abilities and skills	Non-productive	Leadership
Perception	Counterproductive	Rewards
Attitudes		Structure
Personality		Job design

requires that we recognise individual behaviour differences and, when feasible, take them into consideration when managing staff. To understand individual differences, a manager must observe and recognise the differences, study relationships between variables that influence individual behaviour and discover relationships. For example, managers are in a better position to make optimal decisions if they know what the attitudes, perceptions and mental abilities of employees are as well as how these and other variables are related. It also is important to know how each variable influences performance. Being able to observe differences, understand relationships and predict linkages can facilitate managerial attempts to improve performance. The Bob Knowlton Case at the end of the chapter demonstrates how individual differences can arise among several individual-level variables discussed in the chapter and illustrates the impact of these differences on organisational effectiveness.

Case 3

Bob Knowlton

In this chapter, we will start by discussing these two most important explanations of behaviour: individual differences and the work environment. We will consider the limitations of both types of explanation and go on to look at more recent approaches to understanding behaviour. However, a far more important consideration is how we make a choice between these explanations. We will therefore go on to consider the process of *social perception*: how we explain others' behaviour and the systematic errors that we make in these explanations.

THE BASIS FOR UNDERSTANDING WORK BEHAVIOUR

Several variables shape the work behaviour and attitudes of individuals. In this section, we will focus on the role played by individual and organisational factors.

How we explain behaviour has important consequences for both individuals and the organisation. Throughout this book, you will see that theories fall into two groups: those more concerned with the person and those more concerned with the situation. In Chapter 6, we will look at organisational factors that create stress, but also consider how our personality affects the way that we respond to stress. In Chapter 11, we will look at two groups of leadership theories; those that explain good leadership in terms of individual characteristics such as intelligence, and those that focus on how the situation influences leader effectiveness. An important area in which both explanations are considered is job satisfaction. As you can see in the Management Encounter, there is still considerable debate about whether people are happy at work because they have an optimistic personality, or whether they are happy at work because their jobs are challenging.

From a manager's point of view, how we explain behaviour affects how we treat our employees: whether we decide to reward or punish, or whether we decide to make changes to the workplace. From an organisational perspective, how we explain behaviour determines whether we focus on recruiting the 'right' person, or whether we emphasise training once we have hired new staff. In the following sections, we will examine how personality and the situation — separately and together — contribute to our understanding of organisational behaviour, as well as considering how these variables shape the strategies that organisations adopt. We will consider three approaches, summarised in Exhibit 3.2: dispositional, situational and person–organisation fit.

Dispositions, situations and job satisfaction

Dispositions predict job satisfaction

Does the affective state of individuals affect their job satisfaction? According to Barry Staw and his co-workers, individuals who hold a more positive and enthusiastic world view will also report greater job satisfaction, independent of the job that they are doing. Using data from several longitudinal studies that started in the late 1920s and 1930s, these researchers set out to test the extent to which personality could influence job satisfaction. Their data measured personality at five points in time: early and late adolescence and three times during adulthood. In addition, various aspects of career and job satisfaction were measured twice during adulthood. By looking at a small group of individuals for whom they had data at each of the five points in time, Staw and his co-workers were able to establish strong correlations between affect and overall job satisfaction: individuals who reported more positive moods throughout adolescence and adulthood also reported greater overall satisfaction with their jobs.

Implications. Staw argues that these findings have important organisation implications: if personality predicts job satisfaction, then programs such as job redesign waste organisational time and money. These findings imply that selection rather than organisational programs are the key to obtaining a satisfied workforce. Is Staw justified in his conclusions?

Situations predict job satisfaction

Several criticisms can be made of Staw's research. These criticisms suggest that if we consider younger samples and examine how situations and attitudes *change* the results may be different.

And they are. Addressing the first criticism, Newton and Keenan reported that although, across time, the correlation between affective states (anxiety, alienation) and job satisfaction remained high and stable, all measures decreased over time. Second, by including a range of situational factors such as pay, status and job complexity, Gerhart showed that situational factors are able to predict job satisfaction.

More importantly, he also demonstrated that the correlation between affect and job satisfaction was highest when individuals stayed in the same occupation with the same employer; it was lowest when individuals changed both occupations and employers. These findings suggest that at least in part, Staw's results can be explained in terms of an older and more stable work group. Similar findings were also reported by Newton and Keenan: individuals who, over time, remained with the same employer reported stable levels of anger, frustration, hostility, alienation and job satisfaction; however, those who changed employers reported decreases in anger, frustration, hostility and alienation and corresponding increases in job satisfaction.

Implications. This research suggests that Staw has not represented the situation accurately. Based on the work of Gerhart, Newton and Keenan, we must conclude that situational factors *are* able to influence job satisfaction. This implies that organisations should be concerned with conditions of employment and organisational programs such as job redesign that are aimed at improving the quality of working life.

A case for person–organisation fit?

However, the results also suggest that changes in affect and satisfaction are more likely to occur when the workforce is young and mobile. Perhaps a high correlation between affect and job satisfaction reflects high levels of person–organisation fit. Is there evidence that individuals will display more positive affect and higher job satisfaction when they have achieved fit between their values and those of an organisation? What implications might this have for selection and the design of organisation programs?

Source: Gerhart, B. (1987). How important are dispositional factors as determinants of job satisfaction? Implications for job design and other personnel programs, *Journal of Applied Psychology*, **72**, 366–373, Newton, T., & Keenan, T. (1991). 'Further analyses of the dispositional argument in organizational behaviour', *Journal of Applied Psychology*, **76**, 781–787; Staw, B. M., Bell, E. E., Clausen, J. A. (1986). The dispositional approach to job attitudes: A lifetime longitudinal test, *Administrative Science Quarterly*, **31**, 56–77.

Approach	Key Assumptions	Organisational Implications
Dispositional	Personality is the most important determinant of behaviour	Organisations should select staff on the basis of personality traits that maximise satisfaction, motivation and other work attitudes
Situational	Situations provide strong cues for behaviour and are the most important determinants of behaviour	Organisations should alter the environment through programs such as job redesign
Interactional	Both situations and personality act to influence behaviour	Situations can either inhibit or enhance personality
Transactional	Situations and personality shape individual behaviour; individuals also alter situations to suit their personality	Organisational outcomes are improved when there is a match between individual and organisational values; this is achieved through selection *and* training; individuals leave organisations that do not match their needs

Exhibit 3.2 Summary of person, situation and person–environment approaches to behaviour

Dispositional and situational explanations[2]

People generally behave in a regular and predictable way: we know that some of our friends are more optimistic than others, and some more outgoing and extroverted. In the workplace, we know that some of our staff will always be prepared to take on extra work, while others will not. The explanations that we offer for these consistencies affects our behaviour and, as managers, the strategies that we use for dealing with our staff and ensuring organisational effectiveness.

At the simplest level, we might explain these consistencies in two ways: as a consequence of personality, or as the result of the situations that people find themselves in. Briefly, according to personality (*dispositional*) explanations, individuals should display the same characteristics across all situations: they 'possess' enduring characteristics — called *personality traits* — and these characteristics are the major source of influence on individuals' behaviour. We can also consider how individual differences in age, race, educational level, skills and abilities affect behaviour.

In general, this approach implies that managers have little power to change individuals; consequently, organisations must focus on their selection procedures. An alternative view is that personality is far less important than the situations people find themselves in: situations carry with them strong norms for behaviour and people behave consistently only to the extent that situations make similar demands of them. This implies that managers are a major source of influence on behaviour and can alter employees' behaviour by altering the situation. Let's consider these explanations in more detail.

Personality in the workplace

The relationship between behaviour and personality is perhaps one of the most complex matters that managers have to understand. **Personality** is influenced significantly by cultural and social factors. Regardless of how personality is defined, however, certain principles are generally accepted among psychologists. These are:

- Personality is an organised whole; otherwise, the individual would have no meaning.
- Personality appears to be organised into patterns which are, to some degree, observable and measurable.
- Although personality has a biological basis, its specific development is a product of social and cultural environments.[3]
- Personality has superficial aspects, such as attitudes toward being a team leader and a deeper core, such as sentiments about authority or the Protestant work ethic.
- Personality involves both common and unique characteristics. Every person is different from every other person in some respects and similar to other persons in other respects.

These five ideas are included in the following definition of personality:

> *An individual's personality is a relatively stable set of characteristics, tendencies and temperaments that have been significantly formed by inheritance and by social, cultural and environmental factors. This set of variables determines the commonalities and differences in the behaviour of the individual.*[4]

While we think of personality as distinguishing between individuals, more recently researchers have suggested that different cultures have distinct 'personalities'. The Global Encounter in this section gives some examples of how cultural differences may affect personality and behaviour.

Even though personality-based explanations of behaviour have been criticised, there are two personality traits, self-efficacy and self-monitoring, that do seem to have a strong impact on individual behaviour and attitudes over time and we will provide a brief review of these. This is not to say that there are no other personality traits that affect individual responses to their work environment: as you will see in Chapter 6, there are several traits that specifically affect individual responses to stress. Our concern, here, is to examine those traits that seem to influence individual behaviour more generally.

Self-Efficacy. Self-efficacy relates to personal beliefs regarding competencies and abilities. Specifically, it refers to one's belief in one's ability to successfully complete a task. Individuals with a high degree of self-efficacy firmly believe in their performance capabilities. Self-efficacy is an important part of Bandura's social learning theory and comprises three dimensions: magnitude, strength and generality.[5]

Encounter

Cultural forces and personality

One of the important forces working to shape personality is that of culture. Consequently, because nations differ in their cultural values, the personality and behaviour of their citizens may differ as well. One stream of research that has identified differences in cultural values related to behaviour in organisations is that of Geert Hofstede. Three of the cultural dimensions he describes relate to the value placed on *individual* effort and accomplishment versus a collective or *group* orientation; the degree to which uncertainty and ambiguity is accepted (*tolerance*) versus the extent to which it is unwanted (*avoidance*); and the degree to which traditional male values are accepted by the society (*masculine*) versus traditional female values (*feminine*). Hofstede has collected data from forty different countries.

In the light of these cultural differences we should not be at all surprised that there are resulting personality differences. In subsequent studies, Hofstede also found that areas that have a strong Chinese influence are more characterised by a collective orientation than are Western countries. More recently, Huo and Randall have argued that Hofstede's approach ignores more subtle, regional differences within a cultural group. In a study aimed at determining whether subcultural differences can be identified, these researchers compared Chinese managers from four regions: Taiwan, Wuhan, Hong Kong and Beijing. Their results are summarised below and include an added dimension, power distance, that deals with equality, inequality and the extent to which inequality is accepted.

	PDI	UAI	IDV	MAS
Beijing	Low	Avoid	Group	Masculine
Wuhan	High	Tolerate	Individual	Feminine
Hong Kong	High	Avoid	Individual	Masculine
Taiwan	High	Tolerate	Individual	Masculine

PDI: Power distance; **UAI:** Uncertainty and ambiguity; **IDV:** Individual; **MAS:** Masculine

In conducting business in an international environment, individuals who are aware of, and sensitive to, these culturally shaped nuances will have a competitive advantage over those who are not.

Source: Based in part on information in Hofstede, G. (1980). *Culture's Consequence: International Differences in Work-Related Values*, Beverly Hills: Sage Publications. Huo Y. P. & Randall, D. M. (1991). Exploring subcultural differences in Hofstede's value survey: The case of the Chinese, *Asia-Pacific Journal of Management*, **8**, 159–173.

Magnitude refers to the level of task difficulty that individuals believe they can attain. For example, Jim may believe he can put an arrow in the archery range target six times in ten attempts. Sara may feel she can hit the target eight times; thus, Sara has a higher magnitude of self-efficacy regarding this task than Jim. *Strength* refers to whether the belief regarding magnitude is strong or weak. If in the previous example Jim is moderately certain he can hit the target six times, while Sara is positive she can achieve eight hits, Sara is displaying greater strength of belief in her ability than is Jim. Finally, *generality* indicates how generalised across different situations the belief in capability is. If Jim thinks he can hit the target equally well with a pistol and rifle and Sara does not think she can, Jim is displaying greater generality than is Sara.

Beliefs regarding self-efficacy are learned. The most important factor in the development of self-efficacy appears to be past experiences. If over a period of time we attempt a task and are increasingly successful in our performance, we are likely to develop self-confidence and an increasing belief in our ability to perform the task successfully; conversely, if we repeatedly fail in our attempts to perform a task well, we are not as likely to develop strong feelings of self-efficacy. It is important to realise, however, that self-efficacy tends to be task specific; that is, a belief that we can perform very well in one job does not necessarily suggest a corresponding belief in our ability to excel in other jobs.

Gist suggests that the self-efficacy concept has a number of theoretical and practical implications for organisational behaviour and human resource management.[6] Included in the implications she suggests are important relationships between feelings of self-efficacy and performance appraisals, goal setting and the use of incentives. Individuals with high self-efficacy set higher goals and, unlike individuals with low self-efficacy, when they are not meeting their goals they increase their effort.[7] Self-efficacy beliefs may also be important to consider in employee selection and training decisions and in identifying candidates for leadership positions.

Self-monitoring. Self-monitoring describes the degree of adaptability that individuals show in different situations; that is, the extent to which they change their behaviour as they move from one situation to another. Whether or not individuals change their behaviour to suit the situation depends on the cues that they use to guide their behaviour. There are two sources that provide us with cues for how to behave in a particular setting: *external,* for example the situation and what other people are doing, and *internal,* or our own personality and mood. Individuals differ in whether they rely mainly on situational or mainly on dispositional cues to provide information about what behaviours will be appropriate in a particular setting. *High self-monitors* are those people who mainly use the situation and the behaviour of others around them to decide how they will behave. There is little consistency in their behaviour across situations and it is very difficult to predict their behaviour from their attitudes. *Low self-monitors,* in contrast, mainly use their own preferences and moods as cues for their behaviour. These individuals show high consistency in behaviour across situations.[8] Self-monitoring has three major components: high self-monitors behave in an extroverted manner, are highly sensitive to the reactions of others and alter their behaviour to obtain positive reactions from others.[9]

High self-monitors are well suited to jobs that require flexibility and adaptability. Because of their ability to adapt to the needs of different groups, high self-monitors are effective in situations that require boundary spanning: situations in which it is necessary to coordinate groups of individuals, all of whom have different goals, across a range of organisational functions. In addition, high self-monitors appear to have better communication skills and are able to adapt their communication style to match the needs of their audience. Finally, they are more likely to adopt a collaborative approach to resolving organisational conflicts.[10]

Recent research looked at how the different skills of high and low self-monitors affected their careers. Kilduff and Day[11] suggested that because high self-monitors are more skilled in boundary-spanning, leadership, and conflict and impression management, they should be more effective managers; as a result they should obtain more promotions. However, the same traits that result in more promotions also suggest that high self-monitors will be less committed to a job or an organisation: high self-monitors have been described as flexible, pragmatic and utilitarian. According to Kilduff and Day, when these traits are put together, we would expect high self-monitors to be more willing to change jobs, change organisations and change locations to obtain a promotion. By following the careers of 139 Master in Business Administration (MBA) graduates over 5 years, these researchers showed that high self-monitoring managers were more likely than low self-monitoring managers to be promoted within their own company or to a new company, to change jobs and to relocate to another geographical area. The combination of high flexibility and low commitment was a distinct advantage for high self-monitors!

Personality: A final word

When we focus on personality, we assume that these traits will establish consistent patterns of behaviour across time and situations.[12] For example, if individuals display a trait called 'positive affect' we would expect them to be more cheerful and optimistic than individuals who do not display positive affect, independent of the situation that they find themselves in. When we adopt this perspective, we assume that individual differences such as needs, values and personality not only are stable over time, but also are the dominant influence on behaviour across organisational settings.[13] For organisations, this approach implies that personality testing will provide the best means for selecting appropriate staff: if we can match individual personality traits to the requirements of the task, we should have a more effective workforce.

This approach has a number of problems: it is hard to imagine that situations have absolutely no impact on an individual's behaviour; and it is not clear that individual needs, values and personality traits are stable and unchanging. However, the most damaging criticism is that research clearly shows us that personality traits fail to explain large differences in individual behaviour across situations. One of the reasons for this is that situations are also strong influences on behaviour.[14]

Organisations as strong situations

We would be surprised if situations did not also affect our behaviour: situations, because they provide cues for behaviour, are also able to influence us. They vary in how strong and clear those cues are: they may be strong and well defined, providing clear cues for behaviour and little scope for individual differences or they may be weak and ambiguous, providing very few cues for behaviour.[15] For example, going to the theatre is a strong situation, in that there are very clear expectations about how we will behave; however, going to the beach is a relatively weak situation, in that there are far fewer cues about what is appropriate behaviour. Critics of the dispositional approach argue that organisations are strong situations and provide the individual with cues for behaviour that will override individual differences.[16] This argument has three components:[17]

1. Formal organisations institutionalise behaviour. They have rules and procedures that set out how individuals should behave within the organisation. As a result, the effects of personality are minimised.
2. In addition to formal rules and procedures, organisational culture (as it is expressed in mission statements and informal norms) also shapes individuals' behaviour and attitudes. As we will see in Chapter 14, the socialisation process, which instils culture, is critical for organisations.
3. Finally, structural features, such as compensation systems, task design and reward systems, all further influence individual attitudes and behaviour.

This suggests that, directly and indirectly, organisations are able to exert considerable influence on individual behaviour. Indeed, organisational success appears dependent on how responsive individuals are to these forces.[18] One implication of this approach is that organisations should focus their energies, not on selecting the right people, but on ensuring that their practices provide a strong situation that will develop appropriate attitudes and behaviours.

Dispositions and situations together

Like the dispositional approach, explanations of behaviour in terms of the situation alone fail to explain a large amount of the variation in individual behaviour: the same person in the same situation often acts differently. It seems that neither personality nor situations, alone, can satisfactorily explain how and why individual behaviour remains stable across situations. One of the major criticisms of both these approaches is that they ignore the possibility that both personality and the situation act jointly to determine behaviour. The *interactionist* perspective proposes that, since neither personality traits nor situations provide a good explanation of behaviour, we should turn to an examination of their interaction: *both* situations and dispositions provide cues for behaviour and so it is important for us to consider how they act together and to further understand whether and when either the situation or personality may provide the dominant cues for behaviour.[19]

An example of this approach is provided by research investigating how organisational structure and one personality trait — *Machiavellianism* (the desire to influence others) — affect organisational performance. Schultz based his research on laboratory findings that individuals who are highly Machiavellian (strongly motivated to influence others) win more when they are in situations that provide few cues for behaviour than in situations that place many constraints on behaviour. He was interested in seeing whether this finding could be extended to organisational settings, and examined the relative sales performance of staff in two brokering organisations: one tightly structured, the other loosely structured. He expected that when the situation provided few cues and rules governing individual behaviour (loose structure), high Machiavellians would perform better because they would have greater scope for exerting influence and manipulating others. He found that, for two measures of performance, high Machiavellians in loosely structured organisations outperformed all other individuals: they earned higher commissions and maintained more clients than high Machiavellians in tightly structured situations or low Machiavellians.[20]

Transactional approaches

Even the interactional approach has its shortcomings. The main criticism is that, while it accepts that both situations and personality can affect behaviour, it does not recognise that behaviour may alter the situation. This final point provides the foundations for the last approach that we will consider: the *transactional approach*. According to this approach, individuals choose the situations that they are in. This means that, where possible, they attempt to match their personalities to the demands of the situation: individuals who have a competitive nature seek out competitive situations (for example, they may play competitive sports), whereas individuals with a cooperative personality seek out more cooperative situations.

The first assumption of the transactional approach is that individuals attempt to achieve person-environment fit or congruence, between their personalities and the situation. However, this is not always possible, and where there is a mismatch between the person and the situation, individuals attempt to restructure the situation to achieve congruence. The second assumption of this model is that not only do situations shape individual behaviour but also, reciprocally, individuals may alter situations.[21]

Person–organisation fit

Reading 3
Hiring for the
organisation, not
the job

For organisations, this approach has several important implications and our reading at the end of this chapter explores how some organisations are managing for person–organisation fit. This approach suggests that individual performance will be maximised when there is a match between the demands of the environment, the prevailing organisational values and individual skills, abilities and values. What implications does this have for organisations? According to Chatman, organisations need to attend to both selection and training procedures if they are to achieve person–organisation fit and maximise staff performance.[22] The transactional approach is reflected in congruence models of job design, person–environment fit models of workplace stress, some theories of leadership and in the emphasis placed on organisational socialisation.

The values and needs of organisation do not always match. While it is possible for a group of individuals with shared values to alter those of the workplace, it is more likely that organisations will attempt to shape the values of the individual.

Organisations have two strategies for ensuring person–organisation fit. The first is through *selection*: interviews provide the organisation with an opportunity to determine whether individuals will 'fit in' with organisational norms and values; they also allow individuals to assess whether organisational culture matches their value system. Achieving a match leads to greater satisfaction and performance. It is not always possible to select staff whose values match those of the organisation.

The second strategy available to organisations is *socialisation*: the stronger the organisational norms and values, the more effort the organisation must expend in establishing those values in the individual. Induction and training provide two means for doing so. In Chapter 14, we will take a closer look at organisational socialisation practices.[23]

Understanding behaviour

In this section we have looked at the factors that underlie individual behaviour and attitudes at work. Skills and abilities and more enduring attributes such as gender and culture, provided the background for our consideration of two factors: personality and situations. If we look at organisational behaviour theory and research, we can find examples of all these approaches. However, the transactional approach that is currently emerging provides the most useful perspective for us: individuals choose situations that match their personality and, where this is not possible, they try to alter those situations; at the same time, organisations exert strong influences on the individual and try to alter individual attitudes and values to fit with those of the organisation. Overall, both individuals and organisations try to achieve fit between their values. Where this is achieved, both the individual and the organisation benefit.

THE BASIS FOR EXPLAINING BEHAVIOUR

In the last section, we saw that behaviour can be influenced by an individual's personality or the situation. Recent approaches emphasise that both factors play a role in influencing behaviour. The second question that we need to consider is how we use this knowledge. When an employee comes to work late or makes errors when working, what explanation do we offer? And how does our explanation affect our behaviour? Do we conclude that the employee is lazy or incompetent? Or do we conclude that something about the situation, such as the difficulty of the task, influenced that person's behaviour? In this section, we consider how individuals perceive and explain behaviour.

Perception

Perception is the cognitive process by which an individual gives meaning to the environment. Because each person gives his or her own meaning to stimuli, different individuals will 'see' the same thing in different ways. The way an employee sees the situation often has much greater meaning for understanding behaviour than does the situation itself.

Since perception refers to the acquisition of specific knowledge about objects or events at any particular moment, it occurs whenever stimuli activate the senses. Perception involves cognition (knowledge). Thus, perception includes the interpretation of objects, symbols and people in the light of pertinent experiences. In other words, perception involves receiving stimuli, organising the stimuli and translating or interpreting the organised stimuli, so as to influence behaviour and form attitudes.

Exercise 3
Testing your assumptions about people

People select various cues that influence their perceptions of people, objects and symbols. Because of these factors and their potential for imbalance, people often misperceive another person, group or object. To a considerable extent, people interpret the behaviour of others in the context of the setting in which they find themselves. Exercise 3 provides you with an opportunity to experience the influence of various assumptions on your own perceptions.

The way in which we organise and interpret stimuli influences our behaviour. One of the problems that we face is the mass of information that we must process. To help us deal with this information we employ short cuts that help us to quickly organise and interpret stimuli. We will consider two such short cuts: stereotyping and selective perception.

Stereotyping

Stereotyping is a process employed to assist individuals in dealing with massive information-processing demands. In this regard it represents a useful, even essential, way of categorising individuals (or events, organisations and so on) on the basis of limited information or observation. The process of forming stereotypes and placing individuals in certain categories on the basis of these stereotypes is a perceptual one. When we speak of the Germans as efficient, the Italians as great lovers or the French as outstanding cooks, we are engaging in nationality stereotyping. Since many stereotypes relate to ethnic group membership it is important to distinguish between a stereotype and a prejudice. A prejudice is a stereotype that refuses to change when presented with information indicating the stereotype is inaccurate. Stereotypes can be helpful; prejudice is never helpful.

It is often assumed that stereotyping is inherently bad or wrong. This is not the case, however. Stereotyping is a useful process that greatly increases our efficiency in making sense out of our environment. Nonetheless, stereotyping can and does lead to inaccuracies and negative consequences.[24] To the extent that stereotypes create social injustice, result in poorer decision making, stifle innovation or cause underutilisation of organisational human resources, they contribute to ineffectiveness and inefficiency. The solution to perceptual bias created by stereotypes is not to resist forming stereotypes; this is neither practical nor desirable. Rather, it is to:

- be alert to the fact that stereotypes are frequently formed on the basis of very little information and can be extremely inaccurate;
- be receptive to new, additional information that can improve the accuracy of existing stereotypes;
- understand that stereotypes rarely apply well to a specific individual.

Judgements based on personal knowledge of a specific individual are inevitably more accurate than reference to a broad category to which the individual belongs.

Selective perception

The concept of *selective perception* is important to managers since they often receive large amounts of information and data. Consequently, they may tend to select information that supports their viewpoints. People tend to ignore information or cues that might make them feel discomfort. For example, a skilled manager may be concerned primarily with an employee's final results or output. Since the employee is often cynical and negative when interacting with the manager, other managers may conclude that the employee will probably receive a poor performance rating. However, this manager selects out the negative features or cues and rates the subordinate on the basis of results. This is a form of selective perception.

Social perception

It is often said that perception is reality. That is, what an employee perceives to be real is, in fact for that employee, reality. Since behaviour is greatly influenced by our personal interpretation of reality, it is easy to understand why our perceptual processes are potent determinants of behaviour. One approach that provides a basis for understanding the relationship between perception and behaviour is attribution theory. Attribution theory is concerned with the process by which individuals interpret events around them as being caused by a relatively stable portion of their environment.[25] In short, attribution theory attempts to explain the why of behaviour. Returning to our earlier discussion, the attribution process determines whether we explain individual behaviour in terms of personality or situational factors. Exhibit 3.3 displays the attribution process.

Attribution theory

According to attribution theory, it is the perceived causes of events, not the actual ones, that influence people's behaviour. More specifically, individuals will attempt to analyse why certain events have occurred and the results of that analysis will influence their behaviour in the future. As the example in Exhibit 3.3 indicates, an employee who receives a raise will attempt to attribute the raise to some underlying cause. If the employee perceives the explanation for the raise to be the fact that she is a hard worker and consequently concludes that working hard leads to rewards in this organisation, she would decide to continue working hard in the future. Another employee may attribute his raise to the fact that he participates in the company's bowling team and decides it makes sense to continue bowling for that reason. Thus, in both cases employees have made decisions affecting their future behaviours on the basis of their attributions. Subsequent events will be interpreted by these two employees based on their attributions of why these events happened and will be either reinforced or modified depending on future events.

The attribution process also can be important in understanding the behaviour of other people. The behaviour of a subordinate, for example, can be

Exhibit 3.3
The attribution process

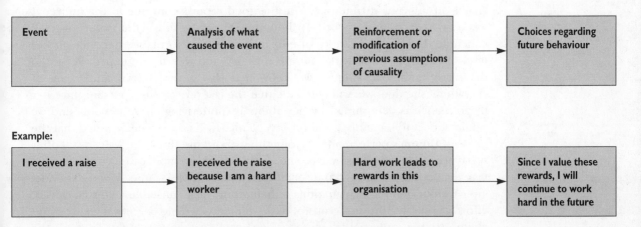

Source: Adapted from Korman, A. (1977). *Organizational Behavior*. Englewood Cliffs, NJ: Prentice-Hall, p. 273.

examined on the basis of its consensus, consistency and distinctiveness. *Consensus* is the degree to which other subordinates engage in the same behaviour. *Consistency* is the degree to which the person in question engages in the same behaviours at different times. *Distinctiveness* is the degree to which the subordinate behaves similarly in other situations. For example, you might observe that a particular subordinate is taking extended rest breaks. If he is the only one in the work group doing this (low consensus), if he is doing this regularly (high consistency) and if he has a history of having taken extended breaks in other work groups he has been part of (low distinctiveness) you might reasonably attribute his behaviour to internal factors (within the employee himself).

On the other hand, you might observe something quite different. Maybe most members of the work group are taking extended breaks (high consensus), and although this subordinate has been doing this regularly since joining the work group (high consistency) you have never known him to do this in other work groups of which he has been a member (high distinctiveness). A reasonable attribution in this scenario might be that there are external factors (in the work group environment) causing this behaviour. We are not suggesting that the behaviour is more or less appropriate in one scenario or the other, or that the subordinate should be held more or less accountable. The point is that whatever attributions the manager makes have direct implications for attempts to correct the problem.

Consistency, consensus and distinctiveness cue us to determining whether another person's behaviour is determined mainly by the situation or mainly by that individual's personality. However, according to Weiner, a second dimension — *stability* — also affects our explanations of behaviour. In addition to asking whether personality or the situation determined someone's behaviour, we also try to determine whether the behaviour will continue; that is, we ask whether the reasons for the individual's behaviour are stable (will persist in the future; can be controlled) or unstable (will not persist in the future; cannot be controlled). Let us imagine that Donna has just handed in an exceptionally good report. If Donna always hands in better reports than your other staff independent of the project that she is working on, we will conclude that she is a good report writer (make an internal attribution). Will the good reports continue in the future? If we know that Donna worked 16 hours every day to finish the report, we will conclude that she put in a lot of effort: since her performance depends on her level of effort, its underlying cause is unstable and we will not expect her to do the same again. However, if we know that she is very bright and excels at everything she does, we will conclude that she is a very capable person: since her performance is determined by her ability its underlying cause is stable and we would expect to see more good reports. Similarly, if we have determined that the cause of Donna's performance is something about the situation, we can still offer two types of explanations: maybe she was lucky (an unstable cause) or maybe the task was an easy one (a stable or at least controllable) cause. Weiner's model gives us four general explanations of behaviour: luck (unstable, external cause), effort (unstable, internal cause), task difficulty (stable, external cause) and ability (stable, internal cause).[26] The Local Encounter looks at how the attributions that we make about success and failure affect our reactions to the changing fortunes of leaders.

Not all attributions are, of course, correct. The situation becomes even more complicated when we realise that we consistently make two errors in our attributions about behaviour.[27] The first is called the **fundamental attribution error**. The fundamental attribution is a tendency to underestimate the importance of external factors and overestimate the importance of internal factors when making attributions about the behaviour of others, and the converse is true when we offer explanations for our own behaviour. An example of this might be a shop floor supervisor who attributes a high injury rate to employee carelessness (a cause internal to the employee) instead of considering the possibility that the equipment is old and in poor repair (a cause external to the employee). Clearly, this error will affect how managers react to the successes and failures of their staff. If they make an internal attribution, they are more likely to reward staff for good performance and punish staff for poor performance, without considering how the situation or task influenced that performance. The second error is the **self-serving bias**. This is reflected in the tendency of people to take credit for successful work (effort or ability) and deny responsibility for poor work (luck or task difficulty). The self-serving bias leads us to conclude that when we succeed it is a result of our outstanding efforts, while when we fail it is because of factors beyond our control.

The managerial implications of an attributional approach to understanding work behaviour are important. In order to influence employee behaviour, the manager must understand the attributions employees make. Further, the manager must be aware that his or her own attributions may be different from theirs. For example, if a manager perceives employee poor performance to be the result of lack of effort, she may attempt to increase motivation levels. On the other hand, if employees perceive performance problems to be attributable to lack of supervisory guidance, the efforts made by the manager are not likely to have the desired effect on performance. Managers cannot assume that their attributions will be the same as their employees'. Knowing this, coupled with an effort to understand what attributions employees make, can greatly enhance the manager's ability to have a positive effect on employee behaviour.

BEHAVIOUR AND ORGANISATIONAL OUTCOMES

Attitudes

Attitudes are determinants of behaviour, because they are linked with perception, personality and motivation. An **attitude** is a mental state of readiness, learned and organised through experience, exerting a specific influence on a person's response to people, objects and situations with which it is related. Each of us has attitudes on numerous topics — unions, jogging, restaurants, friends, jobs, religion, the government and income taxes.

This definition of attitude has certain implications for the manager. First, attitudes are learned. Second, attitudes define one's predispositions towards given aspects of the world. Third, attitudes provide the emotional basis of one's interpersonal relations and identification with others. And, fourth, attitudes are organised and are close to the core of personality. Some attitudes are persistent and enduring. Yet, like each of the psychological variables, attitudes are subject to change.[28]

Politics and entertainment: Do tall poppies get what they deserve?

Wiener's attributional model identifies three factors that affect how we explain people's behaviour: locus (internal or external), stability (stable or unstable) and controllability. We have seen in this chapter that when behaviour is attributed to unstable, external cause we explain outcomes in terms of luck; unstable, internal causes result in attributions of effort; stable, external causes lead to explanations based on task difficulty; and stable, internal causes result in explanations in terms of ability. Weiner extended this model to include our emotional reactions: for example, success due to internal causes should result in feelings of pride; if the causes are also stable, it should increase our expectation that we will succeed again.

More recently, Feather and his co-workers at Flinders University in South Australia have also suggested that how we explain and react to individual successes and failures is influenced by whether we perceive the causes to be internal or external. What is more, our assessment of whether people deserved their fate is influenced by whether they succeed or fail and the behaviour that led to their success or failure. In two investigations of 'tall poppies' Feather and his co-workers examined how we explain the success of tall poppies and how our explanations affect our reactions to their rise or fall.

The fortunes of politicians are more in the public eye than those of many other notable figures. Do they get what they deserve? Feather's surveys show several interesting trends. When Bob Hawke, Janine Haines and Andrew Peacock were compared, Hawke's success was attributed to ability, effort, luck and assistance; Haines' success was attributed to effort and ability alone; while Peacock's success was attributed to luck and assistance. In a second survey, these researchers found that while individuals attributed approximately equal levels of ability and effort to Keating and Hewson, Keating was also seen to have considerably more luck and assistance in attaining his position.

What is more interesting is how individuals responded to the possibility that these political leaders might rise further or fall. When success was attributed to effort and ability alone — as was the case for Janine Haines — individuals believed more strongly that the position was deserved, were more pleased about future rises in position and unhappy about a fall from position than when luck and assistance were thought to play a part in becoming leader. Similarly, individuals believed that Hewson, who was rated as having less assistance and luck than Keating in attaining leadership, was more deserving of his position; individuals also said that they would be more pleased to see him rise further and less pleased to see him fall.

So, in the case of our political leaders, ability and effort make us evaluate their position more favourably and falls from grace less favourably. Is this reaction unique to politics? Also in the spotlight are entertainers. Feather and his co-workers found a similar pattern when they looked at the success of entertainers. In comparison to Kylie Minogue, the success of Paul Hogan and John Farnham was attributed more to effort and ability and less to luck and assistance. As a result, individuals thought that John Farnham and Paul Hogan were more deserving of their success and were more pleased at the thought that their success would increase; they were less pleased about the prospect of a fall.

What conclusions can we draw from this research? Ability and effort are key factors in positive reactions to leaders; however, when success is explained in terms of luck and assistance, we value that success less. As a result, we believe that people who succeed because of ability and effort deserve their success, and we are pleased when they are more successful and unhappy when such individuals fail. But, when we think that luck and help have led to success, we react in the opposite way.

Source: Feather, N. T. (1993). The rise and fall of political leaders: Attributions, deservingness, personality and affect, *Australian Journal of Psychology*, **45**, 61–68; Feather, N. T., Volkmer, R. E. & McKee, I. R. (1991). Attitudes towards high achievers in public life: Attributions, deservingness, personality and affect, *Australian Journal of Psychology*, **43**, 85–91.

Attitudes are intrinsic parts of a person's personality. However, a number of theories attempt to account for the formation and change of attitudes. One such theory proposes that people 'seek a congruence between their beliefs and feelings towards objects' and suggests that the modification of attitudes depends on changing either the feelings or the beliefs.[29] The theory proposes that cognition, affect and behaviour determine attitudes and that attitudes, in turn, determine cognition, affect and behaviour. The *cognitive* component of an attitude consists of the person's perceptions, opinions and beliefs. It refers to the thought processes with special emphasis on rationality and logic. An important element of cognition is the evaluative beliefs held by a person. Evaluative beliefs are manifested in the form of favourable or unfavourable impressions that a person holds towards an object or person.

Affect, the emotional or 'feeling' component of an attitude, is learned from parents, teachers and peer group members. One study displays how the affective component can be measured. A questionnaire was used to survey the attitudes of a group of students towards the church. The students then listened to tape recordings that either praised or disparaged the church. At the time of the tape recordings, the emotional responses of the students were measured with a galvanic skin response (GSR) device. Both prochurch and antichurch students responded with greater emotion (displayed by GSR changes) to statements that contradicted their attitudes than to statements that reflected their attitudes.[30]

The *behavioural* component of an attitude refers to the tendency of a person to act in a certain way towards someone or something. A person can act towards someone or something in a friendly, warm, aggressive, hostile or apathetic way or in any of a number of other ways. Such actions could be measured or assessed to

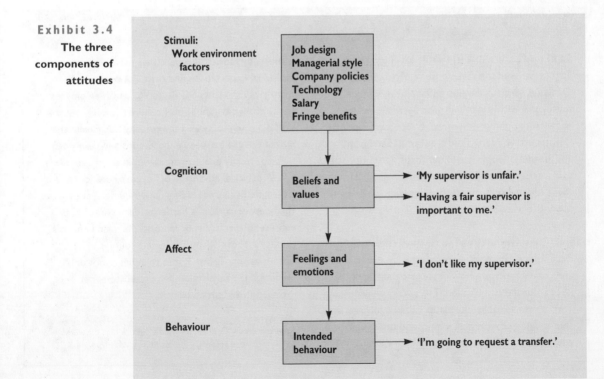

Exhibit 3.4
The three components of attitudes

examine the behavioural component of attitudes. Exhibit 3.4 presents the three components of attitudes in terms of work environment factors such as job design, company policies and fringe benefits. These stimuli trigger cognitive (thought), affective (emotional) and behavioural responses. In essence, the stimuli result in the formation of attitudes, which then lead to one or more responses.

The theory of cognitive, affective and behavioural components as determinants of attitudes has a significant implication for managers. The theory implies that the manager must be able to demonstrate that the positive aspects of contributing to the organisation outweigh the negative aspects. It is through attempts to develop generally favourable attitudes toward the organisation and the job that many managers achieve effectiveness. In an organisational context, an attitude expressed by an employee that other departments in the company ought to develop the degree of teamwork found in the employee's department represents an attitude that expresses the value he or she places on cohesiveness and cooperation. The Organisational Encounter looks at attitude surveys and culture at Toyota.

Changing attitudes

Managers are often faced with the task of changing attitudes because previously structured attitudes hinder job performance. Although many variables affect attitude change, they can all be described in terms of three general factors: trust in the sender, the message itself and the situation.[31] If employees do not trust the manager, they will not accept the manager's message or change an attitude. Similarly, if the message is not convincing, there will be no pressure to change.

ORGANISATIONAL Encounter

Attitudes and culture at Toyota

Toyota has used the seven criteria of the Australian Quality Awards to develop an employee attitude survey that allows it to find gaps between employee expectations and performance. Employees respond to fifty items that address the areas of leadership, policy and planning, people, customer focus, quality, products and service, and organisational performance. Based on these criteria, staff are asked about such issues as product quality, pay, feedback, job satisfaction and supervision.

The survey asks staff to rate each item twice: once, to indicate how important the issue is to them; and once, to indicate how important they think the issue is for the organisation. The results provide Toyota with valuable information: senior managers are able to find out what staff expect and the extent to which Toyota is living up to those expectations. What

is more, by looking at where gaps exist between individual expectations and organisational values, managers can assess the degree to which employees have adopted organisational culture (... and, yes, the staff did rate quality as a top priority ...). Finally, the size of the gap between expectations and reality can help to identify problem areas within the organisation.

A principal advantage of Toyota's questionnaire is its length. Because it is short and all employees answer the questionnaire, it is harder to dismiss results as representing an unhappy minority. Its main benefit is that, by identifying and addressing sources of dissatisfaction, Toyota hopes to improve not only employee job satisfaction but also customer satisfaction and profitability.

Source: Forman, D. (1995) Toyota's culture quiz paves the way to performance reform, *Business Review Weekly*, April 3.

The greater the prestige of the communicator, the greater the attitude change that is produced.[32] A manager who has little prestige and is not shown respect by peers and superiors will be in a difficult position if the job requires changing the attitudes of subordinates so they will work more effectively.

Liking the communicator can lead to attitude change because people try to identify with a liked communicator and tend to adopt attitudes and behaviours of the liked person. Not all managers, however, are fortunate enough to be liked by each of their subordinates. Therefore, it is important to recognise the importance of trust in the manager as a condition for liking the manager.

Even if a manager is trusted, presents a convincing message and is liked, the problems of changing people's attitudes are not easily solved. An important factor is the strength of the employee's commitment to an attitude. A worker who has decided not to accept a promotion is committed to the belief that it is better to remain in his or her present position than to accept the promotion. Attitudes that have been expressed publicly are more difficult to change because the person has shown commitment, and to change would be to admit a mistake.

How much you are affected by attempts to change your attitude depends in part on the situation. When people are listening to or reading a persuasive message, they are sometimes distracted by other thoughts, sounds or activities. Studies indicate that if people are distracted while they are listening to a message, they will show more attitude change because the distraction interferes with silent counterarguing.[33]

Distraction is just one of many situational factors that can increase persuasion. Another factor that makes people more susceptible to attempts to change attitudes is pleasant surroundings. The pleasant surroundings may be associated with the attempt to change the attitude.

Attitudes and job satisfaction

Job satisfaction is an attitude that individuals have about their jobs. It results from their perception of their jobs and the degree to which there is a good fit between the individual and the organisation.[34] Thus job satisfaction stems from various aspects of the job such as pay, promotion opportunities, supervisors and co-workers. Job satisfaction also stems from factors of the work environment such as the supervisor's style; policies and procedures; work group affiliation; working conditions; and fringe benefits. While numerous dimensions have been associated with job satisfaction, five in particular have crucial characteristics.[35] These five dimensions are:

- *Pay* — the amount of pay received and the perceived equity of pay;
- *Job* — the extent to which job tasks are considered interesting and provide opportunities for learning and for accepting responsibility;
- *Promotion opportunities* — the availability of opportunities for advancement;
- *Supervisor* — the abilities of the supervisor to demonstrate interest in and concern about employees;
- *Co-workers* — the extent to which co-workers are friendly, competent and supportive.

Exhibit 3.5
Sample items from
the 72-item Job
Descriptive Index
with 'satisfied'
responses indicated

WORK		SUPERVISION	
N	Routine	Y	Asks my advice
Y	Creative	Y	Praises good work
N	Tiresome	N	Doesn't supervise enough
Y	Gives sense of accomplishment	Y	Tells me where I stand

PEOPLE		PAY	
Y	Stimulating	Y	Income adequate for normal expenses
Y	Ambitious	N	Bad
N	Talk too much	N	Less than I deserve
N	Hard to meet	N	Highly paid

PROMOTIONS	
Y	Good opportunity for advancement
Y	Promotion on ability
N	Dead-end job
N	Unfair promotion policy

Source: The Job Descriptive Index is copyrighted by Bowling Green State University. The complete forms, scoring key, instructions and norms can be obtained from Dr Patricia C. Smith, Department of Psychology, Bowling Green State University, Bowling Green, Ohio 43404. Reprinted with permission.

These five job satisfaction dimensions have been measured in some studies by using the Job Descriptive Index (JDI). Employees are asked to respond 'yes', 'no', or '?' (can't decide) in describing whether a word or phrase reflects their attitudes about their jobs. Of the seventy-two items on the JDI, twenty are presented in Exhibit 3.5. A scoring procedure is used to arrive at a score for each of the five dimensions. These five scores are then totalled to provide a measure of overall satisfaction.

A major reason for studying job satisfaction is to provide managers with ways to improve employee attitudes. Many organisations use attitude surveys to determine the levels of employee job satisfaction. National surveys indicate that, in general, workers are satisfied with their jobs.[36] These types of surveys, though interesting, may not reflect the actual degree of job satisfaction in a specific department or organisation. There is also a problem that arises simply from asking people how satisfied they are. There is a bias towards giving a positive answer, since declaring anything less indicates that the person is electing to stay in an unsatisfying job. Additionally, to say that workers generally are satisfied with their jobs does not identify the fact that there are differences in satisfaction levels across diverse groups.

A company committed to building and maintaining high levels of job satisfaction is Patagonia, a manufacturer of extremely high-quality sportswear and equipment. At Patagonia, employees are expected to put in at least 5 hours a day at the office between the core hours of 9 a.m. and 3 p.m. The remaining 3 hours can be scheduled when and where the employee desires. Consequently, it is not unusual to find people playing volleyball or spending a couple of hours surfing during the middle of the day (Patagonia offices are located about a kilometre and a half from the beach). At the same time, neither is it unusual to see employees, or 'Patagoniacs' as they liked to be called, hard at work in their offices until 9 p.m. or later. Patagonia also realises that such things as challenging jobs and real participation in decision making contribute to organisational commitment and job satisfaction.[37]

Satisfaction and job performance

One of the most widely debated and controversial issues in the study of job satisfaction is its relationship to job performance. Three general views of this relationship have been advanced: satisfaction causes performance; performance causes satisfaction; and the satisfaction–performance relationship is moderated by other variables such as rewards.[38]

The first two views are supported weakly by research. A review of twenty studies dealing with the performance–satisfaction relationship found a low association between performance and satisfaction.[39] This evidence is rather convincing that a satisfied worker is not necessarily a high performer. Managerial attempts to make everyone satisfied will not yield high levels of production. Likewise, the assumption that a high-performing employee is likely to be satisfied is not supported.

Exhibit 3.6
Satisfaction–performance relationships: Three views

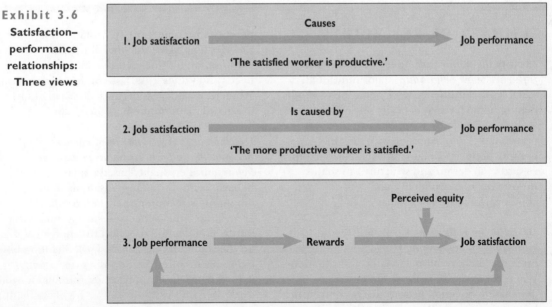

93

The third view suggests that satisfaction and performance are related only under certain conditions. A number of other factors, such as pressure for production, supervisory level, task difficulty and self-esteem, have been posited as moderating the relationship. Most attention, however, has focused on rewards as a key moderator. Generally, this view suggests that the rewards one receives as a consequence of good performance, and the degree to which these rewards are perceived as reasonable or equitable, affect both the extent to which satisfaction results from performance and the extent performance is affected by satisfaction. Exhibit 3.6 shows all three of these viewpoints.

Motivation and behaviour

Now that we have explored the notion of individual differences, it is time we addressed a specific behavioural concern — motivation (Chapter 4). In order to understand such topics as motivation, rewards and stress, the psychological and other variables discussed in this chapter must be a part of the manager's knowledge base. Attempting to motivate employees or to distribute meaningful rewards or to help subordinates cope with the stresses of work life is like groping in the dark if you do not have a sound, fundamental grasp of and insight into abilities, skills, perception, attitudes and personality. The uninformed manager may find her way, but there will be a lot of bumps, bruises and wrong turns. The knowledgeable manager, on the other hand, possesses the insight and wisdom needed to move efficiently, to make better decisions and to be on the lookout for inevitable individual differences among her or his subordinates. As we proceed through the next three individual-level chapters, think about how abilities, skills, perception, attitudes and personality help shape the behaviour and performance of employees.

SUMMARY OF KEY POINTS

Identify the major individual variables that influence work behaviour. Major individual variables that influence work behaviour include demographic factors (e.g. age, sex and race), abilities and skills, perception, attitudes and personality. These combine with various organisational variables (resources, leadership, rewards, job design and structure) to shape productive, non-productive and counterproductive work behaviours.

Describe the influence of personality and situations on behaviour. Two factors influence individual behaviour: personality and situations. When behaviour is explained in terms of personality, selection procedures become critical for organisational effectiveness; when it is explained in terms of situational effects, training

processes become more important. Most current theories emphasise the idea of person–organisation fit: the need to match individual needs and values with those of the organisation. When fit is achieved, organisations benefit from the greater commitment of their staff.

Describe organisational implications of personality and situation-based explanations of behaviour. Personality-based explanations of behaviour imply that organisations should emphasise selection rather than training: according to these theories, such attitudes as job satisfaction depend more on the individual than on the situation (e.g. job design). Situation-based explanations offer the opposing viewpoint: according to these approaches, training or other workplace interventions can be highly influential in shaping work attitudes. More recently, person–organisation fit approaches have emphasised congruence between individual and organisational needs as the key to workplace satisfaction.

Distinguish between stereotyping and prejudice. Stereotyping is a process employed to assist us in dealing more efficiently with massive information-processing demands. It can be a useful, even necessary, perceptual process. A prejudice is a particular form of stereotyping that resists change even in the face of contrary information. Many stereotypes can be helpful; prejudice is never helpful.

Describe how attributions influence our behaviour. Attributions we make about why an event occurs influence our behaviour. The process involves analysing why something has happened (attributing a cause to the event) and fitting that explanation into a general framework that provides a basis for subsequent behaviour. Thus our behaviour is shaped by our perception of why certain things happen.

Explain what an attitude is and identify its three components. An attitude is a learned predisposition to respond favourably or unfavourably to people, objects and situations with which it is related. An attitude consists of a cognitive component (beliefs), an affect component (feelings) and a behavioural component (the individual's behavioural intentions).

Discuss the relationship between job satisfaction and performance. Although the job satisfaction – job performance relationship is a complex one that is not fully understood, it seems clear that these two variables are related under certain conditions. One current view is that the rewards one receives as a consequence of good performance, and the degree to which these rewards are perceived as reasonable, affect both the extent to which satisfaction results from performance and the extent performance is affected by satisfaction.

Identify two important personality factors. Self-efficacy describes the level of confidence of individuals in their ability. It has three components: magnitude, strength and generality. Self-efficacy affects the goals that individuals set as well as their responses to negative feedback.

Self-monitoring describes the level of adaptability that individuals display: high self-monitors change their behaviour to suit the situation whereas low self-monitors tend to display relatively stable behaviours across situations. Self-monitors are especially suited to tasks that require high levels of flexibility and adaptability; they are good communicators and collaborative conflict solvers.

REVIEW AND DISCUSSION QUESTIONS

1. What are the major differences between dispositional, interactional and transactional explanations of behaviour? What are the implications of each approach for the organisation?

2. It seems evident that managers should attempt to match an employee's abilities and skills with job requirements. Is that also true with regard to attitudes and personality? Is it true with regard to demographic factors?

3. In what ways can stereotyping be a helpful process? Can a stereotype be useful even if it is not entirely accurate? Are we better off by getting rid of our stereotypes or by making them more accurate?

4. From the standpoint of managing people effectively, which is more important to the manager: subordinates' perceptions of their behaviour or the actual behaviour itself? Explain.

5. Can you identify attitudes you have about work or school (or this particular course) that affect your job or class performance? How were these attitudes developed and how easily might they be modified?

6. It is frequently said that we see what we want to see. How does attribution theory explain why this statement may be true?

7. A criticism of some organisations is that all their employees have the same personality. Why might this be desirable from the organisation's perspective? How might this be counterproductive?

8. What sort of difficulties might be encountered in doing business in a different culture? What might an organisation do to minimise these difficulties?

9. As a manager, how might you increase a subordinate's feelings of self-efficacy regarding a job assignment? How might you attempt to increase the creativity of your subordinates?

10. So many factors influence an individual's behaviour that it is impossible to accurately predict what their behaviour will be in many situations. Why then should managers take time to understand individual differences?

ENDNOTES

1 Maupin, R. (1993). How can women's lack of upward mobility in accounting organizations be explained? Male and female accountants respond, *Group & Organization Management*, **18**, 132–152.

2 See Snyder, M., & Ickes, W. (1987). Personality and social behavior. In G. Lindzey & E. Aronson (Eds.) *Handbook of Social Psychology* (3rd Ed.). New York: Random House, for a detailed analysis of these positions.

3 Price, R. A., Vandenberg, S. G., Dyer, H., & Williams, J. S. (1982). Components of variation in normal personality, *Journal of Personality and Social Psychology*, **43**, 328–340.

4 This definition is based on Maddi, S. R. (1980). *Personality Theories: A Comparative Analysis.* Homewood, IL.: Dorsey Press, p. 41.

5 Bandura, A. (1977). Self-Efficacy: Toward a unifying theory of behavioral change, *Psychological Review*, **84**, 191–215.

6 Gist, M. E. (1987). Self-Efficacy: Implications for organizational behavior and human resource management, *Academy of Management Review*, 472–485.

7 Baron, R. A., & Greenberg, J. (1993). *Behaviour in Organizations: Understanding and Managing the Human Side of Work* (3rd Ed.). Boston: Allyn Bacon.

8 Snyder, M., & Ickes, W. (1987). Personality and social behavior. In G. Lindzey & E. Aronson (Eds.) *Handbook of Social Psychology* (3rd Ed.). New York: Random House.

9 Briggs, S. R., & Cheek, J. M. (1988). On the nature of self-monitoring: Problems with assessment, problems with validity, *Journal of Personality and Social Psychology*, **54**, 663–678.

10 Baron, R. A., & Greenberg, J. (1993). *Behaviour in Organizations: Understanding and Managing the Human Side of Work* (3rd Ed.). Boston: Allyn Bacon.

11 Kilduff, M., & Day, D. V. (1994) Do chameleons get ahead? The effects of self-monitoring on managerial careers, *Academy of Management Journal*, **37**, 1047–1060.

12 Snyder, M., & Ickes, W. (1987). Personality and social behavior. In G. Lindzey & E. Aronson (Eds.) *Handbook of Social Psychology* (3rd Ed.). New York: Random House.

13 Davis-Blake, A., & Pfeffer, J. (1989). Just a mirage: The search for dispositional effects in organizational research, *Academy of Management Review*, **14**, 385–400.

14 Davis-Blake, A., & Pfeffer, J. (1989). Just a mirage: The search for dispositional effects in organizational research, *Academy of Management Review*, **14**, 385–400; Snyder, M., & Ickes, W. (1987). Personality and social behavior. In G. Lindzey & E. Aronson (Eds.) *Handbook of Social Psychology* (3rd Ed.). New York: Random House.

15 Snyder, M., & Ickes, W. (1987). Personality and social behavior. In G. Lindzey & E. Aronson (Eds.) *Handbook of Social Psychology* (3rd Ed.). New York: Random House.

16 Davis-Blake, A., & Pfeffer, J. (1989). Just a mirage: The search for dispositional effects in organizational research, *Academy of Management Review*, **14**, 385–400.

17 Ibid.

18 Chao, G. T., O'Leary-Kelly, A. M., Wolf, S., Klein, H. J., & Gardner, P. D. (1994). Organizational socialization: Its content and consequences, *Journal of Applied Psychology*, **79**, 730–743; we will consider this point in more detail when we discuss organisational socialisation in Ch. 14.

19 Snyder, M., & Ickes, W. (1987). Personality and social behavior. In G. Lindzey & E. Aronson (Eds.) *Handbook of Social Psychology* (3rd Ed.). New York: Random House.

20 Schultz, C.J. (1993). Situational and dispositional predictors of performance: A test of the hypothesized machiavellianism structure interaction among sales persons, *Journal of Applied Social Psychology*, 23, 478–498.

21 Chatman, J. A . (1989). Improving interactional organizational research: A model of person-organization fit, *Academy of Management Review*, 14, 333–349; Snyder, M., & Ickes, W. (1987). Personality and social behavior. In G. Lindzey & E. Aronson (Eds.) *Handbook of Social Psychology* (3rd Ed.). New York: Random House.

22 Chatman, J. A . (1989). Improving interactional organizational research: A model of person–organization fit, *Academy of Management Review*, 14, 333–349.

23 Ibid.

24 Falkenberg, L. (1990). Improving the accuracy of stereotypes in the workplace, *Journal of Management*, 107–118.

25 Kelly, H. H. (1967). Attribution theory in social psychology. In D. Levine (Ed.) *Nebraska Symposium on Motivation*. Lincoln: University of Nebraska Press.

26 Kanfer, R. (1990). Motivation theory and industrial and organizational psychology. In M. D. Dunnette & L. M. Hough (Eds.) *Handbook of Industrial and Organizational Psychology* (2nd Ed.). Chicago: Rand McNally.

27 Baron, R. A., & Greenberg, J. (1993). *Behaviour in Organizations: Understanding and Managing the Human Side of Work* (3rd Ed.). Boston: Allyn Bacon.

28 Bem, D. J. (1982). *Attitudes, Beliefs and Human Affairs*. Reading, MA.: Brooks-Cole.

29 Rosenberg, M. J. (1960). A structural theory of attitudes, *Public Opinion Quarterly*, 319–340.

30 Dickson, H. W., & McGinnies, E. (1966). Affectivity and arousal of attitudes as measured by galvanic skin responses, *American Journal of Psychology*, 584–589.

31 Freedman, J. L., Carlsmith, J. M., & Sears, D. O. (1974). *Social Psychology*. Englewood Cliffs, N J: Prentice-Hall, p. 271. Also see Coon, D. (1997). *Introduction to Psychology*. St Paul, MN.: West Publishing, pp. 626–629.

32 Ibid, p. 272.

33 Osterhouse, R. A., & Brock, T. C. (1977). Distraction increases yielding to propaganda by inhibiting counterarguing, *Journal of Personality and Social Psychology*, 344–358.

34 Reilly III, C. A., Chatman, J., & Caldwell, D. F. (1991). People and organizational culture: A profile comparison approach to assessing person-organizational fit, *Academy of Management Journal*, 487–516.

35 Smith, P. C., Kendall, L. M., & Hulin, C. L. (1969). *The Measurement of Satisfaction in Work and Retirement*. Skokie, IL.: Rand McNally.

36 DeBats, K. E. (1982). The continuing personnel challenge, *Personnel Journal*, 332–344.

37 See, for example, Cohen, A. (1993). Organizational commitment and turnover: A meta-analysis, *Academy of Management Journal*, 1140–1157.

38 Petty, M. M., McGee, G. & Cavender, J. (1984). A meta-analysis of the relationship between individual job satisfaction and individual performance, *Academy of Management Review*, 712–721.

39 Vroom, V. H. (1964). *Work and Motivation*. New York: John Wiley & Sons.

READING 3 HIRING FOR THE ORGANIZATION, NOT THE JOB

David E. Bowen, Arizona State University-West
Gerald E. Ledford, Jr., University of Southern California
Barry R. Nathan, Southern California Gas Company

Source: *Academy of Management Executive*, 1991, **5**, 4.

Executive overview

This article examines a new approach to selection in which employees are hired to fit the characteristics of an organization, not just the requirements of a particular job. Diverse firms — high and low-tech, US and Japanese owned — are using the approach to build cultures that rely heavily on self-motivated, committed people for corporate success. New, often expensive, hiring practices are changing the traditional selection model. An organizational analysis supplements a job analysis and personality attributes are screened in addition to skills, knowledge, and abilities. We outline the basic steps of the new selection model and present a case description of a manufacturing company that used the model in hiring employees to work in its high-involvement organization. The new model works to its fullest advantage in organizations that allow employees enough freedom to use their unique attributes to influence job performance.

Conventional selection practices are geared toward hiring employees whose knowledge, skills, and abilities (KSAs) provide the greatest fit with clearly defined requirements of specific jobs. Traditional selection techniques rarely consider characteristics of the organization in which the jobs reside. Traditional techniques also ignore characteristics of the person that are irrelevant to immediate job requirements. In common management parlance, the organization hires new 'hands' or new 'heads' — that is, parts of people.

A new model of selection is emerging, however, that is geared toward hiring a 'whole' person who will fit well into the specific organization's culture. It reflects a fundamental reorientation of the selection process toward hiring 'people', not just KSAs, for 'organisations', not just jobs. This leads to hiring practices that seem peculiar and needlessly extravagant, from a traditional human resource standpoint. Consider the hiring practices of three different organizations.

- AFG Industries builds two new float glass plants. The plants use practices such as work teams, extensive training, and skill-based pay that create a high level of employee involvement. The hiring process for factory workers includes screening formal resumes (not job applications), personality testing, pre-employment training that simulates some plant jobs, interviews with panels of managers and/or employees, and a medical exam.
- Sun Microsystems is the fastest-growing US company in the past five years, with annual growth averaging more than 100 percent.[1] Filling open jobs is critical to Sun's effectiveness, phenomenal growth and profitability. Yet, the hiring process is extremely time-consuming and labor-intensive. Potential hires at all levels are brought into the organisation from four to seven times for interviews with up to twenty interviewers. The process is full of ambiguity, lacks formal rules, and demands that all employees engage in problem solving to get themselves hired.
- Toyota (USA) screens 50 000 applications for 3000 factory jobs in the initial staffing of its plant in Georgetown, Kentucky.[2] Each employee hired invests at least eighteen hours in a selection process that includes a general knowledge exam, a test of attitudes toward work, an interpersonal skills assessment center, manufacturing exercise designed to provide a realistic job preview of assembly work, an extensive personal interview, and a physical exam.

As we shall see, these organizations adopt unusual hiring practices to find employees who fit the organization and to encourage those who do not fit to seek employment elsewhere. Although potential hires with skills that meet the demands of specific jobs are not ignored, these companies maintain that the person–job fit needs to be supported and enriched by person–organization fit. These companies are willing to invest substantial resources in rigorously assessing this fit. Why and how organizations approach hiring in this way are explored in this article.

How important are hiring decisions, really? The person-situation controversy revisited

Is individual behavior, such as job performance, a function of the person (attributes of an employee), the situation (characteristics of the work setting), or the interaction of the person and situation? This question is age-old. Proponents of employee selection as a key to human resource effectiveness answer that individual behavior is largely a function of the person. Selection techniques attempt to capitalize on enduring differences between individuals by choosing those individuals who are best suited to the job. Conversely, advocates of socialization and training practices that attempt to mold employees after they are hired assume that the situation is the principal determinant of individual behavior.[3] The majority of researchers and managers subscribe to some form of the interactionist perspective. They assume that both the person and the situation matter, and that the combination of the two determines individual performance and other behaviors.

We argue that both researchers and managers have overemphasized the situation and have paid only lip service to the individual in recent years. In research on organizational behavior, people variables (for example, needs) usually are treated as secondary to situational variables (for example, job designs) and researchers generally are skeptical about the ability of personality variables to predict job performance.[4] Managerial interest in individual testing appears to have dropped sharply after several 1970 court decisions held that invalidated and discriminatory selection procedures were illegal.

An overemphasis on the importance of the situation fits the managerial ideology dominant among American corporations. A basic assumption of bureaucratic organizations is that individuals cannot be trusted to manage their own behavior. Thus, management designs the organization to control employee behavior as tightly as possible, through the managerial hierarchy, impersonal rules and procedures, close supervision, and extensive socialization and training. This curtails the expression of individual differences in behavior. As a result, the organization is designed to be what researchers have called a 'strong situation', the one in which the intensity of the situation suppresses variation in behavior that is attributable to the person.[5] Thus, managers create a self-fulfilling prophesy. The belief that the situation is the most important predictor of behavior leads to the organizational design which suppresses individual differences. This self-fulfilling pattern is further reinforced by basing hiring decisions on a single, brief interview, which has proved to be unreliable and of poor validity.[6] It is not surprising, then, that managers often conclude that the selection system is not a key success factor.

Yet, some organizations are designed as 'weak situations', allowing a range of employee responses to work requirements.[7] These organizations have less control over individuals and the effects of person variables are greater. In such organizations, it is more important than in traditional organizations to do a good job of hiring the right people.

Consider the three organizations we described at the beginning of this article. They are more different than similar. They include high-tech and moderately low-tech, manufacturing-driven and engineering-driven, white collar and blue collar, and US-owned and Japanese-owned firms. Yet these organizations share a set of management assumptions about organizational success. Each is attempting to build a distinctive culture that is intentionally 'fragile', meaning that management relies heavily on self-motivated, committed people for system effectiveness.[8] While all three organizations have a management hierarchy, organizational policies and other tools of external control, all rely to an unusual degree on employees to make the system work effectively. And they use sophisticated selection systems to hire the whole person whose skills and personality fit the type of organization, not just a job.

The new selection model: Hiring for person–organization fit

Exhibit 3.7 presents the new selection model for hiring for person–organization fit. As we shall see, it differs from the traditional selection model in several important ways.[9] Our model represents a synthesis of the steps taken by the organizations mentioned in our opening case examples as well

as by other progressive firms. Although any one firm may not fully implement every step, all of these steps together offer the best guarantee of person–organization fit.

We will describe the steps in the model and then present a case description of a firm where hiring practices are a close match to the ideal. First, however, we clarify the meaning of 'person–organization fit'.

Person–organization fit

The model in Exhibit 3.7 places the selection process in the context of a rich interaction between the person and the organization, both of which are more broadly defined and assessed than in the traditional selection model.

Person–organization fit requires that two types of fit be achieved in the hiring process: (1) between the KSAs of the individual and the task demands or critical requirements for the job; and

---

Exhibit 3.7 A hiring process for person–organization fit

1. Assess the overall work environment
- Job analysis
- Organizational analysis

↓

2. Infer the type of person required
- Technical knowledge, skills, and abilities
- Social skills
- Personal needs, values, and interests
- Personality traits

↓

3. Design 'rites of passage' for organization entry that allow both the organization and the applicant to assess their fit
- Tests of cognitive, motor, and interpersonal abilities
- Interviews by potential co-workers and others
- Personality tests
- Realistic job previews, including work samples

↓

4. Reinforce person–organization fit at work
- Reinforce skills and knowledge through task design and training
- Reinforce personal orientation through organization design

(2) between the overall personality of the individual (e.g. needs, interest and values) and the climate or culture of the organization.

The traditional selection model focuses almost exclusively on the first type of fit (KSAs — job) while tending to ignore or assessing far less rigorously, the second type (personality — climate/culture).[10] The narrow focus of the traditional selection model reflects several factors. One is that managers tend to think of individual job performance as the key outcome of the hiring process and they believe that job performance is a function of the fit between KSAs and task demands. Additionally the traditional selection model is more concerned with finding new employees than with retaining them. There is less attention to whether the whole person finds the organization's culture satisfying enough to stay. Organizations have also been constrained by the unavailability of proven selection technologies for producing the fit between personality and climate/culture. This situation can be improved, we believe, by following the steps for hiring that are described next.

Step One: Assess the work environment

The job analysis of the traditional model of selection is also conducted in the new model. It remains instrumental in achieving the fit between individual KSAs and task demands. Alternative job analysis techniques include the position analysis questionnaire, task inventories, and critical incident techniques.[11]

The purpose of an organizational analysis is to define and assess the work environment in terms of the characteristics of the organization, rather than just in terms of the characteristics of a specific job. It identifies the behaviors and responsibilities that lead to organizational effectiveness, and implies the personal characteristics most likely to be associated with such behaviors and responsibilities. Organizational analysis also is important because job analysis data may quickly become outdated as rapidly changing products and technologies reshape employees' jobs. The organization's overall philosophy and values are likely to be more stable and consequently, the more important long-term focus for fit.

Techniques for organizational analysis are not well-established, largely because there is little research that systematically associates the characteristics of organizations and individual

behavior patterns. Managers need to identify the important dimensions of the organization and their implications for the kinds of employees who would best fit those situations. Although organizational analysis techniques are not nearly as well-developed as job analysis techniques, a variety of methods are available. For example, the training field offers guidelines for conducting an organizational analysis as one component of a training needs analysis. Organization characteristics assessed include short-and long-term goals, staffing needs, properties of the environment (for example, stability) and employee perceptions of organization climate. Organizational culture audits have emerged in the last decade that offer both qualitative and quantitative methods for describing an organization's norms and values.[12] Quite promising is a sophisticated Q-sort methodology that assesses the content, integrity and crystallization of organizational values and matches them with an assessment of individual values.[13] Finally, there is a long-standing approach to diagnosing the characteristics of an organization's four subsystems, (individuals, tasks, organizational arrangements, informal organization) that can yield organizational analysis data.[14]

Organization analysis does not replace job analysis. Rather it ensures that important components of the work context as well as its content are identified and evaluated for their importance to job success. While many job analyses include evaluations of the work context, the person–organization fit model explicitly recognizes that successful employees have knowledge, skills, abilities and other personal characteristics that match both the content and the context of the job.

Step Two: Infer the type of person required

In step two, managers deal with applicants in terms of who they are, not just what they can do. It is still necessary to infer from the job analysis the KSAs that employees need to be technically competent. However, step two also requires inferring, from the organizational analysis, the needs, values and interest — that is, the personality — an employee must possess to be an effective member of the organization. For example, if the organizational analysis reveals that teamwork is a key norm or value in the setting, then selection tools must be used to find people who are team players. Furthermore, social and interpersonal skills will be necessary, in addition to the cognitive and motor abilities that are the dominant skills-focus of the traditional selection model.

The move by some organizations toward hiring the total person coincides with a renewed interest by researchers in personality as a predictor of job attitudes and behaviors. These researchers believe that studies in which personality measures fail to predict job performance often have been plagued by problems such as focusing on personality aspects of questionable relevance to the job, poor research methods, and so on.[15] These problems have given personality a bad name and fostered the impression that the situation matters much more than the person in influencing job attitudes and performance. In contrast, more recent research has yielded such interesting findings that individual personality attributes can predict job satisfaction later — more than fifty years and even for different jobs. The research implies that job satisfaction may be associated with a stable, enduring personality attribute rather than a function of the situation.[16] This indicates that the types of people hired is very important.

Organizations also must pay attention to technical skills needed by the organization. Often applicants with the most appropriate personalities and social skills are not those with the right technical skills. If the organization faces the need to upgrade technical skills quickly, it may be forced to make tradeoffs. Organizations in this situation often place greater weight on personality and social skills, on the grounds that it is easier to train technical skills than change personalities or develop social skills. This can lead to increased short-term training costs and temporary overstaffing. However, if the work technology is complex and training times are long, management may be forced to hire some employees who better fit the organization's technical requirements than its cultural requirements. Douglas Bray, noted pioneer of the AT&T Management Progress Study, considers this tradeoff and suggests that selection decisions about needs, values and interests may be more critical than those for skills.[17] For example, a desire to learn new jobs is an attribute that cannot be taught easily to employees, as job skills can. You either hire people who have this attribute or do without.

Step Three: Design 'rites of passage' that allow the organization and the individual to assess fit

The battery of screens used in the new approach to hiring may seem designed to discourage individuals from taking the job.[18] Yet, these screens have several purposes. First, the use of multiple screening methods, raters, and criteria has long been recommended by researchers as the best approach to hiring.[19] Yet most organizations still hire employees using a single interview with a single interviewer. More sophisticated techniques, if used, typically are reserved for executives and sometimes sales people. Second, multiple screenings not only allow the organization to select employees, but also provide applicants with sufficient realistic information about the work environment so that they can make an informed choice about whether they even want the job. Third, the people who join the organization feel special. They have survived the elaborate rites of passage necessary to join the organization. They experience the sense of accomplishment associated with completing boot camp when entering military service.

A recent *Fortune* article described these fresh approaches as 'The New Art of Hiring Smart'.[20] One ingredient has been increased use of job simulation exercises for assembly workers. These simulations, or work sample tests, help both the person and the organization assess fit. The applicant receives a realistic job preview of the work. The organization has an opportunity to assess applicants' technical skills and, when group interaction is required in an exercise, their interpersonal skills as well. Intelligence tests also seem to be on the rebound.

Sun Microsystems offers a good example of the use of rites of passage to allow mutual assessment of fit. This fast-growing Silicon Valley firm, like many high-technology companies, is constantly changing in response to rapidly developing markets, evolving technologies, and the pace of internal growth. Employees who prefer clear job descriptions, stability, a leisurely pace, and predictability would be unhappy at Sun. The hiring process is such a challenge and so full of ambiguity, that unsuitable applicants tend to give up before the process is completed. Those hired have survived multiple interviews with many different possible co-workers. A joke at Sun is, 'after seven sets of interviews, we put applicants on the payroll whether they've been hired or not'. The hiring process thus introduces prospective employees to the culture of the organization.

Personality tests are another way to assess mutual fit. It appears that 'personality tests are back'.[21] For example, the Meyers-Briggs Type Indicator is used by companies such as Allied Signal, Apple, AT&T, Citicorp, Exxon, G. E., Honeywell and 3M. These tests are used primarily in management development programs. However, personality tests are used increasingly as selection tests, particularly for assembly workers, positions.

There is renewed interest in personality tests even though past efforts to validate them have been largely unsuccessful.[22] However, there is a growing belief that personality tests can be validated under the proper conditions.[23] These include:

1. Using personality measures that are tailored to the work setting. Major personality tests were not developed for work settings, so their poor track record in validation studies is not surprising.
2. Using personality measures to predict global criteria. That is, multi-faceted measures of job attitudes and behaviors, rather than one specific criterion such as quarterly sales.
3. Using measures of personality dimensions that are logically or theoretically associated with the work in the organization. This contrasts with screening for personality attributes that are not job related but hold some particular interest to managers.

Whereas personality tests provide organizations with information about applicants, realistic job previews (RJPs) provide applicants with information about organizations. Examples of RJPs are the Toyota USA job simulations/work sample tests that show applicants the repetitive nature of manufacturing work and the requirements for teamwork. Applicants can then make informed choices about whether they would be satisfied there. 'Turned-off' applicants may drop out of the hiring process. Those hired are more likely to join the organization with a sense of commitment and realistic expectations. Fundamentally, an RJP helps individuals decide if they want to join an organization, based on their own assessment of their personality and how it might fit with a particular type of organization.[24]

Step Four: Reinforce person–organization fit at work

Selection is clearly the first and, arguably, the most important step in implementing a fragile system philosophy. However, the hiring process must be integrated with, and supported by, the firm's other human resource management practices. Japanese-owned plants in the US and high involvement organizations illustrate this point.

Japanese automobile manufacturers operating in the United States provide examples of how to accomplish this. The Japanese 'Auto Alley' in the US provided more than 6000 assembly jobs in 1989. Key operations include Nissan in Smyrna, Tennessee; Toyota in Georgetown, Kentucky: Honda in Marysville, Ohio; Mazda in Flat Rock, Michigan; and Diamond-Star Motors Corporation in Normal, Illinios.[25] The Japanese have attempted to create a certain type of organization, characterized by now-familiar values of teamwork, consensual decision-making, peer control, egalitarianism and non-specialized career paths. Broad job classifications encourage employee flexibility, rather than identification with specific jobs. Extensive on-the-job training and job rotation further increase flexibility. Group activities encourage employees to contribute ideas for organizational improvement and promote teamwork. Employment stability helps the organization realize a return on its training and other investments in human resources and increase employee loyalty to the organization. Thus, a selection system in such organizations typically screens for interest in work variety, social needs and skills, and organization commitment.

High involvement organizations (HIOs) are another class of organization that uses multiple systems to support hiring for person–organization fit. HIOs are a relatively new organizational form; there are perhaps a few hundred examples now existing in the US.[26] HIOs have two key characteristics.[27] First, the organization is designed to create very high levels of employee involvement. Power, information, skills and rewards for performance are pushed down to the lowest level of the organization. Self-managed teams or other structures enable employees to share decision-making power. Extensive training in technical, social and business skills provides team members with the skills needed for effective self-management. Information systems communicate the performance data that teams need to manage themselves. Rewards systems such as skill-based pay and gainsharing motivate needed behaviors, such as learning and problem solving. For obvious reasons, hiring practices in HIOs typically attempt to select employees who prefer working in groups and who have high needs for personal growth and development. Thus, the hiring process is one design element of many that must fit with the overall design.

The following case description of the hiring process in a new HIO illustrates all four steps of the new selection model.

Hiring for person–organization fit: The case of a start-up high involvement organization

The research reported here was conducted as part of an action research project at a new float glass plant in the western United States.[28] The plant is a classic new HIO. Research on the selection system described here is part of a larger, on-going action research effort. Management was interested in developing selection procedures and tools for hiring employees with the necessary job skills, needs and aspirations to fit the organization design. Researchers helped design the hiring process, conducted extensive research on the initial hiring process at the plant and explored the validity of personality measures as possible future selection tools. The overall effort essentially followed the four steps previously discussed for hiring for person–organization fit.

Step One: Assess the work environment

Since the plant was a start-up operation, there were no existing jobs to analyze this initial step. There were individual jobs with comparable content at other organizational sites, but management was committed to designing the new plant as the first high involvement organization in the company. Thus, analyzing the work environment of the existing plants would have been of limited use in designing a hiring process to match the new HIO. Instead top management and two of the researchers/consultants (the second author and Tom Cummings of the University of Southern California) conducted an organizational analysis to assess key desired organizational characteristics, needs and values. This analysis followed standard sociotechnical systems procedures and specifically considered requirements for the level of employee growth and social needs. This led to the development of the management philosophy and practices that would define the new organization. A customized version of the HIO concept, tailored to the needs

of the organization, emerged from this work.

Glass-making lent itself to an HIO design for several reasons. First, there was a great deal of task interdependence which required worker cooperation and teamwork. Second, technical uncertainty was high. Workers were responsible for making immediate decisions about the glass-making process from the procurement to furnace melting of raw materials and various stages of cooling, inspecting, cutting, packing, and storing. The plant's profitability is directly related to production efficiency and glass quality. Quality is directly dependent on workers' ability to maintain a continual, steady flow of glass, by constantly monitoring and regulating the temperature and speed of flow of the product through the system. Deviations from desired parameters must be corrected as soon as possible after detection. Internal control by employees is more responsive to system fluctuations than external control through supervision, rules and procedures.

This work environment led management to adopt a work design that encouraged high levels of employee teamwork and decision making. Employees were organized into self-regulating work teams at each sequential stage of production. Management saw this job design as most appropriate for the relatively high task interdependence and task uncertainty of the plant technology. Management expected that as team members developed technical and social skills, they would make joint decisions about work methods and assignments and solve production problems on the line.

Step Two: Infer the type of person required

Since work in the high involvement glass plant required understanding and becoming involved in the entire production process, selecting on the basis of technical skills was not enough. Basic KSAs, such as motor and arithmetic skills, while necessary, would not be sufficient for organizational success. Workers also had to feel a sense of commitment to working in this type of organization. Furthermore, the jobs were to be dynamic. Over time, employees were expected to learn different skills within their team and in other teams and to take on an increasing share of decision making. Top management expected that the number of supervisors and layers of management would be reduced as the teams matured. A fit between applicant characteristics and the work requirements of a high involvement organization as a whole was required.

In addition to the necessary technical skills, two personality characteristics were especially important to the organization. One was growth need strength. The HIO design placed many demands on employees for continuous learning, decision making, and assuming responsibility for organizational structuring, functioning and performance. For example, employees were required to train each other, give feedback to fellow team members on their performance, and help design organizational changes. Applicants who desired little challenge or learning opportunity and those who prefer narrowly defined jobs would have been misfits with this organization. Conversely, those who valued or had strong needs for personal growth, accomplishment, and personal development would be more committed to working in the new plant.

A second relevant personality characteristic was social needs. This was obvious because self-regulating teams demand cooperation and teamwork. In addition, management planned to make heavy use of special problem-solving groups, committees and task forces. Those who saw working with others as a burden would have been misfits in such a setting, while people with high social needs were expected to prefer group forms of work and group activities.

Step Three: Design 'rites of passage' that allow the organization and the individual to assess fit

The hiring process consisted of several stages that involved multiple methods, raters and criteria. A state agency conducted an initial screen of approximately 100 candidates responding to local advertisements about job openings at the plant, which was then under construction. At this stage applicants received scores for their education and experience, such as a high school degree or GED, manufacturing or related experience, and ability to understand process instrumentation and complete a time card. In addition, tests using potential predictors based on personality and other survey questions also were administered at this time. Personality characteristics were assessed using the Personality Research Form — Form E or PRF, a highly regarded personality assessment instrument.[29] The PRF measure of affiliation needs is very similar to social needs as described previously. Three PRF measures were relevant to

growth needs: achievement, endurance and dominance. (The dominance items measure desire to influence others or social achievement, not oppressiveness.) These two personality dimensions, affiliation and growth needs, were logically associated with the nature of work in an HIO and the PRF measures were moderately tailored to better fit the work setting. Of the 540 applicants who passed the initial screening and were invited to a pre-employment assessment and training program (described below), approximately 500 candidates responded.

Performance was assessed in four half-day sessions of a pre-employment assessment and training program, designed to capture characteristics of work in a high involvement float glass factory. The company used this program both as a selection tool and as a realistic job preview. As an RJP, the program showed how a high involvement organization is designed to operate, technical and social requirements, what it would be like to handle glass (for example, lacerations are common and special protective clothing is used to minimize the likelihood of injury), and various tasks employees would be expected to perform.

The program was divided into two approximately equal segments. One part involved work simulations consisting of handling and packing glass and operating hand tools and equipment required for glass making. Participants were given instructions about work methods, rules and safety procedures, and engaged in glass making and packing tasks as a team. The second part of the training program involved classroom learning and experiential exercises aimed at group decision making. Almost half of the classroom time was used to present information about glass making and the design features of the high involvement plant, including self-regulating groups, participative leadership, egalitarian human-resource practices, skill-based pay, and gainsharing. Participants were given a realistic portrayal of what it would be like to work in a team-based, high involvement structure, including the kinds of work behaviors that would be expected. They also were tested on basic math and measurement skills needed to perform glass making and packaging tasks, as well as given homework covering basic processes and terminology used in making glass as well as the nature of one's work and responsibility in a high involvement organization.

For more than half of the classroom time, participants engaged in exercises designed to simulate the kind of group interaction and decision-making occurring in self-regulating groups. One exercise, for example, involved reaching a group consensus about the ranking of items needed to survive in the rugged outdoors. Another exercise involved role playing a group decision about which department should receive a new piece of equipment. These exercises were followed by extensive debriefing about members' behaviors and interactions and how the learning applies to the work of teams in the plant.

The scoring procedure evaluated applicants from a holistic perspective, that is how well each applicant fitted in a high involvement setting rather than how he or she performed on individual job-related tasks. Applicants were evaluated by managers and supervisors who had received training on how to avoid common rater errors. Classroom activities, group exercises, and work simulations were scored. Applicants were evaluated on the quality and thoroughness of homework assignments and were required to attain minimum passing scores on arithmetic and tape measure reading tests. Group exercises were scored on the degree applicants exhibited participating, negotiating, gatekeeping, and probing behaviors. Finally, work simulations were scored on four factors: absence and tardiness over the four days; safety behavior; responsibility, meaning following instructions and not exhibiting disruptive or distracting behavior; and general behavior, meaning exhibiting team skills, paying attention to instructors, and not breaking plant rules or abusing equipment. Thus the work simulations were not scored on task performance *per se*. Instead, they were scored on behaviors relevant to the overall success of the organization. This focus on behaviors ensured that the selection process could be defended legally, if necessary, in the basis of content validity.

The pre-employment assessment and training program met two important goals. First, it was consistent with technical and professional standards for employment selection. As in assessment centers, job behaviors were sampled systematically across different situations. Multiple and diverse activities and assessment methods afforded evaluators an opportunity to assess how well applicants would fit into an HIO generally, rather than just on how well applicants could perform specific tasks. The use of global criteria satisfied another condition for

successfully validating a personality test as selection tools. Second, the program gave applicants a realistic job preview of what working in a high involvement glass plant would be like. The task activities provided applicants with a preview of the physical and potentially dangerous nature of the work. (One of the authors was present when a piece of tempered glass was mishandled and literally exploded in an applicant's hands.) The classroom activities prepared applicants for the organization's emphasis on working together and taking responsibility for action.

Those who passed this program were invited to a final selection interview with a panel of managers. This structured interview consisted of questions regarding manufacturing experience, education, understanding the high involvement and autonomous work group design, past experience and interest in group activities and other performance skills and creative experiences. Finally, applicants were required to pass a physical examination including a drug screen. Ultimately, 250 applicants of the original 1000 applicants successfully completed these phases and the physical examination.

We subsequently validated the PRF personality test. Specifically, scores on the PRF were significantly correlated with performance in the pre-employment training program and with applicants' anticipated satisfaction with work in the organization.[30] This means that it would be appropriate and legal for the company to use measures of social and growth needs from this test in future hiring decisions. Since the analysis was completed long after most employees had been hired at the site, however, the company did not use the test in hiring decisions.

Step Four: Reinforce person–organization fit at work

The objectives of hiring process were reinforced by various organization design features that emphasized high involvement and team functioning. For example, extensive training was provided, both in technical skills and in social skills such as group decision making. A skill-based pay system gave employees increases in base pay for learning new jobs within their team. This in turn reinforced employees' interest in receiving training, which enabled them to earn pay increases. The plant adopted a gainsharing plan from the beginning that provided generous plant-wide monetary bonuses when plant performance met specific objectives. This reinforced the need for teamwork, since no individual could win a bonus at the expense of another. The gainsharing plan also provided incentives for exemplary performance and for developing improvements in the production process that could result in greater payouts. Extensive business information was routinely shared with employees, in part to make the gainsharing plan work more effectively. Employees were also involved as needed in task forces of various kinds to solve business, personnel, and other problems. In short, there was extensive reinforcement for the behaviors and characteristics that management sought during the hiring process.

The results of the hiring process have been positive. A survey of employees after startup indicated that employee quality of work life, according to various measures of satisfaction, organization commitment, and so on, was very high — a likely indication of person–organization fit. After an initial period of high turnover, turnover has dropped below national norms. On most key performance measures, the plant is one

of the most effective in the company. Its main rival is another new high involvement plant that opened shortly after startup of the plant described here; it was developed on the same HIO model and used a similar hiring process. On the whole, it appears that the plant has been a very effective organization and that hiring for the organization, not just the job, has contributed to that effectiveness.

Benefits and problems from hiring for person–organization fit

Clearly, the new approach to hiring for person–organization fit requires more resources than the traditional selection model. Is it worth the cost? Consider the potential benefits (see Exhibit 3.8).

(1) Employee attitudes. Researchers have long proposed that a fit between individual needs and organizational climates and cultures would result in greater job satisfaction and organization commitment.[31] There is ample data documenting that the realistic job previews typically used in the new selection model are associated with higher on-the-job satisfaction.[32] Greater team spirit also is likely when new employees have shared the experience of moving successfully through the demanding rites of passage that lead to organizational entry.

Survey of applicants in our case example indicated that these favorable attitudes were associated with the hiring process. For example, the majority of applicants felt the pre-employment training program accurately measured how well they could do the job and get along with others, and was a help in subsequent performance on the job and interacting with co-workers. Applicants also felt it provided a realistic preview of working at the plant. An overwhelming seventy seven percent reported that after going through pre-employment training, the work seemed more satisfying than when they first applied for the job. Only two percent thought it would be less satisfying.

(2) Employee behaviors. Studies indicate that high involvement organizations, which typically use the new selection model, have low rates of absenteeism, turnover, and grievances.[33] The data are even clearer that using realistic job previews in Step 3 is associated with lower turnover.[34] We also have presented a strong case that person–organization fit will result in employees

---

Exhibit 3.8 Potential benefits and problems with hiring for person–organization fit

Potential benefits

1. More favorable employee attitudes (such as greater job satisfaction, organization commitment, and team spirit)
2. More desirable individual behaviors (such as better job performance and lower absenteeism and turnover)
3. Reinforcement of organizational design (such as support for work design and desired organizational culture)

Potential problems

1. Greater investment of resources in the hiring process
2. Relatively undeveloped and unproven supporting selection technology
3. Individual stress
4. May be difficult to use the full model where payoffs are greatest
5. Lack of organizational adaptation

displaying more of what have been labelled 'organizational citizenship behaviors'. These are behaviors that employees perform above and beyond explicit job requirements. The thinking here is that fitted employees see themselves as really belonging to the organization and willing to invest their own resources in its on-going maintenance.[35]

(3) Reinforcement of organization design. The effectiveness of Japanese transplants that hire according to this model is common knowledge. HIOs often are very high performers. For example, a study of a large sample of high involvement organizations found that HIOs outperformed their industry on return on sales by an average of 532 percent and outperformed their industry on return on investment by an average of 388 percent.[36] Researchers often argue that the power of such an organization derives from the mutual reinforcement of its parts, including the selection process. The hiring process in HIOs helps select employees who are interested in challenging, responsible, varied jobs and pay systems that reward needed behaviors and performance.

Potential problems

Hiring for person–organization fit may also have its disadvantages (see Exhibit 3.8):

(1) Greater investment in hiring. This model requires a much greater investment of resources in the hiring process. For example, Mazda in Flat Rock, Michigan spends about $13 000 per employee to staff its plant.[37] It appears that organizations hiring within this model are spending the same time and money on hiring an assembly worker as they do in conducting an executive search.

The costs of making revisions in the hiring process also are different in the new model. A traditional hiring process needs to be revised whenever the requirements of the job change significantly. A hiring process for person–organization fit needs to be changed whenever the business, technological, or cultural requirements of the organization change significantly. This means that changes in hiring practices for person–organization fit are likely to be less frequent but much greater in scope than changes in traditional hiring processes. A change in hiring practices for person–organization fit

may well involve a change in how every new employee is hired.

(2) Undeveloped selection technology. The supporting selection technology is still relatively undeveloped and unproven. One problem is the still-thin track record of successfully validating personality tests against job performance. However, the present authors' study in which measures of growth needs and social needs predicted candidates' performance in a pre-employment simulation of high-involvement work demonstrates that personality measures, carefully chosen and developed, can be validated. Yet until personality tests acquire a deeper inventory of successful validation studies, organizations will doubt their usefulness.

In the context of person–organization fit, techniques for assessing people are more developed than those for assessing work environments. Even on the people side, though, the field is not nearly as sophisticated in measuring work-related personality facets as it is in assessing KSAs. Moreover, there is a great need for techniques of organizational analysis that are as sophisticated as those for job analysis (e.g. the PAQ). Overall, the challenge in organizational analysis is to: (a) identify relevant underlying dimensions of settings and how they can be measured, (b) determine the major impact on individual attitudes and behaviors, and organizational effectiveness, and (c) determine how such impacts differ depending upon individuals' personality.[38]

Managers may be concerned about the legality of these developing tools. More broadly, managers may be concerned about whether selecting for organization fit is legal. This concern is groundless, in our view. The legal standards for person–organization fit are no different than those for person–job fit. In general, selection procedures that do not result in adverse impact on protected minorities and women are not illegal. If the selection system does result in adverse impact, then evidence of job-relatedness must be presented. Job-relatedness is based on the content, construct and criterion-related validity of the selection procedures. The procedures we have described establish job-relatedness.

In fact, there may be less adverse impact as a result of hiring for organization fit than in traditional hiring systems. Traditional systems rely mostly on tests of abilities to predict job performance. Intellectual ability tests typically result in adverse impact against minorities, and physical ability tests often result in adverse impact against women. Organization fit, in contrast, is based largely on values, needs and motives that may be more evenly distributed in the population.

(3) Employee stress. Individuals fitted to 'fragile systems' may find their organizational lives to be more stressful. The firms in the Japanese Auto Alley, high-involvement organizations, firms in the Silicon Valley, and so on, which rely on carefully selected people for system effectiveness are also laying substantial claims to those people's lives. This higher level of involvement at work may be associated with experiencing more stress on the job. These workers have reported that they now take work problems home with them and feel the strains more typically associated with managerial roles.[39]

(4) Difficult to use the full model where the benefits are greatest. A new hiring model may offer the greatest potential benefits to new organizations, such as new plants and startup companies. This is because hiring the right kinds of employees can help establish the desired culture of the organization from the very beginning. In existing organizations that are attempting to change their culture, there may be a long period in which the proportion of employees with unwanted attributes drops through attrition, while the proportion of employees with desired attributes gradually increases due to an improved hiring process.

Most of the hiring model we have described can be used in new organizations. However, one component of the model, specifically formal selection testing, often cannot be used appropriately or legally early in the life of the organization because the tests have not yet been validated. By the time the validation studies have been conducted, most of the workforce will have been hired. In some circumstances, it may be possible to avoid this problem by validating the tests before hiring in the new organization. For example, many companies that develop one high involvement organization (or other unusual culture) go on to develop others. It may be possible to validate the tests in an existing location if the culture of the existing organization

and that desired of the new location are similar. AFG Industries, for example, could use the PRF test to hire employees in other plants that are designed as high involvement organizations.

Another way to avoid this problem is taken by Development Dimensions International, a consulting firm that designed the hiring system for Toyota's Kentucky plant as well as other hiring systems aimed at person–organization fit.[40] DDI identifies the desired characteristics of new hires through a diagnosis conducted with senior managers of the organization. Potential hires explicitly are told about the desired characteristics during the orientation process. Then, the new hires complete a Job Fit Inventory, which includes items relevant to the desired qualities of employees in the organization. The instrument intentionally is very 'transparent' and fakeable. Thus, it does not serve the same purposes as personality tests. Rather, it is used to screen out the bottom five to fifteen percent of applicants — those who admit they lack the attributes that they are told explicitly that the company is seeking.

(5) Lack of organizational adaptation. A problem could arise in hiring for the organization if it led to a workforce in which everyone had the same personality profile. The organization might become stagnant because everyone would share the same values, strengths, weaknesses and blindspots. (Obviously, the issue is the same whether employees all tend to have the same point of view because of the selection system or because of training and socialization.) There has been considerable debate about whether a powerful organizational culture, whatever its source, leads to success or leads to dry rot and lack of innovativeness. There is some evidence, for example, indicating that organizations with little internal variability in employee perspectives perform better in the short run but worse in the long run, presumably as a result of inferior adaptation.[41]

However, we expect that significant internal variability will co-exist with person–organization fit. Even the best selection system is still imperfect; we do not succeed in hiring only the 'right types'. More fundamentally, the hiring process still results in variability on the desired characteristics. Even though all those hired may meet minimum standards, some will be higher than others on the desired characteristics. Finally, employees are not clones of one another just because they are similar on some personality dimensions. We would expect considerable variation on demographic, cultural and personality dimensions that were not the basis for selection.

The future of hiring for person–organization fit

What does the future hold for this more sophisticated and elaborate approach to employee selection? Will it be adopted by an increasingly large share of corporations?

We believe that hiring for the organization, not the job, will become the only effective selection model for the typical business environment. The defining attributes of this business environment — such as shortened product life cycles, increasingly sophisticated technologies, growing globalization of markets, shifting customer demands — make for very transitory requirements in specific employee jobs. Organizational success in this environment requires hiring employees who fit the overall organization, not those who fit a fixed set of task demands. Employee personalities must fit the management philosophy and values that help define the organization's uniqueness and its fitness for the future.

We also believe that senior managers must become more 'person-oriented' in their own implicit resolution of the person–situation controversy if hiring for person–organization fit is to become a more common approach to selection. Again, generally speaking, managers tend to believe that tightly controlled situations are more effective in shaping employee performance than less-structured situations that allow the expression of individual differences. Managers who believe this are more inclined to spend resources on creating strong situations via job descriptions, close supervision, and so on than on sophisticated selection procedures.

Finally, we offer an important caveat to 'person-oriented' managers who are committed to hiring for person–organization fit. They must manage a paradox. They must build strong organizational cultures yet, at the same time, design work situations that are weak enough to allow the unique qualities of individual employees to impact work performance. The key ingredient in balancing this paradox is to create a strong organizational culture with values that

empower employees to apply their individual potential to the conduct of their work. In this way, fragile systems release the employee energy necessary to compete in today's business environment.

Endnotes

1 See William E. Sheeline, 'Avoiding Growth's Perils', *Fortune*, August 13, 1990, 55.

2 'Japan's Gung-Ho U.S. Car Plants', *Fortune*, January 30, 1989, 78–85.

3 For a review of the person-situation controversy, see Larry James and Terrence Mitchell (Eds) of several articles in a special forum. 'Situational versus Dispositional Factors: Competing Explanations of Behavior', *Academy of Management Review*, 1988, *14*. In particular, see Jennifer Chatman, 'Improving Interactional Organizational Research' in that issue for implications of the controversy for selection and training.

4 See, for example, Terrence Mitchell 'Organizational Behavior' in M. R. Rosenzweig and L. W. Porter (Eds), *Annual Review of Psychology*, Vol 30 (Palo Alto, CA: Annual Reviews 1979); Howard Weiss and Seymour Adler, 'Personality and Organizational Behavior' in Barry Staw and Larry Cummings (Eds), *Research in Organizational Behavior, Vol 6* (Greenwich, CT-JAI Press, 1984).

5 See, for example, Chatman, op cit., Weiss and Adler, op cit.

6 A number of research reviews have documented the low validity of the employment interview. For example, see R. D. Arvey and J. E. Campion, 'The Employment Interview: A Summary and Review of Recent Research', *Personnel Psychology*, 1982, *35*, 281–322. For an overview of higher validity coefficients reported for appropriately designed, or structured, interviews, see Neal Schmitt and I. Robertson, 'Personnel Selection', in M. R. Rosenzweig and L. W. Porter (Eds), *Annual Review of Psychology*, Vol 41 (Palo Alto, CA: Annual Reviews Inc., 1990).

7 See, for example, Chatman, op cit.; Weiss and Adler, op cit.

8 John P. MacDuffie, 'The Japanese Auto Transplants: Challenges to Conventional Wisdom', *ILR Report*, Fall, 1988, 26 (1), 12–18; Huaro Shlmada and John Paul MacDuffie, 'Industrial Relations and Humanware', Japanese Investments in Auto Manufacturing in the United States'. Working Paper, Sloan School of Management, MIT, 1987.

9   For an overview of the steps in the classic selection model, see Benjamin Schneider and Neal Schmitt, *Staffing Organizations*, Second Edition (USA: Scott Foresman and Company, 1986). The goal of the traditional selection model is to produce a fit between the critical requirements of a particular job and the job-relevant KSAs of job applicants. This approach consists of three steps. First, a job analysis is conducted to determine the critical requirements of a particular job. Second, on the basis of the job analysis the analyst infers the knowledge, skills and abilities that are needed for the job. Finally, selection tests are chosen or developed that are intended to indicate the degree to which job applicants possess the KSAs needed on the job. The tests are administered to all applicants. The tests are validated by collecting data on criteria measures, such as job performance, and then examining the correlation between applicant test scores and criteria measures. A statistically significant and reasonably high correlation indicates that the test is capable of discriminating appropriately between employees who do well and those who do poorly on the criteria measures.

10 See John P. Wanous, *Organizational Entry: Recruitment Selection, and Socialization of Newcomers* (Reading, Mass: Addison-Wesley Publishing Company, 1980) for a more complete discussion of these two types of fit and how both the organization and individual approach them.

11 For more detail on job analysis techniques, see Schneider and Schmitt, op cit.

12 Caren Siehl and Joanne Martin, 'Measuring Organizational Culture: Mixing Qualitative and Quantitative Methods', in M.O. Jones et al. (Eds) *Inside Organizations* (Beverly Hills: Sage 1988).

13 Chatman, op cit.

14 Michael Tushman and David Nadler, 'A Diagnostic Model of Organizational Behavior'.

15 As examples of this thinking, see Barry M. Staw, Nancy E. Bell and John A. Clausen, 'The Dispositional Approach to Job Attitudes; A Lifetime Longitudinal Test', *Administrative Science Quarterly*, 1986, *31*, 56–77; Weiss and Adler, op cit.

16 Staw, et al., op cit.

17 'Doug Bray: You've Got to Pick Your Winners', *Training*, February, 1988, 79–81.

18 Richard Pascale, 'Fitting New Employees into the Company Culture', *Fortune*, May 28, 1984, 28–42.

19 For an overview of this issue, see Schneider and Schmitt, op cit.

20 Brian Dumaine, 'The New Art of Hiring Smart', *Fortune*, August 17, 1987, 78–81.

21 Wilton Woods, 'Personality Tests Are Back', *Fortune*, March 30, 1987, 74–82.

22 For a review of the track record of validation studies of personality tests as selection tools, versus other measures, see R. M. Guion and R. F. Gottier, 'Validity of Personality Measures in Personnel Selection', *Personnel Psychology*, 1965, *18*, 49–65; R. M. Guion, 'Changing Views for Personnel Selection Research', *Personnel Psychology*, 1987, *40*, 199–213; Schmitt and Robertson, op cit; and N. Schmitt, R. Gooding, R. Noe and M. Kirsch, 'Meta-Analysis of Validity Studies Published Between 1964 and 1982 and the Investigation of Study Characteristics', *Personnel Psychology*, 1984, 37, 407–422.

23 Schneider and Schmitt, op cit., 353.

24 See Wanous, op cit.

25 'Japan's Gung-Ho U. S. Car Plants', op cit.

26 Richard E. Walton, 'From Control to Commitment in the Workplace', *Harvard Business Review*, March–April 1985, 76–84.

27 Edward E. Lawler III, *High-Involvement Management* (San Francisco: Jossey-Bass, 1986); S. Mohrman, G. Ledford, Jr., E. E. Lawler III and A. M. Mohrman, 'Quality of Work-Life and Employment Involvement', in C. L. Cooper and I. Robertson (Eds), *International Review of Industrial and Organizational Psychology* (New York: John Wiley & Sons, 1986).

28 The case description is an illustrative overview of the steps and some techniques associated with hiring for the organization, not the job. Readers may contact the authors if they are interested in more details about the hiring process, such as assessment methods, validation strategies, scoring of simulations, and so on.

29 D. N. Jackson, *Personality Research Form Manual*, 3rd Ed. (Port Huron, MI: Research Psychologists Press, 1984). For a review of the PRF, see J. S. Wiggins, *Personality and Prediction: Principles of Personality and Assessment* (Reading, MA: Addison-Wesely, 1973).

30 The significant correlation between scores in the composite growth needs scale and performance in the pre-employment training program was 0.22 (and it was 0.27 after correction for unreliability in the criterion).

This compares favorably to the average validity of 0.15 found in a recent review of research using personality measures (N. Schmitt, R. Z. Gooding, R. A. Noe, & M. Kirsch, 'Meta-Analysis of Validity Studies published between 1964 and 1982 and the investigation of study characteristics', *Personnel Psychology*, 1984, *37*, 407–422). In addition, scores on the social needs measure were significantly correlated (.16) with anticipated satisfaction.

31 See Wanous, op cit, for a discussion of this proposition.

32 For a review of the research findings, see S. C. Premack and J. P. Wanous, 'A Meta-Analysis of Realistic Job Preview Experiments', *Journal of Applied Psychology*, 1985, *70*, 706–719.

33 R. A. Guzzo, R. D. Jotte, & R. A. Katzell, 'The Effects of Psychologically Based Intervention Programs on Worker Productivity: A Meta-Analysis', *Personnel Psychology*, 1985, *38*, 275–291: G. E. Ledford, Jr., T. G. Cummings and R. W. Wright, 'The Structure and Effectiveness of High Involvement Organizations', Working Paper, Center for Effective Organizations, University of Southern California, 1991.

34 Premack and Wanous, op cit.

35 See Chatman, op cit.

36 Ledford et al.

37 William J. Hampton, 'How Does Japan Inc. Pick Its American Workers?' *Business Week*, October 3, 1988, 84–88.

38 For a discussion of these issues, see J. L. Holland, 'Some Speculation About the Investigation of Person–Environment Transactions', *Journal of Vocational Behavior*, 1987, 31, 337–340; R. H. Moos, 'Person–Environment Congruence in Work, School and Health-Care Settings', *Journal of Vocational Behavior*, 1987, *31*, 231–247; and J. B. Rounds, R. V. Davis and L. H. Lofquist, 'Measurement of Person–Environment Fit and Prediction of Satisfaction in the Theory of Work Adjustment', *Journal of Vocational Behavior*, 1987, *31*, 297–318.

39 E. E. Lawler III, 'Achieving Competitiveness by Creating New Organizational Cultures and Structures' in D. B. Dishman and C. Cherniss (Eds.) *The Human Side of Corporate Competitiveness* (Newbury Park: Sage Publications), 69–101.

40 *Assessment Strategies for Selection* (Pittsburgh, PA: Development Dimension International, 1990).

41 D. R. Denison, *Corporate Culture and Organizational Effectiveness* (New York: Wiley, 1990).

EXERCISE 3 TESTING YOUR ASSUMPTIONS ABOUT PEOPLE

Source: Adapted from Fritz, R. (1988). *Rate Your Executive Potential.* New York: John Wiley and Sons, pp. 61–64.

To enable you to examine your assumptions about people, their work and how to get them to do the work that is expected, the following test will be helpful. Simply check the appropriate column beside each of the 15 statements that are presented. Read each statement and *immediately* place a tick in one of the four columns. Because the test is designed to measure your assumptions, not your carefully reasoned responses, answer at once, not after 'qualifying' the statement or looking for the 'right' answer. There are no right or wrong answers and the 'best' answer is the one that describes what you actually believe; any other answer will only cloud the picture this test is trying to obtain — your instinctive pattern of behaviour.

Think of 'people' in a rather general sense, not as specific individuals. You are trying to analyse your general pattern of behaviour — the image that you project to others. It should take you no more than 3 to 4 minutes to complete the quiz.

	Strongly Disagree	Disagree	Agree	Strongly Agree

1. Almost all people could improve their job performance considerably if they really wanted to. _____ _____ _____ _____

2. It is unrealistic to expect people to show the same enthusiasm for their work as for their leisure activities. _____ _____ _____ _____

3. Even when given encouragement by the boss, very few people show the desire to improve themselves on the job. _____ _____ _____ _____

4. If you give people enough money, they are less likely to worry about such intangibles as status or recognition. _____ _____ _____ _____

5. When people talk about wanting jobs that are more responsible, they usually mean that they want more money and status. _____ _____ _____ _____

6. Because most people don't like to make decisions on their own, it is hard to get them to assume responsibility. _____ _____ _____ _____

7. Being tough with people usually will get them to do what you want. _____ _____ _____ _____

8. A good way to get people to do more work is to crack down on them once in a while. _____ _____ _____ _____

9. It weakens people's prestige whenever they have to admit that a subordinate has been right and they have been wrong. _____ _____ _____ _____

10. The most effective manager is one who gets the results expected, regardless of the methods used in handling people. _____ _____ _____ _____

11. It is too much to expect that people will try to do a good job without being prodded by their boss. _____ _____ _____ _____

12. The boss who expects people to set their own standards for performance probably will find that they don't set them very high. _____ _____ _____ _____

13. If people don't use much imagination and ingenuity on the job, it's probably because relatively few have much of either.

_____ _____ _____ _____

14. One problem in asking for the ideas of subordinates is that their perspective is too limited for their suggestions to be of much practical value.

_____ _____ _____ _____

15. It is only human nature for people to try to do as little work as they can get away with.

_____ _____ _____ _____

Total for each column

_____ _____ _____ _____

'Weighting' each column

× 1 _____ × 2 _____ × 3 _____ × 4 _____

Total score

_____

Exhibit 3.9 Your leadership style

Style	60 A	Autocratic	33–30 M	Developmental	15 D
Often called ...		Boss		Leader	
Motivates from ...		Fear		Inspiration	
Supervision is ...		Close		General	

To score the test

Total the number of marks in each column. Obviously, unless you have skipped a question, the four totals should add up to 15. Now 'weight' your answer by multiplying each column total by the figure given (that is, the total in the _strongly disagree_ column × 1, the _disagree_ column total × 2, the _agree_ column total × 3 and the _strongly agree_ column × 4). Enter the answers at the ends of the appropriate columns.

Add together the four weighted column totals to obtain your total score. The total should fall somewhere between 15 and 60. The theory is that your assumptions about people and their work leads you to develop a certain style of management.

Now determine where your score would fall in Exhibit 3.9, place an 'X' along the continuum and circle it.

The range from A to D at the top of the table provides for all possible sets of assumptions regarding people and their work. The segment from A to M represents various degrees of autocratic or authoritarian management styles, while the segment from M to D covers different levels of democratic or developmental styles of management.

CASE 3 BOB KNOWLTON

Source: This case was prepared by Professor Alex Bavelas for courses in management of research and development conducted at the School of Industrial Management, Massachusetts Institute of Technology, Cambridge, and is used with his permission.

Bob Knowlton was sitting alone in the conference room of the laboratory. The rest of the group had gone. One of the secretaries had stopped and talked for a while about her husband's coming induction into the army and had finally left. Bob, alone in the laboratory, slid a little further down in his chair, looking with satisfaction at the results of the first test run of the new photon unit.

He liked to stay after the others had gone. His appointment as project head was still new enough to give him a deep sense of pleasure. His eyes were on the graphs before him, but in his mind he could hear Dr Jerrold, the project head, saying again, 'There's one thing about this place you can bank on. The sky is the limit for a man who can produce!' Knowlton felt again the tingle of happiness and embarrassment. Well, dammit, he said to himself, he had produced. He wasn't kidding anybody. He had come to the Simmons Laboratories 2 years ago. During a routine testing of some rejected Clanson components, he had stumbled on the idea of the photon correlator, and the rest just happened. Jerrold had been enthusiastic: A separate project had been set up for further research and development of the device, and he had got the job of running it. The whole sequence of events still seemed a little miraculous to Knowlton.

He shrugged out of the reverie and bent determinedly over the sheets when he heard someone come into the room behind him. He looked up expectantly; Jerrold often stayed late himself and now and then dropped in for a chat. This always made the day's end especially pleasant for Bob. It wasn't Jerrold. The man who had come in was a stranger. He was tall, thin and rather dark. He wore steel-rimmed glasses and had a very wide leather belt with a large brass buckle. Lucy remarked later that it was the kind of belt the Pilgrims must have worn.

The stranger smiled and introduced himself. 'I'm Simon Fester. Are you Bob Knowlton?' Bob said yes, and they shook hands. 'Doctor Jerrold said I might find you in. We were talking about your work and I'm very much interested in what you are doing.' Bob waved to a chair.

Fester didn't seem to belong in any of the standard categories of visitors: customer, visiting firefighter, stockholder. Bob pointed to the sheets on the table. 'There are the preliminary results of a test we're running. We've got a new gadget by the tail and we're trying to understand it. It's not finished, but I can show you the section we're testing.'

He stood up, but Fester was deep in the graphs. After a moment, he looked up with an odd grin. 'These look like plots of a Jennings surface. I've been playing around with some autocorrelation functions of surfaces — you know that stuff.' Bob, who had no idea what he was referring to, grinned back and nodded, and immediately felt uncomfortable. 'Let me show you the monster,' he said, and led the way to the workroom.

After Fester left, Knowlton slowly put the graphs away, feeling vaguely annoyed. Then, as if he had made a decision, he quickly locked up and took the long way out so that he would pass Jerrold's office. But the office was locked. Knowlton wondered whether Jerrold and Fester had left together.

The next morning, Knowlton dropped into Jerrold's office, mentioned that he had talked with Fester and asked who he was.

'Sit down for a minute,' Jerrold said. 'I want to talk to you about him. What do you think of him?' Knowlton replied truthfully that he thought Fester was very bright and probably very competent. Jerrold looked pleased.

'We're taking him on,' he said. 'He's had a very good background in a number of laboratories and he seems to have ideas about the problems we're tackling here.' Knowlton nodded in agreement, instantly wishing that Fester would not be placed with him.

'I don't know yet where he will finally land,' Jerrold continued, 'but he seems interested in what you are doing. I thought he might spend a little time with you by way of getting started.' Knowlton nodded thoughtfully. 'If his interest in your work continues, you can add him to your group.'

'Well, he seemed to have some good ideas even without knowing exactly what we are doing,' Knowlton answered. 'I hope he stays; we'd be glad to have him.'

Knowlton walked back to the lab with mixed feelings. He told himself that Fester would be good for the group. He was no dunce; he'd produce. Knowlton thought again of Jerrold's promise when he had promoted him — 'the man who produces gets ahead in this outfit.' The words seemed to carry the overtones of a threat now.

That day Fester didn't appear until midafternoon. He explained that he had had a long lunch with Jerrold, discussing his place in the lab. 'Yes,' said Knowlton, 'I talked with Jerry this morning about it and we both thought you might work with us for a while.'

Fester smiled in the same knowing way that he had smiled when he mentioned the Jennings surfaces. 'I'd like to,' he said.

Knowlton introduced Fester to the other members of the lab. Fester and Link, the mathematician of the group, hit it off well together and spent the rest of the afternoon discussing a method of analysis of patterns that Link had been worrying over the last month.

It was 6:30 when Knowlton finally left the lab that night. He had waited almost eagerly for the end of the day to come — when they would all be gone and he could sit in the quiet rooms, relax, and think it over. 'Think what over?' he asked himself. He didn't know. Shortly after 5 p.m. they had almost all gone except Fester and what followed was almost a duel. Knowlton was annoyed that he was being cheated out of his quiet period and finally resentfully determined that Fester should leave first.

Fester was sitting at the conference table reading, and Knowlton was sitting at his desk in the little glass enclosed cubby he used during the day when he needed to be undisturbed. Fester had got the last year's progress reports out and was studying them carefully. The time dragged. Knowlton doodled on a pad, the tension growing inside him. What the hell did Fester think he was going to find in the reports?

Knowlton finally gave up and they left the lab together. Fester took several of the reports with him to study in the evening. Knowlton asked him if he thought the reports gave a clear picture of the lab's activities.

'They're excellent,' Fester answered with obvious sincerity. 'They're not only good reports; what they report is damn good, too!' Knowlton was surprised at the relief he felt and grew almost jovial as he said good-night.

Driving home, Knowlton felt more optimistic about Fester's presence in the lab. He had never fully understood the analysis that Link was attempting. If there was anything wrong with Link's approach, Fester would probably spot it. 'And if I'm any judge,' he murmured, 'he won't be especially diplomatic about it.'

He described Fester to his wife, who was amused by the broad leather belt and brass buckle.

'It's the kind of belt that Pilgrims must have worn,' she laughed.

'I'm not worried about how he holds his pants up,' he laughed with her. 'I'm afraid that he's the kind that just has to make like a genius twice each day. And that can be pretty rough on the group.'

Knowlton had been asleep for several hours when he was jerked awake by the telephone. He realised it had rung several times. He swung off the bed muttering about damn fools and telephones. It was Fester. Without any excuses, apparently oblivious of the time, he plunged into an excited recital of how Link's patterning problem could be solved.

Knowlton covered the mouthpiece to answer his wife's stage-whispered 'Who is it?' 'It's the genius,' relied Knowlton.

Fester, completely ignoring the fact that it was 2:00 in the morning, proceeded in a very excited way to start in the middle of an explanation of a completely new approach to certain of the photon lab problems that he had stumbled on while analysing past experiments. Knowlton managed to put some enthusiasm in his own voice and stood there, half-dazed and very uncomfortable, listening to Fester talk endlessly about what he had discovered. It was probably not only a new approach but also an analysis which showed the inherent weakness of the previous experiment and how experimentation along that line would certainly have been inconclusive. The following day

Knowlton spent the entire morning with Fester and Link, the mathematician, the customary morning meeting of Bob's group having been called off so that Fester's work of the previous night could be gone over intensively. Fester was very anxious that this be done, and Knowlton was not too unhappy to call the meeting off for reasons of his own.

For the next several days Fester sat in the back office that had been turned over to him and did nothing but read the progress reports of the work that had been done in the past 6 months. Knowlton caught himself feeling apprehensive about the reaction that Fester might have to some of his work. He was a little surprised at his own feelings. He had always been proud — although he had put on a convincingly modest face — of the way in which new ground in the study of photon measuring devices had been broken in his group. Now he wasn't sure and it seemed to him that Fester might easily show that the line of research they had been following was unsound or even unimaginative.

The next morning (as was the custom), the members of the lab, including the girls, sat around a conference table. Bob always prided himself on the fact that the work of the lab was guided and evaluated by the group as a whole and he was fond of repeating that it was not a waste of time to include secretaries in such meetings. Often, what started out as a boring recital of fundamental assumptions to a naive listener, uncovered new ways of regarding these assumptions that would not have occurred to the researcher who had long ago accepted them as a necessary basis for his or her work.

These group meetings also served Bob in another sense. He admitted to himself that he would have felt far less secure if he had had to direct the work out of his own mind, so to speak. With the group meeting as the principle of leadership, it was always possible to justify the exploration of blind alleys because of the general educative effect on the team. Fester was there; Lucy and Martha were there; Link was sitting next to Fester, their conversation concerning Link's mathematical study apparently continuing from yesterday. The other members, Bob Davenport, George Thurlow and Arthur Oliver, were waiting quietly.

Knowlton, for reasons that he didn't quite understand, proposed for discussion this morning a problem that all of them had spent a great deal of time on previously with the conclusion that a solution was impossible, that there was no feasible way of treating it in an experimental fashion. When Knowlton proposed the problem, Davenport remarked that there was hardly any use going over it again, and that he was satisfied that there was no way of approaching the problem with the equipment and the physical capacities of the lab.

This statement had the effect of a shot of adrenalin on Fester. He said he would like to know what the problem was in detail and, walking to the blackboard, began setting down the 'factors' as various members of the group began discussing the problem and simultaneously listing the reasons why it had been abandoned.

Very early in the description of the problem it was evident that Fester was going to disagree about the impossibility of attacking it. The group realised this, and finally the descriptive materials and their recounting of the reasoning that had led to its abandonment dwindled away. Fester began his statement which, as it proceeded, might well have been prepared the previous night although Knowlton knew this was impossible. He couldn't help being impressed with the organised and logical way that Fester was presenting ideas that must have occurred to him only a few minutes before.

Fester had some things to say, however, which left Knowlton with a mixture of annoyance, irritation and, at the same time, a rather smug feeling of superiority over Fester in at least one area. Fester was of the opinion that the way that the problem had been analysed was really typical of group thinking and with an air of sophistication which made it difficult for a listener to dissent, he proceeded to comment on the American emphasis on team ideas, satirically describing the ways in which they led to a 'high level of mediocrity'.

During this time Knowlton observed that Link stared studiously at the floor, and he was very conscious of George Thurlow's and Bob Davenport's glances towards him at several points of Fester's little speech. Inwardly, Knowlton couldn't help feeling that this was one point at least in which Fester was off on the wrong foot. The whole lab, following Jerry's lead, talked if not practised the theory of small research teams as the basic organisation for effective research. Fester insisted that the problem could be approached and that he would like to study it for a while himself.

Knowlton ended the morning session by remarking that the meetings would continue and that the very fact that a supposedly insoluble experimental problem was now going to get another chance was another indication of the value of such meetings. Fester immediately remarked that he was not at all averse to meetings for the purpose of informing the group of the progress of its members — that the point he wanted to make was that creative advances were seldom accomplished in such meetings, that they were made by the individual 'living with' the problem closely and continuously, a sort of personal relationship to it.

Knowlton went on to say to Fester that he was very glad that Fester had raised these points and that he was sure the group would profit by re-examining the basis on which they had been operating. Knowlton agreed that individual effort was probably the basis for making the major advances, but that he considered the group meetings useful primarily because of the effect they had on keeping the group together and on helping the weaker members of the group keep up with the ones who were able to advance more easily and quickly in the analysis of problems.

It was clear as days went by and meetings continued that Fester came to enjoy them because of the pattern which the meetings assumed. It became typical for Fester to hold forth and it was unquestionably clear that he was more brilliant, better prepared on the various subjects which were germane to the problem being studied and, more capable of going ahead than anyone there. Knowlton grew increasingly disturbed as he realised that his leadership of the group had been, in fact, taken over.

Whenever the subject of Fester was mentioned in occasional meetings with Dr Jerrold, Knowlton would comment only on the ability and obvious capacity for work that Fester had. Somehow he never felt that he could mention his own discomforts, not only because

they revealed a weakness on his own part but also because it was quite clear that Jerrold himself was considerably impressed with Fester's work and with the contacts he had with him outside the photon laboratory.

Knowlton now began to feel that perhaps the intellectual advantages that Fester had brought to the group did not quite compensate for what he felt were evidences of a breakdown in the cooperative spirit he had seen in the group before Fester's coming. More and more of the morning meetings were skipped. Fester's opinion concerning the abilities of others of the group, with the exception of Link, was obviously low. At times during morning meetings or in smaller discussions he had been on the point of rudeness, refusing to pursue an argument when he claimed it was based on another person's ignorance of the facts involved. His impatience of others led him to also make similar remarks to Dr Jerrold. Knowlton inferred this from a conversation with Jerrold in which Jerrold asked whether Davenport and Oliver were going to be continued on; and his failure to mention Link, the mathematician, led Knowlton to feel that this was the result of private conversations between Fester and Jerrold.

It was not difficult for Knowlton to make a quite convincing case on whether the brilliance of Fester was sufficient recompense for the beginning of this breaking up of the group. He took the opportunity to speak privately with Davenport and with Oliver, and it was quite clear that both of them were uncomfortable because of Fester. Knowlton didn't press the discussion beyond the point of hearing them in one way or another say that they did feel awkward and that it was sometimes difficult for them to understand the arguments he advanced, but often embarrassing to ask him to fill in the background on which his arguments were based. Knowlton did not interview Link in this manner.

About 6 months after Fester's coming into the photon lab, a meeting was scheduled in which the sponsors of the research were coming to get some idea of the work and its progress. It was customary at these meetings for project heads to present the research being conducted in their groups. The members of each group were invited to other meetings which were held later in the day and open to all, but the special meetings were usually made up only of project heads, the head of the laboratory and the sponsors.

As the time for the special meeting approached, it seemed to Knowlton that he must avoid the presentation at all cost. His reasons for this were that he could not trust himself to present the ideas and work that Fester had advanced because of his apprehension as to whether he could present them in sufficient detail and answer such questions about them as might be asked. On the other hand, he did not feel he could ignore these newer lines of work and present only the material that he had done or that had been started before Fester's arrival. He felt also that it would not be beyond Fester at all, in his blunt and undiplomatic way — if he were present at the meeting, that is — to make comments on his [Knowlton's] presentation and reveal Knowlton's inadequacy. It also seemed quite clear that it would not be easy to keep Fester from attending the meeting, even though he was not on the administrative level of those invited.

Knowlton found an opportunity to speak to Jerrold and raised the question. He remarked to Jerrold that with the meetings coming up and with the interest in the work and with the contributions that Fester had been making, he would probably like to come to these meetings, but there was a question of the feelings of the others in the group if Fester alone were invited. Jerrold passed this over very lightly by saying that he didn't think the group would fail to understand Fester's rather different position and that he thought that Fester by all means should be invited. Knowlton immediately said he had thought so, too; that Fester should present the work because much of it was work he had done; and as Knowlton put it, that this would be a nice way to recognise Fester's contributions and to reward him, as he was eager to be recognised as a productive member of the lab. Jerrold agreed and so the matter was decided.

Fester's presentation was very successful and in some ways dominated the meeting. He attracted the interest and attention of many of those who had come, and a long discussion followed his presentation. Later in the evening — with the entire laboratory staff present — in the cocktail period before the dinner, a little circle of people formed about Fester. One of them was Jerrold himself, and a lively discussion took place concerning the application of Fester's theory. All of this disturbed Knowlton, and his reaction and behaviour were characteristic. He joined the circle, praised Fester to Jerrold and to others, and remarked on the brilliance of the work.

Knowlton, without consulting anyone, began at this time to take some interest in the possibility of a job elsewhere. After a few weeks he found that a new laboratory of considerable size was being organised in a nearby city and that the kind of training he had would enable him to get a project-head job equivalent to the one he had at the lab with slightly more money.

He immediately accepted it and notified Jerrold by a letter, which he posted on a Friday night to Jerrold's home. The letter was quite brief and Jerrold was stunned. The letter merely said that he had found a better position; that there were personal reasons why he didn't want to appear at the lab any more; that he would be glad to come back at a later time from where he would be, some 60 kilometres away, to assist if there was any mix-up at all in the past work; that he felt sure that Fester could, however, supply any leadership that was required for the group; and that his decision to leave so suddenly was based on some personal problems — he hinted at problems of health in his family, his mother and father. All of this was fictitious, of course. Jerrold took it at face value but still felt that this was very strange behaviour and quite unaccountable, for he had always felt his relationship with Knowlton had been warm and that Knowlton was satisfied and, as a matter of fact, quite happy and productive.

Jerrold was considerably disturbed, because he had already decided to place Fester in charge of another project that was going to be set up very soon. He had been wondering how to explain this to Knowlton, in view of the obvious help Knowlton was getting from Fester and the high regard in which he held him. Jerrold had, as a matter of fact, considered the possibility that Knowlton could add to his staff another person with the kind of background and training that had been unique in Fester and had proved so valuable.

Jerrold did not make any attempt to meet Knowlton. In a way, he felt aggrieved about the whole thing. Fester, too, was surprised at the suddenness of Knowlton's departure and when Jerrold, in talking to him, asked him whether he had reasons to prefer to stay with the photon group instead of the project for the Air Force which was being organised, he chose the Air Force project and went on to that job the following week. The photon lab was hard hit. The leadership of the lab was given to Link with the understanding that this would be temporary until someone could come in to take over.

Case questions

- What was the major problem that faced Knowlton?
- What ego-defence mechanisms did Knowlton personally use?
- Could Rotter's notion of locus of control be used to analyse Bob Knowlton's situation?

MOTIVATION: AN INDIVIDUAL PERSPECTIVE

Learning objectives

- Describe *the three distinct components of motivation.*

- Distinguish *between three approaches to motivation.*

- Identify *the need levels in Maslow's hierarchy.*

- Describe *four patterns of intrinsic motivation.*

- Define *the key terms in expectancy theory.*

- Identify *the key steps in goal setting.*

- Define *the key components of control theory.*

- Describe *resource-allocation approaches to motivation.*

- Describe *the concept of the psychological contract.*

Chapter

No one questions the central role motivation plays in shaping behaviour and, specifically, in influencing work performance in organisations. Nonetheless, as important as motivation is, it is not the only factor that determines performance. Over the years a variety of other variables thought to play an important role in performance have been suggested. These include ability, instinct and aspiration levels, as well as personal factors such as age, education and family background.

One way of conceptualising the various determinants of performance is illustrated in Exhibit 4.1. As can be seen from this exhibit, job performance may be viewed as a function of the *capacity* to perform, the *opportunity* to perform, and the *willingness* to perform. The capacity to perform relates to the degree to which an individual possesses task-relevant skills, abilities, knowledge and experiences. Unless an employee knows what is supposed to be done and how to do it, high levels of job performance are not possible. Having the opportunity to perform is also a critical ingredient in the performance recipe. An employee assembling a product in a manufacturing plant who constantly experiences equipment failures and a shortage of needed components is clearly going to be unable to perform at the same level as a worker who does not encounter those difficulties. Similarly, an accountant who must make entries in a hand ledger does not have the same opportunity to perform as one who has access to an electronic spreadsheet. Sometimes employees may lack the opportunity to perform not because of poor equipment or outdated technology, but because of poor decisions and outdated attitudes.

The third factor, willingness to perform, relates to the degree to which an individual both desires and is willing to exert effort towards attaining job performance. It is, in other words, motivation and it is what this chapter is about. No combination of capacity and opportunity will result in high performance in the absence of some level of motivation or willingness to perform.

Exhibit 4.1
Determinants of performance

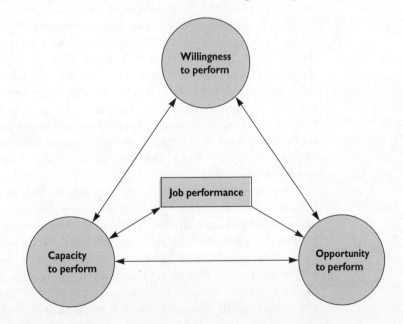

Source: Adapted from Blumberg, M. & Pringle, C. (1982). The missing opportunity in organizational research: Some implications for a theory of work performance, *Academy of Management Review*, October, p. 565.

From a managerial perspective, it is important to realise that the presence of motivation *per se*, coupled with a capacity and opportunity to perform, does not ensure high performance levels. It is a rare manager who has not at some point concluded that performance would be much higher if 'I could just get my people motivated'. In all likelihood, those individuals are already motivated; what that manager really wants is motivation that results in more or different kinds of behaviours. To understand this distinction it is helpful to think of motivation as being made up of at least three distinct components: direction, intensity and persistence.

Direction relates to what an individual chooses to do when presented with a number of possible alternatives. When faced with the task of completing a report requested by management, for example, an employee may choose to direct effort towards completing the report or towards solving the crossword puzzle in the morning newspaper (or any number of other possible activities). Regardless of which option is selected, the employee is motivated. If the employee selects the first alternative, the direction of his or her motivation is consistent with that desired by management. If the employee chooses the second alternative, the direction is counter to that desired by management, but the employee is nonetheless motivated.

The *intensity* component of motivation refers to the strength of the response once the choice (direction) is made. Using the previous example, the employee may choose the proper direction (working on the report) but respond with very little intensity. Intensity, in this sense, is synonymous with effort. Two people may focus their behaviour in the same direction, but one may perform better because he or she exerts more effort than the other. An attribute frequently used to describe an outstanding professional athlete is intensity. When coaches speak of an athlete as playing with a great deal of intensity, they are describing the amount of effort the player invests in the game.

Finally, *persistence* is an important component of motivation. Persistence refers to the staying power of behaviour or how long a person will continue to devote effort. Some people will focus their behaviour in the appropriate direction and do so with a high degree of intensity but only for a short period of time. Individuals who tackle a task enthusiastically but quickly tire of it, or burn out and seldom complete it, lack this critical attribute in their motivated behaviour. Thus, the manager's real challenge is not so much one of increasing motivation *per se* but of creating an environment wherein employee motivation is channelled in the right direction at an appropriate level of intensity and continues over time.

Motivation is an explanatory concept we use to make sense out of the behaviours we observe. It is important to note that motivation is inferred. Instead of measuring it directly, we manipulate certain conditions and observe how behaviour changes.[1] From the changes we observe, we improve our understanding of the underlying motivation. You assumed that your best friend had made a quick stop to eat lunch when you saw his car parked outside a fast-food restaurant. But your inference was not correct because your friend actually was talking to the manager about a weekend job. The lesson is clear: we must always be cautious when making motivational inferences. As more and more information is accumulated, however, our inferences become more accurate because we can eliminate alternative explanations.

THE STARTING POINT: THE INDIVIDUAL

Most managers must motivate a diverse and, in many respects, unpredictable group of people. The diversity results in different behavioural patterns that are in some manner related to needs and goals.

Needs refer to deficiencies an individual experiences at a particular time. The deficiencies may be physiological (e.g. a need for food), psychological (e.g. a need for self-esteem), or sociological (e.g. a need for social interaction). Needs are viewed as energisers or triggers of behavioural responses. The implication is that when need deficiencies are present, the individual is more susceptible to a manager's motivational efforts.The importance of goals in any discussion of motivation is apparent. The motivational process, as interpreted by most theorists, is goal directed. The goals or outcomes that an employee seeks are viewed as forces that attract the person. The accomplishment of desirable goals can result in a significant reduction in need deficiencies.

Exhibit 4.2
The motivational process: An initial model

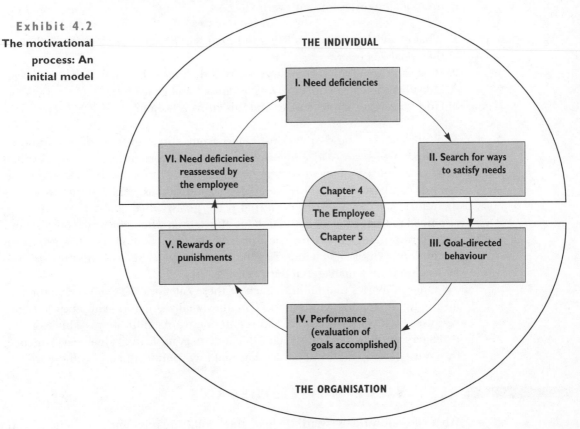

As illustrated in Exhibit 4.2, people seek to reduce various need deficiencies. Need deficiencies trigger a search process for ways to reduce the tension caused by the deficiencies. A course of action is selected and goal-directed (outcome-directed) behaviour occurs. After a period of time, managers assess that behaviour, and the performance evaluation results in some type of reward or punishment. Such outcomes are weighed by the person, and the need deficiencies are reassessed. This, in turn, triggers the process and the circular pattern is started once again.

MOTIVATION THEORIES: A CLASSIFICATION SYSTEM

This framework implies that managers face a number of tasks if they are to motivate employees: to identify the employees' needs, to establish clear links between performance and need fulfilment, and to reward performance. In this chapter, we will consider a range of theories that are concerned with identifying individual needs, and explaining the behaviour–outcome relationship. In Chapter 5, we will consider in more detail strategies for maximising performance, such as the design of reward systems.

What do organisations need to consider if they want to successfully motivate individuals? We have seen that motivation is made up of three components: direction, intensity and persistence. We have also seen that individuals join organisations to meet particular goals and that their long-term behaviour is determined by the need to meet those goals, as well as how organisations respond to those efforts. This suggests that there are three questions that motivational theories must answer:

1. What needs do individuals bring to organisations and how does this influence their goals?
2. How can organisations structure tasks and rewards in a way that encourages individuals to exert effort towards organisational goals?
3. How can organisations ensure that this effort is lasting?

The answers to these questions come from three groups of motivational theories.[2] *Need–motive–value* theories help us to understand different individual needs that must be met in organisations. *Cognitive-choice* theories examine how rewards can be used to influence goals that individuals work towards, as well as the effort that they exert in achieving those goals. Once goals are selected, we also need to understand what maintains effort, even when goals are complex and long term: *self-regulation* theories provide an explanation of this aspect of motivation. Exhibit 4.3 summarises the basic characteristics of these theories of motivation from a managerial perspective.

Often, theories that fall into each of these categories are offered as the one means for increasing motivation. Can they really do this? The answer is no, because each tackles a different component of motivation. Therefore, if managers want to motivate their staff and maximise individual performance, they must develop motivational systems that incorporate aspects of all theories.

NEED–VALUE–MOTIVE THEORIES

What do individuals want? When they join organisations, are they more concerned with pay and job security, or with developing and expanding their skills? When you came to university, was it because you hoped that a degree would guarantee you a job, or because you enjoy learning new things? Need–value–motive theories provide an explanation of how individuals *direct* effort by identifying the needs that they are trying to meet. The focus of these theories has been to identify and describe those factors within the individual that direct, sustain or stop behaviour. In this section, we will consider two such theories: need fulfilment and intrinsic motivation.

Exhibit 4.3 **Managerial applications**

Theoretical Base	Theoretical Explanation	Examples	Managerial Application
Need–Value–Motive	Factors within the person that energise and direct behaviour. Deals with how individuals *direct* effort.	Needs hierarchy Intrinsic motivation	Managers need to be aware of differences in needs, desires and goals.
Cognitive choice	Factors in the environment that energise behaviours. Deals with factors that determine *intensity*.	Expectancy theory	Managers need to understand the factors that affect individual decisions to work hard, as well as how individuals make choices based on preferences.
Self-regulation	Factors within the person that sustain or stop behaviour. Deals with factors that result in *persistence*.	Goal–setting theory Control theory	Managers need to understand the factors that encourage individuals to work towards long-term and complex goals. Making goals clear and specific, and providing timely feedback are important strategies.

Need fulfilment

Maslow, Alderfer and Herzberg[3] have all developed theories that fit into this category. While there are some differences across these theories in terms of how they group needs and the outcomes that they predict, they also share a number of concepts. In particular, they identify three broad categories of needs that individuals strive to meet: those related to *physical* survival, those more concerned with friendship and *social* needs, and those related to the acknowledgement and further *development* of individual skills. We will discuss more fully two of these theories: Maslow's needs hierarchy and Herzberg's two-factor theory. Interestingly, as you can see in our Local Encounter, men and women differ in the needs that they bring to the organisation.

Maslow's needs hierarchy

The crux of Maslow's theory is that needs are arranged in hierarchy.[4] The lowest level needs are the physiological needs and the highest level needs are the self-actualisation needs. These needs are defined to mean the following:

1. *Physiological*: the need for food, drink, shelter and relief from pain;
2. *Safety and security*: the need for freedom from threat, that is, the security from threatening events or surroundings;
3. *Belongingness, social and love*: the need for friendship, affiliation, interaction and love;

4. *Esteem*: the need for self-esteem and for esteem from others;
5. *Self-actualisation*: The need to fulfil oneself by making maximum use of abilities, skills and potential.

Maslow's theory assumes that a person attempts to satisfy the more basic needs (physiological) before directing behaviour toward satisfying upper level needs. Several other crucial points in Maslow's thinking are important to understanding the need-hierarchy approach.

- A satisfied need ceases to motivate. For example, when a person decides that he or she is earning enough pay for contributing to the organisation, money loses its power to motivate.
- Unsatisfied needs can cause frustration, conflict and stress. From a managerial perspective, unsatisfied needs are dangerous because they may lead to undesirable performance outcomes.
- Maslow assumes that people have a need to grow and develop and, consequently, will strive constantly to move up the hierarchy in terms of need satisfaction. This assumption may be true for some employees but not others.

Maslow proposed that the typical adult in society has satisfied about 85% of the physiological need; 70% of the safety and security needs; 50% of the belongingness, social and love needs; 40% of the esteem need; and 10% of the self-actualisation need. Many critics disagree with these figures, however, particularly the 10% figure for self-actualisation. These critics suggest that for blue-collar workers, many of whom are simply trying to survive, the true figure is

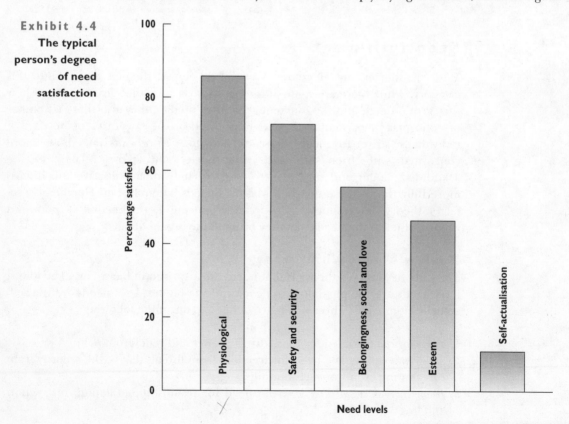

Exhibit 4.4
The typical person's degree of need satisfaction

far closer to zero. Exhibit 4.4 displays, in the form of a bar chart, Maslow's assertions regarding the degree of satisfaction of the five need types.

A number of research studies have attempted to test the need-hierarchy theory. The first reported field research that tested a modified version of Maslow's need hierarchy was performed by Porter.[5] At the time of the initial studies, Porter assumed that physiological needs were being adequately satisfied for managers, so he substituted a higher order need called 'autonomy', defined as the person's satisfaction with opportunities to make independent decisions, set goals and work without close supervision.

Since the early Porter studies, other studies have reported:

- Managers higher in the organisation chain of command place greater emphasis on self-actualisation and autonomy.[6]
- Managers at lower organisational levels in small firms (less than 500 employees) are more satisfied than their counterpart managers in large firms (more than 5000 employees); however, managers at upper levels in large companies are more satisfied than their counterparts in small companies.[7]
- American managers overseas are more satisfied with autonomy opportunities than are their counterparts working in the United States.[8]

Despite these findings, a number of issues remain regarding the need-hierarchy theory. First, data from managers in two different companies provided little support that a hierarchy of needs exists.[9] The data suggested that only two levels of needs exist: one is the physiological level and the other is a level which includes all other needs. Further evidence also disputes the hierarchy notions.[10] Researchers have found that as managers advance in an organisation, their needs for security decrease, with a corresponding increase in their needs for social interaction, achievement and self-actualisation.

Herzberg's two-factor theory

Herzberg developed a theory known as the two-factor theory of motivation.[11] The two factors are called the dissatisfiers–satisfiers or hygiene motivators. The original research which led to the theory gave rise to two specific conclusions. First, there is a set of *extrinsic* conditions, the job context, which result in job dissatisfaction among employees when the conditions are absent. If these conditions are present, this does not necessarily motivate employees. These conditions are the *dissatisfiers* or *hygiene* factors, since they are needed to maintain at least a level of 'no dissatisfaction'. Many of the dissatisfiers fit in to Maslow's idea of lower order needs (physiological and security needs) and include:

- salary;
- job security;
- working conditions;
- status;
- company procedures;
- quality of technical supervision;
- quality of interpersonal relations among peers, with superiors and with subordinates.

What is valued in the workplace?

What do we value in our jobs? Do we expect to have our basic needs met? Or are we looking for jobs that satisfy higher order needs? And, are there any differences in the expectations of men and women in the workplace?

These questions were asked by Lawson Savery at Curtin University in Western Australia. Using staff in a government department, Savery assessed the extent to which men and women differ in their expectations of the workplace. His findings, are summarised below:

Women want:
- greater job security.

Men want:
- better promotion prospects;
- more opportunities to lead;

- greater responsibility;
- higher social status.

Women and men do not differ in the level of the following items that they want:
- pay;
- challenge;
- interest;
- working hours;
- autonomy;
- variety;
- opportunities for learning;
- cooperation from others;
- career development.

Source: Savery, L. K. (1991). Men and women in the workplace: Evidence of occupational differences, *Leadership and Organization Development Journal*, 11, 13–16.

Second, a set of *intrinsic* conditions — the job content — when present in the job, builds strong levels of motivation that can result in good job performance. If these conditions are not present, the job does not prove highly satisfying. The factors in this set are called the *satisfiers* or *motivators*. They fit more clearly with Maslow's higher needs (self-esteem and self-actualisation) and include:

- achievement;
- recognition;
- responsibility;
- advancement;
- the work itself;
- the possibility of growth.

These motivators are related directly to the nature of the job or task itself. When present, they contribute to satisfaction. This in turn can result in intrinsic task motivation.[12]

Herzberg's model assumes that job satisfaction is not a unidimensional concept. His research leads to the conclusion that two continua are needed to correctly interpret job satisfaction. Exhibit 4.5 presents two different views of job satisfaction. Prior to Herzberg's work, those studying motivation viewed job satisfaction as a unidimensional concept; that is, they placed job satisfaction at one end of a continuum and job dissatisfaction at the other end of the same continuum. This meant that if a job condition caused satisfaction, removing it will lead to job dissatisfaction. Similarly, if a job condition caused dissatisfaction, removing it would lead to job satisfaction. Herzberg, however, argues that very different factors lead to satisfaction and dissatisfaction. According to the two-factor theory, removing conditions that cause dissatisfaction will remove the

Exhibit 4.5
Traditional versus Herzberg view of job satisfaction

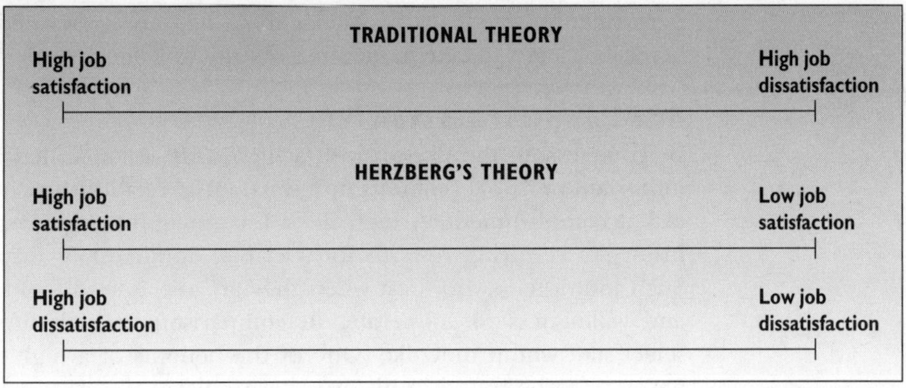

TRADITIONAL THEORY	
High job satisfaction	High job dissatisfaction

HERZBERG'S THEORY	
High job satisfaction	Low job satisfaction
High job dissatisfaction	Low job dissatisfaction

dissatisfaction; however, the removal of these conditions will not lead to satisfaction. To increase satisfaction, it is necessary for managers to focus on — and increase — a different range of factors.

Intrinsic motivation

Intrinsic motivation focuses on the higher order needs identified by need-fulfilment theories. Like need-fulfilment theories, intrinsic motivation identifies a set of stable needs that are held by individuals.[13] According to this theory, our needs are partly determined by our experiences: if we are rewarded for risk taking, we learn to value and seek risks; and if we are rewarded for excellence, we learn to value and seek excellence.[14] Since needs are learned, behaviour that is rewarded tends to recur at a higher frequency. As a result of this process, individuals develop a set of unique needs that affect their behaviour and performance.

Several patterns can be identified.[15] Each is associated with a different set of behaviours and values, and implies that different environmental features will act as motivators. One group of theories is concerned with the curiosity motive, and is related to individual needs for stimulation and arousal from the environment. A second group identifies the need to display competence as the driving force behind individual behaviour. This group stresses such motives as competence, mastery, challenge and effectiveness. It is characterised by two well-known needs: the need for competence (nComp) and the need for achievement (nAch). A third group, emphasising control over the environment, is best exemplified by the need for power (nPow).[16] McClelland identified the need for affiliation (nAff), which reflects a desire to interact socially with people. Individuals characterised by these different patterns of intrinsic motivation value different goals, and display different workplace behaviour.

Need for achievement

Individuals with a high nAch like to take responsibility for solving problems. They work harder when they receive individual recognition for their achievements; tend to set moderate achievement goals to take calculated risks; and desire feedback on performance. These individuals value hard work and expect their staff to display similar attitudes; they select individuals for their technical skills; and their performance is enhanced when they receive detailed performance feedback.[17] Managers who are rewarded for achievement behaviour learn to take moderate risks and to achieve goals.

Need for affiliation

By comparison, the person with a high nAff is concerned about the quality of important personal relationships; thus, social relationships take precedence over task accomplishment. A high need for affiliation or power can be traced to a history of receiving rewards for sociable, dominant or inspirational behaviour. Such individuals work best when they are recognised for their positive attitude and willingness to cooperate. In comparison to high nAch individuals, they select staff whom they like. One of the benefits of a high nAff manager is the harmony to be found in his or her workplace; a cost is that social relationships may be emphasised to the detriment of task performance.[18]

Need for competence

nComp describes a drive to excel, and individuals with high competence motivation develop and apply problem-solving skills to obtain mastery of their environment. They are especially good at overcoming obstacles and constantly improve their skills on the basis of their experience. This group is motivated by the higher order needs (e.g. self-actualisation, self-esteem) and their principal aim is to produce high-quality work. They look for similar values in the people around them and, like high nAch individuals, place less emphasis on interpersonal relationships.[19]

Need for power

A person with a high nPow, meanwhile, concentrates on obtaining and exercising power and authority. He or she is concerned with influencing others and winning arguments. Power has two possible orientations according to McClelland. It can be negative in that the person exercising it emphasises dominance and submission. Or power can be positive in that it reflects persuasive and inspirational behaviour.

COGNITIVE-CHOICE THEORIES

Why do individuals work harder towards some goals than others? What determines the level of effort that they put into particular tasks? Do you work harder for some courses than others? Why? Cognitive-choice theories of motivation provide an explanation of motivational *intensity* by examining the relationship between behaviours, performance and rewards. The two most important theories within this category are expectancy and attribution theory.

Expectancy theory

One of the more popular explanations of motivation was developed by Victor Vroom.[20] Vroom's theory is the best known example of expectancy theory. All of these theories are based on the assumption that individuals aim to maximise positive and minimise negative outcomes. They are used to predict the choices between options that individuals will make, and are focused on specific behaviours in specific situations.[21] Numerous studies have been done to test the

ORGANISATIONAL

Encounter

Avis reaps rewards

In this chapter, we have reviewed several approaches to motivation. Although we have treated them individually, motivating individuals requires us to apply more than one theory. As we will see in Chapter 5 effective reward systems must consider the rewards that individuals want, as well as how those rewards are tied to performance. In this Encounter, we describe how one company — Avis — has used the principles of Maslow's needs hierarchy and Vroom's expectancy theory to stimulate organisational performance.

Maslow identified three higher order needs: social needs, self-esteem and self-actualisation. The last of these is often met in the workplace by increased responsibility; and esteem needs can be met through merit salary increases. At Avis, the company has focused on increasing employee participation as a strategy for improving efficiency. Participation is encouraged through regular meetings of employee suggestion groups. Each location and each department elects a group member and the group has the power to implement plans. This has resulted in several strategies for increasing efficiency and improving customer service. In Sydney, staff have dramatically reduced the amount of water used in car washing; in Melbourne, staff decided to return lost property to clients rather than waiting for clients to collect it; and in Tasmania, staff are providing safety tips in an attempt to cut down the accident rate.

Can this behaviour be maintained? In Avis's case, the answer is probably yes — because these strategies are linked to a bonus system. Avis have met one of the key criteria for effective motivation: it has created strong instrumentalities (Vroom) by establishing clear links between performance and rewards. Staff participate in a pay bonus scheme that can add up to 5% per year to their salaries.

And staff are not the only ones to benefit: Avis has not only doubled its profits, but has also substantially increased market share.

Source: Thomas, T. (1995). How worker involvement pays off for Avis, *Business Review Weekly*, November 20, 71–72.

accuracy of expectancy theory in predicting employee behaviour, and direct tests have been generally supportive.[22] Vroom argues that individual choices are determined by an individual's assessment of the relationship between effort and performance, between performance and the attainment and the value of those rewards.[23] Offering valued rewards, and linking those rewards to performance, is the theme in our Organisational Encounter.

In the work setting, individuals hold an effort–performance expectancy. This expectancy represents the individual's perception of how hard it will be to achieve a particular behaviour (say, completing the budget on time) and the probability of achieving that behaviour. There is also a performance–outcome expectancy. In the individual's mind, every behaviour is associated with outcomes (rewards or punishments). For example, an individual may have an expectancy that if the budget is completed on time, he or she will receive a day off next week. Exhibit 4.6 presents the general expectancy model and includes the two expectancy points (E→P and P→O).

Key terms in expectancy theory

In order to understand expectancy theory, it is necessary to define the terms of the theory and explain how they operate. The four most important terms are: first-level and second-level outcomes, instrumentality, valence and expectancy. According to Vroom, the three components of expectancy theory (expectancy, instrumentality and valence) combine multiplicatively. Thus, if an individual's evaluation of one component is low, overall motivation will be substantially lowered.

First-level and second-level outcomes. Performance is described as a *first-level* outcome if it results from behaviour associated with doing the job itself; this includes productivity, absenteeism, turnover and quality of productivity. The *second-level* outcomes are those events (rewards or punishments) that the first-level outcomes are likely to produce such as merit pay increases, group acceptance or rejection, promotion and termination.

Instrumentality. **Instrumentality** is the perception by an individual that first-level outcomes are associated with second-level outcomes. It refers to the strength of a person's belief that attainment of a particular outcome will lead to (be instrumental in) attaining one or more second-level outcomes. Instrumentality can be negative, suggesting that attaining a second-level outcome is less likely if a first-level outcome has occurred; or positive, suggesting that the second-level outcome is more likely if the first-level outcome has been attained.

Valence. **Valence** refers to the preferences for outcomes as seen by the individual. For example, a person may prefer a 10% merit raise over a relocation to a new facility. An outcome is positively valent when it is preferred and negatively valent when it is not preferred or is avoided. An outcome has a valence of zero when the individual is indifferent to attaining or not attaining it. The valence concept applies to both first-level and second-level outcomes. Thus,

Exhibit 4.6
Expectancy
theory

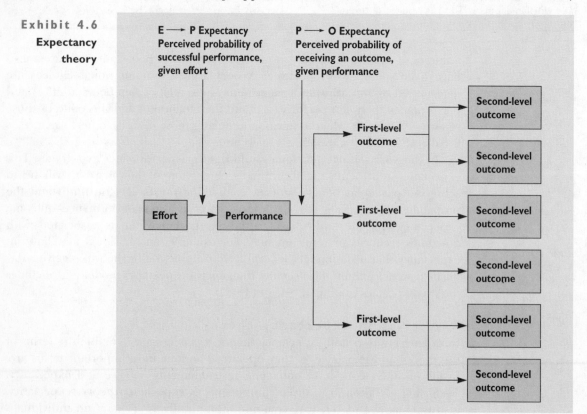

a person may prefer to be a high-performing employee (first-level outcome) because she believes this will lead to a desired merit raise in pay (second-level outcome).

Expectancy. **Expectancy** refers to the individual's belief regarding the likelihood or subjective probability that a particular behaviour will be followed by a particular outcome and it is most easily thought of as a single probability statement. That is, it refers to a perceived chance of something occurring because of the behaviour. Expectancy can take values ranging from 0, indicating no chance that an outcome will occur after the behaviour or act, to +1, indicating perceived certainty that a particular outcome will follow a behaviour or act.

Applying expectancy theory

Expectancy theory attempts to provide a framework for answering the question 'What determines an employee's willingness to expend effort on the job towards the accomplishment of organisational goals and objectives?' To put it another way, the theory assumes that 'people will do what they can do when they want to'.[24] That is, motivation is determined by people's beliefs about effort–performance relationships and the attractiveness of various work outcomes that may result from good (or poor) performance.

There are three points at which managers can intervene to increase motivation.[25]

1. *They can influence and change the belief that effort leads to performance.* Earlier in this chapter, we suggested that even when individuals exert effort they may not perform well because they lack skills or equipment. Managers can increase the strength of the belief that E→P by ensuring that staff have appropriate skills and resources. This can be achieved through the selection of staff or through training programs. Expectancy is also strengthened by setting specific and attainable goals, an issue that we will consider in the next section. We will return to this idea in Chapter 11, in our discussion of path-goal leadership.

2. *They can influence and change the belief that performance leads to rewards.* One of the biggest motivational problems faced by organisations is whether reward systems really have the desired effect: do they increase behaviours valued by the organisation? The most effective means for increasing instrumentality is to clearly link rewards to performance, for example by implementing pay-for-performance plans. When organisations establish such programs, it is important that they implement them in a consistent manner: if employees see the same rewards being given for quite different levels of performance, instrumentality will decrease. We will consider this last issue more closely in Chapter 5.

One means for increasing both expectancy and instrumentality is to implement skill-based pay. In a skill-based plan, employees are paid at a rate based on their personal skills. Typically, employees start at a basic initial rate of pay, and they receive increases as their skills develop. Their pay rates are based on skill levels, no matter which jobs they are assigned: the skills

Exhibit 4.7 Summary of managerial applications of expectancy theory

Expectancy Concept	Employee Question	Managerial Action
Expectancy	'Can I attain the desired level of performance?'	■ Select high-ability employees. ■ Provide adequate training. ■ Provide necessary resource support. ■ Identify desired performance.
Instrumentality	'What outcomes will I attain as a result of my performance?'	■ Clarify the reward system. ■ Clarify performance–reward possibilities. ■ Ensure rewards are contingent upon performance.
Valence	'What value do I place on available performance outcomes?'	■ Identify individual needs and preferences for outcomes. ■ Match available rewards with these. ■ Construct additional rewards as possible and feasible.

developed by employees are the key pay determinants. The skill-based pay plan approximates how professionals are compensated. In skill-based plans, pay increases are not given at any specific time because of seniority.[26] Instead, a raise is granted when employees demonstrate their skills to perform particular jobs.

3. *They can offer valued rewards.* Finally, managers can increase the valence of rewards by offering rewards that are valued by employees. Our discussion of needs theories showed us that different individuals, because they have different needs, may also value rewards differently. We consider reward systems in more detail in Chapter 5. However, we can say now that *cafeteria fringe benefits* provide an excellent tool for offering a range of rewards. In these plans, management places an upper limit on how much the organisation is willing to spend on fringe benefits. Employees then decide how they would like to receive the total fringe benefit amount and develop individual, personally attractive fringe benefit packages. Some employees take all the fringes in cash; others purchase special medical protection plans. The cafeteria plan provides individuals with the benefits they prefer rather than the benefits that someone else establishes for them. Another strategy may be to allow staff to bank time off: employees could earn time-off credits granted for certain levels of performance. That is, a bank of time-off credits could be built up contingent on performance achievements.

Reading 4
Motivation:
A diagnostic
approach

From a managerial perspective, expectancy theory suggests that the manager should develop an awareness of employee thought processes and, based on that awareness, take actions that will influence those processes in a manner that facilitates the attainment of positive organisational outcomes. The reading for this chapter discusses a number of implications that expectancy theory has for organisations in general and managers specifically.

Exhibit 4.7 summarises the potential applications of expectancy theory. As can be seen from the exhibit, the manager can play an active role in influencing employee expectancies, instrumentalities and valences. Exerting such influence encompasses a variety of activities from the initial selection and training of employees to the administration of rewards. To do this effectively requires good (and continuing) communication and listening skills, and knowledge of and sensitivity to employee needs. An important implication here is that motivation programs should be designed with a sufficient degree of flexibility to address the kinds of individual differences discussed in Chapter 3, as well as need differences described earlier in this chapter in the discussion of content approaches to motivation.

Attribution theory

read

See discussion of the attribution theory in Chapter 3.

SELF-REGULATION THEORIES

The last question that we asked was 'What maintains effort?' Obtaining a degree is a long-term goal that requires effort over several years; the final reward is a long way off and many obstacles must be overcome before it can be obtained. So, what keeps you motivated to attend classes and complete assignments? *Self-regulation theories* try to explain individual persistence by considering the mechanisms that keep us focused on our goals. We will look at two theories in this category: goal setting and control theory.

Goal setting

There has been considerable and growing interest in applying goal setting to organisational problems and issues since Locke presented what is now considered a classic paper in 1968.[27] Locke proposed that *goal setting* is a cognitive process of some practical utility. His view is that an individual's conscious goals and intentions are the primary determinants of behaviour.[28] It has been noted that 'one of the commonly observed characteristics of intentional behaviour is that it tends to keep going until it reaches completion'.[29] That is, once a person starts something (e.g. a job, a new project), he or she pushes on until a goal is achieved. Also, goal-setting theory places specific emphasis on the importance of conscious goals in explaining motivated behaviour. Locke has used the notion of intentions and conscious goals to propose and provide research support for the thesis that harder conscious goals will result in higher levels of performance if these goals are accepted by the individual.[30]

Recently, Dave Parkin — coach of the Carlton Football Club in Melbourne — said that if the team won the 1995 premiership, it would be 'the greatest players' premiership ever'. In 1995, the club appointed a psychologist, who advised Parkin to give team members greater responsibility, allowing them to set their own goals. The team worked towards a different goal each month in their efforts to win the premiership. In yet another testimony to the power of goal setting, Carlton won![31]

Descriptions of goal setting

A goal is the object of an action. For example, the attempt to produce four units on a production line or to cut direct costs by $3000 or to decrease absenteeism in a department by 12% are goals. Locke has carefully described the attributes or the mental (cognitive) processes of goal setting. The attributes he highlights are goal specificity, goal difficulty and goal intensity. *Goal specificity* is the degree of quantitative precision (clarity) of the goal. *Goal difficulty* is the degree of proficiency or the level of performance that is sought. *Goal intensity* pertains to the process of setting the goal or of determining how to reach it.[32] To date, goal intensity has not been widely studied, although a related concept, *goal commitment*, has been considered in a number of studies. Goal commitment is the amount of effort used to achieve a goal.

Several features of goal setting have strong similarities to the resource-allocation theories, described in the next section of this chapter. High goals result in high performance because they direct attention and effort towards goal-relevant behaviour and limit the effort expended on tasks that do not contribute to goal attainment. However, an individual's ability to attain a given goal is constrained by a number of factors: high goals increase performance only when coupled with feedback concerning progress towards goals, only if you have the skills and cognitive resources to attain the goal, and when no other situational factors prevent goal achievement.[33]

Exhibit 4.8 portrays applied goal setting from a managerial perspective and the sequence of events for such a goal-setting program. The key steps in applying goal setting are:

1. diagnosis for readiness (determining whether the people, the organisation and the technology are suited for goal setting);
2. preparing employees via increased interpersonal interaction, communication, training and action plans for goal setting;
3. emphasising the attributes of goals that should be understood by a manager and subordinates;
4. conducting intermediate reviews to make necessary adjustments in established goals; and
5. performing a final review to check that the goals have been set, modified and accomplished.

Exercise 4
Goal setting:
How to do it

Each of these steps needs to be carefully planned and implemented if goal setting is to be an effective motivational technique. In too many applications of goal setting, steps outlined in, or issues suggested by, Exhibit 4.8 are ignored. Exercise 4 is designed to let you experience the goal-setting process first hand.

Goal-setting research

Between 1968 and 1996 the amount of research on goal setting increased considerably. Locke's 1968 paper certainly contributed to the increase in laboratory and field research on goal setting. Another force behind the increase in interest and research was the demand of managers for practical and specific techniques that they could apply in their organisations. Goal setting offered such a technique for some managers and it thus became an important management tool for enhancing work performance.[34]

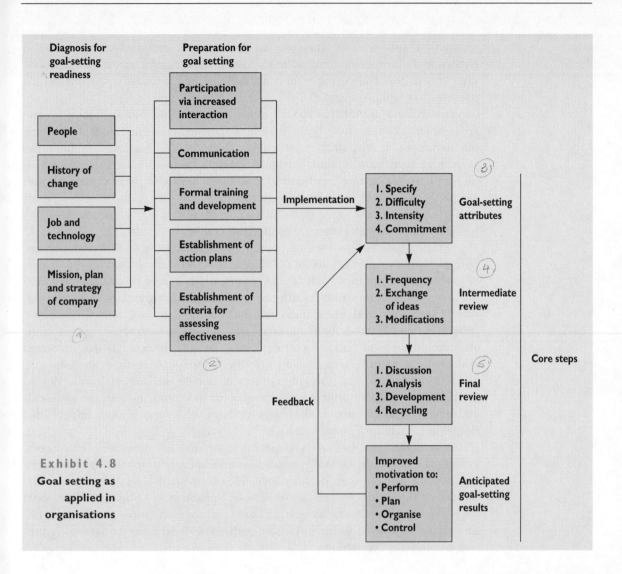

Exhibit 4.8
Goal setting as applied in organisations

Empirical research findings from a variety of managerial and student samples have provided support for the theory that conscious goals regulate behaviour. Yet a number of important issues concerning goal setting must still be examined more thoroughly. One area of debate concerns the issue of how much subordinate participation in goal setting is optimal.[35] A field experiment of skilled technicians compared three levels of subordinate participation: full (the subordinates were totally involved); limited (the subordinates made some suggestions about the goals the superior set); and none.[36] Measures of performance and satisfaction were taken over a 12-month period. The groups with full or limited participant involvement in goal setting showed significantly more performance and satisfaction improvements than the group that did not participate in goal setting. Interestingly, these improvements began to dissipate 6–9 months after the program was started. Some research, however, has failed to find significant relationships between performance and participation in the goal-setting process.[37] One of the reasons for this is that assigned goals appear to be more effective than we might expect. Several reasons for this effect have been suggested: because goals are assigned by individuals with legitimate power, the assignment process may increase an individual's self-efficacy; by posing a challenge it may motivate individuals to develop their skills, and it may stimulate their need for competence; and it defined the standards against which performance will be judged.[38]

Research has found that specific goals lead to higher output than do vague goals such as 'Do your best'.[39] Field experiments using clerical workers, maintenance technicians, marketing personnel, truckers, engineering personnel, typists and manufacturing employees have compared specific versus do-your-best goal-setting conditions.[40] The vast majority of these studies support — partly or totally — the hypothesis that specific goals lead to better performance than do vague goals. In fact, in 99 out of 100 studies reviewed by Locke and his associates, specific goals produced better results.[41]

Certain aspects of goal setting need to be subjected to scientific examination. One such area centres on individual differences and their impact on the success of goal-setting programs. Such factors as personality, career progression, training background and personal health are important individual differences that should be considered when implementing goal-setting programs. Goal-setting programs should also be subjected to ongoing examination to monitor attitudinal and performance consequences. Some research has demonstrated that goal-setting programs tend to lose their potency over time, so there is a need to discover why this phenomenon occurs in organisations. Sound evaluation programs would assist management in identifying success, problems and needs. Finally, research also suggests that goal setting is more effective for simple tasks than for complex tasks.[42]

Goal setting can be a very powerful technique for motivating employees. When used correctly, carefully monitored and actively supported by managers, goal setting can improve performance. However, neither goal setting nor any other technique can be used to correct every problem. No applied motivational approach can be *the* technique to solve all performance problems. This, unfortunately, is what some enthusiastic advocates have turned goal setting into — a panacea for everything.

Control theory

Goal-setting theory has introduced us to the idea that feedback plays an important role in individual performance. One theory that explicitly incorporates feedback into theories about human behaviour is *control theory*.[43] Control theory and its extensions provide a very useful framework for integrating ideas from several theories to describe the factors that affect individual motivation and performance.[44] Four key concepts in control theory are:

1. *referent standard*, which in the context of motivation theories can be seen as the goals or performance standards that individuals are striving to achieve;
2. *input*, which describes the level of effort and performance that the individual is achieving;
3. *comparator*, which compares the current level of performance (input) with the desired level of performance (referent) and identifies discrepancies;
4. *output*, or the individual's responses to any detected discrepancies, especially where these discrepancies suggest that the individual will not attain a desired goal.

These key aspects of control theory are shown in Exhibit 4.9. When applied to people, the theory falls into two components. First, a *cognitive* component describes the goals individuals have, the information available about their current position, and the comparisons that they make between their current position and their goals. Second, an *affective* component describes the consequences of any perceived discrepancies, especially how individuals might change their behaviour to reduce that discrepancy. According to control theory, individuals use goals to monitor their progress. Discrepancies between current performance and goals become especially important when individuals notice that, if they continue on their current course of action, they will fail to achieve a particular goal. According to this theory, motivation is the consequence of individuals noticing such a discrepancy and attempting to reduce it. Carver & Scheier[45] suggest that when individuals notice that they are failing to reach performance targets, they have one of three options: they may keep their goals and increase their level of effort; they may lower their goals and continue working at the same level of effort; or they may reject the goal.

Exhibit 4.9
Control theory model of motivation

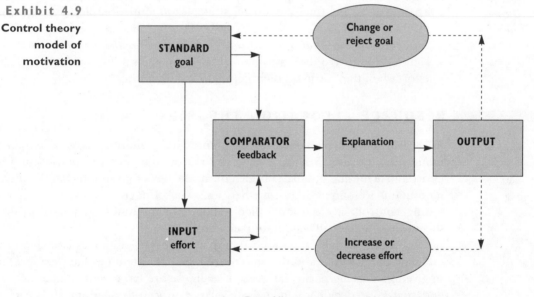

Dotted lines represent possible alternative outputs.

Which of these options we choose will be determined by how we explain our performance (luck, effort, task difficulty or ability) and the value that we place on achieving a particular goal.[46] The attributions that we make directly influence our level of effort: when we explain our performance in terms of stable causes (ability, task difficulty) we are more likely to work harder when we are successful; if we are unsuccessful, the same explanations of our performance will result in a reduction of effort.

Imagine that Sue is not meeting her monthly sales quota. If her bonus is linked to achieving her quota she will consider it important; so she is unlikely to reject the goal (her quota). How can she explain her poor performance? And how does this explanation affect her perception that she can achieve her goal? Let's say that this month the economic outlook has been poor. On this basis, she may explain her performance in terms of task difficulty (a stable, external cause) and we would expect her to reduce her effort. If Sue thought her poor performance was related to the fact that several of her largest clients were away on holidays, she might explain the same performance in terms of luck (an unstable, external cause) and we expect her to continue exerting the same level of effort.

In terms of managing work motivation, control theory suggests three broad strategies. Each of these strategies is closely linked to one of the theories that we have already considered.

1. *Change the value assigned to particular goals: increase attractiveness.* This strategy implies that goals can be more or less desirable as a result of the rewards that they are associated with. If we link goal attainment to highly desirable outcomes, we will increase their desirability. Organisational reward systems have the potential to alter the perceived attractiveness of a goal.
2. *Influence individual assessments of the likelihood that goals can be attained.* This strategy is directly connected to expectancy theory, and is aimed at increasing the belief that effort will lead to performance. This can be accomplished by using any of the strategies identified earlier. One example would be by removing situational constraints on goal attainment.
3. *Influence the explanations that individuals offer for their performance*, that is, to try to change their attributions. We know that individuals will exert less effort when they attribute their failure to stable causes.

RESOURCE ALLOCATION THEORIES

At the start of this chapter, we said that *direction* was an important component of motivation: individuals choose to work towards some goals while putting little effort into achieving others. This idea forms the basis for more recent theories of motivation. Resource allocation theories, which integrate key aspects of goal setting, control and expectancy theories, describe motivation as a decision about the way in which we allocate resources across tasks.

According to these theories, we have a number of resources available to us: our skills and abilities and the amount of time and attention that we are willing to give to achieving particular goals. Usually, we are faced with competing goals and we need to decide which goals we will put effort into achieving and which we will ignore; we also need to decide how we will spread the effort between our goals. Will we give all our effort to one goal? Will we share our effort equally across goals? Or will we put more effort into our more important goals and less effort into less important goals? For example, complex and challenging goals are more demanding and, to meet them, we must allocate more resources. We also need to spend more time checking for discrepancies between these goals and our level of performance; so they also require more attention from us. When will we put effort into complex goals? According to resource-allocation theories, this will depend on a cost–benefit analysis: we will work hard when the benefits of achieving a goal outweigh its costs.

Factors influencing cost–benefit analysis

Resource allocation theories try to explain the factors that influence this cost–benefit analysis. These theories introduce three factors that influence these decisions: performance utility, effort utility and performance–effort utility. Put more simply, resource allocation theories suggest that we ask three questions: How important is this goal (or outcome) to me? How hard do I have to work to achieve this goal? Is the outcome worth the effort?

Performance utility

How important is this goal? We can perform at any one of several levels. For example, an athlete can run a race in 10 minutes, 15 minutes or 20 minutes. A student can pass a course, obtain a credit or obtain a distinction. And an employee can complete a project late, on time or ahead of time. Different levels of performance are associated with different rewards. For example, scoring 50% in a course earns you a pass, while scoring 100% earns you a university prize. The performance-utility describes the *value* that each level of performance has for you, given the reward that you receive (grade, bonus, recognition, or sense of achievement). For example, I may think that a distinction is much more important than just passing, but have no interest in receiving the university prize. An important factor in shaping this evaluation is the strength of the performance–reward relationship (as we saw with the concept of instrumentality).

Effort utility

How hard do I have to work? Different levels of performance are tied to different levels of effort. Whereas you may need to work for only 50 hours to obtain a 50% grade, you may need to work for 200 hours to obtain a 100% grade. The effort utility describes the costs and benefits associated with a particular level of performance. For example, the cost of 50 hours is relatively low in comparison with a fairly high outcome (passing).

Effort–performance utility

Is it worth the effort? This last concept brings together the performance and effort utilities. It suggests that our aim is to minimise costs and maximise outcomes: we are looking for the best outcome with the least effort. We may value obtaining a university prize, but is it worth putting in four times the effort? According to resource-allocation theories, we do not allocate effort to goals for which the costs outweigh the benefits.

Motivation from a resource allocation perspective

An individual's assessment of the relationship between performance and outcomes will determine how resources are allocated across tasks. Feedback loops allow individuals to adjust the allocation of their effort based on *changes* to:

- *total resource capacity*, which may vary as individual skill levels change;
- *preference for outcomes*, which may vary as either the performance or performance–effort utilities associated with specific outcomes change;
- *task resource demands*, which will vary depending on whether tasks are simple or complex, and novel or routine.

MOTIVATION AND THE PSYCHOLOGICAL CONTRACT

A conceptual framework that provides a useful perspective for viewing the topic of motivation is *exchange theory*.[47] In a very general sense, exchange theory suggests that members of an organisation engage in reasonably predictable give-and-take relationships (exchanges) with each other. For example, an employee gives time and effort in exchange for pay; and management provides pleasant working conditions in exchange for employee loyalty. Schein suggests that the degree to which employees are willing to exert effort, commit to organisational goals and derive satisfaction from their work is dependent on two conditions:[48]

1. the extent to which employee expectations of what the organisation will give them and what they owe the organisation in return matches the organisation's expectations of what it will give and receive;
2. assuming there is agreement on these expectations, the specific nature of what is exchanged (effort for pay, for example).

These mutual expectations regarding exchanges constitute part of the psychological contract. The *psychological contract* is an unwritten agreement between the individual and the organisation which specifies what each expects to give to and receive from the other. While some aspects of an employment relationship, such as pay, may be explicitly stated, many others are not. These implicit agreements which may focus on exchanges involving satisfaction, challenging work, fair treatment, loyalty and opportunity to be creative may take precedence over written agreements. Our Management Encounter in this chapter looks at the effects of violating psychological contracts.

In the ideal psychological contract, those contributions the individual was willing to give would correspond perfectly to what the organisation wanted to receive; similarly, what the organisation wanted to give would correspond totally with what the individual wished to receive. Additionally, psychological contracts are not static: either party's expectations can change as can either party's ability or willingness to continue meeting expectations.

Case 4
FAB Sweets
Limited

When there are few or a decreasing number of matches between what each party expects to give and receive in the contract, work motivation suffers. The psychological contract provides a perspective for why this is true. Looking at motivation from a content theory approach, the psychological contract suggests that in return for time, effort and other considerations, individuals desire to receive need gratification. Using Maslow's need hierarchy as an example, if an employee is operating at the self-actualisation level and fails to receive a challenging job which allows for the application of all the capabilities that employee has, motivation will suffer. In other words, the satisfaction of needs is part of the contract; when the expectation of need satisfaction is not matched with the opportunity to achieve such satisfaction, the contract is violated and motivation is negatively affected.

The perspective on motivation provided by the concept of the psychological contract is not limited to content approaches to motivation, however; it is equally applicable to process explanations as well. Adam's equity theory is, in fact, a form of exchange theory. The notion of inputs and outcomes within equity theory is very similar to expectations of giving and receiving in the psychological contract. In the context of an expectancy approach to motivation, performance-outcome

MANAGEMENT

Encounter

Broken contracts

Psychological contracts describe the beliefs that we have about how an organisation will treat us and what we, in return, will give to the organisation. Psychological contracts describe a set of mutual obligations between employers and employees and are usually based on promises that recruiters, human resource personnel and managers make to an individual.

These promises fall into two categories. Employers can make promises in relation to specific employment conditions: for example, promises concerning high pay, rapid promotion and pay-for-performance plans. These relate to immediate and tangible outcomes and are called *transactional* obligations. Employees also have a set of transactional obligations: to warn employers that they plan to leave, to accept transfers to other positions or locations, to protect company information and to not support competitors. These obligations concern *outcomes* and are related to concepts of distributive justice.

A second set of obligations concerns the relationship between employers and employees: they describe the need for treatment that is respectful and fair, establishing trust between employers and employees. On the part of the employer, *relationship obligations* involve guarantees of job security, long-term career prospects, and the provision of training and development. On the part of employees, relationship obligations lead to working long hours, displaying company loyalty, commitment and other organisational citizenship behaviours. These obligations are more concerned with *process* and associated with perceptions of procedural justice.

Obligations change over time

When we join an organisation, we have a clear idea about what we owe the organisation and what it owes us. How do these perceptions change over time? As our relationship develops, do we feel a progressively stronger sense of obligation towards the organisation? Or do we believe that we have exceeded our transactional and relational obligations simply by staying? And does this mean that our expectations of what an organisation should give us in return change? Research shows that this is precisely what happens:

when employees remain with an organisation, they believe that the organisation has greater transactional obligations in the areas of advancement, pay levels, pay-for-performance plans and training. At the same time, they believe that they have fewer obligations in the areas of overtime, loyalty, accepting transfers and giving advance warning of their intentions to leave.

Violations have negative consequences

Individuals enter organisations with a set of beliefs about what they should do for the organisation and what the organisation should do for them. What happens when one party to this contract — either the employee or the employer — fails to fulfil these obligations? When psychological contracts are violated, individuals feel angry and betrayed; violations imply disrespect and reduce the level of trust towards employers. In a recent survey, over half of the employees surveyed reported that their organisations had, at some time, violated their psychological contracts. How do such violations affect organisations?

So far, research has focused on how violations affect employees. The immediate impact of unfulfilled contracts is to decrease the strength of an employee's transactional and relational obligations. If this was the only consequence, perhaps organisations could remain unconcerned. However, when organisations fail to meet their obligations, employees report lower trust, lower satisfaction and less intention to stay. They display fewer organisational citizenship behaviours and a higher turnover rate.

These are all important consequences for organisations. What strategies can you think of to ensure that obligations are met? Will the importance of violations depend on what we value in our relationship with an organisation?

Source: Robinson, S. L. & Morrison, E. W. (1995). Psychological contracts and OCB: The effect of unfulfilled obligations on civic virtue behavior, *Journal of Organizational Behavior*, 16, 289–298; Robinson, S. L. & Rousseau, D. M. (1994). Violating the psychological contract: not the exception but the norm, *Journal of Organizational Behavior*, 15, 245–259; Robinson, S. L., Kraatz, M. S. & Rousseau, D. M. (1994). Changing obligations and the psychological contract: A longitudinal study, *Academy of Management Journal*, 37, 137–152.

expectancies relate directly to the exchange of performance for pay, advancement satisfaction or other outcomes in the psychological contract; likewise, the desire to receive certain considerations in the context of the contract is analogous to positively valent outcomes in expectancy theory.

Managing the psychological contract successfully is one of the more important and challenging aspects of most managers' jobs. The more attuned the manager is to needs and expectations of subordinates, the greater the number of matches that are likely to exist and be maintained in the psychological contract. This, in turn, can positively affect the direction, intensity and persistence of motivation in the organisation. Our Global Encounter provides an example of how the Japanese enhance motivation by maximising the number of matches between employee needs and expectations.

REVIEWING MOTIVATION

In this chapter, several theories of motivation are portrayed. The theories typically are pitted against one another in the literature. This is unfortunate since each approach can help managers better understand workplace motivation. Each approach attempts to organise, in a meaningful manner, major variables associated with explaining motivation in work settings. The content theories are individual-oriented in that they place primary emphasis on the characteristics of people. Each of the theories has a specific orientation. For example, expectancy theory places emphasis on individual, job and environmental variables. It recognises differences in needs, perceptions and beliefs. In contrast, goal-setting theory emphasises the cognitive processes and the role of intentional behaviour in motivation.

If anything, this chapter suggests that instead of ignoring motivation, managers must take an active role in motivating their employees. Four specific conclusions are offered here:

1. Managers can influence the motivation state of employees. If performance needs to be improved, then managers must intervene and help create an atmosphere that encourages, supports and sustains improvement.
2. Managers should be sensitive to variations in employees' needs, abilities and goals. Managers also must consider differences in preferences (valences) for rewards.
3. Continual monitoring of needs, abilities, goals and preferences of employees is each individual manager's responsibility and is not the domain of personnel and human resources managers only.
4. Managers need to work on providing employees with jobs that offer task challenge, diversity and a variety of opportunities for need satisfaction.

In simple terms, the theme of our discussion of motivation is that the manager needs to be actively involved. If motivation is to be energised, sustained and directed, managers must know about needs, intentions, preferences, goals and comparisons and they must act on that knowledge. Failure to do so will result in many missed opportunities to help motivate employees in a positive manner.

GLOBAL

Encounter

Meeting employee expectations Japanese style

While it is not uncommon for an 'us versus them' mindset to characterise labour relations in this country, such an attitude is extremely rare in Japan. Although there are numerous factors involved, it is clear that one reason this is far less often a problem in Japanese companies is that the Japnese do an especially effective job in meeting employee needs and expectations. Japanese executives are unlikely to forget that their organisation's employees — not their equipment or technology—are their most valuable asset. Japanese companies understand that the best way to get employees to meet the company's expectations is to meet their employees' expectations. In other words, Japanese executives are very skilful in building and maintaining what we have called the psychological contract. Japanese workers cooperate with management because management cooperates with them. The welfare of both is inseparable from that of the organisation.

Princeton professor Alan Blinder makes the point that economics identifies an incentive issue known as the principal-agent problem. An example can be found in the relationship between a home owner and the real estate agent hired to sell the home. In whose interest will the agent act? Blinder suggests two major principal-agent problems are common in organisations. How do corporate boards ensure that executives serve the stockholders, and how do managers get workers to put forth their best efforts?

Primarily through large stock options that cause executives and shareholders to have the same interests, US companies have solved the first problem. The Japanese, however, have taken the lead in solving the second problem. They do this by making employees both principals and agents. To a large extent Japanese organisations are run for the benefit of their employees rather than their stockholders. This means, among other things, relatively small salary differentials between executives and workers, managers who start out on the factory floor, and pursuit of growth — even when it is unprofitable — to provide employee job security. These are the types of things Japanese workers expect — and get. In turn, management gets what it expects, highly motivated workers. When Toyota workers think in terms of 'us versus them', 'them' is far more likely to be General Motors or Honda than their own management.

Source: Based, in part, on Blinder, A. S. (1991). How Japan puts the 'Human' in Human Capital, *Business Week*, November 11, 22.

SUMMARY OF KEY POINTS

Describe the three distinct components of motivation. Motivation is made up of at least three distinct components. Direction refers to what an individual chooses to do when presented with a number of possible alternative courses of action. Intensity relates to the strength of the individual's response once the choice (direction) is made. Finally, persistence refers to the staying power of behaviour, or how long a person will continue to devote effort.

Distinguish between three approaches to motivation. The components are reflected in three different approaches to motivation.

Need–value–motive theories are concerned with direction and describe the factors that channel motivation towards particular goals. Cognitive-choice theories focus on intensity, describing the environmental factors that determine how hard individuals work towards their goals. Self-regulation theories are interested in how behaviour/motivation is maintained in the long term, especially when goals are complex — the persistence component of motivation.

Identify the need levels in Maslow's theory. Maslow's theory of motivation suggests that individuals' needs are arranged in a hierarchical order of importance and that a person will attempt to satisfy the more basic (lower level) needs before directing behaviour toward satisfying higher level needs. Maslow's five need levels, from lowest to highest, are (1) physiological, (2) safety and security, (3) belongingness, social and love, (4) esteem, and (5) self-actualisation.

Describe four patterns of intrinsic motivation. The environment shapes individual needs and values: when individuals are reinforced for particular behaviours, the frequency of those behaviours increases. They become a stable part of individuals' interactions with the world. These learned needs are the basis for intrinsic motivation, and research has identified four common patterns. These patterns are the need for achievement, affiliation, competence and power.

Define the key terms in expectancy theory. Key terms in expectancy theory include instrumentality, valence and expectancy. Instrumentality refers to the strength of a person's belief that achieving a specific result or outcome will lead to attaining a secondary outcome. Valence refers to a person's preference for attaining or avoiding a particular outcome. Expectancy refers to a person's belief regarding the likelihood or subjective probability that a particular behaviour will be followed by a particular outcome.

Identify the key steps in goal setting. The key steps in applying goal setting are: (1) diagnosis for readiness; (2) preparing employees via increased interpersonal interaction, communication, training and action plans for goal setting; (3) emphasising the attributes of goals that should be understood by a manager and subordinates; (4) conducting intermediate reviews to make necessary adjustments in established goals; and (5) performing a final review to check that the goals have been set, modified and accomplished.

Define the key components of control theory. Control theory incorporates the idea of feedback and suggests that we alter effort when there is a discrepancy between our goals and a desired level of performance. However, whether we increase or decrease effort depends on how important the goal is to us, as well as the explanations that we offer for performance.

Describe resource-allocation approaches to motivation. Resource-allocation theories incorporate concepts from expectancy, control and goal-setting theories. They introduce the idea that individuals allocate resources (skills, time and attention) based on the desirability of outcomes, the effort required to achieve those outcomes and an evaluation of whether the benefits outweigh the costs of achieving a particular goal.

Describe the concept of the psychological contract. Employee expectations of what the organisation will give them and what they owe the organisation and the organisation's expectation of what it will give to and receive from employees constitute the psychological contract. A psychological contract is an unwritten agreement between the individual and the organisation which specifies what each expects to give to and receive from the other.

REVIEW AND DISCUSSION QUESTIONS

1. Why is it important for a manager to consider the various components of motivation when diagnosing motivation problems? Is any one of the components more or less important than any of the others?

2. Which of the need–value–motive theories discussed in the chapter do you believe offers the best explanation of motivation? Which of the cognitive choice and self-regulation theories? Overall, do you feel that the need–value–motive approach or the cognitive choice and self-regulation approach best explains motivation? Explain.

3. Motivation is just one of several factors that influence productivity. What other factors were discussed in this chapter? What is the relationship between these factors and motivation?

4. Describe the sequence of events involved in the individual motivational process. What would happen to this process if no need deficiencies existed?

5. As a manager, would you rather the people for whom you are responsible be extrinsically or intrinsically motivated? Explain.

6. What would it be like to manage an organisation where all the employees were self-actualised? What kinds of opportunities and problems would this situation present to management?

7. Goal setting can be a difficult system to implement effectively. What kinds of problems might be encountered in attempting to install a goal-setting program in an organisation? As a manager, what would you do to minimise the likelihood you would encounter these problems?

8. Is there a psychological contract between the students enrolled in this course and the instructor? What are some of the specifics of this contract? How was the contract determined?

9. Using any theory described in this chapter, develop a plan for motivating employees.

ENDNOTES

1 Petri, H. (1979). *Motivation: Theory and Research.* Belmont, CA: Wadsworth Publishing, p. 4.

2 Kanfer, R. (1994). Motivation theory and industrial and organizational psychology. In M. D. Dunnette & L. M. Hough (Eds.) *Handbook of Industrial and Organizational Psychology* (2nd Ed.). Palo Alto, CA: Consulting Psychologists Press.

3 For a more detailed discussion of Herzberg's theory see Herzberg, F., Mausner, B. & Snyderman, B. (1959). *The Motivation to Work.* New York: John Wiley & Sons; Dunnette, M., Campbell, J. & Hakel, M. (1967). Factors contributing to job dissatisfaction in six occupational groups, *Organizational Behavior and Human Performance*, p. 147.

4 Maslow, A. H. (1943). A theory of human motivation, *Psychological Review*, 370–396; Maslow, A. H. (1954). *Motivation and Personality*, New York: Harper & Row.

5 Porter, L. W. (1961). A study of perceived need satisfaction in bottom and middle management jobs, *Journal of Applied Psychology*, 1–10.

6 Porter, L. W. (1964). *Organizational Patterns of Managerial Job Attitudes.* New York: American Foundation for Management Research.

7 Porter, L. W. (1963). Job attitudes in management perceived deficiencies in need fulfillment as a function of size of the company, *Journal of Applied Psychology*, 386–397.

8 Ivancevich, J. M. (1969). Perceived need satisfaction of domestic versus overseas managers, *Journal of Applied Psychology*, 274–278.

9 Lawler III, E. E., & Suttle, J. L. (1972). A causal correlation test of the need hierarchy concept, *Organizational Behavior and Human Performance*, 265–287.

10 Hall, D. T., & Nougaim, K. E. (1968). An examination of Maslow's need hierarchy in an organizational setting, *Organizational Behavior and Human Performance*, 12–35.

11 Herzberg, F., Mausner, B., & Snyderman, B. (1959). *The Motivation to Work.* New York: John Wiley & Sons.

12 For a discussion of the importance of intrinsic task motivation, see Thomas, K. W. and Velthouse, B. A. (1990). Cognitive elements of empowerment: An interpretive model of intrinsic task motivation, *Academy of Management Review*, 666–681.

13 Newstrom, J. W. , & Davis, K. (1993). *Organizational Behavior: Human Behavior at Work* (9th Ed.). New York: McGraw-Hill Inc.

14 McClelland, D. C. (1962). Business drive and national achievement, *Harvard Business Review*, July–August, 99–112.

15 Kanfer, R. (1994). Motivation theory and industrial and organizational psychology. In M. D. Dunnette & L. M. Hough (Eds.) *Handbook of Industrial and Organizational Psychology* (2nd Ed.). Palo Alto, CA: Consulting Psychologists Press.

16 Newstrom, J. W., & Davis, K. (1993). *Organizational Behavior: Human Behavior at Work* (9th Ed.). New York: McGraw-Hill Inc.

17 Ibid.

18 Ibid.

19 Ibid.

20 Vroom, V. H. (1964). *Work and Motivation.* New York: John Wiley & Sons. For earlier work, see Lewin, K. (1938). *The Conceptual Representation and the Measurement of Psychological Forces.* Durham, NC: Duke University Press; and Tolman, E. C. (1932). *Purposive Behavior in Animals and Men.* New York: Appleton-CenturyCrofts.

21 Kanfer, R. (1994). Motivation theory and industrial and organizational psychology. In Dunnette, M. D. & Hough L. M. (Eds.) *Handbook of Industrial and Organizational Psychology* (2nd Ed.). Palo Alto, CA: Consulting Psychologists Press.

22 Klein, J. I. (1990). Feasibility theory: A resource-munificence model of work motivation and behavior, *Academy of Management Review*, 646–665.

23 Kanfer, R. (1994). Motivation theory and industrial and organizational psychology. In Dunnette M. D. & Hough L. M. (Eds.) *Handbook of Industrial and Organizational Psychology* (2nd Ed.). Palo Alto, CA: Consulting Psychologists Press.

24 Salancik, G. R. & Pfeffer, J. (1978). A social information processing approach to job attitudes and task design, *Administrative Science Quarterly*, 224–253.

25 Greenberg, J. & Baron, R. A. (1993). *Behaviour in Organizations: Understanding and Managing the Human Side of Work* (4th Ed.). Boston: Allyn and Bacon.

26 Ledford, Jr., G. E. (1985). Skill-based pay: A concept that's catching on, *Personnel*, 20–26.

27 Locke, E. A. (1968). Toward a theory of task motivation and incentives, *Organizational Behavior and Human Performance*, 157–189.

28 For a discussion of the relationship between goals and intentions in motivated behavior, see Tubbs, M. E. and Ekeberg, S. E. (1991). The role of intentions in work motivation: Implications for goal-setting theory and research, *Academy of Management Review*, 180–299.

29 Ryan, T. A. (1970). *Intentional Behavior*. New York: Ronald Press, 1970, p. 95.

30 Locke, E. A., & Latham, G. P. (1990). *A Theory of Goal-Setting and Task Performance*. Englewood Cliffs, NJ, Prentice-Hall

31 Mithen, A. (1995). Players input the key: Parkin, *Age*, September 28.

32 Locke, E. A., Shaw, K. N., Saari, L. M., & Latham, G. P. (1981). Goal setting and task performance: 1969–1980, *Psychological Bulletin*, 129–152.

33 Locke, E. A. & Latham, G. P. (1990). Work motivation and satisfaction: Light at the end of the tunnel, *Psychological Science*, **1**, 240–246.

34 Early, P. C., Northcraft, G. B., Lee, C., & Lituchy, T. R. (1990). Impact of process and outcome feedback on the relation of goal setting to task performance, *Academy of Management Journal*, 87–105.

35 Erez, M., Earley, P. C., & Hulin, C. (1985). The impact of participation on goal acceptance and performance: A two–step model, *Academy of Management Journal*, 50–66.

36 Ivancevich, J. M. (1977). Different goal-setting treatments and their effects on performance

and job satisfaction, *Academy of Management Journal*, 406–419.

37 Shalley, C., Oldham, G., & Porac, J. (1987). Effects of goal difficulty, goal-setting method, and expected external evaluation on intrinsic motivation, *Academy of Management Journal*, 553–563.

38 Locke, E. A. & Latham, G. P. (1990). Work motivation and satisfaction: Light at the end of the tunnel, *Psychological Science*, **1**, 240–246.

39 Locke, E. A. (1968). Toward a theory of task motivation and incentives, *Organizational Behavior and Human Performance*, 157–189.

40 For a complete analysis, see Locke, E. A., Shaw, K. N., Saari, L. M., & Latham, G. P. (1981). Goal setting and task performance: 1969–1980, *Psychological Bulletin*, 125–152.

41 Ibid.

42 For a more detailed discussion of this point, and an attempted resolution, see Wood, R. E. & Locke, E. A. (1990). Goal setting and strategy effects on complex tasks, *Research in Organizational Behavior*, **12**, 73–109.

43 See, for example, Miller, G. A., Galanter E. & Pribram, K. H. (1960). *Plans and the Structure of Behavior*. New York: Holt, Rinehart & Winston, for an early and detailed account of the relationship between plans, feedback and human behaviour.

44 Kanfer, R. (1994). Motivation theory and industrial and organizational psychology. In M. D. Dunnette & L. M. Hough (Eds.) *Handbook of Industrial and Organizational Psychology* (2nd Ed.). Palo Alto, CA: Consulting Psychologists Press; Klein, H. J. (1989). An integrated control theory of work motivation, *Academy of Management Review*, **14**, 150–172.

45 Carver & Scheiers's theory of self-regulation is described more fully in R. Kanfer (1994). Motivation theory and industrial and organizational psychology. In Dunnette, M. D. & Hough, L. M. (Eds.) *Handbook of Industrial and Organizational Psychology* (2nd Ed.). Palo Alto, CA: Consulting Psychologists Press.

46 Klein, H. J. (1989). An integrated control theory of work motivation, *Academy of Management Review*, **14**, 150–172.

47 Ekeh, P. (1974). *Social Exchange Theory*. Cambridge, MA.: Harvard University Press.

48 Schein, H. (1980). *Organizational Psychology* (2nd Ed.). Englewood Cliffs, NJ: Prentice-Hall.

READING 4 MOTIVATION: A DIAGNOSTIC APPROACH

David A. Nadler
Edward E. Lawler III

Source: J. R. Hackman and E. E. Lawler, *Perspectives on Behavior in Organizations* (New York: McGraw-Hill, 1977).

- What makes some people work hard while others do as little as possible?
- How can I, as manager, influence the performance of people who work for me?
- Why do people turn over, show up late to work, and miss work entirely?

These important questions about employees' behavior can only be answered by managers who have a grasp of what motivates people. Specifically, a good understanding of motivation can serve as a valuable tool for *understanding* the causes of behavior in organizations, for *predicting* the effects of any managerial action, and for *directing* behavior so that organizational and individual goals can be achieved.

Existing approaches

During the past 20 years, managers have been bombarded with a number of different approaches to motivation. The terms associated with these approaches are well known — *human relations, scientific management, job enrichment, need hierarchy, self-actualization*, etc. Each of these approaches has something to offer. On the other hand, each of these different approaches also has its problems in theory and practice. Running through almost all of the approaches with which managers are familiar are a series of implicit but clearly erroneous assumptions.

Assumption 1: All employees are alike. Different theories present different ways of looking at people, but each of them assumes that all employees are basically similar in their makeup: Employees all want economic gains, or all want a pleasant climate, or all aspire to be self-actualizing, etc.

Assumption 2: All situations are alike. Most theories assume that all managerial situations are alike, and that the managerial course of action for motivation (for example, participation, job enlargement, etc.) is applicable in all situations.

Assumption 3: One best way. Out of the other two assumptions there emerges a basic principle that there is 'one best way' to motivate employees.

When these 'one best way' approaches are tried in the 'correct' situation they will work. However, all of them are bound to fail in some situations. They are therefore not adequate managerial tools.

A new approach

During the past 10 years, a great deal of research has been done on a new approach to looking at motivation. This approach, frequently called expectancy theory, still needs further testing, refining and extending. However, enough is known that many behavioral scientists have concluded that it represents the most comprehensive, valid and useful approach to understanding motivation. Further, it is apparent that it is a very useful tool for understanding motivation in organizations.

The theory is based on a number of specific assumptions about the causes of behavior in organizations.

Assumption 1: Behaviour is determined by a combination of forces in the individual and forces in the environment. Neither the individual nor the environment alone determines behavior. Individuals come into organizations with certain 'psychological baggage'. They have past experiences and a developmental history which has given them unique sets of needs, ways of looking at the world, and expectations about how organizations will treat them. These all influence how individuals respond to their work environment. The work environment provides structures (such as a pay system or a supervisor) which influence the behavior of people. Different environments tend to produce different behavior in similar people just as dissimilar people tend to behave differently in similar environments.

Assumption 2: People make decisions about their own behavior in organizations. While there are many constraints on the behavior of individuals in organizations, most of the behavior that is observed is the result of individuals' conscious decisions. These decisions usually fall into two categories. First, individuals make decisions about *membership behavior* — coming to work, staying at work, and in other ways being a member of the organization. Second, individuals make decisions

149

about the amount of *effort* they will direct *towards performing their jobs*. This includes decisions about how hard to work, how much to produce, at what quality, etc.

Assumption 3: Different people have different types of needs, desires and goals. Individuals differ on what kinds of outcomes (or rewards) they desire. These differences are not random; they can be examined systematically by an understanding of the differences in the strength of individuals' needs.

Assumption 4: People make decisions among alternative plans of behavior based on their perceptions (expectancies) of the degree to which a given behavior will lead to desired outcomes. In simple terms, people tend to do those things which they see as leading to outcomes (which can also be called rewards) they desire, and avoid doing those things they see as leading to outcomes that are not desired.

In general, the approach used here views people as having their own needs and mental maps of what the world is like. They use these maps to make decisions about how they will behave, behaving in those ways which their mental maps indicate will lead to outcomes that will satisfy their needs. Therefore, they are inherently neither motivated nor unmotivated; motivation depends on the situation they are in, and how it fits their needs.

The theory

Based on these general assumptions, expectancy theory states a number of propositions about the process by which people make decisions about their own behavior in organizational settings. While the theory is complex at first view, it is in fact made of a series of fairly straightforward observations about behavior. (The theory is presented in more technical terms in Appendix A.) Three concepts serve as the key building blocks of the theory:

Performance–outcome expectancy

Every behavior has associated with it, in an individual's mind, certain outcomes (rewards or punishments). In other words, the individual believes or expects that if he or she behaves in a certain way, he or she will get certain things. Examples of expectancies can easily be described. An individual may have an expectancy that if he produces 10 units he will receive his normal hourly rate while if he produces 15 units he will receive his hourly pay rate plus a bonus. Similarly an individual may believe that certain levels of performance will lead to approval or disapproval from members of her work group or from her supervisor. Each performance can be seen as leading to a number of different kinds of outcomes and outcomes can differ in their types.

Valence

Each outcome has a 'valence' (value, worth, attractiveness) to a specific individual. Outcomes have different valences for different individuals. This comes about because valences result from individual needs and perceptions, which differ because they in turn reflect other factors in the individual's life.

For example, some individuals may value an opportunity for promotion or advancement because of their needs for achievement or power, while others may not want to be promoted and leave their current work group because of needs for affiliation with others. Similarly, a fringe benefit such as a pension plan may have great valence for an older worker but little valence for a young employee on his first job.

Effort–performance expectancy

Each behavior also has associated with it in the individual's mind a certain expectancy or probability of success. This expectancy represents the individual's perception of how hard it will be to achieve such behavior and the probability of his or her successful achievement of that behavior.

For example, you may have a strong expectancy that if you put forth the effort, you can produce 10 units an hour, but that you have only a so-so chance of producing 15 units an hour if you try.

Putting these concepts together, it is possible to make a basic statement about motivation. In general, the motivation to attempt to behave in a certain way is greatest when:

a. The individual believes that the behavior will lead to outcomes (performance–outcome expectancy).
b. The individual believes that these outcomes have positive value for him or her (valence).
c. The individual believes that he or she is able to perform at the desired level (effort–performance expectancy).

Given a number of alternative levels of behavior (10, 15 and 20 units of production per hour, for example), the individual will choose that level of performance which has the greatest motivational force associated with it, as indicated by the expectancies, outcomes and valences.

In other words, when faced with choices about behavior, the individual goes through a process of considering questions such as, 'Can I perform at that level if I try?' 'If I perform at that level, what will happen?' 'How do I feel about those things that will happen?' The individual then decides to behave in a way which seems to have the best chance of producing positive, desired outcomes.

A general model

On the basis of these concepts, it is possible to construct a general model of behavior in organizational settings (see Exhibit 4.11 — p. 156). Working from left to right in the model, motivation is seen as the force on the individual to expend effort. Motivation leads to an observed level of effort by the individual. Effort alone, however, is not enough. Performance results from a combination of the effort that an individual puts forth and the level of ability which he or she has (reflecting skills, training, information, etc.). Effort thus combines with ability to produce a given level of performance. As a result of performance, the individual attains certain outcomes. The model indicates this relationship in a squiggly line, reflecting the fact that sometimes people perform but do not get desired outcomes. As this process of performance-reward occurs, time after time, the actual events serve to provide information which influences the individual's perceptions (particularly expectancies) and thus influence motivation in the future.

Outcomes, or rewards, fall into two major categories. First, the individual obtains outcomes from the environment. When an individual performs at a given level, he or she can receive positive or negative outcomes from supervision, co-workers, the organization's rewards systems, or other sources. These environmental rewards are thus one source of outcomes for the individual. A second source of outcomes is the individual. These include outcomes which occur purely from the performance of the task itself (feelings of accomplishment, personal worth, achievement, etc.). In a sense, the individual gives these

rewards to himself or herself. The environment cannot give them or take them away directly; it can only make them possible.

Supporting evidence

Over 50 studies have been done to test the validity of the expectancy-theory approach to predicting employee behavior.[1] Almost without exception, the studies have confirmed the predictions of the theory. As the theory predicts, the best performers in organizations tend to see a strong relationship between performing their jobs well and receiving rewards they value. In addition they have clear performance goals and feel they can perform well. Similarly, studies using the expectancy theory to predict how people choose jobs also show that individuals tend to interview for and actually take those jobs which they feel will provide the rewards they value. One study, for example, was able to correctly predict for 80 percent of the people studied which of several jobs they would take.[2] Finally, the theory correctly predicts that beliefs about the outcomes associated with performance (expectancies) will be better predictors of performance than will feelings of job satisfaction since expectancies are the critical causes of performance and satisfaction is not.

Questions about the model

Although the results so far have been encouraging, they also indicate some problems with the model. These problems do not critically affect the managerial implications of the model, but they should be noted. The model is based on the assumption that individuals make very rational decisions after a thorough exploration of all the available alternatives and on weighing the possible outcomes of all these alternatives. When we talk to or observe individuals, however, we find that their decision processes are frequently less thorough. People often stop considering alternative behavior plans when they find one that is at least moderately satisfying, even though more rewarding plans remain to be examined.

People are also limited in the amount of information they can handle at one time, and therefore the model may indicate a process that is much more complex than the one that actually takes place. On the other hand, the model does provide enough information and is consistent enough with reality to present some clear implications for managers who are concerned

PART 2 The individual in the organisation

with the question of how to motivate the people who work for them.

Implications for managers

The first set of implications is directed toward the individual manager who has a group of people working for him or her and is concerned with how to motivate good performance. Since behavior is a result of forces both in the person and in the environment, you as manager need to look at and diagnose both the person and the environment. Specifically, you need to do the following:

Figure out what outcomes each employee values. As a first step, it is important to determine what kinds of outcomes or rewards have valence for your employees. For each employee you need to determine 'what turns him or her on'. There are various ways of finding this out, including: (a) finding out employees' desires through some structured method of data collection, such as a questionnaire; (b) observing the employees' reactions to different situations or rewards; or (c) the fairly simple act of asking them what kinds of rewards they want, what kind of career goals they have, or 'what's in it for them'. It is important to stress here that it is very difficult to change what people want, but fairly easy to find out what they want. Thus, the skillful manager emphasizes diagnosis of needs, not changing the individuals themselves.

Determine what kinds of behavior you desire. Managers frequently talk about 'good performance' without really defining what good performance is. An important step in motivating is for you yourself to figure out what kinds of performances are required and what are adequate measures or indicators of performance (quantity, quality, etc.). There is also a need to be able to define those performances in fairly specific terms so that observable and measurable behavior can be defined and subordinates can understand what is desired of them (e.g. produce 10 products of a certain quality standard — rather than only produce at a high rate).

Make sure desired levels of performance are reachable. The model states that motivation is determined not only by the performance-to-outcome expectancy but also by the effort-to-performance expectancy. The implication of this

is that the levels of performance which are set as the points at which individuals receive desired outcomes must be reachable or attainable by these individuals. If the employees feel that the level of performance required to get a reward is higher than they can reasonably achieve, then their motivation to perform well will be relatively low.

Link desired outcomes to desired performances. The next step is to directly, clearly and explicitly link those outcomes desired by employees to the specific performances desired by you. If your employee values external rewards, then the emphasis should be on the rewards systems concerned with promotion, pay and approval. While the linking of these rewards can be initiated through your making statements to your employees, it is extremely important that employees see a clear example of the reward process working in a fairly short period of time if the motivating 'expectancies' are to be created in the employees' mind. The linking must be done by some concrete public acts, in addition to statements of intent.

If your employee values internal rewards (e.g. achievement), then you should concentrate on changing the nature of the person's job, for he or she is likely to respond well to such things as increased autonomy, feedback and challenge, because these things will lead to a situation where good job performance is inherently rewarding. The best way to check on the adequacy of the internal and external reward system is to ask people what their perceptions of the situation are. Remember it is the perceptions of people that determine their motivation, not reality. It doesn't matter, for example, whether you feel a subordinate's pay is related to his or her motivation. Motivation will be present only if the subordinate sees the relationship. Many managers are misled about the behavior of their subordinates because they rely on their own perceptions of the situation and forget to find out what their subordinates feel. There is only one way to do this: ask. Questionnaires can be used here, as can personal interviews (see Appendix B for a short version of a motivation questionnaire).

Analyze the total situation for conflicting expectancies. Having set up positive expectancies for employees, you then need to look at the entire situation to see if other factors (informal work groups, other managers, the organization's reward systems) have set up conflicting expectancies in the minds of the employees. Motivation will only be high when people see a number of rewards associated with good performance and few negative outcomes. Again, you can often gather this kind of information by asking your subordinates. If there are major conflicts, you need to make adjustments, either in your own performance and reward structure, or in the other sources of rewards or punishments in the environment.

Make sure changes in outcomes are large enough. In examining the motivational system, it is important to make sure that changes in outcomes or rewards are large enough to motivate significant behavior. Trivial rewards will result in trivial amounts of effort and thus trivial improvements in performance. Rewards must be large enough to motivate individuals to put forth the effort required to bring about significant changes in performance.

Check the system for its equity. The model is based on the idea that individuals are different and therefore different rewards will need to be used to motivate different individuals. On the other hand, for a motivational system to work it must be a fair one — one that has equity (not equality). Good performers should see that they get more desired rewards than do poor performers, and others in the system should see that also. Equity should not be confused with a system of equality where all are rewarded equally, with no regard to their performance. A system of equality is guaranteed to produce low motivation.

Implications for organizations

Expectancy theory has some clear messages for those who run large organizations. It suggests how organizational structures can be designed so that they increase rather than decrease levels of motivation of organization members. While there are many different implications, a few of the major ones are as follows:

Implication 1: The design of pay and reward systems. Organizations usually get what they reward, not what they want. This can be seen in many situations, and pay systems are a good example.[3] Frequently, organizations reward people for

membership (through pay tied to seniority, for example) rather than for performance. Little wonder that what the organization gets is behavior oriented towards 'safe,' secure employment rather than effort directed at performing well. In addition, even where organizations do pay for performance as a motivational device, they frequently negate the motivational value of the system by keeping pay secret, therefore preventing people from observing the pay-to-performance relationship that would serve to create positive, clear, and strong performance-to-reward expectancies. The implication is that organizations should put more effort into rewarding people (through pay, promotion, better job opportunities, etc.) for the performances which are desired, and that to keep these rewards secret is clearly self-defeating. In addition, it underscores the importance of the frequently ignored performance valuation or appraisal process and the need to evaluate people based on how they perform clearly defined specific behaviors, rather than on how they score on ratings of general traits such as 'honesty,' 'cleanliness,' and other, similar terms which frequently appear as part of the performance appraisal form.

Implication 2: The design of tasks, jobs and roles. One source of desired outcomes is the work itself. The expectancy-theory model supports much of the job enrichment literature in saying that, by designing jobs which enable people to get their needs fulfilled, organization can bring about higher levels of motivation.[4] The major difference between the traditional approaches to job enlargement or enrichment and the expectancy-theory approach is the recognition by expectancy theory that different people have different needs and therefore, some people may not want enlarged or enriched jobs. Thus, while the design of tasks that have more autonomy, variety, feedback, meaningfulness, etc., will lead to higher motivation in some, the organization needs to build in the opportunity for individuals to make choices about the kind of work they will do so that not everyone is forced to experience job enrichment.

Implication 3: The importance of group structures. Groups, both formal and informal, are powerful and potential sources of desired outcomes for individuals. Groups can provide or withhold acceptance, approval, affection, skill training, needed information, assistance, etc. They are a powerful force in the total motivational environment of individuals. Several implications emerge from the importance of groups. First, organizations should consider the structuring of at least a portion of rewards around group performance rather than individual performance. This is particularly important where group members have to cooperate with each other to produce a group product or service, and where the individual's contribution is often hard to determine. Second, the organization needs to train managers to be aware of how groups can influence individual behavior and to be sensitive to the kinds of expectancies which informal groups set up and their conflict or consistency with the expectancies that the organization attempts to create.

Implication 4: The supervisor's role. The immediate supervisor has an important role in creating, monitoring and maintaining the expectancies and rewards structures which will lead to good performance. The supervisor's role in the motivation process becomes one of defining clear goals, setting clear reward expectancies, and providing the right rewards for different people (which could include both organizational rewards and personal rewards such as recognition, approval, or support from the supervisors). Thus, organizations need to provide supervisors with an awareness of the nature of motivation as well as the tools (control over organizational rewards, skill in administering those rewards) to create positive motivation.

Implication 5: Measuring motivation. If things like expectancies, the nature of the job, supervisor-controlled outcomes, satisfaction, etc., are important in understanding how well people are being motivated, then organizations need to monitor employee perceptions along these lines. One relatively cheap and reliable method of doing this is through standardized employee questionnaires. A number of organizations already use such techniques, surveying employees' perceptions and attitudes at regular intervals (ranging from once a month to once every year and a half) using either standardized surveys or surveys developed specifically for the organization. Such information is useful both to

the individual manager and to top management in assessing the state of human resource and the effectiveness of the organization's motivational systems.[5] (Again, see Appendix B for excerpts from a standardized survey.)

Implication 6: Individualizing organizations. Expectancy theory leads to a final general implication about a possible future direction for the design of organizations. Because different people have different needs and therefore have different valences, effective motivation must come through the recognition that not all employees are alike and that organizations need to be flexible in order to accommodate individual differences. This implies the 'building in' of choice for employees in many areas, such as reward systems, fringe benefits, job assignments, etc., where employees previously have had little say. A successful example of the building in of such choice can be seen in the experiments at TRW and the Educational Testing Service with 'cafeteria fringe-benefits plans' which allow employees to choose the fringe benefits they want, rather than taking the expensive and often unwanted benefits which the company frequently provides to everyone.[6]

Summary

Expectancy theory provides a more complex model of man [humans] for managers to work with. At the same time, it is a model which holds promise for the more effective motivation of individuals and the more effective design of organizational systems. It implies, however, the need for more exacting and thorough diagnosis by the manager to determine (a) the relevant forces in the individual and (b) the relevant forces in the environment, both of which combine to motivate different kinds of behaviour. Following diagnosis, the model implies a need to act — to develop a system of pay, promotion, job assignments, group structures, supervision, etc. — to bring about effective motivation by providing different outcomes for different individuals.

Performance of individuals is a critical issue in making organizations work effectively. If a manager is to influence work behavior and performance, he or she must have an understanding of motivation and the factors which influence an individual's motivation to come to work, to work hard and to work well. While simple models offer easy answers, it is the more complex models which seem to offer more promise. Managers can use models (like expectancy theory) to understand the nature of behavior and build more effective organizations.

Appendix A: The expectancy theory model in more technical terms

A person's motivation to exert effort towards a specific level of performance is based on his or her perceptions of associations between actions and outcomes. The critical perceptions which contribute to motivation are graphically presented in Exhibit 4.10. These perceptions can be defined as follows:

A. The effort-to-performance expectancy (E→P): This refers to the person's subjective probability about the likelihood that he or she can perform at a given level, or that effort on his or her part will lead to successful performance. This term can be thought of as varying from 0 to 1. In general, the less likely a person feels that he or she can perform at a given level, the less likely he or she will be to try to perform at that level. A person's E→P probabilities are also strongly influenced by each situation and by previous experience in that and similar situations.

B. The performance-to-outcomes expectancy (P→O): and valence (V): This refers to a combination of a number of beliefs about what

the outcomes of successful performance will be and the value or attractiveness of these outcomes to the individual. Valence is considered to vary from +1 (very desirable) to −1 (very undesirable) and the performance-to-outcomes probabilities vary from +1 (performance sure to lead to outcome) to 0 (performance not related to outcome). In general, the more likely a person feels that performance will lead to valent outcomes, the more likely he or she will be to try to perform at the required level.

C. Instrumentality: As Exhibit 4.10 indicates, a single level of performance can be associated with a number of different outcomes, each having a certain degree of valence. Some outcomes are valent because they have direct value or attractiveness. Some outcomes, however, have valence because they are seen as leading to (or being 'instrumental' for) the attainment of other 'second-level' outcomes which have direct value or attractiveness.

D. Intrinsic and extrinsic outcomes: Some outcomes are seen as occurring directly as a result of performing the task itself and are outcomes which the individual thus gives to himself (i.e., feelings of accomplishment, creativity, etc.). These are called intrinsic outcomes. Other outcomes that are associated with performance are provided or mediated by

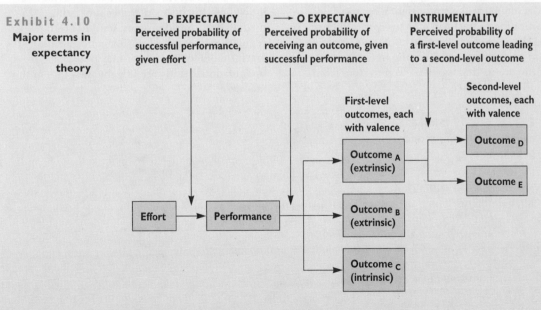

Exhibit 4.10
Major terms in expectancy theory

E → P EXPECTANCY	P → O EXPECTANCY	INSTRUMENTALITY
Perceived probability of successful performance, given effort	Perceived probability of receiving an outcome, given successful performance	Perceived probability of a first-level outcome leading to a second-level outcome

Second-level outcomes, each with valence

First-level outcomes, each with valence

Effort → Performance

Outcome A (extrinsic)

Outcome B (extrinsic)

Outcome C (intrinsic)

Outcome D

Outcome E

Motivation is expressed as follows: M * [E→P] X > [(P→O) (V)]

external factors (the organization, the supervisor, the work groups, etc.). These outcomes are called extrinsic outcomes.

Along with the graphic representation of these terms presented in Exhibit 4.10, there is a simplified formula for combining these perceptions to arrive at a term expressing the relative level of motivation to exert effort towards performance at a given level. The formula expresses these relationships:

A. The person's motivation to perform is determined by the P→O expectancy multiplied by the valence (V) of the outcome. The valence of the first order outcome subsumes the instrumentalities and valences of second outcomes. The relationship is multiplicative since there is no motivation to perform if either of the terms is zero.

B. Since a level of performance has multiple outcomes associated with it, the products of all probability-times-valence combinations are added together for all the outcomes that are seen as related to the specific performance.

C. This term (the summed P→O expectancies times valences) is then multiplied by the E→P expectancy. Again the multiplicative relationship indicates that if either term is zero, motivation is zero.

D. In summary, the strength of a person's motivation to perform effectively is influenced by (1) the person's belief that effort can be converted into performance and (2) the net attractiveness of the events that are perceived to stem from good performance.

So far, all the terms have referred to the individual's perceptions which result in motivation and thus an intention to behave in a certain way. Exhibit 4.11 is a simplified representation of the total model, showing how these intentions get translated into actual behavior.[7] The model envisions the following sequence of events:

A. First, the strength of a person's motivation to perform correctly is most directly reflected in his or her effort — how hard he or she works. This effort expenditure may or may not result in good performance, since at least two factors must be right if effort is to be converted into performance. First, the person must possess the necessary abilities in order to perform the job well. Unless both ability and effort are high, there cannot be good performance. A second factor is the person's perception of how his or her effort can best be converted into performance. It is assumed that this perception is learned by the individual on the basis of previous experience in similar situations. This 'how to do it' perception can obviously vary widely in accuracy and — where erroneous perceptions exist — performance is low even though effort or motivation may be high.

B. Second, when performance occurs, certain amounts of outcomes are obtained by the individual. Intrinsic outcomes, not being mediated by outside forces, tend to occur regularly as a result of performance, while extrinsic outcomes may or may not accrue to the individual (indicated by the wavy line in the model).

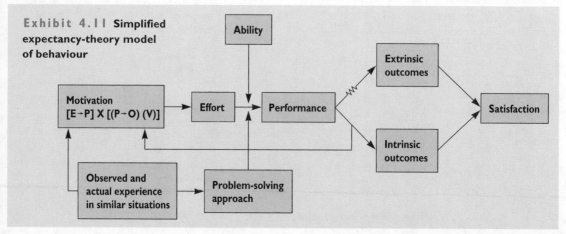

Exhibit 4.11 Simplified expectancy-theory model of behaviour

Exhibit 4.12 Question 1: Here are some things that could happen to people if they do their jobs especially well. How likely is it that each of these things would happen if you performed your job especially well?

	Not at All Likely		Somewhat Likely		Quite Likely	Extremely Likely	
a. You will get a bonus or pay increase.	(1)	(2)	(3)	(4)	(5)	(6)	(7)
b. You will feel better about yourself as a person.	(1)	(2)	(3)	(4)	(5)	(6)	(7)
c. You will have an opportunity to develop your skills and abilities.	(1)	(2)	(3)	(4)	(5)	(6)	(7)
d. You will have better job security.	(1)	(2)	(3)	(4)	(5)	(6)	(7)
e. You will be given chances to learn new things.	(1)	(2)	(3)	(4)	(5)	(6)	(7)
f. You will be promoted or get a better job.	(1)	(2)	(3)	(4)	(5)	(6)	(7)
g. You will get a feeling that you've accomplished something worthwhile.	(1)	(2)	(3)	(4)	(5)	(6)	(7)
h. You will have more freedom on your job.	(1)	(2)	(3)	(4)	(5)	(6)	(7)
i. You will be respected by the people you work with.	(1)	(2)	(3)	(4)	(5)	(6)	(7)
j. Your supervisor will praise you.	(1)	(2)	(3)	(4)	(5)	(6)	(7)
k. The people you work with will be friendly with you.	(1)	(2)	(3)	(4)	(5)	(6)	(7)

C. Third, as a result of the obtaining of outcomes and the perceptions of the relative value of the outcomes obtained, the individual has a positive or negative affective response (a level of satisfaction or dissatisfaction).

D. Fourth, the model indicates that events which occur influence future behavior by altering the E→P, P→0 and V perceptions. This process is represented by the feedback loops running from actual behavior back to motivation.

Appendix B: Measuring motivation using expectancy theory

Expectancy theory suggests that it is useful to measure the attitudes individuals have in order to diagnose motivational problems. Such measurement helps the manager to understand why employees are motivated or not, what the strength of motivation is in different parts of the organization and how effective different awards

are for motivating performance. A short version of a questionnaire used to measure motivation in organizations is included here.[8] Basically, three different questions need to be asked (see Exhibits 4.12, 4.13 and 4.14).

Using the questionnaire results
The results from this questionnaire can be used to calculate a *work-motivation score*. A score can be calculated for each individual and scores can be combined for groups of individuals. The procedure for obtaining a work-motivation score is as follows:

A. For each of the possible positive outcomes listed in questions 1 and 2, multiply the score for the outcome in question 1 (P→0 expectancies) by the corresponding score on question 2 (valences of outcomes). Thus, score *1a* would be multiplied by score *2a*, score *1b* by score *2b*, etc.

Exhibit 4.13 Question 2: Different people want different things from their work. Here is a list of things a person could have on his or her job. How *important* is each of the following to you?

	Moderately Important or Less			Quite Important		Extremely Important	
How important is … ?							
a. The amount of pay you get.	(1)	(2)	(3)	(4)	(5)	(6)	(7)
b. The chances you have to so something that makes you feel good about yourself as a person.	(1)	(2)	(3)	(4)	(5)	(6)	(7)
c. The opportunity to develop your skills and abilities.	(1)	(2)	(3)	(4)	(5)	(6)	(7)
d. The amount of job security you have.	(1)	(2)	(3)	(4)	(5)	(6)	(7)
How important is … ?							
e. The chances you have to learn new things.	(1)	(2)	(3)	(4)	(5)	(6)	(7)
f. Your chances for getting a promotion or getting a better job.	(1)	(2)	(3)	(4)	(5)	(6)	(7)
g. The chances you have to accomplish something worthwhile.	(1)	(2)	(3)	(4)	(5)	(6)	(7)
h. The amount of freedom you have on your job.	(1)	(2)	(3)	(4)	(5)	(6)	(7)
How important is … ?							
i. The respect you receive from the people you work with.	(1)	(2)	(3)	(4)	(5)	(6)	(7)
j. The praise you get from your supervisor.	(1)	(2)	(3)	(4)	(5)	(6)	(7)
k. The friendliness of the people you work with.	(1)	(2)	(3)	(4)	(5)	(6)	(7)

B. All of the 1 times 2 products should be added together to get a total of all expectancies times valences.

C. The total should be divided by the number of pairs (in this case 11) to get an average expectancy-time-valence score.

D. The scores from question 3 (E→P expectancies) should be added together and then divided by three to get an average effort-to-performance expectancy score.

E. Multiply the score obtained in step C (the average expectancy times valence) by the score obtained in step D (the average E→P expectancy score) to obtain a total work-motivation score.

Additional comments on the work-motivation score
A number of important points should be kept in mind when using the questionnaire to get a work-motivation score. First, the questions presented here are just a short version of a larger and more comprehensive questionnaire. For more detail, the articles and publications referred to in the

Exhibit 4.14 **Question 3: Below you will see a number of pairs of factors that look like this:**
Warm weather → sweating (1) (2) (3) (4) (5) (6) (7)
You are to indicate by checking the appropriate number to the right of each pair how often it is
true for you personally that the first factor leads to the second on *your job*. Remember, for each
pair, indicate how often it is true by checking the box under the response which seems most
accurate.

	Never	Sometimes		Often		Almost Always	
a. Working hard → high productivity	(1)	(2)	(3)	(4)	(5)	(6)	(7)
b. Working hard → doing my job well	(1)	(2)	(3)	(4)	(5)	(6)	(7)
c. Working hard → good job performance	(1)	(2)	(3)	(4)	(5)	(6)	(7)

text and footnotes should be consulted. Second, this is a general questionnaire. Since it is hard to anticipate in a general questionnaire what may be valent outcomes in each situation, the individual manager may want to add additional outcomes to questions 1 and 2. Third, it is important to remember that questionnaire results can be influenced by the feelings people have when they fill out the questionnaire. The use of the questionnaire as outlined above assumes a certain level of trust between manager and subordinates. People filling out questionnaires need to know what is going to be done with their answers and usually need to be assured of the confidentiality of their responses. Finally, the research indicated that, in many cases, the score obtained by simply averaging all the responses to question 1 (the P→0 expectancies) will be useful as the fully calculated work-motivation score. In each situation, the manager should experiment and find out whether the additional information in questions 2 and 3 aids in motivational diagnosis.

References

1 For reviews of the expectancy theory research, see T. R. Mitchell, 'Expectancy Models of Job Satisfaction, Occupational Preference, and Effort: A Theoretical, Methodological, and Empirical Appraisal', *Psychological Bulletin* 81 (1974), pp. 1053–77. For a more general discussion of expectancy theory and other approaches to motivation, see E. E. Lawler, *Motivation in Work Organizations* (Belmont, CA: Brooks/Cole, 1973).

2 E. E. Lawler, W. J. Kuleck, J. G. Rhode, and J. F. Sorenson, 'Job Choice and Post-Decision Dissonance', *Organizational Behavior and Human Performance* 13 (1975), pp. 133–45.

3 For a detailed discussion of the implications of expectancy theory for pay and reward systems, see E. E. Lawler, *Pay and Organizational Effectiveness: A Psychological View* (New York: McGraw-Hill, 1971).

4 A good discussion of job design with an expectancy theory perspective is in J. R. Hackman, G. R. Oldham, R. Janson, and K. Purdy, 'A New Strategy for Job Enrichment', *California Management Review*, Summer, 1975, p. 57.

5 The use of questionnaires for understanding and changing organizational behavior is discussed in D. A. Nadler, *Feedback and Organizational Development: Using Data-Based Methods* (Reading, MA: Addison-Wesley Publishing, 1977).

6 The whole issue of individualizing organizations is examined in E. E. Lawler, 'The Individual Organization: Problems and Promise', *California Management Review* 17(2) (1974), pp. 31–39.

7 For a more detailed statement of the model, see E. E. Lawler, 'Job Attitudes and Employee Motivation: Theory, Research, and Practice', *Personal Psychology* 23 (1970), pp. 223–37.

8 For a complete version of the questionnaire and supporting documentation, see D. A. Nadler, C. Cammann, G. D. Jenkins, and E. E. Lawler, eds., *The Michigan Organizational Assessment Package* (Progress Report II) (Ann Arbor: Survey Research Center, 1975).

EXERCISE 4 GOAL SETTING: HOW TO DO IT

Each person is to work alone for at least 30 minutes with this exercise. After sufficient time has elapsed for each person to work through the exercise, the instructor will go over each goal and ask for comments from the class or group. The discussion should display the understanding of goals that each participant has and what will be needed to improve his or her goal-writing skills.

Writing and evaluating goals seem simple, but they are often not done well in organisations. The press of time, previous habits, and little concern about the attributes of a goal statement are reasons why goals are often poorly constructed. Actually, a number of guidelines should be followed in preparing goals.

1. A well-presented goal statement contains four elements:
    a. an action or accomplishment verb;
    b. a single and measurable result;
    c. a date of completion;
    d. a cost in terms of effort, resources or money, or some combination of these factors.
2. A well-presented goal statement is short; it is not a paragraph. It should be presented in a sentence.
3. A well-presented goal statement specifies only what and when and does not get into how or why.
4. A well-presented goal statement is challenging and attainable. It should cause the person to stretch his or her skills, abilities and efforts.
5. A well-presented goal statement is meaningful and important. It should be a priority item.
6. A well-presented goal statement must be acceptable to you so that you will try hard to accomplish the goal.

■ The goal statement model should be:

To (action or accomplishment verb) (single result) by (a date — keep it realistic) at (effort, use of what resources, cost).

■ An example for a production operation:

To reduce the production cost per unit of Mint toothpaste by at least 3% by 1 March, at a changeover of equipment expense not to exceed $45 000.

Examine the next four statements that are presented as goal statements. Below each goal write a critique of the statement. Is it a good goal statement? Why? Discuss your viewpoints in the class group discussion.

To reduce my blood pressure to an acceptable level.

_____
_____
_____
_____
_____
_____
_____

To make financial investments with a guaranteed minimum return of at least 16%.

_____
_____
_____
_____
_____
_____
_____

To spend a minimum of 45 minutes a day on a doctor-approved exercise plan, starting Monday, lasting for 6 months, at no expense.

_____
_____
_____
_____
_____
_____
_____

To spend more time reading non-work-related novels and books during the next year.

_____
_____
_____
_____
_____
_____
_____

CASE 4   FAB SWEETS LIMITED

Source: Case prepared by N. Kemp, C. Clegg, T. Wall, *Case Studies in Organizational Behaviour*, ed. C. Clegg, N. Kemp, & K. Legge, London: Harper & Row, 1985.

Organisational setting

FAB Sweets Limited is a manufacturer of high-quality sweets . The company is a medium-sized, family-owned, partially unionised and highly successful confectionery producer in the north of England. The case study is set within a single department in the factory where acute problems were experienced.

Background to the case

The department (hereafter called HB) produces and packs over 40 lines of hard-boiled sweets on a batch-production system. It is organised in two adjacent areas, one for production staffed by men and one for packing staffed by women. The areas are separated by a physical barrier, allowing the packing room to be air-conditioned and protected from the humidity resulting from production. Management believed this was necessary to stop the sweets from sweating (thus sticking to their wrappers) during storage. Each room has a chargehand and a supervisor who reports to the department manager, who himself is responsible to the factory manager. In total, 37 people work in the department (25 in production, 12 in packing), the majority of whom are skilled employees. Training takes place on the job and it normally takes 2 years to acquire the skills necessary to complete all the production tasks. Exhibit 4.15 presents an outline of the physical layout of the department and the work flow.

The production process is essentially quite simple. Raw materials, principally sugar, are boiled to a set temperature, with 'cooking time' varying from line to line. The resulting batches are worked on by employees who fold and manipulate them so as to create the required texture, while adding colouring and flavourings ('slabbing' and 'mixing'). Different batches are moulded together to create the flavour mixes and patterns required ('make up'). The batch, which by now is quite cool, is then extruded through a machine which cuts it into sweets of individual size. Some products at this stage are automatically wrapped and then passed by conveyor belt to the packing room where they are inspected, bagged and boxed ready for dispatch to retail and wholesale outlets. Other products progress unwrapped into the packing room where they are fed into a wrapping machine, inspected, bagged and dispatched. Several different product lines can be produced at the same time. The most skilled and critical tasks occur early in the process; these include 'cooking' mixtures for different products and 'make up' (e.g. for striped mints). These skills are gradually learned until the operator is able to 'feel' the correct finish for each of the 40 lines. All the tasks are highly interdependent such that any one individual's performance affects the ease with which the next person down the line can successfully achieve his or her part of the production process. Although the work appears quite simple and the management of the process straightforward, the department nevertheless experienced acute problems. These are outlined below.

The problem

In objective terms, the problems in HB were manifest in a high level of labour turnover, six new managers in 8 years, production which consistently fell below targets based on work-study standards, and high levels of scrap. The department was known as the worst in the factory, and its problems were variously characterised in

terms of 'attitude', 'atmosphere' and 'climate'. Moreover, employees had few decision-making responsibilities, low motivation and low job satisfaction, and received little information on their performance. Finally, there were interpersonal problems between the employees in the production and packing rooms, between the two supervisors, and also among the operators, and there were a number of dissatisfactions relating to grading and payment levels.

Experience of the method of working

To understand how HB works and how people experienced their work, it is necessary to recognise the strong drive throughout the organisation for production. Departmental

Exhibit 4.15 **The HB Department: Physical layout and work flow**

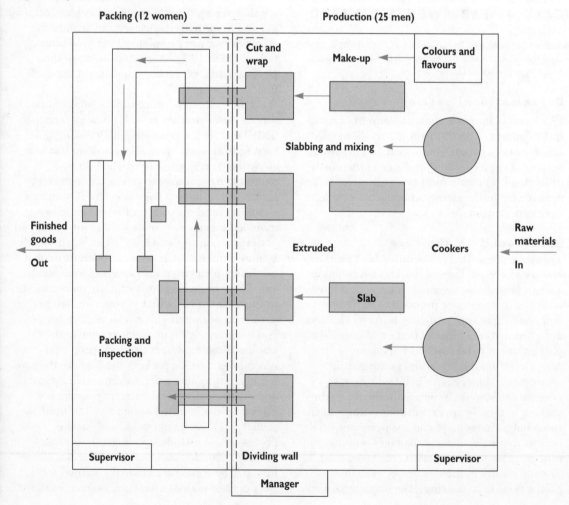

managers are judged primarily in terms of their production levels (against targets) and the efficiency (against work study standards) at which they perform. In HB this pressure was transmitted to the two supervisors. In practice, production levels were the number of batches of sweets processed, and efficiency was the ratio of batches produced to hours used by direct labour.

The production supervisor responded to the pressure for production in a number of ways. First, in an attempt to maximise production, he always allocated people to the jobs at which they performed best. He also determined the cooker speeds. In effect, this set the pace of work for both production and packing. Buffer stocks were not possible in production because the sweets needed processing before they cooled down. If he was falling behind the target, the supervisor responded by speeding up the pace of work. In addition, he regarded his job purely in terms of processing batches and ignored problems in the packing room, which may in fact have resulted directly from his actions or from those of his staff. The supervisory role thus involved allocating people to tasks; setting machine speeds (and hence the pace of work); organising reliefs and breaks; monitoring hygiene, safety and quality standards; maintaining discipline; and recording data for the management information systems. The chargehand undertook these responsibilities in the absence of a supervisor, spending the rest of his time on production.

The men in production complained that they were bored with always doing the same jobs, especially as some were physically harder than others (for example, 'slabbing' involved manual manipulation of batches of up to 50 kilograms). Several claimed that their greater efforts should receive financial recognition. Furthermore, this rigidity of task allocation was in direct conflict with the grading system, which was designed to encourage flexibility. To be on the top rate of pay in the department, an operator had to be capable of performing all the skills for all the lines and hence be able to cover any job. Training schedules matched this. In practice, however, people rarely used more than one or two of their skills. The others decayed through disuse. All the staff recognised that the grading system was at odds with how the department actually worked and tended to be dissatisfied with both. The production supervisor's strict control over the pace of work also proved suboptimal in other

ways. For example, he sometimes pushed the pace to a level regarded as impossible by the staff. Whether this was true or self-fulfilling is a moot point — the net result was an increase in the level of scrap. Also, he ignored the wishes of the staff to work less hard in the afternoon when they were tired: again scrap resulted. In addition, the feeling was widespread among the men in production that management and supervision organised the work badly and would do better if they took advice from the shop floor. Their own perceived lack of control over the job led them to abrogate responsibility when things went wrong ('We told them so!!'). And finally, although the processes of production were highly interdependent, operators adopted an insular perspective and the necessary cooperation between workers was rarely evident, and then only on the basis of personal favours between friends.

The equivalent pressure on the packing supervisor was to pack the sweets efficiently. As her section could pack no more than was produced, her only manipulable variable was hours worked. Thus, to increase her efficiency she could only transfer the packers to 'other work' within her room (e.g. cleaning) or to another department.

The packers for their part resented being asked to work flat out when HB was busy, only to be moved elsewhere when things were slacker. As described above, their own work flow was basically controlled by the speed at which the men were producing. When in difficulty, direct appeals to the men to slow down were unsuccessful and so they channelled their complaints through their supervisor. Because of the insular perspective adopted by the production supervisor (in rational support of his own targets), her approaches were usually ignored ('It's my job to produce sweets'), and the resulting intersupervisory conflict took up much of the department manager's time. In addition the packing room was very crowded and interpersonal conflicts were common.

Finally, production problems throughout the factory were created by seasonal peaks and troughs in the market demand for sweets. These 'busy' and 'slack' periods differed between production departments. In order to cope with market demands, the production planning department transferred staff, on a temporary basis, between production departments. In HB this typically meant that, when they were busy, 'unskilled' employees were drafted in to help, whereas when demand was low HB employees were transferred to other departments where they were usually given the worst jobs. Both of these solutions were resented by the employees in HB.

This description of the department is completed when one recognises the complications involved in scheduling over forty product lines through complex machinery, all of it over 10 years old. In fact, breakdowns and interruptions to smooth working were common. The effects of these on the possible levels of production were poorly understood and in any case few operators were aware of their targets or of their subsequent performance. More immediately, the breakdowns were a source of continual conflict between the department and the maintenance engineers responsible to an engineering manager. The department laid the blame on poor maintenance, the engineers on abuse or lack of care by production workers in handling the machinery. Much management time was spent in negotiating 'blame' for breakdowns and time allowances resulting, since this affected efficiency figures. Not surprisingly, perhaps, the factory-wide image of the department was very poor on almost all counts, and its status was low.

Participants' diagnoses of the problems

Shopfloor employees, chargehands, supervisors, the department manager and senior management were agreed that much was wrong in HB. However, there was no coherent view of the causes and what should be done to make improvements. Many shopfloor employees placed the blame on supervision and management for their lack of technical and planning expertise and their low consideration for subordinates. The production supervisor favoured a solution in terms of 'getting rid of the trouble-makers', by transferring or sacking his nominated culprits. The department manager wanted to introduce a senior supervisor to handle the conflicts between the production and packing supervisors and further support the pressure for production. The factory manager thought the way work was organised and managed might be at the core of the difficulties.

Case questions

rate at which employees are replaced

1. Why is turnover often considered a motivation problem?
2. How would you analyse the department problem using expectancy theory?
3. How would you solve the motivation problem? Be specific.

MOTIVATION:
AN ORGANISATIONAL
PERSPECTIVE

Learning objectives

- Describe *key components of the job characteristics model.*

- Discuss *organisational behaviour management.*

- Describe *several purposes of performance evaluation.*

- Identify *a variety of different evaluation methods.*

- Compare *intrinsic and extrinsic rewards.*

- Describe *key components of equity theory.*

- Discuss *the role of justice in reward systems.*

- Understand *the role rewards play in turnover, absenteeism and performance.*

- Describe *the elements in a model of individual rewards.*

5

Chapter

In the last chapter, we looked at three broad categories of motivational theories. Each category provided us with a different perspective on what motivates the individual and helped us to understand what factors — from an individual's point of view — energise, direct and sustain behaviour. If we think about the determinant of job performance in Chapter 4, we could say that so far we have looked at those factors that affect an individual's willingness to perform. We know, from our consideration of psychological contracts, that this willingness to perform represents only one side of the obligations between employers and employees. We now turn to the obligations that employers have: it is the role of managers and organisational systems to ensure that individuals have the capacity and the opportunity to perform. Employers have the following obligations: in terms of job performance, to provide employees with capacity and opportunity; and in terms of the motivational process, to provide feedback (evaluations) and to reward behaviours in a fair and equitable manner. In this chapter we will consider how such opportunities can be created and our Organisational Encounter describes how one company, Sherlock Holmes Inns, has linked rewards to performance.

IMPROVING PERFORMANCE

Motivational theories give us some insight into how individuals' needs and their perceptions of the environment influence their level of motivation or willingness to perform tasks. The challenge for organisations is to use this knowledge in a way that creates opportunities and increases the capacity of individuals to perform at their best. In this section, we will consider two organisational strategies: job design, which creates opportunities, and organisational behaviour management, which increases capacity.

Job design

Case 5
Vaccino

Job design is most clearly linked to the need–value–motive group of theories that we discussed in Chapter 4. The aim of job design is to create opportunities for individuals to meet their higher order needs of self-esteem and self-actualisation. By focusing on the range of skills that individuals use, the way that those skills are combined and the level of responsibility given to employees, job design strives to create a meaningful and challenging job. In the next section, we will examine three strategies for achieving this goal. Each strategy involves changing the combination of tasks that make up an employee's job. Before looking at these strategies, we need to understand what it is possible to change.

Jobs differ in two ways: their *range*, which describes the number of tasks that individuals perform as a part of their job, and their *depth*, which describes the amount of freedom that a person has in deciding job activities and outcomes. Job range and depth distinguish one job from another not only within the same organisation but also among different organisations. To illustrate how jobs differ in range and depth, Exhibit 5.1 depicts the differences for selected jobs of business firms, hospitals and universities. For example, chiefs of surgery have high job range and significant depth. Chiefs of surgery have significant job range in that they oversee and counsel on many diverse surgical matters. In addition, they are not supervised closely, and they have the authority to influence hospital

Reward systems, pay and motivation

Reward systems are critical to employee motivation and performance: every motivational theory that we have discussed considers how rewards (either intrinsic or extrinsic) can be used to enhance motivation. In the workplace, one of the most obvious means for rewarding staff is through their salaries. What should we aim for? And what are organisations doing?

According to the Australian Institute of Management any salary should have three components: a basic salary that rewards individuals for their particular skills and qualifications; a component that rewards work groups for team performance; and a component that rewards the organisation as a whole when organisation-wide goals are achieved. All of this suggests that, in addition to base salary, organisations need to put together packages and reward systems that draw on strategies such as broadbanding, employee share plans, profit sharing and team-based pay. However, a recent Hay group survey reported in *Business Review Weekly* shows that organisations are not moving with the times: at the individual level, only about 50% reward staff for achieving specific targets or give bonuses when staff learn new skills; and at the organisational level, only 33% have a broadbanding strategy while even fewer (10%) offer some form of profit sharing.

The executive chairman of Sherlock Holmes Inns, a Melbourne-based company, is one exception. John Webb has introduced profit sharing in his chain of pubs. To qualify for the scheme, staff must be with Sherlock Holmes Inns for 12 months; they then receive a slice of company profits that is proportional to their salary (with an adjustment to further reward individual performance). To ensure that there are profits to be shared, staff at Sherlock Holmes Inns are given daily budgets and targets: managers have a high degree of control over staff and other aspects of the workplace and aim to meet daily profit targets. Public postings of profits and targets allow staff to monitor their performance against these targets. And, according to management, staff have responded enthusiastically to this scheme.

However, it is important that such schemes are used to prevent problems rather than to solve them. Organisations should ensure that they match their reward systems to organisational goals: team-based pay will be most efficient when the organisations want self-managing work teams, whereas share plans will be more effective for organisations that value high levels of employee participation.

Source: James, D. (1995). Sherlock Holmes and the case of the profit share, *Business Review Weekly*, March 6; Stickels, G. (1994). Carrots are playing a bigger role in restructuring, *Business Review Weekly*, September 12.

surgery policies and procedures. Examples of jobs with high depth and low range are packaging machine mechanics, anaesthetists and faculty members. Anaesthetists perform a limited number of tasks. They are concerned with the rather restricted task of administering anaesthetics to patients. However, they can decide the type of anaesthetic to be administered in a particular situation, a decision indicative of high job depth. Highly specialised jobs are those that have few tasks to accomplish by prescribed means. Such jobs are quite routine; they also tend to be controlled by specified rules and procedures (low depth). A highly despecialised job (high range) has many tasks to accomplish within the framework of discretion over means and ends (high depth). Within an organisation there are typically great differences among jobs in both range and depth. Although managers have no precise equations to use in deciding job range and depth, they can follow this guideline: Given the economic and technical requirements of the organisation's mission, goals and objectives, what is the optimal point along the continuum of range and depth for each job?

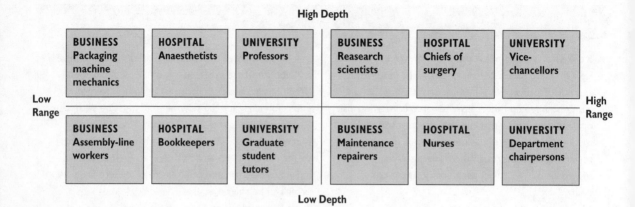

High Depth

| BUSINESS Packaging machine mechanics | HOSPITAL Anaesthetists | UNIVERSITY Professors | BUSINESS Reasearch scientists | HOSPITAL Chiefs of surgery | UNIVERSITY Vice-chancellors |

Low Range   High Range

| BUSINESS Assembly-line workers | HOSPITAL Bookkeepers | UNIVERSITY Graduate student tutors | BUSINESS Maintenance repairers | HOSPITAL Nurses | UNIVERSITY Department chairpersons |

Low Depth

Exhibit 5.1
Job depth and job range

Strategies for job redesign

At the most basic level, we could decide to change either job range or job depth and several strategies used by organisations do just that: job rotation, enlargement and enrichment are able to increase either range or depth. We can also use strategies that will improve both dimensions, and the job characteristics model is the leading strategy for doing this.

Increasing job range. **Job range** describes the number of tasks that an employee performs, and we can increase range by increasing the number of tasks performed at the same level. There are two ways that this goal can be achieved: through job rotation and job enlargement. **Job rotation** describes the practice of rotating an individual from one job to another. In so doing the individual is expected to complete more job activities since each job includes different tasks. Job rotation involves increasing the range of jobs and the perception of variety in the job content. Increasing task variety should, according to expectancy theory, increase the intrinsic valence associated with job satisfaction. However, the practice of job rotation does not change the basic characteristics of the assigned jobs. Critics state that this approach involves nothing more than having people perform several boring and monotonous jobs rather than one.

Job enlargement strategies focus on the opposite of dividing work — they are a form of despecialisation or increasing the number of tasks an employee performs. For example, a job is designed such that the individual performs six tasks instead of three. Although in many instances an enlarged job requires a longer training period, job satisfaction usually increases because boredom is reduced. The implication, of course, is that the job enlargement will lead to improvement in other performance outcomes. Some employees cannot cope with enlarged jobs because they cannot comprehend complexity; moreover, they may not have a sufficiently long attention span to stay with and complete an enlarged set of tasks.

Increasing job depth. You should remember that both rotation and enlargement increase the number of tasks that an employee completes at the same level. Both strategies require an employee to complete more tasks; neither requires the individual to complete more complex or challenging tasks. To tackle the issue of complexity and challenge we must turn to **job depth**, which describes the degree of control and responsibility that a person has. The principal strategy for increasing job depth is job enrichment.

Job enrichment also gives employees more tasks; the difference is that in this strategy we add tasks that are at a higher level. As a result, the individual has greater responsibility in his or her work. This approach is based on Herzberg's two-factor theory of motivation[1] and suggests that control and responsibility are increased when individuals receive feedback, are able to develop new skills, have control over the sequencing of tasks and resources, and are responsible for their outcomes.

The job characteristics model. Job enrichment and job enlargement are not competing strategies. Job enlargement but not job enrichment may be compatible with the needs, values and abilities of some individuals. Yet job enrichment, when appropriate, necessarily involves job enlargement. A promising approach to job redesign which attempts to integrate the two approaches is the job characteristic model devised by Hackman, Oldham, Janson and Purdy.[2]

The job characteristics model grew out of attempts to measure individual perceptions of job content, which identified five core components of jobs:

1. *skill variety*: the range of skills utilised in the job;
2. *task identity*: whether individuals complete an entire process;
3. *task significance*: whether individuals understand how their tasks contribute to organisational or societal goals;
4. *autonomy*: the latitude to make decisions concerning the job;
5. *feedback*: the degree to which the task itself provides performance information.

Exhibit 5.2
The job characteristics model

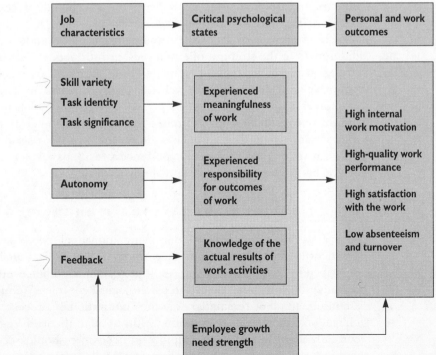

Variety, identity and feedback contribute to job range, while autonomy and significance contribute to job depth. The updated model attempts to account for the interrelationships among certain job characteristics; psychological states associated with motivation, satisfaction and performance; job outcomes; and growth need strength. Exhibit 5.2 describes the relationships among these variables. The core dimensions of the job consist of characteristics first described by Turner and Lawrence. Although variety, identity, significance, autonomy and feedback do not completely describe perceived job content, according to this model, they describe those aspects that management can manipulate to bring about gains in productivity.

We can evaluate a job's motivating potential by rating it on each of these dimensions and calculating a motivating potential score (MPS):

$$\text{MPS} = (\text{skill} + \text{variety} + \text{identity})/3 \times \text{feedback} \times \text{autonomy}$$

Exercise 5

Job design

Use the scales in Exercise 5 to determine how motivating your job as a student is. What are the high points? What are the low points? Calculating a job's MPS provides us with a useful diagnostic tool: it not only tells us how motivating a job is, but also helps us to identify those factors that contribute to low motivation.

The steps management can take to increase the core dimensions include combining task elements, assigning whole pieces of work (i.e. work modules), allowing discretion in selection of work methods, permitting self-paced control and opening feedback channels. Exhibit 5.3 summarises the dimensions that these strategies affect. These actions increase task variety, identity and significance; consequently, the 'experienced meaningfulness of work' psychological state is increased. By permitting employee participation and self-evaluation and creating autonomous work groups, the feedback and autonomy dimensions are increased along with the psychological states 'experienced responsibility' and 'knowledge of actual results'.

The positive benefits of these redesign efforts are moderated by individual differences in the strength of employees' growth needs. That is, employees with strong need for accomplishment, learning and challenge will respond more positively than those with relatively weak growth needs. In more familiar terms, employees who have high need for self-esteem and self-actualisation are the more likely candidates for job redesign. Employees forced to participate in job redesign programs but who lack either the need strength or the ability to perform redesigned jobs may experience stress, anxiety, adjustment problems, erratic performance, turnover and absenteeism.

Organisational behaviour management

So far, we have focused on identifying individual needs and organisational practices to meet those needs. According to the motivational process that we described in Chapter 4, this will result in goal-directed behaviour. In this way, the organisation fulfils its side of the psychological contract. We must now turn our attention to the remainder of the motivational process and employees' obligations to their organisation. Motivational theories suggest that, if we correctly identify and meet employees' needs, we should see high motivation and job performance. When an individual fails to meet her or his obligations,

Exhibit 5.3 **Strategies for increasing the motivating potential of jobs**

If the job is low in ...	Try	Because
Skill variety	Job enlargement	Like job rotation, this increases the number of skills used
	Increasing client contact	Talking to customers adds an additional skill (communication) to tasks
Task identity	Job enlargement	This gives an individual control over a process from beginning to end
	Forming natural work units	This has the same effect as combining jobs, but at the group level
Task significance	Forming work unit	This allows individuals to see where their contribution fits into the performance of a group
Autonomy	Increasing client contact	Direct contact between staff and clients increases their control over the client relationship
	Job enrichment	Adding in more complex tasks increases individual responsibility in the workplace
Feedback	Increasing client contact	Establishing direct relationships gives more immediate performance feedback
	Opening feedback channels	By increasing the number of sources of feedback, we increase feedback

Source: Adapted from Greenberg, J.& Baron, R. A. (1993). *Behaviour in Organizations: Understanding and Managing the Human Side of Work* (4th Ed.). Boston: Allyn and Bacon.

has an organisation failed in the diagnostic procedure? And how can we manage the system to ensure high levels of performance? To answer these questions, we turn to learning theory and organisational behaviour management. In doing so, we will consider two explanations of poor performance:

1. that the organisation has not created sufficiently strong links between an individual's performance and its consequences;
2. that the organisation has not identified sufficiently clearly the levels of performance that are expected.

Learning theory[3]

The basic principle underlying learning theory is that when behaviour is followed by desirable or reinforcing outcomes, we are likely to repeat that behaviour in the future. When behaviour is followed by undesirable or punishing outcomes, we are unlikely to repeat that behaviour in the future. This principle is known as the 'law of effect' and provides us, as managers, with a tool for increasing those behaviours that contribute to organisational performance while decreasing those behaviours that do not. For example, we will try to encourage the performance of job-related tasks, completing reports and coming to work on time by linking them to positive outcomes such as praise, bonuses or promotions. When we do this, we are applying a *reinforcement* strategy. At the same time, we may try to discourage being absent, reading the newspaper, taking too many breaks or making too many errors by disciplinary action such as salary loss, demotion or even dismissal. When we do this, we are applying a *punishment* strategy. Let us take a closer look at these strategies.

Reinforcement. Reinforcement is an extremely important principle of conditioning. Managers often use *positive* reinforcers to influence behaviour. A positive reinforcer is a stimulus which, when added to the situation, strengthens the probability of a behavioural response. Thus, if the positive reinforcer has value to the person, it can be used to improve performance. (It should be noted, however, that a positive reinforcer that has value to one person may not have value to another person.) Sometimes *negative* reinforcers may be used. Negative reinforcement refers to an increase in the frequency of a response following removal of the negative reinforcer immediately after the response. As an example, exerting high degrees of effort to complete a job may be negatively reinforced by not having to listen to the 'nagging' boss. That is, completing the job through increased effort (behaviour) minimises the likelihood of having to listen to a nagging stream of unwanted advice (negative reinforcer) from a superior.

Remember that our aim, when we have a reinforcement strategy, is to increase the likelihood that people will repeat a particular behaviour (such as completing a project on time) because it is associated with a reward (praise). How best can we do this? One obvious way of reinforcing individuals is to do so continuously: every time Martha completes a piece of work, we congratulate her. This will probably increase Martha's effort — until we forget. Continuous reinforcement may be an excellent way to establish a new behaviour, but neglecting to give a reward will also quickly result in Martha's effort decreasing. The problem, for managers, is to strike a balance between giving sufficient reinforcers to encourage a behaviour while ensuring that occasionally forgetting to give a reinforcer will not mean that the new behaviour is lost: we would like Martha to continue to complete her work on time, even if she is not congratulated every time that she does so. How can this be achieved?

There are five ways in which we can give rewards and these strategies are summarised in Exhibit 5.4. Research has shown that the most effective way to administer rewards, to achieve this balance, is to use a *variable ratio* reinforcement schedule. Ratio means that we decide to give a reward after a set number of responses have occurred; for example, we will congratulate Martha every 10th time that she completes a project. *Variable* means that, on average, we will congratulate her every 10th time; in reality, however, we may congratulate her the 3rd, 4th and 30th time that she completes a project. Provided that she is congratulated three times in the course of completing thirty projects, we will have used a variable ratio schedule. Variable ratio schedules have the most long-lasting effects: they not only produce a high and steady rate of behaviour, but also are extremely resistant to extinction. Even if we stop reinforcing a behaviour, it will continue on for quite some time.

Exhibit 5.4 **Reinforcement schedules and their effects on behaviour**

Schedule	Description	When Applied to Individual	When Removed by Manager	Organisational Example
Continuous	Reinforcer follows every response	Faster method for establishing new behaviour	Faster method to cause extinction of new behaviour	Praise after every response, immediate recognition of every response
Fixed interval	Response after specific time period is reinforced	Some inconsistency in response frequencies	Faster extinction of motivated behaviour than variable schedules	Weekly, bimonthly, monthly pay cheque
Variable interval	Response after varying period of time (an average) is reinforced	Produces high rate of steady responses	Slower extinction of motivated behaviour than fixed schedules	Transfers, promotions, recognition
Fixed ratio	A fixed number of responses must occur before reinforcement	Some inconsistency in response frequencies	Faster extinction of motivated behaviour than variable schedules	Piece rate, commission on units sold
Variable ratio	A varying number (average) of responses must occur before reinforcement	Can produce high rate or response that is steady and resists extinction	Slower extinction of motivated behaviour than fixed schedules	Bonus, award, time off

Source: Adapted from Behling, O., Schriesheim, C., & Tolliver, J. (1974). Present theories and new directions in theories of work effort, *Journal of Supplement Abstract Service of the American Psychological Association*, p. 57.

Punishment. Punishment is defined as presenting an uncomfortable or unwanted consequence for a particular behavioural response. Some work-related factors that can be considered punishments include being criticised by a superior, being fired, being suspended, receiving an undesirable transfer or assignment, or being demoted. Using punishment to change behaviour is far more difficult than using reinforcement. First, unlike reinforcement, it must be continuous if we want to change a behaviour. This means that we must punish the unwanted behaviour every time that it occurs. Unless we continually monitor employees this will be very difficult and so our program will fail. However, the greatest risk that we face is that if the punishment does not fit the crime, not only will the behaviour reappear but also the punished employee may develop a strong desire for revenge. If, however, we use punishment within the guidelines for an organisational behaviour management program (described in the next section) we can increase its effectiveness.

Organisational behaviour management

Organisational behaviour management (OBM)[4] programs provide us with a set of guidelines for using either reinforcement or punishment to change behaviour: reinforcement is used to increase desirable behaviours, whereas punishment is used to decrease undesirable behaviours. An important feature of OBM programs is that they focus on specific task-relevant behaviours. Doing this makes it easier to determine whether a problem exists and to isolate the behaviours that must be changed to improve performance. What is more it can be applied to either individuals or work units.

Let us consider Alberta, who provides administrative support to a Staff Training and Development Unit. None of the training staff are happy with Alberta's performance: they complain that the reports and routine administrative tasks that form part of Alberta's duties are neglected or poorly done while Alberta spends time 'playing' on the new computer. According to the principles of OBM, we would deal with the situation in the following way:

1. *Identify behaviours critical to task (organisational) performance.* In Alberta's case we might determine that for her to perform well she must collate information on a weekly basis, compile advertising brochures for courses, ensure that rooms and equipment are available, and undertake routine administrative task.

2. *Establish a performance baseline.* This could be done by documenting the number of times that Alberta performs these critical tasks. This is important, because it helps us to determine whether a problem really exists: it could be that Alberta does all these tasks so efficiently that she has lots of spare time for working on the computer. If there is a problem, we move on to Step 3.

3. *Analyse how the system supports the problem.* This introduces a new concept: the need to consider the causes of Alberta's behaviour. Are her job instructions unclear? Do staff neglect to give her deadlines? If she fails to meet her deadlines, what are the consequences for Alberta? Is she reprimanded, or does someone else do the job for her? In Step 3 we need to consider why the problem behaviours are occurring from two perspectives: first, by asking what features in the environment cause the behaviour; and, second, by asking whether we are unintentionally supporting the unwanted behaviours by associating them with pleasant consequences.

4. *Develop an intervention strategy based on the principles of reinforcement and punishment.* First, we need to change the factors that are causing Alberta's behaviour. For example, we may provide Alberta with clearer instructions and deadlines, and we may stop other people from finishing her jobs for her. We would then reinforce Alberta when she behaves appropriately, to increase the strength of the relationship between desired behaviours and desired outcomes.

5. *Evaluate performance changes.* This is carried out to ensure that the strategies we developed in Step 4 are addressing our Step 2 concerns.

Step 3 highlighted the need to consider not just the link between behaviour and its consequences, but also the contextual or situational factors that cause behaviour. In Alberta's case, it seems that unclear deadlines (cause) mean that she delays doing tasks (behaviour) which are then completed by someone else (positive consequence). Researchers in this area have been especially interested in examining the role of verbal or written instructions as a potential influence on behaviour, and how these instructions are linked to reinforcers. Problem behaviours are interpreted to mean that either the antecedents are unclear, or the link between antecedents and consequences is not clear. Correcting problem behaviours therefore requires that we clearly state the behaviours that we want under specific conditions, and then establish clear links between those behaviours and consequences for the individual.

One line of research within this area has examined how OBM practices might lead to effective supervision. Supervisors not only must supply appropriate consequences but also, in order to do so, must engage in performance monitoring. Effective supervision is the result of regular performance evaluation and ensuring that feedback is contingent on performance. For example, research on supervisory behaviour in an Australian police force shows that, in general, police sergeants engage in more monitoring (behavioural observation), but spend less time establishing antecedents and consequences than other managers. The level of monitoring was correlated with team performance: the higher the level of monitoring, the higher the team performance.[5] Similarly, yachting teams were more likely to win races when their skippers engaged in monitoring and delivered prompt feedback. This research tells us that, for effective supervision and team performance, managers must regularly monitor individual and team behaviour, and regularly provide feedback about performance. This needs to occur irrespective of the many other factors that may be competing for a manager's attention.[6]

EVALUATING PERFORMANCE

In the last section, we suggested that — according to learning theory — we can increase desired behaviours by linking them to rewards. However, before individuals can be rewarded, there must be some basis for distributing rewards. Some rewards may accrue to all individuals simply by virtue of their employment with the organisation. These are what are known as universal or across-the-board rewards. Other rewards may be a function of tenure or seniority. Many rewards, however, are related to job performance. To distribute these rewards equitably it is necessary to evaluate employee performance. Thus, in this section we look at performance evaluation. Developing effective evaluation systems is just as critical to organisational success as developing effective reward systems. Both systems represent efforts to influence employee behaviour. To achieve maximum effectiveness it is necessary to carefully link employee evaluation systems with reward systems.

Virtually every organisation of at least moderate size has a formal employee performance evaluation system. The Local Encounter describes some experiences with evaluation systems. Assessing and providing feedback about performance is considered essential to an employee's ability to perform job duties effectively.[7] In discussing this topic we will identify the purposes performance evaluation may serve, and examine what the focus of evaluations should be. We will also look at a number of different performance evaluation methods, examining their strengths and weaknesses.

Performance appraisal and motivation

Performance appraisal can serve a range of functions from providing a means for rewarding staff through to identifying training needs and performance gaps, and clarifying role expectations.

A survey of eighty-nine New Zealand organisations asked companies to rate the functions that performance appraisal systems served in their organisations, describe how the systems had been implemented and identify problems with their implementation. Organisations were asked to rate the extent to which their appraisal systems served a number of functions. Recognition of individual performance and the provision of feedback received the highest ratings, and performance appraisals were rated as having a strong impact on these factors; they were considered to have little impact on administrative functions.

The majority (61%) of companies conducted appraisals every year, and the major contributors to the final ratings were the appraiser and his or her manager. Where the performance appraisal served a developmental function, the appraisee's contribution had a stronger impact in the final rating than when it served an administrative function. Finally, only 37% of companies gave a general performance rating; however, of those companies a very large proportion (85%) linked this rating to staff salaries. This survey also highlighted several implementation problems: poor performance was not addressed; the appraisal was not used to develop specific performance objectives or to review career and training needs; and there were no mechanisms for an ongoing review of performance between the yearly appraisals.

Especially in organisations that link appraisal to pay, staff need to be confident that appraisal systems are fair; if staff lack confidence in their organisation's appraisal processes the system itself will be less effective. A survey of 103 middle managers in a range of Australian companies examined the extent to which organisational factors, features of the appraisal systems and individual factors affected confidence in the appraisal system. Results showed that organisational factors such as size and structure were unrelated to how employees perceived the appraisal system. However, confidence in the appraisal process was increased when the appraisal process was part of a formalised system conducted on a yearly basis; confidence was also greater when individuals had high self-esteem and an internal locus of control.

This research suggests that, even if performance appraisals are viewed as imperfect by employees, they can serve an important function for organisations. However, since their credibility depends not only on how they are implemented, but also on the characteristics of the appraisee, staff feedback should be delivered in a manner that will increase self-esteem, self-efficacy, effort and performance.

Recent research has also considered whether performance appraisals accomplish their goals: do they encourage supervisors to adopt better management practices and does employee performance increase? Using a government department, Phyllis Tharenou investigated these questions. She found that the introduction of a performance appraisal system increased communication and improved feedback, assisting staff to identify both their strengths and weaknesses. She suggests that formal appraisal programs are especially useful in organisations when communication and feedback processes are poor. In terms of employee reactions, her results showed that when feedback, action planning and supervisory support are part of a formal appraisal program (rather than being spontaneously provided) staff report greater satisfaction with feedback, rewards and training. The moral appears to be that good management is evaluated more positively when it is part of a formal organisational program.

Sources: Saul, P. (1992) Rethinking performance appraisal, *Asia Pacific Journal of Human Resources,* 25–39; Taylor, P., & O'Driscoll, M. (1993). Functions and the implementation of performance appraisal systems in New Zealand organisations, *Asia Pacific Journal of Human Resources,* 20–32; Orpen, C. (1991). Correlates of perceived confidence in performance appraisals, *Psychological Reports,* **68,** 1336–1338; Tharenou, P. (1995). The impact of a performance appraisal program on employee perceptions in an Australian federal agency, Paper presented at the Inaugural Australian Industrial and Organisational Psychology Conference, Sydney, Australia.

Purposes of evaluation

The basic purpose of evaluation, of course, is to provide information about work performance. More specifically, however, such information can serve a variety of purposes. Some of the major purposes are:

1. Provide a basis for reward allocation, including raises, promotions, transfers, lay-offs and so on.
2. Identify high-potential employees.
3. Validate the effectiveness of employee-selection procedures.
4. Evaluate previous training programs.
5. Facilitate future performance improvement.
6. Develop ways of overcoming obstacles and performance barriers.
7. Identify training and development opportunities.
8. Establish supervisor–employee agreement on performance expectations.

These eight specific purposes can be grouped into two broad categories. The first four have a *judgemental orientation,* and the last four have a *developmental orientation.* Evaluations with a judgemental orientation focus on past performance and provide a basis for making judgements regarding which employee should be rewarded, and how effective organisational programs — such as selection and training — have been. Evaluations with a developmental orientation are more concerned with improving future performance by insuring expectations are clear and by identifying ways to facilitate employee performance through training. These two broad categories are, of course, not mutually exclusive. Performance evaluation systems can, and do, serve both general purposes.

The general purpose for which performance evaluations are conducted will also vary across different cultures. So also will the frequency with which evaluations are conducted, who conducts them and a variety of other components. The Global Encounter illustrates some cultural differences in approaches to performance appraisal.

Focus of evaluation

Effective performance evaluation is a continuous, ongoing process and, simply stated, involves asking two questions: Is the work being done effectively? Are employee skills and abilities being fully utilised? The first question tends towards a judgemental orientation, while the second is more developmental in nature. Generally, evaluations should focus on translating the position responsibilities into each employee's day-to-day activities. Additionally, the evaluation should assist the employee in understanding these position responsibilities, the work goals associated with them, and the degree to which the goals have been accomplished.

Performance evaluations should focus on job performance, not individuals. If a word processor operator's work comes to her by written communication and she forwards the work to people with whom she has no personal contact, should the fact that she cannot express herself well when talking to someone be an important factor in judging her performance? If we focus on her verbal ability we are concerned about her as an individual and are evaluating her. But if we look at this in relation to its effect on how well she does her job, we are evaluating her *performance.*

When evaluating employee behaviour it is necessary to ensure not only that the focus of the appraisal remains on job performance, but also that it has proper weighting of relevant behaviours. Relevancy, in the context of performance evaluation, has three aspects — deficiency, contamination and distortion. *Deficiency* occurs when the evaluation does not focus on all aspects of the job. If certain job responsibilities and activities are not considered, the evaluation is deficient. *Contamination* can be said to be the reverse of deficiency. It occurs when activities not part of the job are included in the evaluation. If we evaluate the word processor mentioned in the previous paragraph on her verbal skills, this would be a form of contamination. Finally, *distortion* takes place in the evaluation process when an improper emphasis is given to various job elements. If, for example, placing the phones on automatic answering at the close of each business day is only a small element of a secretary's job, making that activity the major factor in evaluating his performance would be distorting that particular job element. Well-focused performance evaluations avoid deficiencies, contaminations and distortions.

Performance evaluation methods

Most managers can provide at least a general assessment of their employees' performance, even in the absence of a formal system of evaluation. Having a formal system, however, promotes the systematic and equitable collection of performance information, and helps ensure timely and useful feedback. There are a number of different methods available for evaluating employee performance. Each has its own adherents and detractors. In the next few paragraphs we will describe a few of the more commonly used techniques.[8]

Checklists

A checklist, as the name implies, provides a list of job-related behaviours and requires that the individual doing the evaluation check those behaviours that best describe the employee. In some cases, certain behaviours on the list are weighted more heavily than others because of their greater significance or importance in contributing to overall successful performance. Separate check-lists are frequently developed for different jobs since required behaviours vary across jobs. Alternatively, the same form may be used across many jobs, while the behaviours on the checklist that are scored for a particular job are varied.

Critical incidents

The critical-incident technique focuses the evaluator's attention on particularly significant behaviours. These behaviours may be either positive or negative. A real value of the critical-incident technique is that it identifies specific behavioural events, not vague impressions, that affected performance. A list of critical incidents can be extremely effective in demonstrating both desired and undesired behaviours. Since the incidents comprise actual behaviour, it is usually easy for the employee to relate to them and understand how they affected the

GLOBAL   Encounter

Cultural differences and incentives

Do cultural differences affect individual preferences for incentives? Paul Yuo and Richard Steers argue that they do. Drawing on the history of East Asia, they argue that historical differences in the development of East Asian nations result in different cultural characteristics and, as a result, different preferences for incentive systems. They propose the following:

- In politically unstable countries, there is a stronger team spirit so that group-based incentive systems will be preferred.
- When socialist systems have dominated a country's development, the culture will value egalitarianism and consequently stress equality in reward systems.
- Geographically isolated countries will place a stronger emphasis on social needs and therefore will be more responsive to incentive systems that reward social interaction.
- When countries are characterised by a language in which words carry multiple meanings, the culture will have higher tolerance for ambiguity and consequently value imprecise reward systems that do not use objective, public criteria for evaluation.

The allocation of rewards is frequently tied to performance-appraisal systems. Are Yuo and Steers correct in their predictions? Irene Chow compared the preferences of managers in the People's Republic of China with those in Hong Kong. These two groups differed in terms of their perceptions of power-distance relationships and the importance of the group: the Chinese culture is more egalitarian and group-focused than the Hong Kong culture. On this basis, we would expect Chinese managers to prefer equitable and group-based reward systems. Chow investigated several dimensions of performance and performance-appraisal systems. Consistent with their cultural orientation, Chinese managers believed more strongly that performance should be attributed to the group and not the individual; consequently, performance appraisals and rewards should be group based. Chinese managers were also more likely than their Hong Kong counterparts to believe that trust played an important role in the performance-appraisal process and that performance-appraisal sessions should be open, problem-solving sessions (reflecting their more egalitarian orientation). Finally, Chinese managers rated non-work factors as important in the performance-appraisal process: in comparison with Hong Kong managers, they were more prepared to use off-the-job behaviours in performance appraisals. Overall, the trend from these results suggests that consistent with their cultural orientation, managers in the People's Republic of China place greater emphasis on equality and the group in their approach to performance appraisal.

Source: Chow, I. (1994). An opinion survey of performance appraisal practices in Hong Kong and the People's Republic of China, *Asia-Pacific Journal of Human Resource Management*, **33**, 67–79; Huo, Y. P., & Steers, R. M. (1993). Cultural differences in the design of incentive systems: The case of East Asia, *Asia-Pacific Journal of Management*, **10**, 71–85.

overall performance evaluation. Essential to the success of the critical-incident technique is the willingness of the supervisor to maintain an ongoing log of relevant incidents. Otherwise, many of the incidents might be forgotten.

Behavioural anchored rating scales

The behavioural anchored rating scales (BARS) approach combines elements of two techniques: graphic rating scales and critical incidents. BARS resemble graphic rating scales in that both include a number of dimensions to be rated. Unlike the graphic scales, however, the BARS dimensions result from a thorough study to determine specific important areas of performance for a particular job. Each dimension is then anchored with a series of equally specific behaviours representing a range of excellent to unacceptable levels of performance. The anchors are examples of critical incidents which have been shown to be related to various levels of performance. Exhibit 5.5 shows an example of a BARS dimension for an engineer.

BARS advantages include their ease of use, relatively high reliability between raters, and a focus on specific job-related behaviours rather than general traits or characteristics. This latter characteristic tends to make evaluation feedback more acceptable than if a supervisor talked in vague generalities.[9] Also, since the job holders themselves are frequently involved in obtaining examples of relevant critical incidents, there tends to be greater acceptance of the form itself. On the downside, a BARS system can be expensive to develop and maintain. Development takes a great deal of time and must be done for each different job. Additionally, since most jobs change over time, BARS forms must be continually updated to reflect relevant job changes.

Improving evaluations

Developing an effective performance evaluation system constitutes a critical and challenging task for management. This means, among other things, maximising the use and acceptance of the evaluations while minimising dissatisfaction with any aspect of the system. A full treatment of performance evaluation problems and methods of overcoming them is beyond the scope of our discussion here. We offer, however, the following suggestions for improving the effectiveness of virtually any evaluation system:

- Higher levels of employee participation in the evaluation process lead to more satisfaction with the system.
- Setting specific performance goals to be met results in greater performance improvement than discussions of more general goals.
- Evaluating subordinates' performance is an important part of a supervisor's job; they should receive training in the process, and they should be evaluated on how effectively they discharge this part of their own job responsibilities.
- Systematic evaluation of performance does little good if the results are not communicated to employees.
- Performance evaluation feedback should not focus solely on problem areas; good performance should be actively recognised and reinforced.
- Remember that while formal performance evaluation may take place on a set schedule (for example, annually), effective evaluation is a continuous ongoing process.

To the extent that performance is linked with the organisation's reward system, then performance evaluation represents an attempt to influence the behaviour of organisational members. That is, it is an attempt to reinforce the continuation or elimination of certain actions. The basic assumption is that behaviour is influenced by its consequences and that it is possible to affect behaviour by controlling such consequences. We have already discussed this possibility in our consideration of learning theory and OBM. We will now take a closer look at rewards.

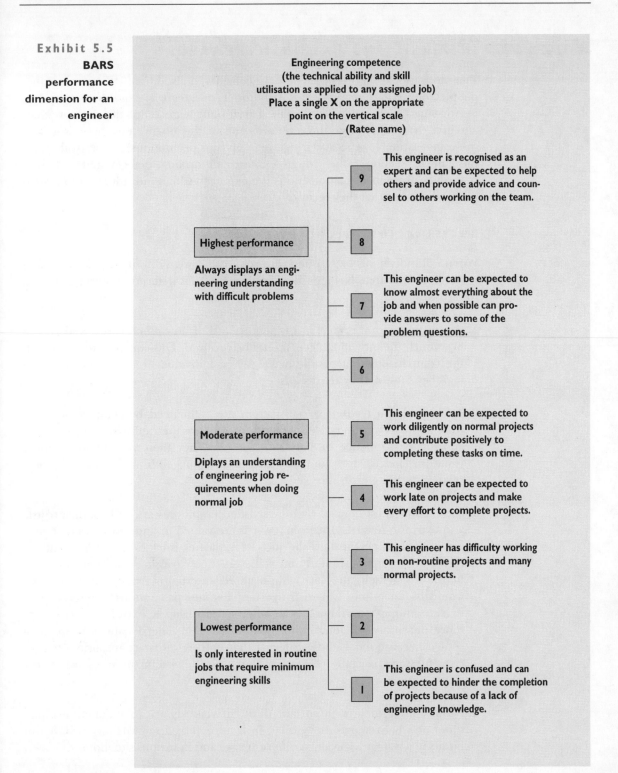

Exhibit 5.5
BARS
performance
dimension for an
engineer

Engineering competence
(the technical ability and skill
utilisation as applied to any assigned job)
Place a single **X** on the appropriate
point on the vertical scale
_____ (Ratee name)

9 — This engineer is recognised as an expert and can be expected to help others and provide advice and counsel to others working on the team.

Highest performance

8

Always displays an engineering understanding with difficult problems

7 — This engineer can be expected to know almost everything about the job and when possible can provide answers to some of the problem questions.

6

Moderate performance

5 — This engineer can be expected to work diligently on normal projects and contribute positively to completing these tasks on time.

Diplays an understanding of engineering job requirements when doing normal job

4 — This engineer can be expected to work late on projects and make every effort to complete projects.

3 — This engineer has difficulty working on non-routine projects and many normal projects.

Lowest performance

2

Is only interested in routine jobs that require minimum engineering skills

1 — This engineer is confused and can be expected to hinder the completion of projects because of a lack of engineering knowledge.

INTRINSIC AND EXTRINSIC REWARDS

The motivational theories that we have considered also identify the rewards that people look for. These rewards fall into two categories: *intrinsic*, related to performing the job and valued in their own right (e.g. completion, achievement and growth), and *extrinsic*, those rewards outside the job given by supervisors and the organisation (e.g. salary, fringe benefits and promotions). As we will see in the next section, the single most important determinant of the reward–performance relationship is the extent to which individuals are satisfied with the rewards that they receive.

Satisfaction with rewards

When will individuals be satisfied with rewards? Lawler, drawing on considerable research in this area, has identified five criteria that determine satisfaction with rewards.

1. Satisfaction with a reward is a function both of how much is received and of how much the individual feels should be received. This conclusion is based on the comparisons that people make. When individuals receive less than they feel they should, they are dissatisfied.

2. An individual's feelings of satisfaction are influenced by comparisons with what happens to others. People tend to compare their efforts, skills, seniority and job performance with those of others. They then attempt to compare rewards. That is, they compare their own inputs with the inputs of others relative to the rewards received.

3. Satisfaction is influenced by how satisfied employees are with both intrinsic and extrinsic rewards. Intrinsic rewards are valued in and of themselves; they are related to performing the job. Examples of intrinsic rewards would be feelings of accomplishment and achievement. Extrinsic rewards are external to the work itself; they are administered externally. Examples of extrinsic would be salary and wages, fringe benefits and promotions. There is some debate among researchers as to whether intrinsic or extrinsic rewards are more important in determining job satisfaction. The debate has not been settled because most studies suggest that both rewards are important.[10] One clear message from the research is that extrinsic and intrinsic rewards satisfy different needs.

4. People differ in how important different rewards are to them. Individuals differ on what rewards they prefer. In fact, preferred rewards vary at different points in a person's career, at different ages and in various situations.

5. Some extrinsic rewards are satisfying because they lead to other rewards. For example, a large office or an office that has carpeting or curtains is often considered a reward because it indicates the individual's status and power. Money is a reward that leads to such things as prestige, autonomy and independence, security and shelter.[11]

We can understand the last three of these criteria in terms of the theories that we have already discussed: Maslow's needs hierarchy and Vroom's expectancy theory. The first two criteria relate to an important theory that we have not yet considered: Adam's equity theory. This theory not only outlines the conditions that result in satisfaction with rewards but also builds a bridge between our understanding of organisational reward systems and their implications for such organisational outcomes as commitment, turnover and absenteeism.

Equity theory

The essence of **equity theory** is that employees compare their efforts and rewards with those of others in similar work situations. Exhibit 5.6 illustrates the equity theory of motivation. According to this theory, the individual works in exchange for rewards from the organisation. Motivation is affected by the extent to which those rewards are distributed equitably within the organisation. According to equity theory, motivation is determined not just by whether we receive rewards but also by how those rewards compare with what others are receiving. The three key concepts that make up equity theory are:

1. *Inputs:* These are the individual characteristics brought to the job. These may be achieved (e.g. skills, experience, learning) or ascribed (e.g. age, sex, race).
2. *Outcomes:* These are what the individual receives from the job (e.g. recognition, fringe benefits, pay).
3. *Comparison other:* This is any group or persons used by the individual as a reference point for assessing the ratio of his or her inputs and outcomes. This may be someone with similar skills and qualification within the same organisation, or someone performing a similar job in a different organisation.

An employee uses the comparison other to provide a reference point for evaluating his or her outcomes, relative to inputs. We find examples of people with similar inputs (skills, qualifications, effort) and compare their outcomes (rewards) with our own. Equity exists when we perceive that the ratio of our inputs to outcomes is the same as that of the comparison other (or group). Inequity exists when there is a perceived imbalance between our inputs and outcomes, and those of the comparison other. There are two types of inequity:

1. *Under-reward inequity* occurs when we perceive ourselves to have higher inputs and lower outcomes than the comparison other. For example, when we work longer hours and obtain less pay than other employees doing the same job.
2. *Over-reward inequity* occurs when we perceive ourselves to be exerting less effort and obtaining better outcomes than our comparison other.

Perceived under-reward inequity is the more serious of the two, as it is likely to result in a reduction of effort. When individuals experience inequity, they have several alternative strategies for restoring a feeling or sense of equity. Some examples of restoring equity are:

- *Changing inputs:* The employee may decide that he or she will put less time or effort into the job. The employee might start working shorter hours or stop engaging in extra-role behaviours.
- *Changing outputs:* The employee may decide, in the case of under-reward inequity, to improve their outcomes by engaging in workplace theft.

183

- *Changing the reference person:* The reference person can be changed by making comparisons with the input:output ratios of some other person. This change can restore equity.
- *Changing the inputs or outputs of the reference person:* If the reference person is a co-worker, it might be possible to attempt to alter his or her inputs or outputs as a way to restore equity. Group norms that limit production are one means for changing the comparison other's inputs.

Research on equity

Most of the research on equity theory has focused on pay as the basic outcome. The failure to incorporate other relevant outcomes limits the impact of the theory in work situations. A review of the studies also reveals that the comparison person is not always clarified. A typical research procedure is to ask a person to compare his or her inputs and outcomes with those of a specific person. In most work situations, an employee selects the comparison person after working for some time in the organisation. Two issues to consider are whether comparison persons are within the organisation and whether comparison persons change during a person's work career.

Several individuals have questioned the extent to which inequity that results from overpayment (rewards) leads to perceived inequity. Locke argues that employees seldom are told they are overpaid. He believes that individuals are likely to adjust their idea of what constitutes an equitable payment to justify their pay.[12]

Exhibit 5.6
The equity theory of motivation

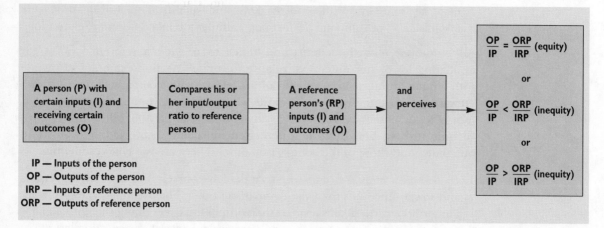

IP — Inputs of the person
OP — Outputs of the person
IRP — Inputs of reference person
ORP — Outputs of reference person

$$\frac{OP}{IP} = \frac{ORP}{IRP} \text{ (equity)}$$

or

$$\frac{OP}{IP} < \frac{ORP}{IRP} \text{ (inequity)}$$

or

$$\frac{OP}{IP} > \frac{ORP}{IRP} \text{ (inequity)}$$

Distributive and procedural justice

Equity theory has a number of important limitations. Of these, the most serious is the inability to take account of other factors that influence perceptions of organisational fairness and organisational outcomes. It became clear that a second dimension affecting these perceptions was related to how reward allocations were made and, in particular, the fairness of the process.[13] For this reason, Adams' equity theory is identified with *distributive* justice or the fairness of outcomes.

Attempts to refine equity theory have resulted in the development of new models. Among these, the Justice Judgement Model is the most dominant. According to this model two criteria may be used to assess outcomes. One is equity, and the other is equality. *Equity* is used for judging fairness when organisations are striving for performance maximisation and organisational reward systems are based on performance. On this criterion the principal means for assessing fairness is based on the level of skill that has earned a specific reward. *Equality* is used when organisational goals emphasise social harmony, and the fairness of outcomes is determined not on individual skills, but on the extent to which a reward system enables individuals to maintain self-esteem.[14]

Even these refinements cannot account for all aspects of perceived fairness. The process by which rewards are allocated is also important. This has led to considerations of *procedural* justice, or the fairness of the process by which the outcomes were reached. A key finding in relation to procedural justice is that fairness is assessed in terms of the degree to which individuals have control over the process by which rewards are allocated. Procedures are judged to be fair when they eliminate bias, establish consistent rules for reward allocation, are based on accurate information, can be changed if unfair and represent all people.[15] Together, distributive and procedural justice determine individual perceptions of fairness. Issues of fairness impact not only on individuals' motivation and job satisfaction, but also on a range of organisational outcomes. The Management Encounter discusses the relationship between justice, individual and organisational outcomes.

REWARDS AFFECT ORGANISATIONAL CONCERNS

Rewards affect employee perceptions, attitudes and behaviour in a variety of ways. In turn, organisational efficiency and effectiveness are affected. Three important organisational concerns that are influenced by rewards are turnover, absenteeism and commitment. We will briefly examine each of these.

Turnover

Some managers assume that high turnover is a mark of an effective organisation. This view is somewhat controversial because a high turnover rate means more expense for the organisation. However, some organisations would benefit if disruptive and poor performers left.[16] Thus, the issue of turnover needs to focus on the *frequency* and on *who* is leaving.

Ideally, if managers could develop reward systems that retained the best performers and caused poor performers to leave, the overall effectiveness of an organisation would improve. To approach this ideal state, an equitable and favourably compared reward system must exist. The feeling of *equity* and *favourable comparison* has an external orientation. That is, the equity of rewards and favourableness involves comparisons with external parties. This orientation is used because quitting most often means that a person leaves one organisation for an alternative elsewhere.

There is no perfect means for retaining high performers. It appears that a reward system based on *merit* should encourage most of the better performers to remain with the organisation. There also has to be some differential in the reward system that discriminates between high and low performers, the point being that the high performers must receive significantly more extrinsic and intrinsic rewards than the low performers.

Absenteeism

Absenteeism, no matter for what reason, is a costly and disruptive problem facing managers.[17] Managers appear to have some influence over attendance behaviour. They have the ability to punish, establish bonus systems and allow employee participation in developing plans. Whether these or other approaches will reduce absenteeism is determined by the value of the rewards perceived by employees, the amount of the rewards, and whether employees perceive a relationship between attendance and rewards. These same characteristics appear every time we analyse the effects of rewards on organisational behaviour.

Organisational commitment

There is little research on the relationship between rewards and organisational commitment. **Commitment** to an organisation involves three attitudes: a sense of identification with the organisation's goals, a feeling of involvement in organisational duties, and a feeling of loyalty for the organisation.[18] Research evidence indicates that the absence of commitment can reduce organisational effectiveness.[19] People who are committed are less likely to leave and accept other jobs.[20] Thus, the costs of high turnover are not incurred. In addition, committed and highly skilled employees require less supervision. Close supervision and a rigid monitoring control process are time-consuming and costly. Furthermore, a committed employee perceives the value and importance of integrating individual and organisational goals. The employee thinks of his or her goals and the organisation's goals in personal terms.

Intrinsic rewards are especially important for the development of organisational commitment. Organisations able to meet employee needs by providing achievement opportunities and by recognising achievement when it occurs have a significant impact on commitment. Thus, managers need to develop intrinsic reward systems that focus on personal importance or self-esteem, to integrate individual and organisational goals, and to design challenging jobs.

A MODEL OF INDIVIDUAL REWARDS

A model that illustrates how rewards fit into the overall policies and programs of an organisation can prove useful to managers. The main objectives of reward programs are to attract qualified people to join the organisation, to keep employees coming to work, and to motivate employees to achieve high levels of performance. Exhibit 5.7 presents a model that attempts to integrate satisfaction, motivation, performance and rewards. Reading the exhibit from left to right suggests that the motivation to exert effort is not enough to cause acceptable performance. Performance results from a combination of the effort of an individual and the individual's level of ability, skill and experience. The performance results of the individual are evaluated either formally or informally by management, and two types of rewards can be distributed: intrinsic or extrinsic. The rewards are evaluated by the individual, and to the extent the rewards are satisfactory and equitable, the individual achieves a level of satisfaction.

MANAGEMENT

Justice at work

In our discussions of equity theory, we described two forms of organisational justice. Distributive justice, which is directly related to equity theory, describes the perceived fairness of outcomes, for example pay. Procedural justice is more concerned with how the outcomes were obtained and focuses on the fairness of organisational procedures. What factors do you think will contribute to a fair process? Research suggests that they include the perception that the process is unbiased, the extent to which decisions arising from the process are consistent, whether they use accurate information, and whether the possibility of changing outcomes — for example through grievance procedures — exists. Two of the areas in which procedural justice is very important to individual and organisational outcomes are dispute resolution and how survivors respond to lay-offs. We will come back to these second outcomes in Chapter 15.

Generally, distributive outcome is thought to be associated with outcome satisfaction; that is satisfaction with the job or salary level. Procedural justice, however, is thought to be more clearly associated with system satisfaction, and therefore linked to organisational outcomes such as turnover, absenteeism and commitment. Is this a fair conclusion? What does research tell us about justice at work? According to research by McFarlin and Sweeney, there is more to it. They examined how perceptions of distributive and procedural justice affected two personal outcomes (pay and job satisfaction) and two organisational outcomes (subordinates' evaluation of managers and organisational commitment). As we would expect, when individuals perceived distributive justice to be low, they were dissatisfied with their pay levels and their job. Other research has similarly found that low distributive justice leads to pay and job dissatisfaction. They also found that when individuals thought that procedural justice was low, they evaluated their supervisors more negatively and reported lower organisational commitment. Again, this finding is supported by other research, which also shows that individuals are more likely to leave organisations in which procedural justice is low. McFarlin and Sweeney, however, also found an interesting pattern: dissatisfaction with pay, jobs and supervisors, as well as organisational commitment, were lowest when individuals perceived both distributive and procedural justice to be low. Satisfaction increased markedly if either of these factors was high.

One implication for organisations is that, depending on whether they are more concerned about organisational or individual outcomes, they should focus on ensuring that either procedural or distributive justice is maintained. However, it seems that when both are low, organisations risk very negative outcomes indeed. If you were responsible for establishing organisational policies concerning pay, performance appraisal and promotion, which type of justice would you focus on? How would you ensure that these forms of justice are met?

Source: Dailey, R. C., & Kirk, D. J. (1992). Distributive and procedural justice as antecedents of job dissatisfaction and intent to turnover, *Human Relations*, **45**, 305–317; Greenberg, J. (1990). Organizational justice: Yesterday, today and tomorrow, *Journal of Management*, **16**, 399–432; McFarlin, D. B., & Sweeney, P. D. (1992). Distributive and procedural justice as predictors of satisfaction with personal and organizational outcomes, *Academy of Management Journal*, **35**, 626– 637; Sweeney, P. D., & McFarlin, D. B. (1993). Workers' evaluations of the 'ends' and 'means': An examination of four models of distributive and procedural justice, *Organizational Behavior and Human Decision Processes*, **55**, 23–40.

The relationship between rewards and satisfaction is not perfectly understood, nor is it static. It changes because people and the environment change. There are, however, some important considerations that managers could use to develop and distribute rewards. First, the rewards available must be sufficient to satisfy basic human needs. Federal legislation, union contracts and managerial fairness have provided at least minimal rewards in most work

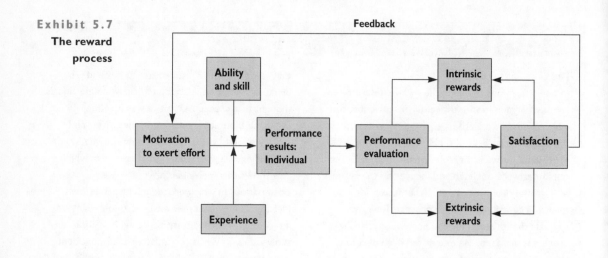

Exhibit 5.7
The reward process

Reading 5
The folly of
rewarding A,
while hoping
for B

settings. Second, individuals tend to compare their rewards with those of others. If inequities are perceived, dissatisfaction occurs. People make comparisons regardless of the quantity of the rewards they receive. Finally, the managers distributing rewards must recognise individual differences.[21] Unless individual differences are considered, invariably the reward process is less effective than desired. To these could be added the very important point made by Steven Kerr in his article accompanying this chapter (Reading 5). For rewards to have their desired effect, they must reward the behaviour that management wishes to encourage. Too often, as Kerr points out, what actually get rewarded are behaviours which the manager is trying to discourage.

SUMMARY OF KEY POINTS

Describe key components of the job characteristics model. The job characteristics model identifies five core characteristics that increase the motivating potential of jobs. These are skill variety, task identity, task significance, autonomy and feedback. Jobs that are rated high on these dimensions are expected to increase motivation; however, this is more likely for individuals who have a high growth need strength. The strategies of job enlargement and job enrichment are two strategies that can be used to increase the motivating potential of jobs.

Discuss organisational behaviour management. Reinforcement theory suggests that behaviour is influenced by its consequences and that it is possible to affect behaviour by controlling such consequences. Desired behaviours are reinforced

through the use of rewards, while undesired behaviours can be extinguished through punishment. These ideas are included in OBM programs. According to OBM, poor performance at work may be the result of unclear or inappropriate links between performance and outcomes, or between instructions and performance. OBM provides a means for analysing each situation of poor performance and determining whether instructions or outcomes need to be clarified or changed.

Describe several purposes of performance evaluation. Among the major purposes which performance evaluation can serve are providing a basis for reward allocation, identifying high-potential employees, validating the effectiveness of employee-selection procedures, evaluating previous training programs, and facilitating future performance improvement.

Identify a variety of different evaluation methods. There are a number of different methods available for evaluating employee performance. Some of the more frequently used methods include checklists, critical incidents, and behavioural anchored rating scales.

Compare intrinsic and extrinsic rewards. Organisational rewards can be classified as either extrinsic or intrinsic. Extrinsic rewards include salary and wages, fringe benefits, promotions, and certain types of interpersonal rewards. Intrinsic rewards can include such things as a sense of completion, achievement, autonomy and personal growth. Both extrinsic and intrinsic rewards can be used to motivate job performance. For this to occur, certain conditions must exist: the rewards must be valued by the employee, and they must be related to the level of job performance that is to be motivated.

Describe key components of equity theory. The essence of equity theory is that employees compare their job inputs and outputs with those of others in similar work situations. *Inputs* are what an individual brings to the job and include skills, experience and effort, among others. *Outputs* are what a person receives from a job and include recognition, pay, fringe benefits and satisfaction among others. Inequity exists when there is a mismatch between inputs and outputs, in comparison to those of others.

Discuss the role of justice in reward systems. Distributive justice describes the perceived fairness of outcomes (as described by equity theory). Procedural justice describes the process by which those outcomes were determined. Both types of justice are important in organisations: individuals are less satisfied with their jobs and pay when distributive justice is low; they are more likely to leave and have lower organisational commitment when procedural justice is low.

Understand the role rewards play in turnover, absenteeism and performance. An effective reward system would encourage the best performers to remain with the organisation, while causing the poorer performers to leave. To accomplish this the system must be perceived as equitable. Additionally, the reward system should minimise the incidence of absenteeism.

Generally, absenteeism will be less if an employee feels that attendance will lead to more valued rewards and fewer negative consequences.

Describe the elements in a model of individual rewards. A useful model of individual rewards would include the suggestion that ability, skill and experience, in addition to motivation, result in various levels of individual performance. The resulting performance is then evaluated by management, who can distribute two types of rewards: intrinsic and/or extrinsic. These rewards are evaluated by the individual receiving them, and to the extent they result in satisfaction, motivation to perform is enhanced.

REVIEW AND DISCUSSION QUESTIONS

1. What are the major organisational purposes served by formal performance-evaluation systems? Are different methods of performance evaluation best suited for each major purpose? Explain.

2. If you were designing a system to evaluate the performance of the instructor in this class, what method, or combination of methods, discussed in this chapter would you use? Why?

3. Evaluations of employees not only should focus on job performance, but also should include proper weighting of relevant behaviours. What are the three aspects of relevancy in the context of performance evaluations? Is any one of these more or less important than the others?

4. From a managerial perspective, why is it impractical to provide continuous reinforcement in work environments? If it were practical, would it be a good idea? Why or why not?

5. The degree of employee satisfaction with the organisation's reward system will significantly affect how successful the system is in influencing performance. Based on the research literature, what do we know about what influences whether individuals will be satisfied with the rewards they receive?

6. Do you think rewards are more important in attracting people to the organisation, keeping people in the organisation, or motivating people to higher levels of performance? Explain.

7. Describe an innovative reward system that will motivate people.

8. Given its costs, under what conditions do you think a BARS evaluation system is a justified approach to evaluating employees? Explain.
9. Should organisations be more concerned with distributive or procedural justice? Describe a reward system that incorporates both principles.

ENDNOTES

1 Herzberg, F. (1974). The wise old Turk, *Harvard Business Review*, September–October, 70–80.

2 Hackman, R .J., Oldham, G., Janson, R., & Purdy, K. (1975). New strategy for job enrichment, *California Management Review*, 57–71; Hackman, R. J., & Oldham, G. (1975). Development of the Job Diagnostic Survey, *Journal of Applied Psychology*, 159–170.

3 For more detailed discussions of how learning theory can be applied to organisational contexts, see Weiss, H. M. (1994). Learning theory and industrial and organizational psychology. In M. D. Dunnette & L. M. Hough (Eds.) *Handbook of Industrial and Organizational Psychology.* (2nd Ed.). Palo Alto, CA: Consulting Psychologists Press.

4 This discussion summarises material in Luthans, F. (1985). *Organizational Behavior* (4th Ed.). New York: McGraw-Hill Book Company.

5 Brewer, N., Wilson, C., & Beck, K. (1994). Supervisory behaviour and team performance amongst police patrol sergeants, *Journal of Occupational and Organizational Psychology*, **67**, 69–78.

6 Komaki, L., Desselles, M. L., & Bowman, E. D. (1989). Definitely not a breeze: Extending an operant model of the effective supervision of teams, *Journal of Applied Psychology*, **74**, 522–529.

7 Nathan, B. R., Mohrman, Jr., A. M., & Milliman, J. (1991). Interpersonal relations as a context for the effects of appraisal interviews on performance and satisfaction: A longitudinal study, *Academy of Management Journal*, 352–369.

8 For a full discussion of various evaluation methods see Ivancevich, J. M. (1992). *Human Resource Management* (5th Ed.). Homewood, IL: Irwin.

9 Klein, J. (1990). Performance reviews that rate an 'A', *Personnel*, 38–40.

10 Mitchell, T. R. (1982). Motivation: New directions theory, research, and practice, *Academy of Management Review*, pp. 80–88.

11 Lawler III, E. E. (1977). Reward systems. In J. R. Hackman & J. L. Suttle (Eds.) *Improving Life at Work.* Santa Monica, CA: Goodyear Publishing, pp. 163–226.

12 Locke, E. A. (1976). The nature and causes of job satisfaction. In M. Dunnette (Ed.) *Handbook of Industrial and Organizational Psychology*, Skokie, IL.: Rand McNally, pp. 1297–1349.

13 Greenberg, J. (1990). Organizational justice: Yesterday, today and tomorrow, *Journal of Management*, **16**, 399–432.

14 Ibid.

15 Ibid.

16 Dalton, D. R., Krackhardt, D. M., & Porter, L.W. (1982). Functional turnover: An empirical assessment, *Journal of Applied Psychology*, 716–721.

17 Blau, G. J., & Kimberly, B. B. (1987). Conceptualizing how job involvement and organizational commitment affect turnover and absenteeism, *Academy of Management Review*, 288–300.

18 Reichers, A. E. (1985). A review and reconceptualization of organizational commitment, *Academy of Management Review*, 465–476.

19 Mowday, R. T., Porter, L. W., & Steers, R. M. (1982). *Employee-Organization Linkages.* New York: Academic Press.

20 Cohen, A. (1993). Organizational commitment and turnover: A meta-analysis, *Academy of Management Journal*, 1140–1157.

21 Lawler, E. E., III. (1977). Reward systems. In J. R. Hackman & J. L. Suttle (Eds.) *Improving Life at Work.* Santa Monica, CA: Goodyear Publishing.

READING 5   THE FOLLY OF REWARDING A, WHILE HOPING FOR B

Steven Kerr

Source: Reprinted with permission from *Academy of Management Journal*, December 1975, pp. 769–83.

Whether dealing with moneys, rats, or human beings, it is hardly controversial to state that most organisms seek information concerning what activities are rewarded, and then seek to do (or at least pretend to do) those things, often to the virtual exclusion of activities not rewarded. The extent to which this occurs, of course, will depend on the perceived attractiveness of the rewards offered, but neither operant nor expectancy theorists would quarrel with the essence of this notion.

Nevertheless, numerous examples exist of reward systems that are fouled up in that behaviors which are rewarded are those which the rewarded is trying to *discourage*, while the behavior he desires is not being rewarded at all.

In an effort to understand and explain this phenomenon, this paper presents examples from society, from organizations in general, and from profit-making firms in particular. Data from a manufacturing company and information from an insurance firm are examined to demonstrate the consequences of such reward systems for the organizations involved, and possible reasons why such reward systems continue to exist are considered.

Societal examples
Politics
Official goals are 'purposely vague and general and do not indicate ... the host of decisions that must be made among alternative ways of achieving official goals and the priority of multiple goals ...' They usually may be relied on to offend absolutely no one, and in this sense can be considered high-acceptance, low-quality goals. An example might be 'build better schools'. Operative goals are higher in quality but lower in acceptance, since they specify where the money will come from, what alternative goals will be ignored, etc.

The American citizenry supposedly wants its candidates for public office to set forth operative goals, making their proposed programs 'perfectly clear', specifying sources and uses of funds, etc. However, since operative goals are lower in acceptance, and since aspirants to public office need acceptance (from at least 50.1 percent of the people), most politicians prefer to speak only of official goals, at least until after the election. They of course would agree to speak at the operative level if 'punished' for not doing so. The electorate could do this by refusing to support candidates who do not speak at the operative level.

Instead, however, the American voter typically punishes (withholds support from) candidates who frankly discuss where the money will come from, rewards politicians who speak only of official goals, but hopes that candidates (despite the reward system) will discuss the issues operatively. It is academic whether it was moral for Nixon, for example, to refuse to discuss his 1968 'secret plan' to end the Vietnam war, his 1972 operative goals concerning the lifting of price controls, the reshuffling of his cabinet, etc. The point is that the reward system made such refusal rational.

It seems worth mentioning that no manuscript can adequately define what is 'moral' and what is not. However, examination of costs and benefits, combined with knowledge of what motivates a particular individual, often will suffice to determine what for him is 'rational'.[1] If the reward system is so designed that it is irrational to be moral, this does not necessarily mean that immorality will result. But is this not asking for trouble?

War
If some oversimplification may be permitted, let it be assumed that the primary goal of the organization (Pentagon, Luftwaffe, or whatever) is to win. Let it be assumed further that the primary goal of most individuals on the front lines is to get home alive. Then there appears to be an important conflict in goals — personally rational behavior by those at the bottom will endanger goal attainment by those at the top.

But not necessarily! It depends on how the reward system is set up. The Vietnam war was indeed a study of disobedience and rebellion, with terms such as *fragging* (killing one's own commanding officer) and *search and evade* becoming part of the military vocabulary. The difference in subordinates' acceptance of authority between World War II and Vietnam is reported to be considerable, and veterans of the Second World War often have been quoted as being outraged at the mutinous actions of many American soldiers in Vietnam.

Consider, however, some critical differences in the reward system in use during the two conflicts. What did the GI in World War II want? To go home. And when did he get to go home? When the war was won! If he disobeyed the orders to clean out the trenches and take the hills, the war would not be won and he would not go home. Furthermore, what were his chances of attaining his goal (getting home alive) if he obeyed the orders compared to his chances if he did not? What is being suggested is that the rational soldier in World War II, *whether patriotic or not*, probably found it expedient to obey.

Consider the reward system in use in Vietnam. What did the man at the bottom want? To go home. And when did he get to go home? When his tour of duty was over! This was the case *whether or not* the war was won. Furthermore, concerning the relative chance of getting home alive by obeying orders compared to the chance if they were disobeyed, it is worth noting that a mutineer in Vietnam was far more likely to be assigned rest and rehabilitation (on the assumption that fatigue was the cause) than he was to suffer any negative consequence.

In his description of the 'zone of indifference', Barnard stated that 'a person can and will accept a communication as authoritative only when . . . at the time of his decision, he believes it to be compatible with his personal interests as a whole'. In light of the reward system used in Vietnam, would it not have been personally irrational for some orders to have been obeyed? Was not the military implementing a system which *rewarded* disobedience, while *hoping* that soldiers (despite the reward system) would obey orders?

Medicine
Theoretically, a physician can make either of two types of error, and intuitively one seems as bad as the other. A doctor can pronounce a patient sick when he is actually well, thus causing him needless anxiety and expense, curtailment of enjoyable foods and activities, and even physical danger by subjecting him to needless medication and surgery. Alternatively, a doctor can label a sick person well, and thus avoid treating what

may be a serious, even fatal ailment. It might be natural to conclude that physicians seek to minimize both types of error.

Such a conclusion would be wrong.[2] It is estimated that numerous Americans are presently afflicted with iatrogenic (physician caused) illnesses. This occurs when the doctor is approached by someone complaining of a few stray symptoms. The doctor classifies and organizes these symptoms, gives them a name, and obligingly tells the patient what further symptoms may be expected. This information often acts as self-fulfilling prophecy, with the result from that day on the patient for all practical purposes is sick.

Why does this happen? Why are physicians so reluctant to sustain a type 2 error (pronouncing a sick person well) that they will tolerate many type 1 errors? Again, a look at the reward system is needed. The punishments for a type 2 error are real: guilt, embarrassment, and the threat of a lawsuit and scandal. On the other hand, a type 1 error (labelling a well person sick) 'is sometimes seen as sound clinical practice, indicating a healthy conservative approach to medicine'. Type 1 errors also are likely to generate increased income and a stream of steady customers who, being well in a limited physiological sense, will not embarrass the doctor by dying abruptly.

Fellow physicians and the general public therefore are really *rewarding* type 1 errors and at the same time *hoping* fervently that doctors will try not to make them.

General organizational examples
Rehabilitation centers and orphanages
In terms of the prime beneficiary classification, organizations such as these are supposed to exist for the 'public-in-contact', that is, clients. The orphanage therefore theoretically is interested in placing as many children as possible in good homes. However, often orphanages surround themselves with so many rules concerning adoptions that it is nearly impossible to pry a child out of the place. Orphanages may deny adoption unless the applicants are a married couple, both of the same religion as the child, without history of emotional or vocational instability, with a specified minimum income and a private room for the child, etc.

If the primary goal is to place children in good homes, then the rules ought to constitute means towards that goal. Goal displacement results when these 'means become ends-in-themselves that displace the original goals'.

To some extent these rules are required by law. But the influence of the reward system on the orphanage's management should not be ignored. Consider, for example, that the:

1. Number of children enrolled often is the most important determinant of the size of the allocated budget.
2. Number of children under the director's care also will affect the size of his staff.
3. Total organizational size will determine largely the director's prestige at the annual conventions, in the community, etc.

Therefore, to the extent that the staff size, total budget, and personal prestige are valued by the orphanage's executive personnel, it becomes rational for them to make it difficult for children to be adopted. After all, who wants to be the director of the smallest orphanage in the state?

If the reward system errs in the opposite direction, paying off only for placements, extensive goal displacement again is likely to result. A common example of vocational rehabilitation in many states, for example, consists of placing someone in a job for which he has little interest and few qualifications, for two months or so, and then 'rehabilitating' him again in another position. Such behaviour is quite consistent with the prevailing reward system, which pays off for the number of individuals placed in any position for 60 days or more. Rehabilitation counselors also confess to competing with one another to place relatively skilled clients, sometimes ignoring persons with few skills who would be harder to place. Extensively disabled clients found that counselors often prefer to work with those whose disabilities are less severe.[3]

Universities

Society *hopes* that teachers will not neglect their teaching responsibilities but *rewards* them almost entirely for research and publications. This is most true at the large and prestigious universities. Clichés such as 'good research and good teaching go together' notwithstanding, professors often find that they must choose between teaching and research-oriented activities when allocating their time. Rewards for good teaching usually are limited to outstanding teacher awards, which are given to only a small percentage of good teachers

and which usually bestow little money and fleeting prestige. Punishments for poor teaching are also rare.

Rewards for research and publications, on the other hand, and punishments for failure to accomplish these, are commonly administered by universities at which teachers are employed. Furthermore, publication-oriented resumés usually will be well received at other universities, whereas teaching credentials, harder to document and quantify, are much less transferable. Consequently it is rational for university teachers to concentrate on research, even if to the detriment of teaching and at the expense of their students.

By the same token, it is rational for students to act based upon the goal displacement which has occurred within universities concerning what they are rewarded for. If it is assumed that a primary goal of a university is to transfer knowledge from teacher to student, then grades become identifiable as a means towards that goal, serving as motivational, control, and feedback devices to expedite the knowledge transfer. Instead, however, the grades themselves have become much more important for entrance to graduate school, successful employment, tuition refunds, parental respect, etc., than the knowledge or lack of knowledge they are supposed to signify.

It therefore should come as no surprise that information has surfaced in recent years concerning fraternity files for examinations, term-paper writing services, organized cheating at the service academies, and the like. Such activities constitute a personally rational response to a reward system which pays off for grades rather than knowledge.

Business-related examples
Ecology
Assume that the president of XYZ Corporation is confronted with the following alternatives:

- Spend $11 million for antipollution equipment to keep from poisoning fish in the river adjacent to the plant; or
- Do nothing, in violation of the law, and assume a 1 in 10 chance of being caught, with a resultant $1 million fine plus the necessity of buying the equipment.

Under this not unrealistic set of choices, it requires no linear program to determine that

XYZ Corporation can maximize its probabilities by flouting the law. Add the fact that XYZ's president is probably being rewarded (by creditors, stockholders, and other salient parts of his task environment) according to criteria totally unrelated to the number of fish poisoned, and his probable course of action becomes clear.

Evaluation of training

It is axiomatic that those who care about a firm's well-being should insist that the organization get fair value for its expenditures. Yet it is commonly known that firms seldom bother to evaluate a new GRID, MBO, job enrichment program, or whatever, to see if the company is getting its money's worth. Why? Certainly it is not because people have not pointed out that this situation exists; numerous practitioner-oriented articles are written each year to just this point.

The individuals (whether in personnel, manpower planning, or wherever) who normally would be responsible for conducting such evaluations are the same ones often charged with introducing the change effort in the first place. Having convinced top management to spend the money, they usually are quite animated afterwards in collecting arigorous vignettes and anecdotes about how successful the program was. The last thing many desire is a formal, systematic, and revealing evaluation. Although members of top management may actually *hope* for such systematic evaluation, their reward systems continue to *reward* ignorance in this area. And if the personnel department abdicates its responsibility, who is to step into the breach? The change agent himself? Hardly! He is likely to be too busy collecting anecdotal 'evidence' of his own, for use with his next client.

Miscellaneous

Many additional examples could be cited of systems which in fact are rewarding behaviors other than those supposedly desired by the rewarder. A few of these are described briefly below.

Most coaches disdain to discuss individual accomplishments, preferring to speak of teamwork, proper attitude, and a one-for-all spirit. Usually, however, rewards are distributed according to individual performance. The college basketball player who feeds his teammates instead of shooting will not compile impressive scoring statistics and is less likely to be drafted by the pros. The ballplayer who hits to right field to advance the runners will win neither the batting nor home run titles, and will be offered smaller raises. It therefore is rational for players to think of themselves first, and the team second.

In business organizations where rewards are dispensed for unit performance or for individual goals achieved, without regard for overall effectiveness, similar attitudes often are observed. Under most Management by Objectives (MBO) systems, goals in areas where quantification is difficult often go unspecified. The organization therefore often is in a position where it *hopes* for employee effort in the areas of team building, interpersonal relations, creativity, etc., but it formally *rewards* none of these. In cases where promotions and raises are formally tied to MBO, the system itself contains a paradox in that it 'asks employees to set challenging, risky goals, only to face smaller paychecks and possibly damaged careers if these goals are not accomplished'.

It is *hoped* that administrators will pay attention to long-run costs and opportunities and will institute programs which will bear fruit later on. However, many organizational reward systems pay off for shorter-run sales and earnings only. Under such circumstances, it is personally rational for officials to sacrifice long-term growth and profit (by selling off equipment and property, or by stifling research and development) for short-term advantages. This probably is most pertinent in the public sector, with the result that many public officials are unwilling to implement programs which will not show benefits by election time.

As a final, clear-cut example of a fouled-up reward system, consider the cost-plus contract or its next of kin, the allocation of next year's budget as a direct function of this year's expenditures. It probably is conceivable that those who award such budgets and contracts really hope for economy and prudence in spending. It is obvious, however, that adopting the proverb 'to him who spends shall more be given', rewards not economy, but spending itself.

Two companies' experience
A manufacturing organization

A Midwest manufacturer of industrial goods had been troubled for some time by aspects of its organizational climate it believed dysfunctional.

For research purposes, interviews were conducted with many employees and a questionnaire was administered on a companywide basis, including plants and offices in several American and Canadian locations. The company strongly encouraged employee participation in the survey, and made available time and space during the workday for completion of the instrument. All employees in attendance during the day of the survey completed the questionnaire. All instruments were collected directly by the researcher, who personally administered each session. Since no one employed by the firm handled the questionnaire, and since respondent names were not asked for, it seems likely that the pledge of anonymity given was believed.

A modified version of the Expect Approval scale was included as part of the questionnaire. The instrument asked respondents to indicate the degree of approval or disapproval they could expect if they performed each of the described actions. A seven-point Likert scale was used, with 1 indicating that the action would probably bring strong disapproval and 7 signifying likely strong approval.

Although normative data for this scale from studies of other organizations are unavailable, it is possible to examine fruitfully the data obtained from this survey in several ways. First, it may be worth noting that the questionnaire data corresponded closely to information gathered through interviews. Furthermore, as can be seen from the results summarized in Exhibit 5.8, sizable differences between various work units, and between employees at different job levels within the same work unit, were obtained. This suggests that response bias effects (social desirability in particular loomed as a potential concern) are not likely to be severe.

Most importantly, comparisons between scores obtained on the Expect Approval scale and a statement of problems which were the reason for the survey revealed that the same behaviors which managers in each division thought dysfunctional were those which lower-level employees claimed were rewarded. As compared to job levels 1 to 8 in Division B (see Exhibit 5.8), those in Division A claimed a much higher acceptance by management of 'conforming' activities. Between 31 and 37 percent of Division A employees at levels 1–8 stated that going along

with the majority, agreeing with the boss, and staying on everyone's good side brought approval; only once (level 5–8 responses to one of the three items) did a majority suggest that such actions would generate disapproval.

Furthermore, responses from Division A workers at levels 1–4 indicate that behaviors geared toward risk avoidance were as likely to be rewarded as to be punished. Only at job levels 9 and above was it apparent that the reward system was positively reinforcing behaviors desired by top management. Overall, the same 'tendencies toward conservatism and apple-polishing at the lower levels' which divisional management had complained about during interviews were those claimed by subordinates to be the most rational course of action in light of the existing reward system. Management apparently was not getting the behaviors it was *hoping* for, but it certainly was getting the behaviors it was perceived by subordinates to be rewarding.

An insurance firm

The Group Health Claims Division of a large Eastern insurance company provides another rich illustration of a reward system which reinforces behaviors not desired by top management.

Attempting to measure and reward accuracy in paying surgical claims, the firm systematically keeps track of the number of returned checks and letters of complaint received from policy-holders. However, underpayments are likely to provoke cries of outrage from the insured, while overpayments often are accepted in courteous silence. Since it often is impossible to tell from the physician's statement which of two surgical procedures, with different allowable benefits, was performed, and since writing for clarifications will interfere with other standards used by the firm concerning 'percentage of claims paid within two days of receipt', the new hire in more than one claims section is soon acquainted with the informal norm: 'When in doubt, pay it out!'

The situation would be even worse were it not for the fact that other features of the firm's reward system tend to neutralize those described. For example, annual 'merit' increases are given to all employees, in one of the following three amounts:

1. If the worker is 'outstanding' (a select category, into which no more than two

Exhibit 5.8 Summary of two divisions' data relevant to conforming and risk-avoidance behaviours (extent to which subjects expect approval)

Dimension	Item	Division and Sample	Total Responses	Percentage of Workers Responding		
				1,2, or 3 (Disapproval)	4	5, 6, or 7 (Approval)
Risk avoidance	Making a risky decision based on the best information available at the time, but which turns out wrong.	A, levels 1–4 (lowest)	127	61	25	14
		A, levels 5–8	172	46	31	23
		A, levels 9 and above	17	41	30	30
		B, levels 1–4 (lowest)	31	58	26	16
		B, levels 5–8	19	42	42	16
		B, levels 9 and above	10	50	20	30
Risk	Setting extremely high and challenging standards and goals, and then narrowly failing to make them.	A, levels 1–4	122	47	28	25
		A, levels 5–8	168	33	26	41
		A, levels 9+	17	24	6	70
		B, levels 1–4	31	48	23	29
		B, levels 5–8	18	17	33	50
		B, levels 9+	10	30	0	70
	Setting goals which are extremely easy to make and then making them.	A, levels 1–4	124	35	30	35
		A, levels 5–8	171	47	27	26
		A, levels 9+	17	70	24	6
		B, levels 1–4	31	58	26	16
		B, levels 5–8	19	63	16	21
		B, levels 9+	10	80	0	20
	Being a 'yes man' and always agreeing with the boss.	A, levels 1–4	126	46	17	37
		A, levels 5–8	180	54	14	31
		A, levels 9+	17	88	12	0
		B, levels 1–4	32	53	28	19
		B, levels 5–8	19	68	21	11
		B, levels 9+	10	80	10	10
	Always going along with the majority	A, levels 1–4	125	40	25	35
		A, levels 5–8	173	47	21	32
		A, levels 9+	17	70	12	18
		B, levels 1–4	31	61	23	16
		B, levels 5–8	18	68	11	21
		B, level 9+	10	80	10	10
	Being careful to stay on the good side of everyone, so that everyone agrees that you are a great guy.	A, levels 1–4	124	45	18	37
		A, levels 5–8	173	45	22	33
		A, levels 9+	17	64	6	30
		B, levels 1–4	31	54	23	23
		B, levels 5–8	19	73	11	16
		B, levels 9+	10	80	10	10

employees per section may be placed):
5 percent.

2. If the worker is 'above average' (normally all workers not 'outstanding' are so rated):
4 percent.

3. If the worker commits gross acts of negligence and irresponsibility for which he might be discharged in many other companies:
3 percent.

Now, since (*a*) the difference between the 5 percent theoretically attainable through hard work and the 4 percent attainable merely by living until the review date is small, and (*b*) since insurance firms seldom dispense much of a salary increase in cash (rather, the worker's insurance benefits increase, causing him to be further overinsured), many employees are rather indifferent to the possibility of obtaining the extra 1 percent reward and therefore tend to ignore the norm concerning indiscrimination payments.

However, most employees are not indifferent to the rule which states that, should absences or lateness total three or more in any six-month period, the entire 4 or 5 percent due at the next 'merit' review must be forfeited. In this sense the firm may be described as *hoping* for performance, while *rewarding* attendance. What it gets, of course is attendance. If the absence-lateness rule appears to the reader to be stringent, it really is not. The company counts 'time' rather than 'days' absent, and a 10-day absence therefore counts the same as one lasting 2 days. A worker in danger of accumulating a third absence within six months merely has to remain ill (away from work) during his second absence until his first absence is more than six months old. The limiting factor is that at some point his salary ceases, and his sickness benefits take over. This usually is sufficient to get the younger workers to return, but for those with 20 or more years' service, the company provides sickness benefits of 90 percent of normal salary, tax-free! Therefore …

Causes
Extremely diverse instances of systems which reward behavior A although the rewarder apparently hopes for behavior B have been given. These are useful to illustrate the breadth and magnitude of the phenomenon, but the diversity increases the difficulty of determining commonalities and establishing causes. However,

four general factors may be pertinent to an explanation of why fouled-up reward systems seem to be so prevalent.

Fascination with an 'objective' criterion
It has been mentioned elsewhere that:
Most 'objective' measures of productivity are objective only in that their subjective elements are (a) *determined in advance, rather than coming into play at the time of the formal evaluation, and* (b) *well concealed on the rating instrument itself. Thus industrial firms seeking to devise objective rating systems first decide, in an arbitrary manner, what dimensions are to be rated, … usually including some items having little to do with organization effectiveness while excluding others that do. Only then does Personnel division churn out official-looking documents on which all dimensions chosen to be rated are assigned point values, categories, or whatever.*

Nonetheless, many individuals seek to establish simple, quantifiable standards against which to measure and reward performance. Such efforts may be successful in highly predictable areas within an organization, but are likely to cause goal displacement when applied anywhere else. Over-concern with attendance and lateness in the insurance firm and with number of people placed in the vocational rehabilitation division may have been largely responsible for the problems described in those organizations.

Overemphasis on highly visible behaviors
Difficulties often stem from the fact that some parts of the task are highly visible while other parts are not. For example, publications are easier to demonstrate than teaching, and scoring baskets and hitting home runs are more readily observable than feeding teammates and advancing base runners. Similarly, the adverse consequences of pronouncing a sick person well are more visible than those sustained by labeling a well person sick. Team-building and creativity are other examples of behaviors which may not be rewarded simply because they are hard to observe.

Hypocrisy
In some of the instances described, the rewarder may have been getting the desired behavior, notwithstanding claims that the behavior was not desired. This may be true, for example, for management's attitude toward apple-polishing in

the manufacturing firm (a behavior which subordinates felt was rewarded, despite management's avowed dislike of the practice). This also may explain politicians' unwillingness to revise the penalties for disobedience of ecology laws, and the failure of top management to devise reward systems which would cause systematic evaluation of training and development programs.

Emphasis on morality or equity rather than efficiency

Some consideration of other factors prevents the establishment of a system which rewards behaviors desired by the rewarder. The felt obligation of many Americans to vote for one candidate or another, for example, may impair their ability to withhold support from politicians who refuse to discuss the issues. Similarly, the concern for spreading the risks and costs of wartime military service may outweigh the advantage to be obtained by committing personnel to combat until the war is over.

It should be noted that only with respect to the first two causes are reward systems really paying off for other than desired behaviours. In the case of the third and fourth causes, the system is rewarding behaviors desired by the rewarder, and the systems are fouled up only from the standpoints of those who believe the rewarder's public statements (cause 3), or those who seek to maximize efficiency rather than other outcomes (cause 4).

Conclusions

Modern organization theory requires a recognition that the members of organizations and society possess divergent goals and motives. It therefore is unlikely that management and their subordinates will seek the same outcomes. Three possible remedies for this potential problem are suggested.

Selection

It is theoretically possible for organizations to employ only those individuals whose goals and motives are wholly consonant with those of management. In such cases the same behaviors judged by subordinates to be rational would be perceived by management as desirable. State-of-the-art reviews of selection techniques, however, provide scant grounds for hope that such an approach would be successful.

Training

Another theoretical alternative is for the organization to admit those employees whose goals are not consonant with those of management and then, through training, socialization, or whatever, alter employee goals to make them consonant. However, research on the effectiveness of such training programs, though limited, provides further grounds for pessimism.

Altering the reward system

What would have been the result if:

1. Nixon had been assured by his advisors that he could not win reelection except by discussing the issues in detail?
2. Physicians' conduct was subjected to regular examination by review boards for type 1 errors (calling healthy people ill) and to penalties (fines, censure, etc.) for errors of either type?
3. The President of XYZ Corporation had to choose between (*a*) spending $11 million for antipollution equipment, and (*b*) incurring a 50–50 chance of going to jail for five years?

Managers who complain that their workers are not motivated might do well to consider the possibility that they have installed reward systems which are paying off for behaviors other than those they are seeking. This, in part, is what happened in Vietnam, and this is what regularly frustrates societal efforts to bring about honest politicians, civic-minded managers, etc. This certainly is what happened in both manufacturing and the insurance companies.

A first step for such managers might be to find out what behaviors currently are being rewarded. Perhaps an instrument similar to that used in the manufacturing firm could be useful for this purpose. Chances are excellent that these managers will be surprised by what they find — that their firms are not rewarding what they assume they are. In fact, such undesirable behavior by organizational members as they have observed may be explained largely by the reward systems in use.

This is not to say that all organizational behaviour is determined by formal rewards and punishments. Certainly it is true that, in the absence of formal reinforcement, some soldiers will be patriotic, some presidents will be ecology-minded, and some orphanage directors will care about children. The point, however, is that in such cases the rewarder is not *causing* the behaviors desired but is only a fortunate bystander. For an organization to *act* upon its members, the formal reward system should positively reinforce desired behaviors, not constitute an obstacle to be overcome.

It might be wise to underscore the obvious fact that there is nothing really new in what has been said. In both theory and practice these matters have been mentioned before. Thus, in many states, Good Samaritan laws have been installed to protect doctors who stop to assist a stricken motorist. In states without laws, it is commonplace for doctors to refuse to stop for fear of involvement in a subsequent lawsuit. In college basketball, additional penalties have been instituted against players who foul their opponents deliberately. It has long been argued by Milton Friedman and others that penalties should be altered so as to make it irrational to disobey the ecology laws, and so on.

By altering the reward system, the organization escapes the necessity of selecting only desirable people or of trying to alter undesirable ones. In Skinnerian terms, 'As for responsibility and goodness — as commonly defined — no one ... would want or need them. They refer to a man's behaving well despite the absence of positive reinforcement that is obviously sufficient to explain it. Where such reinforcement exists, "no one needs goodness"'.

Endnotes

1   Chester I. Barnard, *The Functions of the Executive* (Cambridge, MA: Harvard University Press, 1964).
2   Peter M. Blau and W. Richard Scott, *Formal Organizations* (San Francisco: Chandler, 1962).
3   Fred E. Fiedler, 'Predicting the Effects of Leadership Training and Experience from the Contingency Model', *Journal of Applied Psychology* 56 (1972), pp. 114–19.

EXERCISE 5 JOB DESIGN

Source: Tosi, H. L., & and Young, J. W. (1982). *Management Experiences and Illustrations.* Homewood, IL: Richard D. Irwin, Inc.

Purpose

This exercise illustrates how particular characteristics of work relate to the motivation of those who perform it. Tasks can be thought of as being different on several characteristics:
1. the amount of *task autonomy;*
2. the degree of *variety* of activities;
3. the extent to which one can *identify* their task as a whole unit of work;
4. the *significance* of the job's influence on other people — both within and outside the organisation;
5. the *feedback* which the task itself provides about performance.

This exercise demonstrates how to determine the level of each of these characteristics in a job and how these factors relate to individual motivation.

Time required: 15 minutes to complete the questionnaire. This exercise may also be completed as a homework assignment and brought to class for discussion.

Preparation: Think about the job you now hold or one you have held. Respond to the items on the following questionnaires as they relate to that job.

Job design

Job title _____

(Title of the job to be analysed)

Job description: Briefly describe the major responsibilities of the job.

_____

_____

This part of the questionnaire asks you to describe your job, as *objectively* as you can. *Please do not use the questionnaire to show how much you like or dislike your job.* Questions about that will come later. Make your descriptions as accurate and as objective as you possibly can.

1. How much autonomy is there in your job? That is, to what extent does your job permit you to decide *on your own* how to go about doing the work?

   1 ——— 2 ——— 3 ——— 4 ——— 5 ——— 6 ——— 7

   | Very little; the job give almost no personal say about how and when the work is done. | Moderate autonomy; many things are standardised and not under my control but I can make some decisions about the work. | Very much; the job gives me almost complete responsibility for deciding how and when the work is done. |

2. To what extent does your job involve doing a *'whole' and identifiable piece of work?* That is, is the job a complete piece of work that has an obvious beginning and end? Or is it only a small *part* of the overall piece of work, which is finished by other people or by automatic machines?

   1 ——— 2 ——— 3 ——— 4 ——— 5 ——— 6 ——— 7

   | My job is only a tiny part of the overall piece of work; the results of my activities cannot be seen in the final product or service. | My job is a moderately sized chunk of the overall piece of work; my own contribution can be seen in the final outcome. | My job involves doing the whole piece of work from start to finish; the results of my activities are easily seen in the final product or service. |

3. How much variety is there in your job? That is, to what extent does the job require you to do *many different things* at work, using a *variety of your skills and talents?*

   1 ——— 2 ——— 3 ——— 4 ——— 5 ——— 6 ——— 7

   | Very little; the job requires me to do the same routine things over and over again. | Moderate variety | Very much; the job requires me to do many things using a number of skills and talents. |

4. In general, how much impact on others does your job have? That is, are the results of your work likely to significantly affect the lives or wellbeing of other people?

   1 ——— 2 ——— 3 ——— 4 ——— 5 ——— 6 ——— 7

   | Not very significant; the outcomes of my work are *not* likely to have important effects on other people. | Moderately significant | Highly significant; the outcomes of the work can affect other people in very important ways. |

5. To what extent does *doing the job itself* provide you with information about your work performance? That is, does the actual *work itself* provide clues about how well you are doing — aside from any 'feedback' co-workers or supervisor may provide?

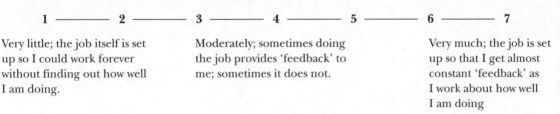

| 1 ——— | 2 ——— | 3 ——— | 4 ——— | 5 ——— | 6 ——— | 7 |

Very little; the job itself is set up so I could work forever without finding out how well I am doing.

Moderately; sometimes doing the job provides 'feedback' to me; sometimes it does not.

Very much; the job is set up so that I get almost constant 'feedback' as I work about how well I am doing

Listed below are a number of statements which could be used to describe a job. You are to indicate whether each statement is an *accurate* or an *inaccurate* description of *your* job. Once again, please try to be as objective as you can in deciding how accurately each statement describes your job — regardless of whether you *like* or *dislike* your job.

Write a number to the left of statement based on the following scale:

How accurate is the statement in describing your job?

1	2	3	4	5	6	7
Very inaccurate	Mostly inaccurate	Slightly inaccurate	Uncertain	Slightly accurate	Mostly accurate	Very accurate

6. The job requires me to use a number of complex or high-level skills.
7. The job is arranged so that I have the chance to do an entire piece of work from beginning to end.
8. Just doing the work required by the job provides many chances for me to figure out how well I am doing.
9. This job is not at all simple or repetitive.
10. This job is one where many other people can be affected by how well the works gets done.
11. The job allows me a chance to use my personal initiative or judgement in carrying out the work.
12. The job provides me the chance to completely finish the piece of work I begin.
13. The job itself provides many clues about whether or not I am performing well.
14. The job gives me considerable opportunity for independence and freedom in how I do the work.
15. The job itself is quite significant or important in the broader scheme of things.

Listed below are a number of characteristics which could be present on any job. People differ about how much they would like to have each one present in their own jobs. We are interested in learning *how much you personally would like* to have each one present in your job.

Using the scale below, please indicate the *degree* to which you *would like* to have each characteristic present in your job.

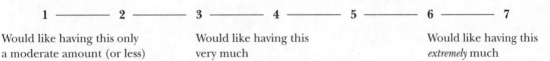

| 1 ——— | 2 ——— | 3 ——— | 4 ——— | 5 ——— | 6 ——— | 7 |

Would like having this only a moderate amount (or less)

Would like having this very much

Would like having this *extremely* much

16. Stimulating and challenging work.
17. Chances to exercise independent thought and action in my job.
18. Opportunities to learn new things from my work.
19. Opportunities to be creative and imaginative in my work.
20. Opportunities for personal growth and development in my job.
21. A sense of worthwhile accomplishment in my work.

Computation work sheet for internal motivating potential

I. Average identity (AVG IDENT)

Question   2 = _____
Question   7 = _____
Question 12 = _____
          Total = _____

$\dfrac{\text{TOTAL} = \_\_\_\_}{3}$ = AVG IDENT

II. Average variety (AVG VAR)

Question   3 = _____
Question   6 = _____
Question   9 = _____
          Total = _____

$\dfrac{\text{TOTAL} = \_\_\_\_}{3}$ = AVG VAR

III. Average significance (AVG SIG)

Question   4 = _____
Question 10 = _____
Question 15 = _____
          Total = _____

$\dfrac{\text{TOTAL} = \_\_\_\_}{3}$ = AVG SIG

IV. Average autonomy (AVG AUTO)

Question   1 = _____
Question 11 = _____
Question 14 = _____
          Total = _____

$\dfrac{\text{TOTAL} = \_\_\_\_}{3}$ = AVG AUTO

V. Average feedback from job (AVG FEED)

Question   5 = _____
Question   8 = _____
Question 13 = _____
          Total = _____

$\dfrac{\text{TOTAL} = \_\_\_\_}{3}$ = AVG FEED

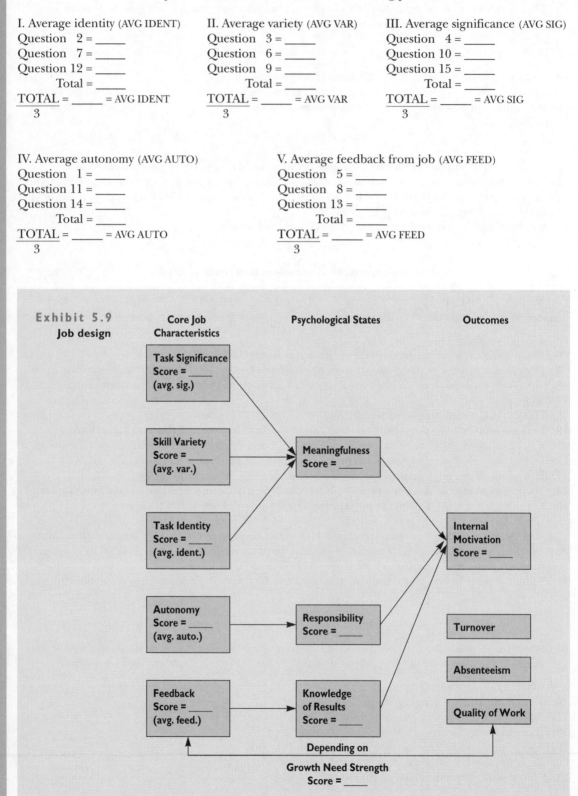

Exhibit 5.9 Job design

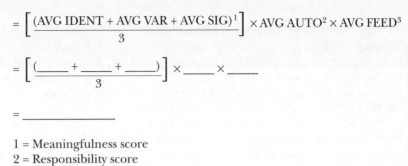

Internal motivating Potential score

$$= \left[\frac{(\text{AVG IDENT} + \text{AVG VAR} + \text{AVG SIG})^1}{3} \right] \times \text{AVG AUTO}^2 \times \text{AVG FEED}^3$$

$$= \left[\frac{(\underline{\qquad} + \underline{\qquad} + \underline{\qquad})}{3} \right] \times \underline{\qquad} \times \underline{\qquad}$$

$$= \underline{\qquad\qquad\qquad}$$

1 = Meaningfulness score
2 = Responsibility score
3 = Knowledge of results score

Growth Need Strength (AVG GNS)
Question 16 _____
Question 17 _____
Question 18 _____
Question 19 _____
Question 20 _____
Question 21 _____
Total = _____
Total ÷ 6 = _____ = AVG GNS

CASE 5   VACCINO

Deborah Watson

Part A

Vaccino is a vaccine manufacturing company which, since 1991, has undergone major changes including the shift from a government statutory authority to a fully privatised company whose shareholders include both individuals as well as major Australian and international institutions. Vaccino management negotiated an enterprise agreement with unions and staff. This agreement will be in existence in its current state until the end of 1995. A pertinent part of the agreement was that all redundancies would remain voluntary.

Research Division

To assist in the changes a new director of research, 55-year-old Neil Bloom, was appointed in mid-1991. Bloom is a world-renowned research scientist with a professorship at the university. He is a public figure with well-developed leadership qualities. However, he has limited commercial experience and an obvious lack of ability to handle people issues; Bloom shows a strong preference for delegating these issues whenever possible. Bloom seemed to surround himself with hard-working individuals who were often considered by other divisions to be 'yes' people.

At the time of his appointment, Bloom's brief included management of all scientific and administrative functions within the Research Division. As well as changing the focus of the science of the division by reducing the number of projects from 112 to 7, he also set about changing the physical layout of the management and administration sections of the division.

When Bloom took charge of the division, the management and administration areas were located on the first floor of the research building. The three administrative secretaries were situated in the same, large office along with the facsimile machine, photocopier, stationery cupboard and so on. Their jobs required that they provide full administrative support to all staff in the division. This included typing and word-processing, photocopying and filing, as well as managing telephone calls, mail and other services.

One of Bloom's first acts, as manager, was to relocate the secretaries to another office about half the size of the original — without consulting them. In the new office, they were provided with work stations set up in an open-plan environment. He then turned the original office into his own office and built a small tearoom and a photocopier room onto the side of his office facing into the hallway to allow easy access for all staff.

Immediately after the physical reorganisation he appointed the laboratory manager, Jean Crickson, as manager of the administrative secretaries and the administrative service. Crickson is a 53-year-old research scientist who has been at Vaccino since 1972. She was moved to the position of laboratory manager because it fitted the company's affirmative action program at the time. Crickson has no administrative experience and her people skills were known to be poor at best and at times quite destructive. However, Crickson worked hard at her job and appeared to be favoured by Bloom because she would do whatever he asked. Crickson's downward management style could best be described as supervisory or command and control, and her upward management as 'yes'. Although hard working, Crickson possessed limited administrative skills and was known to have poor interpersonal skills. Crickson tended to supervise rather than manage her staff and was know to have accused the administrative secretaries of being 'lazy and unable to cope with simple tasks'. Crickson also felt insecure in her position and would not accept suggestions for change from any of her staff.

Over the 12 months from mid-1991 to mid-1992 the administrative services section suffered a 200% staff turnover with only one secretary, Doris Stanford, staying the whole period, and this was mostly due to her length of service with the company and not through any dedication to the current position. Stanford has been with the company 38 years, always as a secretary. She has seen many changes and is somewhat cynical about new ideas. She prefers to be directed in her work but becomes very stubborn when peers try to help or contribute ideas. Although believed by people outside the immediate work team to have a 'heart of gold', Stanford can be loud and overbearing and has been known to make racist remarks.

Some of the comments from the secretaries who decided to leave are:

- 'The work is boring and monotonous and people see us as the typing pool.'
- 'Jean is demanding and rude and never listens to our ideas.'
- 'Jean doesn't know the first thing about administration.'
- 'Neil doesn't understand the area and doesn't care what happens in here.'

- 'Doris is loud and annoying and never wants to try new ideas.'
- 'I'm always having to do the advanced word-processing functions for Doris because she won't learn how to do them herself.'

Senior managers were very concerned at the high staff turnover, estimated to have cost the division about $30 000 in the past 12 months, and the fact that neither they nor their staff received work back from the administrative services on time. Although Bloom believed he knew the main reason behind the problems in administrative services he decided to seek an objective viewpoint, and a consultant was hired to find out the reason the administrative services section was not functioning properly and why there was such a high staff turnover.

The consultant advised Bloom that the laboratory manager should not be in charge of the administrative services area and that a new position should be formed. The new position would be an administrative coordinator and would need to be someone with excellent interpersonal skills and previous experience in administration. The new role would include management of the office and staff, and some duties devolved from the laboratory manager along with additional computing and personnel related areas of responsibility. Bloom accepted the consultant's advice and recruited an administrative coordinator. However, the new position would report to the laboratory manager.

Discussion questions for Part A
1. What factors have contributed to staff turnover?
2. What would you do if you were appointed to this position?
3. How could you apply the principles of job redesign to improve the situation?

Part B
On her apppontement as administrative coordinator, Barbara Kellett took several immediate actions. First, she recruited two permanent secretaries to replace the temporaries. Rani Pajnee, a 27-year-old Indian (Hindu), is a quietly spoken and calm-mannered person. She is well organised and is a skilled PC operator with advanced knowledge of a variety of software packages. Although not overly ambitious, Pajnee would like to develop her

people skills and move into a more senior position. Pajnee enjoys change when it is done for good reason. Pajnee finds Crickson difficult to deal with and her manner very rude. Pajnee has found Stanford to be difficult to fathom because at times she is very helpful and at others she is rude. Kellett believes that Pajnee would make a very good office manager and has a lot of respect for her ability. The second recruit, Catherine Bout, is a 32-year-old Indian (Catholic). She has a bubbly cheerful personality and is very organised and adept at PC software. Bout tends to see issues in black or white with no grey areas. She tackles issues head on, sometimes causing undue distress to the target of her opinions. Bout is the best able to deal with Crickson as she tends to ignore her demands. Bout, however, finds Stanford very difficult to work with, because she is loud and distracts her from her work. Kellett believes that Bout would make a very good executive assistant, but would be too single minded to be an office manager.

Kellett also formed the Administrative Services TQM (Total Quality Management) team. The aim of the TQM team was to identify the major problems within the administrative services office and, as a team, find solutions to the problems. The team reorganised the office to include partitions; developed a work flow system to replace the old ad hoc system; and developed a training program to help ensure that they all had the same level of software skills and were able to undertake personal development training as well. They believed that their aim was, as a team, to provide an efficient, effective and cheerful administrative service to the Research Division. The following 18 months saw the administrative services section become a more cohesive team with no staff turnover and a higher level of service (as assessed by a customer survey).

However, Crickson, who felt threatened by the success of Kellett's techniques, attempted to undermine Kellett by openly asserting her authority and overriding decisions Kellett had made. Although Kellett had managed to become a buffer between Crickson and the administrative secretaries she often bore the brunt of Crickson's temper when she felt she was not getting her work done with priority.

Also during the 18 months, the appointment of two more senior management staff increased the workload by about 35% and conflict developed over individual work distribution within the administrative services team. Rani Pajnee and Catherine Bout, the two other administrative secretaries, felt that they carried most of the workload and that their efforts to create interesting work were thwarted by Doris who seemed opposed to any sort of change — although she is an excellent typist, Doris has a limited ability with advanced or new software. In fact, Stanford's generally lower productivity than the other secretaries became obvious only when the team was starting to function properly. She had been counselled by Kellett but had so far not appeared to be willing to alter her behaviour. Stanford has an ongoing personal dislike of Crickson and firmly believes that Crickson will never change.

Kellett became very frustrated in her job due to Crickson's poor management, the increasingly difficult job trying to nurse Stanford into accepting change, and a limited scope for someone with her level of ambition. Kellett began investigating alternative employment within another division of the company. The rumour of Kellett's possible departure was distressing for the administrative secretaries who feared that their workload would increase yet again and that Crickson would be placed in charge again and all of the changes come to nought. Kellett encouraged them to consider working as a self-directed work team with a rotating system of office manager. Pajnee and Bout felt that this would not work because Doris would not be able to accept them as 'managers' and would ignore any requests they might have.

The month following the initial rumour that Kellett may be leaving saw the emergence and escalation of conflict within the administrative services team — much of which seemed to have racial overtones. The division must now decide how best to run the administrative services team.

Discussion questions for Part B

1. If you were Kellett, how would you manage the three administrative secretaries?
2. Could OBM principles be applied to manage Stanford?
3. What reward systems would provide appropriate incentives for the staff?
4. What factors contributed to Kellett's decision to leave?
5. What problems are now faced by the team?
6. How would you restructure the workplace to ensure high performance and motivation?

OCCUPATIONAL STRESS

Learning objectives

- **Understand** *that the term 'stress' can be defined in a number of different ways.*

- **Describe** *the general adaptation syndrome.*

- **Discuss** *the major variables in an integrative model of stress.*

- **Distinguish** *between several categories of stressors.*

- **Identify** *four important variables that moderate the relationship between stressors and stress.*

- **Discuss** *several individual and organisational approaches to managing stress.*

- **Describe** *the key components of burnout.*

A number of years ago, J. V. Brady, a laboratory psychologist, constructed an experiment in which a monkey strapped to a chair was administered a shock of sufficient voltage to be uncomfortable but not physically harmful.[1] The shock was automatically administered every 20 seconds, unless the monkey pushed a large red button that was within easy reach of its chair. If the monkey did push the button, the 20-second period began anew; thus, it was possible for the monkey to avoid any shock if it stayed alert and made the decision to push the button at least once every 20 seconds. After 3 weeks of doing this 6 hours a day, the monkey died. An autopsy was performed and the monkey was found to have a perforated ulcer.

Brady began the experiment again with a new monkey and within a few weeks the new monkey had died, again with a perforated ulcer. Brady repeated the experiment again, but with an additional component added. This time he used two monkeys side by side. The only difference between the two was that the companion monkey's button did not allow it to avoid the shock. For the third time, the 'executive' monkey (so called because it had to make decisions about when to push the button) died, while the companion monkey remained healthy. The executive monkeys developed ulcers not because of the shock but because they constantly had to make decisions. Compared with the companion monkey, the executive monkeys had extremely stressful jobs.

Since Brady published his work with monkeys, a great deal has been learned about stress in general and the relationship between stress and work specifically. We know, for example, that change can be a powerful contributor to stress. Even the kind of planned change associated with organisational development efforts that we will discuss in Chapter 15 can be responsible for causing dysfunctional stress. Life today is filled with stressors — work overload, a nagging boss, marital disharmony, time deadlines, poorly designed jobs, keeping up with the Joneses and accelerating rates of change. These work and non-work stressors interact and create stress for the individual on and off the job.

This chapter focuses primarily on the individual at work in organisations and on the stress created in this setting. Much of the stress experienced by people in our industrialised society originates in organisations; much of the stress that originates elsewhere affects our behaviour and performance in these same organisations. In the article 'Who beats stress — and how' at the end of this chapter, the author points out that what we do not understand about stress would fill volumes. His point is well taken. One of the complicating issues in understanding stress is the fact that it has been defined in a multitude of ways. We begin this chapter with our definition of stress.

Reading 6
Who beats stress
best — and how

UNDERSTANDING STRESS

Stress means different things to many different people. From a layperson's perspective, stress can variously be described as feeling tense, anxious or worried, or having the 'blues'. Scientifically, these feelings are manifestations of the stress experience, an intriguingly complex programmed response to perceived threat that can have positive and negative results. The term 'stress' has itself been defined in literally hundreds of different ways in the research and professional literature. Virtually all of the definitions can be placed in one of two categories, however; stress can be defined as either a *stimulus* or a *response*.

A stimulus definition treats stress as some characteristic, event or situation in the environment that in some way results in a potentially disruptive consequence. It is, in that respect, an engineering definition of stress, borrowed from the physical sciences. In physics, 'stress' refers to the external force applied to an object, for example a bridge girder. The response is 'strain', which is the impact the force has on the girder.

In a response definition, stress is seen partially as a response to some stimulus, called a **stressor**. A stressor is a potentially harmful or threatening external event or situation. Stress is more than simply a response to a stressor, however. In a response definition, stress is the consequence of an interaction between an environmental stimulus (a stressor) and the individual's response. That is, stress is the result of a unique interaction between stimulus conditions in the environment and an individual's predisposition to respond in a particular way. Using a response definition, we will define **stress** as:

> *An adaptive response, moderated by individual differences, that is a consequence of any action, situation or event that places special demands on a person.*

For our purposes, we think it is useful to view stress as the response a person makes and to identify the stimulus conditions (actions, events or situations) as stressors. This allows us to focus attention on aspects of the organisational environment that are potential stress producers. Whether stress is actually felt or experienced by a particular individual will depend on that individual's unique characteristics. Furthermore, note that this definition emphasises that stress is an adaptive response. The great majority of our responses to stimuli in the work environment do not require adaptation and thus are not really potential sources of stress.

In the context of our definition of stress, it is important to understand that stress is the result of dealing with something that places 'special' demands on the individual. *Special* here means unusual, physically or psychologically threatening, or outside an individual's usual set of behaviours. Starting a new job assignment, changing bosses, having a flat tyre, missing a plane, making a mistake at work, having a performance evaluation meeting with the boss, giving a speech — all of these are actions, situations or events that may place special demands on individuals. In that sense, they are *potential* stressors. We refer to them as potential stressors in recognition of the fact that not all stressors will always place the same demands on all people. For example, having a performance appraisal meeting with the boss may be extremely stressful for Jeff and not in the least bit stressful for his co-worker, Holly — that is, undergoing such a meeting makes special demands on Jeff, for Holly it does not. For Jeff, the meeting is a stressor; for Holly it is not.[2]

In order for an action, situation or event to result in stress, it must be perceived by the individual to be a source of threat, challenge or harm. If there are no perceived consequences — good or bad — there is no potential stress. We will return to this idea when we discuss the appraisal process. At least three additional factors play a role in determining whether what an individual is experiencing is likely to result in stress. These factors are importance, uncertainty and duration.[3] Importance relates to how significant the event is for the individual. For example, let us suppose that an employee is facing a job lay-off. The more significant or important that event is to the individual, the greater the stress potential. If the employee expects such an event to be followed by a period of prolonged unemployment, it will probably be viewed as a more important event than if immediate employment is assured.

Uncertainty refers to a lack of clarity about what will happen. Rumours of an impending lay-off may be more stressful for some people than knowing for certain that they will be laid off. At least in the latter case, they can make plans for dealing with the situation. Frequently, 'not knowing' places more demands on people than knowing, even if the known result is perceived as negative.

Finally, duration is a significant factor. Stressors can be either *acute* or *chronic*. Acute stressors are major events in our lives that have a relatively short time frame. In the next section, the discussion of life events will give you some examples of acute stressors. Getting married, losing your job or failing an exam are all events that have a big impact on us, but they do not endure over time (you don't fail an exam every day). Chronic stressors have a less profound impact on us when they occur, but we are exposed to them on an almost continual basis. They are represented by the daily hassles that we discuss in the next section and fit well with Selye's representation of stress as the 'wear and tear of everyday life'. Such things as shopping, cooking or finding a study space in the library are all minor irritations that we face on an almost daily basis. They may not affect us at the time, but their effects slowly build up over time. Generally speaking, the longer special demands are placed on us, the more stressful the situation. Being given an unpleasant job assignment that lasts for only a day or two may be mildly upsetting, while the same assignment lasting for months may be excruciatingly painful. Although there are some acute stressors in the workplace (job loss or transfer, promotion or demotion, and entering or leaving the job market), most of the workplace stressors that we will consider are better thought of as daily hassles.[4]

THE GENERAL ADAPTATION SYNDROME

Stress includes both psychological and physiological components. Dr Hans Selye, the pioneer of stress research, was the first to conceptualise the psychophysiological responses to stress.[5] Selye considered stress a non-specific response to any demand made upon an organism. He labelled the three phases of the defence reaction that a person establishes when stressed as the *general adaptation syndrome* (GAS). Selye called the defence reaction 'general' because stressors had effects on several areas of the body.

Adaptation refers to a stimulation of defences designed to help the body adjust to or deal with, the stressors. And *syndrome* indicates that individual pieces of the reaction occur more or less together. The three distinct phases, which can be seen in Exhibit 6.1, are called *alarm, resistance* and *exhaustion*.

The *alarm* stage is the initial mobilisation by which the body meets the challenge posed by the stressor. When a stressor is recognised, the brain sends forth a biochemical message to all of the body's systems. Respiration increases, blood pressure rises, pupils dilate, muscles tense up and so forth.

If the stressor continues, the GAS proceeds to the *resistance* stage. Signs of being in the resistance stage include fatigue, anxiety and tension. The person is now fighting the stressor. While resistance to a particular stressor may be high

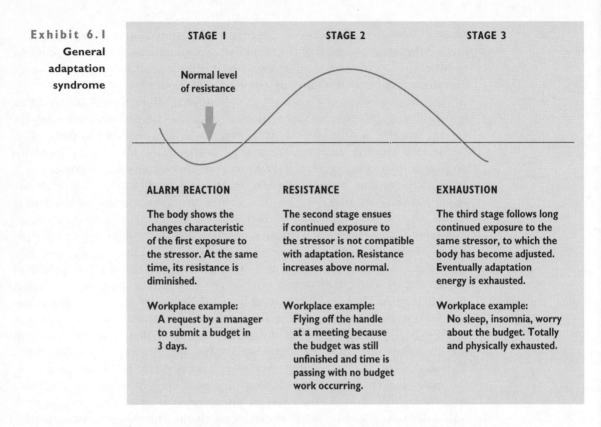

Exhibit 6.1
General
adaptation
syndrome

during this stage, resistance to other stressors may be low. A person has only finite sources of energy, concentration and ability to resist stressors. Individuals are often more illness-prone during periods of stress than at other times.[6]

The final GAS stage is *exhaustion*. Prolonged and continual exposure to the same stressor may eventually use up the adaptive energy available, and the system fighting the stressor becomes exhausted.

It is important to keep in mind that the activation of the GAS places extraordinary demands on the body. Clearly, the more frequently the GAS is activated and the longer it remains in operation, the more wear and tear there is on the psychophysiological mechanisms. The body and mind have limits. The more frequently a person is alarmed, resists and becomes exhausted by work, non-work or the interaction of these activities, the more susceptible he or she becomes to fatigue, disease, aging and other negative consequences.

STRESS AND WORK: A MODEL

For most employed individuals, work and work-related activities, and preparation time, represent more than a 40-hour-a-week commitment. Work is a major part of our lives, and work and non-work activities are strongly interdependent. The distinction between stress at work and stress at home is an artificial one at best. With the explosive increase of dual-career couples in the latter part of the 20th century, even this artificial distinction has become blurred. Nonetheless, our main concern here is with stressors at work.

To better illustrate the link between stressors, stress and consequences, we have developed the model shown in Exhibit 6.2. Recall from our earlier definition that stress is a response to an action, situation or event that places special demands on the individual. These occurrences are represented in Exhibit 6.2 as *work stressors*. We have divided these stressors into three main categories: physical environment, individual, and group and organisational. Bearing in mind that the boundaries between work and home are becoming increasingly blurred, we have also included non-work stressors in the model: life events and daily hassles. In this chapter, however, our focus is on stress at work.

The experience of work-related stress always produces some effects or consequences. We have chosen to categorise these *stress consequences* as primarily individual or organisational in nature. The model suggests that the relationship between stress and stress consequences is not necessarily direct; similarly, neither is the relationship between work stressors and stress. Both of these relationships may be influenced by *stress moderators*. A moderator in some way alters the nature of the relationship; it can change how an individual responds to stress and influence the choice of coping strategies.[7] Moderator variables are extremely important in understanding stress. While numerous moderators have been investigated by organisational stress researchers, we will focus our attention on a small set of representative moderators. We will consider how a small set of variables affects the stressor-stress and stress-consequence relationships: appraisal, personality and social support.

WORK AND LIFE STRESSORS

Stressors are those actions, situations or events that place special demands on a person. Since, in the right set of circumstances, virtually any occurrence can place special demands on a person, the list of potential stressors is infinite. We will limit our examination to a small set of stressors in each of our model's four categories that are relatively common and well researched. Our Global Encounter considers whether we are justified in assuming that culture has little effect on either the causes or consequences of work stress.

Exhibit 6.2
Occupational
stress: A model

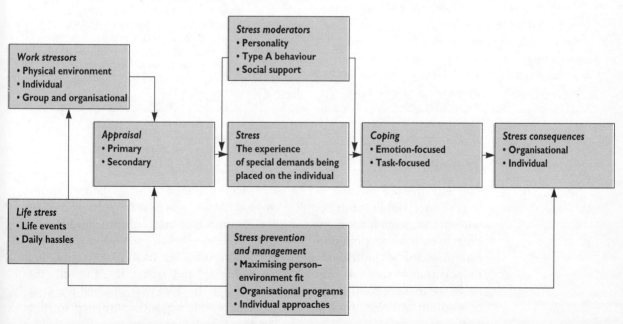

Executive stress in Asia

One of the issues that must be considered, as more and more multinational enterprises appear, is the extent to which research conducted in Western cultures can be generalised to other cultures. Recent research in Asia suggests that while there are many similarities, there are also differences. This implies that managers must adapt their organisational policies and practices to suit cultural needs. In this Encounter, we present some of the causes and consequences of stress for Asian managers.

Leo Sin and Danny Cheng identified six sources of job stress for their sample of Chinese business executives in Hong Kong: job-assigned (overload), responsibility (role clarity); work/organisational climate; career; job-value conflict; and role ambiguity. These not only overlap with the sources of stress that we have identified in this chapter, but also lead to many of the same consequences. Managers who reported high job-assigned stress, role-ambiguity stress and work-organisational culture stress, also reported higher levels of psychological symptoms such as restlessness and forgetfulness. Those reporting high job-assigned and job-value conflict stress reported higher levels of psychosomatic symptoms such as headaches, poor appetite and trouble getting to sleep.

Perrewe, Ralston and Fernandez, in a study of US and Hong Kong managers, found that the two groups reported relatively similar levels of occupational stress. A major difference between the two was that Hong Kong managers reported less financial and family hassles than did American managers. While this might lead us to conclude that the two groups are more alike than different, the organisational consequences of these stressors varied. Whereas work conflict predicted low organisational commitment for both groups, for Hong Kong managers interrole conflict and work hassles also predict low organisational conflict. Similarly, time pressure predicted interrole conflict in both groups. However, for the Hong Kong sample, it was also predicted by environmental hassles (traffic, noise, pollution and crowding) whereas, for the American managers, interrole conflict was predicted by family and health concerns.

Continuing the theme of interrole conflict, research by Aryee at the University of Singapore suggests that family and work roles and stressors impact on perceived work–family conflict and several outcomes: job and life satisfaction, turnover intent and perceived work quality. He found that for a group of married, professional Asian women, work–home conflict increased when they experienced overload, high workload, low autonomy and high commitment to family roles. Following through to the consequences of role stress, Aryee found that, in all cases, individuals reported lower levels of job satisfaction.

Source: Aryee, S. (1992). Antecedents and outcomes of work–family conflict among married professional women: Evidence from Singapore, *Human Relations*, **45**, 813–837; Sin, L., & Cheng, D. (1995). Occupational stress and health among business executives: An exploratory study in an Oriental culture, *International Journal of Management*, **12**, 14–25; Perrewe, P. L., Ralston, D. A., & Fernandez, D. R. (1995). A model depicting the relations between perceived stressors, role conflict and organizational commitment: A comparative analysis of Hong Kong and the United States, *Asia Pacific Journal of Management*, **12**, 1–21.

Group and organisational stressors

The effectiveness of any organisation is influenced by the nature of the interactions within and between groups. Many *group characteristics* can be powerful stressors for some individuals. A number of behavioural scientists have suggested that good relationships among the members of a work group are a central factor in individual wellbeing.[8] Poor relations include low trust, low supportiveness and low interest in listening to and trying to deal with the problems that confront an employee.[9] Studies in this area have reached the same conclusion: mistrust of the person one works with is positively related to high role ambiguity, which leads to inadequate communications among people and low job satisfaction.

One problem in the study of organisational stressors is identifying which are the most important ones. *Participation in decision making* is considered an important part of working within organisations for some individuals. Participation refers to the extent that a person's knowledge, opinions and ideas are included in the decision process. Participation can contribute to stress. Some people may be frustrated by the delays often associated with participative decision making. Others may view shared decision making as a threat to the traditional right of a supervisor or manager to have the final say. Research shows that increased participation results in *role overload*, an additional source of stress for individuals.[10]

Organisational structure is another factor that has rarely been studied. One available study of trade salespeople examined the effects of tall (bureaucratically structured), medium and flat (less rigidly structured) arrangements on job satisfaction, stress and performance. It was determined that salespersons in the least bureaucratically structured arrangement experienced less stress and more job satisfaction and performed more effectively than did salespeople in the medium and tall structures.[11] A number of studies have examined the relationship of organisational level to health effects. The majority of these studies suggest the notion that the risk of contracting such health problems as coronary heart disease increases with organisational level.[12] Not all researchers, however, support the notion that the higher one is in an organisation hierarchy, the greater is the health risk. A study of Du Pont employees found that the incidence of heart disease was inversely related to salary level.

Physical environment stressors

Physical environmental stressors are often termed *blue-collar stressors* because they are more a problem in blue-collar occupations. This group of stressors identifies unsafe working conditions as a source of stress: extreme temperatures, exposure to toxic/chemical substances, physical danger and overexertion. For example, in Victoria, physical stress, falls and being struck by an object account for 60% of WorkCover claims that cost an average of $6338 per person. The highest payments are made for repetition strain injury — RSI ($8750), being caught between objects ($7079), falls ($6839) and physical stress ($6824). Furthermore, approximately forty-one people will die each year as a result of work-related injuries.[13]

Individual stressors

Role stress describes the demands that are placed on an individual in his or her job. This source of stress has been studied more than any other category presented in Exhibit 6.2.

Role conflict is perhaps the most widely examined individual stressor.[14] Role conflict is present whenever compliance by an individual to one set of expectations about the job is in conflict with compliance to another set of expectations.[15] Facets of role conflict include being torn by conflicting demands from a supervisor about the job and being pressured to get along with people

MANAGEMENT   Encounter

Roles, moods and the home–work interface

More and more we are seeing dual-career couples in the workplace. As their number increases, so we must ask what the impact of juggling several roles is on their work and home lives. Do problems at work spill over into home life? Do family problems affect our working life? In recent years, the issue of role and mood spill-over has received a lot of research attention. Research shows that work affects our home lives far more frequently than our home lives impact on work. When work–family conflicts exist, individuals report more depression, job dissatisfaction, higher cholesterol levels and more somatic complaints (e.g. headaches, insomnia and sweaty palms).

What impact does spill-over have? When we feel bad, do we carry those negative feelings between home and work? Is the same true for pleasant feelings? And, how does our involvement either with home or work influence the spill-over process? First, research shows that negative moods spill over far more than positive moods. If we leave work feeling distressed, we will carry that mood home with us; however, if we leave work feeling elated or calm, it will have little impact on how we feel at home. And this effect is far stronger for women than men. Interestingly, the more involved individuals are in their jobs, the less mood spill-over we see.

Overall, research shows that work interferes with family far more than family interferes with work. On this basis, researchers have suggested that organisations could help individuals by assisting in the control and management of their roles. Strategies such as flexible work schedules and on-site child care should enable employees to more easily meet the conflicting demands of work and family. Will employees respond to such strategies? Research shows that when individuals have flexible work schedules and supportive supervisors, they experience significantly greater control over their environment. As a result, work–family conflict and many of the symptoms that we listed at the end of the first paragraph decrease. It is clear that organisations can benefit by implementing 'family friendly' policies. LendLease, Telstra and the Body Shop are among Australian companies adopting such policies.

Source: Thomas, L. T., & Ganster, D. C. (1995). Impact of family supportive work variables on work-family conflict and strain: A control perspective, *Journal of Applied Psychology*, **80**, 6–15; Frone, M. R., Russell, M., & Cooper, M. L. (1992). Prevalence of work–family conflict: Are work and family boundaries asymmetrically permeable?, *Journal of Organizational Behaviour*, **13**, 39–53; Williams, K. J., & Alliger, G. M. (1994). Role stressors, mood spillover, and perceptions of work–family conflict in employed parents, *Academy of Management Journal*, **37**, 837-868; Human Resources Report, Issue 110, 1995.

with whom you are not compatible. Regardless of whether role conflict results from organisational policies or from other persons, it can be a significant stressor for some individuals. For example, a study at Goddard Space Flight Center determined that about 67% of employees reported some degree of role conflict. The study further found that employees who experienced more role conflict also experienced lower job satisfaction and higher job-related tension.[16] It is interesting to note that the researchers also found that the greater the power or authority of the people sending the conflicting role messages, the greater was the job dissatisfaction produced by role conflict.

An increasingly prevalent type of role conflict occurs when work and non-work roles interfere with one another. The most common non-work roles involved in this form of conflict are those of spouse and parent. Balancing the demands of work and family roles is a significant daily task for a growing number of employed adults.[17] Pressure to work late, to take work home, to spend more time travelling and to frequently relocate in order to advance are a few examples of potential sources of conflict between home and work. When both spouses are employed, added conflict potential exists when one partner's career progress may be negatively affected by the career progression of the other. Our Management Encounter takes a more detailed look at the stress created by work–home role conflict.

A second source of role-related stress is **role ambiguity**. This occurs when individuals do not understand the rights, privileges and obligations that a person has for doing the job. In the study at Goddard Space Flight Center, administrators, engineers and scientists completed a role-ambiguity stress scale. The results showed that role-ambiguity was significantly related to low job satisfaction and to feelings of job-related threat to people's mental and physical wellbeing. Furthermore, the more ambiguity a person reported, the lower was the person's utilisation of intellectual skills, knowledge and leadership skills.

A third source of stress for individuals at work is caused by having too much to do. Everyone has experienced work overload at one time or another. This may be of two different types: **quantitative overload** or **qualitative overload**. Having too many things to do or insufficient time to complete a job is quantitative overload. Qualitative overload, on the other hand, occurs when individuals feel that they lack the ability needed to complete their jobs or that performance standards are too high.

From a health standpoint, studies as far back as 1958 established that quantitative overload might cause biochemical changes, specifically elevations in blood cholesterol levels.[18] One study examined the relationship of overload, underload and stress among 1540 executives of a major corporation. Those executives in the low and high ends of the stress ranges reported and had more significant medical problems. This study suggests that the relationship between stressors, stress and disease may be curvilinear. That is, those who are underloaded and those who are overloaded represent two ends of a continuum, each with a significantly elevated number of medical problems.[19] Case 6, 'The case of the missing time', portrays a situation in which overload appears to be a major problem. As you work through this case, it may be helpful to keep in mind that reducing the amount of work that must be completed may not be the only way to deal positively with overload.

Case 6
The case of the missing time

The type of job that we do and the demands that our careers create are a further source of stress. Not surprisingly some jobs are, by their very nature, more stressful than others. Policing, journalism, mining and dentistry are examples of extremely stressful occupations. Only a short way below in the stress stakes are fire and ambulance services. Personnel work, social work, teaching and medical practice are also rated as being very stressful.[20] When our jobs involve *responsibility* for others, we also add to our stress. One study found support for the hypothesis that responsibility for people contributes to job-related stress.[21] The more responsibility for people reported, the more likely the employee was to smoke heavily, have high blood pressure and show elevated cholesterol levels. Conversely, the more responsibility for things the employee reported, the lower were these indicators.

Finally, concerns about our careers can also create stress. We may, for example, be concerned that our skills are no longer required. This type of stress, *obsolescence*, may occur because a once manual job has become automated, because a type of job is considered unnecessary (e.g. middle managers) or because an organisation is changing its functions. People may also question the worth of their job, whether they have fulfilled their potential and whether the sacrifices which they have made are too great. Such *mid-career crises* are prevalent in managers in the 35–45 year group, and can result in depression, excessive use of alcohol, insomnia, headaches, stomach problems, obesity and insecurity.

Life stressors

Common sense holds that when individuals undergo extremely stressful changes in their lives, their personal health is likely to suffer at some point. Research work on this intriguing proposition was initiated by Holmes and Rahe.[22] Their work led to the development of the Social Readjustment Rating Scale (SRRS), which weights the degree of stress caused by specific events. Through research and analysis, Holmes and Rahe weighted the SRRS. An individual is asked to indicate which of the **life change events** he or she has experienced during the past 12 months. The SRRS is presented in Exhibit 6.3. To determine how stressful events are affecting you, tick off those events that you have experienced in the past 12 months and add up the points. Are you over 150? Over 300?

Holmes and Rahe found that individuals reporting life-change units totalling 150 points or less generally had good health the following year. However, those reporting life-change units totalling between 150 and 300 points had about a 50% chance of developing a serious illness the following year. And among individuals scoring 300 or more points, there was at least a 70% chance of contracting a major illness in the following year.

The relationships found between life-change event scores and personal health problems have not been overwhelming.[23] The correlations in most studies between the total score and major health problems the following year have been relatively low.[24] This may be because the SRRS fails to take into consideration the possibility that events can have a positive impact (e.g. marriage) which may offset some of the negative effects of stress. Dohrenwend and Dohrenwend have developed a similar scale that incorporates the magnitude and direction of an event. According to their definition, life events are stressful only if they lead to physical exhaustion, result in the loss of social support, or are perceived as having fateful negative consequences.[25]

Life change events represent acute stress. *Daily hassles*, however, describe the minor (or not so minor) irritations that we face in our everyday lives. The Daily Hassles Scale, developed by Lazarus, identifies a broad range of hassles and individuals rate how frequently these hassles have been experienced over the past few months. They include such events as household hassles (preparing meals), time-pressure hassles (too much to do), inner concerns (loneliness), environmental hassles (pollution, crime) and financial responsibility (debts). Research shows that the level of daily hassles that we report is related to both our physical and psychological wellbeing: the more hassles we experience, the more ill health we report and the lower our sense of wellbeing.[26]

Rank	Life Event	Mean Value
1	Death of spouse	100
2	Divorce	73
3	Marital separation	65
4	Jail term	63
5	Death of a close family member	63
6	Personal injury or illness	53
7	Marriage	50
8	Fired at work	47
9	Marital reconciliation	45
10	Retirement	45
11	Change in health of family member	44
12	Pregnancy	40
13	Sex difficulties	39
14	Gain of new family member	39
15	Business readjustment	39
16	Change in financial state	38
17	Death of close friend	37
18	Change to different line of work	36
19	Change of number of arguments with spouse	35
20	Mortgage over $10 000	31
21	Foreclosure of mortgage or loan	30
22	Change in responsibilities at work	29
23	Son or daughter leaving home	29
24	Trouble with in-laws	29
25	Outstanding personal achievement	28
26	Spouse beginning or stopping work	26
27	Beginning or ending school	26
28	Change in living conditions	25
29	Revision of personal habits	24
30	Trouble with boss	23
31	Change in work hours or conditions	20
32	Change in residence	20
33	Change in schools	20
34	Change in recreation	19
35	Change in church activities	19
36	Change in social activities	18
37	Mortgage or loan less than $10 000	17
38	Change in sleeping habits	16
39	Change in number of family get-togethers	15
40	Change in eating habits	15
41	Vacation	13
42	Christmas	12
43	Minor violations of the law	11

Exhibit 6.3
Social Readjustment Rating Scale

The amount of life stress that a person has experienced in a given period of time, say 1 year, is measured by the total number of life change units (LCUs). These units result from the addition of the values (shown in the right-hand column) associated with events that the person has experienced during the target period.

Source: Holmes, T. H., &. Rahe R. H. (1967). The Social Readjustment Rating Scale, *Journal of Psychosomatic Research*, 213–218.

PERCEIVING, APPRAISING AND COPING WITH STRESS

We have already introduced the idea that stress is an excessive demand placed on the individual, but just what do we mean by 'excessive'? Will the same level of a stressor be excessive for everyone? How each individual defines excess is determined by that person's *adaptation level*: their past experiences and individual preferences. [27] More important than this, however, is how we appraise the event and how we assess our ability to cope with stressors. Lazarus identifies three stages in the appraisal process: primary appraisal, secondary appraisal and reappraisal. *Primary appraisal* describes an individual's initial response to stress and poses the question 'Am I in trouble?' In this phase, individuals may assess the potential stressor as positive (this is good for me), neutral (this has no effect on me) or negative (this is bad for me). Only when we appraise an event as negative, might we experience stress. Once we have appraised an event as negative, we move on to a stage of *secondary appraisal*, in which we search for strategies that will minimise the damage and maximise the benefit to us. We assess the situation in terms of threat (immediate damage), harm (future damage) and challenge (means for overcoming the damage; resources for coping). Only when threat and harm are high, and we further assess our resources for coping with the stressful events as low, do we experience stress.[28]

The process of secondary appraisal is central to how individuals react to stress. In the next section, we will see that individuals differ in the extent to which they are stress-resistant. A common theme across several personality traits is the extent to which individuals emphasise either the threat and harm in the situation or focus on the challenges that the situation presents. One of the stress reduction strategies — *cognitive reappraisal* — specifically aims at altering individual focus and encouraging individuals to emphasise the challenges.

One of the implications of this relates to the types of strategies that individuals employ. When individuals are focused on the threat and harm in a situation, they are more likely to engage in *emotion-focused* coping: to try to ignore or simply reduce the distress associated with the situation. Examples of this type of coping include daydreaming or simply ignoring the problem. However, when individuals focus on the challenge in the situation, they are more likely to employ *problem-focused* coping: to develop specific strategies for dealing with the source of stress. Individuals who engage in problem-focused coping show far fewer signs of strain than those who engage in emotion-focused coping.[29]

STRESS MODERATORS

Stressors evoke different responses from different people. Some individuals are better able to cope with a stressor than others. They can adapt their behaviour in such a way as to meet the stressor head-on. On the other hand, some individuals are predisposed to stress; that is, they are not able to adapt to the stressor.

The model presented in Exhibit 6.2 suggests that various factors moderate the relationship between stressors and stress. A *moderator* is a condition, behaviour or characteristic that qualifies the relationship between two variables. The effect may be to intensify or weaken the relationship. The relationship between the number of litres of petrol used and total kilometres driven, for example, is affected by the variable speed (a moderator). Likewise, an individual's personality may moderate or affect the extent to which that individual experiences stress as a consequence of being in contact with a particular stressor. We will briefly examine three personality variables that moderate stress moderators: Type A behaviour pattern, locus of control and affectivity. We will also consider how social support, a group level moderator, can affect individual reactions to stress.

Type A behaviour pattern

Cardiovascular disease is the leading cause of death. In the 1950s two medical cardiologists and researchers, Meyer Friedman and Ray Rosenman, discovered what they called the **Type A behaviour pattern** (TABP).[30] They searched the medical literature and found that traditional coronary risk factors such as dietary cholesterol, blood pressure and heredity could not totally explain or predict coronary heart disease (CHD). Through interviews with and observation of patients, they began to uncover a pattern of behaviour or traits. They eventually called this the Type A behaviour pattern.

The person with TABP has these characteristics:

- chronically struggles to get as many things done as possible in the shortest time period;
- is aggressive, ambitious, competitive and forceful;
- speaks explosively, rushes others to finish what they are saying;
- is impatient, hates to wait and considers waiting a waste of precious time;
- is preoccupied with deadlines and is work-oriented;
- is always in a struggle with people, things and events.

Exercise 6A
Behaviour Activity Profile — a Type A measure

As a result, individuals who display TABP create stress for themselves.

The converse, Type B individual, is mainly free of the TABP characteristics and generally feels no pressing conflict with either time or persons. The Type B may have considerable drive, wants to accomplish things and works hard, but the Type B has a confident style that allows him or her to work at a steady pace and not to race against the clock. The Type A has been likened to a racehorse; the Type B, to a turtle. Exercise 6A will provide you with an opportunity to assess your Type A or B characteristics.

Exhibit 6.4
Sample items from an early version of Rotter's test of internal–external locus of control

1a	Promotions are earned through hard work and persistence.
1b	Making a lot of money is largely a matter of getting the right breaks.
2a	When I am right, I can convince others.
2b	It is silly to think that one can really change another person's basic attitudes.
3a	In my case, the grades I make are the results of my own efforts; luck has little or nothing to do with it.
3b	Sometimes I feel that I have little to do with the grades I get.
4a	Getting along with people is a skill that must be practised.
4b	It is almost impossible to figure out how to please some people.

More recent research into TABP suggests that not all aspects of the behaviour pattern are equally associated with negative consequences. Specifically, hostility has been identified as the TABP subcomponent most predictive of the development of coronary heart disease among Type As.[31]

The accumulated evidence at this point strongly suggests that managers attempting to manage stress should include TABP in their assessments.[32] Failure to do so would ignore some of the better interdisciplinary research (behavioural and medical) that has been conducted over the past 25 years. Of all the moderators that could or should be included in a stress model, TABP seems to be one of the most promising for additional consideration.

Locus of control and hardiness

The **locus of control** of individuals determines the degree to which they believe their behaviours influence what happens to them.[33] Some people believe they are autonomous — that they are masters of their own fate and bear personal responsibility coming from inside themselves. Rotter calls these people *internalisers*.[34] Rotter also holds that many people view themselves as helpless pawns of fate, controlled by outside forces over which they have little, if any, influence. Such people believe that the locus of control is external rather than internal. Rotter calls them *externalisers*. Rotter devised a scale containing twenty-nine items to identify whether people are internalisers or externalisers.[35] The statements are concerned with success, failure, misfortune and political events. One statement reflects a belief in internal control, and the other reflects a belief in external control. Four pairs of statements on the Rotter scale are shown in Exhibit 6.4. Research shows that when role stressors are present, individuals with an internal locus of control are less likely to experience strain.

Control is also the central concept in Kobasa's hardiness trait. Kobasa proposed that individuals who experienced high life-change unit scores without becoming ill might differ, in terms of personality, from individuals with subsequent health problems.[36] She refers to the personality characteristic as 'hardiness'.[37] In a longitudinal study to test the three-characteristic theory of hardiness, managers were studied over a 2-year period. It was determined the more that managers possessed hardiness characteristics, the smaller was the impact of life-change units on their personal health. Hardiness appeared to offset or buffer the negative impact of life changes. Individuals with a 'hardy' personality seem to possess three important characteristics:

1. *These individuals have an internal locus of control.* That is, they believed that they are able to influence events and outcomes.
2. *These individuals see change as a challenge.* Thinking back to our discussion of appraisal, stress-resistant individuals see stress as an opportunity or challenge rather than as a threat.
3. *These individuals are committed.* These individuals were more involved both with their jobs and other aspects of their lives.

Pessimism, optimism and affectivity

Do optimists have more reasons to be cheerful? According to research they probably do: optimists report lower stress in their lives and, when faced with stress, are less likely to report any of the negative consequences that we have discussed. One of the reasons for this is that, like internalisers, individuals with a positive outlook actively attempt to control their environment and to reduce the stress that they experience.[38] In recent years, the ideas that optimists and pessimists respond differently to stress has received a lot of research attention. Most of the research has focused on two personality traits: positive affectivity (PA) and negative affectivity (NA). That is the disposition to perceive individuals and events in either a generally positive and enthusiastic manner or in a negative manner.[39] These traits exert their influence by affecting individual perceptions of events and outcomes: high NA individuals are more susceptible to events that result in negative experiences or emotions and report greater levels of stressors and strains than do high PA individuals.[40]

What are the implications for organisations? Does this mean that, when recruiting, organisations should screen for pessimists and negative affect individuals? Research identifies a key difference between the two groups: *control*. Individuals with high PA show a greater tendency to actively control their environment, while individuals with high NA are less likely to use direct coping strategies in stressful situations.[41] PA and NA individuals appraise their environment differently and, as shown in the Local Encounter, this affects the coping strategies that are used. This implies that organisational stress management programs should emphasise the development of cognitive reappraisal skills.

Social support

Numerous studies have linked social support with many aspects of health, illness and quality of life.[42] The literature offers a number of definitions of social support. Some of these definitions focus on the exchange of information or material, the availability of a confidant and gratification of basic social needs. **Social support** is defined as the comfort, assistance or information one receives through formal or informal contacts with individuals or groups.[43] This definition would apply to a co-worker listening to a friend who failed to receive a desired promotion, a group of recently laid-off workers helping each other find new employment, or an experienced employee helping a new hiree learn a job.

Social support has been operationalised as the number of people one interacts with, the frequency of contact with other individuals, or the individual's perceptions about the adequacy of interpersonal contact. The limited amount of research using these factors suggests that social support protects or buffers individuals from the negative consequences of stressors. One study showed significant interactions of social support and work stress for factory workers. The support of co-workers moderated the relationship between role conflict and health complaints.[44] The higher the level of social support reported, the fewer were the health complaints reported.

A recent study examined the relationship between social support and locus of control on job stress. In a sample of over 300 police officers and firefighters, the researchers found that social support buffered the effects of job stress on physical health complaints. They further found that the buffering effect of social support was much greater for internal locus-of-control participants than for externals.[45] The best evidence to date on the importance of social support

Coping with stress

Occupational stress is without doubt one of the most widely researched topics, not just in Australia and New Zealand but internationally. Across Australia and New Zealand researchers have been concerned with such issues as how best we can measure stress, the models that best describe the relationship between stress and individual outcomes, as well as the relationship between coping and the experience of stress. In this encounter, we have chosen to focus on the last issue: how individuals define stress at work and how their assessment of these stressors affects the coping strategies that they use.

Michael O'Driscoll, at Waikato University, together with Cary Cooper used a critical incident analysis to determine what stressors are faced by New Zealand workers and how they respond. According to their survey, the three most important sources of stress are organisational conflict, work overload and a lack of resources.

When asked how they coped with these stressors, employees said that they consulted with superiors and others to reduce conflict, worked harder to deal with overload, and found their own solutions when faced with resource restrictions. Overall, this sample reported very direct and task-focused strategies, which they rated as highly effective, in response to organisational problems.

Research at Massey University suggests that this may be because the problems were considered important by the respondents. Lesley Frederiksen and Philip Dewe asked whether it was possible to classify stressors in terms of their importance and frustration and, having done so, to establish a relationship between coping strategies and stressors. Using a small group of government employees, these researchers showed that coping responses fell into one of two groups — avoid the problem or approach the problem — and that which of these strategies was used depended on how stressors were perceived. When a stressful situation was rated as important, employees used direct approach strategies. However, when situations were rated as frustrating, they were more likely to use avoidance strategies. Interestingly, this is also more likely to happen when the frustrating

situation is an unimportant one: after all, why create more stress than you need to?

A different perspective is provided by researchers at the University of Queensland. In several studies examining the responses of Australian managers, Deborah Terry, Victor Callan and their co-workers investigated the relationships between individual differences, coping strategies and two outcomes: psychological wellbeing and job satisfaction. These researchers showed that the use of two emotion-focused coping strategies, escapism and self-blame, predict low psychological wellbeing; what's more, managers who use escapist strategies such as daydreaming also report lower job satisfaction. As was the case in the New Zealand studies, task-focused strategies appear to be more effective: in these studies, managers who use task-focused coping strategies reported higher job satisfaction. Interestingly, this research also found that the use of coping strategies was affected by individual differences: managers with high self-efficacy and an internal locus of control were more likely to use task-focused coping strategies and less likely to use escapist strategies. In summarising their research, Callan and Terry conclude not only that employees should be taught to adopt a more problem-focused coping style, but also that organisations should adopt management practices such as empowerment aimed at increasing employee control.

Source: Callan, V. J., & Terry, D. J. (1994). Coping with work stress and organisational change. In A. Kouzmin, L. V. Still, & P. Clarke (Eds.) *New Directions in Management*. Sydney: McGraw-Hill Book Company; Frederiksen, L. G., & Dewe, P. J. (1995). Stress at work: A longitudinal study of appraisal and coping using repeated measures of stressor, importance, frustration and coping reponse, Paper presented at the Inaugural Australian Industrial and Organisational Psychology Conference, Sydney, Australia; O'Driscoll, M. P., & Cooper, C. (1995). Coping with job-related stress: A critical incident analysis of coping behaviours, Paper presented at the Inaugural Australian Industrial and Organisational Psychology Conference, Sydney, Australia; Terry, D. J., Tonge, L., & Callan, V. J. (1995). Employee adjustment to stress: The role of coping resources, situational factors and coping responses, *Anxiety, Stress and Coping*, **8**, 1–24; Terry, D. J., Callan, V. J., & Sartori, G. (in press). Employee adjustment to an organizational merger: Stress, coping and intergroup differences, *Stress Medicine*.

derives from the literature on rehabilitation, recovery and adaptation to illness.[46] For example, better outcomes have been found in alcohol-treatment programs when the alcoholic's family is supportive and cohesive.[47] Managerial use of social support research in reducing stress will be expanded as more organisationally based research is conducted.[48]

STRESS CONSEQUENCES

The effects of stress are many and varied. Some effects, of course, are positive, such as self-motivation and stimulation to satisfy individual goals and objectives. Nonetheless, many stress consequences are disruptive, counterproductive and even potentially dangerous. Additionally, as we discussed earlier there are consequences associated with too little as well as too much stress. In examining stress consequences, the distinction in our model (Exhibit 6.2) between organisational and individual consequences is somewhat arbitrary. For example, a decrement in job performance due to stress is clearly an individual consequence; it is an individual's performance that is being affected. Just as clearly, however, the organisation experiences important consequences from stress-related performance decrements.

Individual consequences

A recently promoted employee develops an uncharacteristic pattern of Friday and Monday absences. A salesperson begins to lose repeat business; non-renewing customers complain that he has become inattentive and curt in his dealings with them. A formerly conscientious nurse forgets to administer medications, with potentially serious patient consequences. An assembly worker experiences a significant increase in the percentage of her production rejected by the quality-control unit. A laboratory technician displays sudden, apparently unprovoked outbursts of anger. Each of these individuals is experiencing the effects, or consequences, of stress.

Stress can produce *psychological* consequences. These would include frustration, anxiety, apathy, lowered self-esteem, aggression and depression. Some consequences may be *cognitive*. Cognitive consequences would include poor concentration, the inability to make sound decisions or any decisions at all, mental blocks and decreased attention span. Other effects may be *behavioural*. Such manifestations as accident proneness, impulsive behaviour, alcohol and drug abuse, and explosive temper losses are examples. Finally, *physiological* consequences could include increased heart rate, elevated blood pressure, sweating, hot and cold flashes, increased blood glucose levels and elevated stomach acid production.

Among the individual consequences of stress, those classified as physiological are perhaps the most dysfunctional because they can in turn contribute to physical illness. One of the more significant of the physiological consequences and illness relationships is that of coronary heart disease. There is growing medical opinion that job and life stress may be a major contributor to the incidence of heart disease.[49] Several studies have, for example, found a relationship between changes in blood pressure and job stress.[50]

Organisational consequences

While the organisational consequences of stress are many and varied, they share one common feature: stress costs organisations money. As you can see in our Organisational Encounter, stress is becoming one of the most expensive illnesses for which employees are compensated.

These figures do not, however, capture the 'hidden' costs of stress. Excessive stress increases job dissatisfaction. As we have seen from earlier chapters, job dissatisfaction can be associated with a number of dysfunctional outcomes including increased turnover and absenteeism, and reduced job performance. If productivity is reduced just 3%, for example, an organisation employing 1000 staff would need to hire an additional 30 employees to compensate for that lost productivity. If annual employee costs are $40 000, including wages and benefits, stress is costing the company $1.2 million just to replace lost productivity. This does not include costs associated with recruitment and training. Nor does it consider that decreases in quality may be more costly for an organisation than quantity decreases. Customer dissatisfaction with lower quality goods or services can have significant effects on an organisation's growth and profitability.

Burnout: The professional stress syndrome[51]

To finish our discussion of stress consequences, we will turn our attention to one of the most widely researched responses to workplace stress: burnout. **Burnout** is a psychological process, brought about by unrelieved work stress, that is characterised by a group of three symptoms: high *emotional exhaustion*, or the feeling that you are emotionally drained; *depersonalisation*, or feeling negative about or alienated from clients; a sense of low *personal accomplishment*, characterised as a lack of work-related fulfilment or esteem. It is observed largely in professions that involve a high level of interpersonal contact such as nursing, teaching and social work. According to Maslach, individuals in helping professions are especially vulnerable because of the intense nature of client interactions. Staff in these professions not only constantly deal with people and their problems, but also are often seen to have sole responsibility for their clients' wellbeing.

A very important idea implicit in the conceptualisation of burnout relates to job involvement. A high degree of involvement in identification with or commitment to one's job or profession is a necessary prerequisite to burnout. It is unlikely that one would become exhausted doing something to which one does not devote a great deal of effort. Thus, the irony of burnout is that those most susceptible are those most committed to their work; all else being equal, lower job commitment equals lower likelihood of burnout.

Organisations contribute to burnout in a variety of ways. Burnout researchers identify four factors that are particularly important: high levels of work overload, dead-end jobs, excessive red tape and paperwork, and poor communication and feedback, particularly regarding job performance. In addition, factors that have been identified in at least one study as contributing to burnout include role conflict and ambiguity, difficult interpersonal relationships and reward systems that are not contingent on performance.

ORGANISATIONAL   Encounter

The high cost of stress

Whether individuals work for the public or private sector, occupational stress appears to be on the rise. Federal government research shows that 5–6% of all compensation claims can be attributed to stress, while a ComCare survey has shown that stress claims from the public sector have doubled since 1989. Compensation claims are increasing by 20% a year and are expected to reach 3280 by 1998.

Whereas other compensation claims result in the loss of 2.4 working weeks, an average of 7.7 weeks is lost to stress claims. The National Occupational Health and Safety Commission puts the cost of stress claims at around $22 million per year, while ComCare estimates that it will pay out around $50 million in the 1994–95 financial year. The average cost of a stress-related claim is between $25 000 and $30 000 — this makes occupational stress one of the most expensive illnesses for which employees are compensated.

Within the public sector, staff identify many reasons for high stress levels: interpersonal conflict, pressure from work deadlines, organisational change, lack of skills, role ambiguity, and physical or verbal abuse. However, these problems are not confined to the public sector: major banks estimate stress claims to range from 9% to 15% of all compensation claims. Staff at Price Waterhouse recently identified long hours and a lack of time for outside activities as increasing their levels of stress. As a result of time pressure, they tended to eat late, work weekends and eliminate such potentially stress-reducing activities as work-outs. Among their suggestions for combating stress are flexible work hours and the ability to work from home.

What can organisations do? Traditional stress management programs are problematic because their benefits often do not last beyond the training room. Moreover, according to Professor Sharpley at Monash University, just thinking about how stressed you are can make you more stressed! He argues that individuals will better control the situation if they can learn to identify the symptoms of stress and control them. According to his research, training individuals in breathing and relaxation techniques reduced individual reactivity to stress by 93%; more importantly, most people continued to use these techniques in the long term. These are not the only techniques available to individuals: yoga, meditation and boxercise are all gaining popularity as stress management techniques.

Organisations can and should support individual efforts to manage stress. Many companies such as Lend Lease, 3M, Du Pont, Caltex and American Express employ professionals to provide counselling and health services. Others, such as the Australian Taxation Office and the Department of Finance and Treasury, offer stress management courses; perhaps, more importantly, the Department of Finance includes stress management information in supervisory training courses. When organisations face unique stressors, they may need to address the stressors directly. This is the case in the banking industry. Armed hold-ups create special and traumatic problems for staff and the Commonwealth Bank has programs targeted at staff who have been subjected to hold-ups.

Source: Ferguson, A. (1995). Seconds out! The new way to fight executive stress, *Business Review Weekly*, September 5; Hooper, N. (1995). Coping with the modern 'madness', *Business Review Weekly*, April 17; Schmidt, L. (1994). Exhausted staff tell Price Waterhouse how to make them happy, *Business Review Weekly*, August 29.

STRESS PREVENTION AND MANAGEMENT

An astute manager never ignores a turnover or absenteeism problem, workplace drug abuse, a decline in performance, reduced quality in production, or any other sign that the organisation's performance goals are not being met. The effective manager, in fact, views these occurrences as symptoms and looks beyond them to identify and correct the underlying causes. Yet most managers today will be likely to search for traditional causes such as poor training, defective equipment or inadequate instructions on what needs to be done. In all likelihood, stress is not on the list of possible problems. Thus, the very first step in any program to manage stress so that it remains within tolerable limits is recognition that it exists.

How can managers deal with stress? There is an important distinction between *preventing* stress and *managing* stress. Stress prevention focuses on controlling or eliminating stressors that might provoke the stress response. Stress management suggests procedures for helping individuals cope effectively with or reduce stress that is already being experienced. An overview of organisational stress management strategies suggests that the majority intervene once stress is detected rather than engaging in preventative strategies: they seek to alter stressors, to reduce strain, to increase an individual's resistance to stress, or to alter group settings to increase their moderating properties.[52] In this concluding section of the chapter we will discuss organisational programs and individual approaches to stress prevention and management. First, however, we will look at a way of thinking about organisational stress *prevention*.

Maximising person–environment fit

In defining stress earlier in this chapter, we emphasised that stress is the consequence of an interaction between an environmental stimulus (a stressor) and the individual's response. From this perspective organisational stress may be viewed as a consequence of the relationship between the individual and the work environment. While there are numerous ways of thinking about individual–organisational relationships and stress, the concept of person–environment fit is the most widely used.[53]

A person–environment fit (P–E fit) approach generally focuses on two dimensions of fit. One is the extent to which work provides formal and informal rewards that meet or match (fit) the person's needs. Misfit on this dimension results in stress. For example, a job may provide too little job security, insufficient money for the effort expended, or inadequate recognition to meet the individual's needs or preferences. The second type of fit deals with the extent to which the employee's skills, abilities and experience match the demands and requirements of the employer. To the extent that the individual's talents are insufficient for, or underutilised by, job requirements, stress results. By improving the quality of, or maximising, fit between the employee and the organisational environment, potential stressors are eliminated and stress is prevented.

There are numerous strategies for maximising P–E fit. Ideally, the process begins even before an individual joins the organisation. Employee recruitment programs which provide realistic job previews help potential employees determine whether the reality of the job matches their needs and expectations. Selection programs that are effective in ensuring that potential employees possess the requisite skills, knowledge, experiences and abilities for the job are key elements in maximising fit. One of the critical variables for maximising fit and preventing stress is effective organisational socialisation. Socialisation is a process by which individuals learn and internalise the values, expected behaviours and social knowledge that are important for becoming an effective organisational member. We will discuss the socialisation process in more detail in Chapter 14 of this book.

We can also consider fit at the level of the individual and his or her job demands. We can ask whether there is a match between the level of demands placed on the individual, the degree of control that an individual has over the planning and pacing of work, and the variety of skills that are used. Stress occurs when the level of demands is high, the individual has little control over workflow and only a small number of skills are utilised.[54] To deal with this type of misfit, we need to consider job design. We can reduce this type of stress by creating jobs that meet Hackman and Oldham's criteria for motivating work: jobs that have high task significance, variety and identity; are autonomous; and provide feedback. On the basis of this model, we would target skills variety and autonomy.[55]

Organisational stress prevention and management programs

Organisational programs are aimed more broadly at an entire employee population. Organisations may conduct stress management workshops, which aim to provide individuals with the skills to recognise symptoms of stress and to respond appropriately. They may also use other training programs to provide individuals with skills that will help them to manage the environment and reduce the level of stress that they experience: communication skills, conflict management skills, assertiveness training and time management are all examples of such training. However, organisations can do more. In our discussion of the antecedents of stress, we discussed several sources of organisational stress and these also need to be addressed.

Organisational structure and climate

If hierarchical organisations create stress, one means for reducing this type of stress is to decentralise the organisation (remove layers of management). This could involve redesign of work, so that semiautonomous work teams are created, increasing individual control over the environment. In addition, organisations can engage in more participative decision making, so that employees obtain more information and a greater sense of control.[56]

Role characteristics

When individuals have competing or unclear demands made of them, or when there is simply too much (or not enough) to do, they experience stress. One of the simplest means for establishing clear and unambiguous roles is to provide employees with detailed job descriptions. These should not only specify core functions, but also indicate their priority and the specific responsibilities that make up each function. Role analysis and clarification provide a further means for eliminating these stressors: supervisors and employees compare their perceptions of what is expected in a particular job, what resources and information are required to do the job, and potential problem areas. If this process is carried out before an individual starts a job, both the supervisor and the individual should have a much clearer idea of what the goals and functions of each person are.[57]

Interpersonal relationships

Social support is an important means for stress reduction. Therefore, any strategy which improves the relationships between co-workers is likely to foster a less stressful environment. Improving communication will reduce misunderstandings and conflict; however, it also has the potential to remove role conflict and ambiguity. Regular staff meetings, team-building exercises and the development of good interpersonal and organisational communication practices all have the potential to improve interpersonal relationships at work.

Corporate culture

However, none of these strategies will be successful if the organisation does not clearly support a stress-free environment through its actions. At the organisational level, strategies such as sponsoring corporate fitness programs or providing employees with a gym and ensuring that canteens serve healthy food all create an environment in which a key value is employee wellbeing.[58]

Individual stress prevention and management

There are many individual approaches to managing stress. To see this, all you have to do is visit any bookstore and look at the self-improvement section. It will be stocked with numerous how-to-do-it books for reducing stress. We have selected only a few of the more popularly cited methods for individually managing stress. They have been selected because some research is available on their impact, they are widely cited in both the scientific literature and the popular press, and scientifically sound evaluations of their effectiveness are under way.

Behavioural strategies

The first group of strategies available to individuals aims to reduce the strain associated with stress: to reduce muscle tensions, to alleviate headaches and generally to eliminate physical symptoms. Having a drink or a cigarette, or taking a headache tablet or a sedative, can alleviate the immediate symptoms of stress. The major criticism of such strategies is their effects are short term: sooner or later, their effects wear off and the stressor is still there.

A more constructive strategy is to practise *relaxation techniques*. Although they also target symptoms of stress, they can be used to help individuals reduce those symptoms at any time: they help individuals to identify muscle tension and to take preventative action before the situation becomes too extreme. The general purpose of relaxation training is to reduce the individual's arousal level and bring about a calmer state of affairs from both psychological and physiological perspectives. Psychologically, successful relaxation results in enhanced feelings of wellbeing, peacefulness, a sense of being in control and a reduction in felt tension and anxiety; physiologically, decreases in blood pressure, respiration and heart rate should take place. Relaxation techniques include breathing exercises; muscle relaxation; autogenic training, which combines elements of muscle relaxation and meditation; and a variety of mental relaxation strategies, including imagery and visualisation.[59]

Just as stress is an adaptive response of the body, there is also an adaptive antistress response, 'a relaxation response'.[60] Benson reports that in this response, muscle tension decreases, heart rate and blood pressure decrease and breathing slows.[61] The stimuli necessary to produce relaxation include a quiet environment, closed eyes, a comfortable position and a repetitive mental device.

Cognitive techniques

The basic rationale for some individual approaches to stress management, known collectively as *cognitive techniques*, is that people's responses to stressors are mediated by cognitive processes or thoughts.[62] The underlying assumption of these techniques is that people's thoughts, in the form of expectations, beliefs and assumptions, are labels they apply to situations, and these labels elicit emotional responses to the situations. Thus, for example, if an individual labels the loss of a promotion a catastrophe, the stress response is to the label, not to the situation. Cognitive techniques of stress management focus on changing labels or cognitions so that people appraise situations differently. This reappraisal typically centres on removing cognitive distortions such as magnifying, overgeneralising and personalisation.[63] All cognitive techniques have a similar objective: to help individuals gain more control over their reactions to stressors by modifying their cognitions.

Evaluative research of cognitive techniques to stress management is not extensive, although the studies reported to date are generally positive. Representative occupational groups where research has indicated positive outcomes with the use of cognitive approaches include nurses, teachers, athletes and air traffic controllers.[64] The positive research, coupled with the wide range and scope of situations and stressors amenable to such an approach, make cognitive techniques particularly attractive as an individual stress management strategy.

Healthy lifestyle

A healthy lifestyle — eating the right foods and regular aerobic exercise — also has the potential to reduce the impact of stress. Research shows that when individuals engage in regular exercise, they are better able to cope with stress in their lives: when faced with stressful events, they are less likely to become ill than individuals who do not exercise regularly.[65]

Ensuring program success

Simply offering a clinical or organisation-type stress management program does not guarantee positive results for either employees or the sponsoring organisation. While many factors will determine how successful any particular program will be, a number of recommendations, if followed, will increase the likelihood of beneficial outcomes. Among the more important ones are:

- Top-management support, including both philosophical support and support in terms of staff and facilities, is necessary.
- Unions should support the program and participate in it where appropriate.
- The greatest pay-off from stress management comes not from one-shot activities but from ongoing and sustained effort; thus, long-term commitment is essential.
- Extensive and continuing employee involvement would include involvement not only in the initial planning but also in implementation and maintenance.

This is one of the most critical factors for ensuring representative employee participation.

■ Clearly stated objectives lay a solid foundation for the program. Programs with no or poorly defined objectives are not likely to be effective or achieve sufficient participation to make them worthwhile.

■ Employees must be able to participate freely, without either pressure or stigma.

■ Confidentiality must be strictly adhered to. Employees must have no concerns that participation will in any way affect their standing in the organisation.

The last point, that of confidentiality, is particularly critical. It is not only essential for program success, but also helps illustrate that there are important ethical issues involved in the operation of organisation-type stress management programs.

SUMMARY OF KEY POINTS

Understand that the term 'stress' can be defined in a number of different ways. Stress may be viewed as either a stimulus or a response. We view it as an adaptive response, moderated by individual factors, that is the result of any action, situation or event which makes unusual demands on a person.

Describe the general adaptation syndrome. As individuals, we establish a defence reaction to stress. This reaction is termed the general adaptation syndrome (GAS). The three phases of the GAS are alarm, resistance and exhaustion.

Discuss the major variables in an integrative model of stress. Major variables in an integrative model of stress are *stressors* (individual, group organisational and physical environment); *appraisal* (threat, harm and challenge), *coping* (task or emotion focused) and *individual differences* (personality and social support); and *consequences* (subjective, behavioural, cognitive, physiological, health and organisational).

Distinguish between several categories of stressors. There are two groups of stressors that affect individual outcomes. Work stressors include group and organisational factors, the physical environment and individual factors. Life stressors describe both acute (life events) and chronic (daily hassles) stressors.

Identify four important variables that modify the relationship between stressors and strain. Four important variables that moderate the relationship between stressors and strain are the Type A behaviour pattern, locus of control and hardiness, affectivity and social support.

Discuss several individual and organisational approaches to managing stress. Numerous programs initiated and sponsored by organisations are available for managing work-related stress. Organisational programs are aimed more broadly at all employees and may include management by objectives, job enrichment, organisational development programs and a variety of other approaches. Individual intervention programs for managing stress are numerous. The more promising programs of this kind include cognitive techniques, relaxation training, meditation and biofeedback.

Describe the key components of burnout. Burnout describes a stress syndrome experienced by individuals whose jobs require high levels of contact with other people. Three symptoms define burnout: high emotional exhaustion, high depersonalisation and a low sense of personal accomplishment.

REVIEW AND DISCUSSION QUESTIONS

1. Does the kind of definition of stress an organisation uses have implications for its stress management programs? Give an example.

2. Think of a stressful experience that might commonly occur in a work setting. Explain what is happening to the individual experiencing the stress using the general adaptation syndrome model.

3. Why would achieving the goal of eliminating all stress in the workplace be counterproductive for organisations?

4. Exhibit 6.2 suggests that there are several levels of work stressors. The same figure indicates that a number of individual factors moderate the relationship between stressors and stress. Are certain individual factors more or less likely to moderate the effects of certain stressors? Explain.

5. With very few exceptions unions have not been receptive to, or supportive of, stress management programs. Why do you suppose this is true? As a manager, how would you gain the union's cooperation in an organisationally sponsored stress management program?

6. What subcomponents of the Type A behaviour pattern appear to be the most toxic?

7. Many different aspects of one's life may contribute to the formation and maintenance of Type A behaviour. Discuss how each of the following might contribute: the work environment, school, television, and home life as a child.

8. How should an organisation decide whether to offer stress management programs? What sort of issues should be taken into consideration in deciding between a clinical or organisational approach to such programs?

9. Increasingly, workers are being sent on overseas assignments. What stressors might be unique to such assignments? What might organisations do to minimise their impact?

ENDNOTES

1 Brady, J. V. (1958). Ulcers in executive monkeys, *Scientific American*, **199**, 89–95.

2 Matteson, M. T., & Ivancevich, J. M. (1987). *Controlling Work Stress*. San Francisco: Jossey-Bass.

3 Beehr, T. A., & Bhagat, R. S. (Eds.) (1985). *Human Stress and Cognition in Organizations*. New York: Wiley.

4 Kahn, R. L., & Byosiere, P. (1994). Stress in organizations. In M. D. Dunnette & L. M. Hough (Eds.) *Handbook of Industrial and Organizational Psychology* (2nd Ed.). Palo Alto, CA: Consulting Psychologists Press.

5 Selye, H. (1976). *The Stress of Life*. New York: McGraw-Hill; Selye, H. (1974). *Stress without Distress*. Philadelphia, Pa.: J. B. Lippincott.

6 Selye, H. (1974). *Stress Without Distress*. Philadelphia, PA: J. B. Lippincott, p. 5.

7 Holt, R. R. (1982). Occupational stress. In L. Goldberger and S. Breznitz (Eds.) *Handbook of Stress*. New York: Free Press, 419–444.

8 Argyris, C. (1964). *Integrating the Individual and the Organization*. New York: John Wiley & Sons; Cooper, C. L. (1973). *Group Training and Organizational Development*. Basel, Switzerland: Karger.

9 French, J. R. P., & Caplan, R. D. (1970). Psychosocial factors in coronary heart disease, *Industrial Medicine*, 383–397.

10 Ray, E. B., & Miller, K. I. (1991). The influence of communication structure and social support on job stress and burnout, *Management Communication Quarterly*, **4**, 506–527.

11 Ivancevich, J. M., & Donnelly, J. H. (1975). Relation of organizational structure to job satisfaction, anxiety-stress and performance, *Administrative Science Quarterly*, 272–280.

12 Marks, R. V. (1976). Social stress and cardiovascular disease, *Milbank Memorial Fund Quarterly*, 51–107.

13 A statistical profile of occupational health and safety in Victoria, OHSA Commission, 1994.

14 Havlovic, S. J., & Keenan, J. P. (1991). Coping with work stress: The influence of individual differences, *Journal of Social Behavior and Personality*, **6**, 199–212.

15 Leigh, J., Lucas, Jr., G., & Woodman, R. (1988). Effects of perceived organizational factors on role stress-job attitude relationships, *Journal of Management*, 41–58.

16 Kahn, R. L., Wolfe, D. M., Quinn, R. P., Snoek, J. D., & Rosenthal, R. A. (1964). *Organizational Stress: Studies in Role Conflict and Ambiguity*. New York: John Wiley & Sons.

17 Williams, K. J., & Alliger, G. M. (1994). Role stressors, mood spillover and perceptions of work-family conflict in employed parents, *Academy of Management Journal*, 837–868.

18 Margolis, B. L., Kroes, W. M., & Quinn, R. P. (1974). Job stress: An untested occupational hazard, *Journal of Occupational Medicine*, 659–661.

19 Weiman, C. (1977). A study of occupational stressors and the incidence of disease-risk, *Journal of Occupational Medicine*, 119–122.

20 Cooper, C. L., Cooper, R. D., & Eaker, L. H. (1988). *Living with Stress*. London: Penguin Books.

21 French, J. R. P., & Caplan, R. D. (1970). Psychosocial factors in coronary heart disease, *Industrial Medicine*, 383–397.

22 Holmes, T. H., & Rahe, R. H. (1967). Social readjustment scale, *Journal of Psychosomatic Research*, 213–218.

23 Monroe, S. M. (1983). Major and minor life events as predictors of psychological distress: further issues and findings, *Journal of Behavioral Medicine*, 189–205.

24 Perkins, D. V. (1982). The assessment of stress using life events scales. In L. Goldberger and S. Breznitz (Eds.) *Handbook of Stress*. New York: Free Press, 320–331.

25 Kahn, R. L., & Byosiere, P. (1994). Stress in organizations. In M. D. Dunnette & L. M. Hough (Eds.) *Handbook of Industrial and Organizational Psychology* (2nd Ed.). Palo Alto, CA: Consulting Psychologists Press.

26 Greenberg, J. & Baron, R. A. (1993). *Behaviour in Organizations: Understanding and Managing the Human Side of Work* (4th Ed.). Boston: Allyn and Bacon.

27 Mitchell, T. R., Dowling, P. J., Kabanoff, B. V., & Larson, J. R (1988). *People in Organizations: An Introduction to Organizational Behaviour in Australia*. Sydney: McGraw-Hill Book Company.

28 Kahn, R. L., & Byosiere, P. (1994). Stress in organizations. In M. D. Dunnette & L. M. Hough (Eds.) *Handbook of Industrial and Organizational Psychology* (2nd Ed.). Palo Alto, CA: Consulting Psychologists Press.

29 Lazarus, R. S., & Folkman, S. (1984). *Stress, Appraisal and Coping*. New York: Springer. See also footnote 38 for a discussion of the coping strategies of optimists and pessimists.

30 Friedman, M. & Ulmer, D. (1984). *Treating Type A Behavior and Your Heart*. New York: Alfred A. Knopf.

31 Greenglass, E. R., & Burke, R. J. (1991). The relationship between stress and coping among Type As, *Journal of Social Behavior and Personality*, **6**, 361–373.

32 For example, see Schauebroeck, J., Ganster, D. C., & Kemmerer, B. E. (1994). Job complexity, Type A behavior and cardiovascular disorder: A prospective study, *Academy of Management Journal*, 426–439.

33 Spector, P. E. (1982). Behavior in organizations as a function of employee's locus of control, *Psychological Bulletin*, **91**, 482–497.

34 Rotter, J. R. (1966). Generalized expectancies for internal versus external control of reinforcement, *Psychological Monographs*, **609**, 80.

35 Rotter, J. R. (1971). External and internal control, *Psychology Today*, 37.

36 Kobasa, S. C. (1988). Conceptualization and meaurement of personality in job stress research. In J. J. Hurrell, Jnr., L. R. Lawrence, S. L. Sauter, & C. L. Cooper (Eds.) *Occupational Stress: Issues and Developments in Research*. New York: Taylor & Francis.

37 Kobasa, S. C., Maddi, S. R., & Kahn, S. (1982). Hardiness and health: A prospective study, *Journal of Personality and Social Psychology*, 168–177.

38 Scheier, M. F., Weintraub, J. K., & Carver, C. S. (1986). Coping with stress: Divergent strategies of optimists and pessimists, *Journal of Personality and Social Psychology*, **51**, 1257–1264.

39 George, J. (1989). Mood and absence, *Journal of Applied Psychology*, **74**, 317–324; Judge, T. A. (1993). Does affective disposition moderate the relationship between job satisfaction and voluntary turnover?, *Journal of Applied Psychology*, **78**, 395–401; Watson, D., & Clarke, L. A. (1984). Negative affectivity: The disposition to experience aversive emotional states, *Psychological Bulletin*, **96**, 465–490.

40 Brief, A. P., Burke, M. J., George, J. M., Robinson, B. S., & Webster, J. (1988). Should negative affectivity remain an unmeasured variable in the study of job stress?, *Journal of Applied Psychology*, **73**, 193–198; Burke, M. J., Brief, A. P., & George, J. M. (1993). The role of negative affectivity in understanding relations between self-reports of stressors and strains: A comment on the applied psychology literature, *Journal of Applied Psychology*, **78**, 402–412; Ganster, D. C., & Schaubroeck, J. (1991). Work stress and employee health, *Journal of Management*, **17**, 235–271; George, J. M. (1992). The role of personality in organizational life: Issues and evidence, *Journal of Management*, **18**, 185–213; Schaubroeck, J., Ganster, D. C., & Fox, M. L. (1992). Dispositional affect and

work-related stress, *Journal of Applied Psychology*, **77**, 322–335.

41 George, J. (1989). Mood and absence, *Journal of Applied Psychology*, **74**, 317–324; Judge, T. A. (1993). Does affective disposition moderate the relationship between job satisfaction and voluntary turnover?, *Journal of Applied Psychology*, **78**, 395–401; Parkes, K. R. (1990). Coping, negative affectivity, and the work environment: Additive and interactive predictors of mental health, *Journal of Applied Psychology*, **75**, 399–409; Parkes, K. R. (1986). Coping in stressful episodes: The role of individual differences, environmental factors and situational characteristics, *Journal of Personality and Social Psychology*, **51**, 1277–1292.

42 See, for example, J. G. Anderson (1991). Stress and burnout among nurses: A social network approach, *Journal of Social Behavior and Personality*, **6**, 251–272.

43 Wallston, B. S., Alagna, S. W., DeVellis, B. M., & DeVellis, R. F. (1983). Social support and physical health, *Health Psychology*, 367–391.

44 LaRocco, J. M., House, J. S., & French, J. R. P. (1980). Social support, occupational stress and health, *Journal of Health and Social Behavior*, 202–218.

45 Fusilier, M. R., Ganster, D. C., & Mayes, B. T. (1987). Effects of social support, role stress and locus of control on health, *Journal of Management*, 517–528.

46 Mitchell, R. E., Billings, A. G., & Moos, R. H. (1982). Social support and well being: Implications for prevention programs, *Journal of Primary Prevention*, 77–98; Cowen, E. L. (1982). Help is where you find it: Four informal helping groups, *American Psychologist*, 385–395.

47 Gottlieb, B. H. (1983). *Social Support Strategies*. Beverly Hills, CA: Sage Publications.

48 House, J. J. (1981). *Work Stress and Social Support*. Reading, MA: Addison-Wesley Publishing.

49 Glass, D. C. (1977). *Behavior Patterns, Stress and Coronary Disease*. Hillsdale, NJ.: Erlbaum Associates.

50 See, for example, Matthews, K., Cottington, E., Talnbott, E., Kuller, L., & Siegal, J. (1987). Stressful work conditions and diastolic blood pressure among blue collar factory workers, *American Journal of Epedemiology*, 280–291.

51 The discussion of burnout is taken from Cordes, C. L. & Dougherty, T. W. (1993). A review and integration of research on job burnout, *Academy of Management Review*, **18**, 621–658.

52 Kahn, R. L., & Byosiere, P. (1994). Stress in organizations. In M. D. Dunnette & L. M. Hough (Eds.) *Handbook of Industrial and Organizational Psychology* (2nd Ed.). Palo Alto, CA: Consulting Psychologists Press.

53 See, for example, Harrison, R. V. (1985). The person-environment fit model and job stress. In T. A. Beehr & S. Baghat (Eds.) *Human Stress and Cognition in Organzations*. New York: John Wiley and Sons; also, Ganster & Schaubroeck (reference 54).

54 Ganster, D. C., & Schaubroeck, J. (1991). Work stress and employee health, *Journal of Management*, **17**, 235–271.

55 Ibid; Ross, R. R., & Altamaier, E. M. (1994). *Intervention in Occupational Stress*. London: Sage Publications.

56 Ross, R. R., & Altamaier, E. M. (1994). *Intervention in Occupational Stress*. London: Sage Publications.

57 Ibid.

58 Byers, S. K. (1987). Organizational stress: Implications for health promotion managers, *American Journal of Health Promotion*, **2**, 21–27.

59 Matteson, M. T., & Ivancevich, J. M. (1987). Individual stress management interventions: evaluation of techniques, *Journal of Management Psychology*, **1**, 24–30.

60 Benson, H. (1975). *The Relaxation Response*. New York: William Morrow.

61 Benson, H. & Allen, R. L. (1980). How much stress is too much?, *Harvard Business Review*, September–October, p. 88.

62 Kimble, C. P. (1982). Stress and psychosomatic illness, *Journal of Psychosomatic Research*, 63–71.

63 Beech, H. R., Burns, L., & Sheffield, B. (1984). *A Behavioral Approach to the Management of Stress*. New York: John Wiley & Sons.

64 Meichenbaum, D. (1985). *Stress Inoculation Training*. New York: Pergamon Press.

65 Brown, J. D. (1991). Staying fit and staying well: Physical fitness as a moderator of life stress. *Journal of Personality and Social Psychology* **60**, 555–561.

READING 6 WHO BEATS STRESS BEST — AND HOW

Source: 'Who Beats Stress Best — And How', *Fortune*, October 7, 1991, pp. 71–86

In a faster-spinning world, managers are finding new ways to ease stress in workers and themselves. Wisdom comes from surprising sources — like the Army — and pays off.

What we don't understand about stress could fill volumes. And it does. Some books say stress is an invigorating tonic; others, that it's lethal. Stress stands implicated in practically every complaint of modern life, from equipment downtime to premature ejaculation, from absenteeism to sudden death. Some workers in high-stress occupations — bomb deactivators, for example — suffer its effects hardly at all. Yet a man who tastes port for a living lies awake some nights worried that 'the whole business is riding on my palate'. There's enough apparently contradictory information about stress to make any honest seeker after truth, well, anxious.

Isn't there more stress today than ever before? There might be. There might be more love. But neither condition is quantifiable. Diseases to which stress contributes — hypertension, heart attack, ulcers, the common cold — are quantifiable, but since stress isn't their only cause, an increase in them doesn't necessarily signal an increase in stress.

Ask people if they *feel* more stressed and, of course, they say yes. Who would admit, even if it were true, that he feels *less* stressed than he did a year ago? Inner peace is seen to be the prerogative of dweebs. It's hip to be stressed. Earlier this year, Northwestern National Life Insurance questioned a random sample of 600 US workers. Almost half (46 percent) said their jobs were highly stressful; 34 percent said they felt so much stress they were thinking of quitting.

Some of them were telling the truth. Commutes really are growing longer, highways more congested. In more families, both husbands and wives have jobs. And with upsizings, downsizings, rightsizings, takeovers and mergers, the corporate world in recent years has turned upside down more times than James Dean's roadster.

The number of stress-related workers' compensation claims has ballooned in states such as California that compensate for so-called mental-mental injuries. In these, an intangible (mental) injury results from an intangible (mental) cause, such as stress. California courts have awarded compensation to workers who just say they feel hurt. Judith Bradley, a former cake decorator with Albertson's, a supermarket chain, won compensation in part because she said her supervisor had been 'very curt' with her. He had told her to 'get the lead out' and to 'get your butt in high gear', and had reprimanded her for leaving cakes out of the freezer. She was distressed, sued and won.

Though recently the number of stress-related claims has begun to decline in California, dollar costs nationally continue to rise. Donna Dell, manager of employee relations for Wells Fargo Bank, says workers suffering from stress 'typically are out a long, long time and they need lots of rehabilitation', including costly visits to psychiatrists. In medical treatment and time lost, stress cases cost, on average, twice as much as other workplace injuries; more than $15 000 each.

Perhaps the most telling sign of stress's apparent rise: strong business for purveyors of relief. Psychologist Stanley Fisher, a Manhattan hypnotist, says the demise of New York's boom-boom real estate market has sent many relief-seeking former brokers and developers his way. Gene Cooper, a partner at Corporate Counseling Associates (a supplier of corporate employee assistance programs), says, 'It used to be, 3 percent to 5 percent of our calls for counseling were stress related. Now, more like 8 percent to 14 percent'. They come from all levels, clerks to VPs.

There are stress-fighting tapes, goggles that send pulses of white light into your head, vibrating music beds ('not quite like the first time you had sex', says one manufacturer, 'but maybe the second'). Morgan Fairchild has a video out (*Morgan Fairchild Stress Management*, $19.95).

Whenever the status quo gets a good shaking — even where that shaking eventually results in greater opportunity and freedom of choice — stress goes up as people scramble to adapt. Yet if change is a constant and if everyone is susceptible to stress, why doesn't everyone suffer from it equally? Why do some maddeningly healthy people appear not to suffer from it at all?

Not everyone finds the same event stressful. Drop a scorpion into a box of puppies and you get stressed puppies. But drop it into a box of elf owls, which eat scorpions, and you get satisfaction. If a tree falls in the rain forest and nobody from Ben & Jerry's hears it, is there stress? No. Perhaps you think drinking port is fun. Peter Ficklin, wine master of Ficklin Vineyards, a California portmaker, says, 'Sure, it's a pleasure to taste port. But the fortified wine category is down. There's increased competition. In the busy season, sometimes, I have trouble sleeping. The whole business is riding on my palate.'

Some people are protected from stress by buffers. For example, the more mastery or control a person feels he has over circumstances, the less stress he's apt to feel, even if his control extends no further than the power to decide how he's going to feel about change. A surefire recipe for creating stress is to put someone in a job that affords him little decision-making power but carries great responsibility or imposes heavy psychological demands.

Rare is the job where an employee has complete control. Wally Goelzer, a flight attendant for Alaska Airlines, has plenty of control over his schedule — he's got 11 years' seniority. But the workplace limits his freedom: 'Probably the worst incident in the last six months was an alcohol situation. The plane was full of a mixture of tourists and commercial fishermen. I had to tell this guy, one of the fishermen, that we wouldn't serve him any more alcohol. Now these fishermen are out on their boat sometimes six or eight weeks. He wasn't pleased. Yelling. Profanities. People around him were not having an ideal travel experience. "What you're doing", I told him, "is you're being loud now". I didn't want to stir him up too much, since we're all trapped in a tube at 29 000 feet'.

The most potent buffer against stress may well be membership in a stable, close-knit group or community. Example: the town of Roseto, Pennsylvania. Stress researcher Dr Stewart Wolf wondered 25 years ago why Roseto's residents, though they smoked, drank, ate fat and otherwise courted doom, lived free from heart disease and other stress-related ills. He suspected their protection sprang from the town's uncommon social cohesion and stability: It was inhabited almost entirely by descendants of Italians who had moved there 100 years previously from Roseto, Italy. Few married outside the community; the firstborn was always named after a grandparent; ostentation or any display of superiority was avoided, since that would invite 'the evil eye' from one's neighbour.

Wolf predicted Rosetians would start dying like flies if the modern world intruded. It did. They did. By the mid-1970s, Rosetians had Cadillacs, ranch-style homes, mixed marriages, new names, and a rate of coronary heart disease the same as any other town's.

The US Army tries to instill a Rosetian cohesion prophylactically. Says Dr David Marlowe, chief of the department of military psychiatry at the Walter Reed Army Institute of Research: 'If a bond trader feels stress, he can go meditate for 20 minutes. A soldier facing enemy fire can't. So we have to give him the maximum protection ahead of time'. Marlowe says that where stress is concerned, Army research shows the primary issues are organizational. 'You want to build cohesion into a group, by making sure soldiers have good information, that they aren't faced with ambiguity, that they have solid relationships with leaders. If a man feels his squad is listening to him, if he can talk to it about his hopes, fears, anxieties, he's not likely to experience stress'. The Army's No. 1 psychological discovery from World War II, he says, was 'the strength imparted by the small, primary work group'.

Keeping group cohesion strong *after* battle is crucial too, since members, by collectively reliving their experience and trying to put it in perspective, get emotions off their chests that otherwise might leave them stressed out for months or years. The process is called debriefing. Squad members, for example, are encouraged to use travel time en route home from a war zone to talk about their battlefield experience. 'It helps them detoxify', says Marlow. 'That's why we brought them back in groups from Desert Storm. Epidemiologically, we know it works'. Thus, the group emerges both as the primary protector against stress and as the means for relief after a stressful event.

In light of the Army's approach, much of what passes for stress management in US industry looks superficial. Most Fortune 500 companies offer employees either an employee assistance program (EAP), a wellness promotion program, or both. Some of these emphasize stress management. At Liz Claiborne, for example, well-attended lunchtime seminars explain how workers can relax by using mental imagery, muscle relaxation, and a variety of other proven techniques. Why the big turnout? 'Misery loves company', says Sharon Quilter, Claiborne's director of benefits. Honeywell has offered a 45-minute program called Wellness and Your Funny Bone, taught by Sister Mary Christelle Macaluso, RSM (Religious Sister of Mercy), PhD, 'a lecturer/humorist with a PhD in anatomy'.

Ted Barash, president of a company that provides wellness programs, dismisses such approaches to stress reduction as 'Band-Aid happy hours and traveling humor shows'. Professor Paul Roman, a University of Georgia expert on behavioral health who has surveyed EAP programs, says most 'never address the source of the stress. They blame the victim. Our studies at Southwestern Bell and other companies show the single biggest source of stress is poorly trained and inept supervisors'.

External suppliers of EAP programs, such as Corporate Counseling Associates, purveyors of counseling to Time Warner, Digital Equipment, Liz Claiborne, and others, are understandably reluctant to tell clients how to run their own businesses. Says CPA partner Gene Cooper: 'We help employees develop coping mechanisms. We don't reduce the stress itself'. One of Cooper's counselors, asked if she suggests stress-relieving organizational changes to employers, says no, 'that would be presumptuous'.

Stress experts who advocate a more interventionist approach ask how it can possibly make sense for a company to soothe employees with one hand — teaching them relaxation through rhythmic breathing — while whipping them like egg whites with the other, moving up deadlines, increasing overtime, or withholding information about job security. Any company serious about stress management should consider the following steps:

■ *Audit stress.* Dr Paul J. Rosch, president of the American Institute of Stress, thinks any intelligent program must begin and end with a stress audit. Questionnaires typically ask workers and managers to list conditions they find most stressful. Answers can illuminate areas where workers are stressed by boredom, as well as those where they are stressed by overwork. (Rustout, stressmeisters are fond of saying, can be as anxious-making as burnout.) Rosch says, 'An audit may show a need for programs not generally thought of as stress reducing, though

they serve that function'. Examples: child care and flexitime. Follow-up audits show results.

■ *Use EAPs aggressively.* Try to catch stress before it blooms. At McDonnell Douglas, EAP director Daniel Smith uses a program called Transitions to prepare workers for potentially traumatic organizational changes. 'You tell people what they're going to feel before they feel it', he says. 'It prevents more significant problems downstream'.

Case in point: Pete Juliano, head of McDonnell Douglas's 2000-person facilities management operation, knew he would have to flatten and streamline his division to make it more responsive. Specifically, he would have to strip five levels of management with 260 managers down to three levels with 170.

'Nobody was going out the door', he says, 'and nobody was getting a pay cut. They'd all be staying on, though not all as managers. Still, that's a tough nut to crack: One day you're a manager. The next, you're carrying tools. How do you tell your wife and kids? How do you go to work each day and face not being a manager?'

Juliano called in the Transitions team, whose members made a two-hour presentation to the department. They covered such topics as how to face your spouse and peers if you don't continue as a manager, how to recognize denial, how to cope with anger. The counselors also told listeners about career options if they decided to leave the division or McDonnell Douglas. 'It gave them a chance to vent', says Juliano. 'There have been cases of guys committing suicide when they had to go back to carrying tools. But we didn't have any serious problems'.

■ *Examine EAP usage.* If you've got an EAP program, study the usage data that counselors collect: How many employees from what departments are requesting help and for what? For example, if you know that (1) in the past five years nobody from your tax department has ever used the EAP program, (2) half the accountants signed up for stress counseling last week, and (3) it's not mid-April, then you might be seeing evidence of a problem.

■ *Give employees information.* They can't feel in control of circumstances if they lack it. When Donna Dell became manager of employee relations at Wells Fargo Bank last November, she saw there were about 3000 workers' compensation cases outstanding. Accidents accounted for 80 percent; another 10 percent were from workers claiming various injuries from working at video display terminals; and 10 percent were from stress. She wanted to know where the stress claims came from. Were they, for instance, from employees who had been laid off or who had just been through a performance review? There was no correlation to either event. 'I was surprised', says Dell. 'Vengeance, apparently, was not the issue'.

Asbestos was. 'We don't have any claims for asbestosis *per se*', she says, 'but we get stress claims from people who *fear* they may have been exposed. You don't have to prove you were exposed to get workers' comp. The fear is enough. Now we provide instruction at sites where toxic material construction has been scheduled. We go in, in advance, with trainers and explain to the employees what's going to happen. Since we implemented this program about a year and a half ago, we haven't had any more such claims'.

■ *Match employees with jobs they can master.* In his bestselling book, *Flow*, Mihaly Csikszentmihalyi, a psychology professor at the University of Chicago, points out that the least-stressed people often are those who are working flat out on some task that they have selected — something they really love to do. They give themselves so completely that they achieve a kind of precision and grace — what the author calls 'flow'. The chance of your getting such performance from workers goes up, and their stress down, the more choice you give them over assignments.

■ *Be prepared for trauma.* It's easy to forget that stress isn't always the result of a thousand tiny cuts. 'Having a gun put to your head can be upsetting', says Chris Dunning, a trauma expert at the University of Wisconsin at Milwaukee. She ought to know. Her business is de-stressing shot cops, crews of crashed airliners, and, at this writing, the forensic examiners in the Jeffrey Dahmer case ('they're having trouble eating meat').

Abrupt and upsetting things happen in offices. Homicide and suicide — not accidents — now account for 14 percent of male on-the-job deaths and 46 percent of female, reports

psychologist James Turner, an expert on workplace mayhem. At the emergency department of Oakland's Highland Hospital, says chief resident Linda Jenks, mounting stress — with no end in sight — precipitated two suicides. 'A young intern got into her car, numbed up her neck with lidocaine, took out a scalpel, and dissected herself in her rearview mirror. Within a week, a night nurse started an i.v. on herself — injected potassium, which stopped her heart immediately. After that, the hospital said, "Okay, we're ignoring a problem here." It's as if to admit it is a sign of failure.' A suicide, an industrial accident, or any other traumatic event, says Dunning, leaves a lingering psychological strain on survivors: 'It usually takes a good three months to get an organization back on track'.

But, says Mark Braverman, president of Crisis Management Group, a Massachusetts consulting firm, these traumas present management with opportunities as well as problems. 'Management sometimes won't talk about the event or face up to it directly', he says. 'We try to tell them that if they do face up to it and answer workers' questions, they can build a bond that lasts longer afterward'. Even if you can't talk, he says, talk: 'If you can't tell them much because OSHA is still completing an investigation, tell them that'.

Braverman cites an example of trauma handled right: 'A computer company had had a helicopter crash. They'd also had a work site shooting. So they decided, within the structure of their EAP, to create a protocol for dealing with traumatic stress. Later a safety system failed in a plant with 2000 people, killing one. Every work group got together. The international manager of facilities was flown in to answer questions, including the ones on everybody's minds: Why did the system fail? Could it happen again? EAP counselors were available, but it was the information itself that was most stress-relieving'.

Traumatic stress tends to be infectious. Since large numbers of employees are involved, clusters of stress-based workers' comp suits can result. In court, the cases are much harder to defend against than less-dramatic stress cases. Says Jim Turner: 'It behooves you greatly to go in early with counselors, since this will reduce your overall long-term cost'.

At Wells Fargo, where bank robberies rose 37 percent in this year's first quarter, tellers have been traumatized. 'We do get stress claims from robbery incidents and we don't dispute them', says Donna Dell. Instead, the bank dispatches EAP counselors to affected branches, where they conduct group debriefings, much the way the Army does.

Bryan Lawton, head of Wells Fargo's debriefing program, explains how it works: 'The professional asks them things like, where were you when the incident happened, how did you respond, how did the others act? When the employees start to talk, they find out they're not alone, not the only ones who feel the way they do. Everybody else feels guilty or angry over the event. They're told these are normal emotions'. The professional then tells them how they can expect to feel weeks later.

Nobody is sure why debriefings work, but they do. And they are cost-effective. 'All it takes', says Lawton, 'is one case to lead to a significant expense. One person's trauma can wind up costing the bank $100 000'. The figure includes lost time, medical treatment, and retraining cost.

O'Dell Williams, with the bank 16 years, has survived ten robbery situations, the most recent one as a branch manager in Vallejo, California, on May 20. The robbery attempt scared more than 20 of his employees. 'I was afraid we'd lose some afterward', he says. But EAP counselors intervened quickly, and so far nobody has quit. And nobody has filed a workers' comp claim.

■ *Don't forget the obvious.* Managers who want to reduce stress should make sure workers have the tools and training they need to get the job done. Says John Murray, a police bomb deactivator in Florida: 'I'm lucky. I've got the best equipment and the best training. There are departments where all they used to give you was a mattress and a fishhook'. Managers should set realistic deadlines and go out of their way not to change deadlines, once set. What works well for the Army works just as well in the office: Build cohesion through communication. Straighten out managers who like to play the Charles Boyer part from *Gaslight* — who hold sway over subordinates by keeping them confused, by withholding information or by keeping roles and responsibilities ill-defined.

Do all these things, behave flawlessly and your exposure to stress-based lawsuits still remains almost unimaginably broad. Chris Dunning cites a case where an employee, as part of some lunchroom high jinks, got silly and taped

a co-worker's arm to a chair — very lightly, not so it restrained her. She started screaming. Other workers looked at each other in disbelief: What was the woman's problem? It turned out that, as a child, she had been forcibly restrained and raped. The taping of the arm caused her to reexperience the trauma of that and her subsequent disability was judged to be 100 percent the employer's responsibility.

At least this worker's distress was real. Some employees undoubtedly abuse the system and there are lawyers and doctors eager to help them. Listen to Joseph Alibrandi, chairman of Whittaker Corp., an aerospace manufacturer: 'We try to minimize the problems in the physical workplace, to do all we can to reduce *true* stress. But a lot of that seems frustratingly irrelevant. There's always an epidemic of "sore back" after a layoff. Or they say they can't perform sexually. How the hell are you going to defend against that?'

It's almost impossible, of course, but you can try to flag potential claimants early on. New hires can be asked, as part of their medical evaluation, 'Have you ever been off work due to a stress-related illness?' A 'yes' may indicate to the doctor that the employee's assignment should be changed.

Performing a periodic stress audit, or making stress management part of your EAP or wellness program, can pay off in court. Says John M. Ivancevich, dean of the business school at the University of Houston: 'Even a sloppy attempt at stress management can be a legal defence'.

Finally: you. Feeling stressed? Not sure what to do? The first rule, says Dr James Turner, is, Don't quit your job. 'They build these fantasies', he says of stressed-out executives. 'They'll go sailing. They'll open a copy center. Lately, for some reason, they all want to open copy centers'. But sooner or later everyone wants to come back.

Instead of quitting, learn the techniques of coping. You'll find plenty of experts willing to teach them to you for a price, but they're not too complex, and many stressed workers have discovered them without help. Flight attendant Wally Goelzer and plenty of other people use them daily without knowing it. 'Sometimes I put my hands out like a scale', he says. 'I ask myself: How much does this problem matter? I think of a friend of mine who was killed in a plane crash. "Life is too short", I can hear her say. She used to say that and I can see her face'.

Emergency room resident Jenks and bomb deactivator Murray know the stress-relieving power of humor, even when it's of the gallows type. Says Murray: 'Yeah, I get a certain amount of kidding. I've got three daughters and when Father's Day comes around they give me a card with a fuse in it'. Says Jenks: 'We use black humor at work so much that it's gotten so I have to remember to clean up my act when I'm around normal people'.

Then again, you might want to put aside the tricks and strategies, since these change like frocks. You might think about your life. Is it the way you wanted? If not, all the perspective and joking in the world will get you only so far. Mihaly Csikszentimihalyi, who lectures occasionally to 40-ish managers, notes that those who insist on regaining control of their lives, even at what temporarily may seem the peril of their careers, often see an unexpected payoff down the line. 'There comes a point where they're working 70 hours a week and they're not sure why. Their family lives are suffering. Maybe they've never given any thought to setting priorities. Some decide they can't do everything — that they have to step off the fast track to get back their family life or take better care of their health. And then a most interesting thing happens: The ones who do it, most of them, in a year or two, they get promoted'. Dare to be second-rate, if that's how you have to think of it. It may not be what you imagine.

EXERCISE 6A BEHAVIOUR ACTIVITY PROFILE — A TYPE A MEASURE

Copyright © 1982 by Michael T. Matteson and John M. Ivancevich.

Each of us displays certain kinds of behaviours, thought patterns or personal characteristics. For each of the 21 sets of descriptions below, circle the number which you feel best describes where you are between each pair. The best answer for each set of descriptions is the response that most nearly describes the way you feel, behave or think. Answer these in terms of your regular or typical behaviour, thoughts or characteristics.

1. I'm always on time for appointments   7 6 5 4 3 2 1   I'm never quite on time.

2. When someone is talking to me, chances are I'll anticipate what they are going to say, by nodding, interrupting or finishing sentences for them.   7 6 5 4 3 2 1   I listen quietly without showing any impatience.

3. I frequently try to do several things at once.   7 6 5 4 3 2 1   I tend to take things one at a time.

4. When it comes to waiting in line (at banks, theatres, etc.), I really get impatient and frustrated   7 6 5 4 3 2 1   It simply doesn't bother me.

5. I always feel rushed.   7 6 5 4 3 2 1   I never feel rushed.

6. When it comes to my temper, I find it hard to control at times.   7 6 5 4 3 2 1   I just don't seem to have one.

7. I tend to do most things like eating, walking and talking rapidly.   7 6 5 4 3 2 1   Slowly.

TOTAL SCORE 1–7 _____ = S

8. Quite honestly, the things I enjoy most are job-related activities.

7 6 5 4 3 2 1

Leisure-time activities.

9. At the end of a typical work day, I usually feel as though I needed to get more done than I did.

7 6 5 4 3 2 1

I accomplished everything I needed to.

10. Someone who knows me very well would say that I would rather work than play.

7 6 5 4 3 2 1

I would rather play than work.

11. When it comes to getting ahead at work, nothing is more important.

7 6 5 4 3 2 1

Many things are more important.

12. My primary source of satisfaction comes from my job.

7 6 5 4 3 2 1

I regularly find satisfaction in non-job pursuits, such as hobbies, friends and family.

13. Most of my friends and social acquaintances are people I know from work.

7 6 5 4 3 2 1

Not connected with my work.

14. I'd rather stay at work than take a vacation.

7 6 5 4 3 2 1

Nothing at work is important enough to interfere with my vacation.

TOTAL SCORE 8–14 _____ = J

15. People who know me well would describe me as hard driving and competitive.

7 6 5 4 3 2 1

Relaxed and easygoing.

16. In general, my behaviour is governed by a desire for recognition and achievement.

7 6 5 4 3 2 1

What I want to do — not by trying to satisfy others.

17. In trying to complete a project or solve a problem, I tend to wear myself out before I'll give up on it.

7 6 5 4 3 2 1

I tend to take a break or quit if I'm feeling fatigued.

18. When I play a game (tennis, cards, etc.) my enjoyment comes from winning.

7 6 5 4 3 2 1

The social interaction.

19. I like to associate with people who are dedicated to getting ahead.

7 6 5 4 3 2 1

Easygoing and take life as it comes.

20. I'm not happy unless I'm always doing something.

7 6 5 4 3 2 1

Frequently, 'doing nothing' can be quite enjoyable.

21. What I enjoy doing most are competitive activities.

7 6 5 4 3 2 1

Non-competitive pursuits.

TOTAL SCORE 15–21 _____ = H

Impatience (S)	Job Involvement (J)	Hard Driving and Competitive (H)	Total Score (A) – S + J + H

The Behaviour Activity Profile attempts to assess the three Type A coronary-prone behaviour patterns, as well as provide a total score. The three a priori types of Type A coronary-prone behaviour patterns are shown:

Items	Behaviour Pattern	Characteristics
1–7	Impatience (S)	Anxious to interrupt. Fails to listen attentively. Frustrated by waiting (e.g. in line, for others to complete a job).
8–14	Job Involvement (J)	Focal point of attention is the job. Lives for the job. Relishes being on the job. Immersed in job activities.
15–21	Hard driving/ Competitive (H)	Hardworking, highly competitive. Competitive in most aspects of life, sports, work etc Racing against the clock.
1–21	Total score (A)	Total of S + J + H represents your global Type A behaviour.

Score ranges for total score are:

Score	Behaviour Type
122 and above	Hard-core Type A
99–121	Moderate Type A
90–98	Low Type A
80–89	Type X
70–79	Low Type B
50–69	Moderate Type B
40 and below	Hard-core Type B

Percentile Scores

Now you can compare your score to a sample of over 1200 respondents.

Percentile Score	Raw Score	
Percentage of Individuals Scoring Lower	**Males**	**Females**
99%	____140	____132
95%	____135	____126
90%	____130	____120
85%	____124	____112
80%	____118	____106
75%	____113	____101
70%	____108	____ 95
65%	____102	____ 90
60%	____ 97	____ 85
55%	____ 92	____ 80
50%	____ 87	____ 74
45%	____ 81	____ 69
40%	____ 75	____ 63
35%	____ 70	____ 58
30%	____ 63	____ 53
25%	____ 58	____ 48
20%	____ 51	____ 42
15%	____ 45	____ 36
10%	____ 38	____ 31
5%	____ 29	____ 26
1%	____ 21	____ 21

EXERCISE 6B HEALTH RISK APPRAISAL

The Health Risk Appraisal form was developed by the Department of Health and Welfare of the Canadian government. Their initial testing program indicated that approximately one person out of every three who completed the form would modify some unhealthy aspects of lifestyle for at least a while. Figuring the potential pay-off was worth it, the government mailed out over 3 million copies of the questionnaire to Canadians who were on social security. Subsequent checking indicated that their initial projections of the number of recipients altering their behaviour was correct. Perhaps you will be among the one-third.

Choose from the three answers for each question the one answer which most nearly applies to you. The plus and minus signs next to some numbers indicate more than (+) and less than (−). Note that a few items have only two alternatives.

Exercise

_____ 1.   Physical effort expended during the workday: mostly?
(a) heavy labour, walking or housework; (b) ___ ; (c) deskwork

_____ 2.   Participation in physical activities — skiing, golf, swimming, etc. or lawn mowing, gardening, etc.?
(a) daily; (b) weekly; (c) seldom

_____ 3.   Participation in vigorous exercise program?
(a) three time weekly; (b) weekly; (c) seldom

_____ 4.   Average miles [kilometres] walked or jogged per day?
(a) one [one and a half] or more; (b) less than one [one and a half]; (c) none

_____ 5.   Flights of stairs climbed per day?
(a) 10+; (b) 10–; (c) —

Nutrition

_____ 6.   Are you overweight?
(a) no; (b) 5 to 19 lbs [2 to 8.5 kg]; (c) 20+ lbs [9+ kg].

_____ 7.   Do you eat a wide variety of foods, something from each of the following five food groups: (1) meat, fish, poultry, dried legumes, eggs or nuts; (2) milk or milk products; (3) bread or cereals; (4) fruits; (5) vegetables?
(a) each day; (b) three times weekly; (c) —

Alcohol

_____ 8.   Average number of bottles (12 oz.) [340 g] of beer per week?
(a) 0 to 7; (b) 8 to 15; (c) 16+

_____ 9.   Average number of hard liquor (1½ oz.) [42 g] drinks per week?
(a) 0 to 7; (b) 8 to 15; (c) 16+

_____ 10.   Average number of glasses (5 oz.) [140 g] of wine or cider per week?
(a) 0 to 7; (b) 8 to 15; (c) 16+

_____ 11.   Total number of drinks per week including beer, liquor or wine?
(a) 0 to 7; (b) 8 to 15; (c) 16+

Drugs

_____ 12.   Do you take drugs illegally?
(a) no; (b) — ; (c) yes

_____ 13.   Do you consume alcoholic beverages together with certain drugs (_tranquillisers, barbiturates, illegal drugs_)?
(a) no; (b) — ; (c) yes

_____ 14.   Do you use painkillers improperly or excessively?
(a) no; (b) — ; (c) yes

Tobacco

_____ 15.   Cigarettes smoked per day?
(a) none; (b) 10–; (c) 10+

_____ 16.   Cigars smoked per day?
(a) none; (b) 10–; (c) 10+

_____ 17. Pipe tobacco pouches per week?
(a) none; (b) 2–; (c) 2+

Personal health

_____ 18. Do you experience periods of depression?
(a) seldom; (b) occasionally; (c) frequently

_____ 19. Does anxiety interfere with your daily activities?
(a) seldom; (b) occasionally; (c) frequently

_____ 20. Do you get enough satisfying sleep?
(a) yes; (b) no; (c) —

_____ 21. Are you aware of the causes and danger of VD?
(a) yes; (b) no; (c) —

_____ 22. Breast self-examination? _(if not applicable, do not score)_
(a) monthly; (b) occasionally; (c) —

Road and water safety

_____ 23. Mileage [number of kilometres] per year as driver or passenger?
(a) 10 000– [16 000– km]; (b) 10 000+ [16 000+ km]; (c) —

_____ 24. Do you often exceed the speed limit?
(a) no; (b) by 10+ mph [16+ km/h]; (c) by 20+ mph [32+ km/h]

_____ 25. Do you wear a seat belt?
(a) always; (b) occasionally; (c) never

_____ 26. Do you drive a motorcycle, moped or snowmobile?
(a) no; (b) yes; (c) — ;

_____ 27. If yes to the above, do you always wear a regulation safety helmet?
(a) yes; (b) — ; (c) no

_____ 28. Do you ever drive under the influence of alcohol?
(a) never; (b) — ; (c) occasionally

_____ 29. Do you ever drive when your ability may be affected by drugs?
(a) never; (b) — ; (c) occasionally

_____ 30. Are you aware of water safety rules?
(a) yes; (b) no: (c) —

_____ 31. If you participate in water sports or boating, do you wear a life jacket?
(a) yes; (b) no; (c) —

General

_____ 32. Average time watching TV per day _(in hours)_?
(a) 0 to 1; (b) 1 to 4; (c) 4+

_____ 33. Are you familiar with first-aid procedures?
(a) yes; (b) no; (c) —

_____ 34. Do you ever smoke in bed?
(a) no; (b) occasionally; (c) regularly

_____ **35.** Do you always make use of equipment provided for your safety at work?
(**a**) yes; (**b**) occasionally; (**c**) no

To score: Give yourself 1 point for each *a* answer; 3 points for each *b* answer; 5 points for each *c* answer.

Total score:

___ A total score of 35–45 is *excellent*. You have a commendable lifestyle based on sensible habits and a lively awareness of personal health.

___ A total score of 45–55 is *good*. With some minor change, you can develop an excellent lifestyle.

___ A total score of 56–65 is *risky*. You are taking unnecessary risks with your health. Several of your habits should be changed if potential health problems are to be avoided.

___ A total score of 66 and over is *hazardous*. Either you have little personal awareness of good health habits or you are choosing to ignore them. This is a danger zone.

CASE 6   THE CASE OF THE MISSING TIME

Source: 'The Case of the Missing Time', by Thomas J. McNichols, Northwestern University Business School, 1973, pp. 143–148. Reprinted by permission.

At approximately 7:30 a.m. on Tuesday, 23 June, 1959, Chet Craig, manager of the Norris Company's Central Plant, swung his car out of the driveway of his suburban home and headed towards the plant located some ten kilometres away, just inside the Midvale city limits. It was a beautiful day. The sun was shining brightly and a cool fresh breeze was blowing. The trip to the plant took about 20 minutes and sometimes gave Chet an opportunity to think about plant problems without interruption.

The Norris Company owned and operated three printing plants. Norris enjoyed a nationwide commercial business, specialising in quality colour work. It was a closely held company with some 350 employees, nearly half of whom were employed at the Central Plant, the largest of the three Norris production operations. The company's main offices were also located in the Central Plant building.

Chet had started with the Norris Company as an expediter in its Eastern Plant in 1948, just after he graduated from Ohio State University. After 3 years Chet was promoted to production supervisor, and 2 years later he was made assistant to the manager of the Eastern Plant. Early in 1957 he was transferred to the Central Plant as assistant to the plant manager, and 1 month later was promoted to plant manager when the former manager retired.

Chet was in fine spirits as he relaxed behind the wheel. As his car picked up speed, the hum of the tyres on the newly paved highway faded into the background. Various thoughts occurred to him, and he said to himself, 'This is going to be the day to really get things done.'

He began to run through the day's work, first one project, then another, trying to establish priorities. After a few minutes he decided that the open-end unit scheduling was probably the most important, certainly the most urgent. He frowned for a moment as he recalled that on Friday the vice-president and general manager had casually asked him if he had given the project any further thought. Chet realised that he had not been giving it much thought lately. He had been meaning to get to work on this idea for over 3 months. But something else always seemed to crop up. 'I haven't had much time to sit down and really work it out,' he said to himself. 'I'd better get going and hit this one today for sure.' With that he began to break down the objectives, procedures and installation steps of the project. He grinned as he reviewed the principles involved and calculated roughly the anticipated savings. 'It's about time,' he told himself. 'This idea should have been followed up long ago.' Chet remembered that he had first conceived of the open-end unit scheduling idea nearly a year and a half ago, just prior to his leaving Norris's Eastern Plant. He had spoken to his boss, Jim Quince, manager of the Eastern Plant, about it then, and both agreed that it was worth looking into. The idea was temporarily shelved when he was transferred to the Central Plant a month later.

A blast from a passing horn startled him, but his thoughts quickly returned to other plant projects he was determined to get under way. He started to think through a procedure for simpler transport of dies to and from the Eastern Plant. Visualising the notes on his desk, he thought about the inventory analysis he needed to identify and eliminate some of the slow-moving stock items, the packing controls that needed revision, and the need to design a new special-order form. He also decided that this was the day to settle on a job printer to do the simple outside printing of office forms. There were a few other projects he couldn't recall offhand, but he could tend to them after lunch, if not before. 'Yes, sir,' he said to himself, 'this is the day to really get rolling.'

Chet's thoughts were interrupted as he pulled into the company parking lot. When he entered the plant Chet knew something was wrong as he met Al Noren, the stockroom supervisor, who appeared troubled. 'A great morning, Al,' Chet greeted him cheerfully.

'Not so good, Chet; my new man isn't in this morning,' Noren growled.

'Have you heard from him?' asked Chet.

'No, I haven't,' replied Al.

Chet frowned as he commented, 'These stock handlers assume you take it for granted that if they're not here, they're not here, and they don't have to call in and verify it. Better ask Personnel to call him.'

Al hesitated for a moment before replying. 'Okay, Chet, but can you find me a man? I have two cars to unload today.'

As Chet turned to leave he said, 'I'll call you in half an hour, Al, and let you know.'

Making a mental note of the situation, Chet headed for his office. He greeted the group of workers huddled around Marilyn, the office manager, who was discussing her day's work schedule with them. As the meeting broke up, Marilyn picked up a few samples from the clasper, showed them to Chet, and asked if they should be shipped that way or if it would be necessary to inspect them. Before he could answer, Marilyn went on to ask if he could suggest another clerical operator for the sealing machine to replace the regular operator, who was home ill. She also told him that Gene, the industrial engineer he called, was waiting to hear from Chet.

After telling Marilyn to go ahead and ship the samples, he made a note of the need for a sealer operator for the office and then called Gene. He agreed to stop by Gene's office before lunch and started on his routine morning tour of the plant. He asked each supervisor the types and volumes of orders they were running, the number of people present, how the schedules were coming along, and the orders to be run next; helped the folding-room supervisor find temporary storage space for consolidating a carload shipment; discussed quality control with a press operator who had been running poor work; arranged to transfer four people temporarily to different departments, including two for A1 in the stockroom; and talked to the shipping supervisor about pick-ups and special orders to be delivered that day. As he continued through the plant, he saw to it that reserve stock was moved out of the forward stock area, talked to another press operator about his requested change of vacation schedule, had a 'heart-to-heart' talk with a press helper who seemed to need frequent reassurance, and approved two type and one colour-order okays for different press operators.

Returning to his office, Chet reviewed the production reports on the larger orders against his initial productions and found that the plant was running behind schedule. He called in the folding-room supervisor and together they went over the line-up of machines and made several necessary changes.

During this discussion, the composing-room supervisor stopped in to cover several type changes, and the routing supervisor telephoned for approval of a revised printing schedule. The stockroom supervisor called twice, first to inform him that two standard, fast moving stock items were dangerously low, and later to advise him that the paper stock for the urgent Dillion job had finally arrived. Chet made the necessary subsequent calls to inform those concerned.

He then began to put delivery dates on important and difficult inquiries received from customers and salespeople. (The routine inquiries were handled by Marilyn.) While he was doing this he was interrupted twice, once by a sales correspondent calling from the West Coast to ask for a better delivery date than originally scheduled, and once by the personnel vice-president asking him to set a time when he could hold an initial training and induction interview with a new employee.

After dating the customer and salespeople inquiries, Chet headed for his morning conference in the executive offices. At this meeting he answered the sales vice-president's questions in connection with 'hot' orders, complaints, and the status of large-volume orders and potential new orders. He then met with the general manager to discuss a few ticklish policy matters and to answer 'the old man's' questions on several specific production and personnel problems. Before leaving the executive offices, he stopped at the office of the secretary-treasurer to inquire about delivery of cartons, paper and boxes, and to place a new order for paper.

On the way back to his own office, Chet conferred with Gene about two current engineering projects concerning which he had called earlier. When he reached his desk, he lit a cigarette and looked at his watch. It was 10 minutes before lunch, just time enough to make a few notes of the details he needed to check in order to answer knotty questions raised by the sales manager that morning.

After lunch Chet started again. He began by checking the previous day's production reports, did some rescheduling to get out urgent orders, placed appropriate delivery dates on new orders and inquiries received that morning, and consulted with a supervisor on a personal problem. He spent some 20 minutes at the TWX going over mutual problems with the Eastern Plant.

By midafternoon Chet had made another tour of the plant, after which he met with the personnel director to review with him a touchy personal problem raised by one of the clerical employees, the vacation schedules submitted by his supervisors, and the pending job-evaluation program. Following this conference, Chet hurried back to his office to complete the special statistical report for Universal Waxing Corporation, one of Norris's best customers. As he finished the report, he discovered that it was 10 minutes past six and he was the only one left in the office. Chet was tired. He put on his coat and headed through the plant towards the parking lot; on the way he was stopped by both the night supervisor and night layout foremen for approval of type and layout changes.

With both eyes on the traffic, Chet reviewed the day he had just completed. 'Busy?' he asked himself. 'Too much so — but did I accomplish anything?' His mind raced over the day's activities. 'Yes and no' seemed to be the answer. 'There was the usual routine, the same as any

other day. The plant kept going and I think it must have been a good production day. Any creative or special project work done?' Chet grimaced as he reluctantly answered, 'No.'

With a feeling of guilt, he probed further. 'Am I an executive? I'm paid like one, respected like one, and have a responsible assignment with the necessary authority to carry it out. Yet one of the greatest values a company derives from an executive is his creative thinking and accomplishments. What have I done about it? An executive needs some time for thinking. Today was a typical day, just like most other days, and I did little, if any, creative work. The projects that I so enthusiastically planned to work on this morning are exactly as they were yesterday. What's more, I have no guarantee that tomorrow night or the next night will bring me any closer to their completion. This is the real problem and there must be an answer.'

Chet continued, 'Night work? Yes, occasionally. This is understood. But I've been doing too much of this lately. I owe my wife and family some of my time. When you come down to it, they are the people for whom I'm really working. If I am forced to spend much more time away from them, I'm not meeting my own personal objectives. What about church work? Should I eliminate that? I spend a lot of time on this, but I feel I owe God some time, too. Besides, I believe I'm making a worthwhile contribution in this work. Perhaps I can squeeze a little time from my fraternal activities. But where does recreation fit in?'

Chet groped for the solution. 'Maybe I'm just rationalising because I schedule my own work poorly. But I don't think so. I've studied my work habits carefully and I think I plan intelligently and delegate authority. Do I need an assistant? Possibly, but that's a long-term project and I don't believe I could justify the additional overhead expenditure. Anyway, I doubt whether it would solve the problem.'

By this time Chet had turned off the highway onto the side street leading to his home — the problem still uppermost in his mind. 'I guess I really don't know the answer,' he told himself as he pulled into his driveway. 'This morning everything seemed so simple, but now ... ' His thoughts were interrupted as he saw his son running towards the car calling out, 'Mummy, Daddy's home.'

PART 3

Interpersonal influence AND group behaviour

7

Group behaviour

8

Intergroup behaviour and conflict

9

Alternative dispute resolution

10

Organisational power and politics

11

Leadership

*There must be, not a balance of power,
but a community of power ...*
— Woodrow Wilson *Address to the Senate (22 January 1917)*

GROUP BEHAVIOUR

Learning objectives

- Understand *that the term 'group' can be viewed from several different perspectives.*
- Identify *the elements in the process of group formation and development.*
- Compare *formal and informal groups.*
- Discuss *the reasons that people form groups.*
- Describe *two approaches to group development.*
- Describe *the process of group socialisation.*
- Discuss *the concepts of roles and norms.*
- Specify *factors affecting group performance.*

This chapter examines groups in organisations. The existence of groups in organisations can alter the individual's motivation or needs and influence the behaviour of individuals in an organisational setting. Organisational behaviour is more than simply the logical composite of the behaviour of individuals. It is not their sum or product but rather a much more complex phenomenon, a very important part of which is the group. The chapter provides a model for understanding the nature of groups in organisations. It explores the various types of groups, the reasons for their formation, their characteristics and some end results of group membership. The Organisational Encounter in this chapter describes how the concept of work groups has been implemented in Australian organisations; the Global Encounter considers how cultural factors might affect the problem-solving strategies of work groups.

THE NATURE OF GROUPS

Groups are a pervasive part of modern life. All of us have been — and are — members of many different groups. There are school groups, work groups, family groups, social groups and religious groups. There are small groups and large groups, permanent groups and temporary groups, and formal groups and informal groups. Some groups are successful, some are not. Some groups bring out the best in their members, some the worst. These are just a few of the many ways in which groups can be characterised.

One might think that since groups are so commonplace there would be a generally accepted definition of the term **group**. This is not the case. Indeed, there is a wide range of perspectives from which to view, and thus define, groups. Many behavioural scientists would, for example, see a group in terms of perceptions. That is, people who *perceive* themselves to be a group would, from this perspective, constitute a group. Some see a group in terms of organisational characteristics. From this perspective, a group is an *organised system* of individuals who are connected with one another. Still others may see groups in terms of motivation or need satisfaction. From this perspective, a group is a collection of individuals whose collective existence *satisfies needs*.

Each of these perspectives is legitimate. Each focuses on a different aspect of groups, and each leads to a somewhat different definition of what constitutes a group. The authors of this text also have a perspective on groups. Our perspective leads us to the following definition of groups, which we will use throughout this chapter:

Two or more individuals interacting with each other in order to accomplish a common goal.

One way of viewing this definition is to think of it in terms of specifying three minimum requirements that must be met for a group to exist. The first requirement deals with size. There must be *two or more individuals* for there to be a group. One person does not constitute a group. Note that in this definition, while there is a minimum size requirement, there is no maximum.

The second requirement specifies that there must be some form of exchange of communication between these individuals. That is, they must *interact with each other*, in some manner. We usually think of interaction between group members occurring in terms of a face-to-face verbal exchange but that does not have to be

Mark Betts and Gavin Clifford at Monash University recently surveyed twenty-four manufacturing organisations and eleven industry consultants about the implementation of work teams in the manufacturing industry. They found that the use of work teams ranged from highly informal arrangements, through to quality circles, semiautonomous work teams and self-managing work teams. According to their survey, work teams have the potential to increase productivity by 30% when they are well implemented. Their benefits include greater awareness of organisational goals, increased participation and communication, and improvements in occupational health and safety as well as quality and productivity. For senior management, the principal benefit of work teams is the diffusion of decision making across the organisation; this allows senior managers to focus on more long-term and strategic planning.

Best practice in teams

The NSW Mail Service is one example of how work teams improve company performance. The director of this service, John Carnegie, started team-building trials by establishing a team in each of two areas, Delivery and Service, and by helping teams to define simple performance criteria. As a result, since 1990, customer complaints have decreased by 65% and absenteeism has decreased by 75%. What is more, in 1993 the Service's profits rose to $1.5 million. These arrangements were formalised in a 1992 Enterprise Agreement in which all staff in these areas were offered the opportunity to form teams; on this basis, twelve new teams were established. In addition to these workplace teams, a self-managing management team, made up of middle managers, was created. Each manager coaches two or three of the newly established work teams; in turn, the managers have their own team coach. The role of the team coaches is to assist in the implementation of teams, including goal setting and training.

The team project is now being funded by the Australian Best Practice Demonstration Program, winning in the small- and medium-business section. In the first stage of this project, three areas are being considered by teams: goal setting, measurements of customer service and measurement of quality. The teams arrange their own meetings and are working through these issues at their own pace. At the end of this stage, the organisation will move on to developing performance, reward and remuneration systems.

Cross-functional teams

In the NSW Mail Service, team members were all part of the same work area. What happens when team members are brought together from different parts of the organisation with no goal other than to *improve company performance*? These teams, called cross-functional teams, may be given broad goals such as improving company performance or developing a new product; another reason for establishing cross-functional teams is to improve departmental performance by increasing a manager's understanding of the company as a whole. Cross-functional teams face several obstacles: since they are usually short term, individuals have little commitment to their goals; because they involve staff from different functional areas, stereotypes of those areas might make communication more difficult; goals that are framed in terms of benefits for the company may be less motivating; and diffuse goals without clear performance requirements may also reduce motivation. These are all points that need to be addressed for cross-functional teams to be effective.

Source: Work teams in Australian manufacturing organisations, *Benchmark*, 10, 1995; Team development best practice at State Mail Service, *Benchmark*, 11, 1995; Stickels, G. (1995). Personal goals add up to team achievement, *Business Review Weekly*, April 3.

the case. In nominal groups (discussed in Chapter 12), for example, the members might never speak with one another; their interactions are typically in writing. During a football game, the communication between a coach and a full forward may come only in the form of gestures, yet no one would suggest that there was no important interaction taking place. It is certainly true that you can have a collection of individuals who do not interact with one another. They are, however, just that: a collection of individuals, not a group.

The final requirement in our definition of groups is that of attempting to *accomplish a common goal.* If there is no common goal or purpose, there is no group by our definition. A common goal is a goal towards which individual members are willing to work for the benefit of the group. It is different from an individual goal that happens to be shared in common by a number of people. For example, everyone sitting in a medical practitioner's reception area may be waiting to see the doctor. Thus, seeing the doctor may be a goal that everyone in the room has in common, but that is decidedly different from it being a common goal of the group. Each person wants to see the doctor for his or her own individual purposes, not for a common group purpose. Thus, the people in the reception room area, even if they are interacting with each other, do not constitute a group by our definition.

For the most part, our central focus here is on *work groups.* In the context of our definition, the *two or more individuals* are usually employees and the *common goal* is a stated or implied work-related objective of the organisation. Increasingly, the work of organisations is accomplished through the efforts of groups or teams. Some organisational writers and researchers make a distinction between groups and teams. Because we have chosen to define groups in the manner that we have, we will use the two terms interchangeably throughout the remainder of this chapter and book. We will, however, conclude this chapter by taking a brief look at teams at work.

AN INTEGRATED MODEL OF GROUP FORMATION AND DEVELOPMENT

Although every group is different, possessing its own unique attributes and dynamics, it is also true that in many important ways groups tend to display similar patterns of evolution. Exhibit 7.1 presents a model of group formation and development that we will follow in this chapter in discussing this important organisational behaviour and management topic. The model suggests that the end results of group activity are shaped by a number of antecedent variables, each category of which we will examine in this chapter. Indeed, each segment of the model can (and, in reality, does) influence each of the other segments.

TYPES OF GROUPS

An organisation has technical requirements that arise from its stated goals. The accomplishment of these goals requires that certain tasks be performed and that employees be assigned to perform these tasks. As a result, most employees will be members of a group based on their position in the organisation. These are **formal groups**. On the other hand, whenever individuals associate on a fairly continuous basis, there is a tendency for groups to form whose activities may be different from those required by the organisation. These are **informal groups**. Both formal groups and informal groups, it will be shown, exhibit the same general characteristics.

Formal groups

The demands and processes of the organisation lead to the formation of different types of groups. Specifically, two types of formal groups exist: command and task.

Command group

The **command group** is specified by the organisation chart and is made up of the subordinates who report directly to a given supervisor. The authority relationship between a department manager and the supervisors, or between a senior nurse and her subordinates, is an example of a command group.

Task group

A **task group** comprises the employees who work together to complete a particular task or project. For example, the activities of clerks in an insurance company when an accident claim is filed are required tasks. These activities create a situation in which several clerks must communicate and coordinate with one another if the claim is to be handled properly. These acquired tasks and interactions facilitate the formation of a task group.[1] The nurses assigned to duty in the emergency room of a hospital usually constitute a task group since certain activities are required when a patient is treated.

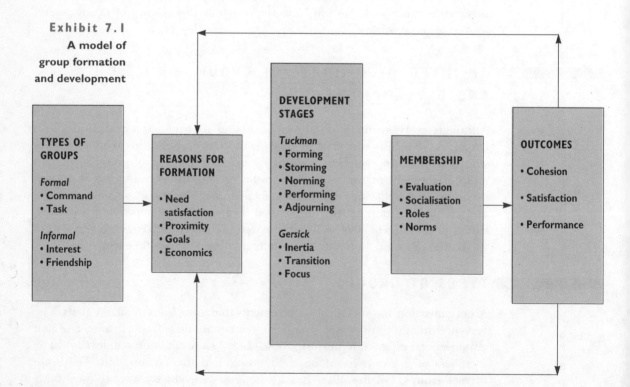

Exhibit 7.1
A model of group formation and development

Informal groups

Informal groups are natural groupings of people in the work situation in response to social needs. In other words, informal groups do not arise as a result of deliberate design. They evolve naturally. Two specific types of informal groups exist: interest and friendship.

Interest groups

Individuals who may not be members of the same command or task group may affiliate to achieve some mutual objective. Examples of **interest groups** include employees grouping together to present a unified front to management for more benefits and waiters 'pooling' their tips. Note that the objectives of such groups are not related to those of the organisation but are specific to each group.

Friendship groups

Many groups form because the members have something in common such as age, political beliefs or ethnic background. These **friendship groups** often extend their interaction and communication to off-the-job activities.

A distinction has been made between two broad classifications of groups—formal and informal. The major difference between them is that formal command and task groups are designated by the formal organisation as a means to an end. Informal interest and friendship groups are important for their own sake. They satisfy a basic human need for association. If employees' affiliation patterns were documented, it would become rapidly apparent that they belong to numerous and often overlapping groups. Why so many groups exist is the question to which we turn next.

JOINING GROUPS

People form groups for a number of reasons, and in joining groups individuals go through various processes.

Why people form groups

Formal and informal groups form for various reasons.[2] Some of the reasons involve needs, goals and economics.

The satisfaction of needs

One of the most compelling reasons that people join groups is because they believe membership in a particular group will help them satisfy one or more important needs. Typical employee needs that can be satisfied to a degree by the affiliation with groups include security, social and esteem needs.

Security needs may be partially met, for example, by membership in an employee group that acts as a buffer between employees and the organisational system. Without such a group, an individual may feel alone in facing management and organisational demands. This aloneness leads to a degree of insecurity which can be offset by group membership. *Social needs* can be satisfied through groups, because the group provides a vehicle for an individual to interact with others. Indeed, it is difficult to imagine being able to fulfil general social needs without participating in at least some groups. *Esteem needs* may be partially met by belonging to a high-status or prestige group, membership in which is difficult to obtain or is based on some noteworthy achievement. An example would be the million-dollar round table in the life insurance business. For people with high esteem needs, membership in such a group can provide much need satisfaction.

Group goals

A group's goals, if clearly understood, can be reasons for an individual to be attracted to it. For example, an individual may join a group that meets after work to become familiar with a new personal computer system. Assume that this system is to be implemented in the work organisation over the next 2 years. The person who voluntarily joins the after-hours group believes that learning the new system is a necessary and important goal for employees.

It is not always possible to identify group goals. The assumption that formal organisational groups have clear goals must be tempered by the understanding that perception, attitudes, personality and learning can distort goals. For example, a new employee may never be formally told the goals of the unit that he or she has joined. By observing the behaviour and attitudes of others, individuals may conclude what they believe the goals to be. These perceptions may or may not be accurate. The same can be said about the goals of informal groups.

Economic reasons

In many cases groups form because individuals believe they can derive greater economic benefits from their jobs if they organise. For example, individuals working at different points on an assembly line may be paid on a group-incentive basis where the production of the group determines the wages of each member. By working and cooperating as a group, the individual may obtain higher economic benefits.

In numerous other instances, economic motives lead to group formation: workers in non-union organisations form a group to exert pressure on top management for more benefits; top executives in a corporation form a group to review executive compensation. Whatever the circumstances, the group members have a common interest — increased economic benefits — that leads to group affiliation.

Becoming a member

In becoming group members, individuals go through three processes: evaluation, commitment and role transition.[3] *Evaluation* is a two-way process, and describes the assessment of costs and benefits that we believe will be obtained from group membership. As we have already discussed, we may join a group to meet one of several needs. To the extent that the group meets those needs, benefits accrue. However, we must also contribute to the group, so there are some costs associated with membership. For as long as the benefits outweigh the costs, we are willing to remain members of the group. Similarly, while a group expects us to meet some of its needs (provide the group with benefits) it too will incur certain costs (for example, we may want the group to change some of its procedures). So, while we evaluate the group and stay for as long as the benefits outweigh the costs, the group is prepared to keep us as members for as long as the benefits to the group outweigh the costs to the group. The second important process is to obtain *commitment*, both from an individual member to the group, and from the group to an individual member. Commitment is increased if members believe they have no alternative, or when they have invested a high level of resources. Groups recognise the importance of commitment, and some groups try to increase commitment through a series of initiation rights. Finally, group membership is achieved by a series of *role transitions*. Outsiders (individuals who do not belong to the group) are described as *non-members*; and those on the periphery of the group — because they are in the process of either joining or leaving — are described as quasi-members. *Full members* identify with the group, and they are committed to and invest energy in group membership. For individuals to be full members, this membership must be recognised by the group.[4]

TWO MODELS OF GROUP DEVELOPMENT

Groups learn just as individuals do. The performance of a group depends both on individual learning and on how well the members learn to work with one another. For example, a new product committee formed for the purpose of developing a response to a competitor may evolve into a very effective team, with the interests of the company being most important. However, it may also be very ineffective if its members are more concerned about their individual departmental goals than about developing a response to a competitor.

This section describes some general stages through which groups evolve and points out the development processes involved.[5] We compare two models that present different perspectives on the developmental process. In considering these models, we must bear in mind that both describe situations in which groups operate over a defined time span and in which membership is stable. This is rarely the case in organisations: in work teams, old members leave and new members join. This means that groups are continuously assimilating and accommodating to membership changes. In Tuckman's terms, this means that groups will spend a considerable amount of time drifting between storming and norming. Bear this in mind as you read through the next two sections. Ask yourself whether this means that, in organisations, groups never perform at their peak.

Tuckman's five-stage model

One widely cited model of group development assumes that groups proceed through as many as five stages of development: forming, storming, norming, performing and adjourning.[6] Although identifying the stage a group is in at a specific time can be difficult, it is nonetheless important to understand the development process. At each stage group behaviours differ and consequently each stage can influence the group's end results.

Forming

The first stage of group development is *forming* and it is characterised by uncertainty (and, frequently, confusion) about the purpose, structure and leadership of the group. Activities tend to focus on group members' efforts to understand and define their objectives, roles and assignments within the group. Patterns of interaction among group members are tried out and either discarded or adopted, at least temporarily. The more diverse the group is, the more difficult it is to manoeuvre through this stage and the longer it takes. That is why this is a particularly sensitive stage in the formation of multicultural groups. Generally, this stage is complete when individuals begin to view themselves as part of a group.

Storming

The *storming* stage of group development tends to be marked by conflict and confrontation. This generally emotionally intense stage may involve competition among members for desired assignments and disagreements over appropriate task-related behaviours and responsibilities. A particularly important part of storming can involve redefinition of the groups' specific tasks and overall goals.

Individually, group members are likely to begin to decide the extent to which they like the group tasks and their degree of commitment to them. While members may accept the group at one level, at another level there may be resistance to the control the group imposes on them. Some group members may begin to withdraw during storming, making this stage a particularly critical one for group survival and effectiveness. It is essential that the conflict that typifies storming be managed, as opposed to being suppressed. Suppression of conflict at this point is likely to create negative effects that can seriously hinder group functioning in later stages.

Norming

While storming is marked by conflict and confrontation, *norming* is characterised by cooperation and collaboration. It is also the stage where group cohesion begins significant development. There tends to be an open exchange of information, acceptance of differences of opinion and active attempts to achieve mutually agreed upon goals and objectives. There is a strong degree of mutual attraction and commitment, and feelings of group identity and camaraderie. Behavioural norms are established and accepted by the completion of this stage, as are leadership and other roles in the group. The specific important impact of norms on group functioning is addressed in a subsequent section on group characteristics.

Performing

The fourth, and what may be the final stage, is performing. *Performing* is that stage where the group is fully functional. The group structure is set, and the roles of each member are understood and accepted. The group focuses its energies, efforts and commitments on accomplishing the tasks it has accepted.

For some groups, this stage marks the attainment of a level of effectiveness that will remain more or less constant. For others, the process of learning and development will be ongoing so that group effectiveness and efficiency continue. In the former case, group performance will be maintained at a level sufficient to ensure survival; in the latter case, the group will record increasingly higher levels of achievement. Which way any particular group will go will depend on a number of variables, particularly how successfully the group completed earlier development stages.

Adjourning

The *adjourning* stage involves the termination of group activities. Many groups, of course, are permanent and never reach the adjourning stage. For temporary groups, however, such as committees, project groups, task forces and similar entities, this stage includes disbandment. Customary task activities are complete and the group focuses on achieving closure. This stage can be marked by very positive emotions centring on successful task accomplishment and achievement. It may also be a source of feelings of loss, disappointment or even anger. The latter may be especially true in the case of permanent groups which fail to survive because of organisational downsizing or bankruptcy.

Gersick's Punctuated Equilibrium Model

Can we use Tuckman's model of group development to understand how groups in organisations form and develop? There are several reasons for thinking that organisational groups may develop differently:[7]

- Short versus long-term focus needs to be considered. Tuckman's model makes it clear that it takes time for groups to function effectively and so provides a useful framework for understanding work teams. However, organisations frequently create short-term groups to work on specific projects. We need to ask whether these groups move through the same phases more quickly, whether they fail to reach the performing stage, or whether they behave differently from long-term groups.
- Organisations provide a much stronger context for groups than was provided for Tuckman's groups. In organisations, groups have rules, information, procedures and guidelines for performing tasks. This means that they do not need to invest time and energy in defining roles, establishing norms, gathering information and developing strategies.
- Most importantly, Tuckman's model does not recognise that most groups are affected by their environment.

It is this last point that has led researchers to suggest that Tuckman's model provides us with no insight about what critical events move a group through the stages, or how long a group may remain in any given stage. Because it ignores the impact that the external environment might have on group development, critics argue that the traditional model is inappropriate for studying groups in organisations.[8] One alternative is provided by Gersick's Punctuated Equilibrium Model.

The Punctuated Equilibrium Model of group development resulted from the study of naturally occurring project groups. By analysing how project teams talked to each other, their performance strategies, relationships between group members and reference to individuals outside the group, Gersick was able to demonstrate a very different pattern of group development. She found that the working life of a group could be divided into two phases, separated at the midpoint of the group's life span by a sharp transition in approaches to work.[9] What is especially interesting is that the transition always occurs at the group's *temporal* midpoint: if the group has 4 weeks to complete the task, the transition occurs after 2 weeks; if the group has 4 months to complete the task, the transition occurs after 2 months, and so on. Simply put, according to this model groups engage in relatively unfocused activity for the first half of their lives and make little progress on their tasks; at the midpoint, they rapidly select a strategy, which is then implemented in the second half of the life cycle. These phases and their key characteristics are described below.

Phase 1: Inertia

During this phase, groups engage in relatively unfocused activity. Group roles and norms are frequently determined by the end of the group's first meeting and these dominate the first half of the group's life. Early in this phase, groups clarify assumptions and define people external to the group who are interested in the outcomes. In this phase the task is defined, strategies for task completion are developed and task-relevant information is collected but, importantly, this is done by relying solely on the resources of group members. Groups do not consider the needs of individuals outside the group, nor do they seek resources from those individuals. The inertia phase is characterised by a rapid definition of the limits of their problem and a focus on a narrow range of alternative approaches.

Midpoint transition

The *transition point* comes halfway through the group's life: progress is evaluated critically and new goals are set. Teams become very conscious of time and also start to look outwards, testing how acceptable solutions will be to other people — especially those who set the task. Finally, during transition, groups agree on specific new plans for how they will tackle the task in Phase 2. During this phase, groups are not at all concerned with interactional problems. As a result, if interpersonal problems are not resolved at the transition point, they worsen considerably in the next phase.

Phase 2: Redirection

In this phase, groups become very task-focused and put into action the plans they develop during the transition period. Like Phase 1, however, once this new course of action has been decided on, groups work on implementing this course of action; there is no further attempt to evaluate the strategy and no new ideas or strategies are introduced.

GROUP ROLES AND NORMS

To become a member of a group and to ensure group survival, it is vital that members understand and conform with group roles and norms. As we will see in the final sections, group norms are critical to the quality of group performance: high performance is evident only when norms encourage excellence. In this section, we consider how roles and norms are learned, before turning to a more detailed discussion of these concepts.

Group socialisation

Socialisation describes the process through which group members learn their roles and the norms of the group. It is, therefore, central to group performance. In this section we describe briefly the process of socialisation. We will look at this process more closely in Chapter 14. There are five stages in the socialisation process: investigation, socialisation, maintenance, resocialisation and remembrance.[10] Of these, we are most concerned with the socialisation and maintenance stages, because it is here that roles and norms are learned.

Before joining a group, individuals engage in a period of *investigation*. Potential members undertake a preliminary investigation of several groups to determine which best suits their needs. In doing so, they try to make sure that the benefits of belonging to a particular group will outweigh the costs. Reciprocally, groups evaluate and weigh up the costs and benefits of potential new recruits. Entry into the group occurs when a group is willing to accept a new member, and the new member wishes to join the group.

In the next stage of *socialisation*, both newcomers and old members must make some adjustments. Newcomers must assimilate (or learn) the group's norms and values, while the group must accommodate (or adapt) the new member's needs. This point has received considerable attention, especially in terms of organisational socialisation. Information is critical to newcomers in this stage, and the socialisation process takes longer when newcomers do not interact with older members of the group, or when older members do not interact with newcomers. The exchange of information is critical to learning roles and norms, and without this information newcomers may not be accepted into the group. Acceptance defines the transition point into the next stage of socialisation.

Because group membership is dynamic, socialisation is an ongoing process In the *maintenance* stage, groups pass through the processes of assimilation and accommodation whenever group membership changes. This means that there is always potential for individual roles within the group to change, and the maintenance period is characterised by role negotiation: efforts to agree on the specific contributions of each member. Problems arise when a member is unwilling to accept a role imposed by the group, or when the member fails to meet group expectations. This may result in transition to the next phase through divergence (a point at which the group and individual cannot reach agreement about the individual's role).

Divergence may be triggered when an individual perceives the costs of group membership to outweigh its benefits, or when the group decides that the costs of maintaining an individual outweigh the contributions that the person is making to the group. Once the point of divergence is reached, individuals have two alternatives. The group may go through a stage of *resocialisation* in which differences are again resolved through assimilation and accommodation. If this occurs, the individual remains a member of the group.

However, if it is not possible to resolve differences, the member will leave. This marks transition into the final stage: *remembrance*. This phase is used to construct a shared story about the individual's time with the group, his or her experiences and the contributions made. Both the individual and the group weigh up what they gained and lost. When the individual and the group agree on this, their story enters into the group's history.

Group roles

Each position in the group structure has an associated role that consists of the behaviours expected of the occupant of that position.[11] For example, the director of nursing services in a hospital is expected to organise and control the department of nursing. The director is also expected to assist in preparing and administering the budget for the department. A nursing supervisor, on the other hand, is expected to supervise the activities of nursing personnel engaged in specific nursing services such as obstetrics, paediatrics and surgery. These expected behaviours generally are agreed on not only by the occupants, the director of nursing and the nursing supervisor, but also by other members of the nursing group and other hospital personnel.

In addition to an *expected role* are also a perceived role and an enacted role. The *perceived role* is the set of behaviours that a person in a position believes he or she should enact. As we discussed in Chapter 3, perception can, in some instances, be distorted or inaccurate. The *enacted role*, on the other hand, is the behaviour that a person actually carries out. Thus, three possible role behaviours can result. Conflict and frustration may arise from differences in these three role types. In fairly stable or permanent groups, there is typically a good agreement between expected and perceived roles. When the enacted role deviates too much from the expected role, the person either can become more like the expected role or leave the group.

Through membership in different groups, individuals perform multiple roles. For example, first-line supervisors are members of a management team but are also members of the group of workers that they supervise. These multiple roles result in a number of expected role behaviours. In many cases, the behaviours specified by the different roles are compatible. When they are not, however, the individual may experience role conflict. In the case of first-line supervisors, for example, top management has a set of expectations that stresses the supervisor's role in the management group. However, the supervisor is part of the group that she is supervising and may have close friendship ties with other members of the group who may be former working peers.[12] Similarly, a scientist in a chemical plant who is also a member of a management group might experience role conflict. In such a situation, the scientist may be expected to behave in accordance with the expectations of management as well as the expectations of professional chemists. A physician placed in the role of hospital administrator may also experience this type of role conflict. Sometimes, the conflict is between the individual's role as a work group member on the one hand and a member of the larger organisational group on the other.

Group norms

Norms are the standards shared by members of a group, and they have certain characteristics that are important to group members. First, norms are formed only with respect to things that have significance for the group. They may be written, but very often they can be verbally communicated to members. In many cases they may never be formally stated but somehow are known by group members. If production is important, then a norm will evolve. If helping other group members complete a task is important, then a norm will develop.

Conversely, if these are not important concerns to the group, no standards for appropriate behaviour in these areas will evolve; group members will feel free to behave in whatever manner seems reasonable to them.

Second, norms are accepted in various degrees by group members. Some norms are completely accepted by all members while other norms are only partially accepted. Third, norms may apply to every group member or they may apply to only some group members. For example, every member may be expected to comply with the production norm, while only group leaders may be permitted to disagree verbally with a management directive.

Groups develop norms for regulating many different aspects of their members' behaviour.[13] In work groups, however, the most common norm relates to productivity and group productivity norms specify production behaviour. It is important to understand that the group's perception of what is an acceptable level of production may be significantly different from management's perception. The group's production norm may differ from management's for a number of reasons including a fear of rate cutting if production is too high or a fear of reprisal if production falls too low.

Exhibit 7.2 illustrates where a group's production norm might fall on a productivity continuum. The zone of acceptance depicted in the exhibit represents minor deviations above and below the group's norm which would be deemed acceptable to the group. Group members greatly exceeding the norm might be referred to as 'rate-busters', while those producing well below group expectations might be known as 'chisellers'.

There are four ways in which norms can develop.[14] It may be that they emerge over time, as a stable pattern of behaviour that is accepted by the group. There are times when we learn group norms because they are explicitly stated; for example, we may be told on our first day in the office that 'we are expected to wear suits to work'. A third means by which norms develop is as a response to a critical and negative event in the group's history. Something happens while the group is together which has negative consequences for the group; the group establishes a norm to prevent the same consequences from occurring again. Finally, we may carry task-knowledge or professional norms from situation to situation, allowing them to govern our behaviour no matter what organisation we are in. This is especially likely to be the case if we have a professional code of conduct to govern our behaviour.

Exhibit 7.2
Hypothetical production norm and its zone of acceptance

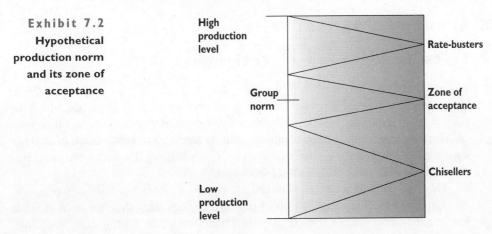

Norm conformity

An issue of concern to managers is why employees conform to group norms.[15] This issue is especially important when a person with skill and capability is performing significantly below his or her capacity so that group norms are not violated. A number of variables may influence conformity to group norms. The *personal characteristics* of the individual play a role. For example, research indicates that people with high intelligence are less likely to conform than less intelligent individuals, and authoritarian personality types conform more than non-authoritarians.[16] *Situational factors* such as group size and structure may influence conformity. For example, conformity may become more difficult in larger groups or in those groups whose members are geographically separated. *Intergroup relationships*, which include such factors as the kind of pressure the group exerts and the degree to which the member identifies with the group, are another potentially important variable.

The degree of conformity with group norms may also be influenced by cultural factors. Some cultures with a more collective tradition may place greater emphasis on the group and on conformity with norms, than might cultures with a more individualistic orientation. Typical examples of these two orientations are Japan and the United States. Groups have traditionally played a far greater role in Japanese society than in American. Consequently, conformity to group norms is given greater emphasis in Japanese organisations.

Potential consequences of conforming to group norms

The research on conformity distinctly implies that conformity is a requirement of sustained group membership. The member who does not conform to important norms is often punished by a group such as by being isolated or ignored. Conformity has some potential negative and positive consequences. On the negative side, conformity can result in a loss of individuality and the establishment of only moderate levels of performance. This type of behaviour can be costly to an organisation that needs above-average levels of performance to remain competitive. Positive consequences can also occur from conformity to group norms. If no conformity existed, a manager would have a difficult, if not impossible, time in predicting a group's behaviour patterns. This inability to estimate behaviour could result in unsuccessful managerial attempts to channel the group's efforts toward the accomplishment of organisational goals.

GROUP PERFORMANCE

Criteria of group effectiveness

Exercise 7
What to do with
Johnny Rocco

Groups exist to accomplish objectives. In the case of work groups, those objectives are generally related to the performance of specific tasks, which in turn are designed to result in attainment of formal organisational outcomes. Measurable production (e.g. number of units assembled, percentage of market captured or number of customers served) is perhaps the most obvious, but certainly not the only, end result of work group activities.

One of the attractive attributes of groups is their potential synergism. *Synergism* is the cooperative action of discrete entities such that the total effect is greater than the sum of the effects taken independently. In the case of groups, discrete entities are individual members of the group. Synergistic groups can create something that is more than the sum total of that produced by individuals. Thus,

$$\text{Potential group performance} = \text{Individual performance} + \text{Synergy}$$

Actual performance, however, may be different. Actual group performance may be expressed by the following equation:

$$\text{Actual group performance} = \text{Potential performance} - \text{Faulty group process}$$

What this suggests is that synergistic gains from groups may be offset by operating failures within the group. If there is intragroup conflict, communication breakdowns, insufficient interaction, political manoeuvring, lack of role clarity, poor decision making, inept leadership or any number of other counterproductive conditions, group performance will most likely be negatively affected. No groups operate smoothly and efficiently all the time. Ensuring that instances of faulty process are minimised is a constant, and extremely critical, challenge for managers and group members alike.

While some form of production output (goods, services, ideas and so on) is typically an important measure of group performance and effectiveness, it is not the only consideration. Organisational researcher Richard Hackman identifies three important criteria of group effectiveness.[17]

1. The extent to which the group's productive output meets the standard of quantity, quality and timeliness of the users of the output is one criterion. For example, a group which produced a product that was unacceptable to a customer could not be considered effective no matter what the group or others thought about the product.

2. The extent to which the group process of actually doing the work enhances the capability of group members to work together interdependently in the future is another criterion. This suggests that even though the group might produce a product that meets the standards mentioned in the first criterion, the group is not effective if that end result was obtained in a manner destructive to future working relationships. The fact that a group is a temporary one, such as a task force or project team, does not negate the importance of this criterion of effectiveness.

3. The third criterion is the extent to which the group experience contributes to the growth and wellbeing of its members. This criterion relates to the end results of development and satisfaction which were specified in Exhibit 7.1. Note that it is not necessary for a group to have member development and satisfaction as a stated objective for this to be a legitimate test of group effectiveness. When group participation does not contribute to personal or professional development and/or does not lead to any personal need satisfaction, this may have negative consequences. It suggests group productivity may not continue over an extended period of time and it may have implications for the quality of group members' participation in subsequent groups.

The principal task, for groups, is to convert group resources (such as members' skills) into tangible outcomes. To the extent that this can be achieved efficiently, group performance should be enhanced. There are, however, several external constraints that might determine how well groups transform resources into performance: resource availability, leadership style and the type of task that individuals are engaged in. Because process losses are due to poor coordination, the type of task that a group is engaged in becomes a critical moderator of the input–output relationship.

Tasks can be of three types: additive, disjunctive and conjunctive. In *additive tasks*, the individual efforts of each group member add up to give total group performance. Examples of such tasks include fruit picking and packing boxes. The critical issue for group performance, in additive tasks, is to ensure that each member works at his or her maximum ability. We will discuss how this might be achieved shortly. *Disjunctive tasks* differ in that group performance is determined by the performance of any one individual: an example of this might be problem solving, where any individual can find the correct solution. In this type of task, the critical issue for group performance is the ability to identify the individual member best able to solve the problem; we will return to this issue in Chapter 12, when we discuss group decision making. Finally, *conjunctive tasks* require all members to work together successfully for the group to succeed. An obvious example of a conjunctive task is any team sport: a football team can win only if the efforts of all the members are coordinated.[18]

Process losses

Process losses refer to the finding that a group's performance is always less than the best possible performance. This can be attributed to poor communication, an inability to correctly identify individual members' resources, and motivational problems such as *free riding* or *social loafing*.[19] In this section, we will consider the phenomenon of social loafing.

Social loafing

Social loafing describes the finding that individuals reduce their effort when they work in groups. Research over several decades has shown that as group size increases, individual output decreases. Three explanations have been given for this effect: output equity, evaluation apprehension and matching to standards.[20]

1. *Output equity.* When we are in a group, we expect others to do less than their fair share. So, to avoid putting in more effort than other group members, we reduce our own level of effort. When everyone thinks this way, we find that groups perform well below their potential. To deal with this, we can provide clear norms for performance.

2. *Evaluation apprehension.* Perhaps people loaf because they are bored. If a task is uninteresting, why put effort into it? One reason is that others would know we are being lazy. However, a group provides the perfect cover. If, for example, a manager is concerned with group output she may not notice that one member of that group is putting in less effort than the other members. To

deal with this situation, managers can remove anonymity so that everyone's contribution is identifiable; another strategy would be to make the tasks themselves more interesting.

3. *Matching to standards.* Standards provide individuals with goals that will motivate performance. If standards are absent, individuals will have less incentive to perform. Consequently, loafing can be reduced by making individual and group goals salient.

In a study of salespeople, George[21] found that task visibility (the extent to which a supervisor could observe you working) was the best predictor of social loafing; however, the relationship between social loafing and task visibility was influenced by the perceived meaningfulness of the task, as well as beliefs about the contribution that an individual made to the organisation.

According to George, there are several strategies that can be used to overcome social loafing:

- *Making each person's contribution identifiable.* Posting information about individual performance results in higher levels of performance than posting information about group performance.
- *Making work more involving.* If people enjoy what they are doing and believe that it is important, fewer are likely to loaf.
- *Rewarding individuals for their contributions to the group.* Reward not just a person's performance but also the extent to which a person helps the group or other members in the group to perform well.
- *Threatening punishment.* Threatening to punish individuals for low levels of group performance can also increase the pressure on an individual to maintain a higher performance standard.[22]

Group cohesion

Formal and informal groups seem to possess a closeness or commonness of attitude, behaviour and performance. This closeness has been referred to as *cohesiveness.* Cohesiveness is typically regarded as a force. It acts on the members to remain in a group and is greater than the forces pulling the members away from the group. A cohesive group, then, involves individuals who are attracted to one another. A group that is low in cohesiveness does not possess interpersonal attractiveness for the members.

Since highly cohesive groups are composed of individuals who are motivated to be together, there is a tendency on the part of management to expect effective group performance. This logic is not conclusively supported by research. In general, as cohesiveness increases, the level of conformity to group norms also increases. But these norms may be inconsistent with those of the organisation. The group pressures to conform are more intense in cohesive groups.

Cohesiveness and performance

The concept of cohesiveness is important for understanding groups in organisations, as is the recognition of the impact of groups on performance.[23] An underlying theme in the discussion of roles and norms is the idea of group cohesiveness: the extent to which group members have a positive attitude towards the group and are strongly attracted to it, and the extent to which they want to belong to the group. Cohesiveness can be established in a number of ways: when a task requires a high level of interaction; when the group has a history of successful task completion; when group members are similar; when initiation into the group has been severe; and, lastly, when groups can perceive a common goal or a common threat or enemy. Our concern here is whether highly cohesive groups are more productive. Can we expect higher performance levels from closely knit groups?

Let's start by considering the factors that influence group cohesion: personal attraction, commitment to the group and group pride. To understand how group cohesiveness influences performance, we need to understand what each of these factors contributes to cohesion. We must ask whether attraction, commitment and pride are all equally important in creating cohesion, or whether one of these factors is dominant. When we can answer these questions, we will be better able to develop strategies for increasing the cohesion–performance relationship. For example, if *interpersonal attraction* dominates the cohesiveness–performance relationship, then strategies that increase group member liking should also increase group performance; if, however, *commitment* is more important, then organisations can increase group performance by ensuring that tasks are enjoyable; and if *group pride* is central to the cohesiveness–performance relationship, then strategies that increase identification with the group will best serve this purpose. Although each of these strategies may be beneficial, research shows us that group commitment, rather than interpersonal attraction or group pride, is critical to the cohesiveness–performance relationship.[24] Underlying the effects of task commitment, we find a norm of excellence. In summarising research in this area, we find that cohesion enhances performance to the extent that standards of excellence are salient for a group; and to the extent that the pursuit of excellence is relevant for the group, as a whole, the link between group cohesiveness and performance will be strengthened.[25] Therefore, organisations wishing to strengthen this relationship must develop strategies for increasing commitment to the task.

A final point for us to consider is that the degree of cohesiveness in a group can have positive or negative effects, depending on how group goals match up with those of the formal organisation.[26] In fact, four distinct possibilities exist, as

Exhibit 7.3
The relationship between group cohesiveness and agreement with organisational goals

		AGREEMENT WITH ORGANISATIONAL GOALS	
		Low	High
DEGREE of GROUP COHESIVENESS	Low	Performance probably oriented away from organisational goals	Performance probably oriented towards achievement of organisational goals
	High	Performance oriented away from organisational goals	Performance oriented towards achievement of organisational goals.

illustrated in Exhibit 7.3. Exhibit 7.3 indicates that if cohesiveness is high and the group accepts and agrees with formal organisational goals, then group behaviour will probably be positive from the formal organisation's standpoint. However, if the group is highly cohesive but has goals that are not congruent with those of the formal organisation, then group behaviour will probably be negative from the formal organisation's standpoint. Exhibit 7.3 also indicates that if a group is low in cohesiveness and the members have goals that are not in agreement with those of management, then the results will probably be negative from the standpoint of the organisation.

TEAMS AT WORK

Although, at the start of this chapter, we suggested that the concepts of groups and teams were interchangeable, in this section we take a closer look at the ways in which teams might differ from groups. Organisations have implemented the team idea in many ways: quality circles and autonomous work groups are two examples. We will consider autonomous work groups in Chapter 16. For the moment, the Local Encounter in this chapter describes research comparing autonomous with traditional work groups. The Global Encounter takes a closer look at whether there are cultural differences in how teams resolve their problems.

Team characteristics

Teams are a special example of groups, characterised by cohesion and high levels of performance. According to Katzenbach and Smith[27], a team is *a small number of people with complementary skills who are committed to a common purpose, performance goals, and approach for which they hold themselves mutually accountable.*

This definition identifies several core characteristics of teams: size, complementary skills, performance goals, commitment to a common purpose and mutual accountability. If you compare this with our definition of groups, you will see that while there is some overlap there are also important differences. We will take a closer look at these differences now.

Complementary skills

It is important that team members offer different skills to the team: If skills are homogeneous, the benefits of working in a group are lost. According to Katzenbach and Smith, teams require three sets of skills: technical, problem solving and decision making, and interpersonal. Successful teams will have complementary technical skills: for example, product development groups will benefit if they have both marketing experts and engineers as members. Perhaps even more important are the interpersonal skills of team members, which again must provide a balance of task- and relationship-focus. Bolman and Deal,[28] in their analysis of a highly successful team at Data General, identified diversity as critical to team success. Creativity in one member was balanced by technical detail-orientation in another; and the aloofness of one was balanced by the warmth and approachability of another. In this case study, it also became clear that balancing humour with seriousness was critical to effectiveness. It not only enabled team members to relax, but also fostered cohesion.

LOCAL

Encounter

Autonomous work groups in Australia

Do different styles of work team organisation affect such organisational outcomes as job satisfaction, organisational commitment and trust in management? To answer this question, John Cordery and his co-workers compared two styles of work group organisation in a mineral-processing plant. By using the implementation of work teams in a new processing plant, they were able to compare these newly formed semiautonomous work groups with more traditional work groups in the same and an older plant.

The semiautonomous work teams differed from traditional teams in several ways: they were given responsibility for allocating work, setting priorities, planning work flow and selecting new members. In addition, the work teams were multiskilled, enabling job rotation. Cordery and his co-workers compared the effects of work organisation on both individual and organisational outcomes. They asked whether this type of work design affected perceptions of the job, perceived autonomy, satisfaction with such things as pay (extrinsic satisfaction) and the job itself (intrinsic satisfaction), organisational commitment, absenteeism and turnover.

For individuals, the benefits of working in a semiautonomous team were clear and positive. Members of autonomous work groups reported that their jobs contained more of the job characteristics that we have identified as increasing intrinsic motivation. Perhaps not surprisingly, they also reported higher intrinsic and extrinsic satisfaction, organisational commitment and trust in management.

From the organisation's perspective, however, results were not as positive. Members of the semiautonomous work teams showed higher levels of absenteeism and turnover. What factors contributed to this behaviour? An obvious answer is that the norms in semiautonomous work groups encouraged this organisationally negative behaviour. However, in this case, the authors note that a large proportion of turnover in these groups resulted from promotions. This suggests that an added advantage for individuals — if not the organisation — is an enlarged range of skills and improved career options.

Source: Cordery, J. L., Mueller, W. S., & Smith, L. M. (1991). Attitudinal and behavioural effects of autonomous group working: A longitudinal field study, *Academy of Management Journal*, **34**, 464–476.

Commitment to a common purpose and approach

As we saw in our definition of a group, teams must have a common goal that cannot be achieved by any individual. Team members must develop a shared meaning of the team's purpose, and must also be able to translate that shared understanding into specific performance goals. Even more importantly, team members must be committed to a common approach: they must agree on just how the team will achieve its goals. As a part of this common approach, work is not delegated. Everyone — including the team leader — does an equal amount of work, contributing to the team's performance. Again, this was evident in Bolman and Deal's case analysis: there were very few rules, and little by way of formal leadership to guide group behaviour. To achieve this requires that individuals and the team understand the strengths and weaknesses of each member and are able to determine how each member can best contribute to the overall purpose of the team.

Mutual accountability

Mutual accountability is perhaps the most important factor that sets teams apart from groups. That is, team members hold themselves accountable to the group, and the team holds itself accountable for its performance. The focus is on what the team, not the individual, can achieve.

MANAGEMENT   Encounter

Teams at work

In our discussion of teams, we identified three factors that set teams apart from groups: commitment and common purpose, mutual accountability and diversity in skills. What implications do these ideas have for the way in which we develop and manage teams?

Commitment and common purpose are central to effective teamwork. Such common purpose may be demonstrated in the development of a common language, as was the case in Bolman and Deal's group. This shared vision, according to Katzenbach and Smith, evolves as individuals discover the range of skills held by group members and determine how individuals will contribute to the team. This means that communication is critical to team performance. Understanding what is meant by 'teamwork' is essential to team performance. According to Rentsch, Heffner and Duffy, experienced and inexperienced teams have a very different understanding of the teamwork concept: experienced teams are much better able to identify the key factors for effective team performance. One implication of this finding is that experienced and inexperienced team members require different types of training: inexperienced team members require more concrete examples of the skills necessary for effective teamwork.

Teams are characterised by mutual accountability and shared roles: self-managing work teams are required to make decisions normally made by managers. Because roles in teams are less well-defined than in work groups, the quality of communication becomes important. Research shows that self-managing teams and traditional work groups differ in several ways: decisions in self-managing teams are more likely to be made by consensus, and cohesiveness, communication and co-worker satisfaction are all higher, as is overall satisfaction. Can we explain these higher levels of communication in terms of the increased cohesion and satisfaction with co-workers? Did people talk more because they got on better? The answer is no: the higher levels of communication in self-managing teams represent a special phenomenon unique to team work. More importantly, the higher level of communication resulted in greater efficiency, as did increased cohesiveness. Overall satisfaction was associated with reduced absenteeism, suggesting that organisations can reap benefits from self-managing work teams.

Reduced absenteeism and increased satisfaction can be obtained in many ways. However, effective teams foster innovation. The team described by Bolman and Deal produced a new, state-of-the-art computer well ahead of any other group in the organisation. According to research by Burningham and West, innovation will occur when teams have shared vision, offer a safe environment for trying out new ideas, have a shared commitment to excellence, and are characterised by norms that support innovation.

Source: Burningham, C., & West, M. A. (1995). Individual, climate, and group interaction processes as predictors of work team innovation, *Small Group Research, 26,* 106–117; Rentsch, J. R., Heffner, T. S., & Duffy, L. T. (1994). What you get is what you know from experience: Team experience related to teamwork schemata, *Group and Organisation Management, 19,* 450–474; Seers, A., Petty, M. M., & Cashman, J. F. (1995). Team member exchange under team and traditional management: A naturally occurring quasi-experiment, *Group and Organisation Management, 20,* 18–38.

Team effectiveness

Organisational context and team development are important factors in team effectiveness[29]. *Organisational context* is important in creating the right atmosphere for team development and functioning. We therefore need to ask whether the organisational culture values autonomy; whether teams are an appropriate form of organisation given the tasks that they must complete; whether they are clear in their goals; whether leaders adopt a style that reinforces autonomy; whether rewards are offered to individuals or the group; and whether the organisation has provided appropriate training in terms of the skills necessary for team work.

Team development is also important. Effective teams must manage interpersonal processes, and provide clear goals and roles, as well as develop problem-solving abilities. Bolman and Deal's analysis suggests that the development of roles and norms —in the process of becoming a team member — is critical to team effectiveness. According to these authors, effective teams develop a high level of cohesiveness. This is maintained through the use of words and phrases that have meaning only for group members; by stories that emphasise team values; and through the use of rituals and ceremonies to ensure that core values are maintained.

GLOBAL   Encounter

Work teams in Japan, Britain and the USA

How do individuals interpret and respond to problems in the workplace? Where do they turn for information? How does this affect organisational performance? Recent research examined how work teams in three countries resolve day-to-day problems and how this affects their performance. An important question posed by this research was whether work teams doing similar work use similar processes (culture-free management) or whether their choice of strategies is somehow determined by their cultural background (culture-specific management). Specifically, this research examined whether reliance on manuals, supervisors and past experience to solve problems could be linked to perceptions of productivity, quality and cooperation and also whether these relationships differed across three countries: Japan, Britain and the USA.

According to Japanese supervisors: work teams are more productive when they use company manuals to resolve unfamiliar problems; they are perceived as more cooperative if they use company manuals to

resolve day-to-day problems; and their work quality is rated as higher when they seek a supervisor's advice to resolve unfamiliar problems. Like Japanese managers, US managers distinguished between familiar and unfamiliar events: work teams were rated as more productive when they used company manuals to resolve unfamiliar problems but as unproductive when the same strategy was applied to day-to-day problems. In contrast to these groups, British supervisors rated work teams as highly cooperative when they avoided using manuals for unfamiliar problems; however, for day-to-day problems the use of manuals and supervisors' advice increased perceived cooperation.

These results show not only that there are differences in the strategies that work teams employ to resolve work-related problems but also that there are cultural differences in the links between strategies and management perception of work team productivity, work quality and cooperation.

Source: Smith, P. B., Peterson, M. F., & Misumi, J. (1994). Event management and work team effectiveness in Japan, Britain and USA, *Journal of Occupational and Organizational Psychology,* **67**, 33–43.

SUMMARY OF KEY POINTS

Understand that the term 'group' can be viewed from several different perspectives. The term 'group' can be viewed from many different perspectives. A group can be thought of in terms of perception, organisation, motivation, interaction or any combination of these. For our purposes a group may be thought of as two or more individuals interacting with each other in order to accomplish a common goal.

Identify the elements in the process of group formation and development. The model of the process of group formation and development presented in the chapter has a number of elements. These include the different types of groups, the reasons that groups are formed, stages in group development, important characteristics of groups and end results of group activity.

Compare formal and informal groups. Formal groups are created to facilitate the accomplishment of an organisation's goal. Command groups, specified by the organisation chart, and task groups, comprised of employees working together to complete a specific project, are two types of formal groups. Informal groups are associations of individuals in the work situation in response to social needs. Interest groups and friendship groups are two types of informal groups.

Discuss the reasons that people form groups. Formal and informal groups exist for a number of reasons. Need satisfaction may be a compelling reason to join a group. Security, social and esteem needs are typical examples. That is, people may form groups because their physical location encourages interaction and they enjoy such interaction. People may also form groups to facilitate the accomplishment of common goals. Finally, some groups form because individuals believe they can derive economic benefits from group membership.

Describe two approaches to group development. The traditional view of groups states that as they form and develop, they tend to go through several sequential stages. These stages are forming, characterised by uncertainty and confusion; storming, marked by conflict and confrontation; norming, where group cohesion begins significant development; performing, where the group becomes fully functional; and for some groups adjourning, which involves the termination of group activities. Gersick's Punctuated Equilibrium Model provides an alternative view. According to this model, groups go through three stages. In the first stage of inertia, they are very task-focused and concerned with obtaining information relevant to the task. The second stage, the transition point, comes at the midpoint of a group's life and acts as a trigger for selecting one strategy. In the final stage, this strategy is implemented.

Describe the process of group socialisation. Before joining groups, individuals investigate groups to determine the costs and benefits of membership. Once they have joined, they must assimilate existing norms while old members must accommodate new members' values. In the central stage of socialisation, roles are defined and negotiated. If there is disagreement over individuals' roles, they may need to be renegotiated. If this is done successfully, group members stay with the group; if it is unsuccessful, members leave.

Discuss group roles and norms. The concept of role is vital to an understanding of group behaviour. A role is the expected behaviour patterns attributed to a particular position. Most individuals perform multiple roles, each with its own role set (expectations of others for the role). An individual involved in many different roles, each having a complex role set, faces the ultimate in complexity of individual behaviour. Norms provide rules for defining acceptable behaviour in groups and increasing the predicability of behaviour. They ensure group survival and are taught during the socialisation process.

Specify factors affecting group performance. Faulty group processes result in groups performing below their potential. One such process is social loafing, in which each individual group member exerts slightly less effort than he or she would if working alone. Problems can be overcome to the extent that groups are cohesive; however, the underlying factor here is whether groups hold a norm of excellence. When groups are committed to their task and have a norm of excellence, group performance is enhanced.

REVIEW AND DISCUSSION QUESTIONS

1. Why is it important for managers to be familiar with the concepts of group behaviour?

2. Are the factors that influence group behaviour the same or different from those that influence individual behaviour? Explain.

3. Describe a case of person-role conflict, intrarole conflict or interrole conflict that you have experienced personally. How did you resolve the conflict? Was the resolution satisfactory?

4. Is it always important for satisfactory end results to be achieved with respect to performance, satisfaction and development? Can you think of a situation where satisfaction and/or development might be more important than performance?

5. Under what circumstances might an organisation encourage the formation of informal employee groups? When might they discourage such groups?

6. Think of a formal group to which you belong. Describe the group in terms of the characteristics of groups discussed in the chapter.

7. Repeat the process in the previous question, this time for an informal group to which you belong.

8. What is the relationship between group norms and group cohesiveness? What roles do both cohesiveness and norms play in shaping group performance?

9. Would you expect the membership of informal groups in organisations to overlap that of formal groups? Why or why not?

ENDNOTES

1   Gersick, C. J. G. (1989). Marking time: Predictable transitions in task groups, *Academy of Management Journal*, **32**, 274–309.

2   Alcorn, S. (1989). Understanding groups at work, *Personnel*, pp. 28–36.

3   Forsyth, D. R. (1990). *Group Dynamics* (2nd Ed.). Pacific Grove, CA: Brooks/Cole Publishing Company.

4   Ibid.

5   For a recent review of group development stages see Bettenhausen, K. L. (1991). Five years of group research: What we have learned and what needs to be addressed, *Journal of Management*, 345–381.

6   Tuckman, B. W. (1965). Developmental sequence in small groups, *Psychological Bulletin*, 384–399; and Tuckman, B. W. & Jensen, M. (1977). Stages of small group development revisited, *Groups and Organization Studies*, 419–427.

7   Gersick, C. J. G. (1988). Time and transition in work teams: Toward a new model of group development, *Academy of Management Journal*, **31**, 9–41.

8   Ibid.

9   Gersick, C. J. G. (1988). Time and transition in work teams: Toward a new model of group development, *Academy of Management Journal*, **31**, 9–41; Gersick, C. J. G. (1989). Marking time: Predictable transitions in task groups, *Academy of Management Journal*, **32**, 274–309.

10   The following description of these stages is based on the descriptions provided by Forsyth, D. R. (1990). *Group Dynamics* (2nd Ed.). Pacific Grove, CA: Brooks/Cole Publishing Company.

11   For an excellent discussion on this and related topics, see Organ, D. (1988). *Organizational Citizenship Behavior: The Good Citizen Syndrome*. Lexington, MA: Lexington Books.

12   For classic discussions of the conflict laden position of foremen see Roethlisberger, F. J. (1965). The foreman: Master and victim of double-talk, *Harvard Business Review*, 23 ff; and Mann, F. C. & Dent, J. K. (1954). The supervisor: Member of two organizational families, *Harvard Business Review*, 103–112.

13   Bettenhausen, K. L., & Murningham, J. K. (1991). The development and stability of norms in groups facing interpersonal and structural challenges, *Administrative Science Quarterly*, 20–35.

14   Feldman, D. C. (1984). The development and enforcement of group norms, *Academy of Management Review*, 47–53.

15   Ibid.

16   Maddi, S. R. (1980). *Personality Theories: A Comparative Analysis*. Homewood, IL.: Dorsey Press, Ch. 7.

17   Hackman, J. R. (Ed.) (1994). *Groups that Work (and Those that Don't)*. San Francisco: Jossey-Bass Publishers, pp. 6–7.

18   Guzzo, R. A. , & Shea, G. P. (1990). Group performance and intergroup relations. In M. D. Dunnette & L. M. Hough (Eds.) *Handbook of Industrial and Organizational Psychology* (2nd Ed.). Palo Alto, CA: Consulting Psychologists Press; Mitchell, T. R., Dowling, P. J., Kabanoff,

B. V., & Larson, J. R. (1988). *People in Organizations: An Introduction to Organizational Behaviour in Australia*. Sydney: McGraw-Hill Book Company.

19 Baron, R. S., Kerr, N., & Miller, N. (1992). *Group Processes, Group Decision, Group Action*. Buckingham: Open University Press; Guzzo, R. A., & Shea, G. P. (1994). Group performance and intergroup relations. In M. D. Dunnette & L. M. Hough (Eds.) *Handbook of Industrial and Organizational Psychology* (2nd Ed.). Palo Alto, CA: Consulting Psychologists Press.

20 Geen, R. G. (1991). Social Motivation, *Annual Preview of Psychology*, **42**, 377–399.

21 George, J. M. (1992). Extrinsic and intrinsic origins of perceived social loafing in organizations, *Academy of Management Journal*, **35**, 191–202.

22 Ibid.

23 George, J. M., & Bettenhausen, K. L. (1990). Understanding prosocial behavior, sales performance, and turnover: A group level analysis in a service context, *Journal of Applied Psychology*, 698–709.

24 Mullen, B., & Copper, C. (1994). The relation between group cohesiveness and performance: An integration, *Psychological Bulletin*, **115**, 210–227.

25 Ibid.

26 It should be noted, of course, that cohesiveness is not the only factor which may influence performance. For just one example, see Wood, W. , Polek, D., & Aiken, C. (1985). Sex differences in group task performance, *Journal of Personality and Social Psychology*, 63–71.

27 Katzenbach, J. R., & Smith, D. K. (1993). *The Wisdom of Teams: Creating High Performance Organizations*. Boston: Harvard Business School Press; Katzenbach, J. R., & Smith, D. K. (1993). This discipline of teams, *Harvard Business Review*, 111–120.

28 Bolman, L. G., & Deal, T. E. (1992). What makes a team work? *Organizational Dynamics,* **21**, 34–44.

29 Sundstrom, E., De Meuse, K. P., & Futrell, D. (1990). Work teams: Applications and effectiveness, *American Psychologist*, **45**, 120–133.

READING 7 THE DESIGN OF WORK TEAMS

J. Richard Hackman

Source: 'The Design of Work Teams' in *Handbook of Organizational Behavior*. J. W. Lorsch, ed. (Englewood Cliffs, NJ: Prentice Hall, 1987), pp. 315, 322–32, 338–39. Reprinted by permission.

In an essay written to commemorate the fiftieth anniversary of the well-known Hawthorne studies at Western Electric Corporation, Harold Leavitt (1975, 76) observed:

Far and away the most powerful and beloved tool of applied behavioral scientists is the small face-to-face group. Since the Western Electric research, behavioral scientists have been learning to understand, exploit, and love groups. Groups attracted interest initially as devices for improving the implementation of decisions and to increase human commitment and motivation. They are now loved because they are also creative and innovative, they often make better-quality decisions than individuals, and because they make organizational life more livable for people. One can't hire an applied behavioral scientist into an organization who within 10 minutes will not want to call a group meeting and talk things over.

Leavitt's paper, entitled 'Suppose We Took Groups Seriously …', raises the possibility that both people and organizations would be better off if groups, rather than individuals, were the basic building blocks in the design and management of organizations. Recent trends in organizational practice — such as the increasing use of quality circles, autonomous work groups, project teams, and management task forces — suggest that groups are indeed becoming a popular way to get things done in organizations.

While groups can yield the kinds of benefits Leavitt discusses, they also have a shady side, at least as they typically are designed and managed in contemporary organizations. They can, for example, waste the time and energy of members, rather than use them well. They can enforce norms of low rather than high productivity (Whyte 1955). They sometimes make notoriously bad decisions (Janis 1982). Patterns of destructive conflict can arise, both within and between groups (Alderfer 1977). And groups can exploit, stress, and frustrate their members — sometimes all at the same time (Hackman 1976).

Clearly, if Leavitt's vision is to be realized, we must expand what we know about how to design, manage, and consult to work groups in organizations. There is currently no well-tested and accepted body of research and theory to guide practitioners in using groups to do work, nor do we have a documented record of success in using behavioral-science techniques to help groups become more effective.

This chapter … provides a conceptual model for integrating and extending that knowledge, and offers some action guidelines for structuring, supporting, and managing groups in contemporary organizations.

A normative model of group effectiveness

The model of work-group effectiveness described in this section is an attempt to bridge between *understanding group behavior* and *doing something to improve it* (the topic of the final section of this chapter).[1] The intent of the normative model is to identify the factors that most powerfully enhance or depress the task effectiveness of a group and to do so in a way that increases the possibility that change can occur. This requires that the variables used in the model be powerful (i.e., they make nontrivial differences in how a group performs), potentially manipulable (i.e., it is feasible to change them in an organization), and accessible (i.e., people can understand them and use them). Moreover, they must be arranged sensibly: the model is not a naturalistic chronological description of what leads to what as a group goes about its work; yet if it is to be useful, it must be plausible.

That is a reasonably tall order, and if we are to have a chance of filling it, we must be very clear about both the kinds of groups to which the model applies and what we mean by 'group effectiveness'.

Scope of the model
Domain
The normative model focuses exclusively on *work groups in organizations*. This means that the model applies only to (1) real groups (that is, intact social systems complete with boundaries and differentiated roles among members); (2) groups that have one or more tasks to perform, resulting in discernible and potentially measurable group

products; and (3) groups that operate within an *organizational context*.

This turns out to be a fairly inclusive statement. The model would apply, for example, to a group of executives charged with deciding where to locate a new plant, a team of rank-and-file workers assembling a product, a group of students writing a case assigned by their instructor, a health-care team tending to the needs of a group of patients, and a group of economists analyzing the budgetary implications of a proposed new public policy.

Nonetheless, many sets of people commonly referred to as 'groups' are excluded. Social groups are out (no task), as are reference groups (not an intact social system), coacting groups (i.e., people who may report to the same manager but who have their own individual tasks to perform — no *group* task), and freestanding groups (no organizational context).

This statement of domain may seem relatively straightforward, but it often is difficult to determine what is a 'real' group, a 'group task', and an 'organizational context'. For a detailed and more formal discussion of these issues, see Hackman (1983).

Group effectiveness defined
In conducting experiments on group performance, researchers try to select tasks for which it is relatively easy to tell how well a group has performed: one can count the number of right answers, or measure how long it takes the group to finish, or see if the group solved the problem correctly. For teams in organizations, effectiveness criteria are more complex. Most organizational tasks do not have clear right-or-wrong answers, for example, nor do they lend themselves to quantitative measures that validly indicate how well a group has done its work. Moreover, one needs to be concerned about more than raw productivity or decision quality when assessing groups in organizations. Unlike participants in laboratory experiments (who come in, do the task, and go home), members of work groups and committees usually continue to relate to one another long after the group task is completed; what happens in the work group can substantially affect their willingness (and their ability) to do so.

For these reasons, we use three criteria to assess team effectiveness. The first deals with the actual output of the group, the second with the state of the group as a performing unit, and the third with the impact of the group experience on individual members.

1. *The productive output of the work group should meet or exceed the performance standards of the people who receive and/or review the output.* If a group's output is not acceptable to its 'clients' and/or to managers charged with evaluating its performance, then it cannot be considered effective. An effectiveness criterion that relies explicitly on assessments made by organization members or clients (rather than on 'objective' indexes of performance) was chosen for two reasons. First, reliable and valid objective criteria are available for only a small proportion of work teams in organizations; to deal only with those teams would restrict radically the domain of the model. In addition, what happens to a group and its members usually depends far more on others' assessments of the group's output than on any objective performance index (even though such assessments may be based, in part, on whatever objective measures happen to be available).[2]

2. *The social processes used in carrying out the work should maintain or enhance the capability of members to work together on subsequent team tasks.* Some groups operate in such a way that the integrity of the group as a performing unit is destroyed; the group 'burns itself up' in the process of performing the task. Even if the product of such a group is acceptable, it would be difficult to argue that the group has been a fully effective performing unit.

3. *The group experience should, on balance, satisfy rather than frustrate the personal needs of group members.* If the primary effect of group membership is to keep individuals from doing what they want and need to do, or if members' predominant reactions to the group experience are disgust and disillusionment, then the costs of generating the group product, at least those borne by individual members, are probably too high.

The inclusion of social and personal criteria in a definition of effectiveness is a departure from tradition — as is the use of system-defined (rather than researcher-defined) assessments of a group's output. Yet the criteria themselves require neither extraordinary accomplishment nor

exemplary social processes. All that is necessary is output judged acceptable by those who receive it, a team that winds up its work at least as healthy as when it started, and members who are at least as satisfied as they are frustrated by what has transpired. The challenge for researchers and practitioners is to develop ways of understanding, designing, and managing groups that help them meet or exceed these modest standards of team effectiveness.

The basic proposition

The normative model presented in the pages that follow rests on the validity of one key proposition. If this proposition is valid (and if its implications are appropriately developed), it should be possible to explain why some groups perform better than others, to assess the strengths and weaknesses of specific groups in organizations, and to determine what needs to be done to help a group become more effective.

Specifically, it is proposed that the overall effectiveness of work groups in organizations is a joint function of:

- The level of *effort* group members collectively expend carrying out task work;
- The amount of *knowledge and skill* members bring to bear on the group task; and
- The appropriateness to the task of the *performance* strategies used by the group in its work.[3]

We will refer to effort, knowledge and skill, and performance strategies as *process criteria of effectiveness*. They are the hurdles a group must surmount to be effective. To assess the adequacy of a group's task processes, then, we might ask: Is the group working hard enough to get the task done well and on time? Do members have the expertise required to accomplish the task, and are they using their knowledge and skill efficiently? Has the group developed an approach to the work that is fully appropriate for the task being performed, and are they implementing that strategy well?

Answers to these questions provide diagnostic data about a group's strengths and weaknesses as a performing unit, and they should enable us to predict with some confidence a group's eventual performance effectiveness. But, as strongly implied by research on interventions that focus exclusively on improving group processes, direct attempts to *manipulate* a group's standing on the process criteria (e.g., by exhortation or instruction) are likely to fail.

A more promising approach is to design and manage a group so that task-effective group processes emerge naturally. Several features of the group and its context can potentially lead to improvements in a group's level of effort, its application of member knowledge and skill, and the appropriateness of its task performance strategies. In particular, we will examine the impact of the following three classes of variables on each of the process criteria.[4]

- The *design of the group* as a performing unit: the structure of the group task, the composition of the group, and group norms that regulate member behavior.
- The *organizational context* of the group: the reward, education, and information systems that influence the group, and the material resources that are put at the group's disposal.
- *Group synergy* resulting from members' interactions as they carry out the task.[5]

Throughout, we will emphasize aspects of group design, context, and synergy that foster both high-quality task behavior and eventual team effectiveness. After completing this analysis, we will explore ways of assessing the standing of a

group on the variables in the normative model, and speculate about the implications of the model for the creation and management of work teams in organizations.[6]

Conditions that support effort

Group members are most likely to work hard on their task if (1) the task itself is motivationally engaging, (2) the organizational rewards system provides challenging performance objectives and reinforces their achievement, and (3) interaction among members minimizes 'social loafing' and instead promotes a shared commitment among members to the team and its work. These factors are illustrated in Exhibit 7.4 and discussed below.

Design of the group

We would expect a group to work especially hard on its tasks when the following conditions are met:

- The group task requires members to use a variety of relatively high-level skills.
- The group task is a whole and meaningful piece of work, with a visible outcome.
- The outcomes of the group's work on the task have significant consequences for other people (e.g., other organization members or external clients).
- The task provides group members with

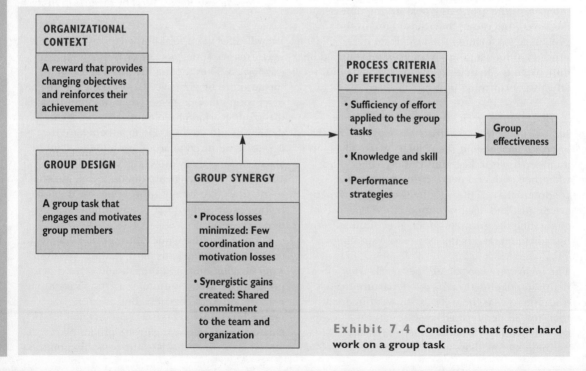

Exhibit 7.4 Conditions that foster hard work on a group task

substantial autonomy for deciding how they do the work — in effect, the group 'owns' the task and is responsible for the work outcomes.

■ Work on the task generates regular, trustworthy feedback about how well the group is performing.

If a group task meets these criteria, it is likely that members will experience their work as meaningful, they will feel collectively responsible for the products they create, and they will know, on a more or less continuous basis, how they are doing. And, extrapolating from Hackman and Oldham's (1980, Chap. 4) model of individual task motivation, a group task with these properties should result in high built-in motivation for a group to try hard to do well (see, for example, Wall and Clegg 1981).

This emphasis on the group task runs counter to traditional wisdom about motivated work behavior. One often hears managers report that some group is 'filled with lazy [or hard-working] people', or that group members 'have a norm of not working very hard [or of always giving their best]'. It is true that people have different chronic energy levels, but there is not much one can do about that. And while norms do emerge in groups that encourage especially high or low effort, such norms usually develop as a reaction to how things are set up, as a means of coping with the group task and work situation.

Thus, if a group's work is routine and unchallenging, of dubious importance, and wholly preprogrammed with no opportunity for feedback, members are likely to develop antiproductivity norms. But if a group task is challenging, important to the organization or its clients, 'owned' by the group, and consequential for group members, then a norm encouraging high effort on the task is likely to emerge. Improving the design of a group's work is usually a better way to foster high collective effort than directly addressing group norms about productivity.

Organizational context

A supportive organizational reward system can reinforce the motivational benefits of a well-designed team task, and a poorly structured reward system can undermine and erode those benefits. Rewards systems that support high effort by work teams tend to have the following three features:

Challenging, specific performance objectives. There is a great deal of research evidence that goal-directed effort is greater when a group accepts moderately difficult performance objectives and receives feedback about its progress in attaining those objectives (Zander 1971, 1980). When the organization specifies a challenging performance target (e.g., a date by which the work must be done, the number of items to be produced, a quality level to be achieved), members often mobilize their efforts to achieve that target. Objectives, however, should supplement rather than replace task-based motivation. A group is unlikely to persist in working toward challenging objectives if its task is inherently frustrating and alienating.

Positive consequences for excellent performance. A reward system that recognizes and reinforces excellent group performance can complement and amplify the motivational incentives of a well-designed group task. People tend to engage in behaviors that are rewarded, and people in groups are no exception (Glaser and Klaus 1966). Which specific kinds of rewards will work best, of course, depends on what group members value. Sometimes simple recognition of excellence will suffice; in other cases, more tangible rewards will be required. But whatever the content of the consequences, their impact on team effort will be greater if members understand that they are contingent on performance — that is, that the group will receive them only if it earns them by performing well.

Rewards and objectives that focus on group, not individual, behavior. When rewards are given to individuals on the basis of managers' judgments about who has contributed most to a group product, dissension and conflict often develop within the group. This is the dilemma of the athletic coach who must try to motivate the team as a whole while simultaneously cultivating and reinforcing individual performance. And it is a problem routinely faced by managers of work teams in organizations where the reward system has traditionally focused on the identification and recognition of excellent *individual* performers.

The destructive effects of rewarding individual contributions rather than team performance can be considerable. Therefore, if it is not feasible to provide performance-contingent rewards to the group as a unit, it may be better to base rewards on the performance of even larger groups (such as a department or division), or not to use contingent rewards at all, than to invite the divisiveness that can develop when members of a team are put into competition with one another for scarce and valued rewards (Lawler 1981).

Group synergy

Group synergy can contribute to effective task behavior in two ways. First, group members can find innovative ways to avoid 'process losses', and thereby minimize waste and misuse of members' time, energy, and talent. Second, members can interact synergistically to create *new* internal resources that can be used in their work — capabilities that did not exist before the group created them. Process losses and synergistic gains that affect how much effort a group applies to its task are discussed below.

Minimizing coordination and motivation losses. There are always some 'overhead costs' to be paid when groups perform tasks. The need to coordinate member activities, for example, takes time and energy away from productive work, resulting in a level of actual productivity that is less than what theoretically would be possible with optimum use of member resources (Steiner 1972). In addition, group productivity often is compromised by what Steiner terms 'motivation decrements' and what Latané (e.g., Latané, Williams, and Harkins 1979) has called 'social loafing'. As groups get larger, the amount of effort each member contributes to the group task decreases — perhaps because each individual feels less responsible for the outcome than would be the case in a smaller group or if one person were doing the task alone.

Some groups suffer much greater coordination and motivation losses than others. And group members can cultivate process skills that help them behave in ways that minimize such losses. But if the group is large or if the task is ill defined or alienating, it may be impossible for the group to avoid serious coordination and motivation losses.

Creating shared commitment to the team and its work. Some groups show great 'spirit': everyone is committed to the team, proud of it, and willing to work hard to make it one of the best. When individuals value their membership in the group

and find it rewarding to work collaboratively with their teammates, they may work considerably harder than they would otherwise. Managers often engage in group-building activities (such as encouraging members of an ongoing team to give the group a name, to decorate their work area, or to participate in an athletic league as a team) in the hope of increasing members' commitment to the group and their willingness to work especially hard on the group task.[7]

Commitment to a team sometimes can result in high effort on the group task even when objective performance conditions are highly unfavorable (e.g., a team that develops a 'can do' attitude and comes to view each new adversity as yet another challenge to be met). It is questionable, however, whether such commitment is sustainable if performance conditions remain poor (e.g., a frustrating or alienating group task, or a reward system that does not recognize excellence).

Conditions that support knowledge and skill

A group is most likely to bring sufficient talent and expertise to bear on its task when (1) the group has an appropriate number of members with a good mix of skills, (2) the education system of the organization offers training or consultation as needed to supplement members' existing knowledge, and (3) group interaction avoids inappropriate 'weighting' of members' contributions and instead fosters sharing of expertise and collective learning. These factors are illustrated in Exhibit 7.5 and discussed below.

Design of the group

A group's composition is the most important condition affecting the amount of knowledge and skill members apply to their tasks. Well-composed groups have the following four characteristics:

Individual members have high task-relevant expertise. The most efficient way to make sure a group has the expertise it needs for its work is simply to assign talented individuals to it. This seemingly obvious principle, however, is not always straightforward in practice. Even when people with ample task-relevant knowledge and skill are available, they may be overlooked — for example, when groups are composed with only political considerations in mind. This can result in a team whose members cover all the right

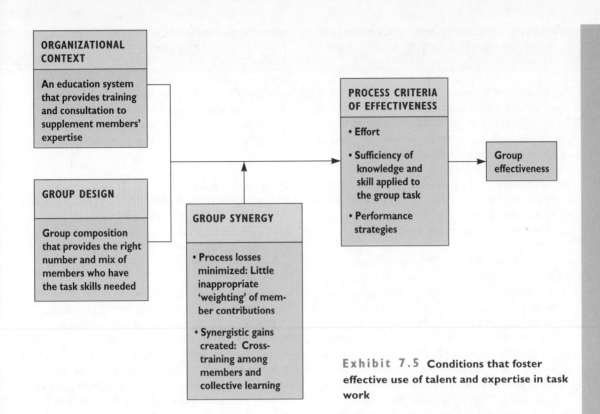

ORGANIZATIONAL CONTEXT

An education system that provides training and consultation to supplement members' expertise

GROUP DESIGN

Group composition that provides the right number and mix of members who have the task skills needed

GROUP SYNERGY

• Process losses minimized: Little inappropriate 'weighting' of member contributions

• Synergistic gains created: Cross-training among members and collective learning

PROCESS CRITERIA OF EFFECTIVENESS

• Effort

• Sufficiency of knowledge and skill applied to the group task

• Performance strategies

Group effectiveness

Exhibit 7.5 **Conditions that foster effective use of talent and expertise in task work**

bases, but one that is not capable of carrying out well the work it was created to do.

The group is just large enough to do the work. If a task required four sets of hands, then there should be four people in the group — but no more than that. The research literature offers abundant evidence documenting the dysfunctions that occur in large groups (see Steiner 1972, Chap. 4, for a review) and establishing the advantages of groups that are slightly smaller than the task technically requires (Wicker et al. 1976). Yet large work groups (especially decision-making committees) are widely used in organizations. Often the decision to put additional people in a group allows managers to avoid difficult personnel choices or sensitive political issues (e.g., how to involve a department in the work of a task force on which it has no representatives), but the cost may be losses in the quality of the group product and the efficiency with which it is produced.

Members have interpersonal as well as task skills. If a group task is well designed (i.e., it provides the group considerable autonomy in managing a challenging piece of work), then at least moderate interpersonal skills are required to bring the *task* skills of members to bear on the group's work — especially if members are diverse (i.e., they come from different demographic groups, represent different organizational units, or have divergent personal views on the matter at hand). Some individuals have little competence in working collaboratively with other people, especially if those people differ from themselves in important ways. Even one or two such individuals can significantly impede the ability of a group to bring members' expertise effectively to bear on the group task.

Membership is moderately diverse. Members of an excessively homogeneous group may get along well together but lack the resources needed to perform the task because the members essentially replicate one another. An excessively heterogeneous group, on the other hand, may have a rich complement of talent within the group but be unable to use that talent well because members are so diverse in values or perspective that they cannot work together effectively. The aspiration in composing a group is to strike just the right balance between homogeneity and heterogeneity: members should have a variety of talents and perspective, yet be similar enough that they can understand and coordinate with one another.[8]

Organizational context

Sometimes a group has within its bounds all the knowledge and skill needed for optimum task performance. More commonly there are aspects of the work for which additional talent or expertise would be helpful. The educational system of the organization can play a useful role in helping the group obtain the outside expertise it needs for its work.

For this potential to be realized, two conditions must be met. First, relevant educational resources (which can include technical consultation as well as training) must exist somewhere in the organization. Second, some sort of 'delivery system' must be in place to make those resources accessible to the group. This may not be a simple matter for rank-and-file teams in organizations where employees have never had the right to call on staff resources.

The particular kind of assistance required will, of course, depend on both the task requirements and the specific needs of the group. And the appropriate form of assistance will vary as well. Sometimes a one-shot technical consultation will suffice, sometimes a continuing consulting relationship will be needed, and sometimes a training program for group members will be more appropriate to build the relevant expertise into the group itself. Whatever the content of the assistance and the vehicle used to provide it, the role of the educational system is the same: to help groups obtain the full complement of knowledge and skill required for excellent task performance.

Group synergy

Minimizing inappropriate weighting of member contributions. The knowledge and skill of group members can be wasted if the group solicits and weights contributions in a way that is incongruent with members' expertise — as when the credence given a member's idea depends on such task-irrelevant considerations as his or her demographic attributes (e.g., gender, ethnicity, or age) or behavioral style (e.g., talkativeness or verbal dominance). This process loss has been well documented in the research literature (e.g., Johnson and Torcivia 1967; Thomas and Fink 1961; Torrance 1954). Groups often have trouble

assessing which members have the special expertise needed for the task, and they appear to have even more difficulty explicitly acknowledging these differences and weighting members' contributions in accord with them. To the extent a group is able to minimize this problem, it will take better advantage of the expertise that was put in the group when it was composed.

Fostering collective learning. When members of a group interact in ways that help them learn from one another, they can increase the total pool of talent available for task work — a synergistic gain from group interaction. The practice of 'cross-training', often encouraged in autonomous work groups in industry, is an example of such behavior, as are more informal activities that involve the sharing of knowledge, expertise, and experience among members. A group that orients itself to collective learning and whose members share what is learned with each other should be far better able to exploit the educational resources of an organization than a group that takes a laissez-faire stance toward the development of its internal talent.

Conditions that support appropriate performance strategies

The likelihood that the group will employ a task-appropriate performance strategy increases when (1) group norms support explicit assessment of the performance situation and active consideration of alternative ways of proceeding with the work; (2) the information system of the organization provides members with the data they need to assess the situation and evaluate alternative strategies; and (3) group interaction results in little 'slippage' when performance plans are executed and instead prompts creative new ideas about ways to proceed with the work. These factors are illustrated in Exhibit 7.6 and discussed below.

Design of group

Group members typically reach agreement on how they will go about performing their task relatively early in their time together. Indeed, for familiar tasks, members may not talk about their strategy at all, because it is obvious to everyone how the task should be done. Once a strategy is agreed to, whether implicitly or explicitly, members tend to behave in accord with it and enforce adherence to it (March and Simon 1958, Chap. 6). Performance strategies thus become part of the fabric of the group, a 'given' that is no more open to questions than the task of the group or who is in the group.

The specific strategies that will be most appropriate for a given group depend both on the task to be done and on the imperatives and resources in the performance situation. No 'one best strategy' can be specified in advance for most task-performing groups in organizations. It is possible, however, to build group norms that increase the likelihood that members will develop task-appropriate performance strategies and execute them well. Such norms have two properties, the first being a prerequisite for the second.[9]

Group norms support self-regulation. Behavior in some groups is so chaotic and subject to individual whim as to approach anarchy. Such groups are unlikely to be able to execute any performance strategy in an orderly fashion, even one that has been specified in detail by management. Thus, a normative structure that enables a group to regulate member behavior is essential to the efficient execution of

performance strategies. This requires that behavioral norms be sufficiently crystallized (i.e., members have consensus about them) and intense (i.e., compliance results in substantial approval or avoidance of substantial disapproval by other members) that individuals will wish to behave in accord with them (Jackson 1965).

Group norms support situation scanning and strategy planning. Groups that actively assess the demands and opportunities in the performance situation and that consider several alternative ways of proceeding with the work tend to develop more appropriate performance strategies than groups that do not (Hackman, Brousseau, and Weiss 1976; Maier 1963). Yet such activities tend not to take place spontaneously. Instead, it appears that the general disinclination of group members to 'talk about process' extends even to discussions about how the work of the group will be carried out.[10]

For this reason, it is necessary somehow to prompt or encourage group members to engage in situation scanning and strategy planning activities. Group norms provide an efficient and powerful way to accomplish this. Such norms focus attention on opportunities and constraints

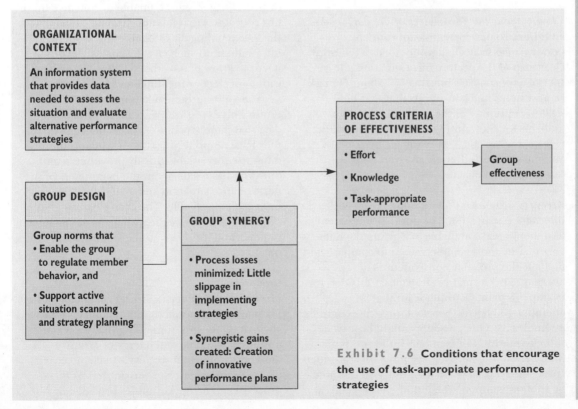

Exhibit 7.6 Conditions that encourage the use of task-appropiate performance strategies

that might otherwise be overlooked and make it difficult for members to fall into familiar or habitual patterns of behavior that may be inappropriate for the particular task at hand.[11]

Group norms governing performance processes can be established when a group is first formed or can be introduced during a hiatus in the work, when members are ready to reconsider how they operate as a team. Regardless of how and when they are developed, the norms that guide a group's performance processes are an important structural feature of the group — an aspect of group design that often has been overlooked by both scholars and managers interested in work-team effectiveness.

Organizational context

The information system of an organization is critical to a group's ability to plan and execute a task-appropriate performance strategy. If a group cannot obtain clear information about its performance situation, or if it does not have access to data about the likely outcomes of alternative approaches to the task, it may develop a way of proceeding that seems reasonable to group members but that turns out, when executed, to be grossly inappropriate.

Clarity about the parameters of the performance situation. To develop a task-appropriate performance strategy, a group needs a relatively clear map of the performance situation. Of special importance is information about (1) task requirements and constraints that may limit strategic options, (2) the material resources available for use, and (3) the people who will receive, review, and/or use the group product and the standards they are likely to employ in assessing its adequacy.

Access to data about likely consequences of alternative strategies. The information system also should make available to a group the data and analytic tools members need to compare and evaluate the probable consequences of alternative performance strategies. Consider, for example, a manufacturing team that is attempting to decide how to approach a complex assembly task. One possibility might be a cyclic strategy, in which all members build components for a period of time, then assemble final products (producing a relative flood of output), followed by another component-building period, and so

on. How would this strategy compare to one in which some members build components continuously while others are dedicated to final assembly? To choose between these strategies, the group needs information about the timing of demand for their product, the availability of space for storing components and completed products, and the cost of obtaining and holding parts for use in batch-component production. It would be quite risky for a group to choose a strategy without data about such matters.

How much information a group needs depends in part on how much latitude it has to manage its own affairs. Groups that have the authority to invent their own strategies and manage their own performance processes will need relatively complete data on both the parameters of the performance situation and the likely consequences of alternative ways of proceeding. Groups with less authority for setting their own directions will have less need for such data.

Managers who control access to performance-relevant information must make sure that data needed by a team are realistically available to it. This is not always easy: the relevant data may not exist, they may be costly to obtain, or the manager may be unable to convince his or her colleagues that it is appropriate to share with the group politically or competitively sensitive information. In such circumstances, the group needs to know that — that it will have to make do with imperfect or incomplete data.[12]

Care also must be taken not to flood the group with excess or irrelevant information — data that members must process but for which they have no present use. Some organizations minimize this risk by initially providing teams only with basic data about the parameters of the performance situation and a guide to the information available. The group has the responsibility for deciding what additional data it requires and for determining when and how to obtain it.

Group synergy
Minimizing slippage in strategy implementation. Plans are never perfectly implemented — there is always a slip or two, something that wastes or misdirects the time and energy of group members, compromising even well-conceived plans. To the extent a group minimizes this process loss, the opportunities provided by norms

that foster strategy planning and by a supportive information system can be well used. But if slippage is high, the group may fail to exploit even a highly favorable performance situation.[13]

Creating innovative strategic plans. On the positive side, groups can develop ways of interacting that occasionally result in truly original or insightful ways of proceeding with the work. For example, a group might find a way to exploit some resources that everyone else has overlooked; it might invent a way to get round a seemingly insurmountable performance obstacle; or it might come up with a novel way to generate ideas for solving a difficult problem. When group members get in the habit of thinking creatively about how they will do their work, interesting and useful ideas can emerge — ideas that did not exist before the group invented them.

Overview and summary

An overview of the normative model is presented in Exhibit 7.7. It shows three major points of leverage for fostering group effectiveness: (1) the design of the group as a performing unit, (2) the supports provided by the organizational context in which the group operates, and (3) the synergistic outcomes of the interaction among group members. The contributions of each of these classes of variables are summarized next in brief.

Design

The design of a group — task structure, group composition, and group norms — should promote effective task behavior and lessen the chances that members will encounter built-in obstacles to good performance. While a good group design cannot guarantee competent group behavior, it does create conditions that make it easier and more natural for task-effective behaviors to emerge and persist.

Context

The organizational context of a group — the reward, education, and information systems of the organization — should support and reinforce the design features. A supportive organizational context gives a group what it needs to exploit the potential of a good basic

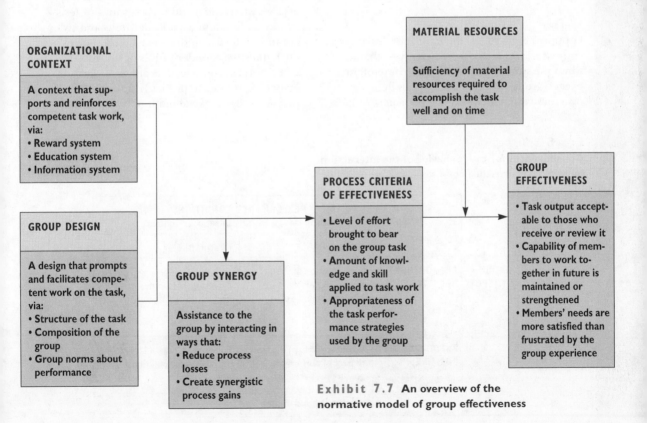

Exhibit 7.7 An overview of the normative model of group effectiveness

design (although it probably cannot compensate for a fundamentally flawed design). An unsupportive organizational context can easily undermine the positive features of even a well-designed team. Excellent group performance requires both a good design for the team and a supportive organizational context.

Exhibit 7.7 shows one important contextual feature not previously discussed — the *material resources* required to do the work. If a group lacks the tools, equipment, space, raw materials, money, or human resources it needs, its performance surely will suffer — even if it stands high on the process criteria of effectiveness. A talented, well-motivated production team, for example, will not perform well if the raw materials it needs to make its products are not available, or if production tools are unsatisfactory. Similarly, a committee formed to select a new agency manager cannot be successful if there are no qualified candidates available. And a group that provides human services to clients may have performance problems if members' work stations are so spread about that they cannot coordinate their activities, or if money is so scarce that needed support staff cannot be obtained.[14]

Synergy

Group synergy 'tunes' the impact of design and contextual factors. Positive synergy — that is, when the synergistic gains from group interaction exceed group process losses — can help a group overcome the limitations of a poor performance situation (e.g., a badly designed group task or an unsupportive reward system). And if performance conditions are favorable, positive synergy can help a group exploit the opportunities those conditions provide. Negative synergy, when process losses exceed synergistic gains, has opposite effects. It can amplify the negative impact of a poor performance situation, and it can prevent a group from taking advantage of favorable circumstances. The relationship between performance conditions (i.e., the group design and the organizational context) and group synergy are illustrated in Exhibit 7.8.[15]

Implications for the management teams

Because this chapter represents a departure from traditional thinking about group performance, it may be appropriate to conclude by briefly highlighting some of the broader management implications of what has been proposed.

On leadership

The research literature is rich with studies of leadership in groups (for reviews, see Hare 1976, Chap. 1, and Stogdill 1974). Most of this research assesses what leaders do *within* groups or tests propositions about what leader traits and styles are most effective under what circumstances. Such questions are derivatives of the approach taken here, because leaders are viewed as exercising influence primarily through the decisions they make about how to frame the

Exhibit 7.8
Consequences for task behavior of the interaction between performance conditions and group synergy

		PERFORMANCE CONDITIONS (Group Design and Organizational Context)	
		UNFAVORABLE	FAVORABLE
GROUP SYNERGY	PREDOMINANTLY NEGATIVE	Amplification of the impact of performance-hindering conditions	Failure by the group to exploit opportunities in the performance situation
	PREDOMINANTLY POSITIVE	Lessening of the negative impact of performance conditions; perhaps transcending their effects for a limited period of time	Full exploitation of favorable performance conditions

group task, how to structure the group and its context, and how to help the group get started up well and headed in an appropriate direction.

Indeed, we have not even discussed whether an internal group leader should be named — let alone how he or she should behave. It often does make sense to have such a role, especially when substantial coordination among members is required, when there is lots of information to be processed (Maier 1967), or when it is advisable to have one person be the liaison with other groups or with higher management. Yet it is rarely a good idea to decide in advance about the leadership structure of a work group. If a group has been designed well and helped to begin exploring the group norms and member roles it wishes to have, questions of internal leadership should appear naturally. And while there invariably will be a good deal of stress and strain in the group as leadership issues are dealt with, when a resolution comes it will have the considerable advantage of being the group's own.

The manager's role, then, is to make sure a group confronts the leadership issue directly (even if members would prefer to deal with it implicitly or avoid it entirely), not to resolve it for the group. To do the latter is to short-circuit an important developmental task in the life of a team and to rob the group of a significant opportunity to organize and develop its own internal resources.

On creating redundant conditions

There are many ways for a group to be effective in performing a task, and even more ways for it to be ineffective. Moreover, different task and organizational circumstances involve vastly different demands and opportunities. Thus it is impossible to specify in detail what specific behaviors managers should adopt to help groups perform effectively. There are simply too many ways a group can operate and still wind up with the same outcome.[16] Attempts to specify contingencies for managerial behavior do not help much, in that they usually result in prescriptions too complex for anyone to follow (Hackman 1984).

Thus, while many models of leadership call for the active manipulation of 'causes' that are assumed to be tightly linked to 'effects', our view of group behavior suggests that the key to effective group management may be to create redundant conditions that support good

performance, leaving groups ample room to develop and enact their own ways of operating within those conditions.

A manager interested in encouraging a group to work hard, for example, would try to make the group task more motivationally engaging. *And* he or she would try to provide more (or more potent) positive consequences contingent on hard, effective work. *And* he or she would work with the group members to improve the efficiency of their internal processes and to build a positive team spirit. And if there were other steps that could be taken to create conditions supportive of high effort, these would be attempted as well.

Group performance does not have clean, unitary causes. To help a group improve its effectiveness involves doing whatever is possible to create multiple, redundant conditions that together may nudge the group towards more competent task behavior and, eventually, better performance.[17]

On managerial authority

The approach taken in this chapter clearly favors the creation of conditions that empower groups, that increase their authority to manage their own work. While this does not imply a diminution of managerial authority, it does suggest that it be redirected.

One critical use of authority, already discussed at some length, is in creating organizational conditions that foster and support effective group behavior. Managers must not view design and contextual features as 'givens' over which they have little control. Instead, influence must be wielded upward and outward in the organization to make organizational structures and systems as supportive of team effectiveness as possible. If a manager does not have the authority to initiate discussions about making such changes, he or she should consider trying to get it, because it will be hard to be a good team manager without it.

Managerial authority also should be used to establish and enforce standards of group behavior and acceptable performance. When a manager defines a piece of work to be done, sets performance standards, and is clear about the bounds of acceptable group behavior, he or she is exercising managerial authority — and concurrently empowering the group that will do the work. To be vague about what is required and expected can be just as debilitating to a group as traditional, hands-on supervision. To enable groups to use their authority well, managers must not be afraid to exercise their own.

On knowing some things

The management behaviors implied by the model of team effectiveness explored in this chapter will seem unfamiliar and awkward to some managers, and may be hard for them to perform well. But any new endeavor can be difficult. Trying to make sense of a balance sheet, for example, or figuring out a good design for a production process can feel just as awkward and be just as hard for an unpracticed manager to do well. Yet for some reason we are far more willing to acknowledge the need for training and experience in these areas than we are in aspects of managerial work related to the effective use of human resources.

Managing work groups is every bit as tough as figuring out what to do about the numbers on a balance sheet. To manage teams well, one needs to know some things, have some skills, and have opportunities to practice. The sooner those requirements are acknowledged, the sooner we will be able to develop a cadre of managers who are expert in creating work teams, developing them, and harvesting the considerable contributions they have to make to organizational effectiveness.

Endnotes

1 The work of Cummings (e.g., 1978, 1981) on the design and management of work groups from a sociotechnical-systems perspective has much in common with what is presented here, although it comes from a rather different intellectual tradition. For an overview of that tradition, see Trist (1981).

2 There are, however, occasions when it may not be sensible to rely on client assessments of a group's output. Consider, for example, a situation in which the legitimate clients of the group are seriously disturbed, ethnocentric, or competitive with the group. The very meaning of 'good performance' under these circumstances is problematic.

3 For example, a group might decide to divide itself into two sub-groups, each of which would do part of the overall task, with the final product to be assembled later. Or it might choose to free associate about task solutions in

the first meeting, reflect for a week about the ideas that came up, and then meet to draft the product. Or it might decide to spend considerable time checking and rechecking for errors after learning that its client cares a great deal about product quality. All of these are choices about task performance strategy.

4 For simplicity, feedback loops among classes of variables in the framework (e.g., how the organizational context may change in response to a team's level of effectiveness) are not shown or discussed here.

5 As applied to group behavior in this chapter, 'synergy' refers to group-level phenomena that (1) emerge from the interaction among members, and (2) affect how well a group is able to deal with the demands and opportunities in its performance situation.

6 Some of the material that follows is adapted from Hackman and Oldham (1980), chaps. 7–8.

7 Such activities are not risk free. 'Team spirit' can evolve into group ethnocentrism and can prompt dysfunctional competition and conflict between groups.

8 A number of scholars have examined the impact of member compatibility on task behavior and performance. See, for example, Belbin (1981); Hewett, O'Brien, and Hornik (1974); and Schutz (1958, 1961).

9 Following Jackson (1965), norms are conceptualized as structural features of a group that summarize members' shared approval (or disapproval) of various behaviors. Norms simplify group influence processes because they make it possible for members to count on certain things being done and other things not being done. For more detailed discussion of how norms structure and channel behavior in a group, see Hackman (1976).

10 Spontaneous strategy planning does, of course, occur if a task is so novel that members are at a loss about how to proceed with it, and is generally more likely when the task is unfamiliar.

11 This analysis presumes that a team has at least some latitude for planning its own strategy. Usually this is the case. In some groups, however, behavior is so completely preprogrammed or closely supervised that members have essentially no strategy choices to make. For such groups, there is little need for a norm supporting scanning and planning because those activities are someone else's

responsibility. All that is needed is the orderly execution of the strategy that has been supplied. The implications of giving a team the authority to devise its own strategies (rather than reserving that authority for management) are explored later in this chapter.

12 Particularly unfortunate are occasions when a manager deliberately withholds performance-relevant information from a group to make sure the group remains dependent on him or her. While this may preserve a manager's feelings of personal power, it can result in inappropriate performance strategies and needlessly poor team performance.

13 One particularly virulent form of this process loss bears special mention. Members of some groups collude with each other in a way that makes it impossible ever to implement performance plans. Such a group may have ample information about the performance situation and may develop a fully task-appropriate performance strategy. But once the plans are complete, they are ignored. When members reconvene, they develop new plans and a new resolve, and the cycle repeats itself. The group acts as if a good strategy is all that is needed for team effectiveness, and its inevitable failures are always well-wrapped in new and better plans for the future. This kind of synergy often is driven by unconscious forces; it is not uncommon in groups that have high-pressure work environments, and it can be lethal to team effectiveness.

14 The importance of mundane aspects of the performance situation such as these are increasingly being recognized as critical to effective work performance (see, for example, Peters and O'Connor 1980, and Peters, O'Connor, and Rudolf 1980). To overlook them is to jeopardize the effort expended to design a team well and provide it with appropriate contextual supports.

15 Although performance conditions and group synergy are placed on separate axes in the figure, they are not independent: positive synergy is more likely under favorable conditions, and negative synergy is more likely under unfavorable conditions. Thus performance spirals can develop. For example, good group performance can lead to management decisions that improve the group's performance situation, which promotes positive synergy, which results in even better performance, and so on. Equally plausible is a negative spiral, in which poor performance begets organizational 'tightening up,' resulting in negative synergy, and so on.

16 Systems theorists call this aspect of organized endeavor 'equifinality' (Katz and Kahn 1978, 30). According to this principle, a social system can reach the same outcome from a variety of initial conditions and by a variety of methods.

17 We see here a key difference between descriptive and action models of behavior in organization. A descriptive model parcels up the world for conceptual clarity; in contrast, a good action model parcels up the world to increase the chances that something can be created or changed. Rather than seek to isolate unitary causes, an action model attempts to identify clusters of covarying factors that can serve as useful levers for change. For related views, see Hackman (1984), Mohr (1982), and Weick (1977).

References and additional readings

Alderter, C. P. 1977. 'Group and Intergroup Relations' in J. R. Hackman and J. L. Suttle, eds., *Improving Life at Work*, Santa Monica, CA: Goodyear.

Argyris, C. 1969. 'The Incompleteness of Social Psychological Theory: Examples from Small Group, Cognitive Consistency, and Attribution Research'. *American Psychologist* 24, pp. 893–908.

——. 1980. *The Inner Contradictions of Rigorous Research.* New York: Academic Press.

——. 1983. 'Action Science and Intervention'. *Journal of Applied Behavioral Science* 19, pp. 115–35.

Bales, R. F. 1950. *Interaction Process Analysis: A Method for the Study of Small Groups.* Cambridge, MA: Addison-Wesley.

——. 1970. *Personality and Interpersonal Behavior.* New York: Holt, Rinehart and Winston.

Bales, R. F., and S. P. Cohen. 1979. SYMLOG: *A System for the Multiple Level Observation of Groups.* New York: Free Press.

Beer, M. 1976. 'The Technology of Organization Development' in M. D. Dunnette, ed., *Handbook of Industrial and Organizational Psychology.* Chicago: Rand McNally.

Belbin, R. M. 1981. *Management Teams: Why They Succeed or Fail.* London: Heinemann.

Bertcher, H. J., and F. F. Maple. 1977. *Creating Groups.* Beverly Hills, CA: Sage.

Blake, R. R., and J. S. Mouton. 1969. *Building a Dynamic Corporation through Grid Organization Development.* Reading, MA: Addison-Wesley.

Colman, A. D., and W. H. Bexton. 1975. *Group Relations Reader.* Sausalito, CA: GREX.

Cooper, C. L. ed. 1975. *Theories of Group Processes.* London: Wiley.

Cummings, T. G. July 1978. 'Self-Regulating Work Groups: A Socio-Technical Synthesis'. *Academy of Management Review* 2, no. 3, pp. 625–34.

——. 1981. 'Designing Effective Work Groups' in P. C. Nystrom and W. H. Starbuck, eds., *Handbook of Organizational Design 2.* London: Oxford University Press.

Dalkey, N. C. 1967. *Delphi.* Santa Monica. CA: Rand.

Davis, J. H. 1973. 'Group Decision and Social Interaction: A Theory of Social Decision Schemes'. *Psychological Review* 80, pp. 97–125.

Davis, J. H. and V. B. Hinsz. 1982. 'Current Research Problems in Group Performance and Group Dynamics' in H. Brandstätter, J. H. Davis, and G. Stocker-Kreichgauer, eds., *Group Decision Making.* London: Academic Press.

Delbecq, A. L., A. H. Van de Ven, and D. H. Gustafson. 1975. *Group Techniques for Program Planning.* Glenview, IL: Scott, Foresman.

Dunnette, M. D., J. Campbell, and K. Jaastad. 1963. 'The Effect of Group Participation on Brainstorming Effectiveness for Two Industrial Samples'. *Journal of Applied Psychology* 47, pp. 30–37.

Dyer, W. G. 1977. *Team Building: Issues and Alternatives.* Reading, MA: Addison-Wesley.

Friedlander, F., and L. D. Brown. 1974. 'Organization Development' in M. R. Rosen-zweig and L. W. Porter, eds., *Annual Review of Psychology* 25. Palo Alto, CA: Annual Reviews.

Gersick, C. J. G. 1983. 'Life Cycles of *Ad Hoc* Groups'. Technical report no. 3. Group Effectiveness Research Project, School of Organization and Management, Yale University.

Glaser, R., and D. J. Klaus. 1966. 'A Reinforcement Analysis of Group Performance'. *Psychological Monographs* 80, whole no. 621, pp. 1–23.

Goodman, P., R. Atkin, and E. Ravlin. 1982. 'Some Observations on Specifying Models of Group Performance'. Paper delivered at a symposium on Productive Work Teams and Groups. American Psychological Association Convention, Washington, DC.

Green, T. B. 1975 'An Empirical Analysis of Nominal and Interacting Groups'. *Academy of Management Journal* 18, pp. 63–73.

Hackman, J. R. 1969. 'Toward Understanding the Role of Tasks in Behavioral Research'. *Acta Psychologica* 31, pp. 97–128.

——. 1976. 'Group Influences on Individuals' in M. D. Dunnette, ed., *Handbook of Industrial and Organizational Psychology.* Chicago: Rand McNally.

——. 1982. 'A Set of Methods for Research on Work Teams'. Technical report no. 1, Group Effectiveness Research Project, School of Organization and Management, Yale University.

——. 1983. 'A Normative Model of Work Team Effectiveness'. Technical report no. 2, Group Effectiveness Research Project, School of Organization and Management, Yale University.

——. 1984. 'Psychological Contributions to Organizational Productivity: A Commentary' in A. P. Brief, ed., *Productivity Research in the Behavioral and Social Sciences.* New York: Praeger.

Hackman, J. R., K. R. Brousseau, and J. A. Weiss. 1976. 'The Interaction of Task Design and Group Performance Strategies in Determining Group Effectiveness'. *Organizational Behavior and Human Performance* 16, pp. 356–65.

Hackman, J. R., and C. G. Morris. 1975. 'Group Tasks, Group Interaction Process, and Group Performance Effectiveness: A Review and Proposed Integration' in L. Berkowitz, ed., *Advances in Experimental Social Psychology.* New York: Academic Press.

Hackman, J. R., and G. R. Oldham. 1980. *Work Redesign.* Reading, MA: Addison-Wesley.

Hare, A. P. 1976. *Handbook of Small Group Research.* 2d ed. New York: Free Press.

——. 1982. *Creativity in Small Groups.* Beverly Hills, CA: Sage.

Heinen, J. S., and E. Jacobson. 1976. 'A Model of Task Group Development in Complex Organizations and a Strategy of Implementation'. *Academy of Management Review* 1, pp. 98–111.

Herold, D. M. 1978. 'Improving the Performance Effectiveness of Groups through a Task-Contingent Selection of Intervention Strategies'. *Academy of Management Review* 3, pp. 315–25.

Hewett, T. T., G. E. O'Brien, and J. Hornik. 1974. 'The Effects of Work Organization, Leadership Style, and Member Compatibility upon the Productivity of Small Groups Working on a Manipulative Task'. *Organizational Behavior and Human Performance* 11, pp. 283–301.

Hoffman, L. R., 1979a. 'Applying Experimental Research on Group Problem Solving in Organizations'. *Journal of Applied Behavioral Science* 15, pp. 375–91.

——, ed. 1979b, *The Group Problem Solving Process: Studies of a Valence Model.* New York: Praeger.

Jackson, J. 1965. 'Structural Characteristics of Norms' in I. D. Steiner and M. Fishbein, eds., *Current Studies in Social Psychology.* New York: Holt, Rinehart and Winston.

Janis, I. L. 1982. *Groupthink.* 2d ed. Boston: Houghton Mifflin.

Johnson, H. H., and J. M. Torcivia. 1967. 'Group and Individual Performance on a Single-Stage Task as a Function of Distribution of Individual Performance'. *Journal of Personality and Social Psychology* 3, pp. 266–73.

Kaplan, R. E. 1979. 'The Conspicuous Absence of Evidence that Process Consultation Enhances Task Performance'. *Journal of Applied Behavioral Science* 15, pp. 346–60.

Katz, D., and R. L. Kahn. 1978. *The Social Psychology of Organizations.* 2nd ed. New York: Wiley.

Katz, R. 1982. 'The Effects of Group Longevity on Project Communication and Performance'. *Administrative Science Quarterly* 27, pp. 81–104.

Latané, B., K. Williams, and S. Harkins. 1979. 'Many Hands Make Light the Work: The Causes and Consequences of Social Loafing'. *Journal of Personality and Social Psychology* 37, pp. 822–32.

Lawler, E. E. 1981. *Pay and Organization Development.* Reading, MA: Addison-Wesley.

Leavitt, H. J. 1975. 'Suppose We Took Groups Seriously …' in E. L. Cass and F. G. Zimmer, eds., *Man and Work in Society.* New York: Van Nostrand Reinhold.

Maier, N. R. F. 1963. *Problem Solving Discussions and Conferences*: Leadership Methods and Skills. New York: McGraw-Hill.

——. 1967. 'Assets and Liabilities in Group Problem Solving: The Need for an Integrative Function'. *Psychological Review* 74, pp. 239–49.

March, J. G., and H. A. Simon. 1958. *Organizations.* New York: Wiley.

McGrath, J. E., 1964. *Social Psychology: A Brief Introduction.* New York: Holt, Rinehart and Winston.

——. 1984. *Groups: Interaction and Performance.* Englewood Cliffs, NJ: Prentice Hall.

McGrath, J. E., and I. Altman. 1965. *Small Group Research: A Synthesis and Critique of the Field.* New York: Holt, Rinehart and Winston.

McGrath, J. E., and D. A. Kravitz. 1982. 'Group Research'. *Annual Review of Psychology* 33, pp. 195–230.

Merry, U., and M. E. Allerhand. 1977. *Developing Teams and Organizations.* Reading, MA: Addison-Wesley.

Mohr, L. B. 1982. *Explaining Organizational Behavior.* San Francisco: Jossey-Bass.

Myers, D. C. and H. Lamm. 1976. 'The Group Polarization Phenomenon'. *Psychological Bulletin* 83, pp. 602–27.

Nagao, D. H., D. A. Vollrath, and J. H. Davis. 1978. 'Group Decision Making: Origins and Current Status' in H. Brandstätter, J. H. Davis, and H. C. Schuler, eds., *Dynamics of Group Decisions.* Beverly Hills, CA: Sage.

Osborn, A. F. 1957. *Applied Imagination.* Rev. ed. New York: Scribner's.

Payne, R., and C. L. Cooper, eds. 1981. *Groups at Work.* Chichester, England: Wiley.

Peters, L. H., and E. J. O'Connor. 1980. 'Situational Constraints and Work Outcomes: The Influences of a Frequently Overlooked Construct'. *Academy of Management Review* 5, pp. 391–97.

Peters, L. H., E. J. O'Connor, and C. J. Rudolf. 1980. 'The Behavioral and Affective Consequences of Performance-Relevant Situational Variables'. *Organizational Behavior and Human Performance* 25, pp. 79–96.

Poza, E. J., and M. L. Marcus. 1980. 'Success Story: The Team Approach to Work Restructuring'. *Organizational Dynamics*, Winter, pp. 3–25.

Roby, T. B. and J. T. Lanzetta. 1958. 'Considerations in the Analysis of Group Tasks'. *Psychological Bulletin* 55, pp. 88–101.

Rubin, I. M., M. S. Plovnick, and R. E. Fry. 1977. *Task-Oriented Team Development.* New York: McGraw-Hill.

Runkel, P. J., and J. E. McGrath. 1972. *Research on Human Behavior.* New York: Holt, Rinehart and Winston.

Schein, E. H. 1969. *Process Consultation.* Reading, MA: Addison-Wesley.

Schutz, W. C. 1958. FIRO: *A Three-Dimensional Theory of Interpersonal Behavior.* New York: Holt, Rinehart and Winston.

——. 1961. 'On Group Composition'. *Journal of Abnormal and Social Psychology* 62, pp. 275–81.

Stasser, G., and J. H. Davis. 1981. 'Group Decision Making and Social Influence: A Social Interaction Sequence Model'. *Psychological Review* 88, pp. 523–51.

Stein, M. I. 1975. *Stimulating Creativity*, vol 2. New York: Academic Press.

Steiner, I. D. 1972. *Group Process and Productivity*. New York: Academic Press.

Stogdill, R. M. 1974. *Handbook of Leadership*. New York: Free Press.

Stumpf, S. A., D. E. Zand, and R. D. Freedman. 1979. 'Designing Groups for Judgmental Decision'. *Academy of Management Review* 4, pp. 589–600.

Thomas, E. J., and C. F. Fink. 1961. 'Models of Group Problem Solving'. *Journal of Abnormal and Social Psychology* 63, pp. 53–63.

——. 1963. 'Effects of Groups Size'. *Psychological Bulletin* 60, pp. 371–84.

Torrance, E. P. 1954. 'Some Consequences of Power Differences on Decision Making in Permanent and Temporary Three-Man Groups'. *Research Studies, State College of Washington* 22, pp. 130–40.

Trist, E. L. 1981. 'The Evolution of Sociotechnical Systems as a Conceptual Framework and as an Action Research Program' in A. H. Van de Ven and W. F. Joyce, eds., *Perspectives on Organization Design and Behavior*. New York: Wiley.

Tuckman, B. W. 1965. 'Developmental Sequence in Small Groups'. *Psychological Bulletin* 63, pp. 384–99.

Vidmar, N., and J. R. Harkman. 1971. 'Interlaboratory Generalizability of Small Group Research: An Experimental Study'. *Journal of Social Psychology* 83, pp. 129–39.

Wall, T. D., and C. W. Clegg. 1981. 'A Longitudinal Field Study of Group Work Design'. *Journal of Occupational Behavior* 2, pp. 31–49.

Walton, R. E., and L. S. Schlesinger. 1979. 'Do Supervisors Thrive in Participative Work Systems?' *Organizational Dynamics*, Winter, pp. 24–38.

Weick, K. E. 1965. 'Laboratory Experimentation with Organizations' in J. G. March, ed., *Handbook of Organizations*. Chicago: Rand McNally.

——. 1977. 'Organization Design: Organizations as Self-Designing Systems'. *Organizational Dynamics*, Autumn, pp. 31–46.

Whyte, W. F. 1955. *Money and Motivation: An Analysis of Incentives in Industry*. New York: Harper.

Wicker, A., S. L. Kirmeyer, L. Hanson, and D. Alexander. 1976. 'Effects of Manning Levels on Subjective Experiences, Performance, and Verbal Interaction in Groups'. *Organizational Behavior and Human Performance* 17, pp. 251–74.

Woodman, R. W., and J. J. Sherwood. 1980. 'The Role of Team Development in Organizational Effectiveness: A Critical Review'. *Psychological Bulletin* 88, pp. 166–86.

Zander, A. 1971. *Motives and Goals in Groups*. New York: Academic Press.

——. 1980. 'The Origins and Consequences of Group Goals' in L. Festinger, ed., *Retrospections on Social Psychology*. New York: Oxford University Press.

EXERCISE 7 WHAT TO DO WITH JOHNNY ROCCO

Source: Adapted from Whetton, D. A. & Cameron, K. S. (1984). *Developing Management Skills*. Glenview, IL: Scott, Foresman and Company, pp. 450–453.

Objectives

1. Participating in a group assignment playing a particular role.
2. Diagnosing the group decision process after the assignment has been completed.

Starting the exercise

After reading the material relating to Johnny Rocco, a committee is formed to decide the fate of Johnny Rocco. The chairperson of the meeting is Johnny's supervisor, who should begin by assigning roles to the group members. These roles (shop steward, head of production, Johnny's co-worker, director of personnel, and social worker who helped Johnny in the past) represent points of view the chairperson feels should be included in this meeting. (Johnny is not to be included.) Two observers should be assigned.

After the roles have been assigned, each role-player should complete the personal preference part of the worksheet, ordering the alternatives according to their appropriateness from the vantage point of his or her role.

Once the individual preferences have been determined, the chairperson should call the meeting to order. The following rules govern the meeting: the group must reach a consensus ordering of the alternatives; the group cannot use a statistical aggregation, or majority vote, decision-making process; members should stay 'in

Worksheet

Personal Preference	Group Decision	
_____	_____	Give Johnny a warning that at the next sign of trouble he will be fired.
_____	_____	Do nothing, as it is unclear that Johnny did anything wrong.
_____	_____	Create strict controls (do's and don'ts) for Johnny with immediate strong punishment for any misbehaviour.
_____	_____	Give Johnny a great deal of warmth and personal attention and affection (overlooking his present behaviour) so he can learn to depend on others.
_____	_____	Fire him. It's not worth the time and effort spent for such a low-level position.
_____	_____	Talk over the problem with Johnny in an understanding way so he can learn to ask others for help in solving his problems.
_____	_____	Give Johnny a well-structured schedule of daily activities with immediate and unpleasant consequences for not adhering to the schedule.
_____	_____	Do nothing now, but watch him carefully and provide immediate punishment for any future misbehaviours.
_____	_____	Treat Johnny the same as everyone else, but provide an orderly routine so he can learn to stand on his own two feet.
_____	_____	Call Johnny in and logically discuss the problem with him and ask what you can do to help him.
_____	_____	Do nothing now, but watch him so you can reward him the next time he does something good.

character' throughout the discussion. Treat this as a committee meeting consisting of members with different backgrounds, orientations and interests who share a problem.

After the group has completed the assignment, the two observers should conduct a discussion of the group process using the group process diagnostic questions as a guide. Group members should not look at these questions until after the group task has been completed.

Johnny Rocco

Johnny has a grim personal background. He is the third child in a family of seven. He has not seen his father for several years and his recollection is that his father used to come home drunk and beat up every member of the family; everyone ran when he came staggering home.

His mother, according to Johnny, wasn't much better. She was irritable and unhappy and she always predicted that Johnny would come to no good end. Yet she worked when her health allowed her to do so in order to keep the family in food and clothing. She always decried the fact that she was not able to be the kind of mother she would like to be.

Johnny quit school in the seventh grade. He had great difficulty conforming to the school routine — misbehaving often, acting as a truant quite frequently, and engaging in numerous fights with schoolmates. On several occasions he was picked up by the police and, along with members of his group, questioned during several investigations into cases of both petty and grand larceny. The police regarded him as 'probably a bad one'.

The juvenile officer of the court saw in Johnny some good qualities that no one else seemed to sense. This man, Mr O'Brien, took it on himself to act as a 'big brother' to Johnny. He had several long conversations with Johnny, during which he managed to penetrate to some degree Johnny's defensive shell. He represented to Johnny the first semblance of personal interest in his life. Through Mr O'Brien's efforts, Johnny returned to school and obtained a high school diploma. Afterwards, Mr O'Brien helped him obtain a job.

Now at age 20, Johnny is a stockroom clerk in one of the laboratories where you are employed. On the whole Johnny's performance has been acceptable, but there have been glaring exceptions. One involved a clear act of insubordination on a fairly unimportant matter. In another Johnny was accused, on circumstantial grounds, of destroying some expensive equipment. Though the investigation is still open, it now appears that the destruction was accidental.

Johnny's supervisor wants to keep him on for at least a trial period, but he wants 'outside' advice as to the best way of helping him grow into greater responsibility. Of course, much depends on how Johnny behaves in the next few months. Naturally, his supervisor must follow personnel policies that are accepted in the company as a whole. It is important to note that Johnny is not an attractive man. He is rather weak and sickly, and shows unmistakable signs of long years of social deprivation.

A committee is formed to decide the fate of Johnny Rocco. The chairperson of the meeting is Johnny's supervisor, who should begin by assigning roles.

Group process diagnostic questions

Communications

1. Who responded to whom?
2. Who interrupted? Was the same person interrupted consistently?
3. Were there identifiable 'communication clusters'? Why or why not?
4. Did some members say very little? If so, why? Was level of participation ever discussed?
5. Were efforts made to involve everyone?

Decision making

1. Did the group decide how to decide?
2. How were decisions made?
3. What criterion was used to establish agreement?
   a. Majority vote?
   b. Consensus?
   c. No opposition interpreted as agreement?
4. What was done if people disagreed?
5. How effective was your decision-making process?
6. Does every member feel his or her input into the decision-making process was valued by the group, or were the comments of some members frequently discounted? If so, was this issue ever discussed?

Leadership

1. What type of power structure did the group operate under?
   a. One definite leader?
   b. Leadership functions shared by all members?
   c. Power struggles within the group?
   d. No leadership supplied by anyone?
2. How does each member feel about the leadership structure used? Would an alternative have been more effective?
3. Did the chairperson provide an adequate structure for the discussion?
4. Was the discussion governed by the norms of equity?
5. Was the chairperson's contribution to the content of the discussion overbearing?

Awareness of feelings

1. How did members in general react to the group meetings? Were they hostile (towards whom or what?), enthusiastic, apathetic?
2. Did members openly discuss their feelings towards each other and their role in the group?

3. How do group members feel now about their participation in this group?

Task behaviour

1. Who was most influential in keeping the group task oriented? How?
2. Did some members carry the burden and do most of the work, or was the load distributed evenly?

3. If some members were not contributing their fair share, was this ever discussed? If so, what was the outcome? If not, why?
4. Did the group evaluate its method of accomplishing a task during or after the project? If so, what changes were made?
5. How effective was our group in performing assigned tasks? What improvements could have been made?

CASE 7 INTERNATIONAL SUPERANNUATION SPECIALISTS

Paul Ackerman

Company background

Australian Financial Advisers Ltd (AFA), a company specialising in superannuation services, is a subsidiary of Amalgamated Insurance Services Ltd (AISL), a large Australian-owned insurance group. AFA was created by AISL in the mid-1980s in response to the growing superannuation industry, which was seen as a potential rival to the group's traditional insurance products.

The company has 320 employees, 250 of whom are located at its Melbourne head office. Despite possessing a good client base and potential investment volumes, AFA has never traded profitably, its last full annual result being a trading loss of $10 million. This poor performance has been attributed to poor cost control, the subordination of AFA's interests to the pursuit of AISL's group goals and a perceived lack of ability to provide independent advice because of its link to AISL products.

Despite the losses, staff morale has been good. Management has been paternalistic and benevolent, and has historically looked after staff needs, although this had begun to change in recent years with increased financial pressure on AISL. AFA's focus was to provide a complete range of financial services under the AISL umbrella to reinforce AISL's market share and organisational prestige, rather than a profit for AFA.

Change of ownership

In 1994, as part of an overall review of the AISL's operations, it was decided to sell AFA. It was bought by International Superannuation Specialists Corporation (ISSC), a US group with extensive international interests in the superannuation/pensions industry, but no previous operations in Australia. The change in ownership was effective from 1 July 1995. In order to emphasise this change, the company has been renamed International Superannuation Specialists (Australia) Ltd (ISSA).

ISSC's corporate culture differs significantly from the existing AFA environment. It is a bottom-line driven, low-overhead operation. While staff are well rewarded, there are high expectations of achievement. There is little head office involvement in local operations, with local management empowered to make decisions and held accountable for performance.

In the first 12 months of its operations, ISCC's priorities are to refocus the identity of the company, reduce administrative and staffing costs, initiate a change to the ISSC culture and integrate the Australian operation into the ISSC worldwide network, particularly its information systems and corporate structure. Apart from some job reductions at the time of takeover, job security has been guaranteed for 12 months. ISSC's objective is for ISSA to be trading at a break-even point within that time frame.

Systems Administration Group

The Systems Administration Group is responsible for the integration of the company's client management systems. Under AISL's ownership, the group was responsible for detailed internal reporting requirements to AISL, as well as its own operational needs. The group comprised a manager and six systems administrators. At the time of the ownership change, the manager transferred to another position within AISL, and two administrators were made compulsorily redundant. This has placed an increased workload on the remaining staff.

ISSC sees the transformation and integration of this area as vital to the overall operation of the company. They have taken the opportunity to appoint an ISSC employee to the vacant manager's position. This person, Amanda Woods, arrived from the US, prior to the formal takeover, in mid-June 1995. Woods is a computer specialist who played a leading role in developing recent changes to the ISSC information technology (IT) systems. Ambitious, company-oriented and hard working, she is highly regarded and respected by ISSC management. She has always worked in a male-oriented environment and is highly task-focused. She has previously been responsible for setting up new systems, and has always implemented those systems under budget and within the time.

Although she has 3 years management experience, this is her first appointment outside the US head office. She has a very direct management style, and expects others to be upfront and speak their mind. She expects that her recommendations regarding the structure of the group will be adopted by ISSC.

Her brief was as follows:

- Improve client service levels on the existing IT system, while integrating the system with ISSC's international standards and requirements. This process is to be completed within 12 months.
- Once integration has been successfully completed, reduce staffing requirements to two administrators consistent with ISSC's international staffing standards, as a result of the improved efficiency of the new system.
- Implement measures necessary to introduce ISSC's corporate culture, with its emphasis on motivated employees and teamwork.

Woods is a career-minded computer professional, committed to meeting ISSC's objectives. She sees this appointment as an opportunity to advance her career within ISSC internationally. She expects high performance from her staff, and finds it difficult to understand employees not totally committed to their work.

One of her first actions after becoming manager was to conduct a staff briefing at which she outlined ISSC's plans for the group, including the reduction in staffing requirements for administrators. She outlined the need for the group to respond to the changes proposed, and emphasised that she would determine who stayed with the group. She indicated that there was little likelihood that alternative employment would be available within the company.

The work performed by the group is generally undertaken in a team environment, and ISSC intends to continue and develop this method of work, which is the basis of their computer operations worldwide.

All staff are tertiary qualified and technically competent, but Woods has become aware they do not always get along well socially. While the younger male administrators, Michael Mann and Billy Campbell, appear to work well together, a female administrator, Jane Reynolds, seems unwilling to work as cooperatively. Woods respects Reynolds's technical ability, and they have had some brief discussions about her career expectations. There also appears to be some conflict between Reynolds and Mann, who seems to resent females in the workplace, including Woods. The final employee, Jason Hansen, does not impress Woods at all. He appears to resent the recent ownership change, and lacks motivation. Attempts to engage him in discussions about the operation of the group have been unsuccessful.

The problem for Woods is that Hansen is the group's specialist in operating and modifying AFA's pre-existing Financial Investment Returns Model (FIRM), a sophisticated program for analysing comparative investment returns. The other administrator familiar with this model was one of those made redundant. This model is highly regarded in the financial community, and was one of the reasons for ISSC's purchase of AFA. It will be integrated into the ISSC system, replacing their existing modelling techniques. To reduce the group's dependence on Hansen, Woods decided to train another employee in the operation of FIRM. She has allocated Campbell to work with Hansen to learn his role, on the recommendation of the previous manager.

In considering how best to achieve her objectives, Woods has prepared brief notes about her staff, based on her observations.

Mann

Mann is a 31-year-old systems administrator who has been with the company since 1989. He is a second generation Australian, from a Southern

European background. Mann is an ambitious person with good technical skills, quite capable of dealing with the systems changes being adopted by ISSC. A protégé of the previous manager, he had expectations of promotion to the manager's position when it became available. He does not like working with women, but is not overt in displaying disapproval. Mann has a tendency to be arrogant with other staff, but gets on well with mates his own age, including Campbell. He intends to be one of the administrators chosen to stay. He is definitely not a team player.

Information not available to Woods: Mann dislikes Woods intensely, and perceives her to be a 'know-all'. He believes that men should hold managerial positions and is unhappy that he was not given Woods's job. He has high career goals and perceives this to be a career set-back. He firmly believes that he is the best person for the systems administrator job.

Reynolds
Reynolds is 26 years old and has been with the company since 1991. She possesses good technical skills, but is reserved and lacks confidence. She prefers to work independently utilising her problem-solving abilities, rather than in a team environment. She interacts with other employees in the group only when it is made necessary by work requirements. Reynolds is a single mother with a 5-year-old child, and her external family responsibilities can sometimes impinge upon work requirements. She is conscious of Mann's disapproval and resentment of her presence in the workplace.

Information not available to Woods: Reynolds likes Woods because Woods has taken an interest in her career. She admires Woods's style and respects the way she is managing the group. She has a strong dislike of Campbell, who she perceived as stupid, unproductive and 'all show'. She finds it difficult to understand why Hansen is training Campbell rather than her. Although she accepts the need for change, and finds the uncertainty frightening, she loves her job and wants to continue her career at ISSC.

Campbell
Campbell is also 26 and, like Reynolds, has been at AFA since 1991. He is a competent administrator who is popular with other staff, and was well regarded by the previous manager. He has good communication skills and works well in team tasks, although his tendency to socialise sometimes affects his work performance. His convivial manner is not well regarded by Woods, who considers it unprofessional. Campbell is not ambitious, but wants to retain his job security. He considers he has the inside running for one of the future positions, especially after being chosen to receive specialist training from Hansen.

Hansen
At 42, and as a long-serving AFA employee (since 1979), Hansen was disappointed he was not offered a position to stay in AISL, and does not see the need for radical change. He has no ambition to stay with ISSC, and has made it no secret that he is already making arrangements to use his likely redundancy pay-out to set up his own business. Lacking motivation, he does the minimum required, but is needed to pass on his specialist knowledge. He finds it difficult to relate to a female manager. He does not like Mann, and is beginning to have doubts about Campbell's competence, but keeps his own counsel.

Information not available to Woods: Hansen has a very dim view of company management. He hates the ideas of efficiency and, despite what he says, is not anxious to take a redundancy pay-out. He is very disappointed that the company has shown no loyalty to long-term staff.

Discussion questions
One of Amanda's objectives is to motivate employees and introduce teamwork.
1. At what developmental stage is this group?
2. What individual needs are being met by group membership?
3. What problems are the group currently facing?
4. What should Amanda do to establish a successful team?

INTERGROUP BEHAVIOUR AND CONFLICT

Learning objectives

- Describe *the concept of interdependence.*

- Discuss *factors affecting cooperation and competition.*

- Explain *the difference between traditional and contemporary views of conflict.*

- Distinguish *between functional and dysfunctional conflict.*

- Describe *the relationship between intergroup conflict and organisational performance.*

- Describe *a model of conflict.*

- Discuss *why intergroup conflict occurs.*

- Identify *several consequences of dysfunctional intergroup conflict.*

- Describe *techniques for managing conflict through resolution.*

- Discuss *several approaches to stimulating conflict.*

Chapter 8

For any organisation to perform effectively, interdependent individuals and groups must establish working relationships across organisational boundaries, between individuals and among groups. Individuals or groups may depend on one another for information, assistance or coordinated action. But the fact is that they are interdependent. Such interdependence may foster cooperation or conflict.

For example, the production and marketing executives of a company may meet to discuss ways to deal with foreign competition. Such a meeting may be reasonably free of conflict. Decisions get made, strategies are developed and the executives return to work. Thus, there is intergroup cooperation to achieve a goal. However, this may not be the case if sales decline because the company is not offering enough variety in its product line. The marketing department desires broad product lines to offer more variety to customers, while the production department desires narrow product lines to keep production costs at a manageable level and to increase productivity. Conflict is likely to occur at this point because each function has its own goals which, in this case, conflict. Thus, groups may cooperate on one point and conflict on another.

The focus of this chapter is on conflict that occurs between groups in organisations.[1] Intergroup problems are not the only type of conflict that can exist in organisations. Conflict between individuals, however, can usually be more easily resolved through existing mechanisms. Troublesome employees can be fired, transferred or given new work schedules.

This chapter begins with a discussion of interdependence, the key to understanding conflict. We outline a model of conflict and this helps in the identification of the causes and consequences of organisational conflict. Finally, we consider various techniques that organisations may use to successfully manage intergroup conflict. The two most common strategies — negotiation and mediation — are considered in more detail in Chapter 9.

INTERDEPENDENCE: THE KEY TO UNDERSTANDING CONFLICT

Exercise 8
Pemberton's dilemma

Why do conflicts occur? Achieving individual, group or organisational goals often depends not just on our actions but also on the actions of other individuals or groups. When other individuals or groups share our goals and are willing to cooperate in goal achievement, conflicts are unlikely to develop. Often, however, individuals find themselves in situations where they must choose between achieving their own goals (competing) or working with others to achieve group goals (cooperating). In this section, we will consider the two keys to conflict — the concepts of social interdependence and mixed motives — as well as the factors that affect individuals' decisions to compete or cooperate. Our understanding of these factors is important in developing strategies for reducing organisational conflict.

Social interdependence

Our understanding of conflict lies in the concept of *interdependence*. Social interdependence describes situations that involve more than one person or group and in which the wellbeing of each individual or group is determined not just by their actions but also by the actions of the other people, or groups, involved. There are occasions when the situation strongly encourages individuals to cooperate; for example, a multidisciplinary research team attempting to find a new drug for the treatment of human immunodeficiency virus (HIV) cannot succeed unless all members of the group contribute their skills. For one person to win, all must win: all members of the research team will benefit when a new drug is found. The goals of the individual and the group coincide and the situation provides a strong incentive for cooperation. When work teams need to finish a project, all will benefit if they are able to cooperate to complete their task.[2] Under such circumstances, the task is one of problem solving and relies on good communication between group members.[3]

At the other extreme, situations can encourage a high degree of competitiveness. The best example of such situations centres around resources: money, computers and staff are all examples of finite resources. In organisations, when one individual or group obtains access to resources it is usually at the expense of another individual or group. If one department hires new staff, it means that another department cannot. Under these circumstances there is considerable incentive to compete, and to try to maximise your own share of the available resources.[4]

Although situations that encourage pure cooperation or pure competition exist, more frequently we find ourselves in situations that are described as *mixed-motive*: situations that encourage us to cooperate while at the same time pulling us towards competition. These kinds of situations are represented by two well-known dilemmas: the Prisoners' Dilemma and the Social Dilemma. Exhibit 8.1 describes the two dilemmas in more detail. These dilemmas present individuals with the choice between maximising individual or joint gain, and create a conflict between short-term benefits for the individual and long-term benefits for the group. Interdependent situations create a paradox that requires individuals to choose between maximising their own outcomes and those of the group. The problem for individuals is twofold: first, there is a strong incentive to compete as this avoids the very worst individual outcome; second, the very best outcomes are obtained by engaging in the high-risk strategy of cooperating. If Dan and Jules' dilemma seems a long way from organisational problems, consider the budget dilemma described at the end of this section.[5] And if Dan and Jules' situation appears complicated, the situation in organisations becomes more complicated because of the larger number of groups involved in such dilemmas.

To the extent that individuals compete, organisational conflicts will increase. If we can find strategies that encourage cooperation, such conflicts can be reduced. In the next two sections, we will consider factors that affect cooperation and competition.

Determinants of competition

How individuals interpret interdependence and the behaviour of others is largely determined by how they perceive themselves in relation to other groups. These perceptions, described as social categorisation, can result in identification at the individual, group or collective level: we may view ourselves as acting on

Consider the situation that faces the two prisoners, Dan and Jules. Their choices are shown in the diagram below. If they view the situation simply from their perspective, both will conclude that their best course of action is to confess. Under the circumstances, this strategy may yield the best individual outcome (not going to jail) and avoids the worst individual outcome (going to jail for 20 years). What is the problem with this strategy? First, to get the best possible individual outcome, Jules must rely on Dan to behave differently from Jules. This seems unlikely; in fact, Dan has been through the same reasoning process and is relying on Jules to behave differently. Consequently, Dan and Jules will spend a total of 10 years in jail, thus achieving a very poor joint outcome. Their best *joint outcome* (2 years in jail) would occur if both remained silent, but this is a high-risk strategy for both. Look at the diagram below to see what would happen to Dan if he stayed silent while Jules confessed. How long would Dan be in prison?

	DAN	
	stay silent	**confess**
stay silent	1, *1*	0, **20**
JULES		
confess	20, *0*	5, **5**

As we increase the number of people involved, so the dilemma becomes more complex and the advantages of competing greater. Social dilemmas describe situations that are similar to the Prisoners' Dilemmas, but involve more people. One example of a social dilemma is the choice we make about whether to drive a car or to take public transport to work. Using public transport will decrease congestion on the roads, reduce pollution and make the environment more pleasant. However, driving a car is more convenient. If everyone were to use public transport, our drive to work would be much quicker. So, relying on others to behave differently from us, we decide to drive to work. So does everyone else. The result: increased congestion and pollution. As we will see, organisations are good examples of social dilemmas.

our own behalf (individual level), on behalf of our work group (group level) or on behalf of the organisation (collective level).[6] Social categorisation is important to our understanding of conflict because it determines our definition of *ingroups* (groups to which we belong) and *outgroups* (groups to which we do not belong)[7] and this definition has several consequences in terms of cooperation. While ingroups serve to decrease both social and psychological distance between group members, outgroups serve to increase that distance.

Outgroup members are perceived as less trustworthy, honest and cooperative; individuals tend to overestimate ingroup effort and underestimate outgroup effort; and communication with outgroup members is infrequent. The consequences of these attributions include the reduction of cooperative behaviour, differences in perceptions of fairness and decreased communication — all vital if conflicts are to be resolved constructively.[8] These factors imply that individuals are more likely to behave competitively towards outgroups and, as we will see in subsequent sections, they also establish the preconditions for dysfunctional organisational conflict.

Determinants of cooperation

Although many factors may influence an individual's decision to cooperate, the most important of these is the ability to communicate with members of an outgroup. Communication allows individuals to better understand another individual's or group's position, especially the intentions underlying their behaviour. It helps to clarify the problem and increases cohesion between previously separate individuals or groups; furthermore, commitment to a cooperative strategy is increased when individuals or groups have made a public commitment to that strategy. As opportunities to communicate increase, so does the probability that individuals will cooperate with outgroup members. Communication breaks down group identification and is an important prerequisite for building trust. As trust grows, cooperative behaviour appears less risky and a major incentive for competing is removed.[9]

In addition to communication, group size plays an important role in determining levels of cooperation: as the number of individuals or groups competing for resources increases, cooperation decreases. There are two reasons for this: the fewer individuals or groups competing for resources, the more easily each individual's or group's behaviour can be identified and monitored; and the impact of taking more than a fair share (cooperating) is more obvious when the number of individuals or groups taking resources from a common pool is small.[10] Past experience also plays a role in determining an individual's (or group's) level of cooperation: cooperation is increased when we have experienced cooperation in the past, and is further increased if other individuals or groups have changed from a competitive to a cooperative strategy.[11] Finally, issues of fairness influence our willingness to cooperate with others: when the outcomes and the processes by which those outcomes are obtained are judged to be fair, individual level of cooperation increases.[12] As we saw in Chapter 5, issues of fairness are important for organisations, not just in relation to conflict but in relation to a whole range of organisational outcomes.

Organisations as resource dilemmas

Organisations, and groups within organisations, cannot function without resources. If individuals within the organisation identified at the collective (or organisational) level, this would not pose a problem. However, organisations — by virtue of the structures that they impose — create categories, and these categories determine the groups that individuals identify with and their interaction patterns. Because of task interdependence, individuals will interact most frequently with other people in their work group and this results in identification at the intergroup level. Consequently, individuals will judge others in their work unit to be more similar, and these individuals will form the ingroup. Other work units will form the outgroup. You should recognise all of these as factors that promote competition. Competition will be further increased as resources become scarce, when individuals attribute this scarcity to internal factors (such as mismanagement) and when the distribution of such resources is judged to be unfair.[13]

To the extent that available resources are finite and groups compete to obtain a share of those resources, organisations provide a good example of a social dilemma. Kramer has described the dominant resource budget dilemma that pervades organisational life. Work units compete for resources such as money, equipment and staff. All recognise that the resource pool is limited and that the organisation would benefit if work groups requested only the resources that they required. However, because the level of resources used in one year determines the level of resources that a work unit receives in the next year, all work units are encouraged to compete: to request and use more resources than they require. Richard Prebble, New Zealand's former Minister for Finance, has described just such situations within the public service (*Weekend Australian*, February 10–11, 1996, p. 2). One example that he gives is of a department that filled a warehouse with collapsible desks, rather than leave money unspent. The consequence is that organisational resources are overutilised, leaving fewer resources for achieving organisational goals or for assisting organisations through economic difficulties. In the long term, this may mean that the organisation cannot survive.

The strategies for altering individual and group behaviour, to change their perceptions of the dilemma, will be outlined at the end of this chapter.

TRADITIONAL VERSUS CONTEMPORARY PERSPECTIVES ON CONFLICT

Since the early part of this century, organisational scholars have gradually changed their perspectives on conflict. Much of this change in thinking relates to assumptions about whether conflict is positive or negative. Two relatively distinct perspectives on conflict can be identified: traditional and contemporary.

The *traditional perspective* asserts that all conflict is bad. Thus, the presence of conflict indicates that something is wrong. This perspective on conflict was probably reinforced by the violent struggles that took place between management and the young labour movement during the first 25 years of this century. One important consequence of this view is that since conflict is inherently bad, it must be eliminated. Typically, attempts to eliminate conflict took the form of suppression. Unfortunately, while suppression might remove the outward appearance of conflict, it does not contribute to resolving the underlying difficulties which led to it.

This traditional perspective on conflict is still held by many people today. Nonetheless, in recent years organisational theorists and practitioners have gradually changed their view of conflict in light of knowledge gained from both research and practice. This has led to what may be described as a more contemporary perspective on conflict.

The *contemporary viewpoint* describes conflict as neither inherently good nor bad but as inevitable. Too much conflict can have negative consequences because it requires time and resources to deal with it and diverts energy that could be more constructively applied elsewhere. Too little conflict, on the other hand, can also be negative in that such a state can lead to apathy and lethargy and provide little or no impetus for change and innovation. If everything is always going smoothly (that is, there is no conflict) people may become too comfortable to want to make changes that could improve organisational effectiveness.

Two important conclusions regarding conflict from the contemporary perspective follow:

1. In many situations conflict can be good because it can have positive results (for example, stimulating innovation and creativity).
2. Since conflict is inherently neither good nor bad and can lead to both positive and negative results, a primary concern should be the management of conflict, rather than its elimination or suppression. This suggests, among other things, that there may be times when conflict is created as a deliberate strategy to stimulate the search for new and better ways of doing things.

A REALISTIC VIEW OF INTERGROUP CONFLICT

Conflict is inevitable in organisations. Intergroup conflict, however, can be both a positive and a negative force. Consequently, management should not strive to eliminate all conflict — only conflict that will have disruptive effects on the organisation's efforts to achieve goals. Some type or degree of conflict may prove beneficial if it is used as an instrument for change or innovation. For example, evidence suggests conflict can improve the quality of decision making in organisations.[14] Thus, the critical issue is not conflict itself but how conflict is managed. Using this approach, we can define conflict in terms of the effect it has on the organisation. In this respect, we shall discuss both functional and dysfunctional conflict.[15]

Functional conflict

A **functional conflict** is a confrontation between groups that enhances and benefits the organisation's performance. For example, two departments in a hospital may be in conflict over the most efficient and adaptive method of delivering health care to low-income rural families. The two departments agree on the goal but not on the means to achieve it. Whatever the outcome, low-income rural families probably will end up with better medical care once the conflict is settled. Without this type of conflict in organisations, there would be little commitment to change, and most groups would be likely to become stagnant. Thus, functional conflict can be thought of as a type of 'creative tension'.

Dysfunctional conflict

A **dysfunctional conflict** is any confrontation or interaction between groups that harms the organisation or hinders the achievement of organisational goals. Management must seek to eliminate dysfunctional conflict. Beneficial conflict often can turn into bad conflicts, but in most cases, the point at which functional conflict becomes dysfunctional is impossible to identify precisely. Certain levels of stress and conflict may help create a healthy and positive movement toward goals in one group. Those same levels, however, may prove extremely disruptive and dysfunctional in another group (or at a different time for the former group). A group's tolerance for stress and conflict can also depend on the type of organisation it serves. Car manufacturers, professional sports teams and crisis organisations, such as police and fire departments, would have different points where functional conflict becomes dysfunctional from organisations such as universities, research and development companies and film production companies.

Conflict and organisational performance

As was indicated earlier, the contemporary perspective on conflict suggests that conflict may have either positive or negative consequences for the organisation, depending on how much exists and how it is managed. Every organisation has an optimal level of conflict that can be considered highly functional — it helps generate positive performance. When the conflict level is too low, performance can also suffer. Innovation and change are less likely to take place and the organisation may have difficulty adapting to its changing environment. If a low conflict level continues, the very survival of the organisation can be threatened. On the other hand, if the conflict level becomes too high, the resulting chaos also can threaten the organisation's survival. An example is the popular press coverage of the results of 'dissension' in labour unions and its impact on performance. If fighting between rival factions in the union becomes too great, it can render the union less effective in pursuing its mission of furthering its members' interests. A further example may be found in the first case at the end of this chapter. The Rainbow Medical Centre case illustrates a number of conflict issues to be discussed in this chapter. The relationship between the level of intergroup conflict and organisational performance that is consistent with a contemporary perspective is presented in Exhibit 8.2 and explained for three hypothetical situations.

A MODEL OF CONFLICT

Several models of the conflict process have been developed. They all capture similar ideas and the model presented in this chapter (shown in Exhibit 8.3) draws on the work of Pondy[16] and Thomas.[17] These models allow us to trace the causes, impact and consequences of conflict at several levels: emotions, attitudes and behaviours. They also highlight two important points about conflict and conflict management. First, as a conflict intensifies, the situation becomes more emotionally charged, attitudes and opinions harden, and communication

Exhibit 8.2 **Relationship between intergroup conflict and organisational performance**

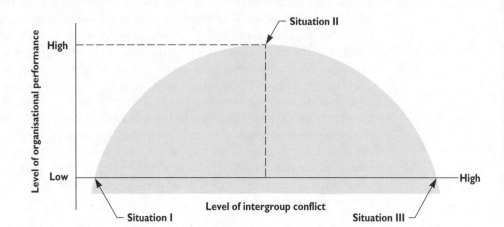

	Level of Intergroup Conflict	Probable Impact on Organisations	Organisation Characterised by	Level of Organisational Performance
Situation I	Low or none	Dysfunctional	• Slow adaptation to environmental changes • Few changes • Little stimulation of ideas • Apathy • Stagnation	Low
Situation II	Optimal	Functional	• Positive movement towards goals • Innovation and change • Search for problem solutions • Creativity and quick adaptation to environmental changes	High
Situation III	High	Dysfunctional	• Disruption • Interference with activities • Coordination difficult • Chaos	Low

gradually breaks down. A cycle of escalating conflict is established. Second, this implies that intervention in the early stages of the conflict results in less destructive or dysfunctional consequences. In the following sections we will consider these stages in more detail, focusing on the changes that take place in intragroup and intergroup processes as conflicts progress. The changes that occur both within and between groups involved in intergroup conflict generally result in either a continuance or an escalation of the conflict.[18]

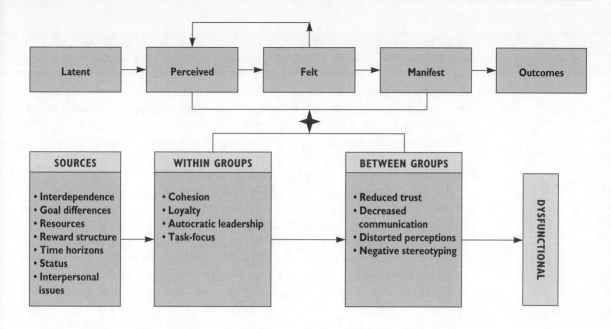

Exhibit 8.3

A model of

conflict

identifying the

group processes

that result in

dysfunctional

outcomes

Stages of conflict

Although some conflicts can become intense and full-blown virtually instantaneously, it is more often the case that intergroup conflicts develop over a period of time. When this happens there are typically several stages of evolution through which the conflict passes.

Latent conflict describes a situation in which the preconditions for conflict exist, but have not yet been noticed by the affected parties. In an organisation this will be when there are power differences, when resources are scarce or when groups hold incompatible goals. In terms of our definition of conflict, although one group has the potential to negatively affect another's outcomes this potential has not yet been realised. Consequently, there are no outward signs of conflict.

Conflicts do not necessarily develop even when the preconditions for conflict exist. They arise when these conditions bring goal differences into focus. This may occur when goal attainment is threatened by other work units, when other groups violate organisational norms or when individuals perceive differences in the way a situation has been defined. **Perceived conflict** exists when there is a cognitive awareness on the part of at least one group that events have occurred or that conditions exist that can create conflict. For example, two units in the same organisation may both want to move into the same space in the company's new office facility. Or perceived conflict may be part of a company's annual budget planning process when each department attempts to maximise the resources it receives, potentially at the expense of every other department. One of the consequences is that groups start to develop negative perceptions of the other parties involved in the dispute.

Although individuals perceive that their goals are in conflict with those of another work unit, perceived conflicts occur at the cognitive level. There is, however, also an emotional component to conflicts, although there is a lag between our cognitive recognition of a conflict and our emotional reactions to it. Perceived conflict may or may not lead to **felt conflict**. The felt stage of conflict represents an escalation that includes emotional involvement: the conflict becomes personalised and we may experience anger or hostility towards the other individual or group. Individuals may also experience increased tension, anxiety or stress. Such negative emotions increase identification with an individual's work unit and make the boundaries of the unit less permeable to other individuals. Because such feelings are generally a source of discomfort, the parties involved may be motivated to reduce the negative emotions. This, in turn, can lead to positive or negative attempts to deal with the conflict. Typically, all parties to a conflict need to experience both perceived and felt conflict to be sufficiently motivated to attempt resolution.

The final conflict stage is **manifest conflict**. Manifest conflict is not only perceived and felt, but also acted upon. That is, at the manifest stage the conflicting groups are actively engaging in conflict behaviour. There may be verbal, written or even physical attacks. In manifest conflict, it is usually very apparent to uninvolved parties that a problem exists. Depending on how the conflict has developed and been managed at previous stages, groups at this stage may choose either a competitive or cooperative strategy. If the conflict has escalated, competition is more likely: individuals or groups will act to prevent 'opponents' from attaining their goals. One means for achieving this is to withdraw support. For example, the information technology division of an organisation may refuse to solve the computer problems of the resources section until they receive further funding. Individuals or groups develop an 'us and them' perspective. Although it is possible to successfully resolve manifest conflict, it is far better to deal with conflict at an earlier stage. Additionally, manifest conflict is more likely to have longer lasting effects than either perceived or felt conflict.

Finally, we must consider how the conflict ends. *Outcomes* will be determined by the strategies that have been employed to end the conflict: it may be resolved, it may escalate further or it may be temporarily suppressed. Of these, suppression is the worst outcome: if we fail to resolve the issues that underlie the conflict, it will resurface at a later time. In the interim, it is likely that individual and group positions and attitudes will harden: not only will there be ongoing difficulties, but when the conflict resurfaces, it will be more difficult to resolve.

WHY INTERGROUP CONFLICT OCCURS

Case 8
Rainbow Medical
Centre

Every group comes into at least partial conflict with every other group with which it interacts. This tendency is known as the 'law of interorganisational conflict'.[19] In this section we consider four factors that contribute to group conflict: work interdependence, differences in goals, differences in perceptions and the increased demand for specialists. Conflict at the interpersonal level is also considered. These sources are also explored in this chapter's Organisational Encounter.

Interdependence

Work interdependence occurs when two or more organisational groups must depend on one another to complete their tasks. The conflict potential in such situations is high. Three distinct types of interdependence among groups have been identified: pooled, sequential and reciprocal.[20]

ORGANISATIONAL   Encounter

Gender and conflict at work

According to Victoria's Equal Employment Opportunity (EEO) Commission, while complaints in all other areas are decreasing those related to employment are on the rise. In 1992–93, 847 (74.7%) employment-related complaints were received; this number increased to 1414 (87.5%) in 1993–94. In both years, the most frequently occurring complaints concerned discrimination on the basis of sex, impairment and race, or were related to sexual harassment in the workplace. In these areas, the sharpest increase in complaints was observed in sexual harassment complaints: whereas 160 (19%) complaints were lodged in 1992–93, 416 (29%) were lodged in 1993–94. Also on the rise were claims of discrimination on the basis of pregnancy (up 2%). However, there were decreases in the number of claims made on the basis of sex (down 4%), impairment (down 5%) and race (down 1%). Does this mean that organisations are changing their human resource management practices?

Recent surveys of larger corporations suggest that this is not necessarily so. In fact, within the accounting profession, it appears that women may prefer to change professions rather than deal with issues of discrimination. Among the larger accounting companies, very few women are partners: two out of fifty-three (Ernst & Young), two out of ninety (Arthur Andersen) and thirteen out of two hundred-and-forty-seven (KPMG Peat Marwick). Among the key issues are a culture that expects staff to work long hours at the office even though a substantial proportion of work could be done from home. Culture change that emphasises flexibility in work practices and the desire of young staff to spend time with their families may help retain women within the accounting profession.

Another company aiming for culture change is Mobil. A recent case in which a manager's pay rise was cut in the performance appraisal process drew attention to the uneasy relationship between Mobil and its female staff. While this case centred around the manager's treatment of an employee returning from maternity leave, it highlighted a number of problems within the organisation. First, on the grounds that customers prefer not to deal with women, women were less likely to be promoted, transferred or given developmental opportunities. Since relocation is central to career progression in Mobil, this means that women were being denied important career opportunities. Second, although staff complained of sexual innuendo and harassment, sexist language and the display of pornographic material, little was done to reprimand the offenders. In fact, the women were advised to 'lighten up'. All of this pointed to a culture that supported sexual discrimination.

How is Mobil dealing with these problems? To achieve culture change and to ensure that all levels of management are responsible for implementing that change, Mobil has reviewed its performance appraisal system. Now, employees rate their managers and this rating contributes 30% to the manager's overall rating; this means that it also contributes 30% to a salary increase (or decrease).

Source: EEO Commission Annual Report; Gome, A. (1994). Breaking down the macho culture, *Business Review Weekly*, May 16; Lyons, M. (1994). The profession moves to retain its women, *Business Review Weekly*, December 12.

Pooled interdependence requires no interaction among groups because each group, in effect, performs separately. However, the pooled performances of all the groups determine how successful the organisation is. For example, the staff of an IBM sales office in one region may have no interaction with their peers in another region. Similarly, two bank branches will have little or no interaction. In both cases, however, the groups are interdependent because the performance of each must be adequate if the total organisation is to thrive. The conflict potential in pooled interdependence is relatively low, and management can rely on standard rules and procedures developed at the main office for coordination.

Sequential interdependence requires one group to complete its task before another group can complete its task. Tasks are performed in a sequential fashion. In a manufacturing plant, for example, the product must be assembled before it can be painted. Thus, the assembling department must complete its task before the painting department can begin painting. Under these circumstances, since the output of one group serves as the input for another, conflict between the groups is more likely to occur. Coordinating this type of interdependence involves effective use of the management function of planning.

Reciprocal interdependence requires the output of each group to serve as input to other groups in the organisation. Consider the relationships that exist between the anaesthesia staff, nursing staff, technician staff and surgeons in a hospital operating room. This relationship creates a high degree of reciprocal interdependence. The same interdependence exists among groups involved in space launchings. Another example is the interdependence among airport control towers, flight crews, ground operations and maintenance crews. Clearly, the potential for conflict is great in any of these situations. Effective coordination involves management's skilful use of the organisational processes of communication and decision making. All organisations have pooled interdependence among groups. Complex organisations also have sequential interdependence. The most complicated organisations experience pooled, sequential and reciprocal interdependence among groups. The more complex the organisation, the greater is the potential for conflict and the more difficult is the task facing management.

Differences in goals

As the subunits of an organisation become specialised, they often develop dissimilar goals. A goal of a production unit may include low production costs and few defective products. A goal of the research and development unit may be innovative ideas that can be converted into commercially successful new products. These different goals can lead to different expectations among the members of each unit. Because of their goals, production engineers may expect close supervision, while research scientists may expect a great deal of participation in decision making. Because of the different goals of these two groups, conflict can result when they interact. Finally, marketing departments usually have a goal of maximum gross income. On the other hand, credit departments seek to minimise credit losses. Depending on which department prevails, different customers might be selected. Here again, conflict can occur because each department has a different goal. There are certain conditions that foster intergroup conflict because of differences in goals.

Limited resources

As we saw in the section on interdependence, goals differences are frequently highlighted when individuals or groups compete for resources. Competition, and consequently conflict, will be increased when resources are scarce. When resources are limited and must be allocated, mutual dependencies increase and any differences in group goals become more apparent. If money, space, the labour force and materials were unlimited, each group could pursue, at least to a relative degree, its own goals. But in virtually all cases, resources must be allocated or shared. When groups conclude that resources have not been allocated in an equitable manner, pressures towards conflict increase.[21]

Reward structures

Reward systems can affect the level of social categorisation. As we saw earlier, the level at which we identify (individual, group or collective) influences our definitions of the ingroup and outgroup, and affects our willingness to cooperate. Intergroup conflict is more likely to occur when the reward system is related to individual group performance rather than to overall organisational performance. When rewards are related to individual group performance, performance is, in fact, viewed as an independent variable, although the performance of the group is in reality very interdependent. For example, in the situation described above, suppose that the marketing group is rewarded for sales produced and that the credit group is rewarded for minimising credit losses. In such a situation, competition will be directly reinforced and dysfunctional conflict will, inadvertently, be rewarded.

Differences in perceptions

The differences in goals can be accompanied by differing perceptions of reality, and disagreements over what constitutes reality can lead to conflict. For instance, a problem in a hospital may be viewed one way by the administrative staff and in another way by the medical staff. Recent disputes over the restructuring of the ambulance service in Victoria provide one example: while the Government views its cost-reduction measures as increasing the efficiency of the service, ambulance workers and the public perceive a reduction in the quality of this critical service. Many factors cause groups in organisations to form different perceptions of reality. The major factors include different goals (previously discussed), different time horizons, status incongruency and inaccurate perceptions.

Different time horizons

Time perspectives influence how a group perceives reality. Deadlines influence the priorities and importance that groups assign to their various activities. Research scientists working for a chemical manufacturer may have a time perspective of several years, while the same company's manufacturing engineers may work within time frames of less than a year. A bank president might focus on 5- and 10-year time spans, while middle managers might concentrate on much shorter spans. With such differences in time horizons, problems and issues deemed critical by one group may be dismissed as not important by another, and conflicts may erupt.

Status incongruency

Conflicts concerning the relative status of different groups are common and influence perceptions. Usually, many different status standards are found in an organisation, rather than an absolute one. The result is many status hierarchies. For example, status conflicts are often created by work patterns — which group initiates the work and which group responds. A production department, for instance, may perceive a change as an affront to its status because it must accept a salesperson's initiation of work. This status conflict may be aggravated deliberately by the salesperson. Academic snobbery is certainly a fact of campus life at many colleges and universities. Members of a particular academic discipline perceive themselves, for one reason or another, as having a higher status than others.

Inaccurate perceptions

Inaccurate perceptions often cause one group to develop stereotypes about other groups. While the differences between groups may actually be small, each group will tend to exaggerate them. Thus, you will hear that 'all women executives are aggressive' or 'all bank trust officers behave alike'. When the differences between groups are emphasised, the stereotypes are reinforced, relations deteriorate and conflict develops. We will return to this issue when we discuss how conflicts affect group processes.

The increased demand for specialists

Conflicts between staff specialists and line generalists are probably the most common type of intergroup conflict.[22] Line managers often lack the technical knowledge to manage all aspects of their departments and thus may become increasingly dependent upon the staff specialist's knowledge. As more organisations turn to specialists for help in improving quality, speeding up product development and improving customer service, specialists are playing increasingly critical roles.[23] As we will see in Chapter 11, specialised knowledge is an important source of power in organisations. That power can come into conflict with the power held by managers in the form of formal authority.

Interpersonal factors

Although organisational conditions are important determinants of organisational factors, it is also necessary to consider how interactions at the interpersonal level might affect conflicts. Such factors as personality clashes, long-lasting grudges, poor communication or differences in values and norms will also affect whether conflicts develop. Critical to conflict at the interpersonal level are the attributions that we make about other individuals' behaviour. Returning to the idea of justice, conflict at the interpersonal level is also more likely to occur when individuals receive inadequate or insincere explanations for behaviour that has negatively affected them.[24]

THE CONSEQUENCES OF DYSFUNCTIONAL INTERGROUP CONFLICT

Behavioural scientists have spent more than three decades researching and analysing how dysfunctional intergroup conflict affects those who experience it.[25] They found that groups placed in a conflict situation tend to react in fairly predictable ways. We will examine a number of the changes that occur within groups and between groups as a result of dysfunctional group conflict. We would expect these changes to become apparent during the perceived, felt and manifest stages of conflict that we described earlier.

Changes within groups

The perception of different goals brings conflict into focus. At the same time that these differences are recognised, tension is generated. When individuals experience negative emotions, conflicts will escalate. Negative emotions reduce trust, result in an oversimplification of the problem into either-or terms, and encourage individuals to view the other group's behaviour negatively.[26] Within groups, this results in a further tightening of group boundaries, while between groups it results in a further reduction of communication. Unfortunately, this generally results in either a continuance or an escalation of the conflict.

Increased cohesiveness

It is clear that when groups are engaged in a conflict their cohesion tends to increase. Competition, conflict or perceived external threat usually result in group members putting aside individual differences and closing ranks. Members become more loyal to the group, and group membership becomes more attractive. This increase in cohesion is necessary to mobilise group resources in dealing with the 'enemy' and tends to result in the suppression of internal disagreements. This tendency toward increased cohesion in the face of threat can be seen in Bosnia. Ethnic groups in the former Yugoslavia have historically had difficulties getting along with each other.

Emphasis on loyalty

The tendency of groups to increase in cohesiveness suggests that conformity to group norms becomes more important in conflict situations. In reality it is not unusual for groups to overconform to group norms in conflict situations. This may take the form of blind acceptance of dysfunctional solutions to the conflict and result in groupthink (discussed in more detail in Chapter 12). In such situations group goals take precedence over individual satisfaction as members are expected to demonstrate their loyalty. In major conflict situations interaction with members of 'the other group' may be completely outlawed.

Rise in autocratic leadership

In extreme conflict situations where threats are perceived, democratic methods of leadership are likely to become less popular. The members want strong leadership. Thus, the leaders are likely to become more autocratic.

Focus on activity

When a group is in conflict, its members usually emphasise doing what the group does and doing it very well. The group becomes more task-oriented. Tolerance for members who 'goof off' is low, and there is less concern for individual member satisfaction. The emphasis is on accomplishing the group's task and defeating the 'enemy' (the other group in the conflict).

Changes between groups

During conflicts, certain changes will probably occur between groups. These changes are likely to prevent communication and increase the distance between groups, making it increasingly difficult to resolve the conflict.

Increased psychological distance

In our discussion of social dilemmas, we emphasised the importance of common goals and perceived similarity to cooperation. As individuals or groups in organisation perceive others to have conflicting goals, values or standards, so they will perceive them to be increasingly dissimilar. Perceptions of dissimilarity will in turn generate decreased trust and restrict communication between the parties. Once another individual or work unit is perceived as an outgroup, individuals search for further information that emphasises differences between the groups. This is likely to result in inaccurate perceptions of the others' intentions and behaviour. When the differences between the groups are emphasised, the stereotypes are reinforced, relations deteriorate and conflict develops.

Distorted perceptions

A second consequence of perceiving incompatible goals is that the perceptions of each group's members become distorted. Group members develop stronger opinions of the importance of their units. Each group displays an *egocentric bias*[27]: it sees itself as superior in performance to the other and as more important to the survival of the organisation than other groups. In a conflict situation, nurses may conclude that they are more important to a patient than physicians, while physicians may consider themselves more important than hospital administrators. The marketing group in a business organisation may think, 'Without us selling the product, there would be no money to pay anyone else's salary'. The production group, meanwhile, will say, 'If we don't make the product, there is nothing to sell'. Ultimately, none of these groups is more important, but conflict can cause their members to develop gross misperceptions of reality.

Negative stereotyping

Inaccurate perceptions often cause one group to develop stereotypes about other groups. While the differences between groups may actually be small, each group will tend to exaggerate them. As conflict increases and perceptions become more distorted, all of the negative stereotypes that may have ever existed are reinforced. A management representative may say, 'I've always said these union guys are just plain greedy. Now they've proved it'. The head of a local teachers' union may say, 'Now we know that what all politicians are interested in is getting re-elected, not the quality of education'. When negative stereotyping is a factor in a conflict, the members of each group see less differences within their unit and greater differences between the groups than actually exist.

Decreased communication

Communications between the groups in conflict usually break down. This can be extremely dysfunctional, especially where sequential interdependence or reciprocal interdependence relationships exist between groups. The decision-making process can be disrupted, and the customers or others whom the organisation serves can be affected. Consider the possible consequences to patients, for instance, if a conflict between hospital technicians and nurses continues until it lowers the quality of health care.

THE CONSEQUENCES OF CONFLICT

The model of conflict has allowed us to examine potential sources of dysfunctional conflict, and to trace the impact that this may have on intergroup and intragroup processes.[28] It has become clear that, at each stage of the process, critical interventions may alter the final outcome, whether the conflict is functional or dysfunctional. These interventions may be structural, and attempt to remove latent and perceived sources of conflict, or they may focus on process, attempting to alter the group processes that can escalate a conflict.[29] Our Management Encounter considers some of the organisational outcomes of workplace disputes.

The effectiveness of these interventions and the ability to obtain functional outcomes will have several important consequences for the organisation. Functional outcomes are more likely to uncover the needs of individuals involved in the conflict and therefore help to resolve conflicts by developing solutions that meet those needs. One effect of this is that the solutions are more

MANAGEMENT Encounter

Workplace conflicts

What happens when supervisors and staff are in conflict? What strategies are most effective? Also, are there differences in the strategies used by supervisors and their staff? Given the choice, will supervisors and staff in conflict use strategies designed to escalate the conflict or will they use strategies that are aimed at cooperation and problem solving? What will be most effective? Is it better to combine strategies or to systematically follow one conflict resolution strategy?

According to recent research, *supervisors* are most likely to try to control the process (direction of the discussion), confront the subordinate or use their power to resolve the situation. They were least likely to avoid the situation, find a halfway point for agreement or to give in to their subordinate's point of view. How effective were these strategies? According to independent observers' ratings, process control and giving in resulted in more effective conflict management than did using power to resolve the situation.

If we consider the situation from the point of view of a *subordinate*, do these findings change? In terms of the strategies that they use, not at all. Again, controlling the process, confronting their manager and using power to resolve the situation are the most frequently used strategies; avoiding the situation,

compromising and giving in were rarely used. However, the perceived effectiveness of these strategies differed. Process control and problem solving emerged as the most effective strategies, while using power or avoiding the conflict emerged as the least effective strategies.

This research provides us with some useful insights into the management of workplace conflicts. Clearly, no matter which side you are on, controlling the process — keeping it focused on the issue — is a highly effective strategy. As we will see in the next chapter, controlling the process reduces the likelihood that the conflict will escalate. On the other hand, using power and authority to resolve the conflict is ineffective no matter whether you are the manager or the subordinate.

There are several questions that this research did not consider. You might like to think about them. Will the effectiveness of conflict resolution strategies differ depending on the source of the conflict? Also, will they differ depending on how far the conflict has progressed?

Source: van de Vliert, E., Euwama, M. C., & Huismans, S. E. (1995). Managing conflict with a subordinate or a superior: Effectiveness of conglomerate behaviour, *Journal of Applied Psychology*, **80**, 271–281.

likely to be stable, and it is less likely that unmet needs will surface in a new conflict. Also, relationships between the disputants will be strengthened and the general community of which the individuals are members (e.g. organisation) will benefit as relationships are improved.[30]

MANAGING INTERGROUP CONFLICT

Reading 8
How to design a conflict management procedure that fits your dispute

Since managers must live with intergroup conflict, they must confront the problem of managing it.[31] In this section, we will examine organisational techniques that have been used successfully in resolving intergroup conflicts that have reached dysfunctional levels. Most of these techniques involve some type of exchange between the conflicting parties, suggesting that resolution may be facilitated by constructive negotiation, a topic treated in detail in the next chapter. What this chapter has said thus far about intergroup conflict is summarised in Exhibit 8.3. The exhibit sets out the stages in escalating conflict. It traces the relationship between sources of conflict, intergroup and intragroup processes, and dysfunctional outcomes. It is also important to keep in mind that views of conflict and approaches to conflict resolution vary across cultures. Our Global Encounter provides an illustration.

Clearly, the most effective means for dealing with conflicts that are generated by perceived structural inequities is to change those inequities or to alter individual perceptions of their impact. Altering the structural variables involves changing the formal structure of the organisation. Structure refers to the fixed relationships among the jobs of the organisation and includes the design of jobs and departments. Interventions at this level may focus on changing organisation structure, altering resource allocation, or changing individual and group definitions of the situation.

GLOBAL   Encounter

Culture and conflict resolution

Rensis Likert, the renowned social scientist and management expert, once observed that the strategies used by a society and its organisations for dealing with conflict reflect the basic values and philosophy of that society. In ideal circumstances conflicts can be difficult to resolve; once the confounding variable of intercultural differences is added, conflict resolution becomes even more complex.

In the next chapter, we will describe five strategies used in conflict resolution: competing, problem solving, avoiding the conflict, yielding to the other party and compromising. We preview these now by taking a look at how they are used by Hong Kong Chinese students and managers. According to Paul Kirkbride and co-workers, the cultural values of this group should result in a strong preference for

compromising or avoiding the conflict, and a low preference for the more contentious strategy of competing. Their research shows that, for this Hong Kong Chinese sample, compromising was the most preferred conflict resolution strategy, followed closely by avoidance. Competing was the least preferred strategy. Their research also showed that preferences were affected by gender and organisational level. Women were less likely to compete and more likely to compromise than men; managers were more likely to collaborate and less likely to yield than were non-managers.

Source: Kirkbride, P. S., Tang, S. F. Y., & Westwood, R. I. (1991). Chinese conflict preferences and negotiating behaviour: Cultural and psychological influences, *Organisation Studies*, **12**, 365–386.

Altering structural variables

If conflicts arise because individuals identify with a particular work unit or because they perceive resource allocations to be unfair, organisations can choose to alter these variables. Organisational boundaries can be changed in order to redefine groups or to reduce interdependence; resource allocation systems can emphasise the processes by which decisions are reached; and organisations can establish grievance processes that allow individuals or groups to have the opportunity to contest unfair decisions.

Changing perceptions of interdependence

Competition is fostered when individuals perceive other work units to have discrepant goals. Structural interventions that alter the level of identification or reduced intergroup polarisation will act to reduce this competition. If individuals identify with collective-level groups, conflict will be correspondingly reduced because the impact of intergroup level identification is weakened. This may, for example, be achieved by reorganising separate work units into one larger unit or by using job design to change the nature of task interdependence. A second means for altering perceptions of interdependence is to ensure that some individuals are members of more than one group. This serves to reduce group cohesion by making group boundaries less clear and provides an important channel for communication between the groups.[32] This cross-cutting group membership may be achieved by transferring, exchanging or rotating members of the groups, or having someone serve as a coordinator, liaison or go-between who keeps groups communicating with one another.

Using symbolic management

How individuals perceive the situation is fundamental to the development of conflicts; consequently, organisations can try to manipulate these perceptions. For example, resource allocations are frequently judged to be unfair because individual work units (displaying an egocentric bias) overestimate their contributions and effort relative to the contributions and effort of other work units. Organisations can attempt to manipulate these estimates by providing information about the efforts of other work groups that compensates for this overestimation. Similarly, if cooperation is more likely to occur when resource scarcity is attributed to external causes, organisations may manipulate attributions by explicitly attributing such scarcities to external factors, such as economic downturn or a lack of competitiveness on the international market.[33]

CONFLICT STIMULATION

Throughout this chapter we have stressed that some conflict is beneficial. This point was first made in the discussion of the contemporary perspective on conflict. We have already examined the situation where conflict is dysfunctional because it is too high; we have said little, however, regarding situations in which there is an insufficient amount of conflict. If groups become too complacent because everything always operates smoothly, management might benefit from

LOCAL   Encounter

Conflict resolution strategies of managers and their subordinates

A survey of large Australia-wide public sector organisations showed that managers and their subordinates had very similar perceptions of the causes of conflict. Although managers identified work performance as the most frequent cause of conflict while subordinates identified resources, both groups agreed that work performance and resources were the major reasons for workplace conflict. In addition, they identified issues relating to work tasks and interpersonal difficulties as creating conflict.

The two groups differed in their preferred conflict resolution strategies. In conflicts with managers, subordinates prefer to adopt an obliging strategy. What's more, subordinates believed that when they used an obliging strategy their managers benefited: superiors increased their reactive advantage, satisfaction and perceived fairness.

Conversely, the less frequently used active styles of conflict resolution (compromising and integrating) predict subordinates' satisfaction as well as the perceived fairness of the process and the relative advantage to themselves. This implies that subordinates believe that superiors obtain the greater benefits in any conflict.

From the perspective of superiors, a somewhat different picture emerges. According to Gaylard's (1994) analysis, superiors believe that any attempt (either active or passive strategies) to manage a conflict will benefit subordinates, increasing their satisfaction, advantage and perceived fairness. Furthermore, passive styles are also seen to be negatively associated with a superior's own outcomes: superiors judged passive styles to lower their satisfaction, decrease their advantage and result in unfair outcomes. Given their preference for more assertive styles (integrating) in such conflicts, this suggests that superiors attempt to maximise their own outcomes.

Kabanoff (1991) places bureaucracies into the elite-dominated organisational type, characterised by unequal power and the use of equity allocation rules. The differences in conflict resolution styles reported by Gaylard (1994) suggest that organisational culture plays a role in determining preferred conflict resolution styles and their relative effectiveness. In particular, the patterns of styles reported by Gaylard (1994) can be interpreted as reinforcing power differences.

Further support for this position is obtained by considering the relationship between strategies and outcomes. Individuals, when considering conflicts with superiors, appear to represent outcomes as being win–lose: active styles are associated with gains to self, passive styles are associated with gains to the superior. Again, this pattern is consistent with an organisation in which there are large (and institutionalised) power differences. So too is the belief that when conflicts are with subordinates, any attempt to resolve them will benefit the subordinate and, furthermore, that passive resolution styles will work against the superior. Although this argument is speculative, it identifies one potential area for research: the need to establish links between organisational culture (especially power differences), preferred conflict styles and the perceived effectiveness of those styles.

Source: Kabanoff, B. (1991). Equity, equality, power and conflict, *Academy of Management Review*, **16**, 416–441; Gaylard, A. (1994). Superior–subordinate conflict management: Predicting process and outcomes. Unpublished Masters dissertation, University of Melbourne.

stimulating conflict. Lack of any disagreement can lead to suboptimum performance, including inferior decision making.

A variety of research supports this conclusion. In one laboratory study, experimental and control groups were formed to solve a problem. The experimental groups had a member, a confederate of the researcher, whose job was to challenge the majority view of the groups he or she had been planted in as the groups attempted to solve the problem. The control groups had no such member. In every case, the experimental groups outperformed the control groups.

There can be a number of benefits from increasing conflict levels. Some conflict is probably necessary to stimulate the critical evaluation of organisational policies and processes, and to lay the groundwork for change. Lack of conflict leads to acceptance of the status quo and discourages innovation. Increasing conflict can be an effective antidote for groupthink. As was suggested in Exhibit 8.2, organisational performance suffers not only when conflict levels are too high, but also when they are too low.

What can management do to stimulate conflict for constructive purposes? We close our discussion of intergroup conflict by looking at four techniques for stimulating conflict.

Bringing outside individuals into the group

A technique widely used to 'bring back to life' a stagnant organisation or subunit of an organisation is to hire or transfer in individuals whose attitudes, values and backgrounds differ from those of the group's present members. Many college faculties consciously seek new members with different backgrounds and often discourage the hiring of graduates of their own programs. This is to ensure a diversity of viewpoints on the faculty.

The technique of bringing in outsiders is also widely used in government and business. Recently, a bank president decided not to promote from within for a newly created position of marketing vice-president. Instead, he hired a highly successful executive from the very competitive consumer products field. The bank president felt that while the outsider knew little about marketing financial services, her approach to, and knowledge of, marketing was what the bank needed to become a strong competitor.

Altering the organisation's structure

Changing the structure of the organisation can not only help resolve intergroup conflicts; it is also excellent for creating conflict. For example, a school of business typically has several departments. One, named the Department of Business Administration, includes all of the faculty members who teach courses in management, marketing, finance, production management and so forth. Accordingly, the department is rather large, with thirty-two members under one department chairman, who reports to the dean. A new dean has recently been hired and he is considering dividing the business administration unit into several separate departments (e.g. departments of marketing, finance and management), each with five or six members and a chairperson. The reasoning is that reorganising in this manner will create competition among the groups for resources, students, faculty and so forth, where none existed before because there was only one group. Whether this change will improve performance remains to be seen.

Stimulating competition

Many managers utilise various techniques to stimulate competition among groups. The use of a variety of incentives, such as awards and bonuses for outstanding performance, often stimulates competition. If properly utilised, such incentives can help maintain a healthy atmosphere of competition that may result in a functional level of conflict. Incentives can be given for least defective parts, highest sales, best teacher, greatest number of new customers, or in any area where increased conflict is likely to lead to more effective performance.

Making use of programmed conflict

Increasingly, organisations are turning to programmed conflict to increase creativity and innovation, and to improve decision making. Programmed conflict is conflict that is deliberately and systematically created even when no real differences appear to exist. It is 'conflict that raises different opinions regardless of the personal feelings of managers'.[34] One popular form of programmed conflict is devil's advocacy. In **devil's advocacy**, someone or some group is assigned the role of critic with the job of uncovering all possible problems with a particular proposal. The role of the devil's advocate is to ensure that opposing views are presented and taken into consideration before any sort of final decision is made.

Numerous organisations use some form of programmed conflict. Royal Dutch Petroleum regularly uses a devil's advocacy approach. Before Anheuser-Busch makes a major decision, such as entering a market or building a plant, it assigns groups the job of making a case for each side of the question. IBM has a system that encourages employees to disagree with their bosses. All of these companies have the same goal: to improve organisational performance by stimulating conflict.

SUMMARY OF KEY POINTS

Describe the concept of interdependence. There are many tasks in which the contributions of several individuals are required to achieve outcomes. Interdependence describes situations in which not only group, but also individual, outcomes depend on the efforts of the group. Many such situations pose a difficult problem for us: should we cooperate for the good of the group, or should we behave more competitively for our own benefit? Our choice of strategy will affect both our own and the group's outcomes.

Discuss factors affecting cooperation and competition. In organisations, we are more likely to behave competitively when we identify closely with our work group rather than the organisation. We are more likely to behave cooperatively when we maintain good communication between ourselves and other work groups, when we have successfully cooperated in the past, and when the processes by which outcomes have been allocated are fair.

Explain the difference between traditional and contemporary views of conflict. The traditional perspective of conflict holds that all organisational conflict is bad, and thus should be eliminated or minimised to the fullest extent possible. The more contemporary view recognises that conflict is neither inherently good nor bad but can be either, depending on how it is dealt with. Rather than eliminating conflict, this view stresses that what is important is that conflict be effectively managed.

Distinguish between functional and dysfunctional conflict. A functional conflict is a confrontation between groups that enhances and benefits the organisation's performance. Functional conflict can contribute to creativity, innovation and improved decision making, among other benefits. Dysfunctional conflict, on the other hand, is that which harms the organisation or hinders the achievement of organisational goals.

Describe the relationship between intergroup conflict and organisational performance. Levels of conflict can be related to overall organisational performance. Too much conflict can be disruptive, creating chaos and damaging interpersonal relations. Too little conflict can also detract from performance. If conflict levels are too low innovation and change are less likely to take place. Each organisation has an optimal level of conflict that can be extremely functional.

Describe a model of conflict. Conflict passes through five stages: latent, in which the preconditions for conflict exist but have not been noticed; perceived, in which individuals within groups identify sources of dissatisfaction or differences between groups; felt, in which individuals experience an emotional reaction to the conditions that they identified in the perceived stage of conflict; manifest, in which groups actively block each other from attaining goals; and aftermath or the consequences of the conflict. Conflicts become progressively more difficult to manage as they progress through these stages. The consequences in the final stage depend on whether individuals have chosen competitive or cooperative strategies for managing the conflict.

Discuss why intergroup conflict occurs. Conflict is inevitable. Every group will sometime come into conflict with one or more other groups. There are numerous factors that contribute to intergroup conflict. Four particularly important ones are the interdependent nature of the relationship between work groups; differences between goals of organisational subunits; different perceptions of people, situations and events; and the increased demand for specialists, which contributes to increasing the incidence of the other three factors.

Identify several consequences of dysfunctional intergroup conflict. Groups involved in dysfunctional conflict tend to react in fairly predictable ways. Some changes occur within the groups involved in conflict; and other changes take place between the groups. Within-group changes include increased cohesiveness, emphasis on group loyalty, a rise in autocratic leadership and a focus on task-oriented activity. Between- group changes include an increase in perceptual distortion, negative stereotyping of the other group and decreased communications.

Describe techniques for managing conflict through resolution. A number of techniques exist for resolving intergroup conflict that has become dysfunctional. Among them are altering structural variables, changing perceptions of interdependence and using symbolic management.

Discuss several approaches to stimulating conflict. Sometimes conflict levels are too low, and the objective becomes to stimulate functional conflict between groups. Techniques available for stimulating conflict include intelligent use of communication channels, bringing outsiders into the group, altering the organisation's structure and creating competition between groups.

REVIEW AND DISCUSSION QUESTIONS

1. What are the differences between the traditional and contemporary perspectives on organisational conflict? What are the management implications of these two different perspectives?

2. What is the difference between functional and dysfunctional conflict? Can conflict that starts off as functional become dysfunctional? Can dysfunctional conflict be changed to functional?

3. Is there a relationship between the level of intergroup conflict and organisational performance? How can an organisation achieve the optimal level of conflict?

4. What are some of the major reasons that intergroup conflict occurs? In your personal experience, what is the most frequent reason?

5. There are a number of possible consequences of dysfunctional conflict. What are these? Are some of these consequences more or less likely to occur in organisational conflict situations?

6. As organisations grow in size and complexity, interdependence increases, goal differences grow, and work and people become more specialised. Does this suggest that conflict in organisations must increase? Does knowledge that these changes are occurring help us better prepare for them. How?

7. Identify and describe the three types of work interdependence discussed in the chapter. Which type is most likely to generate conflict? Which type is least likely to result in conflict?

8. When intergroup conflict occurs, changes take place both within and between the conflicting groups. What are these changes? Which changes generally are positive ones? Which are generally negative?

9. What are the major differences between resolution and stimulation in managing conflict? Could both be appropriate with the same groups at the same time? Explain.

10. Why does it become progressively more difficult to deal with conflicts functionally as they progress? How would you tackle a conflict to ensure that the outcomes will be functional?

ENDNOTES

1 See Alderfer, C., & Smith, K. K. (1982). Studying intergroup relations embedded in organizations, *Administrative Science Quarterly*, 35–64.

2 Grzelak, J. (1988). Conflict and cooperation. In M. Hewstone, W. Stroebe, J-P. Codol, & G. M. Stephenson. *Introduction to Social Psychology: A European Perspective*. Oxford: Basil Blackwell Ltd; Baron, R. S., Kerr, N., & Miller, N. (1992). *Group Processes, Group Decision, Group Action*. Buckingham: Open University Press.

3 Davis, M. (1983). *Game Theory: A Nontechnical Introduction*. New York, Basic Books, Inc.

4 Grzelak, J. (1988). Conflict and cooperation. In M. Hewstone, W. Stroebe, J-P. Codol, & G. M. Stephenson. *Introduction to Social Psychology: A European Perspective*. Oxford: Basil Blackwell Ltd; Baron, R. S. , Kerr, N., & Miller, N. (1992). *Group Processes, Group Decision, Group Action*. Buckingham: Open University Press; Kramer, R. M. (1991). Intergroup relations and organizational dilemmas: The role of categorization processes, *Research in Organizational Behavior*, 13, 191–228.

5 Davis, M. (1983). *Game Theory: A Nontechnical Introduction*. New York, Basic Books, Inc.; Kramer, R. M. (1991). Intergroup relations and organizational dilemmas: The role of categorization processes, *Research in Organizational Behavior*, 13, 191–228.

6 Kramer, R. M. (1991). Intergroup relations and organizational dilemmas: The role of categorization processes, *Research in Organizational Behavior*, 13, 191–228.

7 Hewstone, M., Stroebe, W., Codol, J-P., & Stephenson, G. M. (1988). *Introduction to Social Psychology: A European Perspective*. Oxford: Basil Blackwell Ltd.

8 Kramer, R. M. (1991). Intergroup relations and organizational dilemmas: The role of categorization processes, *Research in Organizational Behavior*, 13, 191–228.

9 Grzelak, J. (1988). Conflict and cooperation. In M. Hewstone, W. Stroebe, J-P. Codol, & G. M. Stephenson. *Introduction to Social Psychology: A European Perspective*. Oxford: Basil Blackwell Ltd; Baron, R. S. , Kerr, N., & Miller, N. (1992). *Group Processes, Group Decision, Group Action*. Buckingham: Open University Press.

10 Ibid.

11 Ibid.

12 Ibid.

13 Kramer, R. M. (1991). Intergroup relations and organizational dilemmas: The role of categorization processes, *Research in Organizational Behavior*, 13, 191–228.

14 Cosier, R. A., & Schwenk, C. R. (1990). Agreement and thinking alike: Ingredients for poor decisions, *Academy of Management Executive*, 69–74.

15 Robbins, S. P. (1992). *Essentials of Organizational Behavior*. Englewood Cliffs, NJ: Prentice-Hall, pp. 182–184.

16 Pondy, L. R. (1967). Organizational conflict: Concepts and models, *Administrative Science Quarterly*, 12, 296–320; Gordon, J. R. (1993). *A Diagnostic Approach to Organizational Behavior*. Boston: Allyn & Bacon.

17 Thomas, K. W. (1994). Conflict and negotiation processes in organizations. In M. D. Dunnette & L. M. Hough (Eds.) *Handbook of Industrial and Organizational Psychology* (2nd Ed.). Palo Alto, CA: Consulting Psychologists Press.

18 The classic work is Sherif, M., & Sherif, C. (1953). *Groups in Harmony and Tension*. New York: Harper & Row. Their study was conducted among groups in a boys' camp. They stimulated conflict between the groups and observed the changes that occurred in group behavior. Also see Sherif, M., & Sherif, C. (1956), Experiments in Group Conflict, *Scientific American*, March, 54–58.

19 See Downs, A. (1968). *Inside Bureaucracy*. Boston: Little, Brown.

20 Thompson, J. (1967). *Organizations in Action*. New York: McGraw-Hill.

21 Kabanoff, B. (1991). Equity, equality, power and conflict, *Academy of Management Review*, 416–441.

22 For a classic discussion, see Allen, L. A. (1955).

The line-staff relationship, *Management Record,* 346–349.

23 See Richman, L. S. (1994). The new worker elite, *Fortune,* August 22, 56–66.

24 Baron, R. A., & Greenberg, J. (1990). *Behavior in Organizations: Understanding and Managing the Human Side of Work.* Boston: Allyn & Bacon.

25 Sherif, M., & Sherif, C. (1953). *Groups in Harmony and Tension.* New York: Harper & Row.

26 Thomas, K. W. (1994). Conflict and negotiation processes in organizations. In M. D. Dunnette & L. M. Hough (Eds.) *Handbook of Industrial and Organizational Psychology* (2nd Ed.). Palo Alto, CA: Consulting Psychologists Press.

27 Ibid.

28 For additional discussion, see Litterer, J. (1966). Conflict in organizations: A reexamination, *Academy of Management Journal,* 178–186; Lorsch, J. W. & Morse, J. J. (1974). *Organizations and Their Members: A Contingency Approach.* New York: Harper & Row; and Schein, E. (1983). Intergroup problems in organizations. In W. French, C. Bell & R. Zawacki (Eds.) *Organization Development: Theory, Practice and Research* (2nd

Ed.). Plano, Tex.: Business Publications, pp. 106–110.

29 Thomas, K. W. (1994). Conflict and negotiation processes in organizations. In M. D. Dunnette & L. M. Hough (Eds.) *Handbook of Industrial and Organizational Psychology* (2nd Ed.). Palo Alto, CA: Consulting Psychologists Press.

30 Pruitt, D. G. (1983). Achieving integrative agreements. In M. H. Bazerman & R. J. Lewicki (Eds.) *Negotiating in Organisations.* Beverly Hills, CA: Sage.

31 For an examination of specific devices for assessing how managers manage conflict see van de Vliert, E. & Kabanoff, B. (1990). Toward theory-based measures of conflict management, *Academy of Management Journal,* 199–209.

32 Kramer, R. M. (1991) Intergroup relations and organizational dilemmas: The role of categorization processes, *Research in Organizational Behavior,* **13**, 191–228.

33 Ibid.

34 Cosier, R. A., & Schwenk, C. R. (1990). Agreement and thinking alike: Ingredients for poor decisions, *Academy of Management Executive,* **71**.

READING 8 HOW TO DESIGN A CONFLICT MANAGEMENT PROCEDURE THAT FITS YOUR DISPUTE

Danny Ertel
Conflict Management, Inc.
Harvard Negotiation Project

Source: Reprinted from Danny Ertel, 'How to Design a Conflict Management Procedure that Fits Your Dispute', *Sloan Management Review,* Summer 1991, pp. 29–42.

In ancient Greece, a tale was told of a roadside inn where a traveler might find lodging for the night, and although the traveler might be tall, short, fat or thin, the inn's bed fit all just the same. The innkeeper, of course, was Procrustes, a giant who tied travelers to the bedstead and either stretched them or chopped their legs to make them fit. Many business disputes seem to be approached this way today: no matter how diverse the parties, issues or stakes, litigation is the answer. And even those managers or counsel who, unlike Procrustes' guests, perceive a choice

among several available 'beds' — litigation, arbitration or even mini-trials — rarely make further attempts to tailor the dispute resolution process to the conflict at hand. Instead they allow the parties to be realigned, the issues reframed, or the stakes redefined.

Managers must deal with a broad range of conflicts, many of which involve parties external to the organization: valuable business partners, threatening competitors, or inquisitive regulators. But scorched-earth litigation followed by an on-the-courthouse-steps settlement is clearly not the answer to every dispute. Dealing with a competitor turned potential alliance partner whose third-level subsidiary may be infringing on a patent calls for a different approach than does responding to a 'professional plaintiff' who has filed a frivolous shareholder derivative suit. Both of these may be different still from how one might want to manage the plausible antitrust claim of a disgruntled distributor.

Sensing the need for a better approach to process selection, both in-house and outside counsel have begun, with the help of academics and specialized professionals, to serve up a choice between traditional litigation and ADR — alternative dispute resolution. But that either-or choice is hardly confidence-inspiring: expensive and disruptive litigation on the one hand, and an enigmatic acronym on the other.

Those who do opt for ADR face another vexing choice: should we go into arbitration, mediation, or a mini-trial? The standard, if somewhat unfair, criticisms of each process are well known: 'arbitrators split the baby in half'; 'mediators never resolve really difficult cases'; 'there is more "trial" than "mini" in mini-trials'. At the other end of the spectrum, ADR partisans indiscriminately and somewhat disingenuously extol the virtues of all ADR processes as uniformly cheaper, faster, and more confidential than the litigation strawman. The choice among the two or three most commercially established ADR mechanisms often feels like the choice offered at a 'new and improved' Procrustean Inn: not one, but three beds, accompanied by the familiar promise of 'an exacting fit'.

Of course, not every dispute requires a custom-designed process any more than every ancient traveler required stretching or hacking. But misdirected attempts to fit the problem to the process exact high tolls in both human and economic terms: wasted time and money, damaged morale, lost opportunity, and unwanted publicity, to name a few. Effective dispute management requires more informed decision making, based on a careful analysis of the conflict and of the means available to resolve it. The

manager responsible for the conflict, whether the disputant or a superior, should probably make these decisions and subsequently design and implement the appropriate process, with the advice and support of legal counsel. This essay, then, is directed at such individuals or teams — the conflict managers.

If no single dispute resolution process can effectively, fairly, and efficiently address all concerns raised by the rich universe of external business disputes, what the conflict managers need is a consistent analytical framework. Instead of refining questionnaires or checklists for choosing between litigation and ADR, and instead of sorting through the benefits and drawbacks of standard litigation alternatives, thoughtful managers should change the question. They should ask not *which* process should we use (suggesting a choice among discrete options), but how can we resolve *this* conflict? They should try to understand the dispute and determine whether designing a more well-suited resolution process is cost effective. Borrowing problem-solving tools from engineering and medicine, conflict managers should attempt to understand what about the conflict has prevented its being quickly and effectively resolved. Only then will they be well equipped to make an informed decision about how to proceed and, if appropriate, to devise a process capable of resolving the conflict.

In this essay, I propose a methodology to allow managers and their counsel to consider

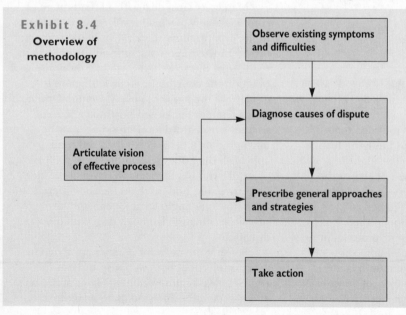

Exhibit 8.4
Overview of methodology

Observe existing symptoms and difficulties

Diagnose causes of dispute

Articulate vision of effective process

Prescribe general approaches and strategies

Take action

systematically either particular conflicts or categories of disputes and then to devise, refine, and implement appropriate procedures for dealing with them.[1] The method, structured as a set of inquiries that the disputants may attempt to answer independently or jointly, starts by positing a standard against which one might measure success. It is a vision of what a good conflict resolution process should look like. The conflict managers can then consider existing difficulties or symptoms against the backdrop of that clear objective. Next they can try to formulate a diagnosis based on their real-world understanding of business disputes and try to prescribe some general approaches or strategies. Finally, they can specify procedures and an implementation plan. At each step of the way, the conflict managers can rely on the articulated measure of success to instruct their analysis and evaluate their prescriptions. Exhibit 8.4 offers a schematic view of the process.[2]

This methodology should prove useful at different levels. Industry groups or professional associations, for example, might devise and publish model procedures for broad classes of disputes. Indeed, the Center for Public Resources, Inc., a New York-based coalition of general counsel, private practitioners, judges and academics has adopted this methodology for designing alternatives to certain types of securities litigation. Parties entering a long-term business relationship such as a strategic alliance have used it to draft sophisticated dispute resolution protocols in anticipation of potential disputes. Ultimately, if disputants either lack or are dissatisfied with available model procedures, they can use this approach to negotiate an appropriate process.

Attributes of an effective conflict management process

Mechanisms for resolving conflict always incorporate some implicit tradeoffs, such as between accuracy and cost, creativity and enforceability, speed and thoroughness. Different conflicts, parties and relationships require different choices. For example, a disagreement among joint-venture partners may call for a highly confidential, forward-looking process that focuses primarily on preventing similar incidents in the future, whereas a dispute with product end users might require litigation to finality, so as to establish a firm precedent. Establishing

consensus among disputants early on with respect to the attributes of a good process will facilitate discussion of the design.

I propose the following interest-oriented process for managing business disputes, based in part on the body of theory being developed at the Harvard Negotiation Project.[3] This seven-element framework is a set of categories for organizing information and ideas about process and for analyzing the tradeoffs between competing priorities. It should help conflict managers diagnose the current process and prescribe a fresh approach.

Clarifies interest

An effective dispute resolution process should help the parties understand their own and each other's interests. Without understanding the basic wants, needs or fears motivating the dispute, the parties will find it difficult to obtain anything but zero-sum, purely distributive results. A process that focuses on the parties' stated position or demands will inevitably leave the parties feeling somewhat dissatisfied with both the process and the outcome. A bluffing contest, however entertaining it may be for buying a used car, cannot be the best way to resolve complex, multi-issue disputes.

While positions may be in conflict, underlying interests need not be. There may be room for dovetailing those interests in such a way that both parties can gain, or at least find themselves distributing a great deal more value than they initially thought was at stake. For example, an engineer who has developed an innovative stamping tool was preparing to retire. He demanded a 3 percent royalty from his former employer for its use. The company, after carefully analyzing the value added to the production process by the tool, and on the advice of its accountants and investment bankers, extended a firm offer of 1.5 percent. After months of haggling, they were no closer.

With some work, a facilitator learned that the engineer had sought 3 percent as a means of insuring himself should he be held personally liable for a young shop worker sustaining injuries from the high-speed stamping tool. After further discussions, the facilitator discovered that the company could bring the engineer under its corporate liability policy, at nominal cost to the company. The company had never offered to do so because it did not understand the interest underlying the engineer's bargaining position. The engineer, upon learning that his retirement could be protected against the unlikely but catastrophic event, was quite satisfied to accept a royalty of around 1 percent.

While most experienced negotiators intuitively recognize the difference between their stated position and their underlying interests, they are often reluctant to disclose their real interests for fear of exposing themselves to extortion. An effective resolution process should allow the parties to share this kind of information without unduly subjecting themselves to such a risk. Absent such a process, the parties may fail to uncover a range of possible agreements that would satisfy their interests without the need to compromise between initial positions.

Builds a good working relationship

The parties to a conflict have some sort of relationship, if only for the purposes of the dispute. And whatever that relationship is, it could probably be better. A good working relationship should enable them to deal effectively and efficiently with the disagreements, large and small, that inevitably arise in any complex interaction between institutions.

A well-designed dispute resolution process should serve two relationship functions. First, it should fill in where the working relationship is breaking down, facilitating the parties' ability to resolve the problem on its merits, as they might have been able to do but for the current breakdown. That might mean, for example, that the process would include mechanisms that temporarily replace the parties' need to trust each other by guaranteeing performance in some easily enforceable manner, or that it would specify use of a third party to help set aside personality issues.

Second, an effective process should also help the parties work purposely toward the kind of relationship they want to have. It may be that the parties want to have no relationship at all and the process should facilitate closure. But if they want a long-term, cooperative relationship in which each feels consulted and accepted, they should probably not follow a purely retrospective process designed to allocate blame.

Both relationship functions add up to the same thing: the process should leave the parties at least slightly better able to deal with each other next time, whenever that happens to be. That

need not mean the corporate equivalent of a long-term love affair, but parties who would find it mutually beneficial to work together should not be prevented from doing so because their dispute resolution process has made it even harder for them to speak to each other.

Generates good options

Most managers would prefer to choose the best course of action from among several options than from a list of one. The more options on the table (within limits, of course), the greater the likelihood of discovering a productive path. What may seem like a foolish or risky approach at first glance may, after reconsideration and refinement by others, develop into a mutually profitable one. An effective dispute resolution process should spur the parties, perhaps with external support or advice, to generate a list of such options before evaluating and choosing among them.

To the extent possible, the process should also orient the parties toward designing options that create value, rather than merely distribute it. By making mutual gain the expressed goal, the options generated are likely to be more creative and value generating.

Is perceived as legitimate

Costly and inefficient as it may be, litigation does incorporate certain norms and rules that society believes are essential to the social order. For example, some liability standards and burdens of proof have been tilted in favor of one party or the other in support of legislative policy goals. For an 'alternate' process to succeed, the parties must believe it will produce a good solution without requiring them to give up substantial rights they would have had in litigation. An alternative process that seemed to shift the balance of power dramatically would most likely meet resistance from at least one party — including possibly their refusal to participate in the process or failure to comply fully with any result. Similarly, an alternate process that negated advances conferred by the legislature on certain classes of parties might well come under powerful criticism as being contrary to the public interest.[4]

No one likes being taken advantage of. A desirable dispute resolution process should instill in the parties a sense that the solution is fair and equitable and was arrived at in a principled fashion. If the new process requires voluntary participation by the disputants, neither the

Exhibit 8.5 Attributes of an effective conflict resolution process

1. Clarifies Interests
- By encouraging the parties to explore the interests underlying their respective bargaining positions
- By facilitating the exploration of common and nonconflicting interests
- By communicating each party's interests to the other without exposing anyone to extortion on the basis of such interests

2. Builds a Good Working Relationship
- By enabling the parties to deal effectively with their differences in the current dispute
- By fostering the type of relationship the parties would have wanted to have but for the present dispute
- By making it easier for the parties to deal with each other next time

3. Generates Good Options
- By spurring the parties to brainstorm many options before evaluating them and choosing among them
- By encouraging the parties to devise ways to create value for mutual gain

4. Is Perceived as Legitimate
- By not being seen to cause the parties to forfeit legal or other rights disproportionately (i.e., the process should not be seen as itself tilting the balance of power)
- By not being perceived as contrary to the public interest
- By instilling in the parties a sense that the solutions it produces will be fair and equitable

5. Is Cognizant of the Parties' Procedural Alternatives
- By allowing both sides to develop realistic assessments of their own and the other side's procedural and substantive alternatives
- By being more attractive to the parties along whatever axis is most important to them (e.g., costs, time, degree of disclosure, nature of outcomes, and quality of compliance)

6. Improves Communication
- By encouraging the questioning and testing of underlying assumptions
- By facilitating the understanding and discussion of partisan perceptions
- By establishing effective two-way communication between decision makers

7. Leads to Wise Commitments
- By enabling the parties to devise commitments that are realistic, operational, and compliance-prone
- By positioning the parties with efficient recourse to litigation in the event they fail to reach agreement or in the event of non-compliance

procedures nor the solutions they produce may be perceived as partisan or arbitrary.

Is cognizant of the parties' procedural alternatives Notwithstanding prior commitments to arbitration, mediation, or some other process, few conflicts arise that cannot at some point and in some form lead to litigation. Given that state of

affairs, a good process permits the parties to assess realistically their own and their counterpart's litigation alternative. In order to be effective, the process must appear, along whatever axis the parties consider most important, to be preferable to litigation. If cost is of principal concern, the new process should be less expensive than litigation; if confidentiality is at issue, it should afford the parties greater control over disclosure; if a long-term relationship is at stake, then perhaps the process should produce forward-looking solutions rather than allocate blame. Ultimately what this means is that the process should generate solutions that are more efficient and satisfying for each side than what they expect litigation could produce. For instance, in a consent-based process the parties might well agree to take more constructive steps than anything a court could order them to do.

Improves communication

Many a dispute escalates because one side misunderstands what the other has said or done. If such misunderstandings are common enough among trusted business partners, they are legion among adversaries and especially their zealous advocates. In the middle of litigation, a simple request for information can be perceived as an attempt to blackmail or coerce, an innocent joke can be taken as an insult, and an attempt to reschedule a meeting as an example of bad faith. Why do we inevitably see the others' action in the worst possible light and expect them to give us the benefit of the doubt? Part of the reason is that we all operate on the basis of many unstated assumptions. One common assumption about adversaries is that they want what we want and that if something is good for them, it must be bad for us. Regardless of whether those assumptions have merit in any given case, acting on them without articulating and testing them is simply unwise. A good dispute resolution process should help the parties articulate and examine their assumptions before they act on them.

Similarly, a great many of us tend to see the facts in the way most favorable to our own side. Once we make up our mind about something, we tend systematically to filter out inconsistent data and to gather as much supporting evidence as possible. It is an inclination well worth resisting, and a good dispute-resolution process should facilitate a discussion of those partisan perceptions and how they might be biasing each side's assessment of the situation. One partner in a large national law firm periodically instructs his young associates to begin research on a particular side of a case without telling them they have actually been engaged to represent the opposite side. When they report back to him with their preliminary research (which is usually quite

favorable), he tells them, 'Remember this well, because this is how strong our opponents think their case is; now prepare our case in response.'

Understanding someone's concerns need not make us agree with them; it should, however, help us persuade them that they do not have to meet their needs at our expense. Good communication between decision makers is essential to effective conflict management. If an executive cannot make herself understood, how can she influence anyone? And if she does not understand her counterpart, how can she craft a persuasive proposition? A good process for resolving disputes should establish and maintain effective communication channels.

Leads to wise commitments

A good process should enable the disputants to craft wise commitments after they have carefully considered all the relevant information and a number of possible options, and after they have determined that their alternatives away from the table are not as good as what they can obtain through a negotiated agreement. Only then will they be able to craft a commitment that is realistic, operational and compliance-prone. To minimize the risk that one party will use the process as an expensive dilatory tactic, an effective process should also position the disputants with efficient recourse to litigation or some other self-help alternative in the event they fail to reach agreement or one party fails to comply with its obligations.

Having identified the attributes of the dispute resolution procedure, the conflict manager can begin examining the problem at hand — whether it is an ongoing or an anticipated dispute or class of disputes — and crating procedures for dealing with it. The design process should be structured and systematic: observe the existing difficulties or symptoms, diagnose their possible causes, and then prescribe general approaches to dealing with them. Finally, make an informed decision about what specific actions to pursue. Exhibit 8.6 illustrates this methodology.

Observe symptoms and difficulties

Before a doctor attempts a diagnosis, she gathers information. She asks the patient to describe his symptoms, to explain in some detail what has brought him into her office in search of a remedy. Good managers, before launching into

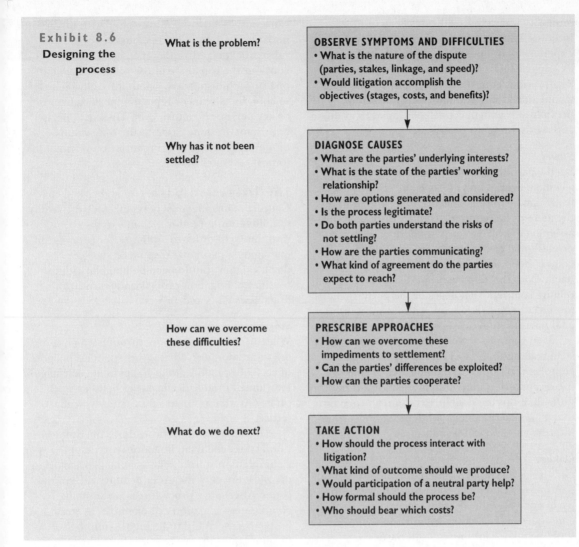

Exhibit 8.6
Designing the process

What is the problem?

OBSERVE SYMPTOMS AND DIFFICULTIES
- What is the nature of the dispute (parties, stakes, linkage, and speed)?
- Would litigation accomplish the objectives (stages, costs, and benefits)?

Why has it not been settled?

DIAGNOSE CAUSES
- What are the parties' underlying interests?
- What is the state of the parties' working relationship?
- How are options generated and considered?
- Is the process legitimate?
- Do both parties understand the risks of not settling?
- How are the parties communicating?
- What kind of agreement do the parties expect to reach?

How can we overcome these difficulties?

PRESCRIBE APPROACHES
- How can we overcome these impediments to settlement?
- Can the parties' differences be exploited?
- How can the parties cooperate?

What do we do next?

TAKE ACTION
- How should the process interact with litigation?
- What kind of outcome should we produce?
- Would participation of a neutral party help?
- How formal should the process be?
- Who should bear which costs?

conflict resolution, should try to understand the conflict as well as possible. Before they can put something right, they must identify what is wrong; in doing so, they should consider both the nature of the dispute and the traditional means of resolving it.

Although categorizing complex business conflicts is no easier than describing everything that can be physically or psychologically wrong with a human being, conflicts do have some characteristics in common that may instruct the resolution design. The methodology described here poses a series of inquiries concerning the parties and the issues. No single answer to a question will determine conclusively the 'best' process to follow; each response will, however, help to identify concerns that should somehow be acknowledged.

The nature of the dispute

The questions that follow are designed to help conflict managers gather and structure information.[5] They should also challenge conflict managers to question their assumptions about their own interests, the other side's intentions, the likely perceptions of third parties and so forth.

Parties

How many parties are there? Are they individuals or institutions? How sophisticated (financially and legally) are they? Is either party a 'repeat player' with respect to this type of conflict or is this likely to be a one-shot experience for both?

By knowing something about the number and relative sophistication and experience of the disputants, the conflict manager can better design a process that addresses each of their interests. Large institutional entities with experienced in-house or outside counsel, for example, may be less likely to require a process that provides education and reality testing than would individuals who have never litigated previously or who may be ill equipped to evaluate complex settlement proposals.

Stakes

Do the parties agree about what is at stake? Is this a dispute over money? If so, is the conflict over a fixed sum, or will a subjective determination of the amount be required? Is this a dispute about assigning the blame for past conduct, or is the primary goal to define permissible future conduct? Is publicity a major concern for either party? Does this dispute primarily concern the relative competitive posture of the parties? Is this merely 'strategic' litigation, with no substantive goal other than to delay or distract?

Understanding what is at stake requires more than reading the prayer for relief in a civil complaint. Without developing a clear sense of the disputants' underlying interests, it will be difficult, if not impossible, to design a procedure that allows each to feel confident that his or her interests can and will be addressed.

Linkage

How is the resolution of this conflict tied to other pending or contemplated disputes between the parties or with others? What collateral consequences will either adjudication or settlement have for one or both parties?

The collateral consequences, whether real or imagined, of resolving a particular dispute are often at least as important as the issue at hand. In designing a procedure, care must be taken to consider whether one or both parties would want the results exported to other disputes, or whether confidentiality of the outcome and avoidance of setting a precedent is the key to resolving the conflict.

Speed

Is speedy resolution important to either party? Would either benefit from delay? Why? Is it simply a matter of the stakeholder enjoying the time value of the money or are other factors at play?

Speed is often one of the first items on the list of ADR advantages. But is it always a good thing? Although overcrowded dockets generally

cause some of the delay associated with litigation, litigants are themselves responsible for substantial delay. Conflict managers must consider the relevance of the passing of time to one or both disputants, whether to allow tempers to cool, fiscal years or reporting periods to close, or key personnel to turn over. These can be as important, in some cases, as the time value of money or the urge to bring unpleasant situations to prompt conclusion.

The litigation path

Conflict managers must generally face the reality that litigation is readily available to the disputants. In order to craft a better process for managing a particular dispute or class of disputes, they should become familiar with the traditional litigation process and learn from litigation's flaws and virtues.

Stages

What are the various stages through which the litigation must go? What is the intended purpose of each? In practice, what happens at each stage? How much time typically passes between each phase? At what point are these suits typically settled, if at all?

Dispute resolution procedures need not be wholly divorced from litigation, nor need they be a complete substitute. The judicial process offers the most effective means of dealing with some issues. Alternative procedures may actually complement litigation, for example, by stream-lining discovery and reducing the number of disputed questions of law or fact. By developing an understanding of the various stages of the traditional litigation path, parties can better design a process tailored to their needs.

Costs and benefits

How expensive is litigation in expended fees and lost productivity? How are expenses incurred over the dispute's life (front-weighted, evenly distributed, end-weighted)? Are the costs evenly borne by the parties? Aside from the actual court award, what other benefits does either party expect from litigation (public vindication, blame shifting, fulfilling fiduciary duty in attempting to recover funds)? Do the costs have proportional impact or significance to the parties?

Litigation, like any other product or service a manager buys, delivers some value. It may produce a favorable outcome, but even if it does not, it at least provides some finality and generally delivers a credible and legitimate result. At a minimum, it often succeeds in shifting responsibility for the outcome from the line executive to the legal department. The key question, however, is at what cost does it accomplish these objectives? Is this a product worth buying, or could the same interests be met for less? The decision to litigate is a business decision. A manager charged with that decision must consider the alternatives and compare how litigation fares with other means of meeting personal and institutional interests.

Diagnose causes

Depending on how one defines ADR, the term may well encompass ordinary negotiation between the parties in the course of preparing to litigate. In that sense, there is nothing new, different or unusual about it — 90 to 95 percent of all civil lawsuits are settled. The key to designing a procedure that will help disputants make better decisions about whether and how to settle, and to generate more attractive choices in the majority of cases, is to focus on what has kept the parties from resolving their conflict until now. Having developed a picture of the conflict, the conflict manager should now ask, 'Why haven't the parties settled yet?'

The range of possible answers to this question is very broad. Any given conflict will generally have multiple barriers to settlement. One or more impediments to resolution may leap out as obvious; others may be more subtle, yet nonetheless significant. The framework for an effective process may serve as an analytical guide to sort through and organize these diagnoses. By comparing the current process with the target process, the conflict manager can generate ideas for remedying the deficiencies.

Interests versus positions

Have negotiations to date focused on demands and concessions? Are the parties being forthcoming about their underlying interests? If pressed, could each party answer the following questions in a manner to which the other would agree: 'What do your counterparts really hope to accomplish in this dispute?' and 'For what purpose?'

One exceedingly common cause of breakdowns in negotiations is that both parties get locked into extreme positions from which neither can easily make concessions. One telltale sign is a pattern of negotiating along single, highly quantifiable variables, such as money. A process that encourages such negotiation exacerbates the zero-sum mentality that generally accompanies bitter disputes. For example, as long as the engineer and the manufacturing company were locked into a positional haggle over the royalty percentage, they could make no progress without one side or the other feeling that it had backed down.

Relationship problems

What relationship did the parties have prior to the dispute? Are they likely to have future dealings? Has one party threatened to terminate the business relationship unless the other gives in?

Another possible cause for the negotiation breakdown could be the parties' working relationship. All too often, personality problems keep the parties from discussing the problem's merits. Sometimes personal trust has broken down so far that the parties cannot even agree to disagree, for fear that the other is trying to pull a fast one. In diagnosing why the dispute has not yet been resolved, it might be useful to know whether the real problem has become the people involved.

Limited generation of options

Who has introduced the options that have been considered so far? Does one party typically take the lead in presenting proposals, or do the parties share the burden? Are the parties reluctant to put the first offer on the table? Do time constraints operate differently on them? Do cost constraints affect the settlement (e.g., might it be easier to settle a suit in a particular fiscal year or under another project's budget)?

Another consequence of negotiation on the basis of position rather than interests is a relative poverty of good options to choose from. If the negotiators perceive their preparation as girding themselves for battle, and their proposals as starting positions to be defended but eventually modified, they will more likely than not craft proposals that are highly favorable to their own side, expecting to make some concessions later. As both sides do this, blithely ignoring their counterpart's interests and constraints as 'their problem', no one is devoting any energy to inventing mutually advantageous options that might bring added value to the table.

Fear of arbitrary, illegitimate outcomes

Do the negotiators have critical constituencies to which they must report their handling of the dispute? Do those constituents expect their agents to follow certain rituals? Are there readily-available standards, within the industry or otherwise, that cover how disputes such as this one are settled?

One reason a party refuses to settle a dispute may have more to do with the dispute resolution process than with the settlement's content. If the process feels arbitrary or coercive, the party may devalue an outcome that it might otherwise have accepted. In baseball, for example, players and owners both accept an arbitrator's award that coincides with their counterpart's final offer more readily than they do if the same salary figure is proposed by the other side in a blustering 'take it or leave it' fashion. Similarly, a party may reject an attractive offer if the terms seem unrelated to any external standards or somehow conjured up out of thin air. Without some supporting rationale, the party might well wonder whether through more strategic negotiating it could do better. A party's inability to explain the logic of a particular settlement to its constituents may well stand in the way of a profitable resolution.

Overestimation of the litigation alternative

Do the negotiators have access to an objective assessment of the dispute, whether internally or outside their institution? Have they done any systematic analysis of the litigation risk? How carefully have they thought through the nonmonetary consequences of not settling?

Sometimes the principal impediment to settlement stems from one or both parties' limited understanding of their procedural alternatives. A failure to grasp the true costs and benefits of litigation can keep one or both parties from settling a case that should never have been litigated. An interesting example arose in an intellectual property dispute. Two parties that shared a profitable market sued and countersued each other over a number of aggressive trade practices, challenging the validity of one's right to exclude the other from certain market segments or from certain applications of the intellectual property. Only after careful analysis did they realize that if *either* prevailed in court on its principal theories, they would open the market to a host of new competitors, to the detriment of both. Without that understanding, however, there had been little room for settlement: each viewed its chances of prevailing at trial optimistically enough that no settlement offer or counter-offer that either could reasonably propose was likely to be acceptable to the other.

Poor communication

What channels do the decision makers use to communicate? Do they always go through lawyers or other agents or do they sometimes communicate directly? How does each party perceive the other's motives? Do the parties disagree on the facts or on the inferences to be drawn therefrom?

If the parties have very different pictures of the conflict and consequently have drawn very different conclusions as to how to resolve it, it may be impossible for them to reach an agreement. A debtor and a creditor may look at the distribution of proceeds from asset liquidation in the same way the pessimist and the optimist observe the proverbial glass of water: one perceives the glass as half empty, posing the problem of how to refill it, while the other perceives it as half full, presenting an opportunity to distribute its contents between the parties.

Differing perceptions may be formed a number of ways — an individual's psychological makeup or a career of working on an emotionally charged issue. Or perhaps each side has access to only part of the information necessary to understand the situation and its context. Depending on the primary reasons for the differing perceptions, the conflict managers might devise procedures for gathering information, testing the objectivity of the parties' perceptions, or facilitating their discussion of such perceptions. To get past the unproductive clash of perceptions, each party must be helped to understand how the other sees it, without feeling that to understand that perspective means it has also to agree with it.

Unclear commitments

Assuming some agreement could be reached, would it require a one-time act, such as a cash payment, or would compliance involve an ongoing commitment to a more complicated program? What issues must a settlement address? Who would have to cooperate in order to make the agreement operational?

If the parties have not considered or discussed with each other what the outline of an agreement would look like, they may develop very different ideas. The more different these images are, the more difficult it will be for them to arrive at a workable resolution. If one views the problem as an imminently bursting dam in need of an immediate stop-gap solution, while the other thinks the dispute is really about the long-term management of a complex navigation and irrigation system, they will be working toward radically different objectives and each will have a tough time understanding the other. Unless the process can help them clarify the nature and scope of the final commitment, they will probably escalate the conflict in an effort to impose a solution. The international diplomacy analogue makes the front pages all too often: in most armed conflicts, the opponents eventually talk about whether and how to cease hostilities. Unless those operational terms are clearly understood by both sides, one side may find its efforts to work toward an interim cease fire frustrated by the other's perception of the demand as a permanent cessation and full demobilization. Consequently, both sides increase combat to 'remind' the other side of how bad things can be in the absence of an agreement.

Prescribe approaches

Now the conflict managers are better prepared to devise a process that can overcome, or at least mitigate, the effect of the impediments described above. They can systematically review their particular diagnoses and devise general approaches to build a process that approximates their view of effective dispute resolution. A few illustrations should help capture the flavor of the task.

Overcome impediments

If the parties are locked into a positional bargaining battle in which substantial concessions seem unlikely, mechanisms to clarify their interests, as distinguished from their positions, may be of value. The classic object of single-variable positional bargaining is money, but underlying a demand for a particular sum are usually other interests that could perhaps be satisfied some other way. An outside facilitator may be able to solicit this kind of information confidentially. When a highly leveraged entrepreneur was attempting to sell one of his magazine properties, his bottom-line asking price was $400 000. No amount of haggling could get him to move, even though no buyer had offered more than $325 000, and independent appraisals had estimated the property's fair market value as somewhere between $280 000 and $325 000. Only after extensive prodding by an outside facilitator did he admit that his problem was not that he needed $400 000, or that he thought the magazine was worth that much. Rather, he felt constrained by a financing clause that treated any write-down of more than $100 000 on any asset as a condition of default. Since all of his financing had cross-default provisions, he could not possibly accept less than $400 000 for a property he had initially purchased at $500 000. Once they understood that, the parties, in consultation with their lawyers and accountants, devised a creative financing scheme that would not trigger a default, but that nonetheless represented real cost to the purchasers of about $310 000.

If both sides are much too willing to take their chances in court, a helpful prescription might afford them a confidential way to develop a realistic assessment of their litigation prospects. The decision-tree and risk-analysis tools long familiar to business decision makers are now being used with some success in analyzing litigation decisions.[6] Such an analysis, carried out independently and confidentially for each side by an outside expert, might inject a useful dose of reality into the process.

If partisan perceptions arising from a disparity in the parties' experience and access to information are impeding communication, the conflict managers may want to devise an information-sharing process that enables one part to 'catch up'. If neither party has sufficient information, perhaps a joint or neutral fact-finding process would help. If one side is concerned that the terms of an agreement will be disclosed, the conflict managers might incorporate into the process some means of managing the flow of information about the agreement.

Sometimes, the greatest impediment to settling a dispute comes from the way in which the conflict has been framed, which in turn contains the types of options the parties consider. To the extent that the parties view the problem as principally involving the distribution of something — money, liability, kudos or blame —

they will conclude that more for one necessarily means less for the other and will proceed to address the problem on that basis. While it is not always possible to settle a dispute by 'enlarging the pie', experience teaches that truly adversarial disputants can always produce a result that leaves less for both, a 'negative sum'. Some conflicts, because of the parties' needs and resource constraints, may never be settled unless someone attempts to generate mutual gains. The small trade magazine that grievously but wholly unintentionally libels the fast-rising entrepreneur may simply not have the ability to make him whole through cash compensation. If he insists on a lump sum payment equivalent to what he might expect to be awarded in court, he may well end up with an unenforceable judgment against a bankrupt company. But a cover story on his visionary leadership in an emerging industry might net him valuable exposure and the publisher an interesting article, made richer and more credible by the subject's full cooperation.

One of the conflict manager's goals, and potentially their greatest contribution, is identifying opportunities for turning the dispute into a positive-sum game. By orienting the parties toward joint problem solving instead of adversarial posturing, and by facilitating communication and information exchange, a well-designed process can help the parties resolve their dispute more profitably for both sides. Two rich sources of value-enhancing potential are the parties' differences and their ability to cooperate.[7]

Exploit differences

Do the parties place different values on possible outcomes or on different goods and services? Do they face different tax or other incentives? Do they have different concerns about publicity? Do the parties have different expectations about contingent events, different attitudes toward risk? Do they have different preferences about the resolution's timing or the performance of the settlement?

One school of thought suggests that the best way to resolve a dispute is to minimize the parties' differences. The more alike the two disputants seem, the more likely they are to reach some accommodation. While that may sometimes be true, it is not always possible to accomplish. Some parties may just have too diverse a set of interests and expectations to be homogenized.

Besides, many differences are valuable and worth preserving. Many a business alliance is struck not because the parties are similar, but precisely because the parties have different strengths or perspectives that they believe make a good fit. A good process for managing conflict should facilitate the way the parties deal with their differences rather than paper over them.

Facilitate cooperation

Is cooperation between the parties a desirable and efficient manner of resolving the problem? Are economies of scale possible? Do the parties have shared interests in some substantive outcome, public good, or public perception of their handling of the dispute? Can one side take steps to benefit the other significantly at minimal cost to itself?

Cooperation with the enemy is usually the last thing disputants consider. Yet it is precisely because that whole class of solutions is so often overlooked that it should be systematically considered in almost every dispute. Sometimes the best way to resolve a problem about past performance is jointly to devise a better mechanism for encouraging, facilitating, and monitoring future performance. Perhaps the prior OEM agreement was not fulfilled because it would have worked better as a full-fledged joint venture. In most business conflicts, there is usually some way that one side could confer substantial value on the other at comparatively low cost, if only in business referrals or good public relations, or more tangibly in at-cost supply contracts or third-party guarantees. The failure to systematically consider those options costs money.

In many business conflicts, there are also activities that both sides would agree constitute a good use of resources and from which both would derive at least indirect benefit; they should consider committing part of what is at stake in the conflict to some such mutually beneficial activity instead of squandering more resources in fighting over how to allocate the nominal stakes between them.

Take action

The analysis thus far has proceeded through the classic problem-solving stages. The first step defined a desired outcome — an effective process for managing business disputes. Second, the conflict managers were encouraged to make observations of the conflict, as yet unresolved by traditional means. The third step encouraged them to diagnose the causes for the parties' failure to settle the case thus far. Fourth, based on these diagnoses, they were to prescribe some general approaches for dealing with the identified problems. Now is the time to take action. What should the conflict managers do next? How do they go from scratchpad to an action plan for resolving this conflict?

Making process choices

Designing a custom dispute resolution process requires making some specific decisions about types of mechanisms to use and how they might fit together. These decisions will vary significantly from one case to another.

The interaction with litigation. If the process replaces traditional litigation, should it aim primarily at facilitating settlement, or would some sort of partial or streamlined adjudication be preferable? How should the alternative procedures interact with the traditional litigation track? Should litigation be temporarily stayed? Should judicial approval of the alternative procedures be sought in advance?

Sometimes the only way to apply sufficient pressure on the parties to reach a productive settlement is to keep litigation going full steam ahead while someone else tries to settle the case on a 'second tract'. Indeed, this is one way to make the parties more comfortable with trying a new approach; they don't have to surrender any perceived advantage in court. Although such an approach does seem to require committing additional resources to the conflict, it may still pay off handsomely in the efficiency and quality of the outcome. If the 'second tract' succeeds, the savings from early termination of the 'litigation tract' alone will easily outweigh the additional expenditures.[8] Other times, in order for an innovative dispute resolution procedure to have a real chance of success, the parties must agree to a temporary cease-fire on the legal battlefield to enable the negotiator to explore a problem-solving approach and exchange information safely.

Expected product. Should the outcome be binding on the parties, or merely advisory? What will be gained or lost in the flexibility of the process, the seriousness with which parties participate, or their willingness to accept the process at all?

The procedures should help the parties craft a solution that meets their interests, feels legitimate, and is preferable to their best alternative away from the table. Such procedures need not impose an outcome on any party; indeed, by definition any such solution will enjoy the support and consent of every party. Yet some nonbinding procedures may lend themselves to bad faith manipulation and may be used solely for delay and intelligence-gathering. For such situations, dispute resolution procedures can be designed to generate a resolution to which all parties will be bound, even if none would have advocated it.

Participation by a neutral. Would a neutral party be of some help? In what capacity? Should a neutral facilitate communication between the parties, evaluate their positions, generate settlement proposals, or ascertain facts? Each of these involves different degrees of intrusion into the process by a stranger to the conflict.

The intervention of a neutral is often charged with tension and anxiety. Some will worry about how the neutral will perceive them and their position and will seek the neutral's approval. Some will worry that outsiders will see the use of a neutral as an admission that they cannot solve their own problems; they will either try to conceal the request for intervention or show public disdain for the neutral's efforts. Often such a public posturing becomes a self-fulfilling prophecy and the neutral, stripped of credibility and trust, cannot help but fail. Before seeking intervention, try to visualize the neutral's role. What procedural deficiencies might the neutral address? Is there some way of addressing them effectively?

Many of the tasks neutrals undertake actually require only someone who does not have a vested interest in the resolution of the conflict, rather than a wholly nonpartisan stranger. In many contexts, it is possible and desirable to overcome barriers to settlement by using 'internal neutrals', that is, individuals within one or both organizations who are not directly involved in the dispute and whose primary interest is in helping manage the conflict. So-called 'wise men' procedures, whereby senior executives within two organizations are designated as process resources to help jointly resolve, for example, a dispute between line managers, are worth considering for any complex, long-term business relationship.

Formality. How formal or informal a process seems best suited to the parties and the dispute? Should rules be specified concerning the stages of the process or their timing? What rules of discovery, if any, should be incorporated? How should the presentation of evidence and testimony (whether to each other or to a neutral) proceed? Should there be avenues of review?

At the risk of turning the design process into a legislative drafting exercise, it is important that the conflict managers think carefully through the operational aspects of the process and the consultative and verification mechanisms that will be necessary to resolve the inevitable procedural disputes. Not only must they think about what process would best help the parties resolve their substantive conflict, but they must consider how to deal with disputes about the process itself. During the discovery phase of traditional litigation, for example, counsel are expected to work out their differences, but if they are unable to do so, they may seek a ruling from the judge, magistrate or special master presiding over that aspect of the case. While that is not to say that one should adopt an adversarial litigious process to resolve disputes about the process, it does mean that these mechanisms require careful attention and that the participation of legal counsel may be especially useful.

Costs. Who should bear the cost of a failure to reach agreement under the new process? In the event the parties reach an agreement, how should costs be allocated among them?

Much has been written about the importance of cost incentives in dispute resolution, both for counsel and their clients.[9] The parties can decide whether they will cover their own costs or allocate costs some other way. Although there may not be an easily identifiable winner in the sense there is in litigation, it may be worth considering whether those responsible for making the parties incur additional costs should bear them. Some dispute-resolution mechanisms in litigation, for example, place the burden on the party declining a good-faith settlement offer to 'do better' by forcing them to bear the risk (in the form of a redistribution of litigation costs) of failing to do so.

Getting started

As noted earlier, the method described in this essay can be applied by professional organizations to draft model procedures for classes of disputes, or by parties to a business venture who want to draft dispute-resolution protocols for future conflicts between them, or by a manager facing a problem that has not been resolved earlier in the process. Whichever the case, conflict managers should make use of as much information as is available.

Although once a conflict arises it may be more difficult to establish the kind of joint problem-solving relationship that might have been available earlier, more facts may be known at that time, and these should permit the parties to devise a process better suited to the specific dispute than to a hypothetical conflict. Mutual consent will generally be required to undertake anything but traditional litigation. The parties will have to negotiate procedures and details and such negotiations may provide an opportunity for the parties to begin to cooperate.

The analysis described here should enable managers facing an escalating conflict to do several things: first, they should be able to decide whether it is worthwhile to structure a custom dispute-resolution process and to discuss the option clearly and systematically with legal counsel; second, even if the conflict managers choose not to negotiate about the process, by having diagnosed the existing problem they should be better prepared to think about how to settle it on the merits; and third, if they decide to approach their counterparts to discuss the possibility of a better process, they will be prepared for negotiating over it.

To initiate such negotiation, managers might try to schedule a meeting with their counterparts to explore conflict management procedures, making it clear that the substance of the dispute is not on the agenda for that meeting. Accompanying the invitation to such a meeting might be a draft of what an effective process should be able to accomplish (rather than what it should look like), along the lines of the attributes described in Exhibit 8.5, and an invitation to revise the draft. A list of attributes of a good dispute resolution process is sufficiently removed from the substance of the conflict that the managers may well be able to approach the problem of designing appropriate procedures much the way they might handle a less adversarial problem-solving session: whatever their respective views of the dispute itself, they have a shared interest in using a process that is tailored to the problem and that might be less painful than letting Procrustes help them into one of those 'one size fits all' beds.

ENDNOTES

1 Based on their experience with labor-management disputes in the coal industry, Ury and Goldberg have come up with a useful and somewhat different checklist of steps that should be included in systems for managing recurring conflicts within an organization. See: W. Ury, J. Brett, and S. Goldberg, *Getting Disputes Resolved* (San Francisco: Jossey-Bass, 1988).

2 This diagnostic approach to designing a dispute resolution process is based in part on the Circle Chart described in R. Fisher and W. Ury, *Getting to Yes* (Boston: Houghton Mifflin, 1981), pp. 68–71.

3 The seven elements of the framework have been described in different forms in a variety of published and unpublished papers. The use of this framework for designing alternatives to litigation is, to my knowledge, original to this essay. For a brief definition, see R. Fisher, 'Negotiating Inside Out', *Negotiation Journal* 5 (1989), pp. 33–41.

4 O. M. Fiss, 'Against Settlement', *Yale Law Journal* 93 (1984), pp. 1073–90.

5 These inquiries have evolved from a related set of considerations outlined in S. Goldberg, E. Green, and F. Sander, *Dispute Resolution* (Boston: Little, Brown & Co., 1985), pp. 545–48; H. Raiffa, *The Art and Science of Negotiation* (Cambridge, MA: Belknap Press, 1982), pp. 14–19; and other works that attempt to identify the 'ADR potential' of a dispute or to produce a classification scheme for disputes.

6 Raiffa (1982); M. Raker, 'The Application of Decision Analysis and Computer Modeling to the Settlement of Complex Litigation' (Cambridge, MA: ILP Symposium, MIT, 1987).

7 D. Lax and J. Sebenius, *The Manager as Negotiator* (New York: The Free Press, 1986), pp. 88–116.

8 R. Fisher, 'He Who Pays the Piper', *Harvard Business Review*, March–April 1985, pp. 150–59; P. Mode and D. Siemer, 'The Litigation Partner and the Settlement Partner', *Litigation*, Summer 1986, pp. 33–35.

9 S. Shavell, 'Suit, Settlement, and Trial: A Theoretical Analysis under Alternative Methods for the Allocation of Legal Costs', *Journal of Legal Studies* 11 (1982), pp. 55–81; J. C. Coffee, Jr., 'Understanding the Plaintiff's Attorney: The Implications of Economic Theory for Private Enforcement of Law through Class and Derivative Actions', *Columbia Law Review* 86 (1986), pp. 669–727.

EXERCISE 8 PEMBERTON'S DILEMMA

Gregory Leck

Introduction

This exercise creates a situation in which you and the other person(s) will be making separate decisions about how to manage your company. In this situation the outcomes (profits and losses) are determined not only by what you do, but also by a number of other factors, such as the goals and motives that you and the other party have, and the communication that takes place between you and the other party.

Advance preparation
None.

Procedure
Step 1: 5 minutes
The class will be broken into six-person groups; three will play the management team of Country Market, and three will play the management team of Corner Store. The teams should sit far enough from each other to allow private meetings.

Step 2: 10 minutes
Read the background information for Pemberton's dilemma below. If you have any questions, clarify them with your instructor at this time.

In this exercise, you will represent your store in discussions with the other store about the hours that each store should open on Sundays. You and the other store will be making decisions simultaneously, and your profits will be directly affected by these decisions. How well you perform will depend in part on your goals, the other store's goals and the communication between you.

Background information

Pemberton is a quaint little town located in the heartland of this country. Although it is only a 30-minute drive to a major metropolitan centre, most of the townspeople prefer to do their shopping at one of the two general stores located in Pemberton. At these stores, one can buy a variety of goods, ranging from groceries to hardware equipment. Both establishments boast a milk bar, which is quite popular among the younger generation as well.

Like most small towns, Pemberton is proud of the fact that it has been able to preserve its many traditions, some of which date back to the 1890s. One of these grand traditions, which became official in 1923 when the local council passed a resolution to this effect, is the cessation of all commercial activity on Sunday. Times have changed, however, and 'Sunday shoppers' are becoming more and more prevalent. In fact, every Sunday there is a mass exodus to the nearby metropolitan centre where Sunday shopping has been permitted for years.

You are a member of the management team from one of the two general stores in Pemberton. Both Country Market and Corner Store have

been consistently losing potential profit as Sunday shopping becomes more popular. Your management team, as well as the team from the competing general store, has recently contemplated opening the store on Sunday, in spite of the municipal resolution that prohibits this.

The ramifications of such decisions are important since the profitability of such an action will depend upon the decision made by the competing store. For instance, if neither store decides to open on Sunday, it will be business as usual, and both stores will make a profit of $20 000 for the week in question.

If only one store decides to open on Sunday, that particular store would enjoy the patronage of all those Sunday shoppers and would manage to make a $40 000 profit for the week. Unfortunately, the store that decided to remain closed on that Sunday would actually incur a loss of $40 000 that week. This would be due to various reasons, most notably the preference of customers to continue to do their shopping throughout the week at the store that remained open on Sunday.

If both stores decided to stay open on the Sunday of a particular week, adverse consequences would be faced by both establishments. Although the local council may be able to turn a blind eye to one store violating the municipal resolution, two stores would be looked upon as a conspiracy against the traditionalists of Pemberton. Eukariah Hampton, Pemberton's mayor and direct descendant of one of the town's founders, would no doubt pressure the local council into levying the highest possible

		Country Market		
		Close Sunday		Open Sunday
Corner Store	**Close Sunday**	Corner: $20 000 Country: $20 000		Corner: −$40 000 Country: $40 000
	Open Sunday	Corner: $40 000 Country: −$40 000		Corner: −$20 000 Country: −$20 000

fine allowable by law. In this case, the penalty would be so excessive that both stores would incur losses of $20 000 each for the week. While your lawyers have suggested that the municipal resolutions prohibiting Sunday shopping in Pemberton might be overturned in a court case, this too would be a costly option. In either case, if both stores open on Sunday, they will each incur losses of $20 000 for the week.

Keeping the above information in mind, your team is to decide each week, for the next 12 weeks, whether your store is to remain open on the Sunday of that week. The decision made for the first week must be made without prior consultation with the management team of the competing store. Subsequent decisions may be made after consulting with your competitors. Both teams shall reveal their decisions simultaneously. Remember, the goal is to maximise profits over the next 12-week period.

Step 3: 10 minutes
Review the details of the situation and understand how you can make or lose money. Familiarise yourself with the profit chart above. Members of each management team should now plan their strategy. There may not be any communication between the teams before the first round.

There will be twelve 1-minute rounds where the stores will either open or close. Each round represents one Sunday, and every fourth Sunday is part of a long weekend. A three-minute planning session separates each Sunday. There may not be any communication between the stores during the planning sessions.

Step 4: 30–45 minutes
The exercise begins when representatives from the stores (one from each) meet and indicate with a card if their store will open or close on the

first Sunday. There may be no communication between the stores before this decision is registered. After each Sunday, representatives from the stores *may* meet and negotiate for 5 minutes before each 3-minute planning session. Negotiations are optional, except after moves four and eight when they are required. If negotiations occur, they will be followed by a 3-minute planning period. If there are no negotiations, the 3-minute planning period will follow the sharing of the previous decision to open or close. Profits and losses are calculated after each Sunday and are cumulative for the 12 weeks.

Each team will record the outcome of each Sunday on their profit chart. The time periods between each Sunday are fixed and may not be altered. Each team will complete a total of 12 moves.

Step 5: 30 minutes
The instructor will record the total profit for each team in each negotiating group. Differences in performance will be noted and possible reasons explored. Participants should describe what happened, particularly in regard to their perceptions of and reactions to the other party. Some suggested questions and issues for discussion are given below.

Discussion questions
1. What were your basic objectives and strategy when you started the exercise? Did they change? What outcomes did you achieve as a result of these plans?
2. What did you talk about after the first round of negotiation?
3. Did the content of your negotiating discussion change? Why?
4. What were the most important things that lead to the outcome of the exercise?

Profit Chart

	Corner Store's Choice	Country Market's Choice	Profit	
			Corner Store	Country Market
15-minute planning period				
1.				
2.				
3.				
4. Double profit				
5-minute required negotiation period				
5.				
6.				
7.				
8. Triple profit				
5-minute required negotiation period				
9.				
10.				
11.				
12. Quadruple profit				

CASE 8 RAINBOW MEDICAL CENTRE

Kathryn Whitfield

Overview

Rainbow Medical Centre (RMC) is an 800-bed, metropolitan-based teaching hospital, with affiliations to the Yarra University Medical and Allied Health Schools. The hospital has a community-based Committee of Management (COM) and chief executive officer (CEO) and is ultimately accountable to the State Health Department for the services it provides. The hospital is organised into a number of functional 'streams' such as Administration, Corporate Services, Casemix and Information Technology, and Clinical Services. Each 'stream' is administered by an executive committee with the CEO or deputy CEO represented on each and is thus directly accountable to the COM. The Clinical Services Executive Committee is responsible for the full range of clinical services and consists of the CEO, medical director, deputy medical director and director of nursing (DON). The actual clinical services are further subdivided into a series of specialties and then into specific departments. For example, the surgical specialty consists of the orthopaedic, general and neurological departments. Within the clinical streams executive the Deputy Medical Director, Dr Jan Green, and the DON, Mary Taylor, have joint responsibility for human resource management issues. In reality though Mary is only concerned with staff issues relating to nurses, with Jan looking after the residual.

Historically, one of the clinical streams, Mental Health, consisted of only one department — that of psychiatry. However, approximately two and a half years ago, it became apparent that as a result of considerable community lobbying, RMC would need to expand Mental Health to create a community-based psychology division. This was encouraged by the Health Department, which offered to assist RMC with additional funding.

The existing Psychiatry Department was headed by Professor Purple. However, the hospital decided that he wasn't a suitable candidate to head a new community-based division. It was intended that this unit be a psychology/community based-program and not a service for the more serious psychiatric disorders that are normally treated by Professor Purple's

Psychiatric Department. Professor Purple, however, resented the fact that the new department was established as an independent unit, outside his control and authority.

A world-renowned specialist, Pam Red, was recruited by the medical director from the United States of America. Pam, albeit of impeccable academic and clinical qualifications, lacks a certain warmth in her dealings with other staff, eschewing social functions and tending to communicate in a very formal way. Professor Purple and Pam very quickly developed a dislike of each other, which manifested itself as a tendency to block each other's plans whenever possible. The psychologists working under Pam's supervision also found her difficult to approach and discuss issues with and considered that she held herself aloof. The staff also quickly realised that Pam was from a different psychology 'school' from them and she seemed to have little regard for the postgraduate studies that all of the staff had either completed or were currently undertaking in the psychoanalytic school they favoured.

Eighteen months after the new department was established, symptoms of these problems began to appear:

- frequent heated (and often personal) discussions between Professor Purple and Pam Red;
- extremely low morale in the Psychology Department demonstrated by poor turnouts to social events and little 'team spirit';
- increased absenteeism and turnover from the Psychology Department;
- increasing numbers associating with the Psychiatry Department (both professionally and socially).

Key characters comment on the problems

Deputy Medical Director Jan Green says ...
Things seemed to be going all right. Although Professor Purple wasn't very supportive of the newly created department, the psychologists were very glad to form their own department. As expected, Professor Purple had a number of clashes with Pam Red. Pam was of equal status and had taken away a full unit from his control. This wasn't of great concern to me because, as professionals, I expected that they would be able to work out any problems for themselves. There

were often management problems in the past, but they always sorted themselves out.

The real problem began when Dan formally approached me and complained about Pam Red. Dan is the most senior person reporting to Pam. In the past, Dan had taken time off work to do supervisory work at the local university. This was supported by Professor Purple, but Pam had directed that this work be done outside work hours. Dan was very upset by this, particularly because Pam had given her decision in writing without him having a chance to discuss the issue. Part of Dan's work was in the wards under Professor Purple's supervision, who gave him permission to continue his teaching during work hours. This was contrary to Pam Red's clear instructions. This really inflamed Pam, who blew up when I tried to discuss the matter with her in an informal manner.

I am concerned with the degeneration of the team spirit within this department. Dan presented with a list of problems with Pam's management approach. He seemed to have the backing of all the other psychologists. I really need to find out what's going on out there.

Therapist Dan Blue says ...

At the age of 24 I suffered a severe nervous breakdown due to stress associated with my profession (I was a bungee-jumping instructor). I was so impressed by the professionalism and helpfulness of the psychological support given to me that I decided that psychology was the career to which I was destined. Since gaining qualifications I have been employed at a number of institutions — most recently RMC for the last several years.

Prior to Pam Red arriving there existed a good working relationship between all professional staff and everyone worked as the one team. I particularly enjoyed the informal, more social events as I found these let me get to know everyone a lot better, and made resolving issues less painful. Being accepted by my peers is very important to me, and I think the best way to resolve any conflict is just to sit down and talk it through. I think it is these aspects of my personality which are always leading me to frustration when I deal with Pam Red.

Pam is forever trying to pull in the opposite direction to what I am. She seems to think the best way to get anything done is to slap a memo onto someone's desk and let them work it out.

She seems to be forever thinking of ideas, and without any consultation thrusting them upon the rest of us and leaving it up to us to overcome the impracticality of it all. She also doesn't seem to think that team morale is important. She doesn't get involved with any social functions which may be organised, and her support for the training scheme for university students is non-existent. I don't know how she thinks this place is going to survive if we can't bring in new people who understand its operations. And how are people going to understand if we don't train them?

It also gets on my nerves (and the nerves of several other members of staff) when Pam (alias Pam the Ram) takes complete control of the secretarial staff, forcing everyone to wait while she gets her multitude of letters, memos and reports typed. She's driving this place to the pits. No one likes her, and we think she's just in it for the short-term personal glory, rather than establishing a coherent team (why else would she appear to do the things she does?).

But I'm not a whinger. I've written letters to Dr Green telling her about the complete incompetence which Pam displays. I don't know if it will do any good but someone has to say something. I'm thinking of applying to work for Professor Purple. At least he seems to care about how his team works, and the long-term future of his unit. I think it would be a good idea if everyone worked for him, leaving Pam Red with no one to send memos to but herself (let her try to find personal glory in that).

Pam Red says ...

When Dr Jan Green decided to talk informally to Dr Pam Red about the complaint made by Dan, Pam felt that here was an opportunity to voice her grievances. Pam said: I feel very strongly about Professor Purple's insidious and malicious undermining of my position of authority over my staff. I also object violently to his direct interference in the administration of my department — he has no right to allow my staff time off from their work roster to be involved in the psychoanalytic course out at Yarra University. Sam Purple is actively working to encourage my staff to insubordination, because he resents me and the professional standing of my department. It is just another example of his typically arrogant and heavy-handed approach to dealing with other people when they are doing something of which he personally, for his own senile reasons, disapproves. He doesn't seem to expect other people to stand up to him — just because he's a medical practitioner, a crony of the medical director and has been working here for umpteen years — and when they do, he does his best to destroy them.

I would not normally have brought this matter to your attention, Jan, as I consider it an internal departmental issue. However, given this opportunity, I feel that the matter has progressed too far. I, as department head, will deal with the issues raised by Dan; however, I consider that you as a member of the Clinical Services Executive Committee should advise Professor Purple to 'back off' and that his interference in a department which he is most definitely not responsible for is both inappropriate, and inexcusable. Although I will say, with respect to the matters you say have been raised by Dan, that I do not consider a continued heavy involvement by the department in the postgraduate studies in psychoanalysis is appropriate, given the shift in the service's focus to a more behaviourist approach — we need to treat people quickly to the point where they are functional and can be discharged, thus increasing throughput. The old style of treatment meant the service being clogged with long-term, dependent clients — it was to change this focus that I was initially recruited to head the new Psychology Department. As to the ridiculous suggestion that I should involve myself in every social event being organised, I actually resent the intrusion into my private life. In reality these complaints are inconsequential, internal to the department and have been exaggerated as a direct result of Professor Purple's 'stirring up trouble' and I will deal with them internally.

Look, Professor Purple clearly has a problem — he seems to resent my position, me personally and the psychologist's autonomy and non-medical focus. Although I admit his right to an opinion I will not tolerate his unwarranted interference, nor should the RMC senior executive unless they want to compromise the Psychology Department's high profile and the valuable work which is being performed in both the outpatient and outreach programs. I expect the full support of the Clinical Services Management Executive — at the very least for the remainder of the term of my contract of employment.

A profile of Head of Psychiatric Services, Sam Purple

Prior to Pam Red's appointment as head of psychology Professor Purple was in charge of all psychiatric and psychological services at RMC. In addition Professor Purple had, for over ten years, taken a hands-on role in mental health training — a role he took great pride in: 'I like to teach. And by crikey the youngsters these days, they sure need it. I've probably forgotten more about the mind than they will ever know'. Following his department's restructuring Professor Purple retained responsibility for psychiatric services while Pam Red assumed responsibility for psychological services.

Professor Purple, or 'Crazy Sammy' as he was affectionately known in his student days (one of the less harmful side effects of a now greatly diminished propensity for high-spirited but very practical experiments with mind-altering substances), had opposed the restructuring of the department, which lead to Pam Red's appointment. Indeed, when he first heard of the restructuring plans he questioned the overall direction the Committee of Management was taking the hospital. 'Have you seen what they're planning to do! I just wish they'd ask some people who have some idea about how this hospital works before committing themselves to a plan like this. They're such a bunch of bloody do-gooders, that they probably wouldn't know the difference between cotton candy and a colonoscopy, without a hands-on demonstration'.

In part his disapproval for the restructuring also stemmed from his general antipathy towards the practice of psychology, a discipline which he regards with more than just a hint of cynicism. Indeed, when Jan Green informed him of Dan Blue's complaint, he said to her, 'I'm not at all surprised you know. I was opposed to the whole thing from the beginning. You have to keep that lot in check you know, otherwise you're bound to end up with chaos.'

His initial opposition to the restructuring had mounted following a number of clashes with Pam Red over hospital policy — in particular in relation to training. Following one such argument, Professor Purple voiced his distaste for Pam Red to one of his colleagues, 'She is such a know-it-all. Always telling me what I'm really thinking and what I really want to be saying. What would she know? Hell, she's from California.'

Professor Purple had tacitly encouraged the drift of psychologists back to his department. When questioned with respect to Dan Blue's complaint, he stated, he 'stood behind Dan all the way.' As he said to Jan Green, 'Dan's a bright guy — he just wants to help other people to get ahead, it's hard to do that these days. There's a lot of competition nowadays. You can't criticise people for wanting to teach.'

Discussion questions

1. At what stage is this conflict?
2. Identify the sources of conflict. How could these sources have been removed?
3. How has the group been affected by the conflict?
4. Could the conflict have been prevented?
5. If you were Pam Red what would you do now?
6. If you were Jan Green, what would you do now?

ALTERNATIVE
DISPUTE RESOLUTION

Learning objectives

- Distinguish *between negotiation and mediation.*

- Describe *four negotiating styles.*

- Distinguish *between distributive and integrative negotiations.*

- Identify *the benefits of integrative negotiations.*

- List *three strategies for integrative negotiating.*

- Describe *factors affecting negotiation outcomes.*

- List *stages in the mediation process.*

9

Chapter

Understanding the sources and causes of organisational conflict can help us to avoid or eliminate them. However, this is not always possible, and so an equally important question is how we might constructively resolve conflicts when they arise. Although there are several strategies that we might use, the two that are most frequently used are negotiation and mediation. *Negotiation* may be viewed as a process in which two or more parties attempt to reach an acceptable agreement in a situation characterised by some level of real or potential agreement. When negotiations break down, it may be necessary to involve an independent third party to help resolve the conflict: to *mediate* the conflict. When third parties are able to make binding decisions, the process is described as *arbitration*. In this chapter, we will be concerned with factors that influence negotiation and mediation, especially the extent to which they will allow us to resolve conflicts constructively rather than destructively.

NEGOTIATION

Joe and Anne share a house. Both have been studying in their rooms all morning, but now find themselves face to face at the fruit basket reaching for an orange. Unfortunately, both Joe and Anne have been too busy to shop and there is only one orange left in the basket. How will Joe and Anne resolve this conflict? They decide that the easiest solution is to share the orange by cutting it in half. Was this the best solution? Joe takes his half of the orange and grates the rind: he had been planning to take a break from studying by baking an orange cake. Now the cake will have less flavour because he has only half the orange. What is Anne doing with her half of the orange? She has taken a juicer from the cupboard and is squeezing herself a small glass of orange juice.[1] Did Joe and Anne make a wise decision when they cut the orange in half? Could they both have had the whole orange? In this case, the answer is yes. If Joe and Anne had stopped to talk about why they wanted the orange both could have had the whole orange.

Although this story may seem a long way from organisations and their conflicts, it demonstrates some very important points about conflict resolution and negotiation:

1. Often in conflicts individuals behave *distributively*: they assume that the only way for one person to improve his or her outcomes is by worsening the other's outcomes.
2. Because of this, individuals fail to recognise the possibility that both people can simultaneously improve their outcomes (the *integrative* potential of the task).
3. This happens when individuals fail to explore the underlying needs of individuals involved in a dispute.
4. This results in the assumption that a compromise (splitting the difference) is the best possible outcome that can be achieved even though there are better outcomes.

Exercise 9
World Bank: An exercise in intergroup negotiation

A definition of negotiation

Negotiation is one process used to resolve conflicts. The principal goal of negotiation is for two (or more) individuals to decide how they will divide resources between them. Along with a conflict of interests, several factors define a negotiation setting: there is some level of interdependence between the parties, so that each is in some way affected by or dependent on the other; the parties involved in the dispute are prepared to communicate with each other; it is likely that the parties will be able to find an acceptable agreement; and the process is one in which negotiators engage in a series of offers and counter offers, none of which is binding, and no outcome is determined until both parties agree.[2] These last two features are important: they mean that one person cannot unilaterally impose her or his solution on the other; this does not, however, mean that the solution will advantage both people equally. Situational factors such as unequal power can still act to advantage a negotiator.

Negotiating styles

What options did Joe and Ann have for resolving the conflict? They chose to *compromise* or split the difference. This is perhaps the most frequently used strategy for resolving conflicts — both people meet some, but not all, of their needs and achieve some level of satisfaction. But is this the best option? In this

---

ORGANISATIONAL   Encounter

Agreement at Sheraton

Negotiation between employees and their unions has long been the way for determining employment conditions. In recent years, however, state and federal legislation in Australia and New Zealand has paved the way for increased flexibility in the bargaining process through the introduction of enterprise agreements and employment contracts. Currently, just over half of the workers employed under federal awards in Australia are covered by enterprise agreements with the majority of agreements representing workers in the manufacturing industry (57%), public and community sector (12.7%) and transport, storage and communications industries (11.7%). Over 60% of these agreements have led to wage increases, with the most common increase being between 4% and 5%.

When is an enterprise agreement a good one? According to *Benchmark*, the enterprise agreement that Melbourne's Sheraton Towers signed in 1992 represents excellence in enterprise agreements; since its implementation, four other Sheraton hotels have adopted the agreement. The agreement, which involved negotiations with the Australian Council of Trade Unions (ACTU) and the Australian Liquor, Hospitality and Miscellaneous Workers Union, aimed to introduce a new approach to human resource management that encompassed the ideals of

empowerment, a customer focus and continuous improvement.

Highlights of the enterprise agreement include:

- **Penalty rates.** Consultation with unions and employees led to loaded hourly rates replacing traditional penalty rates.
- **Classification system.** Existing classifications were replaced by a four-level competency based system.
- **Promotions.** Promotions are tied to competencies, and require demonstration that new skills and competencies have been learned.
- **Salary.** Salary also reinforces the importance of multiskilling.
- **Employment.** Conditions emphasise permanent, full-time employment resulting in a very low number of casual staff.

Sheraton is already reaping the benefits of this new agreement: training and administration costs have been reduced, and also Sheraton has approximately half the turnover rate experienced by other new hotels.

Source: Workplace bargaining is here to stay, *Workplace*, Summer 1995; Enterprise agreement an industry model, *Benchmark*, 11, 1995.

section we consider four strategies for resolving conflicts, as well as their associated costs and benefits.[3]

Inaction

When faced with a conflict, the simplest response is to withdraw or to ignore the conflict. The major benefit of this approach is that it avoids the more unpleasant emotions that we experience when dealing with conflicts. If the issue is unimportant, perhaps this is the best strategy. However, ignored conflicts do not go away. If the issue is important for either party in the dispute, ignoring the conflict simply delays its resolution; while the conflict remains unresolved, the chances are that the issue will intensify. Unless the issue is a trivial one, inaction is not a good strategy.

Yielding

A second option is to yield or give in to the demands of the other person. To do this requires a negotiator to reduce her or his goals and aspirations: that is, the negotiator is prepared to accept less than she or he had initially planned to accept. The principal benefit of this strategy is that it ends the conflict quickly. Again, if the issue is unimportant to one party, this may be the best solution. There are, however, two major pitfalls with yielding. The first, and most obvious, is that when individuals yield they do not meet their needs. If the outcome of the conflict was important to either party, then the party that yields will feel dissatisfied and may seek redress through some other means. The second pitfall is that if both parties yield and end the negotiation rapidly they are unlikely to have discovered the full extent of the resource pool; put more simply, individuals may overlook better solutions in their haste to settle the conflict. In a sense, this is what Joe and Anne did when they cut the orange in half.

Contending

A third option for negotiators is to behave in a contentious manner. Individuals who adopt this strategy make extreme demands, and insist that the other party give in to those demands. As a part of this strategy, negotiators make threats, engage in harassment and make positional commitments. The benefit of this strategy is that it provides the clearest means for meeting one party's needs in the negotiation. The biggest disadvantage occurs when our opponent likewise chooses a contentious strategy. Under these circumstances, there is a risk of creating an escalating conflict spiral that is likely to end in stalemate.

Problem solving

The final strategy available in negotiations is problem solving. Unlike the other strategies, problem solving is more concerned with understanding the underlying positions of an opponent. The greatest benefit of this strategy is that the solutions that are identified are likely to be stable and long-lasting because they meet everyone's needs. Of all the strategies this is the most risky. In order to engage in effective problem solving, it is necessary to give information to our opponent; only if that information exchange is reciprocated will we achieve good agreements. If a negotiating opponent does not reciprocate in information exchange, negotiators leave themselves vulnerable to exploitation.

Both yielding and contending are elements of problem solving. Initial contending is necessary in order to define the limits of the negotiation and to ensure that the full range of solutions is identified. At some point, however, both parties must also be prepared to concede in order to facilitate settlement. Pruitt[4] advocates a strategy of *firm flexibility*: that we be firm about the goals that must be met, but remain flexible about how those goals are achieved. We will return to this point when we look at some more practical tips on how to negotiate wisely.

Factors affecting strategy selection

These four strategies — inaction, yielding, contending and problem solving — form the basis for our thinking about negotiation and many researchers have considered what determines the choice of strategies. Almost all of these researchers have proposed a two-dimensional model as a way of predicting which strategy a negotiator will select. Among the best known of these are Blake and Mouton's Managerial Grid, Thomas' Interpersonal Conflict Style Model and Pruitt's Dual Concern Model.[5] Although these models differ in the way that they describe the two dimensions, all capture similar underlying concepts: the strategic choice of individuals will be determined by the extent to which they value achieving their own outcomes (and therefore behave competitively) and the extent to which they value achieving their opponent's outcomes (and therefore behave collaboratively). These dimensions and their associated strategies are shown in the following account of the Koala Company. Contentiousness is most likely when negotiators value only their own outcomes, yielding is most likely when negotiators place high value on an opponent's outcomes and problem solving occurs when individuals have the dual requirements of maximising both their own and their opponent's outcomes.

Exhibit 9.1
Dual concern model

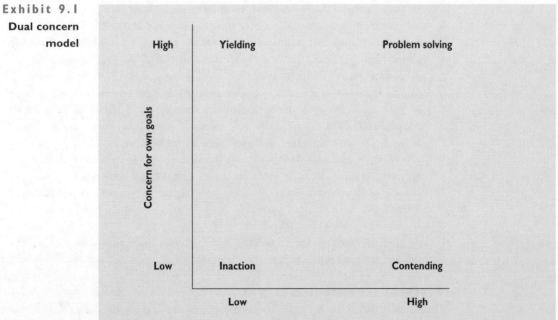

349

Approaches to negotiation

The value that we place on achieving our own goals and those of our opponents is only one determinant of the strategies that we adopt. Another important determinant is how we perceive the situation: do we believe that we can benefit only if the other person 'loses'? Or are we interested in finding a solution that maximises the benefits to both ourselves and the other party? Depending on our perceptions and goals, we will adopt either a *distributive* (win–lose) or *integrative* (win–win) approach to the conflict. Conceding and yielding are examples of strategies that we use in distributive negotiations. Problem solving characterises integrative negotiations.

The next sections will consider the features of both distributive and integrative negotiations, and their implications for conflict resolution. To understand the important issues in distributive and integrative bargaining, we will consider how the Koala Company is managing its employment contract negotiations (see the following account):

> ### Crisis at Koala Company
> *Koala Company is a small company that produces a range of soft toys for children. Union and management have been meeting over the past 4 weeks in an attempt to negotiate an employment contract. The two issues that they are discussing are the hourly rate that staff will be paid and the amount that this will be increased at the end of 12 months. The management offer is an hourly rate of $8.00 with a 1% increase in 12 months. The union has requested an hourly rate of $15.00 with a 10% increase in 12 months. The two parties have been engaged in a protracted dispute over these issues and it appears as though the negotiations have reached a stalemate.*
>
> *To try to facilitate the process, a consultant — Mary Shelley — has been invited to observe the negotiations. In order to understand both parties' claims she interviews the managing director of the company and the union leader. Mary is particularly concerned to understand the value that each party places on the two issues. First, knowing that these claims are likely to hide the true requirements, she asks each party what it would be willing to accept. Management reveals (confidentially) that it would be prepared to offer $13.00 an hour and an increase of 7%; equally confidentially, the union reveals that it would be prepared to accept $10.00 per hour with a 3% increase. Mary now knows the resistance points of the two parties and has established a contract zone.*
>
> *Having done so, she summarises the situation so far. For both parties, the very best outcome would be if the other side agreed to all demands. However, the chances of this happening are not very high. Is there a way around the problem? Think about the two issues separately. Is each worth an equal amount to you, or is one more important than the other?*
>
> *Our Organisational Encounter in this chapter looks more closely at real-life employment contracts.*

Distributive negotiations

Distributive (win–lose) negotiations are characterised by the belief that resources are limited and the aim of the negotiation process is to determine who will receive those resources. Such a win–lose approach characterises numerous negotiating situations. Buying a car is a classic example. As a buyer, the less you pay the less profit the seller makes; your 'wins' (in the form of fewer dollars paid) are the seller's 'losses' (in the form of fewer dollars of profit). Note that in distributive negotiating one party does not necessarily 'lose' in an absolute sense. Presumably the party selling the car still made a profit, but to the extent that the selling price was lowered to make the sale, the profit was lower.

In organisations, distributive negotiating is quite common. It characterises most bargaining involving material goods, such as the purchase of supplies or the manufacturing of raw materials. Distributive negotiating can be seen in universities, where each faculty attempts to negotiate the best budget for itself, invariably at the expense of some other faculty. Frequently, the most visible example of distributive negotiation in organisations is that which takes place between labour and management. Issues involving wages, benefits, working conditions and related matters are seen as conflicts over limited resources.

When individuals believe that their goals are in conflict, that the available resources are limited and that more for 'them' means less for 'us', they will employ the distributive strategies of contending and yielding.[6] This style of bargaining has two goals: to conceal or misrepresent your true needs while convincing your opponent to change his or her position. It is based on the belief that negotiators aim to hide what they really want; its aim is to find out and change this 'bottom line'.

In the Koala Company example, union and management have both started out with tough bids that conceal their real requirements. Management has offered an hourly rate of $8.00 and a 1% increase, while the union has demanded a $15.00 hourly rate and a 10% increase. In distributive negotiations, this range can be thought of as a straight line that defines the range of possible agreements. This range is shown in Exhibit 9.2. These demands of union and management define the end points of the line. At one extreme, point A represents the management demands; at the other extreme, point B represents the union's demands.

We also know that often what negotiators demand is not what they really want. Points C and D show what each side is actually prepared to accept in the negotiation: their bottom line or *resistance point*. You can think about distributive bargaining as a process for determining how this straight line will be divided. Because each party is aiming for a division favourable to itself, the second component of distributive bargaining is to change the opponent's resistance point. Ultimately, the negotiating process will have three aims:[7]

1. *To influence the settlement that an opponent believes is possible.* This will be accomplished if one party misrepresents his or her own resistance point. One means for doing this is to start with extreme demands well removed from the resistance point and to make only small concessions. The management at the Koala Company adopted this strategy by stating that because sales are declining the very best that it can offer is a 1% increase coupled with an hourly rate of $8.00.
2. *To change, and more specifically lower, an opponent's resistance point.* This will increase the contract zone and improve a negotiator's outcomes. Negotiators can achieve this goal by appearing indifferent to delays in the negotiations or by demonstrating that delays will worsen an opponent's

outcomes. Management went on to point out not only that their hourly rate exceeded industry standards and the 1% increase matched inflation, but also that delaying an agreement would advantage management by saving salary costs.

3. *To represent the solution on offer as the best possible settlement option for an opponent.* Finally, management pointed out that if the union pressed for further concessions management would have to 'downsize' the workforce.

The union presented similar arguments in support of its position. At the same time, both sides further concealed their true resistance points by making small concessions. When Mary arrived, management had 'conceded' to an hourly rate of $8.50 and a 1.5% increase, while the union had 'conceded' to a $14.50 hourly rate and a 9.5% increase. Both parties had adopted a tough bargaining style and had discovered one of the disadvantages: they were close to stalemate. If you were Mary, how would you resolve the conflict?

Distributive bargaining is also described as positional bargaining. Negotiators engaged in this type of bargaining often become so involved in defending their position that they do not recognise the potential for agreement that exists. Because 'winning' means changing this other person's position, it involves a lot of argumentation and is therefore very time consuming. It also involves a lot of individual decisions. How big a concession should I make this time? Is the offer that my opponent has just made the best that I am going to get? Should I accept it? At every step the negotiation, offers and counter offers must be assessed, evaluated and responded to.[8] As a consequence, Fisher and Ury describe this type of bargaining as both inefficient and unwise: inefficient because it takes a long time to reach an outcome; and unwise because it fails to obtain the best possible outcomes for everyone.

Exhibit 9.2
Settlement options in negotiations

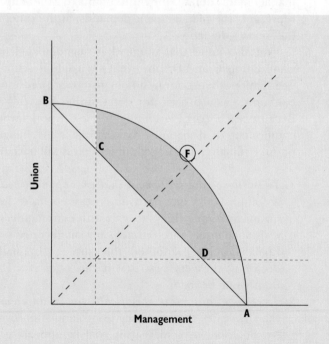

Integrative negotiations

Integrative negotiating brings a different perspective to the process. Remember the Prisoners' Dilemma that we described in the last chapter. The ideas represented by this dilemma — that it is possible for both individuals to achieve good outcomes — is a much better representation of many conflicts that we find ourselves in. When we adopt an integrative (win–win) approach, the chances are that we will all obtain better outcomes — as Joe and Ann might have done.

When individuals believe that they share common goals, recognise that the two groups place different values on issues in the negotiation, and that more for 'them' does not mean less for 'us', they are more likely to improve the outcomes of everyone involved in the conflict. Because these negotiations aim to maximise both parties' outcomes, we would expect them to be characterised by a problem-solving approach. It is important to realise that integrative bargaining does not guarantee that we will get everything we want; we probably won't. The point about this style of bargaining is that the agreement we reach will leave everyone better off than they were before the agreement.

Returning to the Koala Company, recall that while the two parties had been treating hourly rates and increases as separate — and equally important — issues, Mary has encouraged them to rethink this strategy by asking them to consider whether both issues are really of equal value. She has also tried to bring together the two parties by pointing out that the two groups have a common goal: resolve the dispute and avoid a strike, which would be costly to both.

Integrative negotiators will work from this common goal, to try to understand the other party's position. Responding to the consultant's questions, both parties said that the two issues were not equally important. Whereas management identified the hourly rate as its most important issue, union concerns centred around the increase to this rate. The parties differ in the priorities that they place on these issues; these differing priorities have not only created the possibility that the parties can trade off, but also have expanded the resources available to the parties.

This expanded range is shown in Exhibit 9.2. You will see that it is still possible to obtain distributive outcomes, and so points A and B are still in the diagram. However, the negotiations no longer need to be about how the line connecting points A and B will be divided. Recognising their resistance points, the two parties can now look for settlement anywhere in the shaded area; and any settlement above the diagonal line will represent an improved outcome for both parties. In particular, however, we are interested in point F. This point represents an outcome that not only maximises the resources available to negotiators, but also shares these resources equally. Such outcomes are achieved when negotiators completely concede on their low priority issue while maximising their outcomes for their high priority issue. In our example, this would occur if the union accepted an hourly rate of $8.00 and management was prepared to offer the full 10% increase.

As a result, the types of strategies that we expect to be associated with integrative negotiation differ markedly from those associated with distributive negotiations. Integrative negotiations are characterised by a collaborative, problem-solving orientation in which negotiators engage in far less argumentation, start with lower opening bids and are more systematic in their concession making.[9]

Integrative bargaining is also described as principled bargaining.[10] Negotiators engaged in this type of bargaining are no longer concerned with winning. Underlying their actions and strategies is a concern for identifying and meeting the needs of their opponents, while also meeting their own needs. The focus of such negotiations shifts from attacks on the position of the other to attempts to understand the needs underlying those positions. As a consequence, this type of bargaining better meets Fisher and Ury's criteria of wisdom and efficiency.

It may seem as if an integrative approach is always preferable to a distributive approach. Why should there be a winner and a loser if there can be two winners? Realistically, however, not every negotiating situation has an integrative pay-off. Some situations really are distributive: a gain for one side must mean an offsetting loss for the other side. What is important is that we recognise the type of situation we are dealing with. All too often, people assume that they are faced with distributive pay-offs when in fact the situation has integrative potential. We will discuss later the many factors that prevent us from perceiving the integrative potential of negotiations; for now, let us consider the benefits that accrue when we do recognise such potential and the strategies available for maximising the resource pool.

More on integrative bargaining

Integrative bargaining offers many benefits. Pruitt[11] identifies four key advantages if engaging in integrative bargaining:

1. When both parties have high goals or expectations, integrative solutions may offer the only possibility for resolution.
2. Because these solutions meet the underlying needs of both parties, they are more likely to be stable.
3. The relationship between the two parties is strengthened.
4. The broader community will also benefit from the use of more constructive strategies.

Overall, it appears that integrative bargaining has a lot to offer. The next question is: Can we increase the size of the resource pool and improve our integrative bargaining? We will consider three groups of strategies: expanding the pie, concession exchange and solving underlying concerns.[12]

Expanding the pie

The simplest strategy available to us is to increase the resource pool so that everyone can have what he or she wants. For example, if either Joe or Mary had bought another orange, the problem would have been solved. At the Koala Company, management may be able to increase its salary budget and accommodate the union's demands.

Concession exchange

A second way to achieve integrative agreements is to engage in a process of concession exchange in which each party gives large concessions on its low-priority item in return for large concessions on its high-priority item. One example of this was given above: we assumed that hourly rate was less important to the union, while the salary increase after 12 months was less important to management. The two parties can engage in *logrolling* by offering large concessions on their low-priority items, while requesting large concessions for their high-priority items. The Koala Company provides one example of this: management places a lower value on the salary increase while the union places a lower value on the hourly rate. If the two parties engaged in logrolling, management would offer the full 10% salary increase while the union would accept the $8.00 hourly rate.

It may also be possible to obtain an integrative agreement by offering one party something that is not a part of the negotiations. Such *non-specific compensation* gives one party exactly what it wants, while the other party is compensated in some unrelated way. For example, the union is given both the $15.00 hourly rate and the 10% increase; in return, it agrees to a restructure of the workplace that management has been planning for some time.

Finally, a third means for concession exchange can be used when there is only one issue at stake: we can *unbundle* or split that issue to make it into two. Management and the union are still discussing the increases to the hourly rate. If they agree that an initial 7% increase will be granted in 12 months time, while the remaining 3% increase will be delayed for a further 6 months, they have unbundled the issue.

Solving underlying concerns

So far, the strategies have required little, if any, understanding of an opponent's underlying needs. If we understand why parties on a negotiation have adopted a specific position, it becomes possible to develop new solutions that may meet those needs. For example, management may be concerned with containing salary costs because it knows that the organisation is financially strained; the union proposal to take additional days of leave in lieu of overtime may ease this concern and allow management to offer some salary increase. A strategy that addresses the concerns of one party is called *cost cutting*. Management costs in agreeing to the union proposal have been lowered.

Finally, when we consider the concerns of both parties and build new solutions based on those concerns we are engaging in a *bridging* strategy. Mary could also have asked both the parties about the reasons underlying their positions. It may be that the principal concerns identified by management are the joint needs to remain competitive in a difficult industry and to return a reasonable profit to shareholders. The union, on the other hand, is concerned about how inflation will affect real salary over the next 12 months. If the two parties build a new solution that addresses both management and union concerns, they have used a bridging strategy. Perhaps the solution lies in making Koala Company's employees shareholders in the company.

These strategies provide a number of ways for negotiators and mediators to help identify integrative solutions.

Case 9
Olympic
television rights

Factors affecting negotiation outcomes

So far, we have considered the strategies available to negotiators and two broad styles of negotiating: distributive and integrative. We have, however, ignored three important features of the negotiation setting: the context in which

GLOBAL   Encounter

When cultures collide

What happens when negotiators have different cultural backgrounds? Do negotiators employ the same strategies no matter who they are negotiating with? Or do they adapt their negotiation style? And, what role does the source of the conflict play in strategy selection?

When managers from the People's Republic of China (PRC) were compared with Canadian managers, several differences in negotiation style became apparent. PRC managers were more likely to consult superiors or threaten to discontinue negotiations than were Canadian managers; however, they were less likely to delay making a decision. Culture also affected the reasons that managers gave for using particular strategies: PRC managers were more concerned with maintaining self-esteem, and impressing or influencing the other party than were Canadian managers; conversely, Canadian managers emphasised the role of the specific situation in their strategy selection. While who the conflict was with did not affect strategy selection, it did affect perceived outcomes: whereas Canadian managers reported higher satisfaction with outcomes when their negotiating partners were also Canadian, PRC managers reported their lowest level of satisfaction with outcomes when their negotiating partners were also PRC managers. This pattern was reflected in the control that managers felt they had over outcomes: in the case of Canadian managers, perceived control was highest when they negotiated with Canadians; in the case of PRC managers, perceived control was lowest when they negotiated with other PRC managers.

The nature of the conflict also affected strategy selection: when conflicts are related to tasks, individuals are more likely to compromise or seek more information; when they are centred on behaviour, individuals are more likely to threaten to end or actually end negotiations. However, these strategies are affected both by the culture of the individual and the other party in the negotiation. PRC managers are more likely than Canadian managers to consult superiors or be friendly, and less likely to end negotiations when they are task-related. However, there are very few differences in their strategies when conflicts are person-centred. Managers are also more likely to seek information about task-centred conflicts when those conflicts are intracultural.

While this study highlights some differences in negotiating styles, it also identifies similarities. It suggests that negotiators do not adapt their style on the basis of their opponent's cultural background. We will leave it to you to consider whether, in the long run, this is a sound strategy. Or, given the different underlying motivations of different cultural groups, should managers be more sensitive to the negotiating styles of their opponents?

Source: Tse, D. K., Francis, J., & Walls, J. (1994). Cultural differences in conducting intra- and inter-cultural negotiations: A Sino-Canadian comparison, *Journal of International Business Studies*, 537–555.

individuals negotiate, the biases that affect their decision-making processes and the way in which they interpret the situation. All of these further affect individual choices of strategy and their outcomes.

Situational factors in negotiation

Of all the situational factors, the most widely researched is *negotiator power*. This power derives directly from the number of alternatives available to negotiators: the greater the number of alternative sources of supply, the greater a negotiator's power. If, for example, we wish to purchase a car and there is only one dealer in town, we have limited scope for negotiation. As the number of dealers increases, so does our power: we are able to walk away from any particular deal and look for a more favourable one. The best known examples of this type of power are captured in the ideas of 'buyers' markets' or 'sellers' markets'. A buyer's market exists when the number of goods, for example houses, for sale exceeds the number of potential purchasers. Under these circumstances, buyers have many alternatives to choose from and can use this to their advantage when negotiating a price. Not surprisingly, increased power is associated with a greater use of contentious tactics and increased outcomes.[13]

A second factor that affects negotiator performance is the *goals* that negotiators hold. You will remember that we have already seen goals to be a strong motivational force: challenging, specific goals stimulate greater performance from individuals. Similarly, when applied to negotiations, researchers have found that negotiators who hold difficult and specific goals (e.g. I want a $10 000 trade-in for my old car) perform better than individuals who enter negotiations with easy or general goals (e.g. I'll try to get the best possible deal that I can for my old car). In fact, there is a steady improvement in performance when the outcomes of negotiators with specific, easy, moderate and difficult goals are compared. However, as was the case for motivation, goals can be too difficult. If both negotiators enter the situation with very high goals there may not be enough resources — even after all of the integrative strategies have been used in an effort to maximise resources — to allow negotiators to meet those goals. When this happens, negotiator performance is poorer. So, research shows us that goals can stimulate the performance of negotiators provided that the goals are attainable.[14]

Negotiator behaviour is also affected by the specific instructions — *motivational orientations* — that they receive. We can dramatically change individual behaviour simply by instructing negotiators to be concerned only about their own outcomes (an individualistic orientation) or to be concerned about maximising joint outcomes (a cooperative orientation). Again, research shows that these different orientations affect both negotiator strategies and their outcomes. When negotiators are encouraged to cooperate, they show a greater concern for their opponent's needs and greater flexibility in the strategies that they use. They are more likely to recognise the potential for trade-offs and spend less time arguing in support of their position.[15] The result of these strategies is that they uncover integrative solutions: those that maximise joint gain. One benefit is that, typically, this means that they also improve their own outcomes. By comparison, negotiators with an individualistic orientation engage in less information exchange and provide less information about how they value the issues under discussion.[16] Not surprisingly, this means that they fail to find the integrative potential in a negotiation setting, and achieve poorer joint outcomes.

Reading 9
Negotiating rationally: The power and impact of the negotiator's frame

Lastly, a new area in negotiation research considers the role of *affect*. In the chapter on stress, we saw that positive and negative affectivity influence an individual's susceptibility to stress. Although researchers have not investigated the impact of this personality variable on negotiator performance, they have considered how good and bad moods affect the negotiation process. Overall, we find that individuals who are in a positive mood are more likely to engage in cooperative bargaining.[17]

Cognitive biases in negotiation

Throughout this discussion on negotiation we have touched on the idea that negotiator outcomes are improved when individuals communicate with each other and engage in a high level of information exchange. Why is this important? Negotiators are very likely to hold two beliefs that will stand in the way of finding integrative solutions: the *fixed-pie error* and the *incompatibility error*.[18] We have already considered the fixed pie error indirectly. This error describes a common belief among negotiators that the issues most important to them are also the issues most important to the other party. For example, if we return to our union–management example, management would be showing the fixed-pie error if it believed, on the basis of its own preferences, that salary increases were more important to the union than vacations. If we believe that we have exactly opposing interests, we will also assume that no trade-offs are possible. And, as we have seen, the ability to make trade-offs is critical to improving the outcomes of both parties. When negotiators operate from this assumption, they are more likely to behave competitively, and less likely to engage in problem solving. The outcome is poorer solutions for all.[19]

The important point for us to remember is that even when problem solving is possible, negotiators behave as though it is not. Many of the situational factors described above reinforce this belief. How can negotiators challenge this belief? Research has shown that the more information we obtain about our opponents' priorities, the more accurately we can represent the situation from their point of view. As we increase the accuracy of our perceptions, we improve the overall outcomes of the negotiation. Interestingly, it is enough that one negotiator engage in information seeking, as the outcomes of both negotiators will improve.[20]

Negotiator frames

The way negotiators think about their outcomes — their *frame* — also affects their behaviour. The concept of frames will be examined in more detail in the decision-making chapter. For the moment, we can say that negotiators may view their outcomes in terms of potential losses, or in terms of potential gains. When negotiators think about what they might lose in the negotiation, their behaviour becomes more contentious; when they think about what they will stand to gain, their behaviour is more cooperative and they are more prepared to make concessions to an opponent. Research has demonstrated that gain-framed negotiators start negotiations with lower goals, and end their negotiations more quickly than loss-framed negotiators.[21] However, whether differences in frames affect negotiator outcomes is less clear, and the relationship between negotiator frames and their outcomes is affected by several other factors.[22]

Moving towards effective negotiations

Negotiations are difficult and complex interactions in which individuals hold several competing goals: to increase the resource pool and to find creative solutions, but also to ensure that they are not disadvantaged in doing so. One key component, information exchange, requires that negotiators are good communicators. The second key component, generating and selecting the best solution, requires that they are good decision makers. To finish this section on negotiation, let's consider some specific strategies that we can employ to improve our negotiating style.[23]

Communication, cooperation and conflict

In this chapter, we have described two approaches to negotiation — distributive and integrative — and suggested that the approaches are tied to very different outcomes. Researchers at the University of Melbourne are examining just how these approaches differ and how negotiation outcomes are affected. They asked 'Can different outcomes be predicted from the tactics used by negotiators?'.

This research looked for links between the tactics that negotiators use, whether they reach agreement and who benefits from the agreement. The researchers considered four types of outcomes, ranging from those that gave high joint benefit (both parties maximised their outcomes) to stalemates. Poor outcomes were achieved when negotiators engaged in *distributive bargaining*: when they focused on protecting their own position and attacking their opponents' arguments and when they considered issues in the negotiation one at a time. In addition, when negotiations ended in stalemate, negotiators increased the demands that they made as the negotiation progressed. In contrast, negotiators who achieved optimum outcomes engaged in *integrative bargaining*: they were more interested in the underlying needs of their opponents, and introduced far more issues and arguments in the early stages of the negotiation.

To further understand the relationship between tactics and outcomes, the researchers looked at the quality of these optimum outcomes, and found that quality was affected by the sequence in which negotiators used contentious and cooperative tactics. Those negotiators with the very best outcomes showed higher levels of cooperation at the start of the negotiation, and increased their contentiousness towards the end of the negotiation. This research suggests that, contrary to popular belief, starting tough does not benefit negotiators. Negotiators achieve their best outcomes by remaining flexible in their positions, focusing on the needs and priorities of their opponents, starting soft and ending tough.

Source: Olekalns, M., Smith, P. L., & Walsh, T. (1995). The process of negotiating: Tactics, phases and outcomes, *Department of Management & Industrial Relations Working Paper No 85*, University of Melbourne.

Separate the people from the problem

We tend to see the world from our perspective and interpret others' behaviour through this perspective. Remember our tendency to attribute others' behaviour to personality factors rather than situational factors. This can produce a cycle of misunderstanding that creates barriers to good negotiating. Fisher and Ury recommend several strategies to avoid this problem:

- Ensure that you are tackling the problem, not attacking the person. For example, Ann should try to deal with the need for an orange rather than accuse Joe of being greedy.
- Try to see the situation from the other person's point of view. Ask yourself, what is this person looking for? What needs might underlie this problem? It is important to involve the other person in the resolution process, because this will increase his or her commitment to the solution.
- Acknowledge emotions and allow people to let off steam, but do not be sidetracked into a debate about them.
- Communicate well: use active listening, and speak about yourself not the other person.

Using these techniques will ensure that you represent the situation as a joint problem that you need to resolve together, rather than as an adversarial problem in which you are enemies. Represent the situation not as one in which you are opponents, but as one in which you are facing a common problem and need to identify a solution that will meet the needs of both of you.

Focus on interests, not positions

We focus on positions when we become concerned with the specific demands that an individual is making. If Joe had tried to argue with Ann about her need for an orange, or if management had presented arguments about the specific claim presented by the union, the focus would have been on the opponent's position. Focusing on positions can result in impasses, especially when we assume that opposing positions hide opposing interests. We can identify the other party's interests by asking 'Why?' about their proposed solutions and 'Why not?' about rejections of our proposed solutions.

Start with reasons not solutions

When Joe and Ann cut the orange in half they started with a solution; as we know, had they started with reasons, they could both have had the whole orange. This problem can be avoided if negotiators are prepared to be flexible about how their goals can be met. Being certain about your goals, but flexible about strategies to attain those goals, increases the chance of finding integrative solutions.

Generate a range of solutions

As you will learn in the chapter on decision making, a common problem for individuals is to present solutions too early in the problem-solving process. In general, decision makers tend to start evaluating solutions as soon as they are suggested, and try to narrow down the range of solutions as quickly as possible. Both of these strategies should be avoided as they increase the likelihood that we will not find the optimum solution.

Finally, where possible, develop objective criteria for assessing solutions and selecting the best solution.

MEDIATION

Negotiations do not always take place only between the two parties directly involved in the disagreement. Sometimes third parties are called in when the negotiations between the main parties have broken down or reached an impasse. At other times, third parties may be part of the negotiation process from the beginning. In some instances, third party involvement is imposed on the disputing parties; in others, the parties themselves voluntarily seek out third party assistance. In any event, the instances of third party negotiations appear to be increasing.

There are different kinds of third party interventions, and third party involvement has been characterised in many different ways. One such typology suggests that there are four basic kinds of interventions: arbitration, conciliation, consultation and mediation.[24] *Arbitration* is where the third party has the power (authority) to impose an agreement. In conventional arbitration, the arbitrator selects an outcome that is typically somewhere between the final positions of the disputing parties. In final-offer arbitration, the arbitrator is mandated to choose one or other of the parties' final offers, and thus has no real control over designing the agreement.[25] *Conciliation* occurs where the third party is someone trusted by both sides and serves primarily as a communication link between the disagreeing parties. A conciliator has formal authority to influence the outcome. *Consultation* is where a third party trained in conflict and conflict-resolution skills attempts to facilitate problem solving by focusing more on the relations between the parties than on the substantive issues. The chief role of the consultant is to improve the negotiating climate so that substantive negotiations can take place at some time in the future. Finally, **mediation** involves a neutral third party who acts as a facilitator through the application of reasoning, suggestion and persuasion. Mediators facilitate resolution by affecting how the disputing parties interact. Mediators have no binding authority: the parties are free to ignore mediation efforts and recommendations. This section concentrates on the process of mediating and factors affecting the success of mediation.

Stages and strategies in mediating

The mediation process can be divided into three broad stages, each encompassing a different set of tactics. Research shows that mediators move sequentially through these phases; however, the strategies that they select in each phase are linked to the outcomes that they achieve. This section reviews the three basic stages in mediation: setting the stage, problem solving and achieving a workable agreement.[26]

Stage I: Setting the stage

Mediation frequently occurs when individuals have been unable to resolve a dispute through direct negotiations. This implies that communications between the parties are likely to be poor or non-existent, and that mediators will be operating in a hostile and distrustful environment. It may be that only one party is interested in mediation, or that both parties have been forced to participate in the process. Under these circumstances, there will be little trust in the mediator. The first issue for a mediator, therefore, is to establish rapport with the disputants and to set the ground rules for the mediation process.

In addition to developing rapport, at this stage the mediator is focused on clarifying the ground rules for the mediation, gathering information and also controlling the process.[27] Controlling the process is important while levels of hostility are high. It establishes acceptable norms for communication between disputants, and prevents negative behaviours such as attacking, blaming and criticising; and it may also balance out power differences by ensuring that both parties get equal time to speak and present their concerns. In general, reducing disputant hostility is a very important part of successful mediation because hostile behaviour increases contentiousness and decreases problem solving, and the result is that agreements become less likely.[28]

Where levels of hostility are particularly high and there is little attempt at joint problem solving, a mediator may choose to caucus: to separate the parties and talk to each party separately in an effort to reduce hostility.[29] Caucusing is a very useful tool when there is a large power imbalance between the two parties. In such cases the less powerful party might be reluctant to state his or her needs, and might be too willing to accede to a solution that does not meet those needs. This is an important issue in the mediation of sexual harassment cases and the Management Encounter in this section considers some of the special problems that must be faced in such cases.

Stage II: Problem solving

In this stage, mediators move on to help disputants generate possible solutions for the dispute. Mediator tasks during this phase include dealing with underlying issues by helping disputants to uncover those issues, assisting them in setting priorities among those issues, and generating a range of solutions that will deal with the high-priority concerns of both parties.[30]

Stage III: Achieving a workable solution

The final stage is aimed at assisting parties to work towards and accept a specific solution. Mediators have a range of strategies to encourage settlement, varying in how direct and forceful they are. They may simply urge agreement, pointing out that all other options are worse; or they may reduce resistance to conceding by helping one or both parties save face; or they may suggest strategies for implementing a specific solution. At the more extreme end, they may threaten sanctions if disputants fail to agree on a solution.[31]

Improving mediator effectiveness

Mediator effectiveness can be judged on two broad dimensions: substantive, or whether a solution is reached, and procedural, or whether individuals are satisfied with how the solution was reached. *Substantive concerns* deal with the effectiveness and efficiency of the procedure. The extent to which all relevant information is uncovered, whether the source of the dispute is determined, whether resolution is achieved, how stable the resolution is likely to be and how the parties are affected all contribute to the overall effectiveness of the solution. The speed with which this is accomplished, the cost, and how disruptive the process is to the daily lives of the disputants determine how efficient the procedure is. *Procedural concerns* deal with perceived fairness and overall satisfaction with the process. In assessing fairness, individuals consider how neutral the mediator is, the degree of control that disputants have over the process, and the extent to which outcomes are equitable (when compared with outcomes in similar disputes). Participant satisfaction is determined by whether privacy is maintained during the proceedings, the degree to which participants are involved in the process, how committed disputants are to the solution, and whether they benefit from the outcome.[32]

Strategies and substantive outcomes

The most frequently examined of the substantive issues is whether settlement has been reached. Can we identify strategies that are used more frequently in resolved mediations than in mediations that have deadlocked? If this is possible, we may better understand how to increase mediator effectiveness in terms of achieving substantive outcomes. Mediations that end in settlement have greater

Mediating sexual harassment

Power, gender and organisational climate all affect not only the experiences of sexual harassment but also the manner in which individuals choose to respond to that harassment and their satisfaction with how the harassment is resolved. Research shows that power differences and gender affect who is harassed as well as the severity of the harassment. Men are more likely to be harassed by subordinates, who request dates or attempt to establish romantic relationships. Women, on the other hand, are more likely to be harassed by co-workers who make sexist remarks and jokes, attempt seduction or in some way make body contact. Women were more likely than men to seek support from friends and family, a response that was also more likely in an unsupportive organisational climate. Similarly, women and individuals in an unsupportive climate reported less satisfaction with how the harassment was resolved, and satisfaction was also low when there was a large power difference between the harasser and the target.

Obviously, one issue for organisations is how to create a more supportive climate. In this Encounter, we will consider mediation as one tool for the effective management of sexual harassment. According to Harry Gadlin, ombudsperson for a large university, mediation can be an appropriate channel for several reasons, including the large power imbalances between harassers and their targets. According to Gadlin, the concerns of both parties make mediation an ideal tool. However, he also recommends that in cases of sexual harassment, early mediation sessions should be individual rather than joint: this allows both parties to vent strong emotions and bring them to a manageable level when they meet. He describes this as 'shuttle diplomacy'. However, he cautions that each party may try to recruit the mediator's support. For this reason, he also recommends that each party bring a support person to the mediation sessions — to further

redress the power balance and to offset any perceptions of bias. The support person can also be useful in offsetting unrealistic expectations about how the issue will be resolved and in identifying good solutions.

What concerns can mediation address? On the part of the grievant, mediation provides faster resolution than a formal hearing; it is less adversarial and therefore less stressful and it addresses one of the major concerns — that there is no objective evidence. Grievants are often more concerned with ending the harassment, educating the harasser and returning the situation to normal than with punishment. What is more, mediation keeps the process under the grievant's control, guarantees confidentiality and provides an opportunity to re-establish working relationships. Individuals accused of harassment have similar reasons for preferring mediation. They are also concerned about their reputation and fear punishment.

Overall, therefore, mediation provides an excellent tool for dealing with harassment because it addresses the concerns of both parties. This means that there is the possibility of re-establishing trust between the parties — one aim of mediation — and re-establishing their working relationship. One final issue that mediators need to be aware of is that both the victim and the harasser blame the victim — mediators therefore need to be careful that however the harassment is resolved, it is resolved fairly. The danger in everyone agreeing that it is the victim's 'fault' may mean that the victim settles for an unsatisfactory settlement. Here is another role for support people — to ensure that a fair outcome is reached.

Source: Bingham, S. G., & Scherer, L. L. (1993). Factors associated with responses to sexual harassment and satisfaction with outcome, *Sex Roles*, **29**, 239–269; Gadlin, H. (1991). Careful maneuvers: Mediating sexual harassment, *Negotiation Journal*, 139–153; Stamato, L. (1992). Sexual harassment in the workplace: Is mediation an appropriate forum?, *Mediation Quarterly*, **10**, 167–173.

energy invested in the first two stages of the process (establishing rapport and addressing issues), than in the final stage of solution identification. Mediators who resolve disputes are more likely to have established trust in the process[33] and to have managed the process by preventing attacks on one party,[34] assisting in the identification of relevant facts and issues, offering their opinions[35] and structuring the discussions.[36] Mediators who pose problems for the disputants to resolve, challenge disputants to generate new ideas and solutions,[37] identify points of agreement between disputants and assist them in face-saving[38] are more likely to resolve disputes. By contrast, they are highly unlikely to have been actively involved in the process of solution generation:[39] suggestions are effective in resolving disputes only when resistance to mediation is high or when there are no precedents for how such a dispute might be resolved. Also, pressure tactics appear to be effective in settling disputes only when resistance to mediation is high or when there is a precedent for settling this type of dispute.[40] We will see, however, that pressure tactics have negative consequences for satisfaction with the mediation process.

Finally, mediation sessions that resolve a dispute also differ in terms of the way in which strategies are distributed through the phases of mediation. At the start of this section, we described the stages in mediation and the associated strategies. Although research has shown considerable support for this model, a comparison of those disputes that are settled and those that remain unresolved shows differences in how these strategies are used. Although agreement mediators start to identify issues much earlier in the mediation process, they use all the tactics available to them more evenly across the mediation session.[41] In the early and middle stages of the mediation, they emphasise process behaviours such as agenda setting and strategy selection, and spend more time managing communication (by summarising what disputants have said) and establishing rapport (through self-disclosure). Towards the end of the negotiations, they spend more time addressing issues and assisting in the development of proposals, as well as expressing approval of suggestions made by the disputants.[42] So we can see that not only the strategies used by mediators but also their timing is critical in determining whether disputes will be successfully resolved.

Strategies and procedural outcomes

In addition to issues of efficiency and effectiveness, we need to consider how disputants perceive both the process and its outcomes. What factors affect judgements of fairness and individual commitment to the solution? Overall, individuals perceive the process to be fair when mediators invest time in assisting disputants to uncover relevant facts and propose solutions.[43] Disputants express greater satisfaction with the process and more commitment to the solution when mediators manage the process and praise disputants for their solutions;[44] they also perceive that their relationship with the other party has been improved when mediators establish trust and assist in face-saving.[45] Conversely, disputants are less satisfied and committed when mediators assist in the identification of solutions,[46] criticise disputants and exert pressure for agreement.[47]

EFFECTIVE CONFLICT MANAGEMENT

Effective conflict management must address several issues related to justice: *distributive*, or whether the outcomes are perceived as fair; *procedural*, or whether the process itself was fair; and *interactional*, or the quality of the interactions between disputants.[48] Each contributes to the overall satisfaction with outcomes and therefore disputants' commitment to the solution. In Chapter 5 we discussed the concepts of procedural and distributive justice; and some of the implications of injustice were considered in Chapter 5. We can now consider how these concepts of justice contribute to effective conflict management. Together with whether justice criteria are satisfied, effective conflict management systems must consider who will benefit from a particular solution, and how both the outcome and process will impact on the disputants in both the short and long term.

Justice and conflict management

We have already reviewed the factors that contribute to perceptions of both procedural and distributive justice in our discussion of mediation. We have also seen that perceptions of justice contribute to satisfaction with the process and commitment to the outcome. In addition to these criteria, three others may be added: the extent to which the third party is perceived as neutral, the degree to which disputants were able to control the process, and the extent to which the rights of all parties were protected.[49]

Conflict management goals

In addition to meeting criteria of justice, how conflicts are managed will depend on the particular goals that a negotiator or a mediator is attempting to meet. In part, these goals are related to who might benefit from a particular outcome, as well as the time horizon over which such benefits might accrue. In determining goals we may focus on meeting the needs of one *individual* by identifying that person's needs and concerns, by developing skills that will help meet those needs (e.g. assertiveness skills), or by protecting the individual from the demands of the other party. We might also choose to focus on maximising the *joint welfare* of the parties. This approach requires that we identify the needs and concerns of both parties to the dispute and locate a solution that best satisfies all major concerns; the result is what we have described as integrative or win–win solutions. A final consideration might be the *system* or the organisation as a whole. With this goal in mind, conflict resolvers will consider how the conflict and its resolution impact not just on the individuals concerned but on the broader community or organisation. When we attempt to address these issues, we may need to address structural problems that have resulted in the conflict.[50]

How we implement strategies to achieve these goals will also depend on whether we adopt a short- or a long-term focus. When we deal with the immediate situation, we are adopting a short-term focus. The aim is to try to maximise outcomes for the individual, disputants or the system (depending on our goals) by focusing on the process. In doing so, we make it difficult to optimise outcomes and, more importantly, we ignore more systemic factors that may lead to a recurrence of the conflict. While a short-term focus may be necessary to reduce unacceptable levels of conflict intensity, we should combine this with a longer term approach. The benefits of doing so include the ability to identify more generally optimum outcomes and, more importantly, to assess and modify the situation to remove structural factors that lead to conflict.[51] Overall, a short-term focus restricts our thinking to the immediate strategies for managing the conflict while a long-term strategy allows us to consider how we can modify the situation in order to prevent similar conflicts from repeating themselves.

Managing conflicts

This means that any conflict management process needs to consider both substantive and relationship outcomes. *Substantive outcomes* have to do with how the specific issue is settled. To strive to end up with a bigger piece of the pie than the other party is to focus on a substantive outcome. On the other hand, to resolve disputes in a manner designed primarily to maintain good relationships between the parties — irrespective of the substantive result — is to focus on *relationship outcomes*. While the two concerns are not mutually exclusive, the relative importance assigned to them will affect a manager's choice of conflict management strategies. Given the many factors that a manager must balance, and the range of possible conflict management strategies, can we offer a guide for selecting between these strategies? Conflicts vary along three dimensions: the relationship between the parties, the complexity of the issues and the degree to which a manager (or any third party) wants to control the outcome. As issues move from being simple to complex, and as relationships move from being divergent to convergent, so managers should opt for unilateral decision making, arbitration, mediation and collaborative problem solving. However, if the manager requires high control over the outcome, or if the dispute must be resolved immediately, then imposing decisions or arbitrating are more appropriate. When the manager has no solution in mind and if the parties and the organisation would benefit from an improved relationship then either mediation or collaborative problem solving will yield better outcomes.[52]

SUMMARY OF KEY POINTS

Distinguish between negotiation and mediation. Negotiation is a process in which two or more parties attempt to directly resolve a conflict. Mediation describes situations in which negotiations have been unsuccessful and a neutral third party is called on to resolve the conflict.

Describe four negotiating styles. Individuals have four strategies available in negotiations: inaction, or doing nothing; contending, or attempting to get what you want while forcing the other person to give concessions; yielding, or sacrificing your goals in order to end the conflict; and problem solving, in which individuals work together towards an acceptable outcome.

Distinguish between distributive and integrative negotiations. Distributive negotiations adopt a win–lose perspective and are based on the assumption that only one person can obtain his or her goals. They are associated with strategies aimed at obtaining large concessions from the other person. Integrative negotiations adopt a win–win perspective. They are associated with collaborative, problem-solving strategies and aim to find solutions that will meet the needs of all parties.

Identify the benefits of integrative negotiations. Benefits are as follows: integrative negotiations may be the only way to meet everyone's needs, especially if individuals enter negotiations with high expectations; as a result such agreements will be more stable; they improve the relationship between negotiating parties; and they have flow-on benefits for the community of which the parties are members.

List three strategies for integrative negotiating. The three broad strategies that we can use to obtain integrative agreements differ in terms of how well we must understand the other party's needs. Expanding the pie simply requires that we find more resources to divide and so requires no understanding of underlying needs or concerns.

Concession exchange, in which negotiators trade concessions in order to achieve their most important goals, requires a greater level of understanding of underlying needs. Even more understanding is required for the third set of strategies, in which we build new solutions to offset costs for one party in a settlement.

Describe factors affecting negotiation outcomes. Individuals obtain higher outcomes in negotiations when they have greater power or high goals. Outcomes are also influenced by how well we understand our opponents' priorities. Negotiating strategies are affected by whether individuals are concerned with their own needs or the needs of both parties, whether they view the situation in terms of what they stand to gain or lose, and their mood. Negotiators are more cooperative when they are concerned with both parties' needs, when they focus on gains and when they are in a positive mood.

List stages in the mediation process. Mediators must set the stage by encouraging participation, setting ground rules and establishing trust. They assist in problem solving, by helping disputants generate a range of solutions, and they assist in identifying a workable solution that will be accepted by both parties to the dispute.

REVIEW AND DISCUSSION QUESTIONS

1. What are the key differences between integrative and distributive negotiations?
2. What strategies will assist in achieving integrative outcomes? Why are individuals reluctant to use these strategies?
3. Can individuals ignore situational factors in negotiating? How might these factors affect our choice of strategy?
4. How can we overcome the cognitive biases that influence our negotiations?
5. Why do negotiations end in stalemate? How could you prevent this?
6. Describe the stages in the mediation process.
7. Under what circumstances would mediation be an appropriate tool?
8. Design an organisational dispute resolution system. What principles are important in such a system?

9. Managers have two tasks in negotiations: to expand the resource pool and to divide the resource pool. Discuss how they can achieve this.

ENDNOTES

1 Adapted from Follet, M. P. (1924). *Creative Experience.* New York: Longmans, Green.
2 Lax, D., & Sebenius, J. (1986). *The Manager as Negotiator.* New York: Free Press; Thompson, L. (1990). Negotiation behavior and outcomes: Empirical evidence and theoretical issues, *Psychological Bulletin,* **108**, 515–532.
3 Pruitt, D. G. (1983). Strategic choice in negotiation, *American Behavioral Scientist,* **27**, 167–194.
4 Pruitt, D. G. (1981). *Negotiation Behavior.* New York: Academic Press, Ltd.
5 Thomas, K. W. (1994). Conflict and negotiation in organisations. In M. D. Dunnette & L. M. Hough (Eds.) *Handbook of Industrial and Organizational Psychology* (2nd Ed.). Palo Alto, CA: Consulting Psychologists Press.
6 Lewicki, R. J., & Litterer, J. A. (1985). *Negotiation.* Homewood, IL: Irwin.
7 Ibid.
8 Fisher, R. & Ury, W. (1981). *Getting to Yes: Negotiating Agreement Without Giving In.* London: Arrow Press.
9 Pruitt, D. G., & Lewis, S. A. (1975). Development of integrative solutions in bilateral negotiations, *Journal of Personality and Social Psychology,* **31**, 621–630.
10 Fisher, R. & Ury, W. (1981). *Getting to Yes: Negotiating Agreement Without Giving In.* London: Arrow Press.
11 Pruitt, D. G. (1983). Achieving integrative agreements. In M. H. Bazerman & R. J. Lewicki (Eds.) *Negotiating in Organizations.* Beverly Hills: Sage.
12 Carnevale, P. J., & Pruitt, D. G. (1992). Negotiation and mediation, *Annual Review of Psychology,* **43**, 531–582.
13 Northcraft, G. B., & Neale, M. A. (1991). Dyadic negotiation. In B. H. Sheppard, M. H. Bazerman, & R. J. Lewicki (Eds.) *Research on Negotiation in Organizations,* (vol. 2). Greenwich, CT: JAI Press Inc.
14 Neale, M. A., & Bazerman, M. H. (1991). *Cognition and Rationality in Negotiation.* New York: The Free Press.
15 Pruitt, D. G., & Lewis, S. A. (1975). Development of integrative solutions in

bilateral negotiations, *Journal of Personality and Social Psychology*, **31**, 621–630; Weingart, L. R., Bennett, R. J., & Brett, J. M. (1993). The impact of consideration of issues and instruction set in group negotiation process and outcome, *Journal of Applied Psychology*, **78**, 504–517.

16 Carnevale, P. J. D., & Lawler, E. J. (1987). Time pressure and the development of integrative agreements in bilateral negotiations, *Journal of Conflict Resolution*, **30**, 636–659.

17 Baron, R. A. (1990). Environmentally induced positive affect: Its impact on self-efficacy, task performance, negotiation, and conflict. *Journal of Applied Social Psychology*, **20**, 368–384; Kramer, R. M., Newton, E., & Pommerenke, P. L. (1993). Self-enhancement biases and negotiator judgment: Effects of self-esteem and mood, *Organizational Behavior and Human Decision Processes*, **56**, 110–133.

18 Thompson, L., & Hastie, R. (1990). Social perception in negotiation, *Organizational Behavior and Human Decision Processes*, **47**, 98–123.

19 Ibid.

20 Ibid.

21 Neale, M. A., & Bazerman, M. H. (1991). *Cognition and Rationality in Negotiation*. New York: The Free Press.

22 Bottom, W. P., & Studt, A. (1993). Framing effects and the distributive aspect of integrative bargaining, *Organizational Behavior and Human Decision Processes*, **56**, 459–474; Olekalns, M. (1994). Context, issues and frame as determinants of negotiated outcomes, *British Journal of Social Psychology*, **33**, 197–210.

23 Fisher, R. & Ury, W. (1981). *Getting to Yes: Negotiating Agreement Without Giving In*. London: Arrow Press.

24 Fisher, R. J. (1990). *The Social Psychology of Intergroup and International Conflict Resolution*. New York: Springer Verlag.

25 Bazerman, M. H., & Neale, M. A. (1992). *Negotiating Rationally*. New York: The Free Press.

26 Carnevale, P. J., & Pruitt, D. G. (1992). Negotiation and mediation, *Annual Review of Psychology*, **43**, 531–582.

27 Pruitt, D. G., McGillicuddy, N. B., Welton, G. L., & Fry, W. R. (1989). Process of mediation in dispute settlement centers. In K. Kressel, D. G. Pruitt and Associates (Eds.) *Mediation Research: The Process and Effectiveness of Third-Party Intervention*. San Francisco: Jossey-Bass Publishers.

28 Zubek, J. M., Pruitt, D. G., Peirce, R. S., McGillicuddy, N. B., & Syna, H. (1992). Disputant and mediator behaviors affecting short-term success in mediation, *Journal of Conflict Resolution*, **36**, 546–572.

29 Carnevale, P. J., & Pruitt, D. G. (1992). Negotiation and mediation, *Annual Review of Psychology*, **43**, 531–582.

30 Ibid.

31 Carnevale, P. J., & Pruitt, D. G. (1992). Negotiation and mediation, *Annual Review of Psychology*, **43**, 531–582.; Pruitt, D. G., McGillicuddy, N. B., Welton, G. L., & Fry, W. R. (1989). Process of mediation in dispute settlement centers. In K. Kressel, D. G. Pruitt and Associates (Eds.) *Mediation Research: The Process and Effectiveness of Third-Party Intervention*. San Francisco: Jossey-Bass Publishers.

32 Sheppard, B. H., Blumenfeld-Jones, K., & Roth, J. (1989). Informal thirdpartyship: Studies of everyday conflict intervention. In K. Kressel, D. G. Pruitt and Associates (Eds.) *Mediation Research: The Process and Effectiveness of Third-Party Intervention*. San Francisco: Jossey-Bass Publishers.

33 Carnevale, P. J. D., Lim, R. G., & McLaughlin, M. E. (1989). Contingent mediator behavior and its effectiveness. In K. Kressel, D. G. Pruitt and Associates (Eds.) *Mediation Research: The Process and Effectiveness of Third-Party Intervention*. San Francisco: Jossey-Bass Publishers.

34 Donohue, W. A., Allen, M., & Burrell, N. (1988). Mediator communicative competence, *Communication Monographs*, **55**, 104–119.

35 Sheppard, B. H., Blumenfeld-Jones, K., & Roth, J. (1989). Informal thirdpartyship: Studies of everyday conflict intervention. In K. Kressel, D. G. Pruitt and Associates (Eds.) *Mediation Research: The Process and Effectiveness of Third-Party Intervention*. San Francisco: Jossey-Bass.

36 Carnevale, P. J. D., Lim, R. G., & McLaughlin, M. E. (1989). Contingent mediator behavior and its effectiveness. In K. Kressel, D. G. Pruitt and Associates (Eds.) *Mediation Research: The Process and Effectiveness of Third-Party Intervention*. San Francisco: Jossey-Bass Publishers.

37 Zubek, J. M., Pruitt, D. G., Peirce, R. S., McGillicuddy, N. B., & Syna, H. (1992). Disputant and mediator behaviors affecting short-term success in mediation, *Journal of Conflict Resolution*, **36**, 546–572.

38 Donohue, W. A., Allen, M., & Burrel, N. (1988). Mediator communicative competence,

Communication Monographs, **55**, 104–119; Carnevale, P. J. D., Lim, R. G., & McLaughlin, M. E. (1989). Contingent mediator behavior and its effectiveness. In K. Kressel, D. G. Pruitt and Associates (Eds.) *Mediation Research: The Process and Effectiveness of Third-Party Intervention.* San Francisco: Jossey-Bass Publishers.

39 Sheppard, B. H., Blumenfeld-Jones, K., & Roth, J. (1989). Informal thirdpartyship: Studies of everyday conflict intervention. In K. Kressel, D.G. Pruitt and Associates (Eds.) *Mediation Research: The Process and Effectiveness of Third-Party Intervention.* San Francisco: Jossey-Bass.

40 Carnevale, P. J. D., Lim, R. G., & McLaughlin, M. E. (1989). Contingent mediator behavior and its effectiveness. In K. Kressel, D. G. Pruitt and Associates (Eds.) *Mediation Research: The Process and Effectiveness of Third-Party Intervention.* San Francisco: Jossey-Bass Publishers.

41 Donohue, W. A. (1989). Communicative competence in mediators. In K. Kressel, D. G. Pruitt and Associates (Eds.) *Mediation Research: The Process and Effectiveness of Third-Party Intervention.* San Francisco: Jossey-Bass.

42 Jones, T. S. (1988). Phase structures in agreement and no-agreement mediation, *Communication Research,* **15**, 470–495.

43 Sheppard, B. H., Blumenfeld-Jones, K., & Roth, J. (1989). Informal thirdpartyship: Studies of everyday conflict intervention. In K. Kressel, D. G. Pruitt and Associates (Eds.) *Mediation Research: The Process and Effectiveness of Third-Party Intervention.* San Francisco: Jossey-Bass.

44 Zubek, J. M., Pruitt, D. G., Peirce, R. S., McGillicuddy, N. B., & Syna, H. (1992). Disputant and mediator behaviors affecting short-term success in mediation, *Journal of Conflict Resolution,* **36**, 546–572.

45 Carnevale, P. J. D., Lim, R. G., & McLaughlin, M. E. (1989). Contingent mediator behavior and its effectiveness. In K. Kressel, D. G. Pruitt and Associates (Eds.) *Mediation Research: The Process and Effectiveness of Third-Party Intervention.* San Francisco: Jossey-Bass Publishers.

46 Sheppard, B. H., Blumenfeld-Jones, K., & Roth, J. (1989). Informal thirdpartyship: Studies of everyday conflict intervention. In K. Kressel, D. G. Pruitt and Associates (Eds.) *Mediation Research: The Process and Effectiveness of Third-Party Intervention.* San Francisco: Jossey-Bass.

47 Zubek, J. M., Pruitt, D. G., Peirce, R. S., McGillicuddy, N. B., & Syna, H. (1992). Disputant and mediator behaviors affecting short-term success in mediation, *Journal of Conflict Resolution,* **36**, 546–572.

48 Cohen, R. L. (1991). Justice and negotation. In B. H. Sheppard, M. H. Bazerman, & R. J. Lewicki (Eds.) *Research on Negotiation in Organizations,* (vol. 2). Greenwich, CT: JAI Press Inc.

49 Thomas, K. W. (1994). Conflict and negotiation in organisations. In M. D. Dunnette & L. M. Hough (Eds.) *Handbook of Industrial and Organizational Psychology* (2nd Ed.). Palo Alto, CA: Consulting Psychologists Press.

50 Ibid.

51 Ibid.

52 Kolb, D. M., & Glidden, P. A. (1986). Getting to know your conflict options: Using conflict as a creative force. *Personnel Administrator,* **31**, 77–90.

READING 9 NEGOTIATING RATIONALLY: THE POWER AND IMPACT OF THE NEGOTIATOR'S FRAME

M. H. Bazerman and M. A. Neale

Source: Academy of Management (no. 3), August 1992, pp. 42–45. This article is based on the book by M. H. Bazerman, and M. A. Neale, Negotiating Rationally (New York: Free Press, 1992).

Everyone negotiates. In its various forms, negotiation is a common mechanism for resolving differences and allocating resources. While many people perceive negotiation to be a specific interaction between a buyer and a seller, this process occurs with a wide variety of exchange partners, such as superiors, colleagues, spouses, children, neighbors, strangers, or even corporate entities and nations. Negotiation is a decision-making process among interdependent parties who do not share identical preferences. It is through negotiation that the parties decide what each will give and take in their relationship.

The aspect of negotiation that is most directly controllable by the negotiator is how he or she makes decisions. The parties, the issues, and the negotiation environment are often predetermined. Rather than trying to change the environment surrounding the negotiation or the parties or issues in the dispute, we believe that the greatest opportunity to improve negotiator performance lies in the negotiator's ability to make effective use of the information available about the issues in dispute as well as the likely behavior of an opponent to reach more rational agreements and make more rational decisions within the context of negotiation.

To this end, we offer advice on how a negotiator should make decisions. However, to follow this advice for analyzing negotiations rationally, a negotiator must understand the psychological forces that limit a negotiator's effectiveness. In addition, rational decisions require that we have an optimal way of evaluating the behavior of the opponent. This requires a psychological perspective for anticipating the likely decisions and subsequent behavior of the other party. Information such as this can not only create a framework that predicts how a negotiator structures problems, processes information, frames the situation, and evaluates alternatives but also identifies the limitation of his or her ability to follow rational advice.

Rationality refers to making the decision that maximizes the negotiator's interests. Since negotiation is a decision-making process that involves other people that do not have the same desires or preferences, the goal of a negotiation is not simply reaching an agreement. The goal of negotiations is to reach a *good* agreement. In some cases, no agreement is better than reaching an agreement that is not in the negotiator's best interest. When negotiated agreements are based on biased decisions, the chances of getting the best possible outcome are significantly reduced and the probabilities of reaching an agreement when an impasse would have left the negotiator relatively better off are significantly enhanced.

A central theme of our work is that our natural decision and negotiation processes contain biases that prevent us from acting rationally and getting as much as we can out of a negotiation. These biases are pervasive, destroying the opportunities available in competitive contexts, and preventing us from negotiating rationally. During the last 10 or so years, the work that we and our colleagues have done suggests that negotiators make the following common cognitive mistakes: (1) negotiators tend to be overly affected by the frame, or form of presentation, of information in a negotiation; (2) negotiators tend to nonrationally escalate commitment to a previously selected course of action when it is no longer the most reasonable alternative; (3) negotiators tend to assume that their gain must come at the expense of the other party and thereby miss opportunities for mutually beneficial trade-offs between the parties; (4) negotiator judgments tend to be anchored upon irrelevant information — such as an initial offer; (5) negotiators tend to rely on readily available information; (6) negotiators tend to fail to consider information that is available by focusing on the opponent's perspective; and (7) negotiators tend to be overconfident concerning the likelihood of attaining outcomes that favor the individual(s) involved.

Describing the impact of each of these biases on negotiator behavior is obviously beyond the scope of this article. What we will attempt to do, however, is to focus on one particular and important cognitive bias, *framing*, and consider the impact of this bias on the process and outcome of negotiation. The manner in which negotiators frame the options available in a dispute can have a significant impact on their willingness to reach an agreement as well as the value of that agreement. In this article, we will identify factors that influence the choice of frame in a negotiation.

The framing of negotiations

Consider the following situation adapted from Russo and Shoemaker.[1]

You are in a store about to buy a new watch which costs $70. As you wait for the sales clerk, a friend of yours comes by and remarks that she has seen an identical watch on sale in another store two blocks away for $40. You know that the service and reliability of the other store are just as good as this one. Will you travel two blocks to save $30?

Now consider this similar situation:

You are in a store about to buy a new video camera that costs $800. As you wait for the sales clerk, a friend of yours comes by and remarks that she has seen an identical camera on sale in another store two blocks away for $770. You know that the service and reliability of the other store are just as good as this one. Will you travel two blocks to save the $30?

In the first scenario, Russo and Shoemaker report that about 90 percent of the managers presented with this problem reported that they would travel the two blocks. However, in the second scenario, only about 50 percent of the managers would make the trip. What is the difference between the two situations that makes the $30 so attractive in the first scenario and considerably less attractive in the second scenario? One difference is that a $30 discount on a $70 watch represents a very good deal; the $30 discount on an $800 video camera is not such a good deal. In evaluating our willingness to walk two blocks, we frame the options in terms of the percentage discount. However, the correct comparison is not whether a percentage discount is sufficiently motivating, but whether the savings obtained is greater than the expected value of the additional time we would have to invest to realize those savings. So, if a $30 savings were sufficient to justify walking two blocks for the watch, an opportunity to save $30 on the video camera should also be worth an equivalent investment of time.

Richard Thaler illustrated the influence of frames when he presented the following two versions of another problem to participants of an executive development program:[2]

You are lying on the beach on a hot day. All you have to drink is ice water. For the last hour you have been thinking about how much you would enjoy a nice cold bottle of your favorite brand of beer. A companion gets up to make a phone call and offers to bring back a beer from the only nearby place where beer is sold: a fancy resort hotel. She says that the beer might be expensive and asks how much you are willing to pay for the beer. She will buy the beer if it costs as much as or less than the price you state. But if it costs more than the price you state, she will not buy it. You trust your friend and there is no possibility of bargaining with the bartender. What price do you tell your friend you are willing to pay?

Now consider this version of the same story:

You are lying on the beach on a hot day. All you have to drink is ice water. For the last hour you have been thinking about how much you would enjoy a nice cold bottle of your favorite brand of beer. A companion gets up to make a phone call and offers to bring back a beer from the only nearby place where beer is sold: a small, run-down grocery store. She says that the beer might be expensive and asks how much you are willing to pay for the beer. She will buy the beer if it costs as much as or less than the price you state. But if it costs more than the price you state, she will not buy it. You trust your friend and there is no possibility of bargaining with the store owner. What price do you tell your friend you are willing to pay?

In both versions of the story, the results are the same: you get the same beer and there is no negotiating with the seller. Also you will not be enjoying the resort's amenities since you will be drinking the beer on the beach. Recent responses of executives at Kellogg executive training program indicated that they were willing to pay significantly more if the beer were purchased at a 'fancy resort hotel' ($7.83) than if the beer were purchased at the 'small, run-down grocery store' ($4.10). The difference in price the executives were willing to pay for the same beer was based upon the frame they imposed on this transaction. Paying over $5 for a beer is an expected annoyance at a fancy resort hotel; however, paying over $5 for a beer at a run-down grocery store is an obvious 'rip-off!' So, even though the same beer is purchased and we enjoy none of the benefits of the fancy resort hotel, we are willing to pay almost a dollar more because of the way in which we frame the purchase. The converse of this situation is probably familiar to many of us. Have you ever purchased an item because 'it was too good of a deal to pass up', even though you had no use for it? We seem to assign a greater value to the quality of the transaction over and above the issue of what we get for what we pay.

Both of these examples emphasize the importance of the particular frames we place on problems we have to solve or decisions we have to make. Managers are constantly being exposed to many different frames, some naturally occurring and others that are purposefully proposed. An important task of managers is to identify the appropriate frame by which employees and the organization, in general, should evaluate its performance and direct its effort.

The framing of risky negotiations

The way in which information is framed (in terms of either potential gains or potential losses) to the negotiator can have a significant impact on his or her preference for risk, particularly when uncertainty about future events or outcomes is involved. For example, when offered the choice between gains of equal expected value — one for certain and the other a lottery, we strongly prefer to take the *certain* gain. However, when we are offered the choice between potential losses of equal expected value, we clearly and consistently eschew the loss for certain and prefer the risk inherent in the lottery.

There is substantial evidence to suggest that we are not indifferent toward risky situations and we should not necessarily trust our intuitions about risk. Negotiators routinely deviate from rationality because they do not typically appreciate the transient nature of their preference for risk; nor do they take into consideration the ability of a particular decision frame to influence that preference. Influencing our attitudes toward risk through the positive or negative frames associated with the problem is the result of evaluating an alternative from a particular referent point or base line. A referent point is the basis by which we evaluate whether what we are considering is viewed as a gain or a loss. The referent point that we choose determines the frame we impose on our options and, subsequently, our willingness to accept or reject those options.

Consider the high-performing employee who is expecting a significant increase in salary this year. He frames his expectations on the past behavior of the company. As such, he is expecting a raise of approximately $5000. Because of the recession, he receives a $3500 salary increase. He immediately confronts his manager, complaining that he has been unfairly treated. He is extremely disappointed in what his surprised manager saw as an exceptional raise because the employee's referent point is $1500 higher. Had he known that the average salary increase was only $2000 (and used that as a more realistic referent point), he would have perceived the same raise quite differently and it may have had the motivating force that his manager had hoped to create.

The selection of which relevant frame influences our behavior is a function of our selection of a base line by which we evaluate potential outcomes. The choice of one referent point over another may be the result of a visible anchor, the status quo, or our expectations. Probably one of the most common referent points is what we perceive to be in our current inventory (our status quo) — what is ours already. We then evaluate offers or options in terms of whether they make us better off (a gain) or worse off (a loss) from (what we perceive to be) our current resource state.

Interestingly, what we include in our current resource state is surprisingly easy to modify. Consider the executive vice president of a large automobile manufacturing concern that has been hit by a number of economic difficulties because of the recession in the US. It appears as if she will have to close down three plants and the employee rolls will be trimmed by 6000 individuals. In exploring ways to avoid this alternative, she has identified two plans that might ameliorate the situation. If she selects the first plan, she will be able to save 2000 jobs and one of the three plants. If she implements the second plan, there is a one-third probability that she can save all three plants and all 6000 jobs, but there is a two-thirds probability that this plan will end up saving none of the plants and none of the jobs. If you were this vice president, which plan would you select (Plan 1 or Plan 2)?

Now consider the same options (Plan 1 or Plan 2) framed as losses: If the vice president implements Plan 1, two of the three plants will be shut down and 4000 jobs will be lost. If she implements Plan 2, then there is a two-thirds probability of losing all three plants and all 6000 jobs, but there is a one-third probability of losing no plants and no jobs. If you were presented with these two plans, which would be more attractive, Plan 1 or Plan 2?

It is obvious that, from a purely economic perspective, there is no difference between the two choices. Yet managers offered the plans framed in terms of gains select the first plan about 76 percent of the time. However, managers offered the choice between the plans framed in terms of losses only select the first plan about 22 percent of the time. When confronted with potential losses, the lottery represented by Plan 2 becomes relatively much more attractive.

An important point for managers to consider is that the way in which the problem is framed, or presented, can dramatically alter the perceived value or acceptability of alternative courses of action. In negotiation, for example, the more risk-averse course of action is to accept an offered settlement; the more risk-seeking course of action is to hold out for future, potential concessions. In translating the influence of the framing bias to negotiation, we must realize that the selection of a particular referent point or base line determines whether a negotiator will frame his or her decision as positive or negative.

Specifically, consider any recurring contract negotiation. As the representative of Company 'A', the offer from Company 'B' can be viewed in two ways, depending on the referent point I use. If my referent point were the current contract, Company 'B's' offer can be evaluated in terms of the 'gains' Company 'A' can expect relative to the previous contract. However, if the referent point for Company 'A' is an initial offer on the issues under current consideration, then Company 'A' is more likely to evaluate Company 'B's' offer as losses to be incurred if the contract as proposed is accepted. Viewing options as losses or as gains will have considerable impact on the negotiator's willingness to accept side 'B's' position — even though the same options may be offered in both cases.

Likewise, the referent points available to an individual negotiating his salary for a new position in the company include: (1) his current salary; (2) the company's initial offer; (3) the least he is willing to accept; (4) his estimate of the most the company is willing to pay; or (5) his initial salary request. As his referent moves from 1 to 6, he progresses from a positive to a negative

frame in the negotiation. What is a modest *gain* compared to his current wage is perceived as a loss when compared to what he would like to receive. Along the same lines, employees currently making $15/hour and demanding an increase of $4/hour can view a proposed increase of $2/hour as a $2/hour gain in comparison to last year's wage (Referent 1) or as a $2/hour loss in comparison to their stated or initial proposal of $19/hour (Referent 5). Consequently, the location of the referent point is critical to whether the decision is positively or negatively framed and affects the resulting risk preference of the decision maker.

In a study of the impact of framing on collective bargaining outcomes, we used a five-issue negotiation with participants playing the roles of management or labor negotiators.[3] Each negotiator's frame was manipulated by adjusting his or her referent point. Half of the negotiators were told that any concessions they made from their initial offers represented losses to their constituencies (i.e., a negative frame). The other half were told that any agreements they were able to reach which were better than the current contract were gains to their constituencies (i.e., the positive frame). In analyzing the results of their negotiations, we found that negatively framed negotiators were less concessionary and reached fewer agreements than positively framed negotiators. In addition, negotiators who had positive frames perceived the negotiated outcomes as more fair than those who had negative frames.

In another study, we posed the following problem to negotiators:

You are a wholesaler of refrigerators. Corporate policy does not allow any flexibility in pricing. However, flexibility does exist in terms of expenses that you can incur (shipping, financing terms, etc.), which have a direct effect on the profitability of the transaction. These expenses can all be viewed in dollar-value terms. You are negotiating an $8000 sale. The buyer wants you to pay $2000 in expenses. You want to pay less expenses. When you negotiate the exchange, do you try to minimize your expenses (reduce them from $2000) or maximize net profit, i.e., price less expenses (increase the net profit from $6000)?

From an objective standpoint, the choice you make to reduce expenses or maximize profit should be irrelevant. Because the choice objectively is between two identical options, selecting one or the other should have no impact on the outcome of the negotiation. What we did find, in contrast, is that the frame that buyers and sellers take into the negotiation can systematically affect their behavior.[4]

In one study, negotiators were led to view transactions in terms of either (1) net profit or (2) total expenses deducted from gross profits. These two situations were objectively identical. Managers can think about maximizing their profits (i.e., gains) or minimizing their expenses (i.e., losses). These choices are linked; if one starts from the same set of revenues, then one way to maximize profits is to minimize expenses, and if one is successful at minimizing expenses, the outcome is that profit may be maximized. That is, there is an obvious relationship between profits and expenses. So, objectively, there is no reason to believe that an individual should behave differently if given the instructions to minimize expenses or to maximize profits. However, those negotiators told to maximize profit (i.e., a positive frame) were more concessionary. In addition, positively framed negotiators completed significantly more transactions than their negatively framed (those told to minimize expenses) counterparts. Because they completed more transactions, their overall profitability in the market was high, although negatively framed negotiators completed transactions of greater mean profit.[5]

The endowment effect

The ease with which we can alter our referent points was illustrated in a series of studies conducted by Daniel Kahneman, Jack Knetsch, and Richard Thaler.[6] In any exchange between a buyer and a seller, the buyer must be willing to pay at least the minimum amount the seller is willing to accept for a trade to take place. In determining the worth of an object, its value to the seller may, on occasion, be determined by some objective third party such as an economic market. However, in a large number of transactions, the seller places a value on the item — a value that may include not only the market value of the item but also a component for an emotional attachment to or unique appreciation of the item. What impact might such an attachment have on the framing of the transaction?

Let's imagine that you have just received a coffee mug.[7] (In the actual demonstration, coffee mugs were placed before one third of the participants, the 'sellers,' in the study.) After receiving the mug, you are told that in fact you 'own the object (coffee mug) in your possession. You have the option of selling it if a price, to be determined later, is acceptable to you'. Next, you are given a list (see Exhibit 9.3) of possible selling prices, ranging from $.50 to $9.50, and are told that for each of the possible prices, you should indicate whether you would (a) sell the mug and receive that amount in return, or (b) keep the object and take it home with you. What is your selling price for the mug?

Another third of the group (the 'buyers') were told that they would be receiving a sum of money and they could choose to keep the money or use it to buy a mug. They were also asked to indicate their preferences between a mug and sums of money ranging from $.50 to $9.50. Finally, the last third of the participants (the 'choosers') were given a questionnaire indicating that they would later be given an option of receiving either a mug or a sum of money to be determined later. They indicated their preferences between the mug and sums of money between $.50 to $9.50. All of the participants were told that their answers would not influence either the pre-determined price of the mug or the amount of money to be received in lieu of the mug.

The sellers reported a median value of $7.12 for the mug; the buyers valued the mug at $2.88; and the choosers valued the mug at $3.12. It is interesting that in this exercise, being a buyer or a chooser resulted in very similar evaluations of the worth of the mug. However, owning the mug (the sellers) created a much greater sense of the mug's worth. In this case, it was approximately 40 percent greater than the market (or retail) value of the mug.

The explanation for this disparity lies in the fact that different roles (buyer, seller, or chooser) created different referent points. In fact, what seems to happen in such situations is that owning something changes the nature of the owner's relationship to the commodity. Giving up that item is now perceived as a loss and, in valuing the item, the owner may include a dollar value to offset his or her perceived loss. If we consider this discrepancy in the value of an item common, then the simple act of 'owning' an item, however

Exhibit 9.3 The coffee mug questionnaire
For each price listed below, indicate whether you would be willing to sell the coffee mug for that price or keep the mug.

If the price is $0.50, I will sell _____ ;   I will keep the mug _____ .
If the price is $1.00, I will sell _____ ;   I will keep the mug _____ .
If the price is $1.50, I will sell _____ ;   I will keep the mug _____ .
If the price is $2.00, I will sell _____ ;   I will keep the mug _____ .
If the price is $2.50, I will sell _____ ;   I will keep the mug _____ .
If the price is $3.00, I will sell _____ ;   I will keep the mug _____ .
If the price is $3.50, I will sell _____ ;   I will keep the mug _____ .
If the price is $4.00, I will sell _____ ;   I will keep the mug _____ .
If the price is $4.50, I will sell _____ ;   I will keep the mug _____ .
If the price is $5.00, I will sell _____ ;   I will keep the mug _____ .
If the price is $5.50, I will sell _____ ;   I will keep the mug _____ .
If the price is $6.00, I will sell _____ ;   I will keep the mug _____ .
If the price is $6.50, I will sell _____ ;   I will keep the mug _____ .
If the price is $7.00, I will sell _____ ;   I will keep the mug _____ .
If the price is $7.50, I will sell _____ ;   I will keep the mug _____ .
If the price is $8.00, I will sell _____ ;   I will keep the mug _____ .
If the price is $8.50, I will sell _____ ;   I will keep the mug _____ .
If the price is $9.00, I will sell _____ ;   I will keep the mug _____
If the price is $9.50, I will sell _____ ;   I will keep the mug _____ .

briefly, can increase one's personal attachment to an item — and, typically, its perceived value. After such an attachment is formed, the cost of breaking that attachment is greater and is reflected in the higher price the sellers demand to part with their mugs as compared to the value the buyers or the choosers place on the exact same commodity. In addition, we would expect that the endowment effect intensifies to the extent that the value of the commodity of interest is ambiguous or subjective, or the commodity itself is unique or not readily substitutable in the marketplace.

Framing, negotiator bias, and strategic behavior
In the previous discussion, we described the negotiator behaviors that may arise from positive and negative frames within the context of the interaction. In this section, we identify some of the techniques for strategically manipulating framing to direct negotiator performance.

As our research suggests, simply posing problems as choices among potential gains rather than choices among potential losses can significantly influence the negotiator's preferences for specific outcomes.

Framing can also have important implications for how managers choose to intervene in disputes among their peers or subordinates. Managers, of course, have a wide range of options to implement when deciding to intervene in disputes in which they are not active principals. If the manager's goal is to get the parties to reach an agreement rather than having the manager decide what the solution to the dispute will be, he or she may wish to facilitate both parties' viewing the negotiation from a positive frame. This is tricky, however, since the same referent that will lead to a positive frame for one negotiator is likely to lead to a negative frame for the other negotiator if presented simultaneously to the parties. Making use of the effects of framing may be most appropriate when a manager can meet with each side separately. He or she may present different perspectives to each party to create a positive frame (and the subsequent risk-averse behavior associated with such a frame) for parties on both sides of the dispute. Again, if the manager is to effect the frame of the problem in such a way to encourage agreement, he or she may also emphasize the possible losses inherent in continuing the dispute. Combining these two strategies may facilitate both sides' preference for the certainty of a settlement.

Being in the role of buyer or seller can be a naturally occurring frame that can influence negotiator behavior in systematic ways. Consider the curious, consistent, and robust finding in a number of studies that buyers tend to outperform sellers in market settings in which the balance of power is equal.[8] Given the artificial context of the laboratory settings and the symmetry of the design of these field and laboratory markets, there is no logical reason why buyers should do better than sellers. One explanation for this observed difference may be that when the commodity is anonymous (or completely substitutable in a market sense), sellers may think about the transaction in terms of the dollars exchanged. That is, sellers may conceptualize the process of selling as gaining resources (e.g., how many dollars do I gain by selling the commodity); whereas buyers may view the transaction in terms of loss of dollars (e.g., how many dollars do I have to give up). If the dollars are the primary focus of the participants' attention, then buyers would tend to be risk seeking and sellers risk averse in the exchange.

When a risk-averse party (i.e., the seller in this example) negotiates with a risk-averse party (i.e., the buyer), the buyer is more willing to risk the potential agreement by demanding more or being less concessionary. To reach agreement, the seller must make additional concessions to induce the buyer, because of his or her risk-seeking propensity, to accept the agreement. Thus, in situations where the relative achievements of buyers and sellers can be directly compared, buyers would benefit from their negative frame (and subsequent risk-averse behavior). The critical issue is that these naturally occurring frames, such as the role demands of being a 'buyer' or 'seller', can easily influence the way in which the disputed issues are framed — even without the conscious intervention of one or more of the parties.

It is easy to see that the frames of negotiators can result in the difference between impasse and reaching an important agreement. Both sides in negotiations typically talk in terms of a certain wage, price, or outcome that they must get — setting a high referent point against which gains and losses are measured. If this occurs, any compromise below (or above) that point represents a loss. This perceived loss may lead negotiators to adopt a negative frame to all proposals, exhibit risk-seeking behaviors, and be less likely to reach settlement. Thus, negotiators, similar to the early example involving the beach and the beer, may end up with no beer (or no agreement) because of the frame (the amount of money I will pay for a beer from a run-down grocery store) that is placed on the choices rather than an objective assessment of what the beer is worth to the individual.

In addition, framing has important implications for the tactics that negotiators use. The framing effect suggests that, to induce concessionary behavior from an opponent, a negotiator should always create anchors or emphasize referents that lead the opposition to a positive frame and couch the negotiation in terms of what the other side has to gain.

In addition, the negotiator should make the inherent risk salient to the opposition while the opponent is in a risky situation. If the sure gain that is being proposed is rejected, there is no certainty about the quality of the next offer. Simultaneously, the negotiator should also not be persuaded by similar arguments from opponents. Maintaining a risk-neutral or risk-seeking perspective in evaluating an opponent's proposals may, in the worst case, reduce the probability of reaching an agreement; however, if agreements are reached, the outcomes are more likely to be of greater value to the negotiator.

An important component in creating good negotiated agreements is to avoid the pitfalls of being framed while, simultaneously, understanding the impact of positively and negatively framing your negotiating opponent. However, framing is just one of a series of cognitive biases that can have a significant negative impact on the performance of negotiators. The purpose of this article was to describe the impact of one of these cognitive biases on negotiator behavior by considering the available research on the topic and to explore ways to reduce the problems associated with framing. By increasing our understanding of the subtle ways in which these cognitive biases can reduce the effectiveness of our negotiations, managers can begin to improve not only the quality of agreements for themselves but also fashion agreements that more efficiently allocate the available resources — leaving both parties and the communities of which they are a part better off.

References

1 Adapted from J. E. Russo and P. J. Shoemaker, *Decision Traps* (New York: Doubleday, 1989).

2 R. Thaler, 'Using Mental Accounting in a Theory of Purchasing Behavior', *Marketing Science* 4 (1985), pp. 12–13.

3 M. A. Neale and M. H. Bazerman, 'The Effects of Framing and Negotiator Overconfidence', *Academy of Management Journal* 28 (1985), pp. 34–49.

4 M. H. Bazerman, T. Magliozzi, and M. A. Neale, 'The Acquisition of an Integrative Response in a Competitive Market Simulation', *Organizational Behavior and Human Performance* 34 (1985), pp. 294–313.

5 See, for example, Bazerman, Magliozzi, and Neale (1985), op. cit.; Neale and Bazerman (1985), op. cit; or M. A. Neale and G. B. Northcraft, 'Experts, Amateurs and Refrigerators: Comparing Expert and Amateur Decision Making on a Novel Task,' *Organizational Behavior and Human Decision Processes* 38 (1986), pp. 305–317; M. A. Neale, V. L. Huber, and G. B. Northcraft, 'The Framing of Negotiations: Context Versus Task Frames', *Organizational Behavior and Human Decision Process* 39 (1987), pp. 228–41.

6 D. Kahneman, J. L. Knetsch, and R. Thaler, 'Experimental Tests of the Endowment Effect and Coarse Theorem,' *Journal of Political Economy*, 1990.

7 The coffee mugs were valued at approximately $5.00

8 Bazerman, et al. (1985), op. cit.; M. A. Neale, V. L. Huber, and G. B. Northcraft (1987), op.cit.

EXERCISE 9 WORLD BANK: AN EXERCISE IN INTERGROUP NEGOTIATION

Source: Adapted from Jones, J. E., & Pfeiffer, J. W. (Eds.) (1975). *The 1975 Annual Handbook for Group Facilitators.* San Diego, CA: University Associates.

Step 1

The class is divided into two groups. The size of each of the groups should be no more than ten members. Those not in one of the two groups are designated as observers. However, groups should not have less than six members each. The instructor will play the role of the referee/banker for the World Bank.

Step 2

Read the World Bank instruction sheet.

Step 3

Each group or team will have 15 minutes to organise itself and plan strategy before beginning. Before the first round, each team must choose (a) two negotiators, (b) a representative, (c) a team recorder, (d) a treasurer.

Step 4

The referee/banker will signal the beginning of round one and each following round and also end the exercise in about one hour.

Step 5

Discussion. In small groups or with the entire class, answer the following questions:

1. What occurred during the exercise?
2. Was there conflict? What type?
3. What contributed to the relationships among groups?
4. Evaluate the power, leadership, motivation and communication among groups.
5. How could the relationships have been more effective?

World Bank general instruction sheet

This is an intergroup activity. You and your team are going to engage in a task in which money will be won or lost. *The objective is to win as much as you can.* There are two teams involved in this activity, and both teams receive identical instructions. After reading these instructions, your team has 15 minutes to organise itself and plan its strategy.

Each team represents a country. Each country has financial dealings with the World Bank. Initially, each country contributed $100 million to the World Bank. Countries may have to pay further monies or may receive money from the World Bank in accordance with regulations and procedures described below under sections headed 'Finance' and 'Pay-offs'.

Each team is given 20 cards. These are your *weapons*. Each card has a marked side (X) and an unmarked side. The marked side of the card signifies that the weapon is armed. Conversely, the blank side shows the weapon to be unarmed.

At the beginning, each team will place 10 of its 20 weapons in their armed positions (marked side up) and the remaining 10 in their unarmed positions (marked side down). These weapons will remain in your possession and out of sight of the other team at all times.

There will be *rounds* and *moves*. Each round consists of seven moves by each team. There will be two or more rounds in this simulation. The number of rounds depends on the time available. Pay-offs are determined and recorded after each round.

1. A move consists of turning two, one or none of the team's weapons from armed to unarmed status, or vice versa.
2. Each team has 2 minutes to move. There are 30-second periods between moves. At the end of 2 minutes, the team must have turned two, one or none of its weapons from armed to unarmed status, or from unarmed to armed status. If the team fails to move in the allotted time, no change can be made in weapons status until the next move.
3. The length of the 2½-minute periods between the beginning of one move and the beginning of the next is fixed and unalterable.

Each new round of the experiment begins with all weapons returned to their original positions, 10 armed and 10 unarmed.

Finances

The funds you have contributed to the World Bank are to be allocated in the following manner:
- $60 million will be returned to each team to be used as your team's treasury during the course of the decision-making activities.
- $40 million will be retained for the operation of the World Bank.

Pay-offs

1. *If there is an attack*:
  a. Each team may announce an attack on the other team by notifying the referee/banker during the 30 seconds following *any* 2-minute period used to decide upon the move (including the seventh, or final, decision period in any round). The choice of each team during the decision period just ended counts as a move. An attack may not be made during negotiations.
  b. If there is an attack (by one or both teams), two things happen: (1) the round ends, and (2) the World Bank levies a penalty of $5 million for each team.
  c. The team with the greater number of armed weapons wins $3 million for each armed weapon it has over and above the number of armed weapons of the other team. These funds are paid directly from the treasury of the losing team to the treasury of the winning team. The referee/bankers will manage this transfer of funds.
2. *If there is no attack:*
At the end of each round (seven moves), each team's treasury receives from the World Bank $2 million for each of its weapons that is at that point unarmed, and each team's treasury pays to the World Bank $2 million for each of its weapons remaining armed.

Negotiations

Between moves, each team has the opportunity to communicate with the other team through its negotiators.

Either team may call for negotiations by notifying the referee/bankers during any of the 30-second periods between decisions. A team is free to accept or reject any invitation to negotiate.

Negotiators from both teams are *required* to meet after the third and sixth moves (after the 30-second period following that move, if there is no attack).

Negotiations can last no longer than 3 minutes. When the two negotiators return to their teams, the 2-minute decision period for the next move begins once again.

Negotiators are bound only by: (a) the 3-minute time limit for negotiations, and (b) their required appearance after the third and sixth moves. They are otherwise free to say whatever is necessary to benefit themselves or their teams. The teams similarly are not bound by agreements made by their negotiators, even when those agreements are made in good faith.

Special roles

Each team has 15 minutes to organise itself to plan team strategy. During this period before the first round begins, each team must choose persons to fill the following roles. Each team must have each of the following roles, which can be changed at any time by a decision of the team:

- *negotiators* — activities stated above;
- *representative* — to communicate team decisions to the referee/bankers;
- *recorder* — to record the moves of the team and to keep a running balance of the team's treasury;
- *treasurer* — to execute all financial transactions with the referee/bankers.

CASE 9 OLYMPIC TELEVISION RIGHTS

William Oscar Johnson

They want us to be like three scorpions fighting in a bottle. When it's over, two will be dead and the winner will be exhausted.

Thus spoke Roone Arledge, president of ABC Sports, of the way it was when the three major American television networks joined in bitter battle with the government of the former Soviet Union over the US rights to televise the 1980 Summer Olympic Games. It was a Cold War confrontation with an absolutely classic — if also a somewhat comic — cast of adversaries. On one side stood the network executives, representing all that is richest, sleekest, and most glamorous about the free-enterprise system. They came from stately Manhattan skyscrapers, quick-witted, supersophisticated salesmen given to Gucci shoes and manicured hands. If they were not the cream of US business, the network men were certainly from the tip of the vast capitalist iceberg.

On the other side stood a battery of grim Russian bureaucrats — burly, pallid fellows, some former peasants with hands still hard from years of labour in the fields of Mother Russia. They were canny technocrats and politicians from the cold corridors of the Kremlin: some were in their 70s, and their longevity alone made it clear that

they were among the wiliest of men in this land of purges. It also is worth noting that the network representatives were not entirely without this instinct for survival, being no less vulnerable than Soviet politicians to swift turns of fortune that could send them to the Siberias of American business.

So they joined the conflict well matched — the minions of Red Square, Moscow versus the moguls of Sixth Avenue, New York. It would be nice to report that the result was a hard, clean, clear-cut battle between two ideological juggernauts, that two gleaming machines performed in a way that displayed the best of both systems. This did not happen. The big Olympic TV deal became bogged down in misunderstanding, misjudgement, and mistakes.

In fact, during the critical closing phase of negotiations that concluded 3 weeks ago with an astonished National Broadcasting Company (NBC) being presented with the Olympic rights for $85 million, the only real link between the two adversaries was a garrulous little German named Lothar Bock. He is a small-time 'impresario' (the term he uses to describe himself) who had more experience as a booking agent for Georgian saber dancers and Mongolian tumblers than as the indispensable middleman between a bunch of cold-eyed Soviets and high-rolling TV executives. It is true that one network man described Bock as being 'a bit of a klutz,' but it was Bock — and Bock alone — who plodded between Moscow and Manhattan to forge the final bond that gave the Olympics to NBC. In the bargain, he earned himself a million bucks and made his name a household word from the bar at P. J. Clarke's to the boardroom at the A. C. Nielsen Company.

This bizarre situation officially began in Vienna in October 1974, when the International Olympic Committee awarded the Soviet Union the 1980 Summer Olympics. All three networks were there just to shake hands with their new adversaries. No one was selling, no one was buying. Only one network — ABC — was absolutely certain that it would bid for the Moscow Games. Under the masterful guidance of Arledge, ABC had won the rights to six of the last eight Olympics, and it covered each with increasing excellence. But except for sport, the network had been No. 3 in the ratings for many years. That changed in the 1976–77 TV season when ABC burst to the fore, partially because of its hugely successful telecasting of the Montreal Games.

CBS had televised the Rome Olympics of 1960. That was in TV's dark ages, when rights could be purchased for $550 000.* Since then, CBS had never bid successfully — or even seriously — for an Olympics. The network had been rated no. 1 for so long that it seemed to be living on its own Mount Olympus, showing a godlike disdain for the Games of mere mortals. However, in mid-1974, Robert F. Wussler became CBS's vice-president in charge of sports, and he was very interested in the Moscow Games.

As for NBC, it had televised the 1972 Winter Olympics from Sapporo — an aesthetic disaster and a financial disappointment. Top management was at best neutral towards the Moscow Olympics. Carl Lindemann Jr., NBC's vice-president for sports, made a couple of trips to the Soviet capital in the early going but says, 'I was essentially there to wave the flag. Higher network management was ambivalent. I wanted the Games in the worst way. We had lost the Munich Olympics because of a lousy $1 million.' (ABC paid $13.5 million for the rights.)

During 1974 and 1975 the American network executives — Arledge, Wussler, Lindemann, and an ever-growing cast of presidents, board chairmen, lawyers, diplomats, politicians and public-relations men — launched into a lumbering courtship that was intended to win the hearts and minds of the Soviet Olympic hierarchy. In the end, none of it seems to have made any difference in the selection of NBC. Yet the courtship was fervent, relentless — and sometimes quite public.

For example, in the fall of 1975, ABC's faltering morning show 'A.M. America' woke up the nation to a week of reports on life in the Soviet Union that were so uncritical an embarrassed ABC man said, 'We made Moscow look like Cypress Gardens without the water skiers.' In 1976 CBS aired a prime-time bomb that featured a shivering Mary Tyler Moore standing on a wintry Moscow street corner, hosting a show about the Bolshoi Ballet. When Wussler was asked if this was part of his Olympic campaign, he replied, 'No question about it.'

As the time approached for the Montreal Games, there was a constant shuttling of network people to Moscow to wine and dine with Soviet Olympic officials. East and West became palsy-walsy, even kidding each other about whether it was the KGB (secret police of the Soviet Union) or the CIA (Central Intelligence Agency — USA) that was bugging their conversations. Mostly it was social, but in Montreal the plot at last thickened.

The USSR's Olympic Organising Committee glittered with Kremlin stars. The leader was a hulking, dark-haired Ignati Novikov, 70. He had started his career as a labourer in the Ukraine, rising through the ranks until he became one of the top half dozen men in the USSR, the deputy premier in charge of all power construction projects. Second in command was Sergei Lapin, 64, a stern and polished diplomat who had been ambassador to Austria and China and general director of Tass. Now, as Minister of the State Committee for Television and Radio, Lapin became the Soviet Union's head propagandist. They were invariably accompanied by a battery of deputy chairmen, vice commissars, translators and stenographers. The Americans quickly noted a difference between two factions: Novikov, an old Kremlin hand, came on in the intransigent shoe-rapping manner of Nikita Khrushchev, while Lapin and others on the TV-radio committee seemed more subtle.

On a Saturday afternoon in Montreal, the Soviets gave a lavish party on the good ship *Alexander Pushkin*, which was moored in the St Lawrence. The decks were awash with gallons of Stolichnaya vodka and Armenian cognac. The tables groaned beneath platters of cracked lobster, sliced sturgeon and caviar. The event was purely social, even jolly, but Novikov & Co. were in town to do some serious shoe rapping. They contacted the networks one by one and made

* Dollar amounts are expressed in US dollars

their demand: they wanted $210 million. In cash. The networks laughed. An NBC man said to a Russian, '210 million dollars? We were thinking of 210 million *pennies.*' The Soviet representative stalked off in anger, but one of his comrades confided to a CBS representative that no one in Moscow expected more than $65 million.

In fact, none of the numbers meant much of anything. NBC's Lindermann says, 'We all knew the price would be between $70 and $100 million. I think all three of us would have gone to $100 million.' Perhaps so. But the real numbers would come later. The most troubling aspect of the Russian demands in Montreal had to do with the sensitive issue of just how much selling of the Soviet Union a US network would have to do to buy into the Olympics. The fine line between propaganda and news seemed particularly fuzzy to Novikov. Wussler recalls, 'He made it clear to us he expected some kind of favourable political coverage. We said we could *not* compromise CBS news. We might do something like the Mary Tyler Moore show, ice shows, circuses, sports.'

Arledge says, 'I wanted a clause in the contract that said ABC would have total control over our telecast of the Olympics. Novikov had said to me earlier in the year, "If you show things we don't like, we will pull the plug." I doubt they would do that, but the problem of even seeming like a propaganda arm for the Russians is delicate. For example, if you show the subways of Moscow — and they are superb — some people in the United States are going to see it as a selling job for the Soviets just because it isn't something negative.'

The Soviets did not demand specific schedules of pro-USSR programming, but the prospect of having to do such shows hung heavy over the networks throughout the negotiations.

As the Montreal Games ended, the Soviets said they would like to see some preliminary money bids in Moscow that autumn. They would be secret, of course. NBC was particularly careful about security. It wrote a two-sentence bid on a page of company stationery, sealed it in a film can, and sent it by courier to New York's Kennedy Airport where it was given to an airline pilot, who carried it in the cockpit to Moscow. There he gave it to the driver for NBC News, who took it straight to the committee. An hour later in New York Wussler knew NBC's bid.

The early bids received by the Soviets were: NBC $70 million, CBS $71 million, and ABC a surprising $33.3 million for non-exclusive rights, meaning that it was already thinking of the possibility of pool coverage in which all three networks would participate. Arledge later bid $73 million for exclusive rights.

The autumn of 1976 arrived in New York, but in Moscow it seemed suddenly to be the season of CBS. Almost two years earlier Wussler had got enthusiastic encouragement in his Olympic quest from William Paley, the venerable CBS board chairman. Paley said, 'I'm delighted you boys want to go after this, just delighted!' Thus blessed, Wussler and Arthur Taylor, then president of the network's parent company (CBS Inc.), had begun a series of trips between Manhattan and Moscow where they established warm friendships with important committee members. However, nothing they did was as important as the signing of Bock to be CBS's representative in Moscow.

Wussler had first met Bock, 38, in the spring of 1975 as the result of a phone call from film producer Bud Greenspan. 'Bob, if CBS is really serious about the Olympics, the man to get them for you is sitting here in my office,' Greenspan said. Wussler met Bock and invited him to dinner. Later Taylor met Bock in Moscow, and a consulting contract was arranged for him.

Who is Bock? And how did this energetic little fellow with a real-estate salesman's smile ingratiate himself with a pathologically suspicious crowd of Kremlin politicians? The answers are not clear. Was it because Bock arranged a few years ago to have a memorial plaque placed on the house in Munich where Lenin did some of his most important writing? This impressed the Soviets. Beyond that, Wussler says, 'The Russians trust him at least partly because in 1968 Lothar imported a troupe of Russian singers for a tour of West Germany. They were there at the same time the Russians invaded the former Czechoslovakia to crush the uprising. That week the West Germans wouldn't touch anything Russian with a 10-foot pole. Lothar had to eat about a $75 000 loss. And he did. The Russians never forgot that. They thought Lothar showed class. They trusted him.'

There are stories around Munich that contradict this theory. Some people say they cannot understand why the Soviets even let Bock into the USSR because he allegedly once left a troupe of Georgian saber dancers flat broke in Hamburg until the Soviet government sent money to pay their bills. On another occasion, Bock reportedly marooned sixty Mongolian tumblers in a Bavarian country inn, forcing Moscow to come to the rescue again.

Whatever else he may be, Bock is a loquacious chap who is seemingly quite open about himself. Sitting in his office, which is located in the basement of a green bungalow on an unpaved street in a Munich suburb, he explained last week how his prosperous Soviet connection came to be: 'In 1965 I happened to see the Osipov Balalaika Orchestra, and I thought I would bring it to Germany. I wrote to Moscow and got a letter back in Russian. I hardly even speak the language now, and I certainly didn't understand it then. But instead of having it translated, I took the next flight to Moscow. They translated it for me there. It said: "Dear Mr Bock. We are not interested in your offer." But I was insistent, I continued talking to them. After a while, they saw my point, and I have been dealing with them ever since. We are fair and square with each other.'

Pressed further for his formula for gaining friends in the most remote recesses of the Kremlin, Bock said, 'I always tell them I am a capitalist, making no attempt to hide that I am working for profit. They accept it. They love it.'

That seems all too simple. But whatever the reasons, the Soviets trust Bock. As one Russian told Wussler, 'All US networks are bad, but you are less bad, because you know Lothar Bock.' By October 1976, with Bock running interference, Wussler and Taylor felt they were on the brink of closing a deal. 'We had contracts all drawn up between CBS and the organising committee,' says Wussler. They came triumphantly back to New York to tell the network the Olympics were wrapped up, and arranged a big party for the Russians at the International Olympic Committee (IOC) meetings that were scheduled in Barcelona a day later. Wussler was packing to go to Spain when he got the stunning news: Taylor had been fired by Paley.

If there is one thing the Soviets understand with razor-sharp clarity, it is the sudden purge of high-level personnel. And it makes them nervous. 'They were shocked, I mean *shocked*!' says Wussler, who 6 months before had moved up from head of CBS Sports to the presidency of the network. 'I tried to assure them it had nothing to do with the Olympics, but it was hard for them to believe.' Even the sprightly Bock was numb — for a while.

Then he phoned Wussler and said, 'I think if Mr Paley would come to Moscow himself, we could put the deal together again.' Wussler doubted whether Paley would agree, but when he asked him to go, Paley's only question was 'How soon do we leave?' Early in November, the patriarch of American television and a leading patrician of world capitalism was welcomed with almost adoration by the old Ukrainian labourer, Novikov. They toasted each other warmly during a lavish dinner of chicken Kiev fit for a czar. Then, after two long days of meetings, the two old lions had a tête-à-tête in a small room. They toasted each other. They shook hands. Wussler recalls, 'Mr Paley and I left Moscow with the definite feeling that the deal was firm.'

Oddly, nothing further was heard from Moscow until 8 December. Then the networks received a communication outlining the framework under which the final bidding for the rights would take place. It was an amazing document. Only ABC's men had heard anything like it mentioned in Montreal, and nothing resembling it had come up in CBS's private talks. No one was quite sure what it meant.

Nevertheless, all three networks went to Moscow to find out. NBC was planning to seriously enter the fray now. Robert Howard, president of the network, went to Moscow along with Lindemann and nine other executives and technicians. 'Most of our guys had never been to Moscow,' says Lindemann. 'I had been there only four times. I was surprised when Wussler said he had been there eleven or twelve times.'

When the Americans arrived for the showdown on 15 December, two of the networks — CBS and ABC — were dead certain they had been chosen. Only NBC figured it was an underdog, and it was correct. NBC was about as far under as a dog could be. Novikov could never remember the network's call letters; even during the final signing, he twice referred to it as ABC.

Nevertheless, the Soviets treated the three networks exactly the same — like dirt. One by one, they were informed of the new conditions for bidding — which were outrageous. For one thing, the USSR demanded $50 million for equipment and facilities, to be paid in staggering increments of $20 million in 1977 and $30 million in 1978.

All along one of the Russians' most irrational demands had been for huge sums of cash to be paid two or three years before the Games. Recent

Olympics have taken place in such a politically charged atmosphere that it was not unreasonable to fear that an international incident might cancel the Moscow Games, leaving the Soviets with the loot and TV with no programs. But the network executives were less afraid of losing money because of political disruption — after all, in a tightly controlled country like the USSR, the chances of disruption are slim — than because of an old-fashioned business reason.

Though the networks would have no problem raising the money, an enormous amount of interest would be lost if millions of dollars were tied up over such a long period. Arledge figured that if the $50 million for facilities was paid on the timetable the Soviets demanded, $17.5 million in interest would be forfeited.

Along with the ruinous pay schedule for the equipment, the Soviets had decided to hold an auction to sell the actual rights to the Games. In effect, the $50 million was merely an admission ticket to the final round of bidding. Arledge recalls, 'Their plans involved an unending series of bids that went on as long as two guys were able to stand. There was a new sealed bid every 24 hours. The winner would be announced, and then the losers could up the ante by a minimum of 5%. That's when I made the remark about scorpions in a bottle.'

Wussler was most shocked by the USSR proposal. He had a letter with him from Paley reminding Novikov of their deal, and he asked for an audience with the chairman.

They talked for 45 minutes. Novikov was stony. He told Wussler, 'We are here to get the most money possible. That is our sole purpose. We need it for the Games.' Wussler asked him about the agreement with Paley. Novikov replied, 'It is a pity.'

Wussler was appalled. He hurried to his hotel room. It was 4:00 p.m. Moscow time, 7:00 a.m. in the eastern United States. He phoned Jack Schneider, president of CBS Broadcasting, at home in Greenwich, Connecticut, and told him that CBS's deal had collapsed. He suggested that Schneider contact the other networks and arrange a pool. Within 2 hours, CBS, NBC and ABC had agreed to file a brief with the Justice Department, asking it to waive the antitrust laws so the three networks could negotiate as a unified front.

Now it was 7:00 p.m. in Moscow, and the Soviets had decided to throw one last lavish supper before they put the three scorpions into the bottle. It was held in an elegant banquet room of the Hotel Sovietskaya. The party was a mistake. It was the first time that the three networks had been brought together in the same room in Moscow, and they were seething. At this point, no one but Wussler knew that a pool was in the works. The others were shouting angrily about the crude and insulting tactics of the Soviets. Almost immediately there was talk of walking out en masse. The hosts stood against the wall, aghast at the uproar among the Americans. Lindemann says, 'They had figured there was no limit to the manic competitive zeal of the networks. That was insulting, of course. But what bothered me even more was the fact that this wasn't just another ball game, this wasn't a spat with Bowie Kuhn or Pete Rozelle. This was the United States against the Soviet Union — and we just couldn't let this happen.'

The next day, taking a page from the Soviet book on diplomacy, the Americans walked out. At a meeting attended by Arledge, Wussler and Howard, Novikov was impassive. He told them, 'If any of you leave Soviet soil on this day, you will never, *never* be allowed to return.' The three said they had no choice. After leaving Novikov's office, they promised to leave the USSR and they showed each other their airline tickets as a display of good faith.

Arledge had earlier made an appointment for a private session with Novikov. He decided to keep the date. 'I was bound not to negotiate,' says Arledge, 'but I didn't think Novikov understood. He said he would make a deal with me right there on the spot. He said the Olympics were mine. I told him I couldn't take the Olympics at that point if he gave them to me for five million.'

A few days after the networks left, the Soviets announced that the rights now belonged to a mysterious fourth party, an American trading and manufacturing company called SATRA, which does a lot of business with the USSR. This move was — and still is — seen by most network men as both a threat and a face-saving move by the Soviets. But SATRA apparently took it seriously and has filed a $275 million suit against NBC for interfering with its agreement with the Soviets.

Back in Manhattan, each network pledged to have no contact of any kind with the Soviets while the Justice Department considered the pool waiver request. However, Bock was still loose in Moscow. When the networks departed, he was shaken. Technically he was not a network employee, but he still had his contract with CBS. Soon Bock got word to Wussler that Novikov was sorry, and that the Soviets wanted CBS to please come back. Then Novikov sent a telegram to Paley, saying, in effect, that the USSR–CBS deal was still on. Meanwhile, Bock continued to negotiate.

Was this a breach of the agreement between the networks? Wussler claims Bock was working on his own. 'I told him specifically and in person when we left Moscow that he was not to continue any talks with the Russians on our behalf,' Wussler says.

Arledge got disturbing news from Moscow in late December. 'I heard that Lothar was negotiating for CBS,' he says. 'I kept hearing it. Then in mid-January I got word of the terms of a new contract. And I said, "This has gone too far."'

Arledge contacted Wussler and told him, 'The Russians believe Bock is speaking on your behalf.' Wussler said no, he is not. Arledge said that CBS could verify that by sending the Moscow Olympic Committee a telegram stating that Bock had no authorisation to bargain for CBS. Later, ABC indicated it would be satisfied if CBS sent a letter to Bock telling him he could not act on its behalf or sent a letter to ABC saying the same thing. CBS pondered this move for several days, and then out of the blue it announced it was not only dropping out of the pool but also, because of various 'imponderables', would have nothing further to do with the 1980 Olympics.

The shocking decision had been made after a series of CBS senior staff meetings, the last a 24-hour marathon. Bock had indeed brought a letter from Moscow that gave the Olympics to CBS for $81 million; he also brought assurances that a reasonable payment schedule could be worked out. It was a very good deal. Why did CBS quit with the battle at last won? Wussler says, 'We saw nothing but trouble ahead. We couldn't see living with their deviousness. Their refusal to stick to the deal they made with Mr Paley was the most telling point. I figured if they'd go back on a deal with him, how could I ever trust them with anything?'

Some people thought this explanation less than complete — especially after CBS had undertaken such an intense, well-organised 2-year campaign to land the Games. It was suggested that perhaps a more compelling reason was that Bock's unauthorised work in Moscow on CBS's behalf would be embarrassing if it got out. As one network man says, 'They got caught with their hand in the cookie jar.'

Bock was stricken. He pleaded his case with Wussler, and then took a Lear jet to the Bahamas to plead with Paley. The answer was no, although the network arranged for Bock to be paid a little extra cash for his trouble. Bock asked to be released from his CBS contract so he could contact NBC. It was done.

With the CBS pullout, the attempts to form a pool had disintegrated, and both NBC and ABC were free to operate unilaterally. Bock and Lindemann met for breakfast at the Edwardian Room of Manhattan's Plaza Hotel. Lindemann recalls, 'The conversation was remarkably low key, considering its substance. Lothar started telling me his deal. We ordered something to eat. He kept talking. We drank our orange juice, and then it dawned on me what he was saying. He was delivering the Olympics to us. We left without eating.' Within hours, NBC signed a contract with Bock to pay him $1 million, to buy fifteen programs he would produce, and to retain him as a special consultant for 4 years. It was a dazzling package. Bock then delivered his part. A series of phone calls to Moscow clinched the deal that night. A day later Lindemann, Howard and an NBC lawyer were on their way to Moscow for the final negotiating and the formal signing.

NBC had hoped to complete the entire contract in Moscow before ABC learned it was there. It could not be done, even though the Soviets sent a telegram telling Arledge not to come to Moscow. ABC was not dissuaded. Arledge says, 'I knew the Russians were panicky. Novikov made a terrible mistake in December. Even his peers were accusing him of having bungled the deal with CBS. He was faced with the prospect of no American network at all. And by that time, he figured all Americans were crazy anyway, so when Bock said he had NBC, Novikov jumped at it. NBC was never in the Russian plans until CBS quit.

'And Novikov never understood what we were doing about the pool and why I had never contacted him after we walked out. When I finally saw him, he said, "You never phoned, you never wrote. I waited and waited, and you never called." I suppose if I had it to do over, maybe I'd do things differently. But I really felt relieved when it was over. I hated to lose the Games, but I had been wondering way back last summer whether I really wanted to have them.'

ABC's presence at the last minute in Moscow did boost the price considerably. Lord Killanin, president of the previously somnolent IOC (which shares the rights fee with the host country), had heard ABC would go higher, and he had sent a telegram to the Soviets to be certain they were getting top dollar. The deal wound up at $85 million — but there was no demand this time for the kind of pro-Soviet propaganda old Ignati Novikov had once seemed so determined to have.

Now the question is: Who won this confrontation between the USSR and the networks? No one knows. This was just the first skirmish in the conflict. Only late in the summer of 1980, when the Games are over and the NBC cameras and crews have gone home, will we know exactly who sold what, who bought what, and who got the better of whom.

ORGANISATIONAL POWER AND POLITICS

Learning objectives

- Distinguish *between the terms 'influence' and 'power'.*

- Identify *five interpersonal power bases.*

- Distinguish *between positive and negative power.*

- Describe *two forms of organisational power.*

- Discuss *the concept of empowerment.*

- Discuss *factors related to influence.*

- List *organisational influence strategies used by individuals.*

- Describe *five political games played in organisations.*

- Discuss *the criteria for determining ethical behaviour.*

Power is a pervasive part of the fabric of organisational life. Managers and non-managers use it. They manipulate power to accomplish goals and, in many cases, to strengthen their own positions.[1] A person's success or failure in using or reacting to power is determined largely by understanding power, knowing how and when to use it, and being able to anticipate its probable effects. The purpose of this chapter is to examine power and its uses in organisations. We will look at the sources (bases) of power, how power is used, and the relationship between power and organisational politics.

THE CONCEPT OF POWER

The study of power and its effects is important to understanding how organisations operate. It is possible to interpret every interaction and every social relationship in an organisation as involving power.[2] How organisational subunits and individuals are controlled is related to the issue of power and influence. The terms **power** and **influence** are frequently used interchangeably in the organisational behaviour literature; however, there is a subtle, yet important, difference. Influence is a transaction in which person B is induced by person A to behave in a certain way. For example, if an employee works overtime at the boss's request, that employee has been influenced by the boss.

Like influence, power involves a relationship between two people. Robert Dahl, a political scientist, captures this important relational focus when he defines power as A has power over B to the extent that he can get B to do something B would not otherwise do.[3] What is the difference between this definition of power and our earlier definition of influence? Power represents the capability to get someone to do something; influence is the exercise of that capability. Another way of stating the distinction is to say that power is the potential to influence, while influence is power in action. Thus, an individual may have power (the capacity to influence) but not exercise it; on the other hand, an individual cannot influence (induce certain behaviours in another) without power.

As was the case in the definition of power above, we frequently speak of someone having power over someone else. While this is correct, it is important to stress that power is not an attribute of a particular person. Rather, it is an aspect of the relationship that exists between two (or more) people. No individual or group can have power in isolation; power must exist in relation to some other person or group. If A has power over B, it is, in part, because B is willing for that to be an aspect of the relationship between them. If and when B no longer desires that to be part of his or her relationship with A, A will no longer have power over B and no longer be able to influence B's behaviour. Thus, obtaining, maintaining and using power are all essential to influencing the behaviour of people in organisational settings.

There is one other aspect in the concept of power that should be noted. When power is one of the attributes of a relationship, so also is *dependency*. It was noted above that A has power with respect to B only so long as B is willing to allow A to exert influence. B is likely to continue to allow this as long as outcomes B wants can be affected by A. Thus, the amount of power one person has over another is a product of the net dependence of the one over the other. If B depends on A more than A depends on B, A holds the power. If Sam, a night-shift worker who wishes a transfer to the day shift, knows that his boss can veto the request, then he is dependent on the boss with respect to that outcome. Consequently, all else being equal, he is more likely to agree to be influenced by his boss.

SOURCES OF POWER

Power is obtained in a variety of ways. Since it facilitates the organisation's adaptation to its environment, the individuals and groups within the organisation that are able to assist in that adaptation are the ones which will hold power. Such power can be derived from many sources. How power is obtained in an organisation depends to a large extent on the type of power being sought. Power can be derived from either interpersonal or structural bases.

Interpersonal power

In what is considered a classic writing in the management and organisational behaviour literature, John French and Bertram Raven suggested five interpersonal bases of power: legitimate, reward, coercive, expert and referent.[4] We will briefly examine each of these.

Legitimate power

Legitimate power refers to a person's ability to influence because of the position within the organisation that person holds. Legitimate or position power, as it is sometimes called, is derived from the position itself. That is, the organisation has given to an individual occupying a particular position the right to influence — command — certain other individuals. This formal power is what we call **authority**. Orders from a manager in an authority position are followed because they must be followed. That is, persons in higher positions have legal authority over subordinates in lower positions. Not following orders subjects the offender to disciplinary action just as not following society's legal directives subjects one to disciplinary action in the form of arrest and penalty. Organisational authority has the following characteristics:

- It is invested in a person's position. An individual has authority because of the position he or she holds, not because of any specific personal characteristics.
- It is accepted by subordinates. The individual in a legal authority position exercises authority and can gain compliance because he or she has a legitimate right.
- Authority is used vertically. Authority flows from the top down in the hierarchy of an organisation.

Possessing legitimate power, or authority, does not mean that all orders will be followed by those who are subordinate to the individual in authority. For a subordinate to comply with an order from a superior requires that the order fall within the subordinate's zone of indifference. The term 'zone of indifference' may be explained as follows: If all possible orders which might be directed to an individual from a superior were arranged in the order of their acceptability to the individual, some would clearly be acceptable while others might clearly be unacceptable.

For example, a request by a manager that a subordinate complete her expense report might be an acceptable order. It would lie within her zone of indifference; that is, she is relatively indifferent to the request as far as the question of her boss's authority is concerned. However, if the boss were to request that she record expenses she did not incur, or that she otherwise pad the expense report, such a request might well fall outside her zone of indifference. She may elect not to comply because she is no longer indifferent with respect to such an order. A person's zone of indifference may be wider or narrower depending on a number of factors such as the extent to which the boss has a source of power other than authority. Zone of indifference size may also be shaped by cultural factors, as illustrated in the Global Encounter.

Reward power

This type of power is based on a person's ability to reward a follower for compliance. It occurs when someone possesses a resource that another person wants and is willing to exchange that resource in return for certain behaviour. **Reward power** is used to back up the use of legitimate power. If followers value the rewards or potential rewards the person can provide (recognition, a good job assignment, a pay raise, additional resources to complete a job and so on), they may respond to orders, requests and directions. Note, however, that if what a manager is offering as a reward has no value to an individual, it will be unlikely to influence behaviour.

Coercive power

The opposite of reward power is **coercive power** — power to punish. Followers may comply out of fear. A manager may block a promotion or harass a subordinate for poor performance. These practices and the fear they will be used are coercive power. Of course, one need not be in a position of authority to possess coercive power. For example, fear of rejection by co-workers for not complying with what they want represents coercive power even though co-workers have no formal authority.

Expert power

A person has **expert power** when he or she possesses special expertise that is highly valued. Experts have power even when their rank is low. An individual may possess expertise on technical, administrative or personal matters. The more difficult it is to replace the expert, the greater is the degree of expert power he or she possesses. Occasionally, individuals' expertise does not bestow upon them as much ability to influence as they think it does. Expert power is a personal characteristic, while legitimate, reward and coercive power are largely prescribed by the organisation.

Referent power

Many individuals identify with and are influenced by a person because of the latter's personality or behavioural style. The charisma of the person is the basis of **referent power.** A person with charisma is admired because of his or her characteristics. The strength of a person's charisma is an indication of his or her referent power. 'Charisma' is a term that is often used to describe politicians, entertainers or sports figures. However, some managers are regarded as

GLOBAL

Power and influence across cultures

Significant differences in work-related values, attitudes and behaviours exist across a wide variety of different cultures. Geert Hofstede, a Dutch researcher, surveyed managers and non-managers in forty countries and concluded that national culture explained more value, attitude and behaviour differences in organisations than did any other variable. One of the dimensions on which Hofstede found important cross-cultural differences between managers and subordinates was what is referred to as *power distance*.

Power distance is a measure of the extent to which organisational members accept the unequal distribution of power. Specifically, to what extent do subordinates accept that their boss has more power than they do? In high power-distance cultures subordinates are likely to do what the boss asks, without question, because he or she is the boss. In low power-distance cultures, on the other hand, the boss's orders are more likely to be questioned. Low power-distance cultures, because they are more egalitarian, tend to be less accepting of the overt use of power. All else being equal, employees in these societies would be expected to have a narrower zone of indifference. Australia and New Zealand are low power-distance countries, as are Israel, Denmark, Ireland, United States and Canada. Large and high power-distance countries, where subordinates might be expected to have wide zones of indifference, include Mexico, Philippines, Venezuela, India, Yugoslavia, Singapore and Hong Kong.

Does power distance translate to differences in influence strategies? A comparison of Hong Kong Chinese and American managers suggests that it does. Managers from these countries were asked to rate a set of influence tactics for the likelihood that they would be used, the risk associated with them and how ethical they were. The general principle seems to be that when strategies were perceived as carrying low risk and being highly ethical, they were more likely to be used. What differed was the strategies that were perceived to be risk-free and ethical.

In America, the most likely *strategies* were dressing for success, acting to get others' admiration and asking for responsibility on an important project. In Hong Kong, however, managers rated the following as the most likely strategies: developing contacts with people who can provide detrimental information about others, threatening to give valuable information to someone outside the organisation, making others look bad by supplying inaccurate information or withholding information, using blackmail on someone who can help you get ahead, spreading rumours about someone who is blocking advancement and threatening to leave.

Turning to *risk*, Hong Kong managers perceived dressing for success as a risky strategy, along with volunteering for an undesirable task so that you would be more appreciated, demonstrating an ability to get the job done, and helping subordinates to develop new skills. On the other hand, in America, using sexual favours was deemed a high-risk strategy as were many of the information-related strategies described above: developing contacts, spreading rumours, threatening to pass on information, withholding or supplying inaccurate information, blaming someone for your mistakes and blackmail.

Finally, when managers were asked to rate how *ethical* these strategies were, American managers rated working for and building relationships with influential superiors, dressing for success, volunteering for high-profile projects and undesirable tasks, and obtaining responsibility for tasks as ethical. In comparison, Hong Kong managers rated developing contacts, spreading rumours, withholding information, blackmail, blaming others for your mistakes and sexual favours as among the more ethical influence strategies.

Source: Ralston, D. A., Gustafson, D. J., Mainiero, L., & Umstot, D. (1993). Strategies of upward influence: A cross-national comparison of Hong Kong and American managers, *Asia Pacific Journal of Management*, 10, 157–175; Hofstede, G. (1980). *Culture's Consequences: International Differences in Word Related Values*. Beverly Hills, CA: Sage.

extremely charismatic by their subordinates. Certain aspects of charismatic leadership will be discussed in more detail in Chapter 11.

Case 10
Missouri campus bitterly divided over how to reallocate funds

The five bases of interpersonal power can be divided into two major categories: organisational and personal. Legitimate, reward and coercive power are primarily prescribed by the organisation, the position, formal groups or specific interaction patterns. A person's legitimate power can be changed by transferring the person, rewriting the job description, or reducing the power by restructuring the organisation. On the other hand, expert and referent power are very personal. They are the result of an individual's personal expertise or style and, as such, are grounded in the person and not the organisation.

These five types of interpersonal power are not independent. On the contrary, a person can use these power bases effectively in various combinations. Also, the use of a particular power base can affect the others. Some research has suggested, for example, that when subordinates believe a manager's coercive power is increasing, they also perceive a drop in reward, referent and legitimate power held by the manager. Other research suggests that legitimate and reward power are positively related while coercive power is inversely related to legitimate and reward power. Research shows that whether individuals use positional or personal power in their influence attempts has different organisational outcomes. Both managers and subordinates agree that the most frequently used form of power in organisations is positional power. However, the use of positional power is associated only with compliance. To obtain commitment, and to be perceived as effective in their jobs, research shows that managers should use personal rather than positional power bases.[5]

Positive power

The power bases described by French and Raven are based on the assumption that power is a one-way process in which we attempt to influence another's behaviour. However, as we will see in the discussion of empowerment, a more recent view of power suggests that it is something to be shared rather than exerted. Consistent with this view, we need to consider two further bases of power: using participation to build trust and commitment and having a shared or common vision[6] Both are closely associated with charismatic and transformational styles of leadership that we will discuss in Chapter 11. These bases have the following effects:

1. *Participation and trust* encourage commitment by seeking to actively involve individuals in the decision-making process. This strategy has the effect of increasing individuals' commitment to the objective or task.
2. *Shared or common vision* identifies a common vision of the future for the group and strengthens the group's belief that their efforts will succeed in making the vision a reality.[7]

Structural and situational power

Power is primarily prescribed by structure within the organisation.[8] The structure of an organisation is the control mechanism by which the organisation is governed. In the organisation's structural arrangements, decision-making discretion is allocated to various positions. Also the structure establishes the patterns of communication and the flow of information. Thus, organisational structure creates formal power and authority by specifying certain individuals to perform specific job tasks and make certain decisions. Structure also encourages informal power through its effect on information and communication within the system.

We have already discussed how formal position is associated with power and authority. Certain rights, responsibilities and privileges accrue from a person's position. Other forms of structural power exist because of resources, decision making and information.[9]

Resource dependency models

Organisational life is based on the exchange of resources: money, staff, information and equipment all play an important role in organisations. Different areas within an organisation have different responsibilities and control different resources. For example, a manufacturing department must rely on the accounts department for financial resources, the personnel department for staff, and marketing to promote and sell its products. Since not all areas in an organisation have equal access to resources, and since not all resources hold equal value, differences in organisational power can emerge. The more important the resources that one department controls, and the more other departments depend on those resources, the greater is its power. Control over valued resources can increase organisational power.[10]

These resources may be material (e.g. money), control over decisions or information (discussed below). A number of organisational situations can serve as the source of either power or powerlessness (not acquiring power). The powerful manager exists because he or she allocates required resources, makes crucial decisions and has access to important information.[11] He or she is likely to make things happen. The powerless manager, however, lacks the resources, information and decision-making prerogatives needed to be productive. A first-line manager, for example, may display symptoms of powerlessness such as super-vising very closely and not showing much concern about training or developing subordinates. If these symptoms persist, it is likely that the individual is powerless.

Resources. Kanter argues quite convincingly that power stems from access to resources, information and support; and the ability to get cooperation in doing necessary work.[12] Power occurs when a person has open channels to resources — money, human resources, technology, materials, customers and so on. In organisations, vital resources are allocated downward along the lines of the hierarchy. The top-level manager has more power to allocate resources than do other managers further down in the managerial hierarchy. The lower level manager receives resources that are granted by top-level managers. In order to assure compliance with goals, top-level managers (e.g. presidents, vice presidents and directors) allocate resources on the basis of performance and compliance. Thus, a top-level manager usually has power over a lower level manager because the lower level manager must receive resources from above to accomplish goals.

Decision-making power. The degree to which individuals or subunits (e.g. a department or a special project group) can affect decision making determines the amount of power acquired. A person or subunit with power can influence how the decision-making process occurs, what alternatives are considered and when a decision is made.[13] For example, when Richard Daley was mayor of Chicago, he was recognised as a power broker. He not only influenced the decision-making process, but also had the power to decide which decision would be given priority in the city council and when decisions would be made.[14] He was a powerful politician because he was considered to be an expert at controlling each step in important decisions.

Information power. Having access to relevant and important information is power. Accountants generally do not have a particularly strong or apparent interpersonal power base in an organisation. Rather, accountants have power because they control important information. Information is the basis for making effective decisions. Thus, those who possess information needed to make optimal decisions have power. The accountant's position in the organisation structure may not accurately portray the amount of power that he or she wields. A true picture of a person's power is provided not only by the person's position but also by the person's access to relevant information.

Strategic contingencies model

The primary focus to this point has been on individual power and how it is obtained. However, it is also important to consider subunit or interdepartmental power. Subunit power is the focus of the strategic contingency theory developed by Hickson. A **strategic contingency** is an event that is extremely important for accomplishing organisational goals.[15] Crozier, a French sociologist, provided insight into the idea of strategic contingencies. He studied the relationships between workers in the production and maintenance departments of French tobacco-processing plants. Crozier found that the production workers enjoyed job security because of tenure, were protected against unfair disciplinary action, and were not replaced or transferred arbitrarily. The production workers were less skilled than the maintenance workers. The maintenance workers were highly skilled and were recruited and selected only after going through a rigorous screening process.

The production workers were dependent on the maintenance workers. This power differential was explained in terms of the control exercised by the maintenance workers over an important contingency. If machines were shut down, the entire plant came to a halt. Efficiently functioning machines were needed to accomplish output goals. Since the maintenance workers, at the request of the production workers, repaired machines that were down, they possessed significant power.

When machines were down, the job performance of the production workers suffered. Stoppages totally disrupted the work flow and the output of the production workers. Crozier proposed that the maintenance workers controlled a strategically contingent factor in the production process. Crozier's study provided clear evidence of subunit power differences. The study also stimulated other studies that eventually resulted in a strategic contingencies explanation of power differences.[16]

Using the work of Crozier and Hickson and his associates, it is possible to develop a concise explanation of strategic contingencies. The model presented in Exhibit 10.1 suggests that subunit power, the power differential between subunits, is influenced by the degree of ability to cope with uncertainty, the centrality of the subunit and the substitutability of the subunit.

Coping with uncertainty. Unanticipated events can create problems for any organisation or subunit. It is, therefore, the subunits most capable of coping with uncertainty that typically acquire power. There are three types of coping activities. First is coping by *prevention*. Here a subunit works at reducing the probability that some difficulty will arise. One example of a coping technique is designing a new product to prevent lost sales because of new competition in the marketplace. Second is coping by *information*. The use of forecasting is an example. Possessing timely forecasting information enables a subunit to deal with such events as competition, strikes, shortages of materials and consumer demand shifts. Planning departments conducting forecasting studies acquire power when their predictions prove accurate. Third is coping by *absorption*. This coping approach involves dealing with uncertainty as it impacts on the subunit. For example, one subunit might take a problem employee from another subunit and attempt to retrain and redirect that employee. This is done as a favour so that the other subunit will not have to go through the pain of terminating or continuing to put up with the employee. The subunit that takes in the problem employee gains the respect of other subunits, which results in an increase in power. The relation of coping with uncertainty to power was expressed by

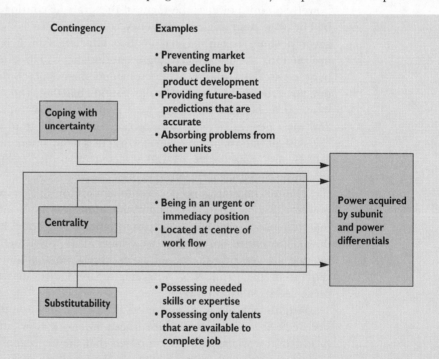

Exhibit 10.1

A strategic contingency model of subunit power

This figure is based on the detailed research work conducted by D. J. Hickson, C. R. Hinnings, C. A. Lee, R. E. Schneck, & J. M. Pennings. (1971). A strategic contingency theory of intraorganizational power, *Administrative Science Quarterly*, June, 216–229; and C. R. Hinnings, D. J. Hickson, J. M Pennings & R. E. Schneck. (1974). Structural conditions of intraorganizational power, *Administrative Science Quarterly*, March, 22–44.

Hickson as follows: 'The more a subunit copes with uncertainty, the greater its power within the organisation.'[17]

Centrality. The subunits that are most central to the flow of work in an organisation typically acquire power.[18] No subunit has zero centrality since all subunits are somehow interlinked with other subunits. A measure of centrality is the degree to which the work of the subunit contributes to the final output of the organisation.[19] Since a subunit is in a position to affect other subunits, it has some degree of centrality and therefore power. Also a subunit possesses power if its activities have a more immediate or urgent impact than that of other subunits. For example, the emergency and trauma treatment subunits in hospitals are extremely important and crucial. They contain significant power within a hospital. Failures in these subunits could result in the death of emergency victims. On the other hand, the psychiatric subunit does important work but not of the crucial and immediate type. Therefore, it has significantly less subunit power than the emergency and trauma treatment subunit.

Substitutability. Substitutability refers to the ability of other subunits to perform the activities of a particular subunit. If an organisation has or can obtain alternative sources of skill, information and resources to perform the job done by a subunit, the subunit's power will be diminished. Training subunits lose power if training work can be done by line managers or outside consultants. On the other hand, if a subunit has unique skills and competencies (e.g. the maintenance workers in Crozier's study discussed above) that would be hard to duplicate or replace, this would tend to increase the subunit's power over other subunits. Hickson et al. capture the importance of substitutability power when they propose that the lower the substitutability of the activities of a subunit, the greater is its power within the organisation.[20]

POSITIVE POWER: EMPOWERMENT

Reading 10
**Leadership:
The art of
empowering
others**

Managers at any level in the organisation can increase the power of subordinates (managers or non-managers) who report to them. This is accomplished through the process of **empowerment**. Empowerment has been defined by Conger and Kanungo as a process of enhancing feelings of self-efficacy among organisational members through the identification of conditions that foster powerlessness and through their removal by both formal organisational practices and informal techniques of providing efficacy information.[21] These researchers suggest that empowerment is a process consisting of five stages.

The first stage involves identifying the conditions existing in the organisation that lead to feelings of powerlessness on the part of organisational members. These conditions could find their origin in organisational factors (such as poor communications or highly centralised resources), management styles (such as authoritarianism), reward systems (non-merit based rewards, low incentive value rewards), or in the nature of the jobs (low task variety, unrealistic performance goals).

The diagnoses completed in the first stage lead to the implementation of empowerment strategies and techniques in the second stage. Use of participative management, establishing goal-setting programs, implementing merit-based pay systems, and job enrichment through redesign are examples of possible empowerment activities. The use of these programs is designed to accomplish two objectives in the third stage. One is simply to remove the conditions identified in the first stage as contributing to powerlessness. The second, and more important, is to provide self-efficacy information to subordinates. Self-efficacy describes a belief in one's effectiveness. Individuals high in self-efficacy tend to be confident and self-assured and feel they are likely to be successful in whatever endeavours they undertake.

Receiving such information results in feelings of empowerment in the fourth stage. This is because increasing self-efficacy strengthens effort-performance expectancies. You will recall from the discussion of expectancy theory in Chapter 4 that this means increasing the perceived probability of successful performance, given effort. Finally, the enhanced empowerment feelings from the fourth stage are translated into behaviours in the fifth and final stage. These behavioural consequences of empowerment include increased activity directed towards task accomplishment.[22]

Thus, by helping organisational members feel more assured of their capability to perform well, and by increasing the linkages between effort and performance, empowerment can result in positive individual and organisational pay-offs.

INTERPERSONAL INFLUENCE AND POLITICS

When individual opinions differ, we create feelings of tension if these differences are made public. Highlighting differences between groups or individuals creates conflict and the need to resolve conflict and reduce the associated tension provides the basis for influence attempts. *Social influence* describes the process by which groups or individuals attempt to resolve differences of opinion and achieve consensus. The aim is to move the opinions of a dissenting individual or minority, so that they are consistent with the majority view.[23]

How does this apply to organisations? In our discussion of social influence, let's consider organisational goals and values to represent the views of the majority. Organisational influence attempts can then be seen as an effort to ensure that individuals conform to organisational goals and values. These can be viewed as legitimate influence attempts. However, in the same way that power can be used to further own, rather than organisational, goals, so influence attempts may also represent efforts to further personal goals. These may be viewed as illegitimate influence attempts. In the following sections, we will consider the mechanisms and processes of social influence, how general influence strategies translate into organisational influence tactics, and what the outcomes of such tactics may be.

The mechanisms of social influence

To understand how influence attempts work, we need to take a closer look at the mechanisms underlying the influence process: uncertainty, authority and reciprocity.

Influence as uncertainty reduction

In our discussion of power, we saw that information and the ability to reduce uncertainty (strategic contingencies model) gave individuals or groups power. There are two ways in which information may influence (and alter) an individual's behaviour. First, when a group provides explicit information about group norms and evaluates negatively behaviour that does not conform to these norms, the group is exerting *normative influence*. It is making clear the behaviours that are (and, more importantly, are not) acceptable to the group and sanctioning acceptable behaviours. This type of influence operates in the socialisation process that we discussed in Chapter 7; the more cohesive the group the stronger is the pressure to conform. A second way to exert influence is to provide individuals with new information that will change their interpretation of the situation or events and, as a consequence, alter their opinions. When groups or individuals hold information, they may use *informational influence* to achieve conformity.[24]

Influence as power

In the last section, we introduced the idea that influence represents a successful use of power to change individual behaviour. When we have authority and individuals depend on us for desirable outcomes (e.g. resource dependency model), we are able to exert influence and alter their behaviour. As we will see in the next section, several organisational influence tactics rely on accessing positional power bases for just this reason. These tactics will be used in downward influence attempts (managers influencing subordinates).

Influence as a reciprocal relationship

There are, however, times when we do not have clear power bases to provide the authority for an influence attempt: when we are trying to influence peers or colleagues (lateral influence) or when we are trying to influence our managers (upward influence). Under these circumstances, we are more likely to rely on personal power and to engage in *interpersonal influence* tactics such as persuasion and negotiation. When we do not have authority, we must ensure that conflicts do not end in the breakdown of communication and impasse. This implies that influence must sometimes be a reciprocal process in which both the influencer and the target alter their opinions or behaviour. At this level, we must recognise that while we may be aiming for consensus, there are few situational factors that force the minority to comply with our influence attempts.[25]

Influence and conformity[26]

Uncertainty reduction, authority and reciprocity provide the basis for influence attempts. The outcome, consensus or agreement can be achieved through one of three processes: normalisation, innovation or conformity. When we achieve consensus through *normalisation*, influence has been through a reciprocal process in which all individuals gradually change their opinions or behaviour in order to establish common norms. This type of process accesses personal power bases, especially those of participation and common vision. *Innovation* is most likely to occur in situations where the minority persistently and actively disrupts majority efforts to alter the minority's opinion. As we will see in the final section, innovation underlies organisational change games: attempts to overthrow the existing power structures. This type of influence attempt must access personal power bases in an effort to increase positional power: personal power maintains a strong minority and successful resistance increases positional power. However, the majority of influence tactics and political games access positional power bases (or attempt to build them), and their aim is conformity.

Conformity aims to resolve the situation or disagreement in favour of the majority view. Where a group has a very strongly held opinion, and makes it clear that this is the only acceptable opinion or goal, individual goals that do not conform are highlighted and tension, for the individual, is increased. To the extent that the majority view is also supported by authority this tension is increased. Consequently, there is overwhelming pressure on the individual to change. What interests us are the consequences of this change: individuals may show either *compliance*, publicly accepting the position but privately disagreeing with it, or *commitment*, both privately and publicly accepting the position. As we will see, not all influence strategies can achieve commitment.

Social influence strategies[27]

Before considering specific organisational influence strategies, let's consider four general influence strategies that we might use to achieve our goals: reciprocity, foot-in-the-door, door-in-the-face and lowball.

Reciprocity, also described as exchange, relies on the principle that social norms require us to return favours. If someone does a favour for us, we expect that at some point we may be asked to return the favour. One means of gaining power, and increasing our ability to influence others, is to do favours and rely on the rule of reciprocity to have those favours returned. For example, we might want to take a week-long holiday, but we know that there is a project that has to be completed within that week. We ask someone else to complete the project, promising that we will 'return the favour'.

Foot-in-the-door describes a strategy in which we make a small request and follow it up with a larger one. It is based on the principle that, having obtained agreement or approval for the small request, it is more difficult for an individual to refuse the larger request. For example, we may approach our manager and ask whether we can have a week's leave. Once our manager has agreed, we may escalate the request, and ask for a month. If our manager has agreed to a week's leave, it becomes more difficult to refuse a month's leave.

Door-in-the-face relies on the reverse principle. We start with a large request that we do not expect to have granted. However, refusing this request induces some level of guilt in the individual. So, when we follow it up with a smaller request, the individual finds it extremely difficult to say no. Continuing the previous example, we might start by saying that we want to take 3 months of long service leave. When this is refused, we ask for what we really wanted, which is a month's leave. It should now be more difficult for our manager to refuse this request.

Lowball strategies are somewhat more interesting. They rely on inducing an attitude change. We start by offering individuals a reward for changing their behaviour. For example, we might offer to give awards to departments that successfully reduce absenteeism over a 1-month period. We monitor absenteeism levels and find that they are decreasing. At the end of the month, we announce that — due to unforeseen circumstances — it will not be possible to give out awards. Research suggests that, even though we are no longer offering incentives for reduced absenteeism, absenteeism will continue to decrease. Over the month, individuals have discovered the benefits of attending work, they have changed their attitudes to work, and as a result the behaviour itself has become rewarding. This strategy should be exercised with caution in organisations: we risk violating equity norms and creating dissatisfaction by offering rewards that do not materialise.

ORGANISATIONAL INFLUENCE AND POLITICS

In the last section, we considered some very general strategies that individuals use when trying to influence others. We will now go on to consider the more specific strategies that individuals use in organisational influence. When individuals use these strategies to achieve their own or subunit, rather then organisational, goals they are said to be engaging in organisational politics.

Individuals and subunits continually engage in politically oriented behaviour.[28] By politically oriented behaviour we mean a number of things:

- behaviour that usually is outside the legitimate, recognised power system;
- behaviour that is designed to benefit an individual or subunit, often at the expense of the organisation in general;
- behaviour that is intentional and is designed to acquire and maintain power.

Exercise 10
How political are you?

As a result of politically oriented behaviours, the formal power that exists in an organisation is often sidetracked or blocked. In the language of organisational theory, political behaviour results in the displacement of power. Exercise 10 allows you to make some judgements regarding the extent to which political processes are involved in organisational decisions and to compare your judgements with others completing the exercise. We are most likely to see individuals engaging in political activity when there is a high degree of uncertainty and there are no clear organisational goals to aid decision making; when the decision involves allocation of scarce resources; and when groups with approximately equal power have different goals and priorities.[29]

Interpersonal influence in organisations

How individuals exert organisational influence has been the subject of considerable research. Among the issues considered by researchers are whether:

- specific strategies are more likely to be used in downward, lateral or upward influence attempts;
- they are most likely to be used alone or in combination with other tactics;
- there are systematic differences in the timing of their use;
- the consequences — commitment and perceived effectiveness — are affected by the strategies that are used.

In Exhibit 10.2 we relate each influence strategy to a power base and summarise the research findings. You will see that most strategies are used more in downward than in lateral or upward influence attempts. Why is this? Why do managers with strong positional power use such a wide range of influence strategies? You might also note the following:

- Strategies accessing personal power bases obtain more commitment and are rated as more effective.
- Softer tactics that access these personal power bases are more likely to be used in combination with other tactics.
- Individuals tend to 'start soft and finish tough'.

Can you think of any reasons for these patterns?

Exhibit 10.2 **Political strategies: How they are used**

Strategy	Power base	Direction of use		Outcome		Sequencing	
		Most	Least	Commit	Effective	Order	Type
Pressure	Coercive	Down	Up	Low, DL	Low, L	Follow-up	
Legitimating	Legitimate	Lateral Down	Up	Low, L	Low, U	Immediate FU	With others
Exchange	Reward	Lateral Down	Up			Immediate FU	
Rational persuasion	Expert	Up	Down	High		Initial	Alone
Inspiration appeal	Referent, common vision	Down	Up	High	High		With others
Personal appeal	Referent	Lateral	Up	High, DL	High	Initial	
Consultation	Participation	Down	Up	High	High	Initial	With others
Ingratiation	Referent	Down Lateral	Up	High, DL			With others
Coalitions		Up Lateral	Down				

D = downward, L = lateral, U = upward, FU = follow-up

Political strategies

Research has identified nine strategies that are commonly used by individuals to influence staff, peers and managers. Like power bases, we can think about these strategies as accessing or building on either positional or personal power bases. Position-oriented strategies access such power bases as reward and coercion; person-centred strategies access what we described as the positive power bases — participation, trust and shared vision. As we will see, the consequences are very different. In this section, we briefly review the political strategies that are regularly used in organisations.[30]

Position-based influence strategies. Several influence strategies rely on our ability to access organisational resources or legitimate power bases. These are exchange, pressure and legitimating (or upward appeals). *Exchange* relies on the principle of reciprocity. This strategy offers, either implicitly or explicitly, some reward or benefit in return for compliance and requires access to reward power. *Pressure* uses threats, coercion or intimidation to gain compliance. To use this tactic, individuals must have access to coercive power bases. The use of pressure tactics can be problematic in the same way that using coercive power is problematic: while it may obtain compliance, it is likely to have negative consequences such as weakening relationships. Pressure is most likely to be used when all other tactics have failed. *Legitimating*, or upward appeal, adds weight to an influence attempt by showing support from senior managers, rules or procedures. This tactic makes use of legitimate power bases.

Person-centred strategies. These are strategies that rely on an individual's characteristics and his or her ability to access expert and referent power bases, or to establish a shared vision. They are rational persuasion, personal appeals, inspirational appeals and consultation. *Rational persuasion*, which is based on expert power bases, uses logical arguments and evidence to gain compliance. This tactic is useful when individuals have shared goals but no agreed means for achieving those goals. *Personal appeals* are based on referent power and draw on existing friendships to gain agreement or favours. *Inspirational appeals* also access a referent power base, appeal to a common vision, and use perceived similarities in goals and values to obtain support or commitment. *Consultation* uses participation in the decision-making process to build trust and commitment by establishing a sense of ownership.

Other strategies. There remain two categories that do not fit neatly into these categories. These are coalition building and ingratiation. *Coalitions* try to increase the force in support of a particular proposal by finding others who agree with it, and then forming a lobby group. This tactic is often used in combination with others, and is most likely to be used when other power bases are weak. *Ingratiation* is a form of impression management and relies on putting the target in a good mood before making a request: praise and flattery are hallmarks of this influence tactic.

The consequences of organisational politics

As was the case with organisational power, the use of organisational influence strategies may differ as a function of target (upward, lateral or downward); and, more importantly, independent of when they are used, some strategies are far more likely to obtain commitment while others actively discourage compliance. At the individual level, strategies — especially ingratiation — are linked to organisational outcomes. For example, some forms of ingratiation improve the quality of leader–member relationships (which we discuss in the next chapter),[31] as well as increasing both intrinsic (job satisfaction) and extrinsic (promotions, salary) success. Before you rush off to ingratiate, be warned that if you choose a strategy that highlights your own performance you may experience less intrinsic and extrinsic success.[32] Also consider that the success of your strategies may differ, depending on whether you are male or female. Men are able to improve their performance appraisals and increase the level of career mentoring by using tough influence tactics designed to take control of the situation. On the other hand, women obtain more psychosocial mentoring when they use weak influence strategies. Our Management Encounter for this chapter considers mentoring as a form of organisational power building.

While we usually think of politics as having negative consequences, the Organisational Encounter shows us that there are times when political strategies can be beneficial.

Playing politics

If anything, the available (yet scanty) research indicates that politics exists in organisations and that some individuals are very adept at political behaviour. Mintzberg and others describe these adept politicians as playing games.[33] Mintzberg identifies four types of games: authority games, played to resist authority; power-base games, played to enhance the scope of organisational power; rivalry games, played to decrease others' power; and change games, played to overturn existing power structures. There are several examples of each game and we will consider a small subset of these.

These examples of political game playing are not offered as always being good or bad for the organisation. They are games that occur in organisations with various degrees of frequency. They occur within and between subunits, and

---

ORGANISATIONAL Encounter

Politics, networks and profits

Small companies are vulnerable; their larger competitors are able to offer more favourable prices, and may eventually take over smaller companies. Not surprisingly, small companies may benefit from employing one type of political strategy: establishing coalitions or networking. According to Greg Hayes, a partner in Sheahan Sims — specialists in small business mergers — the best way for small companies to avoid mergers is to join forces. He gives the example of two small Adelaide graphics and printing companies that, until recently, had been in competition with each other. Because they were competing with each other, resources were being diverted away from tendering for larger printing jobs. Once they merged, they not only increased their skill pool, but also were able to successfully bid for large national contracts. Merging has resulted in decreased operating costs, better management and technical resources, and the ability to compete for large printing jobs.

Another merger success story comes from two small competing companies: the Albion Hat and Cap

Company and the Arcade Badge Embroidery Company. The two companies had a long-standing business relationship and decided that pooling their resources would be of mutual benefit. Shortly after merging (which also made them the largest manufacturer of protective sports equipment in Australia) they also bought out a cricket cap company. Again, this was the result of a long-standing business relationship. A final merger, which resulted in the purchase of an equestrian helmet manufacturing company, has led to the development of a whole line of protective sports equipment. In fact, this much expanded company now manufactures approximately 90% of the world's cricket headgear. To say the least, this string of mergers has been highly successful — boosting turnover from $350 000 in 1980 to $13 million, currently.

Source: Ferguson, A. (1994) Networking the key to company growth, *Business Review Weekly*, June 20; Kennedy, A. (1995) Consider getting into bed with the enemy, *Business Review Weekly*, May 22.

they are played by individuals representing themselves or a subunit. Certainly, political behaviours carried to an extreme can hurt individuals and subunits. However, it is unrealistic to assume that all political behaviour can or should be eliminated through management intervention. Even in the most efficient, profitable and socially responsible organisations and subunits, political behaviours and games are being acted out.

Authority games

The insurgency game is an example of an authority game. This game is played to resist authority. For example, suppose that a plant supervisor is instructed to reprimand a particular worker for violating company policies. The reprimand can be delivered according to the supervisor's feelings and opinions about its worth and legitimacy. If the reprimand is delivered in a half-hearted manner, it probably will have no noticeable effect. On the other hand, if it is delivered aggressively, it may be effective. Insurgency in the form of not delivering the reprimand as expected by a higher level authority would be difficult to detect and correct. Insurgency as a game to resist authority is practised in organisations at all levels.

Power-base games

The sponsorship game is an example of a power-base game. This is a rather straightforward game in that a person attaches himself or herself to someone with power. The sponsor typically is the person's boss or someone else with higher power and status than those of the person. Typically, individuals attach themselves to someone who is on the move. There are a few rules involved in playing this game. First, the person must be able to show commitment and loyalty to the sponsor. Second, the person must follow each sponsor-initiated request or order. Third, the person must stay in the background and give the sponsor credit for everything. Finally, the person must be thankful and display gratitude to the sponsor. The sponsor is not only a teacher and trainer for the person but also a power base. Some of the sponsor's power tends to rub off on the person because of his or her association with the sponsor. Our Management Encounter in this chapter examines a formalised version of this game: mentoring.

The coalition-building game is another power-base game. A subunit such as a personnel/human resources management department or a research and development department may be able to increase its power by forming an alliance or coalition with other subunits. The strength in numbers idea is encouraged by coalition building.[34] When such alliances are formed within the organisation, there is an emphasis on common goals and common interests. However, forming coalitions with groups outside the organisation can also enhance the power of a subunit.

This example of building an internal coalition illustrates how power can be acquired. In most organisations the personnel/human resources department typically has limited power. However, current litigation involving employee relations and employee health problems associated with disability triggered by job stress is becoming a costly expense. Consequently, legal staffs in organisations have acquired power. These legal staffs do not have the information, daily contact with employees and records needed to legally serve

MANAGEMENT | Encounter

The power of the mentor?

Mentoring describes a relationship between a senior and more junior member of staff, established to assist in that person's career development. Mentoring can be either career-related or psychosocial. When individuals engage in *career-related mentoring*, they provide sponsorship, by establishing connections for their protégé; they coach, providing feedback about performance; they provide protection, taking responsibility for mistakes outside the protégé's power; they provide exposure for their protégé's; and they ensure that protégés receive challenging work. Clearly, this has the potential to increase a protégés power. In addition, they may provide *psychosocial mentoring*, acting as role models for the protégé; giving counselling and offering friendship; and providing support for their protégé.

We have argued that mentoring has the potential to increase an individual's power because it aligns that person with a more powerful other. When individuals in a mentor relationship are compared with others,

they report more access to important people, more resource power and a greater ability to influence organisational policy — all forms of organisational power. Does this greater power benefit protégés? Quite a lot of research suggests that it does. Individuals in mentoring relationships not only report higher job satisfaction and lower work alienation but, on the more tangible side, also demonstrate a greater promotion rate and earn higher salaries than individuals who do not have mentors.

On the basis of this research, how desirable is mentoring? What other factors might have affected these results? Do you think that individuals who are more likely to succeed are those selected for mentoring relationships?

Source: Fagenson, E. A. (1988). The power of the mentor: Protégés and nonprotégés' perceptions of their own power in organisations, *Group and Organization Studies*, 13, 182–194; Gordon, J. R. (1993). *A Diagnostic Approach to Organizational Behavior* (4th Ed.). Boston: Allyn and Bacon.

the firm. Skills, abilities and information to cope with employee-based uncertainties are more in the domain of the personnel/human resources department. Therefore, an alliance between the legal staff and the personnel/human resources department would enhance both their power bases. The coalition would enable the organisation to effectively address legal issues.

Building a coalition with an external group can also enhance the power of various groups. The alumni office of most state universities interacts with alumni in fund raising, projecting a positive image and providing service on community projects. The donations of alumni are extremely important for funding and supporting research programs conducted within a university. The alumni office would acquire more power by forming an alliance with major donors who actively support it. The university would be hard-pressed to ignore requests that major donors made to the administration to support the alumni office, the implication being that failing to support the alumni office and its personnel would cause these donors to withhold funds.

Rivalry games

The line-versus-staff game is an example of a rivalry game. The game of line manager versus staff adviser has existed for years in organisations. In essence, it is a game that pits line authority to make operating decisions against the expertise possessed by staff advisers. There are also value differences and a clash of personality. Line managers typically are more experienced, more oriented to the bottom line and more intuitive in reaching decisions. On the other hand, staff advisers tend to be younger, better educated and more analytical as decision makers.[35] These differences result in viewing the organisational world from slightly different perspectives.

Withholding information, having access to powerful authority figures, creating favourable impressions and identifying with organisational goals are tactics used by line and staff personnel. The line-versus-staff clash must be controlled in organisations before it reaches the point at which organisational goals are not being achieved because of the disruption.

Change games

The whistle-blowing game is an example of a change game. Whistle-blowing behaviour is receiving increasing attention.[36] This game is played to bring about organisational change. If a person in an organisation identifies a behaviour that violates his or her sense of fairness, morals, ethics or law, then he or she may blow the whistle. Whistle-blowing means that the person informs someone — a newspaper reporter, a government representative or a competitor — about an assumed injustice, irresponsible action or violation of the law. The whistle-blower is attempting to correct the behaviour or practice. By whistle-blowing, the person is bypassing the authority system within the organisation. This is viewed in a negative light by managers who possess position power. Often, whistle-blowing is done secretly to avoid retribution by the authority system.

Whistle-blowers come from all levels in the organisation.[37] For example, an Eastern Airlines pilot complained to management first and then to the public about defects in his plane's automatic pilot mechanisms. His complaints were attacked by management as being groundless. In another example, a biologist reported to the Environmental Protection Agency that his consulting firm had submitted false data to the agency on behalf of an electric utility company; he was fired. In still another publicised case, an engineer at Ford complained about the faulty design of the Pinto. Unfortunately, this whistle-blower was demoted. Many of the legal costs and settlements from Pinto crash victims might have been avoided if the whistle-blower's message had been taken more seriously.[38]

ETHICS, POWER AND POLITICS

Issues of power and politics often involve ethical issues as well. For example, if power is used within the formal boundaries of a manager's authority and within the framework of organisational policies, job descriptions, procedures and goals, it is really non-political power and most likely does not involve ethical issues. When the use of power is outside the bounds of formal authority, politics, procedures, job descriptions and organisational goals, it is political in nature. When this occurs, ethical issues are likely to be present. Some examples might include bribing government officials, lying to employees and customers, polluting the environment and a general ends-justify-the-means mentality.

Managers confront ethical dilemmas in their jobs because they frequently use power and politics to accomplish their goals. Each manager, therefore, has an ethical responsibility. Recently, researchers have developed a framework that allows a manager to integrate ethics into political behaviour. Researchers recommend that a manager's behaviour must satisfy certain criteria to be considered ethical:[39]

1. *Criterion of utilitarian outcomes:* The manager's behaviour results in optimisation of satisfaction of people inside and outside the organisation. In other words, it results in the greatest good for the greatest number of people.
2. *Criterion of individual rights:* The manager's behaviour respects the rights of all affected parties. In other words, it respects basic human rights of free consent, free speech, freedom of conscience, privacy and due process.
3. *Criterion of distributive justice:* The manager's behaviour respects the rules of justice. It does not treat people arbitrarily but rather equitably and fairly.

What does a manager do when a potential behaviour cannot pass the three criteria? Researchers suggest that it may still be considered ethical in the particular situation if it passes the *criterion of overwhelming factors.* To justify the behaviour, it must be based on tremendously overwhelming factors in the nature of the situation such as conflicts among criteria (e.g. the manager's behaviour

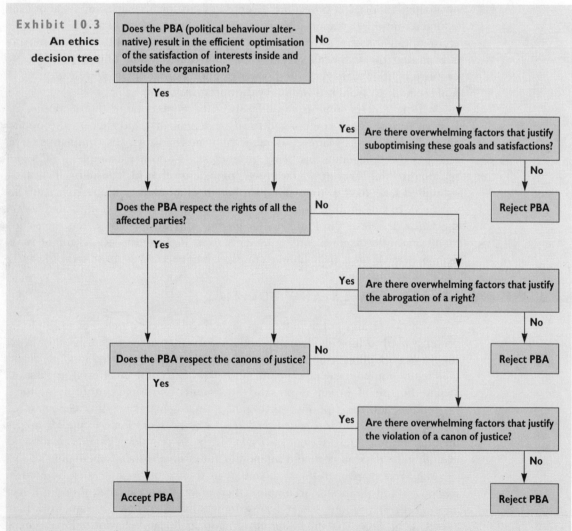

Exhibit 10.3
An ethics decision tree

Source: Adapted from Cavanagh, G. F., Moberg, D .J., & Velasquez, M. (1981). The ethics of organizational politics, *Academy of Management Review*, July, 368.

LOCAL

Encounter

Breaking the glass ceiling

Does understanding organisational politics help your career? According to recent research, women who have broken through the glass ceiling have had to learn some important lessons in organisation politics first. A series of interviews with women executives identified several key lessons that they had learned on the way to the top:

- It is important to understand the corporate culture: what you can say and do.
- Whatever your goals, work within corporate norms to achieve them.
- Work hard and defy the stereotypes.
- Take dramatic action and risks to establish your credibility.
- Build networks, alliances and coalitions.
- Use personal influence and empowerment to build your power. *INFORMAL*

Advancement is affected by three groups of factors: organisational influences, such as training and selection; interpersonal influences, such as establishing networks and obtaining mentors; and individual, non-work factors. Just how do these affect career advancement? According to research by Phyllis Tharenou, at Monash University, these factors have different effects for men and women. Her research showed that, while a number of common factors predicted career advancement, there were also some differences for women and men.

In common, both groups advanced further when they obtained career encouragement and training. Two key differences were that when women were also spouses and parents, they were less likely to advance in their careers than men, whereas men who were parents and spouses were more likely to advance in their careers. In addition, although the nature of the organisational hierarchy did not affect women's career advancement, men working in a male hierarchy received less training, and consequently did not advance as rapidly.

Perhaps the most intriguing finding is that, for men, most of the differences in career advancement could be explained in terms of these factors. However, although these factors predicted career advancement, their impact was not nearly as strong as for women. How can we explain this? Tharenou has assessed organisational and non-work influences on advancement, but not interpersonal influence. Can we conclude that, for women, career advancement is more closely tied to interpersonal influence strategies than it is for men?

Source: Mainiero, L. A. (1994). On breaking the glass ceiling: The political seasoning of powerful women executives, *Organizational Dynamics*, **22**, 5–20; Tharenou, P., Latimer, S., & Conroy, D. (1994). How do you make it to the top? An examination of influences on women's and men's managerial advancement, *Academy of Management Journal, 37*, 899–931.

results in both positive and negative results), conflicts within the criteria (e.g. a manager uses questionable means to achieve a positive result), and/or an incapacity to employ the first three criteria (e.g. the manager acts with incomplete or inaccurate information). Exhibit 10.3 presents a decision-tree approach to the application of these criteria.

Perceptions of political behaviour, and its appropriateness, are affected by gender. As we will see in the next chapter, gender differences in power and politics, as well as leadership style have been researched extensively. Research also suggests that how political activity is evaluated is affected by who is doing what to whom! One experiment asked managers to read a short incident that described an influence attempt. The incidents varied in terms of whether the influencer and the target were male or female. The researchers found that males rated male influencers more favourably, and the manipulation of women as less immoral than the manipulation of men, whereas women rated female influencers more favourably, and the manipulation of men as less immoral than the manipulation of women. In assessing the effects of political behaviour on the organisation, males thought that the manipulation of women was less detrimental to the organisation than the manipulation of men, whereas women reported the exact reverse. Finally, when asked whether they would be willing to engage in similar influence attempts, men were more prepared to manipulate women, and women were more prepared to manipulate men. Overall, the researchers suggested that gender forms the basis for strong ingroup identification within organisations and that manipulation of the outgroup is perceived more favourably than manipulation of the ingroup.[40]

SUMMARY OF KEY POINTS

Distinguish between the terms 'influence' and 'power'. Power is the capability one party has to affect the actions of another party. Influence is a transaction in which one party induces another party to behave in a certain way. Another way of making a distinction is to think of power as the potential to influence, and influence as power in action.

Identify five interpersonal power bases. French and Raven introduced the notion of five interpersonal power bases: legitimate (position based), reward, coercive (punishment based), expert and referent (charismatic). These five bases can be divided into two major categories: organisational and personal. Legitimate, reward and coercive power are primarily prescribed by an organisation, while expert and referent power are based on personal qualities.

Distinguish between positive and negative power. Positive power is based on the principle the power should be shared rather than exerted over other. It relies on strategies such as building trust, establishing a common vision and participative decision making. Negative power, which accesses the power bases described above, is more concerned with obtaining compliance from another individual.

Describe two forms of organisational power. Organisational structure creates power by specifying certain individuals to perform certain tasks. Three important forms of structural power include access to resources, ability to affect decision-making processes, and having access to

relevant and important information. The strategic contingency approach addresses subunit power. A strategic contingency is an event or activity that is extremely important for accomplishing organisational goals. The strategic contingency factors that have been disclosed by research include coping with uncertainty, centrality and substitutability.

Discuss the concept of empowerment. Powerlessness occurs when an individual has little or no access to the bases of interpersonal or structural power. Empowerment refers to a process whereby conditions that contribute to powerlessness are identified and removed. Two important factors in empowerment are helping organisational members feel confident of their ability to perform well, and increasing the linkages between effort and performance.

Discuss factors related to influence. Influence attempts occur when individuals try to reduce uncertainty, establish power or develop norms for behaviour. Often, our aim is to obtain conformity, that is for people to do what we want. General influence strategies include reciprocity, foot-in-the-door, door-in-the-face and throwing a low ball.

List organisational influence strategies used by individuals. Influence strategies used by individuals are exchange, coercion, legitimating, personal appeal, inspirational appeal, consultation, participation, coalition building and ingratiation. They differ in the extent to which they are able to obtain commitment from others, and also the degree to which they are perceived as being effective.

Describe five political games played in organisations. Mintzberg introduced the notion of political game playing in organisations. Examples of political games include insurgency (resisting authority), sponsorship (attaching oneself to someone with power, coalition building (building power bases), line versus staff (defeating rivals) and whistle-blowing (effecting organisational change).

Discuss the criteria for determining ethical behaviour. A manager's behaviour should satisfy certain criteria to be considered ethical. These include the criterion of utilitarian outcomes (the greatest good for the greatest number), the criterion of individual rights (respecting rights of free consent, free speech, privacy and due process) and the criterion of distributive justice (respecting the rules of justice).

REVIEW AND DISCUSSION QUESTIONS

1. Power is an aspect of a relationship between two or more persons. What implications does this fact have for organisational members who wish to increase their power? Decrease the power of others?

2. Is there one particular form of power that is best to have in organisations? Are some forms of power easier (or more difficult) to acquire in organisations?

3. What steps are involved in the empowerment process? Describe how they might be carried out in a situation with which you are familiar.

4. What changes in an organisation's or department's environment would bring about changes in strategic contingencies? How might changes in these contingencies affect power relationships in the unit?

5. Imagine that you want to get a particular job within an organisation. Describe how, using the influence strategies outlined in this chapter, you could achieve your goal.

6. When we influence others we can obtain either commitment or compliance. Is compliance enough in an organisational setting? What would you expect the consequences of compliance and commitment to be?

7. Sometimes playing politics is the most effective way of achieving objectives. Why is this the case? Should organisations be concerned about it?

8. Five of Mintzberg's political games are described in the chapter. How many of them have you witnessed being played in organisations of which you were a member? What other games have you seen played? Which games have you played?

9. The use of power and politics often involve ethical issues. What are the criteria that may be used to determine the extent to which a manager's behaviour is ethical? Are there ever legitimate exceptions to these criteria?

ENDNOTES

1 Cornelius, E. III, & Love, F. (1984). The power motive and managerial success in a professionally oriented service industry organization, *Journal of Applied Psychology*, 32–39.

2 Mintzberg, H. (1984). Power and organizational life cycles, *Academy of Management Review*, 207–224.

3 Dahl, R. (1957). The concept of power, *Behavioral Science*, 202–203.

4 French, J. R. P., & Raven, B. (1959). The basis of social power. In D. Cartwright (Ed.) *Studies in Social Power*. Ann Arbor: Institute for Social Research, University of Michigan, pp. 150–167.

5 Yukle, G., & Falbe, C. M. (1991). Importance of different power sources in downward and lateral relations, *Journal of Applied Psychology*, **76**, 416–423.

6 These power bases are described in Kolb, D. A., Rubin, I. M. & Osland, J. (1991). *Organizational Behavior: An Experiential Approach* (4th Ed.). Englewood Cliffs, NJ: Prentice-Hall International, Inc.

7 Kolb, D. A., Rubin, I. M., & Osland, J. (1991). *Organizational Behavior: An Experiential Approach* (4th Ed.). Englewood Cliffs, NJ: Prentice-Hall International, Inc.

8 Pfeffer, J. (1981). *Power in Organizations.* Marshfield, MA: Pitman Publishing, p. 117; Tjosvold, D. (1985). Power and social context in superior-subordinate interaction, *Organizational Behavior and Human Decision Process*, 281–293.

9 Pfeffer, J. (1981). *Power in Organizations.* Marshfield, MA: Pitman Publishing, pp. 104–122; Kanter, R. M. (1979). Power failures in management circuits, *Harvard Business Review*, 65–75; Taylor, H. R. (1986). Power at work, *Personnel Journal*, 42–49.

10 Greenberg, J. & Baron, R. A. (1993). *Behaviour in Organizations: Understanding and Managing the Human Side of Work* (4th Ed.). Boston: Allyn and Bacon.

11 Cobb, A. T. (1984). An episodic model of power: Toward an integration of theory and research, *Academy of Management Review*, 482–493.

12 Kanter, R. M. (1979). Power failures in management circuits, *Harvard Business Review*, 65–75.

13 For an organizationally oriented, concise and excellent discussion of structural and situationally oriented sources of power, see Hellriegel, D., Slocum, J. W., Jr., & Woodman, R. W. (1986). *Organizational Behavior*. St Paul, MN: West Publishing, 465–468.

14 Royko, M. (1971). *Boss: Richard J. Daley of Chicago*. New York: E. P. Dutton.

15 Crozier, M. (1964). *The Bureaucratic Phenomenon*. Chicago: University of Chicago Press.

16 It should be noted that the strategic contingency theory was developed by D. J. Hickson and his colleagues. Other theorists and researchers have modified and discussed this approach. However, the reader is urged to use the original sources for a discussion of the complete and unmodified theory. See Hickson, D. J., Hinnings, C. R., Lee, C. A., Schneck, R. E., & Pennings, J. M. (1971). A strategic contingency theory of intraorganizational power, *Administrative Science Quarterly*, 216–229; and Hinnings, C. R., Hickson, D. J., Pennings, J. M., & Schneck, R. E. (1974). Structural conditions of intraorganizational power, *Administrative Science Quarterly*, 22–44.

17 Hickson, D. J., Hinnings, C. R., Lee, C. A., Schneck, R. E., & Pennings, J. M. (1971). A strategic contingency theory of intraorganizational power, *Administrative Science Quarterly*, 216–229.

18 Freeman, L. C., Roeder, D. & Mulholland, R. R. (1980). Centrality in social networks: II. Experimental results, *Social Networks*, 119–142.

19 Daft, R. L. (1983). *Organization Theory and Design*. St Paul, MN: West Publishing, 392–398. This source contains an excellent discussion of this strategic contingency perspective in terms of managerial and organisational theory. Daft's discussion is a concise and informative presentation of the original Hickson et al. theory and research.

20 Ibid., p. 40.

21 Conger, J. A. & Kanungo, R. N. (1988). The empowerment process: Integrating theory and practice, *Academy of Management Review*, 474–477.

22 Ibid, pp. 471–482.

23 Moscovici, S. (1987). Social influence and conformity. In G. Lindzey & E. Aronson (Eds.) *Handbook of Social Psychology* (3rd Ed.). New York: Random House.

24 Forsyth, D. R. (1990). *Group Dynamics* (2nd Ed.). Pacific Grove, CA: Brooks-Cole Publishing Company; Moscovici, S. (1987). Social influence and conformity. In G. Lindzey & E. Aronson (Eds.) *Handbook of Social Psychology* (3rd Ed.). New York: Random House.

25 Ibid.

26 This section is based on material contained in Forsyth, D. R. (1900). *Group Dynamics* (2nd Ed.). Pacific Grove, CA: Brooks-Cole Publishing Company; Moscovici, S. (1987). Social influence and conformity. In G. Lindzey & E. Aronson (Eds.) *Handbook of Social Psychology* (3rd Ed.). New York: Random House.

27 See Cialdini, R. (1988). *Influence: Science and Practice* (2nd Ed.). Glenview, IL: Scott, Foresman and Company, for a more detailed discussion of these and other strategies.

28 Velasquez, M., Moberg, D. J., & Cavanagh, G. F. (1983). Organizational statesmanship and dirty politics: Ethical guidelines for the organizational politician, *Organizational Dynamics*, 65–79; and Yoffie, D. & Bergenstein, S. (1985). Creating political advantage: The rise of corporate enterpreneurs, *California Management Review*, 124–139.

29 Greenberg, J. & Baron, R. A. (1993). *Behaviour in Organizations: Understanding and Managing the Human Side of Work* (4th Ed.). Boston: Allyn and Bacon.

30 Yukl, G., & Tracey, J. B. (1992) Consequences of influence tactics used with subordinates, peers, and the boss, *Journal of Applied Psychology*, **77**, 525–535; Yukl, G., & Falbe, C. M. (1991). Importance of different power sources in downward and lateral relations, *Journal of Applied Psychology* **76**, 416–423; Yukl, G., & Falbe, C. M. (1990). Influence tactics and objectives in upward, downward, and lateral influence attempts, *Journal of Applied Psychology*, **75**, 132–140.

31 Deluga, R. J., & Perry, J. T. (1994). The role of subordinate performance and ingratiation in leader-member exchanges, *Group and Organization Management*, **19**, 67–86.

32 Deluga, R. J., & Perry, J. T. (1994). The role of subordinate performance and ingratiation in leader-member exchanges, *Group and Organization Management*, **19**, 67–86.

33 This discussion of games relies on the presentation in Mintzberg, H. (1983*), Power in and around Organizations*. Englewood Cliffs, NJ: Prentice-Hall, pp. 171–271. Please refer to the source for a complete and interesting discussion of political games.

34 Stevenson, W. B., Pearce, J. L., & Porter, L. W. (1985). The concept of coalition in organization theory and research, *Academy of Management Review*, 256–268.

35 Hammond, S. S. III. (1974). The roles of the manager and management scientist in successful implementation, *Sloan Management Review*, 1–24.

36 Near, J. P. & Miceli, M. (1985). Organizational dissonance: The case for whistle-blowing, *Journal of Business Ethics*, 1–16.

37 Dozier, J. & Miceli, M. (1985). Potential predictors of whistle-blowing: A prosocial behavior perspective, *Academy of Management Review*, 823–836.

38 Priest, A. L. (1980). When employees think their company is wrong, *Business Week*, November 24, 2; Pasztor, A. (1980). Speaking up gets biologist into big fight, *The Wall Street Journal*, November 26, 29.

39 Cavanagh, G. F., Moberg, D. J., & Velasquez, M. (1981). The ethics of organizational politics, *Academy of Management Review*, 363–374; and Velasquez, M., Moberg, D. J., & Cavanagh, G. F. (1983). Organizational statesmanship and dirty politics: Ethical guidelines for the organizational politician, *Organizational Dynamics*, 65–79

40 Drory, A., & Beaty, D. (1991). Gender differences in the perception of organizational influence tactics, *Journal of Organizational Behavior*, **12**, 249–258.

READING 10 LEADERSHIP: THE ART OF EMPOWERING OTHERS

Jay A. Conger
McGill University

Source: Reprinted from *Academy of Management Executive* 3(1) (1989), pp. 17–24.

One ought to be both feared and loved, but as it is difficult for the two to go together, it is much safer to be feared than loved … for love is held by a chain of obligation which, men being selfish, is broken whenever it serves their purpose; but fear is maintained by a dread of punishment which never fails.

> The Prince, *Niccolo Machiavelli*

In his handbook, *The Prince*, Machiavelli assures his readers — some being aspiring leaders, no doubt — that only by carefully amassing power and building a fearsome respect could one become a great leader. While the shadowy court life of 16th-century Italy demanded such treachery to ensure one's power, it seems hard to imagine Machiavelli's advice today as anything but a historical curiosity. Yet, interestingly, much of the management literature has focused on the strategies and tactics that managers can use to increase their own power and influence.[1] As such, a Machiavellian quality often pervades the literature, encouraging managers to ensure that their power base is strong and growing. At the same time a small but increasing number of management theorists have begun to explore the idea that organizational effectiveness also depends on the sharing of power — that the distribution of power is more important than the hoarding of power.[2]

While the idea of making others feel more powerful contradicts the stereotype of the all-powerful executive, research suggests that the traditional ways of explaining a leader's influence may not be entirely correct. For example, recent leadership studies argue that the practice of empowering — or instilling a sense of power — is at the root of organizational effectiveness, especially during times of transition and transformation.[3] In addition, studies of power and control within organizations indicate that the more productive forms of organizational power increase with superiors' sharing of power and responsibility with subordinates.[4] And while there is an increasing awareness of this need for more empowering leadership, we have only recently started to see documentation about the actual practices that leaders employ to effectively build a sense of power among organizational members as well as the contexts most suited for empowerment practices.[5]

In this article, I will explore these practices further by drawing upon a recent study of senior executives who proved themselves highly effective leaders. They were selected by a panel of professors at the Harvard Business School and management consultants who were well acquainted with them and their companies. The study included eight chief executive officers and executive vice-presidents of *Fortune* 500 companies and successful entrepreneurial firms, representing industries as diverse as telecommunications, office automation, retail banking, beverages, packaged foods, and management consulting. In each case, these individuals were responsible for either the creation of highly successful companies or for performing what were described as remarkable turnarounds. During my study of these executives, I conducted extensive interviews, observed them on the job, read company and other documents, and talked with their colleagues and subordinates. While the study focused on the broader issue of leadership styles, intensive interviews with these executives and their subordinates revealed that many were characterized as empowering leaders. Their actions were perceived as building confidence and restoring a sense of personal power and self-efficacy during difficult organizational transitions. From this study, I identified certain organizational contexts of powerlessness and management practices derived to remedy them.

In this article I will also illustrate several of these practices through a series of vignettes. While the reader may recognize some of the basic ideas behind these practices (such as providing greater opportunities for initiative), it is often the creative manner in which the leader deploys the particular practice that distinguishes them. The reader will discover how they have been carefully tailored to fit the context at hand. I might add, however, that these practices represent just a few of the broad repertoire of actions that leaders can take to make an empowering difference in their organizations.

A word about empowerment

We can think of empowerment as the act of strengthening an individual's beliefs in his or her sense of effectiveness. In essence, then,

empowerment is not simply a set of external actions; it is a process of changing the internal beliefs of people.[6] We know from psychology that individuals believe themselves powerful when they feel they can adequately cope with environmental demands — that is, situations, events, and people they confront. They feel powerless when they are unable to cope with these demands. Any management practice that increases an individual's sense of self-determination will tend to make that individual feel more powerful. The theory behind these ideas can be traced to the work of Alfred Bandura, who conceptualized the notion of self-efficacy beliefs and their role in an individual's sense of personal power in the world.[7]

From his research in psychology, Bandura identified four means of providing empowering information to others: (1) through positive emotional support during experiences associated with stress and anxiety, (2) through words of encouragement and positive persuasion, (3) by observing others' effectiveness — in other words, having models of success with whom people identified — and (4) by actually experiencing the mastering of a task with success (the most effective source). Each of these sources of empowerment was used by the study executives and will be identified in the practice examples, as will other sources identified by organizational researches.

Several empowering management practices

Before describing the actual practices, it is important to first draw attention to an underlying attitude of the study participants. These empowering leaders shared a strong underlying belief in their subordinates' abilities. It is essentially the Theory Y argument;[8] if you believe in people's abilities, they will come to believe in them. All the executives in the study believed that their subordinates were capable of managing their current situations. They did not employ wholesale firings as a means of transforming their organizations. Rather, they retained the majority of their staff and moved those who could not perform up to standard to positions where they could. The essential lesson is that an assessment of staff skills is imperative before embarking on a program of empowerment. This basic belief in employees' abilities underlies the following examples of management practices designed to empower. We will begin with the practice of providing positive emotional support.

1. The squirt-gun shootouts: Providing a positive emotional atmosphere.

An empowering practice that emerged from the study was that of providing positive emotional support, especially through play or drama. For example, every few months, several executives would stage dramatic 'up sessions' to sustain the motivation and excitement of their staff. They would host an afternoon-long, or a one- or two-day event devoted solely to confidence building. The event would open with an uplifting speech about the future, followed by a special, inspirational speaker. At these events there would often be films meant to build excitement or confidence — for example, a film depicting a mountain climber ascending a difficult peak. The message being conveyed is that this person is finding satisfaction in the work he or she does at an extraordinary level of competence. There would also be rewards for exceptional achievements. These sessions acted as ceremonies to enhance the personal status and identity of employees and revive the common feelings that bound them together.[9]

An element of play appears to be especially liberating in situations of great stress and demoralization. In the study's examples, play allowed for venting of frustrations and in turn permitted individuals to regain a sense of control by stepping back from their pressures for a moment. As Bandura suggests, the positive emotional support provided by something like play alleviates, to some extent, concerns about personal efficacy.[10]

For example, one of the subjects of the study, Bill Jackson, was appointed the head of a troubled division. Demand had outstripped the division's ability to maintain adequate inventories, and product quality had slipped. Jackson's predecessors were authoritarian managers, and subordinates were demoralized as well as paranoid about keeping their jobs. As one told me, 'You never knew who would be shot next.' Jackson felt that he had to break the tension in a way that would allow his staff to regain their sense of control and power. He wanted to remove the stiffness and paranoia and turn what subordinates perceived as an impossible task into something more fun and manageable.

So, I was told, at the end of his first staff meeting, Jackson quietly pulled out a squirt-gun and blasted one of his managers with water. At first, there was a moment of stunned silence, and then suddenly the room was flooded with laughter. He remarked with a smile, 'You gotta have fun in this business. It's not worth having your stomach in ulcers.' This began a month of squirt-gun fights between Jackson and his managers.

The end result? A senior manager's comment is representative: 'He wanted people to feel comfortable, to feel in control. He used waterguns to do that. It was a game. It took the stiffness out of the business, allowed people to play in a safe environment — as the boss says, "to have fun".' This play restored rapport and morale. But Jackson also knew when to stop. A senior manager told me, 'We haven't used waterguns in nine months. It has served its purpose … The waterfights were like being accepted into a club. Once it achieved its purpose, it would have been overdone.'

Interview after interview with subordinates confirmed the effectiveness of the squirt-gun incident. It had been experienced as an empowering ritual. In most contexts, this behavior would have been abusive. Why did it work? Because it is a management practice that fit the needs of subordinates at the appropriate time.

The executive's staff consisted largely of young men, 'rough and ready' individuals who could be described as fun-loving and playful. They were accustomed to an informal atmosphere and operated in a very down-to-earth style. Jackson's predecessor, on the other hand, had been stiff and formal.

Jackson preferred to manage more informally. He wanted to convey, quickly and powerfully, his intentions of managing in a style distinct from his predecessor's. He was concerned, however, that his size — he is a very tall, energetic, barrel-chested man — as well as his extensive background in manufacturing would be perceived as intimidating by his young staff and increase their reluctance to assume initiative and control. Through the squirt-gun fights, however, he was able to (1) relieve a high level of tension and restore some sense of control, (2) emphasize the importance of having fun in an otherwise trying work environment, and (3) direct subordinates' concerns away from his skills and other qualities that intimidated them. It was an effective management practice because he understood the context. In another setting, it might have been counter-productive.

2. The 'I Make a Difference' Club: Rewarding and encouraging in visible and personal ways.

The majority of executives in the study rewarded the achievements of their staffs by expressing personal praise and rewarding in highly visible and confidence-building ways. They believed that people appreciated recognition of their hard work and success. Rewards of high incentive value were particularly important, especially those of person recognition from the leader. As Rosabeth Kanter notes, a sense of power comes '… when one has relatively close contact with sponsors (higher-level people who confer approval, prestige, or backing).'[11] Combined with words of praise and positive encouragement, such experiences become important sources of empowerment.

The executives in the study took several approaches to rewards. To reward exceptional performance, one executive established the 'I Make a Difference Club.' Each year, he selects two or three staff members to be recognized for their excellence on the job. It is a very exclusive club, and only the executive knows the eligibility rules, which are based on outstanding performance. Inductees are invited to dinner in New York City but are not told beforehand that they are about to join the 'I Make a Difference Club'. They arrive and meet with other staff members whom they believe are there for a staff dinner. During dinner, everyone is asked to speak about what is going on in his or her part of the company. The old-timers speak first, followed by the inductees (who are still unaware of their coming induction). Only after they have given their speeches are they informed that they have just joined the club. As one manager said, 'It's one of the most wonderful moments in life.'

This executive and others also make extensive use of personal letters to individuals thanking them for their efforts and projects. A typical letter might read, 'Fred, I would personally like to thank you for your contribution to _____, and I want you to know that I appreciate it'. Lunches and dinners are hosted for special task accomplishments.

Public recognition is also employed as a means of rewarding. As one subordinate commented about his boss,

He will make sure that people know that so-and-so did an excellent job on something. He's superb on giving people credit. If the person has done an exceptional job on a task or project, he will be given the opportunity to present his or her findings all the way to the board. Six months later, you'll get a call from a friend and learn that he has dropped your name in a speech that you did well. It makes you want to do it again.

I found that the investment in rewards and recognition made by many of these executives is unusually high, consuming a significant portion of their otherwise busy day. Yet the payoff appeared high. In interviews, subordinates described these rewards as having an empowering impact on them.

To understand why some of these rewards proved to be so successful, one must understand their organizational contexts. In some cases, the organizations studied were quite large, if not enormous. The size of these organizations did little to develop in employees a sense of an 'I' — let alone an 'I' that makes a difference. It was easy for organization members to feel lost in the hierarchy and for their achievements to be invisible, for recognition not to be received for personal contributions. The study's executives countered this tendency by institutionalizing a reward system that provided visibility and recognition — for example, the 'I Make a Difference Club', presentations to the Board, and names dropped in speeches. Suddenly, you as a member of a large organization stood out — you were special.

Outstanding performance from each of the executive's perspectives was also something of a necessity. All the executives had demanding goals to achieve. As such, they had to tend to subordinates' sense of importance and contribution. They had to structure reward systems that would keep people 'pumped up' — that would ensure that their confidence and commitment would not be eroded by the pressures placed on them.

3. 'Praising the troops': Expressing confidence.

The empowering leaders in the study spent significant amounts of time expressing their confidence in subordinates' abilities. Moreover, they expressed their confidence throughout each day — in speeches, in meetings, and casually in office hallways. Bandura comments that 'people who are persuaded verbally that they possess the capabilities to master given tasks are likely to mobilize greater sustained effort than if they harbor self-doubts and dwell on personal deficiencies when difficulties arise.'[12]

A quote from Irwin Federman, CEO of Monolithic Memories, a highly successful high-tech company, captures the essence and power of a management practice that builds on this process:

If you think about it, we love others not for who they are, but for how they make us feel. In order to willingly accept the direction of another individual, it must make you feel good to do so … If you believe what I'm saying, you cannot help but come to the conclusion that those you have followed passionately, gladly, zealously — have made you feel like somebody … This business of making another person feel good in the unspectacular course of his daily comings and goings is, in my view, the very essence of leadership.[13]

This proactive attitude is exemplified by Bob Jensen. Bob assumed control of his bank's retail operation after a reorganization that transferred away the division's responsibility for large corporate clients. Demoralized by a perceived loss in status and responsibility, branch managers were soon asking, 'Where's our recognition?' Bob, however, developed an inspiring strategic vision to transform the operation. He then spent much of his time championing his strategy and expressing his confidence in employees' ability to carry it out. Most impressive was his personal canvass of some 175 retail branches. As he explained,

I saw that the branch system was very down, morale was low. They felt like they'd lost a lot of power. There were serious problems and a lot of staff were just hiding. What I saw was that we really wanted to create a small community for each branch where customers would feel known. To do that, I needed to create an attitude change. I saw that the attitudes of the branch staff were a reflection of the branch manager. The approach then was a manageable job — now I had to focus on only 250 people, the branch managers, rather than the 3000 staff employees out there. I knew I had to change their mentality from being lost in a bureaucracy to feeling like the president of their own bank. I had to convince them they were special — that they had the power to transform the organization … All I did was talk it up. I was up every night. In one morning, I hit 17 branches. My goal was to sell a new attitude. To encourage people to 'pump iron'. I'd say, 'Hi, how's business?', encourage them. I'd arrange tours of the branches for the chairman on down. I just spent a lot of time talking to these people — explaining that they were the ones who could transform the organization.

It was an important tactic — one that made the branch managers feel special and important. It was also counter-cultural. As one executive told me, 'Bob would go out into the field to visit the operations, which was very unusual for senior people in this industry.' His visits heightened the specialness that branch managers felt. In addition, Bob modeled self-confidence and personal success — an important tactic to build a sense of personal effectiveness among subordinates.[14]

I also watched Jack Eaton, president of a regional telephone company, praise his employees in large corporate gatherings, in executive council meetings, and in casual encounters. He explained his philosophy:

I have a fundamental belief and trust in the ability and conscientiousness of others. I have a lot of good people. You can turn them loose, let them feel good about their accomplishments … You ought to recognize accomplishment as well as build confidence. I generally do it in small ways. If someone is doing well, it's important to express your confidence to that person — especially among his peers. I tend to do it personally. I try to be genuine. I don't throw around a lot of b.s.

This practice proved especially important during the transition of the regional phone companies away from the parent organization.

4. 'President of my own bank': Fostering initiative and responsibility. Discretion is a critical power component of any job.[15] By simply fostering greater initiative and responsibility in subordinates' tasks, a leader can empower organizational members. Bob Jensen, the bank executive, is an excellent example of how one leader created opportunities for greater initiative despite the confines of his subordinates' positions. He transformed what had been a highly constricted branch manager's job into a branch 'president' concept. The idea was simple — every manager was made to feel like the president of his own community bank, and not just in title. Goals, compensation, and responsibilities were all changed to foster this attitude. Existing measurement systems were completely restructured. The value-of-funds-generated had been the principal yardstick — something over which branch managers had only very limited control because of interest rate fluctuations. Managers were now evaluated on what they could control — that is, deposits. Before, branch managers had rotated every couple of years. Now they stayed put. 'If I'm moving around, then I'm not the president of my own bank, so we didn't move them anymore,' Jensen explained. He also decentralized responsibilities that had resided higher in the hierarchy — allowing the branch manager to hire, give money to charities, and so on. In addition, a new ad agency was hired to mark the occasion, and TV ads were made showing the branch managers being in charge, rendering personal services themselves. The branch managers even thought up the ad lines.

What Jensen did so skillfully was recognize that his existing managers had the talent and energy to turn their operations around successfully, but that their sense of power was missing. He recognized their pride had been hurt and that he needed to restore a sense of ownership and self-importance. He had to convince his managers through increased authority that they were no longer 'pawns' of the system — that they were indeed 'presidents' of their own banks.

Another example — this one demonstrating a more informal delegation of initiative — was quite surprising. The setting was a highly successful and rapidly growing computer firm, and the study participant was the vice-president of manufacturing. The vice-president had recently been hired away from another firm and was in the process of revamping manufacturing. During the process, he discovered that his company's costs on its terminal video monitors were quite high. However, he wanted his staff to discover the problem for themselves and to 'own' the solution. So one day, he placed behind his desk a black-and-white Sony TV with a placard on top saying $69.95. Next to it he placed a stripped-down version of the company's monitor with a placard of $125.95. Both placards reflected the actual costs of the two products. He never said a word. But during the day as staff and department managers entered their boss's office, they couldn't help but notice the two sets. They quickly got the message that their monitor was costing twice as much as a finished TV set. Within a month, the manufacturing team had lowered the monitor's costs by 40 percent.

My first impression on hearing this story was that, as a subordinate, I would be hard pressed not to get the point and, more important, I would wonder why the boss was not more direct.

Ironically, the boss appears to be hitting subordinates over the head with the problem. Out of context, then, this example hardly seems to make others feel more competent and powerful. Yet staff described themselves as 'turned on' and motivated by this behavior. Why, I wondered? A little history will illustrate the effectiveness of this action.

The vice-president's predecessor had been a highly dictatorial individual. He tightly controlled his staff's actions and stifled any sense of discretion. Implicitly, his behavior said to subordinates, 'You have no ideas of your own'. He fired freely, leaving staff to feel that they had little choice in whether to accept his orders or not. By his actions, he essentially transformed his managers into powerless order-takers.

When the new vice-president arrived, he found a group of demoralized subordinates whom he felt were nonetheless quite talented. To restore initiative, he began to demonstrate the seriousness of his intentions in highly visible and symbolic ways. For example, rather than tell his subordinates what to do, he started by seeding ideas and suggestions in humorous and indirect ways. The TV monitor is only one of many examples. Through these actions, he was able eventually to restore a sense of initiative and personal competence to his staff. While these examples are illustrative of effective changes in job design, managers contemplating job enrichment would be well advised to consult the existing literature and research before undertaking major projects.[16]

5. Early victories: Building on success. Many of the executives in the study reported that they often introduced organizational change through pilot or otherwise small and manageable projects. They designed these projects to ensure early success for their organizations. For example, instead of introducing a new sales structure nationwide, they would institute the change in one region; a new technology would have a pilot introduction at a single plant rather than systemwide. Subordinates described these early success experiences as strongly reinforcing their sense of power and efficacy. As Mike Beer argues:

In order for change to spread throughout an organization and become a permanent fixture, it appears that early successes are needed ... When individuals, groups, and whole organizations feel more competent than they did before the change, this increased sense of competence reinforces the new behavior and solidifies learning associated with change.[17]

An individual's sense of mastery through actual experience is the most effective means of increasing self-efficacy.[18] When subordinates are given more complex and difficult tasks, they are presented with opportunities to test their competence. Initial success experiences will make them feel more capable and, in turn, empowered. Structuring organizational changes to ensure initial successes builds on this principle.

Contexts of powerlessness

The need to empower organizational members becomes more important in certain contexts. Thus, it is important to identify conditions within organizations that might foster a sense of powerlessness. Certain circumstances, for instance, appear to lower feelings of self-efficacy. In these cases, subordinates typically perceive themselves as lacking control over their immediate situation (e.g., a major reorganization threatens to displace responsibility and involves limited or no subordinate participation),[19] or lacking the required capability, resources, or discretion needed to accomplish a task (e.g., the development of new and difficult-to-learn skills for the introduction of a new technological process).[20] In either case, these experiences maximize feelings of inadequacy and lower self-confidence. They, in turn, appear to lessen motivation and effectiveness.

Exhibit 10.4 identifies the more common organizational factors that affect these self-efficacy or personal power beliefs and contribute to feelings of powerlessness. They include organizational factors, supervisory styles, rewards systems, and job design.

For example, during a major organizational change, goals may change — often dramatically — to respond to the organization's new direction. Rules may no longer be clearly defined as the firm seeks new guidelines for action. Responsibilities may be dramatically altered. Power alliances may shift, leaving parts of the organization with a perceived loss of power or increasing political activity. Certain functional areas, divisions, or acquired companies may experience disenfranchisement as their responsibilities are felt to be diminished or made subordinate to others. As a result, employees'

Exhibit 10.4 Context factors leading to potential state of powerlessness

Organizational Factors:
Significant organizational changes/transitions
Start-up ventures
Excessive, competitive pressures
Impersonal bureaucratic climate
Poor communications and limited network-
    forming systems
Highly centralized organizational resources

Supervisory Style:
Authoritarian (high control)
Negativism (emphasis on failures)
Lack of reason for actions/consequences

Reward Systems:
Noncontingency (arbitrary reward allocations)
Low incentive value of rewards
Lack of competence-based rewards
Lack of innovation-based rewards

Job Design:
Lack of role clarity
Lack of training and technical support
Unrealistic goals
Lack of appropriate authority/discretion
Low task variety
Limited participation in programs, meetings,
    and decisions that have a direct impact on job
    performance
Lack of appropriate/necessary resources
Lack of network-forming opportunities
Highly established work routines
Too many rules and guidelines
Low advancement opportunities
Lack of meaningful goals/tasks
Limited contact with senior management

Source: Adapted from J. A. Conger and R. N.Kanungo, The Empowerment Process: Integrating Theory and Practice, *Academy of Management Review*, July 1988.

sense of competency may be seriously challenged as they face having to accept and acquire new responsibilities, skills, and management practices as well as deal with the uncertainty of their future.

In new venture situations, uncertainty often appears around the ultimate success of the company's strategy. A major role for leaders is to build an inspiring picture of the firm's future and convince organizational members of their ability to achieve that future. Yet, market lead times are often long, and tangible results may be slow in coming. Long work hours with few immediate rewards can diminish confidence. Frustration can build, and questions about the organization's future can arise. In addition, the start-up's success and responses to growth can mean constant change in responsibility, pushing managers into responsibilities where they have had little prior experience; thus, failure may be experienced initially as new responsibilities are learned. Entrepreneurial executives may be reluctant to relinquish their control as expansion continues.

Bureaucratic environments are especially conducive to creating conditions of powerlessness. As Peter Block points out, bureaucracy encourages dependency and submission because of its top-down contract between the organization and employees.[21] Rules, routines, and traditions define what can and cannot be done, allowing little room for initiative and discretion to develop. Employees' behavior is often guided by rules over which they have no say and which may no longer be effective, given the present-day context.

From the standpoint of supervision, authoritarian management styles can strip away subordinates' discretion and, in turn, a sense of power. Under an authoritarian manager, subordinates inevitably come to believe that they have little control — that they and their careers are subject to the whims or demands of their boss. The problem becomes acute when capable subordinates begin to attribute their powerlessness to internal factors, such as their own personal competence, rather than to external factors, such as the nature of the boss's temperament.

Rewards are another critical area for empowerment. Organizations that do not provide valued rewards or simply do not reward employees for initiative, competence, and innovation are creating conditions of powerlessness. Finally, jobs with little meaningful challenge, or jobs where the task is unclear, conflicting, or excessively demanding can lower employees' sense of self-efficacy.

Implications for managers

Managers can think of the empowerment process as involving several stages.[22] Managers might want to begin by identifying for themselves whether any of the organizational problems and characteristics described in this article are present in their own firms. In addition, managers assuming new responsibilities should conduct an organizational diagnosis that clearly identifies their current situation, and possible problems and their causes. Attention should be aimed at understanding the recent history of the organization. Important questions to ask would be: What was my predecessor's supervisory style? Has there been a recent organizational change that negatively affected my subordinates? How is my operation perceived by the rest of the corporation? Is there a sense of disenfranchisement? Am I planning to change significantly the outlook of this operation that would challenge traditional ways of doing things? How are people rewarded? Are jobs designed to be motivating?

Once conditions contributing to feelings of powerlessness are identified, the managerial practices identified in this article and in the management literature can be used to provide self-efficacy information to subordinates. This information in turn can result in an empowering experience for subordinates and may ultimately lead to greater initiative, motivation, and persistence.

However, in applying these practices, it is imperative that managers tailor their actions to fit the context at hand. For example, in the case of an authoritarian predecessor, you are more likely to need praise and confidence-building measures and greater opportunities for job discretion. With demanding organizational goals and tasks, the practices of confidence building and active rewarding, an element of play, and a supportive environment are perhaps most appropriate. The specific character of each practice must necessarily vary somewhat to fit your particular situation. For instance, what makes many of the previous examples so important is that the executives responded with practices that organizational members could relate to or that fit

Exhibit 10.5 **Stages of the empowerment process**

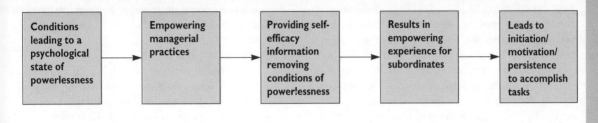

| Conditions leading to a psychological state of powerlessness | → | Empowering managerial practices | → | Providing self-efficacy information removing conditions of powerlessness | → | Results in empowering experience for subordinates | → | Leads to initiation/ motivation/ persistence to accomplish tasks |

Source: Adapted from J. A. Conger and R. N. Kanungo, 'The Empowerment Process: Integrating Theory and Practice', *Academy of Management Review*, July 1988.

their character — for instance, the television and squirt-gun examples. Unfortunately, much of today's popular management literature provides managers with tools to manage their subordinates, yet few highlight the importance of matching the practice to the appropriate contest. Empowering is not a pill; it is not simply a technique, as many workshops and articles would lead us to believe. Rather, to be truly effective it requires an understanding of subordinates and one's organizational context.

Finally, although it is not apparent in the examples themselves, each of the study executives set challenging and appealing goals for their organizations. This is a necessary component of effective and empowering leadership. If goals are not perceived as appealing, it is difficult to empower managers in a larger sense. As Warren Bennis and Burt Nanus argue: 'Great leaders often inspire their followers to high levels of achievement by showing them how their work contributes to worthwhile ends. It is an emotional appeal to some of the most fundamental needs — the need to be important, to make a difference, to feel useful, to be part of a successful and worthwhile enterprise.'[23] Such goals go hand in hand with empowering management practices. They were and are an integral part of the empowerment process I observed in the companies I studied.

A word of caution

In closing, it is important to add a note of caution. First of all, empowerment is not the complete or always the appropriate answer to building the confidence of managers. It can lead to overconfidence. A false sense of confidence in positive outcomes may lead employees and

organizations to persist in what may, in actuality, prove to be tactical errors. Thus, a system of checks and balances is needed. Managers must constantly test reality and be alert to signs of 'groupthink'.

Some managers may be incapable of empowering others. Their own insecurities may prevent them from instilling a sense of power in subordinates. This is ironic, since often these are the individuals who need to develop such skills. Yet, as Kanter argues, 'Only those leaders who feel secure about their own power outward … can see empowering subordinates as a gain rather than a loss.'[24]

Certain situations may not warrant empowerment. For example, there are contexts where opportunities for greater initiative or responsibility simply do not exist and, in some cases, subordinates may be unwilling or unable to assume greater ownership or responsibility. As Lyman Porter, Edward Lawler, and Richard Hackman point out, research 'strongly suggests that only workers with reasonably high strength of desire for higher-order need satisfaction … will respond positively and productively to the opportunities present in jobs which are high in meaning, autonomy, complexity, and feedback.'[25]Others may not have the requisite experience or knowledge to succeed. And those given more than they are capable of handling may fail. The end result will be the opposite of what you are seeking — a sense of powerlessness. It is imperative that managers assess as accurately as possible their subordinates' capabilities before undertaking difficult goals and empowering them to achieve.

Second, certain of the empowerment practices described in this article are not appropriate for all situations. For example, managers of subordinates who require structure and direction are likely to find the example of the manager 'seeding' ideas with the television set an ineffective practice. In the case of a pressing deadline or crisis, such seeding is inappropriate, given its longer time horizons.

When staging playful or unconventional events, the context must be considered quite carefully. What signals are you sending about yourself and your management philosophy? Like rewards, these events can be used to excess and lose their meaning. It is imperative to determine the appropriateness and receptivity of such practices. You may inadvertently mock or insult subordinates, peers, or superiors.

In terms of expressing confidence and rewarding, both must be done sincerely and not to excess. Praising for nonaccomplishments can make rewards meaningless. Subordinates may suspect that the boss is simply flattering them into working harder.

In general, however, empowerment practices are an important tool for leaders in setting and achieving higher goals and in moving an organization past difficult transitions.[26] But remember that they do demand time, confidence, an element of creativity, and a sensitivity to one's context to be effective.

Discussion questions

1. Under what circumstances are organizational members likely to experience powerlessness?
2. In what ways can a leader provide empowering information to others?
3. Describe four empowering leadership practices. In what situations would each be appropriate?

References

1 See, for example, J. P. Kotter, *Power in Management* (New York: AMACOM, 1979); and J. Pfeffer, *Power in Organizations* (Marshfield, MA: Pitman, 1981).

2 See P. Block, *The Empowered Manager* (San Francisco: Jossey-Bass, 1987); W. W. Burke, "Leadership as Empowering Others," in S. Srivastva, ed., *Executive Power* (San Francisco: Jossey-Bass, 1986), pp. 51–77; and R. M. Kanter, *The Change Masters* (New York: Simon & Schuster, 1983).

3 W. Bennis and B. Nanus, *Leaders* (New York: Harper & Row, 1985); and R. M. Kanter, 'Power

Failure in Management Circuits,' *Harvard Business Review*, July–August 1979, pp. 65–75.

4 See Kanter, footnote 3; and A. S. Tannenbaum, *Control in Organizations* (New York: McGraw-Hill, 1968).

5 See J. A. Conger and R. N. Kanungo, 'The Empowerment Process: Integrating Theory and Practice,' *Academy of Management Review*, July 1988; and R. J. House, 'Power and Personality in Complex Organizations,' in L. L. Cummings and B. M. Staw, (eds), *Research in Organizational Behavior: An Annual Review of Critical Essays and Reviews*, vol. 10 (Greenwich, CT: JAI Press, 1988). The author is grateful to Rabindra N. Kanungo for his insights and help in conceptualizing the empowerment process.

6 See Conger and Kanungo, footnote 5.

7 A. Bandura, 'Self-Efficiency: Toward a Unifying Theory of Behavioral Change,' *Psychological Review* 84(2) (1977), pp. 191–215.

8 D. McGregor, *The Human Side of Enterprise* (New York: McGraw-Hill, 1960).

9 See J. M. Beyer and H. M. Trice, 'How an Organization's Rites Reveal Its Culture,' *Organizational Dynamics*, Spring 1989, pp. 4–25.

10 A. Bundura, *Social Foundations of Thought and Action: A Social Cognitive View* (Englewood Cliffs, NJ: Prentice Hall, 1986).

11 See Kanter, footnote 3, p. 66.

12 See Bandura, footnote 10, p. 400.

13 W. Bennis and B. Nanus, *Leaders* (New York: Harper & Row, 1985), pp. 64–65.

14 See Bundura, footnote 10.

15 See Kanter, footnote 3.

16 See J. R. Hackman, 'The Design of Work in the 1980's', *Organizational Dynamics*, Summer 1978, pp. 3–17.

17 M. Beer, *Organizational Change and Development* (Santa Monica, CA: Goodyear, 1980), p. 64.

18 See Bandura, footnote 10.

19 F. M. Rothbaum, J. R. Weisz, and S. S. Snyder, 'Changing the World and Changing Self: A Two Process Model of Perceived Control,' *Journal of Personality and Social Psychology* 42 (1982), pp. 5–37; and L. Y. Abramson, J. Garber, and M. E. P. Seligman, 'Learned Helplessness in Humans: An Attributional Analysis', in J. Garber and M. E. P. Seligman, eds., *Human Helplessness: Theory and Applications* (New York: Academic Press, 1980), pp. 3–34.

20 See Kanter, footnote 2.

21 See Block, footnote 2.

22 See Conger and Kanungo, footnote 5.

23 Bennis and Nanus, footnote 13, p. 93.

24 See Kanter, footnote 3, p. 73.

25 L. W. Porter, E. E. Lawler, and J. R. Hackman, *Behavior in Organizations* (New York: McGraw-Hill, 1975), p. 306.

26 See N. M. Tichy and M. A. Devanna, *The Transformational Leader* (New York: John Wiley, 1986).

EXERCISE 10 HOW POLITICAL ARE YOU?

Source: DuBrin, A. J. (1990). *Winning Office Politics.* Englewood Cliffs, NJ: Prentice Hall, pp. 19–27. Used by permission of the publisher, Prentice Hall/A. Simon & Schuster Company, Englewood Cliffs, NJ.

Mark each of the following statements either mostly true or mostly false. In some instances, 'mostly true' refers to 'mostly agree', and 'mostly false' refers to 'mostly disagree'. We are looking for general tendencies, so don't be concerned if you are uncertain as to the more accurate response to a given statement.

	Mostly true	Mostly false
1. I would stay late in the office just to impress my boss.	_____	_____
2. Why teach your subordinates everything you know about your job? One of them could then replace you.	_____	_____
3. I have no interest in using gossip to personal advantage.	_____	_____
4. Be extra careful about ever making a critical comment about your firm, even if it is justified.	_____	_____
5. I would go out of my way to cultivate friendships with powerful people.	_____	_____
6. I would never raise questions about the capabilities of my competition. Let his or her record speak for itself.	_____	_____
7. I am unwilling to take credit for someone else's work.	_____	_____
8. If I discovered that a co-worker was looking for a job, I would inform my boss.	_____	_____
9. Even if I made only a minor contribution to an important project, I would get my name listed as being associated with that project.	_____	_____
10. There is nothing wrong with tooting your own horn.	_____	_____
11. My office should be cluttered with personal mementos, such as pencil holders and decorations, made by my friends and family.	_____	_____

12. One should take action only when one is sure that it is ethically correct.

_____ _____

13. Only a fool would publicly correct mistakes made by the boss.

_____ _____

14. I would purchase stock in my company even though it might not be a good financial investment.

_____ _____

15. Even if I thought it would help my career, I would refuse a hatchetman assignment.

_____ _____

16. It is better to be feared than loved by your subordinates.

_____ _____

17. If others in the office were poking fun at the boss, I would decline to join in.

_____ _____

18. In order to get ahead, it is necessary to keep self-interest above the interests of the organisation.

_____ _____

19. I would be careful not to hire a subordinate who might outshine me.

_____ _____

20. A wise strategy is to keep on good terms with everybody in your office even if you don't like everyone.

_____ _____

CASE 10 MISSOURI CAMPUS BITTERLY DIVIDED OVER HOW TO REALLOCATE FUNDS

Source: Written by Paul Desruisseaux. Reprinted with permission of *The Chronicle of Higher Education*, copyright © 1982.

On the campus of the University of Missouri, the signs of spring came late and were decidedly makeshift: a white sheet bearing the spray-painted legend 'SOCIAL WORK IS HERE TO STAY' draped from windows in Clark Hall; a crudely lettered placard taped to a glass door in Memorial Union defiantly announcing, 'HELL NO, HOME EC WON'T GO!'

Hasty construction accounted for the homemade quality of the signs, for as the academic year drew quickly to a close, many students and faculty members were surprised to find themselves fighting for their academic lives — the survival of their programs.

In a year in which this campus has had to contend with a host of financial problems — some fabricated, critics allege — April was the cruellest month. It was on 2 April that proposals to 'reallocate' nearly US$12 million in operating funds over the next three years were announced. Among them were recommendations to eliminate two of the university's fourteen colleges and to reduce substantially the offerings in five others.

The ensuing controversy divided the campus. 'It has set department against department and colleague against colleague,' says one dean. 'It's civil war, with everyone trying to gore everyone else's bull.'

In mid-April, the faculty voted to call for the resignation of Chancellor Barbara S. Uehling if she did not withdraw the proposals.

By the time graduating students were preparing for last week's commencement exercises, the subject of their conversations — whether or not they had jobs — also seemed to be a prime topic of talk among many members of the faculty and staff.

What led to this course of events was a decision last summer by President James C. Olson to take action 'to preserve and even enhance the quality of the university in a time of severely limited resources'.

'The university has coped with 10 years of inadequate funding by making cuts across the board,' he says. 'It became clear that a continuation of that policy was a prescription for mediocrity.'

Mr Olson announced last July that the university would attempt to save approximately US$15 million over the next 3 years to finance pay raises as well as library, laboratory and other improvements. He told the chancellors of the four Missouri campuses that their first priority was to be the development of an adequate compensation plan for the university staff. His plan was supported by the university's Board of Curators.

President Olson's goal is to bring salaries at the university up to the average of those at member institutions of the Big 8 and Big 10 athletic conferences — institutions that, he says, 'are comparable to Missouri in mission.' At the start of the 1981–82 academic year, Missouri had the lowest salary average in that comparison group, 8.9% below the midpoint.

Mr Olson instructed the chancellors to find money for salary adjustments 'by reducing the quantity of what you do rather than the quality'.

That met with approval on the Columbia campus, where Chancellor Uehling has said 'the concept of shared poverty is not viable for a competitive university,' and where the faculty has been on the record for 5 years in opposition to across-the-board budget cuts. The 24 000-student campus, biggest in the system, is scheduled for the largest reductions: as much as US$12 million, or about 5% of its operating budget.

The curators adopted procedures for the 'discontinuance' of programs, and the university established four criteria for reviewing them: overall quality, contribution to the university's mission, need for the program and financial considerations. Application of the criteria was left up to the individual campuses.

'On two occasions I identified to the deans the ways in which we might go about this task,' says Provost Ronald F. Bunn, who is faced with reducing the budget for academic programs by US$7 million.

'A quality matrix'

According to Mr Bunn, most of the deans suggested that he take on the task. The Faculty Council recommended the same. 'This was an administrative job,' says David West, the council chairman and a professor of finance. 'We wanted the administration to make its proposals, and then we'd take shots at it.'

Mr Bunn reviewed all of the campus's academic programs himself, rating them according to the four criteria established by the president. He compiled what he calls 'a quality matrix', which resembles the box score of a baseball game. The programs that ranked lowest he proposed reducing.

Specifically, the provost recommended the elimination of the School of Library and Informational Science and the College of Public and Community Services (with the possible retention of its masters-in-social-work program). He also recommended major reductions in the College of Education, the College of Engineering, the School of Nursing, the College of Home Economics, and the School of Health Related Professions. In some cases, the reductions would mean the elimination of one or more departments within those colleges.

All told, campus officials estimated that the cuts in academic programs would affect 2500 students and as many as 200 faculty and staff members. Since tenure regulations require the university to give tenured faculty members 13 months' notice of plans to eliminate their jobs, the reduction proposals would have little effect on the 1982–83 budget.

When university administrators announced their plans on 2 April, those in the academic programs predictably provoked the greatest response.

'It infuriates me'

An ad hoc committee of faculty members and students was charged with reviewing the provost's recommendations and conducting hearings.

Individuals in the targeted programs have been outspokenly critical of Provost Bunn's judgement.

'We are the only accredited library-science program in Missouri, and it infuriates me — as a citizen as much as anything — that the campus, unilaterally, has made the decision to eliminate programs that exist nowhere else in the state,' says Edward P. Miller, dean of the library school. 'I don't think the provost could have done a worse job of abrogating the criteria for review if he tried.'

Bob G. Woods, dean of the College of Education, who supported the idea of programmatic cuts, says he was prepared to reduce his budget by as much as US $500 000, but when he learned that reductions of $1.2 million were required, he changed his mind. 'I want the process to be refuted as unnecessary at this time,' he says.

Officials in the College of Home Economics charge that the recommendations to eliminate two departments there were based on outdated information. 'The decision regarding my program was based on a 3-year-old internal-review document,' says Kitty G. Dickerson, chairman of the department of clothing and textiles, who is in her first year at Missouri. 'I was brought here to strengthen this department. There were thirty-five recommendations in that internal review, and we have already addressed all but three. But there was never an opportunity to let it be known that we have made this enormous progress.'

Martha Jo Martin, assistant dean of home economics, says that eliminating the two departments would cost the college its accreditation and half of its enrolment.

Opposition was not limited to those in programs proposed for reduction. Says Andrew Twaddle, a professor of sociology, 'My main concern is not with the actual targeting of programs but the fact that the administration made these decisions with little input from the faculty, except for a select group of its supporters.'

'I honestly don't know what the university's real fiscal situation is — there are so many conflicting figures flying around, and no one is backing them up very well,' he adds. 'But according to the bylaws of this campus, the faculty is supposed to make academic policy, and when you're talking about what is or is not to be taught at the university, you're talking about policy.'

Others are concerned about the impact of the proposals on women and minorities.

'We are assuming that the university is aware of its commitment to affirmative action,' says W. L. Moore, an assistant professor of education and chairman of the Black Faculty and Staff Organisation. 'But we have not been kept informed, and we are very sceptical of all that is being done in this area.'

Mr Moore says his organisation has determined that the proposed cuts would affect 63% of the black faculty members. The university's Office of Equal Opportunity says the figure is 33%. This discrepancy is due to the administration's inclusion of nonteaching blacks in its figures, says Mr Moore. 'But the precise number doesn't matter, because even 33% is too high a price to pay,' he adds.

Of the campus's 620 black undergraduates, 255 are enrolled in targeted programs, say H. Richard Dozier, coordinator of minority-student services. 'Blacks weren't admitted to this institution until 1950, and they make up only 3.7% of the student body,' he says. 'These cuts would be regressive.'

Blacks on the campus have asked the administration for assurances that the university's 5-year affirmative-action goals will be met.

There is also some feeling on the campus that faculty salary raises are being used as, in the words of one dean, 'a smokescreen' for an attempt to change the institution from a multipurpose university to a research university. One reduction target, home economics, is, according to officials of that college, one of only two areas of study identified in federal farm-bill legislation as being part of the educational responsibility of a land-grant institution.

While some opponents of the proposal were testifying before the review committee, others were mustering support for them. Students, faculty members and alumni mounted massive letter-writing and phone-calling campaigns aimed at state legislators and the university's curators. Rallies were held, petitions circulated and press conferences staged. The Missouri State Teachers Association expressed outrage. The State Senate's Education Committee held a hearing.

On 7 April, the Columbia campus's student senate passed a resolution denouncing the academic review.

On 19 April, the faculty voted 237 to 70 to call for the resignation of the chancellor and the provost if the reduction proposals were not withdrawn. The vote, however, has been criticised

— by, among others, Chancellor Uehling herself — for not being a true representation of the sentiments of the campus's 2038-member faculty. Last November, when the faculty voted against midyear salary increases if they were to come at the expense of campus jobs, more than 800 members cast ballots.

The 'point man'

The author of the resignation resolution, George V. Boyle, says he believes the vote was representative.

'We should not be cannibalising ourselves in order to give people raises,' says Mr Boyle, director of labour education, a program not affected by the provost's proposal. 'When you encounter heavy seas and the best plan the captain offers is to lighten the load by throwing crew members overboard, I think the crew has to try and come up with something better.'

'Our approach to these reductions,' says Provost Bunn, 'required that I become the "point man", and the discussion stage has subsequently become an adversarial one: The source of the recommendations — me — has become as much a subject of debate as the recommendations themselves. It has also become a highly political one, and I think it's unfortunate that the debate has been brought to the legislature and the curators before we have completed the review process on campus.'

Chancellor Uehling also came in for some personal criticism when the campus learned that she was among the final candidates for the chancellorship of the nineteen-campus California State University system. She took herself out of the running for that job last week and announced that she was committed to working for policies that would enable the Columbia campus 'not simply to survive but to carry into the future even greater strength than before.'

The chancellor says she is not surprised by the demonstrations of hostility. 'It's a very frightening and painful process,' she says. 'I can understand the anger on the part of some, but I still think our greater obligation is to the institution as a whole.'

Ms Uehling says that while she will not review or comment on the recommended proposals until they come to her in their final form, she supports the process and is convinced of its necessity.

'For the past 5 years, the State of Missouri has provided the university with budget increases that have amounted to only one-half the rate of inflation,' she says. 'When I came, the faculty was already on the record in opposition to across-the-board cuts to provide salary raises, and we must bring salaries up to attract and retain quality people. We have lost some good people.

'We have no hidden agenda. Our only agenda is our determination to take charge of our own fate. We are trying to anticipate the future so that we won't have to engage in crisis kind of planning. There are enough signs of an impending erosion of our quality to make us want to get ahead and start doing what we do smaller and better.'

There have also been signs that the state can't afford to support the university to any greater extent. Missouri voters in 1980 passed an amendment prohibiting the legislature from increasing appropriations unless there was corresponding growth in the state economy. In 1981, Missouri ranked 46th in state-tax revenue growth, one of the reasons the governor, on two occasions, withheld portions of the university's budget totalling 13%.

Nevertheless, some critics charge that salary increases — if they are essential now — could be provided for next year without eliminating programs, since there has been a slight increase in the state appropriation from what was originally expected, and a 17% hike in student fees.

'If you take a short-term view, it's possible to conclude that we could have an acceptable level of salary adjustment for the coming year,' says Mr Bunn. 'That isn't the case if you're looking ahead. Some on campus feel that it isn't important for us to strengthen our salary structure, but in my judgement that is a very narrow view of the aspirations this campus should have for itself.'

To be sure, there is faculty support for the administration. 'I think the faculty who approved of this strategy previously ought to be heard from again,' says John Kuhlman, a professor of economics. 'I don't think we can afford to sit back and watch a few departments create the big fight with the provost.'

Adds Sam Brown, chairman of the psychology department, 'It would be difficult to find anyone to say they'd favour the cannibalisation of their colleagues' jobs for the sake of a salary raise. But ignoring the source of funds, I can say as a department chairman that one of the major problems I face is insufficient salary increments for faculty.'

Other improvements sought

According to Provost Bunn, when salary raises are given out, they will not be distributed uniformly but will be based on individual merit and the salary market in the particular field.

While salaries will have the highest claim on the 'reallocated' funds, the provost also hopes there will be enough money to strengthen equipment and expense budgets — 'to bring them back to at least the real-dollar level of 3 years ago.'

The provost said he would consider seriously the advice offered by the committee reviewing his proposals. What is not an option, in his view, is to back away from the US$7 million in savings that his proposals would provide.

When it reported to the provost 6 May, however, the review committee announced that it had voted to weaken the effect of all but one of the proposed reductions. Mr Bunn is expected to submit his final recommendation to the chancellor by the end of this week.

The Board of Curators, at meetings on 6 and 7 May, conducted lengthy discussions of the reallocation process underway at the Columbia campus. The result, William T. Doak, president of the board, told the press, was that the curators were so divided on the question that, had a vote been taken on the proposals, they would have been rejected.

'We are trying to plan for a very uncertain future,' says President Olson, 'and I'm not sure we've yet found the mechanism for doing that. We are seeking it.'

Chancellor Uehling is expected to submit her reallocation proposals to President Olson sometime in June. The curators are scheduled to vote on the proposals in July.

'The board's resistance to any program eliminations has certainly given those who favour such a course of action cause for pause,' says the Faculty Council's David West, who has supported the process from the outset. 'There has been much more visible and vocal opposition to the process in the past 4 weeks than there had been support for it up to that time.'

On the Columbia campus, faculty members were circulating petitions calling for votes of confidence and of no confidence in the administration. Mr West says he is advising those faculty members not to call for campus-wide votes at this time.

'There has already been too much confrontation, and faculty votes would just prolong it,' he says. 'I think everyone should try to gather additional information and rethink his position. And try to find some means by which all of this division can be mitigated.'

Case questions

1. How much and what type of power does the faculty possess at the University of Missouri?
2. What does Provost Bunn mean when he claims that he played the role as a 'point man' in this situation?
3. What type of politics is being played in this case? Give and explain examples.

LEADERSHIP

Learning objectives

- **Define** *the terms 'leadership' and 'self-leadership'.*

- **Discuss** *the accuracy of what is called the trait theory of leadership.*

- **Discuss** *the Vroom–Jago model and how it is used to study leadership.*

- **Describe** *the difference in the interpretation of what is referred to as transactional and transformational leadership.*

- **Explain** *the debate concerning whether charismatic qualities of leadership can be learned.*

- **Describe** *what role perceptions play in the attribution theory of leadership.*

- **Discuss** *strategic leadership.*

Chapter

In every group to which you have belonged — family, sports team, social club, study group or work unit — one person was more influential than the others and was probably called a leader. Leaders are important in a variety of organisational settings. Indeed, organisations would be less efficient without leaders and, in extreme cases, they would be unable to accomplish purposeful goals. For these and similar reasons, leadership has been the centre of attention of theorists, researchers and practitioners.

Although leadership is important and has been studied by behavioural scientists for decades, it is still somewhat of a mystery.[1] Even after thousands of studies, there is still a lack of consensus among the experts on exactly what leadership is and how it should be analysed. This chapter examines leadership in organisational settings. Several somewhat distinct perspectives of leadership are presented. Each is explored theoretically and empirically, and from the stand-point of its application value. This type of exploration suggests that leadership is not the same as management; leadership is a complex concept; leadership attributes can be developed through experience, training and analysis; leadership effectiveness depends primarily on the fit between the leader, followers and situations; and leadership is substituted for in various settings and situations — that is, in some situations leadership is not a significant influence.[2]

Leadership is a narrower concept than management. A manager in a formal organisation is responsible for, and entrusted with, such functions as planning, organising and controlling. However, leaders in informal groups are not always formal managers performing managerial functions required by the organisation. Consequently, leaders may or may not be managers.

A distinction between leaders and managers was spelled out by Abraham Zaleznik,[3] a professor at Harvard Business School. He stated that leaders tolerate chaos and lack of structure and are thus prepared to keep answers in suspense. Managers seek order and control and are almost addicted to disposing of problems even before they understand their significance. In a concise way, Zaleznik depicts leaders as having more in common with artists, scientists and other creative thinkers, than they do with managers.[4]

In the formal organisation, roles often have specific responsibilities associated with them. For example, the first-line supervisory role may be one in which the role occupant is responsible for the level and quality of production generated by a particular group of employees. Exactly how the supervisor fulfils this responsibility involves personal style. Some first-line supervisors rely on the *authority* of the position to secure compliance with performance standards; others use a more *participative* approach that involves joint decision making on the part of the leader (manager) and followers (subordinates). What is effective for one leader may not be effective for another. This is, in essence, the crux of the leadership issue: what constitutes effective leadership?

LEADERSHIP DEFINED

With so much interest in leadership, it might be assumed that everyone is in general agreement about what constitutes leadership. Unfortunately, this is not the case. There are numerous interpretations and definitions of leadership. There are definitions that describe leadership as personality, influence, behaviour, power, goal achievement, attribution or relationship development. Each of these definitions offers some insight into how various views conflict, are similar or have no relationship to each other.

Reading 11
Leading learning

A good definition of leadership needs to be broad enough to accommodate different theories, research findings and pragmatic applications.[5] Also, a good definition needs to be specific enough to distinguish leadership from other organisational practices such as the application of rewards, team morale and job design. Thus, we propose that **leadership** is influence in an organisational setting or situation, the effects of which are meaningful and have a distinct impact on, and facilitate the achievement of, challenging organisationally relevant goals.

This definition suggests that a person (e.g. the leader) can influence the behaviour of others (e.g. subordinates, peers and superiors). The situation in which influence plays no role is outside the domain of leadership.

Pfeffer has argued that leadership cannot be distinguished from other forms of influence.[6] He suggests that leadership is redundant and unnecessary. For example, Pfeffer and Salancek propose that changing mayors had little or no effect on the functioning of city government, the implication being that a change in leadership was meaningless.[7] The conclusion may say more about how bureaucracies in city governments blunt any efforts of elected mayors than it does about the irrelevance of leadership.

Certainly, in some situations influence is more important than in other situations.[8] However, in situations in which influence can make a difference to performance or goal achievement, leadership is operating within an organisational setting. Note that our definition emphasises that leadership takes place within an organisation. The organisation contains people, processes and structures upon which influence can be exerted.

A major purpose of exerting leadership influence is to achieve relevant goals. Leaders attempt to influence individuals and groups to achieve important goals. Influencing the behaviour of others to achieve goals outside the organisation is not considered to be leadership.

The attempts to influence leadership can be based on many different factors including personality, behaviour or power. The definition we propose is broad enough to accommodate these and other forms of influence. It is also important to note that our definition indicates that any individual, in any position, at any level of the organisation can exert goal-specific influence on others. The ability to influence does not emerge solely from a person's position in the organisation. In certain situations, non-managers, team members or subordinates in a group can function as influencers of behaviour or as leaders. Leaders can be found everywhere in organisations, and they make themselves stand out when, through the application of influence, relevant goals are achieved.

Is leadership important?

As Exhibit 11.1 suggests, a leader can make a difference in terms of relevant end-result factors: performance, goal attainment, and individual growth and development. However, the degree of difference and the process of using leadership to make a difference are somewhat ambiguous. Some theorists and researchers offer cautious advice about the impact of leadership.

Empirical evidence of the magnitude of the effects of leadership on performance is modest. A number of reasons have been cited for the observed modest effects of leaders on performance and other organisational outcomes.[9] First, those selected as leaders are similar in background, experience and qualifications. The similarity across selected individuals reduces the range of characteristics exhibited by leaders. The similarity of leaders can also produce a self-selection bias: leaders select individuals similar to themselves. Second, even leaders at the highest levels do not have unilateral control over resources. Major decisions require approval, review and suggested modification by others. Third, many factors cannot be controlled or modified by a leader. Labour markets, environmental factors and policies are often outside a leader's direct control. External factors may be overwhelming and uncontrollable, no matter how astute, insightful and influential a leader may be in a job situation.

Some research has specified only a modest effect of leadership on performance. One study of 167 in thirteen industries over a 20-year period has found that the administration factor (a combination of leadership and management) had a limited effect on sales, profits and profit margins.[10] Reanalysis of the same data showed that leadership accounted for more variance in the data than did many of the other variables.[11]

A report by Semler on Brazilian managers again raises doubts about the effect of leaders.[12] Semler believes that democracy, profit sharing and information are more important than a management hierarchy, a power base headed by a leader or the specialisation of work. Instead, employee involvement, salaries instead of wages, circles instead of management hierarchies, and job rotation make leaders almost unnecessary. Semler refers to the organisation of Brazil's largest marine and food-processing machinery manufacturer which manages to be profitable without managers.

Manz and Sims have clearly pointed out a new way of thinking that emphasises the replacement of 'bosses' with teams of employees who serve as their own bosses.[13] The concept has been labelled self-managing teams, empowerment teams and autonomous work groups. Manz and Sims have described 'superleaders', individuals who lead others to lead themselves to higher levels of performance.[14]

The teams described by Manz and Sims may not have bosses, but they do have leaders. As the researchers state, 'No successful team is without leadership'. Team leaders sometimes emerge or are sometimes appointed. They can be called coordinator, facilitator or coach. They exert influence from a position of respect or expertise that is accepted by the other team members.

Bosses are being replaced with leaders or superleaders who exert the type of influence needed to accomplish goals. Using Sims and Manz's concept helps explain Semler's approach. Semler is replacing bosses with leaders, just as Sims and Manz suggest in their research and books.

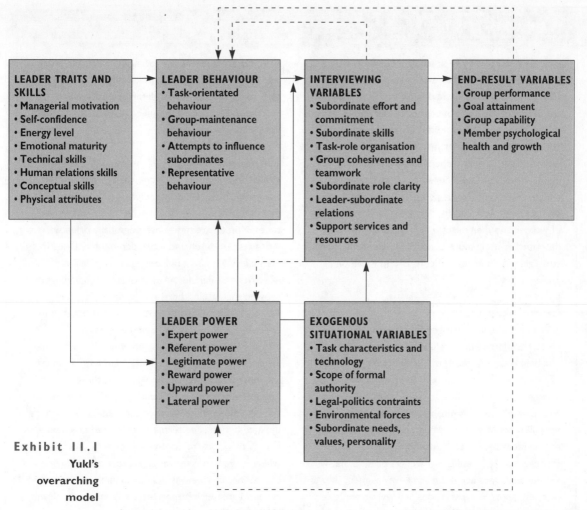

LEADER TRAITS AND SKILLS
- Managerial motivation
- Self-confidence
- Energy level
- Emotional maturity
- Technical skills
- Human relations skills
- Conceptual skills
- Physical attributes

LEADER BEHAVIOUR
- Task-orientated behaviour
- Group-maintenance behaviour
- Attempts to influence subordinates
- Representative behaviour

INTERVIEWING VARIABLES
- Subordinate effort and commitment
- Subordinate skills
- Task-role organisation
- Group cohesiveness and teamwork
- Subordinate role clarity
- Leader-subordinate relations
- Support services and resources

END-RESULT VARIABLES
- Group performance
- Goal attainment
- Group capability
- Member psychological health and growth

LEADER POWER
- Expert power
- Referent power
- Legitimate power
- Reward power
- Upward power
- Lateral power

EXOGENOUS SITUATIONAL VARIABLES
- Task characteristics and technology
- Scope of formal authority
- Legal-politics contraints
- Environmental forces
- Subordinate needs, values, personality

**Exhibit 11.1
Yukl's overarching model**

Source: Adapted from Yukl, G. A. (1981). *Leadership in Organizations.* Englewood Cliffs, NJ: Prentice-Hall, p. 270.

TRAIT THEORIES

The thinking and discussion of leadership has evolved over the years from a trait-based approach to the concept of teams without bosses. In order to examine the various views of leadership, it is necessary to trace some of the historical foundations of a number of approaches. Some of the foundations are considered today to be rather simplistic. On· the other hand, some of the foundations are so complex that practitioners find little value in what is offered.

Much of the early work on leadership focused on identifying the traits of effective leaders. This approach was based on the assumption that a finite number of individual traits of effective leaders could be found. Thus, most research was designed to identify intellectual, personality and physical traits of successful leaders. Our Management Encounter looks at how one such trait — gender — is linked to differences in leadership style and effectiveness.

Leadership styles and effectiveness: Does gender matter?

One of the most researched questions in the area of organisational power, politics and leadership is related to the impact of gender. In this Encounter, we will consider whether gender matters. Do men and women differ in their leadership style and, more importantly, do these differences affect how their effectiveness as leaders is perceived? To provide a starting point, let's consider how the leadership styles of women and men might differ: typically, women are described as using more cooperative and collaborative strategies, focusing less on control and more on problem solving.

Gender does matter

In favour of the idea that gender does matter, researchers argue that we display sex differences in our behaviour as a result of our upbringing and the expectations of our society. These pressures are so strong that, wherever we go, we act in a gender stereotyped way. This means that, in the workplace, we will encounter 'gender role spillover' — the expectation that we act consistently with gender stereotypes. As a result, researchers predict that when women managers act in the same way as men, they are breaking sex-role expectations and will be perceived as less effective.

Gender has no effect

On the other side of the fence, we might argue that organisations are strong situations (remember Chapter 3) that impose their own expectations on individuals. Managers are socialised into leadership roles and, as a result, organisational roles — rather than societal roles — will determine acceptable behaviour. Perceptions of effective leadership should not be affected by gender.

The research findings

Which argument do you think has more merit? After comparing many experiments, researchers have found that men and women do differ in their management styles: women are more interpersonally oriented, more task-oriented and more democratic. Does this matter? Will it affect our perceptions of leader effectiveness? Further analysis of research findings showed that, again, there are gender differences. Although, overall, women were rated as being more effective leaders, men were perceived as more effective in military settings and when they were line supervisors (rather than middle managers). Perhaps the most interesting finding was what these researchers call a *gender congeniality effect*: men were rated as more effective when the leadership role was defined in masculine terms and required task ability, as well as the ability to control and direct others, whereas women were rated as more effective when the leadership role was defined in feminine terms and required greater interpersonal skills and higher levels of cooperation.

Source: Eagly, A. H., Karau, S. J., & Makhijani, M. G. (1995). Gender and the effectiveness of leaders, *Psychological Bulletin*, 117, 125–145; Eagly, A. H., & Johnson, B. T. (1990). Gender and leadership style: A meta-analysis, *Psychological Bulletin*, 108, 233–256.

Intelligence

In a review of thirty-three studies, Stogdill found a general trend indicating that leaders were somewhat more intelligent than their followers.[15] One significant finding was that extreme intelligence differences between leaders and followers might be dysfunctional. For example, a leader with a relatively high IQ attempting to influence a group whose members have average IQs may be unable to understand why the members do not understand the problem. In addition, such a leader may have difficulty in communicating ideas and policies. Being too intelligent would be a problem in some situations.

Personality

Some research suggests that personality traits such as alertness, originality, personal integrity and self-confidence are associated with effective leadership.[16] Edwin Ghiselli reported several personality traits associated with leader effectiveness.[17] For example, he found that the ability to initiate action independently was related to the respondent's level in the organisation. The higher the person went in the organisation, the more important this trait became. Ghiselli also found that self-assurance was related to hierarchical position in the organisation. Finally, he found that people who exhibited individuality were the most effective leaders.

Physical traits

Studies of the relationship between effective leadership and physical characteristics such as age, height, weight and appearance provide contradictory results. Being taller and heavier than the average of a group is certainly not a requirement for achieving a leader position.[18] However, many organisations believe that a physically large person is required to secure compliance from followers. This notion relies heavily on the coercive or fear basis of power. On the other hand, Truman, Gandhi, Napoleon and Stalin are examples of individuals of small stature who rose to positions of leadership.

Do traits predict effectiveness?

Exhibit 11.2 summarises a number of the most researched traits of leaders. Some studies have reported that these traits contribute to leader success. However, leadership success is neither primarily nor completely a function of these or other traits.[19]

Although in some studies traits such as those in Exhibit 11.2 have differentiated effective from ineffective leaders, research findings are still contradictory for a number of possible reasons. First, the list of potentially important traits is endless. Every year, new traits are added to personality, physical characteristics and intelligence. This continual adding on results in

Exhibit 11.2 Traits associated with leadership effectiveness	Intelligence	Personality	Abilities
	Judgement	Adaptability	Ability to enlist cooperation
	Decisiveness	Alertness	Cooperativeness
	Knowledge	Creativity	Popularity and prestige
	Fluency of speech	Personal integrity	Sociability (interpersonal skills)
		Self-confidence	Social participation
		Emotional balance and control	Tact, diplomacy
		Independence (non-conformity)	

Source: Adapted from Bass, B. M. (1982) *Stogdill's Handbook of Leadership.* New York: Free Press, pp. 75–76.

more confusion among those interested in identifying leadership traits. Second, trait test scores are not consistently predictive of leader effectiveness. Leadership traits do not operate singly to influence followers, but act in combination. This interaction influences the leader–follower relationship. Third, patterns of effective behaviour depend largely on the situation: leadership behaviour that is effective in a bank may be ineffective in a laboratory. Finally, the trait approach fails to provide insight into what the effective leader does on the job. Observations are needed that describe the behaviour of effective and ineffective leaders.

Despite its shortcomings, the trait approach is not completely invalid. Kirkpatrick and Locke find evidence that effective leaders are different from other people.[20] Their interesting review of the literature suggests that drive, motivation, ambition, honesty, integrity and self-confidence are key leadership traits. Kirkpatrick and Locke believe that leaders do not have to be great intellects to succeed, but leaders do need to have the 'right stuff' or traits to have a good chance of being effective.

However, after years of speculation and research on leadership traits, we are not even close to identifying a specific set of such traits. Thus, the trait approach appears to be interesting but not very effective for identifying and predicting leadership potential.

PERSONAL-BEHAVIOURAL THEORIES

In the late 1940s researchers began to explore the notion that how a person acts determines that person's leadership effectiveness. Instead of searching for traits, these researchers examined behaviours and their impact on the performance and satisfaction of followers.

The University of Michigan studies: Job-centred and employee-centred leadership

**Exercise 11
Task and people
orientations**

In 1947 Rensis Likert began studying how best to manage the efforts of individuals to achieve desired performance and satisfaction objectives.[21] The purpose of most of the leadership research of the Likert-inspired team at the University of Michigan was to discover the principles and methods of effective leadership. The effectiveness criteria used in many of the studies included:

- productivity per work hour, or other similar measures of the organisation's ability to achieve its production goals;
- job satisfaction of members of the organisation;
- turnover, absenteeism and grievance rates;
- costs and scrap loss;
- employee and managerial motivation.

Studies were conducted in a wide variety of organisations: chemical, electronics, food, heavy machinery, insurance, petroleum, public utilities, hospitals, banks and government agencies. Data were obtained from thousands of employees doing different job tasks, ranging from unskilled work to highly skilled research and development work.

Through interviewing leaders and followers, the researchers identified two distinct styles of leadership, referred to as job-centred and employee-centred. The *job-centred leader* practises close supervision so that subordinates perform their tasks using specified procedures. This type of leader relies on coercion, reward and legitimate power to influence the behaviour and performance of followers. The concern of people is viewed as important but as a luxury that a leader cannot always afford.

The *employee-centred leader* believes in delegating decision making and aiding followers in satisfying their needs by creating a supportive work environment. The employee-centred leader is concerned with followers' personal advancement, growth and achievement. These actions are assumed to be conducive to the support of group formation and development.

The Michigan series of studies does not clearly show that one particular style of leadership is always the most effective. Moreover, it examines only two aspects of leadership — task and people behaviour.

The Ohio State studies: Initiating structure and consideration

Among the several large research programs on leadership that developed after World War II, one of the most significant was headed by Fleishman and his associates at Ohio State University. This program resulted in the development of a two-factor theory of leadership.[22] A series of studies isolated two leadership factors, referred to as initiating structure and consideration. **Initiating structure** involves behaviour in which the leader organises and defines the relationships in the group, tends to establish well-defined patterns and channels of communication, and spells out ways of getting the job done. The leader with a high initiating structure tendency focuses on goals and results. **Consideration** involves behaviour indicating friendship, mutual trust, respect, warmth and rapport between the leader and the followers. The leader with a high consideration overview supports open communication and participation.

The initial premise was that a high degree of initiating structure and a high degree of consideration was most desirable. Since the original research, there have been numerous studies of the relationship between these two leadership dimensions and various effectiveness criteria. Research at International Harvester found some more-complicated interactions of the two dimensions. Supervisors who score high on initiating structure not only had high proficiency ratings from superiors but also had more employee grievances. A high consideration score was related to low proficiency ratings and lower absences.[23]

The simplicity of the initiating structure and consideration view of leadership is appealing. However, most researchers believe that environmental variables play some role in leadership effectiveness. For example, when successful initiating structure behaviour is found, what other variables in the environment are at work? A worker who prefers to have a structured job and needs to have a job is likely to perform effectively under high initiating structure. What situational variables need to be considered? The Ohio State approach does not point out environmental factors.

The Michigan and Ohio State theories have provided practitioners with information on what behaviours leaders should possess. This knowledge has resulted in the establishment of training programs for individuals who perform leadership tasks. Each of the approaches is also associated with highly respected theorists, researchers or consultants, and each has been studied in different organisational settings. Yet the linkage between leadership and such important performance indicators as production, efficiency and satisfaction has not been conclusively resolved by either of the two personal-behavioural theories.[24]

SITUATIONAL THEORIES

The search for the 'best' set of traits or behaviours has failed to discover an effective leadership mix and style for all situations. Thus situational theories evolved that suggest leadership effectiveness depends on a fit between personality, task, power, attitudes and perceptions.[25] A number of situation-oriented leadership approaches have been publicised and researched. Two of the earlier ones are Fiedler's contingency model and House's path-goal theory.

Only after inconclusive and contradictory results evolved for much of the early trait and personal-behavioural research was the importance of the situation studied more closely by those interested in leadership. Eventually, researchers recognised that the leadership behaviour needed to enhance performance depends largely on the situation: what is effective leadership in one situation may be disorganised incompetence in another. The situational theme of leadership, while appealing, is certainly a challenging one to implement.[26] Its basic foundation suggests that a leader must be flexible enough to adapt to differences among subordinates and situations.

Deciding how to lead other individuals is difficult and requires an analysis of the leader, the situation and the group.[27] Managers who are aware of the forces they face are able to modify their styles to cope with changes in the work environment. Three factors that are of particular importance are forces within the managers, forces in the subordinates and forces in the situation.[28] Tannenbaum and Schmidt state the situational theme in this way:

> Thus, the successful manager of men [sic] can be primarily characterised neither as a strong leader nor as a permissive one. Rather, he is one who maintains a high batting average in accurately assessing the forces that determine what his most appropriate behaviour at any given time should be and in actually being able to behave accordingly.[29]

As the importance of situational factors and leadership forces became more recognised, leadership research became more systematic and contingency models of leadership behaviour began to appear. Each model has its advocates and each attempts to identify the leader behaviours most appropriate for a series of leadership situations. Also, each model attempts to identify the leader–situation behaviour patterns important for effective leadership.

The contingency leadership model

The contingency model of leadership effectiveness was developed by Fiedler[30] and postulates that the performance of groups is dependent on the interaction between leadership style and situational favourableness. Leadership style is

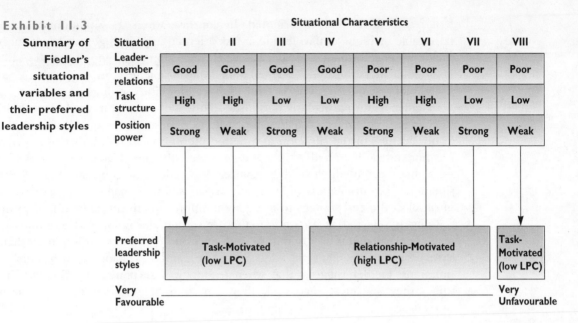

Exhibit 11.3

Summary of Fiedler's situational variables and their preferred leadership styles

Situation	I	II	III	IV	V	VI	VII	VIII
Leader-member relations	Good	Good	Good	Good	Poor	Poor	Poor	Poor
Task structure	High	High	Low	Low	High	High	Low	Low
Position power	Strong	Weak	Strong	Weak	Strong	Weak	Strong	Weak

Preferred leadership styles	Task-Motivated (low LPC)	Relationship-Motivated (high LPC)	Task-Motivated (low LPC)

Very Favourable ———————————————————————— Very Unfavourable

measured by the *Least-Preferred Co-Worker Scale* (LPC), an instrument developed by Fiedler, which assesses the degree of positive or negative feelings held by a person towards someone with whom he or she least prefers to work. Low scores on the LPC are thought to reflect a *task-oriented*, or controlling, structuring leadership style. High scores are associated with a *relationship-oriented*, or passive, considerate leadership style. Initial research, showing that leadership style alone failed to account for group performance resulted in the need to consider how the *situation* influences the relationship between leadership style and group performance.

Fiedler proposes three factors which determine how favourable the leadership environment is, or the degree of *situational favourableness*. **Leader-member relations** refers to the degree of confidence, trust and respect the followers have in their leader. This is the most important factor. **Task structure** is the second most important factor and refers to the extent to which the tasks the followers are engaged in are structured. That is, is it clearly specified and known what followers are supposed to do, how they are to do it, when and in what sequence it is to be done, and what decision options they have (high structure)? Or are these factors unclear, ambiguous and unspecifiable (low structure)? **Position power** is the final factor and refers to the power inherent in the leadership position. Generally, greater authority equals greater position power.

Together, these three factors determine how favourable the situation is for the leader. Good leader–member relations, high task structure and strong position power constitute the most favourable situation. Poor relations, low degree of structure and weak position power represent the least favourable situation. The varying degrees of favourableness and the corresponding appropriate leadership style are shown in Exhibit 11.3.

Fiedler contends that a permissive, more lenient (relationship-oriented) style is best when the situation is moderately favourable or moderately unfavourable. Thus, if a leader is moderately liked and possesses some power, and the job tasks for subordinates are somewhat vague, the leadership style needed to achieve the best results is relationship-oriented. In contrast, when the situation is highly favourable or highly unfavourable, a task-oriented approach generally produces the desired performance. Fiedler bases his conclusion regarding the relationship between leadership style and situational favourableness on more than two decades of research in business, educational and military settings.[31]

Fiedler is not particularly optimistic that leaders can be trained successfully to change their preferred leadership style. Consequently, he sees changing the favourableness of the situation as a better alternative. In doing this, a first step recommended by Fiedler is to determine whether leaders are task- or relationship-oriented. Next, the organisation needs to diagnose and classify the situational favourableness of its leadership positions. Finally, the organisation must select the best strategy to bring about improved effectiveness. If leadership training is selected as an option, then it should devote special attention to teaching participants how to modify their environments and their jobs to fit their styles of leadership. That is, leaders should be trained to change their leadership situations. Fiedler suggests that when leaders can recognise the situations in which they are most successful, they can then begin to modify their own situations.

A critique of Fiedler's model and cognitive resource theory

Fiedler's model and research have elicited pointed criticisms and concerns. First, Graen and associates present evidence that research support for the model is weak, especially if studies conducted by researchers not associated with Fiedler are examined.[32] Second, researchers have called attention to the questionable measurement of the LPC. These researchers claim that the reliability and validity of the LPC questionnaire are low.[33] Third, the meaning of the variables presented by Fiedler is not clear. For example, at what point does an unstructured task become a structured task? Who can define or display this point? Further criticisms are the following:[34]

- The model does not adequately explain the relationship between LPC scores and group performance.
- Although three dimensions of situational favourableness have been identified, the model treats them as one.
- Leader–member relationships may be an outcome of leadership style rather than a moderator in the style-performance relationship.
- Because the model focuses on high- and low-LPC leaders, it ignores its own prediction that moderate LPC leaders (who combine both styles) are expected to be more effective in most situations.

Finally, critics point out that Fiedler's theory can accommodate non-supportive results.

Despite supporters and detractors, Fiedler's contingency model has made significant contributions to the study and application of leadership principles. Fiedler called direct attention to the situational nature of leadership. His view of leadership stimulated numerous research studies and much-needed debate about the dynamics of leader behaviour. He pointed the way and made others uncomfortably aware of the complexities of the leadership process.

As a result of both these criticisms and limited empirical support, Fiedler and Garcia have substantially revised the original theory. *Cognitive resources theory*[35] proposes that the relationship between leadership style and group performance is influenced by two factors — leader intelligence and experience, or the leader's cognitive resources — and is also affected by the level of stress in the situation. Fiedler and Garcia suggest that the impact of directive (hard-nosed) leadership will be greatest when the leader is intelligent and subordinates are inexperienced: intelligent leaders form better plans and strategies and, if this is coupled with a directive style, are better able to communicate those plans to subordinates. When subordinates are inexperienced and their task is complex, an intelligent, directive leader elicits better performance. However, if the task is complex, the group experienced and more intelligent than the leader, performance will be enhanced if the leader behaves participatively.

Stress (which can include role conflict, insufficient resources and interpersonal conflict) can affect the relationship between leaders' cognitive resources and decision quality in two ways. First, the relationship between high intelligence and improved group performance is based on the assumption that intelligent leaders are able to process and integrate large amounts of information; as a result they can formulate better strategies. Stress interferes with their ability to process information. As a consequence, under stress, the quality of their decisions deteriorates. Conversely, experience can offset the effects of stress and improve decision quality. Leaders with a lot of experience are likely to have encountered similar problems in the past. This means that they will have some general procedures for dealing with particular problems (we will return to this idea in Chapter 12, when we look at decision making). When leaders have dealt with similar situations in the past, stress will have less impact on their ability to analyse information and form plans; consequently, experienced leaders will make better decisions under stress. This suggests that experience is able to offset information-processing problems; however, as we will see in Chapter 12 there are some difficulties with this style of decision making.

Cognitive resources theory is relatively new. There is limited research and it has proven difficult to test the relationships suggested by Fiedler and Garcia.[36] However, it raises some interesting ideas about the relationship between leader traits and behaviours, situational factors and group performance.

House's path-goal model

Like contingency leadership, the path-goal model attempts to predict leadership effectiveness in different situations. According to this model, leaders are effective because of their positive impact on followers' motivation, ability to perform and satisfaction. The theory is designated path-goal because it focuses on how the leader influences the followers' perceptions of work goals, self-development goals and paths to goal attainment.[37] The key features of this theory are summarised in Exhibit 11.4.

The foundation of path-goal theory is the **expectancy motivation theory** discussed in Chapter 4. Some early work on the path-goal theory asserts that leaders will be effective by making rewards available to subordinates and by making those rewards contingent on the subordinates' accomplishment of

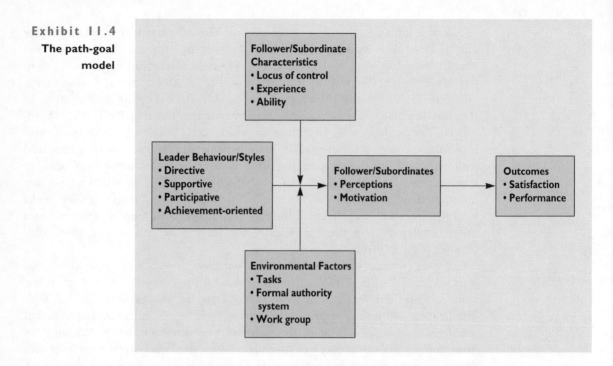

Exhibit 11.4

The path-goal model

specific goals.[38] It is argued by some that an important part of the leader's job is to clarify for subordinates the kind of behaviour most likely to result in goal accomplishment. This activity is referred to as *path clarification*.

The early path-goal work led to the development of a complex theory involving four specific styles of leader behaviour (directive, supportive, participative and achievement) and three types of subordinate attitudes (job satisfaction, acceptance of the leader and expectations about effort-performance-reward relationships).[39] The *directive leader* tends to let subordinates know what is expected of them by providing rules and procedures, as well as coordinating work. The *supportive leader* treats subordinates as equals and focuses on establishing a harmonious work environment. The *participative leader* consults with subordinates and uses their suggestions and ideas before reaching a decision. The *achievement-oriented leader* sets challenging goals, expects subordinates to perform at the highest level and continually seeks excellence in performance.[40]

Two types of situational or contingency variables are considered in the path-goal theory. These variables are the *personal characteristics of subordinates* and the *environmental pressures and demands* with which subordinates must cope in order to accomplish work goals and derive satisfaction.

An important personal characteristic is subordinates' perception of their own ability. The higher the degree of perceived ability relative to the task demands, the less likely the subordinate is to accept a directive leader style. This directive style of leadership would be viewed as unnecessarily close. In addition, it has been discovered that a person's **locus of control** also affects responses. Individuals who have an internal locus of control (they believe that rewards are contingent on their efforts) are generally more satisfied with a participative style, while individuals who have an external locus of control (they believe that rewards are beyond their personal control) are generally more satisfied with a directive style.[41]

The environmental variables include factors that are not within the control of the subordinate but are important to satisfaction or to the ability to perform effectively.[42] These include the tasks, the formal authority system of the organisation, and the work group. Any of these environmental factors can motivate or constrain the subordinate. The environmental forces may also serve as a reward for acceptable levels of performance. For example, the subordinate could be motivated by the work group and receive satisfaction from co-workers' acceptance for doing a job according to group norms.

Although path-goal theory identifies four styles of leadership, research has been limited to examining and developing our understanding of the first two: supportive and directive leadership. According to this model, *supportive leadership* is most effective when the situation is stressful, boring or dangerous. Under these conditions, supportive leaders are able to reduce stress, remove the more unpleasant aspects of the task and increase individuals' self-confidence. In expectancy theory terms, the valence (intrinsic reward) for doing the task is increased as are individual expectancies. The consequence is an increase in effort and satisfaction. By contrast, a *directive leadership* style is better able to reduce role ambiguity and is therefore expected to be effective when tasks are unstructured, there are no clear procedures or guidelines and staff are inexperienced. In expectancy theory terms, the removal of role ambiguity strengthens expectancy (effort-performance link) and consequently increases subordinate effort and satisfaction.[43]

A Critique of the path-goal model

The path-goal model warrants further study because some questions remain about its predictive power. One researcher suggested that subordinate performance might be the cause of changes in leader behaviour instead of, as predicted by the method, the other way around.[44] A review of the path-goal approach suggested that the model has resulted in the development of only a few hypotheses. These reviewers also point to the record of inconsistent research results associated with the model. Additionally, much of the research to date has involved only partial tests of the model.[45]

On the positive side, however, the path-goal model is an improvement over the trait and personal-behavioural theories. It attempts to indicate which factors affect the motivation to perform. In addition, the path-goal approach introduces both situational factors and individual differences when examining leader behaviour and outcomes such as satisfaction and performance. The path-goal approach makes an effort to explain why a particular style of leadership works best in a given situation. As more research accumulates, this type of explanation will have practical utility for those interested in the leadership process in work settings.

Hersey-Blanchard situational leadership theory

Managers often complain that esoteric theories do not help them do a better job on the production line, or in a research and development lab. They request something they can apply and use. Hersey and Blanchard developed a situational leadership theory that has appealed to many managers.[46] Large firms and small businesses have used situational leadership theory (SLT) and enthusiastically endorse its value.

SLT's emphasis is on followers and their level of maturity. The leader must properly judge or intuitively know followers' maturity level and then use a leadership style that fits the level. *Readiness* is defined as the ability and willingness of people (followers) to take responsibility for directing their own behaviour. It is important to consider two types of readiness: job and psychological. A person high in job readiness has the knowledge and the abilities to perform the job without the manager structuring or directing the work. A person high in psychological readiness has the self-motivation and desire to do high-quality work. Again, this person has little need for direct supervision.

Hersey and Blanchard used the Ohio State studies to further develop four leadership styles available to managers:

- *Telling.* The leader defines the roles needed to do the job and tells followers what, where, when and how to do the tasks.
- *Selling.* The leader provides followers with structured instructions but the leader is also supportive.
- *Participating.* The leader and followers share in decisions about how best to complete a high-quality job.
- *Delegating.* The leader provides little specific, close direction or personal support to followers.

By determining followers' readiness levels, a manager can choose from among the four leadership styles. Exhibit 11.5 presents the characteristics of the SLT.

Application of the model works as follows. Suppose that a manager determines that his recently hired followers are unsure of themselves and insecure about how to perform the job. The followers are at the R1 readiness state. By moving vertically from R1 to the leadership style development curve, the intersection of the vertical line would be at the telling style point. That is, an R1 follower requires a leader who is high on task orientation, gives direct instructions and is low on support behaviour. Task behaviour is more needed than supportive behaviour. In fact, research support is available to support the S1 style over any of the others.[47] Some may assume that a participative style (S3) is best. However, asking an insecure follower to participate may result in more insecurity about making a mistake or saying something that is considered dumb.

A follower will be more ready to take on more responsibility as other leadership styles become more effective. For example an R & D lab with expert, experienced scientists who are totally able and willing to do the job would flourish under a delegative (S4) style of leadership. Using the readiness indicator with the four-style model helps the manager conceptualise what is best for followers.

Although managers are attracted to the SLT, there are some serious unanswered questions. The most important may be, does it really work? Testing of the model, over 20 years after its inception, is still limited.[48] Even the originators, Hersey and Blanchard, have failed to provide evidence that predictions can be made and which style is best. Another issue revolves around the notion that a leader can change or adapt her style to fit a follower or group. Are people in leadership positions this flexible? Again, research is needed to validate the flexibility possibility among leaders.[49]

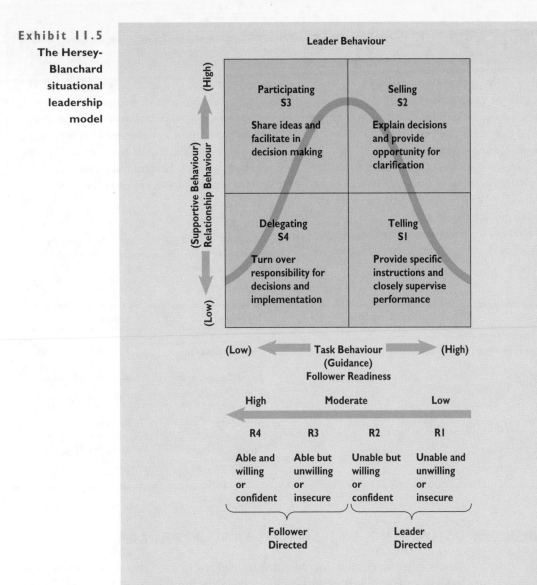

Exhibit 11.5
The Hersey-Blanchard situational leadership model

Source: Hersey, P., & Blanchard, K. H. (1988). *Management of Organizational Behavior: Utilizing Human Resources* (5th Ed.). Englewood Cliffs, NJ: Prentice-Hall, p. 171. The original model published in the first edition in 1969 used the label *maturity* instead of *readiness*.

Despite these words of caution about limited research and flexibility, many managers like SLT. It is thought to be practical, meaningful and useful in training settings. As leadership continues to command attention in organisations, the SLT appears to remain a popular way to express what leaders should be doing at work.

Leadership style and culture

Are leaders the same the world over? Do they show the same behaviours, no matter what country they are in? Or do their styles vary from culture to culture? To answer this question, researchers compared the preferred leadership styles of managers in Australia, United Kingdom, Taiwan and Japan. Their findings are summarised in the table below, which shows the top four styles in these countries.

As you can see, there were two strategies that were used by all managers: bargaining and appeals to higher authority. What power bases were they accessing? Why do you think these are the most popular forms of influence for managers?

You might also notice that, with the exception of Australian managers, the most preferred strategy was one that involved some form of assertiveness. Can you think of any cultural differences that explain why Australian managers prefer a different approach?

Source: Schmidt, S. M., & Yeh, R-S. (1992). The structure of leader influence: A cross-national comparison, *Journal of Cross-Cultural Psychology*, **23**, 251–264.

Australia	United Kingdom	Taiwan	Japan
Friendly reasoning	Bargaining	Applying sanctions	Assertive reasoning
Bargaining	Appeals to higher authority	Assertive reasoning	Appeals to higher authority
Applying sanctions	Forming coalitions	Bargaining	Bargaining
Appeals to higher authority	Assertiveness	Appeals to higher authority	Assertive logic

COMPARING THE SITUATIONAL APPROACHES

Three current models for examining leadership have been presented. These models have similarities and differences. They are similar in that they focus on the dynamics of leadership, have stimulated research on leadership, and remain controversial because of measurement problems, limited research testing or contradictory research results.

The themes of each model are summarised in Exhibit 11.6. Fiedler's model has been the most tested and is perhaps the most controversial. His view of leader behaviour centres on task- and relationship-oriented tendencies and how these tendencies interact with task and position power. The path-goal approach emphasises the instrumental actions of leaders and four styles for conducting these actions — directive, supportive, participative and achievement-oriented.

The situational variables discussed in each approach differ somewhat. There is also a different view of outcome criteria for assessing how successful the leader behaviour has been. Fiedler discusses leader effectiveness; the path-goal approach focuses on satisfaction and performance. SLT extends Fiedler's theory in two ways: by incorporating the concept of follower maturity, and by acknowledging the possibility that leaders can change their leadership style.

Exhibit 11.6 **Summary comparison of three important situational models of leadership**

	Fiedler's Contingency Model	House's Path-Goal Model	Hersey-Blanchard Situational Leadership Theory
Leadership qualities	Leaders are task- or relationship-oriented. The job should be engineered to fit the leader's style.	Leaders can increase followers' effectiveness by applying proper motivational techniques.	Leader must adapt style in terms of task behaviour and relationship behaviour on the basis of followers.
Assumptions about followers	Followers prefer different leadership styles, depending on task structure, leader-member relations and position power.	Followers have different needs that must be fulfilled with the help of a leader.	Followers' maturity (readiness) to take responsibility and ability influences the leadership style that is adopted.
Leader effectiveness	Effectiveness of the leader is determined by the interaction of environment and personality factors.	Effective leaders are those who clarify for followers the paths or behaviours that are best suited.	Effective leaders are able to adapt directing, coaching, supporting and delegating style to fit the followers' levels of maturity.
History of research: problems	If investigations not affiliated with Fiedler are used, the evidence is contradictory on the accuracy of the model.	Model has generated very little research interest in past two decades.	Not enough research is available to reach a definitive conclusion about the predictive power of the theory.

PERSONAL POWER AND LEADERSHIP

Situational approaches to leadership focus on the relationship between specific features of the environment and leader effectiveness. Theories such as the path-goal model emphasise the need for leaders to alter the situation in a way that makes goal attainment easier for individuals. Underlying these theories is the premise that a leader's authority (position power) provides the basis from which she or he can develop strategies for improving subordinate performance. We are now going to examine a somewhat different perspective on leadership: the ability to obtain commitment and effort from followers because of the personal power that individuals possess. Charismatic and transformational leadership styles both rely on a leader's ability to inspire a group of individuals into following a specific vision.

Charismatic leadership

Individuals such as John Kennedy, Winston Churchill, Ghandi and Martin Luther King possessed an attractiveness that enabled them to make a difference with citizens, employees or followers. Their leadership approach is referred to as charismatic leadership. Max Weber suggested that some leaders have a gift of exceptional qualities — a charisma — that enables them to motivate followers to achieve outstanding performance.[50] Such a charismatic leader is depicted as being able to play a vital role in creating change.

Defining charismatic leadership

Charisma is a Greek word meaning 'gift'. Powers that could not be clearly explained by logical means were called charismatic. Presently, no definitive answer has been given on what constitutes charismatic leadership behaviour. House suggests that charismatic leaders are those who have charismatic effects on their followers to an unusually high degree.[51]

Conger's model. Jay Conger proposed a model that illustrates how charisma evolves.[52] Exhibit 11.7 presents his four-stage model of charismatic leadership. In stage one the leader continuously assesses the environment, adapts and formulates a vision of what must be done. The leader's goals are established. It is important that this vision is demonstrably different from the status quo: leaders who propose only small, incremental changes may be effective leaders but will not be described as charismatic.[53] In stage two, the leader communicates his or her vision to followers, using whatever means are necessary. Accessing personal (referent and expert) power and using inspirational appeals are the most effective strategies for obtaining follower commitment at this stage. The stage three segment is highlighted by working on trust and commitment. Often, charismatic leaders use highly unconventional behaviours to achieve their vision. Doing the unexpected, taking risk, and being technically proficient are important in this stage. In stage four, the charismatic leader serves as a role

Exhibit 11.7
Stages in charismatic leadership

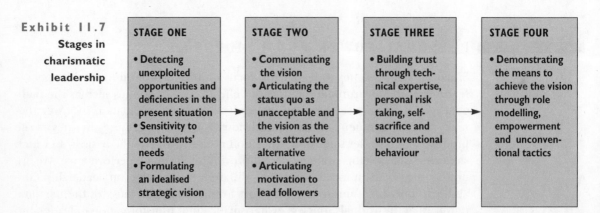

STAGE ONE	STAGE TWO	STAGE THREE	STAGE FOUR
• Detecting unexploited opportunities and deficiencies in the present situation • Sensitivity to constituents' needs • Formulating an idealised strategic vision	• Communicating the vision • Articulating the status quo as unacceptable and the vision as the most attractive alternative • Articulating motivation to lead followers	• Building trust through technical expertise, personal risk taking, self-sacrifice and unconventional behaviour	• Demonstrating the means to achieve the vision through role modelling, empowerment and unconventional tactics

Source: Adapted from Conger, J. A. & Kanungo, R. N. (1988). Behavioral dimensions of charismatic leadership. In J. A. Conger, R. N. Kanungo et al. (Eds.) *Charismatic Leadership*. San Francisco: Jossey-Bass, p. 27.

model and motivator. The charismatic leader uses praise and recognition to instil within followers the belief that they can achieve the vision. In general, two mechanisms seem critical for the success of charismatic leaders. The first is *personal identification*, or the follower's wish to adopt and follow the leader. The second is *internalisation*, or the adoption of the leader's values and ideals in such a way that they establish the norms for individual behaviour.[54]

What constitutes charismatic leadership behaviour? What behavioural dimensions distinguish charismatic leaders from noncharismatic leaders? A criticism of the early work on charismatic leadership is that the explanations of it lacked specificity. Some limited attempts have been made to develop and test specific charismatic qualities such as vision, acts of heroism and the ability to inspire.[55] However, in most cases, clarifying what specifically constitutes charismatic behaviour has generally been ignored. A number of empirical studies have examined behaviour and attributes of charismatic leaders, such as articulation ability, affection for the leader, ability to inspire, dominating personality and need for influence.[56] However, no specific set of behaviours and attributes is universally accepted by theorists, researchers and practitioners. A descriptive behavioural framework that builds upon empirical work has been offered. The framework assumes that charisma must be viewed as an attribution made by followers within the work context.

Two types of charismatic leaders

In most discussions of charismatic leadership, the term 'vision' is highlighted. It is argued that the first requirement for exercising charismatic leadership is expressing a shared vision of what the future could be. Through communication ability, the visionary, charismatic leader links followers' needs and goals to job or organisational goals. Linking followers with the organisation's direction, mission and goals is easier if they are dissatisfied or not challenged by the current situation.

Crisis-based charismatic leaders have an impact when the system must handle a situation for which existing knowledge, resources and procedures are not adequate.[57] The crisis-produced charismatic leader communicates clearly and specifically what actions need to be taken and what will be the consequence of the action.

Crisis management is a growing field of study and inquiry.[58] The crises managers face enable charismatic leadership to emerge. First, under conditions of stress, ambiguity and chaos, followers give power to individuals who have the potential to correct the crisis situation. The leader is empowered to do what is necessary to correct the situation or solve the problem. In many cases, the leader is unconstrained and is allowed to use whatever he or she thinks is needed.[59]

A crisis also permits the leader to promote non-traditional actions by followers. The crisis-based charismatic leader has greater freedom to encourage followers to search for ways to correct the crisis. Some of the methods, procedures and tactics adopted by followers may be disorderly, chaotic and outside the normal boundary of actions. However, the charismatic leader in a crisis situation encourages, supports and usually receives action from followers.[60]

The consequences of charisma

Whether it is positive or negative, charisma can result in poor leadership. The very traits that make charismatic leaders influential also sometimes act to prevent them from behaving effectively. For both positive and negative charismatics, several problems may emerge:[61]

- The use of unconventional behaviours is just as likely to alienate, as to inspire, potential followers; charismatics therefore need to be aware of their potential for creating enemies, especially others who wield organisational influence.
- Because they are focused on long-term goals, charismatics tend to be poor day-to-day managers. As a consequence, when things are going well they ignore administration; and when things are going badly, they become over-controlling.
- Their self-confidence makes them less able to recognise flaws in their vision or the plans for attaining that vision. As a result they are likely to ignore warnings from their followers and may fail to see threats to their goals.
- As part of their impression management strategy, they are likely to take credit for success, failing to acknowledge the part played by followers. When we are dealing with negative charismatics, this extends to failures: negative charismatics are likely to refuse responsibility for failures and, as a consequence, will not learn from their mistakes.
- Charismatics also fail to properly plan for the future. As a consequence, a leadership crisis often follows their demise. This especially applies to negative charismatics, who do not empower their followers.
- Negative charismatics also experience difficulty in maintaining a harmonious working environment, reflecting the fact that their principal concern is with increasing their own power rather than with goal achievement.

Transformational leadership

Transformational leadership has two components. First, this leadership style requires that leaders recognise the needs of individuals, in terms of task and personal requirements. At this level, leaders engage in transactional behaviours: those aimed at helping followers attain their goals. Many leadership theories can be classified as transactional. The key features of such a style are described in the next section. However, in addition to this task focus, transformational leaders add an element of charisma. They differ in the types of visions that they have, their plans for achieving those visions and the power bases that they utilise. The Local Encounter summarises Australian and New Zealand research exploring transactional and transformational leadership.

Transactional behaviours

The exchange role of the leader has been referred to as transactional. The leader helps the follower identify what must be done to accomplish the desired results: better quality output, more sales or services, and reduced cost of production. In helping the follower identify what must be done, the leader takes into consideration the person's self-concept and esteem needs. The transactional approach uses the path-goal concepts as its framework.

LOCAL Encounter

Leadership downunder

The Australian perspective

Transformational leadership builds on transactional leadership and offers individuals not only goal attainment but also less tangible support such as intellectual stimulation and individual consideration. One question that we can ask is whether organisational factors affect the emergence of transformational behaviour, and the effect that such behaviour has on individuals and groups.

Research in New South Wales and Queensland provides us with some preliminary answers. We start by asking 'What factors encourage the use of transformational behaviours?' We might expect that when organisations have few formal rules and procedures and that when individuals are not formally bound to an organisation, there is not only greater scope for employing transformational strategies but also those strategies are critical for obtaining commitment. We might also expect this when work groups are cohesive and individuals better understand their roles and goals. Again under these conditions, transformational leadership behaviours become more important for performance than transactional leadership behaviours.

Is there any support for these ideas? Research suggests that there is. Transformational leadership behaviours are seen more frequently in non-profit organisations where a clear vision assists in recruiting volunteer staff. The use of a transformational leadership style is associated with a greater perception of influence in the decision-making process and better group dynamics (warmth, cooperation and friendliness). What is more, good group dynamics improve group performance and are associated with the use of fewer transactional behaviours.

One interesting finding was that the relationship between transformational leadership behaviours and group dynamics was stronger when individuals perceived their jobs to have low complexity.

The New Zealand perspective

Still on the theme of attributions, Ming Singer and her co-workers at the University of Christchurch examined the relative weight that supervisors and subordinates assign to situational and dispositional variables in explaining behaviour. In particular, they were interested in the degree to which subordinates and supervisors described supervisory behaviours in the same way. Contrary to their expectations, they found that dispositional factors were more important than situational factors, when it came to explaining effective supervisory behaviour: of these, cognitive resources was rated as most important for managerial effectiveness. One difference that emerged was in the value placed on intelligence and management by exception: this was rated more highly by subordinates than by managers themselves. Finally, and perhaps not surprisingly, managers rated themselves to display more charisma and more individualised consideration, and to give more intellectual stimulations and contingent rewards than did their subordinates.

Returning to the theme of organisational factors, Singer and Singer tested the idea that mechanistic organisational structures will support more transactional than transformational behaviours. Within the New Zealand police force, they found not only that staff preferred a transformational style, but also that managers were described as engaging in transformational leadership behaviours, especially individualised consideration. They also found that satisfaction with a leader was affected by leadership style: satisfaction increased as managers used more transformation leadership behaviours; and it decreased as the gap between preferred and actual leadership styles increased.

Source: Cheverton, G. L. (1995). Subordinate perceptions of transformational leadership: A contingency approach, Paper presented at the Inaugural Australasian Industrial-Organisational Conference, Sydney; Singer, M. S., & Beardsley, C. (1990). Attributions about effective leadership behavior and perceptions of actual leader behavior: A comparison between managers and subordinates, *Journal of Social Behavior and Personality,* **5,** 115–122; Singer, M. S., & Singer, A. (1987). Situational constraints on transformational versus transactional leadership behavior, subordinates' leadership preferences, and satisfaction, *Journal of Social Psychology,* **130,** 385–396; Weierter, S. J. M. (1995). Transformational leadership and transactional substitutes, Paper presented at the Inaugural Australasian Industrial-Organisational Conference, Sydney.

In using the transactional style, the leader relies on contingent reward and on management by exception. Research shows that when contingent reinforcement is used, followers exhibit an increase in performance and satisfaction:[62] Followers believe that accomplishing objectives will result in their recovering desired rewards. Using management by exception, the leader will not be involved unless objectives are not being accomplished. Management by exception can take one of two forms: active, in which the leader monitors subordinates and intervenes before a problem occurs to prevent the problem; and passive, in which the leader intervenes after a problem has been identified, to rectify the problem and sanction the subordinate.[63]

Transformational behaviours

An exciting new kind of leader, referred to as the transformational leader,[64] motivates followers to work for transcendental goals instead of short-term self-interest and for achievement and self-actualisation instead of security.[65] In transformational leadership, the employee's reward is internal. By expressing a vision, the transformational leader persuades followers to work hard to achieve the goals envisioned. The leader's vision provides the follower with motivation for hard work that is self-rewarding (internal).

Transactional leaders will adjust goals, direction and mission for practical reason. Transformational leaders, on the other hand, make major changes in the company's or unit's mission, way of doing business and human resource management in order to achieve their vision. The transformational leader will overhaul the entire philosophy, system and culture of an organisation.

The development of transformational leadership factors has evolved from research by Bass.[66] He identified five factors (first three apply to transformational and last two apply to transactional leadership) that describe transformational leaders. They are:

1. *Charisma.* The leader is able to instil a sense of value, respect and pride and to articulate a vision.
2. *Individualised attention.* The leader pays attention to followers' needs and assigns meaningful projects so that followers grow personally.
3. *Intellectual stimulation.* The leader helps followers rethink rational ways to examine a situation. Encourages followers to be creative.
4. *Contingent reward.* The leader informs followers about what must be done to receive the rewards they prefer.
5. *Management by exception.* The leader permits followers to work on the task and does not intervene unless goals are not being accomplished in a reasonable time and at a reasonable cost.

One of the most important characteristics of the transformational leader is charisma. However, charisma by itself is not enough for successful transformational leadership, as Bass clearly states:

> *The deep emotional attachment which characterises the relationship of the charismatic leader to followers may be present when transformational leadership occurs, but we can distinguish a class of charismatics who are not at all transformational in their influence. Celebrities may be identified as charismatic by*

a large segment of the public. Celebrities are held in awe and reverence by the masses who are developed by them. People will be emotionally aroused in the presence of celebrities and identify with them in their fantasy, but the celebrities may not be involved at all in any transformation of their public. On the other hand, with charisma, transformational leaders can play the role of teacher, mentor, coach, reformer or revolutionary. Charisma is a necessary ingredient of transformational leadership, but by itself it is not sufficient to account for the transformational process.[67]

In addition to charisma, transformational leaders need assessment skills, communication abilities and a sensitivity to others. They must be able to articulate their vision, and they must be sensitive to the skill deficiencies of followers.

LEADER ATTRIBUTIONS AND THEIR CONSEQUENCES

The theoretical, empirical and application work provided by the trait, personal behaviour, situational and person-centred approaches has advanced the understanding of leadership in work settings. However, several questions still remain. In this section, we will consider more closely how the attribution process affects leader behaviours. In Chapter 3, we discussed how the ways in which we explain individual behaviour affect our perceptions of those individuals. In this section, we will examine how the attributions that leaders make about their followers might affect leader behaviour.

The attribution theory of leadership

In our discussion of perception in Chapter 3 we introduced the concept of attributions. Attribution theory, we said, was concerned with the process by which individuals interpret events around them and attribute causes to these events. It was suggested that people's behaviour is influenced by the perceived, rather than the actual, causes of events. In short, attribution theory attempts to explain the 'why' of behaviour. Similarly, the emphasis of attribution leadership theory is on why some behaviour has occurred.

Since most causes of subordinate, or follower, behaviours are not directly observable, determining causes requires reliance on perception. In attribution theory, individuals are assumed to be rational and to be concerned about the causal linkages in their environments. The attributional approach to leadership starts with the position that the leader is essentially an information processor.[68] In other words, the leader is searching for information cues that explain why something is happening. From these cues, the leader attempts to construct causal explanations that guide his or her leadership behaviour. The process in simple terms appears to be follower behaviour → leader attributions → leader behaviour.

Leader's attributions

Kelley suggests that the leader's primary attributional task is to categorise the cause of follower, or subordinate, behaviour into one of three source dimensions: person, entity or context. That is, for any given behaviour, such as

Exhibit 11.8

An attributional leadership model

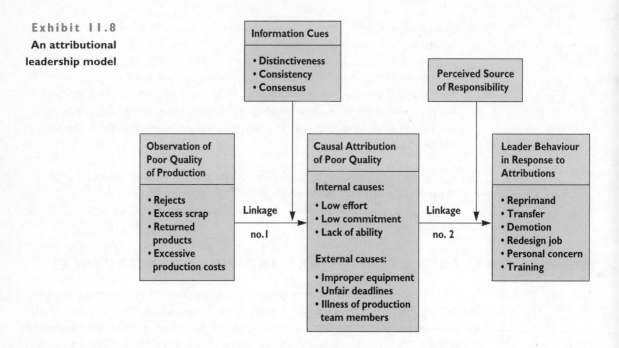

Source: Adapted from Mitchell, T. R. & Wood, R. E. (1979). An empirical test of an attributional model of leader's responses to poor performance. In R. C. Huseman (Ed.) *Academy of Management Proceedings,* p. 94.

poor quality of output, the leader's job is to determine whether the poor quality was caused by the person (inadequate ability), the task or some set of unique circumstances surrounding the event (context).

The leader seeks three types of information when forming attributions about the follower's behaviour: distinctiveness, consistency and consensus. For any behaviour, the leader first attempts to determine whether the behaviour is *distinctive* to the task — that is, whether the behaviour occurs on this task but not on others. Next, the leader is concerned about *consistency,* or how frequently the behaviour occurs. Finally the leader estimates *consensus,* the extent to which others behave in the same way. A behaviour unique to one follower has low consensus; if it is common to other followers, this reflects high consensus.

Leader's perception of responsibility

The judgement of responsibility moderates the leader's response to an attribution. Clearly, the more a behaviour is seen to be caused by some characteristic of the follower (i.e. an internal cause) and the more the follower is judged to be responsible for the behaviour, the more likely the leader is to take some action towards the follower. For example, an outcome (e.g. poor performance) may be attributed to factors outside the control of a person (such as not having the correct tools, or to internal causes (such as lack of effort).

Attributional leadership model

Attribution theory offers a framework for explaining leader behaviour more insightfully than either trait or personal-behaviour theories of leadership. This theory attempts to explain why behaviours are happening, and is able to offer predictions about a leader's response to a follower's behaviour. Attributions are more likely to be made when problems or failure occur.

Exhibit 11.8 presents an attributional leadership model that emphasises two important linkages. At the first linkage point, the leader attempts to make attributions about poor performance. These attributions are moderated by three types of information; distinctiveness, consistency and consensus. The second linkage point suggests that the leader's behaviour, or response, is determined by the attributions that she makes. This relationship between leader attributions and responses is moderated by the leader's perception of responsibility. Is the responsibility external or internal?

Factors affecting leader attributions

In addition to the fundamental attribution error, several other factors may influence leader explanations of their subordinate's performance. First, the quality of relationships between leaders and their followers affects the attribution process. When followers are judged to be similar, leaders are more likely to reverse the normal attributional processes: when leader–member exchange quality is high, leaders are more likely to attribute success to internal factors and failure to external factors.[69] In a sense, good leader–member relationships seem to override this fundamental attribution error. We will consider how such similarity judgements are made in the next section. The attributional process is also affected by leader expectations: when subordinate performance is consistent with leader expectations, leaders are more likely to explain performance in terms of internal causes.[70] Notwithstanding the attributions that leaders make, two further factors influence how they respond: perceived responsibility and subordinate explanations. Even when an internal attribution is made, leaders may perceive different levels of responsibility: while individuals may be held responsible for their personality, they are less likely to be held responsible for their lack of specific skills. As perceived responsibility increases, so does the likelihood that an individual will be either rewarded or punished. Finally, the individual may be able to alter consequences by offering an explanation that redirects attributions away from internal factors and towards situational factors.[71]

Research and attributional leadership

Currently, the research support for the attributional approach to leadership, while positive, is limited, and additional testing of the model is needed, particularly in applied organisational settings.[72] However, Neil Ashkanasy,[73] at Queensland University, has shown that we respond more positively to individuals on all of these dimensions when they have been successful in the past and on other tasks, and when they have succeeded where others have failed. But do we respond differently according to whether individuals succeed or fail? According to this research we do. When individuals are successful, we place greater weight on the role of ability and effort on their performance and, as a result, we hold higher expectations and aspirations; are less likely to supervise them closely; and more likely to give rewards. However, when individuals fail, our attention is drawn to the level of controllability and intentionality in their behaviour; we respond by holding lower expectations and aspirations, and we are more likely to supervise them closely and to give punishments.

Leader–Member Exchange approach

The attributional model of leadership identified leader–member relationships as influencing explanations that leaders offer about subordinate performance. While it is important for understanding explanations of behaviour, research suggests that the quality of leader–member relationships can alter subordinate performance. In this section, we will examine in more detail how good and bad leader–member relationships develop, and the implications of this relationship.

In the personal-behavioural explanation of leadership, it is assumed that a leader's behaviour is the same across all followers.[74] This thinking is similar to assuming that a parent treats or interacts with each of his three children in the same way. Graen, in Leader–Member Exchange Theory (LMX — earlier known as the vertical dyad linkage approach), proposes that there is no such thing as consistent leader behaviour across subordinates. A leader may be very considerate and relaxed towards one follower and very rigid and structured with another subordinate. Each relationship has a uniqueness, and it is the one-on-one relationships that determine the behaviours of subordinates.

The LMX approach suggests that leaders classify subordinates as *in-group* members and *out-group members* (a concept that we discussed in Chapter 8). The in-group members share a common bond and value system and interact with the leader. Out-group members have less in common with the leader and do not share much with him or her. The Leader-Member Exchange Questionnaire, partially presented in Exhibit 11.9, can be used to measure in-group versus out-group status.[75]

Exhibit 11.9
Items that assess leader–member exchange

1. How flexible do you believe your supervisor is about evolving change in *your* job?
   4 = Supervisor is enthused about change; 3 = Supervisor is lukewarm to change;
   2 = Supervisor sees little need to change; 1 = Supervisor sees no need for change.

2. Regardless of how much formal organisational authority your supervisor has built into his position, what are the chances that he would be personally inclined to use his power to help you solve problems in your work? 4 = He certainly would; 3= Probably would; 2 = Might or might not; 1 = No.

3. To what extent can *you* count on your supervisor to 'bail you out', at her expense, when *you* really need her? 4 = Certainly would; 3 = Probably; 2 = Might or might not; 1 = No.

4. How often do you take suggestions regarding your work to your supervisor?
   4 = Almost always; 3 = Usually; 2 = Seldom; 1 = Never.

5. How would *you* characterise *your* working relationship with your supervisor?
   4 = Extremely effective, 3 = Better than average; 2 = About average; 1 = Less than average.

The five items are summed for each participant, resulting in a possible range of scores from 5 to 20.

The LMX explanation suggests that in-group members are likely to receive more challenging assignments and more meaningful rewards. The performance consequences of being in the out-group are likely to be poor. An out-group member is not considered to be the type of person the leader prefers to work with, and this attitude is likely to become a self-fulfilling prophecy. The out-group members receive less challenging assignments, receive little positive reinforcement, become bored with the job and often quit.

The LMX approach rests on the assumption that the leader's perception of followers influences the leader's behaviour, which then influences the follower's behaviour. A clear developmental phase for LMX relationships has been established. In the first stage, *evaluation*, the leader and her or his followers assess each others' values, motives, attitudes and skills. Mutual role expectations develop. Members who form part of the out-group do not progress beyond this stage. In the second stage, *trust*, both parties recognise what can be gained from the other and the exchange process is refined. At this stage, the relationship moves to a base of mutual trust and loyalty; however, it is still governed by self-interest. In leadership terms, this stage is characterised by transactional leader behaviours. In the third and final stage, *commitment*, the base for the relationship moves to one of mutual commitment to a shared goal or vision. At this stage, leader behaviours correspond more closely to a transformational style.[76]

Research has shown several factors to be important in establishing high quality LMX relationships: personal liking, shared values, perceived similarity and the expectation of a positive relationship all contribute to high-quality LMX relationships.[77] Also, individuals with an internal locus of control establish higher quality LMX relationships than do individuals with an external locus of control.[78] Whether LMX relationships are positive or negative also affects a range of organisational outcomes. Subordinates express greater job satisfaction and satisfaction with their managers, perceive greater workplace equity and report higher levels of organisational commitment.[79] Reciprocally, in performance evaluations, managers give higher appraisals to in-group members, irrespective of their actual performance, and are also more likely to attribute in-group success and outgroup failure to internal factors (effort and ability — refer to Chapter 3).[80]

DO LEADERS MATTER?

Such questions and issues as the following are still being debated: Are leaders really needed? Are there substitutes for leadership that affect the performance of followers?

Are leaders necessary?

There are some academic researchers who propose that leadership has become irrelevant in organisations.[81] As we will see in the section on strategic management, there are many organisational and environmental factors that constrain the influence of chief executive officers (CEOs). Committees, boards and review panels all enter into decision making. Shareholders, consumers and government regulators all impose constraints on the CEO. The environment in which a company operates affects a leader's span of discretion. For example, a

CEO in the public utility industry must operate within the rules, policies and constraints imposed by a public utility board or commission. School superintendents have very little control over the enrolments in their district.[82] Birth rates and the district's economic status influence the school budget more than a superintendent's vision or wisdom.

The romance of leadership

Acknowledging these constraints raises questions about the impact of leadership on organisational performance. We see many examples of the belief that leaders are important in determining organisational performance, from changes in football coaches after a bad season to changes in CEOs following low profits. Even if leaders do not affect performance, we attribute considerable power to them. Meindl[83] suggests that individuals search for causal explanations of organisational performance and, although several factors may constrain performance, individuals find leadership the best explanation. He suggests that, at least in part, this is because it increases individual feelings of control over the environment. Summarising several experiments, Meindl points out that we are:

- most likely to attribute organisational performance to leaders when that performance is extreme (either very good or very bad);
- more likely to evaluate organisational performance positively when we can attribute the performance to leaders (rather than regulations, employees or market forces).

Considering how this perspective affects our ideas about leaders and organisations, it suggests that leaders have a powerful effect on the perception of organisational performance and consequently confidence in an organisation. This implies that leaders who are charismatic or transformational are likely to have a strong impact on public perceptions of the organisation. It also suggests that changes in leadership serve a ritual or symbolic function: whether or not leaders actually affect performance, changing leaders is an effective means for signalling an organisation's intent to change.

Substitutes for leadership

A wide variety of individual, task, environmental and organisational characteristics have been identified as factors that influence relationships between leader behaviour and follower satisfaction and performance. Some of these variables (e.g. follower expectations of leader behaviour) appear to influence which leadership style will enable the leader to motivate and direct followers. Other variables function, however, as substitutes for leadership. Substitute variables tend to negate the leader's ability either to increase or decrease follower satisfaction or performance.[84] Some people claim that substitutes for leadership are prominent in many organisational settings.

Exhibit 11.10, based on previously conducted research, provides substitutes for only two of the more popular leader behaviour styles: relationship-oriented and task-oriented. For each of these leader behaviour styles, Kerr and Jermier present which substitutes (characteristics of the subordinate, the task or the

	NEUTRALISES	
Characteristic	**Relationship-Oriented Leadership**	**Task-Oriented Leadership**
Of the subordinate:		
1. Ability, experience, training, knowledge		X
2. Need for independence	X	X
3. 'Professional' orientation	X	X
4. Indifference towards organisational rewards	X	X
Of the task:		
5. Unambiguous and routine		X
6. Methodologically invariant		X
7. Provides its own feedback concerning accomplishment		X
8. Intrinsically satisfying	X	
Of the organisation:		
9. Formalisation (explicit plans, goals and areas of responsibility)		X
10. Inflexibility (rigid, unbending rules and procedures)		X
11. Highly specified and active advisory and staff functions		X
12. Close-knit, cohesive work groups	X	X
13. Organisational rewards not within the leader's control	X	X
14. Spatial distance between superior and subordinates	X	X

Exhibit 11.10 Substitutes for leadership

Source: Adapted from Kerr, S., & Jermier, J. M. (1978). Substitutes for leadership: Their meaning and measurement, *Organizational Behavior and Human Performance*, December, p. 378.

organisation) will serve to neutralise the style.[85] For example, an experienced, well-trained and knowledgeable employee does not need a leader to structure the task (e.g. a task-oriented leader). Likewise, a job (task) that provides its own feedback does not need a task-oriented leader to inform the employee how he or she is doing. Also, an employee in a very cohesive group does not need a supportive, relationship-oriented leader. The group is a substitute for this type of leader.

Admittedly, we do not fully understand the leader–follower relationship in organisational settings. The need to continue searching for guidelines and principles is apparent. Such searching now seems to be centred on more careful analysis of a situational perspective of leadership and on issues such as the cause–effect question, the constraints on leader behaviour and substitutes for leadership. We feel that it is better to study leaders and substitutes for leaders than to use catchy descriptions to identify leaders. This type of study and analysis can result in the development of programs to train, prepare and develop employees for leadership roles.[86]

This chapter has presented the idea that a single, universally accepted theory of leadership is not available. Each of the perspectives covered in the chapter provides insight into leadership. The fact is that various traits of leaders (e.g. intelligence, personality) influence how they behave with followers. Also, situational variables and follower characteristics (e.g. needs, abilities, experience) affect a leader's behaviour. Therefore, trait, personal-behavioural and situational characteristics must be considered when attempting to understand leadership in organisational settings.

PARTICIPATIVE LEADERSHIP

Participative leadership describes a situation in which a leader involves at least one subordinate in a joint decision-making process; and the process does not require more than one subordinate to participate, it does not require that the leader and subordinate participate equally, and the issue of how the participation occurs (what is contributed by each party) is left open.[87] This flexibility in the definition of participative leadership is reflected in the styles of decision procedure that a leader may use: *autocratic* style, in which the leader makes the decision alone; *consultative* style, in which the leader asks subordinates for advice but ultimately makes the decision alone; *joint decisions,* in which leader and subordinates participate in reaching the final decision; and *delegation*, in which the leader passes decision-making responsibility to an individual or group.[88] Of these four styles, consultation and joint decision making fall into the category of participative decision making. Delegation does not because the assignation of decision making responsibilities is made not participatively but by the leader. The two styles of decision making also represent different management philosophies: in terms of Maslow's hierarchy, the aim of participative management is to satisfy individuals' social needs, whereas the aim of delegation (often implemented through job enrichment) is to satisfy growth needs.[89]

Participative leadership has several benefits for the organisation: it can increase morale and satisfaction, resulting in increased productivity and decreased absenteeism and turnover. We can consider several reasons for these outcomes:[90]

- Participative decision making (PDM) makes it easier for individuals to meet their needs.
- By improving organisational communication, it gives individuals a better understanding of specific decisions, and increases coordination and creativity.
- By adding information and developing decision-making skills, decision quality is improved.
- By increasing identification with organisational goals and group pressure, commitment and acceptance of decisions is increased.
- By increasing control over the decision-making environment, acceptance of change is increased.

Clearly, participative leadership offers managers and organisations several advantages. But is participative decision making always the best strategy? Or should managers select from a range of strategies, and use participative decision making only in limited circumstances? To answer these questions, we will consider a prescriptive model for decision making, developed by Vroom and Jago.

The Vroom–Jago model of leadership

Victor Vroom and Philip Yetton initially developed a leadership decision-making model that indicated the situations in which various degrees of participative decision making would be appropriate.[91] In contrast to Fiedler, Vroom and Yetton attempted to provide a normative model that a leader could use in making decisions. Their approach assumed that no single leadership style was appropriate. Unlike Fiedler, Vroom and Yetton assumed that leaders must be flexible enough to change their leadership styles to fit situations. In developing their model, Vroom and Yetton made these assumptions:

- The model should be of value to leaders or managers in determining which leadership styles they should use in various situations.
- No single leadership style is applicable to all situations.
- The main focus should be the problem to be solved and the situation in which the problem occurs.
- The leadership style used in one situation should not constrain the styles used in other situations.
- Several social processes influence the amount of participation by subordinates in problem solving.

After a number of years of research and application, the original model has been revised by Vroom and Arthur Jago in order to further improve its accuracy and predictability.[92] To understand the Vroom–Jago leadership model it is important to consider three elements that are critical components of the model: specification of the criteria by which decision effectiveness is judged, a framework for describing and categorising specific leader behaviours or styles, and key diagnostic variables that describe aspects of the leadership situation.

Critical components of the Vroom–Jago model

Decision effectiveness. Selection of the appropriate decision-making process involves considering two criteria of decision effectiveness: decision quality and subordinate commitment. *Decision quality* refers to the extent to which the decision impacts on job performance. For example, deciding whether to paint the stripes in the employee parking lot yellow or white requires low decision quality because it has little or no impact on job performance. On the other hand, a decision regarding at what level to set production goals requires high decision quality. *Subordinate commitment* refers to how important it is that subordinates be committed to or accept the decision in order that it may be successfully implemented. Deciding which colour paint to use in the parking lot does not really require employee commitment to be successfully implemented; just as clearly, setting production goals at a particular level does require

Exhibit 11.11

**Decision styles
for leadership:
Individuals and
groups**

Individual Level

AI. You solve the problem or make the decision yourself, using information available to you at that time.

AII. You obtain any necessary information from the subordinate and then decide on the solution to the problem yourself. You may or may not tell the subordinate what the problem is in getting the information from him. The role played by your subordinate in making the decision is clearly one of providing specific information that you request rather than generating or evaluating alternative solutions.

CI. You share the problem with the relevant subordinate, getting ideas and suggestions. Then *you* make the decision. This decision may or may not reflect your subordinate's influence.

GI. You share the problem with one of your subordinates, and together you analyse the problem and arrive at a mutually satisfactory solution in an atmosphere of free and open exchange of information and ideas. You both contribute to the resolution of the problem, with the relative contribution of each being dependent knowledge rather than formal authority.

DI. You delegate the problem to one of your subordinates, providing him or her with any relevant information that you possess but giving him or her responsibility for solving the problem alone. Any solution that the person reaches will receive your support.

Group Level

AI. You solve the problem or make the decision yourself, using information available to you at that time.

AII. You obtain any necessary information from the subordinates and then decide on the solution to the problem yourself. You may or may not tell the subordinates what the problem is in getting the information from them. The role played by your subordinates in making the decision is clearly one of providing specific information that you request rather than generating or evaluating solutions.

CI. You share the problem with the relevant subordinates individually, getting their ideas and suggestions without bringing them together as a group. Then *you* make the decision. This decision may or may not reflect your subordinates' influence.

CII. You share the problem with your subordinates in a group meeting. In this meeting you obtain their ideas and suggestions. Then *you* make the decision, which may or may not reflect your subordinates' influence.

GII. You share the problem with your subordinates as a group. Together you generate and evaluate alternatives and attempt to reach agreement (consensus) on a solution. Your role is much like that of chairperson, coordinating the discussion, keeping it focused on the problem, and making sure that the critical issues are discussed. You do not try to influence the group to adopt 'your' solution, and you are willing to accept and implement any solution that has the support of the entire group.

Exhibit 11.12
Rules of thumb underlying the Vroom–Jago model

Rules to improve decision quality:
1. Avoid the use of AI when:
   a. The leader lacks the necessary information.
2. Avoid the use of GII when:
   a. Subordinates do not share the organisational goals.
   b. Subordinates do not have the necessary information.
3. Avoid the use of AII and CI when:
   a. The leader lacks the necessary information.
   b. The problem is unstructured.
4. Move towards GII when:
   a. The leader lacks the necessary information.
   b. Subordinates share the organisational goals.
   c. There is conflict among subordinates over preferred solutions.

Rules to improve decision commitment:
1. Move towards GII when:
   a. Subordinates are not likely to become committed to the leader's decision.
   b. There is conflict among subordinates over preferred solutions.

Rules to reduce decision costs (time):
1. Move toward AI especially if:
   a. A severe time constraint exists.
   b. The problem is unstructured.
2. Avoid use of CII and GII if:
   a. Subordinates are geographically dispersed.
   b. There is conflict among subordinates over preferred solutions.

Source: Abridged from Vroom, V., & Jago, A. (1988). *The New Leadership.* Englewood Cliffs, N.J. Prentice-Hall. Copyright 1987 by V. Vroom and A. Jago. Used with permission of the authors.

commitment. In addition to quality and commitment considerations, decision effectiveness may be influenced by time considerations. A decision is not an effective one, regardless of quality and commitment, if it takes too long to make. Even a decision made relatively quickly, if it is a participative one involving a number of people, may be costly in terms of total time spent. Thus, a decision made at a meeting of fifteen department members and the department manager that takes 2 hours has used 32 work hours. In terms of overall organisational effectiveness, this may represent a larger opportunity cost than can be justified.

Decision styles. The Vroom–Jago model makes a distinction between two types of decision situations facing leaders: individual and group. *Individual decision* situations are those whose solutions affect only one of the leader's followers. Decision situations that affect several followers are classified as *group decisions.* Five different leadership decision styles that fit individual and group situations are available. These are defined in Exhibit 11.11. In the exhibit, A stands for autocratic, C for consultative, G for group and D for delegative. The Roman numerals indicate variants of the same process.

Diagnostic procedure. To determine the most appropriate decision-making style for a given situation, Vroom and Jago suggest that leaders perform a situational diagnosis. To accomplish this they have identified a series of questions that can be asked about the situation.[93]

Each of these questions may be thought of as representing a dichotomy. That is, they may be answered yes or no, or high or low. It is also possible, however, within the framework of the model for responses to fall between the dichotomised extremes. Answers of 'probably' and 'maybe' may reflect subtle differences among situations, particularly those which in some way may be ambiguous or unclear.

Application of the model

Actual application of the Vroom–Jago model can vary significantly in its degree of complexity, sophistication and specificity, depending on the particular purpose for which it is used and the needs of the decision maker. In its simplest form, application of the model can be expressed as a set of decision-making heuristics or rules of thumb. Exhibit 11.12 lists the seven rules of thumb (out of a total of eleven) that apply to the model as discussed here. In contrast, in its most complex form the model requires the use of mathematical formulas too complex to describe here. Using the manager's analysis of the situation represented by the manager's responses to the diagnostic questions, the formulas predict the most appropriate way of handling the situation, the second best way and so forth. The complexity of this approach, however, requires the use of a personal computer and specially developed software.

In between these two approaches is the use of decision trees. Such decision trees can represent the operation of the more complex equations in the model if certain simplifying assumptions are made. Exhibit 11.13 shows one of these trees. The first simplifying assumption is that each question, or problem attribute, can be given a clear yes or no (or high or low) response. The second simplifying assumption is that four of the twelve possible problem attributes are held constant. The decision tree depicted in this figure is what Vroom and Jago label a 'time-driven' decision tree. It is designed for the manager who places maximum weight on saving time. Other trees are available for managers who weight time (and other factors) differently. When the Vroom–Jago model is used in leadership training and development settings, it is not unusual for all three approaches to be used. The rules of thumb help convey the basic logic of the model, the decision trees provide a vehicle for representing various trade-offs among objectives, and the use of a computer efficiently allows for answering numerous 'what if' questions once the basic model itself is understood.

Validity of the model

As was the case with the original model in 1973, the revised model currently lacks complete empirical evidence establishing its validity. Certainly the model is thought to be consistent with what we now know about the benefits and costs of participation. Moreover, it represents a direct extension of the original 1973 model for which ample validation evidence does exist. Nonetheless, without extensive evidence that the use of the model can improve decision effectiveness and, by extension, leadership success, its value as a theoretical contribution and as a practical tool remains open to question.

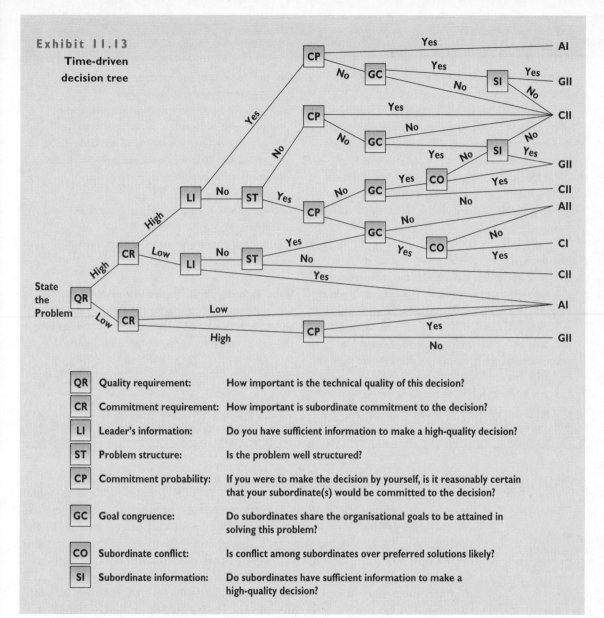

Exhibit 11.13
Time-driven decision tree

QR	Quality requirement:	How important is the technical quality of this decision?
CR	Commitment requirement:	How important is subordinate commitment to the decision?
LI	Leader's information:	Do you have sufficient information to make a high-quality decision?
ST	Problem structure:	Is the problem well structured?
CP	Commitment probability:	If you were to make the decision by yourself, is it reasonably certain that your subordinate(s) would be committed to the decision?
GC	Goal congruence:	Do subordinates share the organisational goals to be attained in solving this problem?
CO	Subordinate conflict:	Is conflict among subordinates over preferred solutions likely?
SI	Subordinate information:	Do subordinates have sufficient information to make a high-quality decision?

STRATEGIC LEADERSHIP

Case 11
The Council of Adult Education

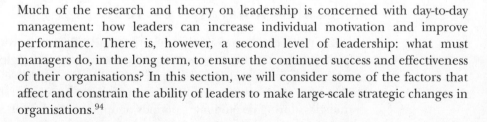

Much of the research and theory on leadership is concerned with day-to-day management: how leaders can increase individual motivation and improve performance. There is, however, a second level of leadership: what must managers do, in the long term, to ensure the continued success and effectiveness of their organisations? In this section, we will consider some of the factors that affect and constrain the ability of leaders to make large-scale strategic changes in organisations.[94]

ORGANISATIONAL Encounter

Banking on the brink

What does it take to turn around a failing organisation? This was the task that faced Don Mercer when he took over the Australia and New Zealand Banking Group Limited (ANZ). At the time that he assumed leadership, the bank faced a $578 million dollar loss; in just one year, Mercer had turned that around and earned a profit of $460 million. What were the problems facing Mercer? How did he handle them?

The problems

The ANZ's problems started with the 'lending binge' that followed deregulation. Banks were operating in a very different environment and were slow to adapt. Among the problems that they encountered for the first time were competition for market share, the sudden emergence of new banks and freedom from exchange rates. Adding to the ANZ's woes was the fact that its assets had been massively overvalued. Mercer's task was to develop a strategy that would turn the situation around.

Key components of the strategy

Key components of the strategy were:

1. creation of a task force to deal with problems of unproductive accounts;
2. philosophy of 'joint and several accountability' that separated the final decision about credit from the staff whose responsibility it was to generate business for the bank;
3. creation of a more conservative, less risk-oriented culture;
4. rebuilding community trust and confidence in banks.

What leader behaviours can you identify? Was Mercer a transactional or a transformational leader? Did he adopt a participative leadership style? And how do his strategies fit in with our ideas of strategic leadership?

Source: Stannard, B. (1992). Mercer's billion-dollar turnaround, *Australian Business Monthly*, April, 60–62.

Organisational performance

Because we assume that leaders are responsible for organisational performance, we also expect that whenever there is a change in corporate leadership, the performance of an organisation will also change. Research suggests that this occurs only when the new leader has skills that are substantially different from those of the old leader: if they are better, performance will improve; however, if they are worse, performance declines. Even if new leaders bring improved skills, situational forces are likely to constrain the leader's ability to make changes and alter organisational performance. Internal constraints such as powerful coalitions and external constraints such as products, markets and stakeholders all act to place constraints on what a leader may do.

Organisational life cycles

Punctuated equilibrium models of organisational change (discussed in more detail in Chapter 15) suggest that organisations go through long periods of stability that are punctuated by rapid upheavals. During stable periods, changes are minor and involve small-scale adjustments to organisational goals and strategies; during revolutionary periods of upheaval both goals and strategies are fundamentally reconceived. Consequently, a top manager's ability to make massive changes may be constrained by where an organisation is placed in this cycle: if it is in a stable period, organisational forces create strong resistance to change and top managers are unlikely to successfully alter organisational goals and strategies. Only if there is a major crisis are they likely to succeed in implementing such changes.

Changes over time

Top managers are most likely to implement changes early in their management period; the longer they are in power, the less likely it is that they will make new changes. Researchers suggest that this is the result of a developmental cycle. At the outset, new managers are concerned with establishing themselves in the organisation. At this stage, there is an expectation that changes will be made, although frequently such changes are localised (confined to a specific area, such as production or marketing). As the new manager acquires information, she or he is able to identify other changes that are required and to determine the impact of early changes. At this point the manager is also developing vision for the organisation and, within the first 2–3 years, the new manager acts to implement strategies that will attain this vision. As commitment to this vision (and its associated strategy increases), managers become progressively more inflexible and further strategic changes are unlikely.

IS LEADER BEHAVIOUR A CAUSE OR AN EFFECT?

We have implied that leader behaviour has an effect on the follower's performance and job satisfaction. There is, however, a sound basis from which one can argue that follower performance and satisfaction cause the leader to vary his or her leadership style. It has been argued that a person will develop positive attitudes toward objects that are instrumental to the satisfaction of his or her needs.[95] This argument can be extended to leader–follower relationships. For example, organisations reward leaders (managers) based on the performance of followers (subordinates). If this is the case, leaders might be expected to develop positive attitudes toward high-performing followers. Let us say that an employee, Joe, because of outstanding performance, enables his boss, Mary, to receive the supervisory excellence award — a bonus of $1000. The expectation then is that Mary would think highly of Joe and reward him with a better work schedule or job assignment. In this case, Joe's behaviour leads to Mary's being rewarded, and she in turn rewards Joe.

In a field study data were collected from first-line managers and from two of each manager's first-line supervisors. The purpose of this research was to assess the direction of causal influence in relationships between leader and follower variables. The results strongly suggested that leader consideration behaviour caused subordinate satisfaction and follower performance caused changes in the leader's emphasis on both consideration and the structuring of behaviour–performance relationships.[96]

The research available on the cause–effect issue is still quite limited. It is premature to conclude that all leader behaviour, or even a significant portion of such behaviour, is a response to follower behaviour. However, there is a need to examine the leader–follower relationship in terms of reciprocal causation. That is, leader behaviour causes follower behaviour and follower behaviour causes leader behaviour.

SUMMARY OF KEY POINTS

Define the terms 'leadership' and 'self-leadership'. Leadership is defined in many different ways. In concise terms, leadership is an attempt to influence the activities (work-related) of followers through the communication process and towards the attainment of some goal or goals. Self-leadership is the concept that individuals will lead themselves or will be self-initiators of acceptable workplace behaviour.

Discuss the accuracy of what is called the trait theory of leadership. Trait theory has for years attempted to identify, classify and apply the traits of effective leaders. Originally, it was assumed that a finite number of individual traits could be identified. This has not been the case. Thus, in terms of accuracy, the trait approach is somewhat questionable.

Discuss the Vroom–Jago model and how it is used to study leadership. The Vroom–Jago model extended a normative model that provides guidance to leaders in presenting appropriate styles to fit specific situations. The model suggests that the amount of subordinate participation depends on the leader's skill and knowledge, whether a quality decision is needed, the degree of structure of the problem, and whether acceptance by followers is needed to implement the decision.

Describe the difference in the interpretation of what is referred to as transactional and transformational leadership. Transformational leadership is considered a special case of transactional leadership. The transactional leader helps the follower identify what must be done to accomplish the desired results. He or she uses the path-goal concepts and approach. Transformational leaders express a vision and are able to persuade followers to work hard to accomplish the goals envisioned.

Explain the debate concerning whether charismatic qualities of leadership can be learned. Whether charismatic qualities can be learned is unknown. There are no specific scientific studies that clearly show that charisma can be acquired via training or executive development.

Describe what role perceptions play in the attribution theory of leadership. Perception plays a major role in the attribution leadership theory. How the leader interprets cues such as worker performance (output or quantity) influences how the leader will respond towards the worker. Interpretation involves the leader's perception.

Discuss strategic leadership. Strategic leadership is concerned with how senior executives manage organisations, rather than with the day-to-day management and motivation of staff. Research in this area has focused on factors that constrain leader behaviour, such as organisational life cycles, stakeholders and markets, as well as how leader behaviours and strategic goals change over time.

REVIEW AND DISCUSSION QUESTIONS

1. Over time the various theories proposed to explain leadership have become increasingly complex. Why has this happened?
2. What are the major differences between attributional and personal-behavioural explanations of leader behaviour?
3. Do organisations do a good job in selecting people for leadership positions? Are there ways in which they could do a better job?
4. Organisations annually spend a great deal of money on leadership training. Is this a wise investment? Are there other, less costly ways of improving leadership?
5. Are leaders really necessary? Does the superleadership concept suggest that leaders are not needed?
6. Realistically, how much control does a leader have over situational favourableness? How might a leader go about trying to improve favourableness?
7. What type of research is needed to validate and further develop the Vroom–Jago model?
8. What charismatic qualities would be important to learn and practise while serving as a leader?
9. The Leader–Member Exchange theory is considered an exchange approach to leadership. Why?
10. Is there a cause-and-effect relationship between leader behaviour and follower performance? What is the nature, or direction, of the relationship?

ENDNOTES

1 Bass, B. M. (1982). In Stogdill, R. M. (Ed.) *Handbook of Leadership*. New York: Free Press.

2 Klein, J. A., & Posey, P. A. (1986). Good supervisors are good supervisors — anywhere, *Harvard Business Review*, 125–128.

3 Zaleznik, A. (1992). Managers and leaders: Are they different?, *Harvard Business Review*, 126–135. Originally appeared in *Harvard Business Review*, 1977.

4 Zaleznik, A. (1992). *Learning Leadership*. New York: Basic Books.

5 See Saal, F. E. & Knight, P. A., (1995). *Industrial/Organizational Psychology*. Pacific Grove, CA.: Brooks/Cole, for an excellent discussion of the influence interpretation of leadership.

6 Pfeffer, J. (1977). The ambiguity of leadership, *Academy of Management Review*, 104–112.

7 Salancek, G. R., & Pfeffer, J. (1977). Constraints on administrator discretion: The budgets, *Urban Affairs Quarterly*, 475–498.

8 Pfeffer, J. (1994). *Competitive Advantage Through People*. Boston: Harvard Business School Press.

9 Pfeffer, J. (1977). The ambiguity of leadership, *Academy of Management Review*, 104–112.

10 Lieberson, S., & O'Connor, J. F. (1972). Leadership and organization performance: A study of large corporations, *American Sociological Review*, 117–130.

11 Weiner, N., & Mahoney, T. A. (1981). A model of corporate performance as a function of environmental, organizational and leadership influences, *Academy of Management Journal*, 453–470.

12 Semler, R. (1989). Managing without managers, *Harvard Business Review*, 76–84.

13 Manz, C. C., & Sims, H. P., Jnr. (1994). *Business Without Bosses*. New York: Wiley.

14 Manz, C. C., & Sims, H. P., Jnr. (1990). *Superleadership: Leading Others to Lead Themselves*. New York: Berkley.

15 Stogdill, R. M. (Ed.) (1974). *Handbook of Leadership*, New York: Free Press, pp. 43–44.

16 For example, see Argyris, C. (1955), Some characteristics of successful executives, *Personnel Journal*, 50–63; and Hornaday, J. A., & Bunker, C. J. (1970). The nature of the entrepreneur, *Personnel Psychology*, 47–54.

17 Ghiselli, E. E. (1963). The validity of management traits in relation to occupational level, *Personnel Psychology*, 109–113.

18 Stogdill, R. M. (1948). Personal factors associated with leadership, *Journal of Applied Psychology*, 35–71.

19 Kenny, D. A., & Zaccaro, S. J. (1983). An estimate of variance due to traits in leadership, *Journal of Applied Psychology*, 678–685.

20 Kirkpatrick, S. A., & Locke, E. A. (1991). Leadership: Do traits matter?, *Academy of Management Executive*, 48–60.

21 For a review of this work, see Likert, R. (1961). *New Patterns of Management*. New York: McGraw-Hill; and Likert, R. (1967). *The Human Organization*. New York: McGraw-Hill.

22 For a review of the studies, Stogdill, R. M. (Ed.) (1974). *Handbook of Leadership*. New York: Free Press, Ch. 11. Also see Fleishman, E. A. (1953). The measurement of leadership attitudes in industry, *Journal of Applied Psychology*, 153–58; Shartle, C. L. *Executive Performance and Leadership*. Englewood Cliffs, NJ: Prentice-Hall; Fleishman, E. A., Harris, E. F., & Burtt, H. E. (1955). *Leadership and Supervision in Industry*. Columbus: Bureau of Educational Research, Ohio State University; and Fleishman, E. A. (1973). Twenty years of consideration and structure. In E. A. Fleishman and J. G. Hunt (Eds.). *Current Developments in the Study of Leadership*. Carbondale, IL: Southern Illinois University Press.

23 Fleishman, E. A., Harris, E. F., & Burtt, H. E. (1955). *Leadership and Supervision in Industry*. Columbus: Bureau of Educational Research, Ohio State University.

24 For a discussion of the relationship between leadership and performance, see, for example, Meindl, J., & Ehrlich, S. (1987). The romance of leadership and the evaluation of organizational performance, *Academy of Management Journal*, 91–109.

25 Fleishman, E. A. (1973). Twenty years of consideration and structure. In E. A. Fleishman & J. C. Hunt (Eds.) *Current Developments in the Study of Leadership*. Carbondale, IL: Southern Illinois University Press.

26 Bellman, G. (1986). *The Quest for Staff Leadership*. Glenview, IL: Scott, Foresman.

27 Carew, D. K., Parisi-Carew, E., & Blanchard, K. H. (1986). Group development and situational leadership: A model for managing groups, *Training and Development Journal*, 46–50.

28 The discussion that follows is based on Tannenbaum, R., & Schmidt, W. H., (1973). How to choose a leadership pattern, *Harvard Business Review*, 162–180.

29   Ibid, p. 180.

30   Fiedler, F. E. (1967). *A Theory of Leadership Effectiveness*. New York: McGraw-Hill.

31   Fiedler, F. E. (1972). How do you make leaders more effective? New answers to an old puzzle, *Organizational Dynamics*, 3–8.

32   Graen, G., Orris, J. B., & Alvares, K. M. (1971). Contingency models of leadership effectiveness: Some experimental results, *Journal of Applied Psychology*, 287–290.

33   Schreisheim, C. A., Bannister, B. D., & Money, W. H. (1979). Psychometric properties of the LPC scale: An extension of Rice's review, *Academy of Management Review*, 287–290.

34   Moscovici, S. (1987). Social influence and conformity. In G. Lindzey and E. Aronson (Eds.) *Handbook of Social Psychology*, (Vol. II), (3rd Ed.). New York: Random House.

35   Yukl, G. (1994). *Leadership in Organizations* (3rd Ed.). Englewood Cliffs, NJ: Prentice-Hall International.

36   Vecchio, R. P. (1987). Situational leadership: An examination of a prescriptive theory, *Journal of Applied Psychology*, **72**, 444–451.

37   House, R. J. (1971). A path-goal theory of Leadership Effectiveness, *Administrative Science Quarterly*, 32–39. Also see House, R. J., & Mitchell, T. R. (1974), Path-goal theory of leadership, *Journal of Contemporary Business*, 81–98, which is the basis for the discussion.

38   Evans, M. G. (1970). The effects of supervisory behavior on the path-goal relationship, *Organizational Behavior and Human Performance*, 277–298. Also see Evans, M. G. (1974). Effects of supervisory behavior: Extensions of path-goal theory of motivation, *Journal of Applied Psychology*, 172–78.

39   House, R. J., & Dessler, G. (1974). The path-goal theory of leadership: Some post hoc and a priori tests. In J. G. Hunt (Ed.) *Contingency Approaches to Leadership*. Carbondale, IL: Southern Illinois University Press.

40   Yukl, G. (1994). *Leadership in Organizations* (3rd Ed.). Englewood Cliffs, NJ: Prentice-Hall International, Inc.

41   House, R. J., & Mitchell, T. R. (1974). Path-goal theory of leadership, *Journal of Contemporary Business*, 81–98.

42   Ibid.

43   Yukl, G. (1994). *Leadership in Organizations* (3rd Ed.). Englewood Cliffs, NJ: Prentice-Hall International, Inc.

44   Green, C. (1979). Questions of causation in the path-goal theory of leadership, *Academy of Management Journal*, 22–41.

45   Faulk, J., & Wendler, E. (1982). Dimensionality and leader-subordinate interactions: A path-goal approach, *Organizational Behavior and Human Performance*, 241–262; For a crititque of this theory see, also, Yukl, G. (1994). *Leadership in Organizations* (3rd Ed.). Englewood Cliffs, NJ: Prentice-Hall International, Inc.

46   Originally published in Hersey, P. & Blanchard, K. H., (1969). *Management of Organizational Behavior*. Englewood Cliffs, NJ: Prentice-Hall, now in 6th edition which first introduced readiness.

47   Yukl, G., & Falbe, C. (1991). Importance of different power sources in downward and lateral relations, *Journal of Applied Psychology*, 416–423.

48   Blank, W., Weitzel, J. R., & Green, S. G. A test of the situational leadership theory, *Personnel Psychology*, 579–597.

49   Vecchio, R. (1987). Situational leadership theory: An examination of a prescriptive theory, *Journal of Applied Psychology*, 444–451; Grafeff, C. L. (1983). The situational leadership theory: A critical view, *Academy of Management Review*, 285–291.

50   Weber, M. (1947). *The Theory of Social and Economic Organization*, trans. A. M. Henderson and T. Parsons. New York: Free Press, originally published 1924.

51   House, R. J. (1977). A 1976 theory of charismatic leadership. In J. G. Hunt and L. L. Larson (Eds.) *Leadership: The Cutting Edge*. Carbondale, IL: Southern Illinois University Press, pp. 189–207.

52   His views of charismatic leadership are clearly presented in Conger, J. A. (1989). *The Charismatic Leader*. San Francisco: Jossey-Bass.

53   Yukl, G. (1994). *Leadership in Organizations* (3rd Ed.). Englewood Cliffs, NJ: Prentice-Hall International, Inc.

54   Ibid.

55   See Willner, A. R. (1984). *The Spellbinders: Charismatic Political Leadership*. New Haven, CT: Yale University Press.

56   Bass, B. M. (1985). *Leadership Performance beyond Expectations*. New York: Academic Press; Bennis, W. G., & Nanes, B. (1985). *Leaders*. New York: Harper & Row; House, R. J., & Baetz, M. L. (1979). Leadership: Some empirical generalizations and new research directions, *Research in Organizational Behavior*, **XX,** 399–401.

57 Bryson, J. M. (1981). A perspective on planning and crisis in the public sector, *Strategic Management Journal*, 181–196.

58 Fink, S. (1986). *Crisis Management*. New York: AMACOM; Mitroff, I. I., Shrivastava, P., & Udivadia, F. E. (1987). Effective crisis management, *Academy of Management Executive*, 283–292.

59 Roberts, N. (1985). Transforming leadership: A process of collective action, *Human Relations*, 1023–1046.

60 Hedberg, B. (1989). How organizations learn and unlearn. In P. C. Nystrom and W. H. Starbuck (Ed.) *Handbook of Organizational Design*. London: Oxford University Press, pp. 3–27.

61 Yukl, G. (1994). *Leadership in Organizations* (3rd Ed.), Englewood Cliffs, NJ: Prentice-Hall International, Inc.

62 Podsakoff, P. M., Tudor, W. D., & Skov, R. (1982). Effect of leader contingent and non-contingent reward and punishment behaviors on subordinate performance and satisfaction, *Academy of Management Journal*, 810–821.

63 Howell, J. M., & Avolio, B. J. (1993). Transformational leadership, transactional leadership, locus of control, and support for innovation: Key predictors of consolidated-business-unit performance, *Journal of Applied Psychology*, **78**, 891–902.

64 Burns, J. M. (1978). *Leadership*. New York: Harper & Row.

65 Avolio, B. J., & Bass, B. M. (1988). Transformational leadership, charisma and beyond. In J. G. Hunt, B. R. Baliga, H. P. Dachler, & C. A. Schriesheim (Eds.) *Emerging Leadership Vistas*. Lexington, MA.: Lexington Books, pp. 29–49.

66 Bass, B. M. (1985). *Leadership Performance beyond Expectations*. New York: Academic Press.

67 Ibid., p. 31.

68 Green, S. G., & Mitchell, T. R. (1979). Attributional processes of leaders in leader-member interactions, *Organizational Behavior and Human Performance*, 429–58.

69 Heneman, R. L., Greenberger, D. B., & Anonyuo, C. (1989). Attributions and exchanges: The effects of interpersonal factors on the diagnosis of employee performance, *Academy of Management*, **32**, 466–476.

70 Mitchell, T. R., Green, S., & Wood, R. (1990). An attributional model of leadership and the poor performing subordinate: Development

and validation. In L.L. Cummings & B. M. Staw (Eds.) *Information and Cognition in Organizations*. Greenwich: JAI Press Inc.

71 Ibid.

72 Martinko, M., & Gardner, W. L. (1987). The leader-member attribution process, *Academy of Management Review*, 235–249.

73 Ashkanasy, N. (1989). Causal attribution and supervisors' response to subordinate performance: The Green and Mitchell attributional model revisited, *Journal of Applied Social Psychology*, **19**, 309–330; Ashkanasy, N. (1988). Supervisors' responses to subordinate performance: Effect of personal-control orientation and situational control, *Journal of Social Psychology*, **131**, 525–544.

74 Graen, G. (1976). Role-making processes with complex organizations. In M. D. Dunnette (Ed.) *Handbook of Industrial Organizational Psychology*. Chicago: Rand McNally, pp. 1210–1259.

75 Graen, G., Liden, R., & Hoel, W. (1982). Role of leadership in the employee withdrawal process, *Journal of Applied Psychology*, 868–872.

76 Yukl, G. (1994). *Leadership in Organizations* (3rd Ed.). Englewood Cliffs, NJ.: Prentice-Hall International, Inc.

77 Liden, R. C., Wayne, S. J., & Stilwell, D. (1993). A longitudinal study in the early development of leader-member exchanges, *Journal of Applied Psychology*, **78**, 662–674.

78 Kinicki, A. J., & Vecchio, R. P. (1994). Influences on the quality of supervisor-subordinate relations: The role of time pressure, organizational commitment, and locus of control, *Journal of Organizational Behavior*, **15**, 75–82.

79 For example, Katerberg, R., & Hom, P. W. (1981). Effects of within-group and between-group variation in leadership, *Journal of Applied Psychology*, **66**, 218–223; Kinicki, A. J., & Vecchio, R. P. (1994). Influences on the quality of supervisor-subordinate relations: The role of time pressure, organizational commitment, and locus of control, *Journal of Organizational Behavior*, **15**, 75–82; Vecchio, R. P., Griffeth, R. W., & Hom, P. W. (1986). The predictive utility of the vertical dyad linkage approach, *Journal of Social Psychology*, **126**, 617–625; Wayne, S. J., & Greene, S. A. (1993). The effects of leader-member exchange on employee citizenship and impression management behavior, *Human Relations*, **46**, 1431–1440.

80 Duarte, N. T., Gordon, J. R., & Klich, N. R. (1993). How do I like thee? Let me appraise the ways, *Journal of Organizational Behavior*, **14**, 239–249; Wilhelm, C. C., Herd, A. M., & Steiner, D. D. (1993). Attributional conflict between managers and subordinates: An investigation of leader-member exchange effects, *Journal of Organizational Behavior*, **14**, 531–544.

81 Pfeffer, J. (1977). The ambiguity of leadership, *Academy of Management Review*, 104–111.

82 Thomas, A. B. (1988). Does leadership make a difference to organizational performance?, *Administrative Science Quarterly*, 388–400.

83 Meindl, J. R. (1990). On leadership: An alternative to the conventional wisdom. *Research in Organizational Behaviour*, **12**, 159–203.

84 Kerr, S., & Jermier, J. M. (1978). Substitutes for leadership: Their meaning and measurement, *Organizational Behavior and Human Performance*, 376–403.

85 Ibid.

86 Manz, C. C. (1986). Self-leadership: Toward an expanded theory of self-influence processes in organizations, *Academy of Management Review*, 585–600.

87 Locke, E. A., & Schweiger, D. M. (1990). Participation in decision-making: One more look. In L. L. Summings & B. M. Staw (Eds.) *Leadership, Participation and Group Behavior*. Greenwich: JAI Press Inc.

88 Yukl, G. (1994). *Leadership in Organizations* (3rd Ed.). Englewood Cliffs, NJ: Prentice-Hall International, Inc.

89 Locke, E. A., & Schweiger, D. M. (1990). Participation in decision-making: One more look. In L. L. Summings & B. M. Staw (Eds.) *Leadership, Participation and Group Behavior*. Greenwich: JAI Press Inc.

90 Locke, E. A., & Schweiger, D. M. (1990). Participation in decision-making: One more look. In L. L. Summings & B. M. Staw (Eds.). *Leadership, Participation and Group Behavior*. Greenwich: JAI Press Inc.; Yukl, G. (1994). *Leadership in Organizations* (3rd Ed.). Englewood Cliffs, NJ: Prentice-Hall International, Inc.

91 Vroom, V., & Yetton, P. (1973). *Leadership and Decision Making*. Pittsburgh: University of Pittsburgh Press.

92 Vroom, V., & Jago, A. (1988*). The New Leadership: Managing Participation in Organizations*. Englewood Cliffs, NJ: Prentice-Hall.

93 Ibid.

94 This section summarises material presented in G. Yukl. (1994). *Leadership in Organizations* (3rd Ed.). Englewood Cliffs, NJ: Prentice-Hall International, Inc., Ch. 13.

95 Katz, D., & Stotland, E. (1959). A preliminary statement to a theory of attitude structure and change. In S. Koch (Ed.) *Psychology: A Study of Science*. New York: McGraw-Hill.

96 Greene, C. N. (1975). The reciprocal nature of influence between leader and subordinate, *Journal of Applied Psychology*, 187–193.

READING 11 LEADING LEARNING

Michael E. McGill
John W. Slocum, Jr.

Source: *The Journal of Leadership Studies* 1, no. 3, June 1994.

1993 was a very good year for the Associates Corporation of North America, the nineteenth consecutive year of increased earnings, growing to total assets of $30 billion. In large part, 1993 was successful because of the contributions of the Consumer Financial Services Division of The Associates, a confederation of consumer lending businesses with branches throughout the US. To recognize the successful efforts of the branch managers, a gala year-end meeting was held in Dallas. Along with the awards banquets, entertainment, and recreational activities, managers and their spouses also were presented with some learning opportunities. Workshops on marketing, managing diversity, benefits, and managing relationships were provided. At many company meetings such as this, especially where spouses are included, attendance at workshops is often sparse at best. This is not the case at The Associates, where the workshops are packed, people take notes, and informal discussions carry topics far beyond the allotted time. There is a genuine and visible involvement in learning.

One reason employees at The Associates are so involved in learning can be found in the behavior of a workshop attendee, Reece A. Overcash, Jr., the 68-year-old chairman and chief executive officer of The Associates. The leader of learning at The Associates, Overcash is adamant about the need for continual learning. He is fond of quoting G. E.'s Jack Welch: 'Are you regenerating? Are you dealing with new things? When you find yourself in a new environment, do you come up with a fundamentally different approach? That's the test. When you flunk, you leave.' Overcash's commitment to learning goes far beyond talking about learning. He leads learning at The Associates in direct and tangible ways. He is a model for learning. Overcash has a seemingly insatiable appetite for new ideas and perspectives. He willingly and frequently puts himself in the role of student and prods other managers to do likewise. At the consumer lender's meeting he attended workshops, took notes, asked questions — he set an example. Overcash is a revered *mentor*; he is constantly teaching. Asking questions, sparking interactions, he seems always to be working toward creating a learning environment. Keith Hughes, president and chief operating officer of The Associates and heir apparent to the top spot upon Overcash's retirement, talks about his relationship with Overcash as a 'tutorial in how to be a CEO'. Like Hughes, every executive in The Associates' hierarchy can point to lessons they've learned from Overcash.

Overcash's leadership of learning at The Associates is not as casual as it may seem. His modeling is personal, but purposeful as well. His monitoring follows an agenda. In short, he *manages* learning at The Associates. Management of learning is seen in the assignment of tasks and responsibilities, the rotation of key individuals through challenging assignments, the use of every opportunity to urge one group or division within the company to look at what another group is doing and learn from their experience.

Finally, Overcash leads learning by *monitoring* the learning going on at The Associates. Like most successful CEOs, Overcash knows the numbers of each of The Associates' businesses backwards and forwards. It is not uncommon for Overcash to ask a division vice president a question about some small detail of his operation. He closely tracks new programs and new pursuits at The Associates, measuring them against their plan and their potential. Beyond the numbers and new ventures, Overcash monitors

relationships. It is his belief that the lending business is a relationship business. On vacations, it is his practice to stop in at branches, greet people by name, ask them about themselves, their business, and what they have learned. Overcash does not micromanage, but instead builds close relationships that help him understand all facets of the business.[1]

As the pace of change in the business world has accelerated, it is apparent that yesterday's accomplishments and even today's successes are no guarantees of tomorrow's success. What managers have known to work in the past, understood to be true, or thought to solve problems is called into question as business conditions differ from one day to the next. Change, the modern-day manager's mantra, has in recent years proven to be an inadequate response. A decade and a half of the pursuit of change has left many organizations scarcely better equipped to deal with their dynamic competitive environments than if they had never changed at all. Smarter organizations learn *to* change and learn *from* change.[2] Smart organizations actively manage the learning process to ensure that it occurs by design rather than by chance. Smarter organizations are learning organizations, able to process their experiences — with customers, competitors, partners, and suppliers — in ways that allow them to create environments in which they can be successful. Learning is their sustainable competitive advantage; leadership makes learning happen.

The purpose of this paper is to capture the behaviors of leaders of learning organizations and, from those behaviors, to outline how to lead learning. Leading learning requires modeling, monitoring, managing, and monitoring learning. We believe that these are the most powerful ways that leaders can influence the behavior of people in their organizations. Leading learning provides a very different perspective on leadership than the styles theory so popular in years past and transformational leadership that currently is in vogue. In order to learn these behaviors, leaders and followers must unlearn much of what they have believed to be true about leadership.

Leaders model learning

One of the most powerful dynamics at work in leadership is what Arnold Toynbee called 'mimesis', literally the process by which people mimic their leaders. When employees look to leaders, however, they often see little change or learning modeled. Those who have reached positions of influence *argue* the need for individual and organizational learning in the face of increasing turbulent environmental conditions. These same leaders often *act* as though their experiences from the past will be an adequate guide. Reflecting in 1987 on his handling of early crises at Apple — the departure of Steve Jobs, 20 percent layoffs, a drop in stock price, bad press — John Sculley described how he responded: 'Well, I found it most useful to be able to fall back on things that I already understood, to define problems in such a way that would let me use solutions that I already had some experience with.'[3] At the same time that Sculley was trying to convince Apple employees that events in the personal computer industry required that they needed dramatically different understandings and actions, Sculley himself was drawing upon a repertoire anchored in his own experience at PepsiCo — acting to establish control, eliminate chaos, maintain distance, in short, to bring the lessons of professional management to Apple. Many managers view it as their job to be a model for learning. G. E.'s Jack Welch says, 'My job is to listen to, search for, think of, and spread ideas, to expose people to good ideas and role models. I'm almost maitre d', getting the crowd to come sit at this table: "Enjoy the food here. Try it. See if it tastes good." And they do.'[4]

Leaders of learning recognize the importance of reflecting on their own experience and the need to periodically retreat from the pace of their office to engage in self-renewal so that they might return reenergized and better able to be a catalyst for others. The notion of renewal or reinvention characterizes the leaders of learning organizations who hold themselves to the same standard that they hold their organizations — 'Are you regenerating?'

Leaders mentor learning

The most effective leaders of learning not only inspire others by their example, they also take a personal interest in the learning of others; they serve as mentors. Borrowing from Greek legend and lexicon where Homer's 'faithful and wise' mentor advised Odysseus and was entrusted with the education of Telemachus, *mentor* has been broadly used to describe the teachers, guides, coaches, helpers, et al., who contribute to an individual's development. Where learning is concerned, the mentoring behaviors of leaders are quite specific: (1) they set learning agendas, targeting particular kinds of learning; (2) they create a learning environment with challenging assignments, assignments in which there is a great deal to be learned, assignments which entail risk-taking; (3) they help process the learning experience, they debrief *what* was learned and *how* it was learned.

The nature of the mentor relationship — interpersonal and intimate — and the dynamics of the mentoring process — intentional and involved — are such that leaders must be very selective in whom they choose to mentor. Leaders set an example for the rest of the organization about the value of mentoring. James E. Burke, former chairman and CEO of Johnson & Johnson, often retells of being mentored early in his career. Six years after Burke went to work for Johnson & Johnson in 1949, he was named director of new products. Burke recalls that, in those days, coming up with new products wasn't the science that it is today. 'We found that only 3 out of 10 new products which reached the marketplace succeeded.' Among Burke's early new products was a children's chest rub promoted as safer and easier to use than those already on the market. The chest rub was designed like today's stick deodorants. It failed, along with new nose drops and cough medicine, and Burke was told to report to the chairman's office. At that time, Robert Wood Johnson, 'the General', son of the founder, was chairman of Johnson & Johnson. 'I was certain that I was going to be fired. I decided to defend myself and was mentally prepared for a good fight. The chairman said to me, "I understand that your product failed." I said, "Yes, sir, that's true." Picking up a piece of blue paper, he said, "Furthermore, I understand it cost this corporation $865 000." I said, "Yes, sir, that's right." He stood up, held out his hand and said, "I just wanted to congratulate you. Nothing happens unless people are willing to make decisions, and you can't make decisions without making mistakes."'

Burke recalls, 'It was during that period that I began to understand the necessity for risk and the realization that you can't grow without it. You simply have to create an environment that encourages risk taking.'[5] Mentored by Johnson in the lessons of risk-taking, it is not surprising that when Burke became CEO he passed these same lessons on to his own protégé, Ralph S. Larsen, who took over the reins from Burke. Asked what he had learned from Burke, Larsen responded, 'Jim has created a culture based on intelligent risk-taking, on not being afraid to fail, on getting everything on the table and arguing if you have to. I love it — it works.'[6]

Through active and purposeful mentoring, leaders enhance the learning of others, helping them to develop their own initiative, strengthening them in the use of their own judgment, and enabling them to grow and to become better contributors to the organization. These learners, by virtue of their learning, then become leaders and mentor to others. In the most effective learning organizations, everyone feels as though they have a mentor, and everyone, in turn, mentors. It starts at the top.

Leaders manage learning

Leaders in learning organizations must do more than set a good example and be a mentor. If the message of learning is to permeate the organization, leaders must also manage learning. Managing learning means leaders must continually focus attention on the learning agenda and institutionalize the learning process.

Employees respond to what leaders attend to and reward. At DuPont, the entire organization became safety conscious when lost-time accidents were written up and given to the chairman daily. At Dell Computer Corporation, customer complaints that aren't fixed in a week go directly to the CEO, Michael S. Dell. This attention assures that employees understand Dell's vision that every customer 'must have a quality experience and must be pleased, not just satisfied'. When leaders focus attention on the learning agenda, employees respond.

At Home Depot, learning sustains their competitive advantage. The dramatic success of Home Depot is due to the training employees receive, training designed and delivered by the leader and CEO, Bernard Marcus. Home Depot's sale staff can offer on-the-spot lessons in tile laying, electrical installations, and other projects. New hires, who are often experienced electricians or carpenters, start with five days of classes that include lessons on everything from company history to how to greet a customer. After class, new staffers spend three weeks tethered to a

department manager learning how to order, stock, and sell. Employees then learn about the rest of the store, which stocks some 30 000 items of hardware, lumber, tools, lighting, and plumbing supplies. Salespeople regularly attend seminars on paint, tile and other merchandise that help them answer customer questions. Nonstop questions from customers are what anyone wearing an orange Home Depot apron can expect. To see to it that they have the answers, the company focuses on nonstop learning.[7]

One way for leaders to effectively and continuously focus attention on learning is to institutionalize the organization's commitment to learning. It is ironic that, faced with a dramatic and dynamic environment that demands change, many managers choose to cut back on the very educational programs that might better prepare their employees to learn. Training and management development programs are often early targets for cost cutting. Such moves may speak ill of a company's commitment to learning, but they might just as well reflect the perceived connection (or lack thereof) between training and development and learning. In learning organizations, both the commitment to learning and the connection are clear.

Since its inception in 1956, G.E. Crotonville, G.E.'s Management Development Institute, has been used as a direct lever for change. When Jack Welch began to transform G.E. in 1981, he told then Crotonville manager James Baughman, 'I want a revolution to start at Crotonville. I want it to be part of the glue that holds G.E. together.' Today Welch uses Crotonville to touch every part of G.E. Since 1989, the energies of Crotonville have been directed toward involving nearly 40 000 G.E. middle managers in learning the workout/reengineering process.[8] Reengineering and workout programs are learning processes particularly applicable to administrative, operating, and human resource systems. By institutionalizing workout in the Crotonville curriculum, Welch has assured that the learning will go on long after managers have left the Crotonville campus.

At Hitachi, the Japanese electronics giant, there can be no mistaking leadership's commitment to learning. Years ago, Hitachi founded the Institute of Management Development, the first in-house institute created in Japan for management education. To maintain

Hitachi's traditions, approximately 70 percent of the instructors at the institute are Hitachi employees. Education is provided for all levels of employees, from recruits to top-level managers.

Programs offered by the institute last one to two weeks and host groups of 16 to 20 employees. All share five objectives for their courses. The first objective is to give managers a clear understanding of Hitachi's management concepts. Managers must understand the company's three maxims — harmony, sincerity, and pioneering spirit — and recognize that the customer comes first. Managers must also be able to lead and develop the employees under them.

The second objective is to acquire an entrepreneurial spirit and innovative thinking since Hitachi relies on creative products to stay ahead of its competition. Managers must grasp the difference between being a 'technology-oriented' business and a 'marketing-oriented' industry.

The third objective is to give managers a broad awareness of the world in order to aid Hitachi's international businesses. Politics, culture, religion, as well as international economics are in the curriculum. This knowledge helps Hitachi conduct harmonious business activities in the global marketplace.

The fourth objective is to unify managers' opinions and sense of direction in order to maintain a common, cohesive outlook. This is especially important for Hitachi since a large number of its group companies and subsidiaries are encouraged to be independent. The intricate web of financial, manufacturing, and distribution relationships makes it imperative that relationships be strong.

Finally, the fifth objective is to improve overall business skills: management, marketing, financial management, human resource management, and so on.

To meet the needs of management in a variety of fields, Hitachi's programs are diverse. But some common threads run through all the courses. For example, company executives are available during the courses to engage in dialogue with the managers. The president attends any course for department managers and above, and the vice presidents attend courses for section managers. Occasionally, presidents of some of Hitachi's group companies serve as instructors. All courses have some of the board officers in attendance as well. Hitachi believes

that people make business and that to respect, develop, and make the most of each individual is the road to success.[9]

Leaders monitor learning

Many fine ideas go unrealized in organizations because no one feels personally responsible for seeing to it that platitudes and pledges are translated into performance and rewards. Managers who are serious about leading learning in their organizations *monitor* learning and, in so doing, make learning everyone's responsibility. Unfortunately, it is not as easy to monitor learning as it is to track production or sales. A leader cannot simply call up on a computer screen the monthly learning figures the way he or she might access production numbers or sales or any one of a number of important financial indicators. To date there is no Lotus 1-2-3 or Windows program for learning. Learning is difficult to monitor because learning is a process, not a product. As such, measurement must be at once more immediate and more intimate. The process must be assessed as it is delivered by those involved. Monitoring organization learning must be built in to the organization's learning. There are two leader behaviors that result in effective monitoring and simultaneously promote learning (1) leaders establish routines for receiving undistorted feedback; and (2) leaders encourage *new* failures.

Without feedback there can be no learning. It is feedback that allows us to adjust our behavior to better attain our goals. In modern organizations, feedback is plentiful, but it is often difficult to get the truth. One significant measure of a learning organization is how much truth the leader hears. There are several dynamics at work in organizations that act to distort feedback to leaders and, therefore, frustrate learning. First, over time there is a tendency for everyone in an organization — especially those at the top — to look alike and think alike. This contributes to 'groupthink', where fitting in and gaining the leader's approval becomes more important than making a meaningful difference. When Ed Whitacre took over as CEO at Southwestern Bell Corporation, he remarked that a habit SBC needed to break was having everyone 'molded into our very image.'[10] Learning organizations value the contribution diversity can make to undistorted feedback. Bill Kaufman, manager of New Areas for Oryx Energy Company, comments on the composition of his group, 'I like to have the lawyer and the marketing guy involved; they bring a different perspective. We're dealing in some parts of the world (Kazakhstan) where "business as usual just isn't going to cut it". The rest of us have been together for a long time and we've been doing what we're doing for a long time. We need somebody to challenge our thinking.'[11]

These remarks suggest the second organizational impediment to undistorted feedback. Many leaders will not harbor dissent, choosing instead to 'shoot the messenger'. The legendary moviemaker, Samuel Goldwyn, presented his key advisors with an unenviable choice when, after a succession of box office bombs, he called them together and demanded, 'I want you to tell me exactly what's wrong with me and MGM, even if it means losing your job.'[12] Many a manager has been faced with the same dilemma — tell the boss what's wrong and risk being fired, or don't tell and risk being fired because what's wrong doesn't get fixed! Leaders in learning organizations encourage dissent, recognizing that dissent promotes learning by forcing people to look at a wider range of possibilities. Some learning leaders even go so far as to structure dissent into the decision-making process and to reward dissenters.

Six months after Apple chairman John Sculley gave the Newton project the go-ahead, Donna Auguste was named software engineering manager. She joined an insulated group. 'There weren't any people who didn't already know people on the Newton team when they joined the group. I didn't think it was healthy.' Auguste set out to increase the diversity and dissent in the Newton group. She began hiring engineers from outside the small circle, bringing in blacks and women in the process. She refined the interviewing process to reach beyond the usual applicants, and looked much farther afield than Apple typically does. With this diversity came dissent which Auguste did not try to smooth away; she used dissent to move the project forward. One of the Newton designers who worked with Auguste recalls, 'She was a lousy diplomat. But this is obviously preferable to the inverse approach that is taken by most managers. They'd much rather think everybody likes them than actually get anything done.' When leaders *use* diversity and dissent, the group learns and things get done.[13]

Some learning organizations have instituted routines for systematically debriefing their management practices. The concept of upward evaluation or 360-degree feedback has become popular in some of America's most admired companies as a mechanism for debriefing employees' experience and giving feedback to leadership. Alcoa, Burlington, General Mills, Hewlett-Packard, Herman Miller, Whirlpool, British Petroleum, 3M, and UPS are all companies that use upward and lateral evaluations along with more traditional downward performance appraisals. The learning potential is tremendous. At UPS, the company learned that its 35 000 managers were not doing a satisfactory job of helping workers to develop their technical and communication skills. Only 48 percent of workers gave their managers satisfactory marks on employee development. Having learned, UPS is now acting to improve the teaching skills of its managers.[14] At Hoechst Celanese Corporation, a key component of the Middle Management Leadership Program is 'Leadership Feedback'. Managers are presented with 360-degree feedback elicited from their boss, their peers, and their subordinates. Reviewing this feedback, they develop action plans for improving their own leadership. These action plans are traced for the individuals and also used as input into curriculum development for future leadership programs. The individual leaders learn from the 360-degree feedback and the organization learns. This kind of learning is possible only because leaders are willing to debrief their own behavior.

Leaders can effectively monitor learning by noting the diversity, dissent, and debriefings present in their own organizations. More of each means, in all probability, more learning. The same is true of failures. The more you have, the more you can learn.

One company that has had a difficult time learning from its failures in recent years is Eastman Kodak Company. Early in the 1970s, Kodak management decided that the future of silver halide technology, the proprietary film coating on which Kodak was founded, was limited. A 20-year period of mostly failed experiments ensued. Then there was Kodak's entry into instant photography in 1976. This was done by stealing Polaroid's technology. The result: heavy losses, a fine of $900 million paid to Polaroid in 1991, and a tarnished reputation.

That debacle was followed by Kodak's entry into reprographics. Kodak's first copying machine was far better than anything Xerox had at the time. But Kodak failed to exploit its competitive advantage, and Xerox regained the edge. In 1991 and 1992, Kodak lost money on its $4 billion (revenues) copier and information systems business.

During the 1980s, Kodak set itself up as a venture capitalist for a number of new technologies. Most did not pay off. It purchased a number of publishing and prepublishing companies. For example, Atex was the premier copy processing system for the publishing industry when Kodak bought the company in 1981. Atex's founders, stifled by Kodak, left; and, 10 years later, Kodak sold Atex. A larger failure by far was Kodak's entry into pharmaceuticals.

Failing to learn the lessons of prior experiences, Kodak purchased Sterling Drug in 1988 for $5.1 billion. Kodak reasoned that its extensive background and knowledge of different chemical-based lab processes would instantly make it a formidable player in the profitable pharmaceutical industry. Because Kodak's blood analyzer, diagnostic equipment, chemical substrates, and film products were already widely used in medical laboratories, its managers thought that Sterling would provide them with an easy entry into a new industry that would not face the same kind of intense competitive pressures that characterized the photographic film industry. Unfortunately, these expectations never materialized. The ability to leverage technologies used in films and imaging did not fit well with the skills required for smooth integration and mastery of the pharmaceutical industry. Kodak eventually placed a major part of its Sterling Drug acquisition into a joint venture with French pharmaceutical giant Sanofi.

Analysts suggest that Kodak's repeated failures have been the result of its own ponderous bureaucracy and the fact that it had neither the skill to manage entrepreneurial companies nor the willingness to admit its own managerial shortcomings. Much of this failure to learn has been laid at the feet of Kodak's CEOs over the last 20 years, all veterans of the Rochester corporate bureaucracy.

George Fisher, of Motorola, has brought new perspectives to Kodak. Instead of seeking external diversification opportunities, Kodak has refocused its efforts to build a strong presence in new, digital-imaging technologies. Now wary of how peripheral businesses can distract the company from its core imaging businesses, Kodak is investing in new products and strategic alliances to extend and renew its imaging-based competencies.[15]

The relevant criticism of Kodak is not that they made mistakes, but that they initially failed to learn from the mistakes they made. Of course, leaders of learning don't actually encourage failures. What they do is encourage experiments by making it clear that it is okay to fail. In most organizations, the costs of failure are so high (often career-ending) that whatever cheerleading managers do on behalf of creativity and risk-taking is not enough to turn employees from the safe and narrow path of making no mistakes. To thwart this inherent conservatism, leaders must often go to the other extreme of seeming to celebrate failures. Ralph C. Stayer, CEO of Johnsonville Foods, used mistakes to stimulate learning. 'Mistakes are road signs along the journey which read "Learning opportunity ahead". Mistakes are the servomechanisms of life. I used to fight or fear them. When I learned to use them to trigger my own learning, both I and my company made progress. I even formed a "Mistake of the Month Club" to stimulate discussions about mistakes made and learn from them. I offered a "Shot in the Foot Award" for the person who made the biggest mistake from which he/she learned the most. It was a coffee cup cast in the form of a foot with a hole in it. I was determined to have individuals see mistakes as an opportunity to learn and try again, not as an act against God's law.'[16]

Conditions for leading learning

Modeling, mentoring, managing, and monitoring are key leader behaviors that promote learning. Here we've described these behaviors as exercised primarily by CEOs, people who have both the position and often the personae of leaders. But nothing about these behaviors makes them the province of members of the executive suite. These leaders may be more visible, but their examples are no more viable than modeling, mentoring, managing, and monitoring done by others elsewhere in the organization. People at every level of an organization have opportunities to model learning, to mentor others' learning, to manage learning, and to monitor learning. In the most effective learning organizations, everyone acts as a learning leader because everyone is learning.

This is not to suggest that these behaviors are easily come by. Leading learning at any level is a challenging task made all the more so because it is an ongoing process. Today it is common to talk of the leadership challenges presented by crises and dramatic changes, where organization and individuals need to be 'transformed'. Leadership may actually be easier in these critical times because the need for change is so obvious and people are looking for lessons to learn.

In 1991, Lawrence Bossidy left his position as vice chairman at G.E. to take over the helm of Allied Signal, the then-troubled $12-billion-a-year manufacturer of aerospace equipment and auto parts. 'The transformation here has been easier than at G.E. because the people of Allied Signal obviously were on a burning platform and they knew from newspaper reports about the struggles of IBM and Sears. They knew Allied Signal would have to be successful to provide them with job security and opportunities.'[17] So much of leadership has come to be associated with fire-fighting that some see the role of a leader as creating, if not crisis, at least the awareness of crisis. Bossidy believes, 'To inaugurate large-scale change, you may have to create the burning platform. You have to give people a reason to do something differently.'

Crises certainly provide an arena for leadership and can test the mettle of any leader. But, in a learning organization, the appropriate measure of leadership is how much learning is going on when things are going well. As difficult as it may be to teach smart people how to learn, it is still more difficult for successful organizations to learn when the platform is not burning.

Ernesto Martens-Rebolledo is the CEO of Vitro, Sociedad Anonima, an 84-year-old Mexican company with over $3 billion in sales and 44 000 employees. One of the largest and most successful of Mexican companies, Vitro, through its subsidiaries such as Anchor Glass Container Corporation and joint ventures with Ford, Corning, Samsonite, and Whirlpool, manufactures everything from glass bottles to washing machines. Martens became Vitro's first nonfamily CEO in 1985. He sees the major challenge before his company now: 'One of the most difficult things to do in a successful company is to convince people that they must change.' He describes specifically the need to change the mind-set of managers from one of complacency to one of continuous improvement. 'The most difficult and probably the most crucial thing we needed to do was change the mind-set of the managers, which is next to impossible to do in a successful company.'[18]

In Martens' view, the problem leaders face is less one of motivation — traditional leadership — than it is one of changing the way the organization reflects upon its own experience — learning. Leaders must help their organization find learning from the commonplace as well as from the critical, from the failures as well as from the successes, and especially from those moments when it seems as though there is nothing to be learned.

Unlearning leadership

In what ways are modeling learning, mentoring learning, managing learning, and monitoring learning different from the kinds of behaviors that leaders typically do? Leading an organization toward learning poses a fundamentally different way of thinking about leadership. It is more concerned with process than with product, aiming more toward commitment and creativity than compliance, intending not to prove, but to improve. The leader as learner and the responsibility of leading an organization's learning mandate new ways of thinking about a leader's role. In order to assume this perspective, leaders and those who would be leaders need to disabuse themselves of certain widely held notions about leadership.

It is popular today to speak of the role of the leader as though *what the leader does* — leader behaviors — can be separated from *who the leader is* — the leader as a person. Most contemporary views of leadership are based upon identifying certain leader behaviors that are appropriate for certain situations. The popular 'leadership styles', 'situational leadership', and 'transactional' approaches of recent years are typical of this view. In each, aspiring leaders are taught how to diagnose organizational situations and how to draw from their repertoire the indicated leader actions. Viewed in this way, leadership is purely an instrumental activity, a study in means. Leaders, thus trained, are not much concerned about modeling behavior. They do not see the way they lead as a reflection of who they are — it is simply a tool they use, a role that they play to achieve specific results. These leaders often are blind to the impact of their own behavior on others and ignorant of how discongruity between their actions and their words may detract from their leadership.

Learning leaders take a more holistic view of leadership. They understand that learning is not just something a person does, it is the way a person is. Leading learning is not a role one plays, it is the way one looks at oneself and the way one processes one's organizational experience. Given this perspective, learning leaders recognize the importance of modeling. They attach much greater importance to congruity between who they are and what they do as perceived by others. They lead learning in large part by learning — not by telling others they *need* to learn, but by showing in their own behavior the value of learning.

Many leaders today pride themselves on their personal detachment. They argue that tough times demand tough people who are able to set aside their personal agendas in favor of fact-finding, objectives analysis, and decision making. We believe that learning occurs through *relational activities*. The effectiveness of learning and of leading learning is, in large part, a function of the effectiveness of the leader's relationships with others in the organization. Nowhere is this more apparent than in mentoring. Mentor/protégé relationships are intensely personal. Who leaders mentor and how they mentor them are choices that have profound effects on learning for individuals and for the organization. Leaders who are 'distant' in an effort to be detached and objective diminish the learning possibilities that could come from their own personal immersion in the process. Many leaders, though distant, are able by virtue of their personalities to evoke an emotional attachment from followers. These charismatic leaders remain detached. They may be the object of a relationship, but they are not involved in the way that leading learning requires.

The personal involvement of the leader serves several learning agendas. It makes the model of learning that the leader presents richer and more reachable for others. The relationships that develop become an important source of honest and thoughtful feedback. The leader's personal involvement with others in learning opens him or her to learning *from* others. Recognizing the need for a personal investment in learning and in others emphasizes that

leadership is not something done to others, but rather a relationship that one enters into *with* others. As much as what the leader does cannot be separated from who the leader is, learners cannot stand apart from their relationships with others. Learning and leading require a personal involvement with others.

Popular approaches present leadership as event-focused, episodic behaviors engaged in at a time and a manner dictated by the situation. Some even speak of 'leadershipping' as though leadership were a skill to be exercised much like planning or budgeting. This perspective comes from our tendency to put the microscope to leadership only when it seems most needed. Crises provide leaders with opportunities to take bold actions. We know that crises are more likely to give rise to charismatic leaders and leaders who are seen as transformational or visionary, in part because at these times followers see a heightened need for leadership and 'sense making'.[19] Many leaders seek out these opportunities to 'be bold'. Who leaders are and what leaders do may be most evident in times of crisis, but the opportunities for learning are not limited to organizational emergencies. Leaders of learning manage learning as an on-going organizational process, not an occasional, extraordinary event. They are *always* looking for the learning opportunity.

Leaders manage learning with: (1) a focus on improving processes over proving performances; (2) an intensity of focus that is always greater than what is sufficient, but less than would be stressful or to the point of distress; (3) a processing of experience close enough in time to correct any problems; (4) an appreciation for individual differences as a means to clarify values. Each of these benchmarks for managing learning underscores the observation that leading learning is a full-time, full-service activity, not a some-time situational option which leaders may or may not exercise.

There is a belief shared by most leaders and all too many followers that the leader is infallible. The practical (political) corollary to this belief is, 'If the leader does do wrong, he or she should not be confronted with the fact'. Leaders who effectively monitor learning will put into place people and processes to generate valid feedback. One of the unintended consequences of effective reengineering programs has been the revelation of the tremendous number of processes and procedures present in organizations, the purpose of which is to prove who or what is right. The majority of these exist at the privilege of leaders at all levels. Ostensibly monitoring mechanisms, these processes and procedures are more commonly used to promote the party line and prompt conformity. The standard defense leaders proffer is, 'I don't want to be surprised'. The pragmatic translation is, 'I don't want to be surprised with feedback which shows me to be wrong'. Learning leaders are serious enough about learning to monitor learning in such a way that all valid information is revealed and reflected upon, *even* if it shows the leader to be wrong, *especially* if it shows the leader to be wrong.

The presumption of leader infallibility presents a particular problem for today's 'transformational' leaders. These leaders, by virtue of their compelling vision, their personal conviction, and their persuasive communication skills, may foster an almost cult-like devotion from employees. Any questioning of the transformational leader's purpose, programs, or processes may be viewed by the leader and by the organization as disloyal. So strong is this feeling that many in these organizations engage in a kind of self-censorship, withholding critical feedback even when it would best serve the leader and the organization to be forthcoming. Leaders blessed with transformational skills must make a special effort to disabuse themselves and their followers of any semblance of leader infallibility. In a learning organization, everyone acknowledges failures — their own, others', and those of the organization. And, because everyone can fail, everyone can learn.

The lesson for leaders

Over 60 years ago, Fritz Roethlisberger, conducting his legendary Hawthorne studies, observed that leaders are characterized by 'A willingness to accept new ideas and a desire to verify them by experience'.[20] How can a leader's willingness and desire be discerned? To our mind, there are four simple tests: (1) Is the leader learning? (2) Is the leader involved? (3) Is the learning and leading constant? (4) Is it okay to say the leader was wrong? The most effective leaders have always been and will always be learners. They lead their organizations by modeling, mentoring, managing, and monitoring learning. To come to this point, leaders at all levels and those engaged in leadership

relationships must unlearn certain contemporary conventional ideas about who leaders are and what leaders do; they must unlearn the role of the leader, personal detachment, leadershipping, and leader infallibility.

Organizations cannot learn unless leaders are learners. The development of a learning organization must begin with development of individual learners who institutionalize learning processes in organizations which, in turn, promote learning communities and a learning society. This seemingly grand, even grandiose, scheme has implications for each of us. Each of us can act to learn and, in so doing, lead the learning of others, whatever our sphere of activity.

References

1 Conversations with Reece Overcash and Keith Hughes, March 18, 1993.
2 M. McGill and J. Slocum, *The Smarter Organization* (New York: John Wiley & Sons, 1994).
3 "John Sculley," INC., October 1987, pp. 49–60.
4 S. Sherman, 'A Master Class in Radical Change,' *Fortune*, December 13, 1993, pp. 82–90.
5 T. Horton, *What Works for Me* (New York: Random House, 1987), pp. 119–120.
6 C. H. Deutsch, 'Taking the Reins from a Legend', *New York Times*, October 30, 1988, p. 24.
7 W. Konrad, 'Cheerleading and Clerks Who Know Awls from Augers', *Business Week*, August 3, 1992, p. 51.
8 N. M. Tichy, 'G.E.'s Crotonville: A Staging Ground for Corporate Revolution', *Academy of Management Executive*, May 1989, pp. 99–106.
9 T. Tanaka, 'Developing Managers in the Hitachi Institute of Management Development,' *Journal of Management Development*, Fall 1989, pp. 27–39.
10 J. D. Judy, 'New Man at the Helm', *Enterprise*, no. 1 (1990), p. 12.
11 Conversation with Bill Kaufman, December 19, 1993.
12 As retold by Warren Bennis, 'Followers Make Good Leaders Good', *New York Times*, December 31, 1989, p. 24.
13 J. Markoff, 'Reprogramming the Hacker Elite', *New York Times*, January 2, 1994, p. 6F.
14 B. Dumain, 'Payoff from the New Management', *Fortune*, December, 1993, p. 110.

15 S. N. Chakravarty and A. Feldman, 'The Road Not Taken', *Forbes*, August 30, 1993, p. 40.

16 J. A. Belasco and R. C. Stayer, *Flight of the Buffalo* (New York: Warner, 1992), p. 321.

17 Sherman, op. cit., p. 84.

18 N. A. Nichols, 'From Complacency to Competitiveness', *Harvard Business Review*, September–October 1993, pp. 163–171.

19 R. J. House, W. D. Spangler, and J. Woycke, 'Personality and Charisma in the U.S.

Presidency: A Psychological Theory of Leader Effectiveness', *Administrative Science Quarterly* 36 (1991), pp. 364–96.

20 F. Roethlisberger, 'Data Concerning the Research Group in Supervisory Training Methods', Section 4.1, 1932 Hawthorne Studies Collection, Harvard University, as reported by Ronald G. Greenwood, 'Leadership Theory: A Historical Look', *The Journal of Leadership Studies* 1, no. 1 (1993), p. 10.

EXERCISE 11   TASK AND PEOPLE ORIENTATIONS

Source: The T/P Leadership Questionnaire was adapted by J. B. Ritchie and P. Thompson in *Organization and People*. New York: West, 1984. Copyright 1969 by the American Education Research Association.

Are you task or people oriented? Or do you have a balanced style of leading? The following items describe the people or task oriented aspects of leadership. Use any past or present experience in leading a group of people as you complete the 34-item scale. Circle whether you would most likely behave in the described way: always (**A**), frequently (**F**), occasionally (**O**), seldom (**S**) or never (**N**).

A F O S N	1.	I would most likely act as the spokesperson of the group.
A F O S N	2.	I would encourage overtime work.
A F O S N	3.	I would allow employees complete freedom in their work.
A F O S N	4.	I would encourage the use of uniform procedures.
A F O S N	5.	I would permit employees to use their own judgement in solving problems.
A F O S N	6.	I would stress being ahead of competing groups.
A F O S N	7.	I would speak as a representative of the group.
A F O S N	8.	I would encourage members for a greater effort.
A F O S N	9.	I would try out my ideas in the group.
A F O S N	10.	I would let members do their work the way they think best.
A F O S N	11.	I would be working hard for a promotion.
A F O S N	12.	I would tolerate postponement and uncertainty.
A F O S N	13.	I would speak for the group if there were visitors present.
A F O S N	14.	I would keep the work moving at a rapid pace.
A F O S N	15.	I would turn the members loose on a job and let them go to it.
A F O S N	16.	I would settle conflicts when they occur in the group.
A F O S N	17.	I would get swamped by details.
A F O S N	18.	I would represent the group at outside meetings.
A F O S N	19.	I would be reluctant to allow the members any freedom of action.
A F O S N	20.	I would decide what should be done and how it should be done.
A F O S N	21.	I would give some members some of my authority.
A F O S N	22.	Things would usually turn out as I had predicted.
A F O S N	23.	I would allow the group a high degree of initiative.
A F O S N	24.	I would assign group members to particular tasks.
A F O S N	25.	I would be willing to make changes.
A F O S N	26.	I would ask members to work harder.

A F O S N	27.	I would trust the group members to exercise good judgement.
A F O S N	28.	I would schedule the work to be done.
A F O S N	29.	I would refuse to explain my actions.
A F O S N	30.	I would persuade others that my ideas are to their advantage.
A F O S N	31.	I would permit the group to set its own pace.
A F O S N	32.	I would urge the group to beat its previous record.
A F O S N	33.	I would act without consulting the group.
A F O S N	34.	I would ask that group members follow standard rules and regulations.

T _____   P _____

The T/P Leadership Questionnaire is scored as follows:

a.   Circle the item number for statement 8, 12, 17, 18, 19, 29, 33 and 34.

b.   Write the number 1 in front of a *circled item number* if you responded **S** (seldom) or **N** (never) to that statement.

c.   Also write number 1 in front of *item numbers not circled* if you responded **A** (always) or **F** (frequently).

d.   Circle the number that you have written in front of the following statements: 3, 5, 8, 10, 15, 18, 19, 21, 23, 25, 27, 29, 31, 33 and 34.

e.   Count the *circled number 1s*. This is your score for concern for people. Record the score in the blank following the letter **P**.

f.   Count the *uncircled numbers 1s*. This is your score for concern for task. Record this number in the blank following the letter **T**.

CASE II   THE COUNCIL OF ADULT EDUCATION

Amanda Sinclair and Jeanette Baird

The Council of Adult Education (CAE) is a unique organisation in Australia. Created in 1946 by the Victorian Parliament as a statutory authority it has endured despite scant government attention to adult education. By the 1990s, with enormous upheaval in the Australian education sector, the CAE is still the largest single short-course provider for adults in Australia and recipient of approximately one-third of recurrent funds distributed by the Victorian Government to adult, community and further education.

However, as Robb Mason, a manager with 20 years experience in the CAE, observes 'we are in a dramatically changed world in which we are no longer in control as we once were … the task has become one of survival'.

With a turnover of around $15 million (41% of which is government funded), and employing 1000 tutors and 160 general staff, the CAE is a substantial enterprise. About 75% of customers and staff are women, the current director is a woman and women outnumber men among the Senior Management Group and on the CAE Board, earning it the label, in some quarters, of a 'women's organisation'.[1]

The publication of the CAE's Program Guide four times a year is a tradition for Victorians, compulsively consumed for the breadth of possibilities it offers. Courses include 'Return to Study' and accredited VCE subjects, as well as programs aimed at developing technical, vocational or professional competence. But balanced against these vocationally oriented courses is an even bigger array which affirm personal development, growth and learning as ends in themselves. In a recent brochure, CAE Director Shirley Randell invites potential customers to 'Select a treat for yourself. Give your body, mind and soul a special present'. The choices are wide: 'Pelvic Potential' is offered alongside 'Asian Noodles', 'Was Your Ancestor a Convict?', 'In Search of the Gods of Ancient Greece', 'Poetry on the Hoof', and 'Zoo Animals at Dusk'. You can go on 'Arts Getaways' and 'Jung and the Workplace' weekends or you can imbibe views on culture and life from tutors such as comedian Max Gillies and radio compere Felix Werder. Randell says that the CAE is 'in the life-changing business'.

Governance structure and political environment

The functions of the CAE, as set out in the *Council of Adult Education Act 1981* (as amended), direct it 'to provide adult learning programs and services designed to contribute to the knowledge and development of individuals and the community'. It is to provide support to other adult, community and further education providers and to participate in the setting of state priorities and policies. The CAE mission 'aims to improve the quality of life and living standards of the people of Victoria through adult education … and assists other agencies providing adult, community and further education' (see also Exhibit 11.14: Values).

The CAE reports to and has a performance agreement with the Victorian Minister for Tertiary Education and Training. Oversight of CAE operations is provided by the fifteen-member CAE Board, whose members are drawn from education, community and business circles and include a member elected by students. One board member is elected by general staff and one by teaching staff of the CAE: both of these members are women, taking the number of women on the board to nine.

Until the 1992–93 state government budget the CAE received separate line funding.

Exhibit 11.14 Values

The CAE:

- believes learning to be a life-long pursuit and that learning programs must be diverse, accessible and responsive to the changing learning needs of adults and the community;
- acknowledges the diversity of motivation adults have in attending learning programs;
- believes that successful learning programs acknowledge the adulthood of students, their individuality and capacity to learn from each other;
- understands that adults have individual learning styles and preferences and that programs should be diverse in format and approach and pay heed to individual differences;
- is committed to assisting all students to reach their learning goals;
- values a learning environment that is welcoming, friendly and supportive;
- believes in adult education processes that are enjoyable, participative, meaningful and life enhancing;
- is committed to adult education that is accessible to all Victorian adults;
- sets high expectations of quality and value in the delivery of its courses and services;
- puts great store on its statutory autonomy as a mechanism for providing an independent, innovative and relevant learning curriculum for the people of Victoria;
- values the government's contribution to and continuing support for the CAE;
- values the contribution of all its staff and aims to provide them with career planning support and effective training and development;
- is committed to equal opportunity policies and practices;
- values research in theory and practice of adult education and the promotion and dissemination of such knowledge within the state, the nation and the region;
- is committed to working cooperatively with other agencies in carrying out its mission;
- values its responsibilities as a corporate citizen of Melbourne to act in a manner consistent with sound environmental practice and to contribute to the life of the city.

Government demarcation of a separate adult education 'sector' in Victoria was marked by the proclamation of the *Adult, Community and Further Education Act 1991*, which established the Adult, Community and Further Education Board (ACFEB) plus a structure of Regional Councils (Exhibit 11.15: CAE Reporting Structure). The creation of ACFEB caused a major re-alignment of relationships among adult education providers in Victoria and was a traumatic experience for the CAE, whose autonomy had been a touchstone since invoked by the CAE's founder[2]. Cross-representation between the ACFEB and the Board of the CAE has been accomplished, after extensive negotiation by the current Director. However, uncertainties remain over how the CAE can achieve consistency with ACFEB policies, while retaining the autonomy perceived by the CAE Board and staff as central to its success.

The CAE's role and the traditional focus of its operations have come under pressure over the past 10 years, following several state inquiries into further education. More recently, a Senate Inquiry, 'Come in Cinderella' (1991), confirmed the value and significance of adult and community education. Although the CAE had for many years offered bridging education for women, these investigations have influenced the CAE's various moves into workplace education, the development of industry programs, the provision of more VCE subjects, and the current focus on accreditation of some courses. In the late-1980s, the CAE's Business Education Centre was set up to provide programs in management, business and computing with a consulting and educational materials development service. With Monash University, the CAE formed the Sir John Monash Business Centre Pty Ltd (SJMBC), to provide management and training programs. Most of these efforts by the CAE to reshape its identify have been successful, though some forays into consulting have been less so.

The CAE's environment has changed enormously since the 1970s when it was 'centre stage' in the Victorian adult education field. Until recently, the director of the CAE had a dual role which included the coordination of all adult education in Victoria. The CAE no longer occupies such a special place — it competes with other more powerful players. Procedures and policies have had to be 'tightened up', to defend against threats from competitors, 'some of whom really hate us', and governments seeking to make the CAE increasingly self-sufficient financially. Although the philosophy of adult education encourages the CAE to collaborate with other providers, such as neighbourhood houses, these organisations are also competitors. The CAE has undertaken initiatives to respond to these changing circumstances, for example services and advice are offered to other providers at a fee and expanding non-fee programs at no additional cost to government. While the CAE has made progress — for every \$1 provided by government the CAE generates a further \$1.27 — securing a 'niche' in this more open and competitive market for adult education is an ongoing challenge.

Mason, now head of Policy and Statewise Liaison, attributes many of the difficulties confronting the organisation to a radical shift in political circumstances and the philosophy of adult education. Up until the mid-1980s, the CAE was, he says, an organisation with 'a free-wheeling style, resource flexibility and doing what we wanted to do. Now we've had to negotiate and fight hard for a position and to maintain that position ... and not being the most significant player by any means.' Now government says 'we have priorities and we want to make sure they are achieved ... we will very tightly tell you what to do and tightly check that you have done it.' Mason also believes that the CAE has been affected by a shift in ideology from socially based and justified adult education to services that are more individually oriented and work-related.

CAE management argue that this more hostile environment demands a more balanced response than simply increased 'dependence on fee for service courses at the expense of our traditional programs'. Ross Gillespie, General Manager Educational Programs, says 'it means we've got to be smarter in establishing clearly the real benefits of the sort of education we offer ... we've got to get smarter at promoting how we benefit the society economically, but we've also got to show how we benefit society socially, politically, culturally.' 'There is enormous economic advantage in ensuring that people are educated and occupied, turning hands to new skills.'

Courses and customers

In 1992, the CAE offered a program of 5000 courses and catered for a total enrolment of over 60 000, including 8500 and 1000 respectively

Exhibit 11.15 Council of Adult Education reporting structure as at 6 October 1992

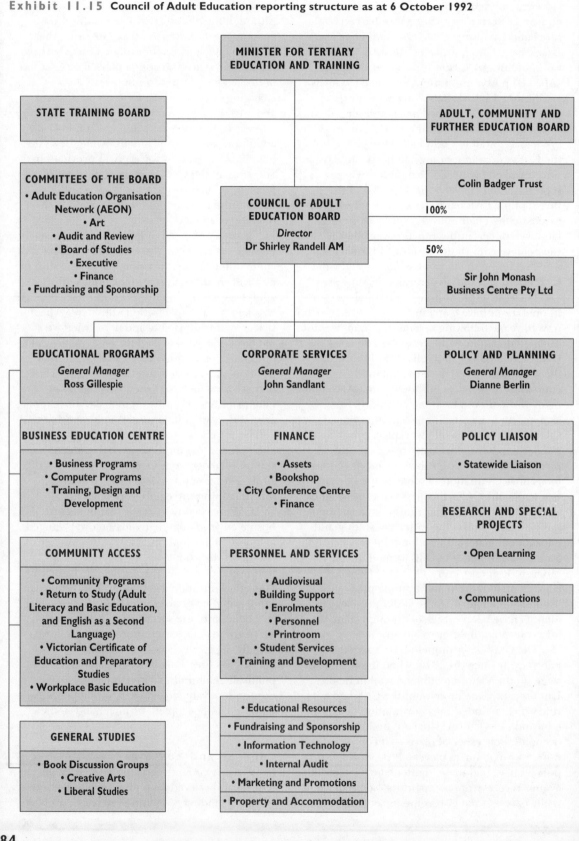

enrolled in book discussion groups and workplace education programs. The University of the Third Age Campus at the CAE had 1200 enrolments.

Diana Bianciardi, who joined the CAE in 1972 and is now Manager, General Studies, recalls the 1970s as halycon years. There were government initiatives directing funds and attention to education and particularly women's retraining: 'women were finding their feet and their voices'. In those days, the scale of operations was much smaller and people involved in programs were generalists, active in the innovation and delivery of a large range of adult education programs, including the first daytime Higher School Certificate — HSC (now Victorian Certificate of Education — VCE) subjects.

The CAE is still renowned for the freshness and relevance of its programs. New program ideas come from three sources. Current or potential tutors approach program coordinators with ideas for new courses, and existing and potential students make suggestions. Coordinators of program areas who have the expertise to initiate and plan new programs evaluate proposals, judge community needs and through their networks stay in touch with new developments. All new courses and new tutors are evaluated. Tutors usually have the opportunity to shape the evaluation forms distributed to students, and those who drop out of courses are followed up. The director and other management staff also enrol in a range of courses both for their own interest and as part of the monitoring process. Programming aims to maintain the quality of traditionally popular courses, such as painting and massage, with flexibility and responsiveness: 'you no sooner see a course than it's over and you never see it again. That's the way we operate'. The high turnover and short span of many courses has fostered a rhythm and minimisation of documentation, which is unlike other providers of technical and further education.

Dianne Berlin, General Manager, Policy and Planning, says the CAE's students have traditionally been those 'short-changed by schooling', 'who don't like tests and rolls' and don't want courses that provide certificates. But statistics reveal the CAE market is increasingly differentiated, with a highly educated group of customers, and there is growing recognition that it must credential courses 'just to provide

students with pathways to go onto TAFE, to more formal study or onto employment'. Many women benefit from these pathways and the companionship the CAE provides as they move from a cookery class to confidence-building courses, then return to study programs, VCE subjects and occasionally return to CAE as a tutor.

Roughly 75% of CAE customers are women and Randell says that the CAE's struggle for adequate funding is partially because it is seen as 'women's business'. The CAE targets women, and runs some women-only courses in activities such as abseiling and rock-climbing, where women might be intimidated by the presence of men. A highly successful Women's Day Program attracts criticism, as well as accolades: 'Every year we get at least one disgruntled member of the Victorian community who thinks we are encouraging lesbianism by running a lesbian course'. Randell responded by asking the tutor and students of that course if she could sit in and she has no qualms about its continuance: 'I am very proud of the Women's Day Program'. She adds 'we also run men-only sewing classes and are committed to increasing male enrolments in our Business Plan.'

CAE customers are stereotyped by some as the 'blue rinse' or 'twin set and pearl set'. Gillespie says: 'The figures actually contradict those stereotypes ... The biggest single group would be the 25–39 year age group, but participants come from all age groups.' 'There is a genuine fondness, a real weight of support out there that I find daunting. You can go anywhere and mention you work for the CAE and someone in the circle with a beer in hand will say "Gee I did a welding course with the CAE" ... The CAE has been all things to all people, quickly and efficiently.'

Many of the CAE's customers keep coming back and a recent quality performance survey indicated 92% satisfaction ('excellent', 'very good' or 'satisfactory' levels) for course content, teaching and value for money[3]. Yet it is the 'untapped market' that bothers John Sandlant, General Manager, Corporate Services: 'the CAE needs to stop saying "We can do all of adult education" and start finding a niche.' 'There are millions of adults in Melbourne. We only have 42 000 of them.' He argues that the CAE's traditional marketing strategy, including the 150 000 copies of the program three times a year and costing around $10 each, only reaches the customers that mirror the demographics of CAE members. 'The strike rate is not big and 70% are repeat customers'. In a bid to go beyond that portion of the market CAE programmers know well, the summer program was launched in a 3AW Caravan adjacent to CAE head office in Degraves St, with the help of local comedian Mark Mitchell, alias 'Marika'. A record number of first day enrolments were taken.

Since January 1991 there have been several increases in fees for CAE courses that have been seen by some CAE staff to jeopardise cherished values of equity and access. While enrolments have not suffered with increasing fees and a concessions policy remains, there is disquiet from some quarters of the organisation about what these more commercially oriented strategies represent.

Staff

The 160 general staff at the CAE are employed directly by the Council, rather than under the *Public Service Act* (now replaced by the *Public Sector Management Act 1991*). Of 137 permanent general staff, 26 are part-time, as are 12 of a further 23 contract staff.

Of the 983 teaching staff, 26 are employed part-time on contract, but almost all are employed on a sessional (casual) basis — employed for brief periods, with little security. They are currently covered by an interim award, though negotiations are underway with the Adult Education Tutors Association to develop an enterprise agreement under the new Victorian Industrial Relations legislation. Many tutors are long-term, with a loyal following and a strong commitment to adult learning. Some are ex-secondary teachers and others retired or semiretired university teachers, who derive satisfaction from teaching adults motivated by the idea of learning rather than by direct career incentives. Among the tutors have been, and continue to be, 'great luminaries'. Gillespie says the CAE has always been bold and cheeky in the search for good tutors, asking 'who is the best in the field?'. They have 'never had trouble recruiting' tutors who are proud to have CAE experience on a curriculum vitae. According to Randell, they 'do it for the love of it'. Berlin says 'they like the CAE ethos and they like the engagement, teaching people who are committed to learning.'

Many of the tutors are ex-secondary and tertiary teachers. Dr Jim Sait, CAE Media Officer, says that tutors have rejected the 'bureaucratic culture' of educational institutions in favour of the 'autonomy and authority' offered by CAE teaching. Managerial initiatives which are perceived to threaten their autonomy are resisted, leaving the program coordinators and managers as 'the meat in the sandwich' who 'have to "interact" with tutors and senior management'. Maintaining cohesion and quality in an organisation predominantly composed of sessional staff also poses particular management challenges, and at times a chasm between 'staff' (general staff) and tutors (teaching staff) has been sharply felt. Now though, Randell observes: 'I think we've healed that a great deal ... I want all staff to be seen as staff. The fact that people are only here for 3 hours in 1 year perhaps, doesn't mean they're any less respected, wanted and important to the organisation.'

The organisation accommodates staff seeking to work part-time or in job share arrangements to accommodate child-rearing responsibilities. Not only tutors, but also other staff including managers, have been able to arrange leave and fractional appointments to spend time with children or to cope with personal crises. The personal aspect is discussed and given legitimacy in various ways in the organisation. Although the director and executive work long hours, they 'do have a personal life'. Randell models a concern with personal priorities and she has taken many of the CAE's courses out of personal interest, in addition to monitoring quality.

Among both general and teaching staff what counts is love of learning and a respect for self-development, whatever that may involve. Some of those in managerial roles in the organisation are also tutors, and opportunities have been there for staff to develop themselves, in whatever way they chose, while doing their jobs. Staff members work either part-time or take time off, also to be artists or historians or writers or parents. Traditionally, in the CAE, there 'were no career paths'. People joined the CAE, not because they were pursuing a managerial career track and there were relatively few men in the organisation, except at the apex. At the same time, staff are far from being dilettantish about their careers in the CAE. Mason observes 'educators are opinionated people. There are lots of disagreements influenced by personal style and personal ambitions'.

The comforting intimacy of the CAE's early years, where program coordinators, tutors and customers mingled, is disappearing. The technology of delivering programs has revolutionised: Bianciardi recalls the days of a 'big cash register and a wooden frame with boxes for each course and paper slips for the number of places'. Although many within the organisation uphold the centrality of the CAE's emphasis on cultural and quality of life education, external changes have imposed organisational changes. Additional layers of management have been inserted, creating new opportunities and clearer career paths for managers but enforcing specialisation and dehumanising some processes. Some innovations were perceived to jeopardise the value placed on equity and ensuring the 'disadvantaged have a voice'. According to some, these are best maintained in the cosy and familiar environment enabling program coordinators to nurture tutors, who in turn nurture students, 'who sometimes take a whole term to find their confidence'. Because 'the ethos of adult education has been non-competitive and learning for learning's sake', it was always important that students progressed on their own terms. This belief that the ethos can be delivered only in small, familiar physical surroundings lingers despite pressures to expand the scope and scale of operations — particularly those that attract generous government subsidy, such as literacy programs.

A more hostile environment, growth and specialisation have also nurtured subcultures, with different 'floors' of the head office building levelling charges against others: 'I am as interested in social justice as my colleagues on the other floor, but I just can't afford to run a special program for these disadvantaged people'. Mason puts this down to more stringent circumstances: 'as soon as you get (funding) cuts, people get defensive. People ask "Why are we doing this, when we should be doing this?" Individuals and departments here have very strong views about what adult education should be about ... What we have now is tension ... and pressure on our people, especially programmers, to generate funds'. Sandlant argues, though, that there is a legacy of territorialism which needs to be overcome: 'They're brilliant people but I think their objectives are not CAE objectives but departmental objectives'.

The CAE is an environment where disparity of views is expected and expressed, though it may appear in various forms. A common complaint is 'we haven't been consulted' and the CAE has become 'too centralist'. Others argue that devolution had produced too many meetings without accountability. Sandlant argues that coordination by committee saps the 'focus' of the CAE: 'There are other ways to communicate apart from meetings'.

Programmers, those who devise and develop educational courses, hold a special place in the organisation and the position of General Manager Educational Programs, has always been a pivotal organisational role. The CAE has been renowned for the creativity and capacity of its programmers and the success of the organisation hinges on these intangible skills. As well as being 'so smart they could sense out and suss out new programs blindfolded' they have been a very stable group. Programmers now face increased workloads and demands for accountability within an ever tightening budget. They are required to deliver new educational initiatives 'without proper consultation and resourcing'. The value of responsiveness in programs has also meant that documentation of programs and curriculum development has been kept to a minimum: 'formal accredited curricula that run for a full 12 months are so out of the culture of this organisation'. There is 'little experience with resourcing, staffing or developing longer term programs'.

The very success of the programming function and culture thus poses some problems for those seeking to introduce change.

From the perspective of Corporate Services, Sandlant sees that the traditional emphasis on educational values continues to threaten the CAE's survival.

I really felt when I walked in here my job would be wiped out ... apart from the finance officer, director and a few others, nobody else in the organisation knew what it meant that we'd had continuing operating deficits, losses every year ... we were effectively bankrupt ... (but) it wasn't permeating throughout the organisation. The management structure still continued to focus on education and expected government to keep picking us up ... The in-ground culture of this organisation is that we are protected.

Gillespie argues that the CAE's adaptiveness is not jeopardised because it 'is steeped in history and culture'. Though he has been with the organisation less than a year, he has long 'reflected on what it would be like to work there'. Infected by 'the scent of the place' when he and his wife did a massage course, Gillespie notes, tongue-in-cheek, that 'I haven't yet done my apprenticeship which I believe lasts around eight to nine years'. But he maintains that the level of commitment and the intellectual calibre of CAE staff 'make it more responsive to change' and the pace of restructuring in the organisation and 'the continual shifting of stacks of responsibility' over the years are evidence. He relishes that working for the CAE is more than just a job: 'People expect you to learn the culture and become committed to it ... You'd find it difficult to get anyone here who is not committed to the ideals of liberal education and social justice'. All those interviewed agree the CAE has a unique warmth as an organisation. Executive Officer Elvie Gothard points out that:

Temporary staff always comment. It's like a big family, a great big family. I was tutoring for a little while in piano and singing. Students come back, the comradeship and friendships are made and carry on long after — between tutors and students as well as between students ... There's something for you, whether you're 16 or 80. Even in the bad times, there's always someone who'll say 'we understand'. There's that feeling, always someone to help, off the cuff support, someone will pop their arm around you, just for two secs. In all the years I've worked [in other places], there was never that.

The CAE home

The CAE is located in the heart of Melbourne, adjacent to Flinders Street Station and with high accessibility, particularly for people from the country and those dependent on public transport. It is a crowded and busy venue. Three lifts are crammed with course customers discussing their classes. People rub shoulders, young and old, in wheelchairs and with strollers, but with evident camaraderie. The floor which houses the management of the CAE is like the other floors — open plan, with dividers located a bit haphazardly, but quite unintimidating and devoid of the sense of corporate hush and clearly defined structure of most executive headquarters. The taped interviews for the case recorded a backdrop of bustle, talk and phones ringing.

Recently the CAE purchased the building with a government guarantee, and was assured of a 'home'. Sandlant says 'There was quite a reaction from government ... They were selling assets, not buying them ... We were directed to consider a lot of ex-school, ex-government offices and we had to argue very strongly that adults coming here day, night and weekends had significant benefits being close to public transport. It had been a way of life for a lot of people'. Staff believe that without the building, the CAE was threatened with banishment 'to the suburbs', a fate equated with organisational death. The current director was also strongly committed, the building becoming a symbol not just of a future for the CAE but of her own contribution as organisational leader and protector. While the treasurer of the day was known to be opposed to the purchase and there was a climate of opinion abroad that the CAE was only for 'middle class, blue rinse women', the CAE managed to persuade government to back the organisation. However, Randell warns staff that this is no guarantee of the CAE's future: 'As always, we live only by how good we are at meeting the needs of two large and interested bodies; our students and the government which funds us'.

Past leaders

With four directors over 47 years, the CAE has a history of leaders with impressively long and devoted terms of duty. Colin Badger retired in 1971 after a quarter of a century in the job — his widely lauded vision for the CAE, though, is still present and is currently being recorded and celebrated through an oral history. The strong and persisting organisational attachment to autonomy is a legacy of his original vision.

Badger was followed by Colin Cave who brought an expansionist strategy and, as a country person, a commitment to country education centres. Another strong personality, he was 'a born educator' with 'great ideas ... off he'd be, way out in front of the organisation ... and all the staff would be complaining about the workload' and he 'blustered about women's studies' though 'gave people their head ... put a lot of faith in CAE staff'. Tony Delves, the third director, brought an administrative focus and experience with the TAFE sector, which served the CAE well for a period. Delves was seen positively, by some CAE staff, for being '*laissez-faire* ... trusting the professionalism of staff and very creative and intelligent'. At the same time, some observers believed that Delves did not pay enough attention to political changes, which left the CAE in an increasingly precarious situation: 'We didn't know who our enemies were'. In the late 1980s with deteriorating economic circumstances and a stringent budgetary regime for government, the CAE's financial management was criticised on several occasions by Victoria's auditor-general. 'In the past the director of the CAE has been a figurehead, somebody supporting the educational role of the organisation'. The CAE now needed a director who would rein in the organisation and provide management discipline and accountability to government, as well as ensuring a future for the CAE in a competitive and vocationally oriented educational climate.

The director

Dr Shirley Randell was appointed at the start of 1991, the fourth director of the CAE and the first woman. Her task was made explicit in her performance agreement:

When I came in, there were two things to get right. The first was the finances, to get Corporate Services up ... We were offside with the Auditor-General, Premier, Finance and Treasury ... and the second relationships in the sector ... the Division of Further Education and the CAE were at loggerheads. They didn't speak to each other.

With a management apprenticeship in the Commonwealth Schools Commission, Department of Prime Minister and Cabinet and the ACT Government, Randell brought her considerable skills as a self-described 'bureaucrat' to the job. She consults widely, seeking advice and support from people in government and education: "When I was in the Commonwealth, I had direct links with Finance, Treasury, Prime Minister and Cabinet. A lot of things happen informally and you can get a lot done by knowing somebody and smoothing the way'.

Not from Victoria, she immediately set out to create these contacts and recruited, as General Manager Corporate Services, someone with an intimate knowledge of the Victorian public service. Her tireless 'networking' is regarded by observers as one of her great strengths. At an official function, one minister marvelled at her capacity to 'work the room', though others feel she overtaxes her connections. In her previous

job as dean in a college, Randell's first actions were to set up two women's networks, one inside the college and one in the town. In her current job her contacts range from politicians through educational institutions, state and federal bureaucracies, and women's networks. She says 'I have lunches regularly, currently with women politicians (in the new government) and women identify immediately with what the CAE is trying to do'.

The task of raising the profile of and building support for the CAE is one Randell has pursued through networks but also through an extensive program of public speaking. Her file of addresses to various groups is extensive and each speech is crafted to each group's interests. In Randell's desire to 'get the message right', her perfectionism is a source of irritation to some staff. Some say that her 'sticking to the script' is due to lack of confidence in speaking publicly. But others see a missionary zeal, which resonates with Randell's early adult experience in New Guinea. And Randell says that public speaking is something she enjoys and does well. Reactions to this leadership emphasis vary, as do perceptions of her performance. Staff members note the priorities: "Shirley is out there ... not nearly as focused on our programs ... but that's because of the times, because she has to be'.

Annual addresses to staff have been instituted, which Randell and her executive draft meticulously. In them is a meshing of public and private domains, a tough business-like tone and affirmation of the personal, spiritual and 'passionate'. Included in the CAE's achievements are seven additions to the 'world population' (babies born to staff), alongside a 92% pass rate for CAE VCE students. Along with the accomplishments of the Finance Department in processing 6000 salary payments and 4500 teacher payments, she cites increasing student confidence and one Access student 'coming to classes for the first time without sunglasses by the end of the year'. These addresses, now a ritual, also evoke contrasting responses.

An owl is the long cherished logo of the CAE. Randell says 'When I came in there would have been twenty different logos, 20 different owls, different sizes and places on the page ... There was no feeling of the organisation as a whole ... There was great dismay about changing the loved owl ... but it really was necessary for us'. By her 1992 address, she quotes the CAE Board Chair in arguing that 'now that we have secured the nest for the owl and its many fledglings, we need to get on with the hard business of lining the nest and producing the owl's eggs'. The familial, domestic and maternal images of the enterprise are frequent, though interspersed with sterner reminders.

Alongside the desire to get things right, and using networks to build support, is a commitment to consultation as a management device. Randell defends this in political terms: 'My strong preference is for my three general managers to know everything I say publicly outside and I always give drafts to them'. She cites a boss from her previous experience who 'would go out and make the most outrageous statements' which would create 'all this political flak'. She adds 'I prefer to consult simply because it makes for better decision making in the longer run. The more heads you can get, within limits, the better it is ... They've all got something to add which improves it, so it's better for the organisation to get it'.

Randell's style of consultation has not been universally embraced by an organisation accustomed to devolution. She likes to 'stay in touch' and 'being on site' is important to her, for example with a difficult student: 'I was able to see my staff handle that in a very quiet and effective manner'. She sets 'personal goals'. In 1991 Randell visited the fifty regional centres which were attached to the CAE through legislation and another goal has been 'spending an hour on the phone in each department every season, giving me an understanding of student inquiries and staff pressures'. She says 'I want to understand the work of the organisation'. She also says that she tries to give feedback to her staff. Randell suffered from a lack of feedback in previous jobs and knows how important it still is to her for someone to say 'That was a good job'. However, the benefit of her feedback is sometimes undercut by her desire to be close to the action and her demand that things be right.

Randell is also regarded as seeking too much advice and hence betraying lack of confidence in herself, while at the same time not devolving enough decision making. Mason recalls that the organisation has been through periods when it was held that 'all things should be decided by everybody'. The organisation still has a powerful mythology around the value of participation: staff expect to be consulted. But Randell is very clear about her own executive responsibility: 'Finally

I'm the one responsible for every decision. It's my job that goes if we don't meet the AG's criticisms and I don't deliver to the board.' On at least two major decisions she has overridden the advice of her senior managers.

While Randell appeals to the traditional CAE values of growth and quality of life, the other part of the job has been to introduce managerial values and controls to the organisation. She admits that she was nervous, accepting the job: 'We were going down the tube', and there was 'no internal auditor and no audit committee'. She saw a slackness of accountability, which she attributed to a view of the organisation of being outside the public service, and she set about redressing it. Apart from appointing the new General Manager, Corporate Services, Randell says: 'I am lucky, I've got a really good board chairperson and finance committee chairperson with good financial experience and I've established an audit committee and I've got a woman who's head of that who is an auditor.'

The determination to improve administration in the organisation has also startled those accustomed to a more relaxed and 'laid-back' approach. She says with satisfaction that it has taken 2 years but 'we've now got thirty procedures and policies' in place.

When I came into the organisation, standards were very sloppy. I didn't get anything that didn't have spelling mistakes ... I rarely got anything that reached the standards of excellence that I require. Staff think that I play games crossing 't's and dotting 'i's. I know how important it is to get it right. Anything that goes to a minister has to be as good as it can possibly be ... but I try to draw back when I am being absolutely unreasonable, and I am sometimes.

The twin desires of the director — to be close to the action and demand that things be right — is read by some staff as overbearing: an observer says 'it is about ticking every box, every box must be ticked'. Her drive is also seen to be at odds with the values of the CAE: 'Not only doesn't she look after herself, but sometimes fails to look after the needs of others, even when they are obviously struggling'. Randell evokes both admiration and unease for being 'upfront, forceful, domineering and demanding, by far the hardest task master'.

Some regard Randell's philosophy as feminist and approach as a manager as an unpalatable mix. In her previous jobs she was typically one woman in an all-male environment — always the one to say 'well, what about the women?'. 'Other people get the impression that you're only interested in one track', though if she waited for one of her male colleagues to raise women's issues or the impact of policies on women 'they never did'. She is now relieved to be in an organisation where she is not the only one giving voice to women's concerns. In fact, she sees the reverse problem in the CAE and now argues that her primary concern is for 'a balanced organisation … If you have the whole range of human experience looking at a problem, you get a balanced perspective'.

People in the organisation are unsure of Randell and her feminism. In some circumstances, such as when the previous Chair, an older person, kept introducing her as 'the new girl on the block' she refrained from comment, but on other issues she goes into battle. She insists on Ms as the title used and has been relentless in instituting Equal Employment Opportunity (EEO) requirements and demands for Koori appointments. Her curriculum vitae is a meticulously presented catalogue of all awards, publications (including many in popular magazines and co-authored), speeches and invitations. Observers note that 'she gets tarred with the over-ambitious woman brush' and some staff regard her promotional efforts as too close to self-promotion, neither as selfless nor as nurturant as a good mother should be. This means that her efforts to connect with staff are sometimes misinterpreted; for example, her public thanks to her staff are not always warmly welcomed. While no one volunteered that working for Randell was complicated by her gender, one staff member admits the appeal of 'just being a weak female with a man to look after me'.

Randell recognises the criticisms she attracts as a leader. She volunteers a feature of her style that is more typical of women: 'I am very conscious of what I don't know. That's something about women'. She acknowledged that adult education was 'very different' and that she acquired her confidence in the job slowly and methodically. Asked whether people judge her more harshly because she is a woman she replies:

In another organisation they might … Because this is a women's … No, no I think you're right. You didn't say

anything but you asked the question. I think people have women managers under much greater scrutiny.

While she would like to think she has learned to live with this, Randell readily admits the difficulties:

I have learned that you don't have to be liked by everybody. That's difficult for women I think to learn. Obviously I'd like everybody to like me, but I know now I can't expect it.

Randell has also learned to protect herself by not admitting mistakes so readily. 'Whereas often women are much more open about sharing the things they don't do quite right' she now avoids admitting and discussing self-perceived mistakes because they are too readily blown up into a disaster by highly competing peers. When asked how something went, she used to say 'Great, although I could have handled one aspect better'. Now she asserts the need for women to market themselves and their organisations more strongly.

This marketing of herself and the organisation is not without tensions, for herself and CAE staff. To those inside and outside the CAE who see her efforts as 'self-aggrandisement' rather than for the CAE, she says:

I've learned that if I don't sing my praises … If I'm the one that says 'I did the bad thing', that is the one thing that is remembered. You learn you've got to be positive about yourself. The other side of that coin is people say 'All she's interested in is herself'. And that is because you are against the model. Traditionally women do not brag, they do not get the limelight so that when they do, they are perceived to be only about self-aggrandisement … If you are convinced that what you are doing is right, you will always get criticism. When you hear it, you look at it and you examine yourself and ask 'for what reason did I do that?' and 'well, yes there was that in it and I'll address that next time'.

Randell cites her commitment to the CAE and to seeing out her 5-year contract. She is aware that this decision may not be in her best career interests, but 'like most women I want to do this job very well indeed … I've never had a career path, foolishly'.

Randell faces particular challenges as a woman leader. She has struggled with and reflected on her own femininity — lack of confidence in some areas, wanting to be liked and needing good feedback, the desire for a personal life while trying to stay on top of a demanding job. Her avowed feminism which is a central part of her public profile has not won universal support internally and she attracts criticism in the way she works — the high demands she places on herself and others. Women in the organisation have regarded her cautiously and not as comfortable to work with as the *laissez-faire*, charisma or paternalism of her male predecessors.

The senior management team and executive

The previous director had inserted an extra layer of seniority into the CAE, in anticipation of further growth and as a reward for personal performance. Randell's belief that the CAE had too many senior managers lead to a difficult dismantling. The Office of the Director became the Executive Team. The executive includes Randell and the three general managers: Berlin, Gillespie and Sandlant. Gillespie and Sandlant were appointments made by Randell and Berlin transferred from Educational Programs to Policy and Planning when Pat Crudden retired (Exhibit 11.16). Elvie Gotthard, the Executive Officer to the Director and the Board, and the secretaries of

the general managers are part of a wider Executive Team on whom Randell relies.

In the appointment of Sandlant as General Manager Corporate Services, Randell was seen to be 'taking on deck the Auditor-General's (AG) criticisms' and the result is the CAE's in 'much better financial shape'. Sandlant's appointment was widely applauded as a 'coup' which Randell worked hard to accomplish — 'she's so persistent ... She kept moving and moving and moving till she got him'. Sandlant is from a different world. With 'some 28 years in government' he has 'an ability to perceive where negotiations might be handled in a better way to optimise results for your department, as well as being very conscious of the way government must be'. But Sandlant is not just a bureaucrat — he runs his own accounting business, and is energetic and entrepreneurial. That he does not share the organisational reverence for adult education has prompted the disapproval of some CAE staff. The new managers have brought with them the language of 'products', 'markets' and 'the bottom line'. These initiatives have sat uneasily for some lower down in the organisation who treat the added administrative burden as additional to their real work of facilitating good teaching. They argue 'Look I just want to get on and organise my classes'.

Exhibit 11.16 Organisational structure: CAE senior management as at 6 October 1992

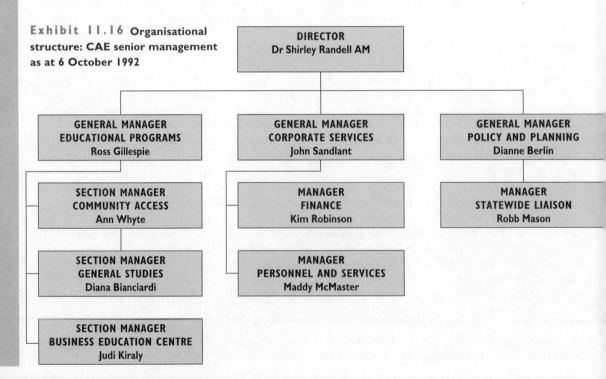

The executive meet every Monday morning. Randell presides, often with a 'piece of paper with things written all over' and works through, 'crossing notes off as she works through them'. General managers see her as firmly in control, 'always a couple of days ahead' of them in her workload. Though the members of the executive have adjacent offices, there is not a high level of informal contact: 'There are three very distinctly different general managers, not only in their modes of operation, backgrounds ... philosophies and values and their understanding about management'. Their interdependency is managed through formal meetings and the director. One of them notes 'we rarely sit together'. The source of their 'lack of caucusing' is privately reflected on — a function of difference, rivalry, workload or Randell's presence — though not discussed by executive members who tend to operate 'autonomously'.

Yet Randell is proud of her creation of 'a really well-balanced team, all new, I've changed all of them in the past 2 years'. She adds that she needs her general managers 'to be better than me'. 'The best people make you look better as a manager. They have to enhance your work'. She saw, in a previous job, a chief executive who was 'frightened by excellence ... didn't like it if any of his staff were better than him in any way'.

The Senior Management Group (SMG) consists of general managers and senior managers, the next level of management. Formerly there were six men and four women in this group. With Randell's own appointment and staff replacements at the next level, this ratio has reversed to six women and four men in the SMG. There are formal weekly meetings of the SMG and comment from senior managers on policies and programs is sought and expected: 'anything that goes out gets circulated'.

Conclusion

The CAE is a Victorian institution. It is 'rooted back where it started' and this belief in its history, some argue, is one of its 'competitive advantages'. Yet the history that is the source of its strength threatens to overpower its capacity to find a contemporary identity or be reborn under new leadership. It is now surrounded by an intensely competitive educational sector in which the value of learning as an end in itself is being trampled in the stampede to make education 'pay' by making it more vocationally oriented and relevant to the

workplace. In this climate the CAE's allies are its students and committed and influential supporters rather than bureaucracies or other institutional friends.

The mythology of the former organisation and former leaders makes the task for the current director a daunting one. And the criteria for success are shifting. History has judged Badger as a great 'educationalist', a man with a vision for adult education. He left an indelible 'imprint', that has been a source of purpose and cohesion. That the CAE is no longer in a position to paint bold visions is a political reality that is resisted by some and reluctantly accepted by many others.

The new CAE, symbolised in the single owl, is seen to be more 'professional', having 'got its act together' and be in much better shape financially. The 1992 Annual Report cites 'an improvement in our operating surplus to $915 000 (from a loss of $232 000 in 1991) together with reduction in working capital deficit'.[4] While this comparative financial health is generally credited to Sandlant, Randell's political astuteness is noted by others: 'As soon as she got here she invited the AG in'. A staff member concedes: 'they'd have to be impressed with Shirley's performance'. Randell 'has taken the tough decisions' and has overseen a turnaround in financial performance, dispensation from the AG's criticisms and a firmer foundation to a future in the education sector. The CAE Board is now well-regarded and Sandlant's appointment, a symbol of financial soundness. Mason says:

I think it's been extremely tough in this sector ... The fact that we're still here, the fact that we still get a fair degree of government funding, the fact that we now own the building, the fact that we maintain an independent charter — and it is at risk — I think is a tribute to Shirley. We've never been so much at risk as we have been in the last four to five years.

Yet Randell's skills in steering the CAE through testing political circumstances are also not universally recognised. An observer noted that personal ambition, regarded as an essential prerequisite for organisational ascendancy in male leadership, is more distasteful and suspiciously regarded in her case. However, when asked if gender influenced the way Randell's performance was judged, those in the organisation argued that it was irrelevant that she was a woman: 'Shirley is just Shirley and she is judged on her leadership style'. While jokes circulate that 'the men feel oppressed', men inside the organisation deny this and are among her more vocal supporters. In spite of the strong value in the CAE about equal employment opportunity, the fact that the CAE is 'a woman's organisation' and 'a women's organisation' remain undiscussed and undiscussable. There is sensitivity in the organisation because of 'an ancient view' in some political and bureaucratic circles that 'adult education is about middle class, blue rinse women'. The CAE has fought hard to rid itself of this label while still affirming that educational programs targeted at women are important. It has also fought the perception that an organisation staffed by women, many on a part-time basis, is 'less professional' and 'low status'. Views of women in organisations and the difficulties of challenging those views are among many issues that Randell and the CAE confronts.

Inside the organisation there are some staff who don't want to embrace the new CAE or the approach of its management. Despite a high level of commitment and intellect among CAE staff, regarded as one of its great assets, there are those who have misgivings about new management priorities, when confronting increased workloads. Staff trained to deliver, with a high degree of autonomy, the CAE's traditional programs are struggling with new priorities of resourcing, documentation and accreditation. Sandlant says 'the CAE has got a significant decision to make about where it's going' and he worries that the commitment of staff that is so inwardly focused is an impediment. 'The perception of staff is we're way up, on top. I don't see that. I think we've come from the floor to the table top, but we have got a long way to go.' He goes on:

The bulk of people here do not understand or do not accept that the CAE's resources should be directed to other than educational programs, such as building international ties or representing government in adult education ... My view is if we do that, that is, restrict our focus to educational provider, we are no more than a TAFE or neighbourhood body ... The CAE would be out the back door in a number of years.

For Gillespie, the task is a balancing one: 'it is a fundamental dilemma in this organisation ... we've got to get the right balance between short course fee-for-service, community access, creative arts, liberal studies focus and the accredited programs that the economy, governments and increasing numbers of our participants are pushing us towards'. For Randell 'the task is one of balancing people too — the educators and the accountants, the dreamers and the doers.'

Endnotes

1   The proportion of women in CAE management and staff, compared with other government and semigovernment agencies, has been assessed favourably against a benchmark of 25%, which few have achieved.

2   For this and other details of the CAE's history and evolution we are indebted to Mason's MEd. Studies thesis 'Council of Adult Education: Policies, Politics and Performance 1947–1987', 1992.

3   Council of Adult Education Annual Report, 1992, p. 7.

4   Council of Adult Education Annual Report 1992, p. 4.

PART 4

Organisational processes

12

Decision making

13

Communication

14

Organisational culture and socialisation

15

Organisational change and development

Leadership and learning are indispensable to each other.

— John Fitzgerald Kennedy

Remarks prepared for delivery at the Trade Mart in Dallas (22 November 1963)

DECISION MAKING

Learning objectives

- Compare *programmed and non-programmed decisions.*

- Describe *dimensions of decision making.*

- Identify *the steps in the decision-making process.*

- Identify *key issues for ill-defined decision problems.*

- Describe *decision rules that are used in*

  well-defined decision problems.

- Explain *factors that prevent rational decision making.*

- Compare *individual and group decision making.*

- Identify *specific techniques for stimulating creativity.*

- List *steps in strategic decision making.*

12

Chapter

The focus of this chapter is on decision making. The quality of the decisions that managers reach is the yardstick of their effectiveness.[1] Sometimes just one or two exceptionally good or exceptionally poor decisions can have significant effects on a manager's career or an organisation's success. Union Carbide management made several poor decisions in the aftermath of the cataclysmic accident involving the release of methyl isocyanate in Bhopal, India, in 1984. This tragic event took the lives of 200 people. The accident itself, as well as the subsequent decisions made regarding the handling of the accident, had profound effects on Union Carbide. Worldwide indignation and censure contributed to a collapse in the value of the company's stock, a downgrading of its credit rating, a hostile takeover attempt (by GAF Corp.) and damage claims totalling billions of dollars.

Because decision making is so very important and can have such significant effects, as illustrated in the Union Carbide example above, it has been suggested that management is decision making. It would be a mistake, however, to conclude that only managers make decisions. Increasingly, important decisions are being made in organisations by non-managers. Thus, while decision making is an important management process, it is fundamentally a *people* process. This chapter, therefore, describes and analyses decision making in terms that reflect the ways in which people make decisions upon their understanding of individual, group and organisational goals and objectives.

TYPES OF DECISIONS

Managers in various kinds of organisations may be separated by background, lifestyle and distance, but sooner or later they must all make decisions. Even when the decision process is highly participative in nature, with full involvement by subordinates, it is the manager who is ultimately responsible for the outcomes of a decision. In this section, our purpose is to present a classification system into which various kinds of decisions can be placed, regardless of whether the manager makes the decision unilaterally or in consultation with, or delegation to, subordinates.

Specialists in the field of decision making have developed several ways of classifying different types of decisions. For the most part, these classification systems are similar, differing mainly in terminology. We use the widely adopted distinction suggested by Herbert Simon.[2] Simon distinguishes between two types of decisions:

1. *Programmed decisions.* If a particular situation occurs often, a routine procedure will usually be worked out for solving it. Decisions are **programmed** to the extent that they are repetitive and routine and a definite procedure has been developed for handling them.
2. *Non-programmed decisions.* Decisions are **non-programmed** when they are novel and unstructured. There is no established procedure for handling the problem, either because it has not arisen in exactly the same manner before or because it is complex or extremely important. Such decisions deserve special treatment.

While the two classifications are broad, they point out the importance of differentiating between programmed and non-programmed decisions. The managements of most organisations face great numbers of programmed decisions in their daily operations. Such decisions should be treated without expending unnecessary organisational resources on them. On the other hand, the non-programmed decision must be properly identified as such since it is this type of decision that forms the basis for allocating billions of dollars worth of resources in our economy every year. Unfortunately, it is the human process involving this type of decision that we know the least about.[3] Exhibit 12.1 presents a breakdown of the different types of decisions, with examples of each type, in different kinds of organisations. The exhibit illustrates that programmed and non-programmed decisions require different kinds of procedures and apply to distinctly different types of problems.

Traditionally, programmed decisions have been handled through rules, standard operating procedures, and the structure of the organisation that develops specific procedures for handling them. Operations researchers — through the development of mathematical models — have facilitated the handling of these types of decisions.

On the other hand, non-programmed decisions have usually been handled by general problem-solving processes, judgement, intuition and creativity. Unfortunately, the advances that modern management techniques have made in improving non-programmed decision making have not been nearly as great as the advances they have made in improving programmed decision making.[4]

Ideally, the main concern of top management should be non-programmed decisions, while first-level management should be concerned with programmed decisions. Middle managers in most organisations concentrate mostly on programmed decisions, although in some cases they will participate in non-programmed decisions. In other words, the nature, frequency and degree of certainty surrounding a problem should dictate at what level of management the decision should be made.

Exhibit 12.1 Types of decisions		Programmed Decisions	Non-programmed Decisions
	Type of problem	Frequent, repetitive, routine, much certainty regarding cause-and-effect relationships	Novel, unstructured, much uncertainty regarding cause-and-effect relationships
	Procedure	Dependence on policies, rules and definite procedures	Necessity for creativity, intuition, tolerance for ambiguity, creative problem solving
	Examples	*Company:* Periodic reorders of inventory *University:* Necessary grade-point average for good academic standing *Health care:* Procedure for admitting patients *Government:* Merit system for promotion of state employees	*Company:* Diversification into new products and markets *University:* Construction of new classroom facilities *Health care:* Purchase of experimental equipment *Government:* Reorganisation of state government agencies

Obviously, problems arise in those organisations where top management expends much time and effort on programmed decisions.[5] One unfortunate result of this practice is a neglect of long-range planning, which is subordinated to other activities, whether the organisation is successful or is having problems. If the organisation is successful, this justifies continuing the policies and practices that have achieved success. If the organisation experiences difficulty, its current problems have first priority and occupy the time of top management. In either case, long-range planning ends up being neglected.

Finally, the neglect of long-range planning usually results in an overemphasis on short-run control. This results in a lack of delegation of authority to lower levels of management, which often has adverse effects on motivation and satisfaction.

UNDERSTANDING DECISION MAKING[6]

Before we go on to consider how decisions are made and what the outcomes might be, we need to understand the dimensions along which decisions and our description of decision making differ. There are three dimensions, relating to how certain we are about outcomes, how well structured the decisions are, and whether we are more interested in *how* decisions are made or *what* those decisions are.

Types of outcomes

Outcomes vary in terms of how certain we are that, if we choose a particular course of action, the outcome that we want will follow. For example, to achieve the outcome of employment you may have chosen to study (your course of action). How certain are you that this course of action will result in employment? Did you choose this course of action because you were absolutely certain that you would get a job, or because you thought that this was the course of action that was most likely to get you a job?

In decision-making, outcomes are classified as being certain, risky or uncertain.

1. *Certain (no risk).* The decision maker has complete knowledge of the outcome of each alternative and the task is to establish preferences among those alternatives.
2. *Risky.* The decision maker has some probabilistic estimate of the outcomes of each alternative. Decision making under conditions of risk is probably the most common situation.[7]
3. *Uncertain.* The decision maker has absolutely no knowledge of the probability of the outcome of each alternative.

In the following sections, we will look at how the level of uncertainty affects both the process and outcomes of decision making.

Types of problems

The three outcomes described above present us with very different types of decision problems. For example, imagine that you must employ a new accountant. You have interviewed three possible candidates, and you must select one. You are, in this example, facing a problem with a certain outcome. You know that if you select Pat from this group of three, then Pat and not one of the other candidates will start work for your company. This is an example of a *well-defined decision problem*. In some cases, you have a fixed set of alternatives available (for example the universities that we can attend). To make your decision, you collect information about these alternatives and, based on this information, make a choice. Well-defined decision problems are associated with certain outcomes and often require programmed decisions to be made.

It is not difficult, however, to imagine a situation in which the outcome is by no means certain. You may, for example, be facing a high level of turnover within your organisation. What strategies do you employ to deal with the situation? And how certain are you that any one of these strategies will be successful? When you face problems for which the solutions are unclear, and you must estimate their likely success, you are facing an *ill-defined decision problem*. Such a decision problem, which is more likely to be associated with uncertain or risky outcomes, requires that we make an unprogrammed decision.

Types of approaches

In attempting to understand decision making, researchers have adopted two approaches: normative and descriptive. *Normative* approaches are concerned with the outcomes that individuals choose. They use models of 'perfect' decision makers to determine the best choice, and then compare real decisions with these perfect choices. These models amply demonstrate that real decision makers rarely behave perfectly or rationally. Such comparisons have raised interesting questions concerning our behaviour as decision makers.

- Do we lack decision-making skills? Would we make perfect decisions if we had better skills? This type of thinking has resulted in efforts to develop better decision aids — expert systems are one example.
- Do our goals differ from those of the perfect decision maker? Is an acceptable decision just as good as the best decision? This has resulted in a distinction between two decision rules — satisfying and optimising — that we will return to later.
- Do we face too much information? Has this led us to develop simple rules of thumb to guide our decisions? We will return to this question when we discuss decision heuristics and biases.
- Are we influenced by motives and emotions that we cannot control? We will return to this when we discuss motivational factors affecting decision making.
- Or are rational models of decision making wrong?

The many problems faced by normative models led researchers to investigate more closely just *how* we go about making decisions. In *descriptive* or *process* models of decision making, we focus on understanding the process by which a decision was made, rather than focusing on the relationship between the conditions under which decisions are made and the outcomes. We will consider both types of approaches in subsequent sections.

In the next section, we describe a model of the decision-making process. In terms of that model, the first steps describing how we define the problem and generate solutions fit better into these descriptive approaches. The final stages in this process, the selection of an alternative, fits better into normative approaches to decision making. To understand the decisions that managers make, we need to understand both the *how* and *what* of decision making.

THE DECISION-MAKING PROCESS

Decisions should be thought of as a means rather than an end. They are the *organisational mechanisms* through which an attempt is made to achieve a desired state. They are, in effect, an *organisational response* to a problem. Every decision is the outcome of a dynamic process that is influenced by a multitude of forces. This process is diagrammed in Exhibit 12.2. The reader should not, however, interpret this outline to mean that decision making is a fixed procedure. It is a sequential process rather than a series of steps. This sequence diagram enables us to examine each element in the normal progression that leads to a decision.

Exhibit 12.2 shows that the decision-making process differs depending on the type of decision problem that we face. The process is considerably more complex when we face ill-defined or uncertain decision problems. In those cases, we are most likely to make unprogrammed decisions. Problems that occur infrequently, with a great deal of uncertainty surrounding the outcome, require that the manager utilise the entire process. For problems that occur frequently, however, this is not necessary. If a policy is established to handle such problems, it will not be necessary to develop and evaluate alternatives each time a similar problem arises.

In this section we will discuss these stages in the decision-making process. In the next two sections, we will go on to consider how the tasks in some of these stages differ, depending on the type of decision that we face. How we go about generating, evaluating and selecting alternatives is determined by whether we are facing ill-defined or well-defined decision problems.

Establishing specific goals and objectives, and measuring results

Goals and objectives are needed in each area where performance influences the effectiveness of the organisation. If goals and objectives are adequately established, they will dictate what results must be achieved and the measures that indicate whether or not they have been achieved. An outstanding example of effectively establishing goals and objectives and measuring results is the well-known Japanese firm Sony. One reason that Sony is so successful is that it closely tracks its progress towards established objectives and responds quickly when such progress is lagging. Sony's specific goals and objectives, coupled with its constant scanning of the environment to detect changes in consumer preferences and competitors' product mix, allow it to make sound decisions rapidly.

Problem identification and definition

A necessary condition for a decision is a problem — if problems did not exist, there would be no need for decisions. Problems typically result from a determination that a discrepancy exists between a desired state and current

Exhibit 12.2
The decision-making process

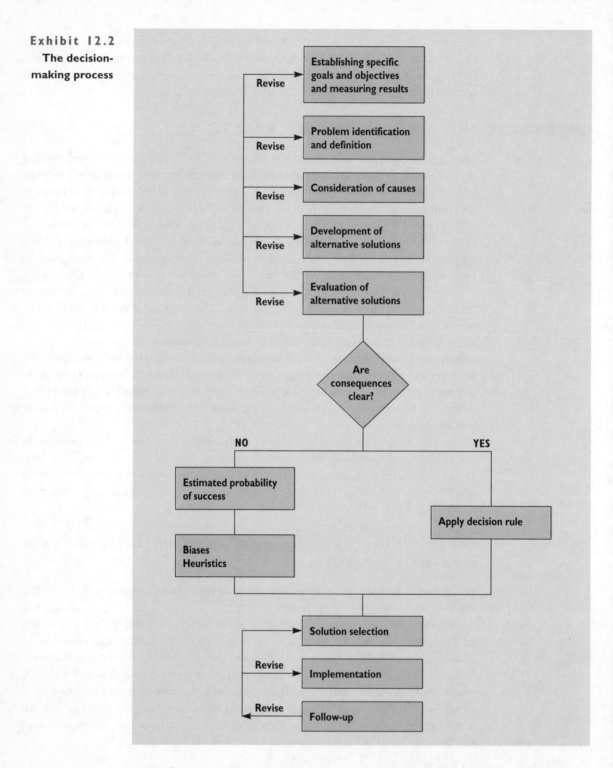

reality.[8] This underscores the importance of establishing goals and objectives. How critical a problem is for the organisation is measured by the gap between the levels of performance specified in the organisation's goals and objectives and the levels of performance attained. Thus, a gap of 20% between a sales volume objective and the volume of sales achieved signifies that some problem exists.

There are two traps for decision makers in this stage: defining the problem in terms of solutions and identifying symptoms as problems. When a sales manager says 'The decrease in profits is due to poor product quality' she has implied a solution: the analysis of the situation carries with it an implication of how the situation should be solved. *Defining the problem in terms of a solution* means that we restrict information search and may develop suboptimum solutions. Similarly, should a manager say 'Our problem is a 32% decrease in orders' he has confused a symptom with the problem. The factors resulting in this decrease — poor quality and change in consumer preferences — are the real problem. *Identifying symptoms as problems* means that we have undertaken a superficial analysis of the situation and therefore our strategies may fail to resolve the problem.

Consideration of causes

While not impossible, it is ordinarily difficult and ill-advised to determine a solution to a problem when the problem cause is unknown. The practice of blood-letting and the use of leeches are examples of solutions that formerly were applied to a variety of medical problems. If the causes of the medical conditions had been known, other solutions would have been implemented. If an organisation wishes to address the problem of declining sales, how can it decide on an appropriate solution if it does not know the reason for the decline? If sales are falling because the product is no longer price competitive, possible solutions will be quite different from the case when there is poor service after the sale. Proper identification of causes helps the decision maker to avoid solving the wrong problem.[9]

Frequently, the search for problem causes leads to a better definition of the real problem. Causes can be turned into new — and better — problem statements. For example, a large metropolitan bank recently began to experience an increase in the number of customers who closed their accounts. Defining the problem as 'loss of accounts' the bank determined the cause was increased customer dissatisfaction with service. This cause then became the basis for a restatement of the original problem. In an effort to determine the cause of the restated problem, the bank contacted several former customers and learned they felt the tellers handling their transactions had gone from being friendly and pleasant to grumpy and irritable. Thus, this cause became the even better defined problem: unfriendly tellers. The problem-to-cause-to-problem sequence was completed when it was determined that a poorly explained change in dress policy requiring all tellers to wear standard blazers was the real problem. It was easily addressed, and a special program for former customers who returned to the bank resulted in recouping virtually all the lost accounts.

Development of alternative solutions

Before a decision is made, feasible alternatives should be developed (actually these are potential solutions to the problem), and the potential consequences of each alternative should be examined. This is really a search process in which relevant internal and external environments of the organisation are investigated to provide information that can be developed into possible alternatives.[10] Obviously, this search is conducted within certain time and cost constraints, since only so much effort can be devoted to developing alternatives.

For example, a sales manager may identify an inadequately trained sales force as the cause for declining sales. The sales manager would then identify possible alternatives for solving the problem, such as a sales training program conducted at the home office by management, a sales training program conducted by a professional training organisation at a site away from the home office, or more intense on-the-job-training.

In this example, the manager faced an ill-defined decision problem, in which he needed to generate a range of alternatives. Ultimately, the quality of his decision will depend on how well he succeeds in this task. We will consider some of the factors that affect this stage in the next section. Had the manager been faced with a well-defined problem for which possible alternatives were known, he would have bypassed this process. However, irrespective of whether solutions are known or must be generated, at the end of this stage managers face a similar task: to evaluate and select one alternative.

Evaluation of solutions

Once alternatives have been developed, they must be evaluated and compared. In every decision situation, the objective is to select the alternative that will produce the most favourable outcomes and the least unfavourable outcomes. This again highlights the necessity of objectives and goals since in selecting from among alternatives, the decision maker should be guided by the previously established goals and objectives. Again, the task faced by managers will differ depending on the type of outcome that they face. Are they certain that a particular strategy will be successful? Is their task simply to select between alternatives with known success rates? Or must they first estimate the likely success of each alternative? In the next two sections, will consider how these factors affect solution evaluation.

On evaluating alternative solutions, two cautions must be kept in mind. First, it is critical that this phase of the decision-making process be kept separate and distinct from the previous step, identifying solutions. This is particularly true in a group decision-making context. When alternatives are evaluated as they are proposed, this may restrict the number of solution alternatives that are identified. If evaluations are positive, there may be a tendency to end the process prematurely by settling on the first positive solution. On the other hand, negative evaluations make it less likely for someone to risk venturing what may be an excellent solution for fear of being criticised.

Reading 12
Agreement and thinking alike: Ingredients for poor decisions

The second caution is to be wary of solutions that are evaluated as being 'perfect'. This is particularly true when the decision is being made under conditions of uncertainty. If a solution appears to have no drawbacks or if, in a group setting, there is unanimous agreement on a course of action, it may be useful to assign someone to take a devil's advocate position. The job of a devil's advocate is to be a thorough critic of the proposed solution. Research supports the benefits of devil's advocacy and the conflict that a devil's advocate may cause, thus forcing a decision maker to reexamine assumptions and information.[11]

Solution selection

The purpose of selecting a particular solution is to solve a problem in order to achieve a predetermined objective. This point is an extremely important one. It means that a decision is not an end in itself but only a means to an end. Although the decision maker chooses the alternative that is expected to result in the achievement of the objective, the selection of that alternative should not be an isolated act. If it is, the factors that led to and lead from the decision are likely to be excluded. Specifically, the steps following the decision should include implementation and follow-up. The critical point is that decision making is more than an act of choosing: it is a dynamic process.

Unfortunately for most managers, situations rarely exist in which one alternative achieves the desired objective without having some positive or negative impact on another objective. Situations often exist where two objectives cannot be optimised simultaneously. If one objective is *optimised*, the other is *suboptimised*. In business organisation, for example, if production is optimised, employee morale may be suboptimised or vice versa. Thus, the multiplicity of organisational objectives complicates the real world of the decision maker.

A situation could also exist where attainment of an organisational objective would be at the expense of a societal objective. The reality of such situations is clearly seen in the rise of ecology groups, environmentalists and the consumerist movement. Apparently, these groups question the priorities (organisational as against societal) of certain organisational decision makers. In any case, whether an organisational objective conflicts with another organisational objective or with a societal objective, the values of the decision maker will strongly influence the alternative chosen.

In managerial decision making, optimal solutions often are impossible. This is because the decision maker cannot possibly know all of the available alternatives, the consequences of each alternative, and the probability of occurrence of these consequences.[12] Thus, rather than being an *optimiser*, the decision maker is a *satisfier*, selecting the alternative that meets an acceptable (satisfactory) standard.

Implementation

Any decision is little more than an abstraction if it is not implemented, and it must be effectively implemented in order to achieve the objective for which it was made. It is entirely possible for a 'good' decision to be hurt by poor implementation. In this sense, implementation may be more important than the actual choice of the alternative.

Since, in most situations, implementing decisions involves people, the test of the soundness of a decision is the behaviour of the people involved relative to the decision. While a decision may be technically sound, it can be undermined easily by dissatisfied subordinates. Subordinates cannot be manipulated in the same manner as other resources. Thus, a manager's job is not only to choose good solutions but also to transform such solutions into behaviour in the organisation. This is done by effectively communicating with the appropriate individuals and groups.[13]

Follow-up

Effective management involves periodic measurements of results. Actual results are compared with planned results (the objective), and if deviations exist, changes must be made. Here again, we see the importance of measurable objectives. If such objectives do not exist, then there is no way to judge performance. If actual results do not match planned results, changes must be made in the solution chosen, in its implementation, or in the original objective if it is deemed unattainable. If the original objective must be revised, then the entire decision-making process will be reactivated. The important point is that once a decision is implemented, a manager cannot assume that the outcome will meet the original objective. Some system of control and evaluation is necessary to make sure the actual results are consistent with the results planned for when the decision was made.

Sometimes the result or outcome of a decision is unexpected or is perceived differently by different people, and dealing with this possibility is an important part of the follow-up phase in the decision process.

The decision-making context

All problems are not created equal. Deciding whether to launch a new product in response to a competitor's move is probably a more significant decision than whether the employee lounge should be repainted. The process of decision making and solution implementation requires resources. Unless the organisation has unlimited resources at its disposal, it is necessary to establish priorities for dealing with problems. This, in turn, means being able to determine the significance level of the problem. Determining problem significance involves consideration of three issues: urgency, impact and growth tendency.

Urgency relates to time. How critical is the time pressure? Putting out a fire in the office is probably more urgent that fixing a stalled lift. On the other hand, the lift is likely to be more urgent than repairing a broken copier. The potential for stopgap measures also impacts on urgency. For example, if there are people in the stalled lift who can be released before the lift is repaired, that reduces the urgency of making repairs. The Local Encounter considers how making decisions under time pressure affects the decision-making process.

Impact describes the seriousness of the problem's effects. Effects may be on people, sales, equipment, profitability, public image, or any number of other organisational resources. Whether problem effects are short term or long term, and whether the problem is likely to create other problems are also questions related to impact.

Growth tendency addresses future considerations. Even though a problem may currently be of low urgency and have little impact, if allowed to go unattended it may grow. The decision to cut back on routine preventive maintenance of plant equipment as a cost-cutting measure may not create a significant problem immediately. Over time, however, major difficulties may arise.

The more significant the problem, as determined by its urgency, impact, and growth tendency, the more important it is that it be addressed. A critical part of effective decision making is determining problem significance.

LOCAL   Encounter

The 'hassled' decision maker

In describing the decision-making process, we identified the importance of generating and evaluating as many alternatives as possible. Incomplete information search means that we are more likely to make less than optimum decisions. Leon Mann, at the Melbourne Business School, has considered how one external constraint — perceived time pressure — affects these all-important early stages in the decision-making process.

In this laboratory study, participants were asked to decide whether or not they would take a job based on the information provided to them. In deciding, they were asked to list the objectives that they needed to meet, list the possible courses of action available to them together with their perceived costs and benefits, and to rate each alternative. After receiving additional information, decision makers were able to change their preferences before making a final decision.

Results showed that time pressure was critical to the early stages of the decision process: individuals who perceived themselves to be under time pressure proposed fewer alternative solutions, generated fewer costs and benefits for each solution and, in the final

stages, made more changes to these consequences than decision makers not under time pressure.

Another interesting finding was that anxiety also related to information search. Those decision makers who were anxious generated fewer objectives for their decision, considered fewer costs and benefits of their strategies, and were less likely to re-evaluate the costs and benefits that they had identified in the light of additional information.

What conclusions can we draw from this study? It appears that time pressure decreases information search. This suggests that, when important decisions are to be made, the deadlines for those decisions should be negotiated to avoid excessive time pressure. However, this may not always be possible: providing individuals with training about how to establish priorities and how to efficiently find information and generate solutions should under these circumstances improve decision making.

Source: Mann, L., & Tan, Charlotte. (1993). The hassled decision makers: The effects of perceived time pressure on information processing in decision making, *Australian Journal of Management*, 18, 197–209.

ILL-DEFINED DECISION PROBLEMS: UNKNOWN OUTCOMES

Most of the complex decisions faced by managers are examples of ill-defined decision problems. Attempting to deal with declining profits, loss of market share and increasingly competitive marketplace, high levels of absenteeism or turnover, or low employee morale all require a decision maker to start by generating a set of solutions and estimating how likely each solution is to solve the problem.

How do decision makers deal with such problems? Essentially, they aim to turn these problems into well-defined problems by creating structure: generating alternatives and estimating the probability of success for each alternative solution. In the next section, we will consider some of the factors that affect our estimates of probability. In this section, we consider just how decision makers tackle these problems. Our focus will be on how decision makers identify and evaluate alternatives.

Structuring the problem

Before a decision is made, feasible alternatives should be developed (actually these are potential solutions to the problem), and the potential consequences of each alternative should be considered. This is really a search process in which the relevant internal and external environments of the organisation are investigated to provide information that can be developed into possible alternatives.[14] Obviously, this search is conducted within certain time and cost constraints, since only so much effort can be devoted to developing alternatives.

How decision makers define the problem affects the identification of alternatives. When decision makers are experienced, they are able to define the problem in terms of similar, past problems. This is known as *structuring by matching*. Decision makers identify key issues in the existing problem and match these issues to other problems that they have faced. For example, we notice that an employee has started to come to work late. We have, in the past, faced this problem several times. We notice certain similarities between this and past situations: the employee has just missed out on a promotion and he has been doing the same job for several years. In the past, we have successfully solved similar problems by offering the employee a special project to work on and we employ this strategy now. One of the advantages of this process is that, having matched the current problem to a familiar problem, decision makers are able to select from a set of ready-made solutions that have been successfully applied in the past. The major disadvantage is that by focusing on particular dimensions of the decision problem that match our experience, we may miss features of this particular problem that are unique.

Decision makers are not always presented with problems that are familiar. When we face unfamiliar problems, we cannot draw on past experience to help us generate alternative solutions. For example, our company may — for the first time in its history — be experiencing a loss. Under these circumstances, we must first try to generate explanations for the problem. This process is known as *structuring by hypothesis generation*. We may speculate that this is the result of a change in economic conditions, the influx of a cheaper product onto the market or the loss of several key staff. Once we have developed a set of plausible explanations, we can start to generate a set of solutions. In this case, because we have no past experience to draw on, we must design new solutions.

It is important to remember that the explanations we offer for a problem constrain the solutions that we consider. For example, once we have decided that an employee's poor performance is a motivational problem, we do not consider strategies for reducing her stress. Or, once we have decided that the loss of staff has resulted in a profit downturn, we no longer develop plans for dealing with the competition. At each stage of the decision-making process, we eliminate possible courses of action as a result of how we analyse and explain the problem.

Solving the problem

As we will see in the next section, when decisions are well defined, this task is simplified because we can apply decision rules. Our question now is how alternatives are evaluated when problems are ill defined. In order to do this, decision makers must establish the criteria that they will use, determine what the likely outcomes of particular strategies will be and also estimate the probability of each outcome. When considering strategies, we try to ascertain how likely it is that a particular strategy will help us achieve our goal: different goals mean that we will focus on different strategies. We also try to estimate the range of outcomes that are associated with a particular strategy. We ask: What is the most likely outcome of this strategy? What is the best possible outcome? What is the worst possible outcome? In this way, we place some limits on the issues that we need to consider.

One of the key issues facing decision makers in this stage is a failure to fully consider all alternatives. Once we have reduced the uncertainty that we face, we may find that one solution seems 'better' than all others. As soon as a preferred solution emerges we change our strategy from acquiring information about all possible courses of action, to obtaining information that supports our preferred alternative. This is known as *confirmatory processing*. In this stage, decision makers weight alternatives and criteria in a way that will support their final decision.

WELL-DEFINED DECISION PROBLEMS: KNOWN ALTERNATIVES

Case 12
Kooyong
appoints a new
vice-principal

Examples of well-defined decisions include choosing which movie to go to, which car to buy, which job offer to accept or which applicant to employ. They are well defined because we have a set of known alternatives. These decisions are certain because we know, for example, that if we choose to see *Star Trek*, we will not see *The Flintstones*. These types of problems are less common in managerial decision making. Frequently, strategies for solving them have been formalised into organisational policies, procedures and manuals. If we face a problem often enough, we develop a standard solution for resolving it. One good example of this type of problem is the selection of new staff: managers must combine the information available to them about each potential new recruit, and on this basis select the best employee.

Well-defined decision problems present us with a set of clear and certain alternatives. Our task as decision makers is to select between these alternatives. In doing so, we gather and weigh up information, developing preferences in the process. Normative models assume that, once we have evaluated all alternatives, we will select the one that is evaluated most highly. However, the way in which we might combine such information has been the subject of considerable research, and we will now turn to an examination of some of the choice rules that individuals employ.

Exhibit 12.3 gives you background information about four individuals who have applied for a job as personnel manager. According to the selection criteria for this job, individuals must have a minimum 3-year university degree, have at least 2 years of relevant experience and have scored at least 250 on your organisation's aptitude test. Who would you pick?

Individual decision rules

In making this choice, we can apply one of several decision rules. These rules differ in how we go about eliminating candidates and therefore who we choose.

Exhibit 12.3		**Michelle**	**Gordon**	**Victoria**	**Miles**
Choosing the right person	Experience	1 year	2 years	10 years	5 years
	Qualification	BComm	BA	VCE	BBus
	Aptitude test	375	275	300	225

Let's take a closer look at these rules. Compare your answer to the choices that we make using these rules. Which rule did you apply?

- *Conjunctive decision rule.* After determining a minimum cut-off for each criterion (described above), we work through the criteria one by one and eliminate anyone who does not meet the cut-off. Starting with qualifications, we eliminate Victoria and Miles. Using experience, we eliminate Michelle. This leaves Gordon, who meets all our criteria.

- *Disjunctive decision rule.* When we apply this rule, we accept any options that meet the minimum cut-off on any one criterion. Using this rule, all applicants are still likely contenders since they all meet our cut-off on at least one criterion.

- *Lexicographic decision rule.* Both the conjunctive and disjunctive decision rules treated all criteria as if they are equally important. However, it may be that one criterion is far more important than the others. For example, we might decide that the aptitude test score is the most important, followed by experience and qualifications. When we focus on only the most important criterion, we are applying a lexicographic decision rule. Using this rule, we pick the person with the highest value on our most important criterion. In this case, it would be Michelle, who has the highest score on our organisation's aptitude test.

- *Elimination-by-aspects decision rule.* We may decide that focusing on our most important criterion is not enough. A slightly more complex approach would be to work through our applicants comparing them first on our most important criterion, then on the second most important criterion, and so. At each step, we would eliminate anyone who failed to meet the minimum cut-off. Using this rule, in the first step we would eliminate Miles, who does not meet the cut-off for our aptitude test. In the second step, we would eliminate Michelle, who does not have the necessary experience. And, in the final step, we eliminate Victoria, who does not have a tertiary qualification. Again, we are left with Gordon. Why do you think this rule gave us the same answer as the conjunctive rule?

- *Compensatory decision rules.* None of the rules that we have discussed so far allow us to make trade-offs. For example, we may decide that Victoria's 10 years of experience compensates for the lack of a degree, and so we may decide to weight experience more heavily in her case. We do not always apply decision rules rigidly, and compensatory rules allow for the fact that we may weight the same criteria differently in different situations.

Applying decision rules

Using these rules results in one solution emerging as the preferred solution. According to rational decision-making models, we should select the preferred solution. Can you think of times when the most rational solution did not appear to be the best solution?

One application of this approach is in the development of decision aids. If we are able to determine how an individual makes decisions — which criteria are given importance, and how information is weighted and combined — we should be able to develop a system for helping individuals to make decisions. Let's think again about selecting an individual for your organisation. Imagine that you had access to personnel records, and were able to compare individuals who were selected with those who were not. By doing so, you would be able to determine which criteria the organisation deemed most important, and how decision makers weighted each criterion. For example, you might discover that aptitude test scores were four times more important than either qualifications or experience, but that experience was only twice as important as qualifications. You could then form a rule which allowed you to give a score to each applicant for the next job:

$$\text{Selection score} = 4(\text{aptitude}) + 2(\text{experience}) + \text{qualification}$$

Using this formula should make each decision easier. Perhaps more importantly, it should allow you to be consistent across several decisions. What do you think are the benefits of this approach? Are there any disadvantages?

LIMITS TO RATIONAL DECISION MAKING

We have already suggested that individuals rarely behave in the way that rational models of decision making predict. Especially when we are faced with ill-defined problems, the process of information gathering and integration leaves scope for many biases. The factors that affect decision making fall into two categories, the first relating to how we estimate probabilities and the second relating to more general motivational issues. We will now turn to a discussion of some of the better known 'errors' that individuals make.

Errors in estimating probabilities[15]

Humans are often described as limited information processors. Because we are unable to systematically deal with all the information that is available to use, we develop rules of thumb — *heuristics* — that help simplify the information. 'First come, first served' is an example of a heuristic: it simplifies the situation by eliminating the need to consider whether different people have different time constraints, whether the needs of some are greater than others, and so on. Most of the time, heuristics are helpful. However, sometimes they introduce *errors* — biases — into the way that we process information. This is particularly evident when we examine how individuals generate and use probabilistic information. In this section, we will consider five biases and heuristics that affect how we process information: availability heuristic, representativeness heuristic, base-rate fallacy, conjunctive fallacy and framing.

Consider the problems described in Exhibit 12.4. Answer the problems before you read on.

Exhibit 12.4

Decision problems

Problem 1

Are there more words in the English language that start with the letter 'k' or that have the letter 'k' as their third letter?

Problem 2

Bill is 34 years old. He is intelligent but unimaginative, compulsive and generally lifeless. In school, he was strong in mathematics and generally weak in humanities.

1. Bill is an accountant.
2. Bill plays jazz for a hobby.
3. Bill is an architect.

Problem 3

A panel of psychologists has interviewed and administered tests to thirty engineers and seventy lawyers. On this basis they have written thumbnail sketches of the engineers and lawyers. Read the thumbnail sketch below. Decide whether it is more likely that Tom is an engineer or a lawyer.

Tom is 45 years old. He is married and has four children. He is generally conservative, careful and ambitious. He shows no interest in political and social issues and spends most of his free time on his many hobbies which include home carpentry, sailing and mathematical puzzles.

Problem 4

Linda is 31 years old, single, outspoken and very bright. She majored in philosophy. As a student she was deeply concerned with issues of discrimination and social justice, and also participated in antinuclear demonstrations.

1. Linda is an insurance salesperson.
2. Linda is a bank teller.
3. Linda is active in the feminist movement.
4. Linda is a bank teller who is active in the feminist movement.

Problem 5

Which do you prefer: a guaranteed $500 or a lottery ticket that gives you a 50–50 chance of winning $1000 or winning nothing?

Which do you prefer: a guaranteed $500 loss or a lottery ticket that gives you a 50–50 chance of losing $1000 or losing nothing?

Problem 6

(adapted from Kahneman & Tversky)

A. Your company is facing a massive downturn on profits and a restructuring that will take 600 jobs. Two alternative programs for implementing the restructure have been proposed, each of which has certain consequences.

Program A saves 200 jobs if adopted.
Program B has a ⅓ chance of saving all 600 jobs, and a ⅔ chance of saving no jobs.

B. Your company is facing a massive downturn on profits and a restructuring that will take 600 jobs. Two alternative programs for implementing the restructure have been proposed, each of which has certain consequences.

Program C	loses 400 jobs if adopted.
Program D	has a ⅓ chance of saving all 600 jobs and, a ⅔ chance that all the jobs will be lost.

Sources: Kahneman, D., Slovic, P., & Tversky, A. (Eds.) (1982). *Judgment under Uncertainty: Heuristics and Biases.* Cambridge and New York: Cambridge University Press; Kahneman, D., & Tversky, A. (1973). On the psychology of prediction, *Psychological Review,* **80**, 237–251; Abelson, R. P., & Levi, A. (1987). Decision making and decision theory. In G. Lindzey & E. Aronson (Eds.) *Handbook of Social Psychology,* vol. II, (3rd Ed.). New York: Random House.

Availability heuristic

In problem 1, if you said that more words start with the letter 'k' than have 'k' as the third letter, you probably allowed the availability heuristic to guide your decision. Put simply, the availability heuristic describes a tendency for us to describe as probable those events that we can most easily imagine. According to this heuristic, to answer the question you would have tried to make a list of words starting with 'k', and those that have 'k' as their third letter. Because it is easier to imagine words that start with 'k', you concluded that it is more probable.

Imagine that you have urgent documents to be delivered. You must decide between posting them, using one of several courier services or hand-delivering them yourself. Which strategy is most likely to guarantee their quick delivery? Applying the availability heuristic, you try to picture the results of each strategy. You recall a recent newspaper article reporting on the efficiency of courier services in the inner city. As a result, you find it very easy to imagine that using a courier service will guarantee the outcome that you want and choose this solution.

Representativeness heuristic

Did you decide that Bill is an accountant? If you did, you have displayed the representativeness heuristic. Because Bill fits our stereotype of an accountant but not our stereotype of an architect or a jazz player, we conclude that he is more likely to be an accountant that either an architect or a jazz player. According to the representativeness heuristic we make probability judgements based on information (stereotypes) that we already hold.

When a situation matches an existing stereotype, we conclude that it is likely to belong to that group of events. In some ways, structuring by matching could be considered an example of the representativeness heuristic in action. When we attempted to diagnose our employee's lateness we hunted through information about lateness. The behaviour pattern best matched our existing stereotype of 'low motivation' and so we concluded that this was the most likely explanation for our employee's behaviour.

Base-rate fallacy

In the third problem, if you said that Tom was an engineer, you demonstrated the base-rate fallacy. You ignored information about the proportion of arts and engineering students on campus — their *base rate*. If you had taken this information into consideration, you would have concluded that Tom was more likely to be a lawyer. Decision makers often ignore the frequency of events in their estimates of what is the most likely outcome. In this case, it is likely that you ignored base-rate information because Tom fits your stereotype of an engineer. This is also an example of the representativeness heuristic in action.

Conjunctive fallacy

In the fourth problem, did you decide that Linda was a feminist and a bank teller? Most people do, and this provides us with an example of the conjunctive fallacy. There are far more feminists than there are feminists who are also bank tellers; there are far more bank tellers than there are bank tellers who are also feminists. So, simply on base rates, it is far more likely that Linda is a bank teller or a feminist, but not both. The combination of two events is always less likely than either of the events alone. However, we frequently conclude the exact opposite: the conjunctive fallacy.

Risk propensity and decision frames

Which outcomes did you choose in problem 5? Most people prefer to gain the cash in hand, but will take the gamble when faced with a loss. However, in objective terms the outcomes are identical. In all cases, your expected outcomes are $500. These types of problems demonstrate that we behave differently, depending on whether we are faced with gains or losses. When we are faced with gains, we tend to behave in a *risk-averse* manner: that is, we prefer a certain outcome. However, when we are faced with losses, we behave in a *risk-seeking* manner: we prefer the gamble. Apparently, when faced with losses a certain loss is unacceptable: we would rather risk a bigger loss when the gamble also offers the possibility that we will lose nothing.

What is interesting for us is that this effect can be obtained by framing decisions as either gains or losses. That is, how we represent a situation — in terms of gains or losses — will affect how we behave. In problem 6, which program did you choose in Part A? What about in part B?. Most people choose Program A when the situation is framed in terms of jobs saved; however, they choose Program D when it is framed in terms of job losses. Although all the outcomes are identical (all offer 200 jobs saved, or 400 lost), *framing the decision* in terms of gains or losses alters individuals' risk propensity.

Motivational factors in decision making

In addition to heuristics and biases, our decision making is influenced by more general motivational factors. In this section, we will consider two major factors — commitment and groupthink — that result in faulty decision making.

Escalating commitment

Are decision makers able to cut their losses? In the face of overwhelming evidence, can decision makers abandon a course of action? Frequently, the answer is no. Imagine that, on behalf of your engineering firm, you have agreed to build a dam for generating hydro-electric power. Its estimated cost is around $5000 million and expected completion is 2 years. At the end of 2 years, the dam is only halfway to completion and it has already cost $4000 million. Do you continue with dam construction? You decide to continue, and receive a geological survey indicating that the dam is being built over a fault line in an earthquake-prone area. The report attracts considerable media attention. Do you abandon the project? You build on. After 4 years, the dam is still incomplete … what do you do?

Although, to an external observer, it seems rational to abandon the project, frequently decision makers persist with a course of action in the face of overwhelming evidence to the contrary. The example above is on a large scale; however, we show the same behaviour in our everyday decisions. This phenomenon is know as **escalating commitment** or 'knee deep in the big muddy'.[16] It describes situations in which decision makers continue with an existing course of action, even though it is clearly failing. Why do they do this? Although several reasons have been advanced, the situational characteristics most likely to result in escalating commitment are:

- *Responsibility.* When individuals have made the first decision, they feel more responsible for it and this increases commitment.
- *Accountability.* When we feel responsible for the consequences of the decision, we also display higher levels of commitment.
- *Publicity.* When our decisions are public and others are evaluating them, we also increase commitment as a means to justify our initial choice.
- *Irreversibility.* When the outcomes are difficult or impossible to undo, we continue with our initial decision in the hope that we can cut our losses.
- *Ability.* If we believe that the poor outcomes will reflect on our abilities, we also display greater commitment.

These conditions also suggest several strategies for minimising commitment.[17] In order to avoid escalating commitment, we can:

- separate the first decision from future decisions by, for example, having different decision makers hire and evaluate an employee;
- provide unambiguous negative feedback, so that the consequences of continuing to follow a course of action are clear;
- deinstitutionalise the decision, by breaking links between the central goals of the organisation and the decision or project;
- provide support for failure, so that the risk — to an individual — of failing is minimised.

Groupthink

In Chapter 8, we considered some of the benefits of highly cohesive groups. There are, however, particular circumstances in which cohesion is detrimental to group performance. In the next section we will consider the relative merits of group and individual decision making. Here, we outline one serious consequence of highly cohesive decision groups: **groupthink**. Our Management Encounter presents an analysis of the space shuttle *Challenger* disaster as an example of this. Groupthink occurs under quite specific conditions and results in strong pressures for agreement with the group's preferred strategy.[18]

MANAGEMENT   Encounter

Groupthink and the space shuttle *Challenger*

The space shuttle *Challenger*, launched on 28 January 1986, exploded 73 seconds after launch killing all on board. In subsequent reviews of the decision to launch it became clear that the National Aeronautics and Space Administration (NASA) had proceeded with the launch despite advice from engineers at Morton-Thiokol, Inc. (MTI). Given the disastrous consequences, why were decision makers at NASA prepared to take the risk? One possibility is that it had displayed all the classic symptoms of groupthink. In this Encounter we present an analysis of the situation from the groupthink perspective. Do you agree that this decision is an example of groupthink? What procedures would you recommend to NASA to ensure that this disaster was not repeated?

Having already aborted one launch, NASA officials were faced with the need to decide whether to proceed. In the evening before the launch, concerns and discussions were focused on the extremely low temperatures and ice on the launch pad.

Let's start by asking whether the preconditions for groupthink were present. It is highly likely that the NASA group was highly cohesive. The launch was supported by top-level managers at NASA (leader preference) and information concerning problems with the O-ring seals was not passed on to top management (insulation from experts), indicating structural problems. In addition, NASA faced an extremely stressful and threatening situation: the number of failed launches put into doubt continued funding for NASA programs. It was critical for NASA to have a success.

Analysis of the decision-making process also provides support for the symptoms of groupthink. Analysis of the Presidential Commission showed that there was considerable pressure for conformity: self-appointed 'mind guards' protected senior officials from conflicting information; NASA exerted pressure on dissenters by requiring a demonstration that it was unsafe to launch (rather than safe to launch); and an illusion of unanimity was seen in evidence as was self-censorship. The commission concluded that, at some point, MTI executives accepted NASA's arguments, reassessed their decision and agreed that the launch was safe. Given their past successes, it is also highly likely that there was an illusion of invulnerability.

In terms of decision-making processes, what was the result? Based on the evidence to the commission, the greatest problem was selective information processing: NASA officials focused on information that supported the launch ignoring efforts from MTI officials to point out problems with their thinking. In general, NASA was more concerned with defending its decision to launch than in reassessing the information or listening to MTI officials. The result ... *Challenger* was launched.

Source: Esser, J. K., & Lindoerfer, J. S. (1989). Groupthink and the space shuttle *Challenger* accident: Toward a quantitative case analysis, *Journal of Behavioral Decision Making*, **2**, 167–177; Moorhead, G., Ference, R., & Neck, C. P. (1991). Group decision fiascos continue: Space shuttle *Challenger* and a revised groupthink framework, *Human Relations*, **44**, 539–550.

Antecedents of groupthink. The preconditions for groupthink include high cohesion, structural problems and a 'provocative' situation. Among the factors that may result in groupthink are structural problems such as isolation of the group from conflicting information, similarity of group members, no precedent for systematic decisions and situational factors such as external threats and recent failures.

Symptoms of groupthink. When the conditions outlined above are present, there is extremely strong pressure for all members to agree on a solution, usually one proposed by the leader. If we analyse decisions made under these conditions, we see the following symptoms of groupthink:

1. *Illusion of invulnerability.* Group members believe that they are invulnerable. As a result, they ignore danger signs and become overoptimistic about their ability to make the decision; this encourages the group to make risky decisions. For example, on the eve of the Cuba invasion, Robert Kennedy stated that with the talent in the group, they could overcome whatever challenged them with 'common sense and hard work' and 'bold new ideas'.

2. *Tendency to moralise.* The group is portrayed as holding the 'right' values and anyone opposing those values is characterised as weak, evil and unintelligent. For example, during the Bay of Pigs incident, the USA was portrayed as the leader of the free world and the opposition as weak, evil and stupid. There is a tendency to negatively stereotype the opposing group by describing them as being too negative to be worth considering. There is a belief in the rightness of the group's position.

3. *Feeling of unanimity.* Members feel that everyone agrees with the decision. Again during the Bay of Pigs incident, the group reported that each member of the executive supported the president's decision. However, later, at least two members reported being uncomfortable with policies that were being developed; at the time, they perceived themselves as being the only group member experiencing any doubts and so were reluctant to voice these doubts for fear of appearing too soft. There is a shared false belief that everyone in the group agrees with the group's opinions, coupled with a reluctance to raise any dissenting ideas and counterarguments.

4. *Pressure towards conformity.* Any expression of dissenting opinions is discouraged, with questions about group loyalty raised whenever dissension occurs. This may be coupled with individuals taking on the role of 'mind guards', and protecting the group from negative or threatening information. They may withhold information, or could privately encourage members not to share dissenting opinions.

5. *Collective rationalisation.* Outside criticism and warning signs are either discredited or ignored; and dissenting opinions are prematurely dismissed.

Consequences of groupthink. Not surprisingly, the above symptoms result in poor decision making processes: the group fails to gather sufficient information or generate a broad range of solutions; it does not focus on the potential risks of the preferred strategy and fails to revisit rejected strategies; and, frequently, the group also fails to have a contingency plan in case of failure.

Groupthink and devil's advocacy. In a group setting, when there is unanimous agreement on a course of action, it may be useful to assign someone to take a devil's advocate position. The job of a devil's advocate is to be a thorough critic of the proposed solution. Research supports the benefits of devil's advocacy and the conflict a devil's advocate may cause, thus forcing a decision maker to reexamine assumptions and information.[19]

GROUP DECISION MAKING

The first parts of this chapter focused on individuals making decisions. In most organisations, however, a great deal of decision making is achieved through committees, teams, task forces and other kinds of groups.[20] This is because managers frequently face situations in which they must seek and combine judgements in group meetings. This is especially true for non-programmed problems, which are novel and have much uncertainty regarding the outcome. In most organisations, it is unusual to find decisions on such problems being made by one individual on a regular basis. The increased complexity of many of these problems requires specialised knowledge in numerous fields, usually not possessed by one person. This requirement, coupled with the reality that the decisions made must eventually be accepted and implemented by many units throughout the organisation, has increased the use of the collective approach to the decision-making process.

Individual versus group decision making

Considerable debate has occurred over the relative effectiveness of individual versus group decision making. Groups usually take more time to reach a decision than individuals do. But bringing together individual specialists and experts has its benefits since the mutually reinforcing impact of their interaction results in better decisions. In fact, a great deal of research has shown that consensus decisions made with five or more participants are superior to individual decision making, majority vote and leader decisions.[21] Unfortunately, open discussion has been found to be negatively influenced by such behavioural factors as the pressure to conform; the influence of a dominant personality type in the group; 'status incongruity,' as a result of which, lower status participants are inhibited by higher status participants and 'go along' even though they believe that their own ideas are superior; and the attempt of certain participants to influence others because these participants are perceived to be expert in the problem area.[22] Additionally, framing effects occur more frequently in groups.[23]

Certain decisions appear to be better made by groups, while others appear better suited to individual decision making. Non-programmed decisions appear to be better suited to group decision making. Usually calling for pooled talent, the decisions are so important that they are frequently made by top management and, to a somewhat lesser extent, by middle managers.

In terms of the decision-making process itself, the following points concerning group processes for non-programmed decisions can be made:

- *In establishing objectives*, groups probably are superior to individuals because of the greater amount of knowledge available to groups.
- *In identifying alternatives*, the individual efforts of group members are necessary to ensure a broad search in the various functional areas of the organisation.
- *In evaluating alternatives*, the collective judgement of the group, with its wider range of viewpoints, seems superior to that of the individual decision maker.
- *In choosing an alternative,* it has been shown that group interaction and the achievement of consensus usually result in the acceptance of more risk than would be accepted by an individual decision maker. In any event, the group

**Exercise 12
Group decision
making**

decision is more likely to be accepted as a result of the participation of those affected by its consequences.

■ *Implementation* of a decision, whether or not made by a group, is usually accomplished by individual managers. Thus, since a group cannot be held responsible, the responsibility for implementation necessarily rests with the individual manager.

Exhibit 12.5 summarises the research on group decision making. It presents the relationship between the probable quality of a decision and the method utilised to reach the decision. It indicates that as we move from 'individual' to 'consensus', the quality of the decision improves. Note also that each successive method involves a higher level of mutual influence by group members. Thus, for a complex problem requiring pooled knowledge, the quality of the decision is likely to be higher as the group moves towards achieving consensus.[24]

Exhibit 12.5
Probable relationship between quality of group decision and method utilised

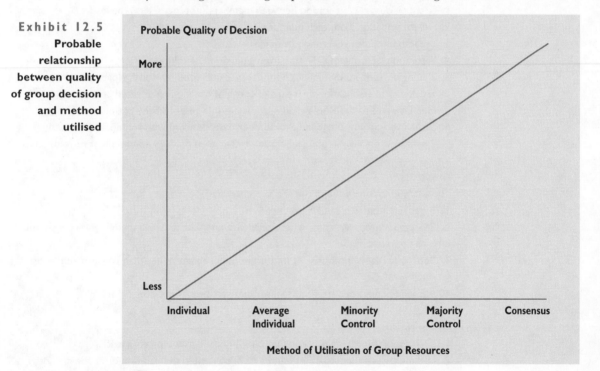

Creativity in group decision making

If groups are better suited to non-programmed decisions than individuals are, then an atmosphere fostering group creativity must be created. In this respect, group decision making may be similar to brainstorming in that discussion must be free-flowing and spontaneous. All group members must participate, and the evaluation of individual ideas must be suspended in the beginning to encourage participation. However, a decision must be reached, and this is where group decision making differs from brainstorming. Exhibit 12.6 presents guidelines for developing the permissive atmosphere that is important for creative decision making.

Exhibit 12.6
Creative group
decision making

Group Structure

The group is composed of heterogeneous, generally competent personnel who bring to bear on the problem diverse frames of reference, representing channels to each relevant body of knowledge (including contact with outside resource personnel who offer expertise not encompassed by the organisation), with a leader who facilitates the creative process.

Group Roles

Each individual explores with the entire group all ideas (no matter how intuitively and roughly formed) that bear on the problem.

Group Processes

The problem-solving process is characterised by:

1. Spontaneous communication between members (not focused on the leader).
2. Full participation from each member.
3. Separation of idea generation from idea evaluation.
4. Separation of problem definition from generation of solution strategies.
5. Shifting of roles, so that interaction that mediates problem solving (particularly search activities and clarification by means of constant questioning directed both to individual members and to the whole group) is not the sole responsibility of the leader.
6. Suspension of judgement and avoidance of early concern with solutions, so that the emphasis is on analysis and exploration rather than on early commitment to solutions.

Group Style

The social-emotional tone of the group is characterised by:

1. A relaxed, non-stressful environment.
2. Ego-supportive interaction, where open give-and-take between members is at the same time courteous.
3. Behaviour that is motivated by interest in the problem rather than concern with short-run pay-off.
4. Absence of penalties attached to any espoused idea or position.

Group Norms

1. Are supportive of originality and unusual ideas and allow for eccentricity.
2. Seek behaviour that separates source from content in evaluating information and ideas.
3. Stress a non-authoritarian view with a realistic view of life and independence of judgement.
4. Support humour and undisciplined exploration of viewpoints.
5. Seek openness in communication, where mature self-confident individuals offer 'crude' ideas to the group for mutual exploration without threat to the individuals for 'exposing' themselves.
6. Deliberately avoid giving credence to short-run results or short-run decisiveness.
7. Seek consensus but accept majority rule when consensus is unobtainable.

Source: Delbecq, A. L. (1967). The management of decision making within the firm: Three strategies for three types of decision making. *Academy of Management Journal*, December, 334–335.

Techniques for stimulating creativity

It seems safe to say that in many instances, group decision making is preferable to individual decision making. But we have all heard the statement: 'A camel is a racehorse designed by a committee'. Thus, while the necessity and the benefits of group decision making are recognised, numerous problems are also associated with it, some of which have already been noted. Practising managers are in need of specific techniques that will enable them to increase the benefits from group decision making while reducing the problems associated with it. We shall examine three techniques that, when properly utilised, have been found to be extremely useful in increasing the creative capability of a group in generating ideas, understanding problems and reaching better decisions. Increasing the creative capability of a group is especially necessary when individuals from diverse sectors of the organisation must pool their judgements and create a satisfactory course of action for the organisation. The three techniques are known as brainstorming, the Delphi technique and the nominal group technique.

Brainstorming

In many situations, groups are expected to produce creative or imaginative solutions to organisational problems. In such instances, **brainstorming** has often been found to enhance the creative output of the group. The technique of brainstorming includes a strict series of rules. The purpose of the rules is to promote the generation of ideas while, at the same time, avoiding the inhibitions of members that usually are caused by face-to-face groups. The basic rules are:

- No idea is too ridiculous. Group members are encouraged to state any extreme or outlandish idea.
- Each idea presented belongs to the group, not to the person stating it. In this way, it is hoped that group members will utilise and build on the ideas of others.
- No idea can be criticised. The purpose of the session is to generate, not evaluate, ideas.

Brainstorming is widely used in advertising where it apparently is effective. In some other situations, it has been less successful because there is no evaluation or ranking of the ideas generated. Thus, the group never really concludes the problem-solving process.

The Delphi technique

The **Delphi technique** involves the solicitation and comparison of anonymous judgements on the topic of interest through a set of sequential questionnaires that are interspersed with summarised information and feedback of opinions from earlier responses.[25] The Delphi process retains the advantage of having several judges while removing the biasing effects that might occur during face-to-face interaction. The basic approach has been to collect anonymous judgements by mail questionnaires. For example, the members independently generate their ideas to answer the first questionnaire and return it. The staff members summarise the responses as the group consensus and feed this summary back along with a second questionnaire for reassessment. From this feedback, the respondents independently evaluate their earlier responses. The underlying belief is that the consensus estimate will result in a better decision after several rounds of anonymous group judgement. While it is possible to continue the procedure for several rounds, studies have shown essentially no significant change after the second round of estimation.

The nominal group technique

The **nominal group technique** (NGT) has gained increasing recognition in health, social service, education, industry and government organisations.[26] The term 'nominal group technique' was adopted by earlier researchers to refer to processes that bring people together but do not allow them to communicate verbally. Thus, the collection of people is a group 'nominally', or in name only. You will see, however, that NGT in its present form combines both verbal and non-verbal stages.

Basically, NGT is a structured group meeting that proceeds as follows: A group of individuals (seven to ten) sit around a table but do not speak to one another. Rather, each person writes ideas on a pad of paper. After 5 minutes, a structured sharing of ideas takes place. Each person around the table presents one idea. A person designated as recorder writes the ideas on a flip chart in full view of the entire group. This continues until all of the participants indicate that they have no further ideas to share. There is still no discussion.

The output of this phase is a list of ideas (usually between eighteen and twenty-five). The next phase involves structured discussion in which each idea receives attention before a vote is taken. This is achieved by asking for clarification or stating the degree of support for each idea listed on the flip chart. The next stage involves independent voting in which each participant, in private, selects priorities by ranking or voting. The group decision is the mathematically pooled outcome of the individual votes.

Both the Delphi technique and NGT have had an excellent record of successes. Basic differences between them are:

- Delphi participants typically are anonymous to one another, while NGT participants become acquainted.
- NGT participants meet face to face around a table, while Delphi participants are physically distant and never meet face to face.
- In the Delphi process, all communication between participants is by way of written questionnaires and feedback from the monitoring staff. In NGT, communication is direct between participants.[27]

Practical considerations, of course, often influence which technique is used. For example, such factors as the number of working hours available, costs and the physical proximity of participants will influence which technique is selected.

Our discussion here has not been designed to make the reader an expert in the Delphi process or NGT. Our purpose throughout this section has been to indicate the frequency and importance of group decision making in every type of organisation. The three techniques discussed are practical devices whose purpose is to improve the effectiveness of group decisions.

Decision making is a common responsibility shared by all executives, regardless of functional area or management level. Every day, managers are required to make decisions that shape the future of their organisation as well as their own futures. The quality of these decisions is the yardstick of the managers' effectiveness. Some of these decisions may have a strong impact on the organisation's success, while others will be important but less crucial. However, all of the decisions will have some effect (positive or negative, large or small) on the organisation.

STRATEGIC DECISION MAKING[28]

Strategic decision making (SDM) describes the processes by which information is collected, integrated, analysed and used to obtain organisational goals and objectives. As we will see, many of the processes parallel those already described in this chapter. The difference between the more general models and SDM models lies in their focus: we are now concerned with particular goals and objectives — those of the organisation. Our Organisational Encounter describes how small companies deal with the issue of strategic planning.

Stages in strategic decision making

Like decision making generally, strategic decision making passes through a series of stages. SDM is best considered as an example of an ill-defined problem, and so we must consider how organisational decision makers attempt to impose structure on such problems. In this section, we will briefly outline the stages in SDM, as well as some of the constraints acting on organisational decision makers.

Mission statement
This stage parallels the goal-identification stage in our decision-making model. Organisational missions provide the standard against which to judge outcomes.

Environmental analysis
Organisational decision makers scan their environment for potential problems, crises or opportunities. Problems and crises suggest that there is a gap between stated and actual goals; and opportunities suggest that there is a means for enhancing organisational performance. In all cases, organisational decision makers must then move on to determining the cause of the problem and generating potential solutions. Problem diagnosis is carried out in relation to competitor behaviour and one commonly used form of diagnosis is a SWOT analysis, which weighs up the Strengths, Weaknesses, Opportunities and Threats facing an organisation. As was the case in our more general model of decision making, how the problem is described determines the solutions that are considered: a different range of solutions is generated depending on whether we view the problem as one of production or skills training.

Strategy development
Following diagnosis of the problem, organisational decision makers must develop strategies to remedy the problem. They have, as we have already seen, two alternatives: either the application of standard solutions or the development

of innovative solutions. How strategies are generated will depend on whether the problem is familiar or novel, and whether the decision makers are experienced or inexperienced.

Strategy selection

All of the factors that we have already discussed influence strategy selection in SDM. However, there is an additional layer of considerations, based on decision makers' evaluation of the environment in which the organisation is operating. In SDM, individuals or teams must also consider such factors as how stable the environment is, where in its life cycle the organisation is, who the competitors are, organisational structure and the flexibility of the organisation. It is at this stage that organisational power and politics come to the fore.

In our discussion of organisational power, we considered the role of information and uncertainty reduction in increasing individual power. In SDM, individuals with information relevant to the problem have the ability to reduce the uncertainty surrounding the decision process, and consequently are able to shape the selection of a strategy. Uncertainty also increases the scope for organisational politics to influence decision making, so that strategy selection is also vulnerable to political tactics such as coalition formation and exchange. In addition, strategies are likely to be considered in terms of their appeal to other stakeholders, as well as an assessment of how competitors will react to those strategies.

ORGANISATIONAL Encounter

Strategic plans for small businesses

What do small businesses have in common with large corporations? Not a lot, if we examine their strategic planning processes. The *Business Review Weekly* reported the results of a poll that showed that while 66% of small businesses had business plans, in the majority of cases those plans were in 'the head of the managing director'. Why the reluctance to engage in strategic planning and develop formal business plans?

According to research at the Southern Cross University in New South Wales, this may be because small, family-owned businesses have very different goals from those of large corporations. These businesses are not focused on goals such as growth, increased exports or even technological advances; nor are they interested in becoming best practice companies. Their goals are more concerned with lifestyle. What implications does this have for planning in small businesses?

In comparison with large corporations, managers in small businesses tend to engage in operational planning — making decisions as they are needed — and make new decisions to deal with problems that arise later. The focus on life goals often means that long-term business goals are put on hold to achieve family goals, and that preference is given to employing family members rather than staff with necessary skills.

Does this mean that the concept of strategic planning has no value for small businesses? Or does it mean that we need to develop different kinds of plans for them? The research suggests that one way of engaging small businesses in the strategic planning process is to link that process to their life goals. 'So, you want to go overseas for six months ... let's look at the profits that you will need to earn to pay for your trip and the salaries of staff replacing you.' When life goals are linked to business performance, strategic planning becomes more palatable for small business managers.

Source: Kennedy, A. (1995). Family or business, the choice is relative, *Business Review Weekly*, August 28.

Implementation and control of strategy

Finally, the new strategies must be incorporated into the everyday management of an organisation. This will mean considering such factors as organisational structure, culture and leadership. The better the fit between these variables and the new strategy, the more likely it is that we will successfully implement a new strategy.

Other issues in strategic decision making

Attempts to describe the SDM process have resulted in the development of several models. Each is based on somewhat different assumptions, and each identifies different issues that need to be addressed. In this section, we will highlight some of the factors that influence SDM.

Incremental adjustment models suggest that SDM is a process of slow change in which we take small steps towards our goal. At each step, we assess whether our strategy is taking us closer to or further from our goals. If we are moving towards our goals, we continue with the next stage of the strategy; if we are moving away from our goal we go back to the beginning of the process and reassess our strategy. This type of approach is most likely to describe SDM in stable environments; in highly unstable environments, organisations must make more rapid decisions concerning strategy if they are to survive.

Bureaucratic models are more concerned with determining where in the organisation decision-making responsibility should lie and in simplifying the decision making process for all other organisational members. Typically, these models argue that individuals at the top of the hierarchy should develop plans for the organisation, which are then implemented by individuals lower in the hierarchy following standardised rules, policies and procedures. The Global Encounter in this chapter examines the relationship between organisational structure and the centralisation of decision making in Japanese factories. This type of approach best suits organisations that are large, stable and face predictable problems.

Contingency models try to integrate several approaches to SDM by suggesting that how we proceed with SDM is determined by two factors: task characteristics and decision-maker characteristics. According to these models, how we approaches decisions is affected by:

- the *decision problem*: familiarity, ambiguity, complexity and stability;
- the *decision environment*: whether the decision will be irreversible, its importance, the degree of accountability that the decision maker has for the decision, and the time and financial constraints that are operating;
- the *decision-maker's* knowledge, ability and motivation.

Essentially, these models suggest that how we approach decision problems should be determined by their characteristics on these dimensions. In terms of the concepts that we introduced earlier, matching strategies and the use of standard solutions are more appropriate when decisions are simple and unimportant and the decision maker is experienced. As tasks become more complex and important, and as decision-maker experience decreases, individuals should rely on more formal rules and procedures in selecting and implementing strategies.

Organisational structure and decision-making style

As we will see in the last chapter, organisations differ in the extent to which authority and, consequently, decisions are centralised: that is, the extent to which decisions are made by senior management and carried out by lower levels of the organisation (as described in the bureaucratic model of strategic decision making). Some of the factors that might affect the level of centralisation include:

- whether the organisation is geographically dispersed;
- how many staff the organisation employs;
- how many hierarchical levels the organisation has;
- whether decisions are programmed or unprogrammed; and
- the extent to which work is automated.

According to Robert Marsh, who investigated the relationship between decision-making styles and organisational structure, centralisation is most likely when the company is geographically dispersed, it is small and has few levels, decisions are programmed and work is automated.

In this research, Marsh surveyed forty-eight Japanese factories ranging in size from 100 to 11 815 employees, and operating in a range of industries. The survey showed that when decisions are new, relate to choosing a market, represent the organisation, or deal with providing welfare facilities, they are made centrally. When decisions concern such issues as overtime, work methods, equipment and task allocation, they are decentralised. In terms of the initial hypotheses, Marsh found considerable support:

- As the number of organisational sites increased, centralisation of all decisions also increased.
- As organisations became larger, decisions concerning personnel (selection, dismissal, promotion, salary), spending unbudgeted money, equipment purchase and use, and task allocation were decentralised.
- As the number of organisational levels increased, decisions concerning provision of welfare facilities, staff salaries, changes to specialist and line departmental responsibilities, output preferences and inspections were decentralised.
- As the nature of decisions become more variable, decisions concerning new products, markets, pricing, personnel selection methods, training methods, overtime, use of equipment and work organisation were decentralised.
- As the task became more automated decisions concerning markets, personnel selection methods, and appointment and promotion of line staff became more centralised.

Source: Marsh, R. M. (1992). A research note: Centralization of decision-making in Japanese factories, *Organization Studies,* **13**, 261–274.

SUMMARY OF KEY POINTS

Compare programmed and non-programmed decisions. Decisions may be classified as programmed or non-programmed, depending on the type of problem. Decisions are programmed to the extent that they are repetitive and routine and a definite procedure has been developed for handling them. Decisions are non-programmed when they are novel and unstructured and there is no established procedure for handling the problem.

Describe dimensions of decision making. The relationship between alternatives and outcomes is based on three possible conditions. Certainty exists when the decision maker has complete knowledge of the probability of the outcome of each alternative. Uncertainty exists when absolutely no such knowledge is available. Risk is an intermediate condition, wherein some probabilistic estimate of outcomes can be made.

Identify the steps in the decision making process. The decision-making process entails following a number of steps. Sequentially, these are: establishing specific goals and objectives and measuring results, problem identification and definition, consideration of causes, development of alternative solutions, evaluation of alternative solutions, solution selection, implementation and follow-up.

Identify key issues for ill-defined decision problems. The key issues for decision makers facing ill-defined problems relate to the process of identifying and evaluating alternative solutions. Alternative identification depends on whether decision makers are experienced or whether they have faced similar problems in the past. Under these conditions, they engage in structuring by matching, and develop solutions based on past experience with similar problems. When problems are novel, decision makers engage in structuring by hypothesis generation: the development of new solutions. In evaluating alternatives, decision makers are guided by their goals and their estimate of what the most likely outcome for any strategy is. Once a preferred solution emerges they engage in confirmatory processing, collecting additional information to support their preferred alternative.

Describe decision rules that are used in well-defined decision problems. Decisions rules vary in whether they aim to meet cut-offs on all or only some criteria, and in whether all criteria are given equal weight. Decision makers can apply one of several rules: conjunctive, disjunctive, lexicographic, elimination-by-aspects or compensatory.

Explain factors that prevent rational decision making. There are two sets of factors that interfere with rational decision making. The first set relates to how we go about estimating probabilities, and identifies several heuristics and biases that result in incorrect estimates: availability heuristic, representativeness heuristic, base-rate fallacy, conjunctive fallacy, risk propensity and framing. In addition, we may be motivated to persist with bad decisions as the result of either escalating commitment or groupthink.

Compare individual and group decision making. Research suggests that decisions made by groups are superior to those made by individuals. However, there are aspects of group decision making that tend to have negative effects. These include pressure to conform and the disproportionate influence exerted by a dominant group member.

Identify specific techniques for stimulating creativity. One of the advantages of group decision making is that it can facilitate the identification of creative and innovative solutions to problems. Three specific techniques for stimulating creativity in groups are brainstorming, the nominal group technique and the Delphi process.

List steps in strategic decision-making. Strategic decision-making processes parallel those described in the more general model of decision-making. They require organisations to develop a mission statement, undertake environmental analysis, develop a strategy, select a strategy, and implement and control the strategy.

REVIEW AND DISCUSSION QUESTIONS

1. 'The source of most of our problems is someone else's solution to an earlier problem.' Do you agree with this statement? What implications does this statement have for organisational decision making?

2. Why is it important to establish priorities among different problems? Under what conditions might it be necessary to re-evaluate priorities?

3. Increasingly today, decisions are made in a global context. Can you think of some techniques that might be employed to reduce the likelihood of difficulties when decision makers from different cultures are working together to solve a problem?

4. Can individuals be trained to make better decisions? What aspects of decision making do you think could be most improved through training decision makers?

5. Think of a reasonably important non-programmed decision you have made recently. Did you employ an approach similar to the decision-making process outlined in Exhibit 12.2? How good was your decision? Could it have been improved by using the decision-making process? Explain.

6. How important a role should ethics play in decision making? Should managers — and organisations — be evaluated on the extent to which they make ethical decisions?

7. Creativity requires non-conformity of thinking. Does that explain why so many organisational decisions are non-creative? Aside from the specific techniques discussed in the chapter, what can be done to stimulate creative decision making in an organisation?

8. What are the relative advantages and disadvantages of individual versus group decision making?

9. 'Decisions should be thought of as means rather than ends.' Explain what this statement means and what effect it should have on decision making.

10. Strategic decision making cannot be a rational process. Discuss.

ENDNOTES

1 Bass, B. M. (1983). *Organizational Decision Making*. Homewood, IL: Richard D. Irwin.

2 Simon, H. A. (1960). *The New Science of Management Decision*. New York: Harper & Row, pp. 5–6.

3 Agnew, N. M. & Brown, J. L. (1985). Executive judgment: The institution/rational ratio, *Personnel*, 48–54.

4 Agor, W. (1986). The logic of institution: How top executives make important decisions, *Organizational Dynamics*, 5–18.

5 Grandori, A. (1984). A prescriptive contingency view of organizational decision making, *Administrative Science Quarterly*, 192–209.

6 This section is based on material discussed in Abelson, R. P. & Levi , A. (1987). Decision making and decision theory. In G. Lindzey & E. Aronson (Eds.) *Handbook of Social Psychology*, (vol.II), (3rd Ed.). New York: Random House.

7 Hodder, J. E., & Riggs, H. E. (1990). Pitfalls in evaluating risky projects, *Harvard Business Review*, 128–135.

8 Cowan, D. A. (1990). Developing a classification structure of organizational problems:

9 Dukerich, J. M. , & Nichols, M. L. (1991). Causal information search in managerial decision making, *Organizational Behavior and Human Decision Processes*, 106–122.

10 Jamison, D. B. (1984). The importance of boundary spanning roles in strategic decision-making, *Journal of Management Studies*, 131–152.

11 Cozier, R. A., & Schwenk, C. R. (1990). Agreement and thinking alike: Ingredients for poor decisions, *Academy of Management Executive*, 69–74.

12 Shrivastava, P. & Mitroff, I. I. (1984). Enhancing organizational research utilization: The role of decision makers' assumptions, *Academy of Management Review*, 18–26.

13 Harrison, T. M. (1985). Communication and participative decision making: An exploratory study, *Personnel Psychology*, 93-116.

14 Jamison, D. B. (1984). The importance of boundary spanning roles in strategic decision making, *Journal of Management Studies*, 131–152.

15 This section is based on material described in Kahneman, D., Slovic, P., & Tversky, A., (Eds.) (1982). *Judgment under Uncertainty : Heuristics and Biases*. Cambridge and New York : Cambridge University Press.

16 Staw, B. M. (1981). The escalation of commitment to a course of action, *Academy of Management Review*, 577–588.

17 Staw, B. M., & Ross, J. (1987). Behavior in escalation situations: Antecedents, prototypes, and solutions, *Research in Organizational Behavior*, **9**, 39–78.

18 Janis, I. L., & Mann, L. (1977). *Decision Making : A Psychological Analysis of Conflict, Choice, and Commitment*. New York : Free Press.

19 Cozier, R. A. , & Schwenk, C. R. (1990). Agreement and thinking alike: Ingredients for poor decisions, *Academy of Management Executive*, 69–74.

20 Crott, H. W., Szilvas, K. , & Zuber, A. (1991). Group decision, choice shift, and polarization in consulting, political, and local political scenarios: An experimental investigation and theoretical analysis, *Organizational Behavior and Human Decision Processes*, 22–41.

21 For examples, see Staw, B. M. (1981). The escalation of commitment to a course of action, *Academy of Management Review*, 577–588; and Bazerman, M. H., & Appelman, A. (1984). Escalation of commitment in individual and

An empirical investigation, *Academy of Management Journal*, 366–390.

group decision making, *Organizational Behavior and Human Decision Processes*, 141–152.

22 Guzzo, R. A., & Waters, J. A. (1982). The expression of affect and the performance of decision making groups, *Journal of Applied Psychology*, 67–74; Tjosvold, D., & Field, R. H. G. (1983). Effects of social context on consensus and majority vote decision making, *Academy of Management Journal*, 500–506; Miner, Jr., F. C. (1984). Group versus individual decision making: An investigation of performance measures, decision strategies, and process losses/gains, *Organizational Behavior and Human Decision Processes*, 112–124.

23 Whyte, G. (1993). Escalating commitment in individual and group decision making: A prospect theory approach, *Organizational Behavior and Human Decision Processes*, 430–455.

24 For a discussion of group decision making in complex problems, see Hart, S., Boroush, M., Enk, G., & W. Hornick (1985). Managing complexity through consensus mapping: Technology for the structuring of group decisions, *Academy of Management Review*, 587–600.

25 Dalkey, N. (1969). *The Delphi Method: An Experimental Study of Group Opinion*. Santa Monica, CA.: Rand Corporation. This is a classic work on the Delphi methods.

26 See Delbecq, A. L., Van de Ven, A. H. & Gustafson, D. H., (1975). *Group Techniques for Program Running*. Glenview, IL.: Scott, Foresman. The discussion here is based on this work.

27 Ibid., p. 18.

28 This section is based on material in Schwenk, C. R. (1995). Strategic decision making, *Journal of Management*, **21**, 471–493; Taylor, R.N. (1994). Strategic decision making. In M. D. Dunnette & L. M. Hough (Eds.) *Handbook of Industrial and Organizational Psychology* (2nd Ed.). Palo Alto, CA: Consulting Psychologists Press.

READING 12 AGREEMENT AND THINKING ALIKE: INGREDIENTS FOR POOR DECISIONS

Richard A. Cosier, Indiana University
Charles R. Schwenk, Indiana University

Source: Richard A. Cosier and Charles R. Schwenk, 'Agreement and Thinking Alike: Ingredients for Poor Decisions', *Academy of Management Executive*, February 1990, pp. 69–74.

Executive overview

People frequently believe that conflict is to be avoided in organizations. They think that meetings and decisions should reflect agreement and consensus. This article suggests that fostering disagreement in a structured setting may actually lead to better decisions. Two techniques for programming conflict into the decision-making process are suggested — the devil's advocate decision program (DADP) and the dialectic method (DM). In particular, evidence indicates that larger firms operating in uncertain environments benefit from encouraging structured conflict in decision making. This article challenges managers to consider either the devil's advocate or dialectic methods to program conflict into important organizational decisions.

Article

Most of us believe that a major objective in organizations is to foster agreement over decisions. After all, agreement indicates cohesion and homogeneity among employees. People who are in agreement with each other are satisfied and secure.

There is growing evidence that suggests conflict and dissent are what organizations really need to succeed.[1] Corporate decisions should be made after thoughtful consideration of counterpoints and criticism. People with different viewpoints must be encouraged to provide thoughts on important decisions. Widespread agreement on a key issue is a red flag, not a condition of good health.

There is an old story at General Motors about Alfred Sloan. At a meeting with his key executives, Sloan proposed a controversial strategic decision. When asked for comments, each executive responded with supportive comments and praise. After announcing that they were all in apparent agreement, Sloan stated that they were not going to proceed with the decision. Either his executives didn't know enough to point out potential downsides of the decision, or they were agreeing to avoid upsetting the boss and disrupting the cohesion of the group. The decision was delayed until a debate could occur over the pros and cons.

Some contemporary managers, however, recognize the benefits of conflict. Gavin Rawl, chief executive officer at Exxon, follows a policy of 'healthy disrespect', according to *Business Week*.

Even as he rose through the Exxon hierarchy, however, Rawl always had a healthy disrespect for bureaucracy. The company was obsessed with consensus. Proposals would wend their way through a maze of committees and task forces, through layers of staff. As Senior Vice President Charles R. Sitter says: 'In a large organization, good ideas have lots of foster parents, and the bad decisions produce lots of orphans.' Consensus, after all, is safer: The footprints are covered.[2]

Another example is the flamboyant Scott McNealy, Sun Microsystems' chief executive officer. McNealy encourages noisy, table-pounding meetings and debate among senior executives. Dissent and opinion is a natural part of the 'controlled chaos'.[3]

These managers, like others, have recognized the need to allow different viewpoints and critical thinking into organizational decisions. The type of conflict that is encouraged involves different interpretations of common issues or problems.[4] This 'cognitive conflict' was noted as functional many years ago by psychologist Irving Janis. Janis, in his famous writings on groupthink, pointed out that striving for agreement and preventing critical thought frequently leads to poor decisions such as those made during the Bay of Pigs invasion and the defense of Pearl Harbor.

Cognitive conflict can arise in two ways: (1) it can reflect true disagreement among managers and surface through an open environment which encourages participation; or (2) it can be programmed into the decision-making processes and forced to surface, regardless of managers' true feelings. Although both methods may be effective, the second is decidedly less common. Given the potential benefits of programmed conflict in organizational decision making, companies would do well to implement it. While elements of both methods of conflict generation are reviewed, means for encouraging programmed conflict is a major focus in this article.

Allowing true disagreement

Allowing disagreement to surface in organizations is exemplified by Jack Welch at General Electric. *Business Week* observed:

Welch, though, is convinced he can reach his aim. Like a man obsessed, he is driving G.E. through drastic fundamental change. Once formal, stable, gentlemanly, the new G.E. is tough, aggressive, iconoclastic. 'It's a brawl,' says Frank P. Doyle, senior vice president for corporate relations. 'It's argumentative, confrontational.' Working there can be a shock to newcomers. 'There's a much higher decibel level here. I told Jack what passes for conversation here would be seen as a mugging by RCA people,' Doyle says.[5]

The planning process involves scrutiny and criticism at G.E. Suggestions are expected and frequently offered and people are encouraged by Welch to speak their minds. This is consistent with organizational case studies that note the value of 'forthright discussion' versus behind-the-scenes politicking in determining organizational strategy. In one case, the vice president for manufacturing and finance at a company showing strong performance stated:

You don't need to get the others behind you before the meeting. If you can explain your view (at the meeting), people will change their opinions. Forefront (the fictitious name of the company) is not political at this point. But, you must give your reasons or your ideas don't count. (VP of manufacturing)

There is some open disagreement — it's not covered up. We don't gloss over the issues, we hit them straight on. (VP of finance)[6]

Several studies on strategic decision making show that, in general, successful companies advocate open discussions, surfacing of conflict, and flexibility in adopting solutions. Other studies, however, suggest that strategy is facilitated by consensus. This contradiction raises an important issue. Consensus may be preferred for smaller, nondiversified, privately held firms competing in the same industry, while larger firms dealing with complex issues of diversification may benefit from the dissent raised in open discussions. Larger firms in uncertain environments need dissent while smaller firms in more simple and stable markets can rely on consensus. In addition, Dess concludes, 'organizations competing within an industry experiencing high growth may benefit from a relatively high level of disagreement in assessing the relative importance of company objectives and competitive methods.'[7]

Example of the benefits of conflict in tactical problem-solving (short-term) situations are also common. Bausch and Lomb has established 'tiger teams' composed of scientists from different disciplines. Team members are encouraged to bring up divergent ideas and offer different points of view. Xerox uses roundtable discussions composed of various functional experts to encourage innovation. Compaq expects disagreement during all stages of new product development. Stuart Gannes, writing in *Fortune*, explains, 'But at Compaq, instead of just arguing over who is right, we tear down positions to reasons. And when you get to reasons you find facts and assumptions.'[8] Apple Computer, Ford Motor Co., Johnson and Johnson, and United Parcel Service are other examples of companies that tolerate conflict and debate during decisions.

In general, successful leaders seem to encourage managers to speak their minds. While this allows conflict into decision making, it carries a potential high cost. Positions are frequently tied to people and competitive 'zero-sum' situations in which perceived winners and losers are likely to develop. Clearly, 'losers' are less likely in future discussions to give their opinions.

Also, unprogrammed conflict is likely to be emotional and involve personal feelings. Lingering dislikes and rivalries are possible after emotional interchanges. Coalitions form and long-term divisiveness ensues.

Corporate time and money may have to be diverted from problem solving to resolving emotional conflicts between managers.

What may, in fact, be needed is programmed conflict that raises different opinions *regardless of the personal feeling of the managers*. Although research exists supporting some options for programmed conflict, few, if any, examples exist in the corporate world.

Programmed conflict
The devil's advocate
What can leaders do to experience the benefits associated with conflict in decision making, while minimizing the cost? Two options with potential are the devil' s advocate and dialectic methods for introducing programmed conflict into organizational decisions.

The usefulness of the devil's advocate technique was illustrated several years ago by psychologist Irving Janis when discussing famous fiascos. Janis attributes groupthink — the striving for agreement instead of the best decision in a group — to decisions such as were made during the Bay Of Pigs and Pearl Harbor.[9] Watergate and Vietnam are also often cited as examples. Janis recommends that everyone in the group assume the role of a devil's advocate and question the assumptions underlying the popular choice. Alternatively, an individual or subgroup could be formally designated as the devil's advocate and present a critique of the proposed course of action. This avoids the tendency of agreement interfering with problem solving. Potential pitfalls are identified and considered before the decision is final.

While Janis' observations are generally well known and accepted, corporate implementation of devil's advocacy as a formal element in decision making is rare. This is despite recent research that supports the benefits of devil's advocacy.[10] The conflict generated by the devil's advocate may cause the decision maker to avoid false assumptions and closely analyze the information. The devil's advocate raises questions that force an in-depth review of the problem-solving situation.

A devil's advocate decision program (DADP) can take several forms. However, all options require that an individual or group be assigned the role of critic. It needs to be clear that the criticism must not be taken personally, but is part of the organizational decision process.

The devil's advocate is assigned to identify potential pitfalls and problems with a proposed course of action. The issue could relate to strategic planning, new product development, innovation, project development, or other problems not amenable to programmed solutions. A formal presentation to the key decision makers by the devil's advocate raises potential concerns. Evidence needed to address the critique is gathered and the final decision is made and monitored. This DADP is summarized in Exhibit 12.7.

It is a good idea to rotate people assigned to devil's advocate roles. This avoids any one person or group being identified as the critic on all issues. The devil's advocate role may be advantageous for a person and the organization. Steve Huse, chairperson and CEO of Huse Food

Exhibit 12.7 A devil's advocate decision program

1. A proposed course of action is generated.

↓

2. A devil's advocate (individual or group) is assigned to criticize the proposal.

↓

3. The critique is presented to key decision makers.

↓

4. Any additional information relevant to the issues is gathered.

↓

5. The decision to adopt, modify, or discontinue the proposed course of action is taken.

↓

6. The decision is monitored.

Exhibit 12.8 The dialectic decision method

1. A proposed course of action is generated.

↓

2. Assumptions underlying the proposal are identified.

↓

3. A conflicting counterproposal is generated based on different assumptions.

↓

4. Advocates of each position present and debate the merits of their proposals before key decision makers.

↓

5. The decision to adopt either position, or some other position, e.g., a compromise, is taken.

↓

6. The decision is monitored.

Group, states that the devil's advocate role is an opportunity for employees to demonstrate their presentation and debating skills. How well someone understands and researches issues is apparent when presenting a critique.[11] The organization avoids costly mistakes by hearing viewpoints that identify pitfalls instead of foster agreement.

Often, a devil's advocate is helpful in adopting expert advice from computer-based decision support systems. Behavioral scientists Cosier and Dalton suggest that computer-based decisions may be more useful if exposed to a critique than simply accepted by managers.[12]

The dialectic

While the DADP lacks an 'argument' between advocates of two conflicting positions, the dialectic method (DM) programs conflict into decisions, regardless of managers' personal feelings, by structuring a debate between conflicting views.

The dialectic philosophy, which can be traced back to Plato and Aristotle, involves synthesizing the conflicting views of a thesis and an antithesis. More recently, it played a principle role in the writings of Hegel who described the emergence of new social orders after a struggle between opposing forces. While most of the world's modern legal systems reflect dialectic processes, Richard O. Mason was one of the first organization theorists to apply the dialectic to organisational decisions.[13] He suggested that the decision maker consider a structured debate reflecting a plan and a counterplan before making a strategic decision. Advocates of each point of view should present their assumptions in support of the argument.

The benefits of DM are in the presentation and debate of the assumptions underlying proposed courses of action. False or misleading assumptions become apparent and decisions based on these poor assumptions are avoided. The value of DM, shown in Exhibit 12.8, for promoting better understanding of problems and higher levels of confidence in decisions is supported by research.[14]

Critics of DM point to the potential for it to accentuate who won the debate rather than the best decision. Compromise, instead of optimal decisions, is likely. Managers will require extensive training in dialectic thinking and philosophy. Supporters of DADP argue that a critique focuses the decision maker on issues while the dialectic focuses more on the process of structural debate. Nevertheless, Cosier and

Dalton suggest the DM may be the best method to use under the worst decision-making condition — high uncertainty and low information availability. The dialectic may be a good way to define problems and generate needed information for making decisions under uncertainty. When information is available and causal relationships are known, computer-assisted or devil's advocate methods are preferred.

Programmed and unprogrammed conflict

It is not a major breakthrough in management advice to suggest that conflict can improve decisions, although it is useful to remind managers of the need to allow dissent. It is, however, uncommon for managers to formally program conflict into the decision-making process. Thus, regardless of personal feeling, programmed conflict requires managers to challenge, criticize, and generate alternative ideas. Compared to conflict that is allowed to naturally surface, programmed conflict may reduce negative emotional byproducts of conflict generation since dissent is no longer 'personal'. It also insures that a comprehensive decision framework is applied to important problems and issues.

Two options for implementing programmed conflict are based on the devil's advocate (DADP) and dialectic (DM) methods. We challenge managers to formally encourage controversy and dissent when making important choices under uncertain conditions. Encouraging 'yes sayers' and complacency promotes poor decisions and lack of innovative thinking in organizations.

Endnotes

1 Conflict has been frequently presented as a positive force in textbooks. See, for example, Peter P. Schoderbek, Richard A. Cosier, and John C. Aplin, *Management* (San Diego: Harcourt, Brace, Jovanovich, 1988), pp. 511–12.

2 'The Rebel Shaking up Exxon', *Business Week*, July 18, 1988, p. 107.

3 'Sun Microsystems Turns on the Afterburners', *Business Week*, July 18, 1988, p. 115.

4 Tjosvold uses the term 'controversy' to describe this type of conflict. He differentiates controversy from conflicts of interest which involve the actions of one person blocking the goal attainment of another person. See Dean Tjosvold, 'Implications of Controversy Research for Management', *Journal of Management* 11 (1985), pp. 22–23.

5 'Jack Welch: How Good a Manager?' *Business Week*, December 14, 1987, p. 94.

6 Kathleen M. Eisenhardt and L. J. Bourgeois, III, 'Politics of Strategic Decision Making in High-Velocity Environments', *Academy of Management Journal* 31 (1989), pp. 751–52.

7 Gregory G. Dess, 'Consensus on Strategy Formulation and Organizational Performance: Competitors in a Fragmented Industry', *Strategic Management Journal* 8 (1987), p. 274.

8 Stuart Gannes, 'America's Fastest-Growing Companies', *Fortune*, May 23, 1988, p. 29.

9 See Irving L. Janis, *Victims of Groupthink* (Boston: Houghton-Mifflin, 1972).

10 See, for example, Richard A. Cosier, 'Methods for Improving the Strategic Decision: Dialectic versus the Devil's Advocate', *Strategic Management Journal* 16 (1982), pp. 176–84.

11 Steve Huse, chairperson and CEO of Huse Food Group Inc., shared these observations in an interview with the senior author.

12 A model is developed which recommends methods of presenting information based upon conditions of uncertainty and information availability in Richard A. Cosier and Dan R. Dalton, 'Presenting Information Under Conditions of Uncertainty and Availability: Some Recommendations', *Behavioral Science* 33 (1988), 272–81.

13 Richard O. Mason, 'A Dialectical Approach to Strategic Planning', *Management Science* 15 (1969), pp. B403–14.

14 Ian I. Mitroff and J. R. Emshoff, 'On Strategic Assumption-Making: A Dialectical Approach to Policy and Planning', *Academy of Management Review* 4 (1979), pp. 1–12.

EXERCISE 12 GROUP DECISION MAKING

Source: Wilderness Survival is reprinted from: Pfeiffer, J. W., & Jones, J. E. (Eds.) (1976) *Annual Handbook for Group Facilitators*. San Diego, CA: University Associates, Inc. Used with permission. The Group Effectiveness Checklist is based on the ideas presented in Janis, I. L. (1971). Groupthink, *Psychology Today*, November; Maier, N. R. F. (1967). Assets and liabilities in group problem solving: The need for an integrative function, *Psychological Review*, 74, 239–249.

Purpose
1. Identify the pros and cons of group versus individual decision making.
2. Experience a group decision-making situation.
3. Practise diagnosing work group effectiveness.

Introduction
Much of the work that takes place in organisations is done in groups. In fact, the more important a task, the more likely it is to be assigned to a group. There is a tendency to believe that groups make better decisions and are better than individuals at solving problems. However, the evidence on this subject is contradictory and seems to suggest that 'it depends'. Groups are more effective under some circumstances and individuals under others. There are assets and liabilities associated with both (Maier, 1967). Because so much important work is done in groups, it is necessary for group members to learn to minimise the liabilities and capitalise on the assets of the group problem solving.

Instructions
1. Read the directions and complete the Wilderness Survival worksheet.
2. Form groups of five to seven people.
3. In groups, read the directions for and complete the Wilderness Survival group consensus task.
4. Calculate your scores using the directions in the Wilderness Survival scoring sheet.
5. Interpret your score.
6. Participate in a class discussion.

Part I: Wilderness Survival worksheet
Directions: Here are 12 questions concerning personal survival in a wilderness situation. Your first task is to *individually* select the best of the three alternatives given under each item. Try to imagine yourself in the situation depicted. Assume that you are alone and have a minimum of equipment, except where specified. The season is autumn. The days are warm and dry, but the nights are cold.

After you have completed the task individually, you will again consider each question as a member of a small group. Both the individual and group solutions will later be compared with the 'correct' answers provided by a group of naturalists who conduct classes in woodland survival.

	Your Answer	*Your Group's Answer*	*Expert's Answer*
1. You have strayed from your party in trackless timber. You have no special signalling equipment. The best way to attempt to contact your friends is to: **a.** Call for help loudly but in a low register. **b.** Yell or scream as loud as you can. **c.** Whistle loudly and shrilly.	_____	_____	_____
2. You are in 'snake country'. Your best action to avoid snakes is to: **a.** Make a lot of noise with your feet. **b.** Walk softly and quietly. **c.** Travel at night.	_____	_____	_____

3. You are hungry and lost in wild country. The best rule for determining which plants are safe to eat (those you do not recognise) is to:
   a. Try anything you see the birds eat.
   b. Eat anything except plants with bright red berries.
   c. Put a bit of the plant on your lower lip for 5 minutes; if it seems all right, try a little more.

4. The day becomes dry and hot. You have a full canteen of water (about one litre) with you. You should:
   a. Ration it — about a capful a day.
   b. Not drink until you stop for the night, and then drink what you think you need.
   c. Drink as much as you think you need when you need it.

5. Your water is gone; you become very thirsty. You finally come to a dried-up watercourse. Your best chance of finding water is to:
   a. Dig anywhere in the stream bed.
   b. Dig up plant and tree roots near the bank.
   c. Dig in the stream bed at the outside of a bend.

6. You decide to walk out of the wild country by following a series of ravines where a water supply is available. Night is coming on. The best place to make camp is:
   a. Next to the water supply in the ravine.
   b. High on a ridge.
   c. Midway up the slope.

7. Your flashlight glows dimly as you are about to make your way back to your campsite after a brief foraging trip. Darkness comes quickly in the woods and the surroundings seem unfamiliar. You should:
   a. Head back at once, keeping the light on, hoping the light will glow enough for you to make out landmarks.
   b. Put the batteries under your airpits to warm them, and then replace them in the flashlight.
   c. Shine your light for a few seconds, try to get the scene in your mind, move out in the darkness, and repeat process.

8. An early snow confines you to your small tent. You doze with your small stove going. There is danger if the flame is:
   a. Yellow.
   b. Blue.
   c. Red.

9. You must ford a river that has a strong
current, large rocks, and some white water.
After carefully selecting your crossing spot,
you should:
   a. Leave your boots and pack on.
   b. Take your boots and pack off.
   c. Take off your pack, but leave your boots
      on.

10. In waist-deep water with a strong current,
when crossing the stream, you should face:
   a. Upstream.
   b. Across the stream.
   c. Downstream.

11. You find yourself rimrocked; your only route
is up. The way is mossy, slippery rock. You
should try it:
   a. Barefoot.
   b. With boots on.
   c. In stockinged feet.

12. Unarmed and unsuspecting, you surprise a
large bear prowling around your campsite.
As the bear rears up about 10 metres from
you, you should:
   a. Run.
   b. Climb the nearest tree.
   c. Freeze, but be ready to back away slowly.

Individual score   _____

Wilderness survival group consensus task

Directions: You have just completed an individual
solution to Wilderness Survival. Now your small
group will decide on a group solution to the same
dilemmas. A decision by consensus is difficult to
attain, and not every decision may meet with
everyone's unqualified approval. There should
be, however, a general feeling of support from all
members before a group decision is made. Do
not change your individual answers, even if you
change your mind in the group discussion.

Outcome	Group 1	Group 2	Group 3
Range of individual scores (low–high)			
Average of individual scores			
Group score			

CASE 12   KOOYONG APPOINTS A NEW VICE-PRINCIPAL

This case study is based on an actual appointment decision. The material was first presented and discussed in an advanced organisational behaviour class in 1995.

There is a vacant position for vice-principal at Kooying High School. Truman, the principal of Kooying, has presented the school council with several reasons for making an internal appointment. He believes that such an appointment would be fair and reasonable; additionally, the procedure would be efficient and it would provide an excellent opportunity to recognise and reward a staff member's commitment and skills. The school council accepted his arguments. Furthermore, Truman convinced the school council to approve a position description which placed more weight on administrative duties, thus effectively dividing the two vice-principal positions into a pastoral position (students' interests and concerns) and an administrative position (school logistics and finances). Two applications only were lodged, from Katsikas and Oakmont. Several staff members commented that the restrictiveness of the job description had discouraged others from applying.

Background of Kooyong High School

The high school services a diverse range of students. Of its 700 students, 25% are Greek, 25% are Vietnamese and the remaining student body contains more than thirty ethnic groups. Of the fifty-five staff, 60% are married women, over 35 years old; 30% are married men, over 35 years old; 10% are unmarried; and 20% come from a non-English-Speaking Background (NESB), predominantly Greek.

The school has been in the midst of turmoil and conflict for several years, starting with the appointment of Ian Couldent as principal in 1983. The decision was a controversial one, as it meant that the vice-principal at the time, Ed Black, was overlooked. The decision was made because of Ed Black's apparent lack of rapport with the staff. Ed felt cheated out of the position, believing he was the better candidate for the job, and from this time onwards he used his influence negatively.

Under Ian Couldent's rule, enrolments dropped from 1000 in 1984, to 450 in 1991. This was the result of Couldent's inability to motivate his staff and initiate policy for the school. Combined with Ed Black undermining his position, this led to his demise.

In 1991 Ian Couldent resigned after 8 years' service to Kooyong High. At his farewell party he said, 'I know I was much better as a teacher than an administrator, I often wished I had stayed as a teacher; maybe some of you can learn from my experience.' The following year, Alan Truman was appointed as principal. Enrolments steadily grew to 700 by 1995; the closure of a neighbouring state school of 300 students helped boost numbers. Resources and staff, however, dropped 15% between 1992 to 1995. A total of 15% of the school's teaching staff accepted voluntary redundancy packages as part of the newly elected government's agenda to reduce the public education system. These reductions led to an atmosphere of uncertainty for the remaining teachers; they feared the cuts would return and would not provide the financial incentives that had existed in the previous voluntary redundancy packages.

Many staff members had applied for the package. The Directorate of School Education indicated that the procedure used to select the successful applicants would be fair and would be applied equally to all staff at all schools with the proviso that the principal had the final say. This meant that the principal was essentially the main authority who approved or disapproved the applications for the package.

Truman's selection of successful applicants was seen by some staff members as a means to rid himself of the troublesome staff members; that is, the staff members who were more willing to challenge his methods and policies regarding the school's best interest. These same staff were also naturally popular among the general staff and attracted a lot of admiration and support from co-workers. Some unsuccessful applicants felt they had been overlooked without good reason, particularly as the selection criteria was supposed to be objective. Some privately thought Truman had used the process for his personal gain and accumulation of power. Truman was aware of speculation from some corners of the staff that he had acted unprofessionally and used every opportunity possible to strenuously deny any implication that he had been anything less than scrupulous; naturally he was backed up by his close associates. Staff had previously enjoyed a close-knit relationship, often socialising outside school hours. Many of those who took the package were the more popular and vibrant teachers who had been more prepared to challenge Truman in regards to his leadership and decision-making style. Truman acknowledges that his staff have low motivation which is adversely affecting their performance and creativity as teachers.

Kooyong High School has maintained its competitiveness in its involvement in the government-initiated Schools of the Future program. When Truman arrived at Kooyong, he had a 'save the school' mentality. He concentrated heavily on highlighting and meeting the needs of the ethnic community. His background and active involvement in the union meant he was also concerned with meeting the union's limit of five NESB students in a class of twenty-five. This limit was intended to ensure that the quality of teaching was maintained for all students and to reduce the stress levels of the teaching staff — an important consideration for a school operating on limited resources.

Over time, however, Truman watered down his commitment to the union's guidelines. Staff noted that he placed a disproportionate emphasis on the 'bums on seats' philosophy rather than on delivering a quality teaching service. This became evident to first year teacher Ruth March. As a result of funding cutbacks and falling teacher numbers, March had a minimum of twelve NESB students in a class of thirty. Although other staff members also taught equally large classes, she was not yet confident of her teaching abilities to be able to effectively teach such a large class, not to mention a class where English was spoken only by about two-thirds of the students. March approached Truman about her concerns; she knew of his union background and thought he would resolve the situation. Truman was sympathetic to March's arguments and acknowledged them as having foundation. At the same time, however, he highlighted the importance the NESB students played in ensuring the school's survival and that although the union's concerns were very real and deserved credit, the bottom line was that it was either the NESB students or the school would close. March realised the futility of trying to convince Truman otherwise and persevered with classes where only

two-thirds of the students understood her, and where many more needed her personal attention.

Truman's vision is to compete directly with the local private schools by offering facilities and programs available at the private schools but without the associated costs. Staff initially supported Truman's demands to be more innovative because they viewed it as a professional challenge, but some have since become drained, particularly as the majority of students are from low socioeconomic backgrounds and their priorities differ from those of the middle classes.

The selection decision
Selection panel

The selection panel comprised:

- Truman — school principal;
- Whistle — principal's nominee;
- Watson — staff representative;
- Livingstone — union representative;

Selection criteria for vice-principal position

The successful applicant should possess the following skills and knowledge:

- assume responsibility and accountability in making decisions when necessary;
- be responsive to the needs and wishes of staff and students;
- be an effective administrator — identify and act on areas which need attention;
- have a clear and practical understanding of and familiarity with budgets and financial matters;
- have a knowledge and understanding of the multicultural issues relevant to the school and its students;
- have the ability to develop in-service education programs for staff in response to students' changing needs;
- have the ability to liaise with staff, students, parents and other community groups and organisations that have contact with the school in a educative, promotional and administrative role.

Case questions

1. Based on staff profiles and what you have read in this case, who would you select for the position of vice-principal? Why?
2. Assess how you have weighted the criteria. What decision rule did you employ in making your choice?

The decision: Transcript of the selection panel

Truman: We need to finalise the decision today.

Whistle: I think it is important to consider that staff are aware that there are only two applicants. They seem to think the position description is pretty limiting and they argue that the position needs more scope so it can get a wider range of applicants.

Truman: The position description was raised before the staff and the union before the applications were lodged. They had every opportunity to offer suggestions or changes then, didn't they Julie?

Livingstone: Yep. Some union members were concerned about parts of the position description, but they seemed quite happy after Alan spoke to all of the staff about the rationale behind the description.

Truman: That's not really the issue at hand now, anyway. We're here to decide who to appoint as vice-principal.

Whistle: A point to consider could be that rumours are flying that if Natalie doesn't get it then she'll leave.

Truman: We just have to ignore rumours and appoint the person on his or her abilities.

Watson: I think Lance deserves it. He's worked for over thirty years and will be retiring next year, so he won't get a second chance. Natalie can apply next year.

Livingstone: That doesn't necessarily mean we make the right decision though. What is the point of making a wrong appointment so that we can make the right appointment next year?

Watson: I just think that Lance should be rewarded for his commitment over the years. Anyway, it is not as if he doesn't fit the selection criteria; he has equal qualifications to Natalie's.

Livingstone: Well if that is the case, then the affirmative action policy should be used and Natalie should get the job.

Whistle: I don't know. I was appointed because of the affirmative action policy to get the gender balance in administration. The policy aims to get a balance. We've got a balance, and so we don't need to apply the policy in this case. Doing so would unreasonably influence the appointment.

Truman: Turning to the selection criteria, let's look at the selection criteria and see how each one matches up against it. What we also need to consider is how the decision will affect the other staff. Claire's appointment was not accepted — unfairly, I might add by some of the senior staff.

We might alienate them if we choose Natalie over Lance. Good morale among the staff is essential if we're going to have enthusiastic teachers and students.

The selection panel votes 3 to 1 in favour of Lance. Julie Livingstone casts the dissenting vote.

Questions on the decision

1. Do your agree with the panel's decision? Why? Why not?
2. How did the panel weight the formal selection criteria?
3. What other factors affected the decision?
4. How could the decision-making process have been improved?

Postcript:
Truman reflects on the decision one week later.

Natalie Katsikas intends to transfer at the end of the year; in the meantime she is not prepared to devote extra time to the newsletter, an important resource which raises issues of concern and interest to the school's community. She has also voiced her disappointment in the decision but not directly towards the selection panel. Natalie was heard to comment to one co-worker: 'I can't understand why Alan asked me to apply for the job when he just turns around and gives it to Lance. I'm the only one who's worked so hard for this school, not him (Lance). If he hadn't got the job, he would have slipped into oblivion as yet another boring, no-ideas man, just like Ian Couldent and Ed Black'.

A school council member has approached Truman about some teachers' concerns that both the vice-principals should be more involved in policy making and not be controlled by him (Truman), saying staff are losing confidence in the school and they believe power should not be so highly concentrated.

Two quality staff members have tendered their resignation, for different reasons:

- 'When Alan came, the school was in a crisis. We gave him full support and power to save it, which he did, but now he should relinquish some of that power and give us back some authority,' Senior Maths teacher, Nick Martin, said. He is leaving the teaching profession.
- 'All the school's resources are going into so many different projects that staff are pushed to

the limit teaching the large and diverse classes. Consequently, they don't have any energy left to deliver quality programs,' Sports Coordinator, Phil Trulove said.

Personality profiles

Alan Truman

Truman is 49 years old, and arrived at Kooyong High School in 1992. His background was as a senior industrial officer with the Teacher's Union. His commitment and experience in the state education system encouraged many staff. Enrolments increased steadily in Truman's first two years as principal.

Truman introduced the Total Quality Management (TQM) Scheme. This consisted of work groups aimed to monitor the progress of various areas ranging from curriculum to attendance.

He gained a reputation as a benevolent dictator. He was often perceived to operate quasi-democratic forums — staff were invited to contribute ideas and opinions on issues which, invariably, were not followed up by Truman. This led to growing frustration and dissatisfaction with him. Many of the staff felt he always had a hidden agenda and would not reveal the whole story or would withhold information that could be relevant to the issue at hand.

Truman has gathered key personnel around him who he relies on to share his vision and who support his style of administration. Outside staff view Truman's coalition as having a stranglehold over key decisions made regarding the school. This has caused staff to feel disempowered and helpless, and morale has subsequently fallen.

Natalie Katsikas

Katsikas is 38 years old and arrived at Kooyong High School in 1985. For the past 3 years she has been the Community Liaison Officer. Katsikas has always worked closely with students from NESB. She has strong links to the local Greek community, which constitutes a prominent ethnic group at the school.

Katsikas is highly committed and well respected as a middle manager and as a competent teacher. She exercises authority and fairness in equal doses. Katsikas's approach to her administrative duties is similar to her classroom manner — friendly, but can be uncompromising.

Both students and staff enjoy a close working relationship with Katsikas; however, staff are aware that she is prone to overwork and consequently 'burn out' from time to time.

Katsikas displays some positive and strong leadership qualities but does have a tendency to work independently of others without seeking a consensus, often citing others' 'casual' approach to work as frustrating. This causes problems with other staff who find Katsikas's unbending style oppressive. For example, she is often unwilling to postpone a test or reschedule a meeting or essay deadline for either staff or students; in fact, she is impatient when asked to be more flexible with others' needs.

Lance Oakmont

Oakmont is 59 years old, and he has taught at Kooyong High School since 1963. He is viewed with equal appreciation and scorn from different quarters; he is sometimes described as the 'paragon of virtue'.

Oakmont has announced he intends to retire when he turns 60 in June 1996. He has held various positions during his time at the school, but most recently he has been the Professional Development Co-ordinator for the past 3 years.

He takes his responsibilities seriously, but lacks initiative and decisiveness. Oakmont is popular with the students and shines in a classroom environment. His general approach to learning and decision making is group-based. Oakmont has nurtured a close and supportive relationship with Truman, promoting Truman's ideas and policies at TQM forums he coordinates. His present role is to ascertain the staff's need for and interest in training in the pastoral and administrative streams. However, staff feel uncomfortable approaching him in this capacity because of his allegiance to Truman. He is therefore viewed as an extension of Truman.

Claire Whistle

Whistle is 48 years old, and arrived at Kooyong High School in 1980. Whistle and Truman had a relationship at teachers' college 30 years earlier. Whistle operates on nervous energy; she diligently returns work to students the following class and has a tendency to respond to events emotionally. This may involve crying, or outbursts of anger or joy in the staffroom with no warning.

Whistle was appointed vice-principal in mid-1992. The position focused heavily on pastoral responsibilities much more than administration work. At the time of the appointment, Whistle was chosen rather than Peter Moran, who was a respected and efficient administrator and an extremely skilled art teacher. This was because Moran lacked a degree of rapport with many of the staff and more importantly because of the school's affirmative action policy designed to balance the gender numbers at the administrative level.

Terri Watson

Watson is 43 years old, and arrived at Kooyong High School in 1990. Watson is the Art and Drama coordinator. She organises theatre productions and art exhibitions at the school and has worked closely with Katsikas in creating links with the local community. Watson and Katsikas have had some differences of opinion concerning deadlines and Truman's willingness, at various times, to relieve Watson of student supervision.

Julie Livingstone

Livingstone is 34 years old, and arrived at Kooyong High School in 1988. Livingstone co-ordinates English for the English as a Second Language (ESL) students and is president of the union branch. This means she follows and pushes the union's line on conditions of employment and fair process in appointments of all teaching staff. She prides herself in having and exercising a strong sense of social justice.

Livingstone is increasingly distrustful of Truman in his covert disrespect for union guidelines, in addition to the overall sense of distrust from a majority of staff members. Currently, Livingstone is organising a branch action against the ratio of ESL students in the classes. The Australian Teachers' Union policy is that there be no more than 25% ESL students in any classes. Truman and Livingstone have had preliminary discussions about the union action and its effect on Kooyong High School.

COMMUNICATION

Learning objectives

- Explain *the elements in the communication process.*

- Identify *blocks to effective sending and receiving.*

- List *strategies for improving interpersonal communication.*

- Compare *the three major directions of communication.*

- Describe *ways in which communication in organisations can be improved.*

- Distinguish *between centralised and decentralised networks.*

- List *benchmarks for excellent communication.*

- Discuss *the importance of multicultural communication.*

The focus of this chapter is the process of organisational communication. Communicating, like the process of decision making discussed in the previous chapter, pervades everything that all organisational members — particularly managers — do. The managerial functions of planning, organising, leading and controlling all involve communicative activity. In fact, communication is an absolutely essential element in all organisational processes.

THE IMPORTANCE OF COMMUNICATION

Communication is the glue that holds organisations together. Communication assists organisational members to accomplish both individual and organisational goals, implement and respond to organisational change, coordinate organisational activities, and engage in virtually all organisationally relevant behaviours. Yet, as important as this process is, breakdowns in communication are pervasive. The anonymous wit who said, 'I know you believe you understand what you think I said, but I am not sure you realise that what you heard is not what I meant' was being more than humorous; he or she was describing what everyone of us has experienced: a failure to communicate.

To the extent that organisational communications are less effective than they might be, organisations will be less effective than they might be. For example, in many companies, new employee orientation programs represent the first important opportunity to begin the process of effective communication with employees. At Marriott International, the worldwide hotel and resort chain, 40% of new employees who leave the organisation do so during the first 3 months of the job. At least that had been true historically. Recently, the rate of departures has been significantly reduced because Marriott has embarked on a concerted effort to improve the content and manner in which it communicates with new employees during orientation. In addition to formally providing more information, each new employee is assigned a 'buddy' who serves as a vital communication link to which the newcomer has unrestricted access. Marriott helps ensure that its front-line service personnel communicate effectively with their guests by first ensuring that Marriott communicates effectively with its employees, starting from their very first day on the job.

It would be extremely difficult to find an aspect of a manager's job that does not involve communication. Serious problems arise when directives are misunderstood, when casual kidding in a work group leads to anger, or when informal remarks by a top-level manager are distorted. Each of these situations is a result of a breakdown somewhere in the process of communication.

Accordingly, the pertinent question is not whether managers engage in communication because communication is inherent to the functioning of an organisation. Rather, the pertinent question is whether managers will communicate well or poorly. In other words, communication itself is unavoidable in an organisation's functioning; only *effective* communication is avoidable. *Every manager must be a communicator.* In fact, everything a manager does communicates something in some way to somebody or some group. The only question is: 'With what effect?' While this may appear an overstatement at this point, it will become apparent as you proceed through the chapter. Despite the tremendous advances in communication and information technology, communication among people in organisations leaves much to be desired.[1]

Communication among people does not depend on technology but rather on forces in people and their surroundings. It is a process that occurs within people.

THE COMMUNICATION PROCESS

Communication experts tell us that effective communication is the result of a common understanding between the communicator and the receiver. In fact, the word **communication** is derived from the Latin *communis*, meaning 'common'. The communicator seeks to establish a 'commonness' with a receiver. Hence, we can define communication as the *transmission of information and understanding through the use of common symbols*. The common symbols may be verbal or non-verbal. You will see later in the context of an organisational structure that information can flow up and down (vertical), across (horizontal) and down and across (diagonal).

The most widely used contemporary model of the process of communication has evolved mainly from the work of Shannon and Weaver, and Schramm.[2] These researchers were concerned with describing the general process of communication that could be useful in all situations. The model that evolved from their work is helpful for understanding communication. The basic elements include a communicator, an encoder, a message, a medium, a decoder, a receiver, feedback and noise. It can be simply summarised as: Who … says what … in what way … to whom … with what effect?[3] Their model is presented in Exhibit 13.1.

Exhibit 13.1
A communication model

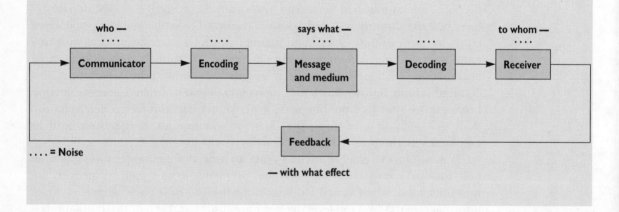

The elements of communication

Communicator-encoding

In an organisational framework, the communicator is an employee with ideas, intentions, information and a purpose for communicating. Given the communicator, an encoding process must take place that translates the communicator's ideas into a systematic set of symbols — into a language expressing the communicator's purpose. For example, a manager often takes accounting information, sales reports and computer data, and translates them into one message. The function of encoding, then, is to provide a form in which ideas and purposes can be expressed as a message.

Message-medium

The result of the encoding process is the message. The purpose of the communicator is expressed in the form of the message — either verbal or non-verbal. Managers have numerous purposes for communicating such as to have others understand their ideas, to understand the ideas of others, to gain acceptance of themselves or their ideas, or to produce action. The message, then, is what the individual hopes to communicate to the intended receiver, and the exact form it takes depends, to a great extent, on the medium used to carry the message. Decisions relating to the two are inseparable.

Not as obvious, however, are unintended messages that can be sent by silence or inaction on a particular issue as well as decisions of which goals and objectives not to pursue and which method not to utilise. For example, a decision to utilise one type of performance evaluation method rather than another may send a 'message' to certain people. Messages may also be designed to appear on the surface to convey certain information, when other information is what is really being conveyed. Related to this are messages designed to protect the sender, rather than to facilitate understanding by the receiver.

The *medium* is the carrier of the message. Organisations provide information to members in a variety of ways, including face-to-face communications, telephone, group meetings, memos, policy statements, reward systems, production schedules and sales forecasts. The arrival of electronic media based upon the computer and telecommunication technologies has increased interest in the role of the medium in various aspects of organisational communications.[4]

Decoding-receiver

For the process of communication to be completed, the message must be decoded in terms of relevance to the receiver. Decoding is a technical term for the receiver's thought processes. Decoding, then, involves interpretation. *Receivers* interpret (decode) the message in light of their own previous experiences and frames of reference. Thus, a salesperson is likely to decode a memo from the company president differently from a production manager. A nursing supervisor is likely to decode a memo from the hospital administrator differently from the chief of surgery. The closer the decoded message is to the intent desired by the communicator, the more effective is the communication. This underscores the importance of the communicator being 'receiver-oriented'.

Feedback

Provision for feedback in the communication process is desirable. *One-way* communication processes are those that do not allow receiver-to-communicator feedback. Addressing a large group, sending a note or an email are examples of one-way communication. One-way communication has several benefits: it is fast and it allows the speaker to be more organised. However, it also increases the potential for distortion between the intended message and the received message. A feedback loop provides a channel for receiver response that enables the communicator to determine whether the message has been received and has produced the intended response. *Two-way* communication processes provide for this important receiver-to-communicator feedback.[5]

For the manager, communication feedback may come in many ways. In face-to-face situations, *direct* feedback through verbal exchanges is possible as are such subtle means of communication as facial expressions of discontent or misunderstanding. In addition, *indirect* means of feedback (such as declines in productivity, poor quality of production, increased absenteeism or turnover, and lack of coordination and/or conflict between units) may indicate communication breakdowns.

Noise

In the framework of human communication, noise can be thought of as those factors that distort the intended message. Noise may occur in each of the elements of communication. For example, a manager who is under a severe time constraint may be forced to act without communicating or may communicate hastily with incomplete information. Or a subordinate may attach a different meaning to a word or phrase from what was intended by the manager.

The elements discussed in this section are essential for communication to occur. They should not, however, be viewed as separate. They are, rather, descriptive of the acts that have to be performed for any type of communication to occur. The communication may be vertical (superior-subordinate, subordinate-superior) or horizontal (peer-peer). Or it may involve one individual and a group. However, the elements discussed here must be present.

Non-verbal messages

The information sent by a communicator that is unrelated to the verbal information — that is, non-verbal messages or **non-verbal communication** — is a relatively recent area of research among behavioural scientists. The major interest has been in the physical cues that characterise the communicator's physical presentation. These cues include such modes of transmitting non-verbal messages as head, face and eye movements; posture; distance; gestures; voice tone; and clothing and dress choices.[6] Non-verbal messages themselves are influenced by factors such as the gender of the communicator.[7]

Some non-verbal messages are spontaneous and unregulated expressions of emotion, while others are conscious and deliberately presented.[8] Through non-verbal behaviour, particularly body movements,

> We say, 'Help me, I'm lonely. Take me, I'm available. Leave me alone, I'm depressed.' We act out our state of being with non-verbal body language. We lift one eyebrow for disbelief. We rub our noses for puzzlement. We clasp our arms to isolate ourselves or to protect ourselves. We shrug our shoulders for indifference, wink one eye for intimacy, tap our fingers for impatience, slap our forehead for forgetfulness.[9]

Non-verbal messages may differ from other forms of communication behaviour in several ways. For example, non-verbal behaviour can be difficult to suppress (e.g. an involuntary frown indicating displeasure). Such unconscious behaviour can contradict the message the communicator is sending verbally. Another way in which non-verbal messages differ from other forms is that they are more apparent to the people who observe them than they are to the people who produce them. This can make it very difficult for the sender to know how successfully she or he produced the non-verbal message that was intended. Finally, many non-verbal messages are susceptible to multiple interpretations.

Smiles may indicate genuine happiness, contempt, deceit, fear, compliance, resignation — even, on occasion, anger.

Research indicates that facial expressions and eye contact and movements generally provide information about the type of emotion, while such physical cues as distance, posture and gestures indicate the intensity of the emotion. These conclusions are important to managers. They indicate that communicators often send a great deal more information than is obtained in verbal messages. To increase the effectiveness of communication, a person must be aware of the non-verbal as well as the verbal content of the messages.

Communication in organisations

The elements of the communication process occur at two levels within organisations: interpersonal and organisational. Good organisational communication rests on good interpersonal communication and a good communication climate. In this chapter, we will start by considering the factors that impede or help good interpersonal communication. We will then go on to consider how these principles apply and are extended in organisational communication.

INTERPERSONAL COMMUNICATION

Within an organisation, communication flows from individual to individual in face-to-face and group settings. Such flows are termed **interpersonal communication** and can vary from direct orders to casual expressions. Interpersonal behaviour could not exist without interpersonal communication. In addition to providing needed information, interpersonal communication influences how people feel about the organisation. For example, as you will see in our Management Encounter, research indicates that satisfaction with communication relationships affects organisational commitment.[10]

Individuals spend much of their time communicating. But, how good are we? Research shows that most of the time, we are very poor communicators: not only do we fail to listen to others, but our responses are aimed at blocking rather than assisting further communication. In this section, we consider some common sending and receiving problems, as well as strategies for improving interpersonal communication.

Blocks to effective sending

As senders, we must make a number of decisions about the message that we plan to send: what information we need to convey, how we will convey it and who the receiver will be. Have you ever had the experience of someone misinterpreting your message? Did you blame the receiver for not listening? Did you check to make sure that your message was clear? As senders, our job is to help the listener understand our message. When we send incomplete messages, we make that task more difficult. What are the major blocks to effective sending?

Frame of reference
Different individuals can interpret the same communication differently depending on their previous experiences. This results in variations in the

encoding and decoding process. Communication specialists agree that this is the most important factor that breaks down the 'commonness' in communications. When the encoding and decoding processes are not alike, communication tends to break down. Receivers interpret messages from their point of view, their experiences and their goals. When experiences and goals differ, it may well be that the meaning given to a message also differs. As a result, distortion often occurs because of differing frames of reference.

People in various organisational functions interpret the same situation differently. A business problem will be viewed differently by the marketing manager and the production manager. An efficiency problem in a hospital will be viewed by the nursing staff from its frame of reference and experiences, which may result in interpretations different from those of the physician staff. Different levels in the organisation also will have different frames of reference. First-line supervisors have frames of reference that differ in many respects from those of vice-presidents. They are in different positions in the organisation structure, and this influences their frames of reference. As a result, their needs, values, attitudes and expectations will differ, and this difference will often result in unintentional distortion of communication. This is not to say that either group is wrong or right. All it means is that, in any situation, individuals will choose the part of their own past experiences that relates to the current experience and is helpful in forming conclusions and judgements.

Filtering

Filtering describes the alteration of information in some way. This block is especially relevant to organisational communication, which often must pass through several layers in the organisational hierarchy before reaching the last receiver. What happens on the way? At each level, individuals summarise (delete) the material, add new information (possibly hoping to make the message clearer), or distort the message by removing or de-emphasising certain aspects of the message. Distortion is especially likely when the message contains bad news: senders are reluctant to pass on such news and may manipulate the information so that the receiver perceives it as a positive. One example in organisations is when subordinates cover up unfavourable information in messages to their superiors. The reason for filtering should be clear; this is the direction (upward) that carries control information to management. Management makes merit evaluations, grants salary increases and promotes individuals based on what it receives by way of the upward channel. The temptation to filter is likely to be strong at every level in the organisation.

In-group language

Each of us undoubtedly has had associations with experts and been subjected to highly technical jargon, only to learn that the unfamiliar words or phrases described very simple procedures or familiar objects. Many students are asked by researchers to 'complete an instrument as part of an experimental treatment'. The student soon learns that this involves nothing more than filling out a paper-and-pencil questionnaire.

Often, occupation, professional and social groups develop words or phrases that have meaning only to members. Such special language can serve many useful purposes. It can provide members with feelings of belongingness, cohesiveness and, in many cases, self-esteem. It also can facilitate effective communication within the group. The use of in-group language can, however, result in severe communication breakdowns when outsiders or other groups are involved. This is especially the case when groups use such language in an organisation, not for the purpose of transmitting information and understanding, but rather to communicate a mystique about the group or its function.

Blocks to effective listening

As listeners, all too often we behave as passive recipients of information. As a result, we fail to attend fully to the message that is being sent. Because we process information far more quickly than it is sent, we have a lot of spare time on our hands while senders are talking. How do we use this time? Bad listeners daydream, prepare their response, monitor for a gap so that they can 'jump in' with their ideas or think about their weekend plans. None of this helps the message to get through. To do this, listeners need to be 'active', as the reading at the end of this chapter highlights. Here are some common blocks to effective listening.

Reading 13
Active listening

Selective listening

Selective listening is a form of selective perception in which we tend to block out new information, especially it if conflicts with what we believe. When we receive a directive from management, we notice only those things that reaffirm our beliefs. Those things that conflict with our preconceived notions we either do not note at all or we distort to confirm our preconceptions.

For example, a notice may be sent to all operating departments that costs must be reduced if the organisation is to earn a profit. The communication may not achieve its desired effect because it conflicts with the 'reality' of the receivers. Thus, operating employees may ignore or be amused by such information in light of the large salaries, travel allowances and expense accounts of some executives. Whether they are justified is irrelevant; what is important is that such preconceptions result in breakdowns in communication.

Value judgements

In every communication situation, *value judgements* are made by the receiver. This basically involves assigning an overall worth to a message prior to receiving the entire communication. Value judgements may be based on the receiver's evaluation of the communicator or previous experiences with the communicator or on the message's anticipated meaning. For example, a hospital administrator may pay little attention to a memorandum from a nursing supervisor because 'she's always complaining about something'. A university professor may consider a merit-evaluation meeting with the department chairperson as 'going through the motions' because the faculty member perceives the chairperson as having little or no power in the administration of the university. A cohesive work group may form negative value judgements concerning all actions by management.

Source credibility

Source credibility is the trust, confidence and faith that the receiver has in the words and actions of the communicator. The level of credibility the receiver assigns to the communicator in turn directly affects how the receiver views and reacts to the words, ideas and actions of the communicator.

Thus, how subordinates view a communication from their manager is affected by their evaluation of the manager. This, of course, is heavily influenced by previous experiences with the manager. Again we see that everything done by a manager communicates. A group of hospital medical staff who view the hospital administrator as less than honest, manipulative and not to be trusted are apt to assign non-existent motives to any communication from the administrator. Union leaders who view management as exploiters and managers who view union leaders as political animals are likely to engage in little real communication.

Case 13
A case of misunderstanding: Mr Hart and Mr Bing

Communication overload

One of the vital tasks performed by a manager in decision making, and one of the necessary conditions for effective decisions, is *information*.[11] Because of the advances in communication technology, the difficulty is not in generating information. In fact, the last decade has often been described as the 'Information Era' or the 'Age of Information.'. Managers often feel buried by the deluge of information and data to which they are exposed and cannot absorb or adequately respond to all of the messages directed to them. They 'screen out' the majority of messages, which in effect means that these messages are never decoded. Thus, the area of organisational communication is one in which more is not always better.

Improving interpersonal communication[12]

The barriers to communication that have been discussed here, while common, are by no means the only ones. In this section, we will outline some strategies that improve interpersonal communication. In considering these, remember that because communication is a two-way process, we take on both the roles of sender and listener.

Obtain feedback

It is important for both senders and listeners to obtain feedback from the other person. Senders should check that their message has been received, while receivers should check that they have understood both the content and the feeling associated with the message. One means for doing this is to paraphrase in your own words the message you think was sent.

Label behaviours and feelings

As senders, it is important that we label both behaviours and feelings. If, for example, we are trying to discuss the late arrival of one of our staff, we should avoid such messages as 'I'm sick of your slack attitude and laziness'. As we saw in our discussion of organisational behaviour management (Chapter 5) this does not provide useful information. By labelling behaviour non-evaluatively — arriving at work late — we make it clear what bothers us. We should add to the message an accurate description of how we feel — are we irritated? Angered? Furious? Puzzled?

Be redundant

Building redundancy into messages is one way of ensuring that they are received. You should be aware that different people process information in different ways. For example, do you prefer to learn by listening to lectures or by reading books? Because we process information differently, different ways of communicating will have different effects. By sending our message through more than one medium we increase the chances that the listener will truly 'hear'.

Ensure congruence of verbal and non-verbal messages

Non-verbal messages are very powerful. So powerful that, according to researchers, no more than 35% of the meaning of messages comes from the meaning of the words that we use; the rest comes from how we sound and how we look. What is more, if there are any discrepancies, we are far more likely to believe non-verbal messages.[13]

Match your listener's frame of reference

Tailor your message to your audience. If you are talking to someone who is new on the job, the language you use should be very different from what you would use in talking to someone with many years experience. Remembering to phrase your messages to match your listener's needs will help eliminate such blocks as in-group language.

Ask the right questions[14]

As a listener, you have a responsibility to help the sender get his or her message across. Usually, we try to do this by asking questions. However, according to Carl Rogers, most of the questions that we ask are attempts to control and direct the conversation rather than sincere efforts to understand the message. According to Rogers, any of the following types of questions and comments are counter-productive:

1. *Evaluating.* This type of response makes a judgement about the value of what the speaker has said or done. It carries with it an implication about what the speaker should do or say next. An example of an evaluative response is something like 'That idea will never work' — it implies that the speaker should abandon the idea and move on.

2. *Interpreting.* Sometimes our responses try to analyse and explain to the speaker what his or her underlying motive is; for example, 'I know you are only doing that to irritate me'.

3. *Supporting.* This is a frequently used strategy whose underlying aim is to avoid the message. Frequently it minimises the feelings reported by the speaker and diverts the speaker from his or her main purpose. 'Don't worry about it, it will all work out' is a good example of support in action.

4. *Probing.* Targeting one component of a message and seeking further information — probing — implies what the speaker should talk about. 'Why do you think you are going to fail?' is a very specific question and one that may — or may not — focus on what concerns the speaker most.

A managerial perspective on interpersonal communication

The day-to-day activities of managers place a high value on effective interpersonal communications. Managers provide *information* (which must be understood); they give *commands* and *instructions* (which must be obeyed and learned); and they make *efforts to influence* and *persuade* (which must be accepted and acted on). Thus, the way in which managers communicate is crucial for obtaining effective performance.[15]

Theoretically, managers who desire to communicate effectively can use both exposure and feedback to enlarge the area of common understanding. As a practical matter, such is not the case. Managers differ in their ability and willingness to use exposure and feedback. At least four different managerial styles can be identified.

Type A

Managers who use neither exposure nor feedback are said to have a Type A style. The unknown region predominates in this style because such managers are unwilling to enlarge the area of their own knowledge or the knowledge of others. Type A managers exhibit anxiety and hostility and give the appearance of aloofness and coldness towards others. If an organisation has a larger number of such managers in key positions, then you would expect to find poor and ineffective interpersonal communications and a loss of individual creativity. Type A managers often display the characteristics of autocratic leaders.

Type B

Some managers desire some degree of satisfying relationships with their subordinates, but because of their personalities and attitude, these managers are unable to open up and express their feelings and sentiments. Consequently, they cannot use exposure and must rely on feedback. The facade is the predominant feature of interpersonal relationships when managers overuse feedback to the exclusion of exposure. The subordinates probably will distrust such managers because they realise that these managers are holding back their own ideas and opinions. Type B behaviour is often displayed by managers who desire to practise some form of permissive leadership.

Type C

Managers who value their own ideas and opinions, but not the ideas and opinions of others, will use exposure at the expense of feedback. The consequence of this style is the perpetuation and enlargement of the blindspot. Subordinates will soon realise that such managers are not particularly interested in communicating, only in telling. Consequently, Type C managers usually have subordinates who are hostile, insecure, and resentful. Subordinates soon learn that such managers are mainly interested in maintaining their own sense of importance and prestige.

Exercise 13
Your communication style

Type D

The most effective interpersonal communication style is one that uses a balance of exposure and feedback. Managers who are secure in their positions will feel free to expose their own feelings and to obtain feedback from others. To the extent that a manager practises Type D behaviour successfully, communication becomes more effective.

COMMUNICATING WITHIN ORGANISATIONS

The design of an organisation should provide for communication in three distinct directions: downward, upward and horizontal. Since these directions of communication establish the framework within which communication in an organisation takes place, let us briefly examine each one. This examination will enable you to better appreciate the barriers to effective organisational communication and the means to overcome them. As our Management Encounter in this chapter shows, the consequences of poor organisational communication affect almost every dimension of organisations: commitment, satisfaction, stress and the acceptance of change.

Downward communication

This type of communication flows downward from individuals in higher levels of the hierarchy to those in lower levels. The most common forms of **downward communication** are job instructions, official memos, policy statements, procedures, manuals and company publications. According to Katz and Kahn,[16] downward communication serves several important organisational functions:

- *job instructions*, telling staff what to do;
- *job rationale*, aimed at increasing individuals' understanding of their role in the organisation and the relationship between their job and organisational goals;
- *procedures and practices*, including policies and regulations;
- *performance feedback* for individuals, groups or departments;
- *establishment of culture*, by informing individuals of the organisation's mission.

In many organisations, downward communication is often both inadequate and inaccurate as evidenced in the often heard statement among organisation members that 'we have absolutely no idea what's happening'. Such complaints indicate inadequate downward communication and the need of individuals for information relevant to their jobs. The absence of job-related information can create unnecessary stress among organisation members.[17] A similar situation is faced by a student who has not been told the requirements and expectations of an instructor.

Issues in downward communication[18]

Three practices can improve downward communication: management attitude, timeliness and quantity. It is important that management demonstrate a positive attitude to communication, being open and willing to share information with staff. Without this attitude, it is unlikely that we can establish good organisational communication. In addition, ensuring that messages are timely and relevant increases the chance that they will be received: time messages so that the information arrives when it is needed and make clear why this information is important. Think about this for a moment: when do you most need to know about exams? If your lecturer gives you this information too early, you ignore it;

Counting the costs of poor communication

What are the consequences of poor organisational communication? Clearly, when we communicate badly, organisational efficiency will deteriorate. However, there is also a high human cost in poor communicating, and one that impacts on the organisation. Dissatisfaction with organisational communication can result in decreased commitment and job satisfaction, lower willingness to accept change, and higher levels of stress and burnout. In this Encounter, we review representative research examining these outcomes.

Organisational commitment

We have already mentioned the importance — for individuals — of getting the information that they think they need. This is also called *communication relationship satisfaction*, and researchers have examined how satisfaction with communication received from top management and supervisors impacts on organisational commitment. Very simply, overall satisfaction is correlated with commitment. However, a closer examination of the relationship suggests that it is the messages of top management that are critical to organisational commitment and emphasises the need for top management to display a positive attitude to communication: to be sincere in their communication efforts and establish trust with staff.

Job satisfaction

Can communication quality increase job satisfaction? According to research this may depend on who is sending the message and just how important your job is to you. When messages are sent by administrative staff, only quality — assessed in terms of timeliness, accuracy and usefulness — matters. However, when the communication comes from individuals with whom you are more involved — supervisors, co-workers and subordinates, then job satisfaction is affected by both the quality of communication and your job involvement. According to this research, communication quality affects your job satisfaction only when your job is very important to you: under these circumstances, poor quality leads to low job satisfaction, whereas high quality leads to high job satisfaction.

Research has also shown that role ambiguity (which we discussed in Chapter 6) is related to job satisfaction: high ambiguity leads to low satisfaction. We also suggested that one means for reducing ambiguity is to improve communication. According to one study, the frequency with which we communicate with others has precisely this effect: the more frequently we communicate with our co-workers, the more supportive they appear. The consequence is lower role ambiguity and higher job satisfaction.

Accepting change

The timeliness of communication also affects employee reactions to change ... along with how the information is delivered and by whom. When the announcement of changes was rated for its effectiveness, researchers found that effective and ineffective messages differed along these three dimensions. Of these dimensions, timing was the most critical: staff resented hearing about changes on the grapevine ahead of formal announcements — or worse still, reading about the changes in the newspaper. Euphemistic messages using terms such as 'downsizing' and written rather than spoken messages also decreased the effectiveness of the announcements. Clearly, ineffective messages violated several of our benchmarks for excellent communicating.

Implications

Imagine that you are developing a communication strategy for an organisation. Based on this research, what would you identify as the critical elements in good organisational communication? What factors other than the communication itself do organisations need to consider?

Source: Frone, M. R., & Major, B. (1988). Communication quality and job satisfaction among nurses: The moderating influence of job involvement, *Group & Organization Studies*, **13**, 5332–5347; Putti, J. M., Aryee, S., & Phua, J. (1990). Communication relation satisfaction and organizational commitment, *Group & Organization Studies*, **15**, 44–52; Ray, E. B., & Miller, K. I. (1991). The influence of communication structure and social support on job stress and burnout, *Management Communication Quarterly*, **4**, 506–527; Smeltzer, L. R. (1991). An analysis of strategies for announcing organization-wide change strategies, *Group & Organization Studies*, **16**, 5–24.

if it arrives too late, you probably feel anxious. Finally, managers should avoid overloading their staff. One response to the complaint that 'no one ever tells us anything' is to send memos, minutes and newsletters in a continuous stream. This strategy guarantees the loss of important information. In this chapter's Organisational Encounter we discuss strategies for reducing information overload by reducing meetings.

Upward communication

An effective organisation needs **upward communication** as much as it needs downward communication. In such situations, the communicator is at a lower level in the organisation than the receiver. Some of the most common upward communication flows are suggestion boxes, group meetings, and appeal and grievance procedures.

Upward communication serves a number of important functions. Organisational communication researcher Gary Kreps identifies several:[19]

- It provides managers with feedback about current organisational issues and problems and information about day-to-day operations that they need for making decisions about directing the organisation.
- It is management's primary source of feedback for determining the effectiveness of its downward communication.
- It relieves employees' tensions by allowing lower level organisation members to share relevant information with their superiors.
- It encourages employees' participation and involvement, thereby enhancing organisational cohesiveness.

Issues in upward communication[20]

One of the biggest problems faced by organisations is that, even though they will benefit from good upward communication, it is difficult to establish. Status differences make it hard to establish the trust necessary to convey information up — especially if the news is bad. Status differences can be perceived as threats by persons lower in the hierarchy, and this can prevent or distort communication. Rather than look incompetent, a nurse may prefer to remain quiet instead of expressing an opinion or asking a question of the nursing supervisor. Many times superiors, in an effort to utilise their time efficiently, make this barrier more difficult to surmount. The governmental administrator or bank vice-president may be accessible only by making an advance appointment or by passing the careful quizzing of a secretary. This widens the communication gap between superior and subordinates. The Local Encounter in this chapter discusses some factors that contribute to this communication gap.

Organisations need to establish formal policies and procedures that encourage upward communication. In order to overcome status differences, organisations can consider such strategies as informal lunches, meetings with staff two levels up and social events. In addition, formal policies that make clear the types of information that should be communicated up remove some of the difficulties concerning the communication of bad news. Finally, employee surveys can be an important and anonymous source of information that overcome both issues of status and trust — the course evaluations that you complete are an example of this communication technique. However, as we will see in our discussion of excellent organisational communication, if the surveys are not acted on staff soon become sceptical.

Horizontal communication

Often overlooked in the design of most organisations is provision for **horizontal communication**. When the chairperson of the accounting department communicates with the chairperson of the marketing department concerning the course offerings in a college of business administration, the flow of communication is horizontal. Although vertical (upward and downward) communication flows are the primary considerations in organisational design, effective organisations also need horizontal communication. Horizontal communication — for example, communication between production and sales in a business organisation and among the different departments or colleges within a university — is necessary for the coordination and integration of diverse organisational functions.

Since mechanisms for assuring horizontal communication do not ordinarily exist in an organisation's design, its facilitation is left to individual managers. Peer–to–peer communication is often necessary for coordination and can also provide social need satisfaction.

ORGANISATIONAL   Encounter

Information overload? Just another meeting...

One of the most frequent tools for disseminating information in organisations is 'the meeting'. Managers spend more of their time than they want in meetings — about 40% — and often do not find the experience an enjoyable one. However, meetings dominate their lives. And one reason for this may be, despite a wide range of alternatives for communicating, that organisations believe holding meetings increases employees' feelings of participation. Meetings are a form of group decision making and therefore, to be effective, should meet the criteria for effective group functioning: they should have clear goals, encourage participation and manage conflicts well. One means for managing meetings is to set beginning and ending times: at Advance Bank, staff are required to book meeting rooms in advance and nominate start and finish times. This should focus them on the goals of the meeting, and also reduce some of the frustration experienced when meetings run on and on ...

But, are meetings necessary? Do all discussions have to take place face to face, or can we utilise the range of new media to communicate at a distance? Group Decision Centres, in which individuals use computers for discussion and voting, are one example of using technology to facilitate meetings. The advantage is that everyone gets a chance to participate, and it reduces meeting time by over a half — perhaps the effort of typing keeps the discussion focused! Using facilitators to manage the process of meetings can also reduce their time and increase their effectiveness.

Are meetings inefficient? Do they overload staff with information? Can you think of ways to use new technology such as e-mail to reduce the need for meetings? Would such strategies increase or decrease the information staff need to process?

Source: Ferguson, A. (1994). How to do away with time-consuming meetings, *Business Review Weekly*, July 25.

LOCAL   Encounter

Organisational communication: How satisfied are we?

Information loss

In our discussion of the benchmarks for excellent communication, we will see that giving staff the information that they want is important. We might expect that the closer we get to the top, the more easily this need is met. Is this so? In an examination of information flow in a recently privatised government processing plant, Frank Sligo at Massey University in New Zealand set out to answer this question. He compared three layers of employees — middle managers, supervisors and non-supervisory staff — in terms of the information that they wanted and the information that they were receiving. He found that although organisational level did not affect what staff wanted to know it did affect what they were told: the three groups differed in what they were told about where their job fitted into the organisation, how work was assessed, how senior management made decisions, the problems facing the organisation and work responsibilities. The biggest differences occurred in two areas — how their job fits into the organisation and how performance is assessed. Surprisingly, supervisors said they were the most poorly informed in terms of the first area; and both supervisors and non-supervisory staff reported inadequate information concerning performance-assessment procedures. Can you think of any reasons for this pattern? Why are supervisors no better informed than their staff?

Communication satisfaction

In the chapter on leadership we considered the possibility that leaders are rated as effective when there is congruence between their leadership style and gender. Victor Callan, at Queensland University, has explored a similar idea in relation to communication style. In his research he examined, first, whether managers and their subordinates agree on the quality and quantity of managerial communication; and,

second, how this is affected by the gender make-up of the dyad and the manager's leadership style. His results show some interesting patterns.

First, managers think that the quantity and quality of their communication are much higher than as perceived by subordinates. The biggest discrepancy occurred for female managers with a task-oriented leadership style: under these conditions, whereas the managers reported high levels of quality and quantity, their subordinates reported exceptionally low levels of both aspects of communication. Could this be because, for task-oriented leaders, any communication seems like a lot of communication?

Second, female staff reported lower quantity and quality than their male counterparts, and this effect was especially pronounced when their managers were also female.

Finally, Callan considered how these factors influenced job satisfaction. He found that in dyads with female managers, job satisfaction was unaffected by quality, quantity and congruence between managers and their subordinates in terms of how they perceived communication or leadership style. However, in dyads with male managers, job satisfaction was higher when the manager was also task-oriented. In addition, when subordinates were female, satisfaction in these dyads was further influenced by the perceived quality of communication and the degree of congruence in terms of communication quantity.

Can you suggest how these findings could be used to improve communication between managers and subordinates?

Source: Callan, V. (1993). Subordinate-manager communication in different sex dyads: Consequences for job satisfaction, *Journal of Occupational and Organizational Psychology*, **66**, 13–27; Sligo, F. (1995). Information loss revisited: How different levels of staff perceive their access to work-related knowledge, *Asia Pacific Journal of Human Resources*, **33**, 60–73.

Diagonal communication

While it is probably the least used channel of communication in organisations, **diagonal communication** is important in situations where members cannot communicate effectively through other channels. For example, the comptroller of a large organisation may wish to conduct a distribution cost analysis. One part of the task may involve having the sales force send a special report directly to the comptroller rather than going through the traditional channels in the marketing department. Thus, the flow of communication would be diagonal as opposed to vertical and horizontal. In this case, a diagonal channel would be the most efficient in terms of time and effort for the organisation.

COMMUNICATION NETWORKS[21]

So far in this chapter, we have considered how information flows from one individual to another. There is, however, a second level at which we can consider communication. In large groups or organisations we need to consider how information flows around the organisation: who gets information and who doesn't? Do the formal and informal communication channels match? Should everyone know everything or should information access be limited?

Communication networks describe the pattern and structure of communication channels within an organisation. In organisations there is always a formal communication chain, as set out in organisation charts; however, such formal networks are usually complemented by informal networks — people establish contacts with others outside of their work area in order to access information more quickly.

Researchers map communication networks by asking individuals to list all of the people they talk to in a day — those to whom they give information and those who provide them with information. This enables researchers to draw up a chart (called a sociogram) showing links between people in the organisation. When we examine communication patterns in this way, we can identify two types of networks: centralised and decentralised. In *centralised networks*, one person holds a key position in the network and all information must flow through that person; this person frequently becomes the leader of the group. We might expect to find this type of network in hierarchically structured organisations. In *decentralised networks*, there is no obvious key figure; information passes from everyone to everyone and no clear leaders emerge. Centralised networks are more suitable for simple problems whereas decentralised problems are more suitable for complex problems. These different types of networks influence the speed and accuracy with which problems can be solved, the number of errors that are made, the number of messages that are sent, and how satisfied individuals feel with the group's work.

Communication networks are determined by several factors, including organisational structure. Structure determines how information will flow around an organisation — up and down, or laterally — and consequently the types of networks that will emerge. Research[22] examining the relationship between organisation structure and information flow has compared mechanistic organisations that are highly structured and hierarchical with organic organisations that are neither, on two dimensions — flow and style of communication. The researchers expected that in mechanistic organisations communication would be one-way, initiating at the top of the organisation and flowing down; they would be aimed at gaining control and would reflect higher levels of conflict. In contrast, they expected that organic organisations would show more flexible patterns of communication, characterised by high levels of two-way interactions and strategies designed to encourage participation. Results showed that in organic organisations managers and subordinates have very similar styles of communication and the focus was on establishing information exchange. Managers reflected a concern for increasing participation by asking subordinates questions and encouraging their participation. However, in mechanistic organisations the pattern of communication was far more competitive: a substantial amount of communication reflected attempts by both parties to gain control of the discussion and, when subordinates made relatively neutral comments, managers responded assertively to regain control of the communication.

IMPROVING COMMUNICATION IN ORGANISATIONS

Managers striving to become better communicators have two separate tasks they must accomplish. First, they must improve their *messages* — the information they wish to transmit. Second, they must seek to improve their own *understanding* of what other people are trying to communicate to them. This means they must become better encoders and decoders. They must strive not only to be understood but also to understand. The techniques discussed here, and summarised in Exhibit 13.2, can contribute to accomplishing these two important tasks.

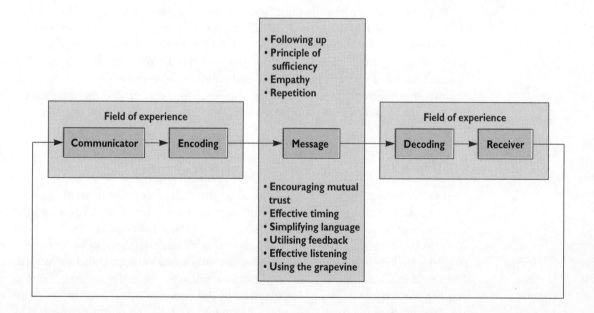

Exhibit 13.2 Improving communications in organisations (narrowing the communication gap)

Following up

Following up involves assuming that you are misunderstood and, whenever possible, attempting to determine whether your intended meaning was actually received. As we have seen, meaning is often in the mind of the receiver. An accounting unit leader in a government office passes on to staff members notices of openings in other agencies. While long-time employees may understand this as a friendly gesture, a new employee might interpret it as an evaluation of poor performance and a suggestion to leave.

Regulating information flow

The regulation of communication can ensure an optimum flow of information to managers, thereby eliminating the barrier of communication overload. Communication is regulated in terms of both quality and quantity. The idea is based on the *exception principle* of management, which states that only significant deviations from policies and procedures should be brought to the attention of superiors. In terms of formal communication, then, superiors should be communicated with only on matters of exception and not for the sake of communication.

Utilising feedback

Earlier in the chapter, feedback was identified as an important element in effective two-way communication. It provides a channel for receiver response that enables the communicator to determine whether the message has been received and has produced the intended response.[23] In face-to-face communication, direct feedback is possible.

In downward communication, however, inaccuracies often occur because of insufficient opportunity for feedback from receivers. A memorandum addressing an important policy statement may be distributed to all employees, but this does not guarantee that communication has occurred. You might expect that feedback in the form of upward communication would be encouraged more in organic organisations, but the mechanisms discussed earlier that can be utilised to encourage upward communication are found in many different organisation designs.

Empathy

Empathy involves being receiver-oriented rather than communicator-oriented. The form of the communication should depend largely on what is known about the receiver. Empathy requires communicators to place themselves in the shoes of the receiver in order to anticipate how the message is likely to be decoded. Empathy is the ability to put oneself in the other person's role and to assume that individual's viewpoints and emotions. Remember that the greater the gap between the experiences and background of the communicator and the receiver, the greater is the effort that must be made to find a common ground of understanding — where there are overlapping fields of experience.

Repetition

Repetition is an accepted principle of learning. Introducing repetition or redundancy into communication (especially that of a technical nature) ensures that if one part of the message is not understood, other parts will carry the same message. New employees are often provided with the same basic information in several different forms when first joining an organisation. Likewise, students receive much redundant information when first entering a university. This is to ensure that registration procedures, course requirements, and new terms such as 'matriculation' and 'quality points' are communicated.

Encouraging mutual trust

We know that time pressures often negate the possibility that managers will be able to follow up communication and encourage feedback or upward communication every time they communicate. Under such circumstances, an atmosphere of mutual confidence and trust between managers and their subordinates can facilitate communication. Managers who develop a climate of trust will find that following up on each communication is less critical and that no loss in understanding will result among subordinates from a failure to follow up on each communication. This is because they have fostered high 'source credibility' among subordinates.

Effective timing

Individuals are exposed to thousands of messages daily. Many of these messages are never decoded and received because of the impossibility of taking them all in. It is important for managers to note that while they are attempting to communicate with a receiver, other messages are being received simultaneously. Thus, the message that managers send may not be 'heard'. Messages are more likely to be understood when they are not competing with other messages.[24] On an everyday basis, effective communication can be facilitated by properly timing major announcements. The barriers discussed earlier are often the result of poor timing that results in distortions and value judgements.

Simplifying language

Complex language has been identified as a major barrier to effective communication. Students often suffer when their teachers use technical jargon that transforms simple concepts into complex puzzles. Universities are not the only place where this occurs, however. Government agencies are also known for their often incomprehensible communications. We have already noted instances where professional people use in–group language in attempting to communicate with individuals outside their group. Managers must remember that effective communication involves transmitting *understanding* as well as information. If the receiver does not understand, then there has been no communication. Managers must encode messages in words, appeals and symbols that are meaningful to the receiver.

Using the grapevine

The grapevine is an important information communication channel that exists in all organisations. It basically serves as a bypassing mechanism, and in many cases it is faster than the formal system it bypasses. The grapevine has been aptly described in the following manner: 'With the rapidity of a burning train, it filters out of the woodwork, past the manager's office, through the locker room, and along the corridors'. Because it is flexible and usually involves face-to-face communication, the grapevine transmits information rapidly. The resignation of an executive may be common knowledge long before it is officially announced.

For management, the grapevine frequently may be an effective means of communication. It is likely to have a stronger impact on receivers because it involves face-to-face exchange and allows for feedback. Because it satisfies many psychological needs, the grapevine will always exist. More than 75% of the information in the grapevine may be accurate. Of course, the portion that is distorted can be devastating. The point, however, is that if the grapevine is inevitable, managers should seek to utilise it or at least attempt to increase its accuracy. One way to minimise the undesirable aspects of the grapevine is to improve other forms of communication. If information exists on issues relevant to subordinates, then damaging rumours are less likely to develop.

Promoting ethical communications

It is incumbent upon organisational members to deal ethically with one another in their communication transactions. Kreps postulates three broad principles which are applicable to internal organisational communications.[25] The first is that organisational members should not intentionally deceive one another. This may not be as simple a principle to conform to as it may seem. While lying clearly violates it, is communicating less than you know to be true a breach of ethics? There is no hard and fast answer. The second principle is that organisation members' communication should not purposely harm any other organisation member. This is known as non–malfeasance, or refraining from doing harm. Finally, organisation members should be treated justly. This too can be difficult, for justice is a relative principle that must be evaluated in a specific context. Of course, internal organisational communications are not the only ones where ethical behaviour is important. Indeed, some of the more ethically challenging communication contexts are those in which the organisation is communicating externally.

BENCHMARKS FOR EXCELLENT COMMUNICATION[26]

Change faces companies worldwide. Poorly managed, it lowers morale, decreases productivity and ultimately may fail. Research has shown that communication can be critical to the change management process: both in terms of timing and the information that is conveyed. A survey of ten companies that have effectively implemented change allowed researchers Young and Post to identify the following seven 'benchmarks' for effective communication.

The chief executive champions communication

If top management has a positive attitude to communication, this is reflected in the behaviour and attitudes of other managers. One effective means for demonstrating this commitment to communication is a willingness to deliver key messages in person.

Actions and words match

Organisations are full not only of official messages but also of implicit messages. You could consider the verbal and non-verbal components of an organisational message — matching them is vital for effective communication. For example, if on the one hand you are emphasising the partnership aspects of joining with another company while on the other hand you are talking about an 'acquisition', you are sending a mixed message.

Be committed to two-way communication

Establishing feedback channels is critical to organisational communication. In this survey, successful companies embraced the concept of two-way communication: interactive television broadcasts were used for communicating with other sites, managers were trained in feedback sheets, and company newsletters contained question–and–answer sheets. Some companies went further and rewarded upward communication.

Face-to-face communication is emphasised

Delivering messages face-to-face makes senior managers more accessible and increases their credibility: they convey a message of concern, indicating that senior managers are prepared to spend time to visit staff and personally answer questions. Excellent companies used this strategy throughout the change implementation process, and as a follow-up established ambassador teams of managers for dealing with outstanding issues once the change had been implemented.

Communication is everyone's responsibility

Clearly defined responsibilities — statements about who should communicate what to whom — assist in improving organisational communication. Ensuring that supervisors, rather than rumours or the grapevine, provide information increases staff satisfaction. When this is combined with communication training, giving and receiving feedback, and problem-solving skills, organisational communication is further enhanced.

Do not avoid bad news

Avoiding bad news does not necessarily improve communication. However, in one exceptionally high performing company the amount of bad news that was communicated was very high. It turned out that this was because company culture valued and encouraged bad news. One effect of communicating bad news is that good news becomes more credible.

Have a communication strategy

The survey identified five key features of communication strategy. These were:

1. *Communicate what, how and why.* A global environment in which we are bombarded with information means that employees feel entitled to information; they want to know why decisions have been made and how they are going to be implemented, not just what those decisions are.
2. *Ensure timeliness.* Trust is increased when information is communicated immediately. This means that managers should not wait until they have worked out every detail — delaying information increases the chance that staff will find out in some other way.
3. *Communicate continuously.* Giving people information all the time makes them feel involved. Even if the news is no news, at least staff know what is happening.
4. *Link the big and little picture.* As well as telling employees how the changes affect their job (the little picture), give them an idea of how these changes fit in with the big picture: how changes in the economy affect the organisation, the job and the employee.
5. *Don't dictate feelings.* People will not all respond to change in the same way, and so telling them how they should feel risks alienating them. Concentrate on the how, what and why, and allow them to experience whatever feelings seem appropriate to them.

GLOBAL   Encounter

Communication and satisfaction in Japan

How does individual culture affect the patterns of communication in organisations? And does it influence the relationship between communication and individuals' satisfaction? Hofstede has shown that cultures can be classified and differentiated along four dimensions: masculinity-femininity, uncertainty avoidance, individualism-collectivism and power distance. Can these dimensions predict differences in the relationship between organisational communication and organisational satisfaction?

These issues were recently addressed in research investigating patterns of communication in Japanese organisations. Researchers argued that Japanese organisations invest considerable effort in upward communications, a reflection of their relatively low *power–distance* score. For the same reasons, Japanese organisations are also thought to establish a climate for open downward communication. Consequently, they predicted — and found — that openness in both upward and downward communication was related to increased satisfaction with the organisation and interpersonal relationships in the organisation.

A second dimension that might affect communication is that of collectivism–individualism. These researchers argued that, because the Japanese culture is rated as collectivist, lateral communication — which aids in group cohesiveness — should also be associated with increased satisfaction. Again, they found that increased openness in lateral communication was associated with greater satisfaction.

These results suggest that, as a consequence of cultural traits, Japanese staff and organisations value openness in communication independent of the direction that it flows. For these companies, greater openness predicts increased organisational and relational satisfaction.

Source: Koike, H., Gudykunst, W. B., Stewart, L. P., Ting-Toomey, S., & Nishida, T. (1988). Communication openness, satisfaction, and length of employment in Japanese organizations, *Communication Research Reports*, **5**, 97–102.

MULTICULTURAL COMMUNICATION

In the international business environment of today — and, even more so, of tomorrow — foreign language training and fluency is a business necessity. It is true that English is an important business language and that many foreign business people speak it fluently. The fact remains, however, that the vast majority of the world's population neither speak nor understand English. Nor is language *per se* the only barrier to effective cross-cultural communications; in fact, it may be one of the easiest difficulties to overcome. There are numerous cultural-related variables that can hinder the communication process, not the least of which is *ethnocentrism.*

Ethnocentrism is the tendency to consider the values, norms and customs of one's own country to be superior to those of other countries. Ethnocentrism need not be explicit to create communication problems. Implicit assumptions based on an ethnocentric view make it less likely that we will have sufficient cultural sensitivity even to be aware of possible differences in points of view, underlying assumptions, interpretation, or a host of other factors that may create communication difficulties. Consider the following true incident involving an Indian and an Austrian.

> When asked if his department could complete a project by a given date, a particular Indian employee said 'Yes' even when he knew he could not complete the project, because he believed that his Austrian supervisor wanted 'yes' for an answer. When the completion date arrived and he had not finished the project, his Austrian supervisor showed dismay. The Indian's desire to be polite — to say what he thought his supervisor wanted to hear — seemed more important than an accurate assessment of the completion date.[27]

Both of the individuals depicted in this incident were operating from their own cultural frame of reference. The Austrian valued accuracy; for the Indian, politeness was the central value. By not being sensitive to the possibility of cultural differences, both contributed to the unfortunate misunderstanding.

Numerous other examples are possible. Words and phrases do not mean the same to all people. If, during an attempt to work out a business deal, for example, an American were to tell another American 'That will be difficult', the meaning would be entirely different if a Japanese were to use that phrase. To the American it means the door is still open, but perhaps some compromise needs to be made. To the Japanese it clearly means 'no'; the deal is unacceptable.[28] As another example, consider eye contact. Australians are taught to maintain good eye contact, and we may unconsciously assume those who do not look us in the eye are dishonest, or at least rude. In Japan, however, when speaking with a superior it is customary to lower one's eyes as a gesture of respect.

In spite of innumerable differences, multicultural communication can be successful. Business people from different cultures effectively and efficiently communicate with each other hundreds, perhaps thousands, of times every business day. By and large, the senders and receivers of those successful communications exhibit some, or all, of the following attributes:

- They have made it a point to familiarise themselves with significant cultural differences that might affect the communication process. They do this through study, observation and consultation with those who have a more direct, or greater, experience with the culture than they do.
- They make a conscious, concerted effort to lay aside ethnocentric tendencies. This does not mean they must agree with values, customs, interpretations or perspectives different from their own; awareness, not acceptance, is what is required to facilitate communications.
- Perhaps most importantly, despite their efforts at doing what is described in the above two points, they maintain a posture of 'knowing they do not know'. This simply means that in the absence of direct, usually extensive, ongoing exposure to another culture there will be nuances in the communication process of which they may well be unaware. Rather than assuming understanding is complete unless demonstrated otherwise, they assume it is incomplete until shown otherwise.

SUMMARY OF KEY POINTS

Explain the elements in the communication process. Communication is one of the vital processes that breathe life into an organisational structure. The process contains five elements: the communicator, who initiates the communication; the message, which is the result of encoding and which expresses the purpose of the communicator; the medium, which is the channel or carrier used for transmitting the message; the receiver for whom the message is intended; and feedback, a mechanism that allows the communicator to determine whether the message has been received and understood.

Identify blocks to effective sending and receiving. There are numerous barriers to effective communication. Among the more significant are frame of reference, selective listening, value judgements, source credibility, filtering, in-group language and communication overload.

List strategies for improving interpersonal communication. Interpersonal communication can be improved by obtaining feedback, labelling behaviour and feelings accurately and non-evaluatively, building redundancy into your messages, matching the listener's frame of reference, and avoiding questions and comments that judge, interpret, divert or probe.

Compare the three major directions of communication. Communication flow moves in one of three directions. Downward communications are the most common, and include job instructions, procedures and policies. They are improved when they are timely, relevant and do not overload staff. An upward flow can be just as important, and may involve the use of suggestion boxes, group meetings or grievance procedures. Horizontal communications serve an important coordinative function.

Describe ways in which communication in organisations can be improved. Improving organisational communications is an ongoing process. Specific techniques for doing this include following up, regulating information flow, utilising feedback, empathy, repetition, encouraging mutual trust, effective timing, simplifying language, effective listening, using the grapevine and promoting ethical communications.

Distinguish between centralised and decentralised networks. Centralised communication networks describe patterns of information flow in which one person receives and distributes all information, and this person is likely to emerge as the group's leader. These networks are highly effective for simple tasks in which information needs to be coordinated. Decentralised networks describe communication networks in which information is shared by everyone. They are better suited to complex tasks in which information needs to be pooled. They are generally associated with higher levels of satisfaction than centralised networks.

List benchmarks for excellent communication. Organisations that have successfully implemented change are effective communicators. To be excellent communicators, the CEO must promote communication, actions and words must match, two-way and face-to-face communication is seen as vital, clear responsibility for communicating is given to managers, bad news is encouraged and the organisation has a clear communication policy.

Discuss the importance of multicultural communication. In the international business environment of today, needing to communicate with members of other cultures is becoming commonplace. In addition to obvious language problems, different cultural customs, values and perspectives can serve to complicate effective communications. A significant barrier is ethnocentrism, which is the tendency to consider the values of one's own country superior to those of other countries.

REVIEW AND DISCUSSION QUESTIONS

1. Can you think of a communication transaction you have been part of when an encoding or decoding error was made? Why did it happen, and what could have been done to avoid it?
2. Why do you think that downward communication is much more prevalent in organisations than upward communication? How easy would it be to change this?
3. Interpersonal style is an important variable in the interpersonal communication process. Are you typically a Type A, B, C or D communicator? Explain.
4. In your experience, which of the barriers to effective communication discussed in the chapter

is responsible for the most communication problems? Which barrier is the hardest to correct?
5. Similarly, in your experience, which of the techniques for improving communication discussed in the chapter would solve the greatest number of problems? Which technique is the most difficult to put into practice?
6. Can you think of reasons why some individuals might prefer one-way communications when they are the sender, and two-way when they are the receiver? Explain.
7. A study once revealed that 55% of our communication time is spent transmitting and 45% is spent receiving. If true, what are the implications of this finding?
8. Organisations should be less concerned with improving communication than with reducing the volume of information they disseminate to employees. Do you agree or disagree with this statement? Explain.
9. How does communication affect the interpersonal influence topics discussed in Chapters 7–10?
10. Have you ever been in a cross-cultural communication situation? How effective was it? What was the most difficult aspect of the situation?

ENDNOTES

1 For a discussion of organizational effects of advanced information technology, see Huber G. (1990). A theory of the effects of advanced information technologies on organizational design, intelligence, and decision making, *Academy of Management Review*, 47–71.
2 Shannon, C., & Weaver, W. (1948). *The Mathematical Theory of Communication*. Urbana: University of Illinois Press; and Schramm,W. (1953). How communication works in W. Scramm (Ed.) *The Process and Effects of Mass Communication*. Urbana: University of Illinois Press, pp. 3–26.
3 These five questions were first suggested in Lasswell, H. D. (1948). *Power and Personality*, New York: W. W. Norton, pp. 37–51.
4 Saunders, C., & Jones, J. (1990). Temporal sequences in information acquisition for decision making: A focus on source and medium, *Academy of Management Review*, 29–46.

5   Watson, C., & Grubb, P. (1985). Beliefs about Performance Feedback: An Exploration of the Job Holder's Perspective. Paper presented at the National Academy of Management Meeting, San Diego, CA.

6   DuBrin, A. J. (1982). *Contemporary Applied Management.* Plano, TX: Business Publications, pp. 127–134.

7   Steckler, N., & Rosenthal, R. (1985). Sex differences in nonverbal and verbal communication with bosses, peers, and subordinates, *Journal of Applied Psychology,* 157–163.

8   DePaulo, B. M. (1992). Nonverbal behavior and self-presentation, *Psychological Bulletin,* 203–243.

9   Fast, J. (1970). *Body Language.* Philadelphia: M. Evans Publishing, p. 7.

10 Putti, J. M., Aryee, S., & Phua, J. (1990). Communication relation satisfaction and organizational commitment, *Group & Organization Studies,* **15**, 44–52.

11 For a review of recent developments in decision making and communication, see Fulk, J., & Boyd B.(1991). Emerging theories of communication in organization, *Journal of Management,* 407–446.

12 This is based on material described in Johnson, D. W. & Johnson F. P.(1987). *Joining Together: Group Theory and Group Skills* (3rd Ed.). Englewood Cliffs, NJ: Prentice-Hall International, Inc.

13 Bolton, R. (1987). *People Skills: How to Assert Yourself, Listen to Others and Resolve Conflicts.* Sydney: Simon & Schuster.

14 Kolb, D. A., Rubin, I. M., & Osland, Y. (1991). *Organizational Behavior: An Experiential Approach* (5th Ed.). Englewood Cliffs, NJ: Prentice-Hall International, Inc.

15 Penley, L. E. , Alexander, E. R. , Jernigan, I. E. , & Henwood, C. I. (1991). Communication abilities of managers: the relationship to performance, *Journal of Management,* 57–76.

16 Katz, D., & Kahn, R. (1978). *The Social Psychology of Organizations* (2nd Ed.). New York: Wiley.

17 Smeed, N. (1985). A boon to employee communications: Letters of understanding, *Personnel,* 50–53.

18 Based on material in Luthans, F. (1985). *Organizational Behaviour* (4th Ed.). New York: McGraw-Hill Book Company.

19 Kreps, G. L. (1990). *Organizational Communication.* New York: Longman, p. 203.

20 Greenberg, J. & Baron, R. A.. (1993). *Behaviour in Organizations: Understanding and Managing the Human Side of Work* (4th Ed.). Boston: Allyn and Bacon.

21 Based on Mitchell, T. R., Dowling, P. J., Kabanoff, B. V., & Larson, J. R. (1988). *People in Organizations: An Introduction to Organizational Behaviour in Australia.* Sydney: McGraw-Hill Book Company.

22 Courtright, J. A., Fairhurst, G. T., & Rogers, L. E. (1989). Interaction patterns in organic and mechanistic systems, *Academy of Management Journal,* **32**, 773–802.

23 Liden, R. C., & Mitchell, T. R. (1985). Reactions to feedback: The role of attributions, *Academy of Management Journal,* 291–308.

24 For a related application, see Peters, T. & Austin, N. (1985). Managing by walking around, *California Management Review,* 83–102.

25 Kreps, G. L. (1990). *Organizational Communication.* New York: Longman, pp. 250–251.

26 Young, M., & Post, J. E. (1993). Managing to communicate, communicating to manage: How leading companies communicate with employees, *Organizational Dynamics,* **22**, 31–43.

27 Adler, N. (1991). *International Dimensions of Organizational Behavior* (2nd Ed.). Boston: PWS-Kent, p. 131.

28 Salacuse, J. (1991). *Making Global Deals.* Boston: Houghton Mifflin.

READING 13 ACTIVE LISTENING

Carl B. Rogers
Richard E. Farson

Source: Reprinted by permission of the Industrial Relations Center, The University of Chicago.

The meaning of active listening

One basic responsibility of the supervisor or executive is the development, adjustment, and integration of individual employees. He tries to develop employee potential, delegate responsibility, and achieve cooperation. To do so, he must have, among other abilities, the ability to listen intelligently and carefully to those with whom he works.

There are, however, many kinds of listening skills. The lawyer, for example, when questioning a witness, listens for contradictions, irrelevancies, errors, and weaknesses. But this is not the kind of listening skill we are concerned with. The lawyer usually is not listening in order to help the witness adjust or cooperate or produce. On the other hand, we will be concerned with listening skills which *will help* employees gain a clearer understanding of their situations, take responsibility, and cooperate with each other.

Two examples

The kind of listening we have in mind is called active listening. It is called active because the listener has a very definite responsibility. He does not passively absorb the words which are spoken to him. He actively tries to grasp the facts and the feelings in what he hears, and he tries, by his listening, to help the speaker work out his own problems.

To get a fuller picture of what is meant by active listening, let us consider two different approaches to the same work problem.

Example No. 1

Foreman: Hey, A1, I don't get this production order. We can't handle this run today. What do they think we are?

Supervisor: But that's the order. So get it out as soon as you can. We're under terrific pressure this week.

Foreman: Don't they know we're behind schedule already because of that press breakdown?

Supervisor: Look, Kelly, I don't decide what goes on upstairs. I just have to see that the work gets out, and that's what I'm gonna do.

Foreman: The guys aren't gonna like this.

Supervisor: That's something you'll have to work out with them not me.

Example No. 2

Foreman: Hey, Ross, I don't get this production order. We can't handle this run today. What do they think we are?

Supervisor: Sounds like you are pretty sore about it, Kelly.

Foreman: I sure am. We were just about getting back to schedule after that press breakdown. Now this comes along.

Supervisor: As if you didn't have enough work to do, huh?

Foreman: Yeah, I don't know how I'm gonna tell the guys about this.

Supervisor: Hate to face 'em with it now, is that it?

Foreman: I really do. They're under a real strain today. Seems like everything we do around here is rush, rush.

Supervisor: I guess you feel like it's unfair to load anything more on them.

Foreman: Well, yeah, I know there must be plenty of pressure on everybody up the line, but — well, if that's the way it is — guess I'd better get the word to 'em.

There are obviously many differences between these two examples. The main one, however, is that Ross, the supervisor in the second example, is using the active–listening approach. He is listening and responding in a way that makes it clear that he appreciates both the meaning and the feeling behind what Kelly is saying.

Active listening does not necessarily mean long sessions spent listening to grievances, personal or otherwise. It is simply a way of approaching those problems which arise out of the usual-day-to-day events of any job.

To be effective, active listening must be firmly grounded in the basic attitudes of the user. We cannot employ it as a technique if our fundamental attitudes are in conflict with its basic concepts. If we try, our behavior will be empty and sterile, and our associates will be quick to recognize this. Until we can demonstrate a spirit which genuinely respects the potential worth of the individual, which considers his rights and trusts his capacity for self-direction, we cannot begin to be effective listeners.

What we achieve by listening

Active listening is an important way to bring about changes in people. Despite the popular notion that listening is a passive approach, clinical and research evidence clearly shows that sensitive listening is a most effective agent for individual personality change and group development. Listening brings about changes in people's attitudes toward themselves and others; it also brings about changes in their basic values and personal philosophy. People who have been listened to in this new and special way become more emotionally mature, more open to their experiences, less defensive, more democratic, and less authoritarian.

When people are listened to sensitively, they tend to listen to themselves with more care and to make clear exactly what they are feeling and thinking. Group members tend to listen more to each other, to become less argumentative, more ready to incorporate other points of view. Because listening reduces the threat of having one's ideas criticized, the person is better able to see them for what they are and is more able to feel that his contributions are worthwhile.

Not the least important result of listening is the change that takes place with the listener himself. Besides providing more information than any other activity, listening builds deep, positive relationships and tends to alter constructively the attitudes of the listener. Listening is a growth experience.

These, then, are some of the worthwhile results we can expect from active listening. But how do we go about this kind of listening? How do we become active listeners?

How to listen

Active listening aims to bring about changes in people. To achieve this end, it relies upon definite techniques — things to do and things to avoid doing. Before discussing these techniques, however, we should first understand why they are effective. To do so, we must understand how the individual personality develops.

The growth of the individual

Through all of our lives, from early childhood on, we have learned to think of ourselves in certain very definite ways. We have built up pictures of ourselves. Sometimes these self-pictures are pretty realistic, but at other times they are not. For example, an average, overweight lady may fancy herself as a youthful, ravishing siren, or an awkward teenager regard himself as a star athlete.

All of us have experiences which fit the way we need to think about ourselves. These we accept. But it is much harder to accept experiences which don't fit. And sometimes, if it is very important for us to hang on to this self-picture, we don't accept or admit these experiences at all.

These self-pictures are not necessarily attractive. A man, for example, may regard himself as incompetent and worthless. He may feel that he is doing his job poorly in spite of favorable appraisals by the company. As long as he has these feelings about himself, he must deny any experiences which would seem not to fit his self-picture — in case any might indicate to him that he is competent. It is so necessary for him to maintain this self-picture that he is threatened by anything which would tend to change it. Thus, when the company raises his salary, it may seem to him only additional proof that he is a fraud. He must hold onto his self-picture because, bad or good, it's the only thing he has by which he can identify himself.

This is why direct attempts to change this individual or change his self-picture are particularly threatening. He is forced to defend himself or to completely deny the experience. This denial of experience and defense of the self-picture tend to bring on rigidity of behavior and create difficulties in personal adjustment.

The active-listening approach, on the other hand, does not present a threat to the individual's self-picture. He does not have to defend it. He is able to explore it, see it for what it is, and make his own decision about how realistic it is. And he is then in a position to change.

If I want to help a man reduce his defensiveness and become more adaptive, I must try to remove the threat of myself as his potential changer. As long as the atmosphere is threatening, there can be no effective communication. So I must create a climate which is neither critical, evaluative, nor moralizing. It must be an atmosphere of equality and freedom, permissiveness and understanding, acceptance and warmth. It is in this climate and this climate only that the individual feels safe enough to incorporate new experiences and new values into his concept of himself. Let's see how active listening helps to create this climate.

What to avoid

When we encounter a person with a problem, our usual response is to try to change his way of looking at things — to get him to see his situation the way we see it or would like to see it. We plead, reason, scold, encourage, insult, prod — anything to bring about a change in the desired direction, that is, in the direction we want him to travel. What we seldom realize, however, is that, under these circumstances, we are usually responding to *our own* needs to see the world in certain ways. It is always difficult for us to tolerate and understand actions which are different from the ways in which we believe we should act. If, however, we can free ourselves from the need to influence and direct others in our own paths, we enable ourselves to listen with understanding and thereby employ the most potent available agent of change.

One problem the listener faces is that of responding to demands for decisions, judgments, and evaluations. He is constantly called upon to agree or disagree with someone or something. Yet, as he well knows, the question or challenge frequently is a masked expression of feelings or needs which the speaker is far more anxious to communicate than he is to have the surface questions answered.

Because he cannot speak these feelings openly, the speaker must disguise them to himself and to others in an acceptable form. To illustrate, let us examine some typical questions and the types of answers that might best elicit the feelings beneath them (Exhibit 13.3).

These responses recognize the questions but leave the way open for the employee to say what is really bothering him. They allow the listener to participate in the problem or situation without shouldering all responsibility for decision making or actions. This is a process of thinking *with* people instead of *for* or *about* them.

Passing judgment, whether critical or favorable, makes free expression difficult. Similarly, advice and information are almost always seen as efforts to change a person and thus serve as barriers to his self-expression and the development of a creative relationship. Moreover, advice is seldom taken and information hardly ever utilized. The eager young trainee probably will not become patient just because he is advised that 'the road to success in business is a long, difficult one, and you must be patient'. And it is no more helpful for him to learn that 'only one out of a hundred trainees reaches a top management position'.

Interestingly, it is a difficult lesson to learn that positive *evaluations* are sometimes as blocking as negative ones. It is almost as destructive to the freedom of a relationship to tell a person that he is good or capable or right, as to tell him otherwise. To evaluate him positively may make it more difficult for him to tell of the faults that distress him or the ways in which he believes he is not competent.

Encouragement also may be seen as an attempt to motivate the speaker in certain directions or hold him off, rather than as support. 'I'm sure everything will work out OK' is

---

Exhibit 13.3 Some typical questions and answers

Employee's Question	Listener's Answer
Just whose responsibility is the tool room?	Do you feel that someone is challenging your authority in there?
Don't you think younger able people should be promoted before senior but less able ones?	It seems to you they should, I take it.
What does the super expect us to do about those broken-down machines?	You're pretty disgusted with those machines, aren't you?
Don't you think I've improved over the last review period?	Sounds as if you feel like you've really picked up over these last few months.

not a helpful response to the person who is deeply discouraged about a problem.

In other words, most of the techniques and devices common to human relationships are found to be of little use in establishing the type of relationship we are seeking here.

What to do

Just what does active listening entail, then? Basically, it requires that we get inside the speaker, that we grasp, *from his point of view*, just what it is he is communicating to us. More than that, we must convey to the speaker that we are seeing things from his point of view. To listen actively, then means that there are several things we must do.

Listen for total meaning.
Any message a person tries to get across usually has two components: the *content* of the message and the *feeling* or attitude underlying this content. Both are important; both give the message *meaning*. It is this total meaning of the message that we try to understand. For example, a machinist comes to his foreman and says, 'I've finished that lathe setup.' This message has obvious content and perhaps calls upon the foreman for another work assignment. Suppose, on the other hand, that he says, 'Well, I'm finally finished with that damned lathe setup.' The content is the same, but the total meaning of the message has changed — and changed in an important way for both the foreman and the worker. Here, sensitive listening can facilitate the relationship. Suppose the foreman were to respond by simply giving another work assignment. Would the employee feel that he had gotten his total message across? Would he feel free to talk to his foreman? Will he feel better about his job, more anxious to do good work on the next assignment?

Now, on the other hand, suppose the foreman were to respond with, 'Glad to have it over with, huh?' or 'Had a pretty rough time of it?' or 'Guess you don't feel like doing anything like that again', or anything else that tells the worker that he heard and understands. It doesn't necessarily mean that the next work assignment need be changed or that he must spend an hour listening to the worker complain about the setup problems he encountered. He may do a number of things differently in the light of the new information he has from the worker — but not necessarily. It's just the extra sensitivity on the part of the foreman which can transform an average working climate into a good one.

Respond to feelings.
In some instances, the content is far less important than the feeling which underlies it. To catch the full flavor or meaning of the message, one must respond particularly to the feeling component. If, for instance, our machinist had said, 'I'd like to melt this lathe down and make paper clips out of it', responding to content would be obviously absurd. But to respond to his disgust or anger in trying to work with his lathe recognizes the meaning of this message. There are various shadings of these components in the meaning of any message. Each time, the listener must try to remain sensitive to the total meaning the message has to the speaker. What is he trying to tell me? What does this mean to him? How does he see this situation?

Not all cues.
Not all communication is verbal. The speaker's words alone don't tell us everything he is communicating. And hence, truly sensitive listening requires that we become aware of several kinds of communication besides verbal. The way in which a speaker hesitates in his speech can tell us much about his feelings. So, too, can the inflection of his voice. He may stress certain points loudly and clearly and may number others. We should also note such things as the person's facial expressions, body posture, hand movements, eye movements, and breathing. All of these help to convey his total message.

What we communicate by listening

The first reaction of most people when they consider listening as a possible method for dealing with human beings is that listening cannot be sufficient in itself. Because it is passive, they feel, listening does not communicate anything to the speaker. Actually, nothing could be farther from the truth.

By consistently listening to a speaker, you are conveying the idea that: 'I'm interested in you as a person, and I think that what you feel is important. I respect your thoughts, and even if I don't agree with them, I know that they are valid for you. I feel sure that you have a contribution to make. I'm not trying to change or evaluate you. I just want to understand you. I think you're worth listening to, and I want you to know that I'm the kind of a person you can talk to.'

The subtle but most important aspect of this is that it is the *demonstration* of the message that works. While it is most difficult to convince someone that you respect him by *telling* him so, you are much more likely to get this message across by really *behaving* that way — by actually *having* and *demonstrating* respect for this person. Listening does this most effectively.

Like other behavior, listening behavior is contagious. This has implications for all communication problems, whether between two people or within a large organization. To ensure good communication between associates up and down the line, one must first take the responsibility for setting a pattern of listening. Just as one learns that anger is usually met with anger, argument with argument, and deception with deception, one can learn that listening can be met with listening. Every person who feels responsibility in a situation can set the tone of the interaction, and the important lesson in this is that any behavior exhibited by one person will eventually be responded to with similar behavior in the other person.

It is far more difficult to stimulate constructive behavior in another person but far more profitable. Listening is one of these constructive behaviors, but if one's attitude is to 'wait out' the speaker rather than really listen to him, it will fail. The one who consistently listens with understanding, however, is the one who eventually is most likely to be listened to. If you really want to be heard and understood by another, you can develop him as a potential listener, ready for new ideas, provided you can first develop yourself in these ways and sincerely listen with understanding and respect.

Testing for understanding

Because understanding another person is actually far more difficult than it at first seems, it is important to test constantly your ability to see the world in the way the speaker sees it. You can do this by reflecting in your own words what the speaker seems to mean by his words and actions. His response to this will tell you whether or not he feels understood. A good rule of thumb is to assume that you never really understand until you can communicate this understanding to the other's satisfaction

Here is an experiment to test your skill in listening. The next time you become involved in a lively or controversial discussion with another

person, stop for a moment and suggest that you adopt this ground rule for continued discussion: Before either participant in the discussion can make a point or express an opinion of his own, he must first restate aloud the previous point or position of the other person. This restatement must be in his own words (merely parroting the words of another does not prove that one has understood but only that he has heard the words). The restatement must be accurate enough to satisfy the speaker before the listener can be allowed to speak for himself.

This is something you could try in your own discussion group. Have someone express himself on some topic of emotional concern to the group. Then, before another member expresses his own feelings and thought, he must rephrase the *meaning* expressed by the previous speaker to that individual's satisfaction. Note the changes in the emotional climate and in the quality of the discussion when you try this.

Problems in active listening

Active listening is not an easy skill to acquire. It demands practice. Perhaps more important, it may require changes in our own basic attitudes. These changes come slowly and sometimes with considerable difficulty. Let us look at some of the major problems in active listening and what can be done to overcome them.

The personal risk

To be effective at all in active listening, one must have a sincere interest in the speaker. We all live in glass houses as far as our attitudes are concerned. They always show through. And if we are only making a pretense of interest in the speaker, he will quickly pick this up, either consciously or unconsciously. And once he does, he will no longer express himself freely.

Active listening carries a strong element of personal risk. If we manage to accomplish what we are describing here — to sense deeply the feeling of another person, to understand the meaning his experiences have for him, to see the world as he sees it — we risk being changed ourselves. For example, if we permit ourselves to listen our way into the psychological life of a labor leader or agitator — to get the meaning which has life for him — we risk coming to see the world as he sees it. It is threatening to give up, even momentarily, what we believe and start thinking in someone else's terms. It takes a great deal of inner security and courage to be able to risk one's self in understanding another.

For the supervisor, the courage to take another's point of view generally means that he must see himself through another's eyes — he must be able to see himself as others see him. To do this may sometimes be unpleasant, but it is far more *difficult* than unpleasant. We are so accustomed to viewing ourselves in certain ways — to seeing and hearing only what we want to see and hear — that it is extremely difficult for a person to free himself from his needs to see things these ways.

Developing an attitude of sincere interest in the speaker is thus no easy task. It can be developed only by being willing to risk seeing the world from the speaker's point of view. If we have a number of such experiences, however, they will shape an attitude which will allow us to be truly genuine in our interest in the speaker.

Hostile expressions

The listener will often hear negative, hostile expressions directed at himself. Such expressions are always hard to listen to. No one likes to hear hostile words. And it is not easy to get to the point where one is strong enough to permit these attacks without finding it necessary to defend oneself or retaliate.

Because we all fear that people will crumble under the attack of genuine negative feelings, we tend to perpetuate an attitude of pseudo peace. It is as if we cannot tolerate conflict at all for fear of the damage it could do to us, to the situation, to the others involved. But of course the real damage is done to all these by denial and suppression of negative feelings.

Out-of-place expressions

There is also the problem of out-of-place expressions — expressions dealing with behavior which is not usually acceptable in our society. In the extreme forms that present themselves before psychotherapists, expressions of sexual perversity or homicidal fantasies are often found blocking to the listener because of their obvious threatening quality. At less extreme levels, we all find unnatural or inappropriate behavior difficult to handle. That is, anything from an off-color story told in mixed company to a man weeping is likely to produce a problem situation.

In any face-to-face situation, we will find instances of this type which will momentarily, if not permanently, block any communication. In business and industry, any expressions of weakness or incompetency will generally be regarded as unacceptable and therefore will block good two-way communication. For example, it is difficult to listen to a supervisor tell of his feelings of failure in being able to 'take charge' of a situation in his department, because all administrators are supposed to be able to 'take charge'.

Accepting positive feelings

It is both interesting and perplexing to note that negative or hostile feelings or expressions are much easier to deal with in any face-to-face relationship than are truly and deeply positive feelings. This is especially true for the businessman, because the culture expects him to be independent, bold, clever, and aggressive and manifest no feelings of warmth, gentleness, and intimacy. He therefore comes to regard these feelings as soft and inappropriate. But no matter how they are regarded, they remain a human need. The denial of these feelings in himself and his associates does not get the executive out of the problem of dealing with them. They simply become veiled and confused. If recognized, they would work for the total effort; unrecognized, they work against it.

Emotional danger signals

The listener's own emotions are sometimes a barrier to active listening. When emotions are at their height, which is when listening is most necessary, it is most difficult to set aside one's own concerns and be understanding. Our emotions are often our own worst enemies when we try to become listeners. The more involved and invested we are in a particular situation or problem, the less we are likely to be willing or able to listen to the feelings and attitudes of others. That is, the more we find it necessary to respond to our own needs, the less we are able to respond to the needs of another. Let us look at some of the main danger signals that warn us that our emotions may be interfering with our listening.

Defensiveness. The points about which one is most vocal and dogmatic, the points which one is most anxious to impose on others — these are always the points one is trying to talk oneself into believing. So one danger signal becomes apparent when you find yourself stressing a point or trying to convince another. It is at these times that you are likely to be less secure and consequently less able to listen.

Resentment of opposition. It is always easier to listen to an idea which is similar to one of your own than to an opposing view. Sometimes, in order to clear the air, it is helpful to pause for a moment when you feel your ideas and position being challenged, reflect on the situation, and express your concern to the speaker.

Clash of personalities. Here again, our experience has consistently shown us that the genuine expression of feelings on the part of the listener will be more helpful in developing a sound relationship than the suppression of them. This is so whether the feelings be resentment, hostility, threat, or admiration. A basically honest relationship, whatever the nature of it, is the most productive of all. The other party becomes secure when he learns that the listener can express his feelings honestly and openly to him. We should keep this in mind when we begin to fear a clash of personalities in the listening relationship. Otherwise, fear of our own emotions will choke off full expression of feelings.

Listening to ourselves

To listen to oneself is a prerequisite for listening to others. And it is often an effective means of dealing with the problems we have outlined above. When we are most aroused, excited, and demanding, we are least able to understand our own feelings and attitudes. Yet, in dealing with the problems of others, it becomes most important to be sure of one's own position, values, and needs.

The ability to recognize and understand the meaning which a particular episode has for you, with all the feelings which it stimulates in you, and the ability to express the meaning when you find it getting in the way of active listening will clear the air and enable you once again to be free to listen. That is, if some person or situation touches off feelings within you which tend to block your attempts to listen with understanding, begin listening to yourself. It is much more helpful in developing effective relationships to avoid suppressing these feelings. Speak them out as clearly as you can and try to enlist the other person as a listener to your feelings. A person's

listening ability is limited by his ability to listen to himself.

Active listening and company goals

- How can listening improve production?
- We're in business, and it's a rugged, fast, competitive affair. How are we going to find time to counsel our employees?
- We have to concern ourselves with organizational problems first.
- We can't afford to spend all day listening when there's a job to be done.
- What's morale got to do with production?
- Sometimes we have to sacrifice an individual for the good of the rest of the people in the company.

Those of us who are trying to advance the listening approach in industry hear these comments frequently. And because they are so honest and legitimate, they pose a real problem. Unfortunately, the answers are not so clear-cut as the questions.

Individual importance

One answer is based on an assumption that is central to the listening approach. That assumption is: The kind of behavior which helps the individual will eventually be the best thing that could be done for the group. Or saying it another way: The things that are best for the individual are best for the company. This is a conviction of ours, based on our experience in psychology and education. The research evidence from industry is only beginning to come in. We find that putting the group first, at the expense of the individual, besides being an uncomfortable individual experience, does not unify the group. In fact, it tends to make the group less a group. The members become anxious and suspicious.

We are not at all sure in just what ways the group does benefit from a concern demonstrated for an individual, but we have several strong leads. One is that the group feels more secure when an individual is being listened to and provided for with concern and sensitivity. And we assume that a secure group will ultimately be a better group. When each individual feels that he need not fear exposing himself to the group, he is likely to contribute more freely and spontaneously. When the leader of a group responds to the individual, puts the individual first, the other members of the group will follow suit and the group will come to act as a unit in recognizing and responding to the needs of a particular member. This positive, constructive action seems to be a much more satisfying experience for a group than the experience of dispensing with a member.

Listening and production

Whether listening or any other activity designed to better human relations in an industry actually raises production — whether morale has a definite relationship to production — is not known for sure. There are some who frankly hold that there is no relationship to be expected between morale and production — that the production often depends upon the social misfit, the eccentric, or the isolate. And there are some who simply choose to work in a climate of cooperation and harmony, in a high-morale group, quite aside from the question of increased production.

A report from the Survey Research Center[1] at the University of Michigan on research conducted at the Prudential Life Insurance Company lists seven findings relating to production and morale. First-line supervisors in high-production work groups were found to differ from those in low-production work groups in that they:

1. Are under less close supervision from their own supervisors.
2. Place less direct emphasis upon production as the goal.
3. Encourage employee participation in the making of decisions.
4. Are more employee-centered.
5. Spend more of their time in supervision and less in straight production work.
6. Have a greater feeling of confidence in their supervisory roles.
7. Feel that they know where they stand with the company.

After mentioning that other dimensions of morale, such as identification with the company, intrinsic job satisfaction, and satisfaction with job status, were not found significantly related to productivity, the report goes on to suggest the following psychological interpretations:

People are more effectively motivated when they are given some degree of freedom in the way in which they do their work than when every action is prescribed in advance. They do better when some degree of decision making about their jobs is possible than when all decisions are made for them. They respond more adequately when they are rated as personalities than as cogs in a machine. In short, if the ego motivations of self-determination, or self–expression, of a sense of personal worth can be tapped, the individual can be more effectively energized. The use of external sanctions or pressuring for production may work to some degree, but not to the extent that the more internalized motives do. When the individual comes to identify himself with his job and the work of his group, human resources are much more fully utilized in the production process.

The Survey Research Center has also conducted studies among workers in other industries. In discussing the results of these studies, Robert L. Kahn writes:

In the studies of clerical workers, railroad workers, and workers in heavy industry, the supervisors with the better production records gave a larger proportion of their time to supervisory functions, especially the interpersonal aspects of their jobs. The supervisors of the lower-producing sections were more likely to spend their time in tasks which the men themselves were performing, or in the paperwork aspects of their jobs.[2]

Maximum creativeness

There may never be enough research evidence to satisfy everyone on this question. But speaking from a business point of view, in terms of the problem of developing resources for production, the maximum creativeness and productive effort of the human beings in the organization are the richest untapped source of power still existing. The difference between the maximum productive capacity of people and that output which industry is now realizing is immense. We simply suggest that this maximum capacity might be closer to realization if we sought to release the motivation that already exists within people rather than try to stimulate them externally.

This releasing of the individual is made possible, first of all, by sensitive listening, with respect and understanding. Listening is a beginning toward making the individual feel himself worthy of making contributions, and this could result in a very dynamic and productive organization. Competitive business is never too rugged or too busy to take time to procure the most efficient technological advances or to develop rich raw-material resources. But these in comparison to the resources that are already within the people in the plant are paltry. This is industry's major procurement problem.

G. L. Clemens, president of Jewel Tea Co., Inc., in taking about the collaborative approach to management, says:

We feel that this type of approach recognizes that there is a secret ballot going on at all times among the people in any business. They vote for or against the supervisors. A favorable vote for the supervisor shows up in the cooperation, teamwork, understanding, and production of the group. To win this secret ballot, each supervisor must share the problems of his group and work for them.[3]

The decision to spend time listening to his employees is a decision each supervisor or executive has to make for himself. Executives seldom have much to do with products or processes. They have to deal with people who must in turn deal with people who will deal with products or processes. The higher one goes up the line, the more one will be concerned with human relations problems, simply because people are all one has to work with. The minute we take a man from his bench and make him a foreman, he is removed from the basic production of goods and now must begin relating to individuals instead of nuts and bolts. People are different from things, and our foreman is called upon for a different line of skills completely. His new tasks call upon him to be a special kind of person. The development of himself as a listener is a first step in becoming this special person.

References

1   'Productivity, Supervision, and Employee Morale', *Human Relations*, Series I, Report 1 (Ann Arbor: Survey Research Center, University of Michigan).

2   Robert L. Kahn, 'The Human Factors Underlying Industrial Productivity', *Michigan Business Review*, November 1952.

3   G. L. Glemens, 'Time for Democracy in Action at the Executive Level' (Address given before the AMA Personnel Conference, February 28, 1951).

EXERCISE 13 YOUR COMMUNICATION STYLE

Source: Lussier, R. N. (1993). *Human Relations in Organisations: A Skill Building Approach.* Homewood, IL: Irwin, pp. 153–156.

To determine your preferred communication style, select the one alternative that most closely describes what you would do in each of the twelve situations below. Do not be concerned with trying to pick the correct answer; select the alternative that best describes what you would actually do. Circle the letter a, b, c or d.

_____   1.   Wendy, a knowledgeable person from another department, comes to you, the engineering supervisor, and requests that you design a special product to her specifications. You would:
   a.   Control the conversation and tell Wendy what you will do for her.
   b.   Ask Wendy to describe the product. Once you understand it, you would present your ideas. Let her realise that you are concerned and want to help with your ideas.
   c.   Respond to Wendy's request by conveying understanding and support. Help clarify what is to be done by you. Offer ideas, but do it her way.
   d.   Find out what you need to know. Let Wendy know you will do it her way.

_____   2.   Your department has designed a product that is to be fabricated by Saul's department. Saul has been with the company longer than you have; he knows his department. Saul comes to you to change the product design. You decide to:

a. Listen to the change and why it would be beneficial. If you believe Saul's way is better, change it; if not, explain why the original idea is superior. If necessary, insist that it be done your way.

b. Tell Saul to fabricate it any way he wants to.

c. You are busy; tell Saul to do it your way. You don't have the time to listen and agree with him.

d. Be supportive; make changes together as a team.

_____ 3. Upper management has a decision to make. They call you to a meeting and tell you they need some information to solve a problem they describe to you. You:

a. Respond in a manner that conveys personal support and offer alternative ways to solve the problem.

b. Respond to their questions.

c. Explain how to solve the problem.

d. Show your concern by explaining how to solve the problem and why it is an effective solution.

_____ 4. You have a routine work order. The work order is to be replaced verbally and completed in 3 days. Sue, the receiver, is very experienced and willing to be of service to you. You decide to:

a. Explain your needs, but let Sue make the other decisions.

b. Tell Sue what you want and why you need it.

c. Decide together what to order.

d. Simply give Sue the order.

_____ 5. Work orders from the staff department normally take 3 days; however, you have an emergency and need the job today. Your colleague Jim, the department supervisor, is knowledgeable and somewhat cooperative. You decide to:

a. Tell Jim that you need it by three o'clock and return at that time to pick it up.

b. Explain the situation and how the organisation will benefit by expediting the order. Volunteer to help any way you can.

c. Explain the situation and ask Jim when the order will be ready.

d. Explain the situation and together come to a solution to your problem.

_____ 6. Danielle, a peer with a record of high performance, has recently had a drop in productivity. Her problem is affecting her performance. You know Danielle has a family problem. You:

a. Discuss the problem; help Danielle realise the problem is affecting her work and yours. Supportively discuss ways to improve the situation.

b. Tell the boss about it and let him decide what to do about it.

c. Tell Danielle to get back on the job.

d. Discuss the problem and tell Danielle how to solve the work situation; be supportive.

_____ 7. You are a knowledgeable supervisor. You buy supplies from Peter regularly. He is an excellent salesperson and very knowledgeable about your situation. You are placing your weekly order. You decide to:

a. Explain what you want and why: Develop a supportive relationship.

b. Explain what you want and ask Peter to recommend products.

c. Give Peter the order.

d. Explain your situation and allow Peter to make the order.

_____ 8. Jean, a knowledgeable person from another department, has asked you to perform a routine staff function to her specifications. You decide to:
   a. Perform the task to her specification without questioning her.
   b. Tell her that you will do it the usual way.
   c. Explain what you will do and why.
   d. Show your willingness to help; offer alternative ways to do it.

_____ 9. Tom, a salesperson, has requested an order for your department's services with a short delivery date. As usual, Tom claims it is a take-it-or-leave-it offer. He wants your decision now, or within a few minutes, because he is in the customer's office. Your action is to:
   a. Convince Tom to work together to come up with a later date.
   b. Give Tom a yes or no answer.
   c. Explain your situation and let Tom decide if you should take the order.

_____ 10. As a time-and-motion expert, you have been called in regard to a complaint about the standard time it takes to perform a job. As you analyse the entire job, you realise the one element of complaint should take longer, but other elements should take less time. The end result is a shorter total standard time for the job. You decide to:
   a. Tell the operator and foreman that the total time must be decreased and why.
   b. Agree with the operator and increase the standard time.
   c. Explain your findings. Deal with the operator and/or foreman's concerns, but ensure compliance with your new standard.
   d. Together with the operator, develop a standard time.

_____ 11. You approve budget allocations for projects. Marie, who is very competent in developing budgets, has come to you. You:
   a. Review the budget, make revisions and explain them in a supportive way. Deal with concerns, but insist on your changes.
   b. Review the proposal and suggest areas where changes may be needed. Make changes together, if needed.
   c. Review the proposed budget, make revisions and explain them.
   d. Answer any questions or concerns Marie has and approve the budget as is.

_____ 12. You are a sales manager. A customer has offered you a contract for your product with a short delivery date. The offer is open for days. The contract would be profitable for you and the organisation. The cooperation of the production department is essential to meet the deadline. Tim, the production manager, and you do not get along very well because of your repeated requests for quick delivery. Your action is to:
   a. Contact Tim and try to work together to complete the contract.
   b. Accept the contract and convince Tim in a supportive way to meet the obligation.
   c. Contact Tim and explain the situation. Ask him if you and he should accept the contract, but let him decide.
   d. Accept the contract. Contact Tim and tell him to meet the obligation. If he resists, tell him you will go to the boss.

To determine your preferred communication style, in the chart below, circle the letter you selected as the alternative you chose in situations 1–12. The column headings indicate the style you selected.

	Autocratic	Consultative	Participative	Laissez-Faire
1.	a	b	c	d
2.	c	a	d	b
3.	c	d	a	b
4.	d	b	c	a
5.	a	b	d	c
6.	c	d	a	b
7.	c	a	b	d
8.	b	c	d	a
9.	b	d	a	c
10.	a	c	d	b
11.	c	a	b	d
12.	d	b	a	c
Total				

CASE 13 A CASE OF MISUNDERSTANDING: MR HART AND MR BING

Source: Reproduced by permission of the President and Fellows of Harvard College.

In a department of a large industrial organisation, there were seven workers (four men and three women) engaged in testing and inspecting panels of electronic equipment. In this department, one of the workers, Bing, was having trouble with his immediate supervisor, Hart, who had formly been a worker in the department. Had we been observers in this department, we would have seen Bing carrying two or three panels at a time from the racks where they were stored to the bench where he inspected them together. For this activity, we would have seen him charging double or triple set-up time. We would have heard him occasionally singing at work. Also we would have seen him usually leaving his work position a few minutes early to go to lunch, and noticed that other employees sometimes accompanied him. And had we been present at one specific occasion, we would have heard Hart telling Bing that he disapproved of these activities and that he wanted Bing to stop doing them.

However, not being present to hear the actual verbal exchange that took place in this interaction, let us note what Bing and Hart each said to a personnel representative.

What Bing said

In talking about his practice of charging double or triple set-up time for panels which he inspected all at one time, Bing said:

This is a perfectly legal thing to do. We've always been doing it. Mr Hart, the supervisor, has other ideas about it, though: he claims it's cheating the company. He came over to the bench a day or two ago and let me know just how he felt about the matter. Boy, did we go at it! It wasn't so much the fact that he called me down on it, but more the way in which he did not. He's a sarcastic bastard. I've never seen anyone like him. He's not content just to say in a manlike way what's on his mind, but he prefers to do it in a way that makes you want to crawl inside a crack in the floor. What a guy! I don't mind being called down by a supervisor, but I like to be treated like a man, and not humiliated like a school teacher does a naughty kid. He's been pulling this stuff ever since he's been promoted. He's lost his friendly way and seems to be having some difficulty in knowing how to manage us employees. He's a changed man over what he used to be like when he was a worker on the bench with us several years ago.

When he pulled this kind of stuff on me the other day, I got so damn mad I called in the union representative. I knew that the thing I was doing was permitted by the contract, but I was intent on making some trouble for Mr Hart, just because he persists in this sarcastic way of handling me. I am about fed up with the whole damn situation. I'm trying every means I can to get myself transferred out of this group. If I don't succeed and I'm forced to stay on here, I'm going to screw him in every way I can. He's not going to pull this kind of kid stuff any longer on me. When the union representative questioned him on the case, he finally had to back down, because according to the contract an employee can use any time-saving method or device in order to speed up the process as long as the quality standards of the job are met.

You see, he knows that I do professional singing on the outside. He hears the people talking about my career in music. I guess he figures I can be so cocky because I have another means of earning some money. Actually, the employees here enjoy having me sing while we work, but he thinks I'm disturbing them and causing them to 'goof-off' from their work. Occasionally, I leave the job a few minutes early and go down to the washroom to wash up before lunch. Sometimes several others in the group will accompany me, and so Mr Hart automatically thinks I'm the leader and usually bawls me out for the whole thing.

So, you can see, I'm a marked man around here: He keeps watching me like a hawk. Naturally, this makes me very uncomfortable. That's why I'm sure a transfer would be the best thing. I've asked him for it, but he didn't give me any satisfaction at the time. While I remain here, I'm going to keep my nose clean, but whenever I get the chance, I'm going to slip it to him, but good.

What Hart said

Here, on the other hand, is what Hart told the personnel representative:

Say, I think you should be in on this. My dear little friend Bing is heading himself into a showdown with me. Recently it was brought to my attention that Bing has been taking double and triple setup time for panels which he is actually inspecting at one time. If effect, that's cheating, and I've called him down on it several times before. A few days ago it was brought to my attention again, and so this time I really let him have it in no uncertain terms. He's been getting away with this for too long and I'm going to put an end to it once and for all. I know he didn't like me calling him on it because a few hours later he had the union

representative breathing down my back. Well, anyway, I let them both know I'll not tolerate the practice any longer, and I let Bing know that if he continues to do this kind of thing, I'm inclined to think the guy's mentally deficient, because talking to him has actually no meaning to him whatsoever. I've tried just about every approach to jar some sense into that guy's head, and I've just about given it up as a bad deal.

I don't know what it is about the guy, but I think he's harbouring some deep feeling against me. For what, I don't know, because I've tried to handle that bird with kid gloves. But his whole attitude around here on the job is one of indifference, and he certainly isn't a good influence on the rest of my group. Frankly, I think he purposely tried to agitate them against me at times, too. It seems to me that he may be suffering from illusions of grandeur because all he does all day is sit over there and croon his fool head off. Thinks he's Frank Sinatra! No kidding! I understand he takes singing lessons and he's working out with some of the local bands in the city. All of which is OK by me; but when his outside interests start interfering with his efficiency on the job, then I've got to start paying closer attention to the situation. For this reason I've been keeping my eye on that bird and if he steps outs of line any more, he and I are going to part ways.

You know there's an old saying, 'You can't make a silk purse out of a sow's ear'. The guy is simply unscrupulous. He feels no obligation to do a real day's work. Yet I know the guy can do a good job, because for a long time he did. But in recent months he's slipped, for some reason, and his whole attitude on the job has changed. Why, it's even getting to the point where I think he's inducing other employees to 'goof-off' a few minutes before the lunch whistle and go down to the washroom and clean up on company time. I've called him on it several times, but words just don't seem to make any lasting impression on him. Well, if he keeps it up much longer, he's going to find himself on the way out. He's asked me for a transfer, so I know he wants to go. But I didn't give him an answer when he asked me, because I was storming mad at the time, and I may have told him to go somewhere else.

Case questions

1. Based on the discussion of the elements of communication in the chapter, where are the breakdowns in communications occurring in this case?
2. What barriers to effective communication are present in this case?
3. What do you think must be done to improve communication between Mr Hart and Mr Bing?

ORGANISATIONAL CULTURE AND SOCIALISATION

Chapter 14

Learning objectives

- **Define** *the terms 'organisational culture' and 'socialisation'.*

- **Explain** *why it is too simplistic to assume that managers can state that they are creating a company's culture.*

- **Describe** *the stages of organisational socialisation.*

- **List** *socialisation strategies and their consequences.*

- **Describe** *six areas of organisational knowledge necessary for socialisation.*

- **Discuss** *the relationship between mentoring and socialisation.*

- **Identify** *specific practices and programs used by organisations to facilitate socialisation.*

Most individuals work for several different organisations over the course of a career. There are growing numbers of people who shift from one occupation to another. A decreasing number of individuals, after finishing their education, start and remain working with one company throughout their careers. When a person moves from one company to another, or even from one department to another in the same company, he or she senses and experiences differences between the environments. Attempting to adjust to these different environments involves learning new values, processing information in new ways, and working within an established set of norms, customs and rituals.

The adaptation to new environments is becoming a common occurrence and is likely to remain so into the 21st century. Although adaptation is difficult, it can be better understood by learning about organisational culture, socialisation and career systems. Organisational life is influenced by each of these concepts.

ORGANISATIONAL CULTURE

When we book into a Sheraton Hotel or a Hyatt Hotel anywhere in Australia — or the world — we know what to expect. Many large chains have a cultural anchor that influences the way employees interact with customers. McDonald's also sends off a powerful cultural message.[1] The 11 000 restaurants in the McDonald's network all pay attention to quality, service and cleanliness. Ray Kroc, the founder, instilled these cultural anchors in McDonald's. He had a significant influence on what McDonald's is throughout the world from Tokyo to Chicago to Moscow. Kroc projected his vision and his openness about what McDonald's would be to customers. He gave McDonald's a purpose, goals and a cultural base. Whether the discussion focuses on a grand hotel that exudes culture or a McDonald's restaurant that projects its founder's vision of the business, culture is a part of organisational life. The Organisational Encounter in this chapter describes how culture is maintained at Conrad Treasury Casino.

Organisational culture defined

Despite being an important concept, organisational culture as a perspective to understand behaviour within organisations has its limitations. First, it is not the only way to view organisations. We have already discussed the goal and systems view without even mentioning culture. Second, like so many concepts, organisational culture is not defined the same way by any two popular theorists or researchers. Some of the definitions of culture are as follows:

- symbols, language, ideologies, rituals and myths;[2]
- organisational scripts derived from the personal scripts of the organisation's founder(s) or dominant leader(s);
- is a product; is historical; is based upon symbols; and is an abstraction from behaviour and the products of behaviour.[3]

Organisational culture is what the employees perceive and how this perception creates a pattern of beliefs, values and expectations. Edgar Schein defined culture as:

ORGANISATIONAL   Encounter

Casino culture

In their efforts to maintain competitiveness within the casino trade, Conrad Casino, Brisbane, has targeted the quality of service provided by its staff. Recognising that the Australian workforce does not have a good reputation for its service delivery, Conrad was determined to establish a service culture. To achieve this goal Andersen Consulting engaged a combination of best-practice and change-management strategies. The casino has kept staff turnover below the industry benchmark of 20% and has lost only ten customers in the first 4 months of operation. What are the keys to its success?

These are as follows:

- **Recruitment.** You will recall that recruitment is important for ensuring a match between individual and organisational needs and values. At Conrad, staff are selected on the basis of their suitability for a service organisation.

- **A service orientation.** The service orientation is emphasised throughout the organisation, and staff are expected to deal with each other as if they were customers. This contributes to increased co-operation through the workplace.

- **Responsibility.** Staff are encouraged to become involved in the business. Quarterly meetings allow them to offer the opportunity to discuss concerns and to offer suggestions for improved service.

- **Communication.** Finally, the importance of communication cannot be overlooked. Everyone in the organisation carries a card that sets out the company's objectives. The aim of this is to provide continual reinforcement of the company's culture.

Source: Ferguson, A. (1995). Casino takes the gamble out of work culture, *Business Review Weekly*, August 7.

> *A pattern of basic assumptions — invented, discovered, or developed by a given group as it learns to cope with the problems of external adaptation and internal integration — that has worked well enough to be considered valid and, therefore, to be taught to new members as the correct way to perceive, think, and feel in relation to those problems.*[4]

The Schein definition points out that culture involves assumptions, adaptations, perceptions and learning. He further contends that an organisation's culture such as Walt Disney's has three layers. Layer I includes artefacts and creations which are visible but often not interpretable. An annual report, a newsletter, wall dividers between workers, and furnishings are examples of artefacts and creations. At Layer II are values or the things that are important to people. Values are conscious, affective desires or wants. In Layer III are the basic assumptions people make that guide their behaviour. Included here are assumptions that tell individuals how to perceive, think about and feel about work, performance goals, human relationships and the performance of colleagues. Exhibit 14.1 presents the Schein three-layer model of organisational culture.

Asking McDonald's or Walt Disney employees about their company's organisational culture is not likely to reveal much. A person's feelings and perceptions are usually kept at the subconscious level. Exhibit 14.2 illustrates how the culture of a company can be inferred by looking at those aspects that are perceptible. For example, four specific manifestations of culture at Walt Disney are shared things (wearing the Walt Disney uniform to fit the attraction), shared sayings (a good 'Mickey' is a compliment for doing a good job), shared behaviour (smiling at customers and being polite), and shared feelings (taking pride in working at Disney).

Exhibit 14.1
Schein's
three-layer
organisational
model

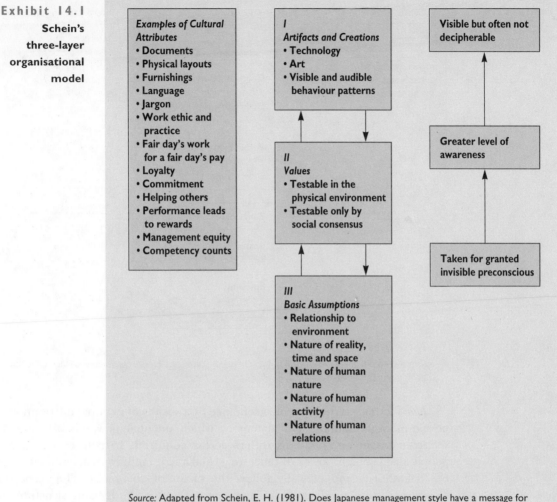

Source: Adapted from Schein, E. H. (1981). Does Japanese management style have a message for American managers?, *Sloan Management Review*, Fall, p. 64.

Societal values and organisational culture

Organisations are able to operate efficiently only when shared values exist among the employees. **Values** are the conscious affective desires or wants of people that guide behaviour. An individual's personal values guide behaviour on and off the job. If a person's set of values is important, it will guide the person and also enable the person to behave consistently across situations.

Values are a society's ideas about what is right or wrong — such as the belief that hurting someone physically is immoral. Values are passed from one generation to the next and are communicated through education systems, religion, families, communities and organisations.[5]

One useful framework for understanding the importance of values in organisational behaviour is provided by Hofstede. The result of his research of 116 000 people in fifty countries has been a four-dimension value framework.[6] He proposes four value dimensions: power distance, uncertainty avoidance, individualism and masculinity.

Reading 14

Levels of culture

Exhibit 14.2

Cultural
relationships

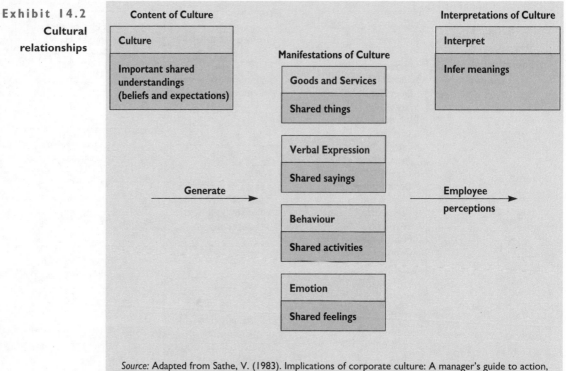

Content of Culture

Culture

Important shared
understandings
(beliefs and expectations)

Generate →

Manifestations of Culture

Goods and Services

Shared things

Verbal Expression

Shared sayings

Behaviour

Shared activities

Emotion

Shared feelings

Interpretations of Culture

Interpret

Infer meanings

Employee
perceptions →

Source: Adapted from Sathe, V. (1983). Implications of corporate culture: A manager's guide to action, *Organizational Dynamics*, Autumn, p. 8.

Power distance is the level of acceptance by a society of unequal distribution of power in organisations. The extent to which unequal power is accepted by subordinates in organisations differs across countries. In countries in which people display high power distance (e.g. Malaysia), employees acknowledge the boss's authority and typically follow the chain of command. The respectful response results, predictably, in more centralised authority and structure. In countries where people display low power distance (e.g. Denmark) superiors and subordinates are likely to regard one another as equal in power, resulting in a more decentralised and less rigid management structure and style.

The concept of *uncertainty avoidance* refers to the extent to which people in a society feel threatened by ambiguous situations. Countries with a high level of uncertainty avoidance (e.g. Japan) tend to have specific rules, laws and procedures. Managers in these countries tend to have a propensity for low-risk decision making, and employees exhibit little aggressiveness. In countries with lower levels of uncertainty avoidance (e.g. Great Britain), organisational activities are less formal, more risk taking occurs and there is high job mobility.

Individualism refers to the tendency of people to fend for themselves and their families. In countries that value individualism (e.g. United States), individual initiative and achievement are highly valued and the relationship of the individual with the organisation is one of independence. In countries such as Pakistan, characterised by low individualism, one finds tight social frameworks and emotional dependence on belonging to 'the organisation'. These countries emphasise collectivism. Japan is a collective society in which the will of the group rather than the individual dominates. Collectivist societies value harmony whereas individualistic cultures value self-respect and autonomy.

Masculinity refers to the degree of traditionally masculine values such as assertiveness and materialism. In comparison, femininity emphasises feminine values, such as a concern for relationships and the quality of life. In highly masculine societies (e.g. Austria), one finds considerable job stress and conflict between the job and family roles. In countries with low masculinity (e.g. Switzerland), one finds less conflict and stress.

The results of Hofstede's research are shown in what he calls maps of the world. The maps show at a glance the similarities and differences in work values across nations. The four cultural value dimensions are interdependent and complex.[7] Consequently, the effects of values on workplace productivity, attitude and effectiveness are difficult to determine. Managers must be cautious about grossly overgeneralising. For example, not all Americans value individualism, a low power distance, moderate uncertainty and masculinity. However, we must bear in mind that a society's values will affect organisational values because of the interactive nature of work, leisure, family and community.

Organisational culture and its effects

Since organisational culture involves shared expectations, values and attitudes, it exerts influence on individuals, groups and organisational processes. Individual members are influenced to be good citizens and to go along. Thus, if quality customer service is important in the culture, then individuals are expected to adopt this behaviour. If, on the other hand, adhering to a specific set of procedures in dealing with customers is the norm, then this type of behaviour would be expected, recognised and rewarded.

Researchers who have suggested and studied the impact of culture of employees indicate that it provides and encourages a form of stability.[8] There is a feeling of stability, as well as a sense of organisational identity, provided by an organisation's culture. Walt Disney is able to attract, develop and retain top-quality employees because of the firm's stability and the pride of identity that goes with being a part of the Disney team.

Australian research suggests that organisational culture can influence human resource management (HRM) systems. Using a two-dimensional category for describing organisational cultures, the HRM practices of companies representing the four organisational cultures were compared. Culture was defined on the basis of power (equal or unequal) and resource (equity or equality) distribution, resulting in organisations described as elite (unequal, equity), meritocratic (equal, equity), leadership (unequal, equality) and collegial (equal, equality). Results showed not only that HRM practices and objectives vary as a consequence of organisational culture, but also that the importance of these practices varies. For example, elite organisations were much less likely to use performance appraisal for developing the individual or determining compensation than were meritocratic or collegial organisations.[9]

It has become useful to differentiate between strong and weak cultures.[10] A strong culture is characterised by employees sharing core values. The more employees share and accept the core values, the stronger the culture is and the more influential it is on behaviour. Religious organisations, cults and some Japanese companies such as Toyota are examples of organisations that have strong, influential cultures.

Popular best seller books such as *Theory Z: How American Business Can Meet the Japanese Challenge,*[11] *In Search of Excellence,*[12] and *Corporate Cultures: The Rites and Rituals of Corporate Life*[13] provide anecdotal evidence about the powerful influence of culture on individuals, group and processes. Heroes and stories about companies are interestingly portrayed. However, theoretically based and empirically valid research on culture and its impact is still quite sketchy. Questions remain about the measures used to assess culture, and definitional problems have not been resolved. There has also been the inability of researchers to show that a specific culture contributes to positive effectiveness in comparison with less effective companies with another cultural profile. Comparative cultural studies are needed to better understand how culture impacts on behaviour.

Creating organisational culture

Can a culture be created that influences behaviour in the direction management desires? This is an intriguing question. An attempt and an experiment to create a positive, productive culture was conducted in a California electronics company.[14] Top managers regularly meet to establish the core values of the company. A document was developed to express the core values as: 'paying attention to detail', 'doing it right the first time', 'delivering defect-free products' and 'using open communications'. The document of core values was circulated to middle-level managers who refined the statements. Then the refined document was circulated to all employees as the set of guiding principles of the firm.

An anthropologist was in the company at the time working as a software trainer. He insightfully analysed what actually occurred in the company. There was a gap between the management-stated culture and the company's actual working conditions and practices. Quality problems existed throughout the company. There was also a strictly enforced chain of command and a top-down only communication system. The cultural creation experiment was too artificial and was not taken seriously by employees.

The consequences of creating a culture in the California company included decreased morale, increased turnover and a poorer financial performance. Ultimately, the company filed for bankruptcy and closed its doors.

The California electronics company case points out that artificially imposing a culture is difficult. Imposing a culture is often met with resistance. It is difficult to simply create core values. Also, when a disparity exists between reality and a stated set of values, employees become confused, irritated and sceptical. They also usually lack enthusiasm and respect when a false image is portrayed. Creating a culture apparently just does not happen because a group of intelligent, well-intentioned managers meet and prepare a document.

Cultures seem to evolve over a period of time as did those of McDonald's and Walt Disney. Schein describes this evolution as follows:

> *The culture that eventually evolves in a particular organisation is ... a complex outcome of external pressures, internal potentials, responses to critical events, and, probably, to some unknown degree, chance factors that could not be predicted from a knowledge of either the environment or the members.*[15]

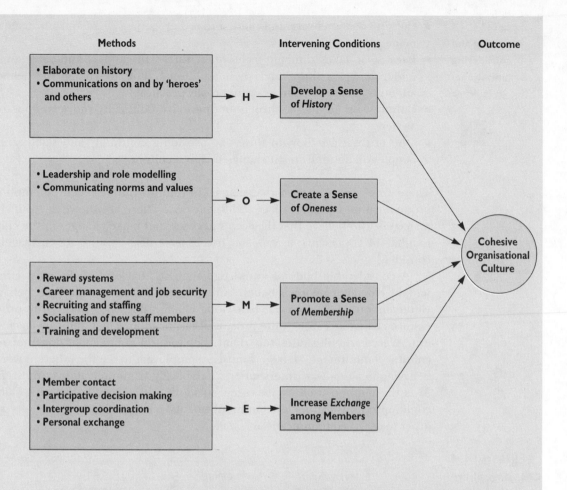

Methods | Intervening Conditions | Outcome

• Elaborate on history
• Communications on and by 'heroes' and others

H → Develop a Sense of *History*

• Leadership and role modelling
• Communicating norms and values

O → Create a Sense of *Oneness*

• Reward systems
• Career management and job security
• Recruiting and staffing
• Socialisation of new staff members
• Training and development

M → Promote a Sense of *Membership*

• Member contact
• Participative decision making
• Intergroup coordination
• Personal exchange

E → Increase *Exchange* among Members

→ Cohesive Organisational Culture

Source: Gross, W., & Schichman, S. (1987). How to grow an organizational culture, *Personnel*, September, pp 52–56, © 1987 *American Management Association*, New York. All rights reserved.

Exhibit 14.3
The evolution of positive culture

A model that illustrates the evolution of culture and its outcome is presented in Exhibit 14.3. The model emphasises an array of methods and procedures that managers can use to foster a cohesive culture. In examining this model, recall the California electronics company and the limited methods it used to generate a quick-fix culture. In Exhibit 14.3 there is an emphasis on the word 'HOME', which suggests the importance of history, oneness, membership and exchange among employees.

Influencing culture change

There is a limited amount of research done on cultural change. The difficulty in creating a culture is made even more complex when attempting to bring about a significant cultural change. Our Local Encounter examines culture change following mergers and acquisitions. The themes that appear in discussing change are these:

Exercise 14
Assessing and considering organisational culture

- Cultures are so elusive and hidden that they cannot be adequately diagnosed, managed, or changed.
- Because it takes difficult techniques, rare skills and considerable time to understand a culture and then additional time to change it, deliberate attempts at culture change are not really practical.
- Cultures sustain people throughout periods of difficulty and serve to ward off anxiety.
- One of the ways they do this is by providing continuity and stability. Thus, people will naturally resist change to a new culture.[16]

These three views suggest that managers who are interested in attempting to produce cultural changes face a difficult task. There are, however, courageous managers who believe that they can intervene and make changes in the culture. Exhibit 14.4 presents a view of five intervention points for managers to consider.[17]

A considerable body of knowledge suggests that one of the most effective ways of changing people's beliefs and values is to first change their behaviour (intervention 1).[18] However, behaviour change does not necessarily produce culture change because of the process of justification. The California electronics example clearly illustrates this point. Behavioural compliance does not mean cultural commitment. Managers must get employees to see the inherent worth in behaving in a new way (intervention 2). Typically, communications (intervention 3) is the method used by managers to motivate the new behaviours. Cultural communications can include announcements, memos, rituals, stories, dress and other forms of communications.

Exhibit 14.4
Changing culture intervention points

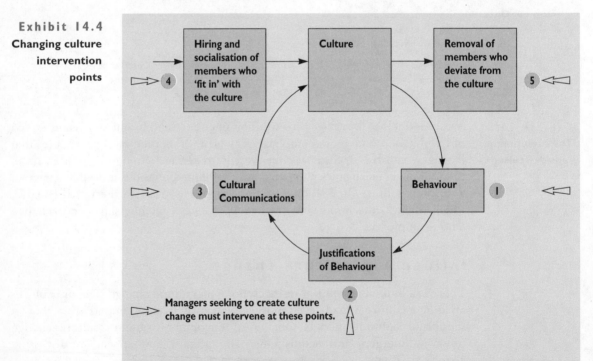

Source: Mainiero, L. A., & Tromley, C. L. (1989). *Developing Managerial Skills in Organizational Behavior.* Englewood Cliffs, NJ: Prentice-Hall, p. 403.

Another set of interventions includes the socialisation of new members (intervention 4) and the removal of existing members who deviate from the culture (intervention 5). Each of these interventions must be done after careful diagnoses are performed. Although some individuals may not perfectly fit the firm's culture, they may possess exceptional skills and talents. Weeding out cultural misfits might be necessary, but it should be done only after weighing the costs and benefits of losing talented performers who deviate from the core cultural value system.

SOCIALISATION AND CULTURE

Socialisation is the process by which organisations bring new employees into the culture. In terms of culture, there is a transmittal of values, assumptions and attitudes from the older to the newer employees. Intervention 4 in Exhibit 14.4 emphasises the 'fit' between the new employee and the culture. Socialisation attempts to make this fit more comfortable for the employee and the organisation. The socialisation process is presented in Exhibit 14.5.

Case 14
The Consolidated
Life case:
Caught between
corporate cultures

The socialisation process goes on throughout an individual's career. As the needs of the organisation change, for example, its employees must adapt to those new needs; that is, they must be socialised. But even as we recognise that socialisation is ever present, we must also recognise that it is more important at some times than at others. For example, socialisation is most important when an individual first takes a job or takes a different job in the same organisation. The socialisation process occurs throughout the career stages, but individuals are more aware of it when they change jobs or change organisations.[19]

Socialisation stages

Although researchers have proposed various descriptions of the stages of socialisation,[20] three stages sufficiently describe it: anticipatory socialisation, accommodation, and role management.[21] Each stage involves specific activities that, if undertaken properly, increase the individual's chances of having an effective career. Moreover, these stages occur continuously and often simultaneously.

Anticipatory socialisation

The first stage involves all those activities the individual undertakes prior to entering the organisation or to taking a different job in the same organisation. The primary purpose of these activities is to acquire information about the new organisation and/or new job. This stage of socialisation corresponds to the prework career stage, and the information-gathering activities include formal schooling, actual work experience, and recruiting efforts of organisations attempting to attract new employees.

People are vitally interested in two kinds of information prior to entering a new job or organisation. First, they want to know as much as they can about what working for the organisation is really like. Second, they want to know whether they are suited to the jobs available in the organisation. Individuals seek out this information with considerable effort when they are faced with the decision to take a job, whether it be their first one or one that comes along by way of

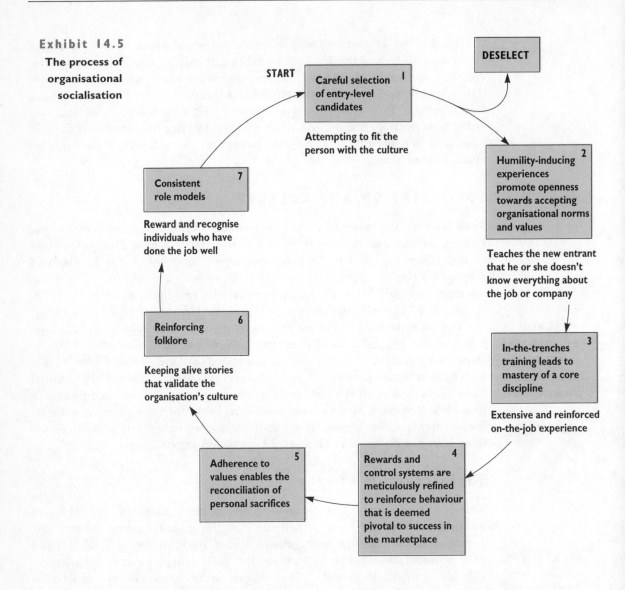

Exhibit 14.5

The process of organisational socialisation

START

Careful selection of entry-level candidates 1

Attempting to fit the person with the culture

DESELECT

Humility-inducing experiences promote openness towards accepting organisational norms and values 2

Teaches the new entrant that he or she doesn't know everything about the job or company

In-the-trenches training leads to mastery of a core discipline 3

Extensive and reinforced on-the-job experience

Consistent role models 7

Reward and recognise individuals who have done the job well

Reinforcing folklore 6

Keeping alive stories that validate the organisation's culture

Adherence to values enables the reconciliation of personal sacrifices 5

Rewards and control systems are meticulously refined to reinforce behaviour that is deemed pivotal to success in the marketplace 4

Source: Pascale, R. T. (1985). The paradox of 'corporate culture': Reconciling ourselves to socialization, *California Mangement Review*, Winter, p. 38. © 1985 by the Regents of the University of California. Reprinted with permission of the Regents.

transfer or promotion. At these times, the information is specific to the job or the organisation. We also form impressions about jobs and organisations in less formal ways. For example, our friends and relatives talk of their experiences. Parents impart both positive and negative information to their offspring regarding the world of work. Although we continually receive information about this or that job or organisation, we are more receptive to such information when faced with the necessity to make a decision.

It is desirable, of course, that the information transmitted and received during the anticipatory stage accurately and clearly depicts the organisation and the job. However, we know that individuals differ considerably in the way they

Mergers, acquisitions and culture shift

Even when organisations have the same function, their cultures may not be compatible. It is, therefore, important to understand what happens when cultures collide: when two organisations with very different cultures merge. Will one culture dominate? Will both cultures change? And what are the determinants of successful mergers? Harrison identified four dimensions of organisational culture: the degree to which power is centralised; the extent to which the organisation is highly bureaucratised; the extent to which team commitment and task achievement are valued; and the extent to which the culture supports personal growth. According to Harrison, successful mergers require an emphasis on personal development, task achievement and standardised procedures in the dominant company coupled with either centralised power or standardised procedures in the minor company.

With this in mind, Neal Ashkanasy and his co-workers at the University of Queensland conducted two case studies focusing on the merger of accounting firms in one, and university libraries in the other. They were interested in determining the extent to which perceptions of organisational culture change over time, as well as in how these changes occur.

Their examination of two accounting firms, over a 27-month period, showed that 2 months after the merger there were substantial differences in how staff in the major and minor firms perceived organisational culture. The minor firm in the merger perceived a greater emphasis on centralised power and little emphasis on task accomplishment — a pattern that Harrison predicts will result in a successful merger. In subsequent surveys, the perceptions of staff in the minor firm changed while those of staff in the major firm remained stable: staff in the minor firm reported an increased emphasis on power and role dimensions, and a decreased emphasis on task and individual needs dimensions. When did perceptions change? Interestingly, the perceptions of all staff changed radically when they relocated into new office accommodation. Not only did the perceptions of culture converge, but there were quite dramatic changes in how the organisational culture was perceived.

A second case study compared changes in organisational culture during library amalgamations. The main finding from this case study was that the biggest changes in perceived organisational culture occurred where the cultures were perceived to be markedly different prior to the merger. When this finding is considered together with the previous findings it suggests that, for mergers to be successful, organisations must redefine themselves. These results imply that we cannot expect a minor partner in a merger to adopt the culture of the dominant partner; rather, the organisation must view itself as a new entity and, consequently, establish new cultural norms.

Based on their findings, these researchers suggest that we can use a two-dimensional typology to define organisational culture. The two dimensions are employee discretion and management support/consideration for employees. This gives us four culture types:

- empowerment, which gives employees complete discretion and support;
- loyalty, which gives support without discretion in return for loyalty to the organisation;
- laissez-faire, in which staff have high levels of discretion but no support from management; and
- obedience, in which staff have neither discretion nor support and are expected to show obedience to management.

Source: Ashkanasy, N. M., & Holmes, S. (1995). Perceptions of organisational ideology following merger: A longitudinal study of merging accounting firms, *Accounting, Organisations and Society*, **20**, 19–34; Ashkanasy, N. M. (1995). Organisational mergers and acquisitions: A natural crucible for research in organisational culture, Paper presented at the Inaugural Conference on Industrial & Organisational Psychology, Sydney; Austen, G., & Ashkanasy, N. M. (in press). Merging tertiary education libraries: Case studies in cultural change, *Australian Academic Research Libraries*; Harrison, R. (1972). How to describe your organization's culture, *Harvard Business Review*, **50**, 119–128.

decode and receive information. Yet if the fit between the individual and the organisation is to be optimal, two conditions are necessary: The first condition is *realism*. Both the individual and the organisation must portray themselves realistically. The second condition is *congruence*. This condition is present when the individual's skills, talents and abilities are fully utilised by the job. Either their overutilisation or underutilisation results in incongruence and, consequently, poor performance.[22]

Accommodation

The second stage of socialisation occurs after the individual becomes a member of the organisation, after he or she takes the job. During this stage, the individual sees the organisation and the job for what they actually are. Through a variety of activities the individual attempts to become an active participant in the organisation and a competent performer on the job. This breaking-in period is ordinarily stressful for the individual because of anxiety created by the uncertainties inherent in any new and different situation. Apparently, individuals who experienced realism and congruence during the anticipatory stage have a less stressful accommodation stage. Nevertheless, the demands on the individual do indeed create situations that induce stress.

Four major activities comprise the accommodation stage: All individuals, to a degree, must engage in establishing new interpersonal relationships with both co-workers and supervisors; learning the tasks required to perform the job; clarifying their role in the organisation and in the formal and informal groups relevant to that role; and evaluating the progress they are making towards satisfying the demands of the job and the role. Readers who have been through the accommodation stage probably recognise these four activities and recall more or less favourable reactions to them.

If all goes well in this stage, the individual feels a sense of acceptance by co-workers and supervisors and experiences competence in performing job tasks. The breaking-in period, if successful, also results in role definition and congruence of evaluation. These four outcomes of the accommodation stage (acceptance, competence, role definition and congruence of evaluation) are experienced by all new employees to a greater or lesser extent. However, the relative value of each of these outcomes varies from person to person.[23] Acceptance by the group may be a less valued outcome for an individual whose social needs are satisfied off the job, for example. Regardless of these differences due to individual preferences, each of us experiences the accommodation stage of socialisation and ordinarily moves on to the third stage.

Role management

In contrast to the accommodation stage, which requires the individual to adjust to demands and expectations of the immediate work group, the role management stage takes on a broader set of issues and problems. Specifically, during the third stage, conflicts arise. One conflict is between the individual's work and home lives. For example, the individual must divide time and energy between the job and his or her role in the family. Since the amount of time and energy are fixed and the demands of work and family seemingly insatiable, conflict is inevitable. Employees unable to resolve these conflicts are often forced to leave the organisation or to perform at an ineffective level. In either case, the individual and the organisation are not well served by unresolved conflict between work and family.

The second source of conflict during the role management stage is between the individual's work group and other work groups in the organisation. This source of conflict can be more apparent for some employees than for others. For example, as an individual moves up in the organisation's hierarchy, he or she is required to interact with various groups both inside and outside the organisation. Each group can and often does place different demands on the individual, and to the extent that these demands are beyond the individual's ability to meet, stress results. Tolerance for the level of stress induced by these conflicting and irreconcilable demands varies among individuals. Generally, the existence of unmanaged stress works to the disadvantage of the individual and the organisation.

SOCIALISATION STRATEGIES

Organisations must make several choices related to how they will socialise new staff. In part, these choices may be determined by the goals that they are attempting to meet. Research by Allen and Meyer[24] shows that socialisation strategies are able to reinforce one of two goals: organisational commitment and role innovation. According to their research, there is a negative relationship between these two goals: if we attempt to obtain high organisational commitment, we will also obtain low role innovation; and if we desire high levels of role innovation, then we need to accept lower levels of commitment. Let's consider how these goals are achieved through the socialisation process.

Van Maanen and Schein[25] describe six dimensions that can be used to classify organisational socialisation tactics: collective–individual, formal–informal, fixed–variable, serial–disjunctive, sequential–random and investiture–divestiture. These dimensions describe different ways in which organisations may approach socialisation.

Collective socialisation occurs when a new group of employees experiences a common training period. For example, many organisations conduct formal induction programs that provide employees with organisational information as well as basic skills. Perhaps one of the most easily recognisable examples of collective socialisation is that experienced by new recruits to the army, police or fire services. In contrast, *individual socialisation* occurs when an organisational newcomer receives one-on-one training or coaching by a more experienced member of staff, for example during an apprenticeship.

Formal programs separate the new recruit from the rest of the organisation during the initial training period. Again, 'boot camp' provides a good example of this process. The need to separate newcomers from experienced staff may also result in symbolic — rather than physical — separation. For example, an apprentice may wear an 'in-training' badge, and trainee nurses may be separated from experienced staff by the colour of their uniforms. When programs are *informal,* this type of separation does not occur and it is difficult to distinguish newcomers from old-timers.

Fixed socialisation strategies set out a specific timetable for new recruits to acquire necessary skills. This may be in the form of training modules that must be completed before newcomers are ready to take on their organisational roles.

Fixed strategies identify a clear end point for the socialisation process, and we could consider professional training programs — accountancy, medicine and dentistry — as examples of fixed programs. By comparison, *variable socialisation* has no clear endpoint.

Serial socialisation occurs when individuals enter into a mentoring relationship with an older and more experienced employee who has, at some point, occupied the same position. This employee serves as a guide and role model for the newcomer. 'Serial' describes a process in which one individual essentially 'passes on' the relevant role demands of a particular job. When socialisation is *disjunctive*, this does not occur.

Sequential strategies require that individuals progress through a series of well-defined stages or experiences, each of which builds on a preceding stage. Again, professional training provides a good example: accounting students must learn the basic principles of accounting before moving on to the more advanced concepts. This type of socialisation is necessary when there is a sequence in which information must be acquired; *random socialisation* occurs when no such sequence is necessary.

Divestiture occurs when the organisation attempts to significantly change the attitudes and values of new employees, for example through humility-inducing experiences. The aim of divestiture strategies is to prepare the individual for attitude change. The basic message is that although the individual's skills may be valued by the organisation, the individual must be willing to assimilate organisational norms. By contrast, *investiture* sends the opposite message: that the organisation must be willing to accommodate the newcomer. Investiture is, therefore, associated with higher levels of innovation than is divestiture.

According to Allen and Meyer, these dimensions can essentially be grouped into strategies that provide *institutionalised socialisation* and those that provide *individualised socialisation*. Institutionalised socialisation is aimed at reinforcing the organisational norms and culture and in shaping individuals to fit that culture. It is represented by tactics that are collective, formal, fixed-variable, serial and sequential, and divest the individual. According to Allen and Meyer, this pattern of socialisation will result in high organisational commitment. Conversely, individualised socialisation has as it goal to encourage high levels of innovation and change, emphasising that the organisation needs to accommodate the individual. It is represented by tactics that are individual, informal, variable, disjunctive and random, and invests the individual. This pattern of socialisation is expected to result in high levels of role innovation.

In their research, Allen and Meyer found that serial socialisation is strongly associated with the level of role innovation: organisations employing serial tactics produce employees who are less willing to experiment and alter the procedures for their jobs than organisations who employ disjunctive strategies. These researchers also found a strong relationship between the process of investiture and organisational commitment: organisational commitment was higher when investiture was used as a socialisation strategy. These findings have interesting implications for organisational socialisation practices: they suggest that organisations must be clear on the goals they wish to achieve, in the long term, and to adapt their strategies accordingly. This research identifies disjunctive socialisation as critical to role innovation, and investiture as critical to organisational commitment.

LEARNING ABOUT THE ORGANISATION

Recent research has focused not on the socialisation tactics that organisations employ, but on the learning that needs to take place for individuals to be effectively socialised. In this section we consider *what* an individual needs to learn; and in our Management Encounter, we consider *how* this learning takes place. According to Chao and her co-workers,[26] socialisation needs to occur in six domains. Individuals in organisations need knowledge in the areas of:

- *performance proficiency*, that is the identification of skill and role requirements;
- *people*, or the establishment of successful relationships with individuals in identifying the right person to provide information about the organisation, tasks and roles;
- *politics*, or the identification of power structures and knowledge bases within the organisation;
- *language*, or the jargon of the workplace;
- *organisational goals and values*, that is understanding both the formal and informal norms and values that govern organisational life;
- *history*, or the traditions, myths and rituals that help define appropriate and inappropriate behaviours.

What consequences does this knowledge have for the organisation and individuals? To answer the first question, Chao and her co-workers compared individuals who left the organisation with those who stayed; they also compared those individuals within the organisation who stayed in the same job with those who found a different job within the organisation. Before they changed jobs, individuals who eventually left an organisation were found to have less knowledge about organisational goals, values and history. This suggests that those individuals who stay are more bound to the organisation — more successfully socialised — and that this may prevent their departure. Clearly, this implies that, in the first instance, organisations should target socialisation at the level of goals, values and history.

When they compared individuals who changed jobs with those who changed organisations, they found that both groups reported having less knowledge about performance proficiency, language and history; in addition, individuals who changed organisations reported knowing less about people and politics in their new organisation. This suggests, for each of these components, not only that there is an organisation-specific dimension but also that there is an area-specific component within organisations,. One consequence of this is that, when individuals change jobs within the same organisation, managers must give consideration to providing socialisation across the three dimensions of performance proficiency, language and history.

And what of the individual? Chao and her co-workers found that the quality of organisational socialisation predicted career outcomes 3 years later. Increased understanding of organisational politics predicted higher salaries; and a better understanding of organisational goals and values predicted greater career involvement and job satisfaction.

MANAGEMENT   Encounter

Learning the ropes

In our discussion of organisational socialisation, we considered the process of assimilation: the need for newcomers to learn their tasks and roles, as well as organisational norms and values. The process of information acquisition is critical to the socialisation process and, as we saw in Chapter 7, when individuals hold themselves aloof from a group their effective socialisation is delayed, perhaps never accomplished. In this chapter, we have already considered some of the information that newcomers must acquire and its consequences for the individual. We now explore this process of information acquisition further.

When individuals join organisations, they must learn about job-related tasks, their work roles, group process and organisational attributes. Where does this information come from? Researchers have identified several potential sources of information. Supervisors, co-workers and mentors all provide interpersonal sources of information. In addition, newcomers may seeks information from non-personal sources: they may examine written material such as policy and procedure manuals, they may simply observe others in the workplace, or they may actively experiment to obtain information or feedback about their performance. Among the issues that researchers are now addressing are whether different sources are better able to provide information in different areas; whether there are preferences for how information is acquired; and what forms of information seeking are linked to increased knowledge.

Research shows that when individuals are seeking information about either their tasks or roles, they use a broad range of strategies: they access all interpersonal sources, and also report using observation and experimentation. When they need information about group or organisational attributes, newcomers report a strong preference for observing others. Remember that interpersonal sources can include supervisors, co-workers and mentors. Are they accessed equally in the quest or information? The answer is no. First when individuals have mentors, they are less likely to use co-workers to obtain information.

Second, individuals prefer to use co-workers to obtain social feedback and supervisors to obtain role-related and task-related information, as well as performance feedback. When individuals obtain information from interpersonal sources (co-workers and supervisors) they report higher levels of satisfaction and stress, and less intention to leave the organisation.

Another interesting finding to emerge relates to the use of experimentation. As a strategy for information acquisition, its use increases over time. This suggests that it is a high-risk strategy and that individuals must be reasonably well assimilated into their organisation before they use this strategy. In addition, together with observation, this strategy is correlated with the perception of much greater knowledge across all domains. This suggests that effortful strategies are more successful in increasing newcomer knowledge. One implication is that highly structured induction programs may not result in well-informed staff in the long term. However, these strategies are also associated with higher levels of stress, suggesting that they take longer to reduce newcomer uncertainty.

Consider the implications that these findings have for organisations. Well-informed staff clearly benefit organisations. If you were responsible for an organisation's induction program, what strategies would you use to ensure that newcomers obtain the information that they need?

Source: Morrison, E. W. (1993). Newcomer information seeking: Exploring types, modes, sources and outcomes, *Academy of Management Journal*, **36**, 557–589; Ostroff, C., & Kozlowski, S. W. J. (1993). The role of mentoring in the information gathering processes of newcomers during early socialisation, *Journal of Vocational Behaviour*, **42**, 170–183; Ostroff, C., & Kozlowski, S. W. J. (1992). Organisational socialisation as a learning process: The role of information acquisition, *Personnel Psychology*, **45**, 849–874.

CHARACTERISTICS OF EFFECTIVE SOCIALISATION

Organisational socialisation processes vary in form and content from organisation to organisation. Even with the same organisation, various individuals experience different socialisation processes. For example, the accommodation stage for a university-trained management recruit is quite different from that of a person in the lowest paid occupation in the organisation. As John Van Maanen has pointed out, socialisation processes are not only extremely important in shaping the individuals who enter an organisation, but are also remarkably different from situation to situation.[27] This variation reflects either lack of attention by management to an important process or the uniqueness of the process as related to organisations and individuals. Either explanation permits the suggestion that while uniqueness is apparent, some general principles can be implemented in the socialisation process.[28]

Effective anticipatory socialisation

The organisation's primary activities during the first stage of socialisation are *recruitment* and *selection and placement programs*. If these programs are effective, new recruits in an organisation should experience the feeling of realism and *congruence*. In turn, accurate expectations about the job result from realism and congruence.

Recruitment programs are directed toward new employees, those not now in the organisation. It is desirable to give prospective employees information not only about the job but also about those aspects of the organisation that affect the individual. It is nearly always easier for the recruiter to stress job-related information to the exclusion of organisation-related information. Job-related information is usually specific and objective, whereas organisation-related information is usually general and subjective. Nevertheless, the recruiter should, to the extent possible, convey factual information about such matters as pay and promotion policies and practices, objective characteristics of the work group the recruit is likely to join, and other information that reflects the recruit's concerns.

Selection and placement practices, in the context of anticipatory socialisation, are important conveyers of information to employees already in the organisation. Of prime importance is the manner in which individuals view career paths in organisations. As noted earlier, the stereotypical career path is one that involves advancement up the managerial hierarchy. This concept, however, does not take into account the differences among individuals towards such moves. Greater flexibility in career paths would require the organisation to consider lateral or downward transfers.[29]

Effective accommodation socialisation

Five different activities comprise effective accommodation socialisation. They are designing orientation programs, structuring training programs, providing performance evaluation information, assigning challenging work, and assigning demanding bosses.

Orientation programs are seldom given the attention they deserve. The first few days on the new job can have very strong negative or positive impacts on the new employee. Taking a new job involves not only new job tasks but also new interpersonal relationships. The new person comes into an ongoing social system which has evolved a unique set of values, ideals, frictions, conflicts, friendships, coalitions, and all the other characteristics of work groups. If left alone, the new employee must cope with the new environment in ignorance, but if given some help and guidance, he or she can cope more effectively.[30]

Thus, organisations should design orientation programs that enable new employees to meet the rest of the employees as soon as possible. Moreover, specific individuals should be assigned the task of orientation. These individuals should be selected for their social skills and be given time off from their own work to spend with the new people. The degree to which the orientation program is formalised can vary, but in any case, the program should not be left to chance.

Training programs are invaluable in the breaking-in stage. Without question, training programs are necessary to instruct new employees in proper techniques and to develop requisite skills. Moreover, effective training programs provide frequent feedback about progress in acquiring the necessary skills. What is not so obvious is the necessity of integrating formal training with the orientation program.

Performance evaluation, in the context of socialisation, provides important feedback about how well the individual is getting along in the organisation. Inaccurate or ambiguous information regarding this important circumstance can only lead to performance problems. To avoid these problems, it is imperative that performance evaluation sessions take place in face-to-face meetings between the individual and manager and that in the context of the job the performance criteria must be as objective as possible. Management by objectives and behaviourally anchored rating scales are particularly applicable in these settings.

Assigning challenging work to new employees is a principal feature of effective socialisation programs. The first jobs of new employees often demand far less of them than they are able to deliver. Consequently, they are unable to demonstrate their full capabilities, and in a sense they are being stifled. This is especially damaging if the recruiter was overly enthusiastic in 'selling' the organisation when they were recruited.

Assigning demanding bosses is a practice that seems to have considerable promise for increasing the retention rate of new employees. In this context, 'demanding' should not be interpreted as 'autocratic'. Rather, the boss most likely to get new hirees off in the right direction is one who has high but achievable expectations for their performance. Such a boss instils the understanding that high performance is expected and rewarded; equally important, the boss is always ready to assist through coaching and counselling.

Socialisation programs and practices intended to retain and develop new employees can be used separately or in combination. A manager is well advised to establish policies most likely to retain those recent hirees who have the highest potential to perform effectively. This likelihood is improved if the policies include realistic orientation and training programs, accurate performance evaluation feedback, and challenging initial assignments supervised by supportive, performance-oriented managers.

Effective role management socialisation

Organisations that effectively deal with the conflicts associated with the role management stage recognise the impact of such conflicts on job satisfaction and turnover. Even though motivation and high performance may not be associated with socialisation activities, satisfaction and turnover are, and organisations can ill afford to lose capable employees.

Retention of employees beset by off-job conflicts is enhanced in organisations that provide professional counselling and that schedule and adjust work assignments for those with particularly difficult conflicts at work and home. Of course, these practices do not guarantee that employees can resolve or even cope with the conflict. The important point, however, is for the organisation to show good faith and make a sincere effort to adapt to the problems of its employees. Exhibit 14.6 summarises what managers can do to encourage effective socialisation.

MENTORS AND SOCIALISATION

In the medical field young interns learn proper procedures and behaviour from established physicians; and PhD graduate students learn how to conduct organisational research from professors who have conducted studies. What about the process of learning or working with a senior person called a *mentor* in work settings? In Greek mythology the mentor was the designation given to a trusted and experienced advisor. Odysseus, absent from home because of the Trojan Wars, charged his servant mentor with the task of educating and guiding his son. In work organisations a mentor can provide coaching, friendship, sponsorship and role modelling to a younger, less experienced protégé. In working with younger or new employees, a mentor can satisfy his or her need to have an influence on another employee's career.

Research has indicated that a majority of managers reported having had at least one mentoring relationship during their career.[31] Kram has identified two general functions of mentoring which she designated as career functions and

	Socialisation Stage	Practice
Exhibit 14.6 **A checklist of effective socialisation practices**	Anticipatory socialisation	1. Recruitment using realistic job previews 2. Selection and placement using realistic career paths
	Accommodation socialisation	1. Tailor-made and individualised orientation programs 2. Social as well as technical skills training 3. Supportive and accurate feedback 4. Challenging work assignments 5. Demanding but fair supervisors
	Role management socialisation	1. Provision of professional counselling 2. Adaptive and flexible work assignments 3. Sincere person-oriented managers

Exhibit 14.7 **Phases of the mentor relationship**

Phase	Definition	Turning Points*
Initiation	A period of 6 months to a year during which time the relationship gets started and begins to have importance for both managers	• Fantasies become concrete expectations. • Expectations are met; senior manager provides coaching, challenging work, visibility; junior manager provides technical assistance, respect and desire to be coached. • There are opportunities for interaction around work tasks.
Cultivation	A period of 2 to 5 years during which time the range of career and psychosocial functions provided expand to a maximum	• Both individuals continue to benefit from the relationship. • Opportunities for meaningful and more frequent interaction increase. • Emotional bond deepens and intimacy increases.
Separation	A period of 6 months to 2 years after a significant change in the structural role relationship and/or in the emotional experience of the relationship	• Junior manager no longer wants guidance but rather the opportunity to work more autonomously. • Senior manager faces midlife crisis and is less available to provide mentoring functions. • Job rotation or promotion limits opportunities for continued interactions; career and psychosocial functions can no longer be provided. • Blocked opportunity creates resentment and hostility that disrupt positive interaction.
Redefinition	An indefinite period after the separation phase, during which time the relationship is ended or takes on significantly different characteristics, making it a more peerlike friendship	• Stresses of separation diminish, and new relationships are formed. • The mentor relationship is no longer needed in its previous form. • Resentment and anger diminish; gratitude and appreciation increase. • Peer status is achieved.

*Examples of the most frequently observed psychological and organisational factors that cause movement into the current relationship phase.
Source: Kram, K. E. (1983). Phases of the mentor relationship, *Academy of Management Journal*, December, p. 622. Used with permission.

psychosocial functions. The career functions include sponsorship, exposure and visibility, coaching, production, and challenging assignments. The psychosocial functions are role modelling, acceptance and confirmation, counselling and friendship.[32]

Although mentoring functions can be important in socialising a person, it is not clear that a single individual must play all of these roles. New employees can obtain valuable career and psychosocial influence from a variety of individuals — managers, peers, trainers and personal friends. At Ford Motor Company, a study was conducted to develop guidelines to socialise new management trainees.

Most mentor–mentee relationships develop over time. There appear to be several distinct phases of mentor-mentee relationships. Exhibit 14.7 presents a four-phase model proposed by Kram. The reasons that cause movement in the relationship are described as turning points. Initiation, cultivation, separation and redefinition cover general time periods of 6 months to more than 5 years.

The benefits that result from mentoring can extend beyond the individuals involved. Mentoring can contribute to employee motivation, retention and the cohesiveness of the organisation.[33] The organisation's culture can be strengthened by passing the core values from one generation to the next generation.

The increasing diversity of the workforce adds a new dimension to the mentor–mentee matching process. People are attracted to mentors who talk, look, act and communicate like them. Gender, race, ethnicity and religion can all play a role in matching. If mentor–mentee matching is left to occur naturally, minority groups may be left out.[34] The under-representation of these groups in management level positions needs to be evaluated in each company that considers using mentor–mentee matching. One study showed that cross-gender mentor relationships can be beneficial. The results of thirty-two mentor–mentee pairings (fourteen male–female; eighteen female–female) found that male–female mentor matchings can be successful.[35]

SOCIALISING A CULTURALLY DIVERSE WORKFORCE

Our society consists of people with many religions, many cultures and many different roots: European, Middle Eastern, Mediterranean, Asian, Pacific Islander and Anglo-Saxon. This gives us a very diverse workforce. It is important that managers learn to value diversity in the workplace. As differences in the workforce increase, managers will have to study socialisation much more closely and intervene so that the maximum benefits result from hiring an increasingly ethnically diverse workforce. Studying the ethnic background and national cultures of these workers will have to be taken seriously. The managerial challenge will be to identify ways to integrate the increasing number and mix of people from diverse national cultures into the workplace. Some obvious issues for managers of ethnically diverse workforces to consider are these:

- coping with employees' unfamiliarity with the English language;
- increased training for service jobs that require verbal skills;
- cultural (national) awareness training for the current workforce;
- learning which rewards are valued by different ethnic groups;
- developing career development programs that fit the skills, needs, and values of the ethnic group;
- rewarding managers for effectively recruiting, hiring, and integrating a diverse workforce;
- spending time not only focusing on ethnic diversity, but also learning more about age, gender, and workers with disability diversity.

Socialising involving an ethnically diverse workforce is a two-way proposition. The manager must learn about the employees' cultural background, but also the employee must learn about the rituals, customs and values of the firm or the work unit.[36] Awareness workshops and orientation sessions are becoming more

GLOBAL   Encounter

Learning about diversity

Learning about other ethnic groups, races and religions has become an important organisational issue in terms of showing understanding about the totality of other people. Let's simply list a number of points that students, managers and people in general should know about.

- What race are Hispanics? Black, white or brown? The correct answer is all of the above. Hispanic refers not only to a race, but also to an origin or an ethnicity. There are Hispanic segments — Cubans, Puerto Ricans, Mexicans, Salvadorans and others who are different in their indigenous ancestry, origins, accents and many other characteristics.
- What is Confucianism? Confucianism is the major religious influence on Chinese, Japanese, Korean and Vietnamese cultures. Confucianism emphasises response to authority, especially parents and teachers; hard work; discipline and the ability to delay gratification; harmony in relationships; and the importance of the group.
- Does the term African-American apply to all blacks? No. Black Americans came from different cultures besides those in Africa, Caribbean, Central

American and South American cultures have provided the USA with many talented blacks. Just as there is in the general population, there is great variety in lifestyle, career choice, educational level attained, and value systems across segments of the over 30 million Black American (includes African and other cultural backgrounds population).

Should a manager know what the terms Hispanic, Confucianism and African-American mean? We think so, and believe that cultural and religious awareness are going to become more important as the workforce increases in terms of race, ethnic and religious diversity. Managers and leaders in organisations need to develop a style and pattern of behaviour that appeals to and reaches all segments of the diverse workforce. Although the USA has never had a homogeneous culture or population, it is now not possible to ignore the mix of diverse workers, colleagues, customers, suppliers and owners facing the organisation.

Source: Adapted from Naisbitt, J. (1994). *Global Paradox*. New York: Morrow, pp.227–235; and Rossman, M. L. (1994). *Multicultural Marketing*. New York: AMACOM, pp. 46–52.

popular every day. Merck began an educational program in 1979 to raise its employees' awareness and attitudes about women and minorities.[37] The program emphasises how policies and systems can be tailored to meet changes in the demographics of the workplace. Procter & Gamble has stressed the value of diversity. The company uses multicultural advisory teams, minority and women's networking conferences, and 'onboarding' programs to help new women and minority employees become acclimatised and productive as quickly as possible. Ortho Pharmaceutical initiated a program to 'manage diversity' that is designed to foster a process of cultural transition within the company. Northeastern Products Company established an on-site English as a Second Language (ESL) program to meet the needs of Asian employees. A buddy system has been established at Ore-Ida. A buddy (English speaker) is assigned to a new employee (first language is not English) to assist him or her with communication problems.

Global competition, like changing domestic demographics, is placing a new requirement on managers to learn about unfamiliar cultures from which new employees are coming. The emphasis on open expression of diversity in the workforce is paralleled by a social movement toward the retention of ethnic roots. The 'new ethnicity', a renewed awareness and pride of cultural heritage, can become an advantage of Australian companies operating in foreign countries.[38] Using the multicultural workforce to better compete, penetrate and succeed in foreign cultures is one potential benefit of managing diversity effectively.

Certainly, claiming that having employees from different cultural backgrounds only provides benefits is misleading. Ethnic and cultural diversity creates some potential problems such as communications, misunderstanding and responding to authority. The managers involved in this socialisation process need to clearly recognise the benefits and the potential problems of working with a more diverse workforce.

SOCIALISATION AS AN INTEGRATION STRATEGY

Our discussion has emphasised the interrelationships between socialisation processes and career effectiveness. Yet it is possible to view socialisation as a form of organisational integration. Specifically, socialisation from the integration perspective is a strategy for achieving congruence of organisational and individual goals. Thus, socialisation is an important and powerful process for transmitting the organisational culture.[39] The content of socialisation strategies are practices and policies that have appeared in many places throughout this text. Here we can not only summarise our discussion of socialisation processes but also cast some important organisation behaviour concepts and theories in a different framework.

Organisational integration is achieved primarily by aligning and integrating the goals of individuals with the objectives of organisations. The greater the congruity between individual goals and organisation objectives, the greater the integration. The socialisation process achieves organisation integration by, in effect, undoing the individual's previously held goals and creating new ones that come closer to those valued by the organisation. In its most extreme form, this undoing process involves debasement techniques such as those experienced by army recruits; less extreme, but having the same purpose, are the initiation rites of many university colleges.

SUMMARY OF KEY POINTS

Define the terms 'organisational culture' and 'socialisation'. Culture is a pattern of assumptions that are invented, discovered or developed to learn to cope with organisational life. Socialisation is the process by which organisations bring new employees into the culture.

Explain why it is too simplistic to assume that managers can state that they are creating a company's culture. Simply declaring that 'this' will be the culture is not realistic. Culture evolves

over a period of time. It can be influenced by powerful individuals such as Ray Kroc at McDonald's, but it typically evolves and becomes real when people interact and work together.

Describe the stages of organisational socialisation. Organisational socialisation passes through three phases. During anticipatory socialisation it involves information gathering on the part of the individual. During this phase, individuals decide whether the values of the organisation match their needs and values, and the organisation makes a similar assessment of the individual. When individuals join an organisation, they enter the accommodation phase of socialisation. In this phase they must learn their roles and identify the skills necessary for performing their job; they must also learn and adapt to the organisational culture. Finally, individuals enter the role management phase of socialisation, in which they must learn to manage conflicts between competing roles, for example between home and work roles.

List socialisation strategies and their consequences. Socialisation strategies fall broadly into two groups: individualised and institutionalised. Individualised programs are less structured and less likely to instil in employees a particular way of doing tasks. In contrast, institutionalised strategies are aimed at developing a high level of conformity with existing organisational practices. Consequently, we see high levels of role innovation when individuals undergo individualised socialisation, but high levels of commitment when they undergo institutionalised socialisation.

Describe six areas of organisational knowledge necessary for socialisation. Individuals need to acquire knowledge in the following areas: performance proficiency — skill and role requirements; people — identifying the right person to provide information about the organisation, tasks and roles; politics — the identification of power structures and knowledge bases within the organisation; language — the jargon of the workplace; organisational goals and values — the formal and informal norms; history — traditions, myths and rituals.

Discuss the relationship between mentoring and socialisation. Senior staff in an organisation can mentor newcomers. In doing so, they provide valuable information concerning role requirements and work norms; they may also create networks and open doors otherwise closed to newcomers. In this way, mentors provide valuable information about the core values of an organisation and assist in the socialisation process.

Identify specific practices and programs used by organisations to facilitate socialisation. The success of socialisation depends on how well the socialisation activities meet the needs of the individual and the organisation at each career

stage. Usual organisational practices such as recruitment, selection and placement can be important parts of an effective socialisation process if management thinks of them as meeting individual as well as organisational needs.

REVIEW AND DISCUSSION QUESTIONS

1. Since the process of organisational socialisation is inevitable, why is it important that it be managed?

2. In Chapter 4 the concept of a psychological contract was introduced. Is there a relationship between the psychological contract and the socialisation process? Explain.

3. Is it likely that individuals can have a successful career in organisations and not be socialised? Does being properly socialised ensure career success?

4. Identify the three stages of socialisation. Which of these stages is the most important for developing high-performing employees? Explain.

5. Organisational socialisation cannot simultaneously create high levels of innovation and high organisational commitment. Discuss.

6. Organisational culture is a difficult concept to diagnose. How would you diagnose the culture of an office or a manufacturing plant?

7. How would you describe the culture of your university? How do you think this affects the organisational practices adopted by the university?

8. Apply the three stages of socialisation to your first year at university. How well socialised are you? What do you think has prevented effective socialisation? What impact has this had on your effectiveness?

ENDNOTES

1   Hoover, G., Campbell, A., & Spain, P. S. (Eds.) (1990). *Profiles of over 500 Major Corporations.* Austin, TX: Reference Press Inc.

2   Pettegrew, A. M. (1979). On studying cultures, *Administrative Science Quarterly*, 579–581.

3   Jongeward, D. (1973). *Everybody Wins: Transactional Analysis Applied to Organizations.* Reading: MA.: Addison-Wesley.

4   Schein, E. H. (1985). *Organizational Culture and Leadership.* San Franscisco: Jossey-Bass.

5 Hofstede, G. (1991). *Culture and Organizations.* New York: McGraw-Hill, pp. 8–10.

6 Hofstede, G. (1983). National cultures in four dimensions, *International Studies of Management and Organization,* 31–42.

7 Ronen, S., & Shenkar, O. (1985). Clustering countries on attitudinal dimensions: A review and synthesis, *Academy of Management Review,* 435–454.

8 Smircich, L. (1983). Concepts of culture and organizational analysis, *Administrative Science Quarterly,* 339–358.

9 Holt, J., & Kabanoff, B. (1995). Organisational value systems and HRM systems: A configurational study. Working Paper Series, School of Industrial Relations and Organisational Behaviour, University of New South Wales.

10 Saffold, G. S., III. (1988). Culture traits, strength and organizational performance: Moving beyond strong culture, *Academy of Management Review,* 546–558.

11 Ouchi, W. (1982). *Theory Z: How American Business Can Meet the Japanese Challenge.* Reading, MA: Addison-Wesley.

12 Peters, T. J., & Waterman, R. H. (1982). *In Search of Excellence.* New York, Harper & Row.

13 Deal, T. A., & Kennedy, A. A. (1982). *Corporate Cultures: The Rites and Rituals of Corporate Life.* Reading, MA: Addison-Wesley.

14 Reynolds, P. C. (1987). Imposing a corporate culture, *Psychology Today,* 33–38.

15 Schein, E. H. (1985). *Organizational Culture and Leadership.* San Franscisco: Jossey-Bass.

16 Trice, H. M., & Beyer, J. M. 1985). Using organizational rites to change culture. In R. H. Kilman, M. J. Saxton, & R. Serpa (Eds.) *Gaining Control of the Corporate Culture.* San Franscisco: Jossey-Bass.

17 Sathe, V. (1983). Implications of corporate culture: A manager's guide to action, *Organizational Dynamics,* 4–13.

18 O'Reilly, C. A., III, Chatman, J., & Caldwell, D. F. (1991). People and organizational culture: A profile comparison to assessing person–organisation fit, *Academy of Management Journal,* 487–516.

19 Feldman, D., & Brett, J. M. (1983). Coping with new jobs: A comparative study of new hires and job changers, *Academy of Management Journal,* 258–272.

20 Wanous, J. P., Reichers, A. E., & Malik, S. D. (1984). Organisational socialisation and group development: Toward an integrative perspective, *Academy of Management Review,* 670–683. This article reviews widely accepted models of socialisation.

21 These stages are identified by Feldman, D.C. (1976), A contingency theory of socialization, *Administrative Science Quarterly,* 434–435. The following discussion is based heavily on this work, as well as D.C. Feldman (1976), A practical program for employee socialization, *Organizational Dynamics,* 64–80; and Feldman, D. C. (1981). The multiple socialization of organizational members, *Academy of Management Review,* 309–318.

22 Feldman, D. C. (1976). A practical program for employee socialization, *Organizational Dynamics,* 64–80.

23 Jones, G. E. (1983). Psychological orientation and the process of organizational socialization: An interactionist perspective, *Academy of Management Review,* 464–474.

24 Allen, N. J., & Meyer, J. P. (1990). Organizational socialization tactics: A longitudinal analysis of links to newcomers' commitment and role orientation, *Academy of Management Journal,* **33**, 847–858.

25 Van Maanen, J., & Schein E. H. (1979). Towards a theory of organizational socialisation. In B. M. Staw (Ed.) *Research in Organizational Behavior,* (vol. 1). Greenwich, CT: JAI Press.

26 Chao, G. T., O'Leary-Kelly, A. M., Wolf, S., Klein, H. J., & Gardner, P. D. (1994). Organizational socialization: Its content and consequences, *Journal of Applied Psychology,* **79**, 730–743.

27 Van Maanen, J. (1978). People processing: Strategies for organizational socialization, *Organizational Dynamics,* 18–36.

28 The following discussion reflects the research findings of Feldman, D. C. (1976). A practical program for employee socialization, *Organizational Dynamics,* 64–80.

29 Hall, D. T., & Hall, F. S. (1976). What's new on career management, *Organizational Dynamics,* 21–27.

30 Fisher, C. D. (1983). The role of social support in organizational socialization, *Academy of Management Proceedings.*

31 Burke, R. J., & McKeen, C. A. (1990). Mentoring in organizations: Implications for women, *Journal of Ethics,* 322.

32 Kram, K.E. (1983). Phases of the mentor relationship, *Academy of Management Journal,* 608–625.

33 Wilson, J. A., & Elman, N. S. (1990). Organizational benefits of mentoring, *Academy of Management Executive*, 88–94.

34 Wilson, J. A., & Elman, N. S. (1990). Organizational benefits of mentoring, *Academy of Management Executive*, 88–94.

35 Brown, R. D. (1986). The role of identification in mentoring female protégés, *Group and Organization Studies*, 72.

36 Cox, T., Jnr. (1991). The multicultural organization, *Academy of Management Executive*, 34–47.

37 Jamieson, D., & O'Mara, J. (1991). *Managing Workforce 2000*. San Francisco: Jossey-Bass.

38 Garfield, C. (1992). *Second to None*. Homewood, IL.: Business One Irwin.

39 Hebden, J. E. (1986). Adopting an organization's culture: The socialization of graduate trainees, *Organizational Dynamics*, 46–72.

READING 14 LEVELS OF CULTURE

Source: Geert Hofstede, *Cultures and Organizations* (New York: McGraw-Hill, 1991, pp. 3–19).

11th juror: (rising) *'I beg pardon, in discussing . . .'*
10th juror: (interrupting and mimicking) *'I beg pardon. What are you so goddamn polite about?'*
11th juror: (looking straight at the 10th juror) ' *For the same reason you're not. It's the way I was brought up.'*
— From Reginald Rose, *Twelve Angry Men*

Twelve Angry Men is an American theatre piece which became a famous motion picture starring Henry Fonda. The play was written in 1955. The scene consists of the jury room of a New York court of law. Twelve jury members who have never met before have to decide unanimously on the guilt or innocence of a boy from a slum area, accused of murder. The quote above is from the second and final act when emotions have reached a boiling point. It is a confrontation between the tenth juror, a garage owner, and the eleventh juror, a European-born, probably Austrian, watchmaker. The tenth juror is irritated by what he sees as the excessively polite manners of the other man. But the watchmaker cannot behave otherwise. After many years in his new home country, he still behaves the way he was raised. He carries within himself an indelible pattern of behaviour.

Different minds but common problems

The world is full of confrontations between people, groups, and nations who think, feel, and act differently. At the same time, these people, groups, and nations, just like our twelve angry men, are exposed to common problems which demand cooperation for their solution. Ecological, economical, military, hygienic, and meteorological developments do not stop at national or regional borders. Coping with the threats of nuclear warfare, acid rain, ocean pollution, extinction of animals, AIDS, or a worldwide recession demands cooperation of opinion leaders from many countries. They in their turn need the support of broad groups of followers in order to implement the decisions taken.

Understanding the differences in the ways these leaders and their followers think, feel, and act is a condition for bringing about worldwide solutions that work. Questions of economics, technological, medical, or biological cooperation have too often been considered as merely technical. One of the reasons why so many solutions do not work or cannot be implemented is because differences in thinking among the partners have been ignored. Understanding such differences is at least as essential as understanding the technical factors.

The objective of this book is to help in dealing with the differences in thinking, feeling, and acting of people around the globe. It will show that, although the variety in people's minds is enormous, there is a structure in this variety which can serve as a basis for mutual understanding.

Culture as mental programming

Every person carries within him or herself patterns of thing, feeling, and potential acting which were learned through their lifetime. Much of it has been acquired in early childhood, because at that time a person is most susceptible to learning and assimilating. As soon as certain patterns of thinking, feeling, and acting have established themselves within a person's mind, (s)he must unlearn these before being able to learn something different, and unlearning is more difficult than learning for the first time.

Using the analogy of the way in which computers are programmed, this book will call such patterns of thinking, feeling, and acting *mental programs*, or, as the sub-title goes, '*software of the mind*'. This does not mean, of course, that people are programmed the way computers are. A person's behavior is only partially predetermined by her or his mental programs: (s)he has a basic ability to deviate from them, and to react in ways which are new, creative, destructive, or unexpected. The '*software of the mind*' this book is about only indicates what reactions are likely and understandable, given one's past.

The sources of one's mental programs lie with the social environments in which one grew up and are collected in one's life experiences. The programming starts within the family; it continues within the neighborhood, at school, in youth groups, at the workplace, and in the living community. The European watchmaker from the quote at the beginning of this chapter came from a country and a social class in which polite behavior is still at a premium today. Most people from that environment would have reacted as he did. The American garage owner, who worked himself up from the slums, acquired quite different mental programs. Mental programs vary as much as the social environments in which they were acquired.

A customary term for such mental software is *culture*. This word has several meanings, all derived from its Latin source, which refers to the tilling of the soil. In most Western languages, 'culture' commonly means 'civilization' or 'refinement of the mind' and in particular the results of such refinement, like education, art, and literature. This is 'culture in the narrow sense': I sometimes call it 'culture one'. Culture as mental software, however, corresponds to a much broader use of the word which is common among social anthropologists: this is 'culture two', and it is the concept which will be used throughout this book.

Social (or cultural) anthropology is the science of human societies, in particular

(although not only) traditional or 'primitive' ones. In social anthropology, 'culture' is a catchword for all those patterns of thinking, feeling, and acting referred to in the previous paragraphs. Not only those activities supposed to refine the mind are included in 'culture two', but also the ordinary and menial things in life: greeting, eating, showing or not showing feelings, keeping a certain physical distance from others, making love, or maintaining body hygiene. Politicians and journalists sometimes confuse culture two and culture one without being aware of it: the adaptation problems of immigrants to their new host country are discussed in terms of promoting folk dance groups. But culture two deals with much more fundamental human processes than culture one; it deals with the things that hurt.

Culture (two) is always a collective phenomenon, because it is at least partly shared with people who live or lived within the same social environment, which is where it was learned. It is *the collective programming of the mind which distinguishes the members of one group or category[1] of people from another.*[2]

Culture is learned, not inherited. It derives from one's social environment, not from one's genes. Culture should be distinguished from human nature on one side, and from an individual's personality on the other (see Exhibit 14.8), although exactly where the borders lie between human nature and culture, and between culture and personality, is a matter of discussion among social scientists.

Human nature is what all human beings, from the Russian professor to the Australian

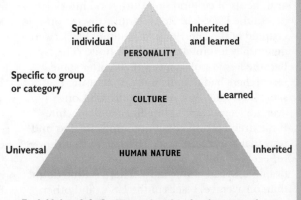

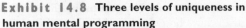

Exhibit 14.8 **Three levels of uniqueness in human mental programming**

Aborigine, have in common: it represents the universal level in one's mental software. It is inherited with one's genes; within the computer analogy it is the 'operating system' which determines one's physical and basic psychological functioning. The human ability to feel fear, anger, love, joy, sadness, the need to associate with others, to play and exercise oneself, the facility to observe the environment and to talk about it with other humans all belong to this level of mental programming. However, what one does with these feelings, how one expresses fear, joy, observations, and so on, is modified by culture. Human nature is not as 'human' as the term suggests, because certain aspects of it are shared with parts of the animal world.[3]

The *personality* of an individual, on the other hand, is her/his unique personal set of mental programs which (s)he does not share with any other human being. It is based upon traits which are partly inherited with the individual's unique set of genes and partly learned. 'Learned' means: modified by the influence of collective programming (culture) *as well as* unique personal experiences.

Cultural traits have often been attributed to heredity because philosophers and other scholars in the past did not know how to explain otherwise the remarkable stability of differences in culture patterns among human groups. They underestimated the impact of learning from previous generations and of teaching to a future generation what one has learned oneself. The role of heredity is exaggerated in the pseudo-theories of *race*, which have been responsible, among other things, for the Holocaust organized by the Nazis during the Second World War. Racial and ethnic strife is often justified by unfounded arguments of cultural superiority and inferiority.

In the USA, a heated scientific discussion erupted in the late 1960s on whether blacks were genetically less intelligent than whites.[4] The issue became less popular in the 1970s, after some researchers had demonstrated that, using the same logic and tests, Asians in the USA on average scored *more* in intelligence than whites. It is extremely difficult, if not impossible, to find tests that are culture free. This means that they reflect only ability, not the differences in, for example, social opportunity. There is little doubt that, on average, blacks in the USA (and other minority and even majority groups in other countries) have fewer *opportunities* than whites.

Cultural relativism

The student of culture finds human groups and categories thinking, feeling, and acting differently, but there are no scientific standards for considering one group as intrinsically superior or inferior to another. Studying differences in culture among groups and societies presupposes a position of cultural relativism.[5] Claude Lévi-Strauss, the grand old man of French anthropology, has expressed it as follows:

Cultural relativism affirms that one culture has no absolute criteria for judging the activities of another culture as 'low' or 'noble'. However, every culture can and should apply such judgment to its own activities, because its members are actors as well as observers.[6]

Cultural relativism does not imply normlessness for oneself, nor for one's society. It does call for suspending judgment when dealing with groups or societies different from one's own. One should think twice before applying the norms of one person, group, or society to another. Information about the nature of the cultural differences between societies, their roots, and their consequences should precede judgment and action.

Even after having been informed, the foreign observer is still likely to deplore certain ways of the other society. If (s)he is professionally involved in the other society, for example as an expatriate manager or development assistance expert, (s)he may very well want to induce changes. In colonial days, foreigners often wielded absolute power in other societies and they could impose their rules on it. In these postcolonial days, foreigners who want to change something in another society will have to negotiate their interventions. Again, negotiation is more likely to succeed when the parties concerned understand the reasons for the differences in viewpoints.

Symbols, heroes, rituals, and values

Cultural differences manifest themselves in several ways. From the many terms used to describe manifestations of culture, the following four together cover the total concept rather neatly: symbols, heroes, rituals, and values. In Exhibit 14.9, these are illustrated as the skins of an onion, indicating that symbols represent the most superficial and values the deepest

Exhibit 14.9 **The 'onion diagram':
Manifestations of culture at different levels
of depth**

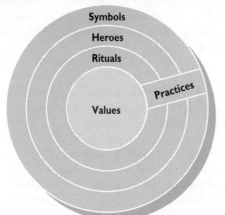

manifestations of culture, with heroes and rituals in between.

Symbols are words, gestures, pictures, or objects that carry a particular meaning which is only recognized by those who share the culture. The words in a language or jargon belong to this category, as do dress, hairstyles, Coca-Cola, flags, and status symbols. New symbols are easily developed and old ones disappear; symbols from one cultural group are regularly copied by others. This is why symbols have been put into the outer, most superficial layer of Exhibit 14.9.

Heroes are persons, alive or dead, real or imaginary, who possess characteristics which are highly prized in a culture, and who thus serve as models for behavior. Even phantasy or cartoon figures, like Batman or, as a contrast, Snoopy in the US, Asterix in France, or Ollie B. Bommel (Mr Bumble) in the Netherlands, can serve as cultural heroes. In this age of television, outward appearances have become more important in the choice of heroes than they were before.

Rituals are collective activities, technically superfluous in reaching desired ends, but which, within a culture, are considered as socially essential; they are therefore carried out for their own sake. Ways of greeting and paying respect to others, and social and religious ceremonies are examples. Business and political meetings organized for seemingly rational reasons often serve mainly ritual purposes, like allowing the leaders to assert themselves.

In Exhibit 14.9, symbols, heroes, and rituals have been subsumed under the term *practices*. As

such, they are visible to an outside observer; their cultural meaning, however, is invisible and lies precisely and only in the way these practices are interpreted by the insiders.

The core of culture according to Exhibit 14.9 is formed by *values*. Values are broad tendencies to prefer certain states of affairs over others. Values are feelings with an arrow to it; they have a plus and a minus side. They deal with:

evil *vs* good
dirty *vs* clean
ugly *vs* beautiful
unnatural *vs* natural
abnormal *vs* normal
paradoxical *vs* logical
irrational *vs* rational

Values are among the first things children learn — not consciously, but implicitly. Development psychologists believe that by the age of 10, most children have their basic value system firmly in place, and after that age, changes are difficult to make. Because they were acquired so early in our lives, many values remain unconscious to those who hold them. Therefore they cannot be discussed, nor can they be directly observed by outsiders. They can only be inferred from the way people act under various circumstances.

For systematic research on values, inferring them from people's actions is cumbersome and ambiguous. Various paper-and-pencil questionnaires have been developed which ask for people's preferences among alternatives. The answers should not be taken too literally; in practice, people will not always act as they have scored on the questionnaire. Still the questionnaires provide useful information because they show differences in answers between groups or categories of respondents. For example, suppose a question asks for one's preference for time off from work versus more pay. An individual employee who states (s)he prefers time off may in fact choose the money if presented with the actual choice, but if in group A more people claim preferring time off than in group B, this does indicate a cultural difference between these groups in the relative value of free time versus money.

In interpreting people's statements about their values, it is important to distinguish between the *desirable* and the *desired*: how people think the world ought to be versus what people want for themselves. Questions about the desirable refer to people in general and are worded in terms of right/wrong, agree/disagree, or something similar. In the abstract, everybody is in favor of virtue and opposed to sin, and answers about the desirable express people's views about what represents virtue and what corresponds to sin. The desired, on the contrary, is worded in terms of 'you' or 'me' and what we consider important, what we want for ourselves, including our less-virtuous desires. The desirable bears only a faint resemblance to actual behavior, but even statements about the desired, although closer to actual behavior, should not necessarily correspond to the way people really behave when they have to choose.

What distinguishes the desirable from the desired is the nature of the *norms* involved. Norms are the standards for values that exist within a group or category of people.[7] In the case of the desirable, the norm is absolute, pertaining to what is ethically right. In the case of the desired, the norm is statistical; it indicates the choices actually made by the majority. The desirable relates more to ideology, the desired to practical matters.

Interpretations of value studies which neglect the difference between the desirable and the desired may lead to paradoxical results. A case in which the two produced diametrically opposed answers was found in the IBM studies (see later in this chapter). Employees in different countries were asked for their agreement or disagreement with the statement 'Employees in industry should participate more in the decisions made by management'. This is a statement about the desirable. In another question, people were asked whether they personally preferred a manager who 'usually consults with subordinates before reaching a decision'. This is a statement about the desired. A comparison between the answers to these two questions revealed that employees in countries where the manager who consults was less popular, agreed more with the general statement that employees should participate more, and vice versa; maybe the ideology served as a compensation for the day-to-day relationship with the boss (Hofstede, 1980, p. 109; 1984, p. 82).

Layers of culture

As almost everyone belongs to a number of different groups and categories of people at the same time, people unavoidably carry several layers of mental programming within themselves, corresponding to different levels of culture. For example:

- A national level according to one's country (or countries for people who migrated during their lifetimes);
- A regional and/or ethnic and/or religious and/or linguistic affiliation level, as most nations are composed of culturally different regions and/or ethnic and/or religious and/or language groups;
- A gender level, according to whether a person was born as a girl or as a boy;
- A generation level, which separates grandparents from parents from children;
- A social class level, associated with educational opportunities and with a person's occupation or profession; and
- For those who are employed, an organizational or corporate level according to the way employees have been socialized by their work organization.

Additions to this list are easy to make. The mental programs from these various levels are not necessarily in harmony. In modern society they are often partly conflicting: for example, religious values may conflict with generation values, gender values with organizational practices. Conflicting mental programs within people make it difficult to anticipate their behavior in a new situation.

National culture differences

Human societies have existed for at least 10 000 years, possibly much longer. Archaeologist believe that the first humans led a nomadic existence as hunter-gatherers. After many thousands of years, some of them settled down as farmers. Gradually, some farming communities grew into larger settlements, which become towns, cities, and finally modern megalopolises like Mexico City with over 25 million inhabitants.

Different human societies have followed this development to different extents, so that hunter-gatherers survive even today (according to some, the modern urban yuppie has reverted to a hunting-gathering state). As the world became more and more populated, an amazing variety of answers was found to the basic question of how people can live together and form some kind of a structured society.

In the fertile areas of the world, large empires had already been built several thousand years ago, usually because the rulers of one part succeeded in conquering other parts. The oldest empire in existence within living memory is China. Although it had not always been unified, the Chinese empire possessed a continuous history of about 4 000 years. Other empires disintegrated: in the eastern Mediterranean and southwestern part of Asia, empires grew, flourished, and fell, only to be succeeded by others: the Sumerian, Babylonian, Assyrian, Egyptian, Persian, Greek, Roman, and Turkish states, to mention only a few. The south Asian subcontinent and the Indonesian archipelago had their empires, such as the Maurya, the Gupta, and later the Moghul in India, and the Majapahit on Java; in Central and South America, the Aztec, Maya, and the Inca empires have left their monuments. In Africa, Ethiopia, and Benin are examples of ancient states.

Next to and often within the territory of these larger empires, smaller units survived in the form of tribes or independent small 'kingdoms.' Even now, in New Guinea most of the population lives in small and relatively isolated tribes, each with its own language, and hardly integrated into the larger society.

The invention of 'nations', political units into which the entire world is divided and to one of which every human being is supposed to belong — as manifested by her or his passport — is a recent phenomenon in human history. Earlier, there were states, but not everybody belonged to one of these or identified with one. The nation system was only introduced worldwide in the mid-twentieth century. It followed the colonial system which had developed during the preceding three centuries. In this colonial period, the technologically advanced countries of Western Europe divided among themselves virtually all the territories of the globe which were not held by another strong political power. The borders between the ex-colonial nations still reflect the colonial legacy. In Africa, particularly, national borders correspond more to the logic of the colonial powers than to the cultural dividing lines of the local populations.

Nations, therefore, should not be equated to *societies*. Historically, societies are organically developed forms of social organization, and the concept of a common culture applies, strictly speaking, more to societies than to nations. Nevertheless, many nations do form historically developed wholes even if they consist of clearly

different groups and even if they contain less-integrated minorities.

Within nations that have existed for some time there are strong forces towards further integration: (usually) one dominant national language, common mass media, a national education system, a national army, a national political system, national representation in sports events with a strong symbolic and emotional appeal, a national market for certain skills, products, and services. Today's nations do not attain the degree of internal homogeneity of the isolated, usually nonliterate societies studied by field anthropologists, but they are the source of a considerable amount of common mental programming of their citizens.[8]

On the other hand, there remains a tendency for ethnic, linguistic, and religious groups to fight for recognition of their own identity, if not for national independence; this tendency has been increasing rather than decreasing in the later part of the twentieth century. Examples are the Ulster Roman Catholics, the Belgian Flemish, the Basques in Spain and France, the Kurds in Iran, Iraq, Syria, and Turkey, and many of the ethnic groups in the Soviet Union.

In research on cultural differences, nationality — the passport one holds — should therefore be used with care. Yet it is often the only feasible criterion for classification. Rightly or wrongly, collective properties are ascribed to the citizens of certain countries; people refer to 'typically American', 'typically German', or 'typically Japanese' behavior. Using nationality as a criterion is a matter of expediency, because it is immensely easier to obtain data for nations than for organic homogeneous societies. Nations as political bodies supply all kinds of statistics about their populations. Survey data, i.e., the answers of people on paper-and-pencil questionnaires related to their culture, are also mostly collected through national networks. Where it is possible to separate results by regional, ethnic, or linguistic group, this should be done.

A strong reason for collecting data at the level of nations is that one of the purposes of the research is to promote cooperation among nations. As was argued at the beginning of this chapter, the (over 200) nations that exist today populate one single world and we either survive or perish together. So it makes practical sense to focus on cultural factors separating or uniting nations.

Dimensions of national cultures

In the first half of the twentieth century, social anthropology has developed the conviction that all societies, modern or traditional, face the same basic problems; only the answers differ. American anthropologists, in particular Ruth Benedict (1887–1948) and Margaret Mead (1901–1978), played an important role in popularizing this message for a wide audience.

The logical next step was that social scientists attempted to identify *what* problems were common to all societies, through conceptual reasoning and reflection upon field experiences, as well as through statistical studies. In 1954, two Americans, the sociologist Alex Inkeles and the psychologist Daniel Levinson, published a broad survey of the English-language literature on national culture. They suggested that the following issues qualify as common basic problems worldwide, with consequences for the functioning of societies, of groups within those societies, and of individuals within those groups:

1. Relation to authority.
2. Conception of self, in particular:
   a. The relationship between individual and society; and
   b. The individual's concept of masculinity and femininity.
3. Ways of dealing with conflicts, including the control of aggression and the expression of feelings. (Inkeles and Levinson, 1969, pp. 447ff.)

Twenty years later I was given the opportunity of studying a large body of survey data about the values of people in over 50 countries around the world. These people worked in the local subsidiaries of one large multinational corporation — IBM. At first sight, it may seem surprising that employees of a multinational — a very special kind of people — could serve for identifying differences in *national* value systems. However, from one country to another they represent almost perfectly matched samples; they are similar in all respects except nationality, which makes the effect of nationality differences in their answers stand out unusually clearly.

A statistical analysis of the answers on questions about the values of similar IBM employees in different countries revealed common problems, but with solutions differing from country to country, in the following areas:

1. Social inequality, including the relationship with authority;
2. The relationship between the individual and the group;
3. Concepts of masculinity and femininity — the social implications of having been born as a boy or a girl; and
4. Ways of dealing with uncertainty, relating to the control of aggression and the expression of emotions.

These empirical results covered amazingly well the areas predicted by Inkeles and Levinson 20 years before. The discovery of their prediction provided strong support for the theoretical importance of the empirical findings. Problems which are basic to all human societies should turn up in different studies regardless of the approaches followed. The Inkeles and Levinson study is not the only one whose conclusions overlap with mine, but it is the one most strikingly predicts what I found.[9]

The four basic problem areas defined by Inkeles and Levinson and empirically found in the IBM data represent *dimensions* of cultures. A dimension is an aspect of a culture that can be measured relative to other cultures. The basic problem areas correspond to dimensions which I named *power distance* (from small to large), *collectivism* versus *individualism*, *femininity* versus *masculinity*, and *uncertainty avoidance* (from weak to strong). Each of these terms existed already in some part of the social sciences, and they seemed to apply reasonably well to the basic problem area each dimension stands for. Together they form a four-dimensional (4-D) model of differences among national cultures. Each country in this model is characterized by a score on each of the four dimensions.

A dimension groups together a number of phenomena in a society which were empirically found to occur in combination, even if at first sight there does not always seem to be a logical necessity for their going together. The logic of societies, however, is not the same as the logic of the individuals looking at them. The grouping of the different aspects of a dimension is always based on statistical relationships, that is, on *trends* for these phenomena to occur in combination, not on iron links. Some aspects in some societies may go against a general trend found across most other societies. Because they are found with the help of statistical methods, dimensions can only be detected on the basis of information about a certain number of countries — say, at least 10. In the case of the IBM research, I was fortunate to obtain comparable data about culturally determined values from 50 countries and three multicountry regions, which made the dimensions within their differences stand out quite clearly.

More recently, a fifth dimension of differences among national cultures was identified, opposing a *long-term orientation* in life to a *short-term orientation*. The fact that it had not been encountered earlier can be attributed to a cultural bias in the minds of the various scholars studying culture, including myself. We all shared a 'Western' way of thinking. The new dimension was discovered when Michael Harris Bond, a Canadian located in the Far East for many years, studied people's values around the world using a questionnaire composed by 'Eastern', in this case Chinese, minds. Besides adding this highly relevant new dimension, Bond's work showed the all-pervading impact of culture; even the minds of the researchers studying it are programmed according to their own particular cultural framework.

The scores for each country on one dimension can be pictured as points along a line. For two dimensions at a time, they become points in a diagram. For three dimensions, they could, with some imagination, be seen as points in space. For four or five dimensions, they become difficult to envisage. This is a disadvantage of the dimensional model. Another way of picturing differences among countries (or other social systems) is through *typologies* instead of dimensions. A typology describes a number of ideal types, each of them easy to imagine. Dividing counties into the First, Second, and Third World is such a typology. A more sophisticated example is found in the work of the French political historian Emmanuel Todd, who divides the cultures of the world according to the family structure traditionally prevailing in that culture. He arrives at eight types, four of which occur in Europe. Todd's thesis is that these historically preserved family structures explain the success of a particular type of political ideology in a country (Todd, 1983).

Whereas typologies are easier to grasp than dimensions, they are still problematic in empirical research. Real cases seldom fully correspond to one single ideal type. Most cases are hybrids, and arbitrary rule have to be made for classifying them as belonging to one of the types. With a dimensional model, on the contrary, cases can always be scored unambiguously. On the basis of their dimension scores, cases can *afterwards* empirically be sorted into clusters with similar scores. These clusters then form an empirical typology. More than 50 countries in the IBM study could, on the basis of their 4-D scores, be sorted into 13 such clusters.[10]

In practice, typologies and dimensional models can be considered as complementary. Dimensional models are preferable for research but typologies for teaching purposes. This book will use a kind of typology approach for explaining each of the five dimensions. For every separate dimension, it describes the two opposite extremes, which can be seen as ideal types. Some of the dimensions are subsequently taken two by two, which creates four ideal types. However, the country scores on the dimensions will show that most real cases are somewhere in between the extremes pictured.

Cultural differences according to region, religion, gender, generation, and class

Regional, ethnic, and *religious* cultures account for differences within countries; ethnic and religious groups often transcend political country borders. Such groups form minorities at the crossroads between the dominant culture of the nation and their own traditional group culture. Some assimilate into the mainstream, although this may take a generation or more; others continue to stick to their own ways. The US as the world's most prominent example of a people composed of immigrants, shows examples of both assimilation (the 'melting pot') and retention of group identities over generations (an example are the Pennsylvania Dutch). Discrimination according to ethnic origin delays assimilation and represents a problem in many countries. Regional, ethnic, and religious cultures can be described in the same terms as national cultures; basically, the same dimensions which were found to differentiate among national cultures apply to these differences within countries.

Religious affiliation by itself is less culturally relevant than is often assumed. If we trace the religious history of countries, then the religion a population has embraced along with the version of that religion seem to have been a *result* of previously existing cultural value patterns as much as a *cause* of cultural differences. The great religions of the world, at some time in their history, have all undergone profound schism: between Roman Catholics, Eastern Orthodox, and various Protestant groups in Christianity; between Sunni and Shia in Islam; between liberals and various fundamentalist groups in Jewry; between Hinayana and Mahayana in Buddhism. Cultural differences among groups of believers have always played a major role in such schisms. For example, the Reformation movement within the Roman Catholic Church in the sixteenth century initially affected all of Europe. However, in countries which more than a thousand years earlier had belonged to the Roman Empire, a Counter-Reformation reinstated the authority of the Roman church. In the end, the Reformation only succeeded in countries without a Roman tradition. Although today most of Northern Europe is Protestant and most of Southern Europe Roman Catholic, it is not this religious split which is at the origin of the cultural differences between North and South but the inheritance of the Roman Empire. This does not exclude that once a religion has settled, it does reinforce the value patterns on the basis of which it was adopted by making these into core elements in its teachings.

Gender differences are not usually described in terms of culture. It can be revealing to do so. If we recognize that within each society there is a men's culture which differs from a women's culture, this helps to explain why it is so difficult to change traditional gender roles. Women are not considered suitable for jobs traditionally filled by men, not because they are technically unable to perform these jobs, but because women do not carry the symbols, do not correspond to the hero images, do not participate in the rituals or foster the values dominant in the men's culture; and vice versa. Feelings and fears about behaviors by the opposite sex are of the same order of intensity as the reactions of people exposed to foreign cultures.

Generation differences in symbols, heroes, rituals, and values are evident to most people. They are often over-estimated. Complaints about youth having lost respect for the values of their elders have been found on Egyptian papyrus scrolls dating from 2000 BC and in the writings of Hesiod, a Greek author from the end of the eighth century BC. Many differences in practices and values between generations will be just normal attributes of age which repeat themselves for each successive pair of generations. Historical events, however, do affect some generations in a special way. The Chinese who were of student age during the Cultural Revolution stand witness to this. The development of technology also leads to a difference between generations which is unique.

Not all values and practices in a society, however, are affected by technology or its products. If young Turks drink Coca-Cola, this does not necessarily affect their attitudes towards authority. In some respects, young Turks differ from old Turks, just as young Americans differ from old Americans. Such differences often involve the relatively superficial spheres of symbols and heroes, of fashion and consumption. In the sphere of values, i.e., fundamental attitudes towards life and towards other people, young Turks differ from young Americans just as much as old Turks differed from old Americans. There is no evidence that the cultures of present-day generations from different countries are converging.

Social classes carry different class cultures. Social class is associated with educational opportunities and with a person's occupation or profession; this even applies in countries which their governments call socialist, preaching a classless society. Education and occupation are in themselves powerful sources of cultural learning. There is no standard definition of social class which applies across all countries, and people in different countries distinguish different types and numbers of class. The criteria for allocating a person to a class are often cultural; symbols play an important role, such as accents in speaking the national language, the use and nonuse of certain words, and manners. The confrontation between the two jurors in *Twelve Angry Men* also contains a class component.

Gender, generation, and class cultures can only partly be classified by the four dimensions found for national cultures. This is because they are not *groups* but *categories* of people. Countries (and ethnic groups too) are integrated social systems. The four dimensions apply to the basic problems of such systems. Categories like gender, generation, or class are only parts of social systems and therefore not all dimensions apply to them. Gender, generation, and class cultures should be described in their own terms, based on special studies of such cultures.

Organizational cultures

Organizational or corporate cultures have been a fashionable topic since the early 1980s. At that time, the management literature began to popularize the claim that the 'excellence' of an organization is contained in the common ways by which its members have learned to think, feel and act. 'Corporate culture' is a soft, holistic concept with, however, presumed hard consequences. I once called it 'the psychological assets of an organization, which can be used to predict what will happen to its financial assets in five years' time'.

Organization sociologists have stressed the role of the soft factor in organizations for more than half a century. Using the label 'culture' for the shared mental software of the people in an organization is a convenient way of repopularizing these sociological views. Yet organizational 'cultures' are a phenomenon *per se*, different in many respects from national cultures. An organization is a social system of a different nature than a nation; if only because the organization's members usually had a certain influence in their decision to join it, are only involved in it during working hours, and may one day leave it again.

Research results about national cultures and their dimensions proved to be only partly useful for the understanding of organizational cultures. The part of this book which deals with organizational culture differences (Chapter 8) is not based on the IBM studies but on a special research project carried out by IRIC, the Institute for Research on Intercultural Cooperation, within 20 organizational units in Denmark and the Netherlands.

Endnotes

1 A *group* means a number of people in contact with each other. A *category* consists of people who, without necessarily having contact, have something in common: e.g., all women managers, or all people born before 1940.

2 The concept of a 'collective programming of the mind' resembles the concept of *habitus*

proposed by the French sociologist Pierre Bourdieu: 'Certain conditions of existence produce a *habitus*, a system of permanent and transferable dispositions. A habitus ... functions as the basis for practices and images ... which can be collectively orchestrated without an actual conductor'. (Bourdieu, 1980, pp. 88–89, translation by GH).

3 'Sociobiology' is an area of study which tries to illustrate how some human social behaviors have analogies in the animal world. From these analogies, sociobiology infers that these social behaviors are biologically (i.e. genetically) determined. See Wilson (1975); for criticisms see Gregory *et al.*, (eds.) (1978).

4 The name of Professor A. R. Jensen is linked with the genetic inferiority thesis.

5 US professor Allan Bloom warns against a cultural relativism in American universities which he calls 'nihilism', but he uses the word 'culture' in the sense of 'culture one'. (Bloom, 1988, first published in the US in 1987.)

6 Translation by GH from Lévi-Strauss and Eribon (1988, p. 229).

7 In popular parlance, the words 'norm' and 'value' are often used indiscriminately, or the twin expression 'values and norms' is handled as an inseparable pair, like Laurel and Hardy. In this latter case, one of the two words is redundant.

8 Some nations are less culturally integrated than others. Examples are some of the ex-colonies and multilingual, multiethnic countries such as Yugoslavia, Belgium, or Malaysia. Yet even in these countries, ethnic and/or linguistic groups which consider themselves as very different from each other may have common traits in comparison to the populations of other countries. I have shown this to be the case for the two language groups of Belgium (1980, pp.335 ff; 1984, pp. 228 ff).

9 See Hofstede (1980 or 1984) for the first analysis covering 40 countries, and Hofstede (1983, pp. 335–55) for a later extension.

10 Hofstede (1980, p. 334; 1984, p. 229) shows 11 clusters among the first 40 countries studied, and the later article in Hofstede (1983, p. 346) extends this to 13 clusters among 50 countries and three regions.

EXERCISE 14 ASSESSING AND CONSIDERING ORGANISATIONAL CULTURE

Listed below are what two researchers refer to as specific manifestations of organisational culture. Enterprises over a period of time illustrate or use these cultural factors to strengthen and perpetuate the culture. Some of the widely publicised companies such as Harley-Davidson, Merck, Nike, Compaq Computer, Bennetton, Honda, Nestlé, Hershey, and Coca-Cola have distinct and strongly influential cultures.

Rite A relatively elaborate, dramatic planned set of activities that combines various forms of cultural expressions and that often has both practical and expressive consequences.

Ritual A standardised, detailed set of techniques and behaviours that manages anxieties but seldom produces intended, practical consequences of any importance.

Myth A dramatic narrative of imagined events, usually used to explain origins or transformations of something; also, an unquestioned belief about the practical benefits of certain techniques and behaviours that is not supported by demonstrated facts.

Saga A historical narrative of some wonderful event that has a historical basis but has been embellished with fictional detail.

Folktale A completely fictional narrative.

Symbol Any object, act, event, quality, or relation that serves as a vehicle for conveying meaning, usually by representing another thing.

Language A particular manner in which members of a group use vocal sounds and written signs to convey meanings to each other.

Gesture Movements of parts of the body used to express meanings.

Physical setting Those things that physically surround people and provide them with immediate sensory stimuli as they carry out culturally expressive activities.

Artifact Material objects manufactured by people to facilitate culturally expressive activities.

The instructor will divide the class into groups of five or six to discuss each of the manifestations in terms of: (1) a company the students have worked in, and (2) a popular company such as the widely publicised enterprises listed above. The groups should also discuss the following:

1. How managers can influence the cultural factors listed in the table.
2. Which of the factors listed in the table apply to the school/university they are now attending.
3. Why culture can influence the morale of employees.

The exercise can be completed in one or two classes (45–90 minutes). After the group discusses the questions and issues in the first class, a second class can be used to review each group's considerations and findings.

CASE 14 THE CONSOLIDATED LIFE CASE: CAUGHT BETWEEN CORPORATE CULTURES

Source: Weiss, J., Wahlstrom, M., & Marshall, E. (1986). *Journal of Management Case Studies*, Fall 238–243.

The authors thank Duncan Spelman and Anthony Buono for their helpful comments on this text.

Part I

It all started so positively. Three days after graduating with his degree in business administration, Mike Wilson started his first day at a prestigious insurance company — Consolidated Life. He worked in the Policy Issue Department. The work of the department was mostly clerical and did not require a high degree of technical knowledge. Given the repetitive and mundane nature of the work, the successful worker had to be consistent and willing to grind out paperwork.

Rick Belkner was the division's vice-president, 'the man in charge' at the time. Rick was an actuary by training, a technical professional whose leadership style was *laissez-faire*. He was described in the division as 'the mirror of whomever was the strongest personality around him'. It was also common knowledge that Rick made US$60 000 a year while he spent his time doing crossword puzzles.

Mike was hired as a management trainee and promised a supervisory assignment within a year. However, because of a management reorganisation, it was only 6 weeks before he was placed in charge of an eight-person unit.

The reorganisation was intended to streamline work flow, upgrade and combine the clerical jobs, and make greater use of the computer system. It was a drastic departure from the old way of doing things and created a great deal of animosity and anxiety among the clerical staff.

Management realised that a flexible supervisory style was necessary to pull off the reorganisation without immense turnover, and so they gave their supervisors a free hand to run their units as they saw fit. Mike used this latitude to implement group meetings and training classes in his unit. In addition he assured all members that they would receive raises if they worked hard to attain them. By working long hours, participating in the mundane tasks with his unit, and being flexible in his management style, he was able to increase productivity, reduce errors, and reduce lost time. Things improved so dramatically that he was noticed by upper management and earned a reputation as a 'superstar' despite being viewed as free spirited and unorthodox. The feeling was that his loose, people-oriented management style could be tolerated because his results were excellent.

A chance for advancement

After a year, Mike received an offer from a different Consolidated Life division located across town. Mike was asked to manage an office in the marketing area. The pay was excellent and it offered an opportunity to turn around an office in disarray. The reorganisation in his present division at Consolidated was almost complete and most of his mentors and friends in management had moved on to other jobs. Mike decided to accept the offer.

In his exit interview he was assured that if he ever wanted to return, a position would be made for him. It was clear that he was held in high regard by management and staff alike. A huge party was thrown to send him off.

The new job was satisfying for a short time but it became apparent to Mike that it did not have the long-term potential he was promised. After bringing on a new staff, computerising the office, and auditing the books, he began looking for a position that would both challenge him and give him the autonomy he needed to be successful.

Eventually word got back to his former vice-president, Rick Belkner, at Consolidated Life that Mike was looking for another job. Rick offered Mike a position with the same pay he was now receiving and control over a fourteen-person unit in his old division. After considering other options, Mike decided to return to his old division feeling that he would be able to progress steadily over the next several years.

Enter Jack Greely; return Mike Wilson

Upon his return to Consolidated Life, Mike became aware of several changes that had taken place in the 6 months since his departure. The most important change was the hiring of a new divisional senior vice-president, Jack Greely. Jack had been given total authority to run the division. Rick Belkner now reported to Jack.

Jack's reputation was that he was tough but fair. It was necessary for people in Jack's division to do things his way and 'get the work out'.

Mike also found himself reporting to one of his former peers, Kathy Miller, who had been promoted to manager during the reorganisation. Mike had always 'hit it off' with Kathy and foresaw no problems in working with her.

After a week, Mike realised the extent of the changes. Gone was the loose, casual atmosphere that had marked his first tour in the division. Now, a stricter, task-oriented management doctrine was practised. Morale of the supervisory staff had decreased to an alarming level. Jack Greely was the major topic of conversation in and around the division. People joked that MBO now meant 'management by oppression'.

Mike was greeted back with comments like 'Welcome to prison' and 'Why would you come back here? You must be desperate!' It seemed like everyone was looking for new jobs or transfers. Their lack of desire was reflected in the poor quality of work being done.

Mike's idea: Supervisors' Forum

Mike felt that a change in the management style of his boss was necessary in order to improve a frustrating situation. Realising that it would be difficult to affect his style directly, Mike requested permission from Rick Belkner to form a Supervisors' Forum for all the managers on Mike's level in the division. Mike explained that the purpose would be to enhance the existing management-training program. The Forum would include weekly meetings, guest speakers, and discussions of topics relevant to the division and the industry. Mike thought the Forum would show Greely that he was serious about both his job and improving morale in the division. Rick gave the OK for an initial meeting.

The meeting took place and ten supervisors who were Mike's peers in the company eagerly took the opportunity to 'Blue Sky' it. There was a euphoric attitude about the group as they drafted their statement of intent. It read as follows:

TO: Rick Belkner
FROM: New Issue Services Supervisors
SUBJECT: Supervisors' Forum

On Thursday, 11 June, the Supervisors' Forum held its first meeting. The objective of the meeting was to identify common areas of concern among us and to determine topics that we might be interested in pursuing.

The first area addressed was the void that we perceived exists in the management-training program. As a result of conditions beyond anyone's control, many of us over the past year have held supervisory duties without the benefit of formal training or proper experience. Therefore, what we propose is that we utilise the Supervisors' Forum as a vehicle with which to enhance the existing management-training program. The areas that we hope to affect with this supplemental training are: (a) morale/job satisfaction; (b) quality of work and service; (c) productivity; and (d) management expertise as it relates to the life insurance industry. With these objectives in mind, we have outlined below a list of possible activities that we would like to pursue.

1. Further utilisation of the existing 'in-house' training programs provided for manager trainees and supervisors, that is, Introduction to Supervision, EEO, and Coaching and Counselling.
2. A series of speakers from various sections in the company. This would help expose us to the technical aspects of their departments and their managerial style.
3. Invitations to outside speakers to address the Forum on management topics such as managerial development, organisational structure and behaviour, business policy and the insurance industry. Suggested speakers could be area university professors, consultants and state insurance officials.
4. Outside training and visits to the field. This could include attendance at seminars concerning management theory and development relative to the insurance industry. Attached is a representative sample of a program we would like to have considered in the future.

In conclusion, we hope that this memo clearly illustrates what we are attempting to accomplish with this program. It is our hope that the above outline will be able to give the Forum credibility and establish it as an effective tool for all levels of management within New Issue. By supplementing our on-the-job training with a series of speakers and classes, we aim to develop prospective management personnel with a broad perspective of both the life insurance industry and management's role in it. Also, we would like to extend an invitation to the underwriters to attend any programs at which the topic of the speaker might be of interest to them.

cc: J. Greely
     Managers

The group felt the memo accurately and diplomatically stated their dissatisfaction with the current situation. However, they pondered what the results of their actions would be and what else they could have done.

Part II

An emergency management meeting was called by Rick Belkner at Jack Greely's request to address the 'union' being formed by the supervisors. Four general managers, Rick Belkner and Jack Greely were at that meeting. During the meeting it was suggested the Forum be disbanded to 'put them in their place'. However, Rick Belkner felt that, if 'guided' in the proper direction, the Forum could die from lack of interest. His stance was adopted but it was common knowledge that Jack Greely was strongly opposed to the group and wanted its founders dealt with. His comment was, 'It's not a democracy and they're not a union. If they don't like it here, then they can leave.' A campaign was directed by the managers to determine who the main authors of the memo were so they could be dealt with.

About this time, Mike's unit had made a mistake on a case, which Jack Greely was embarrassed to admit to his boss. This embarrassment was more than Jack Greely cared to take from Mike Wilson. At the managers staff meeting that day, Jack stormed in and declared that the next supervisor to 'screw up' was out the door. He would permit no more embarrassments of his division and repeated his earlier statement about 'people leaving if they didn't like it here'. It was clear to Mike and everyone else present that Mike Wilson was a marked man.

Mike had always been a loose, amiable supervisor. The major reason his units had been successful was the attention he paid to each individual and how they interacted with the group. He had a reputation for fairness, was seen as an excellent judge of personnel for new positions, and was noted for his ability to turn around people who had been in trouble. He motivated people through a dynamic, personable style and was noted for his general lack of regard for rules. He treated rules as obstacles to management and usually used his own discretion as to what was important. His office had a sign saying, 'Any fool can manage by rules. It takes an uncommon man to manage without any'. It was an approach that flew in the face of company

policy, but it had been overlooked in the past because of his results. However, because of Mike's actions with the Supervisors' Forum, he was now regarded as a thorn in the side, not a superstar, and his oddball style only made things worse.

Faced with the fact that he was rumoured to be out the door, Mike sat down to appraise the situation.

Part III

Mike decided on the following course of action:

1. Keep the Forum alive but moderate its tone so it didn't step on Jack Greely's toes.
2. Don't panic. Simply outwork and outsmart the rest of the division. This plan included a massive retraining and remotivation of his personnel. He implemented weekly meetings, cross training with other divisions, and a lot of interpersonal 'stroking' to motivate the group.
3. Evoke praise from vendors and customers through excellent service and direct the praise to Jack Greely.

The results after 8 months were impressive. Mike's unit improved the speed of processing 60% and lowered errors 75%. His staff became the most highly trained in the division. Mike had a file of several letters to Jack Greely that praised the unit's excellent service. In addition, the Supervisors' Forum had grudgingly attained credibility, although the scope of activity was restricted. Mike had even improved to the point of submitting reports on time as a concession to management.

Mike was confident that the results would speak for themselves. However, a month before his scheduled promotion and a month after an excellent merit raise in recognition of his exceptional work record, he was called into his supervisor's, Kathy Miller's, office. She informed him that after long and careful consideration the decision had been made to deny his promotion because of his lack of attention to detail. This did not mean he was not a good supervisor, just that he needed to follow more instead of taking the lead. Mike was stunned and said so. But, before he said anything else, he asked to see Rick Belkner and Jack Greely the next day.

The showdown

Sitting face to face with Rick and Jack, Mike asked if they agreed with the appraisal Kathy had discussed with him. They both said they did.

When asked if any other supervisor surpassed his ability and results, each stated Mike was one of the best, if not *the* best they had. Then why, Mike asked, would they deny him a promotion when others of less ability were approved. The answer came from Jack: 'It's nothing personal, but we just don't like you. We don't like your management style. You're an oddball. We can't run a division with ten supervisors all doing different things. What kind of a business do you think we're running here? We need people who conform to our style and methods so we can measure their results objectively. There is no room for subjective interpretation. It's our feeling that if you really put your mind to it, you can be an excellent manager. It's just that you now create trouble and rock the boat. We don't need that. It doesn't matter if you're the best now, sooner or later as you go up the ladder, you will be forced to pay more attention to administrative duties and you won't handle them well. If we correct your bad habits now, we think you can go far.'

Mike was shocked. He turned to face Rick and blurted out nervously, 'You mean it doesn't matter what my results are? All that matters is how I do things?' Rick leaned back in his chair and said in a casual tone, 'In so many words, Yes.'

Mike left the office knowing that his career at Consolidated was over and immediately started looking for a new job. What had gone wrong?

Epilogue

After leaving Consolidated Life, Mike Wilson started his own insurance, sales and consulting company, which specialised in providing corporate risk managers with insurance protection and claims-settlement strategies. He works with a staff assistant and one other associate. After 3 years, sales averaged over US$7 million annually, netting approximately US$125 000 to US$175 000 before taxes to Mike Wilson.

During a return visit to Consolidated Life, 3 years after his departure, Mike found Rick Belkner and Jack Greely still in charge of the division in which Mike had worked. The division's size had shrunk by 60% All of the members of the old Supervisors' Forum had left. The reason for the decrease in the division's size was that computerisation had removed many of the people's tasks.

Case questions

1. Can a manager such as Jack have such an impact on the culture of a workplace? Explain.
2. How was the Forum perceived by Jack?
3. What norms of expected behaviour did Mike violate, if any?
4. How could Mike have done a better job of diagnosing the culture at Consolidated Life after Jack had joined the firm?

ORGANISATIONAL CHANGE AND DEVELOPMENT

Learning objectives

- Describe *forces for organisational change.*

- Explain *the change process.*

- Discuss *various approaches for dealing with resistance to change.*

- Distinguish *between evolutionary and revolutionary approaches to change.*

- List *the defining characteristics of organisational development.*

- Describe *targets for organisational change.*

- Identify *specific development programs within the three categories of methods.*

- Understand *the importance of program evaluation.*

- Discuss *the role of change agents.*

The process by which managers sense and respond to the necessity for change has been the focus of much research and practical attention in recent years. If managers were able to design perfect sociotechnical organisations and if the scientific, market and technological environments were stable and predictable, there would be no pressure for change. But such is not the case. As just one example, consider the increasing internationalisation of the business environment and accompanying trends toward globalisation of an organisation's activities. The effective management of increasingly culturally diverse organisational environments that are the result of these changes is critical for maintaining competitiveness.[1]

The literature and practice that deal with the process of organisational change cannot be conveniently classified because of the yet-unsettled nature of this aspect of organisational behaviour. Various conceptualisations and theories, and their meanings and interpretations, are subject to considerable disagreement. Even the traditional assumptions regarding the basic nature of how organisations experience change are being rethought.[2]

In this chapter, we will consider how change can be successfully implemented. Underlying our discussions of organisational change is the assumption that successful change requires an alignment between organisational goals, organisational structure, task design, group processes and individual skills.[3] This approach emphasises the systematic nature of organisations and reminds us that when we change one part of an organisation other parts are affected. For example, if we redesign jobs to increase skill variety we must also train individuals in the new skills that they will need to use. If we decide to adopt a decentralised structure, we must also be prepared to delegate decision-making responsibility to lower levels of the organisation. And, as we will see in the section on resistance to change, we must recognise that disrupting group processes by restructuring an organisation generates a very powerful source of resistance to change. This systems perspective not only emphasises the need to treat the organisation as a whole, but also provides us with a tool for understanding the obstacles that organisations face in the change process.

FORCES FOR CHANGE

The forces for change can be classified conveniently into two groups (summarised in Exhibit 15.1): external forces and internal forces. These forces may be further classified in terms of the extent to which they are anticipated, controllable and result in planned change, or the extent to which they are not anticipated, uncontrollable and result in unplanned change.[4]

External forces

To cope effectively with external changes, an organisation's boundary functions must be sensitive to these changes. These boundary functions must bridge the external environment with units of the organisation. Boundary roles such as marketing research, labour relations, personnel recruiting, purchasing and some areas of finance must sense changes in the external environment and convey information on these changes to managers. In this section we summarise some of the external forces for change.

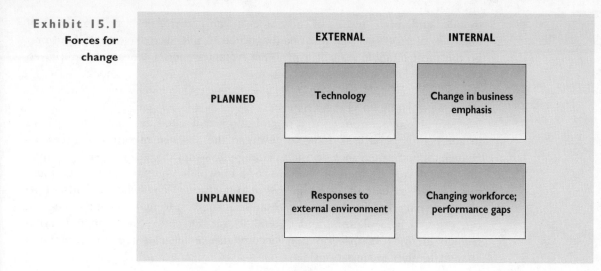

Exhibit 15.1
Forces for
change

Planned external changes

Planned external change describes a situation in which organisations decide to adopt practices that were not developed by the organisation, in order to improve organisational efficiency. Under these circumstances, organisations are able to control how the change is implemented. Probably the best example of a planned change is the introduction of new technology. The knowledge explosion has introduced new technology for nearly every business function. Computers have made possible high-speed data processing and the solution to complex production problems. New machines and new processes have revolutionised the way in which many products are manufactured and distributed. Technological advance is a permanent fixture in the business world and, as a force for change, it will continue to demand attention.

Unplanned external changes

There are occasions on which changes outside of the organisation require an immediate response. These changes were not predicted and the organisation cannot determine the pace at which it will respond to the external changes. For example, competitors introduce new products, increase their advertising, reduce their prices or increase their customer service. The company's products may no longer have customer appeal; or customers may be able to purchase less expensive, higher quality forms of the same products. Or the government may introduce legislation — smoke-free workplaces and Equal Employment Opportunity policies — that must be implemented by a particular date. In all these examples, the organisation must change its practices in order to survive.

Internal forces

Internal forces for change come from within the organisation and can usually be traced to either process or behavioural problems. The process problems include breakdowns in decision making and communication. Decisions are not being made, are made too late or are of poor quality. Communications are short-circuited, redundant or simply inadequate. Tasks are not undertaken or completed because the person responsible 'did not get the word'. Low levels of morale and high levels of absenteeism and turnover are symptoms of behavioural problems that must be diagnosed. A wildcat strike or a walkout may be the most tangible sign of a problem, yet such tactics are usually employed because they arouse management action.

Planned internal changes

We have already mentioned that organisations may need to respond to changes in competitor behaviour. However, even in the absence of external forces for change, organisations may decide to change how they do business. For example, they may decide to open on Sundays, or a chocolate company such as Cadbury may decide to extend its range by manufacturing ice-cream versions of its chocolate bars. Provided your organisation is the first to make such a change, it can proceed in a planned and systematic way. Of course, a planned internal change in one organisation may become the external force for unplanned change in other organisations!

Unplanned internal changes

Changes within the workforce may also signal the need for changes in organisational processes. Perhaps the most readily noticeable change is a gap between desired and actual levels of performance, signalling the need to reassess organisational structure, job design and organisational processes. Changes within the workforce itself also may require adaptation on the part of organisations: a better educated and slightly older workforce brings different expectations, as does a workforce in which women are increasingly returning to work. Organisations must respond to such changes of they are to avoid problems in morale, turnover and absenteeism.

UNDERSTANDING THE CHANGE PROCESS

In this section, we introduce one of the best known models of change: Kurt Lewin's three-stage process. From this model we are able to consider some sources of resistance to change, as well as the issues that need to be addressed for successful change management. Exhibit 15.2 summarises this process.

Exhibit 15.2
A model of the change process

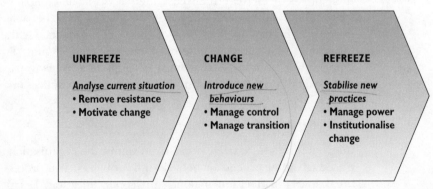

UNFREEZE	CHANGE	REFREEZE
Analyse current situation	*Introduce new behaviours*	*Stabilise new practices*
• Remove resistance	• Manage control	• Manage power
• Motivate change	• Manage transition	• Institutionalise change

Lewin's Field Theory

Have you ever tried to change your behaviour by giving up smoking? Going on a diet? Starting an exercise program? If you have, you will know that changing behaviour is more difficult than you might expect. To understand how we can successfully change behaviour, we need to understand where the motivation for this change is coming from. Think about that exercise program. What factors have motivated you to start exercising? Losing weight, improving body shape or fitness, increasing flexibility or physical wellbeing, or the start of summer are reasons for exercising. However, exercise programs take up time that could be spent socialising, working or relaxing with a book. They are effortful and — in the early stages — may be tiring. The benefits are not immediately apparent. So, we have two sets of forces acting on us: *supporting forces*, or those that are encouraging us to change our behaviour; and *restraining forces*, or those that are encouraging us to continue as we are.

Put simply, Lewin's Field Theory proposes that change occurs when supporting forces outweigh restraining forces. Applied to organisational change, his three-stage model of unfreezing, change and refreezing has been used to focus on how we generate supporting forces and eliminate restraining forces in order to successfully implement change. We will now look at this model in more detail.[5]

Stage 1: Unfreezing

In this stage, we need to generate motivation for change. At an organisational level, we need to demonstrate that the current state of affairs is unsatisfactory. We may provide individuals with statistics related to organisational performance, productivity, turnover or absenteeism as evidence that a change is required. At this stage, it is important that individuals understand the reasons for change. However, we must also deal with several individual concerns: whether there will be a place for individuals in the new organisation and the skills that individuals will require to fit in. The aim of this first stage is to generate dissatisfaction with the current state. The result should be an increase in the forces supporting change.

Stage 2: Changing

If the unfreezing stage has been successful, individuals should be ready for change. In the second stage of Lewin's process, the change is implemented: individuals learn new skills and behaviours, and acquire new values, attitudes and beliefs. These reflect the new organisational goals and lead to changes in performance. As we will see in the next section, this stage — also called the transition phase — is the most difficult and the most vulnerable. During this stage, restraining forces are building: efficiency may decline as new skills are learned, learning a new skill is difficult in its own right, and individuals often experience high levels of stress. Careful management of this phase is critical to successful change.

Stage 3: Refreezing

The final stage deals with the institutionalisation of change: making old what was new. In this stage, new policies, procedures and goals are stabilised. They become the accepted way to do things in the organisation, and individuals are able to implement the new skills that they have learned. Even at this stage, the change process is vulnerable and organisations must address two issues. The first is the reinforcement of new behaviours: a system of incentives and rewards encourages individuals to continue with new practices. The second is the need to monitor for new problems: organisations must anticipate that not all new systems and procedures will work perfectly, and have in place feedback mechanisms for locating and addressing problems.

Field Theory and the implementation of change[6]

Lewin's Field Theory provides us with a framework in which to consider the organisational change process. We can now go on to consider more specifically the tasks and problems that organisations face in implementing change. The three stages described by Lewin represent the desire to move the organisation from its current state (unfreezing) to an improved future state (refreezing). The transition phase (changing), which represents the passage from current to future states, is not only critical to the success of change attempts, but also highly vulnerable. Three issues must be addressed in this phase: resistance, control and power. In the following sections, we describe how the failure to address these issues can block organisational change and we suggest strategies for dealing with each issue.

Resistance to change

Sources of resistance. Individuals resist change for many reasons. Change threatens both security and stability: individuals must fire up old skills and acquire new skills, and also change brings with it the threat of job loss. The Organisational and Management Encounters in this chapter look at the other side of job loss: the impact on survivors. When changes are imposed, they also reduce individual autonomy and control: because they disrupt existing networks, they require individuals to develop new strategies for managing their environment. Finally, individuals may simply not recognise the need for change. Organisations must address all of these issues if they are to successfully implement change.

Motivating change. In order to encourage change, organisations must both eliminate restraining forces and build supporting forces. Of the two processes, the elimination of resistance is the more important. How can organisations do this? As we have already seen, the first strategy is to *generate dissatisfaction with the status quo.* By highlighting discrepancies between desired and actual performance, we can highlight the need for change. A second strategy available to organisations is *participation.* When individuals participate in designing strategies for addressing problems, we not only increase their understanding of the change, but also increase their commitment to change by giving them greater control. Finally, we can also offer *rewards* to individuals who adopt skills and behaviours that support the change. As we will see in the next section, organisations that use pay, appraisal and bonus systems to reward desired behaviours reinforce individuals who support new organisational structures and procedures.

ORGANISATIONAL　　Encounter

The aftermath of change

In the past 2 years, approximately 57% of Australian employers have reduced their workforce; the size of these reductions has ranged from a minimum of 10% to over 20%, with middle management the most vulnerable layer. While the aim of these reductions has been to cut costs, increase productivity and improve communication, few organisations have realised these benefits. While costs may have been cut in about half of these organisations, only about a third report increased productivity and only about one-tenth report improved communication. One of the reasons for this is that, as we will see in the Management Encounter, workforce reductions can reduce the commitment of those employees who are left behind. How do Australian companies manage change?

At Ericsson, the key had been to proceed slowly — evolutionary change has seen the downsizing of the organisation over a 3-year period. What is more, no particular layer of the organisation was targeted in these cuts; instead, all departments were trimmed. This process was accompanied by the training of over 1000 staff to reorient them and change the way that they perceived the task of managing; within the organisation, changes in procedure were accompanied by changes in responsibility at the lower levels of the organisation. The slow pace of change, the use of attrition to reduce staff numbers and training have been instrumental in the management of change at Ericsson.

At Beaurepaires, changes have been more wide sweeping and have resulted in considerable employee dissatisfaction. A reorganisation that resulted in twenty to thirty redundancies also substantially restructured the organisation: management was centralised, the organisation adopted a customer service orientation, and there was a clash between the idea that each Beaurepaires outlet was a profit centre and the strategy of removing some activities from certain outlets. The result was low morale and discontent as old career paths disappeared. To deal with concerns over the loss of business activities, Beaurepaires invested energy in emphasising the new customer service orientation; to reduce concerns about the loss of career paths, it emphasised the central role that store managers would now play; in addition it created a new pay and incentive structure, linking managers' pay to the size of stores and allowing staff to participate in a profit-share scheme. Finally, it has tried to improve organisation communication by having senior managers 'adopt' and visit stores on a regular basis, conducting state conferences and producing an in-house magazine.

Another company that is reorganising is Hewlett-Packard. The human resource manager for Hewlett-Packard has identified five key areas that must be addressed during the reorganisation: the need to clarify what will happen after downsizing, especially what the new roles and tasks will be; the need to keep staff informed about changes, especially by providing feedback about the state of the business; the need to give staff the skills to cope with changes by providing retraining where necessary; the need to plan for the different requirements of the restructured workplace, especially in terms of managing peak workloads and absences; and the need to continue to manage the process after the restructure is complete to ensure that there are no unexpected consequences. You should recognise many of these criteria as fitting into the criteria for effective change that we describe in this chapter.

Source: Forman, D. (1994). Staff need help to overcome the trauma of surviving change, *Business Review Weekly,* 11 July; James, D., & Stickels, G. (1995). Cutting staff numbers is the easy part, *Business Review Weekly,* 10 July.

MANAGEMENT

Survivor sickness: The cost of lay-offs

A lot of attention has been paid to the consequences of job loss and how individuals cope with job loss. More recently, however, researchers have turned their attention to 'survivor sickness': the consequences for those who are left behind.

According to Marks and Mirvis, it is possible to identify three emotional states after mergers: the ready, the wanting and the wrung out. Our concern is with the last two groups. The *wanting* describes that group of individuals who missed out on the job they wanted and who must now adjust to this loss. The *wrung out* are still doing the same job but the organisation has changed around them.

This Management Encounter takes a closer look at the wrung out. What happens when individuals are dissatisfied with the process? Are organisational outcomes affected? According to a series of studies conducted by Joel Brockner and his colleagues, we can expect to see a decrease in organisational commitment and an increased intention to leave the organisation. However, several factors that are under organisational control affect these outcomes. One of the factors that emerges across three studies is the perceived fairness of the decision rule used to determine lay-offs: when the decision rule is perceived as unfair, those individuals who are left behind report lower organisational commitment and a higher intention to leave.

Several other factors affect these outcomes. Prior commitment to the organisation, the adequacy of explanations provided by management, the possibility of future lay-offs, how co-workers respond to the situation, and how attached individuals were to those who lost their jobs all influence commitment and intentions to leave. Perhaps more interesting is the finding that certain combinations of these variables magnify the effects, creating especially low commitment and especially high intentions to leave.

Organisational commitment is especially low when procedural justice is violated in the lay-off process and individuals were highly committed to the organisation before lay-offs. It is also low when decision rules are unfair and managers provide an inadequate explanation of the lay-offs, when survivors had close relationships with those who lost their jobs, and when co-worker reactions were also negative. However, research has also shown that these effects can, to some extent, be offset: survivors are most likely to report lower commitment if they perceive a possibility of losing their jobs; but, organisational commitment remains high if they have the support of their supervisors. Research also suggests that the coping strategies used by survivors are critical in determining commitment: survivors who adopt task-focused coping (described in Chapter 6) report high commitment; those who adopt emotion-focused coping report low commitment.

Turnover intentions were especially high under similar conditions. As was the case for organisational commitment, several factors under organisational control affect turnover intentions. Several coping resources lower the intention to leave: optimism, a sense of mastery, and co-worker and supervisor support all decrease turnover intention, as does the use of task-focused coping strategies. Turnover intention is increased when individuals believe that they may lose their jobs, and when they adopt emotion-focused coping.

Based on these findings, what strategies would you recommend to organisations that want to offset survivor sickness? How important is procedural justice? How important is information and communication? And how can support networks be used to obtain better organisational outcomes?

Source: Armstrong-Stassen, M. (1994). Coping with transition: A study of layoff survivors, *Journal of Organizational Behavior*, **15**, 597–621; Brockner, J. et al. (1990). When it is especially important to explain why: Factors affecting the relationship between managers' explanations of a layoff and survivors' reactions to the layoff, *Journal of Experimental Social Psychology*, **26**, 389–407; Brockner, J. et al. (1992). The influence of prior commitment to an institution on reactions to perceived unfairness: The higher they are, the harder they fall, *Administrative Science Quarterly*, 241–261; Brockner, J. et al. (1993). Interactive effect of job content and context on the reactions of layoff survivors, *Journal of Personality and Social Psychology*, **64**, 187–197; Marks, M. L., & Mirvis, P. H. (1992). Rebuilding after the merger: Dealing with 'survivor sickness', *Organizational Dynamics*, 18–32.

Organisational control

Loss of control. This is the second potential block to effective change. Change disrupts existing control systems, especially those that result from formal organisational procedures. It is likely that a part of the change process will be the restructuring of procedures, with the result that patterns of control will also change. One of the problems that this creates is that it becomes more difficult to monitor performance and to take corrective action when necessary. As a result organisational performance may decline and resistance to change may increase. This is especially likely during the transition phase.

Managing the transition. The critical issue here is to ensure that performance does not deteriorate. Performance can be improved if individuals understand the goals that they are working towards. Remember that in our discussions of control theory (Chapter 4), we said that individuals are able to monitor for discrepancies between actual and desired performance and to make appropriate adjustments. This becomes especially important when formal monitoring systems break down. The first strategy for managing the transition phase is to *provide a clear image of the future.* The second strategy, *using multiple leverage points,* stems directly from the need to maintain fit between the various components of an organisation. Earlier, we said that if we change one aspect of an organisation, for example individual skills, we must also change structure, tasks and processes to support the change in skills. If we do not the pressure for stability will outweigh the pressure for change and individuals will give up their new skills. When we develop plans for change, they should include each component of the organisation and the changes in each component should be mutually supportive. Organisations must put in place *specific plans for the transition.* This is a difficult and vulnerable phase, and organisations should not leave its success to chance. Organisations can use a transition manager, who has responsibility for ensuring that the transition proceeds smoothly; supply resources for training, additional staff, consultants and skilled counsellors to ensure that change is supported; and have a transition plan that allows the organisation to determine progress towards the future state by defining responsibilities of key individuals and groups, and providing benchmarks against which to monitor performance. Finally, organisations must have *feedback mechanisms* that allow managers to determine whether changes have been implemented and also whether there are any unintended negative outcomes of those changes.

Organisational power

Shifts in power. Organisations, as we have seen, are affected by power and politics. The final block to change occurs because individuals and groups all seek to increase their power and enhance their position in an organisation. As we will see in the next section, some researchers argue that major changes represent the overthrow of a dominant power coalition by a new coalition. Even when the change is not dramatic, we can expect shifts in power to create further resistance to change. This means that, during the change process, we can expect an increase in political activity as groups and individuals try to ensure that in the new organisation they will have increased power. One of the problems that this poses is that, if powerful groups do not support the change, it is unlikely to succeed.

Ensuring the success of change. To ensure the success of change we must therefore manage the power and politics of the organisation. The most obvious means for guaranteeing successful change is to *obtain the support of key power groups.* Although different power groups may have different needs, what concerns us is how we can meet those needs and obtain support for change. Our aim is to ensure that a sufficient number of powerful groups offer their support for the change. However, we also need *leaders who support the change.* Leaders provide role models, are in a position to offer rewards and are able to inspire groups to follow their example. They are influential in the change process because they are uniquely placed to emphasise the need for change, create a vision of the future, model appropriate behaviours and reward individuals who successfully change. The third means for dealing with the politics of change is related to the *communication of a vision.* As we saw in the chapter on leadership, charismatic and transformational leaders are able to inspire their followers by creating a shared vision of the future. This helps unite powerful coalitions, and may be able to create new power bases within the organisation. Finally, organisations also need to build in stability. Political activity will continue as long as uncertainty exists. It also creates anxiety and, ultimately, becomes dysfunctional. By establishing a timetable, or by retaining some aspects of the old order, we can create a sense of stability.

Resistance revisited

Individuals require a certain amount of stability and predictability in their lives, and change, particularly major change, may threaten this basic need. Change requires adaptation and, as we saw in Chapter 6, certain adaptation requirements may lead to stress. Organisationally imposed changes in work methods, reporting relationships, task assignments, work schedules, and company policies are but a few of the changes to which employees may be asked to adapt. Thus, overcoming resistance to change is frequently a critical variable in ensuring the success of any organisational change effort.

Since every change situation is unique, each must be carefully analysed to determine the specific forces that may be operating to create resistance to that particular change. Nonetheless, some steps can be taken to minimise that resistance. Kotter and Schlesinger have identified six general approaches for dealing with the problems of resistance to change.[7]

Reading 15
Why transformation efforts fail

1. *Education and communication.* Provide facts and information through increased communication about the change. This may take the form of one-on-one discussions, group presentations, memos and reports to educated individuals prior to the change about the need for and rationale of the change.

2. *Participation and involvement.* Allow those affected by the change to have a voice in how the change will occur by allowing (and encouraging) participation in the change design and implementation. Ad hoc committees or task forces can be useful vehicles for increasing involvement in this approach.

3. *Facilitation and support.* Provide training and socioemotional support for dealing with the change. This can be accomplished by instructional sessions,

effective listening and counselling, and assistance in overcoming performance pressures that frequently arise in change situations.

4. *Negotiation and agreement.* Offer incentives to actual or potential resisters. This may take the form of bargaining over various aspects of the change and making trade-offs to accommodate the concerns of those affected.

5. *Manipulation and cooptation.* Use covert attempts to influence individuals and selectively provide information so that desired changes receive maximum support. It should be noted that this approach can lead to future problems if people feel they are being manipulated.

6. *Explicit and implicit coercion.* Use power and threats of undesirable consequences to resisters if they do not comply with changes. While this can be very successful in overcoming resistance, it is also very risky in that it may result in the formation of undesirable attitudes and subsequent dysfunctional behaviour on the part of those coerced.

Resistance to change is not inevitable. Individuals successfully adapt to change constantly; many changes are in fact sought out and welcomed. Managers who wish to maximise acceptance of organisational change would do well to consider the attributes of changes that individuals voluntarily make and readily accept. Taking a trip abroad, moving to a new house and getting married are all examples of such changes. To varying degrees these changes have a number of attributes in common: They are planned in advance; a great deal of information is available about the change; the change satisfies one or more important needs; there is anticipation that the change will be a positive experience; and it is the individual's choice to experience the change. The greater the extent to which planned organisational change incorporates these attributes, the less likely it is to encounter resistance.

In addition to the general issue of overcoming resistance to change that is so critical to change programs, certain limiting conditions may also significantly affect the success of such efforts. Researchers identify three sources of influence on the outcomes of management development programs, and these can be generalised to cover the entire range of organisational change programs. The three sources are leadership climate, formal organisation considerations, and organisational culture.

Leadership climate refers to the nature of the work environment that results from the leadership style and management practices of superiors. Any program that does not have the support and commitment of management has only a slim chance of success. The *formal organisation* must be compatible with the proposed change. The formal organisation includes the philosophy and policies of top management as well as legal precedent, organisational structure and the systems of control.

Finally, the *organisational culture* refers to the impact on the environment resulting from group norms, values and informal activities. A proposed change in work methods, for example, can run counter to the expectations and attitudes of a work group, and if this is the case, resistance will be encountered.

CHANGE: EVOLUTION OR REVOLUTION?

As you saw in the previous section, there are multiple forces for change acting on organisations. When changes are unplanned, organisations must respond rapidly if they are to survive. However, the nature of the changes that they make can differ.[8] First-order changes are slow and adaptive in nature: they do not require changes in an organisation's fundamental principles, policies, goals or procedures. They may affect only some parts of an organisation, and are described as being linear and continuous. We can consider them as refinements of existing methods. First-order changes are *evolutionary changes*. Second-order changes are more dramatic. They require a fundamental reconceptualisation of how the organisation does its business, possibly even what its business is. They affect all levels of the organisation, and involve changes to organisational goals, procedures and values. Because they overturn existing ways of doing business, second-order changes are described as discontinuous. They represent change by *revolution*.

Whether change by evolution or revolution is more effective depends on the goals that an organisation is trying to achieve. In this section, we consider one model of change by evolution, and also discuss the conditions under which evolutionary and revolutionary change occurs.

Change by evolution

Several models describe the process of change by evolution. This approach to change emphasises the need to proceed slowly, allowing individuals time to adapt to the changes that are being introduced. A key feature of such models is a highly participative approach, designed to obtain the commitment of all individuals affected by the change. The major themes of these models have been summarised into a six-step model of change management:[9]

1. *Joint diagnosis of the problem.* It is important that individuals have an understanding of the problems that have created a need for change. The best way to achieve this is to involve those affected by the problem to determine exactly what that problem is. This stage must therefore involve not only top management but also those individuals who are directly affected by potential changes. At the end of this stage, there should be a shared understanding of the problem.

2. *Develop a shared vision of the future.* In this stage, individuals must develop a clear understanding of how the organisation will look after the changes. More importantly, they must understand where they will fit in: what their new roles and responsibilities will be. A clear vision at this stage allows individuals to assess whether new procedures allow them to achieve the organisational goal; and it also enables them to determine the skills they need to develop in order to work towards new organisational goals.

3. *Create consensus, competence and commitment.* It is important that organisations invest resources in supporting changes. By offering skills training to create competence, and incentives for adopting new organisational goals, organisations can encourage individuals to adopt those goals. A

supportive environment encourages consensus and motivation by providing opportunities to use new skills, and rewarding individuals who do.

4. *Implement changes bottom-up.* This step acknowledges that organisational change cannot be prescriptive. According to this model, different areas will find different strategies and procedures for achieving new organisational goals. Because different areas will adopt different strategies, and because they will vary in the speed with which changes are implemented, change cannot be implemented top-down. According to this model, new organisational structures and processes must be allowed to develop out of the strategies and procedures adopted in work areas. As new roles emerge, so new organisational structures will follow. Management should emphasise the need to achieve new goals, rather than specifying the means for doing so.

5. *Institutionalise the change.* Once individuals and work areas have developed new roles and identified new skills, and are working towards new goals, the organisation must realign itself. At this stage — when individual behaviour has stabilised — the organisation must consider its formal policies and organisational systems. It must address the question of whether these systems support individuals in working towards new goals. Targets for change at this stage include compensation systems, performance appraisal processes, and training and development activities.

6. *Establish feedback and adjustment processes.* As we saw in Chapter 12 on decision making, decision makers are engaged in an ongoing process of matching actual to desired goals, and a continual reassessment of strategy. The same process applies to organisational change. Institutionalisation does not mean that the change process has ended. Organisations must monitor the situation for unintended, negative consequences and new problems, and be prepared to make adjustments to address these issues.

Change as punctuated equilibrium

Gersick[10] provides an alternative perspective on change. She argues that organisations alternate between periods of evolution and revolution, with each stage achieving different goals. Her analysis of organisational change is based on the idea — discussed earlier — that organisations are stable entities that resist change. Structure, policy and procedure all create a high level of inertia that must be overcome for change to take place. As a result, organisations prefer to make small (evolutionary) changes that are less effortful; only when their survival is threatened will they make larger (revolutionary) changes. As a consequence, organisations pass through both evolutionary and revolutionary phases.

Equilibrium periods

Equilibrium periods represent phases of relative stability. Organisations do not question their goals, values or purpose; nor do they question the means for achieving those goals. This does not mean that there is no change; however, we could describe the change as peripheral or incremental. Organisations finetune their procedures in response to internal or external pressures, but do not re-evaluate those procedures. Why are organisations predisposed to equilibrium? According to Gersick's analysis there are three categories of reasons:

1. *cognitive*, or the inability to conceive of doing things differently;
2. *motivational*, related to uncertainty and fear of failure; and
3. *obligations*, or the responsibilities to organisational stakeholders.

Not surprisingly, these categories match the sources of resistance that we identified earlier.

Revolutionary periods

During periods of revolution, organisations reassess their goals, values and procedures. The organisation is thrown into chaos, and from this emerges a new set of values, goals and procedures. Why do organisations succumb to revolution? According to Gersick's analysis, there are two reasons: first, internal changes in one aspect of the organisation result in a misalignment between its components and, consequently, poorer functioning; second, there are external changes that put into doubt the organisation's long-term survival.

Punctuated equilibrium

According to Gersick, organisations display punctuated equilibrium. That is, they show prolonged periods of stability, punctuated by revolutionary change. For as long as possible, organisations will respond to both internal and external forces for change by making incremental adjustments to existing procedures. This is because, among other reasons, incremental adjustments maintain existing power structures. However, the result of such incremental, unplanned and uncoordinated adjustments is that, eventually, all organisational components are misaligned with each other and the environment. At that point, the organisation's efficiency declines and a revolutionary period follows. Once new norms — and possibly new power structures — emerge, the organisation settles into another period of equilibrium.

ORGANISATIONAL DEVELOPMENT: PLANNED CHANGE

Exercise 15
Organisation
development at
J. P. Hunt

Organisation development (OD) describes an approach to organisation change that is both systematic and long-lasting. As we will see in the next section, it takes as its targets all areas of the organisation: the interpersonal and social processes of the organisation; the values, beliefs and attitudes of work groups; and organisational structure and process. It has as its aim the creation of an organisation that is constantly changing and adapting. OD aims to change organisation, group and individual processes to better equip the organisation for diagnosing and solving problems. As a result, it is long-term and system-wide.[11] Specifically, organisation development can be defined as:

a long-range planned effort to improve an organisation's operations through a more effective utilisation of organisational resources.

Three major subobjectives are changing attitudes or values, modifying behaviour, and inducing change in policy and structure.[12] However, it is conceivable that an OD strategy might emphasise one or other of these subobjectives. For example, if the structure of an organisation is optimal in management's view, the OD process might attempt to educate personnel to adopt behaviours consistent with that structure. Such would be the case for leadership training in participative management in an organisation that already has an organic structure. Regardless of whether one, two or all three subobjectives are emphasised, the desired end result of virtually any OD effort is improved organisational functioning.

Organisational development, as the term is used in contemporary management practice, has certain distinguishing characteristics:

- **It is planned.** OD is a data-based approach to change that involves all of the ingredients that go into managerial planning. It involves goal setting, action planning, implementation, monitoring and taking corrective action when necessary.

- **It is problem-oriented.** OD attempts to apply theory and research from a number of disciplines, including behavioural science, to the solution of organisational problems.

- **It reflects a systems approach.** OD is both systemic and systematic. It is a way of more closely linking the human resources and potential of an organisation to its technology, structure and management processes.

- **It is an integral part of the management process.** OD is not something done to the organisation by outsiders. It becomes a way of managing organisational change processes.

- **It is not a 'fix-it' strategy.** OD is a continuous and ongoing process. It is not a series of ad hoc activities designed to implement a specific change. It takes time for OD to become a way of life in the organisation.

- **It focuses on improvement.** The emphasis of OD is on improvement. It is not just for 'sick' organisations or for 'healthy' ones. It is something that can benefit almost any organisation.

- **It is action-oriented.** The focus of OD is on accomplishments and results. Unlike approaches to change that tend to describe how organisational change takes place, the emphasis of OD is on getting things done.

- **It is based on sound theory and practice.** OD is not a gimmick or a fad. It is solidly based on the theory and research of a number of disciplines.[13]

These characteristics of contemporary organisational development indicate that managers who implement OD programs are committed to making fundamental changes in organisational behaviour.

CHANGE THROUGH ORGANISATION DEVELOPMENT[14]

Case 15
Community
Services
Victoria: New
management and
quality of service

The aim of OD interventions is to change organisational outcomes. Essentially, if OD interventions are successful, it is because change agents have successfully altered the work environment. The aim is to change individuals and their behaviour and, as a result, to alter system effectiveness. OD interventions are successful when individuals are able to communicate openly, behave collaboratively and engage in problem solving; are prepared to take responsibility, respect and support others; and are willing to experiment and maintain a shared vision. Managers can increase the chance that OD interventions will succeed by promoting a vision, generating participation and information exchange, and by being willing to develop others.

Consistent with a systems perspective of organisational change, OD interventions target all areas of the organisation. Remember, however, that their aim is to alter the processes that maintain the organisation. With this in mind, we can review possible targets for change, summarised in Exhibit 15.3. OD may target one of four areas: organising arrangements, social processes, technology or physical setting. Within any of these areas, OD may target processes at the individual, group or organisational level. The aim of interventions is to maintain alignment between these four components of the work setting.

Effective organisational change and development requires the active involvement of managers. Managers have a variety of change and development methods to select from, depending on the objectives they hope to accomplish. Although they may target any of the four areas listed above, the most frequent targets for OD interventions are organising arrangements, social factors and technology. In this section, we review strategies that can be used to achieve change in these key areas. The Local and Global Encounters in this chapter consider OD practice in Australia, New Zealand and Asia.

Organising arrangements

Changes to *organising arrangements* can target organisational structure, policies and procedures; goals and strategies; and administrative and reward systems.

Structural development in the context of organisational change refers to managerial action that attempts to improve effectiveness through a change in the formal structure of task and authority relationships. The organisational structure creates the bases for relatively stable human and social relationships, and these relationships can, in time, become irrelevant for organisational effectiveness. For example, the jobs that people do may become obsolete and thus irrelevant. But to change the jobs also changes the relationships among the employees. Members of the organisation may resist efforts to disrupt these relationships.

Structural changes affect some aspects of the formal task and authority definitions. As you have seen, the design of an organisation involves the definition and specification of job range and depth, the grouping of jobs in departments, the determination of the size of the groups reporting to a single manager, and the delegation of authority. Two methods designed to change all or some aspect of the organisational structure are management by objectives and System 4.

Exhibit 15.3 **Targets and OD interventions**

Target	Level				
	Individual	**Interpersonal**	**Intragroup**	**Intergroup**	**Organisational**
Organising arrangements	Flexible work hours	Role analysis	Quality circles	Contingency approach to design	Open systems planning
Social factors	T-Groups	Conflict management	Team building	Collaboration	Culture change
Technology	Job design	Role negotiation	Autonomous work groups	Nil	Sociotechnical systems design

Management by objectives

Management by objectives (MBO) encourages managers to participate in the establishment of objectives for themselves and their units.[15] The process can also include the participation of non-managers in the determination of their specific objectives. Successful use of MBO depends on the ability of participants to define their objectives in terms of their contribution to the total organisation and to be able to accomplish them.

The original work of Drucker[16] and subsequent writings by others provide the basis for three guidelines for implementing MBO:

1. Superiors and subordinates meet to discuss objectives that contribute to overall goals.
2. Superiors and subordinates jointly establish attainable objectives for the subordinates.
3. Superiors and subordinates meet at a predetermined later date to evaluate the subordinates' progress toward the objectives.

The exact procedures employed in implementing MBO vary from organisation to organisation and from unit to unit.[17] However, the basic elements of objective setting, participation of subordinates in objective setting, and feedback and evaluation are usually parts of any MBO program. The intended consequences of MBO include improved contribution to the organisation, improved attitudes and satisfaction of participants, and greater role clarity. MBO is highly developed and widely used in business, health care and governmental organisations.

System 4 organisation

System 4 organisation (so named because it is posited to represent the fourth and highest stage on a theoretical scale of organisation evolution) is an important application in the organic organisational design. Moreover, according to Likert, System 4 is an 'ideal type' of organisation for achieving high levels of performance, and any deviation from the ideal (System 4) represents reduced

The organisation, the expert and the individual: Three perspectives on organisational change

In this Encounter we consider some of the issues related to organisational change: What strategies do organisations use and with what effect? Does culture affect how change is perceived? When is an OD expert effective? How do individuals cope with mergers?

The organisation

Dexter Dunphy and Doug Stace, at the Australian Graduate School of Management, surveyed thirteen Australian service organisations to determine how these organisations approached change and with what effect. These researchers classified change strategies along two dimensions: scale of change and style of management. The scale of change ranged from fine tuning to corporate transformation, and their survey showed that the majority of organisations fell somewhere between: although they aimed for transformational change, it was modular change stopping short of a complete organisational overhaul. The level of collaboration was used to define management style, which ranged from highly collaborative through to coercive. According to this survey, the majority of organisations used a directive management style to implement change. Perhaps the most interesting result was the finding that the degree of change was related to post-change performance. Organisations who, after the change, were identified as poor performers had combined fine tuning with either consultative or directive management strategies. Medium to high performers, who maintained fit with the environment, combined these management strategies with either incremental adjustments or modular transformations. Those organisations that regained their fit did so by effecting major changes through directive or coercive management coupled with corporate transformation. Overall, this suggests that increasing fitness was related to — in Gersick's terms — revolutionary change.

The culture

Changes to power and control are both sources of resistance in the change process. If organisational cultures can be defined in terms of power, then it is likely that the culture itself will affect how individuals perceive and react to change. Boris Kabanoff and co-workers at the Australian Graduate School of Management have examined precisely this issue. They distinguished four types of organisational culture, based on how power (equal or unequal) and resources (equality or equity principles) are distributed within an organisation. The four types are elite (unequal, equity), meritocratic (equal, equity), leadership (unequal, equality) and collegial (equal, equality). These researchers found that only collegial organisations described change in positive terms, emphasising the benefits that would accrue. The remaining organisations all described the impact if change in negative terms: change was seen to result from negative circumstances, and was associated with fear and threat (elite), or stress and pain (leadership). However, even within this negative perspective, the remaining three cultures perceived change somewhat differently. Whereas employees in elite organisations viewed change as a means for increasing organisational strength, leadership organisations tended to associate change with weakness. Moreover, whereas leadership organisations assigned different roles in the change process to managers and non-managers, meritocratic organisations focused on employee participation in what was perceived as a dynamic process.

The expert

In this chapter we consider, in some detail, organisation development as a planned change strategy. We also consider the role of OD experts in this process. Research by Michael O'Driscoll at Waikato University in New Zealand has examined the skills that OD practitioners need in order to be perceived as effective. In a survey of New Zealand and American companies, O'Driscoll and Eubanks first examined the extent to which experts and their clients agree on the skills utilised by OD consultants; they then went on to look at how these skills related to perceived effectiveness. They found that, in comparison to the OD consultants' descriptions of their activities, clients reported that consultants spent more time defining their roles and responsibilities ➤

◀

and less time collecting and interpreting relevant information, managing group processes, implementing the intervention, and maintaining client relationships. They also perceived the interventions to be slightly less effective than did the consultants. There was, however, substantial agreement on the two most important factors for OD effectiveness. These were data utilisation and the setting of specific goals. When OD consultants learned the language and culture of the organisation, used the information that they had collected and broke problems into smaller parts, they were perceived as more effective. This suggests that, independent of how OD activities are perceived, a high level of involvement with the organisation is necessary if interventions are to be effective.

The individual

Finally, Victor Callan and Celia Dickson at the University of Queensland consider how individuals respond to mergers. We have already considered some of the organisational factors related to survivor sickness. In this research, the focus is on individual coping strategies. Their research examined the individual and contextual factors that are associated with different types of coping: appraisal, task-focused and emotion-focused. First, they found that when the

change involved high levels of disruption — changes in location or personnel practices — all coping strategies were invoked more frequently, suggesting that this is the most stressful component of the merger. A second component is the level of uncertainty that the merger creates, and individuals are most likely to deal with this uncertainty by attempting to obtain more information and engaging in problem solving (both task-focused) and outbursts of emotion. When individuals believe they have adequate information, and were satisfied with the information that they received, they are less likely to have emotional outbursts. This implies that uncertainty reduction is an important feature of merger management and that organisations should go to great effort to provide adequate information.

Source: Callan, V. J., & Dickson, C. (1992). Managerial coping strategies during organizational change, *Asia-Pacific Journal of Human Resources*, 47–59; Dunphy, D., & Stace, D. (1993). The strategic management of corporate change, *Human Relations*, **46**, 905–920; Kabanoff, B., Waldersee, R., & Cohen, M. (1995). Espoused values and organizational change themes, *The Academy of Management Journal*, **38**, 1075–1104; O'Driscoll, M. P., & Eubanks, J. L. (1993). Behavioral competencies, goal setting and OD practitioner effectiveness, *Group & Organizational Management*, **18**, 308–327.

levels of performance. Thus, managers should develop their organisations towards System 4 characteristics. According to Likert, an organisation can be described in terms of eight characteristics.[18] They are leadership, motivation, communication, interaction, decision making, goal setting, control and performance.

Furthermore, each of these characteristics can be measured through the use of a questionnaire which members of the organisation (usually managers) complete. The 51-item questionnaire devised by Likert asks respondents to indicate their perceptions or the extent to which the characteristics that define the System 4 organisation are present in their own organisation. Subsequent training programs emphasise the concepts of System 4 and the application of the concepts to the present organisation. According to Likert, higher performance ordinarily should result through the use of supportive, group-oriented leadership, and equalisation of authority to set goals, implement control and make decisions. The improved performance derives from positive changes in employee attitudes that are induced by the changes in organisational structure.

Social factors

Directly, or indirectly, all organisation development efforts involve the individuals in the organisation. However, the technological and structural changes that we have described typically change individual behaviour in a fairly specific and narrow direction. In this section, we will consider development methods designed to result in the far less specific and much broader outcome of helping individuals learn and grow professionally, and perhaps personally. This type of change targets the organisation's *social processes*, including organisational culture and values, intergroup interactions and management style.

A necessary prerequisite to effective, lasting organisational change is individual change. Structural, task and technological transformations will ultimately fail if the individuals involved are not receptive to change. The approaches described in this section help prepare people for ongoing change and learning. The 'learning organisation' philosophy stresses the importance of this. According to Peter Senge, a leading advocate, learning organisations value continuing individual and collective learning.[19] To increase effectiveness, Senge argues, organisational members must put aside their old ways of thinking, learn to be open with others, understand how their company really works, develop plans everyone can agree on, and then work together to achieve those plans.[20] Approaches targeting social processes assist in achieving one or more of those objectives. We will discuss two of the more widely known ones: team building and the managerial grid.

Team building

In recent years organisations have shown renewed interest in effectively using work groups or teams.[21] Anyone who has ever operated a business or organised any kind of project requiring the efforts of several people knows the difficulties involved in getting everyone to pull in the right direction, in the right way and at the right time. One approach to minimising these difficulties is *team building*.[22]

The purpose of team building is to enable work groups to get their work done more effectively, to improve their performance. The work groups may be existing, or relatively new, command and task groups. The specific aims of the intervention include setting goals and priorities, analysing the ways the group does its work, examining the group's norms and processes for communicating and decision making, and examining the interpersonal relationships within the group. As each of these aims is undertaken, the group is placed in the position of having to recognise explicitly the contributions, positive and negative, of each group member.[23]

The process by which these aims are achieved begins with *diagnostic meetings*. Often lasting an entire day, the meetings enable each group member to share with other members his or her perceptions of problems. Subsequently, a *plan of action* must be agreed on. The action plan should call on each of the group members, individually or as part of a subgroup, to undertake a specific action to alleviate one or more of the problems.

Team building is also effective when new groups are being formed because problems often exist when new organisational units, project teams or task forces are created. Typically, such groups have certain characteristics that must be overcome if the groups are to perform effectively. For example:

- Confusion exists as to roles and relationships.
- Members have a fairly clear understanding of short-term goals.
- Group members have technical competence that puts them on the team.
- Members often pay more attention to the tasks of the team than to the relationships among the team members.

To combat these tendencies, the new group could schedule team-building meetings during the first few weeks of its life.

Although the reports of team building indicate mixed results, the evidence suggests that group processes improve through team-building efforts.[24] This record of success accounts for the increasing use of team building as an OD method.[25]

The managerial grid

This OD approach is based on a theory of leadership behaviour.[26] The two dimensions of leadership that the developers of the program, Blake and Mouton, identify are *concern for production* and *concern for people*. A balanced concern for production and people is the most effective leadership style,

---

GLOBAL Encounter

Organisation development in Hong Kong

A recent survey was carried out by Chung-Ming Lau, at the Chinese University of Hong Kong, to assess the extent to which OD is used among leading firms in Hong Kong and to further determine the nature of OD interventions. As we have seen in this chapter, OD intervention can target social factors, technology, or organisational structure and processes. Lau presents two competing views of the factors driving OD interventions in Hong Kong organisations. First, because they are smaller and require less commitment, social factors may be a more desirable intervention in the early stages of organisation development. However, second, because of the Chinese culture, technological approaches may be preferred because they are more impersonal.

Preliminary analysis of survey results showed that most time was spent on people-oriented interventions and these, together with strategic planning, were the most extensively practised OD interventions.

Since many of the organisations surveyed were multinational companies, Lau also considered the possibility that OD practices would be influenced by the parent company's culture. However, this was not the case.

Another factor that may have influenced the nature of OD interventions was industry type. Lau found that there were significant differences in the extent to which OD interventions targeted technology: this was highest in manufacturing companies, decreasing in the banking industry and further decreasing in trading industries. There were no industry-based differences in the time spent on other OD interventions.

Finally, to provide a more fine-grained analysis of these interventions, forty-five managers were surveyed to obtain information about OD practice. The most frequently used intervention at the social level was management training in communication and interpersonal skills and problem solving; when technology was the target, departmental restructuring was the most common intervention; and, at an organisational level, the two most commonly used strategies were the development of organisational mission statements and the implementation of attitude surveys.

Source: Lau, C. M. (1995). Organisation development practices in Hong Kong: Current state and future challenges, *Asia Pacific Journal of Management*, **12**, 101–114.

according to Blake and Mouton. The managerial grid program requires not only the development of this style but also the development of group behaviour that supports and sustains it. The entire program consists of six sequential phases that are undertaken over a period of 3–5 years.

The six phases can be separated into two major segments, and the first two phases provide the foundation for the four later phases.

1. *Laboratory-seminar training.* This is typically a 1-week conference designed to introduce managers to the grid philosophy and objectives. During this period, each participant's leadership style is assessed and reviewed.
2. *Intragroup development.* In this phase, superiors and their immediate subordinates explore their managerial styles and operating practices as a group. Together with Phase I, the objective is to familiarise participants with grid concepts, improve relationships between individuals and groups, and increase managers' problem-solving capacities.
3. *Intergroup development.* This phase involves group-to-group working relationships and focuses on building effective group roles and norms that improve intergroup relationships.
4. *Organisational goal setting.* The immediate objective of this phase is to set up a model of an effective organisation for the future.
5. *Goal attainment.* This phase uses some of the group and educational procedures that were used in Phase I, but the concern is on the total organisation. Problems are defined and groups move towards problem solution using grid concepts and philosophy. .
6. *Stabilisation.* This final phase focuses on stabilising the changes brought about in prior phases. This phase also enables management to evaluate the total program.

The longevity of the managerial grid method, as well as its use in a growing variety of applications,[27] suggests that it is more than a fad to practising managers. Thus, it would appear that more rigorous studies of what it can and cannot accomplish are required. Only by properly studying this approach can those interested in implementing it as a developmental method generally understand how it can change employee behaviour.

Changing technology

The final target for change is *technology*: job and work design, technical procedures, systems and skills. Technological approaches to organisational development focus directly on the work that is performed in the organisation. A task focus emphasises job-design changes, a strategy that we discussed in Chapter 5. Thus, organisations may engage in job enlargement, job enrichment or a combination of both. They may also alter work practices by introducing flexible working hours.

Technological approaches emphasise changes in the flow of work. Such changes could, for example, include new physical plant layouts, changes in office design, and improved work methods and techniques. Many technological changes are related to advances in equipment design and capability. For example, computer aided design (CAD) technology has transformed the job and productivity of draftspeople; laser-guided production equipment has dramatically increased the accuracy of many manufacturing processes; the desktop computer has literally altered millions of jobs; and, on a growing number of factory floors, robots are outnumbering humans. Organisational researchers are just now beginning to examine some of the longer term effects of technological change on individuals.[28]

An important aspect of task and technological approaches to organisational development is training. When jobs are redesigned, when work flow is changed, or when the use of new equipment must be mastered, training programs are an integral tool in providing the necessary new skills and knowledge. In fact, the most widely used methods for developing employee productivity are training programs.[29]

Multifaceted approaches

Not all organisational development interventions fit neatly into one of the three categories of approaches we have just examined. Sometimes techniques from different categories may be used together in a multifaceted approach to development. As an example, a silver-mining company combined team building (social) and MBO (structural).[30] The program was aimed at improving safety and productivity in the mine.

Other OD interventions may be considered multifaceted because the technique used is itself so broad-based that it cuts across two or even all three categories. Currently, the most popular such program is **total quality management** (TQM). TQM is both a philosophy and a system of management which, using statistical process control and group problem-solving processes, places the greatest priority on attaining high standards for quality and continuous improvement. Organisations such as IBM, Xerox, Ford, Johnson & Johnson, and Motorola have adopted some form of TQM. Motorola's program, for example, focuses on achieving 'six-sigma quality'. Six-sigma is a statistical measure that expresses how close a product comes to its quality goal. One-sigma means that approximately 68 % of products reached the quality objective; three-sigma means that 99.7 % have reached that goal; and six-sigma is 99.999997% perfect.

There are many different versions of TQM. In actual operation, one company's TQM program may appear quite different from another company's. In spite of large operational differences, the major components of most TQM programs are similar. One researcher describes key TQM components in the following manner:[31]

- *Goal:* The goal of TQM is to establish quality as a dominant organisational priority, vital for long-term effectiveness.
- *Definition of quality:* Quality is satisfying the customer. All quality improvements must begin with an understanding of customer needs and perceptions.
- *Nature of the environment:* TQM changes the boundaries between the organisation and its environment. Entities formerly considered part of the environment (suppliers and customers) are now considered part of organisational processes.
- *Role of management:* Management's role is to create a system that can produce quality results; managers and the system are responsible for poor quality.

- *Role of employees:* Employees are empowered to make decisions and take necessary steps to improve quality within the system designed by management. Additional training provides needed skills for this broader role.
- *Structural rationality:* The organisation is restructured as a set of horizontal processes that start with suppliers and end with customers. Teams are organised around processes to facilitate task accomplishment.
- *Philosophy toward change:* Change, continuous improvement and learning are necessary. Ideally, all organisational members are motivated towards constant improvement.

TQM represents one of the most comprehensive and far-reaching approaches to improving effectiveness in the half-century history of organisational development. There are very few current or near-future organisational members who have not been or will not be affected in some way by TQM.

IMPLEMENTING THE METHOD

The implementation of the OD method has two dimensions — timing and scope. **Timing** refers to the selection of the appropriate time at which to initiate the method, and **scope** refers to the selection of the appropriate scale. The matter of timing depends on a number of factors, particularly the organisation's operating cycle and the groundwork that has preceded the OD program. Certainly, if a program is of considerable magnitude, it is desirable that it not compete with day-to-day operations; thus, the change might well be implemented during a slack period. On the other hand, if the program is critical to the survival of the organisation, then immediate implementation is in order. The scope of the program depends on the strategy. The program may be implemented throughout the organisation, or it may be phased into the organisation level by level or department by department. The shared strategy makes use of a phased approach, which limits the scope but provides feedback for each subsequent implementation.

The method finally selected is not usually implemented on a grand scale; rather, it is implemented on a small scale in various units throughout the organisation. Not even the most detailed planning can anticipate all the consequences of implementing a particular method. Thus, it may be necessary to experiment and to search for new information that can bear on the program.

EVALUATING THE PROGRAM

An OD program represents an expenditure of organisational resources in exchange for some desired result. The resources take the form of money and time that have alternative uses. The result is in the form of increased organisational effectiveness — production, efficiency and satisfaction in the short run; adaptiveness and development in the intermediate run; and survival in the long run. Accordingly, some provision must be made to evaluate the program in terms of expenditures and results.[32] Generally, an evaluation would follow the steps of evaluative research. The steps include:

1. determining the objectives of the program;
2. describing the activities undertaken to achieve the objectives;

3. measuring the effects of the program;
4. establishing baseline points against which changes can be compared;
5. controlling extraneous factors, preferably through the use of a control group;
6. detecting unanticipated consequences.

The application of this model will not always be possible. For example, managers do not always specify objectives in precise terms, and control groups are difficult to establish in some instances. Nevertheless, the difficulties of evaluation should not discourage attempts to evaluate.[33]

Finally, in addition to being able to determine the extent to which a program or other change effort achieved the desired results, it is important to understand in what ways the change contributed to the results. For example, were all the elements of an OD program essential for obtaining the desired results, or were only some critical? This and similar questions are important to ask and answer.

THE ROLE OF CHANGE AGENTS

Because people have a tendency to seek answers in traditional solutions, the intervention of an outsider is usually necessary. The intervener, or *change agent*, brings a different perspective to the situation and serves as a challenge to the status quo.

The success of any change program rests heavily on the quality and workability of the relationship between the change agent and the key decision makers within the organisation. Thus, the form of intervention is a crucial phase.

To intervene is to enter into an ongoing organisation, or among persons or between departments, for the purpose of helping them improve their effectiveness. [34] A number of forms of intervention are used in organisations. First is the *external* change agent who is asked to intervene and provide recommendations for bringing about change. Second is the *internal* change agent, an individual who is working for the organisation and knows something about its problems. Finally, a number of organisations have used a combination *external–internal* change team to intervene and develop programs. This approach attempts to use the resources and knowledge base of both external and internal change agents.

Each of the three forms of intervention has advantages and disadvantages. On the negative side, the external change agent is often viewed as an outsider by company employees, dictating a need to establish rapport between the change agent and decision makers; the change agent's views on the problems faced by the organisation are often different from those of the decision maker, leading to problems in establishing rapport; and differences in viewpoints often result in a mistrust of the external change agent by all, or a segment of, the policymakers. On the other hand, arguments in favour of external agents include their objectivity, independence and specialised skill in introducing change.[35]

The internal change agent is often viewed as being more closely associated with one unit or group of individuals than with any other, and this perceived favouritism leads to resistance to change by those who are not included in the internal change agent's circle of close friends. The internal change agent, however, is familiar with the organisation and its personnel, and this knowledge can be valuable in preparing for and implementing change.[36]

The third type of intervention, the combination external–internal team, is the rarest, but it seems to have an excellent chance for success. In this type of intervention, the outsider's objectivity and professional knowledge are blended with the insider's knowledge of the organisation and its human resources. This blending of knowledge often results in increased trust and confidence among the parties involved. The ability of the combination external–internal team to communicate and develop a more positive rapport can reduce the resistance to any change that is forthcoming.

Regardless of the form of intervention, the role of the change agent is critical. Change agents facilitate the diagnostic phase by gathering, interpreting and presenting data. If the diagnostic part of the process is faulty, the remainder of the OD process is significantly flawed.

More importantly, the change agent must leave the organisation more flexible and adaptable than it was before the intervention. According to Argyris,[37] the change agent serves three functions:

1. *Collect valid information.* This should provide the client with publicly verifiable information concerning the factors underlying organisational problems; it must take into consideration all dimensions of the organisation, so that future problems can be predicted and controlled; and it must identify those issues that are within the control of the client.
2. *Allow free choice.* Once the information is provided, the responsibility for making decisions and selecting solutions must be given to the client. However, it is the responsibility of a change agent to ensure that the decision is well informed. She or he must therefore resist organisational pressure for a 'quick fix'.
3. *Obtain internal commitment.* At the end of the process, the client must feel a high level of ownership for the solution, and responsibility for the consequences of his or her choice.

SUMMARY OF KEY POINTS

Describe forces for organisational change. The motivation for change can come from four sources, classified along two dimensions. Forces may be external (arising from factors outside of the organisation) or internal (related to changes within the organisation). The second dimension classifies these as either planned (changes that the organisation can anticipate and control) or unplanned (changes that the organisation must respond to).

Explain the change process. According to Lewin's Field Theory, we pass through three stages in change: unfreezing, freezing and refreezing. The change — or transition — phase is the most vulnerable to failure and

organisations must manage issues concerning resistance, control and power. Only if these are effectively managed will a change succeed.

Discuss various approaches for dealing with resistance to change. Change requires adaptation, and consequently resistance to change is a potential impediment to the change process. Approaches for dealing with the resistance problem include education and communication, participation and involvement, facilitation and support, negotiation and agreement, manipulation and co-optation, and various forms of coercion.

Distinguish between evolutionary and revolutionary approaches to change. Changes can occur in one of two ways. They may be slow, involve all individuals in a participative process, and result in small incremental adjustments to organisational practices. These changes are described as first-order or evolutionary. However, changes may also completely overturn organisation missions, values and practice. When changes involve a fundamental restructuring, they are described as second-order or revolutionary changes.

List the defining characteristics of organisational development. Organisation development is planned, is problem-oriented, reflects a systems approach, is an integral part of the management process, is not a 'fix-it' strategy, focuses on improvement, is action-oriented, and is base on sound theory and practice.

Describe targets for organisational change. Organisational development can target change at one of four levels: organising arrangements, social processes, technology and the physical setting. The first three of these are the most common targets.

Identify specific development programs within the three categories of methods. Organising structure interventions attempt to introduce change through formal policy and procedure, for example management by objectives and System 4 organisations. Technological approaches to OD focus directly on the work that is performed in the organisation and introduce job and work design, as well as improved work methods. Social level interventions are designed to prepare individuals and groups for ongoing change and learning, and include such activities as team building.

Understand the importance of program evaluation. Evaluation of OD programs is essential. Without such evaluation there is no way to determine whether the expenditure of effort and resources is worthwhile. Additionally, evaluation is important in helping to understand in what ways the program contributed to the changes that occurred.

Discuss the role of change agents. Change agents play a key role in organisational interventions. They may be external and assist in collecting and interpreting information; they may be internal, and provide an organisational perceptive on the

information; or organisations may form teams of internal and external change agents. Their ultimate aim is to provide the organisation with skills that increase the adaptability of the workforce to ongoing demands.

REVIEW AND DISCUSSION QUESTIONS

1. What characteristics of planned change distinguish it from unplanned change? Are these characteristics more likely to increase or decrease people's receptivity to organisational change?
2. Think of an organisation with which you are familiar. What are the external and internal forces operating on the organisation to bring about change?
3. 'Only revolution can lead to long-lasting organisational changes.' Discuss.
4. What key issues must be addressed during the transition phase? How can organisations manage this phase to ensure the successful implementation of change?
5. Which of the OD methods discussed in this chapter would improve the effectiveness of the university that you attend?
6. Do you think that organisations might differ in their receptivity to OD efforts as a function of the industry of which they are a part? The skill level of their workforce? The condition of the global economy?
7. 'Change must be introduced very carefully because you can never go back to the way things were before you made the change.' What does this statement mean? What implications does it have for organisational development?
8. How might an organisation overcome resistance to change? To what extent would the types of change being implemented affect the method(s) chosen to reduce resistance?
9. Why is it important to evaluate change efforts and why are such evaluations difficult to do?
10. Discuss the relative merits of using internal and external change agents.

ENDNOTES

1 Cox, T., Jr., & Blake, S. (1991). Managing cultural diversity: Implications for organizational competitiveness, *Academy of Management Executive*, 45–56.

2 See, for example, Gersick, C. (1991). Revolutionary change theories: A multilevel exploration of the punctuated equilibrium paradigm, *Academy of Management Review*, 10–36.

3 Nadler, D. A. & Tushman, M. L. (1979). A diagnostic model of organizational behavior. In J. R. Hackman et al. (Eds.) *Perspectives on Behavior in Organizations*. New York: McGraw-Hill.

4 Narayanan, V. K., & Nath, R. (1993). *Organization Theory*. Homewood, IL: Irwin.

5 Lewin, K. (1947). Frontiers in group dynamics, *Human Relations*, 5–41; Mitchell, T. R., Dowling, P. J., Kabanoff, B. V., & Larson, J. R. (1988). *People in Organizations: An Introduction to Organizational Behaviour in Australia*. Sydney: McGraw-Hill Book Company.

6 This discussion is based on material contained in Nadler D. A. (1981). Managing organizational change: An integrative perspective, *Journal of Applied Behavioural Science*, **17**, 191–211.

7 Kotter, J., & Schlesinger, L. (1979). Choosing strategies for change, *Harvard Business Review*, 102-121.

8 Porras, J. I., & Robertson, P. J. (1994). Organizational development: Theory, practice and research. In M. D. Dunnette & L. M. Hough (Eds.) *Handbook of Industrial and Organizational Psychology* (2nd Ed.). Palo Alto, CA: Consulting Psychologists Press.

9 Beer, M., Eisenstat, R. A., & Spector, B. (1990). Why change programs don't produce change, *Harvard Business Review*, 158–166.

10 See, for example, Gersick C. (1991). Revolutionary change theories: A multilevel exploration of the punctuated equilibrium paradigm, *Academy of Management Review*, 10–36.

11 French, W. L., Bell, C. H., & Zawacki, R. A. (Eds.) (1983). *Organization Development: Theory, Practice, and Research*. Plano, TX: Business Publications.

12 Winn, A. The laboratory approach to organisation development: A tentative model of planned change. Cited in R. T. Golembiewski (1969). Organizational development in public agencies: Perspective on theory and practice, *Public Administration Review*, 367.

13 Margulies, N., & Raia, A. P. (1978). *Conceptual Foundations of Organizational Development*. New York: McGraw-Hill, p. 25.

14 Porras, J. I., & Robertson, P. J. (1994). Organizational development: Theory, practice and research. In M. D. Dunnette & L. M. Hough (Eds.) *Handbook of Industrial and Organizational Psychology* (2nd Ed.). Palo Alto, CA: Consulting Psychologists Press; Porras, J. I., & Silvers, R. C. (1991). Organization development and transformation, *Annual Review of Psychology*, **42**, 51–78.

15 Original statements of MBO may be found in Drucker , P. (1954). *The Practice of Management*. New York: Harper & Row; Odiorne, G. (1965). *Management by Objectives*. New York: Pitman Publishing; and Reddin, W. J. (1970). *Effective Management by Objectives*. New York: McGraw-Hill.

16 See Greenwood, R. G. (1981). Management by objectives: As developed by Peter Drucker, assisted by Harold Smiddy, *Academy of Management Review*, 225–230.

17 Muczyk, J. P., & Reimann, B. (1989). MBO as a complement to effective leadership, *Academy of Management Executive*, pp. 131–138.

18 Likert, R. (1967). *The Human Organization*. New York: McGraw-Hill.

19 Senge, P. (1990). *The Fifth Discipline*. New York: Doubleday Publishing Company.

20 Dumaine, B. (1994). Mr Learning Organization, *Fortune*, October 17, 147–157.

21 Ancona, D. (1990). Outward Bound: Strategies for team survival in an organization, *Academy of Management Journal*, 334–365.

22 Larson, C., & LaFasto, F. M. J. (1989). *Teamwork*. Newbury Park, CA.: Sage.

23 Hughes, R. L., Rosenbach, W. E., & Clover, W. H. (1983). Team development in an intact, ongoing work group, *Group and Organizational Studies*, 161–181.

24 de Meuse, K. P., & Liebowitz, S. J. (1981). An empirical analysis of team-building research, *Group and Organizational Studies*, 357–358.

25 For a recent example of the use of team building, see Hardaker, M., & Ward, B. (1987). How to make a team work, *Harvard Business Review*, 112–120.

26 Blake, R. R. & Mouton, J. S. (1982). *The Versatile Manager*. Homewood, IL.: Richard D. Irwin.

27 For an example, see van de Vliert, E., & Kabanoff, B. (1990). Toward theory-based measures of conflict management, *Academy of Management Journal*, 199–209.

28 See, for example, Burkhardt M. E. (1994). Social interaction effects following technological change: A longitudinal investigation, *Academy of Management Journal*, 869–898.

29 Michael, S.R. (1982). Organisational change
    techniques: Their past, their future,
    Organizational Dynamics, 67–80.

30 Buller, P. F., & Bell, C. H. (1986). Effects of
    team building and goal-setting on productivity:
    A field experiment, *Academy of Management
    Journal*, 305–328.

31 Spencer, B.A. (1994). Models of organization
    and total quality management, *Academy of
    Management Review*, 446–471.

32 Vicars, W. M., & Hartke, D. D. (1982).
    Evaluating OD evaluations: A status report,
    Group and Organizational Studies, 402–417.

33 French, W. (1983). A checklist for organizing
    and implementing an OD effort. In W. L.
    French, C. H. Bell, Jr., & R. A. Zawacki (Eds.)
    *Organization Development: Theory, Practice and
    Research*. Plano, TX.: Business Publications, pp.
    451–459; and Woodman, R. & Wayne, S.,

    (1985). An investigation of positive-findings bias
    in evaluation of organization development
    interventions, *Academy of Management Journal*,
    889–913.

34 French, W. L., & Bell, Jr., C. H. (1984).
    *Organizational Development: Behavioral
    Science Interventions for Organizational
    Improvement*. Englewood Cliffs, NJ:
    Prentice-Hall.

35 Armenakis A., & Burdg, H. (1988).
    Consultation research: Contributions to
    practice and directions for improvement,
    Journal of Management, 339–365.

36 Harper, S.C. (1989). The manager as change
    agent: 'Hell no' to the status quo, *Industrial
    Management*, 8–11.

37 Argyris, C. (1983). Action science and
    intervention, *Journal of Applied Behavioral Science*,
    19, 115–140.

READING 15 WHY TRANSFORMATION EFFORTS FAIL

by John P. Kotter

Source: John P. Kotter, 'Leading Change: Why
Transformation Efforts Fail', *Harvard Business Review*,
March–April 1995, pp. 59–67.

Over the past decade, I have watched more than
100 companies try to remake themselves into
significantly better competitors. They have
included large organizations (Ford) and small
ones (Landmark Communications), companies
based in the United States (General Motors) and
elsewhere (British Airways) and corporations that
were on their knees (Eastern Airlines) and
companies that were earning good money
(Bristol-Myers Squibb). These efforts have gone
under many banners: total quality management,
reengineering, right sizing, restructuring,
cultural change, and turnaround. But, in almost
every case, the basic goal has been the same: to
make fundamental changes in how business is
conducted in order to help cope with a new,
more challenging market environment.

A few of these corporate change efforts have
been very successful. A few have been utter

failures. Most fall somewhere in between, with a
distinct tilt towards the lower end of the scale.
The lessons that can be drawn are interesting and
will probably be relevant to even more
organizations in the increasingly competitive
business environment of the coming decade.

The most general lesson to be learned from
the more successful cases is that the change
process goes through a series of phases that, in
total, usually require a considerable length of
time. Skipping steps creates only the illusion of
speed and never produces a satisfying result. A
second very general lesson is that critical mistakes
in any of the phases can have a devastating
impact, slowing momentum and negating hard-
won gains. Perhaps because we have relatively
little experience in renewing organizations, even
very capable people often make at least one big
error.

Error #1: Not establishing a great enough sense of urgency

Most successful change efforts begin when some
individuals or some groups start to look hard at a
company's competitive situation, market position,
technological trends, and financial performance.
They focus on the potential revenue drop when
an important patent expires, the five-year trend
in declining margins in a core business, or an
emerging market that everyone seems to be

ignoring. They then find ways to communicate this information broadly and dramatically, especially with respect to crises, potential crises, or great opportunities that are very timely. This first step is essential because just getting a transformation program started requires the aggressive cooperation of many individuals. Without motivation, people won't help and the effort goes nowhere.

Compared with other steps in the change process, phase one can sound easy. It is not. Well over 50 percent of the companies I have watched fail in this first phase. What are the reasons for that failure? Sometimes executives underestimate how hard it can be to drive people out of their comfort zones. Sometimes they grossly overestimate how successful they have already been in increasing urgency. Sometimes the lack patience: 'Enough with the preliminaries; let's get on with it'. In many cases, executives become paralyzed by the downside possibilities. They worry that employees with seniority will become defensive, that morale will drop, that events will spin out of control, that short-term business results will be jeopardized, that the stock will sink, and that they will be blamed for creating a crisis.

A paralyzed senior management often comes from having too many managers and not enough leaders. Management's mandate is to minimize risk and to keep the current system operating. Change, by definition, requires creating a new system, which in turn always demands leadership. Phase one in a renewal process typically goes nowhere until enough real leaders are promoted or hired into senior-level jobs.

Transformations often begin, and begin well, when an organization has a new head who is a good leader and who sees the need for a major change. If the renewal target is the entire company, the CEO is key. If change is needed in a division, the division general manager is key. When these individuals are not new leaders, great leaders, or change champions, phase one can be a huge challenge.

Bad business results are both a blessing and a curse in the first phase. On the positive side, losing money does catch people's attention. But it also gives less maneuvering room. With good business results, the opposite is true: convincing people of the need for change is much harder, but you have more resources to help make changes. But whether the starting point is good performance or bad, in the more successful cases

---

Exhibit 15.4 Eight steps to transforming your organization

1. Establishing a Sense of Urgency.
Examining market and competitive realities.
Identifying and discussing crises, potential crises, or major opportunities.

2. Forming a Powerful Guiding Coalition.
Assembling a group with enough power to lead the change effort.
Encouraging the group to work together as a team.

3. Creating a Vision.
Creating a vision to help direct the change effort.
Developing strategies for achieving that vision.

4. Communicating the Vision.
Using every vehicle possible to communicate the new vision and strategies.
Teaching new behaviors by the example of the guiding coalition.

5. Empowering Others to Act on the Vision.
Getting rid of obstacles to change.
Changing systems or structures that seriously undermine the vision.
Encouraging risk taking and nontraditional ideas, activities, and actions.

6. Planning for and Creating Short-Term Wins.
Planning for visible performance improvements.
Creating those improvements.
Recognizing and rewarding employees involved in the improvements.

7. Consolidating Improvements and Producing Still More Change.
Using increased credibility to change systems, structures, and policies that don't fit the vision.
Hiring, promoting, and developing employees who can implement the vision.
Reinvigorating the process with new projects, themes, and change agents.

8. Institutionalizing New Approaches.
Articulating the connections between the new behaviors and corporate success.
Developing the means to ensure leadership development and succession.

I have witnessed, an individual or a group always facilitates a frank discussion of potentially unpleasant facts: about new competition, shrinking margins, decreasing market share, flat earning, a lack of revenue growth, or other relevant indices of a declining competitive position. Because there seems to be an almost universal human tendency to shoot the bearer of bad news, especially if the head of the organization is not a change champion, executives in these companies often rely on outsiders to bring unwanted information. Wall Street analysts, customers, and consultants can all be helpful in this regard. The purpose of all this activity, in the words of one former CEO of a large European company, is 'to make the status quo seem more dangerous than launching into the unknown'.

In a few of the most successful cases, a group has manufactured a crisis. One CEO deliberately engineered the largest accounting loss in the company's history, creating huge pressures from Wall Street in the process. One division president commissioned first-ever customer-satisfaction surveys, knowing full well that the results would be terrible. He then made these findings public. On the surface, such moves can look unduly risky. But there is also risk in playing it too safe: when the urgency rate is not pumped up enough, the transformation process cannot succeed and the long-term future of the organization is put in jeopardy.

When is the urgency rate high enough? From what I have seen, the answer is when about 75 percent of a company's management is honestly convinced that business-as-usual is totally unacceptable. Anything less can produce very serious problems later on in the process.

Error #2: Not creating a powerful enough guiding coalition

Major renewal programs often start with just one or two people. In cases of successful transformation efforts, the leadership coalition grows and grows over time. But whenever some minimum mass is not achieved early in the effort, nothing much worthwhile happens.

It is often said that major change is impossible unless the head of the organization is an active supporter. What I am talking about goes far beyond that. In successful transformations the chairman or president or division general manager, plus another 5 or 15 or 50 people, come together and develop a shared commitment to excellent performance through renewal. In my experience, this group never includes all of the company's most senior executives because some people just won't buy in, at least not at first. But in the most successful cases, the coalition is always pretty powerful in terms of titles, information and expertise, reputations and relationships.

In both small and large organizations, a successful guiding team may consist of only three to five people during the first year of a renewal effort. But in big companies, the coalition needs to grow to the 20 to 50 range before much progress can be made in phase three and beyond. Senior managers always form the core of the group. But sometimes you find board members, a representative from a key customer, or even a powerful union leader.

Because the guiding coalition includes members who are not part of senior management, it tends to operate outside the normal hierarchy by definition. This can be awkward, but it is clearly necessary. If the existing hierarchy were working well, there would be no need for a major transformation. But since the current system is not working, reform generally demands activity outside of formal boundaries, expectations, and protocol.

A high sense of urgency within the managerial ranks helps enormously in putting a guiding coalition together. But more is usually required. Someone needs to get these people together, help them develop a shared assessment of their company's problems and opportunities, and create a minimum level of trust and communication. Off-site retreats, for two or three days, are one popular vehicle for accomplishing this task. I have seen many groups of 5 to 35 executives attend a series of these retreats over a period of months.

Companies that fail in phase two usually underestimate the difficulties of producing change and thus the importance of a powerful guiding coalition. Sometimes they have no history of teamwork at the top and therefore undervalue the importance of this type of coalition. Sometimes they expect the team to be lead by a staff executive from human resources, quality, or strategic planning instead of a key line manager. No matter how capable or dedicated the staff head, groups without strong line leadership never achieve the power that is required.

Efforts that don't have a powerful enough guiding coalition can make apparent progress for a while. But, sooner or later, the opposition gathers itself together and stops the change.

Error #3: Lacking a vision

In every successful transformation effort that I have seen, the guiding coalition develops a picture of the future that is relatively easy to communicate and appeals to customers, stockholders, and employees. A vision always goes beyond the numbers that are typically found in 5-year plans. A vision says something that helps clarify the direction in which an organization needs to move. Sometimes the first draft comes mostly from a single individual. It is usually a bit blurry, at least initially. But after the coalition works at it for 3 or 5 or even 12 months, something much better emerges through their tough analytical thinking and a little dreaming. Eventually, a strategy for achieving that vision is also developed. In one midsize European company, the first pass at a vision contained two-thirds of the basic ideas that were in the final product. The concept of global reach was in the initial version from the beginning. So was the idea of becoming preeminent in certain businesses. But one central idea in the final version — getting out of low value-added activities — came only after a series of discussions over a period of several months.

Without a sensible vision, a transformation effort can easily dissolve into a list of confusing and incompatible projects that can take the organization in the wrong direction or nowhere at all. Without a sound vision, the reengineering project in the accounting department, the new 360-degree performance appraisal from the human resources department, the plant's quality program, the cultural change project in the sales force will not add up in a meaningful way.

In failed transformations, you often find plenty of plans and directives and programs, but no vision. In one case, a company gave out four-inch-thick notebooks describing its change effort. In mind-numbing detail, the books spelled out procedures, goals, methods, and deadlines. But nowhere was there a clear and compelling statement of where all this was leading. Not surprisingly, most of the employees with whom I talked were either confused or alienated. The big, thick books did not rally them together or inspire change. In fact, they probably had just the opposite effect.

In a few of the less successful cases that I have seen, management had a sense of direction, but it was too complicated or blurry to be useful. Recently, I asked an executive in a midsize company to describe his vision and received in return a barely comprehensible 30-minute lecture. Buried in his answer were the basic elements of a sound vision. But they were buried — deeply.

A useful rule of thumb: if you can't communicate the vision to someone in five minutes or less and get a reaction that signifies both understanding and interest, you are not yet done with this phase of the transformation process.

Error #4: Undercommunicating the vision by a factor of ten

I've seen three patterns with respect to communication, all very common. In the first, a group actually does develop a pretty good transformation vision and then proceeds to communicate it by holding a single meeting or sending out a single communication. Having used about .0001 percent of the yearly intracompany communication, the group is startled that few people seem to understand the new approach. In the second pattern, the head of the organization spends a considerable amount of time making speeches to employee groups, but most people still don't get it (not surprising, since vision captures only .0005 percent of the total yearly communication). In the third pattern, much more effort goes into newsletters and speeches, but some very visible senior executives still behave in ways that are antithetical to the vision. The net result is that cynicism among the troops goes up, while belief in the communication goes down.

Transformation is impossible unless hundreds or thousands of people are willing to help, often to the point of making short-term sacrifices. Employees will not make sacrifices, even if they are unhappy with the status quo, unless they believe that useful change is possible. Without credible communication, and a lot of it, the hearts and minds of the troops are never captured.

This fourth phase is particularly challenging if the short-term sacrifices include job losses. Gaining understanding and support is tough when downsizing is a part of the vision. For this reason, successful visions usually include new growth possibilities and the commitment to treat fairly anyone who is laid off.

Executives who communicate well incorporate messages into their hour-by-hour activities. In a routine discussion about a business problem, they talk about how proposed solutions fit (or don't fit) into the bigger picture. In a regular performance appraisal, they talk about how the employee's behavior helps or undermines the vision. In a review of a division's quarterly performance, they talk not only about the numbers but also about how the division's executives are contributing to the transformation. In a routine Q&A with employees at a company facility, they tie their answers back to renewal goals.

In more successful transformation efforts, executives use all existing communication channels to broadcast the vision. They turn boring and unread company newsletters into lively articles about the vision. They take ritualistic and tedious quarterly management meetings and turn them into exciting discussions of the transformation. They throw out much of the company's generic management education and replace it with courses that focus on business problems and the new vision. The guiding principle is simple: use every possible channel, especially those that are being wasted on nonessential information.

Perhaps even more important, most of the executives I have known in successful cases of major change learn to 'walk the talk'. They consciously attempt to become a living symbol of the new corporate culture. This is often not easy. A 60-year-old plant manager who has spent precious little time over 40 years thinking about customers will not suddenly behave in a customer-oriented way. But I have witnessed just such a person change, and change a great deal. In that case, a high level of urgency helped. The fact that the man was a part of the guiding coalition and the vision-creation team also helped. So did all the communication, which kept reminding him of the desired behavior, and all the feedback from his peers and subordinates, which helped him see when he was not engaging in that behavior.

Communication comes in both words and deeds, and the latter are often the most powerful form. Nothing undermines change more than behavior by important individuals that is inconsistent with their words.

Error #5: Not removing obstacles to the new vision

Successful transformations begin to involve large numbers of people as the process progresses. Employees are emboldened to try new approaches, to develop new ideas, and to provide leadership. The only constraint is that the actions fit within the broad parameters of the overall vision. The more people involved, the better the outcome.

To some degree, a guiding coalition empowers others to take action simply by successfully communicating the new direction. But communication is never sufficient by itself. Renewal also requires the removal of obstacles. Too often, an employee understands the new vision and wants to help make it happen. But an elephant appears to be blocking the path. In some cases, the elephant is in the person's head, and the challenge is to convince the individual that no external obstacle exists. But in most cases, the blockers are very real.

Sometimes the obstacle is the organizational structure: narrow job categories can seriously undermine efforts to increase productivity or make it very difficult even to think about customers. Sometimes compensation or performance-appraisal systems make people choose between the new vision and their own self-interest. Perhaps worst of all are bosses who refuse to change and who make demands that are inconsistent with the overall effort.

One company began its transformation process with much publicity and actually made good progress through the fourth phase. Then the change effort ground to a halt because the officer in charge of the company's largest division was allowed to undermine most of the new initiatives. He paid lip service to the process but did not change his behavior or encourage his managers to change. He did not reward the unconventional ideas called for in the vision. He allowed human resource systems to remain intact even when they were clearly inconsistent with the new ideals. I think the officer's motives were complex. To some degree, he did believe the company needed major change. To some degree, he felt personally threatened by all the change. To some degree, he was afraid that he could not produce both change and the expected operating profit. But despite the fact that they backed the renewal effort, the other officers did virtually nothing to stop the one blocker. Again, the reasons were complex. The company had no history of confronting problems like this. Some people were afraid of the officer. The CEO was concerned that he might lose a talented executive. The net result was disastrous. Lower-level managers concluded that senior management had lied to them about their commitment to renewal, cynicism grew, and the whole effort collapsed.

In the first half of a transformation, no organization has the momentum, power, or time to get rid of all obstacles. But the big ones must be confronted and removed. If the blocker is a person, it is important that he or she be treated fairly and in a way that is consistent with the new vision. But action is essential, both to empower others and to maintain the credibility of the change effort as a whole.

Error #6: Not systematically planning for and creating short-term wins

Real transformation takes time, and a renewal effort risks losing momentum if there are no short-term goals to meet and celebrate. Most people won't go on the long march unless they see compelling evidence within 12 to 24 months that the journey is producing expected results. Without short-term wins, too many people give up or actively loin the ranks of those people who have been resisting change.

One to two years into a successful transformation effort, you find quality beginning to go up on certain indices or the decline in net income stopping. You find some successful new product introductions or an upward shift in market share. You find an impressive productivity improvement or a statistically higher customer-satisfaction rating. But whatever the case, the win is unambiguous. The result is not just a judgment call that can be discounted by those opposing change.

Creating short-term wins is different from hoping for short-term wins. The latter is passive, the former active. In a successful transformation, managers actively look for ways to obtain clear performance improvements, establish goals in the yearly planning system, achieve the objectives, and reward the people involved with recognition, promotions, and even money. For example, the guiding coalition at a US manufacturing company produced a highly visible and successful new product introduction about 20 months after the start of its renewal effort. The new product was selected about six months into the effort because it met multiple criteria: it could be designed and launched in a relatively short period; it could be handled by a small team of people who were devoted to the new vision; it had upside potential; and the new product-development team could operate outside the established departmental structure without practical problems. Little was left to chance, and the win boosted the credibility of the renewal process.

Managers often complain about being forced to produce short-term wins, but I've found that pressure can be a useful element in a change effort. When it becomes clear to people that major change will take a long time, urgency levels can drop. Commitments to produce short-term wins help keep the urgency level up and force detailed analytical thinking that can clarify or revise visions.

Error #7: Declaring victory too soon

After a few years of hard work, managers may be tempted to declare victory with the first clear performance improvement. While celebrating a win is fine, declaring the war won can be catastrophic. Unit changes sink deeply into a company's culture, a process that can take five to ten years, new approaches are fragile and subject to regression.

In the recent past, I have watched a dozen change efforts operate under the reengineering theme. In all but two cases, victory was declared and the expensive consultants were paid and thanked when the first major project was completed after two to three years. Within two more years, the useful changes that had been introduced slowly disappeared. In two of the ten cases, it's hard to find any trace of the reengineering work today.

Over the past 20 years, I've seen the same sort of thing happen to huge quality projects, organizational development efforts, and more. Typically, the problems start early in the process: the urgency level is not intense enough, the guiding coalition is not powerful enough, and the vision is not clear enough. But it is the premature victory celebration that kills momentum. And then the powerful forces associated with tradition take over.

Ironically, it is often a combination of change initiators and change resistors that creates the premature victory celebration. In their enthusiasm over a clear sign of progress, the initiators go overboard. They are then joined by resistors, who are quick to spot any opportunity to stop change. After the celebration is over, the resistors point to the victory as a sign that the war has been won and the troops should be sent home. Weary troops allow themselves to be convinced that they won. Once home, the foot soldiers are reluctant to climb back on the ships. Soon thereafter, change comes to a halt, and tradition creeps back in.

Instead of declaring victory, leaders of successful efforts use the credibility afforded by short-term wins to tackle even bigger problems. They go after systems and structures that are not consistent with the transformation vision and have not been confronted before. They pay great attention to who is promoted, who is hired, and how people are developed. They include new reengineering projects that are even bigger in scope than the initial ones. They understand that renewal efforts take not months but years. In fact, in one of the most successful transformations that I have ever seen, we quantified the amount of change that occurred each year over a seven-year period. On a scale of one (low) to ten (high), year one received a two, year two a four, year three a three, year four a seven, year five an eight, year six a four, and year seven a two. The peak came in year five, fully 36 months after the first set of visible wins.

Error #8: Not anchoring changes in the corporation's culture

In the final analysis, change sticks when it becomes 'the way we do things around here', when it seeps into the bloodstream of the corporate body. Until new behaviors are rooted in social norms and shared values, they are subject to degradation as soon as the pressure for change is removed.

Two factors are particularly important in institutionalizing change in corporate culture. The first is a conscious attempt to show people how the new approaches, behaviors, and attitudes have helped improve performance. When people are left on their own to make the connections, they sometimes create very inaccurate links. For example, because results improved while charismatic Harry was boss, the troops link his mostly idiosyncratic style with those results instead of seeing how their own improved customer service and productivity were instrumental. Helping people see the right connections requires communication. Indeed, one company was relentless, and it paid off enormously. Time was spent at every major management meeting to discuss why performance was increasing. The company newspaper ran article after article showing how changes had boosted earnings.

The second factor is taking sufficient time to make sure that the next generation of top management really does personify the new approach. If the requirements for promotion don't change, renewal rarely lasts. One bad succession decision at the top of an organization can undermine a decade of hard work. Poor succession decisions are possible when boards of directors are not an integral part of the renewal effort. In at least three instances I have seen, the champion for change was the retiring executive, and although his successor was not a resistor, he was not a change champion. Because the boards did not understand the transformations in any detail, they could not see that their choices were not good fits. The retiring executive in one case tried unsuccessfully to talk his board into a less seasoned candidate who better personified the transformation. In the other two cases, the CEOs did not resist the board's choices, because they felt the transformation could not be undone by their successors. They were wrong. Within two years, signs of renewal began to disappear at both companies.

There are still more mistakes that people make, but these eight are the big ones. I realize that in a short article everything is made to sound a bit too simplistic. In reality, even successful change efforts are messy and full of surprises. But just as a relatively simple vision is needed to guide people through a major change, so a vision of the change process can reduce the error rate. And fewer errors can spell the difference between success and failure.

EXERCISE 15 ORGANISATION DEVELOPMENT AT J.P. HUNT

Objective

To experience an OD technique — in this case the use of survey feedback — to diagnose strengths and weaknesses and develop an action plan.

Starting the exercise

Set up four to eight members for the 1-hour exercise. The groups should be separated from each other and asked to converse only with members of their own group. Each person should read the following:

J. P. Hunt department stores is a large retail merchandising outlet located in Boston. The company sells an entire range of retail goods (e.g. appliances, fashion, furniture and so on) and has a large downtown store plus six branch stores in various suburban areas.

Similar to most retail stores in the area, employee turnover is high (i.e. 40 to 45% annually. In the credit and accounts receivable

Exhibit 15.5 Survey results for J. P. Hunt department store: Credit and accounts receivable department

Variable	Survey Results*			Industry Norms*		
	Managers	Supervisors	Non-supervisors	Managers	Supervisors	Non-supervisors
Satisfaction and rewards						
Pay	3.30	1.73	2.48	3.31	2.97	2.89
Supervision	3.70	2.42	3.05	3.64	3.58	3.21
Promotion	3.40	2.28	2.76	3.38	3.25	3.23
Co-workers	3.92	3.90	3.72	3.95	3.76	3.43
Work	3.98	2.81	3.15	3.93	3.68	3.52
Performance-to-intrinsic rewards	4.07	3.15	3.20	4.15	3.85	3.81
Performance-to-extrinsic rewards	3.67	2.71	2.70	3.87	3.81	3.76
Supervisory behaviour						
Initiating structure	3.42	3.97	3.90	3.40	3.51	3.48
Consideration	3.63	3.09	3.18	3.77	3.72	3.68
Positive rewards	3.99	2.93	3.02	4.24	3.95	3.91
Punitive rewards	3.01	3.61	3.50	2.81	2.91	3.08
Job characteristics						
Autonomy	4.13	4.22	3.80	4.20	4.00	3.87
Feedback	3.88	3.81	3.68	3.87	3.70	3.70
Variety	3.67	3.35	3.22	3.62	3.21	2.62
Challenge	4.13	4.03	3.03	4.10	3.64	3.58
Organisational practices						
Role ambiguity	2.70	2.91	3.34	2.60	2.40	2.20
Role conflict	2.87	3.69	2.94	2.83	3.12	3.02
Job pressure	3.14	4.04	3.23	2.66	2.68	2.72
Performance evaluation process	3.77	3.35	3.19	3.92	3.70	3.62
Worker cooperation	3.67	3.94	3.87	3.65	3.62	3.35
Workflow planning	3.88	2.62	2.95	4.20	3.80	3.76

*The values are scored from 1, very low, to 5, very high.

department, located in the downtown store, turnover is particularly high at both the supervisor and subordinate levels, approaching 75% annually. The department employs approximately 150 people, 70% of whom are female.

Due to rising hiring and training costs brought on by the high turnover, top department management began a turnover analysis and reduction program. As a first step, a local management consulting company was contracted to conduct a survey of department employees. Using primarily questionnaires, the consulting company collected survey data from over 95% of the department's employees. The results are

shown in Exhibit 15.5, by organisational level, along with the industry norms developed by the consulting company in comparative retail organisations.

The procedure
1. Individually, each group member should analyse the data in the exhibit and attempt to identify and diagnose department strengths and problem areas.
2. As a group, the members should repeat step 1 above. In addition, suggestions for resolving the problems and an action plan for feedback to the department should be developed.

CASE 15 COMMUNITY SERVICES VICTORIA: NEW MANAGEMENT AND QUALITY OF SERVICE

This case was prepared by Dr Amanda Sinclair, Jeanette Baird and John Alford from previous case studies, as a basis for class discussion rather than to illustrate either effective or ineffective handling of an administrative situation. © 1992 University of Melbourne. Distributed by Melbourne Case Study Services, at the Graduate School of Management, University of Melbourne, 200 Leicester Street, Carlton, Victoria 3053. All rights reserved to the contributors.

John Paterson's appointment
Dr John Paterson took up his appointment as Director General of Community Services Victoria (CSV) on 3 July 1989, at a time when the Department was regarded as accident prone, if not actually jinxed.

As an expert in resource economics and a self-styled 'managerialist', he had been aware that his appointment to CSV would alarm some people. Many believe a person from the welfare field would be best placed to take account of the complex moral and social issues underlying CSV's work. Patterson recognised this criticism but was clear: 'I wasn't brought in because I know about social work ... but because I know a bit about organisation'. Paterson had come from the newly created Victorian Department of Water Resources (DWR), where his task was to rationalise the functioning of a myriad of small rural water boards. He arrived at DWR — and

then at CSV — with a reputation from his time at the Hunter District Water Board.

The job at Hunter District, in northern New South Wales, was a new experience for Paterson, who had graduated from the University of Melbourne with a commerce degree and completed his PhD at ANU. After working for a white-collar union body, and running his own consultancy company during the 1970s, he joined the engineering and town planning consultancy firm Pak Poy, later moving to the NSW Department of Environment and Planning. He commented to a reporter: 'I held fairly dry views during the 70s, which weren't at the height of fashion then ... I was pretty much in favour of being in the marketplace and that kind of stuff.'

The Hunter District Water Board was described by Paterson as 'a celebrated basket case', an institution where 'the atmosphere of corruption, demoralisation and decay was everywhere — apparent in every artefact of organisational life'. Paterson retired many senior managers and fired others. He introduced a user-pays system for water. Most importantly, he set in a train a major reorientation of the organisation's culture. His approach engendered considerable hostility, but also much admiration.

He also had firm views on his role as chief executive of a government agency. Of his agreeing to take on CSV, he said:

When I was approached about coming over here I actually had a sit down with the then Minister and we talked it through. I said I believe I can probably sort the department out for you, but only if there's a clear recognition of roles. Yours will be to tell us what the priorities are, to see the groups that have an interest, to meet the delegations, to deal with your Cabinet colleagues, and the party apparatus and so on. I'll stay right out of that; that is not my business. But I would expect to be left alone to deal with my own industrial matters, with personnel matters, with operational stuff, with investment or lack thereof in systems and that kind of thing . . .

I think the Minister's intentions and the government's intentions when I was sent over here were quite clear. I wasn't sent here to contribute to policy thought in the welfare field. I was sent here to get under control an outfit that was seen to be in more and more trouble. So I've never seen it as my business to say whether we should be putting more emphasis on child care and less on kindergartens, or more emphasis on family support and less on protective services and that kind of stuff. In the absence of hard effectiveness indicators, I would regard that as a matter for political choice. And then it's for me, having been given a budget and given powers, to make them work as best I can . . .

It's not something that one states once and then it's settled forever. Issues arise day to day, then we talk about who should resolve it and what the respective roles are. I would never seek to abrogate the political choice role of the Minister but would wish to be clear about political choice matters. For example, unions might come to the Minister on a disciplinary issue, when we take action against a staff member who's doing the wrong thing. And I would be absolutely adamant that that has absolutely nothing to do with the Minister, unless the Minister wants to bear responsibility for the consequences of bad behaviour or bad practice, which no minister does.

Breaking the ice

Paterson's early reaction to CSV was a sense of surprise. As he subsequently observed:

I'd never personally seen a sick organisation where everyone was absolutely hyperactive. That was a very unusual thing and it's not something I'd expected or been prepared for. To see a huge amount of energy going to no purpose was a new experience for me . . .

I got an impression of a place where management as such had been devalued, and which showed all the consequent effects of that: enormous misdirection of energy; a lot of things that the professional manager would regard as important that got little attention; other matters got overwhelming attention that one would have thought two or three people doing a competent job could have sorted out for the whole department . . .

There were a lot of well-intentioned people. If ever there was a case of the path to hell being paved by good intentions, this Department was on it . . .

His first move was swift and, for those not involved in the process, painless. At 11 a.m. on a Wednesday morning, after two days in the job, Paterson gave the most senior staff a set of parameters on which to base a 'recut' of the Executive, to be completed by Friday. The organisation structure was to be flattened by abolishing the two Deputy Director General positions. Further, the Executive was to be reduced from ten to seven, including the Director General. The Policy Development and Regional Support Divisions were also abolished. As Paul Bartholomew, who became General Manager of Community Programs, described it:

There were three decision rules. One was that all the six General Managers had to have both operations and program responsibilities. There was a fair degree of flexibility in that — you might have one region, or six. Another was that the span of control should be a maximum of eight. And, that work should be divided roughly according to what you get paid.

And he basically then sent us away to sort out what the best proposals were, so there was a lot of negotiation between us, and a recommendation was put to John, and he didn't disagree with it. By the end of the week we had a new top structure in place. (See Exhibit 15.6.)

The restructure served a number of purposes, as Paterson observed. 'It immediately had an impact on the balance of political power between Head Office and the regions. It had massive symbolic content, but it also had massive impact on the direct operation of day-to-day executive authority and the access of people at the operating level to people with senior executive power in the department.'

In late July Paterson issued the first of a series of departmental broadsheets, bordered in red and headed STOP PRESS. It was an open letter to staff in which Paterson kept an earlier promise to outline the rationale behind the new reporting arrangements. He also laid down some early thoughts on CSV.

'Since my appointment', Paterson wrote, 'I have received calls from literally scores of well-wishers. The general burden of their remarks has been that I face a herculean task. Typical comments have been "snake pit", "can of worms",

Exhibit 15.6
CSV reporting arrangements

Source: Community Services Victoria

CSV REPORTING ARRANGEMENTS
as at 15 March 1990

MINISTERIAL STAFF

MINISTER HON. PETER SPYKER

DIRECTOR-GENERAL DR JOHN PATERSON

Director, Office of the Director-General — *Karen Cleave*
- Executive Co ordination
- Legislation & Legal Services
- CSV Promotions Unit
- Media Unit
- Planning & Budget Dvlpt
- Policy & Special Projects
- Operational Research
- Freedom of Information

GENERAL MANAGER CHILD PROTECTION & MAJOR PROJECTS — Peter Allen

Regions	Programs
• North West (metro.) Linda Martin (A)	• IDS State Plan Teri Whiting
• Central Highlands David Volk	• Child Protection Branch Robin Clark
• Wimmera Graeme Smith	• Adoptions
• Caloola Doug Dalton	• Children & Young Persons Act Vic Coull

GENERAL MANAGER COMMUNITY PROGRAMS — Paul Bartholomew

Regions	Programs
• Inner West (metro.) Jude Munro	• HACS Diane Sisely
• Western (metro.) Margaret Wagstaff	• Community Support Diana Batzias
• W. Port (metro.) Mick Ellis (A)	• Phys. & Sensory Disability State Plan Judy Tyers
• Central Gipps. Mark Diamond	
• East Gipps. Andrew Gagalowicz	
• Barwon Bill Joyce	

GENERAL MANAGER RESOURCES — Alan Clayton

Regions	Programs
• Southern (metro.) Ron Tiffen (A)	• Budget & Financial Mgt Ken Taylor
• Upper Murray Tom Keating	• Personnel & Industrial Relations Syma Stern
	• Personnel Jenny Alvin
	• Staff Dev. Katherine Henderson
	• Info. Tech. Joe Wilding
	• Facilities & Adm. Services Gabrielle Levine
	• Mngt Review Peter Stoppa

GENERAL MANAGER FAMILY & YOUTH SERVICES — Ken Williams

Regions	Programs
• Outer East (metro.) John Leatherland (A)	• Extended Family Care Allan Stewart
• Goulburn David Robinson	• Adoption Information Service
	• Statewide Services Redev.
	• Youth Sppt Vaughan Duggan
	• Youth Parole Board
	• Special Needs

GENERAL MANAGER CHILDREN'S & FAMILY SERVICES — Barbara Spalding

Regions	Programs
• Inner Urb. (metro.) Pat Semmens (A)	• Children's and Family Services Ray Judd
• Loddon Campaspe Chris Fyffe	• Vic. Fam. & Ch. Serv. Council Meredith Edgar
• Mallee John Beasy	
• Glenelg Michael Clanchy	

GENERAL MANAGER OFFICE OF INTELLECTUAL DISABILITY SERVICES — Alan Rassaby

Regions	Programs
• North East (metro.) Heather Scovell	• Programs and Program Support Alan Hall
	• Service Pln. & Redev. Wayne Kinrade (A)
	• Statewide Issues Plp Wisdom
	• Nursing Advisory Unit

"the Beirut of bureaucracy", "one long talk fest", and "everyone is so busy being across every thing that they do nothing", and so on. Not one caller had a positive overall perception of CSV.'

He went on to note that his experience had not confirmed these views. 'I know from first hand experience what a genuinely sick organisation looks, feels and smells like ... At CSV we do have some square pegs in round holes, some systems which are primitive relative to contemporary best practice, and some opacity of structure and function when greater transparency is needed. However, the current limits to our performance appear primarily to be the cumulative effects of a *multitude of small shortcomings*, rather than of fundamental flaws.'

Within CSV, reactions to the restructure were generally positive, once the shock had subsided. A common explanation for the crises in early 1989 was that there had been organisational structural problems; that the regions and operational staff had become too remote from the centre. The position of Deputy Director General Regional Services was acknowledged as problematic: four or five people had tried to fill it before Paul Bartholomew, who had often felt himself to be the lone voice on the CSV Executive raising regional concerns.

The groundwork

Paterson moved quickly to stop uncertainty among other management levels. According to Barbara Spalding, the then General Manager of Children's and Family Services:

He did a number of things to reassure people very quickly. I think what would have been in their minds was that he'd make changes with regions. But he very quickly said 'I do not intend to do anything about that, I'm quite satisfied for the time being with the way it is'. So once people understood that — and he did reassure them of that quickly — then they stopped wasting energy on worrying about their own position, and were able to actually receive the messages about the organisation, which was a very skilful sort of move really.

Some people, however, *were* worried about their positions: managers working in program areas. Paterson publicly described their jobs as 'piss and wind'. On the other hand, Regional Directors saw the restructure as leading to a better appreciation of their very diverse roles. As Jude Munro, Director of Inner Eastern Region, put it: 'I've got

the role of a fix-it person. And a generator of resources — my job is to generate resources for clients, from a scarce resource base.' And, as Paul Bartholomew remarked:

Everything reflects itself at the regional level. The regional issues are everything we deal with, and the nature of the business we're in is such that when you are dealing with people who are in fairly precarious or difficult life situations themselves, then the judgements our caseworkers make are very difficult and complex ones with a high degree of risk. And that requires fairly understanding and supportive management structures.

Corporate services were further strengthened under the new regime. Many managers had viewed the systems with concern for some time: 'the nature and sophistication of the welfare system had changed, and the systems weren't there'. Paterson sent Alan Clayton, General Manager of Resources, to look at information systems in child welfare agencies overseas, in the hope of adapting an existing package to CSV's needs.

He also created an Office of the Director General, responsible for executive co-ordination, legislation and legal services, Freedom of Information, media and publicity, budget development and planning, and special projects. Karen Cleave, who had worked previously with Paterson in Water Resources, took over as Director of the Office in February 1990. Her position was a powerful one and some staff were initially threatened by her proximity to Paterson. Although Regional Directors provided support for her work, others, she felt, had adopted a 'hands-off' policy. John Paterson had quickly introduced a media liaison position and assistance to journalists seeking human interest stories took on greater importance. CSV began to actively seek 'good news' stories to counterbalance the 'disaster' reports that could erupt unexpectedly.

Paterson instituted a number of cost-effectiveness studies: a Service Costing Study aimed to uncover costs per client, and model work flows and decision points, in several program areas. There were also plans for institutional and regional equity reviews, and by mid-1990 the draft of a corporate plan was under way. New legislation was also contemplated and an Industry Study was commenced, to explore the size and resource base of non-government service agencies, many of which were funded in part by CSV. Karen Cleave observed of the planning role:

What this organisation has not done is to clearly articulate our principal roles and to articulate where CSV sits in the bureaucracy, where it sits in the community, and its relationship to non-government service providers. While planning is seen to be important, especially in the urban growth areas, it has not been based on answers to these key questions. Existing planning concentrates on service models and service delivery, rather than on their effectiveness and relevance to the community. I don't believe you can really do long-term planning on that basis.

CSV staff of some years standing recalled unfortunate experiences with previous corporate planning exercises:

There was a lot of developing of six-inch tomes that never got anywhere, and a real reluctance to bring disparate parts of the organisation together and say this is where we're going. When Peter Spyker came in as Minister and said 'These are the three things we have to deliver on' it was the first time anyone had said that. And it wouldn't have mattered what they were, but actually being clear about a number of areas to move on was enough.

Tackling CSV's culture

Paterson viewed the 'culture' of CSV as 'a lot of zealous people with strong belief systems', 'a number of contending and warring groups, often highly opinionated and highly motivated to achieve what they thought were proper ends, but with very little sense of corporate purpose or corporate affiliation'. As he saw it:

Belief systems tended to be locally focused. People in child care were about child care; people in IDS were about intellectual disability services. Relatively little cross-programmatic influence ... And within those groups one could say the Head Office self-absorption was often marked, even within programs, with emphasis on doctrinal matters ... The corporate resource that the whole provided was not something which was widely recognised.

Paterson boosted staff development and training from the outset. 'It was something he brought as a given', Barbara Spalding said. She described this approach as 'a reorganisation of priorities':

... a very high priority to things like staff development and training which were there before but it was really just ploughing on doing a job. But now staff have really been given a commission that says 'You're crucial. Get people trained up for their work.' And this is extremely high priority. Particularly management training, but also right across the board, professional task-related training ...

I have a strong view that a lot of people who view themselves as having a professional interest that is in conflict with a management interest actually do have to be assisted and trained to rethink their priorities. And part of the management training that's being offered now is to help people to see that.

The second issue of Stop Press began with a lecture: 'To be across is not to be', a reference to a phrase in common use among welfare workers. Paterson's remarks focused on the role and function of committees. He pointed out that abundant communication did not necessarily make for good communication. To be clear about what you are doing, he noted, you need to be clear in the use of words:

The use of 'to be across' has no place in the English language, let alone in the vocabulary of organisation. Please never use it again at work. The penalty for infringement will be to write out 100 times by hand: TO BE ACROSS IS NOT TO BE.

CSV staff also discussed training with social work departments in tertiary institutions, seeking what General Manager Peter Allen described as: 'a better working relationship, with a clearer understanding on their part of what we want as an employer, and a clearer involvement with them about what the reasonable expectations are, what's appropriately funded in training, and what's post-vocational'.

Getting hold of the levers

In November 1989, Paterson and all SES staff went to a two-day Portfolio Planning Workshop at Ballarat. After working furiously all through the first night, Paterson produced an analysis of the causes of some of the problems in CSV. These included 'client capture', when clients became 'owned' by one program area although requiring services from several programs, and CSV's 'first-come, first served' approach. Using the travel industry as a metaphor, Paterson proposed the idea of a One Stop Shop which, like the travel agent's office, would provide 'a *window* into an *enormous* … system of facilities and services'.

Three strategic areas were identified by Paterson as critical to the achievement of change. The first of these was the Shopfront concept, designed to provide one point of client contact to the department, through which clients could access the full range of services offered. The second challenge was overcoming problems caused by professional and workplace demarcations; and the third was the use of information technology, including a generic case management system. Each of these three 'strategic drivers', as Paterson labelled them, were communicated to staff through Stop Press, a process of 'corporate planning in action':

Shopfront: a new front-end, client-focused presentation of all CSV services

Paterson's vision for Shopfront involved redesigning CSV services to provide greater visibility and accessibility, both in a physical but also in a 'service' sense. The major aim was to help clients of any type to find quickly the services that best fitted their needs, either by streaming initial inquiries to local government or non-government services, or by mixing up individual 'prescription' from CSV's range of services. In Paterson's words, Shopfront would 'put a friendly, helpful and efficient face on what has been until now a faceless, and at times menacing, welfare bureaucracy'.

Shopfront, Paterson said later, 'endorsed a service philosophy which contrasts greatly with the compartmentalisation and client capture philosophy that was absolutely rampant here, even when I started. People then start responding to that … Even without doing anything myself, local services start changing. Integrated youth officer and intellectual disability service officer functions have been developed for a group of kids on the margins of the Corrections program and the Intellectual Disability program. So, a new regional initiative occurred simply by giving the green light to cross-program integration in an abstract sense.'

New career opportunities: A framework for staff development and career mobility

The November Workshop had drawn attention to the number of job classifications in CSV: Social Worker, Mental Retardation Nurse, Intellectual Disability Services Officer, Youth and Child Care Officer, to name only a few. Staff turnover was also a major concern. Paterson proposed the development of a broadened Human Services Worker job structure to subsume existing occupational categories. All staff would have opportunities for extended career development and lateral mobility, in contrast to current categories where 'para-professionals' such as Youth and Child Care Officers and Intellectual Disability Service Officers had very limited career paths.

CSV, Paterson stated, would also produce an integrated approach to training, combining on-the-job experience, in-service training and formal education. He created as well a new peak Staff/Management Consultative Council to replace existing union/management committees. 'Talk about the ideas with your colleagues and think about the issues of workplace representation' he advised. 'Most people are members of a union. Perhaps this is the time to become active and participate in the development of CSV. We still have a long way to go and many choices to make. Many minds are better than a few.'

Information technology: New technology focusing on client information and case management

Much wider use of new information systems would be a key element in improving CSV performance. Client-based accounting and performance measurement, and the use of systems rather than client 'ownership' to track both cases and money flowing through the department, were the major aims.

The Paterson style

These initiatives promoted thinking and some self-scrutiny among staff. The immediate upshot of the Shopfront idea, as General Manager Peter Allen noted: 'was to generate a big query in the minds of staff. They have always been committed to client service, and they were trying to make sense of what a more client-oriented department would be like, and what's the appropriate response to that idea.'

Paterson also sought ideas for new program initiatives, in a process known as the Second Step. Staff were set to work developing these for trial in the more enthusiastic regions. Paterson said 'We got a lot of ideas, about 170 or so. It turned out that 51 of them were things people were already doing in the regions but not telling Head Office because they thought they'd be stomped on.'

Although a popular view was that Head Office staff were simply scared of Paterson, it was generally agreed that his personal qualities added enormously to the impact of the messages: 'He's got tons of charisma, he's personable, aggressive — willing and even eager to adopt a confrontational stance'. According to Alan Clayton:

John took on the role of setting a new management style that was about quick decision making, minimising meetings, stop wanking, And because he's so articulate and entertaining, he created a real interest. In the SES meetings you'd be lucky to get a lot turning up in the old days — now it's standing room only. And he's allowed all the institutional managers to attend, and you get a clear statement of what his expectations and standards are.

Among middle management and more junior staff, reactions to Paterson's broadsides were mixed, especially once the initial excitement died down. One manager suggested that 'he did a number of things that kept everyone thinking while he actually formulated a view about what needed to be done.' Senior managers appreciated being given some elbow room. 'He really doesn't want to get involved in individual issues, whereas in the past I think my work was actually increased by having to brief others who were getting personally involved, as well as dealing with the issue.'

Staff in several cases took the messages very literally. 'They stopped having any meetings', one program manager said, adding that 'there's a tendency for him to upset them by using travel industry analogies.' And, as one regional worker said, 'I've talked to staff out in the field, and it was all interesting in the beginning, but in reality they're saying "Well, life goes on, the services are the same." It hasn't affected services.' Some staff were more critical:

There are some downsides to his management style, which could be detrimental to the organisation ... You do need to treat people in such a way that they're going to give their best for you. This is human services and we ought to look after our own. That process stuff is also important.

The question is really whether John's thrown out the baby with the bath water, in the sense that if it's all operationally based, nuts and bolts stuff, the value bases may not be as apparent.

Paterson himself placed great store on exemplary conduct. He had little tolerance of slipshod performance, buck-passing or abuse of power: 'I do believe that I have a very serious regard to matters of probity, to the conventions of the Westminster system in its modified form. For individual responsibility and all those kinds of things.' By 1990, attention to disciplinary issues had become a major part of Paterson's attempts to 'sort out' CSV. Efforts to deal with 'slackness, wrong-doing and criminal acts by staff' resulted in disciplinary actions increasing from an average of 10.5 per year during the 1980s to 77 in 1990–91. 'In the past', Paterson remarked, 'people often found it much easier to forget about the wrongdoers than wield the axe.'[1]

Various communication techniques were used to re-focus CSV, in addition to Stop Press and Paterson's regular visits to regions. According to Paterson:

Other forms of communication are in some ways more potent. For example, I came in here and said we will back line management if they're trying to do the right thing. Now a lot of bad things happened in our institutions, community residential units and other facilities. But management that's tried to deal with it has very often become the victims. And so on a number of disciplinary matters that came up where I was confident we were on strong ground, I backed management even in the face of industrial stoppages and so on, to see it through. And the message from that is very potent: if you try and do the right thing and do it competently, you'll get backing rather than becoming a burnt offering.

The tasks ahead

John Paterson's job at CSV, as he saw it, was to 'get it under control'. In quick succession CSV acquired a new structure, new priorities and a new language. The new Director-General gave the department a blueprint for the future, and provided symbols to point staff in the right direction. By late 1991 organisational relations had been substantially realigned and many staff had embraced new ways of thinking. Paterson was able to observe 'the management ethos is now remarked on'.

But staff at the frontlines still harbour concerns over the ultimate worth of better management practices. Some argue that streamlining CSV's processes won't necessarily produce superior outcomes. One commented that the response to Baby Kajal had been 'to set up a whole lot of procedural things that will stop it happening … [But] good practice will not be created only by procedures … ultimately you can't make the decision on a checklist'. Others see the department as a 'classic bureaucracy' in which even someone with Paterson's widely recognised ideas and energies has only limited impact at the local level.

Paterson's earliest efforts emphasised management reforms, but he would increasingly turn directly to matters of professional practice. New efforts in this direction included the development of Consensus Documents negotiated among practitioners and representatives of CSV and other agencies. Targeted at professionals, these documents attempt to bring together varying strands of policy and practice in a manual endorsed by government and non-government services, central and regional offices. As an example, the Consensus Document for Protective Services was based on a belief that the search for common ground could be used to develop better client services. It contains a philosophy of child protection and definitions of terms such as child abuse. Categories of maltreatment, management responsibilities, agreed objectives and co-ordinating mechanisms are also specified.

For Paterson, 'effective practice is the practice which produces the best client outcomes', though for some professionals the process of defining and reproducing it remains more problematic. Paterson was appalled to hear in his discussions with the recognised best practitioners in CSV that they had needed to 'unlearn' major elements of their undergraduate education. Undaunted, he has embarked on 'an attempt to identify best practice and bottle it'.[2]

Endnotes

1   *Herald*, 3 October 1990.
2   Foreword to CSV Annual Report 1990–91.

PART 5

Organisational structure AND design

16

Organisational structure and design

Who has seen the wind? Neither you or I:
But when the trees bow down their heads,
The wind is passing by.
— Christina Georgina Rossetti *'Who Has Seen the Wind?'*, st. 2

ORGANISATIONAL STRUCTURE AND DESIGN

Chapter 16

Learning objectives

- **Identify** *the choices which must be made in designing an organisation structure.*

- **Define** *what is meant by the term 'division of labour'.*

- **Discuss** *the role of delegation of authority in design decisions.*

- **Describe** *several forms of departmentalisation.*

- **Explain** *the importance of span of control.*

- **Define** *three important dimensions of structure.*

- **Compare** *mechanistic and organic organisational design.*

- **Identify** *the major advantages of matrix organisation design.*

- **Discuss** *multinational organisation structure and design issues.*

Organisational structure and design have always been important factors influencing the behaviour of individuals and groups that comprise the organisation; the new rules of operating in today's global business environment make structure and design considerations even more critical.[1] Through the design of the structure, management establishes expectations for what individuals and groups will do to achieve the organisation's purposes. But before these purposes can be accomplished, somebody must do some work. People must not only do some work, but also do the right work. And that brings us to organisational structure, because through organisation managers decide how the purposes will be accomplished.[2]

Managers achieve coordinated effort through the design of a structure of task and authority relationships.[3] Design, in this context, implies that managers make a conscious effort to predetermine the way employees do their work. Structure refers to relatively stable relationships and processes of the organisation. Organisational structure is considered by many to be 'the anatomy of the organisation, providing a foundation within which the organisation functions'.[4] Thus, the structure of an organisation, similar to the anatomy of a living organism, can be viewed as a framework. The idea of structure as a framework 'focuses on the differentiation of positions, formulation of rules and procedures, and prescriptions of authority'.[5] Therefore, the purpose of structure is to regulate, or at least reduce, uncertainty in the behaviour of individual employees.

Organisations are purposive and goal-oriented, and so it follows that the structure of organisations also is purposive and goal-directed. Our concept of organisational structure takes into account the existence of purposes and goals, and our attitude is that management should think of structure in terms of its contribution to organisational effectiveness, even though the exact nature of the relationship between structure and effectiveness is inherently difficult to know. Structure alone, however, is only one part of the organisation. This chapter examines structural and design variables in the context of a total organisation system.

DESIGNING AN ORGANISATIONAL STRUCTURE

Managers who set out to design an organisational structure face difficult decisions. They must choose among a myriad of alternative frameworks of jobs and departments. The process by which they make these choices is termed *organisational design*, and it means quite simply the decisions and actions that result in an organisational structure. This process may be explicit or implicit, it may be 'one-shot' or developmental, or it may be done by a single manager or by a team of managers.[6] However the actual decisions come about, the content of the decisions is always the same. The first two decisions focus on individual jobs, and the next two decisions focus on departments or groups of jobs.

1. Managers decide how to divide the overall task into successively smaller jobs — divide the total activities of the task into smaller sets of related activities. The effect of this decision is to define jobs in terms of specialised activities and responsibilities. Although jobs have many characteristics, the most important one is their degree of specialisation.

2. Managers distribute authority among the jobs. Authority is the right to make decisions without approval by a higher manager and to exact obedience from designated other people. All jobs contain some degree of right to make decisions within prescribed limits, but not all jobs contain the right to exact obedience from others. The latter aspect of authority distinguishes managerial from non-managerial jobs. Managers can exact obedience; non-managers cannot.

The outcomes of these two decisions are jobs which management assigns to individuals. The jobs will have two distinct attributes: activities and authority. The third and fourth decisions affect the manner in which the jobs are grouped into departments.

3. Managers decide the bases by which the individual jobs are to be grouped together. This decision is much like any other classification decision, and it can result in groups containing jobs which are relatively homogeneous or heterogeneous.

4. Finally, managers decide the appropriate size of the group reporting to each superior, and this decision involves determining whether spans of control are relatively few or many.

Thus, organisational structures vary depending on the choices that managers make. If we consider each of the four design decisions to be a continuum of possible choices, the alternative structures can be depicted as follows:

	Specialisation	
Division of labour:		
	High	Low
	Delegation	
Authority:		
	High	Low
	Basis	
Departmentalisation:		
	Homogeneous	Heterogeneous
	Number	
Span of control:		
	Few	Many

Generally speaking, organisational structures will tend towards one extreme or the other along each continuum. Structures tending to the left are characterised by a number of terms including *classical, formalistic, structured, bureaucratic, System 1,* and *mechanistic.* Structures tending to the right are termed *neoclassical, informalistic, unstructured, non-bureaucratic, System 4* and *organic.*[7] Exactly where along the continuum an organisation finds itself has implications for its performance as well as for individual and group behaviour.

DIVISION OF LABOUR

Division of labour concerns the extent to which jobs are specialised. Managers divide the total task of the organisation into specific jobs having specified activities which define what the person performing the job is to do. For example, the activities of the job 'accounting clerk' can be defined in terms of the methods and procedures required to process certain types of quantities of transactions during a period of time. Using the same methods and procedures, one accounting clerk could be processing accounts receivable while others process accounts payable. Thus, jobs can be specialised both by method and by application of the method.

Exercise 16
Paper Plane
Corporation

The economic advantages of dividing work into specialised jobs are the principal historical reasons for the creation of organisations.[8] As societies became more and more industrialised and urbanised, craft production gave way to mass production. Mass production depends on the ability to obtain the economic benefits of specialised labour, and the most effective means for obtaining specialised labour is through organisations. Although managers are concerned with more than the economic implications of jobs, they seldom lose sight of specialisation as the rationale for dividing work among jobs.[9]

DELEGATION OF AUTHORITY

Managers decide how much authority is to be delegated to each job and each job older. As we have noted, authority refers to the right of individuals to make decisions without approval by higher management and to exact obedience from others. It is important to understand that delegation refers specifically to making decisions — not to doing work. A sales manager can be delegated the right to hire salespersons (a decision) and the right to assign them to specific territories (obedience). Another sales manager may not have the right to hire but may have the right to assign territories. Thus, the degree of delegated authority can be relatively high or relatively low with respect to both aspects of authority. For any particular job there is a range of alternative configurations of authority delegation, and managers must balance the relative gains and losses of these alternatives. Let us evaluate some of them.

First, relatively high delegation of authority encourages the development of professional managers. As decision-making authority is pushed down (delegated) in the organisation, managers have opportunities to make significant decisions and to gain skills that enable them to advance in the company. By virtue of their right to make decisions on a broad range of issues, managers develop expertise that enables them to cope with problems of higher management. Managers with broad decision-making power often make difficult decisions. Consequently, they are trained for promotion into positions of even greater authority and responsibility. Upper management can readily compare managers on the basis of actual decision-making performance. The advancement of managers on the basis of demonstrated performance can eliminate favouritism and personality conflicts in the promotion process.

Second, high delegation of authority can lead to a competitive climate within the organisation. Managers are motivated to contribute in this competitive atmosphere since they are compared with their peers on various performance

671

measures. A competitive environment in which managers compete on how well they achieve sales, cost reduction and employee development targets can be a positive factor in overall organisational performance. Competitive environments can also produce destructive behaviour if the success of one manager occurs at the expense of another. But regardless of whether it is positive or destructive, significant competition exists only when individuals have authority to do those things which enable them to win.

Finally, managers who have relatively high authority are able to exercise more autonomy and thus satisfy their desires to participate in problem solving. This autonomy can lead to managerial creativity and ingenuity which contribute to the adaptiveness and development of the organisation and managers. Opportunities to participate in setting goals can be positive motivators. But a necessary condition for goal setting is authority to make decisions.

These are only three of the benefits associated with delegated authority. But these advantages are not free of costs. Some of the costs are:

1. Managers must be trained to make the decisions that go with delegated authority. Formal training programs can be quite expensive, and the costs can more than offset the benefits.
2. Many managers accustomed to making decisions resist delegating authority to their subordinates. Consequently, they may perform at lower levels of effectiveness because they believe that delegation of authority involves losing control.
3. Administrative costs are incurred because new or altered accounting, rating and reporting systems must be developed to provide top management with information about the effects of their subordinates' decisions.

These are, of course, only some of the costs. As is usually the case in managerial decisions, whether to centralise or decentralise authority cannot be resolved simply and can be guided only by general questions.

DEPARTMENTALISATION

Departmentalisation, or the process of defining the activities and authority of jobs, is analytical; that is, the total task of the organisation is broken down into successively smaller ones. But then management must combine the divided tasks into groups of departments.

The rationale of grouping jobs rests on the necessity for coordinating them. The specialised jobs are separate, interrelated parts of the total task, and accomplishing the task requires the accomplishment of each of the jobs. But the jobs must be performed in the specific manner and sequence intended by management when they were defined. As the number of specialised jobs in an organisation increases, there comes a point when they can no longer be effectively coordinated by a single manager. Thus, to create manageable numbers of jobs, they are combined into smaller groups, and a new job is defined — that of manager of the group. The crucial managerial consideration when creating departments is the determination of the bases of grouping jobs. These bases are termed *departmentalisation bases*, and some of the more widely used ones are described in the following sections.

Functional departmentalisation

Managers can combine jobs according to the functions of the organisation. Every organisation must undertake certain activities in order to do its work, and these necessary activities are the organisation's functions. The necessary functions of a manufacturing firm include production, marketing, finance, accounting and personnel — activities necessary to create, produce and sell a product. The necessary functions of a commercial bank include taking deposits, making loans and investing the bank's funds. The functions of a hospital include surgery, psychiatry, housekeeping, pharmacy, nursing and personnel.[10] Each of these functions can be a specific department, and jobs can be combined according to them. The functional basis is often found in relatively small organisations providing a narrow range of products and services. It is also widely used as the basis of divisions of large multiproduct organisations.

The Oldsmobile Division of General Motors is structured on a functional basis as depicted in Exhibit 16.1. General Motors management decided on eight functions — engineering, manufacturing, reliability, distribution, finance, personnel, public relations, and purchasing — as the bases for combining the jobs of the Oldsmobile Division. Other divisions of General Motors use different functional bases depending on management decisions. The specific configuration of functions that appear as separate departments varies from organisation to organisation.

Exhibit 16.1
Organisational structure of Oldsmobile Division

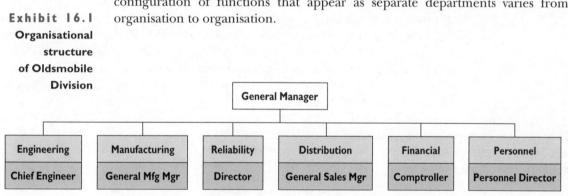

The principal advantage of the functional departmentalisation basis is its efficiency. That is, it seems logical to have a department consisting of experts in a particular field such as production or accounting. By having departments of specialists, management creates highly efficient units. An accountant is generally more efficient when working with other accountants and other individuals who have similar backgrounds and interests. They can share expertise to get the work done.

A major disadvantage of this departmental basis is that because specialists are working with and encouraging each other in their area of expertise and interest, the organisational goals may be sacrificed in favour of departmental goals. Accountants may see only their problems and not those of production or marketing or the total organisation. In other words, the culture of and identification with the department are often stronger than identification with the organisation and its culture.

Territorial departmentalisation

Another commonly adopted method for departmentalising is to establish groups on the basis of geographical area. The logic is that all activities in a given region should be assigned to one manager who would be in charge of all operations in that particular geographical area.

In large organisations territorial arrangements are advantageous because physical dispersion of activities makes centralised coordination difficult. For example, it is extremely difficult for someone in Sydney to manage salespeople in Perth. It makes sense to assign the managerial job to someone in Perth.

Territorial departmentalisation provides a training ground for managerial personnel. The company is able to place managers in territories and then assess their progress in that geographical region. The experience that managers acquire in a territory away from headquarters provides valuable insights about how products and/or services are accepted in the field.

Product departmentalisation

Many large diversified companies group jobs on the basis of product where all jobs associated with producing and selling a product or product line are placed under the direction of one manager. As a firm grows by increasing the number of products it markets, it is difficult to coordinate the various functional departments, and it becomes advantageous to establish product units. This form of organisation allows personnel to develop total expertise in researching, manufacturing and distributing a product line. Concentration of the authority, responsibility and accountability in a specific product department allows top management to coordinate actions.

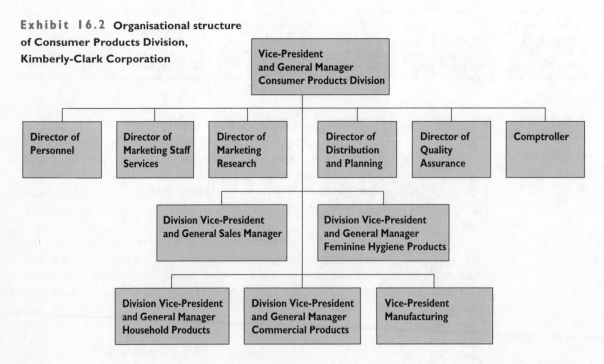

Exhibit 16.2 Organisational structure of Consumer Products Division, Kimberly-Clark Corporation

The Consumer Products Division of Kimberly-Clark reflects product departmentalisation. The specific product groups shown in Exhibit 16.2 include feminine hygiene, household and commercial products. Within each of these units we find production and marketing personnel. Since managers of product divisions coordinate sales, manufacturing and distribution of a product, they become the overseers of a profit centre. In this manner profit responsibility is implemented in product-based organisations. Managers are often asked to establish profit goals at the beginning of a time period and then to compare actual profit with planned profit.

Product-based organisations foster initiative and autonomy by providing division managers with the resources necessary to carry out their profit plans. But such organisations face the difficult issue of deciding how much redundancy is necessary. Divisional structures contain some degree of redundancy because each division wants its own research and development, engineering, marketing and production personnel. Thus, with technical and professional personnel found throughout the organisation at the division levels, the cost can be exorbitant. In companies with a large number of divisions, coordination also can be extremely difficult.

Customer departmentalisation

Customers and clients can be bases for grouping jobs.[11] For example, educational institutions have customer-oriented divisions such as regular (day and night) courses and extension divisions. In some instances a professor will be affiliated solely with one or the other. In fact, the titles of some faculty positions often specifically mention the extension division.

Another form of customer departmentalisation is the loan department in a commercial bank. Loan officers are often associated only with industrial, commercial, or agricultural loans, and the customer will be served by one of these three loan officers.

Some department stores are set up to a degree on a customer basis with groupings such as university shops, men's and boys' clothing departments, and bargain floors. Organisations with customer-based departments are better able to satisfy customer-identified needs than organisations that base departments on non-customer factors.[12]

Mixed and changing departmentalisation

The bases for departments do not remain unchanged in organisations. Because of the importance of departments, managers change the bases as conditions warrant. An organisation chart should be viewed much like a snapshot of a moving object. The action is frozen for a moment, but the viewer understands that the object continued in motion. Over time organisations will use a mix of bases — at some time using function and at other times using product, territory and customer bases. Moreover, within the same organisation will be different bases at different levels of management. For example, the departmental basis at the corporate level of General Motors is by product type — compact and full-size cars — with an executive vice-president heading up each division. The general managers of the Chevrolet and Pontiac divisions report to the compact car vice-president; and the general managers of the Buick, Oldsmobile and Cadillac divisions report to the full-size-car vice-president. But below the general managers, function is on the departmental basis as we noted in Exhibit 16.1.

SPAN OF CONTROL

The determination of appropriate bases for departmentalisation establishes the kinds of jobs that will be grouped together. But that determination does not establish the number of jobs to be included in a specific group. That determination is the issue of span of control. Generally, the issue comes down to the decision of how many people a manager can oversee; that is, will the organisation be more effective if the span of control is relatively wide or narrow? The question is basically concerned with determining the volume of interpersonal relationships the department's manager is able to handle. Moreover, the span of control must be defined to include not only formally assigned subordinates but also those who have access to the manager. A manager may be placed in a position of not only being responsible for immediate subordinates but also being the chairperson of several committees and task groups that take time.

The number of potential interpersonal relationships between a manger and subordinates increases geometrically as the number of subordinates increases arithmetically. This relationship holds because managers potentially contend with three types of interpersonal relationships: direct single, direct group, and cross. Direct-single relationships occur between the manager and each subordinate individually in a one-on-one setting. Direct-group relations occur between the manager and each possible permutation of subordinates. Finally, cross relationships occur when subordinates interact with one another.

The critical consideration in determining the manager's span of control is not the number of potential relationships. Rather it is the frequency and intensity of the actual relationships that is important. Not all relationships will occur, and those which do will vary in importance. If we shift our attention from potential to actual relationships as the basis for determining optimum span of control, at least three factors appear to be important: required contact, degree of specialisation and ability to communicate.

Required contact

Research and development, medical and production work have a need for frequent contact and a high degree of coordination between a superior and subordinates. The use of conferences and other forms of consultation often aid in the attainment of goals within a constrained time period. For example, the research and development team leader may have to consult frequently with team members so that a project is completed within a time period that will allow the organisation to place a product on the market. Thus, instead of relying on memos and reports, it is in the best interest of the organisation to have as many in-depth contacts with the team as possible. A large span of control would preclude contacting subordinates so frequently, and this could have detrimental effects on completing the project. In general, the greater the inherent ambiguity that exists in an individual's job, the greater the need for supervision to avoid conflict and stress.[13]

Degree of specialisation

The degree of employee specialisation is a critical consideration in establishing the span of control at all levels of management. It is generally accepted that a manager at the lower organisational level (e.g. first-line supervisor) can oversee more subordinates because work at this level is more specialised and less complicated than at higher levels of management (e.g. president). Management can combine highly specialised and similar jobs into relatively large departments because the employees may not need close supervision.

Ability to communicate

Instructions, guidelines and policies must be communicated verbally to subordinates in most work situations. The need to discuss job-related factors influences the span of control. The individual who can clearly and concisely communicate with subordinates is able to manage more people than one who cannot do so. Even though it is possible to identify some of the specific factors that relate to optimal spans of control, the search for the full answer continues.[14]

DIMENSIONS OF STRUCTURE

The four design decisions (division of labour, delegation of authority, departmentalisation and span of control) result in the structure of organisations. Researchers and practitioners of management have attempted to develop their understanding of relationships between structures and performance, attitudes, satisfaction and other variables thought to be important, but this has been hampered by the complexity of the relationships themselves as well as by the difficulty of defining and measuring the concept of organisational structure.

Although universal agreement on a common set of dimensions that measure differences in structure is neither possible nor desirable, some suggestions can be made. At the present time three dimensions — formalisation, centralisation and complexity — are often used in research and practice to describe structure.[15]

Formalisation

The dimension of **formalisation** refers to the extent to which expectations regarding the means and ends of work are specified and written. In a highly formalised organisational structure, rules and procedures prescribe what each individual should be doing. Such organisations would have written standard operating procedures, specified directives and explicit policies.[16] In terms of the four design decisions, formalisation is the result of high specialisation of labour, high delegation of authority, the use of functional departments and wide spans of control.

ORGANISATIONAL   Encounter

The de-layering of organisations

As we saw in Chapter 15 on organisational change, one of the most common responses to a changed environment is the flattening of organisational structures. In this Encounter, we look at one consequence of flatter structures — a poorer career path — and consider how organisations can deal with this issue.

First, let's consider just how big an issue restructuring and the loss of organisational layers is. A recent article in *Business Review Weekly* shows us that many of the largest organisations have been engaged in serious restructuring over the past decade.

What are the aims of restructuring? According to human resource managers in these organisations, the aim of 'delayering' is to encourage managers to develop cross-functional skills, create greater accountability and have employees accept greater responsibility for their development. In many organisations, this has meant a culture shift, with a new culture that emphasises communication, collaboration, team work and employee involvement.

This does, however, also mean that employees face a less clear career path. Consequently, many organisations — Telstra, Boral and BHP — now say that staff must give up the traditional idea of moving up, and exchange vertical moves for horizontal moves. The skills important for this new breed of management include cross-functional and networking skills, the ability to be a team player and excellent communication skills.

For the organisation, there are two problems that follow this type of restructuring. The first is to find a new way to motivate and reward staff. Motivational strategies such as providing job variety and challenge, coupled with feedback, have taken on a new importance in these organisations. The second is to select and retain 'star performers'. While recognising the greater mobility and flexibility of the workforce, organisations must also be acutely aware of the need to retain a small core of talented employees who will be groomed for senior management. Rotation, interdivisional and international transfers are among the strategies used to ensure that star performers do not change organisations to enhance their career prospects.

Source: James, D. (1995). The end of the career path, *Business Review Weekly*, March 6.

The company ...	then ...	and now
General Electric	• Up to 80 management layers	• 4 layers between a worker at Dandenong and the CEO (Jack Welch, in USA)
IBM	• 406 000 staff • 10 management layers • Manager controls 6	• 250 000 staff • 4 management layers • Manager controls 12
Hewlett Packard	• 12 management layers	• 4 management layers
Pacific BBA		• 70% reduction in management
Dow Chemical		• Devolve management responsibility • Create broad job classifications • Change function of line managers

Although formalisation is defined in terms of written rules and procedures, it is important to understand how these are viewed by the employees. In organisations with all the appearances of formalisation — thick manuals of rules, procedures and policies — employees may not perceive the manuals as affecting their behaviour. Thus, even though rules and procedures exist, they must be enforced if they are to affect behaviour.[17]

Centralisation

Centralisation refers to the location of decision-making authority in the hierarchy of the organisation. More specifically, the concept refers to the delegation of authority among the jobs in the organisation. Typically, researchers and practitioners think of centralisation in terms of decision making and control.[18] But despite the apparent simplicity of the concept, it can be complex.

The complexity of the concept derives from three sources. First, people at the same level can have different decision-making authority. Second, not all decisions are of equal importance in organisations; for example, a typical management practice is to delegate authority to make routine operating decisions (i.e. decentralisation) but retain authority to make strategic decisions (i.e. centralisation). Third, individuals may not perceive that they really have authority even though their job descriptions include it. Thus, objectively they have authority, but subjectively they do not.[19]

Complexity

Reading 16
The new enterprise architecture

Complexity is the direct outgrowth of dividing work and creating departments. Specifically, the concept refers to the number of distinctly different job titles or occupational groupings, and the number of distinctly different units or departments. The fundamental idea is that organisations with a great many different kinds and types of jobs and units create more complicated managerial and organisational problems than those with fewer jobs and departments.

Complexity, then, relates to differences among jobs and units. It is therefore not surprising that differentiation is often used synonymously with complexity. Moreover, it has become standard practice to use the term **horizontal differentiation** to refer to the number of different units at the same level; vertical differentiation refers to the number of levels in the organisation. The degree of **vertical differentiation** determines how 'flat' or 'tall' the organisation will be. In recent years there has been a tendency to reduce vertical differentiation, or flatten organisations. Since this reduces the number of levels in the organisation such restructuring activities can displace employees. Thus, important questions of company values and ethical issues may be involved in restructuring. The discussion of the relationships between dimensions of organisational structure and the four design decisions is summarised in Exhibit 16.3. The figure notes only the causes of high formalisation, centralisation and complexity. However, the relationships are symmetrical: the causes of low formalisation, centralisation and complexity are the opposite of those shown. In completing Exercise 16, think about the dimensions of structure as you compete with other groups.

Exhibit 16.3	Dimensions	Decisions
Organisation dimensions and organisational decisions	High formalisation	1. High specialisation 2. Delegated authority 3. Functional departments 4. Wide spans of control
	High centralisation	1. High specialisation 2. Centralised authority 3. Functional departments 4. Wide spans of control
	High complexity	1. High specialisation 2. Delegated authority 3. Territorial, customer and product departments 4. Narrow spans of control

ORGANISATIONAL DESIGN MODELS

As we have seen, organisational design refers to managerial decision making aimed at determining the structure and processes that coordinate and control the jobs of the organisation. The outcome of organisational design decisions is the framework or structure of the organisation. However, design decisions are not permanent. Organisation designs are continually adapted to deal more effectively with changing conditions.[20] Earlier in this chapter, we examined a number of factors and dimensions that influence the structure which ultimately emerges. In this section, we briefly examine two general organisational design models that have had significant impact on management theory and practice. While there is little uniformity in the terms used to designate the models, we refer to them as *mechanistic* and *organic*.[21] In a later section in the chapter, we review an emerging organisational design: the matrix.

The mechanistic model

During the early part of the 20th century a body of literature emerged that considered the problem of designing the structure of an organisation as but one of a number of managerial tasks, including planning and controlling. The objective of the contributors to that body of literature was to define principles that could guide managers in the performance of their tasks. Numerous theorists and management practitioners made contributions to this literature, including such names as Fayol, Follet and Weber. While each contributor made a unique contribution, they all had a common thread. They each described the same type of organisation, one that functioned in a machinelike manner to accomplish the organisation's goals in a highly efficient manner. Thus, the term 'mechanistic' aptly describes such organisations.

Mechanistic organisations emphasise the importance of achieving high levels of production and efficiency through the use of extensive rules and procedures, centralised authority and high specialisation:

- Activities are specialised into clearly defined jobs and tasks.
- Persons of higher rank typically have greater knowledge of the problems facing the organisation than those at lower levels. Unresolved problems are thus passed up the hierarchy.
- Standardised policies, procedures and rules guide much of the decision making in the organisation.
- Rewards are chiefly obtained through obedience to instructions from supervisors.[22]

The mechanistic model achieves high levels of efficiency due to its structural characteristics. It is highly complex because of its emphasis on specialisation of labour; it is highly centralised because of its emphasis on authority and accountability; and it is highly formalised because of its emphasis on function as the primary basis of departmentalisation.

The organic model

The **organic model of organisational design** stands in sharp contrast to the mechanistic model. The organisational characteristics and practices that underlie the organic model are distinctly different from those that underlie the mechanistic model. The most distinct differences between the two models result from the different effectiveness criteria that each seeks to maximise. While the mechanistic model seeks to maximise efficiency and production, the organic model seeks to maximise flexibility and adaptability:

- There is a de-emphasis on job descriptions and specialisation. Persons become involved in problem solving when they have the knowledge or skill that will help solve the problem.
- It is not assumed that persons holding higher positions are necessarily better informed than those at lower levels.
- Horizontal and lateral organisational relationships are given as much or more attention as vertical relationships.
- Status and rank differences are de-emphasised.
- The formal structure of the organisation is less permanent and more changeable.[23]

The organic organisation is flexible and adaptable to changing environmental demands because its design encourages greater utilisation of the human potential. Managers are encouraged to adopt practices that tap the full range of human motivations through job design which stresses personal growth and responsibility. Decision making, control and goal-setting processes are decentralised and are shared at all levels of the organisation. Communications flow throughout the organisation, not simply down the chain of command. These practices are intended to implement a basic assumption of the organic model, which states that an organisation will be effective to the extent that its structure is 'such as to ensure a maximum probability that in all interactions and in all relationships with the organisation, each member, in the light of his background, values, desires, and expectations, will view the experience as supportive and one which builds and maintains a sense of personal worth and importance'.[24]

An organisational design that provides individuals with this sense of personal worth and motivation and that facilitates flexibility and adaptability would have the following characteristics:

- It would be relatively simple because of its de-emphasis on specialisation and its emphasis on increasing job range.
- It would be relatively decentralised because of its emphasis on delegation of authority and increasing job depth.
- It would be relatively informal because of its emphasis on product and customer as bases for departmentalisation.

Which of the two models is better? The answer is neither and both. Neither is better for any and all situations. Both can be better depending on the situation.[25] Because of management's interest in designing organisations that have the advantages of both models, the matrix model has emerged as a promising alternative.

MATRIX ORGANISATION DESIGN

A **matrix organisation design** attempts to maximise the strengths and minimise the weaknesses of both the mechanistic and organic designs. In practical terms the matrix design combines functional and product departmental bases.[26] Companies such as American Cyanamid, Avco, Carborundum, Caterpillar, Hughes Aircraft, ITT, Monsanto, NCR, Prudential Insurance, TWR, and Texas Instruments are only a few of the users of matrix organisation. Public sector users include public health and social service agencies.[27] Although the exact meaning of matrix organisation is not well established, the most typical meaning sees it as a balanced compromise between functional and product organisation, between departmentalisation by process and by purpose.[28]

The matrix organisational design achieves the desired balance by superimposing, or overlaying, a horizontal structure of authority, influence and communication on the vertical structure. The arrangement can be described as in Exhibit 16.4. Personnel assigned in each cell belong not only to the functional department but also to a particular product or project. For example, manufacturing, marketing, engineering and finance specialists will be assigned to work on one or more projects or products. As a consequence, personnel will report to two managers — one in their functional department and one in the project or product unit. The existence of a dual-authority system is a distinguishing characteristic of matrix organisation.

Matrix structures are found in organisations which require responses to rapid change in two or more environments, such as technology and markets; which face uncertainties that generate high information-processing requirements; and which must deal with financial and human resources constraints.[29] Managers confronting these circumstances must obtain certain advantages which are most likely to be realised with matrix organisation.[30]

Exhibit 16.4
Matrix
organisations

Project, Products	Functions			
	Manufacturing	Marketing	Engineering	Finance
Project or product A				
Project or product B				
Project or product C				
Project or product D				
Project or product E				

Advantages of matrix organisation

A number of advantages can be associated with the matrix design. Some of the more important ones are as follows:

Efficient use of resources

Matrix organisation facilitates the utilisation of highly specialised staff and equipment. Each project or product unit can share the specialised resource with other units rather than duplicating it to provide independent coverage for each. This is particularly advantageous when projects require less than the full-time efforts of the specialist. For example, a project may require only half a computer scientist's time. Rather than having several underutilised computer scientists assigned to each project, the organisation can keep fewer of them fully utilised by shifting them from project to project.

Flexibility in conditions of change and uncertainty

Timely response to change requires information and communication channels that efficiently get the information to the right people at the right time.[31] Matrix structures encourage constant interaction among project unit and functional department members. Information is channelled vertically and horizontally as people exchange technical knowledge, resulting in quicker response to competitive conditions, technological breakthroughs, and other environmental conditions.

Technical excellence

Technical specialists interact with other specialists while assigned to a project. These interactions encourage cross-fertilisation of ideas such as when a computer scientist must discuss the pros and cons of electronic data processing with a financial accounting expert. Each specialist must be able to listen, understand and respond to the views of the other. At the same time, specialists maintain contact with members of their own discipline because they are also members of a functional department.

Freeing top management for long-range planning

An initial stimulus for the development of matrix organisations is that top management increasingly becomes involved with day-to-day operations. Environmental changes tend to create problems that cross functional and product departments and cannot be resolved by the lower level managers. For example, when competitive conditions create the need to develop new products at faster than previous rates, the existing procedures become bogged down. Top management is then called upon to settle conflicts among the functional managers. Matrix organisation makes it possible for top management to delegate ongoing decision making, thus providing more time for long-range planning.

Improving motivation and commitment

Project and product groups are composed of individuals with specialised knowledge to whom management assigns, on the basis of their expertise, responsibility for specific aspects of the work. Consequently, decision making within the group tends to be more participative and democratic than in more hierarchical settings. This opportunity to participate in key decisions fosters high levels of motivation and commitment, particularly for individuals with acknowledged professional orientations.

Providing opportunities for personal development

Members of matrix organisations are provided considerable opportunity to develop their skills and knowledge. Placed in groups consisting of individuals representing diverse parts of the organisation, they come to appreciate the different points of view expressed and become more aware of the total organisation. Moreover, the experience broadens each specialist's knowledge not only of the organisation but also of other scientific and technical disciplines — engineers develop knowledge of financial issues; accountants learn about marketing.

Different forms of matrix organisation

Matrix organisation forms can be depicted as existing in the middle of a continuum with mechanistic organisations at one extreme and organic organisations at the other. Organisations can move from mechanistic to matrix forms or from organic to matrix forms. Ordinarily, the process of moving to matrix organisation is evolutionary. That is, as the present structure proves incapable of dealing with rapid technological and market changes, management attempts to cope by establishing procedures and positions which are outside the normal routine.

This evolutionary process consists of the following steps:

Task force

When a competitor develops a new product that quickly captures the market, a rapid response is necessary. Yet in a System 1 organisation, new product development is often too time-consuming because of the necessity to coordinate the various units that must be involved. A convenient approach is to create a task force of individuals from each functional department and charge it with the responsibility to expedite the process. The task force achieves its objective and then dissolves, and members return to their primary assignment.

Teams

If the product or technological breakthrough generates a family of products that move through successive stages of new and improved products, the temporary task force concept is ineffective. A typical next step is to create permanent teams consisting of representatives from each functional department. The teams meet regularly to resolve interdepartmental issues and to achieve coordination. When not involved with issues associated with new product development, the team members work on their regular assignments.

Product managers

If the technological breakthrough persists so that new product development becomes a way of life, top management will create the roles of product managers. In a sense, product managers chair the teams, but they now are permanent positions. They have no formal authority over the team members but must rely on their expertise and interpersonal skill to influence them. Companies such as General Foods, Du Pont and IBM make considerable use of the product management concept.

Product management departments

The final step in the evolution to matrix organisation is the creation of product management departments with subproduct managers for each product line. In some instances the subproduct managers are selected from specific functional departments and would continue to report directly to their functional managers. Considerable diversity in the application of matrix organisation exists, yet the essential feature is the creation of overlapping authority and the existence of dual authority.

Exactly where along the continuum an organisation stops in the evolution depends on factors in the situation. Specifically and primarily important are the rates of change in technological and product developments. The resultant uncertainty and information required vary.

MULTINATIONAL STRUCTURE AND DESIGN

As we have seen previously, four design decisions regarding division of labour, delegation of authority, departmentalisation and span of control shape the design of organisational structures. These decisions, in turn, are affected by a variety of factors. Foremost among them are the social, political, cultural, legal and economic environments in which the organisation is operating. Because of their very nature, multinational corporations frequently exist in very divergent environments. A multinational corporation may be categorised as consisting of a group of geographically dispersed organisations with different national subsidiaries.[32]

One approach to setting up a foreign subsidiary is that of *replication*. That is, the same organisation structure and operating policies and procedures that exist in the existing domestic organisation are used. For example, when establishing its foreign subsidiaries, Procter & Gamble created an 'exact replica of the United States Procter & Gamble organisation' because they believed that using 'exactly the same policies and procedures which have given our company success in the United States will be equally successful overseas'.[33] The potential difficulty with such a practice is that it may result in the reliance upon organisational designs and management practices that are simply unsuitable for the environment of the host country. This may explain why there is a tendency for foreign subsidiary organisational structures to evolve over time as the company becomes more internationalised.[34]

For multinational corporations there are a number of factors which may have important implications for structure and design decisions, as well as general operating policies. We will briefly examine four of these.[35]

- *National boundaries are an important force in defining organisational environments.* This is similar to the point we made at the beginning of this discussion. For many elements of structure, crossing national boundaries creates a necessity for carefully assessing the nature and extent of environmental differences.

- *National boundaries are of varying importance for different elements of organisational structure and process.* Not all effects are equal. Some aspects of an organisation may be significantly affected by distinct aspects of the environment of the host country. Other aspects may be affected by global or regional factors that are independent of a particular nation. Still other aspects may be relatively environment free.

- *Subsidiaries of multinational corporations can act as conduits that introduce changes into the host country's environment.* In some cases this may mean the direct replication of elements of a particular structure heretofore not used in the host country. More often, however, it relates to operating procedures that emanate from the subsidiary organisation. An example would be Marriott Corporation's introduction of their 5-day work week into Hong Kong, a setting in which a 6-day work week is the norm.[36]

- *Subsidiaries of multinational corporations can act as conduits by which features of the host country's environment are introduced throughout the organisation.* This is the reverse of the previous point. It strongly suggests that beneficial changes can — and do — flow both ways. Organisations should be structured to facilitate both directions of change.

Of course, while there can be important cross-country differences that dictate making adaptations in structure, policy and management practices, there can also be a great deal of similarity even between widely divergent countries. One of the challenges to organisational researchers is to provide data to help better understand the degree of similarity and difference across national boundaries that have implications for organisational operations.

ORGANISATIONAL DESIGN AND ORGANISATIONAL BEHAVIOUR

In our discussions of organisational behaviour, we repeatedly emphasised the importance of person-environment fit: the need for organisations and individuals to have common values, needs and skills. When we turned to a discussion of organisation development, we again considered the need for organisational change efforts to ensure good fit between the four components of organisations: structure, tasks, individuals and groups. In this chapter, we have considered several options for organisational design. However, we must bear in mind that the design choices that we make have an effect of task design group processes and the demands made of individuals. It is therefore important that we remember the consequences of structure for other components of the organisation, and make sure that there are no unintended consequences of our design decisions. Let's review some of the relationships between individuals and organisational design. You might like to think about some of the organisational design implications of the issues raised in this section.

Job and work design

In Chapter 5 we described the Job Characteristics Model as a tool for increasing the motivating potential of individual jobs. This approach can be extended to the organisational level by considering *work design*. Rather than focusing on the individual, we can focus on the work group in redesigning tasks. One strategy for improving the motivating potential of work is the use of the self-managed team (SMT), which represents a job enrichment approach to redesign at the group level. An SMT is a relatively small group of individuals who are empowered to perform certain activities based on procedures established and decisions made within the group, with minimum or no outside direction. SMTs can take many forms, including task forces, project teams, quality circles and new venture teams.[37] Typically, SMTs determine their own work assignments within the team and are responsible for an entire process from inception to completion. It is not unusual for SMTs to select their own members and to evaluate their performance, even though such activities are usually management functions.

Occupational stress

Our discussion of stress identified several workplace sources of stress for the individual. However, in our discussion of contextual factors we also mentioned several organisation-level factors that affect individual experiences of stress. Whether organisational are 'tall' or 'flat', and the degree of participation that they encourage, affects stress. The small amount of research examining these factors suggests that, generally, individuals experience less stress in organic, 'flat' organisations, and in organisations that encourage participation in the decision-making process. In addition, we saw that stress is most likely to occur when there is a mismatch between the demands being placed on individuals and the level of responsibility and decision-making power that they hold. Clearly job and work design hold solutions to these forms of stress.

Organisational communication

Although good individual communication skills form the basis for excellent organisational communication, we also saw — in Chapter 13 — that organisational structure affects the type and direction of communication. Our discussion of networks showed that flow is affected by whether networks are centralised and match more closely mechanistic organisations, or decentralised and match more closely organic structures. We discussed research that showed that speed, error rate, leader emergence and satisfaction were all affected by communication network structure. We also saw that in mechanistic organisations power dominance issues seemed to underlie all communication efforts, whereas in organic organisations a more open and participative communication climate existed.

Justice and conflict at work

Organisational structure also links in to the types of justice that organisations emphasise, and consequently their preferred means for conflict resolution.[38] Organisational cultures and structures are linked to different leadership styles, and consequently to a differing emphasis on the roles of equity and equality in organisational procedures, including dispute resolution.

Organisational change and innovation

Finally, in Chapter 15 on organisational change we discussed the need to ensure that organisational structures match and support the changes implemented elsewhere in the organisation. At another level, we can ask how organisations — through their structure — can support a culture of change. According to Kanter,[39] innovation is most likely to occur in organisations that have high complexity, low formalisation and low centralisation. It is not difficult to understand how high formalisation and centralisation stifle innovation: existing rules and procedures make it more difficult to implement changes as does the need to protect power hierarchies within the organisation. However, according to Kanter, high complexity encourages innovation because it encourages specialisation. The result is that staff are well informed about current advances in their area and more able to generate the motivation for change. However, this must be coupled with loose structures that encourage the crossing of organisational boundaries, broad job definitions that assign goals but not procedures for achieving those goals, and cross-fertilisation across inter- and intra-organisational boundaries. And, of course, innovations require sponsors: open communication, well-established links across organisational boundaries and the ability to shift power bases are all critical to organisational innovation.

A FINAL WORD

Managers must consider many complex factors and variables to design an optimal organisational structure. We have discussed several of the more important ones in this chapter. As we have seen, the key design decisions are division of labour, departmentalisation, span of control and delegation of authority. These decisions which reflect environmental and managerial interactions are complex, and matching the appropriate structure to these factors to achieve strategic performance outcomes is not an easy task.

Organisational design remains an important issue in the management of organisational behaviour and effectiveness. As we approach the 21st century, organisational design will become even more important. As is apparent, strategies which have been successful in the past will prove ineffectual in the face of the new international competition, technological change and the shifting patterns of industrial development. As organisations experiment with new strategies, they will be forced to experiment with new configurations, such as triangular design.[40] These designs will bear closer resemblance to organic than to mechanistic designs. Organisations of the future are likely to be flatter, less hierarchical and more decentralised.[41]

Organisational structures differ on many dimensions. Regardless of the specific configuration of the parts, however, the overriding purpose of organisational structures is to channel the behaviour of individuals and groups into patterns which contribute to organisational performance.

SUMMARY OF KEY POINTS

Identify the choices which must be made in designing an organisation structure. Four key managerial design decisions determine organisational structures. These decisions are concerned with dividing the work, delegating authority, departmentalising jobs into groups and determining spans of control.

Define what is meant by the term 'division of labour'. The term 'division of labour' concerns the extent to which jobs are specialised. Dividing the overall task of the organisation into smaller related tasks provide the technical and economic advantages found in specialisation of labour.

Discuss the role of delegation of authority in design decisions. Delegating authority enables an individual to make decisions and extract obedience without approval by higher management. Like other organising issues, delegated authority is a relative, not an absolute, concept. All individuals in an organisation have some authority. The question is whether they have enough to do their jobs.

Describe several forms of departmentalisation. There are several forms of departmentalisation. Functional departmentalisation groups jobs on the basis of the function performed, for example marketing, accounting and production. Territorial departmentalisation groups jobs on the bases of geographical location. Product departmentalisation groups jobs on the basis of a department's output. Customer departmentalisation groups jobs on the basis of the users of the goods or services provided.

Explain the importance of span of control. Span of control relates to the decision regarding how many individuals a manger can oversee. It is an important variable because managerial effectiveness can be compromised if spans of control are too large. Additionally, span of control affects the number of levels in an organisation: the wider the span, the fewer the levels.

Define three important dimensions of structure. Three important dimensions of structure are formalisation, centralisation and complexity. Formalisation refers to the extent to which rules, policies and procedures exist in written form; centralisation refers to the extent to which authority is retained in the jobs of top management; and complexity refers to the extent to which the jobs in the organisation are relatively specialised.

Compare mechanistic and organic organisational design. Two important organisational design models are termed mechanistic and organic. Mechanistic design is characterised by highly specialised jobs, homogeneous departments, narrow spans of control and relatively centralised authority. Organic designs, on the other hand, include relatively despecialised jobs, heterogeneous department, wide spans of control and decentralised authority.

Identify the major advantages of matrix organisation design. Matrix designs offer a number of potential advantages. These include efficient use of resources, flexibility in conditions of change and uncertainty, technical excellence, freeing top management for long-range planning, improving motivation and commitment, and providing good opportunities for personal development.

Discuss multinational organisation structure and design issues. It is important to be particularly attentive to structure and design considerations in multinational organisations. Differences in the social, political, cultural, legal and economic environments of countries hosting subsidiaries of domestic organisations can dictate the need for different answers for design questions.

REVIEW AND DISCUSSION QUESTIONS

1. What choices must be made by management when designing an organisational structure?
2. 'The more authority that is delegated to non-managers, the less authority managers have'. Is this a necessarily true statement? Discuss.
3. What are the most common bases for departmentalisation? On what basis is a university typically organised? What other type of departmentalisation might you suggest for a university?
4. What are some of the factors that have important implications for structure and design decisions in multinational corporations?
5. Characterise the following organisations in their degree of formalisation, centralisation and complexity: the university you are attending, the federal government, and a local branch of a national fast-food franchise.

6. Can you think of a particular company or type of industry that tends towards a mechanistic design? What advantages and disadvantages could you see if that organisation or industry adopted a more organic form?
7. What is the difference between organisational structure and design?
8. What cues might a manager have that suggest a problem with the design of an organisation? Is changing an organisation a different task from designing a brand new structure? Explain.
9. Changes in organisation size affect structure. In what ways might growth (increasing size) affect an organisation's structure? In what ways might decreasing size affect structure?
10. What are some of the potential advantages of matrix designs? What are some of the potential problems of the dual-authority concept of such designs?

ENDNOTES

1 Borucki, C., & Barnett, C. K. (1990). Restructuring for survival: The Navistar Case, *Academy of Management Executive*, 36.
2 Miller, D. (1987). The genesis of configuration, *Academy of Management Review*, 691–692.
3 Huber, G. P., & McDaniel, R. R. (1986). The decision-making paradigm of organizational design, *Management Science*, 573.
4 Dalton, D. R., Todor, W. D., Spendolini, M. J., Fielding, G. J., & Porter, L. W. (1980). Organization structure and performance: A critical review, *Academy of Management Review*, 49.
5 Ranson, S., Hinings, B., & Greenwood, R. (1980). The structuring of organizational structures, *Administrative Science Quarterly*, 2.
6 Heiner, R. A. (1988). Imperfect decisions in organizations: Toward a theory of internal structures, *Journal of Economic Behavior and Organization*, 25–44.
7 Tosi, H. (1985). *Theories of Organization*. New York: John Wiley & Sons.
8 Kopelman, R. E. (1985). Job redesign and productivity: A review of the literature, *National Productivity Review*, 239.
9 Campbell, D. J. (1988). Task complexity: A review and analysis, *Academy of Management Review*, 40–52.
10 Leatt, P. & Schneck, R. (1984). Criteria for grouping nursing subunits in hospitals, *Academy of Management Journal*, 150–164.

11 Chase, R. B., & Tansik, D. A. (1983). The customer contact model for organization design, *Management Science*, 1037–1050.

12 Cornish, F. (1988). Building a customer-oriented organization, *Long-Range Planning*, June, 105–107.

13 Chonko, L. B. (1982). The relationship of span of control to sales representatives, experienced role conflict and role ambiguity, *Academy of Management Journal*, 452–456; Van Fleet, D. D. (1983). Span of management research and issues, *Academy of Management Journal*, 546–552.

14 Dewar, R. D., & Simet, D. P. (1981). A level-specific prediction of spans of control examining the effects of size, technology, and specialization, *Academy of Management Journal*, 5–24.

15 Blackburn, R. S. (1982). Dimensions of structure: A review and reappraisal, *Academy of Management Review*, 59–66.

16 Walsh, J. P., & Dewar, R. D. (1987). Formalization and the organizational life cycle, *Journal of Management Studies*, 215–232.

17 Walton, E. J. (1981). The comparison of measures of organization structure, *Academy of Management Review*, 155–160.

18 See, for example, Alexander, J. A. (1991). Adaptive change in corporate control practices, *Academy of Management Journal*, 162–193.

19 Ford, J. D. (1979). Institutional versus questionnaire measures of organizational structure, *Academy of Management Journal*, 601–610.

20 McCann, J. E. (1991). Design principles for an innovating company, *Academy of Management Executive*, 76–93.

21 Burns, T., & Stalker, G. M. (1961). *The Management of Innovation*. London: Tavistock Publications.

22 Gullet, C. R. (1975). Mechanistic vs. organic organizations: What does the future hold? *Personnel Administrator*, 17.

23 Ibid.

24 Likert, R. (1961). *New Patterns of Management*. New York: McGraw-Hill; Likert, R. (1967). *The Human Organization*. New York: McGraw-Hill.

25 Kazanjian, R. K., & Drazin, R. (1987). Implementing internal diversification: Contingency factors for organization design choices, *Academy of Management Review*, 342–354.

26 Galbraith, J. R., & Kazanjian, R. K. (1986). Organizing to implement strategies of diversity and globalization: The role of matrix organizations, *Human Resource Management*, 37–54; Krusko, D., & Cangemi, R. R. (1987). The utilization of project management in the pharmaceutical industry, *Journal of the Society of Research Administrators*, 17–24.

27 Knight, K. (1976). Matrix organization: A review, *Journal of Management Studies*, 111.

28 Ibid., p. 114.

29 Lawrence, P. R., Kolodny, H. F., & Davis, S. M. (1977). The human side of the matrix, *Organizational Dynamics*, 47.

30 The following discussion is based upon Knight, K. (1976). Matrix organization: A review, *Journal of Management Studies*, 111.

31 Best, C. K. (1988). Organizing for new development, *Journal of Business Strategy*, 34–39.

32 Ghoshal, S. , & Bartlett, C. A. (1990). The multinational corporation as an interorganizational network, *Academy of Management Review*, 603–625.

33 Bartlett, C. A. , & Ghoshal, S. (1989). *Managing across Borders: The Transnational Solution*. Boston: Harvard Business School Press, p. 38.

34 Ricks, D. A. , Toyne, B. , & Martinez, Z. (1990). Recent developments in international management research, *Journal of Management*, 219–253.

35 The following discussion is based upon Rosenzweig, P. M. & Singh, J. V. (1991). Organizational environments and the multinational enterprise, *Academy of Management Review*, 340–361.

36 Ibid., p. 354.

37 Barry, D. (1991). Managing the bossless team: Lessons in distrbuted leadership, *Organizational Dynamics*, 31–47.

38 Kabanoff, B. (1991). Equity, equality, power and conflict, *Academy of Management Review*, **16**, 416–441.

39 Kanter, R. M. (1983). *The Change Masters*. New York: Simon & Schuster.

40 Keidel, R. W. (1990). Triangular design: A new organizational geometry, *Academy of Management Executive*, 21–37.

41 Drucker, P. F. (1988). The coming of the new organization, *Harvard Business Review*, 45–53.

READING 16 THE NEW ENTERPRISE ARCHITECTURE

Source: William A. Band, *Touchstones*, (New York: John Wiley, 1994), pp. 59–76.

The ubiquitous Tom Peters predicts the imminent 'disappearance of the organization as we know it'. Is this a prescription for his brand of 'liberation management' or a descent into chaos? One fact is certain: never before have so many enterprise leaders questioned the fundamental principles of traditional organization structures as during this turbulent period of the value decade. The pressure to become more customer-driven, and to manage horizontally with greater attention to core business processes, is creating the need to rethink the way we configure enterprises. New forms of 'organizational architectures' are emerging that are fundamentally different from the 'command-and-control' structures of the past. This third competency of the high-performing enterprise is to design an enterprise architecture that is consistent with the demands of becoming a superior value-delivering business.

An example of an enterprise that can cope with rapid change and that shows tremendous flexibility is Ross Perot's former company, Electronic Data Systems (EDS). EDS's goal is to 'help define and exploit fast-changing markets'. EDS is unique in that it is quite possibly the world's biggest and best professional service firm. What's different about EDS is an organizational structure that looks nothing like the typical corporate hierarchy that most people in the business world are used to. EDS considers itself to be in the 'knowledge extraction, integration, and application business'. It operates almost entirely on the basis of 'projects'. In other words, the company's 72 000 employees, in 28 countries, are organized primarily around the completion of client projects rather than into business functions.

In 1984, when the company became a wholly owned subsidiary of General Motors, it registered a profit of $71 million on $950 million in revenue. By 1991, the numbers were up to $548 million in profit derived from $7.1 billion in revenue. The rapid growth of the company is a reflection tremendous growth of information technology around the world. EDS 'offers information systems consulting, total information systems development, information systems integration, and total information systems management for clients'.

The company is divided into 38 strategic business units (SBUs), each responsible for its own profit; these are subdivided into 32 vertical industry units dealing with such sectors as finance, manufacturing, transportation, and communications. There are also six horizontal SBUs that deal with specific, across the board client information systems capabilities.

For each client project, EDS assigns 8 to 12 employees who work together for a time span that ranges between 9 and 18 months. Some members of the group work with the customer on a full-time basis. 'Though the project's product/result is buttoned down, the formal structure of the project team is murky ... Who reports to whom is not critical. Getting the job done is.' However, there are usually three discernible 'ranks' within project groups: (1) the individual performer, (2) the subproject team leader, and (3) the project manager. Individual performers will often become subproject leaders when their skills match certain requirements. Then they will return to performer status on subsequent projects. An individual performer will qualify for project manager status after displaying project management skills in his or her work. All of these designations are extremely informal in nature to everyone but the customer. 'The ball, when it comes to on-time, on-budget results, is clearly in the leader's court, formal designation or not,' says Barry Sullivan, EDS's marketing head:

EDS is 'loose and flexible,' says one EDS executive — but damned disciplined. Accountability is unmistakable. If you're assigned a job, you're expected to get it done, even if nothing is written down, even if your 'authority' doesn't come close to matching your 'responsibility.'

EDS demonstrates many of the characteristics of the new organizational structures of the future: customer-focused, team-based work units; temporary work assignments; high levels of employee autonomy based on demonstrated skill competencies; and a clear accountability to 'get the job done.' The traditional command-and-control model for organizational structure is giving way to a looser, flexible, and more freewheeling style. The 'adaptive' organization in the value decade:

... will bust through bureaucracy to serve customers better and make the company more competitive. Instead of looking to the boss for direction and oversight, tomorrow's employee will be trained to look closely at the work process and to devise ways to improve upon it ...

Raymond Miles, management professor at the University of California, Berkeley, likens the adaptive organization to ' ... a network where managers work much as switchboard operators do, coordinating the activities of employee, suppliers, customers, and joint-venture partners'.

Apple Computer takes this idea to extraordinary lengths through its 'Spider' system. This network of personal computers, with a videoconferencing system and a database of Apple employee records, provides project team managers with a record of every employee's skills, location and position, plus color photographs. When a manager wishes to form a team to get something done, he or she is able to access Spider to identify and select employees from around the world.

What will the enterprise of the future look like? Former Harvard economist and now Secretary of Labor Robert Reich believes that, in the future, ' ...every big company will be a confederation of small ones. All small organizations will be constantly in the process of linking up with big ones'. Welcome to the world of 'no boundaries', 'shamrocks', and 'clusters'.

'Boundaryless'
The requirements of the value decade place a premium on enterprise innovation and change. Your task is to design a more flexible organization, to break down the internal boundaries that make the enterprise rigid and unresponsive. However, as traditional organizational boundaries crumble, a new set of 'psychological boundaries' must be successfully managed. These new dimensions can be identified as 'authority', 'task', 'political', and 'identity' boundaries. Each is rooted in one of four dimensions common to all work experiences, and each poses a new set of managerial challenges in the new work environment.

1. The authority boundary: 'Who's in charge of what?' Even in the most 'boundaryless' company, some people lead and others follow; some provide direction and others are responsible for

execution. When managers and employees take up these roles and act as superiors and subordinates, they meet each other at the authority boundary and will want to know: 'Who's in charge of what?' Traditionally structured organizations don't find this question difficult to answer, but more flexible organizations do. For example, the individual with the formal authority is not necessarily the one with the most up-to date information about a business problem or customer need. In addition, to be an effective follower means that subordinates have to challenge their superiors, to push for the best solutions to business problems. When leaders and subordinates fail to communicate at the authority boundary, they can't work together to achieve common goals.

2. The task boundary: 'Who does what?' Work in complex organizations requires a highly specialized division of labor. Yet, the more specialized the work becomes, the harder it is to give people a sense of a common goal. This contradiction between specialized tasks and the need for shared purpose helps explain why teams have become such a popular form of work organization in recent years. Teams provide a mechanism for bringing people with different but complementary skills together and tying them to a single goal. If teams are to succeed, however, decisions have to be made to address 'Who does what?' People at the task boundary divide up the work they share and then coordinate their separate efforts so that the resulting product or service has integrity. Again, in a traditional organization, 'Who does what?' was an easy question to answer. In a more flexible environment, the old standby, 'It's not my job,' doesn't work anymore. To work effectively in teams, workers must take an interest not only in their own jobs but also in their coworkers'.

3. The political boundary: 'What's in it for us?' Just because an organization does away with traditional boundaries, it doesn't mean that it's suddenly 'one big, happy family'. There will always be politics, because each group within the enterprise has different interests. This is normal and healthy because it ensures that all aspects of the enterprise are being 'looked out for'. For example, R&D has an interest in long-term research; manufacturing, in the producibility of a product; marketing, in customer acceptance; and so on. A director of a research lab who tries to protect his or her scientists from intrusions from marketing is engaged in a necessary political agenda. The only time the political boundary doesn't work is when negotiating and bargaining fail and people can't reach a mutually beneficial solution. This is the difference between a win/lose and a win/win situation.

4. *The identity boundary: 'Who are we?'* When traditional functional or departmental boundaries are abandoned, a more common identify for all employees in the enterprise can be fostered. Having fewer boundaries helps to break down the 'us against them' thinking that leads to conflicts within the organization. However, when the identity boundary is strong, 'team spirit' strengthens. Groups within the enterprise need to feel that 'they are the best' without devaluing the potential contribution of other teams. When this seemingly paradoxical balance is achieved, people feel loyal to their own groups and also maintain a healthy respect for others. In other words, healthy pride prevails.

Shared authority

A more fluid, boundaryless organization will create more blurred roles for workers, and will require new types of skills of the senior executives of the enterprise. Authority will have to be exercised in new ways.

Authority in the corporation without boundaries is not about control but about containment — containment of the conflicts and anxieties that disrupt productive work … In the corporation without boundaries … creating the right kind of relationships at the right time is the key to productivity, innovation, and effectiveness.

Here's an example of how one human resources executive exercised authority and leadership in the collaborative style that is becoming more common in the flexible organizations emerging in the 1990s. This vice president of a high-tech components manufacturer was faced with managing a massive downsizing and reorganization as a result of a shift in his company's strategic plan. He also had to figure out how his own department could best serve the company's new strategy while laying off 20 people — 40 percent of the staff in the department.

He decided to ask his subordinates to help him design a new and smaller human resources

department. By asking them to help plan the cutback, he felt the layoffs might feel less arbitrary and impersonal. Meanwhile, those who did leave could do so in dignity.

He divided eight people into two teams. He asked both teams to come up with a wide range of possible configurations for the new human resources department and to recruit some of their own subordinates as team members. The teams considered issues such as reporting relationships, spans of control, organizational structure, and new combinations of functions. At the same time, the new departments had to operate with 40 percent fewer people, while taking on additional responsibilities called for under the company's strategic plan. By asking each team to design several alternatives, he was able to avoid potentially explosive turf wars among team members, who, in essence, were designing themselves out of a job. The teams were encouraged to think through all options without becoming wedded to one solution.

The VP gave the teams less than a month to come up with their plans. This was done to create a sense of urgency and to establish a momentum to break free from the inertia of day-to-day activities. He also offered to meet with each participant privately, to discuss his or her own future in confidence. This allowed each team member to openly vent frustrations and connect personally to the VP. Every participant was given the opportunity to discuss how he or she might fit into the new organizational structure or even how the VP might help with the search for a new job.

Nine proposals were presented, and, although discussions were stormy, each team collaborator was committed to the task at hand — even if it meant supporting a plan that eliminated his or her job. In the end, the VP sketched-out a new organization that drew on elements from all nine plans.

The downsizing and implementation went smoothly for everyone involved. Each team member felt that all viewpoints had been heard and a fair and effective solution had been reached.

The vice president never wavered from the goal of establishing a smaller department. However, he created a way in which conflicts could surface and be dealt with in a productive manner. He managed the 'psychological boundaries' of the group effectively.

Shamrocks and portfolio people

Besides enterprises 'without boundaries', what other forms might an enterprise take in the value decade? Management observer Charles Handy proposes an unusual metaphor to illustrate his predicted organizational structure: the 'shamrock', an enterprise that resembles a four-leaf clover.

The first leaf contains core workers — qualified professional technicians, and managers; people essential to the firm. The second leaf contains contract workers. Nonessential work is contracted out to people who specialize in one particular task and who did it well at low cost. The third leaf features the flexible work force, the part-time and temporary workers used as the organization expands and contracts its services to match customers requirements.

External customers form the fourth leaf. The customer is not viewed as separate from the organization, but as an integral part of the overall 'shamrock'.

The shamrock framework envisions relatively temporary links connecting everyone involved except the 'professional core.' As a consequence, Handy strongly believes that the worker of the future will have to be adaptive and flexible. The new worker won't have just a job, but a 'work portfolio' made up of many different types of work. *Wage (salary)/ fee work* will be done where money is paid for time expended or upon the completion of a particular job. *Homework* will include such things as cooking and cleaning. *Gift work* will be done for charity, for neighbors, or for the community. *Study work* will include the learning or training necessary to keep other work skills up-to-date and relevant.

Portfolio people will see themselves as 'minibusinesses', continually contracting their skills where there is the greatest demand, then moving on when the assignment is finished.

Vineyards

D. Quinn Mills suggests, in his provocative book, *Rebirth of the Corporation,* the preferred architecture of the future will be 'the cluster organization'.

He defines this concept as 'a group of people so arranged as if growing on a common vine, like grapes'. In business, the common vine is the vision; the employees are in groups arranged by the vision; and the vine and clusters together produce the wine of business success.

Clusters succeed because they make it possible for a firm to hire the best people, develop an ongoing commitment to quality, be quickly responsive to shifts in the marketplace, and provide a process of rapid revitalization when performance declines.

In Mill's vision, people will be drawn from different disciplines to work together on a semi-permanent basis. The six types of clusters are:

1. *A core team.* Comprised of top management; has the central leadership role and is akin to European management committee.
2. *Business units.* Clusters with customers external to the firm; they conduct their own business, deal directly with customers, and may be profit centers. Their flexibility, responsiveness and autonomy allow a complex company to move at the same pace as far smaller firms.
3. *Staff units.* Clusters with customers internal to the firm, such as accounting, personnel, and legal. These units may price services to internal customers, and may evolve into business units with external customers.
4. *Project teams.* Assembled for a specific project. They lack the ongoing business orientation of the business unit, but projects may last a long time, and teams may appear semipermanent.
5. *Alliance teams.* Today's version of the joint venture. Teams involving participants from different corporations are becoming common in marketing, sales and product development fields.
6. *Change teams.* Created for the purpose of reviewing and modifying broad aspects of firms' activities, their objectives are limited to achieving a specific end-result.

Even more variations

Boundaryless enterprises, shamrock-shaped organizations, and companies that resemble clusters of grapes are only a few of the new forms of enterprise structures that are emerging. What other types of architecture might you consider for your company? The choice is wide, but the common denominator is a focus on flexibility and responsiveness.

■ *Autonomous work teams.* These self-managed units are responsible for an entire piece of work or a complete segment of a work process. They provide their own supervision, cross-train and trade work tasks, and are empowered to take responsibility for the work process and results.

They are used extensively in factories and will become more prevalent in knowledge-intensive work.

- **'*Spinouts.*'** Rather than lose innovators who supply more opportunities than there is time to take advantage of, companies will 'stake' entrepreneurs in the creation of new organizations in which they will retain equity. Spinouts may evolve into joint ventures, become fully independent companies, or continue to be associated with the parent, but will usually not end up fully integrated. In the future, there will be many 'satellite' operations of this nature, with various degrees of coupling to the core business.
- **Networks.** Companies will evolve into a combination of wholly owned operations, alliances, joint ventures, spinouts, and acquired subsidiaries. These networks will be linked together through shared values, people, technology, financial resources, and operating styles.

Teams of specialists

The important components of the 'new enterprise' architecture are small task-oriented collections of people who carry out essential enterprise activities, using team-based structures as the 'linchpin' for delivering value to a clearly defined customer group. Noted management writer Peter Drucker models the new organization after a soccer team or a doubles tennis team; team members have designated positions on the field of play, but they also have the mobility to move into another area if that will produce the optimum result. Drucker writes:

Because the modern organization consists of knowledge specialists, it has to be an organization of equals, of colleagues and associates. No knowledge ranks higher than another; each is judged by its contribution to the common task rather than by any inherent superiority or inferiority. Therefore the modern organization cannot be an organization of boss and subordinate. It must be organized as a team.

A highly skilled, more knowledgeable workforce brings new pressures on an enterprise. Unless the environment in the organization fosters innovation, creativity, and flexibility, the 'knowledge worker', who has transportable skills, can easily leave and find an organization better suited to his or her needs. Team-based organizations work well in satisfying the needs of

knowledge workers and improving business process efficiency.

As discussed in *Touchstone Two,* Hallmark is a good example of how team-based organizational structures work to better harness the talents of specialized technicians and creative workers. Approximately 700 writers, artists, and designers are responsible for creating the 40 000 new cards and other items Hallmark produces each year. The company recently reexamined its organizational structure because, although it was happy with the cards being produced, it took too long to turn an initial idea into a salable item. The long gestation period was caused by the sequence of sketches, approvals, cost estimates, and proofs that had to be completed as the product ideas moved from one from one department to another.

Hallmark staff members are now assigned to separate 'holiday and occasions' teams. A Valentine's Day team, for example, consists of artists, writers, designers, lithographers, merchandisers, and accountants. At the head office in Kansas City, team members have been relocated for a closer physical proximity that allows them to work more intimately as a unit. A single card can now move through the production stages faster. This new way of organizing the work at Hallmark has cut cycle times in half, saved money, and made the company more responsible to its customers' changing tastes.

Hired help

As employees within the enterprise become more specialized, a trend to hire outside subcontractors is emerging. Leading organizations are investing heavily in the training and development of their core staff — in building core competencies. They then 'buy in' the expertise and services of outside specialists who can perform noncore tasks more effectively than in-house staff. This approach improves organizational flexibility and drives down costs. But new skills are required to smoothly mesh the efforts of outsiders with full-time employees.

Xerox Canada's former Director, Communications, Monica Burg, made subcontracting an integral part of her department. She restructured Xerox's marketing department and explored nontraditional partnerships with advertising agencies and other suppliers, such as printers, graphics companies, and individual copywriters. In what she termed 'best of breed, best of price', Burg handpicked a cross-section of experts and put them together in a Xerox 'partnership.' The result: competitors became collaborators. Burg even went to the extent of making an agreement with her advertising agency of record (Young & Rubicam) to have a few of the agency's employees work out of Xerox's offices and cross-train with Xerox staff. Xerox benefited from the expertise of dozens of companies instead of going to only one agency for every service. Burg therefore eliminated the problem of mediocre services at high prices. 'For the same budget that gave us one commercial last year, I did six commercials, a corporate video, and a national print campaign.'

Subcontractors can be involved at all levels of the enterprise, including research and development. Apple Computer has maintained the lion's share of its 'thinking function' at home, but utilizes software writers by the thousands, and hires independent contractors to help with its research and development.

It's important to treat your subcontractors as your own people. Train, share values, share information, and invite them to participate in your enterprise, just as Xerox Canada has. But there's a catch. Although outsiders must be given access to virtually all information, if 'insiderization' becomes extreme, you lose the element of a fresh approach — the main purpose behind subcontracting in the first place. Innovation is imperative. Keep your enterprise 'scouring the world for subs' who unexpectedly leapfrog your current partners' offerings.

Finally, don't 'sub your soul'. Determine what's special or unique about your organization, and make sure it doesn't get subcontracted out.

Self-management

For core tasks that must be retained within your enterprise, how should the teams of employee specialists be governed? 'Self-management' seems to be the answer for many innovative companies in the value decade. Self-management is not a new idea. For example, there are Proctor & Gamble factories that have been worker-run since 1968, unbeknownst to competitors and even to some people at corporate headquarters!

Thomas A. Stewart predicts, in *The Search for the Organization of Tomorrow*, that the organization of the 21st century will be created through the convergence of three streams of reasoning:

1. A new emphasis on managing business processes rather than functional departments like purchasing and manufacturing;
2. The evolution of information technology to the point where knowledge, accountability, and results can be distributed rapidly throughout the organization; and
3. 'The high-involvement workplace' where self-managing teams and empowered employees are the rule.

A classic example of self-managed work teams that has received wide attention is Johnsonville Foods. Johnsonville, a family-owned sausage-making company, was growing rapidly in 1988, but CEO Ralph Stayer still thought something was wrong. He looked around and found that none of his employees was having any fun; they were simply carrying out his orders. This discovery led Stayer to launch a program where self-managed work teams have become the rule.

To better prepare them for self-management, Johnsonville workers were encouraged to broaden their skills in any way they wished, with the company picking up the tab. Workers could take drama courses, painting or karate, or upgrade their personal computer skills. The choice didn't matter, so long as each worker felt enriched as an individual.

Johnsonville workers are among the one percent or less in the United States who are encouraged, with company financial support, to study anything — job related or not.

One Johnsonville 'member' says:

Look, anything you learn means you're using your head more. You're engaged. And if you're engaged, then the chances are you'll make a better sausage.

Self-management continues to be the backbone of Johnsonville Foods. As for the company's self-managed team formula, the following ingredients are included in Johnsonville's 'recipe':

- Each team recruits, hires, evaluates, and fires its own people;
- Team workers regularly acquire new skills as the company sees fit, and train one another as necessary;
- Teams formulate, track and adjust their own budgets;

- Teams make capital investment proposals as needed after completing support analyses, visits to equipment vendors, and so on;
- Teams handle quality control, inspection, subsequent troubleshooting, and problem solving;
- Teams are constantly improving every process and product;
- Teams develop and monitor quantitative standards for productivity and quality;
- Teams suggest and develop prototypes of possible new products, packaging and other components;
- Teams in the plant routinely work with their counterparts from sales, marketing and product development; and
- Teams participate in 'corporate-level' strategic projects.

Johnsonville revenue has grown from around $7 million in 1981 to about $130 million in 1991. Stayer believes great results come about because 'people want to be great'. This CEO wants all of his employees to develop to their full potential, 'to be the instrument of their own destiny. It is unconscionable for people not to have the chance to use their full talents'.

Focus on process
Organizing people around processes, as opposed to functions, permits greater self-management and allows companies to dismantle unneeded supervisory structures. This kind of structure also improves communication and eliminates the 'crabgrass' that often grows between departments, 'Purchasing buys parts cheap, but manufacturing needs them strong. Shipping moves goods in bulk, but sales promised them fast.' Organizing around processes helps ensure that the overall goals of the enterprise are reached with greater ease.

Says Xerox's Richard Palermo, Vice President for Quality and Transition:

If a problem has been bothering your company and your customer for years and won't yield, that problem is the result of a cross-functional dispute, where nobody has total control of the whole process; people who work in different functions hate each other.

Here are ten ideas for promoting a more horizontal structure:

1. Organize primarily around processes, not tasks;
2. Flatten the hierarchy by minimizing subdivision of processes;
3. Give senior leaders charge of processes and performances;
4. Link performance, objectives and evaluation of all activities to customer satisfaction;
5. Make teams, not individuals, the focus of organizational performance and design;
6. Combine managerial and nonmanagerial activities as often as possible;
7. Emphasize that each employee should develop several competencies.
8. Inform and train people on a just-in-time, need-to-perform basis;
9. Maximize supplier and customer contact with everyone in the organization; and
10. Reward individual skill development and team performance instead of individual performance alone.

High-performance work systems
The work systems of superb value-delivering enterprises are designed for high performance. David A. Nadler, Marc S. Gerstein, and Robert B. Shaw define high performance work systems (HPWS) as:

An organizational architecture that brings together work, people, technology, and information in a manner that optimizes the congruence or 'fit' among them in order to produce high performance in terms of effective response to customer requirements and other environmental demands and opportunities.

This sounds like a sensible idea, but what is the most superior configuration? There are two conflicting schools of thought about the 'best' enterprise structure. Some observers promote the 'melting pot' solution, which gives employee teams the freedom to organize themselves as they see fit; structure and hierarchy are secondary, if not irrelevant, to this view. Another group argues that somewhere 'out there' is a perfect solution to your organizational problem. The solution can take any shape — hierarchical, matrix, parallel, team-based, or fashioned after a symphony orchestra. Whatever your own bias toward organizational design, keep these HPWS design principles in mind:

- Perfect structure is in the eye of the beholder.
- Complex problems sometimes demand complex solutions.

- In a turbulent world, structures must be flexible enough to allow 'fleet-of-foot' responses to strategic opportunities and competitive challenges.
- Determining what does and doesn't work largely depends on the competency and attitude of leaders.
- Continuous assessment and improvement should be a way of life.
- The two key tests of an effective structure are: (1) the customer's needs are being met; and (2) the structure stimulates learning at all levels of the organization.
- There is a strong correlation between market responsiveness and flat structure.

The Zoological Society of San Diego illustrates the HPWS principles in action. Its management practices are as unique as the species it houses. With 1200 year-round employees, $75 million in revenues, and 5 million visitors annually, the San Diego Zoo directly competes with amusement park heavyweights such as Disneyland. In addition to maintaining high technical standards, the zoo also champions environmentally sound business practices.

In 1988, the zoo remodeled its displays according to 'bioclimatic zones'. This was a radical change from its former method of display, which grouped types of animals together according to their species, such as primates and pachyderms. As a result of the new display philosophy, the zoo had to change its internal management structure as well. The old zoo was managed through 50 departments — animal keeping, horticulture, maintenance, food service, fund-raising, and so on; a traditional functional management structure was used. For example, if a groundsman, responsible for keeping paths clear of trash, was rushed or tired, he would sweep garbage under a bush, suddenly transforming his trash into the 'gardener's problems'.

After the Zoo's redesign, the departments became invisible. Each bioclimatic section is run by a team of mammal and bird specialists, horticulturists, and maintenance and construction workers. The team tracks its own budget on a separate personal computer that is not hooked up to the zoo's mainframe. Team members are jointly responsible for their displays, and it's difficult to tell who is from which department. When, for example, the path in front of one of the buildings needed fixing one autumn, both the construction person and horticulturist did it. As team members learned one another's skills, teams have been gradually trimmed in size from 11 to 7. It became apparent, when some staff left the zoo, that it was not necessary to replace them.

Because the teams are self-managed, zoo executives, who were once burdened with petty managerial tasks, have much more free time to focus on increasing attendance. In 1991, although the Gulf War and the recession had depressed California tourism overall, the San Diego Zoo enjoyed a 20 percent increase in attendance. Management attributes this success to the employees' new sense of ownership and their effort to improve the zoo attractions for visitors.

'High-performing TV'
Other interesting examples of high-performing design principles can be seen in the television industry.

When the Cable News Network (CNN) went on the air on June 1, 1980, it had secured access to only 1.7 million cable subscribers, far short of the 7.5 million 'minimum' founder Ted Turner needed to cover 50 percent of operating costs. By 1992, the number had grown to almost 60 million in the US alone.

Turner's dream was to revolutionize televised news programming by 'delivering news on demand'. Traditionally, newspapers and established TV networks delivered the news according to *their* schedules. Morning newspapers are delivered at about the same time each day regardless of when a major story breaks. Televised newscasts appear on air at exactly the same time each day and night, regardless of the events being covered. Only news announcements that have profound national or international consequences are aired immediately. Otherwise, it is rare for the major television networks to preempt regularly scheduled programming.

From the start, CNN was run contrary to established TV network practices. CNN's first president, Reese Schonfeld, advised everyone to 'avoid slickness at all costs'. Decisions that would take the major networks and newspapers hours to make were routinely handled by CNN executives in minutes. Furthermore, committees aren't part of the CNN decision-making process.

This formula continues. At CNN, the news is the 'star', not the anchor persons. Unlike the major networks, which require an entire team of people for a remote news report, CNN operates leaner and meaner. CNN 'video journalists' (VJs) will often write, direct, and report a story solo. A VJ may even be responsible for sound; the only other CNN team member may be the camera person. VJs may be required to be on air 'live' for many hours on end when a major story breaks in their area. (This was the case for Bernard Shaw, who reported live from Baghdad during the Gulf War.) Atlanta, Georgia, is the hub for all the network's activities, and CNN's key decision makers are found there. The staff at this highest level has been organized in an extremely flat structure, and each member of the core group is very familiar with the others. However, the structure of remote video journalists and assignment desks pushes the responsibility for the live stories away from the 'core'.

CNN is a superb example of radical centralization and radical decentralization — at once. Everyone at CNN is encouraged to take the initiative for split-second decisions. People on or close to the firing line have extraordinary autonomy, yet they must buy into the vision and understand how their piece fits into the larger puzzle.

Turner's vision has become a reality and a money maker. By 1984, he had lost $77 million in launching CNN. In 1985, the organization was in the black for the first time, recording profits of $13 million on $123 million in revenue. In 1991, CNN generated $479 million in revenue and $167 million in profit.

Fashion television

Another high-performance success story is found in the design of CITY TV, a television station in Toronto. The unique aspect of CITY TV is that the station operates with no studios. Cameras are not 'hard-wired' to studios and control rooms. A network of 32 exposed 'hydrants' connects audio, video, intercom, and lights, and 90 miles [145 kilometres] of cable. Literally, any corner of the station can be on-air within minutes. All programming is casually broadcast from the desks and workspaces of CITY TV staff. CITY successfully creates live, interactive programming using workspaces, offices, or the station's lobby, roof, or parking lot as a living 'set'.

CITY TV's unorthodox and flexible organizational design has spawned several thriving 'niche television magazines', the most successful of which is *Fashion Television* (FT). Although produced and edited locally in Toronto, the show uses the latest technology to combine and use 'on-location' footage from all over the world. *Fashion Television* reports on sophisticated haute couture trends as well as on pop culture and other art forms. The flexible style of the show gives viewers the feeling they are 'on the inside' with the latest fashion trends.

An architecture that is right for you

Where does all this leave your enterprise? Your task is to find the right framework — one that is responsive to the turbulence of the value decade. Four organizational components must be in fine working order if your organization is to achieve long-term success: (1) the work — the basic tasks to be done by the organization and its parts; (2) the people — the characteristics of individuals in the organizations; (3) the formal organization — the various structures, processes and methods created to get individuals to perform tasks; and (4) the informal organization — the emerging arrangements regarding structures, processes, and relationships. Here are some design tips for creating a high-performing enterprise:

1. *Customer-focused design.* The design should start from outside the organization, beginning with customers and their requirements and then moving back to the work and organizational processes. The core purpose is to enable sets of people working together to deliver products and services that meet customer requirements in a changing environment.

Xerox, formly a traditional company — with separate vertical functions such as R&D, marketing, and sales — recently adopted a new, horizontal structure.

The new design creates nine businesses aimed at markets such as small businesses and individuals, office document systems, and engineering systems. Each business will have an income statement and a balance sheet, and an identical set of competitors.

Each business will be run by teams with a strong emphasis on the customer. Says Paul Allaire, Xerox CEO, 'We've given everyone in the company a direct line of sight to the customer.'

2. *Empowered and autonomous units.*
Organizational units should be designed around whole pieces of work — complete products, services or processes. The goal is to maximize interdependence within the unit and minimize interdependence among units, and the aim is to create loosely coupled units that have the ability to manage their relationships with each other. Teams, rather than individuals, are the basic organizational building blocks.

3. *Clear direction and goals.* Great latitude should be given in how work is done, but there is a great need for clarity about the requirements of the output. A clear mission, defined output requirements, and agreed-on performance measures provide the necessary guidance.

4. *Control of variance at the source.* Work processes and units should be designed so that variances (errors) are detected at the source, not outside the unit; information and tools required for early detection must be built in.

5. *Sociotechnical integration.* Social and technical systems should be inexorably linked. The design's purpose is to achieve effective integration between the two.

6. *Accessible information flow.* Members of autonomous units need to have access to information about the market, their output, and the performance of their work processes. The flow of information must allow members to create, receive, and transmit information as needed.

7. *Enriched and shared jobs.* The strength of a group effort is fortified if people are cross-trained in a variety of skills. Broader jobs increase individual autonomy, learning, and internal motivation. The unit's ability to reconfigure is enhanced, as is people's ability to participate in the design and management of the entire work process. Learning becomes an important driver for individuals.

8. *Empowering human resources practices.* There should be practices consistent with autonomous, 'empowered' work units, such as locally controlled staff selection, skilled-based pay, peer feedback, team bonuses, and minimization of rank and hierarchy.

Ralph Heath, president of Ovation Marketing, Inc., of La Crosse, Wisconsin, discovered that the path to 'empowerment' isn't always easy. In the past, purchase requisitions and travel budgets had to be approved by both middle management and himself. This was time-consuming, for Heath in particular. Heath made a decision: employees were told to approve their own expenses.

Two weeks later, however, Heath was still being swamped with purchases and expenses submitted to him for approval. Heath realized that his employees weren't comfortable with this responsibility and didn't trust that he was willing to let them operate without constant approvals. So, he called a meeting and explained again that requisitions were now an individual responsibility. He then set fire to his stack of purchase orders to prove how serious he was!

Not only hasn't he received any more purchase orders or expenses for approval, but six months later, Ovation's travel expenses were down 70 percent; entertainment expenses dropped 39 percent; car mileage dropped 46 percent; and office supply expenses dropped 18 percent. Ovation's profits went up 16 percent in 1991, compared to profits a year earlier. The 'empowerment' of employees has paid off.

9. *Empowering management structure, process, and culture.* Ensure that the larger 'host' system is supportive of the empowered autonomous unit. There will be different approaches in each unit to planning and budgeting, modes of decision making, management styles, types of information systems, and management processes. These differences should be acknowledged and accepted.

10. *Capacity to reconfigure.* The enterprise should be designed to anticipate and respond to changes quickly. Work units need the ability to act on their learning, either through continuous improvement or through large leaps of design.

Organizations in the future will clearly be flatter. The high-performing enterprise will comprise small units linked together into networks. The team will be the basic building block of the firm, and the most-prized enterprise skill will be effective collaboration. Above all, the high involvement of all members of the workforce will be critical to success in the value decade.

EXERCISE 16 PAPER PLANE CORPORATION

Source: Louis Potheni in Luthan, F. (1985). *Organizational Behavior.* New York: McGraw-Hill, p. 655.

Objectives

1. To illustrate how division of labour can be efficiently structured.
2. To illustrate how a competitive atmosphere can be created among groups.

Starting the exercise

Unlimited groups of six participants each are used in this exercise. These groups may be directed simultaneously in the same room. Approximately a full class period is needed to complete the exercise. Each person should have assembly instructions (Exhibit 16.5) and a summary sheet, which are shown, and ample stacks of paper (210 by 297 centimetres). The physical setting should be a room large enough so that the individual groups of six can work without interference from the other groups. A working space should be provided for each group.

- The participants are doing an exercise in production methodology.
- Each group must work independently of the other groups.
- Each group will choose a manager and an inspector, and the remaining participants will be employees.
- The objective is to make paper aeroplanes in the most profitable manner possible.

- The facilitator will give the signal to start. This is a 10-minute, timed event utilising competition among the groups.
- After the first round, everyone should report their production and profits to the entire group. They should also note the effect, if any, of the manager in terms of the performance of the group.
- This same procedure is followed for as many rounds as there is time.

Paper Plane Corporation: Data sheet

Your group is the complete workforce for Paper Plane Corporation. Established in 1943, Paper Plane has led the market in paper plane production. Presently under new management, the company is contracting to make aircraft for the US Air Force. You must establish an efficient production plant to produce these aircraft. You must make contact with the Air Force under the following conditions:

1. The Air Force will pay $20 000 per aeroplane.
2. The aircraft must pass a strict inspection made by the facilitator.
3. A penalty of $25 000 per aeroplane will be subtracted for failure to meet the production requirements.
4. Labour and other overhead will be computed at $300 000.
5. Cost of materials will be $3000 per bid plane. If you bid for 10 but only make 8, you must pay the cost of materials for those you failed to make or which did not pass inspection.

Exhibit 16.5

Step 1: Take a sheet of paper and fold it in half, then open it back up.

Step 2: Fold upper corners to the middle.

Step 3: Fold the corners to the middle again.

Step 4: Fold in half.

Step 5: Fold both wings down.

Step 6: Fold tail fins up.

Completed aircraft

Summary Sheet:

Round 1:
Bid: _____ Aircraft @ $20 000.00 per aircraft = _____
Results: _____ Aircraft @ $20 000.00 per aircraft = _____
Less: $300 000.00 overhead; _____ x $3000 cost of raw material; _____ x $25 000 penalty
Profit: _____

Round 2:
Bid:_____ Aircraft @ $20 000.00 per aircraft = _____
Results: _____ Aircraft @ $20 000.00 per aircraft = _____
Less: $300 000.00 overhead; _____ x $3 000 cost of raw material; _____ x $25 000 penalty
Profit: _____

Round 3:
Bid:_____ Aircraft @ $20 000.00 per aircraft = _____
Results:_____ Aircraft @ $20 000.00 per aircraft = _____
Less: $300 000.00 overhead; _____ x $3000 cost of raw material; _____ x $25 000 penalty
Profit: _____

Appendix A

SELECTED FUNCTIONS OF MANAGEMENT

This Appendix is designed to provide text users with a general background of the practice of management.[1] The skills managers use, the roles managers must perform, and those crucial functions of managing within organisations are also concisely introduced. The Appendix is intended to serve as a refresher or as a brief introduction to managerial practice.

Managers who are also viewed as leaders are tremendous resources for helping organisations, individuals and work teams accomplish meaningful objectives. Effectiveness in an organisation does not just happen. Dedicated and skilful managers and non-managers carrying out specific roles make it happen. Managers influence effectiveness by defining objectives, recognising and minimising obstacles to the achievement of these objectives, and effectively planning, organising, leading and controlling all available resources to attain high levels of effectiveness. The skilful manager is able to manage and monitor effectiveness in such a way that objectives are achieved because he or she is action-oriented and does not simply sit back and let things happen.

The term *productivity* has been used to indicate specifically what is being accomplished. Productivity is defined in a general sense as the relationship between real inputs and real outputs, or the *measure* of how well resources (human, technological, financial) are combined and utilised to produce a result desired by management. Productivity is a component of performance, not a synonym for it. As the highest order of resources, human beings are responsible for utilising all other resources. People design and operate the technology and work flow; they purchase and use raw materials; they produce the product or service; and they sell the product or service. People make a company effective or ineffective and they must be skilfully managed if an organisation is to function and survive.

A successful manager possesses certain qualities in applying his or her skills and carrying out various managerial roles. One insightful study conducted by Harbridge House, a Boston consulting company, identified the qualities of a successful manager.[2] The profile seems to fit managers regardless of age, sex, industry, size of organisation or corporate culture. The study identified the following qualities:

1. *Provide clear direction.* Effective managers need to establish explicit goals and standards for people. They must communicate group goals, not just individual goals. Managers must involve people in setting these goals and not simply dictate them. They must be clear and thorough in delegating responsibility.

2. *Encourage open communication.* Managers must be candid in dealing with people. They must be honest and direct. 'People want straight information from their bosses,' the study says, 'and managers must establish a climate of openness and trust'.

3. *Coach and support people.* This means being helpful to others, working constructively to correct performance problems, and going to bat with superiors for subordinates. This last practice 'was consistently rated as one of the most important aspects of effective leadership'.

4. *Provide objective recognition.* Managers must recognise employees for good performances more often than they criticise them for problems. Rewards must be related to the quality of job performance, not to seniority or personal relationships. 'Most managers don't realise how much criticism they give,' the study says. 'They do it to be helpful, but positive recognition is what really motivates people.'

5. *Establish ongoing controls.* This means following up on important issues and actions and giving subordinates feedback.

6. *Select the right people to staff the organisation.*

7. *Understand the financial implications of decisions.* This quality is considered important even for functional managers, such as those in

personnel/human resources and research and development, who do not have responsibility for the bottom line.

8. *Encourage innovation and new ideas.* Employees rate this quality as important in even the most traditional or conservative organisations.

9. *Give subordinates clear-cut decisions when they are needed.* 'Employees want a say in things,' the report says, 'but they don't want endless debate. There's a time to get on with things, and the best managers know when that time comes.'

10. *Consistently demonstrate a high level of integrity.* The study shows that most employees want to work for a manager they can respect.

If any one quality stood out in the study, it was the importance of open and honest communication. Above all other things, managers must be honest when dealing with employees.

The management system

As any organisation increases in size and complexity, its management must adapt by becoming more specialised. This section addresses some results of specialisation of the management process.

Types of managers

The history of most ongoing firms reveals an evolution through which the management cadre has grown from one manager with many subordinates to a team of many managers with many subordinates. The development of different types of managers has occurred as a result of this evolution. Three broad categories of managers exist in most organisations (e.g. over 100 employees).

First-line management

These managers coordinate the work of others who are not themselves managers. Those at the level of *first-line management* are often called *supervisors* or *office managers*. These are typically the entry-level line positions of recent university graduates. The subordinates of a first-line manager may be blue-collar workers, salespersons, accounting clerks or scientists, depending on the particular tasks that the subunit performs — for example, production, marketing, accounting or research. Whatever the

case, first-line managers are responsible for the basic work of the organisation according to *plans* provided by their superiors. First-line managers are in daily contact with their subordinates, and they are ordinarily assigned the job because of their ability to work with people. They must work with their own subordinates and with other first-line supervisors whose tasks are related to their own.

Middle management

The middle manager is known in many organisations as the departmental manager, plant manager or director of operations. Unlike first-line managers, those in *middle management* plan, organise, lead and control the activity of other managers; yet, like first-line managers, they are subject to the managerial efforts of a superior. The middle manager coordinates the activities (e.g. marketing) of a subunit.

Top management

A small cadre of managers, which usually includes a chief executive officer, president, or vice-president, constitutes the *top management*. Top management is responsible for the performance of the entire organisation through the middle managers. Unlike other managers, the top manager is accountable to none other than the owners of the resources used by the organisation. Of course, the top-level manager is dependent on the work of all of his or her subordinates to accomplish the organisations' goals and mission.

Managerial skills

Regardless of the level of management, managers must possess and seek to further develop many critical skills. A *skill* is an ability or proficiency in performing a particular task. Management skills are learned and developed. Various skills classifications have been suggested as being important in performing managerial roles.

Technical skills

Technical skill is the ability to use *specific* knowledge, techniques and resources in performing work. Accounting supervisors, engineering directors or nursing supervisors must have the technical skills to perform their management jobs. Technical skills are especially important at the first-line management level, since daily work-related problems must be solved.

Analytical skills

This skill involves using scientific approaches or techniques to solve management problems. In essence, it is the ability to identify key factors, and understand how they interrelate and the roles they play in a situation. An analytical skill is actually an ability to diagnose and evaluate. Such skills are needed to understand the problem and to develop a plan of action. Without analytical proficiency, there is little hope for long-term success.

Decision-making skills

All managers must make decisions or choose from alternatives, and the quality of these decisions determines their degree of effectiveness. A manager's decision-making skill in selecting a course of action is greatly influenced by his or her analytical skill. Poor analytical proficiency will inevitably result in inefficient, spotty or inadequate decision making.

Computer skills

One of the most profound and far-reaching trends in the world is the interconnection of individual computers. The information age which is sweeping the world requires managers who understand and can use the products of computers. Computer abilities are important because using computers substantially increases a manager's productivity. Computers can perform in minutes tasks in financial analysis, human resource planning and other areas that otherwise take hours, even days, to complete. The computer is an especially helpful tool for decision making. The computer instantly places at a manager's fingertips a vast array of information in a flexible and useable form.

Software enables managers to manipulate the data and perform 'what if' scenarios, looking at the projected impact of different decision alternatives.

Human relations skills

Since managers must accomplish much of their work through other people, their ability to work with, communicate with and understand others is most important. The human relations skill is essential at every organisational level of management; it is a reflection of a manager's leadership abilities.

Communication skills

Effective communication — the written and oral transmission of common understanding — is vital for effective managerial performance. The skill is critical to success in every field, but it is crucial to managers who must achieve results through the efforts of others. Communication skills involve the ability to communicate in ways that other people understand, and to seek and use feedback from employees to ensure that one is understood.

Conceptual skills

These skills consist of the ability to see the big picture, the complexities of the overall organisation, and how the various parts fit together. Recall that in our discussions of the systems approach as a way to thinking about organisations, we stressed the importance of knowing how each part of the organisation interrelates and contributes to the overall objectives of the organisation.

While the above skills are all-important, the relative importance of each will vary according to the level of the manager in the organisation.

Exhibit A.1 Managerial skills and management level

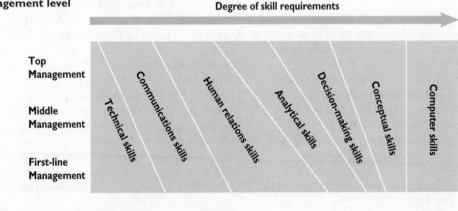

Exhibit A.1 illustrates the skills required at each level. For example, note that technical and human relations skills are more important at lower levels of management. These managers have greater contact with the work being done and the people doing the work. Communication and computer skills are equally important at all levels of management. Analytical skills are slightly more important at higher levels of management where the environment is less stable and problems are less predictable. Finally, decision-making and conceptual skills are extremely critical to the performance of top managers. Top management's primary responsibility is to make the key decisions that are executed or implemented at lower levels. This requires that top management sees the big picture in order to identify opportunities in the environment and develop strategic plans to capitalise on these opportunities. The need for the many skills required of an effective manager is one of the reasons so many individuals find the field so challenging.

Managerial roles

We know that managers perform at different hierarchical levels and require an array of skills. At this point, we want to examine what managers actually do and how they spend their time. One of the most frequently cited studies of managerial roles was conducted by Henry Mintzberg. He observed and interviewed five chief executives from different industries for a 2-week period. He determined that managers serve in ten different but closely related roles.[3] These are illustrated in Exhibit A.2. The figure indicates that the ten roles can be separated into three categories: interpersonal roles, informational roles, and decisional roles. Exhibit A.3 briefly describes each role and lists the specific activities each comprises.

Interpersonal roles

The three roles of figurehead, leader and liaison grow out of the manager's formal authority and focus on interpersonal relationships. By assuming these roles, the manager is also able to perform informational roles which, in turn, lead directly to the performance of decisional roles.

All managerial jobs require some duties that are symbolic or ceremonial in nature. Some examples of the *figurehead role* include a faculty dean who hands out diplomas at graduation,

Exhibit A.2 Managerial roles

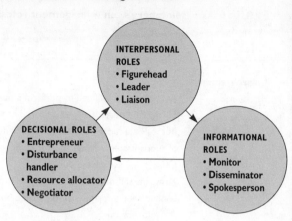

a shop supervisor who attends the wedding of a subordinate's daughter, and a mayor of Melbourne who gives the key to the city to a sportsperson.

The manager's *leadership role* involves directing and coordinating the activities of subordinates. This may involve staffing (hiring, training, promotion, dismissing) and motivating subordinates. The leadership role also involves controlling — making sure that things are going according to plan.

The *liaison role* involves managers in interpersonal relationships outside of their area of command. This role may involve contacts both inside and outside the organisation. Within the organisation, managers must interact with numerous other managers and other individuals. They must maintain good relations with the managers who send work to the unit as well as those who receive work from the unit. For example, a faculty dean must interact with individuals throughout a university campus, a supervisory nurse in an operating room must interact with supervisors of various other groups of nurses, and a production supervisor must interact with engineering supervisors and sales managers. Managers also often have interactions with important people outside the organisation. It is easy to see that the liaison role can often consume a significant amount of a manager's time.

Informational roles

The informational role establishes the manager as the central point for receiving and sending non-routine information. As a result of the three

Exhibit A.3 Mintzberg's ten management roles: Description and activities

Roles	Description	Identifiable Activities
Interpersonal		
Figurehead	Symbolic head; obliged to perform a number of routine duties of a legal or social nature	Ceremony, status, requests, solicitations
Leader	Responsible for the motivation and activation of subordinates; responsible for staffing, training and associated duties	Virtually all managerial activities involving subordinates
Liaison	Maintains self-developed network of outside contacts and informers who provide favours and information	Acknowledgements of mail, external board work, other activities involving outsiders
Informational		
Monitor	Seeks and receives wide variety of special information (much of it current) to develop a thorough understanding of the organisation and environment; emerges as nerve centre of internal and external information of the organisation	Handling all mail and contacts, which are primarily informational, such as periodical news and observational tours
Disseminator	Transmits information received from outsiders or from subordinates to members of the organisation, some information factual, some involving interpretation and integration	Forwarding mail into the organisation for informational purposes; verbal contacts involving information flow to subordinates including review sessions and spontaneous communication
Spokesperson	Transmits information to outsiders on the organisation's plans, policies, actions and results; serves as expert on the organisation's industry	Board meetings; handling mail and contacts involving transmission of information to outsiders
Decisional		
Entrepreneur	Searches the organisation and its environment for opportunities and initiates 'improvement projects' to bring about change; supervises design of certain projects as well	Strategy and review sessions involving initiation or design of improvement projects
Disturbance Handler	Responsible for corrective action when the organisation faces important, unexpected disturbances	Strategy and review involving disturbances and crises
Resource Allocator	Responsible for the allocation of organisational resources of all kinds — in effect, the making or approving of all significant organisational decisions	Scheduling: requests for authorisation; any activity involving budgeting and the programming of subordinates' work
Negotiator	Responsible for representing the organisation at major negotiations	Negotiation

Adapted from Mintzberg, H. (1980). *The Nature of Managerial Work.* Englewood Cliffs, NJ: Prentice-Hall, pp. 91–92.

interpersonal roles discussed above, the manager builds a network of interpersonal contacts. The contacts aid him or her in gathering and receiving information as a monitor and transmitting that information as the disseminator and spokesperson.

The *monitor role* involves examining the environment in order to gather information, changes, opportunities and problems that may affect the unit. The formal and informal contacts developed in the liaison role are often useful here. The information gathered may be competitive moves that could influence the entire organisation or knowing whom to call if the usual supplier of an important part cannot fill an order.

The *disseminator role* involves providing important or privileged information to subordinates. The managing director of a company may learn during a lunch conversation that a large customer of the company is on the verge of bankruptcy. Upon returning to the office, the managing director contacts the director of marketing, who in turn instructs the sales force not to sell anything on credit to the troubled company.

In the *spokesperson role*, the manager represents the unit to the other people. This representation may be internal when a manager makes the case for salary increases to top management. It may also be external when an executive represents the organisation's view on a particular issue of public interest to a local civic organisation.

Decisional roles

Developing interpersonal relationships and gathering information are important, but they are not ends in themselves. They serve as the basic inputs to the process of decision making. Some people believe decisional roles — entrepreneur, disturbance handler, resource allocator and negotiator — are a manager's most important roles.

The purpose of the *entrepreneur role* is to change the unit for the better. The effective first-line supervisor is continually looking for new ideas or new methods to improve the unit's performance. The effective faculty dean is continually planning changes that will advance the quality of education. The effective marketing manager continually seeks new product ideas.

In the *disturbance handler role*, managers make decisions or take corrective action in response to

pressure that is beyond their control. Usually the decisions must be made quickly, which means that this role takes priority over other roles. The immediate goal is to bring about stability. When an emergency room supervisor responds quickly to a local disaster, a plant supervisor reacts to a strike, or a first-line manager responds to a breakdown in a key piece of equipment, they are dealing with disturbances in their environment. They must respond quickly and must return the environment to stability.

The *resource allocator role* places a manager in the position of deciding who will get what resources. These resources include money, people, time and equipment. Invariably there are not enough resources to go around, and the manager must allocate the scarce goods in many directions. Resource allocation, therefore, is one of the most critical of the manager's decisional roles. A first-line supervisor must decide whether an overtime schedule should be established or whether part-time workers should be hired. A faculty dean must decide which courses to offer next semester, based on available staff. The Government must decide whether to allocate more to defence and less to social programs.

In the *negotiator role*, a manager must bargain with other units and individuals to obtain advantages for his or her unit. The negotiations may concern work, performance, objectives, resources or anything else influencing the unit. A sales manager may negotiate with the production department over a special order for a large customer. A first-line supervisor may negotiate for new typewriters, while a top-level manager may negotiate with a labour union representative.

Mintzberg suggests that recognising these ten roles serves three important functions. First, they help explain the job of managing while emphasising that all the roles are interrelated. Neglecting one or more of the roles hinders the total progress of the manager. Second, a team of employees cannot function effectively if any of the roles is neglected. Teamwork in an organisational setting requires that each role be performed consistently. Finally, the magnitude of the ten roles points out the importance of managing time effectively, an essential responsibility of managers if they are to successfully perform each of the ten roles.

The skilled manager performing the ten roles engages in carrying out specific management functions. Four of the most important functions are planning, organising, directing and controlling. Leadership is the focus of the directing functions, and is thoroughly treated in Chapter 11. Similarly, Chapter 6 addresses multiple aspects of the organising function. The remaining planning and controlling functions of management will be discussed in this Appendix. A more detailed and complete discussion of these functions is available in James H. Donnelly, James L. Gibson, and John M. Ivancevich's text entitled *Fundamentals of Management* (Burr Ridge, IL: Irwin, 1995). This text focuses on management and the historical evolution of managerial practices in a global world. This and other up-to-date management textbooks provide, in much more detail, a complete picture of managerial issues, successes and failures. That is, a realistic picture of how management is practised is available in many excellent textbooks, readers and professional books.

Planning

Planning is a keystone management function. Although some environments are less predictable than others, all organisations operate in uncertain environments. For an organisation to succeed, management must somehow cope with, and adapt to, change and uncertainty. Planning, if used properly, offers management help in adapting to change. If an organisation does no planning, its position and fate in the future will mostly be the result of any momentum built up previously and of luck (hopefully, good). On its own, the organisation would follow some kind of course during the next 5 years. If management wishes to have any control over that course, however, it must plan. Otherwise, it will have to rely on defensive reactions rather than on planned actions. Management will be forced to respond to current pressures rather than the organisation's long-run needs.

In one way or another, every manager plans. However, the approach to planning, the manner of arriving at plans and the completeness of plans can differ greatly from organisation to organisation. Formal planning (as distinguished from the informal planning that we do in thinking through proposed actions prior to their execution) is an activity that distinguishes managers from non-managers. Formal planning also distinguishes effective managers from ineffective ones.

If you want to effectively manage the performance of individuals, groups and organisations, you must understand the concept of, and the necessity for, planning. Planning is that part of the management process which attempts to define the organisation's future. More formally, *planning includes all the activities that lead to the definition of objectives and the determination of appropriate courses of action to achieve those objectives.*

To justify the time and resources expended in planning, distinct benefits must accrue to the planner. The major benefits include the following:

1. Planning forces managers to think ahead.
2. It leads to the development of performance standards which enable more effective management control.
3. Having to formulate plans forces management to articulate clear objectives.
4. Planning enables an organisation to be better prepared for sudden developments.

Understanding the need for planning

You cannot develop a sound plan at any level of an organisation without first understanding and appreciating the necessity for planning. If a manager does not believe in the value of planning (and some managers do not), it is unlikely that he or she will develop a useful plan.

To better appreciate the need for planning, consider the following three important factors.

1. *Increasing organisation complexity.* As organisations become more complex, the manager's job also becomes bigger and more complicated by the interdependence among the organisation's various parts. It is virtually impossible to find an organisation (or even a division of an organisation) in which the decisions of the various functions, such as research and development, production, finance and marketing, can be made independently of one another. The more products an organisation offers and the more markets it competes in, the greater the volume of its decisions.

Planning enables each unit in the organisation to define the job that needs to be done and the way to go about doing it. With such a blueprint of objectives, there is less likelihood of changing direction, costly improvising or making mistakes.

2. Increased external change. A major role of managers has always been that of change initiator. A manager must be an innovator and doer, someone in constant search for new markets, businesses and expanded missions. Rapid rates of change in the external environment will force managers at all levels to focus on larger issues rather than solely on solving internal problems. The faster the pace of change becomes, the greater the necessity for organised responses at all levels in the organisation. And organised responses spring from well-thought-out plans.

3. Planning and other management functions. The need for planning also is illustrated by the relationship between planning and other management functions. We already know that planning is the beginning of the management process. Before a manager can organise, or control, he or she must have a plan. Otherwise, these activities have no purpose or direction. Clearly defined objectives and well-developed strategies set the other management functions into motion.

The effect of planning on the other management functions can be understood by considering its influence on the function of control. Once a plan has been translated from intentions into actions, its relationship to the control function becomes obvious. As time passes, managers can compare actual results with the planned results. The comparisons can lead to corrective action.

The elements of planning

The planning function requires managers to make decisions about four fundamental elements of plans. They are:

1. objectives;
2. actions;
3. resources;
4. implementation.

Objectives are integral to plans because they specify future conditions that the planner deems satisfactory. For example, the statement 'The company's objective is to achieve a 12% rate of return on invested capital by the end of 1997' refers to a future, satisfactory condition.

Actions are the specified, preferred means to achieve the objectives. The preferred course of action to lead to a 12% return might be to

engage in a product development effort so that five new products are introduced in 1996.

Resources are constraints on the course of action. For example: 'The total cost to be incurred in the development of five new products must not exceed $10 million'. A plan should specify the kinds and amounts of resources required, as well as the potential sources and allocations of those resources. Specifying resource constraints also involves *budgeting* — identifying the sources and levels of resources that can be committed to planned courses of action.

Finally, a plan must include ways and means to implement the intended actions. *Implementation* involves the assignment and direction of personnel to carry out the plan.

Establishing objectives and prescribing actions also require *forecasting* the future. A manager cannot plan without explicit consideration of future events and contingencies that could affect what it will be possible to accomplish.

Although the four elements of the planning function are discussed separately, they are in fact intertwined. Objectives must be set according to what is possible, given the forecasts of the future and the budgets of resources. Moreover, availability of resources can be affected by the very actions that management plans. In the previous example, if a 12% return is not achieved, $10 million may not be available, because stockholders, bondholders or other sources of capital will not invest the funds. Then, other action may not be feasible.

In some organisations, planning is the combined effort of managers and staff personnel. In other organisations, planning is done by the top-management group. In still others, it is done by one individual. Planning activities can range from complex, formal procedures to simple and informal ones. Although the form of planning activities varies from organisation to organisation, the substance is the same. Plans and planning inherently involve objectives, actions, resources and implementation directed toward improving an organisation's performance in the future.

Strategic planning

Because changes in the internal and external environments of organisations are occurring so rapidly, there is increased pressure on top management to respond. In order to respond more accurately, on a more timely schedule, and with a direction or course of action in mind, managers are increasingly turning to the use of strategic planning. Strategic planning is a process that involves the review of market conditions; customer needs; competitive strengths and weaknesses; sociopolitical, legal and economic conditions; technological developments; and the availability of resources that lead to the specific opportunities or threats facing the organisation. In practice, *the development of strategic plans involves taking information from the environment and deciding upon an organisational mission and upon objectives, strategies and a portfolio plan.*

As indicated, to develop a unity of purpose across the organisation, the strategic planning process must be tied to objectives and goals at all levels of management.

The basic questions that must be answered when an organisation decides to examine and restate its mission are 'What is our business?' and 'What should it be?' While the questions may appear simple, they are in fact such difficult and critical ones that the major responsibility for answering them must be with top management.

The environment of strategic planning

Any strategic planning effort requires an analysis of those factors in the organisation's environment which may have an influence on the selection of appropriate objectives and strategies. Also, some organisations must survive in more uncertain environments than others. In fact, an important goal of a strategic planner is to anticipate change that is beyond the control of the organisation so that change within the organisation's control can be initiated.

The strategic planning process

The output of the strategic planning process is the development of a strategic plan. There are four components to such plans: mission, objectives, strategies and the portfolio plan.

The organisation's environment supplies the resources that sustain the organisation, whether it is a business organisation, a college or university, or a governmental agency.

In exchange for these resources, the organisation must supply the environment with goods and services at an acceptable price and quality. In other words, every organisation exists to accomplish something in the larger environment, and that purpose or mission is

usually clear at the start. As time passes, however, the organisation expands, the environment changes and managerial personnel change. And one or more things are likely to occur. First, the original purpose may become irrelevant as the organisation expands into new products, new markets and even new industries. Second, the original mission may remain relevant, but some managers begin to lose interest in it. Finally, changes in the environment may make the original mission inappropriate. The result of any or all of these three conditions is a 'drifting' organisation, without a clear mission or purpose to guide critical decisions. When this occurs management must renew the search for purpose or restate the original purpose or mission.

The mission statement should be a long-run vision of what the organisation is trying to become — the unique aim that differentiates it from similar organisations. The need is not for a stated purpose (such as 'to fulfil all the cosmetic needs of women') that would enable stockholders and managers to feel good or to promote public relations. Rather, the need is for a stated mission that provides direction and significance to all members of the organisation, regardless of their level.

A critical phase of planning is the determination of future outcomes that, if achieved, enable the organisation to satisfy the expectations of its relevant environment. These desired future outcomes are objectives. Organisational objectives are the end points of an organisation's mission and are what it seeks through the ongoing, long-run operations of the organisation. The organisational mission is defined into a finer set of specific and achievable organisational objectives.

As with the statement of mission, organisational objectives are more than good intentions. In fact, if formulated properly, they will accomplish the following:

1. They will be capable of being converted into specific actions.
2. They will provide direction. That is, organisational objectives serve as a starting point for more-specific and detailed objectives at lower levels in the organisation. Each manager will then know how his or her objectives relate to those at higher levels.
3. They will establish long-run priorities for the organisation.

4. They will facilitate management control because they will serve as standards against which overall organisational performance can be evaluated.

Organisational objectives are necessary in any and all areas that may influence the performance and long-run survival of the organisation. When an organisation has formulated its mission and developed its objectives, it knows where it wants to go. The next management task is to develop a 'grand design' to get there. This grand design constitutes the organisational strategies. The role of strategy in strategic planning is to identify the general approaches that the organisation will utilise to achieve its organisational objectives.

Achieving organisational objectives comes about in two ways. They are accomplished by better managing what the organisation is presently doing and/or finding new things to do. In choosing either or both of these paths, it must then decide whether to concentrate on present customers, to seek new ones, or both.

The final phase of the strategic planning process is the formulation of the organisational portfolio plan. In reality, most organisations at a particular time are a portfolio of businesses. For example, an appliance manufacturer may have several product lines (such as televisions, washers and dryers, refrigerators, stereos) as well as two divisions (consumer appliances and industrial appliances). A college or university will have numerous schools (e.g. education, business, law, engineering) and several programs within each school. The YMCA has hotels, camps, spas and schools.

Managing such groups of businesses is made a little easier if resources and cash are plentiful and each group is experiencing growth and profits. Unfortunately, providing larger and larger budgets each year to all businesses is rarely feasible. Many are not experiencing growth, and profits and/or resources (financial and non-financial) are becoming more and more scarce. In such a situation, choices must be made, and some method is necessary to help management make the choices. Management must decide which businesses to build, maintain or eliminate or which new businesses to add.

Controlling

The controlling function consists of actions and decisions managers undertake to ensure that actual results are consistent with desired results. The key to effective controlling is to plan for specific results. Unless managers decide in advance what level of performance they want, they will have no basis for judging actual performance. As described in earlier chapters, when managers plan, they establish the ways and means to achieve objectives. These objectives are the targets, the desired results, that management expects the organisation to achieve.

After planning, managers must deploy their organisations' resources to achieve results. And although resources can be allocated and activities can be planned, managers must recognise that unforeseen events such as fuel shortages, strikes, machine breakdowns, competitive actions, and new governmental regulations or tax law changes can sidetrack the organisation from its initial plans. Thus, managers must be prepared and able to redirect their organisations' activities toward accomplishing the original objectives. To do this, managers must understand the concept of necessary conditions for control.

Effective control requires three basic conditions: *standards* that reflect the ideal outcomes, *information* that indicates deviations between actual and standard results, and *corrective action* for any deviations between actual and standard results. The logic is evident. Without standards, there can be no way of knowing the situation; and without provision for action to correct deviations, the entire control process becomes a pointless exercise.

Standards

Standards are derived from objectives and have many of the same characteristics. Like objectives, standards are targets; to be effective, they must be clearly stated and be logically related to objectives. Standards are the criteria that enable managers to evaluate future, current or past actions. They are measured in a variety of ways, including physical, monetary, quantitative and qualitative terms. The various forms standards take depend on *what* is being measured and on the *managerial level responsible* for taking corrective action.

As a manager is promoted in the organisation, the standards for which he or she is accountable become more abstract, and the causes for deviation become more difficult to identify. Chief executive officers gauge the success of their organisations against standards such as 'service to the public', 'quality health care' and 'customer satisfaction'. These abstract criteria have no obvious method of measurement. But managers at the top of an organisation are not the only ones who must deal with difficult-to-measure standards. For example, managers of staff units that provide service to line units also have problems determining standards to guide their units' actions.

Information

Information that reports actual performance and permits appraisal of that performance against standards is necessary. Such information is most easily acquired for activities that produce specific results. For example, production and sales activities have easily identifiable end products for which information is readily obtainable. The performance of legal departments, research and development units, or human resources management departments, is more difficult to evaluate, however, because the outputs of these units are difficult to measure.

Corrective action

Corrective action depends on the discovery of deviations and the ability to take necessary action. The people responsible for taking the corrective action must know that they are indeed responsible and that they have the assigned authority to take those steps. The jobs and position descriptions must include specific statements clearly delineating these two requirements. Otherwise, the control function will probably fall short of its potential contribution to organisational performance. Responsibilities that fall between the jobs of two individuals are undesirable, but sometimes unavoidable. Managers who work in organisations facing uncertain and unpredictable environments often confront unanticipated situations — the kinds not stated in job descriptions.

The control function involves implementing methods that will provide answers to three basic questions: What are the planned and expected results? By what means can the actual results be compared to the planned results? What corrective action is appropriate from which authorised person?

Control methods can be classified according to their foci. Three different types of control methods are precontrolled, concurrent and feedback (see Exhibit A.4).

Precontrol

Precontrol methods increase the possibility that future actual results will compare favourably with planned results. Policies are important

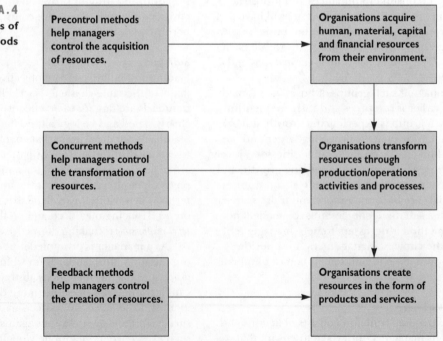

Exhibit A.4
Three types of control methods

Precontrol methods help managers control the acquisition of resources.

Organisations acquire human, material, capital and financial resources from their environment.

Concurrent methods help managers control the transformation of resources.

Organisations transform resources through production/operations activities and processes.

Feedback methods help managers control the creation of resources.

Organisations create resources in the form of products and services.

precontrol methods since they define appropriate future action. Other precontrol methods involve human, capital, and financial resources.

Precontrol of *human resources* depends on job requirements. Job requirements predetermine the skills needed by the job holders. How specific the skills must be will depend on the nature of the task. At the shop level, for example, the skills needed may include specific physical attributes and degrees of manual dexterity. On the other hand, the job requirements for management and staff personnel can be more difficult to define with concrete measurements.

Concurrent control

Concurrent control consists primarily of actions by supervisors who direct the work of their subordinates. Direction refers to the acts managers undertake to instruct subordinates in the proper methods and procedures, and to oversee the work of subordinates to ensure that it is done properly. Direction follows the formal chain of command, since the responsibility of each manager is to interpret for subordinates the orders received from higher echelons. The relative importance of direction depends almost entirely on the nature of the tasks performed by subordinates. The manager of an assembly line that produces a component part requiring relatively simple manual operations may seldom engage in direction. On the other hand, the manager of a research and development unit must devote considerable time to direction. Research work is inherently more complex and varied than manual work and requires more interpretation and instruction.

Feedback

Feedback control employs historical outcomes as bases for correcting future actions. For example, a company's financial statement can be used to evaluate the acceptability of historical results and to determine if changes should be made in future resource acquisitions or operational activities. Four feedback methods are widely used in business: financial statement analysis, standard cost analysis, employee performance evaluation and quality control.

A company's accounting system is a principal source of information from which managers can evaluate historical results. Periodically, managers receive financial statements which usually include a balance sheet, an income statement, and a sources-and-uses-of-funds statement. These statements summarise and classify the effects of transactions in terms of assets, liabilities, equity, revenues and expenses — the principal components of the company's financial structure.

Standard cost accounting systems are a major component of scientific management. A standard cost system provides information that enables management to compare actual costs with predetermined (standard) costs. Management can then take appropriate corrective action or assign others the authority to take action. The first uses of standard cost accounting were concerned with manufacturing costs. In recent years, however, standard cost accounting has been applied to selling expenses and general and administrative expenses.

The most difficult feedback control method is *performance evaluation*. Yet good performance evaluation is important because people are the most crucial resource in any organisation. Effective business organisations, hospitals, universities and governments must have people who are effectively performing their assigned duties. Evaluating individual or group performance can be very difficult, however, because the standards for performance seldom are objective and straightforward. Furthermore, many managerial and non-managerial jobs do not produce outputs that can be counted, weighted, and evaluated in objective terms.

Each control method, whether precontrol, concurrent control or feedback, requires the same three fundamental elements: standards, information and corrective action. Of the three, information is the element most critical for effective control. Managers act on the basis of information — reports, documents, position papers and analyses. Without information, standards could not be set and corrective action could not be taken.

This Appendix is intended to provide the basics of management. These basics apply to any organisational setting — domestic or global. The millions of managers practising around the world each add their own personality, intellect and style to interactions with peers, superiors, subordinates and constituents of the enterprise. As this text will illustrate, there is no one best management or leadership approach. There is, however, the need for every manager to plan, organise and control. How effective he or she is in carrying out these functions is not always accurately assessed or determined. The importance, however, of planning, organising, directing and controlling will become clearer as you proceed with the text and classroom discussion.

References

1 Comprehensive and up-to-date viewpoints of what constitutes management are presented in Donnelly, J. H., Jr., Gibson, J. L., &. Ivancevich, J. M. (1995). *Fundamentals of Management.* Burr Ridge, IL: Irwin; and Ivancevich, J. M., Lorenzi, P., Skinner, S. J., & and Crosby, P. B. (1994). *Management: Quality and Competitiveness.* Burr Ridge, IL: Irwin.

2 A checklist of qualities that make a good boss. (1984). *Nation's Business,* November, p. 100.

3 Mintzberg, H. (1980). *The Nature of Managerial Work.* Englewood Cliffs, NJ: Prentice-Hall.

QUANTITATIVE AND QUALITATIVE RESEARCH TECHNIQUES FOR STUDYING ORGANISATIONAL BEHAVIOUR AND MANAGEMENT PRACTICE

Sources of knowledge about organisations

The vast majority of the research reports and writing on organisations are contained in technical papers known as journals. Examples of these journals are the *Australian Journal of Management*, the *Australian Journal of Psychology*, the *Asia-Pacific Journal of Human Resources* and the *Asia-Pacific Journal of Management*. Some journals, such as the *Academy of Management Review*, are devoted entirely to topics of management and organisation, while journals such as *Organisational Behaviour and Human Decision Processes* are largely devoted to the results of laboratory studies. Such journals as the *Harvard Business Review* are general business journals, while the *American Sociological Review* and the *Journal of Applied Psychology* are general behavioural science journals. These business and behavioural science journals often contain articles of interest to students of management. Exhibit B.1 presents a selective list of journals.

The sources in Exhibit B.1 provide information, data and discussion about what is occurring within and among organisations. This knowledge base provides managers with available research information that could prove useful in their own organisations or situations.

History as a way of knowing about organisations

The oldest approach to the study of organisations is through the history of organisations, societies and institutions. Throughout human history, people have joined with others to accomplish their goals, first in families, and later in tribes and other, more sophisticated, political units. Ancient peoples constructed pyramids, temples and ships; they created systems of government, farming, commerce and warfare. For example, Greek historians tell us that it took 100 000 men to build the great pyramid of Khufu in Egypt. The project took more than 20 years to complete. It was almost as high as the Washington Monument and had a base that would cover eight football fields.

Remember, these people had no construction equipment or computers. One thing they did have, though, was organisation. While these 'joint efforts' did not have formal names such as 'XYZ Corporation', the idea of 'getting organised' was quite widespread throughout early civilisations. The literature of the times refers to such managerial concepts as planning, staff assistance, division of labour, control and leadership.[1]

The administration of the vast Roman Empire required the application of organisation and management concepts. In fact, it has been said that 'the real secret of the greatness of the Romans was their genius for organisation.'[2] This is because the Romans used certain principles of organisation to coordinate the diverse activities of the empire.

If judged by age alone, the Roman Catholic Church would have to be considered the most effective organisation of all time. While its success is the result of many factors, one of these factors is certainly the effectiveness of its organisation and management. For example, a hierarchy of authority, a territorial organisation, specialisation of activities by function, and use of the staff principle were integral parts of early church organisation.

Finally, it is not surprising that some important concepts and practices in modern organisations can be traced to military organisations. This is because, like the church, military organisations were faced with problems of managing large, geographically dispersed groups. As did the church, military organisations adopted early the concept of staff as an advisory function for line personnel.

Knowledge of the history of organisations in earlier societies can be useful for the future manager. In fact, many of the early concepts and practices are being utilised successfully today. However, you may ask whether heavy reliance on the past is a good guide to the present and future. We shall see that time and organisational setting have much to do with what works in management.

Exhibit B.1 Selected sources of writing and research on organisations

Academy of Management Executive
Academy of Management Journal
Academy of Management Review
Administrative Science Quarterly
Advanced Management Journal
American Sociological Review
Asia–Pacific Journal of Human Resources
Asia–Pacific Journal of Management
Australian Journal of Management
Australian Journal of Psychology
Business Horizons
Business Management
California Management Review
Decision Sciences
Fortune
Hospital and Health Services Administration
HR Focus
Human Organization
Human Resource Management
Industrial and Labor Relations Review
Industrial Engineering
Industrial Management Review
Journal of Applied Behavioral Science
Journal of Applied Psychology
Journal of Business
Journal of International Business Studies
Journal of Management
Journal of Management Studies
Management International Review
Management Review
Management Science
Organizational Behavior and Human Decision Processes
Organizational Dynamics
Personnel
Personnel Journal
Personnel Psychology
Public Administration Review
Sloan Management Review
Strategic Management Journal
Training and Development Journal

Experience as a way of knowing about organisations

Some of the earliest books on management and organisations were written by successful practitioners. Most of these individuals were business executives, and their writing focused on how it was for them during their time with one or more companies. They usually put forward certain general principles or practices that had worked well for them. Although using the writings and experiences of practitioners sounds 'practical', it has its drawbacks. Successful managers are susceptible to the same perceptual phenomena as each of us. Their accounts, therefore, are based on their own preconceptions and biases. No matter how objective their approaches, the accounts may not be entirely complete or accurate. In addition, the accounts may also be superficial since they often are after-the-fact reflections of situations in which, when the situations were occurring, the managers had little time to think about how or why they were doing something. As a result, the suggestions in such accounts are often oversimplified. Finally, as with history, what worked yesterday may not work today or tomorrow.[3]

Science as a way of knowing about organisations

We have noted that a major interest in this book was the behavioural sciences which have produced theory, research and generalisation concerning the behaviour, structure and processes of organisations. The interest of behavioural scientists in the problems of organisations is relatively new, becoming popular in the early 1950s. At that time, an organisation known as the Foundation for Research on Human Behaviour was established. The objectives of this organisation were to promote and support behavioural science research in business, government and other types of organisations.

Many advocates of the scientific approach believe that practising managers and teachers have accepted prevalent practices and principles without the benefit of scientific validation. They believe that scientific procedures should be used whenever possible to validate practice. Because of their work, many of the earlier practices and principles have been discounted or modified, and others have been validated.

Research in the behavioural sciences

Research in the behavioural sciences is extremely varied with respect to the scope and methods used. One common thread among the various disciplines is the study of human behaviour through the use of scientific procedures. Thus, it is necessary to examine the nature of science as it is applied to human behaviour. Some critics believe that a science of human behaviour is unattainable and that the scientific procedures used to gain knowledge in the physical sciences cannot be adapted to the study of humans, especially humans in organisations.

The authors do not intend to become involved in these arguments. However, we believe that the scientific approach is applicable to management and organisational studies.[4] Furthermore, as we have already pointed out, there are means other than scientific procedures that have provided important knowledge concerning people in organisations.

The manager of the future will draw from the behavioural sciences just as the physician draws from the biological science. The manager must know what to expect from the behavioural sciences, their strengths and weaknesses, just as the physician must know what to expect from bacteriology and how it can serve as a diagnostic tool. However, the manager, like the physician, is a practitioner. He or she must make decisions in the present, whether or not science has all the answers, and certainly cannot wait until it finds them before acting.

The scientific approach

Most current philosophers of science define 'science' in terms of what they consider to be its one universal and unique feature: *method*. The greatest advantage of the scientific approach is that it has one characteristic not found in any method of attaining knowledge: *self-correction*.[5] The scientific approach is an objective, systematic and controlled process with built-in checks. These checks control and verify the scientist's activities and conclusions to enable the attainment of knowledge independent of the scientist's own biases and preconceptions.

Most scientists agree that there is no single scientific method. Instead, there are several methods that scientists can and do use. Thus, it probably makes more sense to say that there is a scientific approach. Exhibit B.2 summarises the major characteristics of this approach. While only an 'ideal' science would exhibit all of them, they are nevertheless the hallmarks of the scientific approach. They exhibit the basic nature — objective, systematic, controlled — of the scientific approach, which enables others to have confidence in research results. What is important is the overall fundamental idea that the scientific approach is a controlled rational process.

Exhibit B.2 Characteristics of the scientific approach

1. *The procedures are public.* A scientific report contains a complete description of what was done to enable other researchers in the field to follow each step of the investigation as if they were actually present.

2. *The definitions are precise.* The procedures used, the variables measured and how they were measured must be clearly stated. For example, if examining motivation among employees in a given plant, it would be necessary to define what is meant by motivation and how it was measured (for example, number of units produced, number of absences).

3. *The data collecting is objective.* Objectivity is a key feature of the scientific approach. Bias in collecting and interpreting data has no place in science.

4. *The finding must be replicable.* This enables another interested researcher to test the results of a study by attempting to reproduce them.

5. *The approach is systematic and cumulative.* This relates to one of the underlying purposes of science, to develop a unified body of knowledge.

6. *The purposes are explanation, understanding and prediction.* All scientists want to know 'why' and 'how'. If they determine 'why' and 'how' and are able to provide proof, they can then predict the particular conditions under which specific events (human behaviour in the case of behavioural sciences) will occur. Prediction is the ultimate objective of behavioural science as it is of all science.

Source: Berelson, B., & Steiner, G.A. (1964). *Human Behavior: An Inventory of Scientific Findings.* New York: Harcourt Brace Jovanovich, pp. 16–18.

Methods of inquiry used by behavioural scientists

How do behavioural scientists gain knowledge about the functioning organisations?[6] Just as physical scientists have certain tools and methods for obtaining information, so do behavioural scientists. These usually are referred to as research designs. In broad terms, three basic designs are used by behavioural scientists: the case study, the field study and the experiment.

Case study

A case study attempts to examine numerous characteristics of one or more people, usually over an extended time period. For years, anthropologists have studied the customs and behaviour of various groups by actually living among them. Some organisational researchers have done the same thing. They have worked and socialised with the groups of employees they were studying.[7] The reports on such investigations are usually in the form of a case study. For example, a sociologist might report the key factors and incidents that led to a strike by a group of blue-collar workers.

The chief limitations of the case-study approach for gaining knowledge about the functioning of organisations are:

- Rarely can you find two cases that can be meaningfully compared in terms of essential characteristics. In other words, in another company of another size, the same factors might not have resulted in a strike.
- Rarely can case studies be repeated or their findings verified.
- The significance of the findings is left to the subjective interpretation of the researcher. Like the practitioner, the researcher attempts to describe reality, but it is reality as perceived by one person (or a very small group). The researcher has training, biases and preconceptions that can inadvertently distort the report. A psychologist may give an entirely different view of a group of blue-collar workers than would be given by a sociologist.
- Since the results of a case study are based on a sample of one, the ability to generalise from them may be limited.[8]

Despite these limitations, the case study is widely used as a method of studying organisations. It is extremely valuable in answering exploratory questions.

Field study

In attempts to add more reality and rigour to the study of organisations, behavioural scientists have developed several systematic field research techniques such as personal interviews, observation, archival data and questionnaire surveys. These methods are used individually or in combination. They are used to investigate current practices or events, and with these methods the researcher does not rely entirely on what the subjects say. The researcher may personally interview other people in the organisation — fellow workers, subordinates, and superiors-to gain a more balanced view before drawing conclusions.[9] In addition, archival data, records, charts and statistics on file may be used to analyse a problem or hypothesis.

A very popular field study technique involves the use of expertly prepared questionnaires. Not only are such questionnaires less subject to unintentional distortion than personal interviews, but they also enable the researchers to greatly increase the number of individuals participating. Exhibit B.3 presents part of a questionnaire used in organisations to evaluate ratee perceptions of a performance appraisal interview program. The questionnaire enables the collection of data on particular characteristics that are of interest (for example, equity, accuracy and clarity). The seven-point scales measure a person's perceptions of the degree to which the performance appraisal interviews possess a given characteristic.

In most cases, surveys are limited to a description of the current state of the situation. However, if researchers are aware of factors that may account for survey findings, they can make conjectural statements (known as hypotheses) about the relationship between two or more factors and relate the survey data to those factors. Thus, instead of just describing perceptions of performance evaluation, the researchers could make finer distinctions (e.g. distinctions regarding job tenure, salary level or education) among groups of ratees. Comparisons and statistical tests could then be applied to determine differences, similarities or relationships. Finally, longitudinal studies involving observations made over time are used to describe changes that have taken place. Thus, in the situation described here, we can become aware of changes in overall ratee perceptions of appraisal interviews over time, as well as ratee perceptions relating to individual managers.[10]

Exhibit B.3 Scale for assessing GANAT appraisal interviews

Part A: Appraisal Interview

The following items deal with the formal appraisal interview used in conjunction with the GANAT project program. Please circle the number that best describes your opinion of the most recent interview session.

	Very False						Very True
1. The appraisal interview covered my entire job.	1	2	3	4	5	6	7
2. The discussion of my performance during the appraisal interview was covered equitably.	1	2	3	4	5	6	7
3. The appraisal interview was accurately conducted.	1	2	3	4	5	6	7
4. I didn't have to ask for any clarification.	1	2	3	4	5	6	7
5. The interview was fair in every respect.	1	2	3	4	5	6	7
6. The interview really raised my anxiety level.	1	2	3	4	5	6	7
7. The interview's purpose was simply not clear to me.	1	2	3	4	5	6	7
8. The appraisal interview really made me think about working smarter on the job.	1	2	3	4	5	6	7
9. The interview was encouraging to me personally.	1	2	3	4	5	6	7
10. I dreaded the actual interview itself.	1	2	3	4	5	6	7
11. The boss was totally aboveboard in all phases of the interview.	1	2	3	4	5	6	7
12. The interview gave me some direction and purpose.	1	2	3	4	5	6	7
13. The interview really pinpointed areas for improvement.	1	2	3	4	5	6	7
14. The interview was disorganised and frustrating.	1	2	3	4	5	6	7
15. I disliked the interview because the intent was not clear.	1	2	3	4	5	6	7
16. The appraisal interviewer (boss) was not well trained.	1	2	3	4	5	6	7
17. The interview has been my guide for correcting weaknesses.	1	2	3	4	5	6	7
18. I understood the meaning of each performance area better after the interview.	1	2	3	4	5	6	7
19. The interview time was too rushed.	1	2	3	4	5	6	7
20. I received no advanced notice about the interview.	1	2	3	4	5	6	7
21. The interview analysed my performance fairly.	1	2	3	4	5	6	7
22. I was often upset because the interview data were not accurate.	1	2	3	4	5	6	7
23. My record as it was introduced in the interview contained no errors.	1	2	3	4	5	6	7

Source: This interview appraisal form was developed by John M. Ivancevich and sponsored by research funds provided by the GANAT Company.

Despite their advantages over many of the other methods of gaining knowledge about organisations, field studies are not without problems. Here again, researchers have training, interests and expectations that they bring with them.[11] Thus, a researcher may inadvertently ignore a vital technological factor when conducting a study of employee morale while concentrating only on behavioural factors. Also, the fact that a researcher is present may influence how the individual responds. This weakness of field studies has long been recognised and is noted in some of the earliest field research in organisations.

Experiment

The experiment is potentially the most rigorous of scientific techniques. For an investigation to be considered an experiment, it must contain two elements — manipulation of some independent variable and observation or measurement of the results (dependent variable) while maintaining all other factors unchanged. Thus, in an organisation, a behavioural scientist could change one organisational factor and observe the results while attempting to keep everything else unchanged.[12] There are two general types of experiments: laboratory experiments and field experiments.

In a *laboratory experiment*, the environment is created by the researcher. For example, a management researcher may work with a small, voluntary group in a classroom. The group may be students or managers. They may be asked to communicate, perform tasks or make decisions under different sets of conditions designated by the researcher. The laboratory setting permits the researcher to control closely the conditions under which observations are made. The intention is to isolate the relevant variables and to measure the response of dependent variables when the independent variable is manipulated. Laboratory experiments are useful when the conditions required to test a hypothesis are not practically or readily obtainable in natural situations and when the situation to be studied can be relocated under laboratory conditions. For such situations, many schools of business have behavioural science laboratories where such experimentation is done.

In a *field experiment*, the investigator attempts to manipulate and control variables in the natural setting rather than in a laboratory. Early experiments in organisations included manipulating physical working conditions such as rest periods, refreshments and lighting. Today, behavioural scientists attempt to manipulate a host of additional factors.[13] For example, a training program might be introduced for one group of managers but not for another. Comparisons of performance, attitudes and so on could be obtained later at one point or at several different points (a longitudinal study) to determine what effect, if any, the training program had on the managers' performance and attitudes.

The experiment is especially appealing to many researchers because it is the prototype of the scientific approach. It is the ideal towards which every science strives. However, while its potential is still great, the experiment has not produced a great breadth of knowledge about the functioning of organisations. Laboratory experiments suffer the risk of artificiality. The results of such experiments do not often extend to real organisations. Teams of business administration or psychology students working on decision problems may provide a great deal of information for researchers. Unfortunately, it is questionable whether this knowledge can be extended to a group of managers or non-managers making decisions under severe time constraints.[14]

Field experiments also have drawbacks. First, researchers cannot control every possible influencing factor (even if they knew them all) as they can in a laboratory. Here again, the fact that a researcher is present may make people behave differently, especially if they are aware that they are participating in an experiment. Experimentation in the behavioural sciences and, more specifically, experimentation in organisations are complex matters.

In a *true experiment*, the researcher has complete control over the experiment: the who, what, when, where and how. A *quasi-experiment*, on the other hand, is an experiment in which the researcher lacks the degree of control over conditions that is possible in a true experiment. In the vast majority of organisational studies, it is impossible to completely control everything. Thus, quasi-experiments typically are the rule when organisational behaviour is studied via an experiment.

Finally, with each of the methods of inquiry utilised by behavioural scientists, some type of measurement is usually necessary. For knowledge to be meaningful, it must often be compared with or related to something else. As a result, research questions (hypotheses) are usually stated in terms of how differences in the magnitude of some variable are related to differences in the magnitude of some other variable.

The variables studied are measured by research instruments. Those instruments may be psychological tests, such as personality or intelligence tests; questionnaires designed to obtain attitudes or other information, such as the questionnaire shown in Exhibit B.3; or in some cases, electronic devices to measure eye movement or blood pressure.

It is very important that a research instrument be both *reliable* and *valid*. Reliability is the consistency of the measure. In other words, repeated measures with the same instrument should produce the same results of scores. Validity is concerned with whether the research instrument actually measures what it is supposed to be measuring. Thus, it is possible for a research instrument to be reliable but not valid. For example, a test designed to measure intelligence could yield consistent scores over a large number of people but not be measuring intelligence.

Research designs

A number of designs are used in experiments to study organisational behaviour. To illustrate some of the available designs, we shall use the example of a training program being offered to a group of first-line supervisors. Suppose the task of the researchers is to design an experiment that will permit the assessment of the degree to which the program influenced the performance of the supervisors. We will use the following symbols in our discussion:

S = the subjects — the supervisors participating in the experiment

O = the observation and measurement devices used by the researchers (that is, ratings of supervisors' performance by superiors)

X = the experimental treatment, the manipulated variable (that is, the training program)

R = the randomisation process[15]

One-shot design

If we assume that all supervisors go through the training program, it will be difficult for the researchers to evaluate it. This is because the researchers cannot compare the group with another group that did not undergo the training program. This design is called a one-shot design and is diagrammed as follows:

$$X \; O$$

The letter X stands for the experimental treatment (that is, the training program), and the letter O for the observation of performance on the job. The measure of performance could be in

---

Exhibit B.4 **Some sources of error in experimental studies**

Factor	Definition
1. History	Events other than the experimental treatment (X) that occurred between pretest and posttest.
2. Maturation	Changes in the subject group with the passage of time that are not associated with the experimental treatment (X).
3. Testing	Changes in the performance of the subjects because measurement of their performance makes them aware that they are part of an experiment (that is, measures often alter what is being measured).
4. Instrumentation	Changes in the measures of participants' performance that are the result of changes in the measurement instruments or the conditions under which the measuring is done (for example, wear on machinery, boredom, fatigue on the part of observers).
5. Selection	When participants are assigned to experimental control groups on any basis other than random assignment. Any selection method other than random assignment will result in systematic biases that will result in differences between groups that are unrelated to the effects of the experimental treatment (X).
6. Mortality	If some participants drop out of the experiment before it is completed, the experimental and control groups may not be comparable.
7. Interaction effects	Any of the above factors may interact with the experimental treatment, resulting in confounding effects on the results. For example, the types of individuals withdrawing from a study (mortality) may differ for the experimental group and the control group.

the form of an average score based on ratings of superiors. However, the researchers in no way can determine whether performance was influenced at all by the training program. This experimental design is rarely used because of its weaknesses.

One-group pretest-posttest design

The previous design can be improved upon by first gathering performance data on the supervisors, instituting the training program, and then remeasuring their performance. This is diagrammed as follows:

$$O_1 \quad X \quad O_2$$

Thus, a pretest is given in time period 1, the program is administered, and a posttest is administered in time period 2. If $O_2 - O_1$, the differences can be attributed to the training program.

Numerous factors can confound the results obtained with this design. For example, suppose new equipment has been installed between O_1 and O_2. This could explain the differences in the performance scores. Thus, a *history factor* may have influenced our results. Other factors could influence our results. The most recurrent factors are listed along with their definitions in Exhibit B.4.[16] Examination of Exhibit B.4 indicates that results achieved in this design also may be confounded by *maturation* (the supervisors may learn to do a better job between O_1 and O_2, which would increase their performance regardless of training), *testing* (the measure of performance in O_1 may make the supervisors aware that they are being evaluated, which may make them work harder and increase their performance), and *instrumentation* (if the performance observations are made at different times of the day, the results could be influenced by fatigue). Each of these factors offers explanations for changes in performance other than the training program. Obviously, this design can be improved upon.

Static-group comparison design

In this design, half of the supervisors would be allowed to enrol for the training. Once the enrolment reached 50% of the supervisors, the training program would begin. After some period of time, the group of supervisors who enrolled in the program would be compared with those who did not enrol. This design is diagrammed as follows:

$$\begin{array}{cc} X & O \\ & O \end{array}$$

Since the supervisors were not randomly assigned to each group, it is highly possible that the group that enrolled consists of the more highly motivated or more intelligent supervisors. Thus, *selection* is a major problem with this design. However, note that the addition of a *control group* (comparison group) has eliminated many of the error factors associated with the first two designs. The problem here is that the subjects were not randomly assigned to the experimental group (undergoing training) and the control group (no training). Therefore, it is possible that differences that are not related to the training may exist between the two groups.

The three designs discussed thus far (one-shot, one-group pretest-posttest, and static-group comparisons) have been described as 'pseudo-experimental' or 'quasi-experimental' designs. When true experimentation cannot be achieved, these designs (especially the last two) are preferred over no research at all or over relying on personal opinion. The following three designs can be considered true experimental designs because the researcher has complete control over the situation in the sense of determining precisely who will participate in the experiment and which subjects will or will not receive the experimental treatment.

Pretest–posttest control group design

This design is one of the simplest forms of true experimentation used in the study of human behaviour. It is diagrammed as follows:

$$\begin{array}{cccc} R & O_1 & X & O_2 \\ R & O_1 & & O_2 \end{array}$$

Note that this design is similar to the one-group pretest-posttest design except that a control group has been added and the participants have been randomly assigned to both groups. Which group is to receive the training (experimental group) and which will not (control group) is also randomly determined. The two groups may be said to be equivalent at the time of the initial observations and at the time the final observations are made and are different only in that one group has received training while the other has not. In other words, if the change from O_1 to O_2 is greater in the experimental group than in the control group, we can attribute the difference to the training program rather than selection, testing, maturation and so forth.

The major weakness of the pretest-posttest control group design is one of *interaction* (selection and treatment), where individuals are aware that they are participating in an experiment. In other words, being observed the first time makes all of the participants work more diligently, both those who are in the training group and those who are in the control group. Here, the participants in the training program will be more receptive to training because of the pretest. This problem of interaction can be overcome by using a posttest-only control group design.

Posttest-only control group design

In this design, the participants are randomly assigned to two groups, the training is administered to one group, and the scores on the posttests are compared (performance evaluated). It is diagrammed as follows:

$$R \quad X \quad O$$
$$R \qquad\;\; O$$

This eliminates the problem of the previous design by not administering a pretest. However, the dependent variable (performance) is an ultimate rather than a relative measure of achievement. Also, the researcher does not have a group that was pretested and posttested without receiving the experimental treatment (training program). Such a group can provide valuable information on the effects of history, maturation, instrumentation and so on. However, where a pretest is difficult to obtain or where its use is likely to make participants aware that an experiment is being carried on, this approach may be much preferred to the pretest-posttest control group design.

Solomon four-group design

This design is a combination of the previous two designs and is diagrammed as follows:

Group 1	R	O_1	X	O_2
Group 2	R	O_1		O_2
Group 3	R		X	O_2
Group 4	R			O_2

Where gain or change in behaviour is the designed dependent variable, this design should

be used. This design is the most desirable of all the designs examined here. While it does not control any more sources of invalid results, it does permit the estimation of the extent of the effects of some of the sources of error. In our example here, the supervisors are randomly assigned to four groups, two of which will receive the training, one with a pretest and one without. Therefore, the researcher can examine, among other things, the effects of history (Group 1 to Group 2), testing (Group 2 to Group 4), and testing-treatment interaction (Group 2 to Group 3). Clearly, this design is the most complex, utilising more participants, and it will be more costly. The added value of the additional information will have to be compared to the additional costs.[17]

Qualitative research

Instead of using experimental designs and concentrating on measurement issues, some researchers use qualitative research procedures. The notion of applying qualitative research methods to studying behaviour within organisations has recently has been addressed in leading research outlets.[18] The term *qualitative methods* is used to describe an array of interpretative techniques that attempt to describe and clarify the meaning of naturally occurring phenomena. It is by design rather open-ended and interpretative. The researchers' interpretation and description are the significant data collection acts in a qualitative study. In essence, qualitative data are defined as those whose meanings are subjective, that are rarely quantifiable, and that are difficult to use in making quantitative comparisons.

Using both quantitative and qualitative methods in the same study can, in some cases, achieve a comprehensiveness that neither approach, if used alone, could achieve.[19] Another possible advantage of the combined use of the quantitative and qualitative methods is that the use of multiple methods could help check for congruence in findings. This is extremely important, especially when prescribing management interventions on the base of research.[20]

The quantitative approach to organisational behaviour research is exemplified by precise definitions, control groups, objective data collection, use of the scientific method and replicable findings. These characteristics were presented in Exhibit B.2.

The importance of reliability, validity and accurate measurement is always stressed. On the other hand, qualitative research is more concerned with the meaning of what is observed. Since organisations are so complex, a range of quantitative and qualitative techniques can be used side by side to learn about individual, group and organisational behaviour.[21]

Qualitative methodology uses the experience and intuition of the researcher to describe the organisational processes and structures being studied. The data collected by a qualitative researcher requires him or her to become very close to the situation or problem being studied. For example, one qualitative method is called the ethnographic method by anthropologists.[22] Here the researcher typically studies a phenomenon for long periods of time as a participant-observer. The researcher becomes part of the situation being studied to feel what it is like for the people in that situation. The researcher becomes totally immersed in other people's realities.

Participant observation usually is supplemented by a variety of quantitative data collection tools such as structured interviews and self-report questionnaires. A variety of techniques is used so that the researcher can cross-check the results obtained from observation and recorded in field notes.

In training researchers in the ethnographic method, it is a common practice to place them in unfamiliar settings. A researcher may sit with and listen to workers on a production line, drive around in a police car to observe police officers, or do clean-up work in a surgical operating room. The training is designed to improve the researcher's ability to record, categorise and code what is being observed.

An example of qualitative research involvement is present in Van Maanen's participant-observer study of a big-city police department. He went through police academy training and then accompanied police officers on their daily rounds. He functioned with police officers in daily encounters. Thus, he was able to provide vivid descriptions of what police work was like.[23]

Other qualitative techniques include content analysis (e.g. the researcher's interpretation of field notes), informal interviewing, archival data surveys and historical analysis, and the use of unobtrusive measures (e.g. data whose collection is not influenced by a researcher's presence). An example of the last would be the wear and tear on a couch in a cardiologist's office. As reported in the discussion of Type A Behaviour Pattern in Chapter 6, the wear and tear was on the edges of the couch, which suggested anxiety and hyperactive behaviour. Qualitative research appears to rely more on multiple sources of data than on any one source. The current research literature suggest a number of characteristics associated with qualitative research.[24]

1. *Analytical induction.* Qualitative research begins with the close-up, first-hand inspection of organisational life.
2. *Proximity.* Researchers desire to witness first hand what is being studied. If the application of rewards is what is being studied, the researcher would want to observe episodes of reward distribution.
3. *Ordinary behaviour.* The topics of research interest should be ordinary, normal, routine behaviours.
4. *Descriptive emphasis.* Qualitative research seeks descriptions for what is occurring in any give place and time. The aim is to disclose and reveal, not merely to order data and to predict.
5. *Shrinking variance.* Qualitative research is geared towards the explanation of similarity and coherence. Greater emphasis is placed on commonality and on things shared in organisational settings than on things not shared.
6. *Enlighten the consumer.* The consumer of qualitative research could be a manager. A major objective is to enlighten without confusing him or her. This is accomplished by providing commentary that is coherent and logically persuasive.

Researchers and managers do not have to choose either quantitative or qualitative research data and interpretation. There are convincing and relevant arguments that more than one method of research should be used when studying organisational behaviour. Quantitative and qualitative research methods and procedures have much to offer practising managers. Blending and integrating quantitative and qualitative research are what researchers and managers must do in the years ahead to better understand, cope with and modify organisational behaviour.

References

1 For an excellent discussion of organisations in ancient societies, see George, C. S., Jr. (1968). *The History of Management Thought.* Englewood Cliffs, NJ: Prentice-Hall, pp. 3–26.

2 Mooney, J. D. (1939). *The Principles of Organization.* New York: Harper and Row, p. 63.

3 Mitroff, I. I. (1985). Why our old pictures of the world do not work anymore. In E. E. Lawler III, et al. (Eds.) *Doing Research That Is Useful for Theory and Research.* San Francisco: Jossey-Bass, pp. 18–44.

4 A similar debate has taken place for years over the issue of whether management is a science. For relevant discussions, the interested reader should consult Gribbons, R. E. & Hunt, S. D. (1978). Is management a science? *Academy of Management Review,* January, 139–143; Behling, O. (1978). Some problems in the philosophy of science of organizations, *Academy of Management Review,* April, 193–201; and Behling, O. (1980). The case for the natural science model for research in organizational behavior and organization theory, *Academy of Management Review,* October, 483–490.

5 See Kerlinger, F. N. (1973). *Foundations of Behavioral Research.* New York: Holt, Rinehart & Winston, p. 6.

6 A cross-section of papers on gaining knowledge about organisations can be found in Bateman, T. S., & Ferris, G. R. (1984). *Methods and Analysis in Organizational Research.* Reston, VA: Reston Publishing.

7 See Chinoy, E. (1955). *The Automobile Worker and the American Dream.* Garden City, New York: Doubleday; and Roy, D. (1960). Banana time — job satisfaction and informal interaction, *Human Organization,* 158–169.

8 Based in part on House, R. J. (1970). Scientific investigation in management, *Management International Review,* 141–142. The interested reader should see. Morgan, G., & Smircich, L. (1980). The case for qualitative research, *Academy of Management Review,* October 491–500; and Jauch, L. R., Osborn, R. N. & Martin, T. N. (1980). Structured content analysis of cases: A complementary method for organizational research, *Academy of Management Review,* October, 517–526.

9 See Salancik, G. R. (1979). Field stimulations for organizational behavior research, *Administrative Science Quarterly,* December, 638–649, for an interesting approach to field studies.

10 The design of surveys and the development and administration of questionnaires are better left to trained individuals if valid results are to be obtained. The interested reader might consult Sudman, S., & Bradburn, N. M. (1992). *Asking Questions: A Practical Guide to Questionnaire Design.* San Francisco: Jossey-Bass.

11 For an excellent article on the relationship between what researchers want to see and what they do see, consult Nettler, G. (1973). Wanting and knowing, *American Behavioral Scientist,* July, 5–26.

12 For a volume devoted entirely to experiments in organisations, see Evan, W. M. (Ed.) (1971). *Organizational Experiments: Laboratory and Field Research.* New York: Harper & Row. Also see Walters, J. A., Salipante, P. F., Jr,. & Notz, W. W. (1978). The experimenting organization: Using the results of behavioral science research, *Academy of Management Review,* July, 483–492.

13 See an account of the classic Hawthorne studies in Roethlisberger, F. J., & Dickson, W. J. (1939). *Management and the Worker.* Boston: Division of Research, Harvard Business School. The original purpose of the studies, which were conducted at the Chicago Hawthorne Plant of Western Electric, was to investigate the relationship between productivity and physical working conditions.

14 For a discussion of this problem, see Weick, K. W. (1977). Laboratory experimentation with organizations: A reappraisal, *Academy of Management Review,* January, 123–127.

15 Helmstader, R. H. (1970). *Research Concepts in Human Behavior.* New York: Appleton-Century-Crofts; Scott, W. C., & Mitchell, T. R. (1976). *Organization Theory: A Structural and Behavioral Analysis.* Homewood, IL: Richard D. Irwin; and Emory, D. W. (1980). *Business Research Methods.* Homewood, IL: Richard D. Irwin.

16 Ibid.

17 For a complete coverage of this area, see Kerlinger, *Foundations of Behavioral Research,* pp. 300–376; Helmstader, *Research Concepts in Human Behavior,* pp. 91-121; and Emory, *Business Research Methods,* pp. 330–365.

18 Van Maanen, J. (Ed.) (1983). *Qualitative Methodology.* Beverly Hills, CA: Sage Publications.

19 Stone, C. (1985). Qualitative research: A viable

psychological alternative, *Psychological Reports*, Winter 63–75.

20 Goodwin, L. D. & Goodwin, W. L. (1984). Qualitative vs. quantitative research, or qualitative and quantitative research, *Nursing Research*, November–December, 378–380.

21 Daft, R. L. (1983). Learning the craft of organizational research, *Academy of Management Review*, October 539–546.

22 Wallace, A. F. C. (1972). Paradigmatic processes in cultural change, *American Anthropologist*, 267–278.

25 Van Maanen, J., Dobbs, J. M., Jr., & Raulkner, R. R. (1982). *Varieties of Qualitative Research*. Beverly Hills, CA: Sage Publications.

24 Van Maanen, *Qualitative Methodology*, pp. 255–256.

Ability. A trait, biological or learned, that permits a person to do something mental or physical.

Adaptation level. Individuals' differences in tolerance for stressors, as a consequence of past experiences and individual characteristics.

Adaptiveness. A criterion of effectiveness that refers to the ability of the organisation to respond to change that is induced by either internal or external stimuli. An equivalent term is *flexibility*, although adaptiveness connotes an intermediate time frame, whereas flexibility ordinarily is used in a short-run sense.

Affectivity. A tendency for individuals to view the world in either a generally positive and enthusiastic way (positive affect) or a negative and pessimistic way (negative affect). Negative affectivity is associated with higher levels of stress.

Appraisal processes. Individuals' assessment of stress. Primary appraisal establishes whether an event is positive, neutral or negative. Secondary appraisal establishes whether a negative event carries harm, threat or a challenge. Stress occurs when harm and threat are assessed as high and skills and resources are assessed as low.

Attitudes. Mental states of readiness for need arousal.

Authority. Authority resides in the relationship between positions and in the role expectations of the position occupants. Thus, an influence attempt based on authority is generally not resisted because, when joining an organisation, individuals become aware that the exercise of authority is required of supervisors and that compliance is required of subordinates. The recognition of authority is necessary for organisational effectiveness and is a cost of organisational membership.

Availability. The tendency for individuals to perceive as likely those events that they can imagine most easily.

Banking time off. A reward practice of allowing employees to build up time-off credits for such things as good performance or attendance. The employees then receive the time off in addition to the regular vacation time granted by the organisation because of seniority.

Baseline. The period of time before a change is introduced.

Behaviour. Anything a person does, such as talking, walking, thinking or daydreaming.

Behaviour modification. An approach to motivation that uses the principles of operant conditioning.

Boundary-spanning role. The role of an individual who must relate to two different systems, usually an organisation and some part of its environment.

Brainstorming. The generation of ideas in a group through non-critical discussion.

Burnout. A psychological process brought about by unrelieved work stress, resulting in emotional exhaustion, depersonalisation and feelings of decreased accomplishment.

Cafeteria fringe benefits. The employee is allowed to develop and allocate a personally attractive fringe-benefit package. The employee is informed of what the total fringe benefits allowed will be and then distributes the benefits according to his or her preferences.

Centralisation. A dimension of organisational structure that refers to the extent to which authority to make decisions is retained in top management.

Classical design theory. A body of literature that evolved from scientific management, classical organisation and bureaucratic theory. The theory emphasises the design of a preplanned structure for doing work. It minimises the importance of the social system.

Classical organisation theory. A body of literature that developed from the writings of managers who proposed principles of organisation. These principles were intended to serve as guidelines for other managers.

Coercive power. Influence over others, based on fear. A subordinate perceives that failure to comply with the wishes of a superior would lead to punishment or some other negative outcomes.

Cognition. This is basically what individuals know about themselves and their environment Cognition implies a conscious process of acquiring knowledge.

Cognitive choice theories of motivation. These theories focus on explaining why individuals work harder for some goals than for others. They provide an explanation of motivation intensity. See **expectancy theory of motivation**.

Cognitive dissonance. A mental state of anxiety that occurs when there is a conflict among an individual's various cognitions (eg. attitudes and beliefs) after a decision has been made.

Cognitive resources theory. An extension of Fiedler's contingency theory of leadership. Suggests that leaders' cognitive resources (skills, abilities, and experience) affect work group effectiveness.

Command group. A group of subordinates who report to one particular manager constitutes the command group. The command group is specified by the formal organisation chart.

Commitment. A sense of identification, involvement and loyalty expressed by an employee towards the company.

Communication. The transmission of information and understanding through the use of common symbols.

Communication networks. Patterns of communication flow through organisations. They identify who talks to whom. Networks may be centralised, with all information passing through one person, or decentralised, with information flowing freely around the network.

Complexity. A dimension of organisational structure that refers to the number of different jobs and/or units within an organisation.

Compressed work week. An alternative work arrangement in which the standard 5-day, 40-hour work week is compressed. The most popular form is four 10-hour days.

Confrontation conflict resolution. A strategy that focuses on the conflict and attempts to resolve it through such procedures as the rotation of key group personnel, the establishment of superordinate goals, improving communications, and similar approaches.

Conscious goals. The main goals that a person is striving towards and is aware of when directing behaviour.

Consideration. Acts of the leader that show supportive concern for the followers in a group.

Contingency approach to management. This approach to management is based on the belief that there is no one best way to manage in every situation but that managers must find different ways that fit different situations.

Contingency design theory. An approach to designing organisations where the effective structure depends on factors in the situation.

Continuous reinforcement. A schedule that is designed to reinforce behaviour every time the behaviour exhibited is correct.

Control theory. A theory that combines concepts of feedback and goals to provide an explanation of motivation. It argues that we monitor for gaps between desired and actual performance. Discrepancies stimulate effort to reduce the size of gaps.

Coping styles. Individual styles for dealing with stress. Task- or problem-focused coping is aimed at reducing or eliminating the source of stress. Emotion-focused coping is aimed at offsetting the negative emotional consequences of stress.

Counterpower. Leaders exert power on subordinates, and subordinates exert power on leaders. Power is a two-way flow.

Decentralisation. Basically, this entails pushing the decision-making point to the lowest managerial level possible. It involves the delegation of decision-making authority.

Decision. A means to achieve some result or to solve some problem. The outcome of a process that is influenced by many forces.

Decision acceptance. An important criterion in the Vroom–Jago model that refers to the degree of subordinate commitment to the decision.

Decision quality. An important criterion in the Vroom–Jago model that refers to the objective aspects of a decision that influence subordinates' performance aside from any direct impact on motivation.

Decision rules. How information is combined to select between alternatives when decisions are well defined.

Decoding. The mental procedure that the receiver of a message goes through to decipher the message.

Defensive behaviour. When an employee is blocked in attempts to satisfy needs to achieve goals, one or more defence mechanisms may be evoked. These defence mechanisms include withdrawal, aggression, substitution, compensation, repression and rationalisation.

Delegated strategies. Strategies for introducing organisational change that allow active participation by subordinates.

Delegation. The process by which authority is distributed downward in an organisation.

Delphi technique. A technique used to improve group decision making that involves the solicitation and comparison of anonymous judgements on the topic of interest through a set of sequential questionnaires interspersed with summarised information and feedback of opinions from earlier responses.

Departmentalisation. The manner in which an organisation is structurally divided. Some of the more publicised divisions are by function, territory, product, customer and project.

Development. A criterion of effectiveness that refers to the

organisation's ability to increase its responsiveness to current and future environmental demands. Equivalent or similar terms include *institutionalisation*, *stability*, and *integration*.

Devil's advocacy. A form of programmed conflict in which someone or some group is assigned the role of critic whose job is to uncover all possible problems with a particular proposal.

Diagonal communication. Communication that cuts across functions and levels in an organisation.

Discipline. The use of some form of sanction or punishment when employees deviate from the rules. Using whips and chains to maintain control.

Dispositional explanations of behaviour. These attribute differences in individual behaviour to internal factors such as personality. They argue that personality results in consistent behaviour across situations. See also **situational explanations of behaviour**, **interactional explanations of behaviour**, **transactional explanations of behaviour**, and **person–environment fit**.

Distributive negotiations. Negotiations in which resources are a fixed sum: one individual's gain must be the other's loss. In such negotiations, the aim of individual negotiators is to lower an opponent's resistance point while hiding their own.

Downward communication. Communication that flows from individuals in higher levels of the organisation's hierarchy to those in lower levels.

Dysfunctional conflict. A confrontation or interaction between groups that harms the organisation or hinders the achievement of organisational goals.

Dysfunctional intergroup conflict. Any confrontation or interaction between groups that hinders the achievement of organisational goals.

Effectiveness. In the context of organisational behaviour, effectiveness refers to the optimal relationship among five components: production, efficiency, satisfaction, adaptiveness and development.

Efficiency. A short-run criterion of effectiveness that refers to the organisation's ability to produce outputs with minimum use of inputs. The measures of efficiency are always in ratio terms, such as benefit/cost, cost/output, and cost/time.

Employee assistance program. An employee benefit program designed to deal with a wide range of stress-related problems, including behavioural and emotional difficulties, substance abuse, and family and marital discord.

Employee stock ownership plans (ESOPs). An employee reward program in which organisations make contributions of company stock (or cash to purchase stock) to employees. Stock allocation is typically, but not always, based on seniority.

Empowerment. Encouraging and/or assisting individuals and groups to make decisions that affect their work environments.

Encoding. The conversion of an idea into an understandable message by a communicator.

Environmental certainty. A concept in the Lawrence and Lorsch research that refers to three characteristics of a subenvironment that determine the subunit's requisite differentiation. The three characteristics are the rate of change, the certainty of information, and the time span of feedback or results.

Environmental diversity. A concept in the Lawrence and Lorsch research that refers to the differences among the three subenvironments in terms of certainty.

Environmental forces. Forces for change beyond the control of the manager. These forces include marketplace actions, technological changes, and social and political changes.

Equity theory of motivation. A theory that examines discrepancies within a person after the person has compared his or her input/output ratio to that of a reference person.

Escalation of commitment. An impediment to effective decision making, it refers to an increasing commitment to a previous decision when a rational decision maker would withdraw. It typically results from the need to turn a losing or poor decision into a winning or good decision.

Eustress. A term made popular by Dr Hans Selye to describe good or positive stress.

Expectancy. The perceived likelihood that a particular act will be followed by a particular outcome.

Expectancy theory of motivation. In this theory, the employee is viewed as faced with a set of first-level outcomes. The employee will select an outcome based on how this choice is related to second-level outcomes. The preferences of the individual are based on the strength (valence) of desire to achieve a second-level state and the perception of the relationship between first- and second-level outcomes.

Experiment. To be considered an experiment, an investigation must contain two elements — manipulation of some variable (independent variable) and observation of the results (dependent variable).

Expert power. Capacity to influence related to some expertise, special skill or knowledge. Expert power is a function of the judgement of the less powerful person that the other person has ability or knowledge that exceeds his or her own.

Extinction. The decline in the response rate because of non-reinforcement.

Extrinsic rewards. Rewards external to the job such as pay, promotion, or fringe benefits.

Felt conflict. The second stage of conflict which includes emotional involvement. It is 'felt' in the form of anxiety, tension and/or hostility. See also **perceived conflict** and **manifest conflict**.

Field experiment. In this type of experiment, the investigator attempts to manipulate and control variables in the natural setting rather than in a laboratory.

Field theory. Kurt Lewin's explanation for successful change. It argues that change occurs in three stages: unfreezing, change and refreezing. For change to occur, supporting forces must outweigh resisting forces.

Fixed-internal reinforcement. A situation in which a reinforcer is applied only after a certain period of time has elapsed since the last reinforcer was applied.

Fixed-pie error. A belief frequently held by negotiators that resources are a fixed sum when they are a variable sum. This leads to the use of competitive strategies and an unwillingness to search for joint solutions. See also **distributive negotiations** and **integrative negotiations**.

Flexitime. An arrangement that provides employees with greater individual control over work scheduling. In a flexitime schedule employees can determine, within some limits, when they will go to work. In most flexitime plans, employees may vary their schedule day-to-day, provided they work a specific number of hours per week.

Formal group. A group formed by management to accomplish the goals of the organisation.

Formalisation. A dimension of organisational structure that refers to the extent to which rules, procedures and other guides to action are written and enforced.

Free riding. A group phenomenon in which one individual benefits from the actions of the group without making a contribution to the efforts of the group.

Friendship group. An informal group that is established in the workplace because of some common characteristic of its members and that may extend the interaction of its members to include activities outside the workplace.

Functional conflict. A confrontation between groups that enhances and benefits the organisation's performance.

Functional job analysis. A method of job analysis that focuses attention on the worker's specific job activities, methods, machines and output. The method is used widely to analyse and classify jobs.

Fundamental attribution error. A tendency to underestimate the importance of external factors and overestimate the importance of internal factors when making attributions about the behaviour of others.

Gainsharing. A reward system in which employees share in the financial benefits the organisation accrues from improved operating efficiencies and effectiveness. Gainsharing can take many forms including cash awards for suggestions and bonus plans.

General adaptation syndrome (GAS). A description of the three phases of the defence reaction that a person establishes when stressed. These phases are called alarm, resistance and exhaustion.

Goal. A specific target that an individual is trying to achieve; a goal is the target (object) of an action.

Goal approach to effectiveness. A perspective on effectiveness that emphasises the central role of goal achievement as the criterion for assessing effectiveness.

Goal commitment. The amount of effort that is actually used to achieve a goal.

Goal difficulty. The degree of proficiency or the level of goal performance that is being sought.

Goal orientation. A concept that refers to the focus of attention and decision making among the members of a subunit.

Goal participation. The amount of a person's involvement in setting task and personal development goals.

Goal setting. The process of establishing goals. In many cases, goal setting involves a superior and subordinate working together to set the subordinate's goals for a specified period of time.

Goal specificity. The degree of quantitative precision of the goal.

Graicunas's model. The proposition that an arithmetic increase in the number of subordinates results in a geometric increase in the number of potential relationships under the jurisdiction of the superior. Graicunas set this up in a mathematical model:
$$C = N \left(\frac{2^N}{2} + N + 1 \right)$$

Grapevine. An informal communication network that exists in organisations and short-circuits the formal channels.

Grid training. A leadership development method proposed by Blake and Mouton that emphasises the balance between production orientation and person orientation.

Group. Two or more employees who interact with one another in such a manner that the behaviour and/or performance of one member is influenced by the behaviour and/or performance of other members.

Group cohesiveness. The strength of the members' desires to remain in the group and the strength of their commitment to the group.

Group norms. Standards shared by the members of a group.

Groupthink. The deterioration of the mental efficiency, reality testing and moral judgement of the individual members of a group in the interest of group solidarity.

Hardiness. A personality trait that appears to buffer an individual's response to stress. The hardy person assumes that he or she is in control, is highly committed to lively activities and treats change as a challenge.

Hawthorne studies. A series of studies undertaken at the Chicago Hawthorne Plant of Western Electric from 1924 to 1933. The studies made major contributions to the knowledge of the importance of the social system of an organisation. They provided the impetus for the human relations approach to organisations.

Health promotion program. See **Wellness program**.

Heuristics. The rules of thumb adopted by decision makers attempting to estimate the probability that a particular solution will be successful. See **availability** and **representativeness**.

History. A source of error in experimental results. It consists of events other than the experimental treatment that occur between pre- and post-measurement.

Horizontal communication. Communication that flows across functions in an organisation.

Horizontal differentiation. The number of different units existing at the same level in an organisation. The greater the horizontal differentiation, the more complex is the organisation.

Ill-defined decision problems. Decision problems for which solutions are unknown. Decision makers must generate a range of solutions and estimate the probability that these solutions will be successful. See also **well-defined decision problems**.

Impression management. A political strategy which refers to actions individuals take to control the impressions that others form of them. It represents a deliberate attempt to leave a desirable impression on others. The desired impression may or may not be an accurate one.

Incentive plan criteria. To be effective in motivating employees, incentives should be related to specific behavioural patterns (for example, better performance), be received immediately after the behaviour is displayed, and reward the employee for consistently displaying the desired behaviour.

Influence. A transaction in which a person or a group acts in such a way as to change the behaviour of another person or group. Influence is the demonstrated use of power.

Informal group. A group formed by individuals and developed around common interests and friendships rather than around a deliberate design.

Information flow requirements. The amount of information that must be processed by an organisation, group or individual to perform effectively.

Initiating structure. Leadership acts that imply the structuring of job tasks and responsibilities for followers.

Instrumentality. The relationship between first- and second-level outcomes.

Instrumentation. A source of error in experimental results. In this type of error, changes in the measure of participants' performance are the result of changes in the measurement instruments or the conditions under which the measuring is done (for example, wear on machinery, fatigue on the part of observers).

Integrative negotiations. Negotiations in which resources are a variable sum: it is possible for both individuals to gain and to maximise joint outcomes. In such negotiations, the aim is to uncover underlying needs and the develop solutions that meet those needs.

Interaction. Any interpersonal contact in which one individual acts and one or more other individuals respond to the action.

Interaction effects. The confounding of results that arises when any of the sources of errors in experimental results interact with the experimental treatment. For example, results may be confounded when the types of individuals withdrawing from any experiment (mortality) may differ for the experimental group and the control group.

Interactional explanations of behaviour. These attribute differences in individual behaviour to a combination of internal factors such as personality and external or situational factors. See also **dispositional explanations of behaviour**, **situational explanations of behaviour**, **transactional explanations of behaviour** and **person–environment fit**.

Interdependence. Situations in which an individual's actions do not determine his or her outcomes. Outcomes are determined by the joint activities of two or more people.

Interest group. A group that forms because of some special topic of interest. Generally, when the interest declines or a goal has been achieved, the group disbands.

Intergroup conflict. Conflict between groups; can be functional or dysfunctional.

Internal forces. Forces for change that occur within the organisation and that usually can be traced to process and to behavioural causes.

Interpersonal communication. Communication that flows from individual to individual in face-to-face and group settings.

Interpersonal orientation. A concept that refers to whether a person is more concerned with achieving good social relations as opposed to achieving a task.

Interpersonal rewards. Extrinsic rewards such as receiving recognition or being able to interact socially on the job.

Interpersonal style. The way in which an individual prefers to relate to others.

Interrole conflict. A type of conflict that results from facing multiple roles. It occurs because individuals simultaneously perform many roles, some of which have conflicting expectations.

Intervention. The process by which either outsiders or insiders assume the role of a change agent in the OD program.

Intrapersonal conflict. The conflict that a person faces internally, as when an individual experiences personal frustration, anxiety, and stress.

Intrarole conflict. A type of conflict that occurs when different individuals define a role according to different sets of expectations, making it impossible for the person occupying the role to satisfy all of the expectations. This conflict is more likely to occur when a given role has a complex role set.

Intrinsic rewards. Rewards that are part of the job itself. The responsibility, challenge and feedback characteristics of the job are intrinsic rewards.

Job analysis. The description of how one job differs from another in terms of the demands, activities and skills required.

Job content. The factors that define the general nature of a job.

Job definition. The first subproblem of the organising decision. It involves the determination of task requirements of each job in the organisation.

Job depth. The amount of control that an individual has to alter or influence the job and the surrounding environment.

Job description. A summary statement of what an employee actually does on the job.

Job descriptive index. A popular and widely used 72-item scale that measures five job satisfaction dimensions.

Job enlargement. An administrative action that involves increasing the range of a job. Supposedly, this action results in better performance and a more satisfied workforce.

Job enrichment. An approach developed by Herzberg that seeks to improve task efficiency and human satisfaction by means of building into people's jobs greater scope for personal achievement and recognition, more challenging and responsible work, and more opportunity for individual advancement and growth.

Job evaluation. The assignment of dollar values to a job.

Job range. The number of operations that a job occupant performs to complete a task.

Job relationships. The interpersonal relationships that are required of or made possible by a job.

Job rotation. A form of training that involves moving an employee from one work station to another. In addition to achieving the training objective, this procedure is also designed to reduce boredom.

Job satisfaction. An attitude that workers have about their jobs. It results from their perception of the jobs.

Job sharing. A form of alternative work arrangements in which two or more individuals share the same job. One job holder might work in the mornings, while a second job holder works in the afternoon. Job sharing increases employee discretion.

Job specification. A product of job analysis. A job specification identifies the minimum acceptable qualifications that a job holder must have to perform the job at an acceptable level. It may include specifications for educational level, knowledge, skills, aptitudes and previous experience.

Justice. An extension of equity theory, describing the perceived fairness of rewards. Distributive justice is concerned with the share that an individual receives; procedural justice is concerned with the process by which allocation decisions are made.

Laboratory experiment. The key characteristic of laboratory experiments is that the environment in which the subject works is created by the researcher. The laboratory setting permits the researcher to control closely the experimental conditions.

Leader-member relations. A factor in the Fiedler contingency model that refers to the degree of confidence, trust and respect that the leader obtains from the followers.

Leadership. Using influence in an organisational setting or situation, producing effects that are meaningful and have a direct impact on accomplishing challenging goals.

Learning. The process by which a relatively enduring change in behaviour occurs as a result of practice.

Learning transfer. An important learning principle that emphasises the carry-over of learning into the workplace.

Legitimate power. Capacity to influence derived from the position of a manager in the organisational hierarchy. Subordinates believe that they 'ought' to comply.

Life change events. Major life changes that create stress for an individual. The work of Holmes and Rahe indicates that an excessive number of life change events in one period of time can produce major health problems in a subsequent period.

Linking-pin function. An element of System 4 organisation that views the major role of managers to be that of representative of the group they manage to higher level groups in the organisation.

Locus of control. A personality characteristic that describes as internalisers people who see the

control of their lives as coming from inside themselves. People who believe their lives are controlled by external factors are externalisers.

Management by objectives (MBO). A process under which superiors and subordinates jointly set goals for a specified time period and then meet again to evaluate the subordinates' performance in terms of the previously established goals.

Manifest conflict. The final stage in conflict. At the manifest conflict stage, the conflicting parties are actively engaging in conflict behaviour. Manifest conflict is usually very apparent to uninvolved parties. See also **perceived conflict** and **felt conflict**.

Matrix organisational design. An organisational design that superimposes a product- or project-based design on an existing function-based design.

Maturation. A source of error in experimental studies. The error results from changes in the subject group with the passage of time that are not associated with the experimental treatment.

Mechanistic model of organisational design. The type of organisational design that emphasises the importance of production and efficiency. It is highly formalised, centralised and complex.

Mediation. The use of a neutral third party for resolving disputes.

Mission. The ultimate, primary purpose of an organisation. An organisation's mission is what society expects from the

organisation in exchange for its continuing survival.

Modelling. A method of administering rewards that relies on observational learning. An employee learns the behaviours that are desirable by observing how others are rewarded. It is assumed that behaviours will be imitated if the observer views a distinct link between performance and rewards.

Modified or compressed work week. A shortened work week. The form of the modified work week that involves working 4 days a week, 10 hours each day, is called a 4/40. The 3/36 and 4/32 schedules are also being used.

Mortality. A source of error in experimental studies. This type of error occurs when participants drop out of the experiment before it is completed, resulting in the experimental and control groups not being comparable.

Motion study. The process of analysing a task to determine the preferred motions to be used in its completion.

Motivator-hygiene theory. The Herzberg approach that identifies conditions of the job that operate primarily to dissatisfy employees when they are not present (hygiene factors — salary, job security, work conditions and so on). There are also job conditions that lead to high levels of motivation and job satisfaction. However, the absence of these conditions does not prove highly dissatisfying. The conditions include achievement, growth and advancement opportunities.

Multiple roles. The notion that most individuals play many roles simultaneously because they occupy many different positions in a variety of institutions and organisations.

Need for power. A person's desire to have an impact on others. The impact can occur by such behaviours as action, the giving of help or advice, or concern for reputation.

Need hierarchy model. Maslow assumed that the needs of a person depend on what he or she already has. This in a sense means that a satisfied need is not a motivator. Human needs are organised in a hierarchy of importance. The five need classifications are physiological, safety, belongingness, esteem and self-actualisation.

Need-value-motive theories of motivation. These identify internal needs that stimulate action on the part of the individual. They identify the factors that direct effort. See **need hierarchy model**.

Needs. The deficiencies that an individual experiences at a particular point in time.

Negotiating styles. Negotiators may do nothing, compete, yield, or engage in problem-solving. Problem-solving is recognised as providing the best means for identifying lasting solutions.

Negotiation. A process for conflict resolution in which two individuals (or two groups) attempt to find a satisfactory solution to a problem. See also **negotiating styles**, **integrative negotiations** and **distributive negotiations**.

Noise. Interference in the flow of

a message from a sender to a receiver.

Nominal group technique (NGT). A technique to improve group decision making that brings people together in a very structured meeting that does not allow for much verbal communication. The group decision is the mathematically pooled outcome of individual votes.

Non-programmed decisions. Decisions required for unique and complex management problems.

Non-verbal communication. Messages sent with body posture, facial expressions, and head and eye movements.

Norms. The standards of behaviour shared by members of a group.

Operant. Behaviours amenable to control by altering the consequences (rewards and punishments) that follow them.

Optimal balance. The most desirable relationship among the criteria of effectiveness. Optimal, rather than maximum, balance must be achieved in any case of more than one criterion.

Organic model of organisation. The organisational design that emphasises the importance of adaptability and development. It is relatively informal, decentralised and simple.

Organisational behaviour. The study of human behaviour, attitudes and performance within an organisational setting; drawing on theory, methods and principles from such disciplines as

psychology, sociology and cultural anthropology to learn about individual perceptions, values, learning capacities and actions while working in groups and within the total organisation; analysing the external environment's effect on the organisation and its human resources, missions, objectives and strategies.

Organisational behaviour modification. An operant approach to organisational behaviour. This term is used interchangeably with the term **behaviour modification**.

Organisational climate. A set of properties of the work environment, perceived directly or indirectly by the employees, that is assumed to be a major force in influencing employee behaviour.

Organisational culture. The pervasive system of values, beliefs and norms that exists in any organisation. The organisational culture can encourage or discourage effectiveness, depending on the nature of the values, beliefs and norms.

Organisational development. The process of preparing for and managing change in organisational settings.

Organisational politics. The activities used to acquire, develop, and use power and other resources to obtain one's preferred outcome when there is uncertainty or disagreement about choices.

Organisational processes. The activities that breathe life into the organisational structure. Among the common organisational processes are communication, decision making, socialisation and career development.

Organisational structure. The formal pattern of how people and jobs are grouped in an organisation. The organisational structure is often illustrated by an organisation chart.

Organisations. Institutions that enable society to pursue goals that could not be achieved by individuals acting alone.

Participative management. A concept of managing that encourages employees' participation in decision making and on matters that affect their jobs.

Path-goal leadership model. A theory that suggests it is necessary for a leader to influence the followers' perception of work goals, self-development goals and paths to goal attainment. The foundation for the model is the expectancy motivation theory.

Perceived conflict. The first stage of the conflict process. Perceived conflict exists when there is an awareness on the part of at least one party that events have occurred or that conditions exist favourable to creating overt conflict. See also **felt conflict** and **manifest conflict**.

Perception. The process by which an individual gives meaning to the environment. It involves organising and interpreting various stimuli into a psychological experience.

Performance. The desired results of behaviour.

Person–environment fit. A match between the needs and

characteristics of the individual and the needs and characteristics of the situation or organisation.

Person-role conflict. A type of conflict that occurs when the requirements of a position violate the basic values, attitudes and needs of the individual occupying the position.

Personal-behavioural leadership theories. A group of leadership theories that are based primarily on the personal and behavioural characteristics of leaders. The theories focus on what leaders do and/or how they behave in carrying out the leadership function.

Personality. A stable set of characteristics and tendencies that determine commonalities and differences in the behaviour of people.

Personality test. A test used to measure the emotional, motivational, interpersonal and attitude characteristics that make up a person's personality.

Pooled interdependence. Interdependence that requires no interaction between groups because each group, in effect, performs separately.

Position analysis questionnaire. A method of job analysis that takes into account the human, task and technological factors of job and job classes.

Position power. A factor in the Fiedler contingency model that refers to the power inherent in the leadership position.

Power. The ability to get things done in the way one wants them to be done.

Process. In systems theory, the process element consists of technical and administrative activities that are brought to bear on inputs in order to transform them into outputs.

Process losses. Situations in which groups are less effective that individuals. See **free riding** and **social loafing**.

Production. A criterion of effectiveness that refers to the organisation's ability to provide the outputs the environment demands of it.

Programmed decisions. Situations in which specific procedures have been developed for repetitive and routine problems.

Progressive discipline. Managerial use of a sequence of penalties for rule violations, each penalty being more severe than the previous one.

Psychological contract. An unwritten agreement between an employee and the organisation which specifies what each expects to give to and receive from the other.

Punctuated equilibrium (change). A model of change. According to this model, change proceeds through cycles of evolution and revolution. During evolutionary cycles, small changes to existing procedures are made. During revolutionary cycles, organisational systems are overturned and new procedures are implemented.

Punctuated equilibrium (groups). An alternative explanation of how groups work. It proposes that the working life of groups can be divided into two phases with a transition point halfway in the group's life. The transition marks a shift from inactivity and inertia to activity and problem solving.

Punishment. Presenting an uncomfortable consequence for a particular behaviour response or removing a desirable reinforcer because of a particular behaviour response. Managers can punish by application or punish by removal.

Qualitative overload. A situation in which a person feels that he or she lacks the ability or skill to do a job or that the performance standards have been set too high.

Quality circle. A small group of employees who meet on a regular basis, usually on company time, to recommend improvements and solve quality-related problems. Frequently a part of **total quality management** efforts.

Quantitative overload. A situation in which a person feels that he or she has too many things to do or insufficient time to complete a job.

Reciprocal causation of leadership. The argument that follower behaviour has an impact on leader behaviour and that leader behaviour influences follower behaviour.

Reciprocal interdependence. Interdependence that requires the output of each group in an organisation to serve as input to other groups in the organisation.

Referent power. Power based on a subordinate's identification with a superior. The more powerful individual is admired because of certain traits, and the subordinate is influenced because of this admiration.

Representativeness. The use of stereotypes to assist in estimating probabilities.

Resource allocation theories. An integrated approach to motivation combining aspects of expectancy, goal-setting and control theory. It suggests that motivation is a decision about where to allocate resources (effort, energy) on the basis of a cost–benefit analysis of the relationship between particular outcomes and the effort required to attain those outcomes.

Reward power. An influence over others based on hope of reward; the opposite of coercive power. A subordinate perceives that compliance with the wishes of a superior will lead to positive rewards, either monetary or psychological.

Role. An organised set of behaviours.

Role ambiguity. A person's lack of understanding about the rights, privileges and obligations of a job.

Role conflict. Arises when a person receives incompatible messages regarding appropriate role behaviour.

Role set. Those individuals who have expectations for the behaviour of an individual in a particular role. The more expectations, the more complex is the role set.

Satisfaction. A criterion of effectiveness that refers to the organisation's ability to gratify the needs of its participants. Similar terms include *morale* and *voluntarism.*

Scalar chain. The graded chain of authority created through the delegation process.

Scientific management. A body of literature that emerged during the period 1890–1930, which reports the ideas and theories of engineers concerned with such problems as job definition, incentive systems, and selection and training.

Scope. The scale on which an organisational change is implemented (for example, throughout the entire organisation, level by level, or department by department).

Selection. A source of error in experimental studies. The error occurs when participants are assigned to experimental and control groups on any basis other than random assignment. Any other selection method will cause systematic biases that will result in differences between groups that are unrelated to the effects of the experimental treatment.

Self-efficacy. Confidence about our ability to perform well.

Self-managed team (SMT). A relatively small group of individuals who are empowered to perform certain activities based on procedures established and decisions made within the group, with minimum or no outside direction. They may take many forms including task forces, project teams, quality circles and new venture teams.

Self-monitoring. A personality trait that describes how responsive individuals are to situational cues. High self-monitors adapt behaviour to each situation; low self-monitors do not.

Self-regulation theories of motivation. These theories attempt to explain how motivation is sustained over time in order to achieve complex goals. See **goal setting** and **control theory**.

Self-serving bias. A frequent attribution error that is reflected in the tendency people have to take credit for successful work and deny responsibility for poor work.

Sensitivity training. A form of educational experience that stresses the process and emotional aspects of training.

Sequential interdependence. Interdependence that requires one group to complete its task before another group can complete its task.

Shared approach. An OD strategy that involves managers and employees in the determination of the OD program.

Shared strategies. Strategies for introducing organisational change that focus on the sharing of decision-making authority among managers and subordinates.

Situational explanations of behaviour. These attribute differences in individual behaviour to external factors. They argue that situations create strong norms that determine situations and override the influence of personality. Organisations are seen as strong situations. See also **dispositional explanations of behaviour, interactional explanations of behaviour, transactional explanations of behaviour** and **person–environment fit**.

Situational theory of leadership. An approach to leadership advocating that leaders understand their own behaviour, the behaviour of their subordinates, and the situation before utilising a particular leadership style. This approach requires diagnostic skills in human behaviour on the part of the leader.

Skills. Task-related competencies.

Social influence. The strategies used to obtain either compliance or commitment from other individuals.

Social loafing. When, in a group, individuals exert slightly less effort than when they are on their own. As a result, a group of ten people (for example) never achieves quite as much as ten individuals on their own might.

Social support. The comfort, assistance or information an individual receives through formal or informal contacts with individuals or groups.

Socialisation processes. The activities by which an individual comes to appreciate the values, abilities, expected behaviours, and social knowledge essential for assuming an organisational role and for participating as an organisation member.

Span of control. The number of subordinates reporting to a superior. The span is a factor that affects the shape and height of an organisational structure.

Status. In an organisational setting, status relates to positions in the formal or informal structure. Status is designated in the formal organisation,

whereas in informal groups it is determined by the group.

Status consensus. The agreement of group members about the relative status of members of the group.

Stereotyping. A means for reducing large amounts of information. By placing individuals or events in a category (stereotype) we can reduce the amount of information that we need to process.

Strategic contingency. An event or activity that is extremely important for accomplishing organisational goals. Among the strategic contingencies of subunits are dependency, scarcity of resources, coping with uncertainty, centrality and substitutability.

Strategic decision making. The process of determining organisational goals and objectives, and ensuring that those goals and objectives are met.

Strategic leadership. This differs from supervision in that it is concerned less with the day-to-day management of staff and more with the long-term direction that an organisation should follow.

Stress. An adaptive response, moderated by individual differences and/or psychological processes, resulting from any environmental action, situation, or event that places excessive psychological and/or physical demands on a person.

Stressor. An external event or situation that is potentially harmful to a person.

Structure. The established patterns of interacting in an organisation and of coordinating the technology and human assets of the organisation.

Structure (in group context). Used in the context of groups, the term *structure* refers to the standards of conduct that are applied by the group, the communication system, and the reward and sanction mechanisms of the group.

Substitutability. The ability of various work units to perform the activities of other work units.

Superordinate goals. Goals that cannot be achieved without the cooperation of the conflicting groups.

Survey. A survey usually attempts to measure one or more characteristics in many people, usually at one point in time. Basically, surveys are used to investigate current problems and events.

System 4 organisation. The universalistic theory of organisation design proposed by Likert. The theory is defined in terms of overlapping groups, linking-pin management and the principle of supportiveness.

Systems theory. An approach to the analysis of organisational behaviour that emphasises the necessity for maintaining the basic elements of input-process-output and for adapting to the larger environment that sustains the organisation.

Task group. A group of individuals who are working as a unit to complete a project or job task.

Task structure. A factor in the Fiedler contingency model that refers to how structured a job is with regard to requirements, problem-solving alternatives and feedback on how correctly the job has been accomplished.

Technology. An important concept that can have many definitions in specific instances but that generally refers to actions, physical and mental, that an individual performs upon some object, person or problem in order to change it in some way.

Telecommuting. An alternative work arrangement in which an employee works at home while being linked to the office via a computer and/or fax machine.

Testing. A source of error in experimental studies. The error occurs when changes in the performance of the subject arise because previous measurement of his performance made him aware that he was part of an experiment.

Time orientation. A concept that refers to the time horizon of decisions. Employees may have relatively short- or long-term orientations, depending on the nature of their tasks.

Time study. The process of determining the appropriate elapsed time for the completion of a task.

Timing. The point in time that has been selected to initiate an organisational change method.

Tolerance of ambiguity. The tendency to perceive ambiguous situations or events as desirable. On the other hand, intolerance of ambiguity is the tendency to perceive ambiguous situations or events as sources of threat.

Total quality management (TQM). A philosophy and system of management which, using statistical process control and group problem-solving processes, places the greatest priority on attaining high standards for quality and continuous improvement.

Trait theory of leadership. An attempt to identify specific characteristics (physical, mental, personality) associated with leadership success. The theory relies on research that relates various traits to certain success criteria.

Transactional explanations of behaviour. These attribute differences in individual behaviour to both internal factors such as personality and external factors such as the situation. They extend interactional approaches by proposing that while situations influence individual behaviour, individual behaviour also influences and changes situations. See also **dispositional explanations of behaviour**, **interactional explanations of behaviour**, **situational explanations of behaviour**, and **person–environment fit**.

Type A behaviour pattern. Associated with research conducted on coronary heart disease. The Type A person is an aggressive driver who is ambitious, competitive, task-oriented, and always on the move. Rosenman and Friedman, two medical researchers, suggest that Type As have more heart attacks than do Type Bs.

Type A managers. Managers who are aloof and cold towards others and are often autocratic leaders. Consequently, they are ineffective interpersonal communicators.

Type B behaviour pattern. The Type B person is relaxed, patient, steady and even-tempered — the opposite of the Type A.

Type B managers. Managers who seek good relationships with subordinates but are unable to express their feelings. Consequently, they usually are ineffective interpersonal communicators.

Type C managers. Managers who are more interested in their own opinions than in those of others. Consequently, they usually are ineffective interpersonal communicators.

Type D managers. Managers who feel free to express their feelings to others and to have others express their feelings. Such managers are the most effective interpersonal communicators.

Unilateral strategies. Strategies for introducing organisational change that do not allow forparticipation by subordinates.

Universal design theory. A point of view that states there is 'one best way' to design an organisation.

Upward communication. Upward communication flows from individuals at lower levels of the organisational structure to those at higher levels. Among the most common upward communication flows are suggestion boxes, group meetings, and appeal or grievance procedures.

Valence. The strength of a person's preference for a particular outcome.

Values. The guidelines and beliefs that a person uses when confronted with a situation in which a choice must be made.

Vertical differentiation. The number of authority levels in an organisation. The more authority levels an organisation has, the more complex is the organisation.

Vroom–Jago model. A leadership model that specifies which leadership decision-making procedures will be most effective in each of several different situations. Two of the proposed leadership styles are autocratic (AI and AII); two are consultative (CI and CII); and one is oriented towards joint decisions (decisions made by the leader and the group, GII).

Well-defined decision problems. Decision problems for which solutions are known. Decision makers must combine information and select the 'best' solution by using decision rules.

Wellness program. An employee program focusing on the individual's overall physical and mental health. Wellness programs may include a variety of activities designed to identify and assist in preventing or correcting specific health problems, health hazards or negative health habits.

Whistle-blowing. The process in which an employee, because of personal opinions, values or ethical standards, concludes that an organisation needs to change its behaviour or practices and informs someone about that conclusion.

Work module. An important characteristic of job redesign strategies. It involves the creation of whole tasks so that the individual senses the completion of an entire job.

INDEX

A

Ability, 515
Absenteeism, 186
Accommodation socialisation, 594, 599–600
Accountability, 515
Achievement need, 129
Acquisitions and cultural change, 593
Action style, 66
Active listening, 569–77
Adaptation to stress, 209–10, 218
Administrative style, 66
Affect, 357
Affiliation need, 130
Alternative conflict resolution, 17
  conflict management, 364–6
  mediation, 360–4
  negotiation, 346–60, 370–7
Anheuser-Busch, 320
Anticipatory socialisation, 591–2, 599
Arbitration, 360–1, 366
Arthur Andersen culture change, 309
Assimilation, 598
Attitudes, 87, 89–90
  changing, 90, 91
  and job satisfaction, 91–3
Attribution theory, 85–7, 88
  leadership, 451–5
Australia and New Zealand Banking Group Limited (ANZ), 464
Authority
  delegation, 671–2
  games, 403, 428
Autocratic leadership style, 458
Autonomous work groups, 270
Avis
  application of motivation theory, 131

B

Base-rate fallacy, 514
Beaurepaires, 629
Behaviour
  general model and implications, 151–4
  labelling, 550
  transactional, 448, 450
  transformational, 448, 450
  Type A behaviour pattern, 219–20, 239–42
  Type B behaviour pattern, 219
Behavioural anchored rating scales (BARS), 179–80, 181
Behavioural science, 25
Blue-collar stressors, 213
Body language, 546
Bridging strategy, 355
Bureaucratic models, 525
Burnout, 224

C

Centrality, 395
Change. see also Organisational development (OD)
  in Australia, 629
  and communication, 554
  cultural, 593
  evolutionary, 634–5
  external forces, 624–5
  games, 405
  internal, 625–6
  motivating, 628
  process
    Lewin's Field Theory, 627–8
    model, 626
  as punctuated equilibrium, 635–6
  rapidity of, 3
  resistance to, 628, 629–33
  revolutionary, 636
  structural, 638
  success of, 632

Change agents, 647–8
Charisma, 389, 391
  consequences, 448
  definition, 446
Charismatic leadership, 445–8
Classical approach to organisational behaviour, 22
Coalition-building game, 403–4
Coalitions, 401
Cognitive reappraisal, 218
Cognitive resource theory, 439
Cohesiveness, 267–9, 313
Collective rationalisation, 517
Collective socialisation, 595
Command groups, 254
Commitment
  escalating, 514–15
  organisational, 554, 630
  subordinate, 186, 268, 270, 398, 455, 459
Communication. see also Interpersonal communication
  benchmarks, 562–4
  case study: misunderstanding, 580–1
  costs of poor, 554
  definition, 544
  diagonal, 558
  downward, 553, 555, 560
  elements, 544–6
  ethical, 562
  as factor of cooperation, 302
  horizontal, 556
  Japan, 564
  model, 544
  multicultural, 565–6
  networks, 558–9
  organisational, 688
  overload, 550
  process, 18, 544–7
  strategy, 564
  upward, 555–6

Companies
  leading Australian, 34
Compensation, 355
  Competence need, 130
Competition, 299, 303, 317
  determinants, 300–2
  for resources, 310
  stimulating, 319–20
Compliance, 398
Conceptual style, 65–6
Concession exchange, 354–5
Conciliation, 361
Conflict. *see also* Intergroup
    conflict
  basis of, 299
  case study: Rainbow Medical
      Centre, 341–4
  contemporary, 303, 304
  cycle of escalating, 306
  exercise, 337–40
  and gender, 309
  intragroup, 265
  and organisational structure,
      688
  programmed, 320, 531–3
  stages of, 307–8
  traditional perspective, 303
  types of, 304–5
  unprogrammed, 533
Conflict management, 16–17,
    364–6
  design of procedures, 316,
      323–37
  litigation, 330–1, 335
Conflict resolution
  and culture, 316
  process, 325–9
  strategies, 318
Conflict stimulation, 317, 318–19
Conformity
  influence and, 397–8
  norm, 264
  pressure towards, 517
Conger's charisma model, 446–7
Conjunctive fallacy, 514
Conrad Casino, 584
Consideration, 435
Consultation, 361, 401

Consultative leadership style, 458
Contamination, 178
Contending, 348, 349
Contingency leadership model,
    436–8
Contingency models, 525
Controlling function, 713–16
Cooperation, 299, 300
  determinants, 302
Coping
  emotion-focused, 218
  problem-focused, 218
  research into, 222
Corporate culture
  and stress management, 228
Cost cutting, 355
Cost–benefit analysis, 141
Creativity, 519–21
Crisis management, 447
Cultural diversity
  and socialisation, 604
Cultural relativism, 610
Culture processes, 19

D

Daily Hassles Scale, 216
Deadlines, 311
Decision effectiveness, 459
Decision frames, 514
Decision making. *see also* Group
    decision making; Strategic
    decision making
  approaches, 500
  case study: Kooyong High
      School, 537–41
  context of, 506
  devil's advocacy, 320, 504, 517,
      529, 531–2
  dialectic method, 529, 532–3
  ethical, 406
  follow-up, 506
  goals and objectives, 501
  implementation, 505
  limits to rational, 511–17
  motivational factors, 514–17
  non-programmed, 497, 498
  and organisational structure,
      526

outcomes, 499
  problems, 499–500, 507–9, 512
  process, 18–19, 501–7
  programmed, 497–9
  rules, 509–11
Decision quality, 459
Decision styles, 460, 461
Deductive approaches, 66
Deficiency, 178
Delphi technique, 521–2
Departmentalisation, 672–6
Development processes, 19
Developmental orientation, 177
Devil's advocacy, 320, 504, 517,
    529, 531–2
Diagnostic procedure, 462
Dialectic method, 529, 532–3
Distortion, 178
Distributive bargaining
    (win–lose), 350–2, 354, 359
Distributive justice, 184, 187, 364,
    365, 406
Division of labour, 671
Dow Chemical, 678
Du Pont
  health risk factors study, 213
Dual concern model, 349
Dual-career couples, 214–15

E

Ecology, 193–4
Effective management, 33
Effective performance
  controlling, 49–50
  leading, 48
  organising, 47
  planning, 46–7
Effectiveness
  and adaptiveness, 43–4
  corrective action, 50
  criteria, 41
  culture, 49
  and development, 44
  and efficiency, 43
  history, 35–40
  information, 50
  managerial, 49
  and productivity, 43

and quality, 41–3
and satisfaction, 43
standards, 50
systems theory, 37–9
time dimension model, 40–1
Effort utility, 141
Effort–performance utility, 141, 150
Egocentric bias, 314, 317
Emotion-focused coping, 218
Empathy, 560
Employee-centred leadership, 434–5
Employees
absenteeism, 186
attribution process, 85–7
degree of specialisation, 677
employer view of, 3
empowerment, 395–6
expectations in Japan, 145
Hawthorne studies, 8–9
information needs, 237
matched to jobs, 237
organisational commitment, 186
performance evaluation, 175, 177–8
rewards systems, 186, 187, 188
socialisation, 597–605
turnover, 185
Empowerment
concept, 412
definition, 395–6
and leadership, 395–6, 412–21
management practices, 412–17
Enterprise architecture, 692–701
Environmental analysis, 523
Environmental dependencies, 45
Equality, 185
Equity theory, 142, 183–5
Ericsson, 629
Ernst & Young
culture change, 309
Ethics
in communication
transactions, 562
power and politics, 405–6, 407–8

Ethics decision tree, 406
Ethnocentrism, 565
Evaluation apprehension, 266–7
Exception principle, 560
Exchange, 401
Exchange theory, 142
Expectancy, 133
Expectancy theory, 130–5, 144, 150–9, 183, 439
implications for organisations, 153–4
key terms, 131–3
managerial application, 133–5
measuring motivation, 157–9
model, 155–7

F
Fairness
as factor of cooperation, 302
Fallacy, 514
Feedback
in controlling function, 715–16
in interpersonal
communication, 550
in learning, 474–5
and managerial style, 552
need for, 545–6, 631, 635
utilising, 560
Feelings
labelling, 550
Felt conflict, 307–8
Fiedler's leadership model, 436–9, 445
Fixed socialisation, 595–6
Formal groups, 16, 17, 253, 254
Frame of reference
(communication), 547–8, 551
Free riding, 266
Friendship groups, 255
Functional conflict, 304

G
Gender
and conflict, 309
leadership style, 432

and organisational politics, 407–8
General adaptation syndrome
(GAS), 209–10
General Electric, 678
General Motors, 675–6
Glass ceiling, 407
Global competition, 3, 13
Goal approach, 35, 37
Goal setting
application, 136, 137
control theory, 138–40
description, 136
exercise, 160–1
research, 136–8
Goals
in conflict management, 365
differences as cause of conflict, 310
effect on negotiator power, 357
establishing, 501
organisational definition, 46–7
Goddard Space Flight Center
study, 214, 215
Grapevine (communication), 562
Group behaviour, 15, 16
Group cohesion, 267–9
Group decision making
brainstorming, 521
creativity, 519–21
Delphi technique, 521–2
versus individual decision
making, 518–19
nominal group technique
(NGT), 522–3
Group performance, 20
Group pride, 268
Group size
as factor of cooperation, 302
Group synergy, 280, 282, 284–5, 286
Groups
autonomous work, 270
case studies
International
Superannuation
Specialists, 295–7
Johnny Rocco, 292–5

Groups *(continued)*
changes within, 313
changes without, 313–14
collective-level, 317
commitment to, 257
decisions styles, 460, 461
definition, 251, 252–3
evaluation by members, 256–7
formation and development
Gersick's Punctuated
Equilibrium Model,
259–60
integrated model, 253, 254
reasons for, 255–6
Tuckman's five-stage model,
257–9
goals, 256
membership process, 256–7
normative model of
effectiveness, 276–88
norms, 260–1, 262–4, 283
performance, 264–9
revitalisation of, 319
roles within, 260–2
socialisation, 261
synergistic, 264–5
tasks, 266
types of, 253–5
Groupthink, 515–17

H
Hardiness (personality), 220
Hawthorne studies, 8–9
Health Risk Appraisal, 242–5
Healthy lifestyles, 229
Hersey-Blanchard situational
leadership theory (SLT),
441–4, 445
Heuristics, 511, 513
Hewlett-Packard, 629, 678
Home–work interface, 214–15
Human relations
approach to organisational
behaviour, 22–3
Human resource management
(HRM), 24
and organisational culture,
587

Human resources
power of, 3

I
IBM, 320, 678
Inaction, 348, 349
Incentives
cultural differences, 179
Incremental adjustment models,
525
Individual performance, 20
Individualism, 586
Individuals
characteristics, 13, 14
decisions styles, 460, 461
motivation, 15
needs, 123
revitalising groups, 13, 14, 319
rights, 406
socialisation, 595, 596
Inductive approaches, 66
Industrialisation, 6
Influence
conformity and, 397–8
cultural differences, 390
definition, 387
interpersonal, 399–400
as power, 397
as a reciprocal relationship,
397
social, 396–9
Informal groups, 16, 17, 253, 255
Information
filtering, 548
loss, 557
overload, 550, 556
regulating flow, 560
Information power, 393
Ingratiation, 401
In-groups, 301, 303, 311, 454
language, 548–9
Initiating structure, 435
Innovation, 397–8, 688
Input-output cycle, 39
Insightful style, 66
Inspirational appeals, 401
Institutionalised socialisation, 596
Instrumentality, 132

Insurgency game, 403
Integration strategy, 605
Integrative bargaining (win-win),
349, 353–5
Interdependence
as cause of conflict, 308–10
changing perceptions, 317
social, 299–300
task, 303
types of, 309–10
Interest groups, 255
Intergroup conflict
causes of, 308–12
change in organisational
structure, 319
dysfunctional, 305
consequences of, 312–14,
315
functional, 304
managing, 16–17, 316–17
and organisational
performance, 305–8
and social interdependence,
299–300
Interpersonal attraction, 268
Interpersonal behaviour, 15–16
Interpersonal communication
barriers to, 547–50
managerial perspective, 552–3
Interpersonal factors, 312
Interpersonal influence, 397,
399–400
Interpersonal relationships, 228
Interpersonal style, 66
Intragroup conflict, 265, 315
Irreversibility, 515

J
Japan
employee's expectations, 145
Job depth, 166–7, 168–9
Job Descriptive Index (JDI), 92
Job design
case study: Vaccino, 203–5
exercises, 170, 199–203
as motivating factor, 166–70,
687
range and depth, 166–70

strategies for redesign, 168
Job enlargement, 168
Job enrichment, 169
Job range, 166–7, 168, 170
Job rotation, 168
Job satisfaction, 75
    and attitudes, 91–3
    and communication, 91–3
    Herzberg's view, 129
    and performance, 93–4
Job-centred leadership, 434–5
Jobs
    characteristics model, 169
    defining activities and
        authority, 672–6
    frame of, 55–6
    grouping, 47–8, 672–6
    motivating potential, 171
    nature and content of, 47
    people in, 54–5
    specialisation, 671, 677
Judgemental orientation, 177
Justice, 184–5, 187, 688
Justice Judgement Model, 184–5

K

Kimberly-Clark Corporation, 674
KPMG Peat Marwick
    culture change, 309

L

Language, 561
Latent conflict, 307
Lay-offs, 630
Leader–Member Exchange
        approach (LMX), 454–5
Leaders
    attributions, 451–5
    change oriented, 632
    charismatic, 447
    definition, 428
    intelligence, 431, 432
    learning and, 471–7
    member relations, 437
    organisational behaviour,
        10–12
    personality, 433
    physical traits, 433

types of, 428, 435, 440–1, 442,
    447
Leadership, 17
    attributional theory, 451–5
    Australian perspective, 449
    autocratic, 313
    case study: The Council of
        Adult Education, 481–94
    charismatic, 445–8
    contingency leadership model,
        436–8
    cultural differences, 444
    definition, 395–6, 429
    employee-centred, 434–5
    and empowerment, 411–21
    Fiedler's contingency model,
        436–9, 445
    impact of, 430
    impact of gender, 432
    job-centred, 434–5
    New Zealand perspective, 449
    overarching model, 431
    participative, 458–63
    path-goal theory, 436, 439–44,
        445
    and personal power, 445–51
    personal-behavioural theories,
        434–6
    romance of, 456
    situational theories, 436–45
    strategic, 463–5
    substitutes for, 456–8
    traits, 431–4
    transformational, 445, 448,
        450–1
    two-factor theory, 435
    unlearning, 477–9
Leadership climate, 633
Learning
    cultural diversity, 604
    organisations, 597–8
Learning theory, 171–3
Least-Preferred Co-Worker Scale
    (LPC), 437, 438
Legitimising, 401
Levi Strauss & Co., 33, 34–5
Life-change events, 216
Line generalists

conflicts with specialists, 312
Line-*versus*-staff game, 404–5
Listening
    active, 569–77
    barriers to, 549–50
Locus of control, 220, 221, 440
    Rotter's internal–external test,
        219
Logrolling, 355
Loyalty, 313

M

Machiavellianism, 81
Management
    definition, 46
    effective, 33
    by exception, 450
    functions, 7–8, 14, 44–50,
        704–16
    history, 6–7
    scientific, 6–7
    social context, 5
Management by objectives
    (MBO), 639
Management practice, 717–28
Management response, 45
Managerial authority, 287–8
Managerial ideologies, 25
Managerial roles, 707–10
Managerial skills, 705–7
Managerial styles, 65–7
    opportunistic, 56
Managers
    attribution process, 85–7
    characteristics of successful,
        704–5
    comparison with leaders, 428
    decisional roles, 709–10
    definition, 428
    delegation of authority, 671–2
    design of conflict management
        procedures, 323–37
    effective communication, 543
    empowerment, 395–6
    and ethics, 405–6, 407–8
    implications of expectancy
        theory, 133–5
    informational roles, 707, 709

Managers *(continued)*
  interpersonal roles, 707
  and motivation, 144
  and organisational design,
      669–70
  product, 685
  and stress management, 225–6
  types of, 552–3, 705
Managing
  action, 62–4
  by information, 58
  through people, 60–2
Manifest conflict, 308
Marriott International, 543
Masculinity, 587
Matrix organisational design,
    682–5
McDonald's, 583, 584, 588
Mediation
  outcomes, 362, 364
  sexual harassment, 363
  stages in, 361–2
Mediators, 361, 362, 363–4
Medicine
  rewards systems and, 192
Men
  and conflict, 309
  leadership style, 432
  motivation, 128
  and organisational politics,
      407–8
Mental programming, 608–10
Mentoring, 402, 404, 601–3
Mentors, 601
Mergers
  and cultural change, 593
  small business, 402
Merit reward system, 185
Messages
  decoding, 545, 548
  distorted (noise), 546
  encoding, 544, 548
  improving, 559
  medium, 545
  non-verbal, 546–7, 551
Mintzberg's management roles,
    708
Mission, 46

Mission statement, 523
Mixed motive situations, 299, 300
Mobil
  culture change, 309
Motivating potential score (MPS),
    170
Motivation. *see also* Expectancy
      theory
  and behaviour, 94
  case study: Fab Sweets Limited,
      161–4
  components, 122
  diagnostic approach, 134–5,
      149–55
  factors in decision making,
      514–17
  gender differences, 128
  intrinsic, 129
  Japanese style, 145
  measuring, 154, 157–9
  and performance appraisal,
      176
  process model, 123
  psychological contract, 142–4
  reward systems, 167
  role of managers, 144
  theories, 170–1
    Adam's equity, 142, 183
    classification system, 124
    cognitive-choice, 124, 125,
        130–35
    exchange, 142
    Herzberg's two-factor,
        127–9, 169
    managerial application, 125
    Maslow's needs hierarchy,
        125–7, 131, 142, 183
    need–value–motive, 124–30,
        166
    resource allocation, 140–1
    self-regulation, 124, 125,
        135–40
    Vroom's expectancy, 130–5,
        144, 150–9, 183
Motivational losses, 266–7
Motivational orientations, 35
Multicultural communication,
    565–6

Multinational corporations, 4,
    685–6

N

NASA (National Aeronautics and
    Space Administration), 516
National culture, 612–15
Need fulfilment, 125–9
Negotiation
  definition, 346–7
  distributive (win–lose), 350–2,
      354
  dual concern model, 349
  integrative (win–win), 349,
      353–5
  interpersonal conflict style
      model, 349
  managerial grid, 349
  strategies, 347–9
Negotiations
  case studies
    Olympic television rights,
        379–85
    World Bank, 377–9
  cognitive biases, 357–8
  cultural differences, 356
  effective processes, 358, 359–60
  endowment effect, 374–5
  framing, 370–4, 375–7
  settlement options, 352
  situational factors, 356–7
Negotiators
  frames, 358
  power, 356–7
Neo-Human Relations, 28
Networking, 402
Networks
  communication, 558–9
Nominal group technique (NGT),
    522–3
Non-malfeasance, 562
Non-programmed decision
    making, 497, 498
Normalisation, 397
Normative influence, 397
Norms
  group, 260–1, 262–4
  hypothetical production, 263

O

Objectives, 47
Obligations, 143
Obsolescence
 cause of stress, 215
Occupational stress. *see* Stress
Ohio State leadership studies, 435–6
Organisational behaviour
 classical approaches, 22
 leaders, 10–12
 origins, 8–9, 22–9
 processes, 17
 research techniques, 717–28
 studying, 9–10, 14
 systems thinking, 23–4
 theorists, 24
Organisational behaviour
  management (OBM),
  guidelines, 173–5
Organisational change, 19
 expert perspective, 640–1
 failures in, 651–7
 individual perspective, 641
 and innovation, 688
 organisation perspective, 640
Organisational commitment, 186, 630
Organisational communication, 687
Organisational culture, 617
 case study: Consolidated Life, 619–22
 and change, 589–91, 633, 640
 creating, 588–9
 definition, 583, 584
 and human resource
  management (HRM), 587
 national differences, 586–7
 socialisation, 591–605
Organisational design, 19, 20
 matrix, 682–5
 mechanistic model, 680–1
 multinational, 685–6
 new enterprise architecture, 692–701
 organic model, 680, 681

Organisational development (OD)
 aim, 638
 characteristics, 636–7
 Community Services Victoria, 659–66
 evaluation, 646–7
 Hong Kong, 643
 implementation, 646
 management by objectives (MBO), 639, 641
 managerial grid, 643–4
 social factors, 642
 structural, 638
 team building, 642
 technology, 644–5
 total quality management (TQM), 645–6
Organisational effectiveness
 studying, 50–1
Organisational integration, 605
Organisational life cycles, 464–5
Organisational management
 origins of, 8–9
Organisational performance, 20
 and intergroup conflict, 305–8
Organisational research
 history, 36
Organisational structure, 19–20
 centralisation, 679, 680
 change resolving conflicts, 319
 complexity, 679–80
 and decision making, 526
 departmentalisation, 672–6
 design, 669–70, 680–5
 dimensions, 677–80
 flattening, 678
 formalisation, 677, 679, 680
 horizontal differentiation, 679
 relationship to stress, 213, 227
 span of control, 676–7
 vertical differentiation, 679
Organisations
 communication within, 553–64
 environment of, 12
 greening, 4
 individualising, 154
 individuals in, 12–13

learning about, 597–8
 power shifts, 631
 purpose of, 5
 social context, 5
 stress prevention and
  management programs, 226–7, 229–30
 types of, 45
 visions for, 632
Orphanages
 rewards systems and, 192–3
Outcomes, 132
 in conflict management, 366
Out-groups, 301–2, 303, 311, 454
Output equity, 266
Overarching model, 431

P

Pacific BBA, 678
Participative approach, 428, 442
Participative leadership
 Vroom–Jago model, 459–63
Path-goal theory, 436, 439–41, 445
Pay, 167
Perceived conflict, 307
Perceptions
 attribution theory, 85–7
 definition, 83–4
 differences causing conflict, 311, 312
 distorted, 314
 of interdependence, 317
 selective, 84
 social, 85–7
 stereotyping, 84
Performance
 determinants, 121
 evaluation, 600
 leadership and organisational, 464
 outcomes, 20
 variables, 121
Performance evaluation. *see also*
  Motivation
 behavioural anchored rating
  scales (BARS), 179–80, 181
 checklists, 178

Performance evaluation
(continued)
critical incidents, 178–9
focus of, 177–8
improving effectiveness, 180–1
purposes of, 177
reasons for, 175
Performance utility, 141
Performance–outcome
expectancy, 150
Personal appeals, 401
Personality
case study: missing time, 245–7
and cultural forces, 78
definition, 77
generality, 78
'hardy,' 220
interactionist perspective, 81
locus of control, 219, 220
optimists, 220, 221
pessimists, 221
relationship to behaviour, 77, 80
self-efficacy, 77, 78–9
self-monitoring, 79–80
transactional approaches, 82
Personality traits, 76
affectivity, 221
Person–centred strategies, 401
Person–environment fit, 226–7
Person–organisation fit, 82,
98–109
Placement practices, 599
Planning function, 710–13
Politics
and gender, 407–8
and organisational influence,
399–405
playing, 402, 403, 404–5
and rewards systems, 191
strategies, 400
Pooled interdependence, 309
POSDCORB, 60, 66
Position power, 437
Position-based influence
strategies, 401
Power
case study: Missouri University,
422–6

coercive, 389
cultural differences, 390
decision-making, 392–3
definition, 17, 387–8
expert, 389
information, 393
interpersonal, 388–9
positive, 391
referent, 389, 391
reward, 389
structural, 391–3
Power distance, 586
Power need, 130
Power-base game, 403
Powerlessness, 417–18
Principled bargaining. see
Integrative bargaining
Probabilities, 511
Problem identification, 501–3
Problem solving, 348, 349, 362
Problem-focused coping, 218
Procedural concerns, 362
Procedural justice, 184, 185, 187,
364, 365
Process losses, 266–7
Procter & Gamble, 686
Programmed conflict, 531–3
Programmed decision making,
497–9
Psychological contract, 3, 142–3,
142–4
Psychological distance, 314
Publicity, 515
Punctuated Equilibrium Model,
259–60
Punishment, 172, 173–4

Q
Questioning, 551

R
Rational persuasion, 401
Rationality, 370
Reciprocal interdependence, 310
Recruitment, 599
Rehabilitation centres
and rewards systems, 192–3
Reinforcement, 173–4

schedule, 172–3
theory, 172
Relationship outcomes, 366
Relationship-orientated
leadership style, 437, 457
Replication, 685
Resource allocation
and integrative bargaining, 354
motivational perspectives of,
140–1
Resource dependency models,
392–3
Resources
factor of power, 392
Responsibility
as cause of stress, 215
for decision making, 515
Reward structures
as factor in conflict, 311
Rewards, 15
extrinsic, 182
individual model of, 186, 187,
188
intrinsic, 182, 186
valued, 134
Rewards system, 167, 180
and ecology, 193–4
impact on
absenteeism, 186
organisational commitment,
186
turnover, 185
and medicine, 192
and orphanages, 192–3
and politics, 191
and rehabilitation centres,
192–3
and universities, 193
and war, 191–2
Risk avoidance behaviours, 196
Risk propensity, 514
Rivalry games, 404–5
Role ambiguity, 215
Role analysis, 227
Role characteristics, 227
Role conflict, 213, 214
Role management socialisation,
594–5, 601

Roles
    group, 260–2
Royal Dutch Petroleum, 320

S

Schein's three-layer organisational
        model, 583, 584, 585
Selection interviews, 82
Selection programs, 599
Selective listening, 549
Self-managed teams, 430, 687
Sequential interdependence, 310
Serial socialisation, 596
Situational leadership theories,
        436–45
Situations
    and dispositions, 80
    organisations as strong, 80
Small business
    mergers, 402
    strategic plans, 524
Social categorisation, 300, 301,
        311
Social engineering, 25
Social influence, 396–7
    strategies, 398–9
Social interdependence
    and conflict, 299–300
Social loafing, 266
Social perception, 85–7
Social Readjustment Rating Scale
        (SRRS), 216, 217
Social science, 25
Social support, 221, 223, 228
Socialisation, 82
    characteristics, 599–601
    culturally diverse workforce,
        603–5
    group, 261
    as integration strategy, 605
    and learning, 597–8
    and mentors, 601–3
    processes, 19, 591–5
    strategies, 595–6
Societal values, 585
Solutions in decision making,
        503–6

Sony, 501
Source credibility, 549–50
Space shuttle *Challenger*, 515, 516
Span of control, 676–7
Specialists
    conflicts with line generalists,
        312
Sponsorship
    as a political game, 403
Standards, 713–14
Status incongruency, 311–12
Stereotyping, 84, 314
Strategic contingency
    definition, 393
    model, 393–5
Strategic decision making (SDM),
        523–5
Strategic plans, 524
Stress, 15
    adaptation to, 209–10, 218
    appraisal, 218
    burnout, 224
    case study: missing time,
        245–7
    and change, 207
    coping with, 218
    cost of
        Australia, 225
        United States of America,
            234
    definitions, 207–8
    'excessive,' 218
    executive, in Asia, 212
    general adaptation syndrome
        (GAS), 209–10
    model, 211
    moderators, 218
    monkey experiments, 207
    organisation structure factor,
        687
    positive effects, 223
    research, 222
Stress audits, 236
Stress consequences, 211, 223
    individual, 223
    organisational, 224
Stress moderators, 211
    definition, 218

Stress prevention and
        management, 225–30
    cognitive techniques, 229
    healthy lifestyle, 229
    individual approaches, 228
    maximising
        person–environment fit,
            226–7
    relaxation techniques, 228–9
Stressors
    definition, 208
    environmental, 213
    group, 212–13
    individual, 213–16
    level of, 216, 217–18
    life, 211, 216
    moderating, 218–23
    organisational, 212, 213
    types of, 208–9
    work, 210–11
Substantive concerns, 362
Substantive outcomes, 366
Substitutability, 395
Supervisors
    role of, 154
Synergism, 264–5
Systems theory, 37–9

T

Task groups, 254
Task structure, 437
Task-orientated leadership style,
        437, 457
Teams
    best practice, 252
    building, 642
    commitment, 270, 271
    common purpose, 270, 271
    complementary skills, 269
    cross-functional, 252
    definition, 269
    development, 272
    effectiveness, 271–2
    mutual accountability, 270
    self-managing, 430, 687
    work
        Britain, 272
        design of, 275–88

Teams, work *(continued)*
    Japan, 272
        United States of America,
            272
Technology, 646
Time dimension model, 40–1
Time perspectives, 311
Total quality management
    (TQM), 645–6
Toyota, 587
    attitude and culture, 90
Training
    altering rewards system, 198–9
    evaluation of, 194
Transactional behaviour, 448, 450
Transformational behaviour, 448,
    450
Transformational leadership, 445,
    448, 450–1
Trust, 455, 561
Turnover, 185
Type A behaviour pattern
    (TABP), 219–20, 239–42

Type A managers, 552
Type B behaviour pattern , 219
Type B managers, 552
Type C managers, 552
Type D managers, 552–3

U

Uncertainty
    coping with, 394
    influence reducing, 397
Uncertainty avoidance, 586
Understanding, 559, 561
Union Carbide, 497
Universities
    rewards systems and, 193
University of Michigan leadership
        studies, 434–5, 436
Unprogrammed conflict, 533

V

Valence, 132–3, 150
Value judgements, 549
Values, 585

W

Walt Disney, 584, 587, 588
War, and rewards system,
        191–2
Whistle blowing, 405
Women
    and conflict, 309
    leadership style, 432
    motivation, 128
    and organisational politics,
            407–8
Work
    agenda, 56
    scheduling, 56
Work overload, 215
Work teams. *see* Teams
Worker–employer
    psychological contract, 3
Workforce
    culturally diverse, 3

Y

Yielding, 348, 349